LINCOLN THE PRESIDENT

MIDSTREAM to the LAST FULL MEASURE

Courtesy of F. H. Meserve

THE GARDNER FULL FIGURE—1863

One of several photographs taken by Alexander Gardner in his Washington studio on Sunday, November 15, 1863, a few days before the Gettysburg address.

LINCOLN
THE PRESIDENT

MIDSTREAM
TO THE
LAST FULL MEASURE

VOLUME TWO

BY

J. G. Randall

AND

Richard N. Current

ILLUSTRATED

DA CAPO PRESS • NEW YORK

Library of Congress Cataloging in Publication Data

Randall, J. G. (James Garfield), 1881-1953.
Lincoln the president / by J. G. Randall.
p. cm.
Originally published: New York: Dodd, Mead & Co., 1946, 1952, 1955.
Includes bibliographical references and index.
Contents: v. 1. Springfield to Gettysburg–v. 2. Midstream to the last full measure.
ISBN 0-306-80754-8 (v. 1: alk. paper).–ISBN 0-306-80755-6 (v. 2)
1. Lincoln, Abraham, 1809-1865. 2. Presidents–United States–Biography. 3. United States–Politics and government–1861-1865. 4. United States–History–Civil War, 1861-1865. I. Title.
E457.R2 1997
973.7'092–dc20 96-36026
[B] CIP

First Da Capo Press edition 1997

This Da Capo Press paperback edition of volume two of *Lincoln the President* is an unabridged republication of *Lincoln the President: Midstream* by J. G. Randall, first published in New York in 1952, and *Lincoln the President: Last Full Measure* by J. G. Randall and Richard N. Current, first published in New York in 1955, supplemented by a new introduction by Richard N. Current. It is reprinted by arrangement with the estate of J. G. Randall and with Richard N. Current.

Published by Da Capo Press, Inc.
A Subsidiary of Plenum Publishing Corporation
233 Spring Street, New York, N.Y. 10013

Manufactured in the United States of America

To Ruth Painter Randall
biographer of Mrs. Lincoln

INTRODUCTION TO THE DA CAPO EDITION

WHEN THE FOUR volumes of J. G. Randall's *Lincoln the President* first appeared (1945, 1952, 1955), they received the enthusiastic acclaim of experts in the Lincoln field, who recognized Randall as the preeminent living authority. This work, they said, was "basic Lincoln literature." It was "the best portrayal of Lincoln and his difficult role as President." Indeed, it was "one of the most impressive works of historical scholarship ever written in America."

Randall had already established his reputation with *Constitutional Problems under Lincoln* (1926) and *The Civil War and Reconstruction* (1937). From 1920 to 1950 he also provided inspiration and guidance for a large number of historians who gained their doctorates from the University of Illinois at Urbana-Champaign. The most illustrious of his disciples is David Herbert Donald, prize-winning biographer of Lincoln, Herndon, and Sumner.

Conceiving of his Lincoln volumes as both history and biography, Randall provided a fairly broad coverage of wartime events as well as intimate pictures of life in the White House. Despite his title *Lincoln the President,* he included six chapters dealing with the pre-presidential years and an appendix appraising the Ann Rutledge romance. He deliberately excluded the assassination, avowing: "This biography knows only the living Lincoln."

Actually, the four volumes do not present continuous history or biography so much as they do a series of historiographical essays. Randall proposed to clear away existing misconceptions and thus make a "historical restoration" that would reveal the underlying truths about Lincoln and his times. This involved analyzing and synthesizing a vast quantity of both original and secondary sources and disagreeing with much that had been taken for granted in scholarly or in popular literature. Upon both the general reader and the Lincoln scholar, these essays had a refreshing, astringent effect.

So it was, for example, with Randall's treatment of William H. Herndon's stories of Lincoln's love for Ann Rutledge and difficulties with Mary Todd. Randall concluded that the supposed love affair with Ann was unproved in its essentials and disproved in its elaborations, and that Lincoln's later home life with Mary was pretty much that of a typical American family man.

Other conclusions were equally iconoclastic for the time. The Lincoln-Douglas debates revolved about insubstantial and purposely confused issues; the participants only "*seemed to differ.*" Lincoln as President-elect did not block the path to sectional compromise in 1860-61, though he did bungle the delicate task of conciliating the upper South. He was innocent of the charge that he sent an expedition to Fort Sumter with the ulterior aim of maneuvering the Confederates into firing the first shot. He left foreign affairs largely to his secretary of state, William H. Seward, and was something less than the diplomat in carpet slippers that he had been depicted. Yielding to pressure, he let General George B. McClellan down and thus brought disaster upon the Army of the Potomac. Randall did not share the feeling of some of the older biographers that justice to Lincoln required the berating of McClellan or, for that matter, James Buchanan and Stephen A. Douglas.

Lincoln, according to Randall, was closer to the Rebels than to the Radicals, the extreme antislavery members of his own Republican party. His famous proclamation of January 1, 1863 failed to set the slaves definitely free. The assurance of freedom awaited the Thirteenth Amendment, which he helped to guide through Congress. "Of the stereotypes concerning Lincoln one of the most unhistorical is the stock picture of the Emancipator sitting in the White House and suddenly striking the shackles from millions of bondmen at a stroke of the presidential pen."

Slavery was not, however, the basic issue of the Civil War, as Randall viewed the matter. He assumed that the war was neither an "irrepressible conflict" nor a contest between right and wrong. Its "causes" were unreal, and there was right and wrong on both sides. The war resulted from the propaganda of politicians and agitators, North and South, particularly the abolitionists of the North.

This approach troubled some critics, even some who otherwise were favorable, at the time the volumes appeared. It was "doughface" history and "historical sentimentalism," they said. Slavery as a moral question was deeply involved, they insisted, and the issues of Union and freedom were not only real but fundamental.

Since that time, Lincoln scholars have questioned other judgments of Randall's besides his view that the Civil War was both undesirable and unnecessary, the work of a "blundering generation." Herndon has been rehabilitated to the extent that his view of the Lincoln marriage is now widely accepted, along with the Ann Rutledge story, at least in its essentials. According to some of the more recent scholarship, the Lincoln-Douglas debates revealed sharp differences between the participants in regard to human rights. Lincoln must have known that his Sumter expedition might provoke a warlike response. No Southerner at heart, he became increasingly a Radical Republican himself, and if he had lived he would probably have adopted a Radical policy in dealing with the postwar South.

These and other issues pertaining to *Lincoln the President* remain controversial. If Randall were writing in the 1990s, he would likely treat some of the topics differently, though not necessarily all of them. As the author of *The Civil War and Reconstruction*, he said of himself in 1937: "He has tried to avoid being unduly impressed by the mere newness of this or that historical contribution, and, while recognizing—indeed welcoming with keenest pleasure—the work of revisionists, he has at times suspected that some day the revisionists themselves may be revised." Randall's interpretations may be no less credible than some of the more recent ones, and in any case his views need to be considered if the controversies are to be fully understood.

But his volumes have much more in them than controversy. Quite apart from his stand on historical disputes, these books contain a full and accurate account of the events in which President Lincoln had a part, as well as a lively picture of the man himself and of the people with whom he was associated. Though *Lincoln the President* bears the marks of its time, it still has much to offer the reader interested in Lincoln and the Civil War period.

—RICHARD N. CURRENT
August 1996

PREFACE

THIS study of President Lincoln finds the nation's Chief in the midst of his crucial administration. In a great complexity of public affairs attention is focused on the man and his work. Biography is an interplay of character and incident, of the person and the world about him. Lincoln's world was a vast stage. It was not merely the United States—certainly not merely "the North" or Washington—but the larger world in terms of that fundamental democracy envisaged at Gettysburg. To Lincoln the American ideal was based on no narrow concept. In speeches and writings before and during the presidency he repeatedly interpreted the American experiment in its bearing upon the cause of free government in the world.

Two questions, reciprocal in nature, arise as to Lincoln. What effect did the war, the appalling crisis, and the challenge of many problems have upon his personality? And in what respects were the developments of that troubled era different because it was Lincoln, and not another man, in the presidential chair? There are, of course, other questions. In biography there is always the factor of an impression, or portrait, of the man. How near we can come to a recovery of the real Lincoln it is not easy to say; for these pages the effort at recovery has been a matter of primary record, contemporary portrayal, and direct evidence. Such portrayal is not easy for the inner man—perhaps that is why Mark Twain considered biography to be little more than "clothes and buttons"—but for Lincoln there is more revelation of his deepest thought than is usually realized. It is desirable to seek historical appraisal in terms of large perspective, but that is not the whole task. There remains the close-up view—the mobile face, gesture, playful quip, laugh or sigh, small talk and off-duty jest. Both the broad picture and the complete limning of the immediate portrait may be unattainable in the full sense. Inadequate presentation of Lincoln is all too common. The subject has been voluminously treated without being "exhausted." Yet a new delineation may have value without aspiring to finality.

The theme is not one for hasty conclusions. One could easily emphasize the many contradictions that pervade the inquiry, yet such is the nature of historical investigation. A distinction is not worthless because it breaks down at the border, and a showing of unlike factors does not invalidate essential truth. The multiplicity of claims for Lincoln, or the numerous appropriations of his name for sponsorship of this or that view or faction, should not lead to the assumption that Lincoln himself was inconclusive or incapable of being associated with particular movements or ideals. The very intensity of opposition to him within his own party is evidence that he was taking a stand and asserting his position.

If, therefore, one discovers opposites in Lincoln research, if a generalization is worked up only to be followed by the finding of counteracting evidence, that should be taken as indicating that the subject itself is many-sided. A seeming inconsistency should not greatly disturb the mature student. Some would have said that Lincoln "saw everybody"; yet often he was inaccessible. He had a dignity and appropriateness, yet an "irresistibly ludicrous" informality. He dripped with sadness, yet exploded with laughter and anecdote. Among all our Presidents he was one of the most resourceful and eloquent in his use of the English language, yet he often slipped back into the cruder dialect of untutored folk. One could quote him for high eloquence but also for frivolity. He was denounced as a dictator; yet he was the very opposite of the militarist and the supposition that he trampled on civil rights needs to be reëxamined. There were those who from lack of understanding assailed him as a war maker; yet in his inaugural of 1861 he spoke with pathetic earnestness for peace, and in the interview with Mrs. Gurney he said that if he had had his way the war would never have begun. Some writers picture Lincoln as a great strategist or a supreme military genius; others point to incompetence and lack of effective control in military administration as directed from Washington. Instead of being upset by such contradictory elements one learns to reserve judgment, to give the second look, to keep in mind that history is not always reducible to easy generalization, and to remember that, for Lincoln as for every President, the adoption of a "general policy" did not preclude the necessity for many an individual adjustment.

For the most part the bibliography for the first two volumes serves for the present work. Other titles, however, original and secondary, are given in the annotations. Perhaps in general, footnotes should be held guilty unless proved innocent, but in these pages it is hoped they will not obtrude. They indicate sources, and for a treatment that continually calls for the showing of credentials such verification can hardly be ignored. It is believed also that they serve other purposes, but enough! The intent here is not to unloose a disquisition on historical evidence.

It has been considered desirable, in fact indispensable, to give some account of the Lincoln papers opened to investigators in July 1947; this topic has been set off to itself in an appendix. It is not claimed that the importance of that vast collection has been adequately indicated or its unique flavor conveyed; only an extended account of the many thousands of items could serve that purpose. While writing this volume the author has been, as it were, caught between two editions of Lincoln's writings. Previously it has been necessary to rely upon the so-called *Complete Works* of Lincoln edited by Nicolay and Hay (in two large volumes, later in twelve small ones); but as the present book "goes to press" (with all the finality of that dread phrase) the important new edition known as *The Collected Works of Abraham Lincoln,* in preparation for many years under the editorship of the Abraham Lincoln Association, is nearing its day of publication. Because of imperfect editing and great incompleteness, the Nicolay-Hay edition is plainly outmoded, yet the new set is still awaited. In this situation, though some references to Nicolay and Hay are kept, the actual words of Lincoln have been collated with photostats (of originals) in the files of the Abraham Lincoln Association.

Of necessity the author's many acknowledgments must be briefly and inadequately expressed. The University of Illinois has supplied the services of an assistant and has acquired extensive bodies of microfilms and photostats. The rich holdings of its library on the Lincoln theme, built up over many years, have been in constant use. These resources have been greatly enhanced by the generous donation of one of the greatest private Lincoln collections, that of Harlan Hoyt

Horner of Albany, New York.

To the noble profession of librarians a great debt is due. This is especially true of that important national institution, the Library of Congress, not only for the notable Robert Todd Lincoln Collection long kept in faithful custody and opened in 1947, but for a vast amount of other original material on Lincoln and his time. The resources of the National Archives, a voluminous treasure for which guidance and skilled access is essential, have yielded significant results; this has been made possible by the aid, counsel, and serviceableness of its willing staff. The author is also grateful to the Harvard Library, the Massachusetts Historical Society, the Boston Public Library, the New York Public Library, the New York Historical Society, Brown University, the Detroit Public Library, the University of Wisconsin Historical Society. Institutional service, of course, is always human service, as shown by the personal and scholarly contribution of Robert Gerald McMurtry of Harrogate, Tennessee, editor of the *Lincoln Herald* and director of the department of Lincolniana at Lincoln Memorial University. Of special value has been the Lincoln National Life Foundation at Fort Wayne, where elaborate files have been opened and interpreted by the friendly helpfulness of Dr. Louis A. Warren. Closer home, access has been given to the manuscripts of the Chicago Historical Society (including new-found Lincoln letters), the Illinois State Historical Library, and the Abraham Lincoln Association. Only by using that Association's full set of sources (in photostat), the Historical Library's rich collection of Lincoln originals, and similar depositories over the country, can one appreciate how largely Lincoln's own handwritten form for the great bulk of his writing is now available. The competent help of Dr. Roy P. Basler, secretary of the Abraham Lincoln Association and editor of the forthcoming set of Lincoln's works, is sincerely acknowledged while it cannot be fully recorded.

The Pratts—Harry E. Pratt of the Illinois State Historical Library and Mrs. Marion Bonzi Pratt of the Abraham Lincoln Association—stand high among the author's distinguished benefactors by reason of their incomparable knowledge, able guidance, and unstinting service. All who use the Illinois State Historical Library are familiar with the superior service of Miss Margaret Flint; to her a special recognition is due. In the Far West the Lincoln theme has been a matter of active interest and rewarding fellowship. The University of California at Berkeley has given helpful service through its Bancroft Collection, while at San Marino in the Los Angeles area the superb Henry E. Huntington Library seems to have been made for the combination of hard work with thrilling enjoyment. On both of these counts the author has profited by the assistance and understanding advice of the Huntington staff. To mention one member of that staff, Miss Norma Cuthbert, is to call to mind a scholar who has combined a high standard of librarianship with Lincoln authorship in her own right.

Carl Sandburg—that eloquent voice, eminent Lincoln writer, and beloved interpreter of the American spirit—has given encouragement and specific assistance. Indeed, in looking over the pages of this volume the author sees the footprints of friends in every chapter. He wishes herewith to record his indebtedness to Paul M. Angle, Lincoln authority and director of the Chicago Historical Society; to Theodore L. Agnew, Jr. of Stillwater, Oklahoma, for material on that redoubtable but elusive Peter Cartwright; to Miss Margaret C. Norton of the department of archives of the State of Illinois for search in original state documents; to David Rankin Barbee of Washington for the friendly sharing of material; and to that well known figure in the Lincoln fraternity, Ralph G. Newman of the Abraham Lincoln Book Shop in Chicago, whose establishment is a mecca for Lincoln devotees and who has been especially thoughtful in offering material and giving suggestions from his skilled experience. Writers often depend on collectors and in this sense as well as in friendship the author makes special acknowledgment to Alfred W. Stern, Foreman M. Lebold, and the late Oliver R. Barrett of Chicago. The important Barrett Collection, recently sold at auction in New York, is fortunately not lost to students; institutions have much of it and private collectors are usually generous with photostats. The Lincoln field is fortunately not a closed corporation.

For further response and assistance the author is grateful to S. L. M. Barlow of New York City; to Allan Nevins, editor of the series, *American Political Leaders;* to Frank Freidel of the University of Illinois, authority on Lieber; to Miss Marie K. Hochmuth of the department of speech of the University of Illinois for her penetrating study of Lincoln's 1861 inaugural; to George Winston Smith of the University of New Mexico, author of highly useful articles; and to that friend of Lincoln students in search of pictures, Frederick H. Meserve. Southerners also have helped, and the assistance of Mr. William H. Townsend of Lexington, Kentucky, has been a source of real delight. David Donald of Columbia University, in critically reading many galleys of proof, performed an invaluable service of friendship and of scholarship.

In preparing the typed manuscript Miss Lida E. Voight has given excellent service. Several graduate students of the University of Illinois have assisted in the heavy duty of research and checking. The vigorous work of some of these young colleagues has been cited in earlier volumes; more recently the author has been greatly benefited by the indispensable support of Maurice G. Baxter now of Indiana University, Lavern M. Hamand of Arkansas Polytechnic College (Russellville), and Wayne C. Temple, now pursuing his work for the doctor's degree at the University of Illinois. Each of these men, on his own, has made significant contributions in the Lincoln field. For example, the colorful personality and career of Noah Brooks is being ably studied for a doctoral dissertation by Mr. Temple. The author is especially grateful to Mrs. Helen Metz of Elmwood, Illinois, for the superior quality of her assistance in preparing the index.

The author's wife, Ruth Painter Randall, after years of research and with newly used material, has completed a life of Mrs. Lincoln which is soon to be published. Since it is the history of a marriage—a double biography—it is valuable for an understanding of the man as well as of the wife. Her book deals fully with the personal life of Lincoln. The writing of this competent biography during the period when the present third volume has been in preparation, has been of great advantage.

J. G. R.

Urbana, Illinois
May 31, 1952

CONTENTS

PART ONE: MIDSTREAM

PART TWO: LAST FULL MEASURE

ILLUSTRATIONS AND MAPS

PART ONE

PART TWO

LINCOLN THE PRESIDENT

MIDSTREAM

CHAPTER I

PRESIDENTIAL DAYS

THE year 1863 was a tremendous period for Lincoln. That was the year of the emancipation proclamation, of the first nationwide draft, of draft riots, of Missouri troubles, of Copperhead turbulence, of Vallandigham agitation, of important international dealings, and of hard military campaigns in which the nation's fate was wavering. One needs only to mention Chancellorsville, Gettysburg, Vicksburg, Chattanooga, Chickamauga, and Missionary Ridge to realize how desperate was the growing contest on the war fronts, while mention of the Laird rams, of Napoleon III, and of Maximilian will serve to suggest the complications that arose in foreign fields.

At home it was, to an intense degree, a year of "politics." Politics was never adjourned during the whole war—though the loyal-opposition policy of Douglas would have been a factor toward such adjournment—and the year 1863 witnessed sharp and bitter contests in state and congressional elections which were of vital concern to the Lincoln administration. Finally, as the turbulent middle year drew to a close, the statesmanship of Lincoln rose vigorously to the greatest challenge of his age as he delivered his immortal Gettysburg address and turned from that, amid illness and critical fighting, to one of the most famous of his messages—the annual message to Congress of December 1863. In that message and in a simultaneous proclamation to the people, the President gave the outline of his formula for restoration. With more foresight than that of Congress he put forth a program of peace and genuine union without which the "honored dead" would have "died in vain" and the fearful conflict would have been meaningless. The whole crowded year could have been epitomized in Lincoln's phrase "environed with difficulties."

Fully to recover the inner story and over-all significance of the Lincoln administration is impossible, since the upheavals and emotions of that age, with their complexities and simultaneous manifestations, are beyond recall. To understand any one of Lincoln's major problems in its intensity and entirety was not even within the reach of his contemporaries. To get a merely approximate view of such things now is a large order. It may be for this reason that Lincoln is often cast in less than his full mold. It is not that the task of historical restoration can be completely performed, yet the effort for some restoration must be made.

It is in that sense that we shall try to see Lincoln struggling with his problems, adjusting his difficulties, reaching for solutions, watching a number of fronts at one time, and always keeping his eye on the main goal. The present volume will be concerned with this midstream phase, though with the necessity of omitting many factors in so complex a story. It may be well to begin with some of the things close at hand, to note the routine of presidential days, and to catch a glimpse of duties which the President could not evade.

I

Among the stories that have come down to us is that of Lincoln's remark when a friend from back home asked him "How does it feel to be President of the United States?" In reply, so the story goes, he referred to a man who was tarred and feathered and ridden out of town on a rail. When some one in the crowd asked how he enjoyed it, the tarred-and-feathered one answered: "If it were not for the honor of the thing, I'd much rather walk." The story might be apocryphal, but the point of the yarn is our present concern. There is hardly any country in which the highest office has such a dazzling preeminence as that of President of the United States. To those who seek the honor it is the supreme goal. What of those who attain it? It is not of record that Washington enjoyed the position, which brought him a world of grief and kept him away from his beloved Mount Vernon.

What of Lincoln? Was he exalted and elated by the fame and prestige of his great office? There is little record of any such feeling. He suffered unmerciful and unending abuse, much of it from his own party. At one time, as already noted, he said while President that he was more distressed than at any time in his life.[1] He is reported to have looked forward happily to the day when the burdens of office could be laid down. At times he might actually have wished to relinquish the position before his term expired, except for one factor: no man of character wants to be a quitter when he has a great task to perform. The realization that he must not fall short, must not fail the country or shirk responsibility, was always more of a motive with Lincoln than any personal pleasure in the holding of high office.

When he went to Gettysburg in November 1863 he was put on the program as an afterthought. The initial idea had been to emphasize the states, not the nation. There was little of presidential fanfare; indeed there was actual insult to Lincoln on the part of a heckler in a street audience. The orator of the day was the polished Everett. The President was invited after Everett. His convenience was but incidental, if it was considered at all. It was as if he were playing second fiddle, and it was unforeseen that his presence and his distinguished words would have great significance.[2] In making the trip to Gettysburg he had inadequate secretarial assistance, even in the scheduling of the journey. Stanton proposed that the President leave Washington at six o'clock of the day of dedication, travel laboriously via Baltimore, reach Gettysburg at noon, leave Gettysburg at six in the evening, and arrive at Washington at midnight, "thus doing all in one day."

Lincoln objected. He wrote: "I do not wish to so go that by the slightest accident we fail entirely, and, at the best, the whole to be a mere breathless running of the gauntlet."[3] The plan was accordingly changed and the presidential party arrived at Gettysburg the day before the ceremony. He gave his famous dedicatory speech to an audience tired by much standing and prolonged oratory. There was something in the occasion, or in his own sense of inadequacy, that gave him a feeling of depression and disappointment, as if he had not risen to the demands of the hour.

---

1 *Lincoln the President,* II, 243.

2 In the first annual report of the organization which promoted the Gettysburg dedication, signed by David Wills, Governor Curtin is emphasized and Everett featured as the orator, but Lincoln is not even mentioned.

3 Lincoln's endorsement on note of Stanton, Nov. 17, 1863, Nicolay and Hay, *Works,* IX, 208.

Not long after returning from Gettysburg to Washington he became ill. The disease was reported as varioloid, a mild form of smallpox. The illness came at the Thanksgiving season, and at a time when the President was heavily engaged in preparing his important annual message to Congress with its accompanying proclamation.[4] People wondered about the disease, about which they were not well informed, and whether the President could die of it. There had been, as Stoddard later explained, slight thought of the President's health. Assassination fears were so familiar as to be "worn out," but another possible cause of death had hardly been contemplated. The White House was under a kind of half-quarantine, resulting not only in an unwonted loneliness, but in public apprehension. It was feared that Hamlin "could not step into Mr. Lincoln's shoes, and something of inestimable value would be lost to the country, even if Mr. Hamlin were twice as large a man as he is believed to be." It was characteristic of the clamor for office and public favors that "something like engineering" was required to protect the sick President from intruders. One of them, thought Stoddard, may have been thinking that "Lincoln could appoint him to-day and die to-morrow." The President continued to attend to official business in spite of his irritating illness. He even made it a subject of jest, suggesting the advantage of scaring office seekers by the statement that he had the smallpox, and wishing that his office might be in one of the smallpox hospitals, then reflecting on further thought that this would give him no relief. "They'd all go and get vaccinated, and they'd come buzzing back . . . ."[5]

---

[4] There are numerous records of Lincoln's illness. He explained to a governor why a response had been delayed, and reassured Mrs. Lincoln by daily telegrams while she was in New York (*Works*, IX, 216–217, 254). Various diarists mentioned the illness: "The President quite unwell" (Hay, Nov. 26); "The President has been sick ever since thursday" (Bates, Monday, Nov. 30); "The President returned ill [from Gettysburg], and . . . it was ascertained he had the varioloid" (Welles, Dec., 1863, otherwise undated). Account is taken of the sickness in the Lincoln Papers (R. T. L. Coll., 28719) and in newspapers of the day (*Nat. Repub'n*, Nov. 28; Cincinnati *Daily Gazette*, Nov. 30; N.Y. *Daily Tribune*, Dec. 2 and 10). Dr. Milton H. Shutes writes: "Lincoln became ill on the train leaving Gettysburg, so it is known that he was sick from the very day of the ceremony, November 19, until about the middle of December. . . . Varioloid is a mild form of smallpox acquired by the partially immune, ..." *Lincoln and the Doctors*, 85.

[5] Stoddard, *Inside the White House*, 190–192.

II

Any day's run at the White House was crowded, tiring, and strenuous. According to Ben: Perley Poore,[1] the President was an early riser. In the morning he would devote two or three hours to correspondence, with a glance at the newspapers. He would have breakfast about nine, then walk over to the war department building, a few steps from the White House. Returning to the White House, he would go through the morning's mail with his private secretaries.[2] The preliminary screening of the mail, and the discarding of crank missives, was the function of W. O. Stoddard.[3] Some of the letters would be endorsed and sent to the appropriate department. Others were entrusted to a secretary who would make a note of Lincoln's suggestions for a reply. Still others would be retained by the President to be answered by himself. Nicolay and Hay were important and efficient helpers, but it is no disparagement of their valuable assistance to say, what is not fully realized, that Lincoln gave close and careful attention to his correspondence. He often wrote a letter twice (the first draft and the final copy) in his own hand, and was even known to draft entirely in his handwriting a letter to be issued over Hay's name.[4] "Every letter," wrote Poore, "receives attention"; he added that all that were "entitled to a reply" received one, "no matter . . . how inelegant the chirography might be." [5]

Letter writing over, the rest of the day would be taken up with manifold activities—social, official, ceremonial, often trivial, and al-

1 Poore's account is in Cincinnati *Daily Gazette,* Dec. 12, 1863, p. 1, c. 4.

2 For Nicolay's duties as secretary, see Helen Nicolay, *Lincoln's Secretary,* esp. chap. 7.

3 "There was a river of documents . . . . The larger number of the epistles belonged in one or another of the two tall wastebaskets which sat on either side of me . . . . It did seem to me as if the foulest blackguards on earth had made up their minds that they could abuse the President through the mails . . . . Added to these were the lunatics." "Face to Face With Lincoln," by his secretary, William O. Stoddard, ed. by William O. Stoddard, Jr., 135 *Atl. Mo.,* 333 (Mar., 1925).

4 A letter signed by John Hay and directed to J. C. Welling (July 25, 1864) was written by Lincoln himself. A draft of the letter in full is found in the Lincoln Papers, entirely in the President's handwriting. *Works,* X, 173–174; R. T. L. Coll., 34756. The matter in hand pertained to the hostile attitude of a certain Mr. Gibson. It was a difficult personal situation in which the President watched closely the wording of the letter that went out from the executive office, though he preferred that it be sent as a communication from his secretary. This is almost like ghost writing in reverse.

5 Cincinnati *Daily Gazette,* Dec. 12, 1863, p. 1, c. 4.

ways time consuming. About four o'clock the President would decline seeing any more callers. He and Mrs. Lincoln would then go for a drive, or sometimes he would ride horseback. Dining at six, he was usually joined by personal friends. His visits to the war office were for a variety of purposes: chatting with a general (often Halleck), reading the military telegrams as they came over the wires (though of course these messages could have been brought to him), hearing what was new so that he could tell it, exchanging funny stories, enjoying the peculiar argot of the telegraph office, holding informal conferences, escaping White House crowds, and seeking a retreat to avoid interruption when composing an important state paper. The vivid account by David Homer Bates indicates that Lincoln found enjoyment in these war department intervals. "His tall, homely form," wrote Bates, "could be seen crossing the well-shaded lawn between the White House and the War Department day after day with unvaried regularity. . . . He seldom failed to come over late in the evening before retiring, and sometimes would stay all night in the War Department." [6] "Three or four times daily," wrote Gideon Welles, "the President goes to the War Department and into the telegraph office to look over communications." [7] It was natural for Welles to feel that he had less of a share in the President's daily attention than was due to a member of the cabinet and the head of the navy department.

The war-department retreat was even referred to by Lincoln as his "office." In a telegram on an October day in 1864 he wired former Secretary of War Cameron: "Am leaving office to go home." The telegram was dated: "War Department, October 11, 1864." It implied a distinction between the "office" in the war and navy building and "home," which meant the White House.[8]

Lincoln's self-forgetfulness and his informal intimacy with private secretaries sometimes made an amusing picture. In his diary of April 30, 1864, Hay noted: "A little after midnight . . . the President came into the office laughing, with a volume of Hood's works in his hand, to show Nico[lay] and me the little caricature 'An unfortunate Bee-ing,' seemingly utterly unconscious that he with his short shirt

---

[6] David Homer Bates, *Lincoln in the Telegraph Office*, 7.

[7] Welles, *Diary*, II, 16.

[8] Lincoln to Cameron, Oct. 11, 1864, photograph, A. Lincoln Assoc.

hanging above his long legs & setting out behind like the tail feathers of an enormous ostrich was infinitely funnier than anything in the book he was laughing at. What a man it is! Occupied all day with matters of vast moment, deeply anxious about the fate of the greatest army in the world, with his own fame & future hanging on the events of the passing hour, he has such a wealth of simple bonhommie & good fellowship that he gets out of bed & perambulates the house in his shirt to find us that we may share with him the fun of one of poor Hood's queer little conceits." [9]

A glimpse of a harassed Executive unable to escape interruption even after going to bed appears in the following diary entry by Hay (November 2, 1863): "Tonight Schenck sent for copies of the correspondence between the President and Bradford. The Tycoon came into his room with the despatch in his hands, clad in an overcoat pure & simple reaching to his knees, & sleepily fumbled for the papers in his desk till he found them & travelled back to bed. I took the letters to the telegraph office & sent them off about midnight." [10]

III

When the President went about he did not want body guards to accompany him, and there was in that day no regular force of secret service men comparable to that of a later day. Once he wrote to Secretary Stanton: "On reflection I think it will not do as a rule for the Adjutant General to attend me wherever I go: not that I have any objection to his presence, but that it would be an uncompensating incumbrance both to him and me. When it shall occur to me to go anywhere, I wish to be free to go at once, and not to have to notify the Adjutant General, and wait till he can get ready." Lincoln added: "It is better too, for the public service, that he shall give his time to the business of his office, and not to personal attendance on me." The correspondence indicates that the suggestion had come

---

[9] Tyler Dennett, ed., *Lincoln and the Civil War in the Diaries and Letters of John Hay,* 179 (Apr. 30, 1864). Hereafter cited: Dennett, ed., . . . *Diaries* . . . *of John Hay.*

[10] *Ibid.,* 115. The correspondence with A. W. Bradford, governor of Maryland, concerned the state-and-Federal problem of giving protection to loyal men at the polls when voting for state officers. Major General Robert C. Schenck was in command in Maryland. *Works,* IX, 196–198 (Nov. 2, 1863).

from the secretary of war; one wonders, not at the proposal for guarding the President, but at Stanton's impractical suggestion that the adjutant general should be the official assigned to that duty.[1]

It is not to be supposed that Lincoln was altogether unprotected or that the problem of his bodily safety was ignored. It was rather that the guarding of the President was irregular, haphazard, and inefficient, and that perhaps he preferred it so. This caused considerable worry, as shown by the advice of an anxious soul, who wrote: "You are accustomed in riding out, to be escorted by a Body guard, and you invariably take a distance ahead; and generally any number of persons follow you, either in Vehicles, or Horseback, and your habit is, to frequently ride out to your Summer retreat Soldiers Home . . . . I cannot help, but warn you. If you value your life! *do* I entreat of you discontinue your visits out of the City. Unless, less conspicuously." [2]

If this anonymous writer was concerned about the President's safety, what about his wife? It was a constant and painful worry to Mrs. Lincoln. She would insist that he have some protection—a cavalry guard, for example—as he went back and forth to or from the Soldiers' Home. (It appears that such protection was occasional rather than regular or invariable.) He would brush her off, though far from relieving her fears. "All imagination," he was quoted as saying. "What does any one want to harm me for? Don't worry about me, mother, as if I were a little child, ..." [3]

Along with his strong distaste for being escorted or guarded, Lincoln paid little attention to fears of assassination. Since there were "a thousand ways" of getting at him, he believed that guards could not effectively ward off the danger; if anyone wanted to kill him, he would do it. (Not a comforting principle for those genuinely concerned for his safety.) Early in the administration General Charles P. Stone, by his own report, took careful, though unostentatious, measures for the guarding of the Executive Mansion and grounds.

---

1 Lincoln to Sec. of War, Jan. 22, 1862, copy, photostat, A. Lincoln Assoc. This questionable suggestion was one of the very first acts of Stanton on assuming the headship of the war department.

2 The name of this writer, who was otherwise anonymous, was signed "Lizzie." Robert Todd Lincoln Collection, Lib. of Cong., 34900-01 (July 1864). This great collection of the papers of Lincoln will hereafter be given the short citation: R. T. L. Coll.

3 Elizabeth Keckley, *Behind the Scenes,* 119.

He placed sentries in the shrubbery, put an armed guard in the basement, and put this guard in touch with Captain Lockwood Todd, cousin of Mrs. Lincoln. In addition to these precautions, service in guarding the President was done by a considerable number of alert volunteers, among whom were Cassius M. Clay and Jim (General James H.) Lane. These men, for a brief time, did nightly guard in the East Room. Part of the earlier arrangements included a cavalry guard at the White House gates, but Lincoln got rid of it. Sometimes he rode to and from the Soldiers' Home with a mounted escort. Frequently, however, he went about, even at night, "unguarded, and often alone, in his open carriage." [4]

There were incidents when the danger to the President's life was shown to be real enough. In April 1862, on his return from the Navy Yard, there was a minor accident in which horses drawing the President's carriage became unmanageable, creating alarm and compelling a change of carriage. Lincoln was unhurt. One August night, as the record has come down to us, a shot was fired as the President, riding horseback alone, approached the Soldiers' Home. A startled horse, we are told, tore into the grounds bearing a hatless President. A guard, on investigation, found the Chief's tall silk hat with a "*bullet-hole* through the crown." [5]

According to the recollection of Ward Lamon, this incident was told by Lincoln himself, but with an air of playful levity and without any apprehension that it involved danger to himself. He made it an amusing joke as he told how his horse, "Old Abe," his "erratic namesake," made a reckless bound and, as he put it, "separated me from my eight-dollar plug-hat, with which I parted company without . . . assent . . . ." The President seemed unwilling to attach any importance to the affair. He concluded that the shot "was the result of an accident." Dismissing that aspect of the matter, he went on to compare Old Abe's performance with the "historic ride of John Gilpin, and [Senator] Henry Wilson's . . . equestrianship on the stray army mule from the . . . battle of Bull Run." In the delayed Lamon version we have Lincoln's further comment: "I can truthfully say that one of the Abes was frightened on this occasion, but modesty forbids my mentioning which of us is entitled to that

[4] Francis F. Browne, *Every-Day Life of Abraham Lincoln,* 310.
[5] *Ibid.,* quoting a body-guard, John W. Nichols, 541–542.

distinguished honor." The President went on to make it clear that he wanted no publicity given to the event. It seemed to Lamon that the Chief Executive sometimes "acted an unnatural part" in order to forget the agonizing loss of his son Willie.[6]

When in February 1865 certain Union officers were captured by a guerrilla band at Cumberland, Maryland, Thomas Ewing wrote to Stanton: "I am surprised that it was not the President and yourself [that were captured] in Washington. The President could be seized any reception evening, in the midst of the masses assembled round him, and carried off by fifty determined men armed with bowie knives and revolvers, and once out could be put into a market wagon guarded by a dozen horsemen, and borne off at will,—the conspirators having first set a dozen or twenty hacks in motion to distract attention —look out for some such dash soon." [7]

It is known that at about this time the Booth plan to kidnap Lincoln was actually being plotted and the date set, though not so elaborately as the Ewing letter would suggest. Another expression of uneasiness, very close to the time of the assassination, came from a correspondent of Ward H. Lamon. On April 4, 1865, W. H. Hanna of Bloomington, Illinois, wrote: "I hope the President will keep out of danger, . . . Mr. Lincoln's personal safety is of such vast importance to the country . . . that his friends feel more or less solicitous when they read of his 'going to the front.' But he has made a glorious trip this time." [8]

IV

In what would now be called "off the cuff" speaking Lincoln showed restraint and reluctance. He disliked commonplace utterance in public; if he spoke at all, he wanted his words to be effective and

[6] Dorothy Lamon Teillard, ed., *Recollections of Abraham Lincoln, 1847–1865, by Ward Hill Lamon,* 266–269. In the Lamon account the date of this startling incident seems to be August 1862; in the Browne-Nichols account (see preceding note) it is given as August 1864. Lamon had a special responsibility for guarding the President, but he was not present at the Soldiers' Home. In addition to the difference as to date, the Lamon account makes no mention of the bullet hole in the hat. Yet there is similarity in the two accounts.

[7] Thomas Ewing to Stanton, Feb. 22, 1865, Ewing MSS., Lib. of Cong.

[8] W. H. Hanna to Ward H. Lamon, Bloomington, Ill., April 4, 1865, Lamon MSS., Huntington Lib.

not too repetitious. On one occasion, being taken by surprise at a serenade, he asked Fenton of New York to precede him and give him "a peg to hang on." Achieving a "peculiarly quaint" remark which "raised a good laugh," he considered it a happy exit line and withdrew.[1]

When in May 1862 he spoke to the soldiers of the Twelfth Indiana Regiment, he began by saying, "It has not been customary heretofore, nor will it be hereafter, for me to say something to every regiment passing in review. It occurs too frequently for me to have speeches ready on all occasions." After thanking the men for their satisfaction as to his own performance "in the difficulties which have surrounded the nation," he added that it was the soldiers who were more to be thanked. The nation, he said, "is more indebted to you, and such as you, than to me. It is upon the brave hearts and strong arms of the people of the country that our reliance has been placed in support of free government and free institutions." [2]

The speech just mentioned included all fighting men while showing special recognition to those who faced him; for the boys who thus heard and saw their President it was an incident to remember, a high spot in their war experience. Again in late October 1864 Lincoln favored a regiment with a speech. Addressing the 189th New York, and not forgetting that he was speaking just prior to a presidential election, he praised the soldiers for sustaining his administration, recognizing that they had "not only fought right," but "voted right." [3]

There could be no neglecting, or dodging, of serenades. They could happen when least expected, but they could certainly be expected because of an outstanding or notable event. When told that a serenade "was coming" just after the emancipation proclamation of September 1862, and asked if he "would make any remarks,"

---

1 "It was just when General Sherman was *en route* from Atlanta to the sea, and we had no definite news as to his safety or whereabouts. After one or two sentences, rather commonplace, the President . . . said he had no war news other than was known to all . . . ; that 'we all knew where Sherman went in, but none of us knew where he would come out.' This last remark was in the peculiarly quaint, happy manner of Mr. Lincoln, and created great applause." (In print the remark seems quite ordinary; there must have been something in the President's look or manner that produced the audience response.) R. E. Fenton, in Rice, *Reminiscences of Abraham Lincoln,* 71.

2 Speech to Twelfth Indiana Regiment, New York *Evening Post,* May 15, 1862.

3 New York *Times,* Oct. 25, 1864, p. 1, c. 5.

Lincoln said "No"; yet he did say a few words. Referring to himself as "environed with difficulties," and avoiding any comment in support of his proclamation, he shifted the emphasis, and the glory, from himself and his administration to "those who, upon the battle field, are endeavoring to purchase with their blood and their lives the future happiness and prosperity of this country." Speaking at a time of military deliverance (just after South Mountain and Antietam), he mentioned "battles bravely, skillfully and successfully fought" and called for three cheers for the "brave officers and men who fought those successful battles." [4]

This call for cheers, seemingly a little thing, gave the President a graceful cue to bow out. It fitted perfectly the mood of the crowd, which was in "glorious humor" [5] that night, serenading and demanding speeches not only from Lincoln, but also from Secretary Chase, Cassius M. Clay, and Attorney General Bates.

On the whole Lincoln did not perform badly in response to serenades. "The speeches of the President at the last two serenades," wrote Hay in November 1864, "are very highly spoken of." [6] There were times when some of his most quotable and epigrammatic phrases were delivered in such offhand speeches, though they presented unusual difficulties, not only as to preparation and delivery, but also as to reporting in the papers. A serenade response by Seward was "horribly butchered" in the *Chronicle,* and in order to avert a similar fate Hay wrote out one of Lincoln's night speeches "after the fact" (it was Lincoln's; Hay watched the reporting of it), while for the next serenade the President carefully wrote his words in advance and read them from manuscript.[7]

V

How did the lanky President look on horseback? Very well, according to Nicolay; awkward and careless, according to others. When a "grand review" of the army was held near Washington on Novem-

---

4 Reply to serenade, Sep. 24, 1862, New York *Tribune,* Sep. 25, 1862.

5 On this occasion of the post-Antietam serenade, Hay thought the President's "half a dozen words" were said "with great grace and dignity." Dennett, ed., . . . *Diaries . . . of John Hay,* 50.

6 *Ibid,* 239.

7 *Ibid.,* 238–239; Nicolay and Hay, *Works,* X, 261–265 (Nov. 9 and Nov. 10, 1864).

ber 20, 1861, with fifty thousand men in line, the President rode out in his carriage, then mounted his horse. "Seward I think," wrote Nicolay, "remained in his carriage." The occasion was something of an endurance test, Cameron giving out and dismounting midway in the performance, "while the President went through the whole without the least symptom of fatigue." He rode up and down before the standing troops; then he and the officers took their stand on an acclivity while the soldiers marched past. "Hay and I," wrote Nicolay, "started home near sundown and the columns had not yet finished passing." "The President," he noted, "rode erect and firm in his saddle as a practised trooper—he is more graceful in his saddle than anywhere else I have seen him." [1]

In contradiction of this—a minor example of the contradictions that run all through the Lincoln subject—we have a critical and ludicrous (indirect) account of Lincoln's technique when reviewing troops. A gentleman wrote from Wall Street, New York, to admonish the President as to "the receiving of military citizens (as all the volunteers are)." He thought it was a serious matter whether the Chief Executive pleased them or not; "soldiers write home to their friends in this town with reference to their disappointment in your bearing and manners when reviewing them—"

They say [he continued] when you are on horseback, and platoons of men marching by you, that you lean about and turn your head to talk with people behind you, when they claim that you should sit erect & talk to nobody and look straight at the saluting soldiers—that you ought to assume some dignity for the occasion even though your breeding has not been military— It makes but little difference whether the demand is reasonable or not—it dont require half so much sacrifice on your part, to rectify it as it does of the men to go from their homes for the hardship they undertake—

And when you are passing lines of soldiers, reviewing them, afoot, they say you take your boys along, and straddle off as if you were cutting across lots, to get somewhere in the quickest time you can, and pay a good deal more attention to your own getting along, than to the soldiers whom you start out to review—

These things dont sound well at all— The influence is bad here— The complaint may be frivolous and based on a mistake: but such things are written home here and fortify Raymond in his position of advertising for

---

1 MS., Ill. State Hist. Lib., published in Pratt, *Concerning Mr. Lincoln*, 89–90. See also Nicolay and Hay, *Lincoln*, IV, 469.

a "Leader"— He has got over that, rather, but there is no need of your being so infernally awkward, if these things are true— For God's sake consult somebody, some military man, as to what you ought to do on these occasions in military presence— Nobody will volunteer advice, probably, and if you are arbitrary and conceited on these little things, as Webster used to be, you will alienate your friends and go where he went and John Tyler too, towit where a man has no party—I dont mean a political party, but a great and universal body guard of men who speak well of you and will do anything to bear aloft and above reproach your administration—

The gentleman informed the President that the people cared "a mighty sight" about their soldiers. Even an autocrat would have to give attention to army evolutions and to let the soldiers know that, in reviewing them, he appreciated the business in hand. He would have the President know that his manner was as important as his talk. A lawyer in his office could rest his feet on a table, but not the Commander in Chief of the Armies of the United States. He must "pretend" to be a soldier even if his knowledge was deficient. The letter continued:

You had better let some officer put you through a few dress parades in your leisure moments, if you can get any, and get some military habit on you so you shall feel natural among military men— Dont let people call you a goose on these *very, very* important relations to the Army—

Mrs Lincoln is growing popular all the while, because people say she is mistress of her situation— She aptly fits herself to the times— The dinner service she bought at Houghout's makes people think she is "in town"—they like to talk about her and say she has a good deal of sense and womanly wit about her—she is coming into excellent reputation in this naturally prejudiced city against you and her both—

My impression is that you will do well by paying more attention to your manners and make less effort at wit and story telling— All well enough in private but publicly it is a nuisance— Your talent is conceded—be a gentleman and courtly in your manners when you ought to be— Now I dont care whether you take this well or ill— I voted for you and have a desire to be proud of your administration and I dont wish to see you over slaughed by these damaging stories when you could prevent it so easily—[2]

Walt Whitman, who saw Lincoln frequently in Washington days, thought that the President and his cavalry guard, with sabres drawn, made "no great show in uniforms or horses." Whitman lived on the

[2] Robert Colby to Lincoln, 47 Wall Street, New York, May 18, 1861, R. T. L. Coll., 9943–9949.

MRS. LINCOLN

As to the Lincolns being a loving and thoroughly devoted couple there can be no doubt on the part of those who know their story.

LINCOLN FAMILY

Upper left: Mrs. Lincoln. (Courtesy of Lincoln National Life Foundation.)
Upper right: Robert Todd Lincoln. (Brady photograph, National Archives.)
Center: Lincoln with Tad. (Brady photograph, National Archives.)
Lower left: Willie (William Wallace Lincoln). (Meserve Collection.)
Lower right: Tad (Thomas Lincoln). (Brady photograph, National Archives.)

route the President took to and from the Soldiers' Home. "Mr. Lincoln," he wrote, "on the saddle, generally rides a good-sized, easy-going gray horse, is dressed in plain black, somewhat rusty and dusty; wears a black stiff hat, and looks about as ordinary . . . as the commonest man. . . . Sometimes one of his sons, a boy of ten or twelve [Tad was ten in 1863], accompanies him, riding at his right on a pony." [8]

VI

Combining his function as ceremonial head of state with that of responsibly active Chief Executive, Lincoln found increasingly heavy demands on his time. Visiting the Navy Yard, he "personally and minutely inspected" its foundries and workshops where six hundred men were employed.[1] One night at the observatory he "took a look at the moon & Arcturus." [2] Pausing at the Capitol on one of his rides, he viewed the newly placed statuary of the east pediment. This evoked a bit of presidential art criticism; he "objected to Powers's statue of the Woodchopper, as he did not make a sufficiently clean cut." [3] Fairs sought him out for a speech, a personal visit, a gift, or a written statement. The president of the Sanitary Commission, returning from California, brought and personally handed him "a present of great beauty and value from a few citizens of that state"—a gold box bearing the letters "A L" and containing "a number of singularly beautiful golden crystals . . . embedded in fine velvet." [4]

Another "interesting ceremony . . . at the White House" was the "presentation to President Lincoln of a truly beautiful and superb vase of skeleton leaves, gathered from the battlefield of Gettysburg." They had been gathered by the ladies of the Philadelphia Sanitary Fair, at which over a million dollars had been raised for soldier welfare. Gettysburg was an exalted theme; tribute to the nation's defenders at Bloody Angle had already been paid. The speaker of the Gettysburg address was now called upon to sound the same note; and that, shortly after the death of Edward Everett. It was one more among countless demands upon the President's time and energy, but

[8] Rice, *Reminiscences,* 469–470.
[1] Washington *Daily Chronicle,* Apr. 7, 1861, p. 3, c. 6.
[2] Dennett, ed., . . . *Diaries* . . . *of John Hay,* 82.
[3] *Ibid.,* 79.
[4] Washington *Daily Chronicle,* Oct. 29, 1864, p. 2, c. 6.

the occasion could not be passed off lightly. Though the event was reported as "wholly unexpected," Lincoln responded with a speech. It was like being asked to paint the lily. "So much," wrote Lincoln, "has been said about Gettysburg, and so well said, that for me to attempt to say more may, perhaps, only serve to weaken the force of that which has already been said." Lincoln did not paint the lily. He acknowledged the gift "with emotions of profoundest gratitude," referred handsomely to the departed Everett, paid appropriate tribute to the women of America, and gave assurance that the "kind wishes" extended to him were sincerely reciprocated.[5]

Personal tragedies of the war were repeatedly brought home to the President in the funerals at which his attendance was required. A service for Col. Elmer E. Ellsworth, shot down in Alexandria early in the war, was held in the White House, May 26, 1861. Known to the nation as the dashing commander of a volunteer regiment of zouaves, and as the first striking example of a martyr to the Union cause, he was further known to Lincoln as a youth of zest and gusto who had studied law in the Springfield office, had participated in the 1860 presidential campaign, and had accompanied the President Elect on his trip to Washington. Lincoln was present at the rites for General Amiel W. Whipple who fell in battle at Chancellorsville, in May 1863, and at the ceremony for fifteen victims of an accident at the arsenal grounds in June 1864. On the latter occasion it was estimated that 25,000 people attended, coming by boat and every type of conveyance. When it was found in January 1864 that Lincoln could not attend the funeral of John Hughes, Catholic archbishop of New York, a letter was sent in the President's behalf by Secretary Seward in which the distinguished prelate's national service was acknowledged and tribute was paid to his loyalty, fidelity, and practical wisdom.[6]

At times the President would honor an occasion by being part of

[5] Reply to a committee, Washington *Daily Chronicle,* Jan. 25, 1865. Everett had died on January 15; Lincoln's reply was on January 24.

[6] A letter was sent by Seward on Lincoln's behalf. After expressing regret for inability to attend the funeral of the archbisnop, Seward continued: "The President formed the acquaintance of the Archbishop in the earlier period of our national troubles, and highly appreciated his counsels and advice. At a conjunction of deep interest the Archbishop went abroad and did the nation a service there, with all the loyalty, fidelity, and practical wisdom which, on so many other occasions, illustrated his great ability for administration." Washington *Daily Morning Chronicle,* Jan. 21, 1864, p. 2, c. 2.

an audience. He attended the lecture on the battle of Gettysburg delivered by Dr. J. R. Warner in May 1864 in the hall of the House of Representatives,[7] and was present in the same hall when Anna E. Dickinson, abolitionist girl orator, spoke for the benefit of the Freedmen's Aid Association.[8] His attendance was duly announced to stimulate the sale of tickets. He also attended when Bayard Taylor, in December 1863, delivered his lecture on "the geographical, social, political and economic history of Russia." [9] On the numerous occasions when the President's attendance was requested but had to be declined, the declination required a letter from himself or a secretary; at times such a communication took on the nature of a state paper.

Despite constant demands in Washington Lincoln was to a considerable extent a traveling President. Besides the well known speaking occasions at Gettysburg and Baltimore, the record of his presidential travels, if compiled, would include an expedition to Norfolk and Fort Monroe (May 1862), where he actually took a hand in directing operations,[10] various trips through Hampton Roads and up the James, the famous conference at Hampton Roads, a hurried visit to West Point to consult General Winfield Scott, a visit by boat to Mount Vernon, excursions on the Potomac, a trip to Point Lookout, many visits to soldier camps and to the headquarters of McDowell, McClellan, Hooker, Meade, and Grant, and notable visits late in the war to City Point and Richmond. Sometimes he would take Tad with him, sometimes Mrs. Lincoln, or one of his private secretaries, or Ward Lamon, or Noah Brooks. Where a cabinet secretary accompanied the President, it would usually be Seward or Stanton, or less frequently Bates or Chase.

Of his visits to the army one of the most extended and noteworthy was that of April 4–10, 1863, when he combined recreation and duty by spending six whole days at Hooker's headquarters for the Army of the Potomac at Falmouth, Virginia. In the party were the President, Mrs. Lincoln, their beloved Tad, Dr. A. G. Henry, Noah

---

[7] Rev. J. R. Warner of Gettysburg delivered his lecture on the battle of Gettysburg in the hall of the House of Representatives on May 18, 1864. "President Lincoln and many other distinguished gentlemen . . . were present." *Nat. Intelligencer,* May 21, 1864, p. 3, c. 4.

[8] James Harvey Young, *Anna Elizabeth Dickinson and the Civil War* (abstract of doctoral dissertation, Univ. of Illinois, 1941), 6.

[9] Washington *Daily Chronicle,* Dec. 19, 1863.

[10] *Lincoln the President,* II, 78–80.

Brooks, a Mr. Crawford, and Attorney General Bates. There were several reviews, in grand style, of what was considered the finest and biggest army in the world. Henry was very sure that the nation had the right man (Hooker) and that he would promptly "take his army into Richmond" and "to New Orleans if necessary." It was reported that 15,000 well mounted cavalry, 300 pieces of field artillery, and "about 150,000 of the finest looking, & best disciplined Infantry . . . ever seen in one Army" passed before the reviewing President, whose visit would "add intensity to their zeal and confidence." [11]

Noah Brooks's pen added color to the spectacle. The President wore a high hat and rode "like a veteran." Tad rode with the cavalry in charge of a mounted orderly, "his gray cloak flying in the gusty wind like the plume of Henry of Navarre." "It was a grand sight to look upon, this immense body of cavalry, with banners waving, music crashing, horses prancing, as the vast column came winding like a huge serpent over the hills past the reviewing party, and then stretching far away out of sight." After the review the President insisted on going through the hospital tents, "Stopping and speaking to nearly every man . . . and leaving a kind word as he moved from cot to cot." When the party rode from camp to headquarters, "tremendous cheers rent the air from the soldiers, who stood in groups, eager to see the good President." [12]

Welles thought the President traveled too much. In his "intense anxiety" concerning the military situation in June 1864 the President visited Grant at his headquarters. Welles disapproved of "these Presidential excursions" and tried to discourage them, though Stanton and Chase, he said, favored them. "He can do no good," thought Welles. "It can hardly be otherwise than harmful, even if no accident befalls him. Better for him and the country that he should remain at his post here. It would be advantageous if he remained away from the War Department and required his Cabinet to come to him." [13]

Travel was arduous and a good deal of time was thus consumed, but business was attended to on some of these trips, and they may have afforded variety, diversion, and much needed recreation to a cruelly burdened President. They gave him direct contacts outside Washing-

---

[11] A. G. Henry to his wife, Washington, Apr. 12, 1863, MS., Ill. State Hist. Lib.

[12] Noah Brooks, *Washington in Lincoln's Time,* 48–49.

[13] Welles, *Diary,* II, 55 (June 20, 1864).

ton (contacts inside the capital being rather uninspiring); at times they would enable him to skip a cabinet meeting. At an early stage in the war the New York *Times* informed its readers that the President was "given to unannounced journeying." "His trip from Harrisburg about fifteen months since took the nation by surprise [the secret night ride through Baltimore to Washington in February 1861]; his recent visit to the army and navy yard at Fortress Monroe and Norfolk was as unexpected as it was significant; and the last excursion, taking the whole North by storm, is but one of a similar series." [14]

[14] New York *Times,* June 26, 1862. "In the latter part of June [1862] the President . . . had made . . . a visit to General Scott in his retirement [the general was then at West Point] to ask his counsel. It is probable that at this . . . interview the appointment of Halleck as general-in-chief was . . . suggested by General Scott." Nicolay and Hay, *Lincoln,* VI, 2.

CHAPTER II

LONELY WHITE HOUSE PAIR

THROUGHOUT his life as President, though this has not been sufficiently understood, one should think not alone of Lincoln, but always of the Lincolns. They were a close-knit couple—not that all their tastes were similar; it was rather that they were united; their concerns were mutual. Their children meant everything to them. The welfare of each was inseparable from that of the other. Mrs. Lincoln wrote: ". . . my husband told me that I was the only one he had ever thought of, or cared for." [1] (Referring as a young man to his feeling for Mary Owens, whom he knew before he met Mary Todd, Lincoln had written that he was "a little in love with her.") As to the Lincolns being a loving and thoroughly devoted couple there can be no doubt on the part of those who know their story.

I

Mrs. Lincoln, not being of a blasé temperament, was elated by her high position, enjoyed it (at first), and plunged into the dazzling new life with buoyancy and enthusiasm. One of her sisters even referred to her "court." Her first duty as she saw it was to make a suitable and properly furnished abode out of the sadly unpresentable White House. No informed person could deny the need for such a transformation. There was a congressional appropriation of $20,000 for fitting out the President's mansion and when she undertook the expenditure of this seemingly large amount she had her first lesson in the intricate economics of officialdom.

In her love of beautiful things and her honest wish to perform her task suitably, she was flattered by merchants, carried away by her

---

1 Mrs. Lincoln to Mrs. Gideon Welles, Dec. 6, 1865, Welles MSS.

own quick approval of the purchases she wanted, and victimized by the rather general tendency to gouge that impersonal entity known as "the Government." Mrs. Lincoln did not perform badly in what she bought, but in the lack of a proper check on her ordering she did exceed the appropriation. At the moment of purchase the problem of budgeting was not her main thought. (There was more to it than that; it seemed beyond Mary Lincoln's power to think straight about money matters.) She was in tears when she realized what she had done: tears of penitence and also of distress when she saw that she was creating a difficulty for her overworked husband.

To Lincoln the need for all this refurbishing did not register as with her, and when the matter was brought up by the commissioner of public buildings—B. B. French—the President was indignantly disgusted. He stood ready to pay the excess—about $7,000 over the appropriated amount—but the matter was adjusted by Congress with deficiency appropriations.[2] Of course this business of exceeding an appropriation and appealing to Congress to make it up, while undesirable in terms of finance, was a familiar procedure. It is a procedure which has not yet been outmoded.

This episode of the expenditures was but one of many which brought heartaches for Mary Lincoln. The White House, with humanity crowding its doors, was becoming a lonely and a hostile place. As the months passed the bitter extent and depth of that hostility became a sore trial to this lady of unstable health. Her physical strength was never adequate to these demands of public life. She was shaken by chills and fever, had devastating migraine headaches, and suffered a severe head injury in a carriage accident. Emotional instability and (beginning with the presidency) a species of irrationality, were parts, though minor parts, of her constitution, along with an unsteadiness of nerves. Was she to blame for this? A fully explanatory answer to this question cannot be easily given. All the conditions involved, and all the balancing factors including fine attributes, would have to be considered. To give the answer has not been within the reach of superficial writers—certainly not of Herndon. It would take a physician and a well informed and understanding one at that. A sudden noise—the slamming of a door—would send her nerves quiv-

---

2 For the details, see Harry E. Pratt and Ernest E. East, "Mrs. Lincoln Refurbishes the White House," *Lincoln Herald*, Feb., 1945.

ering. Calmness had not been her forte. She had always had a timidity, a tendency toward panic in a storm, and a sense of insecurity. These qualities did not make for the fullest self control in an emergency. Yet speaking generally as to her public conduct she did show poise, mastery, and control; her social deportment was excellent.[3]

II

Social occasions in the President's mansion were elaborate and stately, though often overcrowded. Shortly after the 1861 inauguration the Lincolns held their first "levee or reception." Among those attending was William H. L. Wallace, an attorney of Ottawa, Illinois, on an office-seeking visit to Washington. He wrote to his wife: "The throng was immense. Ladies crinoline suffered mercilessly. The crowded [White House] was thickly sprinkled with the gay uniforms of the army & navy & the diplomatic corps. Mr. Lincoln wore white kid gloves & worked away at shaking hands with the multitude, with much the same air & movement as if he were mauling rails. Mrs. Lincoln seemed from the happy glance I had of her, to be doing her part of the honors with becoming grace." [1]

For her at least, since she was not well during the White House years, something was done to ease the strain on these exacting occasions. William O. Stoddard, whose post of duty was by Mrs. Lincoln's side, relates that she stood some steps to the right of the President and farther back; much of the procession would sweep past without shaking the hand of the First Lady. "Her hand," wrote Stoddard, "is not so hard as his, and could not endure so much grasping and shaking. Even his iron fingers weary sometimes." [2]

The general party in March 1863, at the close of the winter social season, was typical. People formed in line awaiting entrance. Long before 8:30, the hour set for the opening, it was reported that "crowds of ladies and gentlemen" filled the approaches to the entrance of the mansion. In an effort to keep the crowd under some control a file of

---

3 There was one sad exception which would be greatly misunderstood if taken as typical. It came near the end of Lincoln's life and involved an unfortunate scene created by Mrs. Lincoln (at City Point in March 1865) who was angered by a general's wife (Mrs. Ord) riding horseback beside the President.

1 Pratt, *Concerning Mr. Lincoln,* 70–71.

2 Stoddard, *Inside the White House in War Times,* 92.

soldiers was stationed at the doors. "Mr. Lincoln stood in the reception room, with Mrs. Lincoln on his right, and after the ladies and gentlemen were presented to the President and his lady they passed on and entered the East room, where the promenading took place." So wrote the reporter, first person plural, for the Washington *Chronicle*. He continued: "In the latter room we noticed several distinguished officers, both of the civil and military departments of the Government, accompanied by their wives, daughters, and friends. . . . The ladies endeavored to rival each other in the brilliancy of dress, and it would take a *Jenkins* to decide which was the belle of the evening . . . ."[3]

Next year another of the huge levees was described as surpassing all its predecessors. "The reception last evening, being the last of the season, attracted an overflowing attendance; indeed, the 'oldest inhabitant' would be at a loss to name one in the history of Washington so densely crowded. It is within bounds to state that thousands, on account of the immense throng, were unable to pay their respects to the President and Mrs. Lincoln, the latter of whom was exquisitely attired, and excited general admiration."

"The President," wrote the reporter, "was, as usual, affable and urbane to every one who approached him, bestowing upon all a friendly smile and cordial grasp of the hand, and to his official and social intimates a warm salutation and a pleasant word." The "distinguished personages" who were present in "large number" included members of the cabinet, senators, representatives, officers of army and navy, and foreign ministers.[4]

New Year's Day was regularly the occasion of a general public reception. For this event in 1862 the newspaper accounts glittered with journalistic superlatives. The affair was "very brilliant." The people who attended in large numbers were "of the first order of Society." "The President never appeared in finer spirits, and Mrs. Lincoln, supported by a bevy of the fairest of the metropolis, received with grace and elegance." Then came a mention of the man with whom Lincoln almost fought a duel in 1842. "General Shields [James Shields of Illinois, former senator, brigadier general of volunteers] made his appearance at the levee, and being originally from Illinois, and an

---

[3] Washington *Daily Morning Chronicle,* Mar. 3, 1863, p. 3, c. 1.

[4] *Ibid.,* Apr. 20, 1864, p. 2, c. 8.

acquaintance of the President and his family, was the special object of attention by Mr. and Mrs. Lincoln." After this levee was over, "a choice party was invited to listen to several patriotic songs from the Hutchinson Family in the red room." [5]

The first day of 1863 is remembered in history for the definitive proclamation of emancipation, but for Lincoln the hours and moments as they passed were harassing and exhausting. In addition to the public handshaking (or jerking) the President had a distressing interview with Burnside (who was getting nowhere in Virginia) and was confronted with the resignations of the highest ranking army leaders: Halleck, general in chief, and Burnside, commander of the Army of the Potomac. The trouble was temporarily patched up and the two resignations withdrawn (which did not solve the Burnside problem, or the Halleck one either), but on the historic day when they were proffered, those resignations were ugly facts.[6] One of the features of the New Year's Day reception of 1864 was the attendance of the diplomatic body with "felicitations . . . as cordial as they were demonstrative." The entire corps were present with the exception of the minister from Nicaragua; detained by illness, he sent his "most friendly apology." [7]

After officers, diplomats, and special groups had been received in the morning, a kind of free-for-all party followed. About noon, "the doors were thrown open, and the crowd surged in, trampling on one another's heels and toes, and doing some considerable damage to hats, bonnets and fine dresses." Entering at the front (the north door) of the White House, and moving first to the right, the sweeping mass of humanity pushed "through the Green, Blue and Reception rooms; and near the west door of the latter stood President Lincoln, and with a smile for all, [he] shook hands with his visitors of high and low degree." Ward Hill Lamon, marshal of the District of Columbia, made the presentations to the President; B. B. French, commissioner of public buildings, the introductions to Mrs. Lincoln. In the meantime the Marine Band "discoursed excellent music." Visitors passed into the great East Room, and "thence out by a substantial platform through one of the windows onto the pavement." "Coverings were

---

[5] New York *Herald,* Jan. 8, 1862, p. 10, c. 2.

[6] *Lincoln the President,* II, 252–253.

[7] Cincinnati *Daily Gazette,* Jan. 4, 1864, p. 3, c. 5.

placed over the elegant carpets in all the rooms, in order to prevent them being soiled by the mud." The throng of army officers, estimated at "between five and seven hundred," had assembled in the lower hall of the war department building, "completely jamming its entire space." In orderly formation "they proceeded at 11¼ A. M. to the Executive Mansion on their errand of courtesy, headed by the distinguished General-in-Chief [Halleck]." [8]

For Gideon Welles, ever ready to see that his diary was informed on such matters, the undignified wedging and squeezing at these functions reflected no credit on the Chief's household organization. Describing one of the large parties, he wrote: "It was a jam, not creditable in its arrangements to the authorities." Observing that the "multitude were not misbehaved, farther than crowding together in disorder and confusion," he added: "Had there been a small guard, or even a few police officers, present, there might have been regulations which would have been readily acquiesced in and observed. There has always been a want of order and proper management at these levees or receptions, which I hope may soon be corrected." [9] The big reception to open the year 1865, however, showed the same lack of order. It was held on Monday, January 2, and the people enjoyed it, but Welles thought a "little more system at the President's would improve matters." [10]

So it went: dinners, receptions, matinees, concerts, perhaps a picnic for Negroes on the White House lawn, serenades, introductions, parades, reviews, generals to greet, foreign dignitaries to receive, crowds shaking the President's hand, studio pictures to be posed for, delegations or committees to be heard and answered, Sanitary Fairs to be attended or addressed by letter, speeches to be made, soldiers to be visited in camp or hospital, presentations, openings, dedications, inspections—no end to the continual round, while through it all the nation's existence and fate depended on the manner in which the gravest and most serious problems were faced and handled by the President.

A casual or random glance would find Lincoln speaking to a regiment, reading a prepared address of welcome to a diplomat, attending a funeral, visiting an observatory, testing a new gun, attending

[8] *Ibid.*, Jan. 7, 1864, p. 2, c. 2.

[9] Welles, *Diary*, II, 15 (Apr. 20, 1864).

[10] *Ibid.*, II, 219.

a lecture, or visiting the Capitol to observe progress on the construction of the unfinished dome.

Unusual interest in Washington society attached to the wedding of the famous belle, Kate Chase, daughter of the secretary of the treasury, to Senator (former Governor) William Sprague of Rhode Island. On this occasion "a large and brilliant concourse of guests thronged the hospitable mansion of Secretary Chase . . . . The President of the United States, members of the Cabinet, the diplomatic corps, eminent officers of the army and navy, with citizens of Washington and friends invited from a distance, lent distinction to the scene, as their wives and daughters shed grace and beauty on the gay assemblage." [11]

These incidental and miscellaneous duties collected their toll of energy, time, and thought. To be constantly called upon to say and do the appropriate thing on innumerable occasions, giving attention to each small duty without revealing boredom, is one of the exacting trials of a public man. Yet the people wanted to see their President. They pressed their attentions upon him. It was out of the question, nor was it desired by Lincoln, to deny them access. For thousands it was precisely these small occasions for which Lincoln in person was remembered.

An impressive lady reformer has left a unique first-hand account of President and Mrs. Lincoln. Mrs. Jane Grey Swisshelm was a journalist, an aggressive abolitionist, vigorous newspaper editor, and lecturer. For a time she conducted at Pittsburgh the antislavery paper, the *Saturday Visiter;* at times she contributed to Greeley's *Tribune;* later at St. Cloud, Minnesota, she published the St. Cloud *Democrat.* Coming to Washington in January 1863, and in spite of being a Republican, she did not wish to meet President and Mrs. Lincoln, regarding Lincoln as an "Obstructionist" to the cause of abolition. She resisted various opportunities to meet the Lincolns, but at last she was persuaded to attend a levee at the White House (April 2, 1863). The notable alteration of her impressions of the Lincolns when she met them face to face was recorded in her words as follows:

"I watched the President and Mrs. Lincoln receive. His sad, earnest, honest face was irresistible in its plea for confidence, and Mrs. Lin-

---

[11] Cincinnati *Daily Gazette,* Nov. 20, 1863, p. 1, c. 4.

coln's manner was so simple and motherly, so unlike that of all Southern women I had seen, that I doubted the tales I had heard. Her head was not that of a conspirator. She would be incapable of a successful deceit, and whatever her purposes were, they must be known to all who knew her.

"Mr. Lincoln stood going through one of those dreadful ordeals of hand-shaking, working like a man pumping for life on a sinking vessel, and I was filled with indignation for the selfish people who made this useless drain on his nervous force. I wanted to stand between him and them, and say, 'stand back, and let him live and do his work.' But I could not resist going to him with the rest of the crowd . . . ." [12]

Later Mrs. Swisshelm attended a Union meeting (March 31, 1863) attended by the President and his cabinet. She gave her record of the scene as follows: "He is very tall, and very pale. He walked quickly forward, bowed and took his seat. He was dressed in a plain suit of black which had a worn look; and I could see no sign of watch chain, white bosom or color. But all men have some vanity, and during the evening I noticed he wore on his breast, an immense jewel, the value of which I can form no estimate. This was the head of a little fellow ["Tad" Lincoln], about seven years old, who came with him and for a while sat quietly beside him in one of the great chairs, but who soon grew restless and weary under the long drawn out speeches . . . , and who would wonder [wander] from one Member of the Cabinet to another, leaning on him and whispering to him, no doubt asking when that man was going to quit and let them go home; and then would come back to father, come around, whisper in his ear, then climb on his knee and nestle his head down on his bosom."

Mrs. Swisshelm was impressed by the simplicity of the President forming one of the audience and by the picture of the father with his boy. She wrote: "As the long, bony hand spread out over the dark hair, and the thin face above rested the sharp chin upon it, it was a pleasant sight. The head of a great and powerful nation, without a badge of distinction, sitting quietly in the audience getting bored or applauding like the rest of us; soothing with loving care the little

---

12 Jane Grey Swisshelm, *Half a Century*, 236.

restless creature so much dearer than all the power he wields—a power greater than that exercised by any other human being on earth." [18]

III

When a dinner was given, or some other party which was invitational, the Lincolns, like all presidential couples, were sure to encounter grief on the question as to whom to invite. In this respect one of the White House functions was described in the New York *Herald* as a "blunder." To the one who used this phrase it meant that the "wrong people" had been invited, the "right" ones neglected. Later, however, S. P. Hanscom of the *Herald* was able to inform his illustrious editor, James Gordon Bennett, that "corrections" had since been made. "Some of the first families in the country have been invited who were before neglected, while it is a fact that parties were invited who would not be admitted to the first circles in New York, Boston, or Philadelphia. The whole programme has changed in regard to the lines drawn with reference to the Diplomatic *Corps,* Brigadier Generals, and some Colonels, such as Mr. Astor &c., who were ruled out." [1]

As topics of general discussion, White House affairs were comparable to crises in foreign relations. "Next to the British question," wrote one of the journalists, "the forthcoming party at the White House is the principal subject of comment. The limitation of the number of invitations to only five hundred and fifty occasions many disappointments and heart burnings." The "general expression of disapprobation," he added, "makes it very questionable whether the gratification afforded to the five hundred and fifty favored guests will compensate for the sore disappointment and chagrin occasioned to five thousand five hundred who believe themselves equally entitled to the distinction of an invitation. The whole affair is regarded as a social blunder much to be regretted." [2]

This dispatch was written on February 2, 1862, but soon the correspondent had come to see things in a different light. Next day he wrote:

---

[18] St. Cloud (Minn.) *Democrat,* April 9, 1863.

[1] S. P. Hanscom to James Gordon Bennett, "private," Wash., D.C., Feb. 4, 1862, Bennett MSS.

[2] New York *Herald,* Feb. 3, 1862, p. 1, c. 2.

"The wise course which is being pursued by Mrs. Lincoln, in returning to the customs of the early days of the republic, in her manner of receiving visitors, is applauded by all excepting some few envious individuals who are unable to procure invitations. It is fully time that festivities at the residence of the President of the United States should cease to be infested by crowds of individuals, neither whose manners, habits, nor antecedents entitle them to a place in respectable society. It cannot be expected, crowded as Washington is, that every candidate for office, every petty placemonger, every contract seeker, every quidnunc, whose time hangs heavily on his hands of an evening, should feel entitled as one of the 'great unterrified,' to while away his hours in companionship with the ladies who compose the refined circle of the accomplished lady of our excellent President. It was not so in the days of Washington and Adams . . . . The party [here he referred to the large reception to be held on February 5, 1862] . . . is the uppermost topic of conversation. Over eight hundred invitations have already been issued. The preparations are upon a scale of the greatest magnificence." [3]

It is unimportant to speculate on the reason for the change of tone in the *Herald* correspondent's dispatches of the second and third of February. Perhaps by the latter date he had received his invitation. When he presented his lavish report of the party as held, he marshaled his best adjectives to describe "a truly brilliant array of fashion, beauty and manliness." He went on: "Such a display of elegance and taste and loveliness has perhaps never before been witnessed within the walls of the White House. . . . The President . . . greeted the guests with courteous warmth, and chatted familiarly with many whom he recognized as old friends. He was attired in a plain suit of black." Mrs. Lincoln, the reporter added, was "in half mourning for Prince Albert." [4] To take this newspaper account of this fifth-of-February party in 1862 would be most inadequate. As will be seen later, the occasion was to become a ghastly memory for the Lincolns.

William O. Stoddard of the President's secretarial staff had a *bon mot* for that type of formidable occasion that was called a "ball." When, because of the crowding masses of people, there was no dancing, he thought the affairs could have been so called only by those

---

[3] *Ibid.*, Feb. 4, 1862, p. 1, c. 3.

[4] *Ibid.*, Feb. 6, 1862, p. 5, cc. 4–5.

who were "thinking of cannon balls." After considering all the cabinet members, judges, diplomats, admirals, generals, and governors, with their wives, he measured the floors with a tape line to estimate "standing-room." Custom, he said, required for each President a "routine of official dinners, dull, stately, costly affairs, . . . in a wearisome string through the season." In addition to the usual worries attending such affairs there was, in the case of the Lincolns, "the perpetual peril of having some official jollification set down beforehand for the evening after the arrival of stunning news from the army." [5]

It was not a matter of Washington people only. Over the country, "great society people," together with "the would-be great," wrote in for invitations. Many "applications" had to be rejected, which swelled "the storm of absurd disapprobation . . . aroused by this unfortunate 'reception with refreshments.' " [6]

Not merely admission, but recognition of personal importance, was demanded. The desire was not merely to be accommodated but received as specially favored gentlemen, with cards of invitation second to none. This business of inviting people "as gentlemen," or in such manner as to recognize degrees of personal prestige, could not fail to be serious in a democracy where human worth and equality was emphasized in principle. It was evident that in social invitations equality was not wanted in practice. Men could be invited as officials; that was not always easy, but at least it was a recognized principle. Where, however, cards of invitation were given to officials, others—e. g., reporters—might "be admitted," though without cards. The trouble was that this would not satisfy certain "proudly indignant" individuals. If they could not attend "as gentlemen" they would not attend at all. They had to be told that everyone who had a card of invitation received it by reason of official character, not because of "social position." The reporter of a leading paper would, of course, not be excluded, but he was to understand that he "had no more right to an invitation [by official card] than . . . any hod-carrier on Pennsylvania Avenue." As a precedent (not precisely an analogous one), Stoddard mentioned the prideful conduct of Charles Dickens,

---

[5] Stoddard, *Inside the White House in War Times*, 193–194.

[6] *Ibid.*, 195.

who "refused to perform his theatricals before the Queen, at her command, because he was not a gentleman of England, and could not be received at court." Such situations bring to mind the fact that to the exclusive minded the word "gentleman" connotes superiority, and that many who theoretically praise democratic "equality" do not at all object to exclusiveness so long as they are within the chosen circle.

The presence or absence, also the manner and facial expression, of diplomats was a matter of special observation. In a period of strained relations between the United States and Britain it was noted that no difficulty could have been guessed from the deportment of Lord Lyons, British minister. "No American," it was noted, "has shaken hands more heartily than he with the President . . . ." On the same occasion Stoddard observed: "France is not here, and it is understood that he will not come to-night; but if his absence has any ominous diplomatic meaning the hint is utterly lost upon Mr. Lincoln." The White House was "not a good workroom for intrigue." [7]

IV

Of the three living Lincoln sons—Robert, Willie, and Tad—only two were part of the daily White House scene; for Robert, who came of age in the summer of 1864, was attending college at Harvard. It was Willie and Tad, with their exuberance and pranks, who gladdened, while they also complicated, home life in the presidential household, if home life it could be called. Abraham and Mary Lincoln loved their little sons with a love that was ardently reciprocated. Yet with official business conducted in the mansion—endless conferences, visitings, and interviews—there was little chance to enjoy family life.

Willie, their third son, was ten years old when his father became President. Well endowed, good looking, and lovable, he was the center of animated boy life, which included parties in which his mother took a special interest. "Willie Lincoln," wrote his playmate Julia Taft Bayne, "was the most lovable boy I ever knew, bright, sensible, sweet-tempered and gentle-mannered." Willie and Tad, she wrote, "were two healthy, rollicking Western boys, never accustomed to

[7] *Ibid.*, 94–95. (For Stoddard's reference to Dickens, see p. 197.)

restraint, and the notice which their father's station drew upon them was very distasteful. Willie would complain, 'I wish they wouldn't stare at us so. Wasn't there ever a President who had children?' "[1]

In the wretched unhealthiness of Washington, with its shocking lack of adequate sanitation, Willie caught a serious illness, and it was announced on February 8, 1862, that "the usual Saturday reception at the White House and the levee on Tuesday would be omitted, on account of the illness of the second son [he was really the third son] of the President, an interesting lad of about eight years of age [another error], who has been lying dangerously ill of bilious fever [at another time reported as typhoid] for the last three days. Mrs. Lincoln has not left his bedside since Wednesday night [February 5], and fears are entertained for her health."[2]

Days passed while the Lincoln household was plunged in anxious gloom. It was reported on February 11 that the lad had been "very ill," but was "much improved."[3] Next day it was stated that the "little son" was "reported out of danger." In the altered tempo of life at the White House not only the levee, but the "usual Cabinet meeting" was dispensed with, while the President was often at the bedside. On February 18 Attorney General Bates noted in his diary: "The Prest.'s 2d. son, Willie, has lingered on for a week or 10 day[s], and is now thought to be *in extremis*[.] The Prest. is nearly worn out, with grief and watching."[4]

As the grieving President and his wife continued their agonized vigil it was announced that the boy was "pronounced past all hope of recovery."[5] Next came the report: "The White House is still overspread with the gloom of the expected death of the President's second son, who is reported more easy to-day, but no hope of his recovery is entertained. The President and Mrs. Lincoln are overwhelmed with grief."[6] In the midst of all this it was noted that Tad was "now threatened with a similar sickness."[7] In his unceasing solicitude for his sons

---

1 Julia Taft Bayne, *Tad Lincoln's Father*, 8–9.

2 "News from Washington," New York *Herald*, Feb. 10, 1862, p. 5, c. 3.

3 *Ibid.* (news dated Feb. 11), Feb. 12, 1862, p. 5, c. 4.

4 Bates made the common error of referring to Willie as the Lincolns' second, instead of their third-born son.

5 New York *Herald*, Feb. 19, 1862, p. 1, c. 3.

6 *Ibid.*, Feb. 20, 1862, p. 1, c. 4.

7 Helen Nicolay, *Lincoln's Secretary: A Biography of John G. Nicolay*, 132. (Quoted from a letter by Nicolay to Therena Bates, his future wife.)

Lincoln "gave them their medicines and spent as much time as possible in the sickroom." [8]

V

In a letter written at the time it was reported of Mrs. Lincoln: "She is . . . just now sadly affected both of her little boys are down with fever, and one is very dangerously sick. She & the president have been watching for ten days, & she looks haggard enough." [1]

On February 20 there was the "same routine," with the President "very much worn and exhausted." As Nicolay wrote: "At about five o'clock this afternoon [February 20] I was lying half asleep on the sofa in my office when his entrance roused me. 'Well, Nicolay,' said he, choking with emotion, 'my boy is gone—he is actually gone!' and, bursting into tears, turned and went into his own office." [2]

"Me and father" had been pals or companions in frolic, travel, and adventure, as well as at home. When he was but eight years old, in June 1859, Willie had written to a friend from Chicago: "This town is a very beautiful place. . . . Me and father have a nice little room to ourselves. We have two little pitcher[s] on a washstand. The smallest one for me the largest one for father. We have two little towels on a top of both pitchers. . . . [etc.]" [3]

To those who have a feeling for the Lincolns as a family there has come the thought—if Willie had lived. He was thus described by Mrs. Elizabeth Todd Grimsley: "Willie, a noble, beautiful boy of nine years, of great mental activity, unusual intelligence, wonderful memory, methodical, frank and loving, a counterpart of his father, save that he was handsome. He was entirely devoted to Taddie who was a gay, gladsome, merry, spontaneous fellow, bubbling over with innocent fun, whose laugh rang through the house, when not moved to tears. Quick in mind, and impulse, like his mother, with her naturally sunny temperament, he was the life, as also the worry of the household. There could be no greater contrast between children."

---

[8] *Ibid.*

[1] Unidentified letter, signed James, to "My dearest Mary," Washington, Feb. 16, 1862, photostat of ms., Abr. Lincoln Assoc.

[2] Nicolay, *Lincoln's Secretary*, 132–133.

[3] Willie Lincoln to "Dear Henry" [Remann], Chicago, June 6 [?], 1859, MS., Univ. of Chicago Lib. The name Remann is verified by Mrs. Mary Edwards Brown of Springfield, who formerly owned the letter.

Mrs. Grimsley continued: "Our first Sunday in the White House, we all went to the New York Avenue Presbyterian Church, Dr. Phineas D. Gurley's, which had been decided upon as the church home, and ever after, the boys attended the Sabbath School, Willie conscientiously, and because he loved it, Tad as a recreation, and to be with Willie." [4]

Tad recovered, though his illness was no slight matter. He was now the one boy living in the White House. It is impossible to put on paper the depth and intensity of Lincoln's grief, of Mary Lincoln's, and of Tad's. On March 2 Mrs. Ninian W. Edwards, Mary's sister, visiting the White House, wrote in a letter to her daughter: "It is enough to feel . . . that my presence here, has tended very much to soothe, the excessive grief, that natures such as your Aunt's experience. And moreover to aid in nursing the little sick Tad, who is very prostrated with his illness and subdued with the loss he evidently suffers from, yet permits no allusion to. His mother has been but little with him, being utterly unable to control her feelings." On March 12 Mrs. Edwards wrote again: "Your Aunt Mary still confines herself to her room . . . and at times, gives way to violent grief. . . . Tad is still feeble, can barely walk a few steps at a time. He deeply feels the loss of his loving brother." [5]

Another touching record of Tad's grief remains. In the series of home letters just mentioned, Mrs. Edwards referred to a trunk she was sending home to Springfield. In it Tad was sending two toy railroad cars to a little cousin. Mrs. Edwards wrote "It [the trunk] contained *two cars* that belonged to Willie. Tad insisted upon sending them to Lewis [Edward Lewis Baker, grandson of Mrs. Edwards], saying he could not play with them again." [6]

VI

It was in this month of February 1862 that a favorable turning point was reached in the bitter war, with the important western vic-

---

4 Elizabeth Todd Grimsley, in *Journal*, Ill. State Hist. Soc., XIX, nos. 3–4, 48–49 (1926–27).

5 For the use of these original letters of Mrs. Ninian W. Edwards the author is indebted to the kindness of one of her descendants.

6 This letter, though undated, was evidently written to her daughter, Mrs. Edward Lewis Baker, by Mrs. Edwards from the White House in April 1862. See previous note.

tories at Fort Henry and Fort Donelson. It was stated in the papers that the "rebellion . . . [was] receiving fatal blows" under Lincoln's administration. Much was to be made of Washington's Birthday that year. Meetings for public celebration all over the country had been planned. "As a patriot and as President of the United States," wrote one of the journalists, "Mr. Lincoln has occasion to feel the proudest satisfaction in the success of our arms on land and sea; while, as a father, he is called to endure the severest domestic calamity. There is an indescribable gloom in the White House. The muffled bell, and the profound silence in those noble rooms . . . produce a strange effect upon the visitor who goes there to look upon the lifeless form of the pretty boy, . . . the sprightly, sweet tempered and mild mannered child, ... To-day the obsequies of little Willie took place. . . . Mrs. Lincoln . . . was too ill . . . to be present at the funeral ceremonies. . . . Here [in the East Room] were seated in a circle President Lincoln and his oldest son Robert, and the members of his Cabinet. . . . Mr. Lincoln was bowed down with grief and anxiety, and looked as if nearly worn out with watching." [1]

In New Hampshire a former President, who would not ordinarily have been moved to write to Lincoln, broke silence to send a touching letter of sympathy and condolence. On the eve of taking office in 1853, Franklin Pierce had suffered a devastating bereavement when his eleven-year-old son, Benny, had been killed before his eyes in a railway accident. On matters concerned with the spiritual life he had been reticent. Now came the following letter in Pierce's hand:

Concord N. H.
March 4, 1862

My dear Sir,

The impulse to write you, the moment I heard of your great domestic affliction was very strong, but it brought back the crushing sorrow which befel me just before I went to Washington in 1853, with such power that I felt your grief to be too sacred for intrusion.

Even in this hour, so full of danger to our Country, and of trial and

1 New York *Herald*, Feb. 26, 1862, p. 10, cc. 3–4. News in this dispatch was reported as of February 24, the day of the funeral. The minister who conducted the service was Dr. Phineas D. Gurley, pastor of the New York Avenue Presbyterian church in Washington. Departments were closed; both houses of Congress adjourned as a token of respect; government buildings were not illuminated on Washington's Birthday.

anxiety to all good men, your thoughts will be, of your cherished boy, who will nestle at your heart, until you meet him in that new life, when tears and toils and conflict will be unknown.

I realize fully how vain it would be, to suggest sources of consolation.

There can be but one refuge in such an hour,—but one remedy for smitten hearts, which, is to trust in Him "who doeth all things well", and leave the rest to—

"Time comforter & only healer
When the heart hath bled"

With Mrs Pierce's and my own best wishes—and truest sympathy for Mrs Lincoln and yourself

I am, very truly,
yr. friend
Franklin Pierce [2]

His Excy—
A. Lincoln
Presdt &c
&c &c

VII

For Mary Lincoln the death of Willie came as a crushing and shattering blow. Social functions were sharply curtailed. Never again would the life of the First Lady have the glamor of its first brief phase. When a lady nurse, quickly summoned to attend the broken woman, arrived, she found the President where one could have expected to find him, by the bedside of his sick wife.

It was his habit to be constantly solicitous of her, sending daily telegrams when she or he was away, keeping her informed of military movements (knowing her deep interest in the progress of national events), and constantly striving to have some sister or cousin on hand to assist and keep her company. For her part she found numerous ways of helping him: contriving to overcome his moods of depression, suppressing her own complaints to avoid worrying him with them, offering relaxation, watching out for his meals (which he neglected), and instituting the practice of a daily carriage ride. Thought for his safety amid the lurking dangers and cruel burdens of his position was with her a constant anxiety.

Deprived of any element of joy by the death of her beloved son, the White House became for Mrs. Lincoln a storm center and a kind of dismal trap. Whatever she did or omitted to do, she was sure to

---

[2] R. T. L. Coll., 14792.

be criticized. An example was the expensive and elaborate party (on February 5th) at the White House within the period when Willie lay ill. It had been planned well in advance and when Mrs. Lincoln considered canceling it, which would have been her wish, she was assured of her son's recovery while of course she could not forget her function as hostess. She was in an agony of suspense while the party was on as she realized that the boy was not improving; afterward she had to endure the stabbing injustice of a devastating set of verses, misnamed a poem, on the "Lady President's Ball," a savage piece of misplaced sarcasm put in the supposed mouth of a dying soldier and scoring her thoughtless extravagance and gaiety while men of the army were writhing and dying in neglect. The false implication that she did not care as to the welfare of soldiers—anyone who knew her realized that she cared very deeply—was of a piece with the incredible campaign of abuse of which she was the victim. Yet if she omitted social functions, she was equally denounced for that. Parties and dinners were not in general omitted in Washington in war time, and when she cut down on them in those months of '62 following Willie's death, she had to bear the accusation that she was denying her people that to which they were entitled. She was even accused of being a "rebel" at heart and a Confederate spy in the White House. No one in the nation was a more firm and earnest Unionist than she. It should be added that she showed notable friendliness and understanding toward the colored people. The enduring tradition among those people of worshipful friendliness to her has vastly more validity than the fabrication of some—alas, too many—among the whites.

There were two things that somewhat sustained her in her prostrating grief: first, her realization that Lincoln suffered too and that it was her duty to hearten him; and in addition her service in soldier hospitals. It was an impressive sight to see her ministrations as she visited the sickbeds of the wounded, brought them delicacies from the White House kitchen, and by her presence and conversation reanimated the spirits of the men who on their part—so different from the alleged soldier in the poem—gave her a sincere and grateful response. In her sensitiveness to suffering she was deeply affected by the painful scenes she encountered, but this, together with the constant danger of contagion to herself, she heeded not. It was W. O. Stoddard's view that she missed a chance in public relations by not deliberately publicizing this hospital service. That was not her nature. In her own person she did not seek the limelight. Her feeling about the matter, in addition to the impulse to help, was that without these humane employments her heart would have been broken by the loss of her child.

Unscrupulous men wormed their way into the mansion, gained access to the lady of the house, and made her an unsuspecting victim of their low intrigues. Such a man was one John Watt, the White House gardener whose extracurricular activities and juggling as to payrolls revealed him to be a disloyal cheat. Another impostor was the fabulous Henry Wikoff, an unprincipled adventurer who had been dismissed from Yale and had seen the inside of prison. He was a traveler extraordinary, wealthy idler, courtier, amateur diplomat, frequenter of foreign courts, supposed authority on Napoleon III, and purveyor-in-chief of various kinds of fancy gossip. The name "Chevalier Wikoff" became attached to him because of an unimportant decoration he had received in Spain. This disreputable but socially attractive man ingratiated himself in Mrs. Lincoln's favor for the furthering of his own intrigues, one of which had to do with the smuggling of unauthorized information to James Gordon Bennett's *Herald.* (That Bennett denied the connection with Wikoff was to have been expected both of Bennett and his type of journalism.) The story of Wikoff's machinations need not be given in detail here; the time came, none too soon, when he was told by the President to leave the White House and never return.

VIII

It did not help matters in Mary Lincoln's "furnace of affliction" (to use her own phrase) that Lincoln's secretaries, Nicolay and Hay, could exchange letters belittling her—Hay going so far with his over-clever pen as to call her a "Hell-cat." To say the least, a greater respect should have been shown by the secretaries for the President's own wishes and attitudes; he was not ignorant of her imperfections, but he dealt with her in kindness and understanding. A private secretary, to serve adequately, should be an aide to the President. Mrs. Lincoln had her difficulties with these secretarial youths on matters of the household payroll and of social invitations.

To know this side of the story from the standpoint of the Lincolns will enable one better to realize why it was that the President planned differently for 1865. These young men were slated to be provided for by appointments abroad and it was arranged that Noah Brooks should be private secretary for the second presidential term. One of the ablest men in Washington, Brooks was the correspondent of the Sacramento *Union*. He has importance in the Lincoln story for his reportorial records and for his specially intimate relation with the President; he was one of the few spirits of whom Lincoln was genuinely fond and with whom he felt comfortably at ease. It is Brooks who has given us one of the most striking comments on the vicious weapons aimed against Mrs. Lincoln. He knew and indignantly resented the abusive slanders of the Washington rumor-factory; he knew better, for he knew Mrs. Lincoln as she was. Brooks wrote:

"The wife of the President has been so frequently and cruelly misrepresented and slandered that, though hesitating to approach so delicate a subject, your correspondent cannot refrain from saying a word in strict justice to this distinguished and accomplished woman. When the present administration came into power, the National Capital was infested as well as besieged by rebels, and every conceivable means was adopted to render the members of the new Administration unpopular. To this end slanders innumerable were circulated concerning the habits of the President and his family; and it is not many months since when candid and loyal men were to be found believing that our temperate President drank to excess, and that Mrs. Lincoln was a vulgar, ill-bred woman. Such stories are scandalous, and though time has done justice to the President, who is seen and read of all men, Mrs. Lincoln is denied the privilege of defense, and in the privacy of a household clad in mourning has not yet had justice done her by the public."

To Brooks's mind the inexcusable outrage was that "loyal people, more shame to them, without knowing the truth of what they repeat, still allow themselves to become the media for the dispersion of scandals as base as they are baseless." Feeling most keenly that a correction was long overdue, he continued:

"It is not a gracious task to refute these things, but the tales that are told of Mrs. Lincoln's vanity, pride, vulgarity and meanness ought to put any decent man or woman to the blush, when they remember they do not *know* one particle of that which they repeat, and that they would resent as an insult to their wives, sisters or mothers that which they so glibly repeat concerning the first lady in the land. Shame upon these he-gossips and envious retailers of small slanders. Mrs. Lincoln, I am glad to be able to say from personal knowledge, is a true American woman, and when we have said that we have said enough in praise of the best and truest lady in our beloved land."

This comment was part of a long article giving at some length a first-hand description of life as it was lived in the White House, a subject on which Brooks could speak with assurance. He was letting his far-off Pacific coast readers share with him the inside view of the mansion: its ante-room for those seeking the President, its parlors, upholstery and fittings, satin and damask, "profusion of ormulu work," vases and the like bought or presented during the administrations of Madison and Monroe, its grand piano, its full length portrait of Washington, its richly colored hangings. Most people, he said, admired the blue room, "formed in the graceful curves of a perfect ellipse," its windows commanding "a lovely view of the grounds in the rear of the house and of the Potomac."

No part of the mansion seems to have escaped him. He wrote of the family apartments, dining room, conservatory, servants' rooms, kitchen, and basement. There was no "Kitchen Cabinet," he noted, "but the present presiding lady of the White House has caused a terrible scattering of ancient abuses . . . below stairs." There had been "suckers" who stole from kitchen and conservatory, "spies in every room in the house." When they were dispersed, they "circulated innumerable revengeful yarns . . . and there were . . . credulous people who believed them." He noted how vandals had snipped off bits of lace, drapery and carpet as relics; he wondered how they could have the "cheek" to exhibit these objects to friends at home with accounts as to how they were stolen.

After all this elaborate description and this indignant refutation of fabricated yarns, the observant Brooks concluded: "Republican simplicity and Republican virtues [upper case in the newspaper] reign at the home of the American President; thousands of private citizens in our prosperous country are more luxuriously lodged, and more daintily fed; but, search the wide nation over and you will not find a more united household or a more noble and loving family than that which to-day dwells in all of the anxious cares of the White House." [1]

What was said by Noah Brooks was made evident by another close and competent observer, Ben Perley Poore, who wrote: "The President's wife . . . ought not to be left unmentioned, although there is little of interest to chronicle in her daily round of serving, reading and visiting hospitals, which occupies the time of Mrs. Lincoln. She may have made mistakes—who does not? in her invitations, and thereby have provoked envious criticisms. Neither do those of the Democratic [party] era admit there can be any courtesy displayed here now-a-days. But I am sure that since the time that Mrs. Madison presided at the White House, it has not been graced by a lady so well fitted by nature and by education to dispense its hospitalities as is Mrs. Lincoln. Her hospitality is only equaled by her charity, and her graceful deportment by her goodness of heart." [2] Not all the mud slinging and shameful abuse can rob Mrs. Lincoln of that which was admitted by contemporary writers not governed by prejudice: her performance as hostess and First Lady. She served with dignity in all the exacting social world of the presidency.[3]

---

1 Letter from Washington, signed "Castine," Nov. 7, 1863, in Sacramento *Union*, Dec. 4, 1863. The excellent reporting in this article was typical of the work of Noah Brooks.

2 "From Our Regular Correspondent," Washington, Nov. 30, Boston *Journal*, Dec. 1, 1863, signed "Perley."

3 The author has been greatly assisted by studying in manuscript the biography of Mary Lincoln by his wife, Ruth Painter Randall. Many points in the life and personality of Mrs. Lincoln, used in this chapter, are to be amplified and fully documented in Mrs. Randall's book which is scheduled for early publication.

CHAPTER III

ATTENTION OF THE PRESIDENT

I

FEW men of his time understood the extent of Lincoln's presidential burden. Patronage, dealings with Congress, public relations, civil and military duties, and an appalling amount of detailed business pertaining to the army, crowded upon his waking hours and robbed him of sleep. The unceasing demands upon him as the court of high appeal in numerous personal cases took heavy toll of his time and energy, of his patience and emotional endurance.

On hundreds of private requests the President had to give or refuse permission. What about the case of "Sue and Charlie"—Mr. and Mrs. Charles Craig, cousins of John Todd Stuart? Dislodged from their home by war's desolation, they wanted to go back and cultivate their farm near Helena, Arkansas. They needed a pass through the lines and assurance of non-molestation by the military authorities. Accompanied by Henry T. Blow of St. Louis ("old friend" of Lincoln, successful business man, and leading Republican), Sue called at night at the White House, saw Lincoln, and presented her request. Writing on a Sunday, Stuart informed his wife that "Mr. Lincoln . . . granted all Sue's wishes and promised to have the papers made out for her by tomorrow." This bit of personal business involved "influence" of prominent men, use of the President as errand boy, the writing of an official "A D S" (autograph document signed) by the President, the making out of various papers, and due attention to the details by the proper authorities. The matter was mentioned along with the problem of "a permit for *Cousin Ann* [Mrs. Ann Todd Campbell of Boonville, Missouri, cousin of Mrs. Lincoln] to trade in Cotton down the Mississippi." Stuart thought the affairs of sundry cousins were going well. "How *we apples swim!*" he remarked.[1]

An "old lady of genteel appearance" called with a "piteous appeal." Having fitted up portions of the old Duff Green building in order to take in boarders, and having engaged members of Congress to board there, she was given an eviction notice with a quick deadline; aside from the "ruin" occasioned by the loss of her financial outlay, she could find no other shelter for her head. Her appeal was given personal consideration by the President, resulting in his "A L S" (autograph letter signed) to Secretary Stanton in the lady's behalf.[2]

Were these trivial matters? Of course they were matters that should never have been brought up to the President, but if one is studying Lincoln's presidential days and how they were spent, the accumulated weight of such things cannot be ignored; Lincoln's time was continually devoted to precisely such appeals. A loyal Mississippi lady had taken the Federal oath of allegiance and had leased her plantation "to parties of unquestioned loyalty." By military sanction it had been leased to other parties. So Lincoln had to write to Adjutant General Thomas to have the matter, about which he knew nothing, straightened out.[3] Could something be done about the request of Dr. William Fithian, friend of Lincoln and substantial citizen of Danville, Illinois, who wished to recover the remains of a stepson in Missouri? Lincoln did what he could, wiring to General Samuel R. Curtis, asking that the necessary facilities be extended.[4] Was there a Confederate prisoner named Joseph J. Williams confined at Camp Chase, Ohio? Or was he at Camp Douglas near Chicago? Would the officer in charge "tell him his wife is here, and allow him to Telegraph her." [5]

Sometimes the request was for a recommendation. Though he had "but slight personal acquaintance" with Mrs. Lotty Hough, Lincoln knew of her by reputation and had "never heard ought against her." She was struggling to support herself and little boy. The President hoped that opportunities to succeed would be afforded her.[6]

---

1 John T. Stuart to his wife, Dec. 29, 1863, MS., Ill. State Hist. Soc.; Pratt, *Concerning Mr. Lincoln*, 105–106.

2 Lincoln to Stanton, Jan. 1, 1863, photostat, A. Lincoln Assoc.

3 Case of Mrs. Eugenia P. Bass. Lincoln to Lorenzo Thomas, Jan. 15, 1864. Lincoln MSS., Lib. of Cong.

4 Nicolay and Hay, *Works*, VIII, 144.

5 *Ibid.*, VII, 10.

6 *Ibid.*, X, 238 (corrected by photostat, A. Lincoln Assoc.).

In unnumbered personal cases the President sought to relieve distressed human beings of the harassments of war. In a generalized letter of instruction to commanding officers in West Tennessee he wrote: "It is my wish for you to relieve the people from all burdens, harassments, and oppressions, so far as is possible, consistently with your military necessities; . . . the object of the war being to restore and maintain the blessings of peace and good government, I desire you to help, and not hinder, every advance in that direction." [7]

It is remarkable that so many hardship cases and personal appeals came up to Lincoln himself. A Unionist-minded lady was reported to be seeking separation from her husband who was in the Confederate army. The President would not offer her, or any wife, "a temptation to a permanent separation from her husband," but if her mind was "independently and fully made up to such separation," he wished certain "property . . . to be delivered to her, upon her taking the oath" of loyalty. A lady with her six daughters wished to go to her father in Richmond, Kentucky; Lincoln directed the officer in command at Knoxville, Tennessee, to allow the trip. A poor widow had a son in the army, who for some offense had been sentenced "to serve a long time without pay, or at most, with very little pay." Lincoln wrote to his secretary of war: "I do not like this punishment of withholding pay—it falls so very hard upon poor families." [8]

Sometimes an individual appeal would involve a broad public policy. Frequently the problem would be an excessive use of military authority in matters appropriate for the courts. A provost marshal, for example, seized a building, with premises and furniture, belonging to a lady whose husband "went off in the rebellion," though she was the owner of the property, independently of her husband. The basis of the seizure was vague, and the property was not taken for any military object. "The true rule for the Military," wrote the President, "is to seize such property as is needed for Military uses and reasons and let the rest alone." The case involved complicated and serious legal questions—whether either husband or wife was a traitor, which one owned the property, and whether the wife's prop-

---

[7] To commanding officers in West Tennessee, Feb. 13, 1865, photostat, A. Lincoln Assoc.

[8] For these cases see Nicolay and Hay, *Works*, X, 27–29, 72–73 (photostats, A. Lincoln Assoc.).

erty was confiscable for the treason of her husband—"all which," wrote Lincoln, "it is ridiculous for a provost-marshal to assume to decide." He directed that the case be adjusted and revised on these principles.[9]

II

Often the thing desired of Lincoln was his signature. One jovial visitor stated that he would prefer it "at the foot of a commission." [1] A lady wrote a "complimentary poem" to the President and asked for his autograph. Lincoln wrote: "I thank you for it, and cheerfully comply with your request." [2] A bride-to-be, signing her name as Polly Peachblossom, asked the busy President for an autograph on an enclosed piece of silk, to be placed in her wedding quilt. "All the other Peachblossoms," she wrote, "had a silk quilt ready for their wedding and why should not I?" [3] These little requests were satisfied with a sense of form suited to the occasion. When a wish for his autograph was expressed by Lady Villiers, Lincoln wrote: "I beg that her Ladyship will accept the assurance of my sincere gratification at this opportunity of subscribing myself Very truly Her Ladyship's obedient servant A. Lincoln." [4]

There were numerous pleas for notes of introduction. And there was the case of "a fair, plump lady" of Dubuque. Just before a cabinet meeting she pressed forward, saying she "was passing East and came from Baltimore expressly to have a look" at the President.[5] Among other questions he was asked to approve a benefit raffle. So a presidential telegram went to Mother Mary Gonyeag of Keokuk: "The

---

[9] Lincoln to Gen. Joseph J. Reynolds, Jan. 20, 1865, photostat, A. Lincoln Assoc. (Erroneously given in Nicolay and Hay, *Works,* IX, 287–288, as Jan. 20, 1864.)

[1] Rice, *Reminiscences of Abraham Lincoln* . . . , 229–230.

[2] *Works,* X, 253 (Oct. 26, 1864).

[3] R. T. L. Coll., 32804 (Apr. 4, 1864). The lady who presented this "modest request" put it up to the President: there could be no wedding without the quilt, and no quilt without the autograph. She enclosed a poem, "The Maul," depicting Lincoln as a rail-splitting young hero who rose under his "Star of Fame" till his pen became "the heaviest maul" of all. This Victorian effusion is printed in Moore, *Rebellion Record* ("Poetry and Incidents"), IX, 13–14, under the name Mary E. Nealy. See also Ruth Painter Randall, "Little Stories from the Lincoln Papers," *Lincoln Herald,* vol. 50, 26–27 (Feb. 1948).

[4] Photostat, A. Lincoln Assoc. (May 20, 1862).

[5] Welles, *Diary,* I, 528.

President has no authority as to whether you may raffle for the benevolent object you mention. If there is no objection in the Iowa laws, there is none here." [6] Sometimes in this endless round there would be a flash of homely kindness and human sympathy. Toward laboring people especially the President showed particular consideration. He held an interview with a committee of Philadelphia working women to hear their complaints. In the sewing that these women did they had a poor pittance which was "reduced one-half to gratify and enrich a class of grasping contractors." In the Forney press of Washington and Philadelphia we find the comment: "It is rather a unique spectacle to find the chief of a great Republic . . . quietly and patiently hearing the complaints of a committee of plain and humble women, ... This, however, is one of the most beautiful examples of a republican Government. The voice of the poor is not often heard by the politician, and particularly the voice of poor women, who have no votes and no influence in primary conventions. . . . These persecuted women go to the President with their grievances, and tell him their story with the simple, homely way of the housewife. And the result is precisely what was anticipated by all who know Abraham Lincoln and his great, good heart. . . . The sewing women will hereafter receive justice. . . . The poor men and women will find that their greatest friend is the President, and that when their errand is justice, no one will be more patient, and sincere, and prompt than the laboring man of Illinois who sits in the Executive chair at Washington." [7]

It might be a new invention that the President would be asked to pass upon. Often it was a personal request for employment. Perhaps it was the disunionists of Maryland or the Unionists of Eastern Tennessee who required attention. A congressman would offer his services. A governor would demand an explanation. Serious Indian troubles in Minnesota in the summer of 1862, "involving official frauds on the one hand and Indian depredations on the other," required an arduous trip by John G. Nicolay to the scene of turmoil, so that Lincoln might have at that distant point "an unprejudiced observer"

[6] *Works,* IX, 259 (Dec. 15, 1863).

[7] Washington *Daily Morning Chronicle,* Jan. 28, 1865, p. 2, c. 2 (reprinting from the Philadelphia *Press* of Jan. 27).

Courtesy of the New Hampshire Historical Society

FRANKLIN PIERCE

The Pierce story has relevance to the Lincoln presidency in two connections: a preposterous accusation of disloyalty which turned out to be a hoax, and a most beautiful but slightly known letter which the ex-President wrote to Lincoln after the death of Willie.

CARL SCHURZ

Brave German revolutionary, distinguished German-American, diplomat, brilliant speaker, Union major general. In the center picture the trappings (busby, pelisse, cape, saber—complete with riding whip and cigar) are not those of any identified uniform. (Center, upper left, and lower right photographs are by courtesy of the State Historical Society of Wisconsin; lower left, of Federick H. Meserve of New York; the others, of the National Archives, Washington.)

who could be, if not an *alter ego,* at least a kind of domestic presidential envoy. In performing this duty—meeting with United States officials and conferring with Chippewa chief Hole-in-the-Day—Nicolay was absent for an extended period during which he wondered whether his scalp was safe. Next summer there was a flare-up of Indian trouble in Colorado, and again Lincoln sent Nicolay, this time "to accompany the Governor of Colorado Territory down to Connejos in the San Juan Valley and to conclude a treaty with the Utes." The secretary "looked upon that visit to Colorado as one of the rare experiences of his life." "A little black notebook that he carried in his pocket fairly explodes with adjectives praising the beauty of the scenery, the fantastic grades at which alleged roads climbed steeple-like peaks, only to drop again into valleys in a way to make a traveler's head swim." [8]

Such things can be voluminously listed—it is like going over a file of government papers—but when that is done it is still difficult to recover an adequate picture of the executive job as it existed under Lincoln. To enumerate his diverse "problems" is not enough. One problem alone might be supercharged with vexation and annoyance; yet to analyze the intricacies of his tasks, or explore their limits and boundaries, is impracticable. In his routine of duties Lincoln had to have eyes and ears for all parts of the country and for matters within every department. Decisions had to be made as to the Almedan mine in California.[9] Attention had to be directed to the breaking of ground for the Union Pacific Railroad, the restoration of Virginia, espionage in the Confederate capital, American participation in the London "exhibition of the products of industry of all nations" (1862), the bringing of produce through the military lines, "the subject of a Reciprocity Treaty with the Sandwich [Hawaiian] Islands," [10] and to the request that Brigham Young be authorized to raise a force to protect the property of the telegraph and overland mail companies in Utah Territory.

---

8 Helen Nicolay, *Lincoln's Secretary,* 151–155, 172–174.

9 Bates, *Diary,* 303, 338; Welles, *Diary,* I, 397, and II, 338; Leonard Ascher, "Lincoln's Administration and the New Almedan Scandal," *Pacific Hist. Rev.,* V, 38–51 (1936); Milton H. Shutes, "Abraham Lincoln and the New Almedan Mine," *Calif. Hist. Soc. Quar.,* XV, 3–20 (1936).

10 Lincoln to the Senate of the United States, Feb. 5, 1864, photostat, A. Lincoln Assoc.

The President's time, as he himself wrote, was subject to "constant and unexpected requisitions." [11] At another time he referred to "the multitude of cares" claiming his "constant attention" because of which he had been "unable to examine and determine the exact treaty relations between the United States and the Cherokee Nation." [12] One becomes accustomed to the unusual, and inmates of the White House, as Stoddard called them, became familiar with "this strange, unnatural, wartime atmosphere." "Mr. Lincoln," he wrote, "bears it better than could another man in his place, perhaps, but it is telling upon him perceptibly. . . . All kinds of people come on all kinds of errands, and most of them, nowadays, besiege the Capitol and the Departments, but there is a long list of persistent visitors who hang around the White House and wait for chances to see the President, even after they are assured that he cannot and will not see them." [13]

III

In the face of all these demands the accessibility of the President and his willingness to meet people was a source of wonder, even though by many it was taken for granted. If, however, some found him "hard to see," that was but another evidence of the extent of his burdens. The White House staff sought as far as possible to protect him. There were "guards or footmen" whose duty it was to divert the many who called from curiosity or without sufficient business.[1] Sometimes, because of this, those who had serious business could not see him. Charles D. Drake, chairman of a delegation from Missouri, having submitted documents "of great length," waited for three days seeking a conference in order to get the President's answer to some very serious and vexing questions pertaining to the muddled situation in Missouri. He remained in Washington for that purpose alone. Failing to see Lincoln, he left; then it turned out that this was a matter requiring such detailed and extended study that Lincoln wrote a long and involved answer, over two thousand words, in

11 Lincoln to J. R. Fry, Apr. 30, 1864, R. T. L. Coll., 32709–10.

12 Lincoln to John Ross, Chief of the Cherokee Nation, Sep. 25, 1862, photostat, A. Lincoln Assoc.; R. T. L. Coll., 18626.

13 Stoddard, *Inside the White House in War Times,* 37.

1 R. T. L. Coll., 25610.

the nature of a substantial state paper.[2] So much concentration was required by Lincoln when he got round to this task that others who sought audience with him had to be disappointed. "The President," it was reported, "excluded all visitors to-day. The Missouri delegation think he is at work on a reply to them." [3]

Another caller wrote: "I called for a personal interview, & have done so many times since, but found you engaged with some Major General, cabinet officer, member of the Senate or House: or the throngs pressing upon you, their varied claims or propositions; & so . . . retired for a more favorable opportunity." [4]

Often it required a good deal of endurance to succeed in meeting the nation's Chief, but the main point is that Lincoln wanted to see people, disapproved of anything that kept them away from him, submitted to constant annoyance, and actually did see an amazing number. Of course he had assistance and time-saving devices. Secretaries were at hand, ready for the immediate sending of telegraphic messages, a bell at his touch for summoning needed help, a clerk to sign land warrants [W. O. Stoddard], and authorities on many subjects ready to respond with specialized advice, as when George Bancroft was asked for historical information, or the storehouse of official lore was tapped for points as to procedures of earlier Presidents reaching back to Jefferson and even to Washington. The march of data into and out of Lincoln's mind would make an impressive procession. He was not as unmethodical as is sometimes supposed, was aware of the importance of files, and in tricky or serious matters was prudently careful to keep records of what he said and of the precise extent of his commitments.

None of his manifold problems came singly. They were tossed into the President's lap in heaps, with nagging persistence and exhausting repetition, bursting at times, or threatening to burst, into acute crises. Easier things—those for which a ready answer could be found—could be handled as department matters, or dealt with by subordinates. It was the bothersome, baffling, or painfully difficult aspects of a case, or questions involving larger trends of governmental ac-

---

[2] Lincoln to Charles D. Drake and Others, Oct. 5, 1863, *Works,* IX, 155–164.

[3] Cincinnati *Daily Gazette,* Oct. 5, 1863, p. 3, c. 3.

[4] A. F. Williams (seeking the non-existent office of commissioner of emancipation) to Lincoln, Mar. 7, 1864, R. T. L. Coll., 31364.

tion, that would reach the President. Broad trends, however, or what was called general policy, could never suffice for all the decisions Lincoln had to make. The very concept of "general policy" was somewhat illusory. The particular case, the human aspects of a situation brought before his eyes, had always to be considered.

To "see" Lincoln and shake hands with him was not the same as knowing him or having contact with his mind. The outward Lincoln, when people met him socially, might be playful, friendly, or seemingly relaxed. Finding him so, people would, in the fuller sense, not meet Lincoln at all. Leaving his presence they could have said something of his face and figure, his clothes, his smile, his manner of bowing and greeting; but they would not have known the burdens and perplexities of the Chief Executive within those clothes, nor would they have glimpsed the feelings and emotional stresses of the inner man.

It was fortunate that strength and patience were given to Lincoln beyond the usual measure. His rugged features were furrowed with anxiety. When Grant's army was hacking its way through the Wilderness there was a week when it was said that "he scarcely slept at all." Carpenter the artist met him in the "main hall of the domestic apartment on one of these days, . . . clad in a long morning wrapper, pacing back and forth a narrow passage leading to one of the windows, his hands behind him, great black rings under his eyes, his head bent forward upon his breast,—altogether such a picture of . . . sorrow, care, and anxiety as would have melted the hearts of . . . adversaries, who so mistakenly applied to him the epithets of tyrant and usurper." [5] There was an irregularity about his eating habits; trays would be carried upstairs, but left untouched for long intervals. The "weary air . . . became habitual during his last years . . . and no rest and recreation . . . could relieve it." As he expressed it, the remedy "seemed never to reach the *tired* spot." [6] The significant thing about all this strain and anxiety is that Lincoln endured it. It did not break him. His was not one of those "high-wrought nervous organizations" as has been said of Jefferson Davis.[7] His nerves were under balance and control, and unlike Davis he had a great American sense of humor.

---

[5] Carpenter, *Inner Life*, 30–31. [6] *Ibid.*, 217.

[7] Gamaliel Bradford, *Lee the American*, 51.

The whole nation, with constant attention to its great future, occupied his thought. Problems were not timed to suit his convenience; matters of peaceful development crowded in with the wretched tasks of war. Lincoln had to be mindful, not only of preserving the nation, but of the kind of nation he was preserving. A war was on, but affairs could not be static for that reason. Industrial growth, foreign relations, and westward advance required as much thought certainly as they had under Buchanan. Even the non-war activities under Lincoln were not "ordinary." Things that were formative, and would be effective for decades to come, aside from the battles and campaigns, took shape in Lincoln's four years.

IV

It is known of Arthur Hugh Clough that he wrote distinguished poetry. It is also known that he spent many hours wrapping and mailing brown paper parcels for Florence Nightingale.[1] If biography is a story of how a man's life was spent, everyday things cannot well be omitted. In August 1862 Abraham Lincoln was watching for his chance—i. e., a victory—so that he might issue the emancipation proclamation. In that month, on August 9, he also gave his attention to a snuff-box presented by the son of Henry Clay.[2] Perhaps the snuff-box, a memento of him who spoke "for the Union, the Constitution, and the freedom of mankind," was not such a small object to Lincoln, nor the service for Florence Nightingale a trivial thing for Clough. If an incident *seemed* small, it may have had real meaning. It could not be considered altogether insignificant that on May 30, 1864, Lincoln handed a little boy a note: "This little gentleman has seen me, and now carries my respects back to his good father, Gov. Hicks." [3]

That was Lincoln's side of the correspondence on this small matter. The incident is of sufficient interest to justify us in noticing the circumstances on the Hicks side. The governor of Maryland had well served the Union cause in the severe crisis of secession, for which

1 Lytton Strachey, *Eminent Victorians,* 174.

2 Lincoln to John M. Clay, Aug. 9, 1862. The President, as in numerous other cases, wrote this letter twice: in a worksheet (R. T. L. Coll., 17537), and in final smooth form (photostat, A. Lincoln Assoc.).

3 MS., Ill. State Hist. Lib.

Lincoln had a lasting gratitude; after that he served usefully in the United States Senate. There is a quality of respect and dignity in the letters he wrote to Lincoln which one finds, in legible handwriting, in the Lincoln papers. In 1863 his ankle was so severely injured that the foot had to be amputated. He therefore paid his personal respects to the President through the assistance of his son. On the day of Lincoln's note just quoted, Hicks wrote to the President, concluding with the words: "I sit at yr door in carriage until I hear your determination. Wish I could climb the stair way as formerly, and see yr Honor myself. yr obt. Servant, Tho. H. Hicks." [4]

Nor was it an unimportant detail when President Lincoln wrote to John H. Bryant of Princeton, Illinois (brother of William Cullen Bryant), concerning a monument to the memory of Owen Lovejoy, whose brother (Elijah P.) had fallen a martyr to the antislavery cause. In the late fifties the managers of the Republican party (notably David Davis) had worked hard, largely behind the scenes, to counteract the influence of such as Owen Lovejoy, who was an upstanding and fearless leader against slavery.[5] Now, in May 1864, Lincoln wrote beautifully of his "increasing respect and esteem" for the man who "bravely endured the obscurity which the unpopularity of his principles imposed." It would indeed have taken a man of the highest principles and character to have earned the carefully phrased tribute which Lincoln paid. The President continued: "Throughout my heavy, and perplexing responsibilities here, to the day of his death, it would scarcely wrong any other to say, he was my most generous friend. Let him have the Marble Monument, along with the well-

---

[4] R. T. L. Coll., 33420.

[5] As revealed in the R. T. Lincoln Collection, Republican leaders in the prewar period were animated by drives for party success and not by antislavery zeal. The result was that those who were moved by strong abolitionist sentiment and who wished to use the party for that purpose were deliberately repelled. Whig support was courted, also that of "Americans"—those who were moved by prejudice against men of foreign birth. (W. H. Gray to Lincoln, Carlyle, Ill., May 31, 1858, R. T. L. Coll., 816.) "Less of the [slavery] discussion," wrote W. M. Chambers from Charleston, Illinois (July 22, 1858), "and less of the favoring of negro equality" (*ibid.*, 1009). David Davis wrote on ". . . in Bureau and Lasalle [counties] success will enure to you if conservative men are nominated. If out & out abolitionists . . . are nominated, then I should fear trouble" (*ibid.*, 1118). Again, August 3, 1858, David Davis wrote, "All the [Republican] orators should distinctly & emphatically disavow *negro suffrage*—negro[es] holding office, serving on juries & the like. . . . For God's sake dont let [Owen] Lovejoy go into Tazewell" (*ibid.*, 1130).

assured and more enduring one in the hearts of those who love liberty, unselfishly, for all men." [6]

When the ladies in charge of the Northwestern Fair for the Sanitary Commission asked the President to donate the original draft of the emancipation proclamation, Lincoln sent it, thus parting with a manuscript which he valued highly. He wrote: "I had some desire to retain the paper; but if it shall contribute to the relief or comfort of the soldiers, that will be better." [7] The paper was "offered for sale [as stated by Isaac Arnold] at the Sanitary Fair held at Chicago, in the autumn of 1863. It was purchased by Thomas B. Bryan, Esq., and by him presented to the Chicago Historical Society . . . ." [8] In the great Chicago fire of 1871 this valuable Lincoln original was burned; had Lincoln kept the document, it would presumably have remained with his papers, which are now safely kept in the Library of Congress.[9]

The personal attention of the President was also required in connection with the children's petition that he "would free all slave children," sponsored by Mrs. Horace Mann and handed to Lincoln by Senator Sumner.[10] The thought that went into the writing of this letter to one of the notable Peabody sisters was Lincoln's own; the petition was preserved in his papers.

In addition to broad national causes—soldier relief, emancipation, and the like—requests kept piling up for merely local or personal favors. One such was mentioned by Secretary Welles: "The

---

6 Lincoln to John H. Bryant, May 30, 1864, photostat, A. Lincoln Assoc. One of Lincoln's carefully written letters. Where Lincoln wrote "Throughout my heavy . . . responsibilities," etc., Nicolay and Hay (*Works*, X, 111) erroneously give "very" instead of "my."

7 Lincoln to Ladies having charge of the North Western Fair, Oct. 26, 1863, photostat, A. Lincoln Assoc.

8 Isaac N. Arnold, *Life of Abraham Lincoln*, 266 n.

9 Bryan was a "Chicago philanthropist and business man," active in promoting the fair. Having paid $3000 for the document, he gave it to the Soldiers' Home. It was securely kept there for several years, placed temporarily in a bank vault, and then moved to the new building of the Chicago Historical Society, where it was so firmly framed and fastened to the wall that it could not be rescued from the 1871 fire. Either at the Soldiers' Home or at the bank it would have escaped. Owing to Mr. Bryan's thoughtfulness, however, a number of lithograph copies were made. For these and other interesting details, with illustrations, see Paul M. Angle, "How Emancipation Manuscript Was Lost," *Chicago Sunday Tribune Grafic Magazine*, Feb. 8, 1948.

10 Lincoln to Mrs. Horace Mann, Apr. 5, 1864, photostat, A. Lincoln Assoc.

President sends me a strange letter from [Vice President] Hamlin, asking as a *personal* favor that prizes may be sent to Portland [Maine] for adjudication." The Secretary of the Navy did not like this. Such a matter "was not to be disposed of on personal grounds or local favoritism"; other New England ports would have equal claims; additional prize courts would be expensive; Portland had no navy yard or station, nor did it have facilities for examining captured vessels, or for confining prisoners. But, said Welles, Hamlin was not moved by such considerations; he wanted all this extra paraphernalia to be set up at Portland "and solicited them of the President, as special to himself personally." [11]

Perhaps this language was a bit strong, though Welles was correct in principle. Nor can it be forgotten that Lincoln himself had played the politician, promoting merely local interests by way of log rolling, while in the legislature of Illinois. Where great advantage was attainable in wartime expenditures, facilities, and appointments, it was natural for many localities to seek their shares of that advantage, but it was essential that the nation's effort be not dissipated by such demands. Here was a case where Lincoln, under constant pressure from such appeals, was careful to refer the matter to the appropriate minister even in a request that was hard to deny because of the personal influence of the Vice President.

V

After one considers the seemingly small matters that had real significance, there remain hundreds that were small only, having no other meaning than to show how Lincoln was harassed, badgered, and importuned in innumerable requests that, to say the least, fell short of the national or patriotic motive. People continually tried to exploit him. He was asked to recommend cotton traders to the military authorities—i. e., to advise that particular men seeking profit in cotton trading be given military facilities. The answer came that the President could not write "that class of letters." [1] Yet in some cases, where trading in enemy territory was represented to him in the best light, he did give permission.[2] Lobbyists for special interests crowded

---

[11] Welles, *Diary*, I, 366–367.

[1] *Works*, X, 71 (Apr. 7, 1864).

[2] *Ibid.*, XI, 48–50 (Mar. 8, 1865). For a scheme of Orville H. Browning, James Hughes,

the hotel bars and could by no means be kept out of the White House. One of these is portrayed by W. O. Stoddard as coming out of Lincoln's room, propelled by a large foot. Some of those who sought to use Lincoln, wrote Stoddard, were "thieves, counterfeiters, blacklegs—the scum and curse of the earth." [3] Toward such men Lincoln was not kindly. He was decidedly blunt.

As to the vast unceasing flow of these miscellaneous requests the reader must be spared, though Lincoln was not. A few instances will indicate the type. There came a request for the use of blockade vessels to bring out a "lady-relative" of a Chicago friend; [4] for permission to a Mrs. Keenan for "her and her little nephew to pass our lines and go to her father in Rockingham, Virginia"; [5] for cadets by the hundred to be appointed to West Point.[6] So tormented was Lincoln "by visitors seeking interviews for every sort of frivolous and impertinent matter [wrote Francis F. Browne], that he resorted sometimes, in desperation, to curious . . . inventions to rid himself of the intolerable nuisance." One of "these bores" was scared off by the pointed statement that the President's varioloid was "very contagious." "'Some people,' said the President, 'said they could not take very well my proclamation; but now, I am happy to say, I have *something that everybody can take.*'" [7] When an editor of a small weekly called at the White House claiming to have been the first to suggest Lincoln's nomination for the office of President, the busy

---

and James W. Singleton, for bringing Southern produce through the lines with prospects of some private profit, see Browning, *Diary*, II, 1–3, 7, 14, 15, 17. Arrangements were completed by Charles H. Ray of Chicago and others, late in the war, to "give the rebels whiskey for cotton" and in general to exchange a variety of Northern goods for Southern products to be obtained from the interior of Mississippi and Alabama. It was stated that the articles taken down could be disposed of (exchanged for cotton) at four times their New Orleans value. C. H. Ray to Lincoln, Vicksburg, April 11, 1865, Ray MSS., Huntington Lib. Other letters in this collection in the Huntington Library give additional details concerning this venture, which was approved by military authorities, by C. A. Dana (assistant secretary of war), and by the President. If fully treated, this Northern trading within Southern lines would be a vast subject.

3 Stoddard, *Inside the White House in War Times*, 58.

4 Lincoln to the Secretary of the Navy, May 28, 1861, Naval Records, National Archives, photostat, A. Lincoln Assoc.

5 *Works*, X, 73.

6 West Point records in the National Archives at Washington contain numerous brief notes and endorsements by President Lincoln, showing his careful and minute attention to cadetships at the United States Military Academy. Photostats are in the files of the Abraham Lincoln Association.

7 Browne, *Every-Day Life of Abraham Lincoln*, 459–460.

Chief sought to escape him by saying he was going over to the war department to see Stanton. The editor then offered to walk over with him and Lincoln said "Come along." "When they reached the door of the Secretary's office, Mr. Lincoln turned to his visitor and said, 'I shall have to see Mr. Stanton alone, and you must excuse me,' and taking him by the hand he continued, 'Good-bye. I hope you will feel perfectly easy about having nominated me; don't be troubled about it; *I forgive you.*' "[8]

VI

That the presidency under Lincoln was not limited to legally official acts was shown by his leadership in the observance of Thanksgiving. It was through him that the day became for the first time a matter of regular annual proclamation by the President. By so using his position he was widening the reach of the presidency itself, making it an institution touching the hearts and expressing the emotions of the American people.

The religious ceremony of giving thanks for the harvest and for other blessings was, of course, an old American custom, as old as the early days of the Plymouth colony. Down the years the custom had become established with special importance in New England, yet before Lincoln's administration there was no regularly recurring annual proclamation by the President. Washington, John Adams, and Madison had called upon the people for specified days of public thanks or prayer, but these earlier presidential calls were not annual and were not associated with the harvest festival, nor with any particular time of the year. The days set aside ranged through January, February, April, May, August, September, and November. The occasions had to do with such matters as the establishment of the Constitution in 1789, the suppression of the whiskey insurrection in 1795, and the making of peace with Britain in 1815.

While the Thanksgiving custom was becoming more firmly established and was spreading to the South, it was the governors who issued the proclamations and indicated the days to be observed in their states. This was not fully satisfactory and in the 1840's a prominent and tireless editress, Sarah Josepha Hale ("Madonna in Bustles") began a campaign of persistent appeals year by year in *Godey's*

8 *Ibid.*, 461.

Lady's Book urging that the governors concur in proclaiming a uniform date, the last Thursday in November. This idea took hold, though not completely; then in 1863 she had another plan. Would not a proclamation by the President, unvarying as to date from year to year, be the best device to establish Thanksgiving Day along with Washington's Birthday and the Fourth of July in the calendar of holidays? The President, she proposed, would proclaim a day of national thanksgiving for the District of Columbia, the territories, the army and navy, and American citizens abroad. Also she hoped he would "appeal" to the state governors to unite with him in proclaiming the same date so that the nationwide festival would become not only a common event for all, but also a great force for the Union. She continued this agitation through the fifties, though in the unenlightened politics of that decade the Union emphasis became inaudible in the noise and clamor of sectional agitation.

Mrs. Hale's letter to Lincoln, embodying her idea that the President should proclaim Thanksgiving, was written on September 28, 1863. Five days later Lincoln issued his eloquent proclamation. In the midst of "a civil war of unequaled magnitude" he noted that peace with other nations had prevailed and that the year had been "filled with the blessings of fruitful fields and healthful skies." Noting the continuance of peaceful industry amid war, he declared: "No human counsel hath devised, nor hath any mortal hand worked out these great things. They are the gifts of the . . . most high God . . . . I do, therefore, invite my fellow-citizens in every part of the United States, and also those who are at sea and those who are sojourning in foreign lands, to set apart and observe the last Thursday of November next as a day of thanksgiving and praise." The editress's appeal was repeated in 1864, and on October 20 of that year Lincoln issued the second regular annual presidential proclamation of Thanksgiving. He recommended "fervent prayers" to God for "inestimable blessings." (On July 15, 1863, Lincoln had issued a proclamation for national thanksgiving, setting August 6 as the date, but this was for notable recent victories; it was a special proclamation, not to be confused with the annual autumn custom.)

Lincoln had done it in his own way. Mrs. Hale's idea had been that the President should proclaim the event for those under national (as distinct from state) jurisdiction and should appeal to the governors for concurrence as to date. Instead of that procedure—which seemed confined to a pattern of jurisdiction, legal authority, and official right—Lincoln simply invited all his "fellow-citizens" to join in the common observance. So far as the President's proclamation was concerned the governors were not brought into the picture. The state executives, of course, also issued their own proclamations and it is of interest to note in the Lincoln Papers the handsome crop of gubernatorial proclamations of Thanksgiving in 1863 and 1864. The newer and more sparse the state or territory, the more elaborate was the printed proclamation. It was a matter in which the governors took pride.

It was fitting that the nationalizing of Thanksgiving should be associated with the man who led the country through what Allan Nevins has called the "Ordeal of the Union." The custom has been continuously followed by all subsequent Presidents,[1] but in the case of its originator it had special significance. In making the proclamation Lincoln was acting not in terms of legal duty or appointed function, but rather as a focus of national thought, as the man to whom the people turned, the spokesman of the nation. The President does various things which cannot be encompassed if one has in mind only his official duties assigned by law. There is an irreducible core of presidential tasks, but beyond that there is a wider field of presidential spokesmanship, and it is worth while to remember how Lincoln performed, how he initiated certain manifestations of leadership, in this broader dimension. We are dealing here with a matter of public relations, with emotional and intangible elements of the national Union, with the virtue and merits of unity itself, and with the President as the embodiment of that unity.[2]

---

1 From the time of Lincoln the fixing of the holiday was a matter of annual presidential proclamation until 1941. In that year Congress for the first time enacted that Thanksgiving Day should thereafter be "a legal public holiday," and that the date should be "the fourth [not the last] Thursday of November." Though Congress has fixed the date, the President continues the customary proclamation which Lincoln originated. *U.S. Stat. at Large,* vol. 55, pt. 1, 862 (Dec. 26, 1941).

2 The subject of Lincoln and Thanksgiving has been treated by the author in *Lincoln Herald,* October 1947. Annotations of that article are not repeated here.

CHAPTER IV

THE GIFT OF LAUGHTER

I

A MAN might recall Lincoln only partially, yet remember his laugh. An old-timer in Springfield wrote to Robert Todd Lincoln: "I remember only the general form of your father as I saw him in the office of Bledsoe and Baker, his height, his length of limb, the cheery laugh in response to a salutation seems to sound in my ears yet." His laugh has also been described as "boisterous," "ringing," "happy," "joyous," and "the President's life preserver." Henry Villard wrote: "A high-pitched laughter lighted up his otherwise melancholy countenance with thorough merriment. His body shook all over . . . and when he felt particularly good over his performance, he followed his habit of drawing his knees, with his arms around them, up to his very face . . . ." Though a laugh is curative and wholesome, there is an even warmer quality in a smile. A newspaper comment in 1860 was: "when he smiles heartily it is something good to see." [1]

Without smile and laughter it would not have been Lincoln. He was born to a sense of humor. As a lad in the Pigeon Creek neighborhood of southern Indiana he had amused his friends, on the sly, with those salty verses, the "Chronicles of Reuben." Forney recalled that

[1] For these descriptive touches the citations are scattered: Samuel Willard, quoted in *Chicago History*, II, 205 ("cheery"); Hay, in *Century Mag.*, Nov. 1890, p. 37 ("boisterous"); Carpenter, *Inner Life*, 150 ("ringing"); Keckley, *Behind the Scenes*, 168 ("happy"); Mrs. Lincoln to David Davis, Chicago, Mar. 4, 1867, MS., Ill. State Hist. Lib. ("joyous"); Carpenter, 161 ("life preserver"); Villard, *Memoirs*, I, 143 ("high pitched," etc.); Helen Nicolay, *Lincoln's Secretary*, 44 ("something good to see"). The quotation from Mary Lincoln, just cited, deserves a further word. Commenting on the "malignity" of Herndon's playing up of the Ann Rutledge romance, Mrs. Lincoln wrote: "Nor did his [Lincoln's] life or his joyous laugh, lead one to suppose that his heart, was in any unfortunate woman's grave."

he "liked the short farce." [2] He was conversant with the humorists of his day. He could anticipate a joke in the making and see how it would be played by such a man as Orpheus C. Kerr. (This pseudonym, a play on "office seeker," was the trade mark of Robert H. Newell.) When General Meigs once inquired who this individual was, Lincoln remarked that his papers were in two volumes and that any one who had not read them "must be a heathen." He enjoyed them best when they poked fun at Welles or Chase. Some of those aimed at himself "rather disgusted him." [3] A sufficient reason for this would have been the dull or misfit quality of some of the anti-Lincoln thrusts.

Lincoln knew also the works of Petroleum V. Nasby (David R. Locke). The humorist himself wrote: "The 'Nasby Letters' . . . attracted his attention . . . . He read them regularly. He kept a series in a drawer in his table, and it was his wont to read them on all occasions to his visitors, no matter who they might be, or what their business was. He seriously offended many of the Republican Party in this way." [4]

He particularly enjoyed a piece in which Nasby ridiculed the opposition of men in the border states to the use of Negro soldiers, and the quick change of opinion on this subject when they realized the advantage of having colored men serve as substitutes for unwilling whites. (It would not have been necessary to associate this attitude with the border region. The same sentiment appeared in New England and elsewhere.) On one occasion, when Noah Brooks spent a night at the Soldiers' Home, the "President, standing before the fireplace, recited the whole of Nasby's letter" which most people had forgotten.

Part of it ran: "Arowse to wunst! . . . Rally agin the porter at the Reed House! Rally agin the cook at the Crook House! . . . Rally agin Missis Umstid! Rally agin Missis Umstid's childern by her first husband! Rally agin Missis Umstid's childern by her sekkund husband! . . . Rally agin the saddle-kulurd gal that yoost 2 be hear! Ameriky fer white men!" [5] If such a passage does not seem very funny now, it may be because one cannot recapture its flavor when written. Satire must have a target, and in this passage the target, now largely

---

[2] John W. Forney, *Anecdotes of Public Men*, I, 38.

[3] Welles, *Diary*, I, 333 (June 17, 1863). [4] Rice, *Reminiscences*, 447–448.

[5] Noah Brooks, *Washington in Lincoln's Time*, 108–110.

forgotten, was the inconsistency of contemporary anti-Negro attitudes.

A great favorite with Lincoln, of course, was Artemus Ward (Charles Farrar Browne), the foremost professional humorist of his day. It was Ward's "High Handed Outrage in Utica" that Lincoln chose for reading to his impatient cabinet on the day when he presented his emancipation proclamation to them.[6] Ward's humor, like Nasby's, was thoroughly dated. Much of its flavor has evaporated. The droll spectacle of Ward in action could be enjoyed only by the immediate audience as they watched him exhibit his wax works or hold forth with bland irrelevance on "The Babes in the Wood."

Lincoln never met Ward, whose highly advertised contacts with the President were fictitious, but he did meet Jeems Pipes of Pipesville, who instructed his hearers on "Eating Roast Pig with the King of the Cannibal Islands." Pipes was the guest of Lincoln in the White House, and an account has come down to us of the President suggesting a bit of stage business for an act imitating a stammering man. Suiting the action to the stammer, Lincoln showed how "irresistibly ludicrous" it would be if Pipes would punctuate his limping speech with an occasional whistle. There is complete lack of dignity in the sound-picture that comes before us: the President turned comedian, the humorist catching on and rehearsing a trick of his trade, their hilarious laughter at this bit of burlesque ringing through the corridors of the Executive Mansion.[7]

II

There is no need to box the compass as to Lincoln's stories. Some of them were reminiscent of boyhood days in Indiana, a state famous for fun and humor. Others, told with equal nostalgic relish, brought back the Illinois prairie days. Amusing incidents that he knew of personally would be stored in his retentive memory and brought to the front of conversation when needed. When some senators demanded a wholesale shake-up of the cabinet because one change had been made, the President was reminded of the farmer who went after seven skunks with a shotgun. "I took aim," said the farmer (as Lincoln retold

[6] Diary of S. P. Chase (*Annual Report*, Am. Hist. Assoc., 1902, II), 87.

[7] Ruth Painter Randall, in *Lincoln Herald*, 50, 27–28 (Feb. 1948); R. T. L. Coll., 33567–9.

it), "blazed away, killed one, and he raised such a fearful smell that I concluded it was best to let the other six go." [1]

Of course Lincoln did not invent all, or most, of the stories he told. Some of them were old acquaintances, and many of the tales or quips attributed to him were not his at all, but were merely pinned on him. The story about Grant's whiskey drinking (Lincoln wanted some of the "same brand" for his other generals) is one of the most familiar, but it was disclaimed by Lincoln, who probably wished he had told some of the good ones for which he was credited. It has been suggested that one should thank a New York *Herald* writer, not the President, for this Lincoln story,[2] and David Homer Bates mentions the Grant-and-whiskey remark as belonging to the category of stories that were current in former times, saying: "Lincoln disclaimed the story in my hearing . . . ." [3] A similar remark in a slightly different form has been attributed to King George II. When some one mentioned that General Wolfe was mad, the King's reported comment was: "Mad, is he? Then I wish he would bite some of my other generals." [4]

It was the view of W. O. Stoddard that Lincoln had "never so much as heard" the vast number of "so-called jokes" attributed to him. When a bit of foul humor was accredited (or debited) to him, the President's face would "flush and darken." [5] In that sense there was hazard in the President's fame as a "funny man." Altogether unjustly, his humor was associated with thoughtless indifference or even with vulgarity. Not all the yarns gratuitously given him were harmless and the general reputation of being a joker was used against him. There were stories which he indignantly denied because they were forgeries made up by his enemies,[6] and others which he disowned simply because they were not his.

There is, however, an ample supply remaining after one has winnowed out the chaff and rejected the spurious. The story about being

---

1 Rice, *Reminiscences*, 236.

2 F. L. Paxson, in *Amer. Hist. Rev.*, XLIII, 168 (Oct. 1937).

3 Bates, *Lincoln in the Telegraph Office*, 197.

4 C. R. L. Fletcher, *An Introductory History of England from the Restoration to the Beginning of the Great War* [1660–1792], 214. (A similar remark has been attributed to more than one king.)

5 W. O. Stoddard, *Inside the White House in War Times*, 55.

6 As to a certain story told against him in 1860, Lincoln wrote: "it is a forgery out and out." Lincoln to H. J. Raymond, Dec. 18, 1860 ("Confidential"), photostat, A. Lincoln Assoc.

"within one mile of Hell" [7] (that far from the Capitol) can be contemporaneously traced, and the one about Negro Joe's dilemma between two roads is found in the Welles diary. This story was an example of a Lincoln anecdote which "clicked" perfectly because of its appositeness to the problem in hand. Deliberation in cabinet had turned upon the Dominican problem as of early 1864, in which Lincoln wisely chose to avoid the blundering policy which Grant unsuccessfully attempted a few years later, and which "almost wrecked" the Republican party.[8] In a milieu of local tyranny, civil war, and military action by Spain to recover control over the Dominican republic, the question arose as to whether the United States should intervene and perhaps annex this island domain. To seize control or intervene would have angered Spain; to make a point of refusing to do so would have created resentment among Negroes and their sympathizers.

Having decided to keep clear of this explosive and dangerous entanglement, Lincoln, in cabinet meeting, told of an interview between two Negroes. One of them, a preacher, admonished his friend: "There are two roads for you, Joe. . . . One . . . leads straight to hell, de odder go right to damnation." Joe answered: "I go troo de wood." The Welles diary continues: " 'I am not disposed to take any new trouble,' said the President, 'just at this time, and shall neither go for Spain nor the Negro, but shall take to the woods.' " [9]

Welles is also authority for an uncomplimentary but humorous remark of Lincoln's concerning Greeley, another of those Lincoln sayings that have the reminiscent western flavor. Lincoln recalled that in early Illinois, with few mechanics and small means, it was customary to make a pair of shoes wear as long as possible with much mending, but the time would come when the leather was so rotten that "the stitches would not hold." He thought Greeley was like an old shoe; "the stitches all tear out." [10] It would be a mistake, however, to evolve a broad conclusion from a casual remark of this nature; Lincoln gave repeated expression of a high regard for Greeley.[11]

Sometimes the origin of a Lincoln story is clouded while at the same time the clouding does not indicate that the story was necessarily un-

---

[7] See below, p. 132.

[8] Allan Nevins, *Hamilton Fish,* 250.

[9] Welles, *Diary,* I, 520 (Feb. 2, 1864).

[10] *Ibid.,* II, 112.

[11] Archer H. Shaw, ed., *Lincoln Encyclopedia,* 142–143.

true. So it was with the President's oft-quoted remark that he "hadn't much influence with this administration." [12] This famous quip is supported by reminiscences of contemporaries, yet Noah Brooks doubted that Lincoln ever said it as usually reported—i. e., with special reference to Secretary Stanton and the war department.[13] It was a familiar item of Washington chit-chat, the more so because of its frequent and pointed applicability. It sounds so much like Lincoln that if he did not originate it he probably wished he had.

Yet, as would naturally be true with such a many sided subject, the applicability of this remark was only partial and should not be taken as giving the whole tone of Lincoln's administration. When, for instance, it was suggested that Lincoln should dismiss the postmaster general from his cabinet, he stated clearly that he himself would be "the judge as to when a member of the Cabinet shall be dismissed." [14]

Other Lincolnian items, of varying quality, are substantiated by contemporary record. There was the President's pun at the time when a young captain was arraigned by court martial as a Peeping Tom; Lincoln remarked that he should have been elevated "to the peerage." There was also the devastatingly sarcastic remark apropos of the political principle that you should "be always on the side of your country in a war." The President said: "Butterfield of Illinois was asked at the beginning of the Mexican War if he were not opposed to it; he said, 'No, I opposed one war. That was enough for me. I am now perpetually in favor of war, pestilence and famine.'" To hear such items is like participating in Lincoln's informal and unpremeditated conversation, listening in, as it were, on his table talk, and catching his unrehearsed or spontaneous witticisms, as when he said that troops "dwindled on the march like a shovelful of fleas pitched from one place to another." Once in a rather atrocious pun, Lincoln was quoted as saying that he was "thin as a shad (yea, worse—as thin as a shadder.)" Pun making was a habit, or disease, of the age, and that remark was not so bad as some atrocities that appeared, for instance, in *Punch.*

Sometimes a story would be associated with Lincoln by context, his own words being quoted along with those of other men. There

---

12 J. P. Usher, in Rice, *Reminiscences,* 100; John N. Kasson, *ibid.,* 379.

13 Brooks, *Washington in Lincoln's Time,* 29.

14 Lincoln to Stanton, July 14, 1864, photostat, A. Lincoln Assoc.

was, for instance, in a string of random jottings on Lincoln, a recording by Hay of Ben Wade's remark that in praying for the prolongation of Taney's life (to outlast Buchanan's administration) he was afraid he had "overdone the matter." Similarly there was a well pointed story—one that Lincoln probably enjoyed—attributed to General Spinner at the time when Richmond papers were going so far as to call Morgan's raid a "success." "Genl Spinner: 'They remind me of a little fellow whom I saw once badly whipped by a bigger man, who was on top of him & jamming his head on the floor. The little cuss, still full of conceit & pluck, kept saying, '*Now,* damn you, will you behave yourself?' " Lincoln, his generals, his intimates, and some at least of his people, were going through the tragic war, certainly with no thought of flippancy, but with jests on their lips.[15]

Noah Brooks, later to become a friend of Mark Twain and Bret Harte, was a skilled raconteur, and when he told a Lincoln anecdote it usually had point and flavor as well as closeness to the original. Brooks was considerably amused at the President's brand of diplomacy when dealing with one of the White House "corps of attaches of Hibernian descent." "One morning the President happened to meet his Irish coachman at the door, and asked him to go out and get the morning paper. The Jehu departed, but, like the unfilial party of whom we read in Scripture, he said, 'I go,' but went not, and the anxious President went out himself and invested five cents in a *Morning Chronicle.* It afterwards transpired that the coachman did not consider it his business to run errands, which coming to the President's ears he ordered up the carriage the next morning at six o'clock . . . ." This summons at an uncomfortably early hour, presumably for an important presidential purpose, could not be ignored. Instead of using the carriage himself, however, the President "sent a member of his household in the equipage to the Avenue, where he bought a paper and rode back, with the mortified coachee on the box."

Another anecdote via "Castine" (Brooks's pen name) pertained to a gentleman who had "been waiting around Washington for three months" in order to obtain a pass to Richmond. Finally he applied "as a *dernier resort,* to the President for aid." "I would be most happy

[15] For random witticisms in this and the preceding paragraph, see Dennett, ed., . . . *Diaries* . . . *of John Hay*, 53, 79–80.

[said Lincoln] to oblige you if my passes were respected; but the fact is I have within the last two years given passes to more than two hundred and fifty thousand men to go to Richmond, and not one of them has got there yet in any legitimate way." [16]

III

Of all the humorous recordings the best are to be found in Lincoln's own works. This goes far to explain the endless fascination of his writings, even down to the commonest jottings or incidental endorsements. It might be the humor of a sharp dig, homely simile, clownish fun, or play acting. It might be nonsense, to which the best humorists have descended, or rather risen; for if we were to omit delightful nonsense we should have to discard the gems of Gellett Burgess, of Edward Lear, and of Lewis Carroll. That Lincoln shared the joyousness of nonsense was shown in 1848 when he was speaking in Congress on internal improvements. Favoring such improvements and supporting huge governmental expenditures for the purpose, he was refuting the objection that they should be financed, not by the Federal government, but by "tonnage duties, under state authority, with the consent of the General Government." He continued: "How could we make any entirely new improvement by means of tonnage duties? How make a road, a canal, or clear a greatly obstructed river? The idea that we could, involves the same absurdity as the Irish bull about the new boots. 'I shall niver git em on,' says Patrick 'till I wear em a day or two, and stretch em a little.' We shall never make a canal by tonnage duties until it shall already have been made awhile, so the tonnage can get into it." [1] Similarly, applying the idea of absurdity, Lincoln said of Douglas that he was using the horsechestnut style of argument. By this Lincoln meant "a specious and fantastic

[16] "A Pair of Lincoln Anecdotes," Sacramento *Daily Union,* May 27, 1863, p. 1, c. 5. In the Castine letters that appeared in the Sacramento *Union* one finds a rich storehouse of authentic source material on Lincoln. Inadequate attention has been paid to Brooks. A careful historical study is given in Wayne C. Temple, "Noah Brooks—Friend of Lincoln," master's dissertation, Univ. of Ill., 1951.

[1] Speech on internal improvements, House of Rep., June 20, 1848, photostat of Lincoln's autograph MS., A. Lincoln Assoc. (Nicolay and Hay, *Works,* II, 41–42.) Lincoln's logic may not have been quite up to his humor if he implied that a bridge or road ought never to be financed on the basis of anticipatory tolls. Such a basis has been proved sound. His whole speech, however, on internal improvements (of which this passage was a small part) was an effective and logically constructed argument.

arrangement of words, by which a man can prove a horse-chestnut to be a chestnut horse." [2]

The continual interweaving of good fun in his writings and speeches shows that humor was no mere technique, but a habit of his mind. When, as he thought, Polk was mistakenly appealing to a declaration by Thomas Jefferson, Lincoln showed that Jefferson's true position was against that of Polk. Then he added: "this opinion of Mr. Jefferson, in one branch at least, is, in the hands of Mr. Polk, like McFingal's gun: 'Bears wide, and kicks the owner over.' " [3] Using exaggerated ridicule to destroy Douglas's position on slavery in the territories (a position which Lincoln considered a "sort of do-nothing sovereignty . . . that is exercised by doing nothing at all"), he considered it "as thin as the homeopathic soup that was made by boiling the shadow of a pigeon that had starved to death." [4] And when thinking of courts—how they should be set up—Lincoln dreaded a "Puppy Court"—i. e., petty local judges, too many of them, and with "salaries so low as to exclude all respectable talent." [5]

Politics aside, one should note Lincoln's whimsical twist in asking a renewal of a railroad pass. "Says Tom to John 'Heres your old rotten wheelbarrow.' 'I've broke it, usin on it' 'I wish you would mend it, case I shall want to borrow it this arter-noon.' Acting on this as a precedent, I say 'Heres your old "chalked hat." I wish you would take it, and send me a new one, case I shall want to use it the first of March.' " [6]

At times a Lincolnian figure of speech would be chosen for its universality and homely appeal: Buchanan after the election of Pierce in 1856, was, said Lincoln, like "a rejected lover making merry at the wedding of his rival." [7] Or the Lincoln phrase would be one that every farmer would understand—e. g., his self-depreciating comment that his speech at Gettysburg would "not scour," [8] or that under John

---

2 Nicolay and Hay, *Works,* III, 229 (Aug. 21, 1858); see also *ibid.,* IV, 212.

3 Speech, June 20, 1848, photostat, A. Lincoln Assoc. (Nicolay and Hay, *Works,* II, 38–39).

4 *Ibid.,* IV, 379–380 (Oct. 13, 1858).

5 Tracy, *Uncollected Letters,* 23 (June 24, 1847).

6 Lincoln to R. P. Morgan, Feb. 13, 1856, photostat of facsimile, A. Lincoln Assoc.

7 Speech at Republican banquet, Chicago, Dec. 10, 1856, *Ill. State Jour.,* Dec. 16, 1856.

8 "He said to me on the stand, immediately after concluding the speech [at Gettysburg]: 'Lamon, that speech won't *scour.*' " Lamon, *Recollections,* ed. by Dorothy Lamon Teillard, 173. (In colloquial farmer language a good plough "scours" when it cuts cleanly through the soil.)

Quincy Adams the post office service "cut its own fodder." He could use current patter (Burnside's "mud march"), or classical mythology ("Procrustean bed"), or Shakespearean metaphor ("a shelled peascod," referring to Pierce).[9]

On the question whether Lincoln's jokes were sometimes risqué, reports and reminiscences differ. One finds diametrically opposite statements, but on the whole the answer would be that Lincoln's humor was sometimes as exquisite as the tooled binding of a volume de luxe, while at other times he fell into expressions that were none too choice and anecdotes that were not intended for the parlor. Such robust yarns occurred off duty, on occasions for which they were not, or their hearers thought they were not, unsuited. After meeting informally with Lincoln in Springfield, Donn Piatt reported Lincoln's manner of talking with "those good honest citizens, who fairly worshiped their distinguished neighbor." Giving way to his natural bent for fun, Mr. Lincoln, reported Piatt, "told very amusing stories, always in quaint illustration of the subject under discussion, no one of which will bear printing." [10]

Some people like risqué stories; some do not; some like them without admitting it. There are degrees, moods, and tenses of unparlorable humor, and a story may be amusingly risqué without being offensively vulgar. It is known that Lincoln's thoughts and conduct were clean. Most of his humorous chit-chat has evaporated and is impossible to recover. Much of it was off the record. What then? If we had all of it barring none, and if parts here and there would need expurgating, one would still ask, to whom should the task of expurgation be assigned? And after all the purification had been accomplished there would remain for undignified sinners a lively demand for the unexpurgated edition.

IV

Lincoln's humorous diversions were not always appreciated or well received. There were contrasting attitudes in American folkways. American wit was irreverent, and religion itself, if too unbending, "provoked the irreverence of professional jokers." [1] There remained

---

[9] Speech at Republican banquet, cited above.

[10] Donn Piatt, in Rice, *Reminiscences,* 485. [1] Sandburg, *War Years,* III, 301.

in America something of a holdover from the days, even of Shakespeare, when Puritans made war upon the theater and other forms of amusement. Religion was unimaginative, somber, and rigidly repressive. "The Devil was as real as the Red Indian." [2] To minds under such a killjoy spell, Lincoln's quips seemed almost sinful—or at best profitless frivolity. In his cabinet, when he read some tomfoolery by Artemus Ward, the heavy burden of the occasion—discussion of the emancipation proclamation—was to Lincoln all the more reason for a bit of preliminary playfulness, while to Chase's Puritan mind such levity on a serious occasion was incomprehensible. As a young man Chase had continually chided himself on his unworthiness, had suffered miserably from religious self distrust, had repeated psalms when bathing or dressing, and had considered it a sin to waste time. There was a charming young lady with whom, as he wrote in his diary, he would have fallen in love if she had not been "fond of the gay world" and "disinclined to religion," which he valued "more than any earthly possession." [3]

Much of the contrast between Lincoln and Stanton is revealed by the comment that if Lincoln would be telling a rich story and Stanton would enter, the story and the laughter would die.[4] If the President got along better personally with Seward than with others of his cabinet, it may have been partly because Seward had a sense of humor, as when he said: "Did you ever hear Webster's recipe for cooking cod? 'Denude your cod of his scales, cut him open carefully, put him in a pot of cold water, heat it until your fork can pass easily through the fish, spread good fresh butter over him liberally, sprinkle salt on the butter, pepper on the salt, and—send for George Ashmun and me.' " [5]

Among those who had no ear for Lincoln's humor was Henry Wilson, Republican senator from Massachusetts. When Wilson and Goldwin Smith, with several English friends, were conferring with the President, conversation turned on the subject of battle losses, which the distinguished Englishman illustrated by reciting statistics of killed, wounded, and missing. No one was more emotionally moved

---

2 *Ibid.*

3 Robert B. Warden, *Private Life and Public Services of Salmon Portland Chase,* 190.

4 Stoddard, *Inside the White House,* 165.

5 Dennett, ed., . . . *Diaries . . . of John Hay,* 196.

by these human tragedies than Lincoln; but, crossing his long legs, he solemnly observed that as to such matters one should apply darky arithmetic. The visitor did not know of two systems of arithmetic, upon which the President offered to illustrate the point by a "little story," much to the embarrassment of the senator; "had he [Wilson] known a thousand stories he would not have told one of them to Prof. Smith and his grave-looking British friends; and he was mortified that the President, who in all things had few superiors in easy dignity of manner [this is the comment of W. D. Kelley], should so inopportunely indulge in such frivolity."

Lincoln went on with the story. Darky Jim wanted to know "what is 'rithmetic?" It's when you add up things, explained the other. " 'When you have one and one, and you put them together, they makes two. And when you subtracts things. When if you have two things, and you takes one away, only one remains.' 'Is dat 'rithmetic?' 'Yes.' 'Well, 'tain't true den; it's no good.' Here a dispute arose, when Jim said: 'Now, you s'pose three pigeons sit on that fence, and somebody shoot one of dem, do t'other two stay dar? I guess not, dey flies away quicker'n odder feller falls.' " The trifling story seemed to the President to illustrate the arithmetic to be used in estimating the actual losses resulting from great battles. "The statements you refer to [he said, turning to the Professor] give the killed, wounded and missing at the first roll-call after the battle, which always exhibits a greatly exaggerated total, especially in the column of missing." [6]

Petroleum V. Nasby wrote: "Grave and reverend Senators who came charged to the brim with important business—business on which the fate of the nation depended—took it ill that the President should postpone the consideration thereof while he read them a letter from 'Saint's Rest, wich is in the state of Noo Jersey,' especially as grave statesmen, as a rule, do not understand humor, or comprehend its meaning or effect." [7]

There were those, such as Adam Gurowski, who simply could not understand Lincoln's language. The ferocious old Count considered Lincoln a "brat" and worse: "he is no fit for be President." [8] Even

[6] William D. Kelley in Rice, *Reminiscences,* 286–288.

[7] David R. Locke, *ibid.,* 448.

[8] Dennett, ed., . . . *Diaries . . . of John Hay,* 177; see also LeRoy H. Fischer, "Lincoln's Gadfly—Adam Gurowski," *Miss. Vall. Hist. Rev.,* XXXVI, 415–434 (Dec. 1949).

old-time associates, who comprehended Lincolnian humor readily enough, found occasionally (though not often) that it grated on them. When O. M. Hatch and Jesse K. Dubois asked for a certain appointment, Lincoln wired in 1863: "What nation do you desire Gen. [Robert] Allen to be made quarter-master-general of? This nation already has a Quarter-Master-General." [9] Hatch and Dubois then wrote to Lincoln explaining their request. Allen had notified Governor Yates that there was to be "a new Quarter Master General" and had asked "will you go for me," asking also that he wire the President and get other state officers to do the same. Yates was absent, and, "supposing that General Allen *knew what he said,* . . . and believing him competent," these men (Hatch was secretary of state for Illinois; Dubois was state auditor) had telegraphed Lincoln urging the appointment. They added: "We profess to be your friends and have no desire to embarrass you, . . . We trust the same spirit governs you —though we confess your despatch read harshly to us." [10]

Lincoln's humor had misfired, and he was quick to correct the first impression. On receiving the Hatch-Dubois letter he at once telegraphed: "The particular form of my despatch was jocular, which I supposed you gentlemen knew me well enough to understand. Gen. Allen is considered here as a very faithful and capable officer; and one who would be at least thought of for Quarter-Master-general if that office were vacant." [11]

V

It was a sad thing that Lincoln's fondness for stories and his enjoyment of humor were so inscrutable. His biographer, William H. Herndon, had it all physiologically accounted for. We have a remarkable Herndonian passage in which the humorless partner-biographer mounted his unbridled steed and dashed off on an analytical gallop to clarify the profound subject of Lincoln's laughter. The passage illustrates a curious combination of qualities—a ridiculous approach which has no importance for a serious biographer, combined with a curious readability.

---

[9] Lincoln to J. K. Dubois and O. M. Hatch, telegram in cipher, Sep. 15, 1863, photostat, A. Lincoln Assoc.

[10] O. M. Hatch and Jessie K. Dubois to Lincoln, Springfield, Ill., Sept. 16, 1863; R. T. L. Coll., 26310–1.

[11] Lincoln to O. M. Hatch and J. K. Dubois, Sep. 22, 1863, photostat, A. Lincoln Assoc.

Lincoln, explained Herndon, had a low and feeble circulation. His "whole organism moved slowly to the influences of all kinds of stimuli." His body and mind "needed oiling." He had spells of gloom and melancholy. "This state of Mr. Lincoln made him . . . unconscious of his surroundings and to arouse that somewhat dormant consciousness he needed a stimulant and that was found in a story and tell it he would."

There follows a readable passage in which Herndon vividly pictures Lincoln in a typical story-telling scene with an unappreciative secretary. It comes out as a lifelike portrayal of such a situation (though at second hand, because Herndon knew practically nothing directly about Lincoln as President), but it is all mixed up with one of Herndon's own inventions—a theory of Lincoln's laughter which is something of a howler.

"This story telling [continued Herndon]—this stimulant, sending more blood to the brain, aroused the whole man to an active consciousness . . . . Grave men in grave times, sometimes his ministers, would approach him in order to state the urgency of some matter that needed his immediate attention. Mr. Lincoln would look up to his minister half sleepily—dreamily, saying—'Mr Secretary take a chair': he would, in a moment or two, after the secretary had stated his errand, tell some story much to the disgust of his minister, who would censuringly say—'Mr President, this is no time for story telling—the times are grave and full of war, and the country is fast drifting to ruin.' Mr. Lincoln would good naturedly reply—'Come Mr Secretary, sit down—sit down—I have a perfect and profound respect for you and were it not for these stories I should die; they are rents through which my sadness—gloom and melancholy escape.' Mr. Lincoln would thus arouse his half dormant consciousness into activity . . . ; and after he had been thus aroused he would listen to what the . . . minister eagerly told him, like a philosopher and in a short moment he would make his answer . . . so wisely and earnestly as to convince the man that that point . . . had been . . . maturely considered before, long, long before this moment of meeting."

In this immediate passage, describing Lincoln's manner with a humorless cabinet member, Herndon gives something like a reasonable treatment of Lincoln's joking, but what follows indicates the peculiar kind of hash that he was so apt to dish up. "This state of Mr Lincoln [he wrote], particularly so if it was accompanied by a mental & nervous exhaustion, produced by long and intense study, caused him to have delusions—saw apparitions—specters & the like." Lincoln's laughter was thus associated with something supposedly abnormal, as if he was not himself when in good humor. Lincoln, wrote his partner, was usually "a gloomy & melancholy man, but at exceptional times a momentarily happy one." To follow this line of reasoning would be to identify Lincoln's humor with a kind of illusion, as if the laughter-loving Lincoln were seeing things.

Poor Lincoln! He was so beset, or so physiologically sluggish, that he had to whip up these jokes and stories. We ought to understand it and not be too hard on the man. The passage continues: "Let no man blame Mr Lincoln for being sad or seeing apparitions: his sadness and his gloom came naturally out of his organism and his apparitions from the same source somewhat and from nervous & mental exhaustion. Let no man rudely censure Mr Lincoln for his story telling . . . ." [1] And so on.

It is fair to add that we are dealing here with one of Herndon's numerous and voluminous letters to his literary collaborator, Jesse Weik. In these letters, frankly given as something very different from a finished product, Herndon simply poured out his thoughts and ruminations as they rushed through his mind. He didn't try to check them. Sometimes he would admit that they were to be taken only in part, and only for what they might be worth, and that Weik was to be the judge. "Draw on your imagination and fill up [he once wrote]: it will please the people . . . . Pick out what you like and cast away the balance. I have no time to elaborate—amplify &c &c nor correct." [2]

This quality of Lincoln, thought Herndon, was good for the country. Had Lincoln been ardent, "with swift and strong volumes of blood pouring through his brain," had he been impulsive and rash, the national cause would have failed. "This feeble low circulation —this slow irritability which slowly responded to stimuli—this organism . . . [etc.] saved the nation from disunion and consequent ruin." Herndon knew that his collaborator disliked "such stuff ter-

[1] "Lincolns nature—one side," Herndon to Weik, Dec. 22, 1888, Herndon Weik MSS.
[2] Herndon to Weik, Nov. 13, 1885, *ibid.*

ribly, and yet some persons may like it." [8] He now had Lincoln's humor vivisected. It was explainable. He had cleared up what might have remained a permanent mystery. The great man's story telling actually had its good side! Herndon could reconcile it. It was about like saying that sunshine should not be too much regretted and if a man had his happier moments his friends should do their best to endure it.

Herndon, who was bored by Lincoln's story telling, was explaining Lincoln's humor, as on other occasions, unbeliever that he was, he "explained" Lincoln's religion. This was the biographer who had so much to do in setting Lincoln, and Mary Lincoln, before the world in a manner which the world has too largely accepted. In the whole passage, which has to be read carefully to be believed, the emphasis is on two things: in elucidating his hero's humor Herndon stresses, above all, his utter gloom, sadness, and melancholy; and, physiologically speaking, he puts the stress on the man's sluggish circulation of blood. It did not seem to occur to him that there must have been something other than gloom in a man who could brighten a conversation as Lincoln did, and that the quickening of circulation could just as well have been a cause as a result of mirth.

VI

When one thinks of Lincoln as a man of humor (perhaps a better term than "humorist" which suggests a calling or occupation), one thinks also of Mark Twain. As one develops the comparison—which has already been drawn and need not be repeated here [1]—the life and personality of the man Lincoln, set against the man Clemens, becomes a theme of major import. Starting with Pigeon Creek and Holliday (Cardiff) Hill, the subject unfolds till it embraces the human race and touches the mysteries of life. One can show how Lincoln and Clemens were alike and how they differed. Both were of Southern origin, both knew the border between North and South, and both lived their formative years in a pioneer, or near-pioneer society. They shared the same type of native background, folkways,

---

[8] Herndon to Weik, Dec. 22, 1888, *ibid.*

[1] Dixon Wecter, "Lincoln, Mark Twain, and the Human Race," *Abr. Lincoln Quar.*, II, 157–175 (Dec., 1942); Bernard DeVoto, *The Portable Mark Twain* (intro.), 5.

and dialect. Both had a minimum of conventional education and formed their characters and intellects in the school of experience. Both had the advantage—for them—of growing up as poor boys. Both knew the rude horseplay, the side-splitting jest, the practical joke, and the preposterous tall tale of the West. Both were close to nature, with a tenderness for animals, though that was hardly a backwoods characteristic.

The same fascination, spell, and adventurous lure of the river stirred in their hearts. Clemens became a licensed river pilot and produced masterpieces of river literature. Lincoln's love of the river produced no literary results, but his biography would be incomplete without his river experiences. Coming down the Sangamon River in a large canoe was "the manner of A's [Abraham's] first entrance into Sangamon County." [2] His early introduction to the majesty of a local court was related to a boyhood river incident, his specialization in river navigation was of early political importance, and his inventive genius turned to the problem of easing a steamboat over shoals.

Each was to become, in a supreme sense, the very embodiment of that combination of qualities that we call "American." Both were "stamped unforgetably with the American brand." [3] Both had a sympathy for the Negro, and both gave poignant expression (Twain with devastating satire) to a sense of outrage at the mistreatment of the colored race. Both felt a kind of collective guilt on this subject and a long overdue debt which the white race owed to the colored. And of all the traits which they had in common, the most dominant and deeply felt was an overwhelming sense of protest against social abuse and human injustice.

There were, of course, contrasts between them. Lincoln's soul endured the fiery ordeal, and in the heat of war's crisis his leadership was shaped and his character forged. Clemens sat out the war, so to speak, or escaped it in a part of the far West that was, as Lincoln said, "undisturbed by the civil war." [4] They had a similar lack of enthusiasm for military "glory." Both Sam and Abraham recalled their brief army experiences as matters of burlesque and comedy. There was the obvious fact that Clemens was not a political leader and Lincoln

[2] Autobiography, June 1860, R. T. L. Coll., 3219.
[3] Wecter, in *Abr. Lincoln Quar.,* II, 157.
[4] *Works,* VIII, 99 (annual message to Congress, Dec. 1, 1862).

not (in the professional sense) a man of literature; but that did not mean that Twain ignored matters of statesmanship in his thinking, or that the President lacked the gift of expression. Mark could have written something like Lincoln's contribution to the Rebecca "Lost Township" letters or some of his less serious speeches, and Lincoln could have done some of the paragraphs of the *Gilded Age.* Mark Twain's comments on political life in Washington, on the party spirit (which he characterized with sharp bitterness), and on the meaning of patriotism, showed how much his mind was occupied with fundamentals of political and social democracy. One of their strongest traits in common was a deep-seated conviction of the need for self criticism in a democracy. For each the intolerable thing was imprisonment of the human mind. One of the faults which they both despised was a smug and unrealistic complacency in the face of crying abuses, North and South.

Lincoln's contrast to Clemens can be extended, both as to environment and as to personality. Clemens's association with men of wealth, his impracticality, his Sellers-like speculative dreams, restless travel, theatrical poses, boyish display, extravagance, craving for applause, and fastidiousness of dress set him apart from the homely lawyer and unpretentious President. And, as Dixon Wecter has pointed out, the ultimate philosophical outlook of Twain was, or seemed, the opposite of Lincoln's.

That is to say, Lincoln developed a serenity of optimism and democratic faith to which he gave classic expression, while Clemens seemed (or professed) to have a low opinion of the "damned human race," and, as his writings would indicate, became in the darkened evening of life bogged and tangled in a jungle of fatalism and despair. To each, of course, had come great personal tragedy—to Lincoln in the death of mother, sister, father, and two boys; to Clemens in a whole series of family casualties, including the terrible death of his brother Henry, the loss of children, and the passing of his beloved Olivia. It was Lincoln whose spirit was better able to recover from, though never to forget these sorrows; and, though both had disgust for conventional creeds and dogmas, it was Lincoln who was better able to grasp for his own personal uplift the eternal assurances of Christianity.

Looking over the whole subject, one realizes that Lincoln and Clemens would have understood each other if they had met and conversed, which they never did. It has been remarked that they would have enjoyed the same jokes, which was true; but that is a small part of the subject. Each had a spirit sensitized to the tragedies of Adam's breed. The bonds of personality that would have united them were their Americanism, their humor, and their understanding of the human heart.

VII

There are factors in life which need not so much to be explained as to be appreciated and accepted. It is those who have relish for Lincoln's humor who come nearest to understanding Lincoln the man.

There is little profit, however, in disquisitions on the cause and purpose of Lincoln's humor. The best place to seek his humor is not in a cheap collection such as *Old Abe's Jokes, Fresh from Abraham's Bosom . . .*.[1] Humor is like caviar or *hors d'oeuvres.* One should not make a meal of it. The passing moment has much to do with the matter. The success of a joke is not always predictable. The mood must be right, also the delivery, timing, and congeniality with the listener. Humor in action or in running discourse is better than humor in bottles with labels, or piled up in joke books. By contemporary accounts Lincoln's humor was successful. It was not of the labored, limping variety which makes the inveterate jokester something of a nuisance.

It was in fact notably successful. People enjoyed Lincoln the better, and had more of a fellow feeling for him, as they repeated tales of how he rode a galloping thunderstruck cow, or how he outwitted a judge in a horse trade by swapping a saw-horse for the judge's sorry-looking nag. His playfulness, in the western tradition, became in his own lifetime at once a mark of popularity and a factor in American folklore.

It was true, of course, that sometimes his humor was turned against him in denunciation or ridicule. For the campaign of 1864 there appeared the following: "Only Authentic Life of Abraham Lincoln, Alias 'Old Abe.' A Son of the West. With an account of his birth and

[1] Monaghan, *Lincoln Bibliography,* no. 335. This collection, published in 1864, was the first of a considerable category. The subtitle ran on: "Containing all his Issues, Excepting the 'Greenbacks,' to call in some of which, this work is issued."

education, his rail-splitting and flat-boating, his joke-cutting and soldiering, with some allusions to his journeys from Springfield to Washington and BACK again. Sold by all Newsdealers in the Country." [2]

The journey *back to Springfield* was to have its unspeakable pathos after April 15, 1865, but in this 1864 leaflet the suggestion was only that Lincoln would be defeated in the coming election. As to making fun of his soldiering, one would need only to quote Lincoln himself. "By the way, Mr. Speaker [said Lincoln in Congress, in his rollicking speech in ridicule of Cass in the campaign of '48], did you know I am a military hero? Yes, sir; in the days of the Black Hawk War I fought, bled, and came away. Speaking of Gen. Cass' career, reminds me of my own. I was not at Stillman's defeat, but I was about as near it, as Cass was to Hulls surrender; and, like him, I saw the place very soon afterwards. It is quite certain that I did not break my sword, for I had none to break; but I bent a musket pretty badly on one occasion. . . . If Gen Cass went in advance of me in picking huckleberries, I guess I surpassed him in charges upon the wild onions. If he saw any live, fighting indians, it was more than I did; but I had a good many bloody struggles with the musquitoes . . . ." [3]

One should not bother too much to settle the questions as to how Lincoln "used" his mirth and pleasantry. One may think of it as part of him, indeed as part of his greatness. Tyrants and dictators do not laugh, nor do they induce genuine laughter. Popular jokes become associated with them, but the dictator is the butt or target, not the participant or raconteur, of the jest. Lincoln's anecdotes were human, close to the soil, and drawn from life. A famous example was his parable-like reference in 1858 to Stephen, James, Franklin, and Roger producing timbers which fitted together so perfectly as to convince the ordinary man that they had worked in collusion.[4] He knew that this type of illustration would make his point against Douglas and others memorable. It is always a question how many statements people will preserve in memory from a speech which they hear, but it is a

[2] *Ibid.*, no. 336.

[3] Speech in House of Representatives, July 27, 1848, photostat of Lincoln's autograph MS., A. Lincoln Assoc. (Nicolay and Hay, *Works,* II, 75–76.)

[4] *Works,* III, 10 (house divided speech, June 16, 1858). This simile was subject to criticism, since no such conspiracy between Douglas, Buchanan, Pierce, and Taney existed; see *Lincoln the President,* I, 108.

rather safe bet that they will recall the homely example or the concrete instance.

Chauncey M. Depew wrote: "His power of managing men, of deciding and avoiding difficult questions, surpassed that of any man I ever met. A keen insight of human nature had been cultivated by the trials and struggles of his early life. He knew the people and how to reach them better than any man of his time. I heard him tell a great many stories, many of which would not do exactly for the drawing-room; but for the person he wished to reach, and the object he desired to accomplish with the individual, the story did more than any argument could have done.

"He said to me once, in reference to some sharp criticisms which had been made upon his story-telling: 'They say I tell a great many stories; I reckon I do, but I have found in the course of a long experience that common people'—and repeating it—'common people, take them as they run, are more easily influenced and informed through the medium of a broad illustration than in any other way, and as to what the hypercritical few may think I don't care.' "

". . . He said that, 'riding the circuit for many years and stopping at country taverns where were gathered lawyers, jurymen, witnesses and clients, they would sit up all night narrating to each other their life adventures; and that the things which happened to an original people, in a new country, surrounded by novel conditions, and told with the descriptive power and exaggeration which characterized such men, supplied him with an exhaustless fund of anecdotes which could be made applicable for enforcing or refuting an argument better than all the invented stories of the world.' " [5]

It was characteristic of Lincoln's joking while President that the very darkest and stormiest of times would set off an explosion of humor. "A frontiersman," he was quoted as saying, "lost his way in an uninhabited region on a dark and tempestuous night. The rain fell in torrents, accompanied by terrible thunder and more terrific lightning. To increase his trouble his horse halted, being exhausted with fatigue and fright. Presently a bolt of lightning struck a neighboring tree, and the crash brought the man to his knees. He was not an expert in prayer, but his appeal was short and to the point: 'Oh,

[5] Chauncey M. Depew, in Rice, *Reminiscences,* 427–428.

good Lord, if it is all the same with you, give us a little more light, and a little less noise!' "[6]

An appeal was once made to the President on behalf of a lieutenant who was accused of embezzling government money. It was charged that the officer had corruptly received while on duty the sum of forty dollars. "Why, Mr. Lincoln," exclaimed the officer, "it wa'n't but thirty dollars." This reminded Lincoln of an Indianian who got into a quarrel with a neighbor. "One charged that the other's daughter had three illegitimate children. 'Now,' said the man whose family was so outrageously scandalized, 'that's a lie, and I can prove it, for she only has two.' This case is no better [said Lincoln]. Whether the amount was thirty dollars or thirty thousand dollars, the culpability is the same. Then, after reading a little further, he said: 'I believe I will leave this case where it was left by the officers who tried it.' "[7]

A good story that has come down pertained to Lincoln's droll remark about one of his generals. As remembered by Ward Lamon, the President, arousing himself from meditation, remarked: " 'Do you know that I think General —— is a philosopher? He has proved himself a really great man. He has grappled with and mastered that ancient and wise admonition, 'Know thyself;' he has formed an intimate acquaintance with himself, knows as well for what he is fitted and unfitted as any man living. Without doubt he is a remarkable man. This war has not produced another like him.' "

" 'Why is it, Mr. President' asked his friend, 'that you are now so highly pleased with General ——? Has your mind not undergone a change?'

" 'Because,' replied Mr. Lincoln, with a merry twinkle of his eye, 'greatly to my relief, and to the interests of the country, *he has resigned.* And now I hope some other dress-parade commanders will study the good old admonition, "Know thyself," and follow his example.' "[8]

VIII

By easing into a story Lincoln could change the climate of an interview. He could carry the ball, shape the trend, and control the

---

[6] Rufus Rockwell Wilson, *Intimate Memories of Abraham Lincoln,* 423.

[7] Lamon, *Recollections of Abraham Lincoln,* ed. by Dorothy Lamon Teillard, 83.

[8] *Ibid.,* 125–126.

direction of a conference. Conversation may be partly a matter of holding the floor. Lincoln would do this by bland good nature, his partner or opponent in discussion hardly realizing just how or why the breeze was shifting; then the President would conclude the conference with a smiling face without actually agreeing; or, in a crowd or reception, would slip away behind a barrage of merriment.

Lincoln's joking usually had pertinence to the subject in hand, but to think of every bit of his humor as serving a purpose or carrying a point would be a mistake. His laughter was a kind of release. It was Seward's impression that he "had no notion of recreation as such; enjoyed none; went thro' levees &c purely as a duty—found his only recreation in telling or hearing stories in the ordinary way of business—often stopped a cabinet council at a grave juncture, to jest a half-hour with the members before going to work; joked with every body, on light & on grave occasions. This was what saved him." [1]

Lincoln's humor was not "put on"; it was never artificial. A glimpse of the manner in which his fun making belonged to the daily, or hourly, Lincoln is seen in a newspaper item pertaining to Mrs. Lincoln who was visiting an ocean resort in the summer of '61. When she left for Washington a *Herald* reporter wrote that it was largely because she thought Lincoln was lonely. He needed some one to listen to his fun making. She said that he always joked and jested at the supper table "no matter what the labors and fatigues of the day"; he was always "[l]ively, sociable, and agreeable." [2]

The by-play of laughter was part of Lincoln's knack of being good company. It was an attribute of his magnetism. He was the man around whom fellow lawyers and courthouse loungers would cluster. Though his published works were usually serious, dignified, and well polished, humor served him as a kind of popular language. More than that, it was an actual resource in thought and deliberation; for the man of humor is superior in mental tools. He does not stop with the obvious stereotype or the conventional stock phrase. He takes another look at a problem, turns it over, gives it a new relevance. He frees himself from uninspired literalness. Characterizing a well known

---

1 Henry W. Bellows to his wife (reporting a conversation with Seward), Apr. 23, 1863, Bellows MSS., Mass. Hist. Soc.

2 New York *Herald,* Aug. 25, 1861, p. 2, c. 4; article dated at Long Branch, N.J., Aug. 23, 1861.

type, Robert Louis Stevenson remarked that "Some people swallow the universe like a pill." [3] These are the folk who take what is ladled out to them, who "fall for" partisan ballyhoo, who accept the politician at face value (which is more than politicians themselves do), and who believe what they see in print. But in a democracy the type of opinion that is vitally needed is of the sort that sees behind the demagogue's façade, or punctures the pompous orator's dignity. Such an attitude, stimulated by Lincolnian humor, is thus actually an element in the formation, or conditioning, of opinion.

To say that playfulness for Lincoln was a life-saver was no exaggeration. It was therapy of the spirit. Turning from dark worry to laughter was not, as Herndon ponderously supposed, a kind of deliberate or laborious setting-up exercise to induce circulation of the blood. Often it was an easing down, a relaxation, a healthy release from mental imprisonment. It is the man who can find such release who has the free intellect. To understand this fully is to attempt to realize, or perceive, pretty much the whole of Lincoln's wartime task, with all of its care, anxiety, immense responsibility, and unending pressure. Remembering this from direct observation of Lincoln, Depew wrote: "He knew the whole situation better than any man in the administration, and virtually carried on in his own mind not only the civic side of the government, but all the campaigns. And I knew when he threw himself (as he did once when I was there) on a lounge, and rattled off story after story, that it was his method of relief, without which he might have gone out of his mind, and certainly would not have been able to have accomplished anything like the amount of work which he did." [4]

For the rest, his lighter moods were a means of disarming (or winning over) an antagonist, of getting a hearing, of assuring popularity, of keeping the common touch, of enriching and enlivening the day's work. Even had there been no more to the subject—and there was vastly more—it would be enough to remember that anecdotes and jests were for Lincoln a source of enjoyment.

---

[3] R. L. Stevenson, "Crabbed Age and Youth," *Virginibus Puerisque and Other Papers,* 102.

[4] Rice, 428–429.

CHAPTER V

CAPITOL HILL

I

IN 1833 an English observer penned a description of the American Congress. The principal object of the members, he said, was to impress constituents by long, meaningless speeches to be printed and sent home. Debate, rambling on from one topic to another, was confusing to listeners. There was, he thought, a certain difference between the two houses, with the Senate gaining, but only slightly, by the comparison. In the upper chamber, though there were some outstanding men such as "Livingstone [*sic*], . . . , Webster, . . . Hayne, . . . [etc.]," he found "the same loose, desultory, and inconclusive mode of discussion . . . but . . . less talking for the mere purpose of display, and less of that tawdry emptiness and vehement imbecility which prevails in the Representatives." [1]

Thirty years later Gideon Welles, recalling his visit to the Senate in the year 1829, contrasted his old-time memories with what he knew of the upper house in 1863. "There is [he said] an impotent and ridiculous attempt at self-sufficient and presuming airs, an exhibition of lame and insolent arrogance, on the part of many Senators towards men who are, to say the least, their equals in every good quality." "If the present room is larger [than thirty-four years earlier]," he wrote, "the Senators seem smaller." At another time he observed: "The demagogues in Congress disgrace the body and the country. Noisy . . . professions, with no useful policy or end, exhibit themselves daily." [2]

---

1 *Annual Register* [London], 1833, 467–470. Allowing for the unescapable truth in these observations, one is nevertheless reminded of Lowell's essay "On a Certain Condescension in Foreigners," *Atl. Mo.*, XXIII, 82–94 (1869).

2 Welles, *Diary,* I, 224, 244, 206.

This was a familiar *motif*—the theme that the quality of Congress had deteriorated. Another observer who recorded the same impression was Carl Schurz, writing of the time when Charles Sumner entered the Senate. It was a new era (about the end of 1851); the voices of Calhoun, Clay, and Webster were no longer to be heard in that famous body. Schurz wrote: "What was left of the old generation of public men was mediocrity and commonplace—country lawyers grown up in the politics of their localities and had [*sic*] a slight smattering of general knowledge gathered from the reading of some of the standard histories—tobacco-chewing statesmen with dull and heavy minds, uncouth manners and pompous airs." [3]

On this matter, of course, opinions differed, and encomiums on Congress in Lincoln's day were not lacking. One of the members, A. G. Riddle, remarked on the Thirty-Seventh Congress (1861–63) that history does not "show any large body of men surprised by a great emergency, which ever met it more unitedly or with a more determined spirit." The Congress of those days, he wrote, was "a huge committee of ways and means, where should work the brain, and the controlling will, and whence should issue the law, the mandates, the sinews, which together should accomplish the real purpose to be wrought out by the war itself." He thought the President and the armies were on a less important level. "In this view the President merely executed the expressed will of Congress. The great armies, with their generals, . . . were the mere mechanics of the struggle." [4]

On another page Riddle left a different set of impressions. In casting his eye over members of the House, his first thought was "wonder as to how half the men ever got there." "One is next impressed," said Riddle, "by the audacity, or serene stupidity, which enables so many men to be willing to occupy these seats." He wondered whether there was anywhere in the world "so melancholy a book as *The Political Register and Congressional Directory* . . . by Ben: Perley Poore?" [5]

---

[3] Arthur Reed Hogue, ed., *Charles Sumner: An Essay by Carl Schurz,* 8 (intro.). This is from Schurz's first draft; the passage was considerably weakened when redrafted.

[4] Albert G. Riddle, *Recollections of War Times,* 36, 42.

[5] *Ibid.,* 222.

II

It was in 1861, Lincoln's first year as President, that the Republican party had for the first time in American history a majority in the Congress. It was called, however, a "rump Congress." Of the thirty-four commonwealths in the United States it included members from only twenty-three that adhered to the Union. (In addition, what was called "restored Virginia" was represented, and Senator Andrew Johnson of Tennessee retained his seat for some months after his state seceded. Later in the war West Virginia and Nevada were admitted.) If the Congress had been fully national—i. e., if the eleven seceded states had been represented—the Republicans would not have had a majority.[1]

Under these circumstances it was but natural that the 1861 Congress consisted chiefly of new men. "From Maine every representative was a new man; of the thirty-three members from New York, only eight had held seats in the last Congress; of the five representatives from New Jersey, three were new men. Two thirds of the entire delegation in the House consisted of men who had never before held seats in Congress." [2]

A glance at the roster of members in the period 1861 to 1865 proves puzzling now; so many of the names strike no chord. Who was Socrates N. Sherman of New York? Or Ambrose W. Clark or Burt Van Horn from the same state? Few would be able to identify such men as Portus Baxter of Vermont, George T. Cobb or John L. N. Stratton of New Jersey, Sydenham E. Ancona or John P. Verree of Pennsylvania or Robert H. Nugen of Ohio.[3]

This newness, inexperience, and obscurity on the part of many members tended toward submissiveness, giving expanded influence

---

1 Coöperationists in the South in the crisis of 1860–61, noting that Lincoln was not an abolitionist and "not in harmony with the extremists of his party," argued further that "even if he wished to encroach upon the South, he would be unable to do so, because majorities in both branches of Congress would be against him." In the Senate, supposing all the states represented, the opposition to Lincoln was estimated to have a majority of eight; in the House, a majority of twenty-one. Dwight L. Dumond, *The Secession Movement, 1860–1861,* 130–131.

2 *Harper's Pictorial History of the Civil War,* I, 184.

3 *Biographical Directory of the American Congress (House Doc. No. 783,* 69 Cong., 2 sess.), 266–274.

to a few leaders or managers. That these managers were anti-Lincoln is constantly to be borne in mind in any study of the wartime situation. It was the leading managers who stayed on; otherwise there was a considerable turnover of congressional membership. The Republicans did not fare well by the election of 1862,[4] and the consequence was described as follows by one of the members: "Seldom has the personnel of a House been so completely changed without a change of parties." [5]

As times changed it might have been said that America had passed from the period of senatorial grandeur—the era of Webster, Calhoun, Clay, and Benton—but had not outlived the age of grandiloquence. In the sixties the spreadeagle style, often in decadent form, was still in vogue. Much was mere oratory, designed not so much to promote legislation as to offer a sounding board for particular members. The attention of those who (presumably) would read the speeches when mailed to them, and the approval of the galleries, were seldom disregarded. The floor of Congress was more the scene of exhibitionist performance than of serious business.

It was said of President Lincoln's first Congress, as well as of himself and his cabinet, that they were chosen "to do anything, everything, except what fell to them to do—fight the greatest civil war of history, one of the enormous wars of modern times." [6] This task "came upon them as an utter surprise. . . . The great contest passed . . . through all stages—moral, political, legislative, judicial—and no man of the North (and perhaps few of the South) was at first in the least aware of the tendency, until, armed, they stood confronting each other, neither believing the other intended very war." [7]

The House of Representatives, thought Riddle, was "unquestionably the worst place in America for a man to speak in." What with members sauntering in and out, loafing, telling stories, and creating a general air of confusion and inattention, it became necessary for the member who (in a manner of speaking) had "the floor" to raise his voice to so high a volume (for the reporters) "as to preclude all free mental action." [8] Sometimes the Congress was enveloped with the

---

[4] *Lincoln the President,* II, 232–234. [5] Riddle, 249. [6] *Ibid.,* 37.
[7] *Ibid.,* 37–38. That Lincoln did not intend war is brought out by Riddle (38–39).
[8] *Ibid.,* 223.

"lurid atmosphere" of battle, with artillery actually shaking the walls of the Capitol. Whether that battle setting was literally present or not, the national legislature "was an arena in which men could not win distinction or secure the attention of the press or public." [9] "During the entire war [wrote Riddle] the American people knew little, saw little of the men in Congress, and cared only that they should create and supply the needed money, and back Mr. Lincoln and the Secretary of War." [10] The point of all this is that, while men spoke for display, and while full galleries indicated popular curiosity, the people neither cared much for Congress nor were conversant with its proceedings.

Riddle found it hard to understand "the attachment that men form for Congressional life." It seemed strange to him that some members were so "bitten of it" that after ceasing to be members they would work hard to be appointed sergeant-at-arms, doorkeeper, or postmaster "where once they were masters." This Ohio member spoke with loathing of the title "Honorable" prefixed to members' names. His comment brings to mind Congressman Lincoln's request in 1848 that his wife avoid the title in her letters to him. As for the volumes of the *Globe,* they aroused in Riddle no more enthusiasm than a retiring congressman's "scrapbook filled with newspaper laudations and criticisms." Taking satisfaction in the fact that he had at least escaped personal injury, Riddle remarked: "No man has ever served through three congresses and returned healthfully to take up his old . . . pursuits." As for the upper house, he thought, "nobody cares much for the Senate save to get into it." [11]

The very building, its passageways and odors, had become offensive to Riddle, and in the years following his brief congressional service, if he visited the Capitol—he was then practising law in Washington—he found that "the old dismaying flavor assails me, bringing momentary heart failure." His friendships had not been confined to men of his own party. He remarked: "Indeed, I have always found disinterested friends [he also called them "assured" friends] among the Democrats, and have observed among politicians that the warmest personal ties are usually across party lines." [12]

---

[9] *Ibid.,* 32. [10] *Ibid.,* 40. [11] *Ibid.,* 40, 224–225. [12] *Ibid.,* 226–227.

III

Of one thing there was no doubt: members of Congress in Lincoln's day were picturesque individuals. Their habits, clothes, visages, posturings, and verbal displays offered many a theme for the artist and the reporter. Curiosity as to seeing public men in person and watching them perform has long been an American trait, as shown by the visitors who regularly crowded the galleries of House and Senate. In the upper chamber on a typical day there were about forty or less in attendance. Total membership was forty-eight, including two from Virginia (the "restored" government set up at Wheeling). Some of the senators—such as Lafayette S. Foster of Connecticut, Richard S. Field of New Jersey, Anthony Kennedy of Maryland, and Robert Wilson of Missouri—made only a slight impression. Those who were "well known" numbered hardly more than a dozen. Leaders who were largely effective in actually shaping public affairs were still fewer.

One of "the few men whom visitors to the Senate galleries first asked to have pointed out" was Charles Sumner of Massachusetts. Conscious of his superiority, meticulously careful in pose and dress, this successor of Webster was the very model of an important senator. "His favorite costume was a brown coat and light waistcoat, lavender-colored or checked trousers, and shoes with English gaiters," otherwise known as spats. It has been reported from his own lips that "he never allowed himself, even in the privacy of his own chamber, to fall into a position which he would not take in his chair in the Senate." In that seat and on the floor he was "studiously dignified." Preparation for his speeches was made weeks in advance, and prying youngsters, with no respect for his privacy, could see him in his rooms, "before a pier-glass . . . , studying the effect of his gestures by the light of lamps placed at each side of the mirror." [1]

Though his manner was pedantic, he was assisted by a "magnificent voice" and genuine learning. Lincoln is said to have remarked that Sumner was his idea of a bishop.[2] The senator "regarded his position

---

1 Noah Brooks, *Washington in Lincoln's Time,* 24–25.

2 Frank Maloy Anderson, ed., *The Mystery of "A Public Man": A Historical Detective Story,* 216. Lincoln may or may not have made the remark, but it describes Sumner and it has a Lincolnian flavor.

as Chairman of the Committee on Foreign Relations as superior to all others in Congress, while he was unquestionably the leader of the Abolition wing of the Republican party." [3]

In the camps of leading generals the feeling toward Sumner and men of his kind was not always favorable. From Meade's headquarters Colonel Theodore Lyman wrote as follows on March 5, 1864: "I find that politicians, like Sumner and company, have a way of saying of officers who have had their very clothes shot off their back and have everywhere displayed the utmost skill and courage, that 'their hearts are not in the cause,' or 'they are not fully with us'; meaning that these officers do not happen to fully agree with every political dogma the party may choose to enunciate." He added: "it would appear that Washington people often think the best test of faithfulness is to stay away from the fighting and make a good many speeches to people who entirely agree with your sentiments." [4]

Some of Sumner's associates considered him dictatorial and insufferable. His speaking perfection was carried to an extreme; it was like an overindulgence in "fine writing." He was too scholarly and precise; his rehearsed performance and self-conscious emphasis smacked of the oracular, while his "fastidiousness," even in matters of ordinary routine, "provoked injurious comments." [5]

All told, however, Sumner was a man worth noting; there were times (notably in the *Trent* affair) when the country would have been poorer without his public service and achievement. Fully to appraise him, one must remember that the principles in which he ardently believed—international peace, antislavery, rights for Negroes—were, for him, burning and compelling impulses; he was not animated, as many were, by the commoner motives of the politician. Into the advocacy of these principles he put tremendous—albeit pompous and self-righteous—effort. He felt and believed, deeply and sincerely, in what he was working for. Though rhetorical to excess, he was by no means a mere orator. One cannot study his life fully without realizing that he was fearless, disdainful of upper-class petting or praise, outspoken in dealing with matters on which others were timid (e. g., the shocking denial of civil rights in the fugitive slave act of 1850), and earnestly

---

[3] Poore, *Perley's Reminiscences*, II, 98. [4] Agassiz, ed., *Meade's Headquarters*, 78–79.
[5] Brooks, 23–24.

conscious of moral imperatives. The regret is that he was difficult—some would have said impossible—to get along with. In his "Crime against Kansas" he was terribly at fault in his abuse of Southerners; that his message was clothed in a superior garb of ostentatious learning and misplaced similes made the abuse no easier to bear. (Preston Brooks was vastly more at fault in thinking that the answer to Sumner was to assault him with a cane and give him a severe beating. Nor did Brooks's answer gain true validity by its guise of "honorable" conduct.)[6]

Sumner and his partner from Massachusetts were sometimes mentioned in the same breath,[7] but in personal characteristics they were of different mold. Henry Wilson had none of Sumner's elegance. As described by Noah Brooks he was "rather loose and ramshackle in his manner of speech; his enunciation was not distinct, his delivery was slipshod, and he was neither precise nor fortunate in his choice of words . . . ." He was not handsome or prepossessing, but "stout, florid, dark-haired, and of a portly figure."[8]

Wilson was, however, one of the key men in the Senate. He was more concerned with congressional business and formulative labor than with oratory or showmanship. As chairman of the committee on military affairs, with a background as brigadier general of Massachusetts state militia, he had an active part in devising, explaining, and promoting legislative measures touching the raising and organizing of the army. This is not to say, however, that his measures were always well chosen.

No study of the wartime Senate, especially in the latter part of Lincoln's administration, is adequate without frequent reminders of the prominence of Benjamin F. Wade of Ohio and Zachariah Chandler of Michigan.[9] Wade was described as of the "Cromwellian type," a man "of rugged, fierce, and vindictive feeling."[10] Noah Brooks al-

---

6 See the work by E. L. Pierce (4 vols.), and the briefer account by Moorfield Storey. Sumner's voluminous papers are in the Harvard library. David Donald, author of *Lincoln's Herndon,* is preparing a full-length biography. Carl Schurz's eloquent essay on Sumner, unfinished at Schurz's death, remained buried for many years. It has been brought to light and edited by Arthur Reed Hogue (Univ. of Ill. Press, 1951).

7 For Gurowski's withering comment on Sumner and Wilson, see *Lincoln the President,* II, 209.

8 Brooks, 23.

9 *Lincoln the President,* II, 209–210.

10 Cox, *Three Decades of Federal Legislation,* 88.

lowed that the Ohio senator was "tender-hearted" and "lovable," "the embodiment of the high qualities that he possessed—manliness, courage, vehemence, and . . . bulldog obduracy . . . ." Having said this, Brooks noted further that his "impatience" with the Lincoln administration "betrayed him into frequent exhibitions of bad temper, . . . and his intense radicalism too often hurried him into complications with the more conservative Union politicians . . . ." Brooks thought that "he did not always extricate himself from these entanglements with credit to himself." [11] In one of his thumbnail portraits Ben: Perley Poore wrote: "Then there was bluff Ben Wade, of Ohio, whose honesty was strongly tinged by ambition, and who looked at the contest with the merciless eyes of a gladiator about to close in a death-grip." [12]

Much the same mixture of eulogy and denunciation is to be found in accounts of Zach Chandler. George F. Hoar of Massachusetts found him "strong as a rock, true as steel, fearless and brave, honest and incorruptible." In a glowing passage, too long to repeat here, Hoar went on to speak of the senator's plain spoken simplicity, scorn for elegant phrases, and disregard "for fine sentiment or the delicacies of a refined literature." Without such men as Chandler, Hoar believed that "the Union never would have been saved, or slavery abolished, or the faith kept." [13]

Such a comment indicated, what is well known, that Chandler had his partisans. If one thinks, however, of Lincoln and of his chances for success with Congress, the quality for which Chandler became most conspicuous, and in which he was most influential, was his "distrust," [14] or rather his acrimonious hostility, to presidential policies, and toward the President himself as a leader. The senator's vindictive aggressiveness on domestic problems was matched, as is often the case, with startling jingoism in international outlook. The partisanship of the man, directed toward the utter dominance of a faction within a party, was to appear in later years. His success as a politician rested

---

[11] Brooks, 26.

[12] *Perley's Reminiscences,* II, 100. A. G. Riddle, Wade's eulogist and biographer, called him "the first man in the Senate." Riddle, *Recollections,* 40.

[13] Hoar, *Autobiography of Seventy Years,* II, 75 ff. Hoar, however, admitted that Chandler had "great faults" (p. 77), and wrote, as did others, of his vigorous control of patronage.

[14] McClure, *Men of War-Times,* 62.

on questionable use of patronage to build up his political control in Michigan.

IV

In judging of the House of Representatives one needs to distinguish between the façade, or showcase, and the unpublicized situation behind the scenes. In terms of later standards one might have regarded the office of speaker as of great importance, but during the Lincoln administration that office lacked the dominance that it was to acquire in the days of Thomas B. Reed or Joseph G. Cannon. Yet some of the most exciting episodes in the House wing were connected with the election of the speaker. In the last prewar Congress it had taken eight long weeks of wrangling and balloting to elect to the speakership William Pennington of New Jersey, a man of little distinction.[1] The Republican choice for the Thirty-Seventh Congress (1861–1863), Galusha A. Grow of Pennsylvania, was known for pioneer vigor, physical impressiveness. combativeness toward Southerners, and earnest agitation for free homesteads, but he was not destined to become outstanding in the history of the speakership.

Of Schuyler Colfax it might be said that he was the stuff of which vice presidents are made.[2] Not that he should be written off as altogether a minor figure; indeed he was one of the best known men of his time. He was described as "neat, nimble, shiny, on his face a constant smile which might easily have been called a smirk." [3] This smile was a trademark; he was known as "Smiler Colfax." It was observed that in presiding over the House his manner "left something to be desired." He performed "like an auctioneer." [4]

James A. Garfield of Ohio belonged to the small group of men—

---

[1] In this Congress the first vote for speaker was taken on the first day, December 5, 1859, the eventual winner (Pennington) receiving one vote, that of John Sherman of Ohio. *Cong. Globe,* 36 Cong., 1 sess., 2. On the forty-fourth and last ballot, Feb. 1, 1860, Pennington received 117 votes, the minimum necessary to a choice. *Ibid.,* 655. He could not have been chosen but for Knownothing votes, and should not be regarded as a leading contender for the speakership; that designation should be applied to McClernand on the Democratic side and Sherman on the Republican.

[2] In 1868 Schuyler Colfax was nominated as Republican candidate for Vice President after five ballots in the national convention. He was elected and served during Grant's first administration, but for the second term he was rejected in favor of Henry Wilson. Edward Stanwood, *History of the Presidency,* I, 321, 328, 348.

[3] D. B. Chidsey, *The Gentleman from New York: A Life of Roscoe Conkling,* 64.

[4] Brooks, 21.

including Edward D. Baker, Frank P. Blair, Jr., and Robert Schenck —who alternated between a military and a congressional career. Such men, though something of a problem for Lincoln, attracted particular attention, as when Garfield entered upon his service in the House (December, 1863) in the uniform of a brigadier general, soon to be exchanged for civilian clothes. In 1861, with no previous military experience, he had left the principalship of the institute that later became Hiram College in Ohio to form a regiment, of which he became colonel and in which a large portion of his student body enlisted. Brigadier general at the age of thirty, and shortly thereafter major general and congressman, he was well started, though that was hardly suspected at the time, on the road to the presidency.[5]

Henry Winter Davis of Maryland, Republican radical, is chiefly remembered for his sharp hostility toward Lincoln's policy for restoration of the South. This was bitter enough, but his opposition to the existing administration did not end there. He extended his activity to other fields, including the international. In 1864 he introduced a resolution intended as a rebuke and check upon Secretary Seward, and designed to give the lower house control of foreign policy. His resolution asserted that Congress "has a constitutional right to an authoritative voice in declaring and prescribing the foreign policy of the United States" and "it is the constitutional duty of the President to respect that policy . . . in diplomatic negotiations." When a matter was pending in Congress, his resolution continued, it was "not a fit topic of diplomatic explanation with any foreign Power." [6] Incidentally, remembering the declaration of the House in 1861 in approving the unauthorized act of Wilkes, the Davis principle would have made it impossible for Lincoln to have adjusted the *Trent* affair, thus seriously endangering the nation, besides robbing the Lincoln government of a significant diplomatic success.

"Having turned Radical, for a purpose," wrote Edward Bates, "he [Davis] seems to ignore all former doctrines, and stakes his all on the struggle for leadership of his faction." Bates noted how "peremptory,"

[5] Robert Granville Caldwell, *James A. Garfield: Party Chieftain.*

[6] Davis's resolution died with the session. It was offered on June 27, 1864; the session ended on July 2. To have voted on the resolution in the existing parliamentary situation would have required a suspension of the rules. How far Davis expected a vote is doubtful; he supposed "the House will probably be too impatient to give it much consideration." *Cong. Globe*, 38 Cong., 1 sess., 3309 (June 27, 1864).

yet how "conveniently vague," Davis's resolution was. He predicted that the Marylander would "kill himself off." "The original radicals will not trust him—His knavery is of a different sort from theirs." [7]

Gideon Welles looked upon Davis's drive for power as part of a "disposition to make the legislative . . . the controlling power of the government." "Davis," he said, "never has been, and never will be, a useful Member of Congress. Although possessing talents, he is factious, uneasy, and unprincipled." Welles bracketed Davis with "a clique of malcontents" which he also characterized as an "embryo party." [8]

Davis was a member of the Thirty-Eighth Congress (1863–65), but not of the Thirty-Seventh (1861–63). We have the following description by Noah Brooks: "At that time he was about forty-five years of age [forty-seven in 1864], . . . with a round, boyish head, sandy hair and mustache. He had a high, clear, ringing voice, and a manner of speaking which was peculiar in its sharpness and firmness. He was a brilliant speaker, but not a ready debater . . . . Garfield once said of him that his eloquence was 'clear and cold, like starlight.' " In summing up his appraisal of Davis, Brooks observed that he had "not left any lasting trace of his public career" except for one thing—"his record as a persistent and violent critic of Lincoln's reconstruction policy." [9]

Conspicuous among the "politicos" was Roscoe Conkling of New York. Handsome and well endowed, he was superb in masculine beauty, with well modeled head, full beard, and pendant curl atop his forehead. Like Garfield, John Sherman, and Blaine, his chief prominence was to be reached in garish postwar decades. With his striking appearance, unbounded confidence, oratory, and talent for politician-like management, he was to ride the crest of triumphant Republicanism almost to the presidency, while he was also to contribute to the intraparty factionalism so evident in the eighties. "Possibly like Pooh Bah," writes his biographer, "he was *born* sneering." "He was touchy, temperamental . . . , incalculably conceited." Though he became a boss, he was not the friendly "mixer" type. Rather he was "haughty, supercilious, aloof." As for crowds, he

---

7 Bates, *Diary*, 380 (June 28, 1864).

8 Welles, *Diary*, II, 202 (Dec. 19, 1864).

9 Brooks, 18.

wanted them "in front of him and a little below, respectfully listening." He was a Beau Brummell "in the exact sense that while he did not originate fashions he sported them incomparably." [10] Known as a successful lawyer, in which capacity he was famous for "bullying witnesses," [11] the gentleman from upstate New York was a formidable fighter in controversial, even hateful, episodes. In certain obvious matters he and the President were in apparent or alleged agreement.

When Lincoln wrote in 1864 that "no one could be more satisfactory" [12] to him than Conkling, he may have had in mind the congressman's vigorous support of emancipation and of measures friendly to the Negro race. Also it should be remembered that the choice was limited to men who were actually available, and that the Republican faction opposed to Conkling was unfriendly to the President.

Conkling, in fact, developed a reputation as a "staunch supporter" of Lincoln, also as being the "legatee of Seward." [13] This was misleading. His attitude toward Southern reconstruction was the opposite of Seward's, while his support for Lincoln was belied by his friendliness toward Thad Stevens, his similarity to Henry Winter Davis, his prominence in the formation of the committee on the conduct of the war, his severe denunciation of General Charles P. Stone, his vindictiveness, and his full assortment of "radical" [14] tendencies. It is hard to see how in the full accounting he should have been deemed an upholder of Lincolnian policies. Here was something of a paradox. The successful invoking of Lincoln's name (where convenient) by a man such as Conkling was one of the misleading signs of the times. Both Henry Winter Davis and Roscoe Conkling were

---

10 Chidsey, *Roscoe Conkling,* 1–2, 4–5.

11 *Ibid.,* 11.

12 If Lincoln praised Conkling here it was indeed faint praise. He added: "I do not mean to say there [are] not others as good as he in the district; but I think I know him to be at least good enough." Lincoln to Ward Hunt, Aug. 16, 1864, photostat, A. Lincoln Assoc.

13 Alfred R. Conkling, *The Life and Letters of Roscoe Conkling, Orator, Statesman, Advocate,* 188, 204. This is a worshipful eulogy by a nephew. For a colorful, modern, and highly readable treatment, see the biography by Donald Barr Chidsey, cited above.

14 The reader, of course, will not be misled by the term "radical" applied to Conkling. While belonging to the group specifically known as "radicals" (Thaddeus Stevens, Henry Winter Davis, and their kind), he was conservative on economic and social questions, undemocratic, supporter of Grant against "Liberal Republicans," and in later life "a prosperous corporation lawyer with some unsavory but rich clients." Chidsey, *Roscoe Conkling,* 364.

considered good Republicans; yet the Marylander was famous for assailing Lincoln, while it was said of the New Yorker that "the mantle of the late Winter Davis" had fallen upon him.[15]

V

Of the "peace Democrats" in the House, the most conspicuous, not to say notorious, were Clement L. Vallandigham of Ohio and Fernando Wood of New York. The Ohioan came to be shunned and scorned by men of his own party.[1] His attitude was complex and not susceptible of easy definition. He denied the allegation that he was anti-Union. What can be said with assurance is that, from the standpoint of the Union cause promoted as a war movement against the Southern Confederacy, he was regarded as disloyal (this again being a charge that he would have stoutly denied). His opposition to the Lincoln administration was made abundantly clear, as was also his belief that the war was wicked, atrocious, and futile.

Vallandigham was dangerous in that he used the time-honored traditions of civil rights as weapons against the existing government. He was "altogether a personable man," with regular features, complexion "fresh and fair," manner "agreeable and prepossessing." Though he spoke with great excitement and convulsive gestures, he was described as "a good speaker—smooth, plausible, and polished, . . . well versed in literature, history, and politics." He had high nuisance value in "filibustering" tactics. At a "wave of his hand" the Vallandigham faction in the House would "scud into the . . . cloakrooms"; at another signal they would rush back to their seats when needed." [2] (This is not to imply that they accomplished much on the floor of the House.) Sometimes a movement with which a man

15 Conkling's sarcastic personal enemy, James G. Blaine, could not endure this comparison. "The resemblance is striking," he said. "Hyperion to a satyr, . . . mud to marble, . . . a singed cat to a Bengal tiger, a whining puppy to a roaring lion. Shade of the mighty Davis, forgive the almost profanation of that jocose satire!" *Cong. Globe*, 39 Cong., 1 sess., 2299 (Apr. 30, 1866).

1 The Vallandigham element proved a serious embarrassment to McClellan in 1864, and when Democrats and moderate Republicans were promoting the Philadelphia convention of August 1866, designed to develop sentiment for non-vindictive reconstruction, Democratic leaders made it clear that they did not want Vallandigham to be associated with the movement.

2 Brooks, 18–19.

is indelibly associated embraces more than the man himself, and that was true of Vallandigham. As will be noted in another chapter, the whole subject of Lincoln's "arbitrary" rule on the one side, and wartime civil rights on the other, was dramatized and focused in the Vallandigham case.[3] In the long run he probably increased the number of pro-Lincoln votes.

Fernando Wood of New York was for good reason regarded as an ally of Vallandigham, but the two men were very different in personality. The Ohioan was nervous and fiery, the New Yorker polished, restrained, and calculating. Adept in Manhattan "politics," Wood had achieved influence in Tammany Hall, but he became much more prominent by organizing "Mozart Hall," a vigorous rival of the Tammany Society.[4] Much of his life was involved in the roaring factionalism of metropolitan politics in the days of "Dead Rabbits," "Bowery Boys," and other riotous gangs.[5] He was a "democrat" with the small letter, battling against Whig conservatism, opposing nativist intolerance, and favoring free trade in opposition to the protective tariff. In several terms as mayor of New York City he promoted movements for a better and more efficient city administration. In the secession crisis of 1860–61, having naturally opposed the election of Lincoln, Wood took the view that Southern withdrawal was inevitable, remembered that New York City was joined by many business links with the South, and declared that the metropolis ought to secede from the United States and set itself up as a "free city." This novel idea produced a flurry of discussion but went no further.

For a time, just after the Sumter outbreak, Wood spoke for vigorous and non-partisan support of the Union, but in a few months he was bitterly denouncing the Lincoln administration, opposing conscription, favoring peace negotiation with Southern leaders, and, by the admission of his friendly biographer, coming "dangerously close to treason." [6] As congressman in the years 1863 to 1865 he continued

---

[3] See below, chap. ix.

[4] For a thorough and detailed study, revealing the intricacies of metropolitan, state, and national Democratic politics, see *Fernando Wood of New York,* by Samuel A. Pleasants (1948). Though admitting Wood's defects, including conduct that "approached the line of disloyalty during the Civil War," this biographer urges (p. 201) that "a comprehensive estimate of the man should note more creditable features as well."

[5] Pleasants, *Fernando Wood,* 80, 81.

[6] *Ibid.,* 120.

the agitation of Vallandigham, who was not in Congress during that period.

Described as a "born politician," Wood is said to have "depended far more upon . . . the sharing of drinks and the manifestations of a warm personal interest in the ordinary voter, than upon the more orthodox methods." [7] It was said that he "knew every longshoreman in his district by name." [8] As portrayed by Brooks, he "was always calm, cool, and collected. His hair and mustache were dyed black, and his thin, spare face, elegant manners, and precise method of speech, gave him the appearance of a refined and scholarly man. He never lost his temper, was always agreeable, polite and even courtly." [9]

The full story of these two stinging gadflies—Vallandigham and Wood—cannot be told in a paragraph. It is true that Wood worked with Vallandigham and that the pair were thought of as a team of "peace Democrats." It is also true, however, that Wood "did not like Vallandigham, and on more than one occasion he held long conversations with President Lincoln in regard to the notorious Ohio Copperhead. He was especially anxious that Lincoln should not make a martyr of Vallandigham . . . ." [10] On the question of peace, and of the return of the Southern states to the Union, he wrote challenging letters to Lincoln, worrying the President with nagging demands that the President's own letters, meant to be confidential, should be published.[11]

Also prominent among the outspoken anti-Lincoln Democrats was the "Tall Sycamore of the Wabash," Daniel W. Voorhees, representative from Indiana. His virulent speaking was the more effective because of his striking appearance, natural talent for eloquence, and mastery of invective. In his strong dislike of abolitionists and of the Republican party he was sometimes bracketed with Vallandigham and Wood, but his career was not always negative and obstructionist. He was vigorous in denouncing arbitrary arrests and was described by an admirer and colleague as "an eloquent tribune of the people." [12]

A vivid personality among the House Democrats was S. S. ("Sunset") [13] Cox of Ohio. He was not a man to be overlooked, being often

---

[7] *Ibid.*, 27. [8] *Ibid.*, 202. [9] Brooks, 19–20. [10] *Ibid.*, 20.

[11] To be treated in a later volume, in connection with peace discussions of 1864.

[12] Cox, *Three Decades*, 224.

[13] So called because of his vivid passage describing a sunset.

on the floor, and was known for witty, facetious, and emphatic speeches. Though personally friendly toward Vallandigham, his general attitude was that of a loyal Democrat supporting measures to uphold the Union cause, and coming forward with constructive proposals for the adjustment of the *Trent* affair, the abandonment of privateering, and the honorable treatment of crews and officers on captured Confederate ships. It was he, according to his own statement, who "nominated [William T.] Sherman to President Lincoln as the first choice of Ohio for a brigadier general." [14] Cox's long career was remarkable not only in politics. He was a distinguished lawyer and was interested in western development. With his flair for writing, he was known also for achievement in journalism and literature.

VI

Thaddeus Stevens of Pennsylvania was well understood to be the Republican leader in the House of Representatives. It is true that he disclaimed the role of party spokesman, saying rather that he was "ahead of the party" and that he did "not speak the sentiments of this [Republican] side of the House." When Maynard of Tennessee pointed out that the Pennsylvanian's remarks would be taken as "those of a representative of his party," Stevens replied: "I speak for myself only." Maynard's rejoinder was: "it will not be so understood." [1] From this colloquy it will appear (1) that Stevens's power in the House was so widely known that he was recognized as the spokesman of the Republican party; and (2) that this spokesmanship was so ill defined, vague, and unauthorized that all responsibility could be easily brushed aside. The House could not control Stevens; yet (not always, but as a regular thing) Stevens went far toward controlling the House. It was not a matter of leadership duly organized and officially determined, but rather of a forceful man imposing his will by methods of his own upon a working majority of the House.

Stevens's official status was that of chairman of the committee on ways and means, whose duty it was to study what would now be called the budget (a word not much used then) and to prepare tax legisla-

---

14 Cox, *Three Decades,* 208.

1 *Cong. Globe,* 37 Cong., 3 sess., 240 (Jan. 8, 1863).

tion, but he got tangled up on tax questions [2] and his activities could not be described in terms of committee functions. In what sense, then, was Stevens a "leader"? Who made him a leader? He was not speaker of the House, nor was he majority leader in the fully recognized sense. If it suited him he would speak for the House; otherwise he would claim to speak only for himself. Yet people came to look to him as more of a spokesman of the party than Lincoln. Since it was the party in control, his word passed as that of the most numerous branch of the national Congress.

What was called Stevens's leadership was strongly flavored with boss rule. On one side of the coin one sees Stevens with his forceful scowl and domineering personality. The reverse of the coin was a kind of weakness or follow-the-leader habit on the part of large droves of Republicans in the House. Power was exerted by the making of "deals," by party caucus, by informal agreements, and by striking the fear of the Lord into the hearts of any who might stand up against him. In July 1861 Stevens maneuvered it so that Galusha A. Grow, whom he could manage, was chosen speaker instead of Frank Blair, Jr., whom he hated. Blair, besides being friendly to Lincoln, was by far the more forceful man; Stevens's hand in the affair made all the difference.[3] In December 1863, at the opening of the Thirty-Eighth Congress, a visitor to the House would have noted that Washburne of Illinois nominated his rival, Colfax of Indiana, for speaker, and that with the smoothness of a well oiled machine Colfax was easily chosen. What was not evident on the surface was that this was by Stevens's design. It had all been worked out by backstage combinations and bargains among House Republican members.

Stevens's coarse manner and rough bluster were among his means of control. On one occasion, when debate was to end at a certain time, a Republican member, Ashley of Ohio, yielded to permit a further half-hour of Democratic discussion. With a big gallery, everyone excited, and nerves on edge, a large group of angry Republicans including Stevens gathered round Ashley's seat. As a journalist recorded it: "There was Thad. Stevens, got up in full fighting trim . . . , shaking his finger at Mr. Ashley for giving way and reading him a

---

[2] *Ibid.*, 238–240.
[3] William E. Smith, *The Francis Preston Blair Family in Politics*, II, 118.

lecture. Stevens's face looked fire, while Ashley's was as red as a fresh cut of beef." It was not as if Ashley was the kind of man to stand up to Stevens. The significance of the incident lay in the fact that he was controllable by Stevens's steam-roller tactics.[4]

Stevens's technique was manifest in his relations with the House committee on military affairs. It might have been supposed that that committee, of which Frank Blair, Jr., was chairman, would work up plans for military legislation, as was true of the corresponding committee of the Senate headed by Wilson of Massachusetts. Stevens, however, ignoring Blair's committee, presented his own military bill to the House in 1861. When asked by Mallory of Kentucky why the military committee was not allowed to perform its proper functions, Stevens had the rudeness to reply that if Blair reported a different bill it should be rejected at once. Though Blair was regarded as a friend and supporter of the President, the bill of Stevens was railroaded through.[5]

On another occasion, when Republicans in the House were faltering and threatening to revolt on a measure which Stevens was determined to have passed, A. K. McClure sat by him and watched his methods during the moments before the session formally opened. ". . . I heard a leading Pennsylvania Republican approach him," wrote McClure, "to protest against committing the party to that policy." Stevens did not plead, argue, or seek to persuade. He simply commanded the "trembling suppliant" to do as he was told and vote for the measure. The dissenting member obeyed. Had he not done so, said McClure, he "would have been proclaimed to his constituents, over the name of Stevens, as a coward, and that would have doomed him to defeat." [6]

Toleration and caution, important with Lincoln, were not in the "Commoner's" vocabulary. It stands to his credit that he used his power for such liberal causes as Negro suffrage in the District of Columbia and abolition of slavery by constitutional amendment, but it was also used for measures associated with hatred and war hysteria, proscription of Southerners, sweeping confiscation of their

---

4 Richard Nelson Current, *Old Thad Stevens: A Story of Ambition,* 206; New York *Herald,* Feb. 2, 1865. See also A. K. McClure, *Abraham Lincoln and Men of War-Times,* 277 ff.

5 *Cong. Globe,* 37 Cong., 1 sess., 72 (July 11, 1861); Smith, *Blair Family,* II, 121.

6 McClure, 280–281.

property, denial of civil rights, reconstruction on a pattern opposed to Lincoln's, and (at a later time) for irregular and unfair procedure in the impeachment of Andrew Johnson.[7]

In addition to his terrifying manner and ruthlessness of party control, Stevens had supporting qualities. His parliamentary competence was of a high order. When he spoke, members listened to him as to a manipulator who was pulling the ropes and an oracle who knew how the pending matter of business was going to turn out. Contrary debate was merely tolerated if permitted at all. Where others were bewildered, Stevens's mind was made up. At all times he knew the status of legislative proposals as they wended their way through the intricate parliamentary maze, which could have been said of very few members. He was sarcastic to the point of insolence, but this very coarseness made him formidable. He was "a born dictator in politics." [8] In his unrefined way he was a capable speaker, though his persuasiveness, some thought, was that of the highwayman. When schemes for special interests arose, he would block some and promote others as he wished. He opposed and defeated a canal project in which Washburne of Illinois was interested, but was watchful of interests close to his own Caledonian Iron Works. The linking of the Republican party with capitalistic interests, one of the chief economic features of the time and of later decades, was a central factor of Stevens's policy. Party control of the government, and business support of the party, constituted the Stevens pattern as interlocking factors of a neatly working scheme. "With such a champion as Stevens," writes Richard N. Current, "Northern industrialists were

[7] After the 1867 "investigation," or testimony hunting in which perjured testimony was sought and used, the resolution to impeach President Johnson was decisively voted down in the House. The 1868 impeachment proceeding began, not with an investigation, nor even with the presentation of charges, but with the Covode resolution which declared that Johnson "be impeached of high crimes and misdemeanors," without naming even one instance of such a crime or misdemeanor. This resolution was referred, not to the committee on the judiciary, but to Stevens's committee on reconstruction. It was quickly passed; then a committee (loaded against Johnson) was appointed, not to investigate, but to "report articles of impeachment" against the President. This was *after* he had already been "impeached" without consideration of the reasons therefor. The committee was interested, not in justice to Johnson, but in the value of each article for producing conviction in the Senate. This 1868 matter is pertinent here for its bearing upon the spirit and method of the anti-Lincoln Stevens when attacking the President who sought to fulfill Lincoln's restoration program. It was the same Stevens. Randall, *Civil War and Reconstruction,* chap. xxxiv.

[8] McClure, 280.

steadily intrenching themselves in the favor of a generous government . . . . And he was interesting himself in policies . . . which, by keeping Republican politicians and their allies in power, would assure to them . . . the fruits of peace." [9]

The relations between this most powerful man in the House and Abraham Lincoln were, wrote McClure, "seldom cordial," though "always friendly." Stevens did not prefer Lincoln for President in 1860 or 1864, was not "enthusiastic in Lincoln's cause," "believed him weak," and "never saw Lincoln during the war except when necessity required it." He "often grieved" the President, and, to the recollection of McClure, spoke only once in "positive and enthusiastic commendation of Lincoln, and that was when he issued his Emancipation Proclamation in 1862." The two men, said McClure, a competent observer, were "seldom in actual harmony." [10]

These remarks by McClure, though clearly showing the lack of cordiality between Stevens and Lincoln, may be set down as understatements. The full extent of the radical leader's enmity to the President is not easy to measure. It has been suggested that under certain circumstances Stevens would not have withheld the weapon of impeachment against Lincoln.[11] Ward Hill Lamon, who knew Lincoln well, believed that Stevens's "demand for the head of 'that man at the other end of the Avenue,' would not have been a whit less ferocious" against Lincoln than in fact it turned out to be against Johnson. Believing that Lincoln could not have been made "a tool and an instrument" of the radicals, Lamon wrote: "Mr. Thaddeus Stephens [*sic*] was to the best of my knowledge the only leading man in the [Republican] party shameless and impudent enough to avow his hostility to the Union. He was not the exponent of our views and he represented not even a fractional part of the honest millions who cast their votes, spent their money and shed their blood to bring back the Government of their fathers." [12]

It is perhaps unnecessary to probe Lamon's meaning as to Stevens's hostility to the Union. It is obvious that Old Thad did not favor restoring the Union on the prewar basis, with slavery preserved and

---

9 Current, *Old Thad Stevens,* 197.

10 McClure, 281, 284.

11 Current, *Old Thad Stevens,* 305 n.

12 Ward H. Lamon to Andrew Johnson, Wash., Feb. 26, 1866, Johnson MSS., 9550–9555.

with the rights of Southern states remaining as before. In this attitude Stevens was sincere. What needs to be borne in mind in these pages is the incompatibility between the Lincoln program and that of the Pennsylvanian. Where he was to blame from the Lincolnian standpoint, it was not for being antislavery, but for the unfairness, intolerance, and hatefulness of his manner and method. He was spoiling a good cause. On the famous Crittenden resolution in the House, July 22, 1861, declaring that restoration of the old Union was the purpose of the war, Stevens did not vote. That resolution, regarded as law and gospel by Lamon, expressed the very opposite of the Pennsylvanian's policy.

VII

The way of a senator towards another senator was one of the quaint things under the Washington sun. The most devastating statements could be uttered if they were given in formal or superficially respectful phrasing. It would not do for Wilson of Massachusetts, a Republican, to say of Cowan of Pennsylvania, another Republican, that he was a liar or didn't know what he was talking about. He would not even use the name Cowan. He would put it thus: "I desire to say a . . . word to the Senator from Pennsylvania before I sit down. I was sorry to hear him say . . . what is said so often without . . . being sustained by the facts . . . ."[1] When Wade of Ohio had a colloquy with this same Cowan, he did not blurt out that Cowan was a traitor, doing all in his power to aid and abet the enemy of his country. The Ohioan merely suggested that Jefferson Davis would pray "for just such an advocate" as the senator from Pennsylvania.[2] Cowan replied that Davis would pray "for just such a statesman as the honorable Senator from Ohio, the most effective ally he ever had or could have."

Hale of New Hampshire did not say that Cowan was absurd, mentally fogged, and the victim of delusions. He gave his colleague a qualified compliment, then followed it with language of polite debate. Once the meaning of his language was apprehended, however, it had all the sting of a verbal blackjack. He said: "My friend from Pennsylvania is a man, whatever may be said of his politics, of re-

[1] *Cong. Globe,* 38 Cong., 1 sess., 3307 (June 27, 1864).
[2] *Ibid.,* appendix, 136 (June 27, 1864).

markably clear intellect; and where he has not suffered his intellect to be led away by the absurdities of black-letter English law, I have no doubt is a good lawyer . . . ."[3]

No one could have said that Reverdy Johnson was disrespectful toward Charles Sumner. He did not say that this scholar in politics was a learned fool. He pointed out that "the honorable member" from Massachusetts "reads everything that comes out that is worth reading." Then he added: "he will pardon me for saying he sometimes reads what is not worth reading."[4]

It was not always easy to tell when a member passed the bounds of parliamentary etiquette. Clever members managed well enough within those bounds. Riddle of Ohio referred to an opponent's utterances as "slobbering balderdash." When Holman of Indiana quoted from an Ohio journal, Riddle was indignant that the Hoosier member "flaunted a soiled rag of a newspaper in our faces." "Ohio," he remarked, "will select her own organs, and we will answer . . . without the officious aid of any meddler from outside."[5]

Sometimes this backbiting would take the form of a legislative resolution. With near unanimity (105 to 1) the House passed a resolution of Morrill of Vermont, declaring that it was "the duty of all loyal American citizens . . . [and] of every department of the Government—the legislative branch included—as a unit, to . . . unitedly strike down the assassins . . . who have conspired to destroy our Constitution, our nationality . . . [etc.]."[6] Cox, Ohio Democrat, then offered an "explanatory" resolution. He would have the House resolve that "the word 'assassins,' used in the resolution this day offered by the member from Vermont . . . is intended . . . to include all men, whether from the North or the South, who have been instrumental in producing the present war, and especially those in and out of Congress who have been guilty of flagrant breaches of the Constitution, and who are not in favor of the establishment of the Union as it was and the Constitution as it is." Cox's resolution, aimed at Republicans, was tabled, 85 to 41.[7]

A great deal of forensic heat was engendered in proceedings look-

---

[3] *Ibid.*, 3308 (June 27, 1864).
[4] *Ibid.*, 2900 (June 13, 1864).
[5] Riddle, *Recollections*, 212.
[6] *Cong. Globe*, 37 Cong., 3 sess., 14–15 (Dec. 5, 1862).
[7] *Ibid.*, 15 (Dec. 5, 1862).

ing to the expulsion or censuring of individual members. One target of such an attack was Alexander Long, an Ohio congressman to whom little attention had been previously attracted. His offense was that he had favored recognizing the Confederacy. No bare account of the "proceedings" could convey an idea of the dramatic intensity of this incident. As described by Noah Brooks it was one of several "field-days in Congress," with Garfield comparing Long to Benedict Arnold, while Speaker Colfax's voice "trembled with emotion" as he urged a resolution of expulsion. In the midst of the excitement a Maryland "Peace Democrat," Benjamin G. Harris, got up and endorsed the views of Long, believing his proposal to be the only method of obtaining peace. The House was now "in the wildest confusion, and a score of members were on their feet shouting to the Speaker and endeavoring to be recognized." In a "stentorian voice" which rose above the tumult, Washburne of Illinois moved to expel Harris, as Colfax had moved in the case of Long, whereupon Fernando Wood "tried to slide in a little speech" to the effect that he, too, agreed with Long and was alike deserving of expulsion.

The debate raged on. Washburne shouted that Wood should also be put out, Long delivered an impressive speech of defense, and Thad Stevens, having come from a sick bed, "arose like a column of iron" to vindicate his Union-saving attitude against aspersions that had been cast during his absence. When an opponent tried to offer some words in reply, "the stern old Pennsylvanian waved him down by a motion of his hand." [8] After long drawn out and excited discussion the motions to expel Long and Harris failed for want of the necessary two-thirds vote. Instead of expulsion, both men were then stigmatized by severe votes of censure.[9]

Where members actually entered Confederate military service they were naturally dropped from Congress at Washington. In the House this was true of John W. Reid and John B. Clark, both of Missouri; in the Senate, Waldo P. Johnson and Trusten Polk of Missouri and John C. Breckinridge of Kentucky.[10] For a different

---

[8] Brooks, *Washington in Lincoln's Time,* 98 ff.

[9] For the prolonged and elaborate debate, see *Cong. Globe,* 38 Cong., 1 sess., 1505–1635 (Apr. 9 to 14, 1864).

[10] On Clark, see *Cong. Globe,* 37 Cong., 1 sess., 116–117 (July 13, 1861); on Johnson and Polk, *ibid.,* 37 Cong., 2 sess., 263–264 (Jan. 10, 1862); on Breckinridge, *ibid.,* 37 Cong., 2 sess., 9–10 (Dec. 4, 1861); on Reid, *Biog. Cong. Direc.,* 1452. Reid's case is almost that

reason Senator Jesse D. Bright of Indiana was expelled after an elaborate debate of nearly three weeks. His offense was that before the war (March 1, 1861) he had written a minor letter of recommendation to Jefferson Davis. It was remarked that the expulsion vote in the case of Bright "was based perhaps as much on personal and political opposition as on the charge of treason." [11] Having expelled him for treason against the United States, very few senators would have seriously expected him to be tried and convicted in the courts for that offense on the basis of the accusation and evidence concerning the unimportant letter to Davis.

VIII

The formula "be it enacted" implies a determined and collective will. It is a legislative imperative and may be regarded as the essence of a legislative "act." If, however, one goes behind the record, in diaries and correspondence, he begins to wonder what is the actual significance of legislative "intent" as embodied in completed legislation. Much the same is true if he takes the open record itself and seeks to correlate discussion with final enactment. One cannot very well enact a stump speech. When varying purposes simmer down to a legislative act, the end result may indeed evoke a majority of affirmative votes, but such affirmation may often fall short of genuine concurrence of thought. A resolution may be a kind of catch-all, so that partial consent as to sections may be misleading if interpreted as total consent for the whole measure. With disorder prevailing and attention lacking, with management in the hands of a few party leaders, and with the attitude of members largely predetermined, the content of unremembered debates would seem a minor factor.

In any parliamentary situation, of course, as in a popular election, composite concurrence of a majority may be difficult to break down in terms of individual approval of specific provisions and interpretations. Compromise and adjustment of differing views are normally expected as regular aspects of democratic procedure. Yet in some cases individual doubts or imperfections of understanding may be so

---

of a vanishing congressman; it is stated that he "withdrew" from the House on August 3, 1861, and joined the Confederate army.

[11] *Dic. of Amer. Biog.*, III, 46.

serious that one may consider the "intent" of Congress as little more than an abstraction. After a bill was passed in the upper house, one senator remarked that a colleague had "entirely misapprehended" what it was all about.[1] When the habeas corpus law was passed, March 3, 1863, it was claimed that incorrect procedure had been used in forcing the vote, while the language of the act was so ambiguous as to admit of diametrically opposite meanings.[2] Matters would get into such a jam at the end of a short session that important bills would be lost for no good reason while others would be passed in sheer exhaustion. Secretary Welles noted that a bill affecting the navy department (concerning an "advisory board") was passed without the secretary of the navy having even seen it. When asked about the matter Senator Grimes reported that "the bill had never been discussed; he did not approve of it; . . . he had expected it would be killed in the House." Another bill, wrote Welles, "must have been got through surreptitiously."[3]

On the subject of the American Constitution in its relation to the existing emergency congressional minds differed widely. The idea of adhering strictly to constitutional provisions was emphatically urged by anti-Lincoln Democrats who were shocked at what they called the President's disregard of the nation's fundamental charter. When men spoke of adhering to the Constitution, of course, they meant such adherence to be understood in terms of their own interpretation. There were those, however, who believed that the Constitution should be ignored or evaded. Sometimes this would amount to a deliberate and conscious violation of plain constitutional provisions. There were times when the men of Congress found their constitutional problem too much of a task, and at such times there was a tendency to enact or repeat the words of the Constitution and let the Supreme Court figure out what they meant. Pure reasoning or deduction, or detached legal exposition, of the Constitution was rare. Comments on the meaning of the great document were usually colored by the motive back of each man's attitude. This situation was brought out by a Massachusetts member when he declared that

1 Senator Ira Harris of New York made this statement concerning Senator Trumbull's understanding of the confiscation bill. *Cong. Globe,* 37 Cong., 2 sess., 3381 (July 16, 1862).

2 Randall, *Constitutional Problems Under Lincoln,* 130–131.

3 Welles, *Diary,* I, 245.

"not a man will oppose this bill [making paper money legal tender] . . . upon constitutional grounds, unless he is opposed to it for other and satisfactory reasons." [4]

To some the idea was that they were voting and acting *in extremis.* The classical smartness of the phrase lent dignity to this type of reasoning. If it had a Latin name it could not be wholly bad; at least it could be labeled, recognized, and related to ancient precedent. Some, however, objected to applying this principle except where dire extremity actually required it. In 1862 Wright of Pennsylvania said: ". . . I voted, during the extra session of Congress [July–August 1861], to affirm the act of the President . . . in the suspension of the writ of *habeas corpus.* I voted also to approve his act by which he declared . . . seaports in a state of blockade. I also voted to approve his act declaring the establishment of military law. I did it for the sole reason that . . . the exigency had arisen which justified us and the President . . . in violating a constitutional provision. It was a vote *in extremis.* . . . [He also approved presidential seizure of the railroads because that was an extreme case.] And now we are called upon . . . to . . . declare it to be . . . legal to make paper itself money." This, he felt, was going too far. "I call upon gentlemen to show me how, when, and where, in what particular, we have power, under the Constitution, to make anything, except gold and silver, a legal tender?" To do this, he felt, would be to set "all . . . precedents at defiance." [5]

There were some who favored changing the Constitution. Such a change, however, presented practical difficulties, especially in a period of civil war, and the tendency was to attempt the process of amendment only as a kind of compulsion when the constitutional obstacle was insurmountable for a measure which was plainly a necessity. It was realized, of course, that a time of unbalance and emotional tension did not offer the best atmosphere for the task of revising a nation's enduring constitutional instrument. It was also considered questionable to make such alterations at a time when a large Southern area was outside the Union.

Where constitutional thinking seemed to smack of casuistry there were cautious minds that objected to the idea of constitutionalism be-

---

[4] *Cong. Globe,* 37 Cong., 2 sess., 659 (Feb. 5, 1862).

[5] *Ibid.,* 37 Cong., 2 sess., 662–663 (Feb. 5, 1862).

coming whatever the members chose to make it. The aged Crittenden of Kentucky, whose years of prime belonged to the period of Monroe and John Quincy Adams, deeply regretted the legislative "doctrine which makes the end justify the means." "The argument here," he said, "is exactly the argument of the Jesuit—fix your mind and attention upon one object which you think a lawful one, and then all the means are lawful." [6]

In the face of these constitutional discussions Thaddeus Stevens showed a blunt impatience, both against those who held back because of negative constitutional scruples and those who went to great lengths to square their affirmative votes with the Constitution. He wanted neither objections nor constitutional justifications. He declared: "I say that you cannot justify nine out of ten of the acts of the Government, or of our own acts here, if you consider the Constitution a valid and binding instrument with reference to those in arms in the rebellious States." On that theory, said Thomas of Massachusetts, "we are every day passing unconstitutional acts, we are every day violating our oaths recorded in heaven to support the Constitution of the United States." To Olin of New York, however, it seemed that nothing but obedience to the Constitution could justify the prosecution of the war. It was his view that if there remained "but a single man . . . loyal to the Constitution in any one of the seceded States, he . . . [was] entitled to all the rights, . . . privileges, and . . . immunities granted to any citizen in any loyal State." [7]

Stevens would not allow to the people of the South any constitutional rights. He would tax them though they were not in the Union; at the same time he would take from them "every particle of property, real and personal." [8] Then he would "sell" that property for the benefit of the nation. To carry out Stevens's scheme and confiscate all the property of the people in "these conquered provinces" and sell it, would have been a gigantic affair. Uncle Sam would have been going into the real estate business, not to mention personal property, on a colossal scale.

---

[6] *Ibid.*, 37 Cong., 3 sess., 1290 (Feb. 25, 1863).

[7] For references in this paragraph, see *Cong. Globe*, 37 Cong., 3 sess., 240–242 (Jan. 8, 1863).

[8] *Ibid.*, 37 Cong., 3 sess., 240 (Jan. 8, 1863).

IX

To contemplate a large representative assembly, and study the manner in which measures take shape in such an assembly, is a primary problem of political scientists and a necessary task for all who would understand the actual workings of democracy. Congress may be considered collectively, as a "branch" of the government. At any particular time, however, the nation's legislature consists of human beings, of politicians—or, it may be hoped, of statesmen. Sometimes men of no more than ordinary capacity may be brought to high achievement by able leadership. If the nation has a vigorous and competent President, the matter of his leadership as to Congress will necessarily arise. One may ask: If the President does not lead, who does? One may also ask: Who among our capable Presidents has felt that his function as leader in legislative matters could be neglected? As issues were drawn in Lincoln's day, the need to turn to Congress, and to wait upon measures passed by Congress, was a continuing factor. This being so, the peculiarities of its members, suggested only in part in this chapter, had to be kept in mind, for these were the men with whom Lincoln had to deal. In such dealing he had often to conceal his exasperation and muster up a tact and skill in which many of the honorable gentlemen were deficient.

The relation of Congress and the President to the American "two-party system" also comes into view. If one speaks of party leadership he must of course recognize the President as a leader. The following comment, though recent, has a general significance: "The history of American politics has been that when the President lost control of his party we had no effective government." [1] It has been pointed out, however, that at times the two-party system, as to Congress, seems rather meaningless.[2] What was called Republican policy, 1861 to

---

1 Philip Willkie, in New York *Times*, editorial page, Oct. 26, 1949.

2 In discussing recent aspects of party organization in Congress, Clarence A. Berdahl has pointed to the lack of clear-cut party responsibility, the "coalition" of a few Democrats with a major portion of the Republicans, and the fact that "party organizations in Congress are almost completely independent of the national party organizations." He mentions the "extraordinary looseness in party performance" that coexists with "passionate attachment to party labels." As to the situation in 1948 it is shown that "Governor Dewey, as the Republican Presidential candidate, felt obliged to urge strongly the election of Republican candidates for the Senate and House, even though those men were opposed to the Dewey policies and would presumably so vote in Con-

1865, in the congressional sense was not Lincoln's policy, though Lincoln was a Republican President. These are but a few of the difficulties and complexities of a subject that cannot be fully discussed in this book, but which will receive further treatment in some of its phases in the next chapter.

---

gress." Thus Dewey was campaigning "for men who were actually his political opponents." One can readily see the analogy of this situation to that existing under Lincoln, when many Republicans in Congress, a majority of them, were voting against Lincoln's views and measures. For Berdahl's illuminating analysis, see *Amer. Pol. Sci. Rev.*, XLIII, especially pp. 309, 732, 733.

CHAPTER VI

PRESIDENT AND CONGRESS

I

THE difficulty of using war as an instrument of policy, and of controlling a particular war in order to adhere to a solemn declaration made at the outset, was illustrated whenever Congress got round to discussing the purpose and meaning of the growing struggle. In the passing of the Crittenden resolution that the war was not waged for any other purpose than restoring the Union (mentioned in a previous volume),[1] we find only the first phase of congressional attitude concerning war aims. That was in the summer of 1861 (July 22), but by the summer of 1862 a marked change had come about. Crittenden's resolution, passed just after the defeat at first Bull Run, was soon abandoned, and the policy of confiscation and punitive emancipation was adopted.[2] As the war unfolded far beyond its foreseen outline, earlier declarations of purpose receded into the unrecoverable past. It was obvious that institutions would be shaken and that slavery would be treated with no gentle hand. This was not surprising. Perhaps the surprising thing was that, with the "radical" spirit on the march, more was not done by way of dispossessing Southerners and punishing "traitors."

Time and again some member, in one form or another, would propose a reaffirmation of the Crittenden declaration, but always without success. An example was in December 1863, when Finck of Ohio offered a resolution that the war was not being carried on in any spirit of oppression, but to defend the Constitution. When finally this resolution was disposed of (April 11, 1864), it was laid on the

1 *Lincoln the President,* II, 127–128.

2 *Cong. Globe,* 37 Cong., 2 sess., Appendix, 412–413 (July 17, 1862).

table in the House by vote of 81 to 64. A similar resolution was defeated, 88 to 66, under the leadership of Thaddeus Stevens.[3] On this question of the purpose of the war, border-state members, Democrats generally, and the less vindictive Republicans were voted down by the radical Republican majority. As these tendencies increased there were those who felt that the party in power was multiplying the enemies of the Union cause and that serious wedges of factional difference were dividing the North.

What were called "war aims" were, of course, in reality peace aims. The purpose of war itself is to kill, maim, destroy, break down morale, annihilate enemy fighting power, and produce victory by force. What that victory shall signify, and what a nation is "fighting for," can never be achieved except by peace, and by conditions and attitudes as they persist during years of peace. There were honest souls who felt, as did Lincoln, that it would be most unfortunate for the country to continue to be divided by sectionalism and partisanship after the conclusion of a war whose avowed purpose was the reuniting of the nation.

This matter of purpose that looked beyond war to long eras of peace was properly a function of both Congress and the President. If there could be harmony between executive and legislative minds, and if that harmony could be kept on a high level, something constructive might be accomplished. If not, there would be a sorry sequel to Lincoln's high resolve that the nation's dead should not have died in vain.

The whole issue of so-called "war aims" involved a serious clash of ideologies. Divisions on this subject were stubborn and obstinate; tempers were hateful and intense. Those who honestly differed with the radicals and desired a moderate policy were branded as traitors or as sympathizers with treason who "prate learnedly about the Constitution." [4] In a war against disunion the gulf was widening within the Union itself. Vindictiveness was growing. It had been supposed, early in the war, that there was room for agreement by which men at Washington would stand together with loyal men at the South. Instead of that, as Cowan of Pennsylvania remarked in the Senate,

---

[3] *Ibid.*, 38 Cong., 1 sess., 1532 (Apr. 11, 1864); 22 (Dec. 14, 1863).

[4] Thaddeus Stevens in House of Representatives, *ibid.*, 37 Cong., 2 sess., 440 (Jan. 22, 1862).

hardly a day passed that some bill was not introduced that increased the animosity and added to the irritation.[5] How far and how deep would the fury extend? Said Thomas of Massachusetts: "You cannot . . . carry on a war with a fierceness and severity that would destroy life as rapidly as it germinates." Whoever talked of "a war of extermination," he said, was "mad." [6]

Those who favored a reasonable vision as to aims agreed with Lincoln; but, as the war seemed to be failing of its pacifying purpose as stated by the President, the words of Lincoln were thrown back at him. Strongly partisan anti-Lincoln speeches were made by way of denouncing a vindictive war for which Lincoln was blamed, though in all conscience he of all men wished an end to vindictiveness. This meant that Lincoln was assailed for opposite reasons. Some attacked him on the ground that harsh measures were being used which amounted to a violation of civil rights. Such denunciation ignored the fact that, for a war President, Lincoln was in practice lenient. Others attacked him for that very leniency and for a broad policy that was considered too generous toward "rebels" and too trustful of Southerners' good intentions.

Loyal border-state men, vigorously favoring the Union which was so important for Kentucky, West Virginia, and their neighbors, were saying that there had been no sufficient provocation in terms of Northern aggression, that the South had suffered no serious grievance. Senator Waitman T. Willey of Virginia [7] declared in December 1861: "Mr. President, how utterly absurd are all the pretexts of the insurgents for their rebellion. . . . If the South had remained loyal to their Government, . . . what could your President or your party have accomplished prejudicial or objectionable to the South." He compressed his views into a resolution (not passed) which declared that the war had been "forced upon the country by the States in rebellion, without justifiable cause or provocation . . . ." [8]

With congressional oratory, however, becoming ever more heated,

---

5 *Ibid.*, 37 Cong., 2 sess., 2993 (June 28, 1862).

6 *Ibid.*, 37 Cong., 3 sess., 651 (Jan. 31, 1863).

7 Willey was United States senator from "restored Virginia." He was chosen by the "reorganized" legislature (claiming to act for the yet unbroken state) in its special session at Wheeling in July 1861.

8 For Willey's resolution and his long, formidable speech in its support, see *Cong. Globe*, 37 Cong., 2 sess., appendix, 32 ff.

it appeared that grievances, which men such as Willey considered lacking in the prewar sense, were being offered in increasing supply. Part of the trouble was the continual tendency of some Northern members to identify Southernism with slavery, so that a denunciation of the peculiar institution was likely to take the form of a tirade against what was broadly called "the South."

But could one ignore antislavery voices? Could there be such a thing as guaranteeing slavery absolute immunity from the war? Should the antebellum past be kept upon the throne? Was slavery worth saving? Was it not slavery that had "caused" the war? Was the opportunity for extinguishing the evil of human bondage to be neglected? What if the war did become a crusade? [9] Some thought the conflict unjustified unless it were exactly that. Was not freedom a lofty cause?

These were potent considerations, though it should not be forgotten that moderate policy to a large extent allowed for abolition, not by one stroke or immediately, but by progressive steps. The main problem was whether other freedoms were to be kept while freedom from slavery was established. The issue to be decided was whether policy against slavery should be constructive rather than vindictive, corrective rather than punitive. Should not the hand of reform be laid upon slavery as an institution, not upon Southerners as persons? Should not enlightened Southern coöperation be welcomed? It was not contemplated by the best moderates that an unchanging "Old South" was to be projected into an indefinite future, but that liberation when it should come, as come it would, should not be marred by partisanship or frustrated by narrow sectionalism. Moderates believed that a postwar regime could be better launched by men who would coöperate with well disposed Southerners than by those who would perpetuate the war mind, crystallize sectionalism in party terms, and make resentment permanent. As early as 1861, and continuously throughout the war, Lincoln showed deep concern that the

[9] When he voted against the Crittenden resolution in July 1861, A. G. Riddle of Ohio was angrily assailed and urged to change his vote. In "white heat," as reported by himself, he retorted: "Not a man of you believes that slavery is eternal. . . . You all believe that it is to go out, when it does go, through convulsion, fire, and blood. That convulsion is upon us. The man is a delirious ass who does not see and realize this." Riddle, *Recollections*, 43.

nation's purpose should "not degenerate into a violent and remorseless . . . struggle." [10]

II

This basic question of policy and method, of broad plans for future years, of clarifying the issue as to what the war was about, was distressingly illustrated in connection with the problem of the confiscation of Southern property. In the records of the time, entombed in the *Congressional Globe,* one finds an excessive flow of language on this vexatious subject. Every member, it seemed, had a confiscation speech in his pocket. It was, however, the kind of unenlightened and rambling debate that leaves the reader (if any) in doubt as to the design and purpose of congressional oratory. With discussion remaining so long at a tentative stage and with members sometimes betraying ignorance of the bill or the motion on which they were presumably speaking, it can hardly be said that the cause of legislation was notably promoted by what was said on the floor or what was spread forth in the appendix of the *Globe* with "leave to print."

The bill for confiscation was started in the Senate by Trumbull of Illinois, but the measure as passed, though he voted for it, was not Trumbull's. The roving debate, or congressional maneuvering, extended all the way across the long session of the Thirty-Seventh Congress, from the opening day, December 2, 1861, when the question was first presented, to the last day, July 17, 1862, when final action was taken. Some of that final action was mere patchwork. Trumbull's bill provided for "absolute and complete forfeiture forever to the United States of every species of property . . . belonging to persons beyond the jurisdiction of the United States" who should "take up arms against the United States, or . . . aid or abet the rebellion." [1] What happened from the point where Trumbull presented his bill was a long-drawn-out story. Weeks passed; then the Senate committee on the judiciary, of which Trumbull was chairman, reported its bill, which resembled Trumbull's. Liability to confiscation under this bill derived from participation in the "rebellion," but Trumbull had a limited idea as to reaching the offender's property.

[10] Nicolay and Hay, *Works,* VII, 51.

[1] *Cong. Globe,* 37 Cong., 2 sess., 18 (Dec. 5, 1861).

"Where the rebel can be reached by judicial process," said he, "the punishment for his crimes can be visited upon him personally, and this bill does not propose to interfere with his property at all." [2] It was explained that this manner of approach was for the purpose of avoiding constitutional difficulties concerning the punishment for treason. The method of his bill—directed against those who could not be reached by the Federal courts—was punitive in a non-judicial sense; the property of offenders was simply to be seized by the military authorities without any judicial process whatever.

As the Trumbull bill, with its substitutes and amendments, wended its tortuous way through the congressional jungle, it encountered unexpected obstacles. Inherently the problem of confiscation was bad enough with all its ramifications, but the trouble was enhanced by inconsistencies in the bill itself and by discordant arguments put forth by its sponsor as against the declarations of the many who participated in the debate. Forfeiture was intended as punishment for crime—the crime of "rebellion." Yet the punishment, according to Trumbull, was to be inflicted by the military authorities without judicial hearing to determine the individual's guilt. Moreover, as he proceeded, Trumbull seemed to forget the principle of domestic insurrection (or rebellion) for which forfeiture was to be decreed as a penalty. Warming to his theme, he put the bill in the category of strictly military or belligerent measures, as if it were merely a matter of invoking a rule of war. If confiscation had been an established and unquestioned rule of war, and if the existing conflict was a regular war between recognized belligerents, no special law of Congress would have been necessary. Trumbull was supposed to be an authority on constitutional matters, as his position at the head of the judiciary committee would imply, but as the months passed his analysis of perplexing constitutional problems was neither accurate nor conclusive. At one time he spoke as though he intended the punitive forfeiture of *all* property of offenders. At another time he referred to the property of Southerners as "prize of war," as if the situation were analogous to maritime capture, for which the law is international with personal guilt of the owners left out of the picture.

---

[2] *Ibid.*, 942 (Feb. 25, 1862).

On both sides of the debate there was great diversity of motive and intent. Some arose to oppose the measure with friendliness toward the Lincoln administration. These were among the most reasonable men in Congress. Others opposed it with the bitterest feeling of antagonism to Lincoln. Affirmative speakers were really in favor, not so much of the particular confiscation bill, as of a confiscation policy. Wide ranging speeches on confiscation in the broad sense were more often a kind of exhibition than a specific contribution to the difficult legislative process. Some favored the measure because of its bearing upon treason, some because of the (ineffective) emancipating feature, others because of the colonization clause, still others because of confiscation itself.

To assume that confiscation as enacted was a clear matter of legislative purpose would be to imply that the majority voted for the bill in knowledge of its content, visualizing its practical effect when administered, favoring it as an act necessitated by the existing emergency, and justifying it as a constitutional measure. It would be very questionable to assert that any such genuine majority existed. Some of the members admitted that they did not like certain features of the bill, but cast their votes for it because their Republican brothers were voting that way and they felt it expedient to follow the party line. There were motions to substitute radically different measures for the bill in hand, motions to refer, to amend the bill, to amend the amendment, to lay on the table, and to force the previous question. Finally, as noted in a previous volume,[8] Lincoln wrote out a veto message stating his objections to the confiscation bill which very obviously he disliked.

Then an extraordinary thing happened. Determined that a forfeiture bill be passed, the leaders of Congress, instead of altering the text of the bill which the President, so to speak, was in the act of vetoing, hastily prepared what was called an "explanatory joint resolution" to the effect that the bill was not intended to work forfeiture of real estate beyond the natural life of the offender. This did not by any means correct all, or the most important, of the features of the bill to which Lincoln objected. In particular there was no correction

---

[8] *Lincoln the President*, II, 228–229.

of the provision which required the condemnation of property without allowing a personal hearing to the "supposed criminal." That presidential objection was left unanswered.

At this point Lincoln himself did a most unusual thing—something without precedent and with no later matching instance in executive procedure. He approved the distasteful measure to which he had so convincingly objected, and signed the bill and the explanatory resolution as "substantially one." Then he transmitted to Congress the veto message expressing disapproval of the bill he had signed. Thus he put on record his statement of presidential judgment, and sought to clinch the point that any parts of the bill inconsistent with the resolution—which, by the way, was not an amending measure—were of no force. It appears that he never intended a vigorous enforcement of the act. Certainly the attorney general, Edward Bates, had no stomach for such enforcement, even if the ill drafted measure had been capable of practical execution.[4]

III

In January 1864 there was a curious sequel to the 1862 proceedings in Congress concerning confiscation. James F. Wilson, representative from Iowa, offered a resolution (January 13) to "amend" the last part of the explanatory joint resolution, the part that had been added to avoid forfeiture beyond the offender's life. In place of the words of the explanatory resolution, Wilson moved to substitute the words of the Constitution itself, as follows: "The Congress shall have Power to declare the Punishment of Treason, but no Attainder of Treason shall work Corruption of Blood or Forfeiture, except during the Life of the Person attainted." [1] Just why an act of Congress should reënact a provision of the Constitution was not clear, nor why a congressional measure should contain the words "The Congress shall have Power," etc. Congressman Wilson explained: "We do not propose by resolution to determine the question of the legislative construction of the Constitution, whether we may provide

[4] The tangled and amazing history of the second confiscation act of July 17, 1862, is treated in Randall, *Constitutional Problems Under Lincoln,* 276–280. In addition the author has drawn upon his own unpublished MS., "Confiscation of Property during the Civil War," doctoral dissertation, University of Chicago, 1911.

[1] *U.S. Constitution,* art. III, sec. 3.

for forfeiture of fee or confiscation of the real estate during life. The pending resolution leaves the whole matter to the court. In other words, we simply submit the section of the Constitution relating to the forfeiture of real estate to the courts . . . to determine whether forfeiture may be in fee or only for life." [2] This bit of proposed legislation—a joint resolution to amend a joint resolution explanatory of an act—was submitted by Wilson as coming from the House committee on the judiciary. It was thus the work of that committee of the House whose duty it was to interpret and apply the Constitution in legislative matters.

As questions piled up, it was evident that the members were facing complexities with which they could not cope. Would not the Wilson proposal render the whole meaning of the confiscation act doubtful? Would it not show that Congress did not even profess to know the meaning of its own law and was for that reason leaving the matter to the courts? Every law, of course, has to be interpreted and applied by the courts, but it is an odd proceeding for Congress in the very act of legislating to dodge the meaning and intended effect of what it was doing. What about persons buying an estate under confiscation proceedings? How could they know what they were buying, and how avoid the possible loss of the value they were paying?

What, after all, was meant by the words of the Constitution: "except during the Life of the Person attainted"? Did this phrase mean that confiscation should be only temporary, terminating with the condemned person's death, or (which would be rather doubtful) that a lasting forfeiture was to be effected, so long as the court decree of forfeiture was completed and issued during the offender's life? Part of the difficulty was that some members were assuming a double punishment of both confiscation and death being visited upon the same victim, and of an interpretation which would absurdly allow confiscation to apply only during the interval between the imposing of the sentence and the day of execution.[3] This would become even

[2] *Cong. Globe,* 38 Cong., 1 sess., 185 (Jan. 13, 1864).

[3] This point was threshed out in the House by Godlove S. Orth of Indiana who asked: "Did our Constitution, else so redolent with wisdom . . . , intend . . . such a farce as that the property of the traitor should be forfeited . . . only for that brief . . . time . . . between the day of the sentence and the day of execution?" *Cong. Globe,* 38 Cong., 1 sess., 187–188 (Jan. 13, 1864).

more absurd if the sale of the real estate would require forty days while the unfortunate defendant would be executed thirty days after sentence.[4]

In brave efforts to master such problems the deliberation got bogged down in a semantic morass, and "Sunset Cox" of Ohio rose in the House of Representatives to dispute what he called a point of "technical logomachy." Mustering the authorities ("Worcester, Webster, and all other dictionaries"), descanting upon "progressive philology," citing Justice Story, and tracing the word "except" to the Latin *ex* and *capio,* he led up through an elaborate passage to what was expected to be a clinching pronouncement. Then he said: "There are some clauses which interpret themselves. Discussion only obscures and does not elucidate their meaning. This clause is one of them." [5]

Discussion ran on and one wonders how a visitor could have understood the ponderous language emitted on a typical afternoon of confiscation discussion—on January 14, 1864, for instance, the legalistic and lexicographical field day on which the points of "technical logomachy" were elucidated by Cox. After protracted debate the House of Representatives resolved to change the wording of the explanatory joint resolution of July 17, 1862, striking out the words which were intended to limit the forfeiture to the offender's life and putting in a solemn provision that there should be no forfeiture "contrary to the Constitution of the United States." This resolution, which dodged the question as to what the Constitution meant (the very ques-

---

4 This question of the duration of the forfeiture—whether the property should fully be taken in fee, leaving the heirs no rights, or whether the offender surrendered only a life interest—was one of the many problems with which the Supreme Court struggled in its elaborate interpretations of the confiscations acts. As to the act of 1861, directed only against the property, it was held by the Court (as in cases of smuggling) that the whole title was surrendered, so that nothing could be recovered by the heirs. Kirk *vs.* Lynd, 106 U.S. 315. On the other hand, in forfeitures under the act of 1862, based on the guilt of the owner and directed against him as a punishment, the Court decided that a decree of condemnation and order of sale conveyed only a "right . . . terminating with the life of the person for whose act it had been seized." Bigelow *vs.* Forrest, 9 Wall. 339. (All of this implied, of course, that confiscation should be imposed, but not confiscation and death.) The effect of the Court's ruling was that heirs of the offender would, even during his life, have a future interest in the property, and that they could fully inherit the estate when the offender died. Such considerations, however, only faintly suggest the Court's perplexities in applying confiscation. Randall, *Constitutional Problems Under Lincoln,* 275–341 (as to the duration of the forfeiture, 286 ff.).

5 *Cong. Globe,* 38 Cong., 1 sess., 211 (Jan. 14, 1864).

tion on which the whole tedious debate had hinged), was passed by the House by a vote of 83 to 74.[6]

The parliamentary situation at this point was as follows. Congress had passed the confiscation bill of July 17, 1862. Lincoln had objected to it, partly because he considered it unconstitutional. Thinking to repair that defect, Congress had hastily enacted an explanatory resolution in order to make the law conform to the Constitution. This was done to avert a presidential veto, for which an able veto message had been prepared by Lincoln. Now, in 1864, Congress in a lengthy debate was floundering and stumbling as to the meaning of the explanatory resolution which it had enacted. Then, instead of explaining what was meant, the House resolved that nothing was intended that was contrary to the Constitution.

After all this, when the matter came up in the Senate, Trumbull moved that the explanatory resolution of July 17, 1862, on which Lincoln's reluctant signature of the confiscation bill had hinged, be *repealed,* offering his motion as an irrelevant "rider" on the bill to establish the freedmen's bureau.[7] This trick would have caught the President in a position where he could not have vetoed the repeal without vetoing the whole measure concerning the care of freedmen. The Senate was then off to another wordy debate on confiscation, in which grave constitutional doubts were raised and Trumbull subjected to embarrassing questions. Carlile of Virginia [8] said:

> . . . it was made known to Congress that that bill [the confiscation bill] could not receive the approval of the President, and could only become a law by the passage of this very joint resolution, a portion of which is now proposed to be repealed, and that portion, too, which the President required should be adopted before he would approve it. . . . Well may the Senator from Massachusetts [Sumner] . . . ask the Senator from Illinois [Trumbull] not to load his [freedmen's bureau] bill with this proposition. Unless the President has reread his constitutional duties, . . . he never can sign this bill with this proposition in it.[9]

Senate discussion now became still more complicated, involving not merely the question of the advisability of Trumbull's "rider,"

---

[6] *Ibid.,* 38 Cong., 1 sess., 501, 519 (Feb. 4–5, 1864).

[7] *Ibid.,* 38 Cong., 1 sess., 3304 (June 27, 1864).

[8] John S. Carlile was one of the senators from "restored Virginia" (not the new state of West Virginia). *Biog. Cong., Direc.,* 273.

[9] *Cong. Globe,* 38 Cong., 1 sess., 3306 (June 27, 1864).

but also the basic problem as to whether confiscation was a wise policy, whether it was approved under international law as a belligerent right, and whether Congress was justified in "adding a new provision to the laws of nations and of war." After proceedings which Cowan of Pennsylvania thought were "enough to drive a sane man mad,"[10] the Senate passed, as a rider to the freedmen's bureau bill, the Trumbull amendment to repeal the joint resolution "amendatory" of the confiscation act. The amendment failed of enactment because of postponement in the House; later the House passed its own repealing section. That repealing provision, however, was not actually enacted, despite each house going on record in favor of it; this was because the two chambers did not agree on an identical wording of the measures which they severally voted.

In the final analysis the amount of property actually confiscated in the Federal courts in accordance with the act of July 17, 1862, was so small as to make those members seem ridiculous who had glibly predicted that confiscation would serve as a means of financing the war.[11] As to the features of the bill which pertained to emancipation, that part of the act was poorly drawn. It was lacking as to procedure to make freedom legally effective; the result was that in actual practice the enforcement of this antislavery portion, which certain voting members considered its main feature, was utterly negligible. Emancipation arrived nowhere by the confiscation route.[12] Taking it all in all, it can hardly be said that in the field of confiscation the men of Congress presented a very efficient performance. Showing scant regard

---

[10] *Ibid.*, appendix, 137 (June 27, 1864).

[11] It was reported by the solicitor of the treasury in 1867 that proceeds of confiscation under the act of July 17, 1862, had been deposited in the United States treasury in the amount of $129,680.67. (*Sen. Doc. No. 58,* 40 Cong., 2 sess.) This report omits proceeds under the confiscation act of 1861, which were small, and does not include confiscations in Virginia, Kansas, and elsewhere. There were defaults and irregularities, and the full total is a somewhat obscure matter, but it has been estimated that if allowance is made for these factors, the total proceeds from confiscation sales would probably not exceed $300,000. This amount, roughly speaking, was comparable to the value of two estates such as Lee's Arlington. Arlington itself, however, was seized, not under the confiscation acts, but under the Federal direct tax in the South. Ultimately the United States government paid $150,000 to the Lee heirs, and it is upon this basis (i. e., purchase) that title to Arlington has rested. Randall, *Constitutional Problems Under Lincoln,* 288–292, 320–322.

[12] Commenting on the ineffectiveness of the second confiscation act of July 17, 1862, Lincoln wrote: ". . . I cannot learn that that law has caused a single slave to come over to us." Reply to a committee, Sep. 13, 1862, *Nat'l Intelligencer,* Sep. 26, 1862 (Nicolay and Hay, *Works,* VIII, 30).

for the President's well considered but modestly presented advice, the law makers made something of a muddle of their own measure.

IV

The manner of congressional deliberation was further revealed in connection with the subject of Negro troops. None of these debates can be fully summarized, but it may be worth while to glance at some of the ideas expressed.

Crittenden of Kentucky: ". . . shall we, sir, stigmatize . . . our brothers, the white free-born men of this land, as being so degenerate as to shrink from this contest, and compel you to appeal to your own black men to defend the liberties of the white men? . . . You stigmatize them, while you invite them into the field. . . . You employ them as soldiers to fight your battle, but give them only one half pay, and exclude them from command . . . ."[1]

Cox of Ohio: "Now, the present pending law . . . is intended to place the African soldier upon a perfect equality in every regard with the white soldier . . . ."[2]

Stevens of Pennsylvania: "I have not said so. I said the object was to put them upon an equality as to the protection which the President could afford them. I do not mean to say that they are to be put upon a social and political equality."[3]

This unwillingness to give genuine equality to Negroes even when using them as troops was indicated by the House of Representatives when it passed, July 16, 1862, a measure providing that the pay for Negro troops should not be above $10 a month, while the pay of the white private was $13 a month.[4] One would have expected those who opposed the use of Negro troops to show an unwillingness to extend equal treatment. The surprising thing is to note the ungracious arguments put forth by those who favored their use. In presenting to the House a resolution for a more vigorous policy to enlist persons of African descent "at an early day and in larger numbers," Josiah B. Grinnell of Iowa made the point that the more extended employment of colored persons would be "a relief to our northern

1 *Cong. Globe,* 37 Cong., 3 sess., appendix, 73 (Jan. 29, 1863).

2 *Ibid.,* 599 (Jan. 29, 1863).

3 *Ibid.*

4 *Ibid.,* 37 Cong., 2 sess., 3398 (July 16, 1862).

soldiers, unacclimated and unused to manual labor" and that it would "lessen the number [of white men] to be taken from their homes and from the industrial pursuits . . . where there is now an unusual demand for labor." [5]

Speaking of the manner in which the conscription act served to "elevate the sentiment of this nation," Senator Wilson of Massachusetts pointed out that when the act was passed there was "a wild, unreasoning prejudice against using a black man to fight the battles of our country." Then he added: "But when people who were filled with these prejudices saw they must go themselves, and bare their bosoms to the shot and shell of the enemy, they learned that the black man's blood was no more sacred than their own, and that they would as soon have a black man stand up and fight the battles of the country as to do it themselves. The most popular thing to-day is to crowd black men into our armies." [6] Again Senator Wilson said: ". . . if there be anything in the prosecution of this war that the people are in favor of, it is the raising of black troops to fight the battles . . . . Everybody now demands it." [7]

Senator Grimes of Iowa agreed with him. Get more colored men into the army, was Grimes's policy. If that had been done, he said in 1864, "we need not have required a single new white soldier to enter the army." [8] This motive for obtaining colored troops was confirmed by Senator Fessenden of Maine. Asking for "what purpose" they were procured, he said: "Is it not to relieve . . . the country of the necessity of furnishing white men?" [9]

One aspect of this movement in Congress to promote the further enlistment of colored men was to give "credit" to certain Northern states in such a way as to reduce their liability to conscription. A military curiosity of the time—one of many—was the practice by which men of color, recruited in the South, were credited to Northern states. There were recruiting agents of these Northern states operating in the South for this purpose, a doubtful state activity in connection with a nationally enacted and administered program of conscription. Senator Doolittle of Wisconsin offered an amendment providing that colored troops mustered into the service of the United States should

[5] *Ibid.*, 38 Cong., 1 sess., 427 (Feb. 1, 1864).
[6] *Ibid.*, 80 (Dec. 22, 1863).
[7] *Ibid.*, 160 (Jan. 12, 1864).
[8] *Ibid.*, 162.
[9] *Ibid.*, 240 (Jan. 16, 1864).

"be credited upon the quota of the State within which they are enlisted, and not upon the quota of any other State." [10] The measure passed the Senate,[11] but it is significant to note that among those voting against it were Senators Dixon of Connecticut, Fessenden of Maine, Harris of New York, Howard of Michigan, Sprague of Rhode Island, and both Sumner and Wilson of Massachusetts.[12]

V

Recruitment and conscription were frequent subjects of discussion. In a remarkable debate in the upper house on January 8, 1864, the point of deliberation was a sensible amendment, brought up from Senator Wilson's committee on military affairs, that so much of the conscription (or enrollment) act of 1863 as authorized the exemption of drafted men on payment of $300 "be, and the same is hereby, repealed." [1]

So it began, but before the deliberation concluded or halted, Sumner moved to amend the amendment. This was after a good deal of discussion. More discussion ensued; then Sumner modified his amendment to the amendment to the statute.[2] Days passed, and the Massachusetts senator came up with yet another modification.[3] After thousands of words had poured forth, Sumner's proposal (his altered modification of his amendment) was voted down.[4] This having been done, the question was now upon the committee's original amendment for repeal of the $300 exemption or commutation clause.

The idea of Sumner's much battered amendment was that, instead of a flat sum of $300 as the price of exemption from the draft, the amount should be ratable according to a man's income. Sumner felt that a wealthy man, being well able to do so, should pay at a higher rate "as a commutation for the service which the country has a right to expect from him." [5] He mentioned twenty per cent (of

---

10 *Ibid.*, 38 Cong., 1 sess., 246 (Jan. 16, 1864).

11 As it went into the statute book the law provided that "men of color . . . , while they shall be credited upon the several states, or subdivisions of states, wherein they are . . . drafted, enlisted, or shall volunteer, shall not be assigned as state troops, but shall be mustered . . . as United States colored troops." *U.S. State at Large,* XIII, 11; act of Feb. 24, 1864, sec. 24.

12 *Cong. Globe,* 38 Cong., 1 sess., 247 (Jan. 16, 1864).

1 *Cong. Globe,* 38 Cong., 1 sess., 139 (Jan. 8, 1864).

2 *Ibid.*, 141 (Jan. 8, 1864).

3 *Ibid.*, 154 (Jan. 12, 1864).

4 *Ibid.*, 159 (Jan. 12, 1864).

5 *Ibid.*, 140 (Jan. 8, 1864).

a year's income), pointing out that this would be a small contribution, considering the immense benefit of relief from military service. He emphasized that the Senate must vote whether the rich man who was drafted should pay more than the poor man. Sherman, however, dashed cold water on the proposal by showing that Sumner's amendment would amount to "a new income tax, to be imposed only upon those who are drafted." If the scheme amounted to a tax, thought Sherman, it ought to be imposed "upon all wealthy citizens." Every man, he said, held his property subject to the nation's taxing power, and every able-bodied man was also subject to whatever military service was required by law, but he did not favor mixing the two systems.

Proceeding further in his argument, Sherman showed the dilemma of the conscription policy in terms of avoiding the draft by a money payment. Retain the commutation clause, he showed, and you may exhaust the basis of future drafts and reënforcements. (It was generally agreed in the discussion that volunteering was insufficient.) On the other hand, said Sherman, "if you make your draft arbitrary and require every one to render military service, you will incite resistance to the draft." Nothing, he added, could justify resistance, but it might nevertheless "excite it." [6]

In addition to the basic misconception of putting a money price on exemption from military service—making it a kind of sales arrangement between the government and the conscript and constantly emphasizing procedures by which service could be avoided—the unwisdom of the enrollment act was shown also in connection with the question of substitutes. Clark of New Hampshire reminded the Senate that the conscription act had been passed so that the government could get men. Then came the idea, said Clark, "that a man should either go himself or furnish a substitute, or give the Government money enough to obtain a substitute for him." Clark was speaking of this aspect of the system favorably; he referred to the fact that in his state "we furnished more men under the draft than any other State in the Union; we furnished fifty per cent. of the call." [7]

---

[6] *Ibid.*, 154 (Jan. 12, 1864).

[7] *Ibid.*, 140 (Jan. 8, 1864). According to the army report the number called for in New Hampshire in the draft of July 1863 was 8002. To meet this call 181 were "personally held" (drafted), and 2240 substitutes were furnished. Thus the total for the state brought into the army by the draft amounted to 2421. (In addition there were 571 who

Here was an odd type of thinking. If men were drafted and "could not well go themselves" (these were Clark's words, as if going into the army were a kind of convenience), the curious supposition was that they would be doing approximately the equivalent if they "furnished" substitutes to serve for them. If a man went into the military service, exposing himself to the hazard of being killed or wounded, and if he added effectiveness to the army, his service was the significant thing, not the fact that so-and-so had "furnished" him. It is hard to see the merit that attaches to army "service" by proxy.

And what type of thinking was it to suppose that the *buying* of soldiers as "substitutes" could be done by the government itself, if a drafted individual but furnished the money! If the conscripted person could get a substitute and pay for him, he could *select* him. This meant bargaining, for often the amount paid for a substitute was a good deal more than $300. The next step, as it worked out, was that a "substitute broker" would do the actual bargaining, buying, and selecting. But if all these methods failed (though quite a few men actually preferred furnishing substitutes to paying commutation money, feeling somehow they were making more of a contribution), the drafted man might pay $300. In that case, such was the reasoning of certain congressional minds, the government, coming in as a kind of last resort, might select and buy the substitute.

By that time, the idea that a soldier so procured could be considered a "substitute" at all, was absurd. In any case the government must take a man if he goes into the service; if the government takes him, he should be regarded as serving in his own right. But according to the procedure of exempting for money and bargaining for "substitutes," the government would be excusing the originally drafted able-bodied man for a period of three years, and thus reducing by so much the basis for future drafts. This gem of congressional thinking was indeed a far cry from modern concepts of military duty and selective service.

At last the unsatisfactory $300 provision was repealed, but in the Senate the repealing motion barely carried by a close vote of 18 to 17, with such influential men as Henderson, Hendricks, Sherman,

paid commutation money; in army statistics they were included when figuring the "total accepted.") These records do not seem to harmonize with Senator Clark's statement as to furnishing fifty per cent of the call, but they do emphasize the large number of "substitutes" obtained by the system of conscription used in 1863. *Offic. Rec.*, 3 ser. V, 730–732.

and Trumbull voting in the negative, and fourteen senators absent.[8] In the lower house, where the repeal was carried by 65 to 53, it was opposed by such men as J. G. Blaine and Thaddeus Stevens.[9] Among other things, this showed the manner in which comparatively few men did the effective voting; sixty-five men in the House amounted to little more than a third of the membership from the Union states.

VI

How did Lincoln feel about the Congress which the people—or the politicians—had given him? He once said concerning a maneuver of Republican senators: "They wish to get rid of me, and I am sometimes half disposed to gratify them." On hearing of the proceedings of this group he added: "I have been more distressed than by any event of my life." [1] "I am to be bullied by Congress, am I?" he once asked.[2] Again, referring to appeals for clemency, he said: "Congress has . . . left the women to howl about me." [3] Ward Lamon recalled that he once found the President in the private room of the White House lying on a sofa, "greatly disturbed and . . . excited." Jumping up, according to Lamon, Lincoln said: "I am President of one part of this divided country . . . ; but look at me! I wish I had never been born! . . . With a fire in my front and rear; having to contend with the jealousies of the military commanders, and not receiving that cordial co-operation and support from Congress which could reasonably be expected; with an active and formidable enemy in the field threatening the very life-blood of the government,—my position is anything but a bed of roses." [4]

There were occasions—just a few—on which Lincoln was asked to take a hand in intraparty contests for nominating a representative in Congress. In 1864 a particularly hot campaign was waged within Republican ranks to prevent the renomination of Isaac N. Arnold of Chicago, who was serving as congressman and desired another term. It was represented to the President that John L. Scripps, known for his connection with the Chicago *Tribune* and his authorship of a

---

[8] *Cong. Globe*, 38 Cong., 1 sess., 3491 (July 2, 1864).
[9] *Ibid.*, 3525 (July 2, 1864).
[1] Browning, *Diary*, I, 600–601.
[2] Rice, 93.
[3] *Ibid.*, 489.
[4] Lamon, *Recollections*, 182–183.

campaign biography of Lincoln in 1860, was using his position as postmaster in Chicago "to defeat Mr. Arnold's nomination to Congress." Lincoln thereupon wrote to Scripps, saying that he was "well satisfied" with Arnold, and asking Scripps not to constrain any of his subordinates in the exercise of his vote for congressman. The matter developed into a considerable row in the period when Lincoln's prospects for his own reëlection were at the lowest ebb. Scripps, himself a candidate for the congressional nomination, denied using post-office control for his own ends, but went on in a complaining letter to denounce Arnold, accusing him of seeking support among Federal office-holders, boosting Frémont, and taking measures that would lead to the choice of John Wentworth, whom Scripps deemed undesirable. After a considerable flow of denunciatory statements, Scripps asked Lincoln to oppose the selection of Arnold. Meanwhile Arnold was hurt and offended by the episode and freely expressed his feelings in letters to the overworked President. According to Arnold's account he had hoped for a "friendly understanding" by personal interview in Chicago but was met by a "storm of rage and passion" on the part of Scripps.

The upshot of this bickering within the party was that Arnold withdrew, pointing out that both the *Tribune* and the post office were against him. As a result John Wentworth was nominated and elected as a Republican to the Thirty-Ninth Congress.[5] In terms of the purposes of President Lincoln it was no small matter to lose the support of such a man as Arnold.[6]

Commenting on the radical attitude, with emphasis upon Wade, Joshua Giddings wrote of the manner in which senators were de-

---

[5] John Wentworth ("Long John") was a vigorous and colorful Chicago leader, Democratic in former background, antislavery in sentiment but not bitterly vindictive. He had a distinguished career as editor, civic leader, early promoter, picturesque character, and mayor of Chicago. In an excellent short biography (*Dic. of Amer. Biog.*, XIX, 657–659) Carl Sandburg wrote that he "had striven with the generations who found Chicago a swamp mudhole and saw it made into an audacious metropolis." In the 1864 congressional race, Wentworth, on the Union (Republican) ticket, defeated the Democratic candidate, Cyrus H. McCormick, noted inventor and producer of the reaper. The Congress chosen in 1864 did not, of course, meet until after Lincoln's death.

[6] On the Scripps-Arnold controversy, see Nicolay and Hay, *Works*, X, 141–142 and 168 (two letters of Lincoln to Scripps, deploring the use of official power in the post office "to defeat Mr. Arnold's nomination to Congress"); R. T. L. Coll., 34223, 34498, 34544, 35854. For similar rows concerning Roscoe Conkling in New York, and William D. Kelley in Philadelphia, see Nicolay and Hay, *Lincoln*, X, 362–363.

nouncing Lincoln; then he generalized: "The truth is that from that day [early in 1861] to the present [January of 1862] Congress has been the theatre for making Presidents and not to carry on the war." [7] One of the milder comments, typical of the radicals, was that of Senator Chandler: "The President is a weak man." [8] Lying "in wait" [9] against the President, these men opposed him on confiscation, on war aims, on methods and pacing as to slavery, on Southern rights, on cabinet composition, on amnesty, on the election of 1864 (in which they would have preferred another man), and on reconstruction.

According to an incident reported in Washington in 1862, a senator once called at the White House and vehemently denounced the President for his "calm and moderate views," ending with the words: "Sir you are within one mile of Hell!" To this Lincoln offered no dissent, but with a gentle nod of his head as if talking to himself, replied: "Yes, yes it is just one mile to the Capitol!" [10]

VII

Some concept of Lincoln's difficulties with Congress may be obtained by studying that organization known as the joint committee on the conduct of the war.[1] This congressional group collected and caused to be printed a huge mass of testimony, six volumes of it exceeding 4000 pages, about two million words. Yet only a few of the military episodes were investigated; attention was focused chiefly on the Army of the Potomac, and, as to that army, the 1862 campaign on the Peninsula. Much less interest was shown in the Maryland campaign.

The effort of the committee was not to get a well rounded account of military events or to hear both sides of a given controversy equally.

---

7 Giddings to G. W. Julian, Montreal, Canada, Jan. 28, 1862, Giddings-Julian MSS.

8 Zachariah Chandler to his wife, Dec. 18, 1862, Chandler MSS., Lib. of Cong.

9 Bates, *Diary*, 241.

10 The remark about "one mile from Hell" became a topic of familiar chitchat and has been often quoted. See, for instance, Browne, *Everyday Life*, 503. The above form of the joke is found in a letter from A. J. Bleeker to B. Galbraith of New York, July 14, 1862, James Gordon Bennett MSS. This manuscript reference to the incident in mid-July of 1862 has special significance; this was a period of special stress and of serious difficulty between President and Congress, especially on the subject of confiscation.

1 For the formation of the committee, its character, membership and activity, see *Lincoln the President*, II, 20 n., 62–64 (with bibl.), 80–83, 87–88.

In the committee's activities there was always a slant, a preconceived notion of who was to blame, an effort to shape the proceedings so as to fasten blame upon particular scapegoats, these being especially Democratic generals. The harrying of victims was not confined to actual committee proceedings which were relentless enough; there was also an accompaniment of wild rumor and irresponsible publicity. The group served the purposes of a faction—the radicals—and the nature of its maneuvers may be illustrated by its atrocious handling of the case of General Charles P. Stone. That officer, a Democrat, was blamed for the minor Union disaster at Ball's Bluff (October 21, 1861) at which Colonel Edward D. Baker was killed. Stone's special duty was guarding the city of Washington and vicinity; he was a man of admirable record; reliable observers resented the drive to put the blame for Ball's Bluff upon him. In its long drawn out "investigation" the committee gave ear to worthless stories of the man's alleged disloyalty, caused him to be arrested (through Stanton), refused to inform him as to charges and witnesses, denied him the right to be heard, and subjected him to a continued ordeal of vague defamation. It was not until February 1863, a year after his arrest, that the committee gave Stone a copy of the charges against him; his answer was so convincing that he was restored to command, but the vindication never caught up with the defamatory campaign. Sick and broken in spirit, with an entirely undeserved blot upon his character, Stone resigned from the army in September 1864; after the war he served for a time in the Egyptian army. It was the conclusion of J. G. Blaine that the testimony regarding Stone was not sifted by the committee, that the case was "prejudiced," and that the drive against the general was conducted in an atmosphere of rumor and "victim-hunting mania." [2]

The committee with its publicized reputation for vigilant watchfulness to prevent or expose military mistakes, had certain targets, such as McClellan, Stone, Fitz-John Porter, and Franklin, and it had also its favored pets such as Frémont and Butler. It showed by no means a uniform record of severity toward military incompetence. As to the investigation of the operation at Fort Fisher (December

[2] Blaine, *Twenty Years of Congress,* I, 381–395. "Rumors and exaggerations filled the newspapers; and the public, in that state of credulity which is an incident of victim-hunting mania, accepted everything as true" (*ibid.,* 382).

1864), one of Butler's failures, the following observation has been made: "The inquisitors had already prejudged the case, and their only purpose was to assemble evidence which would help the general. . . . Butler was given the widest latitude in his answers, and his testimony consisted of a series of long prepared statements. There was no cross-examination." [3]

If one asks how the officious maneuvers of this committee affected the President, the first observation is that the prominently active members were anti-Lincoln men such as Wade, Chandler, and Julian. The committee was strongly favored by Stevens and, from a different party angle, Vallandigham.[4] There is no doubt that the group was a pain to Lincoln. In a conversation with Ward Hill Lamon the President is reported to have said: "I have never faltered in my faith of being ultimately able to suppress this rebellion and of reuniting this divided country; but this improvised vigilant committee to watch my movements and keep me straight, appointed by Congress and called the 'committee on the conduct of the war,' is a marplot, and its greatest purpose seems to be to hamper my action and obstruct the military operations." [5]

The attitude of committeemen toward the President may be judged by the remark of Chandler to his wife: "Folly, folly folly reigns supreme. The President is a weak man . . . & these fool or traitor Generals rule wasting precious time & yet more precious blood in indecisive battles and in avoidable delays." Again he wrote: "The Cabinet is weak & Lincoln weaker . . . ." [6] One might ask what did the committee accomplish? It recommended no legislation and the generals that it favored were by no means the efficient ones. The committee's air of omniscience in military matters was matched only by the lack of military experience on the part of its members. It dealt in partisanship and in the kind of "flagrant wrong" of which, as Blaine has written,[7] General Stone was the victim.

---

[3] T. Harry Williams, *Lincoln and the Radicals,* 366–367.

[4] In supporting the resolution to set up the committee Vallandigham congratulated the country that "gentlemen of the majority" were falling back upon his own (Vallandigham's) principles. *Ann. Cyc.,* 1862, 304.

[5] Lamon, *Recollections,* 183.

[6] Zachariah Chandler to his wife, Dec. 18, 1862, and Feb. 10, 1863, Chandler MSS., Lib. of Cong.

[7] Blaine, *Twenty Years of Congress,* I, 395.

VIII

Students of the American government will find in the Lincoln administration no such coöperation between President and Congress, and no such presidential leadership in legislation as existed under Wilson [1] or under Franklin D. Roosevelt in the earlier New Deal years. Lincoln's chief effort to promote a specific project of legislation —i. e., to obtain Federal approval and practical financial help to support state emancipation—fell flat despite the President's earnest appeals, conferences with legislators, formal messages, and presidential drafting of a sample bill. In military leadership, in the blockade, in international dealings, and in such matters as the presidential proclamation of emancipation, treatment of disloyal persons, reconstruction, and other important measures, the President either went his way regardless of Senate and House, or was actually checked and angrily challenged by Congress.

As a matter of regular procedure (legitimate, and proper enough if not abused) President Lincoln was questioned by one or the other house of Congress, or requests were sent to him for information. The President usually transmitted the desired documents,[2] almost as a matter of routine, but there were times when requests were refused. He explained the refusal on the ground, traditional in such cases reaching back to the time of Washington, that response to the congressional request would be "incompatible with the public interest." [3] The withholding of information under such circumstances was done with full respect to Congress and no issue was made of it; in-

---

1 In the general picture Woodrow Wilson's leadership was notably effective in Congress, both in domestic and foreign matters. The great exception—a deeply unfortunate one for the United States and the world—was the defeat, by a minority of the Senate, of Wilson's program for adherence to the League of Nations. For a summary, see *Lincoln the Liberal Statesman,* chap. vii ("Lincoln's Peace and Wilson's").

2 *Works,* VI, 334.

3 *Ibid.,* VI, 335; VIII, 188–191. In Lincoln's assertion of his right to choose whether or not to submit certain information to Congress, there was a close analogy to the withholding of information by Washington on the pending Jay treaty with Great Britain. Washington declared that he would not withhold information which "the public good shall require to be disclosed," but under the circumstances he considered that a concession of the right then demanded by the House of Representatives "as a matter of course" would constitute a "dangerous precedent." He justified his interpretation by the intention of the Constitution framers. Washington to the House of Representatives, Mar. 30, 1796, Richardson, *Messages and Papers of the Presidents,* I, 194–196.

deed, members were sometimes careful to point out that questioning the President was not to be construed as a vote of censure.[4]

At times, however (aside from requests for information), the Congress came near to censuring the President, and there were frequent occasions when lack of confidence in the Executive was the dominant sentiment. The fact that censure or want of confidence was not formally voted seems to have been chiefly for the reason that such votes are not a parliamentary custom in the United States. Such lack of formal censure, however, was small comfort to a President having to deal with an uncoöperative body whose members gave out frequent censure in their own statements. A few examples of such statements must suffice:

Julian of Indiana, House of Representatives, December 11, 1861: "I . . . infer that the general policy of the Administration . . . renders necessary some action on the part of Congress, looking to a change of that policy." [5]

Thaddeus Stevens of Pennsylvania, House of Representatives, December 16, 1861: "I do not understand where the President gets his facts which he states in this respect [on conditions in Kentucky]. I believe he has been misled. I believe he is laboring under a hallucination of mind upon this subject, as fatal as that of Samson under the manipulation of Delilah." [6]

Hale of New Hampshire, Senate, December 16, 1861: ". . . I venture to predict . . . that if the American people . . . shall find in the future that they have been trifled with . . . there will be such a storm come upon your heads as history has never yet recorded; and it does not want a very great degree of faith to hear the distant rumblings of that thunder-storm that will overwhelm the Administration and the party in power if they do not see the things that belong to the day and the hour before they are hidden from their eyes." [7]

These criticisms, however, were mild when compared to such a document as the "Wade-Davis Manifesto" (August 5, 1864), a scorching denunciation of the President in the midst of the campaign for

---

[4] Trumbull was an example. *Cong. Globe,* 37 Cong., 2 sess., 95 (Dec. 16, 1861).

[5] *Ibid.,* 37 Cong., 2 sess., 59.

[6] *Ibid.,* 103.

[7] *Ibid.,* 93.

his reëlection. This hostile declaration, issued by men of importance in congressional leadership, had a bearing chiefly upon the subject of reconstruction and will be discussed in that connection.

IX

It might have clarified the situation if those who were so vigorously denouncing Lincoln had faced up to the necessity of going on record in an actual vote of censure. The consequences of such a vote would have been serious, but that very fact might have had a sobering effect upon some of those who were hounding the nation's leader. Absence of formal censure should not obscure the fact that, as George W. Julian said concerning one occasion, "the action of the President [as to confiscation] was inexpressibly provoking to a large majority of Congress." [1]

Though there were ups and downs in his popularity, Lincoln stood continually in need of support. People who could not see the whole picture, and could not appreciate the Executive's paramount emphasis upon the Union, would express their impatience with the President. Intemperance of language seemed characteristic of this type of person. At the time of Lincoln's first regular annual message to Congress in December 1861 an Illinois radical wrote: "Not *one single manly, bold, dignified* position taken . . . . No response to the popular feeling . . . but . . . a timid, timeserving, commonplace sort of an abortion of a message, cold enough with one breath, to *freeze* h—ll over." [2] He thought Lincoln must have looked southward when he wrote it.

On those rare occasions when the Chief Magistrate was commended in Congress he would, like as not, be praised in an unfortunate sense. It was like getting applause in the wrong places. Early in the war, when Lincoln's arrests were being discussed in the Senate, Wilson of Massachusetts remarked that "the loyal people of this country were electrified; they felt that they had a government that was ready to exert its power to save the country." Wilson's next remark gave the whole passage a dubious twist: ". . . they rejoiced [at the

1 Rice, *Reminiscences*, 58.

2 S. York to Lyman Trumbull, Paris, Ill., Dec. 5, 1861, Trumbull MSS.

arrests] as they did when Mason and Slidell were clutched from the deck of a British vessel, and imprisoned at Fort Warren . . . ." [3] Since the Lincoln administration was finding the seizure of Mason and Slidell most unfortunate, and was doing its best to work out a solution which ultimately involved the release of the envoys, this sort of senatorial approval gave no comfort. Wilson's declaration (December 16, 1861) came while the vexing problem of what to do with Mason and Slidell was pending; so far as the troubled administration was concerned, it struck the wrong note.

Referring to the attitude of "the leading men of the two Houses," A. G. Riddle wrote: "he [Lincoln] . . . became the theme of criticism . . . [and] reproach on the part of these gentlemen. The New York *Tribune* was largely the organ of these congressional critics, and . . . Mr. Greeley . . . was diligently searching . . . for a man to succeed him [i. e., to succeed Lincoln]. To such extent did this condemnation reach, that, at the end of the Thirty-seventh Congress [March 1863], there were in the House but two men, capable of being heard, who openly and everywhere defended him—Mr. Arnold of Illinois, and Mr. Riddle of Ohio." [4]

This astounding statement—that the President had only two unwavering defenders (if indeed the two mentioned could be so described)—need not be taken too literally, but Riddle was a keen observer. His statement has significance as indicating the general attitude of the House, which was that of opposition to, or divergence from, the views of Lincoln. If one goes so far as to assume that Riddle and Arnold were the only men in the House of Representatives who were really friendly to Lincoln, it should be remembered that neither of these men was reëlected in 1864. Riddle did not seek reëlection, and Arnold, despite his appeal to Lincoln to help him in seeking another term, was stopped in his efforts to remain in Congress. The situation becomes the more remarkable when one remembers Riddle's eulogistic friendliness toward Senator Wade, a bitter and powerfully active opponent of the President.

To document his statement that he was a supporter of the President, Riddle referred to a speech he had made in the House on Feb-

[3] *Cong. Globe,* 37 Cong., 2 sess., 94 (Dec. 16, 1861).

[4] Riddle, *Recollections,* 218 n.

ruary 28, 1863, concerning the bill to indemnify the President—i. e., to afford protection for those who had made irregular arrests and seizures in accordance with presidential orders. In that speech Mr. Riddle had declared:

> . . . How easy it is to abuse, traduce, and denounce. That it requires neither wit, grace, or truth, is illustrated by the assaults of those gentlemen on the President. . . .
>
> Sir, the Executive is the arm of the people under our Constitution, and with it only can we deal a blow upon the rebellion. . . . Whoever strengthens this arm, strengthens the national cause; whoever weakens it strengthens the enemy. . . . You cannot separate the Executive from the *personale* of the President; and whatever detracts from him personally weakens the Executive force . . . .
>
> The President, without the people, and all of them, can no more conduct this war to a successful issue than can the people without him. . . . With a united people he is irresistible, spite of mistakes and accidents. A united people and President can control fate and compel success. They must stand together; and woe unutterable to the wretches whose words or deeds shall separate them. . . . They [i. e., millions of the people] will discuss the events and management of the war. . . . But I submit if the just limit of criticism and manly debate has not been brutally outraged in the fierce denunciation of the President by gentlemen on this floor, and which have been caught up and reëchoed by their partisan press?
>
> . . . .
>
> . . . If any man here distrusts the President, let him speak forth here, . . . and no longer offend the streets and nauseate places of common resort with their . . . clamor. . . . He [the President] may not have in excess that ecstatic fire that makes poets and prophets and madmen; he may not possess much of what we call heroic blood, that drives men to stake priceless destinies on desperate ventures, and lose them; he may not in an eminent degree possess that indefinable something that school-boys call genius, that enables its possessor through new and unheard-of combinations to grasp at wonderful results, and that usually ends in failure . . . . He is an unimpassioned, cool, shrewd, sagacious, far-seeing man, with a capacity to form his own judgments, and a will to execute them; and he possesses an integrity pure and simple as the white rays of light that play about the Throne. It is this that has so tied the hearts and love of the people to him, that will not unloose in the breath of all the demagogues in the land. It is idle to compare him with Washington or Jackson. Like all extraordinary men, he is an original, and must stand in his own niche.

. . . contemplate, if you can, . . . the fearful responsibilities imposed upon this man. Is it not a marvel . . . that he sustains them so well? [5]

It is not surprising that Lincoln welcomed the days and months when there was no assembled Congress. When, after a long session, the Senate adjourned in July 1862, the New York *Herald* remarked that this would relieve the President of embarrassment; he could carry on without senatorial annoyance and hindrance.[6] Some of the solons, however, wanted Congress to remain in permanent session. It is significant that many of Lincoln's principal executive measures were taken when Congress was not sitting. This was true of the initial call for troops in April 1861, the blockade, the enlargement of the regular army, the overruling of Frémont, the suspension of the habeas corpus privilege, the preliminary proclamation of emancipation, and the important speech of April 11, 1865, on postwar policy. If Lincoln had had a coöperative Congress, most if not all of these measures ought to have been the combined product of the legislative and executive branches.

At one of those periods when Lincoln was having particular difficulty with an uncoöperative Congress, his friend Orville Browning of Illinois called on him at the White House. The day was July 15, 1862. The President was trying to check the course that leaders of Congress were taking on the question of confiscation. At the same time he was shaping up his emancipation policy and was struggling with a military situation that led to the elevation of Halleck and Pope over McClellan. As if this were not enough, the international situation and the coming congressional election were on his mind.

The President, as Browning wrote in his diary, "was in his Library writing, with directions to deny him to every body. I went in a moment. He looked weary, care-worn and troubled. I shook hands with him, and asked how he was. He said 'tolerably well' I remarked that I felt concerned about him—regretted that troubles crowded so heavily upon him, and feared his health was suffering. He held me by the hand, pressed it, and said in a very tender and touching tone —'Browning I must die sometime', I replied 'your fortunes Mr President are bound up with those of the Country, and disaster to one

[5] *Cong. Globe,* 37 Cong., 3 sess., 1400 (Feb. 28, 1863). Though the speech is reproduced in Riddle's book, the text as here given is based on the *Globe*.

[6] New York *Herald,* July 13, 1862, p. 4, c. 6; p. 5, c. 1.

would be disaster to the other, and I hope you will do all you can to preserve your health and life.' He looked very sad, and there was a cadence of deep sadness in his voice. We parted I believe both of us with tears in our eyes." [7]

It is not argued here that Lincoln's depression was altogether attributable to the difficulties he was having with Congress. It is rather that, when tribulations from many a quarter were piling up their accumulated weight, Congress added its bit by rebuffing his suggestions and pursuing policies of which he strongly disapproved. As the second session of the Thirty-Seventh Congress neared its close, Senator Fessenden of Maine, conversing with Browning of Illinois, indicated doubts as to the wisdom of his colleagues. "During recess met Fessenden [wrote Browning on July 16, 1862], and in a conversation about the confiscation bill he said very emphatically that he thought with me it would have been better not to have legislated upon the subject . . . at all." [8]

We are dealing here, of course, with the disharmony between Lincoln and the radicals, which has been pointed out earlier as a pervasive dualism running throughout the Lincoln administration,[9] and which was a primary factor in the President's unsatisfactory dealings with Congress. In this respect the two factors were that Republican radicals came increasingly into control of Congress; and that, in the minds of these radicals, opposition to Lincoln rose steadily in an embittering crescendo. These were "the men to whom the nation . . . turned as the great representative men of the new political power." They "did not conceal their distrust of Lincoln, and he had little support from them at any time during his administration." Except for some of the younger leaders, declared A. K. McClure, "he would have been a President without a party." McClure added that the "one man who rendered him [Lincoln] the greatest service of all at the beginning of the war was Stephen A. Douglas, his old competitor of Illinois." Speaking of the manner in which Republican leaders "were hesitating and criticising their President," McClure remarked upon "the general distrust and demoralization that existed among men who should have been a solid phalanx of leadership in the crisis that confronted them." [10]

[7] Browning, *Diary*, I, 559–560.
[8] *Ibid.*, I, 560.
[9] *Lincoln the President*, II, 1–2.
[10] McClure, 62.

Since Congress and the President were not traveling the same path, Lincoln simply took over certain powers without regard to Congress. "The President was . . . compelled to decide for himself in the multitude of conflicting counsels what policy the administration should adopt, and even a less . . . conservative man than Lincoln would have been compelled . . . to move with the utmost caution." [11] When, in addition to all this, it is remembered that the President got little comfort and much interference from his cabinet, that his generals were often a trial to him, and that few of the state governors were genuinely enthusiastic for him, one can understand Lincoln's loneliness in his lofty office.

X

The question arises: Were there constructive and hopeful factors at work in Congress? The answer, of course, is in the affirmative. The very fact that Congress existed—that it was not abolished, intimidated, prorogued, or suppressed—was evidence that the nation was not under a dictatorship and that the principle of representative government still endured. The whole government, including the armed forces and the civil establishment, depended upon Congress. Bureaus and departments, courts, military systems—all such things existed by congressional enactment. Vital matters of finance, the raising of the army, specific appropriations for a thousand purposes, rested with the men on Capitol Hill. (Such a thing as executive expenditures from the Federal treasury without congressional appropriation, though it did occur,[1] was highly exceptional.) Since Congress possessed the power of the purse, together with the broad function of determining what branches should or should not exist, it was central in the whole governmental structure. It is true, of course, that Congress could administer virtually nothing. Practical management of the nation's business, execution of the laws, administrative tasks, belonged to the executive branch; but in any comprehensive view it would be a great mistake to underestimate the legislative role.

It is the judgment of J. F. Rhodes that "the senators and representatives labored with zeal, sagacity, and effect." Referring to the

[11] *Ibid.*, 63.

[1] *Lincoln the President*, I, 375.

long session of the Thirty-Seventh Congress (December to July, 1861–1862), he wrote: "The laws of this session show how much an able and honest Congress may accomplish when possessed of an earnestness and singleness of purpose that will prevail against the cumbrous rules which hedge about the action of a democracy's legislative body, unfitting it for the management of a war." [2]

A noteworthy aspect of the war period was the continuing concept of the nation's greatness and permanence which animated both President and Congress. War measures were perforce the chief preoccupation of the law makers. Through all this, however, and beyond it, there was the thought of an enduring nation whose peaceful growth and prosperity was, in the long run, the government's main concern. As a relief from the many episodes that showed the excesses of the war mind, it is well to note those moments of deliberation which envisaged a nation that would survive its internal struggle, promote the vital task of restoration, and go on from there to normal peaceful advance and improvement.

It is true that such deliberation left much to be desired, so that the "Gilded Age" was to be a time of extravagance and coarseness, but no history of Lincoln's day is complete without noticing lasting accomplishments that pertained to non-war pursuits and developments. For the first time in the nation's history a department was created in the United States government for the promotion of agriculture. In his annual message of December 1861 Lincoln called attention to this need. "Agriculture," he said, "confessedly the largest interest of the nation, has not a department, nor a bureau, but a clerkship only, assigned to it in the government." Congress acted to create the department of agriculture on May 15, 1862, and President Lincoln appointed as its head one of the nation's most devoted and competent public servants, Isaac Newton. A personal friend of Lincoln, Newton was serving in the agricultural division of the patent office of the department of the interior. With a department of his own he now went ahead to organize a highly serviceable agency, so that in December 1862 Lincoln reported the establishment of "an extensive system of correspondence and exchanges, both at home and abroad, which promises to effect highly beneficial results in the development of a correct knowledge of recent improvements in agri-

---

2 J. F. Rhodes, *History of the United States,* IV, 57–58.

culture . . . ." [3] He went on to comment on specific services of the new department, such as the collection of agricultural statistics, the introduction of new products, and the distribution of seeds, plants, and cuttings.

Lincoln's interest in agriculture is an extensive subject in itself. He had spoken prominently before the Wisconsin Agricultural Society at Milwaukee on September 30, 1859, this being one of his major addresses. As in the case of Jefferson, he associated agricultural activity with democracy, and in this spirit, in 1864, he referred to Newton's department as "peculiarly the people's department, in which they feel more directly concerned than in any other." [4]

There was more in this than agriculture, great as that was. In such matters the Lincoln administration was treating the function of government broadly, as involving more than the restricted sphere of keeping order and suppressing crime. Rather, the instruments of government were to be devoted in a broad sense to serving the people's needs, developing the resources of the country, promoting general prosperity, improving the means of livelihood, stamping out pests, and performing those functions that are beyond the reach of individual or merely local effort.

This purposeful, rather than negative, use of government was illustrated in other fields. Realizing a scheme projected by Jonathan B. Turner, earnest and public spirited professor at Illinois College at Jacksonville, Illinois, Congress enacted and Lincoln signed a far reaching law in 1862. It is one of the landmarks in American education. Known as the Morrill land-grant-college act, this statute set up a plan for the establishment of colleges to promote agriculture and the mechanic arts with the aid of public lands donated by the Federal government. The act took its name from one of its legislative sponsors, Senator Justin S. Morrill of Vermont. While it was passed in the midst of war, this law had more than wartime importance. Its significance as a national project to be projected far into the future was illustrated after the war when its benefits were extended to those states which, in Lincoln's day, were in the Confederacy, as well as

---

[3] Annual message to Congress, Dec. 1, 1862, MS. in clerk's hand, Nat. Archives; photostat, A. Lincoln Assoc. (Nicolay and Hay, *Works,* VIII, 109).

[4] Annual message to Congress, Dec. 6, 1864, photostat, A. Lincoln Assoc. (Nicolay and Hay, *Works,* X, 302).

to commonwealths still to enter the Union. Liberal donations of public lands and other forms of government aid were also employed by Congress in the launching of ambitious railroad projects designed to reach the Pacific and complete the span of transportation across the continent.

The notable homestead act of 1862 belonged in this category of welfare measures enacted during the Lincoln administration. In the campaign of 1860 a great deal of Republican emphasis was placed upon the theme that every man should "possess the means of gaining a fair living and bringing up his family respectably." For that reason it was urged that *"A homestead should be granted . . . to every poor man who needs it, desires it, and will cultivate it."* Arguments were raised against the undemocratic regime that results "whenever an excessive share of land has been accumulated in the hands of any person or class of persons." [5]

The homestead act, signed by the President on May 20, 1862, was one of the most significant of all the non-war measures enacted during the Lincoln administration. It provided that one hundred sixty acres, a quarter-section, of land was to be given out of the public domain to a bona fide homesteader on payment of a nominal fee after five years of actual residence. The effect of the law on American social and economic development, though it needs to be rejudged by the fuller findings of recent writers,[6] was far reaching. As a measure frankly devoted to welfare, and not to the more restricted functions of government, it is an early landmark.

These developments would have been enough to cause the Lincoln administration to be remembered for its permanent contributions, altogether apart from the war and the nobly great question of emancipation, but the constructive story does not end here.[7] Industry was promoted in numerous ways. Prejudice against "aliens" was avoided. Immigration was encouraged. Foreign laborers were brought in under the contract system, whose later exploitive aspects were at

5 Hartford *Evening Press* (pro-Lincoln), Oct. 25–26, 1860, reprinted in Howard C. Perkins, ed., *Northern Editorials on Secession*, I, 63.

6 Paul Gates, "The Homestead Law in an Incongruous Land System"; Fred A. Shannon, "The Homestead Act and the Labor Surplus." For these two papers, see *Amer. Hist. Rev.*, XLI, 637–681 (1936).

7 J. Duane Squires, "Some Enduring Achievements of the Lincoln Administration, 1861–1865," *Abr. Lincoln Quar.*, V, 191–211 (1948).

variance with the original intent of the law. Sympathy toward men of other countries was stimulated. Valuable progress was made in surgery, medicine and nursing. New devices were used in public finance and in the much needed national regulation of banking. The National Academy of Sciences was set up by Congress (March 3, 1863), such distinguished scientists as Joseph Henry and Asa Gray being original members. The Capitol at Washington was completed under Lincoln. In the relation of the President to the governors, in state and Federal coöperation, and in the general emphasis upon the human importance of government, the period 1861 to 1865 still stands out as an era of great significance. It amounted, in fact, to a new orientation. Never again would the relation of the people to the government be so detached, so restricted and undeveloped, as in the age that ended with Buchanan.

Part of this congressional activity was trial and error; in certain aspects the result was frustration; permanent effectiveness did not always attach to the legislation of the time. Some of the "resolutions" of Congress fell flat. Confiscation accomplished almost nothing at all —certainly nothing that was constructive. Generals were pilloried by the committee on the conduct of the war. Attacks upon the cabinet led to no beneficial result. Republican "reconstruction" was abandoned by its own sponsors in 1877. The optimism that greeted the homestead act—the assumption that free land in the West would relieve the congestion and distress of a labor surplus in the East— proved illusory. The fine purposes of the homestead law met with disappointment in later decades because of fraud and shameful exploitation by profit seeking interests.[8] Despite these factors, which belong to sordid postwar years, it is nevertheless true that in those moments when Congress was at its best, measures were launched which, though attracting minor attention in contemporary history and memoirs, were planned on lines of a progressive design and were indicative of a hopeful and forward looking outlook even in the nation's darkest hours.

It is in this sense that one should read Lincoln's messages to Con-

[8] Paul W. Gates, "The Homestead Law in an Incongruous Land System," *Amer. Hist. Rev.*, XLI, 652–681 (1936). For the later situation which "made a mockery of the presumed intention of the Homestead Act," see Fred A. Shannon, *America's Economic Growth* (3rd ed., 1951), 376 ff.

gress. They reveal a sense of time, an unwavering concept of a nation with a future. Matters just treated—agriculture, the homestead system, aid to education, railroads to the Pacific, immigration, scientific improvement, and so on—were called to the attention of Congress by Lincoln.

Naturally a great deal of space in his messages to Congress was devoted to the Union cause, to the distress and challenge of war making, to undoing (partially) of the effects of the war, to slavery and emancipation, and to the high ideal of "freedom disenthralled." [9] These were affairs of immediate urgency. Yet it is remarkable to observe how often and how confidently he spoke of matters that were natural and peaceful. At times he became so inspired with visions of the country's growth that his predictions turned out to be overstatements. There were men then living, he thought, who would live to see the United States contain a population of 250 millions.[10] He did not, however, think merely of numbers. He drew attention to America's health and harvests, its abundant resources, and, as the war progressed, to "the improved condition of our national affairs." [11] In the western territories he saw regions untouched by war, areas of hope, with prospects for new States in the Union.[12] In a significant passage he described and extolled the Middle West, which he called "the great body of the republic." He recognized in "this great interior region" natural advantages which made it "one of the most important in the world." He could not bear the idea that so vast and centrally located an area should be "cut off," as it would be if there should be a separation of "our common country into two nations." [13]

In terms of lasting adjustment he wrote eloquently of labor and capital, with marked emotional emphasis on the dignity of labor.[14] Public works, public lands, postal and telegraphic arrangements, internal improvements, Indian affairs, participation in "the exhibition of the industry of all nations to be holden at London in the year 1862" —all such topics were treated by Lincoln on more than a perfunctory

[9] Last sentence, message of Dec. 8, 1863, photostat, A. Lincoln Assoc.

[10] Last paragraph, message of Dec. 3, 1861.

[11] First paragraph, message of Dec. 8, 1863, photostat.

[12] Message of Dec. 1, 1862, photostat.

[13] Message, Dec. 1, 1862 (Nicolay and Hay, *Works,* VIII, 113–115).

[14] On various occasions Lincoln dealt at some length with labor's indispensable contribution and its relation to capital. Examples are his agricultural address at Milwaukee, Sep. 30, 1859, and his annual message of Dec. 3, 1861.

level. Above the ruin and abnormality of war the President was looking forward to the time when the nation's concern would be with healing, making whole, restoration, and healthy growth. It was in this sense that he viewed the function of government, of the Union itself. Referring in December 1861 to the growth of the nation's population since 1790, he declared that the "increase of those other things which men deem desirable has been even greater." He considered this an argument for democracy, showing "at one view, what the popular principle applied to government, through the machinery of the States and the Union, has produced in a given time; and also what, if firmly maintained, it promises for the future." "The struggle of today," he concluded, "is not altogether for today . . . ."[15]

---

[15] Concluding paragraph, message of Dec. 3, 1861, photostat, A. Lincoln Assoc.

CHAPTER VII

DEMOCRACY AND THE WAR POWER

WARTIME procedures under Lincoln offer many a text in politics and philosophy. When the government of a democratic nation chooses harsh methods as an alternative to extinction there will be sincere protest and criticism, and there will be slurs upon democracy itself. This criticism will come if the nation survives, but suppose it does not survive. Suppose it goes down by reason of division, dissension, or treason within the walls? In that case there will be worse criticism stressing the weakness and inadequacy alleged to be characteristic of a democratic nation in an emergency.

In facing this situation Lincoln was in a position where he would be condemned either way. If he did not preserve all the niceties of the Constitution he would be assailed not only by those who genuinely valued civil liberty, but also by enemies and opponents whose motive was criticism itself and whose animus was partisanship. Far heavier would have been the denunciation if the whole experiment of the democratic American Union had fallen as it seemed possible that it might fall. If such a disaster had come, where would have been the use of the Constitution whose procedures had been adhered to?

Such in part was Lincoln's problem, but to state the case in this way does not exhaust the subject. Suppression is a matter of degree. To use a discreet amount of it does not imply the utmost of brutality, severity, and despotism. Things regarded as severe in Lincoln's time would have seemed soft and "decadent" to a Hitler, a Heydrich, or a Himmler. It becomes, therefore, a matter of importance to examine the Lincoln procedures, to perceive them for what they were, to study them against the background of those threatening times, and to note the qualifications, concessions, compromises, and ameliorations that appeared in the human application of measures that looked harsh on the books.

To speak of the government as Lincoln's is in part true and in part a matter of rhetoric. Everything pertaining to the United States was Lincoln's in the language of the secessionist press: it was Lincoln's government, Lincoln's army, Lincoln's navy, his hirelings, Hessians, raw head and bloody bones. One cannot of course identify everything in the United States of 1861–65 with Lincoln. One may, however, speak of what happened "under Lincoln" as denoting in point of time the period of Lincoln's rule. Much that happened was indeed shaped by the personality, discretion, and executive procedure of the President. Yet things were done, by Congress and by military leaders, of which Lincoln disapproved.

In managing the government Lincoln acted. He took authority; he was out in front; he did not depend upon Congress; he did not take his cues from the courts; he made the presidency, to a large extent though not completely, the dominant power, certainly more so than it had normally been. He came to a major clash with Congress because he attempted to exert his leadership in the shaping of postwar policy. In this sense, and in others in which the radicals opposed him, his will did not prevail. The intent, pattern, and method of that administration in its emergency aspects must now be examined.

I

It is a traditional Anglo-Saxon principle that rulers must not be arbitrary. A citizen is entitled to redress. He may appeal to the courts. If they find that officials have wronged him in person or property by measures beyond the bounds of legitimate government, not only is reparation due, but rulers and administrators may themselves be brought to book.[1] No American official is above the law. Military power is by no means unlimited.[2] Down through the decades the curtailing of army authority has had repeated emphasis, from the Virginia Declaration of Rights (1776) on down to the Milligan decision (1866) and beyond. It is not merely that, until recent years, a large standing army in time of peace has been considered undesirable and

1 *Constitutional Problems Under Lincoln*, esp. chaps. ii, vii, viii, xx.
2 *Ibid.* (foreword to revised ed., 1951), xvii–xx.

has not been the American policy.[3] It is also true that with their dislike of military excess Americans have had definite concepts of the limits beyond which army power must not go.

Time of war is different, but even then it is a mistake to suppose that all the basic safeguards are to be shattered. We are familiar with the idea "necessity knows no law," the maxim "inter arma silent leges," and the oft-repeated phrase "military necessity." But it would be a great mistake to argue, by using such phrases, that anything and everything can be justified by the demands of war. "Necessity knows no law" is a dangerous half-truth. If it has a kernel of genuine meaning, being applicable to a situation of utmost extremity, it should always be watched as to how it is applied. If a commander appeals to "military necessity," which he would not do except for something wrongful or irregular, he should be ready to show that the main object is justified. (Beginning an aggressive war, as in the attack upon Belgium in 1914, would not be such an object.) He should also show that the case is desperate, that the public urgency is imperative, that the means used are not excessive, and that these means are conducive to order. No reputable commander even in war will do a deeply dishonorable thing. Proper military rule leaves some space for civilian rights. One can understand the characterization that war is crime, yet wanton criminality has no place in the procedures of a reputable government drawn into war. What has been called phony currency is not to be tolerated. Mass killings, genocide, brutal collective reprisals, the rounding up of hostages, slaughter of refugees, torture chambers, camps of horror, labor enslavement, annihilation of whole villages—such procedures are not to be justified because war is on. The kind of government to use such practices would be the kind to start a war.[4]

Martial law is a kind of by-passing of law. It is the commander's will in a situation so unusual that ordinary rules do not and cannot

---

[3] As late as 1910 the regular army of the United States numbered only 80,718, with the national guard (119,660) as an imperfect reserve. Peacetime conscription, well established in Europe, was not used in the United States until 1940, a time of world upheaval. At the mid-century (1950) compulsory universal military training had not been adopted as a permanent peacetime program, while the postwar draft and huge defense program (from 1945 on) have been obviously related to the abnormal stress of a wretched world crisis.

[4] Randall, "Civil and Military Relationships Under Lincoln," *Pa. Mag. of Hist. and Biog.*, vol. 69, 201–202 (July 1945); *Constitutional Problems Under Lincoln* (revised ed., 1951), foreword, xxix–xxxi.

apply.[5] Yet one should note how seldom such measures have actually been found "necessary" by the American national government. Up to Lincoln's day there was very little Federal use of martial law. Up to March 1863 Congress never approved the general suspension of the habeas corpus privilege. It did so then with reluctance and ambiguity. No such suspension was declared under Woodrow Wilson or Franklin Roosevelt.[6]

When one considers the kind of man Lincoln was—considerate, tolerant, and regardful of civil liberty—one realizes forcibly the dilemma he faced in assuming war power. He to whom democracy was fundamental and precious became the target for attack by those who called him a despot. He became the wielder of such expanded executive authority that he was referred to as a "dictator." He was compared to Nero or Caligula. It has been noted in an earlier volume how, in the eighty days between the April call for troops and the meeting of Congress on July 4, 1861, Lincoln performed a whole series of important acts by pure assumption of presidential power.[7] He proclaimed, not "civil war" in those words, but the existence of "combinations too powerful to be suppressed by the ordinary course of judicial proceedings." He called forth the militia to "suppress said combinations" which he commanded "to disperse and retire peacefully" to their homes. Congress has the constitutional power to declare war, but suppression of rebellion has been recognized as an executive function, for which the power of setting aside civil pro-

---

5 British and American citations on martial law are given at length in *Constitutional Problems Under Lincoln,* 144 n. For a short selection of American authorities one may cite: G. B. Davis, *Military Law of the U.S.;* W. S. Holdsworth and H. Earle Richards, in *Law Quar. Rev.,* XVIII; H. W. Ballantine, in *Yale Law Rev.,* XXIV and *Columbia Law* Rev., XII; *Ex parte* Milligan, 71 U. S. 2.

6 Under Franklin Roosevelt there were instances when military executions were not overruled by invoking the right of habeas corpus, but that right itself was not set aside. An example is the Yamashita case (327 U. S. 1). The courts were available for inquiring into military procedures, trials, and punishments. If one goes farther back he finds that civil procedures were retained and martial law avoided under Washington in the Whiskey Insurrection, under John Adams in the Fries Rebellion, and under Jefferson in the Burr Conspiracy. Jackson's use of martial law in Louisiana during the War of 1812—his actual imprisoning of a judge and a district attorney who tried to stop him—was disapproved in the regular courts and the famous general subjected to a fine. The remission of the fine many years later by Congress was a personal tribute to Jackson when on the eve of the grave, not a justification of his act as a sound precedent. All of these factors point up the exceptional nature of the procedure under Lincoln, but of course the Civil War happened only once.

7 *Lincoln the President,* I, chap. xiii.

cedures has been placed in the President's hands. In this initial phase Lincoln also proclaimed a blockade, suspended the habeas corpus privilege, increased the size of the regular army, and authorized the expenditure of government money without congressional appropriation. He made far reaching decisions and commitments while Congress was not in session.

The irregularity, or at least the unusual character, of these measures, was indicated by Senator John Sherman's statement, "I never met any one who claimed that the President could, by a proclamation, increase the regular army." [8] Sherman's statement referred, not to the April call for 75,000 militia to serve for three months, but to a further call (May 3, 1861) directing "that the regular army of the United States be increased . . . , making . . . a maximum aggregate increase of twenty-two thousand seven hundred and fourteen officers and enlisted men . . . ." [9]

Lincoln did not deny that he had stretched his constitutional power. "These measures," he declared, "whether strictly legal or not, were ventured upon, under what appeared to be a popular demand, and a public necessity; trusting then, as now, that Congress would readily ratify them." [10] Lincoln thus confronted Congress with a *fait accompli*. It was a case of a President deliberately exercising legislative power, and then seeking congressional approval or legalization after the event. There were those who believed that in doing so he had carried his authority too far.

II

These constitutional questions—the validity of initial war measures, the legal nature of the conflict, Lincoln's assumption of war power—came up to the Supreme Court in one of the most fundamental cases ever heard by that tribunal. The decision, in the *Prize Cases*,[1] came in March 1863, though the specific executive acts had been performed in 1861. The particular question before the Court pertained to the seizure of vessels for violating the blockade, whose

---

[8] New York *Tribune*, Aug. 23, 1861, p. 7, c. 6.

[9] Call for 42,034 volunteers, May 3, 1861, photograph of original, A. Lincoln Assoc.

[10] Message of July 4, 1861, *Sen. Exec. Doc. No. 1*, 37 Cong., 1 sess., p. 9.

[1] 67 U. S. 635.

legality had been challenged since it was set up by presidential proclamation without congressional declaration of war. The problem, however, had much broader aspects, since the blockade was only one of the emergency measures taken by Lincoln in the "eighty days" by his own authority.

It was argued in the *Prize Cases* (in which proceedings for a number of captured ships were joined) that Congress alone has power to declare war, that the President has no right to institute a blockade until after such a declaration, that war did not lawfully exist when the seizures were made, and that judgments against the ships in lower Federal courts were invalid. Had the high court in 1863 decided according to such arguments, it would have been declaring invalid the basic governmental acts by which the war was prosecuted in its early months, as well as the whole procedure (in terms of law and authority) by which the government at Washington had met the 1861 emergency. In some minds the matter went further and it was supposed that a decision adverse to the President's power would have overthrown, or cast into doubt, the legality of the whole war.

Pondering such an embarrassment to the Lincoln administration, the distinguished lawyer Richard Henry Dana, Jr. wrote to Charles Francis Adams: "Contemplate, my dear sir, the possibility of a Supreme Court deciding that this blockade is illegal! What a position it would put us in before the world . . . ! It would end the war, and how it would leave us with neutral powers, it is fearful to contemplate!" [2]

Under these circumstances it was a great relief to the Lincoln administration when the Court sustained the acts of the President, including the blockade. A civil war, the Court held, does not legally originate because it is declared by Congress. It simply occurs. The "party in rebellion" breaks its allegiance, organizes armies, and commences hostilities. In such a case it is the duty of the President to resist force by force, to meet the war as he finds it "without waiting for Congress to baptize it with a name." As to the weighty question whether the struggle was an insurrection, or a "war" in the full sense (as if between independent nations), the Court decided (here and elsewhere) that it was both. Justice Grier, who delivered the opinion,

2 R. H. Dana, Jr. to Charles Francis Adams, Mar. 9, 1863, quoted in Adams, *Richard Henry Dana,* II, 267.

showed a dislike of legal refinements on this point, as he had earlier shown an impatience (1861) with legalistic efforts to justify the treatment of Confederate privateersmen as "pirates." [3] He refused to approve any "such anomalous doctrine" as that "a war levied on the Government . . . to dismember and destroy it, is not a *war* because it is an *insurrection*."

Lincoln's acts were thus held valid, the blockade upheld, the convenient double-nature theory of the war announced, and the condemnation of the ships sustained. But all this was by a narrow escape. The decision, which was handed down on March 10, 1863, was five to four, the Chief Justice (Taney) being among the dissenters. The five constituting the majority were Grier of Pennsylvania, Wayne of Georgia, Swayne of Ohio, Miller of Iowa, and Davis of Illinois. The minority included Taney of Maryland, Nelson of New York, Catron of Tennessee, and Clifford of Maine. This was weighty dissent, all the more so when one remembers the traditional policy of the Court to avoid smashing pronouncements on "political" questions, as well as the urgency of sustaining a government in time of desperate war. On analyzing the situation further it is found that three of the five justices who sustained Lincoln's acts, where every one of the five was essential to a majority, were men of his own appointing (Swayne, Miller, and Davis), while another (Wayne) was of the deep South.

This situation gives particular importance to James Moore Wayne of Georgia and to the special service which he performed in terms of his sincere adherence to the Union. He had remained on the Court despite the secession of his state, unlike Campbell of Alabama, also a man of great sincerity, who, though not himself a secessionist, resigned from the Supreme Court when his state seceded. Wayne's career was that of "legislator, mayor of Savannah, judge of the Eastern Circuit of Georgia, congressman during the Jackson era, president of two constitutional conventions in his State, [and] associate justice of the Supreme Court of the United States for thirty-two years . . . ." [4] Appointed by President Jackson in 1835, he remained on the Court until his death in 1867, his service falling within the period of eleven Presidents. Of the justices who served with John Marshall he was the last to survive. Wayne's strong Unionism is

[3] Randall, *Civil War and Reconstruction*, 586–587.

[4] Alexander A. Lawrence, *James Moore Wayne: Southern Unionist*, vii.

clearly shown by his biographer, who writes: "On the night that his State seceded Benjamin H. Hill shut out the light of the bonfires from his room and grieved in darkness for the shattered Union. Herschel V. Johnson left Milledgeville sick at heart. But none was more heartbroken than Mr. Justice Wayne. And none saw more clearly the disaster which lay ahead." [5]

In recognizing, however, the full seriousness of the governmental situation touching the *Prize Cases* in their bearing upon the legality of Lincoln's war measures, it is important to avoid exaggeration. The idea that the war policy would have broken down and the war have ended if the decision had gone the other way, is not merely an over-dramatization; it is an erroneous supposition as to the substance of the decision. The matter in legal doubt was the validity of presidential war measures prior to July 13, 1861; [6] it was then that Congress, in the words of dissenting Justice Nelson, "recognized a state of civil war." [7] After this July date there was no serious question. The whole Court agreed that after the congressional authorization the President was properly invested with the war power. They divided, with the venerable Chief Justice in the minority, on the validity of Lincoln's measures before that time.

III

It was not, however, the enemy in arms, but rather the condition of internal agitation and dissension, that caused the most heated and serious constitutional disputes under Lincoln.[1] Confronted with a startling threat to law and order at home—a threat to the very existence of the national government—Lincoln chose to set aside civil guarantees. In a series of proclamations and orders he suspended the privilege of the habeas corpus writ, that ancient and respected procedure by which the civilian is protected against arbitrary arrest.

The first act of Lincoln for such suspension was his communication to General Scott:

---

5 *Ibid.*, 179.

6 The act of July 13, 1861, for collection of duties "and for other Purposes," authorized the President to declare a state of insurrection. *U.S. Stat. at Large,* XII, 255–258.

7 67 U. S. 696.

1 For "Copperhead" disloyalty and the like, see below, chap. viii.

The Commanding General Army of the United States:

You are engaged in repressing an insurrection against the laws of the United States. If at any point on or in the vicinity of any military line which is now or which shall be used between the city of Philadelphia and the city of Washington you find resistance which renders it necessary to suspend the writ of habeas corpus for the public safety, you personally or through the officer in command at the point where resistance occurs are authorized to suspend that writ.[2]

The date of this early proclamation was April 27, 1861; the purpose was to deal with the isolation of the nation's capital, the severing of communications, the serious situation growing out of the mob attack upon Federal troops in Baltimore (April 19), and the widespread confusion and fear of violence occasioned by anti-government leaders and agitators. Born of a startling emergency, this Lincoln policy was at first experimental, tentative, and undeveloped. As explained in a later official pronouncement of Secretary of War Stanton "By order of the President," defection and treason pervaded the very government itself. "Treason was flagrant,"—thus read Stanton's order. "The capital was besieged, and its connection with all the States cut off." It was further stated that secret societies were forming, passions were highly excited, arms and war supplies were assembled, army and naval officers were deserting their posts, and garrisons were being betrayed or abandoned. Congress was not in session. In its previous session (before the war, to be sure) the national legislature had not anticipated or provided for the emergency.[3]

Aside from Washington itself, this sharp emergency at the outset of the war was most startling in the state of Maryland. It was there that the earliest incidents occurred in the suspension of civil guarantees by the Lincoln administration. If control of Maryland had been seized by the secessionists as an "inside job," the nation's capital city would have been surrounded by the enemy. Short of this, which was a real threat, there was also great danger that powerful activities of a disloyal nature would be continually conducted in Maryland, partly as an underground movement, but also as open defiance and resistance. It would be a faulty method to treat the subject in the ab-

---

[2] *Offic. Rec.*, 2 ser. II, 19; 1 ser. LI, pt. 1, 337; Nicolay and Hay, *Works*, VI, 258.

[3] Nicolay and Hay, *Works*, VII, 100–104 (Feb. 14, 1862).

stract, or in its merely legal aspects, without an awareness of these difficult facts.

There was, of course, genuine Southern sympathy in the state and especially in Baltimore. The mayor and chief of police of that city were pro-Confederate and anti-Lincoln. The failure to prevent the murderous and disorderly mob attack upon Federal troops as they passed through the city in April of 1861 showed both an inadequacy and a lack of diligence on the part of the city authorities. It was not that Maryland in general was "disloyal." Confederate trouble makers, however, were numerous, inflammatory, destructive, and sufficiently active (and local officials sufficiently inactive) so that Union authorities, as they viewed the situation with no chance for long-drawn-out deliberation, decided that they had to resort to arrests, seizures, and emergency measures. One can hardly visualize the turbulent situation: a "thousand conflicting stories and rumors," [4] bridges destroyed for the deliberate purpose of obstructing the passage of troops, such destruction justified by local officials, anti-administration newspapers whipping up disunion sentiment, and, most threatening of all, the legislature about to meet with an active element of that body planning to have the state secede from the Union, thus seeking by political action to extend the boundaries of the Confederacy northward, deep within Union lines. It is not to be intelligently supposed that Maryland could have been "neutral" if it had seceded. A seceded government of Maryland would have been a pro-Confederate government, in all probability proclaimed as a part of the Confederacy. Perhaps a rival pro-Union government might also have been formed, but the existence of two conflicting governments in the state would have been most embarrassing and confusing.

On the Union side Lincoln watched the government's step, being determined to avert an explosion, avoid undue severity, and yet, above all, to save the national cause. Governor Thomas H. Hicks, loyal and pro-Union, was nevertheless apprehensive lest suppressive measures should misfire. Others in the Maryland drama were Secretary Seward, directing the arrests (until early in 1862); Cameron, secretary of war, not a very prominent figure; and such generals (in one capacity or another) as Scott, McClellan, Butler, Cadwalader, Banks, and Dix.

---

[4] *Offic. Rec.*, 2 ser. I, 571.

Also in the picture were R. B. Marcy, Lafayette C. Baker, Frederick Seward, and a secretive person who signed his name as E. J. Allen, better known as Allan Pinkerton. Scott was the aged general in chief. McClellan was given chief command of the armies in July 1861 and succeeded Scott in November. Butler, Cadwalader, Banks, and Dix, in that order, were Union commanders in the Baltimore area.[5] Lafayette C. Baker, later a vigorous secret agent of Stanton's war department, was acting in that general capacity for Seward, watching to see what secessionists—for instance, in Canada—should be arrested. Pinkerton and Marcy were on McClellan's staff.

Out of this situation there grew a number of prominent Maryland arrests. There was, for example, the case of the mayor of Baltimore, George William Brown, which loomed large in the voluminous record and correspondence. Though General Dix considered Mayor Brown an amiable person, "the dupe rather than the willing accomplice" [6] of trouble makers, the mayor was arrested in mid-September 1861, held in various Federal forts including Fort Warren at Boston, released for thirty days, recommitted, transferred from the state to the war department, and set free after the Maryland storm had subsided. At the time of the April excitement (April 21, 1861) Lincoln had conferred with Brown in Washington, along with General Scott and the cabinet, as to the best way to move troops through Maryland and yet avoid a collision.[7]

George P. Kane, Baltimore chief (marshal) of police, described as "notoriously in deep sympathy with the rebels," [8] was arrested as "a measure of military precaution" on June 27, 1861. Four days later other members of the Baltimore board of police commissioners were also arrested on suspicion of disloyalty and collusion with the enemy.

Even more spectacular was the arrest of members of the Maryland legislature. On September 11, 1861, Secretary Cameron wrote General Banks: "The passage of any act of secession by the Legislature of

---

[5] This command, known for early months as the Department of Annapolis, covered "a vital corridor from the free states to the Union capital." F. H. Harrington, *Fighting Politician: Major General N. P. Banks*, 56. With headquarters at Baltimore, it was commanded successively by B. F. Butler, George Cadwalader, and N. P. Banks. By early August 1861 John A. Dix was commanding at Baltimore over a larger area known as the Department of Pennsylvania. *Offic. Rec.*, 2 ser. I, 567–589.

[6] *Offic. Rec.*, 2 ser. I, 645. For a summary on Brown, see *ibid.*, 619.

[7] Nicolay and Hay, *Lincoln*, IV, 130–131.

[8] *Offic. Rec.*, 2 ser. I, 620.

Maryland must be prevented. If necessary all or any part of the members must be arrested. Exercise your own judgment as to the time and manner, but do the work effectively." [9] It was believed at this time that "at the coming session" some effort would be made "on the part of the 'Tory' majority to convulse the State and force it into an attitude of hostility to the Government." [10]

Even if such belief was unfounded, it was felt that a grave risk existed, that prevention was what the loyal citizens of the state desired, and that arrests were a justifiable safeguard. Directing that "any meeting of this Legislature at any place or time" was to be prevented, General Banks ordered the arrests, indicating how it should be done, and how those taken should be conveyed by special train to Annapolis, and thence by steamer to the place of detention. Banks reported that nine legislators were arrested on September 17, these being "all the members of the Maryland Legislature assembled at Frederick City on the 17th instant known or suspected to be disloyal." [11] In addition, the chief clerk of the senate was arrested. It was explained that "the opening of the session was attended chiefly by Union men and . . . but nine secession members were found in the city." [12]

There have been conflicting opinions as to whether this arrest of legislators was a wise move. If it is not certain that this is what turned the trick, at least the trick was turned. Governor Hicks, a man who greatly respected the fundamentals of law and order, concurred in what was done. He wrote to Banks: "We see the good fruit . . . produced by the arrests. We can no longer mince matters with these desperate people." [13] Men of the time felt that a hands-off policy of gentleness and of full freedom as in peace time for dangerous plotters was not among the methods practically open to them. Use of stern measures, they felt, was their only choice. Secessionists themselves were none too scrupulous about full democracy. Perhaps Maryland could have been saved without these arrests; that seems probable. If so, the error was a misjudgment as to facts and probabilities. Such misjudgment may have been unfortunate, but the arrests were not made with evil intent. Severity in the Maryland case is to

---

[9] *Ibid.*, 678–679. [10] *Ibid.*, 679. [11] *Ibid.*, 684.

[12] Dix made one or two other arrests. Some of the prisoners were promptly released. Hicks referred (Sep. 20, 1861) to the arrest of "some eight or ten" legislators. *Ibid.*, 685.

[13] *Ibid.*, 685.

be appraised as part of the whole picture which included, after all, more leniency than brutality.

IV

In this urgent situation in Maryland, at a time when it was felt that a desperate and violent minority at the very door of the capital city was aiming a pistol at the heart of the government, there had arisen a famous arbitrary arrest and a notable judicial pronouncement in the case of one John Merryman. This otherwise unimportant individual was arrested by military authority on May 25, 1861, near Cockeysville, Maryland (north of Baltimore), "charged with various acts of treason and with . . . holding a commission as lieutenant in a company having in their possession arms belonging to the United States and avowing his purpose of armed hostility against the Government." [1] It was asserted that his readiness to coöperate with the enemy could be clearly established. The prisoner was confined in Fort McHenry and came under the custody of General George Cadwalader commanding at Baltimore, though that general did not order, nor was he responsible for, the original arrest.

Roger B. Taney, Chief Justice of the United States, now came into the picture. Taney being on circuit duty, General Cadwalader was commanded to appear before him. This was done by writ of habeas corpus which Taney issued. In the language of the writ the command was: ". . . that you have with you the body of John Merryman . . . and make known the day and cause of the capture and detention . . . , and that you then and there do submit to . . . whatsoever the . . . court shall determine . . . [etc.]." [2]

The fact that the judicial writ was issued, that it was the Chief Justice who issued it, that the general was commanded to hold himself subject to the court, and that in reality the high authority of the President was being challenged, gave the case unusual, indeed sensational, importance. Merryman was one among hundreds, but, thus singled out, his became a test case. Failure to sustain the executive (military) power would have caused the whole system of "political arrests" to break down.

[1] *Ibid.*, 2 ser. I, 576.

[2] *Offic. Rec.*, 2 ser. I, 575; *Ex parte* Merryman, 17 Fed. Cas. 144.

It was not, however, a case before the Supreme Court. It was a proceeding before one justice, Taney, who heard and granted the petition for the habeas corpus writ while on duty in the United States circuit court at Baltimore. (It was not that a whole court was in session; the proceeding was before Taney alone.) Cadwalader was under instructions from Washington to decline to produce prisoners in answer to all such writs. He answered that he was "duly authorized by the President . . . in such cases to suspend the writ . . . ."[3]

It was a clash of authority, but actual physical clash was out of the question. Orders of a court may be enforced by a marshal, if need be with the aid of a *posse comitatus;* but such a *posse* is seldom used,[4] and this type of procedure presupposes a broad and peaceful regime of law and order. To deal with widespread violence or disturbance is an executive function. It was not seriously proposed that Taney should have ordered his marshal to call out the citizenry in opposition to the President and army of the United States.

That, however, to his mind, did not mean that he could ignore his duty in the matter of civil rights. He could announce the law. Accordingly he put on file a long and impressive opinion, replete with historical and constitutional argument, emphasizing that the power to suspend the writ, which should only be done with "extreme caution," belonged only to Congress, and not to the President.

V

Taney was dealing here with one of the most controversial questions in American constitutional history.[1] The Constitution of the United

---

[3] *Offic. Rec.,* 2 ser. I, 576.

[4] The question how far a marshal of a United States court may go in using a *posse* of citizens as a large force to maintain order arose in Kansas in 1858–59. W. P. Fain, marshal of the territory of Kansas, being confronted with serious violence on the part of lawless desperadoes, took the unusual course of keeping a standing *posse* continuously in the field for months in order to arrest the lawbreakers or drive them out. Several hundred men were assembled; they carried on until disbanded on orders from Washington. It was made clear in this case that a marshal is a ministerial officer for executing judicial writs or orders, and is not authorized to maintain a quasi-military force or keep a large body of men in the field for an indefinite period in order to break up an insurrection. Documents on this subject (Attorney General's papers, now in the National Archives) are cited in *Constitutional Problems Under Lincoln,* 160 and n.

[1] *Constitutional Problems Under Lincoln,* chap. vi.

States contains the following provision: "The Privilege of the Writ of Habeas Corpus shall not be suspended, unless when in Cases of Rebellion or Invasion the public Safety may require it." This statement has produced volumes of discussion. The privilege may be suspended—that is clear enough—in the specified emergency and for the indicated purpose: to guard the public safety in cases of rebellion or invasion. The prohibitory emphasis of the Constitution, with the monitory tone of the clause, shows that such suspension was considered highly exceptional. But if suspension should occur, who was to judge of the occasion or necessity? Was the power exclusive with Congress, exclusive with the Executive, or concurrent between them? Could the authority be delegated to subordinates? Would rebellion in one part of the country justify suspension in a remote and loyal part? Even if suspension were provided by Congress, did not the President have considerable importance in the ordering and controlling of arrests? Suspension would be a legal condition. What about the acts performed under that condition? If a summary regime were instituted, there would have to be executive discretion as to how, when, and where arrests should be made, what should be done with prisoners, when the regime should be terminated, and so on. But if the President could do nothing at all in setting aside the privilege, that would be a significant limitation on presidential and military power. To many it would have seemed a beneficial limitation.

Having developed his constitutional argument that the power of suspension belonged only with Congress, and never with the President, Taney went considerably further. He wrote:

> . . . And even if the privilege of the writ of habeas corpus was suspended by act of Congress and a party not subject to the rules and articles of war was afterwards arrested and imprisoned by regular judicial process he could not be detained in prison or brought to trial before a military tribunal, ... [This was because of the sixth amendment requiring jury trial and various other safeguards in criminal prosecutions.]
>
> And the only power therefore which the President possesses where the "life, liberty or property" of a private citizen is concerned is the power and duty . . . which requires "that he shall take care that the laws be faithfully executed." He is not authorized to execute them himself or through agents or officers civil or military appointed by himself, but he is to take care that they be faithfully carried into execution as they are expounded and adjudged by the coördinate branch of the Government to

which that duty is assigned by the Constitution. It is thus made his duty to come in aid of the judicial authority if it shall be resisted by a force too strong to be overcome without the assistance of the executive arm. But in exercising this power he acts in subordination to the judicial authority, ...

Taney therefore declared: ". . . I can see no ground whatever for supposing that the President in any emergency or in any state of things can authorize the suspension of the privilege of the writ of habeas corpus or arrest a citizen except in aid of the judicial power." To suppose such a thing, thought Taney, was to suppose that the Constitution "conferred upon him [the President] more regal and absolute power over the liberty of the citizen than the people of England have thought it safe to intrust to the Crown—a power which the Queen of England cannot exercise at this day and which could not have been lawfully exercised by the sovereign even in the reign of Charles the First."

Such in brief was Taney's reasoning in this celebrated case. In his conclusion he noted that if the President had the power in question "the people of the United States are no longer living under a government of laws, but every citizen holds life, liberty and property at the will and pleasure of the army officer in whose military district he may happen to be found."

What, then, was the duty of the nation's highest judicial official, and what was his disposition of the case? His duty, wrote Taney, "was too plain to be mistaken." He had done all he could, but his power had "been resisted by a force too strong" for him to overcome. Taney therefore caused the record and opinion in the case to be filed in the Federal circuit court, and a copy to be transmitted under seal to the President of the United States. "It will then remain [he wrote] for that high officer, in fulfillment of his constitutional obligation to 'take care that the laws be faithfully executed,' to determine what measures he will take to cause the civil process of the United States to be respected and enforced." [2]

Beyond the case books in law, and the famous Taney opinion, Merryman is a forgotten man. All students of American constitutional law know of the Merryman "case," but very few could tell what happened to him. (It is often so with celebrated cases. The

---

[2] *Offic. Rec.*, 2 ser. I, 585; 17 Fed. Cas. 153.

Supreme Court's pronouncement is the accepted climax; beyond that the "follow-up" is lost.) As a matter of fact, Citizen Merryman did not suffer for long. Secretary of War Cameron, visiting Fort McHenry on July 4, promised the prisoner a "parole," and on July 12 Cameron sent a letter to General N. P. Banks, who commanded the Department of Annapolis, directing him to cause Merryman to be delivered to the marshal of the district court when that should be demanded on lawful warrant. Actual release of the prisoner from military custody to civil authority occurred on July 13, forty-nine days after his arrest.[3] Merryman was now under the control of the district court of the United States at Baltimore, as Chief Justice Taney said he ought to have been from the beginning. He was under a wordy indictment for treason; it was charged that "he did intend to levy war and carry on war, insurrection, and rebellion against the United States of America." He was not held in confinement, however, being released (July 13, 1861) upon entering into a recognizance in the sum of $20,000 for his appearance in the United States Circuit Court at Baltimore, to which the case was handed over. It went no further. The recognizance was "respited"; the case was continued by order of the court; there was no prosecution; the matter faded from the record as Merryman had already faded from notice as a person.[4]

Thus, so far as Merryman was concerned, though historical and legal treatises usually ignore this aspect of the affair, the processes of judicial protection and civil procedure were actually complied with —not immediately nor by honoring the Chief Justice's writ, but within a fairly short time after the prisoner was seized. There was nothing done judicially to punish him, and this fact gives some point to the contention of the Lincoln administration that the courts were too slow and clumsy for handling the dangerous situation. It could also be said, however, that Lincoln was not going all the way with the "usurpation" which Taney charged. Arbitrary punishment for treason was not the main executive purpose. Military detention,

---

[3] E. G. Campbell (assisted by Elizabeth B. Drewry), War Records Section, National Archives, Wash., D. C., to the author (citing specific documents in the Archives), Jan. 16, 1950.

[4] For these obscure details of the case, after Merryman's military release, information was kindly supplied by Arthur L. Spamer, clerk of the U. S. district court at Baltimore, in a letter to the author, Feb. 6, 1924. *Constitutional Problems Under Lincoln,* 162 n.

though arbitrary—and serious enough, to be sure—was only temporary. For the acute and brief emergency at Baltimore for which it was used, such detention, so it could be argued, served the presidential purpose.

VI

For many months, while sharp controversy raged, Congress made no declaration of legislative will on the disputed question as to the authority for suspension. In the short special session of July–August 1861 certain emergency orders of the President were ratified, but the habeas corpus privilege was not specifically mentioned in this connection (though the matter had been debated), and the ratifying provision was inconspicuously and irrelevantly tucked away as a "rider" in an act to increase the pay of privates in the army.[1] What is more remarkable is that in the long session from December to July, 1861–62, no law was enacted on this much discussed subject. The issue dragged on while lawyers and agitators poured out elaborate discussions. Then, in the closing hours of the short session which ended on March 3, 1863, the "habeas corpus act" was passed.

This act was railroaded through, said its opponents. What happened was that in each chamber there was a lively filibuster against the measure. In the House, for instance, obstruction took the form of numerous excuses for absence on the ground of being "unwell" and the like, in the course of which Colfax of Indiana, rising to a point of order, was told that he was "absent." Despite the filibuster the bill passed the House on March 2, by vote of 99 to 44.[2]

The following night produced a prolonged and confused session in the Senate. Powell of Kentucky, Bayard of Delaware, and others —men of genuine purpose, not mere obstructionists—struggled to keep the floor, occupy time, and prevent a vote, holding forth with lengthy speeches, which rang the changes on Magna Carta, Shakespeare, Cowper, Molière, Marshall, Webster, and other authorities and poets. Meanwhile Trumbull and other friends of the bill used all their strength to keep awake, maintain a quorum, prevent adjournment, and seize the floor for a motion to concur in a conference re-

[1] *U. S. Stat. at Large,* XII, 326 (act of Aug. 6, 1861).

[2] *Cong. Globe,* 37 Cong., 3 sess., 1479 (Mar. 2, 1863).

port and thus get the bill enacted into law. During these maneuvers the yeas and nays were taken on the question of adjournment five times.

Finally, at about five o'clock in the morning of March 3, 1863, the presiding officer (Senator Pomeroy) unexpectedly put a *viva voce* vote amid great confusion. He then announced that the bill had passed, denied the floor to senators who insisted it had not passed, and, against the vociferous protests of filibusterers (who shortly before had been demanding adjournment), declared the Senate adjourned.[3]

The measure so enacted declared in oracular phrase that "during the present rebellion, the President of the United States, whenever, in his judgment, the public safety may require it, is authorized to suspend the privilege of the writ of habeas corpus in any case throughout the United States, or any part thereof." [4]

Did this settle it? Who, then, had the power to suspend? Diametrically opposite interpretations were given as to the essence and meaning of this action. The measure passed was in fact a masterpiece of legislative ambiguity. The oracular statement—"the President . . . is authorized to suspend"—might be interpreted to mean that this was a power which Congress was *recognizing* as rightly belonging to the President; or on the other hand it could mean that the power to suspend, as Taney said, was purely legislative, and that this function of legislative suspension was then being exercised by *conferring* upon the President, for the emergency, authority which otherwise he did not have.

Congress had spoken; so had the Chief Justice of the United States. Yet neither the Taney opinion in the Merryman case nor the habeas corpus act of 1863 controlled the government. The Lincoln administration did not regard the Taney opinion in the Merryman case as a binding or final declaration of the law. This is evident from statements of cabinet members after the decision was issued. On January 31, 1863, Attorney General Bates, in an unpublished and confidential communication to Stanton, showed not only that he considered the basic question undecided, but also that he did not want the matter pushed to a conclusion. There had been a Wisconsin decision

---

[3] *Ibid.*, 1477.

[4] *U. S. Stat. at Large*, XII, 755.

challenging the President's power to suspend,[5] and word had come to Bates that Stanton was intending to have the case brought up for review before the Supreme Court of the United States. In an emphatic statement Bates advised against it. A decision of the highest court pronouncing arbitrary arrests to be illegal, he said, would "do more to paralyze the Executive . . . than the worst defeat our armies have yet sustained." He also considered that such an adverse opinion was not unlikely, in view of the "antecedents and present proclivities" of a majority of the Court, taken in connection with the expressed opinion of some of the justices.[6]

Throughout the war two things were evident as to the executive attitude in this matter: (1) the Chief Executive intended to assert and exercise the presidential power of suspension; (2) there was an uneasy apprehension that the administration would be seriously embarrassed if the matter came up for final decision by the Supreme Court. As to the first of these points, it is to be noted that Lincoln, on September 15, 1863, six months after the passage of the habeas corpus act, issued a proclamation that "the privilege of the Writ of Habeas Corpus is suspended throughout the United States," and that "this suspension will continue throughout the duration of the . . . rebellion, or until . . . modified or revoked."[7] A similar proclamation had been issued on September 24, 1862; this confirmation of executive policy made the matter more emphatic.

Cabinet uneasiness as to a possible Supreme Court decision was shown late in the war by a statement of Gideon Welles concerning a consultation between Lincoln and his attorney general, James Speed. They were conferring over "an apprehended decision of Chief Justice Chase, whenever he could reach the question of the suspension of the writ of *habeas corpus.*"[8] Speed, noted Welles, "is apprehensive Chase will fail the Administration" on this question.[9] Whether Chase "would have" decided against the administration and

[5] A state judge in Wisconsin held that the Federal Constitution "knows no 'political' . . . cause of imprisonment," that there "must be a 'process of law,'" that the President did not have the "political powers" which had been claimed for him, and that Lincoln had acted illegally in suspending the privilege. *In re* Kemp, 16 Wis. 396.

[6] Bates to Stanton ("Confidential"), Jan. 31, 1863, Stanton MSS., 52223.

[7] Proclamation suspending writ of habeas corpus, Sep. 15, 1863, photostat, A. Lincoln Assoc.

[8] Welles, *Diary,* II, 242 (Feb. 21, 1865).

[9] *Ibid.,* II, 245.

whether that would have been the decision of the Court, is not clear,[10] but at least the statements of Bates and Welles indicate that at the end of the war the question of the President's suspending power was still a matter on which the Supreme Court had not given a pronouncement. It was also abundantly clear that the ponderous habeas corpus act of 1863, passed after so much ado in Congress, was not regarded as having settled the matter of the exclusive power of Congress to suspend, or of the alleged illegality of Lincoln's course.

But this was not the only matter that lawmakers had failed to settle. It was supposedly the intention of Congress, in the habeas corpus act of 1863, to grasp and deal with the administrative matter of arbitrary arrests. The law set up a kind of compromise between camp and bench. The President's power to suspend was recognized (or, some would have said, conferred); military officers were relieved of the obligation to answer the writ; and (as an important feature of what came to be called the "indemnity act" as well as the "habeas corpus act") officers who might be prosecuted for searches, seizures, arrests, or imprisonments in compliance with an order of the President or "under his authority," were to be indemnified and given the benefit of Federal court protection. To military officers and administrators high and low this was important. Damages or imprisonment or fines for false arrests would have ruined them. Under such prosecutions "Stanton said he would be imprisoned a thousand years at least." [11]

On the other hand, as concessions to the bench, lists of political prisoners were to be furnished to the Federal courts; then, where grand juries found no indictments against them, they were to be discharged from military custody *by judicial order* upon taking the oath of allegiance. If such lists were not furnished (a congressional confession of doubt as to their law being obeyed), it was provided that a Federal justice might discharge a prisoner on habeas corpus petition.

10 Even with Taney on the Court, there had been a five-to-four decision in support of the President's war power in the *Prize Cases*. Those five justices were still on the Court at the end of the war, and there is reason to suppose (though the opposite result was apprehended) that, if the matter had come up at any time during the war, the Court would have sustained Lincoln on the question of arrests, as it had on the extraordinary use of the war power between April and July of 1861. Substitution of Chase for Taney obviously did not make for greater Court opposition to the President's war powers.

11 Welles, *Diary,* II, 206.

Only a superficial reading of history, however, would leave the matter here, for on careful search it is found that, like other congressional measures of the time, the habeas corpus law was largely a dead letter. When Stanton directed that lists of prisoners of state be sent to district and circuit justices, Judge Advocate General Holt reported that the lists had "not been furnished within the twenty days specified in the act." Such lists as were furnished were incomplete, omitting important facts—e. g., "what the offense was or charge." Holt then went on to criticize the law itself. "The act [he wrote] does not appear to have been carefully framed and has been found to be extremely difficult of construction." Holt therefore did his own construing; he did not believe the act was intended "to invite attention to cases of persons charged with purely military offenses or . . . suffering under sentences of military tribunals." [12] In the Milligan decision the Supreme Court was to hold that the act should properly have applied to citizens under such sentence, which was declared illegal in non-military areas, but this decision did not come until after the war; it was the Holt interpretation (later discredited) which fixed the pattern during the war.

The truth was that the executive, not the legislative or judicial, branch determined policy as to arrests and imprisonments, both before and after the passage of the habeas corpus act in which Congress presumably fixed the pattern. It does not appear that things were changed by this law. Numerous arrests—including the most famous of all, that of Vallandigham—were made after the act was passed. Moreover, where prisoners were released after that act, it was done not by Federal judges but by authority of the war department. Since the act confirmed the President's power to suspend and provided legal immunity for those acting under his orders, the policy as to political prisoners was understood to have a stronger sanction and legal force than before. A clerk of one of the district courts after examining the record reported that he could find no instance of a list of prisoners having been turned over to the court by the war department, and no record of any order of judicial release.[13] It should be

12 *Offic. Rec.*, 2 ser. V, 765–766.

13 Clerks of the United States district courts at Indianapolis and Cleveland reported to the present writer that they found no wartime cases of lists being supplied or of prisoners judicially released, thus signifying that the act was not observed. Similar re-

added that civil procedures during this period were not fully destroyed. They were rather dormant. The military itself showed some restraint (Lincoln saw to that), but so long as the war continued the army was the dominant power.

VII

The extent of that dominant power of the President appears more fully when some of the half-forgotten procedures of the period are recalled. Such was the expansion of the executive power under Lincoln that, in addition to other wartime increases of authority within the executive branch, there were considerable instances when the legislative function was controlled by the President, and also when judicial duties were taken over by the executive.

In important respects the President got along without Congress, though this was perhaps overbalanced by the extent to which Congress thwarted him on the issue of reconstruction. So far did he take over legislative functions that one could speak of some of his acts as "presidential legislation." [1] It is obvious that the two emancipation proclamations trenched upon the legislative sphere. As another example, Lincoln issued a set of "regulations" for the enforcement of the militia act of July 17, 1862. Actual conscription was not specifically provided in the law as passed by Congress, yet conscription was used to raise troops. It was done simply under executive regulations. The matter went even further, for under these regulations governors of the states could set up their own systems of compulsory service as an alternative to following the President's orders. There has been considerable discussion of Lincoln's exercise of legislative power when, beginning in December 1863, he promulgated and later developed his presidential system of reconstruction.

It could also be said that a function belonging to Congress was performed by Lincoln when he issued a whole elaborate code for the governing of the armies in the field. This important code had

---

sults appeared in other courts, and a special search in the war department failed to reveal any measures taken in compliance with the act, other than Judge Advocate General Holt's letter to Stanton, June 9, 1863 (above cited), in which it was indicated that the law was given a strict war-department construction and that compliance was slight. *Constitutional Problems Under Lincoln,* 163–168, especially 166 n.

[1] *Ibid.,* 37.

a significant history. Two men were especially active in its preparation—Henry W. Halleck, general in chief of the Union armies, and Francis Lieber, noted German-American expert in political science. Born in Germany, Lieber had served at Waterloo, lying all night on that battlefield (a fact he often recalled in later life), had been wounded at Namur (1815), had previously dreamed of assassinating Napoleon, had studied and traveled in Europe, and had come to the United States in 1827. He wrote elaborate treatises and became a distinguished authority on public law. After productive literary work at Boston and Philadelphia he served for twenty-one years as professor in South Carolina College at Columbia. His important works included his *Manual of Political Ethics* and his famous work *On Civil Liberty and Self Government.* From 1857 he served on the faculty of Columbia College in New York.[2]

With a friendliness toward radical Republicans, a hatred of slavery, and a strong ethical sense, Lieber had a comprehensive understanding of law and government throughout the world and down the ages. Having three sons in the army (one in Confederate service), Lieber knew the agony of scanning casualty lists and the personal tragedy of learning that one of his sons was killed in the war and another severely wounded. His interest in military practices was not merely academic as he observed the lack of adequate system concerning the usages of war. A variety and multiplicity of questions called for clarification: the distinction between soldiers and guerrillas or bushwhackers, the problem of runaway slaves (whose return by McClellan aroused Lieber's indignation), pillage, espionage, the proper penalty for spies (should it be death?), retaliation, flags of truce, treatment of prisoners of war, exchange of prisoners, stealing, burning of homes, attitude toward non-combatants, seizure and destruction of private property, compensation for such destruction, occupation of enemy territory, and—as a subject of special interest—the wartime problem of Negro emancipation.

Coming up through Lieber's elaborate study and his voluminous correspondence with Halleck, the military code took shape with the assistance of a special board of army officers headed by General E. A. Hitchcock, and was issued in May 1863. It appeared as "General Or-

[2] Frank Freidel, *Francis Lieber: Nineteenth Century Liberal.*

ders No. 100: Instructions for the Government of the Armies of the United States in the Field." [3]

One may speak of this as an instance of presidential legislation. It is difficult to trace Lincoln's personal attention to the actual codification, but here was an essentially legislative duty performed entirely within the executive domain. The Lieber code could have been adopted by Congress and if so adopted it would have been considered a proper exercise of the congressional power, under the Constitution, to "make Rules for the Government and Regulation of the land and naval Forces." Congress, however, despite all its elaborate attention to the "conduct" of the war, did not perform the task, or even undertake it. It was through the executive branch that the great talents of Lieber were utilized, and thus one of the most important legal tasks of the war was accomplished by expert skill under presidential authority. Through the decades since the Civil War the code has undergone modification and development as regulations for the armies and manuals for service schools. Its basic principles have reappeared in Hague conventions. The fact that military practices in "World War I" and "World War II" have departed from the declared standards of these conventions (though they have not been formally revoked) is no disparagement of the work of Lieber.[4]

After considering presidential legislation (sketched here only in part) one may turn to the subject of presidential justice. It was under the executive, not the judiciary, that wartime judicial functions were performed in occupied portions of the South. It required years for normal business of Federal courts to be reëstablished in regions recovered from enemy control. State courts carried on in part during the occupation, but their duties were limited.[5] It was felt at times that

---

[3] *Offic. Rec.*, 3 ser. III, 148–164; 2 ser. V, 671–682.

[4] The author has studied, in original manuscript, the elaborate two-sided correspondence between Francis Lieber and General Halleck (Lieber MSS., Henry E. Huntington Library); he has also had access to the highly useful notes of Professor Frank Freidel of the University of Illinois. The authoritative account is Frank Freidel, *Francis Lieber: Nineteenth Century Liberal,* chap. xiv. For General Orders No. 100, see *Offic. Rec.*, 3 ser. III, 148 ff. See also Brainerd Dyer, "Francis Lieber and the American Civil War," *Huntington Libr. Quar.*, II, 449–467 (1939); Frank Freidel, "General Order 100 and Military Government," *Miss. Vall. Hist. Rev.*, XXXII, 541–556 (1946).

[5] It was held that a soldier of the United States who committed murder in Tennessee while that state was under Federal occupation was not subject to prosecution by a Tennessee court. Coleman *vs.* Tenn., 97 U.S. 509. Yet it was also held that insurrection and war do not loosen the bonds of society, and on this principle the Supreme Court treated

provost-marshal justice, or military-governor justice, was carried too far. There was resentment when General Butler exercised his military power at Norfolk in a manner which infringed upon the judicial authority of the Unionist state government under Pierpoint. On this point Attorney General Bates wrote: "I have heretofore forborne too much, to avoid a conflict of jurisdiction, but it only makes the military usurpers more bold and insolent."[6] It was, of course, a general situation which Bates resented, not merely a matter of concern at Norfolk. In North and South the executive power of courts martial controlled the process of justice as to men in the armed services (which was normal), while the military commissions, also purely executive, claimed and exercised unusual powers not only over civilians guilty of military offenses (such as destroying bridges), but also (though this power was seldom used in the North) over civilian deeds coming broadly under the category of disloyal acts. Aside from these military tribunals, whose sentences were reviewable by the President and whose operation was under the executive rather than the judicial branch, it should be added that "special war courts" were set up—e. g., in Louisiana—by presidential authority. One such was the "provisional court of Louisiana" which was created by President Lincoln in December 1862. It had almost unlimited jurisdiction, its powers being confined only "by the limits of human acts and transactions capable of becoming subjects of judicial investigation." It exercised both Federal and state functions.[7] In addition, judicial powers were grasped by administrative bureaus or executive agencies. The treasury department had much to do with matters of trade and land tenure in Southern regions, and local judicial activity on an extensive scale was assigned to the freedmen's bureau under the war department. (The bureau hardly got under way until after Lincoln's death, but the bill creating the agency was passed in March 1865 and was signed by Lincoln.)

These are but examples. The full situation would amply justify the generalization that the Civil War President, for what he deemed

---

the ordinary acts of states within the Confederacy (for maintaining police regulations, punishing crime, protecting property, etc.) as valid and binding. *Constitutional Problems Under Lincoln,* 237–238.

[6] Bates, *Diary,* 401 (Aug. 20, 1864).

[7] Judge Charles A. Peabody, "United States Provisional Court for . . . Louisiana, 1862–1865," *Annual Report,* Amer. Hist. Assoc., 1892, 199–210; *Ann. Cyc.,* 1864, 480 ff.

necessary and unavoidable reasons, extended his sphere of activity throughout the whole government—civil and military, state and Federal, legislative and judicial as well as executive. In the economic field, of course, the scale of governmental activities under Lincoln was in no sense comparable to that under Wilson or Franklin Roosevelt. The principle, however, of expanded national economic power was illustrated in such affairs as the national banking system, the deep penetration of taxation, the support of economic enterprise by United States bonds, army efforts to control working conditions, new regulations as to bringing laborers in from abroad, and governmental seizure of railroads and telegraph lines.

VIII

The general question as to where the war power resided arose in Congress (June 25, 1862) and was debated in the Senate by Browning of Illinois and Sumner of Massachusetts. Sumner argued that the war powers of Congress were virtually without limit. "There is not one of the rights of war," he said, "which Congress may not invoke. There is not a single weapon in its terrible arsenal which Congress may not grasp." [1] Browning, on the other hand, contended that rights of war were by their very nature matters of emergency and military necessity; for that reason he urged that they belonged to the executive arm. Browning went so far as to "defy . . . any man to point to one single word . . . in the Constitution which confers upon Congress any power to do any act in the exigency of war which it cannot do in times of peace." [2]

Whatever may have been the merits of the senatorial arguments, the result was that both Congress and the President exercised war powers. The President did it first at the outset of the struggle and repeatedly throughout the contest. Lincoln believed that he had powers in time of war that Congress did not have. In July 1864 (in a state paper concerning the Wade-Davis bill [3] which he killed by a pocket veto) he proclaimed that he was "unprepared . . . to de-

---

1 *Cong. Globe,* 37 Cong., 2 sess., 2919. 2 *Ibid.,* 2923.

3 Sponsored by Benjamin F. Wade in the Senate and Henry Winter Davis in the House, this bill provided for reconstruction in terms very different from those favored by Lincoln.

clare a constitutional competency in Congress to abolish slavery in States . . . ."[4] Yet his own definitive emancipation proclamation had been issued a year and a half earlier.

Initiative, decision, and important action was chiefly executive; yet a listing of the war powers exercised by Congress would cover a considerable range—confiscation, conscription, dealing with crimes (rebellion, conspiracy, obstructing the draft), creating the state of West Virginia, legalizing privateering, authorizing (or recognizing) the suspension of habeas corpus, levying a direct tax against Southerners, extending the jurisdiction of Federal courts, giving the President the authority (already mentioned) to take possession of railroad and telegraph lines, and, in the military field, setting up the busily active, officious committee on the conduct of the war. As to reconstruction, it was there, perhaps, that we find the most far-reaching powers that any Congress ever assumed, including the creation of a military regime in the South by which the functions of state governments were superseded.

It was not as if Lincoln had been eager to seize arbitrary power. So far as the President's purpose was concerned, if it was a matter of circumspectly watching to avoid abuse, he did not stand in need of Taney's admonition in the Merryman case. (Even so, Taney's strong conviction that a government of laws should be preserved is a worthy part of American constitutional history. Lincoln was no despot, but neither could it be said that the Chief Justice in advising against military despotism, was asserting a vain principle.)

The matter is so important that one should notice how and why Lincoln acted. His suspension of civil guarantees was announced with great reluctance. Only a qualified suspension was ordered in 1861 when the emergency was undeniably alarming. Military authorities were enjoined to use the power sparingly. The President's action was taken during a recess of Congress, and at its first convening the matter was laid before that body in Lincoln's message of July 4, 1861. In one of the passages of that important message he gave what may be called his answer to Taney.

It is instructive to note the workings of Lincoln's mind as he thought through the preparation of that message. This becomes more

---

[4] "A Proclamation," July 8, 1864, photograph, A. Lincoln Assoc.

striking as we compare the original handwritten draft of the document with the finished product as finally submitted. The two forms are given below in parallel columns.[5]

Original Autograph Draft	*Published Form*
Soon after the first call for militia, I felt it my duty to authorize the Commanding General, in proper cases . . . to suspend the privilege of the writ of habeas corpus. . . . At my verbal request, as well as by the Generals own inclination, this authority has been exercised but very sparingly.	it was considered a duty This authority has purposely been exercised . . . sparingly.
Nevertheless, . . . I have been reminded from a high quarter that one who is sworn to "take care that the laws be faithfully executed" should not himself be one to violate them.	the attention of the country has been called to the proposition, [etc.]
Of course I gave some consideration to the questions of power, and propriety, before I acted in this matter.	. . . some consideration was given . . . before this matter was acted upon.
The whole of the laws which I was sworn to . . . [execute] were being resisted, . . . in nearly one third of the states.	The whole of the laws which were required to be . . . executed.
Must I have allowed them to finally fail of execution . . . ? To state the question more directly, are all the laws, *but one,* to go unexecuted, and the government itself go to pieces, lest that one be violated? . . .	Must they be allowed to finally fail of execution . . . ?
But, . . . I was not, in my own judgment, driven to this ground. In my opinion I violated no law. The provision of the Constitution . . . is equivalent to a provision . . . that [the] privilege may be suspended when, in cases of rebellion, or invasion, the public safety *does* require it.	But it was not believed that this question was presented. It was not believed that any law was violated.
I decided that we have a case of rebellion	It was decided, [etc.]

[5] The autograph draft has been checked with the original in the Lincoln Papers (R.T.L. Coll., 10503–42); the official printed form with *Sen. Exec. Doc. No. 1,* 37 Cong., 1 sess., pp. 1–17.

The working draft shows the questioning and struggling that went on in Lincoln's mind. The decision as to arbitrary power troubled him. Any suggestion or appearance of dictatorship caused him concern and pain. When the matter was presented to Congress the wording was impersonal: "Some consideration was given"; "the attention of the country has been called . . ."; "the laws . . . were required to be executed" and so on. But as he first thought it out, these problems were his own; they touched him closely: "I gave some consideration to the question . . ."; "I have been reminded from a high quarter . . . [the reference was to Chief Justice Taney]"; "the laws which I was sworn to [execute]." The finished form was, as Nicolay and Hay have pointed out, a "state paper"; [6] the early working draft reflected the mind of the man in the White House meeting and coping with the duty of his office.

IX

The preciousness of civil rights even in time of war has produced a great deal of emphasis upon the guarding of those rights in the courts. It is a healthy sign in a democracy to have such emphasis. Yet in treating the Lincoln administration it would be an error to put all the stress on presidential power in terms of harshness or unjustifiable cruelty. Lincoln's regime was no juggernaut. Restraints were applied. The war was actually conducted *in vinculis,* which is not only democratically necessary but is preferable to a militarized state. (The opposite tendency would lead at its worst extreme to a Dachau or a Buchenwald.) Throughout the struggle in Lincoln's day there was a constant tempering of severe rules. Deserters were sometimes executed, but by far most of them were spared. Killing in battle was done by duly organized forces in military operations. (Predatory or criminal activities of guerrilla warfare, as in Missouri, were among the irregular by-products of the war. They were unauthorized and completely lawless.) Where men were put to death in the exercise of military discipline, this was done by court-martial trial under competent control. Seizure of property by the armies was done *as a rule* in an orderly and non-predatory manner. (Plundering by Sherman's

[6] Nicolay and Hay, *Lincoln,* IV, 177–178.

"bummers" in his "march" through Georgia and the Carolinas was exceptional. It was an unfortunate example of soldier conduct getting out of hand.) Prisoners of war were treated under the rules of war. Death for treason, much talked of, was not applied.[1] Discretion was exercised in carrying out orders against disloyal persons; escape from penalties was made possible by taking the oath of loyalty; first offenses were passed over; excuses were considered; the shooting of sentries was disapproved; [2] even spies were released on acceptance of stipulated terms.

By comparison with other regimes, political prisoners were mildly treated. Vallandigham, arrested contrary to the President's judgment, was not the brutally persecuted victim he was represented to be. Many thousands who sympathized with Vallandigham were not molested at all. Crews of Confederate ships were called "pirates," and the penalty for piracy was death; but this was a matter of language, not of action. It is true that Lincoln issued a proclamation (April 19, 1861) declaring that any person acting under "pretended authority," who should "molest a vessel of the United States" (e. g., resist the blockade) would be held "amenable to the laws of the United States for the prevention and punishment of piracy." [3] This policy, however, of punishing Confederate crewmen for piracy was not carried out, either by the courts or by the executive branch. The main purpose seems to have been to uphold the theory that the Confederate States could not be "recognized," that their naval vessels were not legitimate warships, that their letters of marque and reprisal were invalid, and that theirs was only a "pretended" government with no rightful standing.

Judicial embarrassment over this problem arose in the case of the *Petrel,* a privately owned schooner (formerly a U. S. revenue cutter) commissioned as a Confederate privateer. This vessel was sunk in a fight with a U. S. warship and its crew became Federal prisoners.[4]

---

1 The case of William B. Mumford, executed by sentence of a military commission in New Orleans in 1862 for having torn down the United States flag, was an exceptional and isolated case, being altogether out of keeping with presidential and judicial policy. It was an episode in the eccentric rule of Benjamin F. Butler, who was removed from his New Orleans command by Lincoln in December 1862 and replaced by N. P. Banks.

2 For denunciation of the practice of shooting sentries—"insignificant atoms of armies" —see *Harper's Weekly,* V, 407 (June 29, 1861).

3 Proclamation of blockade, Apr. 19, 1861, photograph of original, A. Lincoln Assoc.

4 William M. Robinson, Jr., *The Confederate Privateers,* 125–127.

They were taken to Philadelphia and were indicted—thirty-five in number—in the United States circuit court for treason, their offense being also denoted as "piracy," the equivalent of treason. There was immense popular excitement as the case, along with other cases of "treason," was brought up, but the justices who had to deal with the problem, not as theory but as human facts, were disgusted. Justice Grier of the United States Supreme Court, on circuit duty at Philadelphia, blurted out that he did not "intend to try any more of these cases." "I have other business to attend to," he said, "and do not mean to be delayed . . . from day to day in trying charges against a few unfortunate individual men here out of half a million that are in arms against the government." The "laws of war [he added] must be observed, or you will lay it open to the most horrid reactions that can possibly be thought of; hundreds of thousands of men will be sacrificed upon mere brutal rage. . . . I will not sit on another case." [5] In general neither treason nor piracy cases were pursued to completion in the United States courts. There were indictments, but the cases were simply continued on the dockets and eventually dropped. In the few cases where convictions for treason resulted, they were considered an embarrassment. Judgment was suspended and the men were ultimately released.

As with the courts, so with the executive. A study of the Lincoln Papers shows that the purpose of the government was not to convict and punish any individuals for treason because of service for, or aid to, the Confederacy. The purpose of arrests was to uphold respect for the law and give protection against disloyalty in its effect upon the war effort. The object of the administration was precautionary, not punitive. Seizure and temporary detention of dangerous characters —rather than pursuing the whole course of indictment, trial, conviction, sentence, possible appeal, and eventual execution—was the administration's view of the appropriate and practical method.

If Confederate privateersmen and naval men had actually been punished for piracy—i. e., executed as traitors—, retaliation would have resulted. Union captives were in fact held as hostages by Confederate authorities, and if the utmost penalty had been used as had

[5] J. Hubley Ashton, assistant district attorney for eastern Pennsylvania, to Attorney General Bates, Nov. 4, 1861 (enclosure), Attorney General's papers, MSS., National Archives.

been announced *on paper,* the conduct of the war would have degenerated into a kind of savage orgy below the "civilized" level. This was one of many problems making necessary the codification of the usages of war (above treated) by Francis Lieber. In the case of captured Confederate officers and crewmen of privateering vessels the solution adopted was to treat them as merchant marine personnel. Trials, as in the case of the *Petrel* crew, were accordingly dropped, the crews being released and sent South.[6] The war was grim, but regard for civilized opinion was always a factor with Lincoln.

Part of the confusion on this and other subjects was due to an aspect of governmental policy which was essentially abstract. There was a constant and stubborn refusal to "recognize" the Confederacy. Technically, diplomatically, and formally that government was never given recognition by the United States. (Nor, except as a belligerent, was it ever recognized by any foreign power.) Language of the department of state and formal procedures of the government at Washington were carefully watched to avoid such recognition. Yet, when this subject is analyzed realistically in terms of actualities, it will be found that this denial of recognition was hardly more than a stickling for theory. It was precisely the theory that was deemed important. Language had to be correct; etiquette and procedure had to be watched; protocol had to be observed. Deeds were another matter. In practical affairs pertaining to the conduct of armies the usages in the main were the same as would have prevailed if the conflict had been waged between two fully recognized independent nations. The Union government *treated* the Confederates as regular belligerents though it did not *recognize* them as such.

The attitude of the Washington government toward that at Richmond, as generally applied and fully matured, was about as follows. To the Confederate army belligerent rights were "conceded, in the interest of humanity." These rights, by the statement of the Supreme Court, were "such . . . as belonged, under the laws of nations, to the armies of independent governments engaged in war against each other." The Court also stated that "The Confederate States were belligerents in the sense attached to that word by the law of nations [international law]." [7] The subject is to be understood, not in terms

[6] Robinson, *Confederate Privateers,* 150–151.

[7] Ford *vs.* Surget, 97 U. S., 605, 612.

of consistency, but of variance between language and deed, between form and substance, between diplomatic punctilio and essential conduct. In the view of the Washington government secession was a nullity and the whole Southern nation illegal. Those who took part in the Confederacy were insurgents warring against their rightful government. They were technically traitors and were theoretically amenable to the municipal power in the same sense that the Whiskey insurgents during Washington's administration were amenable. In addition, they were "enemies" in the sense used in international war. The area declared by the constituted authorities to be in insurrection was "enemies' territory" and all persons residing in the designated area were liable to be treated as "enemies." [8] Both belligerent and sovereign powers could be brought into play in dealing with such areas —e. g., the belligerent power of blockade and the sovereign power of punishing for treason. Yet to avoid cruelties and inhuman practices, soldiers and officers of the "rebel" army were accorded all rights connected with the mode of prosecuting "lawful war." Confederate officers and privates were not held to individual responsibility. Confederate authority might be considered a mere usurpation and Confederate acts invalid, but those in military service who proceeded under such authority were not in fact held to account. Nor, ultimately, were those in civil authority held personally to account. Jefferson Davis after the war was held in military custody for two years and (after military release) was indicted in the United States circuit court at Richmond for treason under the law of 1790, where the penalty was death; but no other Confederate official was given anything like so long a military detention, most of them being allowed to go free, and Davis's case in court was allowed to drag on without trial till finally the prosecution was dropped.[9] In general the postwar "flight into oblivion" of certain Confederate leaders was unnecessary if regarded as an escape from severe treatment.

Throughout all these complex problems of war power the historian must constantly recognize that pronouncements of law, which can be cited on both sides of every issue, were lacking in finality. Though a lawyer of great shrewdness, capable of supporting a cause by impres-

[8] *House Report No. 262,* 43 Cong., 1 sess., 6 ff.

[9] Roy F. Nichols, "The United States *vs.* Jefferson Davis," *Amer. Hist. Rev.,* XXXI, 266–284; Randall, *Constitutional Problems Under Lincoln,* chap. v.

sive legal reasoning, Lincoln, after all, made his decisions in terms of what he thought was needed to support and maintain the government. On a point of governmental relations he could uphold a principle—for instance, refusing recognition to the Confederacy—without the embarrassment of getting out on a legalistic limb. When he had made up his mind on a matter of presidential conduct whose legal aspects he had canvassed, he was neither disrespectful toward legal opposition nor upset by it. Taney differed with him fundamentally on questions of war power; yet the difference consisted only of dignified assertion of opposite views. The President and the Chief Justice never came to an unseemly open break or personal clash. The Supreme Court in general, partly by a kind of avoidance, gave support to the President.

CHAPTER VIII

"COPPERHEADS" AND PRISONERS OF STATE

I

DISCUSSION of suppressive measures leads unavoidably into the subject of so-called "Copperhead" activity.[1] Throughout the war years (especially in 1863 and 1864) the Lincoln administration constantly faced the perplexing problem of disunity, underground activity, and violence, always considerably mingled with politics and amounting at times—so it was claimed—to disloyalty or treason. The remedy was not simple. A complicated problem was posed which required administrative resourcefulness and demanded something other than the crude method of seizure and incarceration for matters of opinion.

As one seeks reliable generalizations on this subject he notes an inexactness in the use of terms. Dissent was to be expected. There were sincere differences of judgment and opinion. Disagreement was rife, and desertion was startlingly extensive in the army. Disaffection behind the lines was widespread. In using the terms "disloyalty," "conspiracy," "rebellion," and "treason" people were employing a familiar vocabulary without stopping to put into these terms a definite content

1 On the "Copperheads" and related activities, see: Wood Gray, *The Hidden Civil War: The Story of the Copperheads;* George Fort Milton, *Abraham Lincoln and the Fifth Column;* J. F. Rhodes, *Hist. of the U.S.*, V, 317 ff.; *War of the Rebellion: Official Records,* esp. 2 ser. II, and 2 ser. VII; *Report of the Judge Advocate General on "The Order of American Knights," Alias "The Sons of Liberty,"* . . . (Wash., Chronicle Print., 1864 [same report in *Offic. Rec.*, 2 ser., VII, 930–953]); Nicolay and Hay, *Lincoln,* VIII, chap. 1; Paul B. Smith, "First Use of the Term 'Copperhead,'" *Amer. Hist. Rev.*, XXXII, 799–800; Ollinger Crenshaw, "Knights of the Golden Circle: The Career of George Bickley," *ibid.*, XLVII, 23–50.

with reference to solid acts, or even as to general attitudes. The difficult subject becomes no easier when ethics, philosophy, and ultimate values are brought into consideration.

Was it treasonable to be for peace? Or, to turn the phrase around (from the standpoint of a man such as Joseph Holt or Burnside), were not "peace men" the promoters and abettors of treason? Certainly the "anti-war" rallies and the "peace agitation" of the period were at the opposite pole from the "Union rallies," the Union League meetings, and the voluminous literature of the Loyal Publication Society. According to their own claim, these "Union Leagues" held in a kind of partisan monopoly the standard of loyalty and patriotism.

Could the national effort be so easily reduced to a party label? To take one example among hundreds, was John Scott Harrison of Ohio, son of one President and father of another, disloyal because he accepted in 1861 the Democratic nomination for lieutenant-governor of his state? The question is absurd, but precisely such absurdity—i. e., the tendency to pin the label of disloyalty upon members of one of the major parties—was shockingly prevalent in that period. First causes and ultimate objectives were a matter of some confusion. Motives were mixed and finality was not so certain a factor as leaders and publicists would imply. Opinion for or against the Lincoln administration, or the Republican party, or "the cause" in the sense of war against the South, was a matter of contributing factors, of antecedents and sympathies, of party preference, and of ups and downs when elections impended, as they did in every year of the war, or when military fortunes shifted.

There were broad regions—as in southern Ohio, Indiana, and Illinois—where disaffection prevailed at least in the sense of opposition to Republicanism, and to the Lincoln government.[2] One need not go back into the remote past of glaciers to explain it, but scientists would no doubt find a correlation between geological backgrounds, with their resulting soil conditions, and those human elements which became manifest in party affiliation. In the Middle West, as Wood Gray has pointed out, the "people of the less favored southern third tended to be envious of their more fortunate neighbors to the north." [3] Variations in agricultural wealth bore a demonstrable relation to

2 Well treated in H. C. Hubbart, *The Older Middle West,* 1840–1880.

3 Wood Gray, *The Hidden Civil War: The Story of the Copperheads,* 17.

differences in political attitudes. Immigration into these middle states had left a marked pattern: people of the more southerly counties were both geographically close to the South and humanly akin as descendants of Southerners if not Southerners themselves by birth.

There was a constant tendency to oversimplify, and this was especially true as to the position of parties, in which oversimplification became falsehood or misrepresentation. Not all Republicans were genuinely pro-Lincoln. Certainly the "anti-war" attitude in the sense of being anti-Union was emphatically repudiated by the Democratic party. The difficulty was to come to grips with reality. The peace group—those who agitated for an immediate cease-fire order looking to "negotiation" with the Confederacy—would be represented as anti-Union and as supporting the enemy; but they would deny these imputations and would maintain that war could never succeed in restoring the Union, but that negotiation could do so. Southerners, it was said, could not work with Republicans, but could coöperate with Northern friends.

When, however, such men took the next step, they posed a serious question; they stoutly maintained what the administration considered a fallacy, that Confederate leaders would end the war by negotiation on the basis of reunion. This was supposing that Southern leaders would voluntarily liquidate their own Confederacy. This was made to sound plausible, but there was an element of unreality in such a policy. There were, of course, Southerners who were ready to accept reunion, but armistice and negotiation required an official Southern instrument. The Confederate government, fully committed to disunion and separation, was the agency that ruled the South and the only agency with which the United States government could negotiate, since it controlled the armies. Obviously it was not a suitable mouthpiece for those Southerners who were ready to call off the war without victory and rebuild the United States as a reunited nation.

II

The matter of labels only added to the confusion. On the one hand the name "Union" was increasingly appropriated by one party at the North. On the other hand the term "Copperhead" took hold rapidly and became a common word, or byword, in the political glossary. By the summer of 1862 it was a familiar term; it had been used by the New York *Tribune* as early as July 20, 1861.[1] Spoken, written, or flashed on a cartoon, the word "Copperhead" became a devastating term of reproach, suggesting always the slimy and venomous snake. Efforts to give it a favorable connotation by linking it with the copper penny, the coin of the common people, were ineffectual, though cut-out heads of the penny were worn by some who thought to adopt the term as their own.

Like other labels of scorn and hate, the word came to be so inexactly used as to lose all genuine meaning and to become a mere trick of name-calling. So far as the word had a justifiable, specific significance it may be said to have denoted secret, subversive, pro-Confederate, or treasonable groups at the North. To put it in other words—where there were such groups it was understandable to stigmatize them with this word of burning scorn. Then came the next step: the label came to have such crushing force as a whiplash of reproach that it offered a cheap advantage to those who would use it irresponsibly to smirch political opponents. The ancient legend of the Trojan horse was not much used in this connection, nor the modern "fifth column," nor the term "underground" in the sense of the nineteen-forties and after. Perhaps this was because, while there were secret organizations and mysterious conclaves, much of the anti-war agitation—very much indeed—was carried on in the open. It should also be remembered that these movements were really Northern. Some few Southern spies were sent North to work with them, but that was only a minor factor. The groups that worked against prosecution of the war might be "pro-Southern," but for the most part they were under Northern organization, leaders, and agitators, rather than under Confederate agents. There were, it is true, a few such agents,[2] and Confederate spies were daringly active in the North, but subversive activities did not on any large scale take on the nature of a Trojan horse.

Though groups actually subversive could properly have been called

1 After mentioning this use of the term in the *Tribune,* Wood Gray points out that "it had in fact been used as a general term of opprobrium long before the war." He adds: "Since it was purely an epithet, it never had any definite range of application, being sometimes used to refer only to those believed to be actively in sympathy with the Confederates but on other occasions fixed on the Democratic party as a whole." *Ibid.,* 140–141.

2 For Confederate agents—e. g., Thomas H. Hines—working with Northern plotters, see *ibid.,* 167 ff., 181 ff., and *passim.*

"Copperheads," the term came soon to be applied to "peace Democrats." Then with shameless disregard of obvious truth the serpent label was attached to Democrats in general; this became a kind of Republican trick to disseminate the idea that to be a Democrat was to be disloyal! After the war the meaningless use of the term was part of the "bloody shirt" tradition characteristic of the vituperative politics of a whole generation. A careful scholar has written: "The disloyalty, real or unreal, of . . . Southern sympathizers at the North created a detestation for Democrats which lasted, like an incurable cancer, long years after the war ended—often terminating only with the death of the haters and the hated." [3]

When speaking of organizations deemed subversive one thinks first of the Knights of the Golden Circle. Taking the full story of its origin and history, it is amazing how small was the sum-total of its proved accomplishments. Ollinger Crenshaw has elaborately shown how the organization began before the Civil War as an ambitious yet abortive Southern filibustering venture to promote ideas of "young America" and "manifest destiny" in the proslavery sense. The order was founded by G. W. L. Bickley, a versatile Southerner who intended it as a scheme to colonize, "Texasize," or annex Mexico, and thus extend powerfully the cause of proslavery domination over the United States. If this annexation could have been accomplished, it was hoped that "fifty new slave state senators would one day appear in Washington and sixty or more new members of the House of Representatives." (Or perhaps this wholesale annexation could be effected by a "Southern Confederacy.")

The esoteric and aggressive order which Bickley founded was strongly militaristic, being conceived and organized as a kind of private "army." (That fact alone, as to the private army, would stamp the group as essentially un-American, however much it flaunted the phrases of Americanism. In this sense it was like the Ku Klux Klan and other similar groups whose professional patrioteering have masked ulterior and sinister motives. Private armies, with ambitious leaders seeking control of affairs, have no place in the American polity.) With its high-sounding ritual, codes, secrets, and flamboyant titles, its castles and lodges, its appeal to "chivalry" combined with expansive promises

---

[3] William A. Russ, Jr., in *Pa. Hist.*, V, 245 (1938).

of Mexican land (640 acres for a private), and its affiliation with shipping and financial agencies, the prewar K. G. C. was calculated to have an alluring attraction for human ambition, swaggering vanity, misapplied "patriotism," and cupidity.[4] In its fraternal aspect it could exploit the joining urge so characteristic of Americans. Like other similar organizations it was double-faced, having an impressive front and sonorous declarations of purpose which half-concealed its undemocratic and conspiratorial activity.

III

In describing these secret orders it would not be hard to paint a lurid picture. One could tell of their hide-outs, their guarded meetings, their grapevine intelligence, warning signals, hailing signs, countersigns, inner-door passwords, and cryptic markings on houses. Members were armed and under impressive oaths with terrible penalties for violation. "In all correspondence by the members," so it was reported, a device would be used which "reverses the whole matter; so they write one thing when they mean another." To write: "You are not in 33" would mean: "You are in danger." It was testified by a former member of the K. G. C. that their object was "to oppose everything the Administration may do toward putting down the rebellion; oppose all war measures whatever, such as preventing enlistments, encouraging desertions, &c." He added: "The promulgation of treason against the Government is the business of every member." He added: "I have heard leading men say at their meetings that Jeff. Davis had violated no rights that they claim in this Government; that he was a better man than Lincoln, and that John Morgan [Confederate cavalry leader] was as good." None but the "leading members," it was pointed out, understood "the true meaning and intentions of the K. G. C.s." In Missouri, where lodges were numerous, it was reported that a prominent leader, "thoroughly disloyal," was "in constant communication with Price's [Confederate] army." [1]

In the local scene the activities of these secret societies took the form of recruiting for the enemy, discouraging Union enlistment, aiding desertion, distributing disloyal literature, resisting the draft, destroy-

[4] Ollinger Crenshaw, in *Amer. Hist. Rev.,* XLVII, 23 ff.

[1] *Offic. Rec.,* 2 ser. VII, 741 ff., esp. 742–744, 747, 753.

ing enrollment lists, and demolishing government property. On the larger scale there were reports of ambitious and far reaching plots to assist "rebel" raids from the rear, to form a great "Northwest Confederacy" that would unite with the South, to liberate Confederate prisoners, and to split the North in such a way as to facilitate Confederate victory. There were schemes to assassinate Union officers, there was talk of hanging Lincoln,[2] and there were conspiracies for using Canadian soil as hatching ground and base for pro-Confederate raids into the United States.

Testimony as to these Copperhead plottings is voluminously available, but the story becomes anti-climactic when the grandest and darkest of these schemes are reduced to completed accomplishment or even fair prospects of accomplishment. These orders were a menace, but the assessment of their importance should be approached as a matter of realistic history. Their strength should be neither exaggerated nor underestimated. Statements on the subject are not always exact or specific. Deponent for the government would often use such phrases as "I have heard," "they say," "some claim," "My own belief is . . . ," or "I think . . . but am not certain." [3]

On closer inspection the ineffectiveness of these gentry is revealed. Many of the knights were ignorant of the intentions of the lodges and it was believed that a large number "would leave the order if they were not deceived by the officers and leading men." [4] Such a condition hardly gave the basis for a determined fighting force of daring rebels with the will to win. One man who joined the K. G. C. swore under oath: "I claim to be a Douglas Democrat, but my Democracy has ever taught me to be always on the side of my country, willing to aid in putting down conspiracies instead of sustaining them." [5] Investigators on the hunt for members of these groups, though aided by spies and informers, would sometimes report that in certain supposedly disaffected localities they found few or none. As to their military organization, there were companies for drill and military "districts" with "district commanders," but squad organization was emphasized, and it was said to be understood that if a "general war" should take place

[2] A Chicago commission merchant "said [as reported] they intended to go down and hang Abe Lincoln, his Cabinet, and all the abolitionists." (What "they" would have done after that was not stated.) *Ibid.*, 2 ser. VII, 747.

[3] *Ibid.*, 746–747. [4] *Ibid.*, 744. [5] *Ibid.*

the squads would "act separately, the guerrilla mode of warfare being adopted." That does not sound like much of a plan for a "general war," whatever that might mean. Civil war experience showed that warfare in guerrilla fashion could be a cursed annoyance, but it never became a major menace.

As for a rising to help a Confederate raid into the North, the facts did not bear out the supposed menace. When Morgan swept into southern Indiana and Ohio in the summer of 1863 the expectation that men of these secret societies would help the enemy was doomed to utter disappointment. A captain who rode with Morgan wrote: "The Copperheads turned out and fought by the side of their loyal neighbors and no aid in any shape was afforded the raiders." [6] The historian of that raid, Basil W. Duke, writes: "the 'Copperheads' and 'Vallandighammers' fought [on the Union side] harder than the others." [7] The "Democrats were disgusted with Morgan," writes J. F. Rhodes. When he plundered shops or took food he did not stop to inquire whether he was robbing Republicans or Democrats. "Whatever they might do it was almost certain that they [members of the K. G. C.] would not rise with arms in their hands to give assistance to the invading enemy in his work of ravaging the Northern States." [8]

A fact to be remembered is that there were government spies within the order—men operating in the cause of Lincoln, or agents of a governor such as Morton—and this considerably nullified the value of an elaborately studied secrecy that often proved deceptive. One hears much of plans for a general "rising" in the North or Northwest (perhaps that was what their term "general war" signified), but it is only a matter of conjecture to suppose that large numbers of knights who enjoyed their local out-of-the-way meetings in the woods would actually have "risen" in force. It is also mere conjecture to say that, if they had done so, they would have had any chance of success. If Copperheads had risen, nothing was more certain than that Union-minded citizens would also have done so, having the home guard, militia, army, and authority of constituted government on their side, which would have been an enormous advantage. When the knights talked of rising they had in mind, as motive, something political or partisan,

---

6 *The Southern Bivouac,* Dec. 1886, 442; quoted in Rhodes, *Hist. of the U. S.,* V, 316 n.
7 Basil W. Duke, *History of Morgan's Cavalry,* 439.
8 Rhodes, *Hist. of the U. S.,* V, 317.

which is what they had chiefly in mind on the whole accounting. They would, or thought they would "rise" if this or that thing should happen—for example, if another attempt (say in 1864) should have been made to arrest Vallandigham, or if Lincoln should have forcibly interfered in the elections.[9]

These plots, of course, could not be ignored. The point is that since the Union intelligence system, never of course perfect, was operating, the government knew about these orders. That being so, the avoidance of what might be called all-out suppressive measures against them was a calculated avoidance. It was not due to ignorance or inadvertence. The Lincoln government, with its shrewdness in recognizing realities, would have done much more to "crack down" on these groups than it did, if that had been deemed necessary. On the whole it was considered wiser to let a horrendous, colossal plot fizzle out than to create trouble by taking it too seriously.

With continued war, mounting radicalism, shocking casualties, profiteering, conscription, arrests, and doubtful prospects for a military decision, more was heard of these conspiratorial groups, but the Knights of the Golden Circle, under that name, faded into the background. By 1863 a new fraternity, the Order of American Knights, was carrying on the work. That it largely absorbed the K. G. C. was due to its compactness, centralized organization, and "new militancy." [10] Then in February 1864 "a so-called national meeting of its moving spirits took place in New York in which the name was changed to the Sons of Liberty, thus claiming spiritual kinship with the patriotic society of the Revolutionary period." [11] It was this organization of which Clement L. Vallandigham was chosen supreme grand commander. The over-all number of the organization has been given as 500,000, or even one million, but J. F. Rhodes shows that even the halfway figure was "an obvious exaggeration." [12] In the three states where it was strongest in numbers—Ohio, Indiana, and Illinois—"it may have counted 175,000." If one adds two other states—Kentucky and Missouri—the total would hardly have exceeded a quarter of a million. Outside of the five states named the number of "Knights" or "Sons" was "inconsiderable." [13]

---

[9] *Offic. Rec.*, 2 ser. VII, 747. [10] Gray, *Hidden Civil War*, 164. [11] *Ibid.*, 166.
[12] Report of judge advocate general, in *Offic. Rec.*, 2 ser. VII, 935; Rhodes, V, 318.
[13] Rhodes, V, 318.

An explanation of the purpose and nature of the order in other than disloyal terms was given in a long letter to Lincoln in 1865. The writer, a high official of the Sons of Liberty in Illinois, attributed most of the accusations of wrongful acts leveled against the society to "the suppositions . . . understandings . . . guesses, and loose generalizations of a portion of the witnesses." The organization, he wrote, was not intended to aid rebellion but to serve as an auxiliary to the Democratic party, as an "offset to the secret organization called the 'Union League,' and as a safeguard of the personal . . . rights of Democrats." [14]

This partisan motive must constantly be kept in mind in order to understand these orders. The brothers all had their instructions how to vote—as did the Union Leagues—and any history that would ignore this aspect would be most imperfect. In Indiana, where the knights or their successors were especially notorious, it has been said that Governor Morton "was undoubtedly more afraid that his Democratic opponent, Joseph E. McDonald, would defeat him for Governor in the October election of 1864 than that the Sons of Liberty would rise and depose him from power." [15] If one looks at the subject somewhat obliquely, Morton might have thanked these "Sons." Though bitterly and savagely anti-Republican, such *sub rosa* groups actually helped the dominant party. Republicans could denounce treason, point to these "treasonable" groups, and show, which was true, that the efforts of these societies were directed toward Democratic success. In this they would conveniently omit to show that in the whole broad picture Democrats were overwhelmingly loyal, patriotic, and firm for the Union. Copperheads—if one uses this inexact term to apply to men who were obstructing the existing national effort—were not really helping the Democratic party. If Copperheads were Democrats, that did not mean that all Democrats were Copperheads. Yet many people lacked the elementary intelligence to detect the obvious fallacy of this kind of reasoning.

---

[14] S. Corning Judd to Lincoln, Washington, Mar. 3, 1865 (endorsed on envelope in Lincoln's hand), Nicolay and Hay MSS. (VIII: 1), Ill. State Hist. Lib. Judd, a lawyer of Lewistown, Fulton County, Illinois, was active in Democratic politics. During the war "he was a determined opponent of the war policy of the Government." Bateman and Selby, *Hist. Encyc. of Ill.*, I, 310.

[15] Rhodes, V, 319–320.

IV

It has been seen how the executive policy of arbitrary arrests under Lincoln began at the very outset of the war, how the alarming situation in Maryland claimed chief attention at first, and how a major legal controversy—one of the most famous in American history—developed over the presidential power of suspension, with the Chief Justice officially denying the validity of that power, while Congress delayed for years and then dodged the main issue. It becomes necessary now to look further into the activities of the government with regard to prisoners of state.

In the first year of the war the problem was handled, not by considered planning, but by improvisation. The attorney general's tiny staff was unable to cope with the situation, while the secretary of state, though his office pertained to international affairs, was ready to assume executive responsibilities and was conveniently available as a kind of factotum for a variety of duties on the domestic front. Thus it came about that William Henry Seward, through most of the first year of the war, had the responsibility for the detection, arrest, examination (if any), and confinement of "political prisoners"—an unusual term in American vocabulary.

Seward threw himself into this "arbitrary, largely secret, and altogether unusual" business with a good deal of vigor, and the activities of his department were on a wide scale as he set up a "personal blockade," required passports for those who departed the country, directed the disposition of prisoners, determined punishment, and where he thought proper, ordered releases.[1] Arrests were sometimes effected by Seward's confidential agents, sometimes by local police on direct order of Seward, or at other times by military authorities or marshals of Federal courts.

Those taken were not told why they were seized. It was not a matter of clearly formulating, much less substantiating, the charges prior to arrest. The state department, as Frederic Bancroft shows, "never made up its case." [2] "If Seward," writes Bancroft, "had carried on his system in time of peace, he would have been the most despicable tyrant of the

1 Bancroft, *Life of Seward,* II, 259 ff.; see also 254–280.

2 *Ibid.,* II, 276.

century. Its sole moral justification must rest upon its necessity."[3] The victim would often be "seized at night, searched, borne off to the nearest fort, deprived of his valuables, and locked up in a casemate, or in a battery generally crowded with men that had had similar experiences."[4] To get a hearing by the secretary was difficult; to obtain a release was often a matter of "political and personal pressure."[5]

The general hue and cry against "traitors" and spies gave the occasion for irresponsible accusation and abuse. One of the most flagrant instances of this was the case of ex-President Franklin Pierce of New Hampshire, who was the victim of an anonymous letter and of the thoughtless manner in which the affair was handled by Seward and his staff. The writer, embellishing his letter with meaningless cryptic symbols, wrote: "President P—— in his passage has drawn many brave and influential men to the league." (This was supposed to refer to the Knights of the Golden Circle; the man was assumed to be Pierce.) The letter came into the hands of Federal officials, and as a result Seward wrote to the ex-President suggesting the need for an "explanation."

Furiously indignant, Pierce wrote to Seward expressing surprise that, on such a flimsy basis, this incoherent and meaningless "extract from the vagaries of an anonymous correspondent . . . should have been sent for explanation to one who during his whole life has never belonged to any secret league, society, or association." Pierce added: "Nothing but the gravity of the insinuation, the high official source whence it emanates, and the distracted condition of our recently united, prosperous, and happy country could possibly lift this matter above ridicule and contempt."

This drew from Seward a clumsy apology in which the secretary expressed regret and explained that he had devolved upon a department clerk the duty of preparing a note to Pierce. (The note had been signed by Seward.) In this he supposed that he was rendering the ex-President a "service." Pierce answered with a cold but dignified letter showing that he could not pass over the matter as blithely as Seward suggested. "You will excuse me," he wrote, "if I regard even a suggestion from a source so eminent that I am 'a member of a secret league, the object of which is to overthrow this Government,' as rather too grave to have been sent off with as little consideration as a note of

---

[3] *Ibid.*, II, 259. [4] *Ibid.*, II, 261. [5] *Ibid.*, II, 279.

rebuke might have been addressed to a delinquent clerk of one of the departments." Pierce's name had not appeared in the anonymous extract (only "President P——"); yet Seward had referred to it as an "injurious aspersion on your fair fame and loyalty." Pointing to a serious defect in procedure, Pierce wrote: "I think you will . . . arrive at the conclusion that the whole ground upon which the allegation is repeated should, as a simple act of justice, have been placed before me."

This slanderous bit of trash did not merit an explanation, but, since the correspondence would become a part of the government files, and because Pierce wanted no ambiguity in the record, he wrote: ". . . it is proper—perhaps it is my duty—to add that my loyalty will never be successfully impugned so long as I enjoy the constitutional rights which pertain to every citizen of the Republic, and especially the inestimable right to be informed of the nature and cause of accusation and to be confronted face to face with my accusers."

After this preposterous accusation of Pierce had been taken up in the Republican press, and in Congress (where Seward was asked to submit the correspondence but omitted part of it until a senator called it to his attention),[6] the whole libelous affair was shown to have been a fabrication and a hoax. The perpetrator, a certain Dr. Guy S. Hopkins of North Branch, Michigan, was accused of secessionist leanings, but this he flatly denied. To cut the long story short, he was a Democrat who had noted with disgust frequent paragraphs in Detroit papers charging Democrats with treason and referring to a pro-Confederate secret league.[7] The worst accusations were being directed against men whom he "admired as statesmen and loyal Americans." He therefore concocted the letter, with its reference to "President P——" and a good deal else, with the expectation "that it would be sent to one of the treason-shrieking presses, and when exploded would produce lots of fun." The "universal reign of suspicion" and the manner in which disgraceful stories were being used to blast the reputation of well-intentioned men had so irritated him that it entered his mind "to sell the Detroit [Republican] press by writing a letter full of dark innuen-

6 *Cong. Globe,* 37 Cong., 2 sess., 1370–71 (Mar. 26, 1862).

7 The K. G. C. was of slight importance in Michigan, especially in 1861 when the fabrication as to Pierce was perpetrated. The statement of the judge advocate general that the later order of O. A. K. had "about 20,000" members in Michigan was given as of 1864 and was an exaggerated guess. *Offic. Rec.,* 2 ser. VII, 935.

does and hints, but which in reality would mean nothing." Later he deeply regretted his trick, which he referred to as "one moment's indiscretion," "this fanciful practical joke," and "that doubly-accursed letter." With detectives on the alert and all sorts of accusations flying around, it was not remarkable that the letter should have been held for investigation, but by the time the hoax was revealed (which required no extraordinary sleuthing) the harm had been done through unfortunate publicity and Seward's bungling. Refutation could not catch up with accusation, the slander could not be easily wiped off, and the senseless injury lingered.[8]

The defects of Seward's system may have been due to the alarming emergency, the hasty improvisation, the lack of organization, and the unfamiliarity of this kind of treatment in American experience. Whatever may have been the excuses, the fact was that the use of these crude methods gave the policy of summary arrests an unfortunate turn at its earliest stage. With far less than the requisite attention to so difficult a matter, a machinery had been set up for catching the innocent with the guilty, while the methods of release were capricious and unpredictable. Frederic Bancroft mentions the current story "that Seward boasted to Lord Lyons that he could ring a little bell and cause the arrest of a citizen of Ohio or order the imprisonment of a citizen of New York, and that no one on earth except the President could release the prisoner." [9]

If a man is quoted as having made a certain remark, it may be difficult to prove that he did not make it. The point is, rather, to find proof *for* the remark; otherwise, to consider it unproved. After reporting an elaborate search in the sources, in which no evidence for this bit of Seward conversation was found, J. F. Rhodes notes that it became a stock Democratic argument, was referred to in Marshall's *American Bastile* as "undisputed historical truth," and as such was quoted by S. S. Cox in *Three Decades*.[10] On reading the record, and the summary by Bancroft, one gathers that the question of Seward's oft-quoted remark is less important than the fact of his far-reaching one-man power and the manner in which he used it. Bancroft con-

[8] For the Pierce episode see *Offic. Rec.*, 2 ser. II, 1244–1267 (for Hopkins's explanation of the hoax, 1250–51); Bancroft, *Seward*, II, 271–276; Roy F. Nichols, *Franklin Pierce*, 519–520. The Seward-Pierce correspondence extended from December 20, 1861, to January 7, 1862.

[9] Bancroft, *Seward*, II, 280.

[10] Rhodes, *Hist. of the U. S.*, IV, 413 n.

cludes that, while Seward was "almost as free from restraint as a dictator or a sultan," he did not act like one. He writes: ". . . in the great mass of documents on the subject of political prisoners there are no manifestations of improper motives or of extreme prejudice or of personal considerations except in the Pierce episode."

It is hard to make a final appraisal on so complex a subject. There were plots behind the lines, the military threat to Washington was startlingly serious, the very life of the nation was at stake, and the persistence of pro-enemy activity, if unchecked, would have weakened the confidence of European countries in the ability of the government to survive. On the other hand, any large program for arresting political prisoners is open to abuse, and even in the case of so easy going a secretary as Seward it has been conceded that he "sought and was given too much responsibility." [11]

V

In the evolution of Lincoln's policy—or that of the Lincoln government—concerning arbitrary arrests, the year 1862, and especially February of that year, was marked by several important administrative steps. For one thing, control over arrests was shifted from the department of state under Seward to the war office under Stanton. In a war department order (February 14) over the signature of Stanton ("By order of the President") it was indicated that the startling aspects of the emergency were now past, that "a favorable change of public opinion" had occurred, and that the whole situation had improved. In view of these facts (so the order read) the President directed that all political prisoners held in military custody "be released on their subscribing to a parole engaging them to render no aid or comfort to the enemies in hostility to the United States." (Exceptions from this release could be made by the secretary of war at his discretion in the case of spies "or others whose release . . . may be deemed incompatible with the public safety.") It was announced in this order that presidential amnesty for past offenses was granted to those released if they kept their paroles. Also, as illustrating the increasing importance of the war department, it was declared, "Ex-

---

11 Bancroft, *Seward,* II, 280.

traordinary arrests will hereafter be made under the direction of the military authorities alone." [1]

All this looked like governmental relaxation as to arrests, but against that supposition there were several factors to consider. The February order came near the beginning of Stanton's administration of the war department. Soon the government would have within that tightening department, a detective bureau and a secret service. The head of that secret police service, La Fayette C. Baker—colonel (later brigadier general) and special provost marshal—became famous, or rather notorious, for his snooping, his disregard of due process, his raking-in of perjured testimony, his accumulation of a fortune for himself, his "habitual carelessness in mixing truth and fiction," [2] and the whole rapid pace of his melodramatic career.[3] He is best known for his later activities in the man hunt after Lincoln's assassination, his amazing "documents" in connection with the impeachment of Johnson, his secretive methods of combating the hidden system of Confederate espionage, and his trailing of deserters, Negro-stealers, and bounty jumpers. Of this branch of the service Perley Poore wrote: "How they watched and waited at official doors till they had bagged the important secret of state they wanted; how they stole military maps from the War Department; how they took copies of official documents; how they smuggled the news of the Government's strength in the linings of honest-looking coats; and how they hid army secrets in the meshes of unsuspected crinoline—all these became familiar facts, almost ceasing to excite remark or surprise." [4] As Seward gave way (in the seizure and control of prisoners) to the newly appointed Stanton, a so-called "premier" who has been compared to a dictator and whose office had done a shocking injustice to an ex-President, was relinquishing his "dangerous machinery" [5] to an official who was prepared to use it with the resources of a much greater and more specialized staff, but with no less severity.

---

1 Order issued by war department, Feb. 14, 1862, signed by Stanton, secretary of war, Nicolay and Hay, *Works*, VII, 100–104.

2 Thomas Denton McCormick, in *Dic. of Amer. Biog.*, I, 523.

3 *Secret Service, By Gen. La Fayette C. Baker, Organizer and First Chief of the Secret Service of the United States* (Washington, 1898). This self-important book has the cheap paper, lurid illustrations, and racy style of a dime novel or popular thriller.

4 Ben: Perley Poore, *Perley's Reminiscences of Sixty Years in the National Metropolis*, II, 110–111.

5 Bancroft, *Seward*, II, 278.

In applying the policy of release under Stanton a special commission was set up, consisting of Edwards Pierrepont and John A. Dix, to examine the cases of political prisoners and determine whether they should be discharged, kept in military custody, or turned over to the civil authorities for trial. Of this two-man commission, Pierrepont was a distinguished New York lawyer and judge, while Dix, in his sixty-third year when the war opened, was a soldier, lawyer, former senator, and prominent Civil War general. Both Pierrepont and Dix were Democrats and both strong Unionists.[6] The creation of the commission was evidence of the need for more system in the process of release, but the commission acted under orders from Stanton, who was still in command of this whole business, by "authority of the President."

In the first year and a half of the war suspension of the habeas corpus privilege had proceeded by specific orders of limited coverage; then came an order which in effect made of these arbitrary arrests a kind of normal wartime procedure. On September 24, 1862, two days after the preliminary edict of emancipation, President Lincoln issued a proclamation:

> . . . be it ordered, first, that during the existing insurrection . . . , all Rebels and Insurgents, their aiders and abettors within the United States . . . [etc.] shall be subject to martial law and liable to trial and punishment by Courts Martial or Military Commission.
>
> Second. That the Writ of Habeas Corpus is suspended in respect to all persons arrested, or who are now, or hereafter . . . shall be, imprisoned . . . by any military authority or by the sentence of any Court Martial or Military Commission.[7]

Here was an indication that policy as to arrests was being tightened rather than relaxed under Stanton.[8] The war secretary has

---

[6] For correspondence of the Pierrepont-Dix commission see *Offic. Rec.*, 2 ser. II *passim;* for sample list of prisoners examined and released, 277–279.

[7] Proclamation suspending writ of habeas corpus, Sep. 24, 1862, photostat, A. Lincoln Assoc.

[8] In addition to Lincoln's proclamation of September 24, 1862, which has elicited the most discussion, there were other presidential orders of a general nature covering the suspension of the famous privilege. In particular, one should note his proclamation of September 15, 1863 (suspending the privilege under the specific authority of the statute of March 3, 1863), and his instruction to military officers, September 17, 1863 (in which he presupposed that the writ should issue, and that the military officer should make "proper return thereto," but that the prisoner should not be produced). See below, p. 223.

been credited with greater caution in the invasion of personal liberty than Seward; it has been said that he traced his authority to Lincoln's suspension while feeling that such suspension "in no wise justified arrests not required by the public safety." [9] It must be remembered, however, that the number of arrests under Stanton was far greater than those under Seward, that Baker's secret service was a Stanton institution, that its methods were highly surreptitious, and that the Baker papers in the war department have been closed to investigators, so that the whole subject is considerably hidden. The vast series of volumes known as the *Official Records of the Union and Confederate Armies* contains elaborate and detailed accounts of political prisoners under Seward,[10] but no such detailed report of Baker's, or Stanton's, arrests has been issued. Furthermore, Stanton is one of those leading figures of the Lincoln period for whom we have no adequate biography.

VI

Though the number of political prisoners under the Lincoln administration has been greatly exaggerated, the total was undoubtedly large. No definite, all-inclusive estimate seems possible to find, but the records of the commissary general of prisoners contain the names of 13,535 citizens arrested and confined in military prisons between February 1862 and the end of the war. To this one would have to add those confined before that date, being under the state department, those arrested under naval authority, and those held in prisons and penitentiaries of the several states.[1] The statement that the arrests totaled 38,000 is only an exaggerated guess.[2]

How were these thousands of prisoners treated? For an answer to this question the pages of *American Bastile,* by John A. Marshall,

---

9 George C. Gorham, *Life . . . of Edwin M. Stanton,* I, 262–263.

10 See esp. 2 ser. II.

1 "Notwithstanding the many mentions of . . . political or citizen prisoners in the . . . *Official Records,* . . . I do not believe that it will ever be possible for any one to gather from any source an approximately definite estimate of the total number of such prisoners held by Federal authorities during the Civil War." Major General Robert C. Davis, Adjutant General of the United States, to the writer, June 26, 1925, quoted (with additional data) in *Constitutional Problems Under Lincoln,* 152–153 (footnote).

2 An estimate based on this guess was given by Alexander Johnston. See the article "Habeas Corpus," in J. J. Lalor, *Cyclopaedia of Political Science . . .* [etc.]; see also Rhodes, IV, 230 ff.

published in 1869, must be considerably discounted without being fully discarded. The book reads like the bitterest anti-Lincoln wartime propaganda. Its author was the historian of the "Association of State Prisoners," chosen by that organization in convention assembled. Along with voluminous abuse of the Lincoln government the volume gives numerous case histories of particular prisoners whose tribulations are presented in the author's rhetorical phraseology, with a kind of horrifying embellishment. The uprightness of Lincoln's opponents, their heroism, their sacrifices for the cause of freedom, and their suffering are thrown in contrast to the coarse cruelty of Lincoln's agents and the black despotism of his methods. Liberty Bell, Magna Carta, and the Constitution are referred to in ironic emphasis to show how the free principles of the founding fathers had become in Lincoln's day an idle boast. The book has a kind of fractional authenticity in the sense that there were thousands of prisoners (vastly more than the cases mentioned), that they did suffer, that normal civil guarantees were in fact denied them, and that the concentrated bitterness dripping from these pages was a mental fact, being not only part of the war mind, but also an element of well-intentioned protest.

Prisoners of state, according to Marshall's mordant book, were housed in a stable, made to sleep in the open air on a "cold and dreary night upon the frozen ground," kept in rooms "not fit for . . . human beings," inhaled "fetid . . . atmosphere," were plundered "in a hundred different ways" (as by the sale of articles of poor quality at a "profit of five hundred per cent."), and were "in danger of being shot" by frenzied guards. In the case of one prisoner it was stated: "His Republican creditors bankrupted him while in prison, and left his helpless family in destitution." [3] Frederic Bancroft writes: "Month after month many of them were crowded together in gloomy and damp casemates . . . . Many had committed no overt act. There were among them editors and political leaders of character and honor, but whose freedom would be injurious to the prosecution of the war." [4]

Yet on a fair generalization it must be recognized that prisoners were not brutally treated. Comforts were allowed them and they

[3] Marshall, *American Bastile* (for quoted portions, see pp. 124, 133, 160–161, 329, 691).
[4] Bancroft, *Seward,* II, 277.

were permitted to receive articles sent by friends and relatives. Under inspection they could transmit and receive letters, obtain newspapers, and receive visitors. Even Marshall, with all his abuse, reveals, under careful reading, that prisoners, where in camp, sometimes had housekeeping privileges, that one of them was allowed to board himself in a nearby town, that "hospital accommodations were, with some exceptions, as good [in the Old Capitol Prison] as could be expected in a place conducted without regard to system," that prisoners were allowed some recreation, and that, after the election of November 1862, "the condition of the prison [Old Capitol] became somewhat improved." [5] Any period of being held in custody, even with some freedom of movement, is a hardship, and it is not to be denied that these imprisonments were a grievous experience.

The harsh features, however, were due rather to lack of space and to general conditions of prison management (not all of which have even yet been remedied) than to deliberate cruelty. Most of those seized were imprisoned for short periods. Prisoners were often men of proud spirit, keen upholders of right principle as they understood it—too proud, many of them, to purchase their liberty by taking an oath of allegiance which would put their previous conduct in the wrong (as they thought), and which their consciences could not approve. Personal attention was given by Seward to "the comfort of the prisoners" at Fort Lafayette, while at Fort Warren the instruction was given "That the prisoners be securely held and . . . allowed every privilege consistent with this end." [6] Though the whole system was in many respects deplorable and regrettable, a book as long as Marshall's could be made up to show moderation and a fair amount of leniency in the actual treatment of prisoners.

VII

To give case histories of the many prisoners, or even a representative sampling, is impracticable, but a passing word as to a few of them may be appropriate. F. Key Howard, prominent lawyer and editor of the Baltimore *Exchange,* was arrested on the night of September 12–13, 1861, being "publicly known to be in deep sympathy

---

[5] Marshall, *Amer. Bastile,* 124, 125, 328, 331.
[6] *Offic. Rec.,* 2 ser. II, 118, 111.

with the rebels." His paper (according to the state department "Record Book") "zealously advocated their cause." [1] In his possession was found a large quantity of manuscripts, "mostly of a decided secession character." He could not see how the Union could be preserved against majority Southern opposition and said so.[2] In effecting his arrest one sees the fine hand of Allan Pinkerton, under authority of General Dix. After being confined in Forts McHenry, Monroe, Lafayette, and Warren—a rather familiar itinerary—he was released on November 27, 1862.

Henry May of Maryland, member of Congress (successful competitor against Henry Winter Davis, Republican), was arrested at the same time as Howard. May was suspected of criminal intercourse with the enemy in connection with a visit to Richmond in July 1861. The judiciary committee of the House of Representatives investigated his case but found no evidence to prove matters charged against him; the accusations or suspicions were based only on newspaper reports. He was released on December 2, 1861.[3]

William H. Winder, a citizen of Philadelphia, was arrested on September 11, 1861, charged with treasonable correspondence with the Confederates. He admitted having "condemned without stint . . . the abolition wing of the Republican party," and was shocked at what he considered the "barbarity" of Lincoln's emancipation proclamation. He stubbornly defended the rightness of his conduct, and one of the difficulties of his case was his proud refusal to take the oath of allegiance. Contending that he had done no wrong and that the whole system of arrests was unconstitutional, he looked for an "unconditional release" and a full acquittal. "To be called upon [he wrote] to take an oath to support the Constitution, &c., as a condition of my release is by my own act to indorse my arrest and imprisonment as being deserved." [4] Had it not been for such an implication, he would willingly have sworn to support the Constitution as in fact he had done in joining the Philadelphia Home Guard. Secretary Seward offered a modified oath which Winder also refused,

---

[1] *Ibid.*, 2 ser. II, 778–779. [2] Marshall, 700.

[3] *Offic. Rec.*, 2 ser. II, 790 ff.; *Cong. Globe*, 37 Cong., 1 sess., 196 ff. (July 20, 1861).

[4] *Offic. Rec.*, 2 ser. II, 730. For the Winder case in general, see *ibid.*, 721–747; Marshall, 268–289.

as he said it would render him "tongue-tied under the grossest imputations." There was an elaborate correspondence on the case of Winder, who was befriended by distinguished Boston lawyers, such as Benjamin R. Curtis, Sydney Bartlett, Samuel Dexter Bradford, and George S. Hillard. On November 27, 1862, he was given what he had demanded—an unconditional release at Fort Warren.

Others among the thousands of prisoners—though there is no space to treat them—included Charles J. Faulkner of Virginia, minister to France under Buchanan, arrested for supposed disloyalty, held as a hostage, and as such released in return for Confederate release of Alfred Ely, congressman from New York; George W. Jones of Iowa, minister resident at Bogotá (sympathizer with Jefferson Davis); Judge Richard Bennett Carmichael of Maryland's Eastern Shore; Charles S. Morehead, Kentucky governor and congressman (he also refused to take the oath of allegiance but was nevertheless released on parole); and William M. Gwin, senator from California, Confederate sympathizer, arrested in November 1861 and released after two weeks. The roll of state prisoners also included John S. Emerson (steamboat captain suspected of spying but soon released); Tench Schley, similarly suspected; and such well known women spies of the Confederacy as Catherine Virginia Baxley, Rose O'Neal Greenhow, and Belle Boyd. It would fill hundreds of pages to tell only the stories of these clever and daring women—their underground connections, ruses, courage, and biting hatred of Yankees in general and Seward and Stanton in particular.

Some of the charges, such as being a "noisy secessionist," selling Confederate "mottoes and devices," or "hurrahing for Jefferson Davis," seem trivial and insignificant. Yet, as one reads the record, it appears that most of those summarily arrested were seized because they were suspected of serious offenses. It was shown or believed that they had been acting as Confederate agents, furnishing supplies to the enemy, encouraging desertion from the service of the United States, committing outrages upon Unionists, stealing military stores, destroying bridges, engaging in bushwhacking, making drawings of fortifications, conveying "treasonable" correspondence, or otherwise assisting the enemy. Many of them were actual spies.

If one takes the list of prisoners of state confined in the famous

Old Capitol Prison in the shadow of the Capitol at Washington (on ground now occupied by the Supreme Court building), the designations read as follows: carrying goods South, violating blockade, bushwhacker, contrabandist, guerrilla, sutler robber, sutler robber and guerrilla, blockade runner, disloyalty and stoning guards, rebel mail carrier, rebel spy, and using altered pass.

The list goes on: awaiting sentence for treason, refugee, refugee drunk, dealer in Confederate money, sending recruits to the insurgents, attempting to escape to the insurgents after taking the oath of allegiance, murdering and robbing Federal soldiers, being a spy and holding a commission in the insurgent army, persecuting Union men, attempting to go South in violation of the President's proclamation, furnishing information which led to the murder of Federal pickets, being an officer in the Confederate signal corps, "held until army moves," deserter and spy, kidnapper, following the army without pass, showing "secesh" sentiments, causing the arrest of Union men, "rabid rebel," smuggler, suspicious character, one of a party who made a raid, aiding the enemy in raid at Catlett's Station, scout for Mosby and White, and forging soldier's discharge paper.

The enumeration becomes at times repetitious, but the more surprising thing is the variety of offenses and the extent to which the sins of these men (and women) are particularized without repetition. Some of the causes in addition to those already listed are: refuses to take the oath, abusive language to Col. Drew, crazy wanderer, harboring guerrillas, damaging draw on Long Bridge (near Washington), burning commissary stores, aiding and piloting deserters, burning barges, "held for Sec. of War," "committed by Sec. of War," "Turned over to L. C. Baker," "scold for a time," kidnapping negroes, citizen of Richmond conscript, defrauding government, horse thief, notorious blockade runner, within our lines—no pass, held as witness by order of Sec of War, subject to orders from Genl L. C. Baker (a considerable number of these), "charged with passing himself for Brig Genl USA & having forged papers in his possession," committed by War Dept (many such), news boy sent out of lines, furnishing citizen clothes to soldiers, "knowingly enlisting an enlisted man," laborer with ball and chain, and so on. The term "hidden Civil War" comes to mind when one peruses this kind of list and tries to imagine the full stories of these numerous men who were

Brady photographs, National Archives

TWO VIEWS OF THADDEUS STEVENS

Radical, anti-Lincoln politician; master of the House of Representatives; advocate of vindictive, punitive, and avowedly partisan measures; prominent in his opposition to the policies of reconstruction which President Lincoln favored.

THOSE GUILLOTINES.—A LITTLE INCIDENT AT THE WHITE HOUSE.

SERVANT. "If ye plase, Sir, them Gilliteens has arove."
MR. LINCOLN. "All right, MICHAEL.——Now, Gentlemen, will you be kind enough to step out in the Back Yard?"

UNIVERSAL ADVICE TO ABRAHAM.
DROP 'EM!

CARTOONIST'S VIEW OF HIGH MILITARY LEADERSHIP AFTER FREDERICKSBURG

Both cartoons appeared in *Harper's Weekly:* the one at the left on January 3, 1863; that at the right on January 10, 1863. The theme is the same: after Burnside's shattering defeat in the battle of Fredericksburg, December 1862, it is suggested that top military command in Washington is hopeless and that Halleck and Stanton must be dropped.

caught.[5] Though one seldom reads about this type of activity in detail, it was a large part of the wartime story.

VIII

That Lincoln would have avoided these arbitrary arrests if he could, and that, permitting them, he wished them held under curb, is evident from a careful study of his sayings and acts. Harsh things were done reluctantly; their harshness did not extend to the worst extremes; as for those measures which proved most unfortunate, they were not done by Lincoln nor in terms of his intent. In some respects—especially as to military repression—what is called the "Lincoln administration" should be called the Stanton administration, or (in 1861) the Cameron administration.

Take the question of arresting the members of the Maryland legislature. When this problem arose at the outset of the war Lincoln wrote to General Scott recognizing the danger that this legislature, about to convene at Annapolis, would act "to arm the people of that State against the United States." Should the general in view of this truly alarming situation, "arrest, or disperse the members of that body"? Lincoln answered: "I think it would *not* be justifiable; nor, efficient for the desired object." The President thought that these legislators had a legal right "to assemble." It could not be known in advance that their action would "not be lawful, and peaceful." If arrested, they would become prisoners, but not for long; when liberated, they would reassemble and proceed as if never imprisoned; if dispersed, they would reassemble somewhere else. Lincoln would, indeed, use strong measures if the legislature should "arm their people against the United States," but he disapproved of a premature and perhaps unnecessary use of such measures.[1] As seen above, a few of the legislators were arrested in September 1861; but this action was more the work of Cameron, Banks, and Dix (with the reluctant concurrence of Governor Hicks) than of Lincoln. At least the government did not rush hastily into that kind of measure; moreover,

---

[5] "Prisoners of State: Old Capitol Prison, vol. 303, Dept. of Washington," MSS., War Dept., National Archives. (Even where quotation marks are omitted in the above enumeration, the wording has been taken from the archival original.)

[1] Lincoln to Scott, April 25, 1861, R. T. L. Coll., 9404–06.

that episode of arrest was not only exceptional but unique. When it did occur, the views of Lincoln were in favor of great governmental caution and restraint. In a published quotation of his words the President was reported at the time as assuring the people of Maryland: "In no case has an arrest been made on mere suspicion, or through personal or partisan animosities, but in all cases the Government is in possession of tangible and unmistakable evidence, which will, when made public, be satisfactory to every loyal citizen." [2]

Another clue as to how Lincoln felt about these matters came up in the case of one of the arrested police commissioners of Baltimore. The President took the ground that this commissioner, at the time of his arrest or "at any time" later, could have obtained release "by taking a full oath of allegiance to the government of the United States." If the gentleman refused the oath, then, wrote Lincoln: "If Mr. Davis is still so hostile to the Government, and so determined to aid its enemies in destroying it, he makes his own choice." [3]

In a revealing letter (a private one) to Reverdy Johnson of Maryland in 1862, Lincoln recalled Maryland events in 1861, and showed that he had not miscalculated in counting on the strength of Union sentiment in that state. He had been warned, the day after the Baltimore riot in April, "that it would crush all Union feeling in Maryland for me to attempt bringing troops over Maryland soil to Washington." "I brought the troops notwithstanding [he added], and yet there was Union feeling enough left to elect a Legislature the next autumn which in turn elected a very excellent Union U.S. senator!" (Johnson would have no difficulty in guessing who that senator was.)

"I am a patient man," continued Lincoln, "—always willing to forgive, on the Christian terms of repentance; and also to give ample *time* for repentance. Still I must save this government if possible. What I *cannot* do, of course I *will* not do; but it may as well be understood, once for all, that I shall not surrender this game leaving any available card unplayed." [4]

---

[2] *Ann. Cyc.*, 1861, 448. This statement is not to be taken as proof that there were no ill considered arrests. It harmonizes, however, with Bancroft's conclusion that improper motives did not appear except in the Pierce instance (*Seward*, II, 280), and in any case these words show the President's wish and judgment as to how these matters should be handled.

[3] Endorsement on letter of John W. Davis, [Sep. 15?] 1861, photostat, A. Lincoln Assoc.

[4] Lincoln to Reverdy Johnson, July 26, 1862, copy in Hay's hand, photostat, A. Lincoln Assoc.

IX

When rightly considered, loyalty is a thing that runs deep, a thing of the spirit. It is a matter, not merely of sworn fealty, but of a man's very nature. To speak of loyalty is to speak of one's soul or good name. A man without loyalty is a lost soul. There may be loyalty oaths for a governmental purpose—and Lincoln favored such oaths if kept simple and not abused—but loyalty at its best is like devotion or affection; it is not a thing of compulsion.

Horace Bushnell, distinguished Congregational minister whose place in religious thought stands high, wrote in 1863: "Loyalty then is no subject of law or legal definition. It belongs entirely to the moral department of life. It is what a man thinks and feels and contrives, not as being commanded, but of his own accord, for his country and his country's honor—his great sentiment, his deep and high devotion, the fire of his habitual or inborn homage to his country's welfare. It goes before all constitutions, ..."[1]

The hard thing is where two honest loyalties conflict. This was a problem—North and South reading the same Bible and praying to the same God—that Lincoln pondered with tolerant recognition of the difficulty of saying the final and all-conclusive word, though he perceived a certain rightness in devotion to the United States and to human freedom which he did not perceive in slavery and disunion.

There is, of course, such a thing as corporate loyalty, and it is there that a species of compulsion may come into view. That is to say, the compulsion of human society, of organic social life, the vital necessity of cohesion in the great body of a nation if that nation is to survive, cannot be ignored. A criminal is not to be tolerated merely because he has his code, nor left unchecked on the principle that there is "honor among thieves." If a man actually serves the enemies of his country, his alien type of adherence, which should not in this connotation be termed loyalty, may be justified in his own reasoning, but the corporate bonds of society require that the traitor be held answerable as a supreme criminal. Such corporate loyalty, however, pertains to the great enduring fundamentals; it does not pertain to a party or a faction. It presupposes unanimity of homage to the na-

---

1 Horace Bushnell, in *New Englander*, XXII, 565 (July 1863).

tion's cause, but it allows for democratic differences of opinion as to policies, procedures, and administrations. Furthermore, it is broadly corporate in the sense of belonging to the whole body of the people. Its enforcing is not a self-appointed function of a group, a clique, a secret society, a "front," a Klan, or a partisan league.

If serious cracks or faults should develop in this fundamental adhesion, then indeed, thought Lincoln, the nation would be in danger of destruction; but, as he believed, it would be self-destruction. The mature Lincoln thought thus, but so also did the young Lincoln, who had more maturity than is usually supposed. In his lyceum address in 1838 he said: "At what point . . . is the approach of danger to be expected? I answer, if it ever reach us it must spring up amongst us. It cannot come from abroad. If destruction be our lot, we must ourselves be its author and finisher. As a nation of freemen, we must live through all time, or die by suicide." That was why Lincoln was horrified at the wild passions of his time in America—at the hanging of Negroes, the murder of white citizens, at "dead men . . . dangling from the boughs of trees," at a "mulatto man by the name of McIntosh . . . seized in the street, dragged to the suburbs of the city [St. Louis], chained to a tree, and actually burned to death." When mob law ran riot, Lincoln realized that its effects were pervasive; "the innocent [he said], those who have ever set their faces against violations of law in every shape, alike with the guilty, fall victims to the ravages of mob law; and thus it goes on, step by step, till all the walls erected for the defence of the persons and property of individuals, are trodden down, and disregarded." [2]

When Lincoln thought in war time of testing and demanding loyalty, he did not think in terms of name calling or of witch hunts. Where accusations of disloyalty were raised, he set down his idea of fairness in construing an act of Congress for that purpose: the accused, he wrote, "are not to be punished [under the treason, or confiscation, act of July 17, 1862] without regular trials in duly constituted courts under the forms and all the substantial provisions of law and of the Constitution applicable to their several cases." [3] These

[2] "The Perpetuation of our Political Institutions," speech before Young Men's Lyceum, Springfield, *Sangamo Journal*. Feb. 3, 1838. If one wonders why, in terms of current facts in 1838, Lincoln spoke thus of the wild, undemocratic disorders of his time, a certain light of disillusionment will come by reading *Fettered Freedom* by Russell Nye.

[3] Message, July 17, 1862.

forms of law, to be sure, were not applied in the case of those arbitrarily arrested, but as to his feeling with regard to this abnormal procedure, Lincoln expressed real distaste. He wrote: "thoroughly imbued with a reverence for the guaranteed rights of individuals, I was slow to adopt the strong measures which by degrees I have been forced to regard as being within the exceptions of the Constitution, and as indispensable to the public safety." Part of his distaste was due to his realization that "instances of arresting innocent persons might occur, . . . and then a clamor could be raised . . . which might be . . . of some service to the insurgent cause." [4]

[4] Lincoln to Corning and Others, June 12, 1863, Nicolay and Hay, *Works,* VIII, 302–303.

CHAPTER IX

THE VALLANDIGHAM CASE

WHAT was called "Copperhead" agitation, with all its repercussions in popular emotion and governmental policy, was focused and personalized in the case of Clement L. Vallandigham. It was the *cause célèbre* of the Lincoln administration. This handsome Ohio politician, whose fiery yet plausible oratory has already been noted, was the leading spirit among Northern antiwar Democrats. His strength—or power for mischief—lay in his handsome appearance, eloquence, marked ability, fearless defiance, apparent readiness to go all the way to martyrdom, and vigorous championship of civil rights. He also had points of weakness or of irritation. He denounced the war as a method of maintaining the Union so vigorously that he was accused—unjustly, he insisted—of being opposed to the Union. The effect of his agitation was to arouse civil disturbance, promote disobedience, discourage enlistment, confuse the public mind, and spread disunity. It was alleged that he was a conscious and deliberate instrument of the Confederacy. He denied this, but at least his course of conduct tended toward breaking down all organized forcible opposition to Jefferson Davis and the Confederate movement.

It has sometimes been made to appear that the whole prewar problem of peace instead of war could be centered in Vallandigham. Vallandigham would have avoided war. So would Lincoln. But Vallandigham's accusation that Lincoln and his friends were wholly responsible for the war, and that when the Union was broken nothing (by way of using armies) should be done about it, was too oversimplified, too plausible and fluent, to be taken as the last word. The cause of possible Union-saving conciliation in the great sectional crisis is to be judged in terms of all its broad and complicated factors, not in terms of Vallandigham's speechmaking or wartime anti-Lincoln agitation.

I

As of 1863 Vallandigham's career had been that of lawyer, legislator, officer in the Ohio militia, Democratic organizer, and orator. He had served in Congress before the war and during the early part of the conflict, but had not been reëlected in 1862, though the congressional election of that year had gone against the Republicans, especially in Ohio, whose delegation to the lower house of the Thirty-Eighth Congress (1863–65) was predominantly Democratic.

Putting together his statements in Congress and on the stump, in resolutions, conversations, and convention deliberations, Vallandigham's avowed views were substantially as follows. He favored, as he said, Union, peace, and harmony of the sections. Before the war he desired, not disruptive sectionalism and conflict, but friendliness toward "our brethren of the South." He considered the Democratic party the best upholder of the Union, favored it as an instrument of progress in the West, and deeply deplored the prospect, at Charleston in 1860, that the party would be split apart. As a result of such a split, if it should occur, he foresaw "one of the bloodiest civil wars on record, the magnitude of which no one can estimate." [1] He took the ground that he was not for the North nor for the South, but for the whole country, with emphasis on the hope-filled West. In the 1860 convention at Charleston Vallandigham had favored Douglas as the Democratic candidate who was most truly national. (This should not be taken as implying that his course in time of war was harmonious with the views of Douglas or of like-minded men.)

He looked to the day when Americans should hear no more of sections. He despised abolitionists because of the disintegrating effect of their agitation, and he opposed the Republicans as the Northern party of disunion. Put an end to the Republicans and abolitionists, he urged, and "the extreme Southern pro-slavery 'fire-eating' organization of the Cotton States (its offspring) will expire in three months."

---

[1] James L. Vallandigham, *A Life of Clement L. Vallandigham,* 138.

(This, to say the least, was rather an underestimate of the intensity of proslavery, Yankee-hating opinion, and of its dominance in the South.) In November 1860 he declared that, as congressman, "he never would . . . vote one dollar of money whereby one drop of American blood should be shed in a civil war." [2]

When the war came, which he blamed on the Republicans and the abolitionists,[3] he declared that "the Union as it was must be restored," that the conflict must not be perverted into a war of subjugation or conquest, that extinguishing any of the states or moving "toward the declaring of a dictator" would be a "high crime." [4]

With such background and views the Ohio agitator proceeded according to form as the war progressed, denouncing the Lincoln administration for promoting an unjust war, for refusing reasonable peace, destroying the Union of the fathers, and suppressing fundamental civil liberties.

Throughout the Vallandigham subject there are two kinds of emphasis, and in the stress of these opposite contentions one can visualize much of the internal civil war in the North. Newspapers friendly to the agitator made his statements appear patriotic, pro-Union, orderly, and proper as dignified protest. On the other hand, citizens of Butler County, Ohio, who had heard him on the twelfth of October 1861, believed his speech calculated "to render aid and comfort to the traitors now in hostility against the Government of the United States." In its general tone, they reported, it "was just such a speech as might very well have been addressed to and been applauded by an audience of rebels." The arrest and "safe-keeping" of Vallandigham was therefore recommended by these protesting citizen many months before that arrest occurred.[5]

S. S. Cox, a Democratic colleague of a different type and trend from Vallandigham, said: "No man has been more thoroughly misunderstood and abused than Clement L. Vallandigham, of Ohio. There never was a man in public life who had a greater devotion to the Constitution and institutions of his country than he. His motto

---

[2] *Ibid.*, 141.

[3] The concept that Republicans were one with the abolitionists, though many earnest Americans would have wished to have it so, was quite contrary to the whole practical emphasis of Republican managers and leaders. Incoming letters in the Lincoln papers (R. T. L. Collection)—e. g., for 1858—make this abundantly clear.

[4] *Ann. Cyc.*, 1863, 234–235.

[5] *Offic. Rec.*, 2 ser. II, 128.

was to do right, to trust in God, in truth, and the people." [6] By contrast, the following was said by Roscoe Conkling of those who defended Vallandigham: "Now I am entirely of opinion . . . that we ought not . . . even to seem . . . to give one single inch to the rant and fustian and clamor of these men. . . . They would array popular passion and prejudice against this Administration, ... I know they are hypocrites and they know they are." [7]

II

The Vallandigham case arose in the following manner. General Burnside, commanding the "Department of the Ohio" with headquarters at Cincinnati, issued an order, April 13, 1863, which was intended to suppress Northern disloyal agitation. In this document ("General Orders, No. 38") the commanding general announced that "all persons found within our lines who commit acts for the benefit of the enemies of our country will be tried as spies or traitors, and, if convicted, will suffer death." To this he added: "The habit of declaring sympathy for the enemy will not be allowed in this department. Persons committing such offenses will be at once arrested, with a view to being tried as above stated, or sent beyond our lines into the lines of their friends." [1]

In deliberate and open defiance of this order, Vallandigham delivered a fiery speech on May 1, 1863, at Mount Vernon, Ohio. The occasion was a rousing Democratic mass meeting with the trimmings of a popular gathering—decorated wagons in procession, hickory poles, American flags, and heads cut from copper pennies.

Four days after the speech General Burnside caused the orator to be arrested at his home in Dayton, Ohio. A military commission was then convened under Burnside's order and the prisoner was haled before that tribunal. The charge against him was that of publicly expressing sympathy for those in arms against the United States, "declaring disloyal sentiments," and violating Order No. 38. In the specification to support the charge various phrases of the Mount Vernon speech were presented.

---

[6] Cox, *Three Decades,* 80–81.

[7] Alfred R. Conkling, *Life and Letters of Roscoe Conkling,* 192–193.

[1] *Offic. Rec.,* 1 ser. XXIII, pt. 2, 237.

As a lawyer's problem the Vallandigham case involved three stages: (1) trial, conviction, and sentence by the military commission; (2) Federal court hearing on habeas corpus petition; (3) the proceeding, months later, before the Supreme Court of the United States.

At the military trial Vallandigham offered no plea, contending that such a court had no jurisdiction to try him, but a plea of "not guilty" was entered for him by direction of the commission.[2] The proceedings of the commission were not those of a drumhead court-martial; neither were they according to the standards of a court with due process of law. The accused was allowed counsel, permitted personally to cross-examine witnesses, and given the advantage of compulsory attendance of witnesses in his favor. If, however, a regular court had been trying him because of that speech, they could have found no statutory basis for indicting or convicting him. Testimony by officers in civilian clothes concerning what was said in the speech was followed by Vallandigham's own cross examination of these witnesses. It is in this testimony and the questions and answers that followed it, that we have the record, such as it is, of the famous speech. As J. F. Rhodes has written, these "are the only reports of the speech, and are of little value as historical evidence, for detached sentences and isolated remarks fail to give the tenor of a discourse." Rhodes adds that the address was sharply anti-Lincoln, and "went as near giving 'aid and comfort to the rebellion' as any talk could that proceeded from a good lawyer who knew the law." [3]

According to this testimony, Vallandigham denounced the wicked and cruel war, denied that restoration of the Union was the purpose, and asserted that the Union could have been saved without war if certain reasonable plans had been adopted or French mediation accepted. The administration, he was quoted as saying, was seeking to suppress public meetings. He expressed contempt for such power as was indicated in General Order No. 38; he trampled on it; he did not ask Tod (governor of Ohio) or Lincoln or Burnside for his right to speak. He was resolved never to submit to a military dictator prohibiting free discussion. The people, he allegedly said, should remember that this was not a war for the preservation of the Union, but "a wicked abolition war." It was "a war [he was quoted as saying] for the libera-

---

[2] *Ibid.*, 2 ser. V, 635.

[3] Rhodes, *Hist. of the U. S.*, IV, 247.

tion of the blacks and the enslavement of the whites." As for him, he would "never be a priest to minister upon the altar upon which his country was being sacrificed."

Other testimony or summaries of the speech exhibited further statements. The country had been told that the war would be terminated in three months, then in nine months, then again in a year, but there was still no prospect of its being ended. Richmond was not taken, nor Charleston nor Vicksburg; "the Mississippi was not opened and would not be so long as there was cotton on its banks to be stolen or . . . contractor or officers to enrich." The administration had been rebuked in the election of November 1862; "no more volunteers could be had." Such were a few of the orator's reported assertions. As to the tone of his speech, it may be judged by quoted epithets or catchwords—"King Lincoln," "Lincoln's minions" (army officers), and the like.[4]

Those who wish to follow the proceedings in detail (which cannot be done here) would be interested to read Vallandigham's examination of hostile witnesses. In that cross examination the following points were brought out by the accused, being admitted by witnesses: Vallandigham, in urging peace, did not favor disunion; he believed the military commission unconstitutional; persons if guilty of treason ought to be tried by a judicial court and a jury. It was admitted that one of the witnesses made no notes of the speech, but "made minutes" of the discourse after returning to his hotel. S. S. Cox, the well known Democratic congressman who had been a speaker at the same meeting as Vallandigham, testified that Vallandigham applied no "epithet" to Burnside, that he opposed any attempts to restore peace by a separation of the states, that he denounced applause given to Jefferson Davis, and that he "counseled no resistance except such as might be had at the ballot-box."[5]

A curious aspect of the case was that on May 6, while Vallandigham was in prison awaiting trial, Cox, according to his own statement, "was informed by General Burnside that Mr. Vallandigham would not be convicted" and was "requested to so advise Mrs. Vallandigham, who was in great distress." Another queer feature was that, by some mistake of reporting, Cox's words were given "as the words of Val-

4 *Offic. Rec.*, 2 ser. V, 633 ff., esp. 636, 641.

5 *Ibid.*, 2 ser. V, 642–644.

landigham." [6] The evidence was not clear as to what the prisoner had said about the conscription act. Cox testified that, to the best of his recollection, Vallandigham "did not say a word about the conscription." He added that reference was made to French conscription, by Cox himself, not by the accused.[7]

III

The military commission found Vallandigham guilty—i. e., guilty "Of the charge—" [1] and sentenced him to be imprisoned during the continuance of the war. The proceedings, findings, and sentence were confirmed by General Burnside. It was evident that this was not an Ohio matter or a Burnside matter only, but a serious problem, and an embarrassing one, for President Lincoln and his administration. Embarrassment increased as the case grew more complicated, and on May 29, 1863, Burnside sent the President a despatch referring to differences between himself and the administration. Convinced, he said, that his action had been a "source of embarrassment" to Lincoln, but unchanged in his views, except that he preferred increased instead of diminished rigor, he wrote that he would "be glad to be relieved" if the public service required it.[2] To this Lincoln answered by wire: "Your despatch of to-day received. When I shall wish to supersede you I will let you know. All the cabinet regretted the necessity of arresting, for instance, Vallandigham—some perhaps, doubting, that there was a real necessity for it—but, being done, all were for seeing you through with it." [3]

Under the circumstances Lincoln felt that he could not release Vallandigham,[4] whose arrest he would not have approved. Neither

---

[6] Cox, *Three Decades*, 83. [7] *Offic. Rec.*, 2 ser. V, 643.

[1] He was found not guilty as to certain words attributed to him in the "specification," but guilty "Of the charge." The evidence was not clear as to the words used. *Ibid.*, 2 ser. V, 646.

[2] *Offic. Rec.*, 2 ser. V, 717.

[3] Lincoln to Burnside (telegram in cipher), May 29, 1863, photostat, A. Lincoln Assoc.

[4] Certain writers have concluded that Lincoln made a mistake in not simply releasing Vallandigham, since he disapproved of the arrest and did not intend to enforce the sentence of imprisonment. Had this release been effected, the Ohioan would have had to make a contest to obtain the Democratic nomination for governor of Ohio in 1863. As it was, delegates who disagreed with him voted for him because he had become a kind of symbol or test case for important rights, and he was nominated by acclama-

did he wish the sentence of the military commission enforced. Commuting the sentence, as was his presidential function, he directed through Stanton that the orator be sent to the headquarters of Rosecrans "to be put . . . beyond our military lines." In case of his return, he was "to be arrested and kept in close custody for the term specified in his sentence." Rosecrans was notified by Stanton (by order of the President) that the prisoner was to be put beyond Union lines, "and if he returns within your command you arrest and keep him in close custody during the war or until further orders." [5]

Turning the pages of Vallandigham's voluminous biography written by his brother, we read of the exile's ride under military escort and flag of truce to the Confederate outposts, his "proposition" to General Rosecrans that he be allowed to address the Union soldiers, his prediction that by his words they would be moved to "tear Lincoln . . . to pieces," and his nomination for the governorship of Ohio on the Democratic ticket. Reading further, we learn of his escape to Canada after a dash through the blockade, his sojourn at Windsor, his addresses "to the people" in which he rebuked the "weak despots at Washington," his elaborate reply to visiting students from the University of Michigan (one wonders whether the students did not regard the affair as a lark), and his determination to "recover his liberties or perish in the attempt." Under a Falstaffian disguise, aided by a thick mustache and a large pillow, he returned to the States. Then he threw off the disguise and participated prominently in the screaming campaign of 1864.[6] After this return from Elba his speeches were as violent as before, but Lincoln's sense of humor was still in working order and he allowed Vallandigham to go unmolested. The terms of the banishment, and the specific orders in the case, called for reimprisonment in case of return, but Vallandigham in jail would have done more harm to the Lincoln government than Vallandigham free.

Since it was a matter of opinion, Lincoln made it so. Opinion was allowed to take its sway. A clear test of free opinion came in 1863 in

---

tion. G. H. Porter writes: "Much better would it have been, had Mr. Lincoln rescinded the sentence of the military commission and allowed Vallandigham to go free . . . ." *Ohio Politics during the Civil War*, 177. See also, for criticism of Lincoln, Rhodes, *Hist. of U.S.*, IV, 250–255.

5 *Offic. Rec.*, 2 ser. V, 657.

6 J. L. Vallandigham, *Life of Vallandigham*, 297–365.

the defeat of Vallandigham for governor of Ohio. In that election Vallandigham and his friends gave all they had in appeals to the people; the people voted; Lincoln's Union policy was sustained and Vallandigham defeated.[7] The 1864 situation still remained. That is another story, to be treated when it comes up; it too involved a sharp defeat of all that Vallandigham stood for, but it was a defeat with Vallandigham in the open, which made it all the more effective.

A curious and remarkable feature of the Vallandigham case appears when we consider the part played by Captain J. Madison Cutts, a Democrat, a brother-in-law of Stephen A. Douglas, and an officer on Burnside's staff. He, of all men, was the judge advocate at the military trial—thus becoming the chief instrument in the actual prosecution—yet he strongly disapproved of the whole proceeding. What is even more surprising is that this same Cutts—a minor figure who gains importance because of certain personal difficulties and especially because of an exquisite reprimand by Lincoln—went so far as to send the President the following telegram: "To His Excellency Abraham Lincoln President of the United States (Private & in cipher.) I advise you to relieve Major Genl A. E. Burnside from command of the Department of the Ohio *immediately*, by Telegraph. He has been plausibly pressing a policy hostile and adverse to your wishes and instructions, and those of the Secretary of War and General in Chief." Cutts added: "Order 38 has kindled the fires of hatred and contention —and Burnside is foolishly and unwisely excited and if continued in command will disgrace himself, you and the country, as he did at Fredericksburg. . . . I am absolutely right. Douglas was my preceptor." [8]

Later, on July 26, 1863, Cutts wrote to Lincoln: "In my opinion that policy of Genl. Burnside's which developed itself without your previous knowledge or consent, in the trial of Mr Vallandigham has inflicted a lasting injury upon *your administration* . . . . I do now state that the first step should be the immediate withdrawal of Ambrose E. Burnside from the command of this Department. I have always been opposed to General Burnside's policy. . . . I was forced to enforce it, but determined I would do so with as much judgment as possible, and so as to inflict as little harm as possible."

---

[7] See below, chap. xi, espec. pp. 273–274. [8] R. T. L. Coll., 25018–19.

Cutts filled his letter with further details. Then he wrote: "Ambrose E. Burnside has refused to do that which would have remedied the *evils of his own creation.* There *was perfect quiet, peace* and good feeling among all parties before he came to this Department. He still persists in the same *bad policy.* . . . Who is the President of the United States, and what are his duties, his power, and his authority? I again advise you to send some thoroughly brave man to take his place—and I have strong reasons for recommending Hooker. I pronounce myself a determined unwavering War Democrat." [9] Just how much attention Lincoln paid to this advice of Cutts is not known. We know, however, that Burnside did not long remain in Cincinnati. He was shifted to command of combat operations in east Tennessee, and by the first week in September we find him established with headquarters at Knoxville. His unimportant successor in the command of the Department of the Ohio was General John G. Foster.

IV

To return to the course of events in the Vallandigham case, after the famous prisoner had been found guilty and sentenced by the military commission, the next step was a civil proceeding, a hearing before Judge Humphrey H. Leavitt of the United States circuit court at Cincinnati, on an application for a writ of habeas corpus. Here was a problem: Could a Federal court review, and possibly overrule, the proceedings of a military commission? If military rule was carried to the point of arresting, trying, and sentencing a civilian for the expression of certain opinions, could the civil courts intervene?

In this habeas corpus proceeding for Vallandigham it was argued that the writ should be issued "as of right" (or as "of course") at once, and that the hearing, including the response of General Burnside, should occur "when the body of the prisoner should be brought into court." This meant that the purpose of the writ was not necessarily to release the prisoner—gruesomely referred to as the "body"—but to have a hearing to see whether he should be ordered released. Instead of this manner of handling the case, Judge Leavitt decided to "hear

[9] *Ibid.* (eight-page letter), 25144–48. In studying the activities of Cutts in relation to the Vallandigham affair and other matters, the author has made use of an extensive file in the National Archives.

the argument on the application"—i. e., to hold up his decision whether the writ should issue until the answer—usually considered a response to the writ itself—should be presented.[1]

Burnside submitted a lengthy answer. We were in a state of war, he pointed out. Criticisms of the government were demoralizing the army. It was his duty to prevent or stop it. An enemy delivering speeches to demoralize the troops would be "tried and hung if found guilty." Why should our public men be spared? The emergency required suppressive measures. The constituted authorities had the power "to inaugurate a war policy," and he was determined to support "their policy." Fear as to the people "losing their liberties" was but "the cry of demagogues." The army was part of the people and was educated in the love of civil liberty. It was not to be feared that our "citizen soldiery" would ever support a "military despotism." On this basis Burnside justified order No. 38 and the military proceedings concerning Vallandigham. As to the trial by the military commission, the general merely alluded to it without indicating its outcome. "The result of that trial [he stated] is now in my hands." [2]

In denying the writ of habeas corpus Judge Leavitt did not consider it necessary to "notice the charges" directed against the prisoner; nor was the court informed whether he had been condemned or acquitted on those charges. "Whether the military commission [he said] . . . was legally constituted and had jurisdiction of the case is not a question before this court." He pointed to the desperate crisis in the country and the constitutional power "to arrest persons who by their mischievous acts of disloyalty . . . endanger the military operations . . . ." "The sole question [he continued] is whether the arrest was legal, and as before remarked its legality depends on the necessity . . . for making it, and of that necessity . . . this court cannot judicially determine."

Justice Leavitt's main purpose seemed to be to indicate the things he could not decide. He considered that the situation was beyond the judiciary, and as he thought rightly so. In contrast, Taney had considered that an arbitrary arrest was beyond the judiciary not as a matter of right, but only of superior force. Habeas corpus, according to Leavitt, ought not to impede the military, even if that were

---

1 *Offic. Rec.*, 2 ser. V, 574, 576 ff.

2 *Ibid.*, 575–576.

possible. He could not "judicially pronounce the order . . . for the arrest of Vallandigham as a nullity." [3] He found no sufficient ground for granting the writ.

If as noted above the writ had issued as of right, that would have been similar to judicial approval of a motion to begin the hearing of a case. To institute a hearing is the purpose of the writ. In such a hearing the judge would consider the military officer's answer or "return." If that answer should prove satisfactory, no further judicial action would follow. Should the judge find no adequate basis for holding the prisoner he could order his release; if, then, the officer in charge should prove contumacious, a possible procedure would be an order holding him guilty of contempt of court. Lincoln's orders had not stated that the writ was suspended; it was rather the "privilege of the Writ," which is the wording of the United States Constitution. Presidential orders seemed to allow that the writ should issue, but that executive suspension of the privilege should constitute an adequate answer. This manner of handling the military "return" was later specifically prescribed in the President's instruction of September 17, 1863. Instead of upholding Leavitt's interpretation—i.e., that presidential suspension meant that the writ should not issue—this document by Lincoln indicated exactly the opposite. Lincoln's instruction was: "Please order each military officer of the United States, that, whenever he shall have in his custody any person, by the authority of the United States and any writ of *habeas corpus* shall be served upon him, commanding him to produce such person before any court or judge, he, the said military officer, make known to the court or judge issuing such writ, by a proper return thereto, that he holds such person by the authority of the President . . . ." This instruction also directed that the officer refuse to "produce such person according [to] said writ" and that any enforcing effort by the judge be resisted by force.[4]

If the procedure thus indicated by the President had been followed in the Vallandigham case, Burnside still could have given the answer which he did submit, but it would have been done as a "return" to the writ, which is the usual custom, instead of a military

---

[3] *Ibid.*, 576–584.

[4] The original, all in Lincoln's hand, is in the National Archives, Washington (WR RG 110: Pro. Mar. Bur., vol. II, H 319 [1863]); photostat, A. Lincoln Assoc.

statement bearing upon the application. The point is that it belongs to the judge to decide whether a judicial inquiry shall be made. The layman would hardly be aware of this point, but to a defense lawyer or a legal authority it would have more than technical significance. Lincoln's instruction showed his proper understanding of the law.

V

It is hard to convey an idea of the immense outcry in the country occasioned by Lincoln's policy of arbitrary arrests. Editors, lawyers, agitators, politicians, generals, members of Congress, poured out a stream of protest. John M. Palmer of Illinois, referring to the administration's "letters de cachet," was shocked at the power claimed (in January 1862) by the secretary of state, which "simply converts this Constitutional Republic into a despotism." [1] There was extended discussion in Congress. Senator Bayard of Delaware asked whether sympathy was "to be the ground on which a man is to be hung." "Suppose [he said] a man believes that the restoration of the Government . . . over the revolted States cannot be effected by war; the Administration may say that is an evidence of sympathy with rebellion, and hang a man for that!" [2] (The administration, of course, was doing nothing of the sort. There were no such hangings.) Sherman of Ohio said that "we cannot afford these arrests." [3] Cox of Ohio, always vigorous in denunciation of what he considered the despotic acts of the executive branch, presented in the House of Representatives a resolution "that the House . . . do hereby condemn all such arrests . . . as a usurpation of power [etc.]." By vote of 80 to 40 his resolution was laid on the table.[4] Similar resolutions were voted down. Senator Latham of California said: "I see no necessity for trampling upon the Constitution in order to maintain it. I see no necessity for violating all law . . . in order to preserve the laws." [5]

Though arrests were military, it is not to be supposed that outstanding generals always approved of them. Seizure of persons by military authority at Shawneetown, Illinois, for example, elicited protest from U. S. Grant in 1861.[6] John Pope, who later commanded

1 John M. Palmer to Lyman Trumbull (postscript), Jan. 1862, Trumbull MSS.

2 *Cong. Globe,* 37 Cong., 3 sess., 19 (Dec. 8, 1862). 3 *Ibid.,* 30 (Dec. 9, 1862).

4 *Ibid.,* 2 (Dec. 1, 1862). 5 *Ibid.,* 37 Cong., 2 sess., 95 (Dec. 16, 1861).

6 Protest against military arrests, signed by U. S. Grant and others, Nov. 5, 1861. Reavis MSS., Chicago Hist. Soc.

the principal Union army in the East, wrote in December 1861: "I dread to witness the rapid strides toward despotism which we have made during the past six months." [7]

Nor should it be supposed that complaints as to summary military procedures in disregard of civil guarantees came only from extreme agitators, partisans, or men of the recognizable "anti-Lincoln" type. When Lincoln had issued his suspending proclamation of September 24, 1862, Benjamin R. Curtis, former justice of the United States Supreme Court, strongly assailed the President in a pamphlet, *Executive Power,* published in 1862 in Boston.[8] Newspaper criticism on the same theme was emphatic. Historians have noted that the suspending edict was a factor in the setback to Lincoln and the Republican party in the congressional election of 1862. Lincoln's oldtime law partner at Springfield, John Todd Stuart, considered the proclamation, along with the emancipation edict, "most unfortunate." Senator Fessenden of Maine was quoted as saying that "the proclamation suspending the privilege . . . of Hab: Corp: in the loyal states where no insurrection existed was an exercise of despotic power which he [Lincoln] did not possess, and very dangerous." A similar view was held by old Thomas Ewing, who "said the Presidents emancipation and Habeas Corpus proclamations had ruined the Republican party in Ohio." [9]

Lincoln's dilemma in the Vallandigham case—his disapproval of Burnside's course weighed against the practical consequences of overruling and weakening the military power—was shown by his own statements, and by the record of cabinet discussion. When the incident came up in cabinet meeting, according to Welles, "All regretted the arrest, but, having been made, every one wished he had been sent over the lines to the Rebels . . . ." [10]

A meeting of Union-supporting Democrats was held at Albany, New York, on May 16, 1863, while the case was hot. The Democrats, so the meeting resolved, had loyally supported the war and had suffered great sacrifices as evidence of their patriotism, but liberties of the citizen must be recognized and the Constitution maintained. In

---

[7] John Pope to Lyman Trumbull, Otterville, Mo., Dec. 31, 1861 (typed), Trumbull MSS.

[8] *Lincoln the President,* II, 175–176.

[9] For the views of Stuart, Fessenden and Ewing, see Browning, *Diary,* I, 585, 588, 592 (Nov. 12, Nov. 28, Dec. 5, 1862).

[10] Welles, *Diary,* I, 306 (May 19, 1863).

view of these principles the meeting denounced "the recent assumption of a military commander to seize and try a citizen of Ohio, Clement L. Vallandigham, for no other reason than words addressed to a public meeting . . . ."[11] The document was directed to the Vallandigham case, but was in fact a protest against the whole policy of arbitrary arrests.

This Albany meeting drew from Lincoln one of those dignified, carefully worded statements addressed to a person or occasion, but intended as a kind of state paper. In a long letter (to Erastus Corning and Others, June 12, 1863) the President used the language of utmost courtesy toward those who were criticising his policy. He noted their patriotic promise to support "our common Government and country." If they differed with him, it was not as to purpose, but only as to "the choice of means." From this beginning the President launched into a defense of his policy concerning military arrests. Enemies of the government, he argued, were seeking to destroy the Constitution while relying on its guarantee to protect them. Civil courts, suited for quiet times and for trials of individuals "on charges of crimes well defined in the law" were "utterly incompetent" to deal with the problems arising out of the existing rebellion and the serious threat posed by immense numbers of insurgents and their sympathizers. The Constitution itself, permitting the setting aside of the habeas corpus privilege "in case of rebellion," attested "the understanding of those who made the Constitution that ordinary courts . . . are inadequate" to such an emergency, and that in such a crisis the regular safeguards could be suspended.

The arrests, he noted, were not for treason nor for defined crimes committed. They were "preventive" rather than "vindictive." The government had been lenient, as shown by the fact that notable leaders "now occupying the very highest places in the rebel war service" had been allowed to go free though it had been within the power of the government to arrest them. As to Vallandigham, Lincoln refused to admit that he was arrested "for no other reason than words addressed to a public meeting." He was seized, said the President, because of his hostility to the war for the Union, and because he was "laboring, with some effect, to prevent the raising of troops; to en-

11 McPherson, *Rebellion,* 163.

courage desertions from the army; and to leave the rebellion without an adequate military force to suppress it."

Lincoln was dealing with the fact of war, and with the need of military force to suppress the rebellion. These ugly facts were not agreeable to him, nor was the arrest of Vallandigham. But he assumed that the Albany meeting was in favor of using the army to overcome the enemy and maintain the Union. Armies "cannot be maintained unless desertion shall be punished by the severe penalty of death." Then followed Lincoln's famous question: "Must I shoot a simple-minded soldier boy who deserts, while I must not touch a hair of a wily agitator who induces him to desert? This is none the less injurious when effected by getting a father, or brother, or friend, into a public meeting, and there working upon his feelings till he is persuaded to write the soldier boy that he is fighting in a bad cause, for a wicked Administration of a contemptible Government, too weak to arrest and punish him if he shall desert."

Lincoln believed certain things to be constitutional in cases of rebellion or invasion which are not applicable "in times of profound peace and public security." The Constitution itself made this distinction. He then added a point which showed that he was sensitive on the subject of civil rights and felt as keenly as anyone the necessity of preserving those rights in normal times. "Nor am I able," he said, "to appreciate the danger . . . that the American people will, by means of military arrests during the rebellion, lose the right of public discussion, the liberty of speech and the press, the law of evidence, trial by jury, and *habeas corpus* throughout the indefinite peaceful future which I trust lies before them, any more than I am able to believe that a man could contract so strong an appetite for emetics during temporary illness as to persist in feeding upon them during the remainder of his healthful life."

It "gave me pain," said Lincoln, "when I learned that Mr. Vallandigham had been arrested—that is, I was pained that there should have seemed to be a necessity for arresting him—and . . . it will afford me great pleasure to discharge him so soon as I can, by any means, believe the public safety will not suffer by it." As the war progressed, Lincoln believed that opinion and action, then in confusion, would "take shape and fall into more regular channels." In that case he thought that the necessity for strong dealing would decrease. He closed on a conciliatory note. "I have every reason to desire that it should cease altogether, and far from the least is my regard for the opinions and wishes of those who like the meeting at Albany, declare their purpose to sustain the Government . . . ." [12]

VI

The Vallandigham case ultimately reached the Supreme Court of the United States on a petition (for a writ of *certiorari*) to review the sentence of the military commission.[1] The opinion (Ex parte Vallandigham) was announced on February 15, 1864.[2] In Vallandigham's behalf it was urged by his counsel, George E. Pugh, that military commissions have a limited function and that this one had exceeded its jurisdiction in trying a civilian unconnected with the armed forces. The argument against Vallandigham was presented by Judge Advocate General Holt, and this argument became the basis for the Court's decision handed down by Justice Wayne.[3] The substance of the opinion was a denial of authority in the premises. A military commission was not a "court" within the meaning of existing laws for the Federal judiciary. The Supreme Court, therefore, "cannot . . . originate a

12 This is the reply as published at the time. McPherson, *Hist. of the Rebellion,* 163–167. The text in Nicolay and Hay, *Works,* VIII, 298–314, shows only minor differences; Lincoln's original draft (R. T. L. Coll., 23995–24071) is substantially the same as the final published version, variations being minor matters of form with one exception. In his finished letter, in the statement that the arrest of Vallandigham gave him pain, Lincoln inserted the words: "that is, I was pained that there should have seemed to be a necessity for arresting him." In adding this qualification, indeed in the whole letter, the President was attempting the most careful and precise definition of his difficult position as a man appreciative of civil rights, and at the same time as chief of state in a time of great turbulence and danger.

1 Attorney General Bates, who had a low opinion of Vallandigham and who supported the President's power of military arrest without civil process, objected strongly to the proceedings before the Supreme Court. He considered the motion for *certiorari* "so utterly without law & so clearly against law" that he found it "hard to guess the object, . . ." "It may be only a peg on which to hang a denunciatory speech against the administration generally & the war in particular." Bates to Stanton, Attorney General's Office, Jan. 19, 1864, Stanton MSS., 54025. Lawyers continually differ, but in view of the Milligan decision of 1866 one may question Bates's air of finality in saying that the motion was "so clearly against law."

2 68 U. S. 243.

3 In "The Supreme Court during the Civil War" (doctoral dissertation, Univ. of Ill., 1940) David M. Silver has shown how, in the Vallandigham opinion, Justice Wayne not only took his arguments, but also his phraseology, from Holt's brief. This is shown conclusively by parallel columns.

writ of *certiorari* to review . . . the proceedings of a military commission."

In the published report it is stated that Nelson, Grier, and Field "concurred in the result" of the opinion by Wayne and that Miller, having not been present at the argument (which occurred on January 22, 1864), took no part.[4] Of the ten justices on the Court in this period, all except Taney were present, as shown by the unpublished minute book, on February 15, 1864. These nine were Wayne, Catron, Nelson, Grier, Clifford, Swayne, Miller, Davis, Field. The statement that Nelson, Grier, and Field concurred in the result signifies that they agreed in what the Court did—i. e., in denying the petition—though not concurring in all of Wayne's wording; it should not be taken to signify that none of the other justices participated. The proper inference—so the author is reliably informed—is that all participated in the decision except Taney and Miller, and that those not mentioned as having done otherwise (Catron, Clifford, Swayne, Davis) presumably concurred with Wayne. There is no record that any justice dissented; had there been any dissent, it would have been recorded. Just what were the reasons that caused Nelson, Grier, and Field to concur only in the result remains an unanswered question. They did not, as did various justices in the Dred Scott case, submit individual concurring opinions.[5]

The effect of this action, or non-action, by the highest court of justice was that the military proceeding was sustained by the simple process of denying the right to examine into it. The merits of the case—the charges against the prisoner, his guilt under those charges, the competence of the military commission, and the appropriateness of the sentence—were not considered. Arguments against the fairness of a proceeding, though not refuted, become unavailing when a court decides that it is without authority to act.

One should notice the cumulative effect of the Wayne decision when added to the earlier Leavitt decision. Neither case recognized any judicial function to inquire into the essential issue or the substance of the question. Leavitt was not concerned whether the military

---

[4] 68 U. S. 254.

[5] In studying how the justices stood, the author has been greatly assisted by an informative letter (with a copy from the minute book) from Helen Newman, librarian of the Supreme Court of the United States, July 12, 1951.

authority had acted legally or illegally. It had acted, and nothing judicially could be done about it. Wayne's position was not that the military commission had acted rightly, but that there was no rightful jurisdiction on the part of the Supreme Court to supply a remedy. And all these disclaimers on the part of Federal justices, when traced to the origin of the case, pertained to a military prosecution which was not the action of the President and was not approved by him, but was rather the order of one of the generals—a man, by the way, who did not long continue to retain the confidence of the Washington administration in his command of the Department of the Ohio.

In two respects the contemporary view of the Vallandigham case was faulty if judged by the long-range view. In the first place, the proceeding against Vallandigham was inevitably associated with "the Executive," despite the fact that the arrest and the trial were not correctly attributable to the President's true intention. The press of the day did not fail to note the significance of the Vallandigham decision as a factor upholding the arm of the President. The New York *Times,* observing that the "Copperheads" had not hitherto abused the Court, seeming to imagine "that it had proclivities in their favor," remarked that there had been no warrant for this supposition. "In no single instance," declared the *Times,* "has its opinion been at variance with the executive action of the President." [6]

In the next place, the whole point of law which was announced in the decision soon became outmoded. It took but two years (and especially the ending of the war) to demonstrate that the Vallandigham decision did not set the pattern of ruling law in the United States. The Court's position on the principle involved was reversed (1866) in the famous Milligan case. In October 1864 Milligan and his associates were placed under arrest in Indiana, tried on the charge of conspiracy and membership in disloyal organizations, and found guilty. Milligan was sentenced to be hanged and the day fixed at May 19, 1865. Execution was suspended, and in 1866 the Supreme Court, through Justice David Davis, announced a decision which was the opposite of that given in the Vallandigham case. "If there was law to justify this military trial," said the Court, "it is not our province to interfere; if there was not, it is our duty to declare the nullity of the

[6] Editorial, Feb. 16, 1864, p. 4, c. 3. (Chief Justice Taney's opinion in the Merryman case had not been that of the Supreme Court.)

whole proceedings." "Martial law [so the opinion continued] cannot arise from a *threatened* invasion. The necessity must be actual and present; the invasion real, such as effectually closes the courts and deposes the civil administration. . . . Martial rule can never exist where the courts are open, and in the proper and unobstructed exercise of their jurisdiction." [7]

One does not need to defend the Ohio politician for all that he was doing, nor agree with him in his attacks upon Lincoln, in order to perceive and emphasize the foremost point in the whole Vallandigham case—namely, the precious principle of freedom of speech. Not that freedom of speech has no limits, but the Lincoln practice was to permit such freedom in general, even to the point of tolerating the most vociferous and bitter denunciation of the government. Lincoln had no need to place reliance upon such methods as those of General Burnside. Arrests for speech making were so far from the regular procedure under Lincoln that aside from Vallandigham there was hardly an instance of an arrest for that reason. Furthermore, in the latter part of the war, even though the reëlection of Lincoln was at stake, the speaker was unmolested. There were honest protests against arrests in the war period and of the denial of habeas corpus, but that is not to say that all the excessive complaints of Vallandigham and his followers were justified. In a dictatorship Vallandigham would have been far more severely treated. He would doubtless have been liquidated.

Going back over the decades, though opposite examples come to mind, it will be found that the curtailing of military power has had more emphasis than the stretching of army control. The time honored principle that the military power is subordinate to the civil was not forgotten by the Lincoln administration. This well known principle made all the more painful the many episodes under Lincoln which involved clashes of military with civil authority. It might be a local imbroglio or a tempest in a teapot, but at times the trouble reached great proportions, even threatening civil war behind the Union lines. A kind of *opera bouffe* conflict between Ward Lamon and General Wadsworth on the matter of slaves fleeing from Maryland into the District of Columbia, has been treated in an earlier volume.[8] Atten-

[7] *Ex parte* Milligan, 71 U. S. 119, 127.

[8] *Lincoln the President,* II, 134–135.

tion has also been given to the Frémont incident in Missouri in 1861, in which the general imposed such military severity upon the lives and property of civilians that his orders had to be overruled by the President, the more so because Frémont had exceeded his proper military authority, had issued orders outside his competence, and had shown a tendency to appeal for popular favor in opposition to the government at Washington. The issue was not merely the question of emancipation—a matter of high policy which the President was keeping in his own hands—but the serious implications of an order that said in effect that Frémont was the state and that the military power superseded the civil.[9] If one were to follow up this matter of the stretching of military authority even with regard to one general only—let us say Benjamin F. Butler—he could fill a book which would show the unusual character, and the un-Lincolnian tone, of some of the commanders.

VII

As a subject of public discussion—in speeches, pamphlets, legal treatises, and editorials—the problem of arrests and of civil guarantees during Lincoln's presidency became one of the most notable controversies in American history. In the Congress the administration was defended by such men as Dixon of Connecticut, Wilson of Massachusetts, Hale of New Hampshire, and, to a certain extent, by Browning of Illinois.[1] In and out of Congress the names of Cox, Pugh, and Vallandigham of Ohio, Voorhees of Indiana, Richardson and Singleton of Illinois, Seymour and Wood of New York, and Bayard of Delaware, come readily to mind among those who assailed Lincoln, but it is not feasible to enumerate the men of this group. The President's course was defended by the Philadelphia lawyer Horace Binney in an elaborate legal and historical treatise on habeas corpus,[2] and officially by Edward Bates, the attorney general. Bates's opinion was a legal essay of more than five thousand words, of which the keynote was the statement: "The power to do these things [suspend the habeas

[9] *Ibid.*, II, 16–23.

[1] *Ann. Cyc.*, 1862, 285; *ibid.*, 1863, 236; Browning, *Diary*, I, 554 n.; *Cong. Globe*, 37 Cong., 2 sess., 2943–2953.

[2] Horace Binney, *The Privilege of the Writ of Habeas Corpus under the Constitution* (Phila., 1862).

corpus privilege, etc.] is in the hand of the President, placed there by the Constitution and the statute law as a sacred trust to be used by him in his best discretion in the performance of his great first duty—to preserve, protect and defend the Constitution. . . . He is the chief civil magistrate of the nation and being such *and because he is such* [author's italics] he is the constitutional Commander in Chief of the Army and Navy, and thus within the limits of the Constitution he rules in peace and commands in war and at this moment he is in the full exercise of all the functions belonging to both those characters." [8]

In the best statements in support of Lincoln's policy the militaristic type of argument was notably absent. The bearded, conservative attorney general was as unbelligerent an individual as one could find. In that very document supporting the executive policy of arrests which has just been quoted, Bates indicated that the main purpose of investing the President with the function of Commander in Chief was to uphold the supremacy of the civil over the military authority. It is not the military arm that controls the government, but the government that controls the military.

VIII

The Vallandigham case was not Burnside's only non-Lincolnian act of military severity. From his attack on freedom of speech he proceeded to a sensational move against freedom of the press. On June 1, 1863, he issued the following order: "On account of the repeated expression of disloyal and incendiary sentiments, the publication of the newspaper known as the Chicago Times is hereby suppressed." [1] There had been sore provocation. The paper had been praising Vallandigham, assailing Burnside, and bitterly criticizing the policy of prosecuting the war. It was described as "the foul and damnable reservoir which supplied the lesser sewers with political filth, falsehood, and treason." [2] The act of seizure occurred on June 3 when a detachment of soldiers from Camp Douglas under Captain Putnam occupied the *Times* establishment, stopped publication, and put the premises under guard.

---

[8] *Offic. Rec.*, 2 ser. II, 29; *Constitutional Problems Under Lincoln*, foreword to revised ed. (1951), xix.

[1] *Offic. Rec.*, 1 ser. XXIII, pt. 2, 381.

[2] Rhodes, *Hist. of the U. S.*, IV, 253 n.

The reaction of public opinion was immediate. Some Chicagoans favored the suppression, but a public meeting was held in the court-house square on the evening of the 3rd, where "Twenty thousand loyal citizens of Illinois" resolved that law was the bulwark of liberty, that infringement of freedom of the press was a blow at the Constitution, and that "military power is and must remain subordinate to the civil power." "If the 'Times' or any other public journal has exceeded the limits of lawful discussion or criticism," so read the resolution, "the civil tribunals, and they alone, are the competent and lawful judges of its crime." [3]

To make effective this appeal to the courts an application had been made to Judge Drummond of the United States circuit court at Chicago for an injunction to restrain Captain Putnam from interference with the newspaper; that judge at once issued a restraining order while entertaining the question of a permanent injunction.[4]

This use of the judicial authority over the military power, however, became unnecessary, and the Drummond proceedings went no further. President Lincoln, having had enough embarrassment from Burnside's unauthorized measures, took prompt action. On the day of Burnside's order of suppression (June 1) and two days before the actual seizure, Stanton wrote to the general: ". . . the President has been informed that you have suppressed the publication or circulation of the Chicago Times in your department. He directs me to say that in his judgment it would be better for you to take an early occasion to revoke that order. The irritation produced by such acts is in his opinion likely to do more harm than the publication would do. The Government approves of your motives and desires to give you . . . support. But while military movements are left to your judgment, upon administrative questions such as the arrest of civilians and the suppression of newspapers not requiring immediate action the President desires to be previously consulted." [5] In this, as in the arrest and trial of Vallandigham, Burnside had acted without the approval of Washington. "The President—and I think every member of the Cabinet—[wrote Gideon Welles] regrets what has been done." [6]

Final responsibility, however, was with the President. That is an

---

[3] *Ann. Cyc.*, 1863, 424.
[4] *Constitutional Problems Under Lincoln*, 493–494.
[5] *Offic. Rec.*, 2 ser. V, 724.
[6] Welles, *Diary*, I, 321 (June 3, 1863).

inescapable duty of the presidency: to be saddled with the effects and the blame of what is done by scores and hundreds of men who see only the smaller or more immediate aspects of a problem as it affects their headquarters or their particular departments. It is one thing to see an abuse; it is quite another to shape the remedy. It was realized at the White House that, while the *Times* was a thorn in the flesh, misusing the protection of the laws and the shielding influence of the President, yet it would be unwise to strike impatiently at the abuse, and thoughtful men could only lament, as Welles wrote, "that our military officers should, without absolute necessity, disregard those great principles on which our government and institutions rest." [7]

The fault in Burnside's procedure appears in the fact that, if he had consulted Washington first, the order of suppression would not have been issued. Nor would it have been issued if Stanton's above-quoted communication telling of Lincoln's strong disapproval had been sent by telegraph instead of by mail. The President, in his function of undoing the mistaken work of subordinates, held a cabinet meeting at which it was decided that Burnside's suppression order must be revoked. Word was flashed to Burnside at Cincinnati, and by his command the revocation was ordered (June 4) by "direction of the President." [8] Actual suppression had lasted two days, Wednesday and Thursday, June 3 and 4, 1863.[9]

Meanwhile a lesser Burnside, General Milo S. Hascall at Indianapolis, had issued "General Orders, No. 9" proclaiming suppressive action in accord with Burnside's "No. 38," against newspapers and speakers counseling resistance to conscription or bringing the war policy of the government "into disrepute." [10]

Hascall's order "No. 9" set off an explosive tempest in Indiana, as well it might in the supercharged politics of 1863. That military gentleman, practically unknown till then, got himself more and more deeply involved as he sought to follow up the original order which, as was to be expected, was openly defied. For example, from his Indianapolis headquarters of the "District of Indiana" (under Burnside) the general on May 8 sent a peremptory order to the editor of the Columbia City (Ind.) *News*. The editor was bluntly told to do one of two things: recant his resistance to order "No. 9" or discon-

[7] *Ibid.*, I, 322.

[8] *Offic. Rec.*, 2 ser. V, 741.

[9] *Ann. Cyc.*, 1863, 424.

[10] *Offic. Rec.*, 2 ser. V, 485.

tinue publication "until further orders." [11]

If anything was designed to show up Burnside's policy, making it intolerably obnoxious and a bit absurd in Indiana, the Hascall treatment was so calculated. Lincoln's emphatic disapproval was made clear, though in doing so the President knew that he had to tread carefully so as not to offend the dignity of state executives. As expressed through Stanton in a despatch to Burnside, the President's answer was discreet and tactful, but firm and unmistakable: "Whatever dissatisfaction there may exist . . . within your department is liable to be increased by the presence of an indiscreet military officer, who will unnecessarily interfere with the political condition of the State and produce irritation by assuming military powers not essential to the preservation of the public peace." On recommendation from Washington, Hascall was promptly shifted to duty elsewhere and his rather useless military command at Indianapolis was terminated. His "No. 9" was revoked.[12] One of the surprising things about the Hascall episode is that his interference with newspapers began in mid-April and had reached such a crisis by May 27, 1863, that David Davis, then at Indianapolis, notified Stanton that his "immediate removal" was "demanded by the honor and interests of the Government." [13] Yet after this, and with Hascall's record before him, Burnside issued the order suppressing the Chicago *Times*. He knew this kind of conduct was not approved at Washington.

IX

In a fair historical appraisal it is important to avoid misunderstanding the Vallandigham case. It was bound in the shallows of wartime politics, but it is not correct to treat as proved all the familiar assumptions. One should not assume that this agitator was truly representative of the main body of Northern Democrats. It was to a large extent the faulty machinery of party management (through the unsatisfactory workings of the Ohio Democratic convention), plus the reaction against his arrest, that gave him more prominence than he would otherwise have had. It is worth remembering that in the con-

[11] *Ibid.*, 725. Similar orders were issued to other Indiana editors.

[12] *Ibid.*, 752, 759; Stampp, *Indiana Politics during the Civil War*, 202.

[13] *Offic. Rec.*, 1 ser. XXIII, pt. 2, 369. On the same date, May 27, Governor Morton wrote Stanton asking that Hascall be removed "at once" (*ibid.*).

gressional election of 1862, though that was overwhelmingly a Democratic year in Ohio, Vallandigham was a candidate but was defeated; certainly in that year he was not synonymous with the party; certainly also he was no asset to the party. In Ohio as elsewhere Democrats claimed always to be "devoted friends of the Constitution and the Union."[1] If this is brushed off as a party statement, then the opposite effort to make all Democrats appear as traitors should be taken no more seriously than the general run of party propaganda. Much of the fallacy was in equating two things that were not at all the same—the cause of the Union was being promoted (e. g., by the Union League) as if it were the precise equivalent of Republicanism. Democrats could hardly be blamed for resenting that theory. Yet when all is said, the Democrats were out of luck. They were inept, poorly led, and quite vulnerable to the rough and clumsy weapons used against them. To be saddled with Vallandigham was their chief wartime misfortune,[2] and it was their party managers that did the saddling.

Having noted these things, one should also avoid wrong assumptions as to Lincoln. Where he approved of irregular measures it was because in his opinion, under the terrific stress of war, he had to. To deny the ordinary course of civil justice was, for him, to play an unwelcome and unnatural role. It would seem superfluous to repeat that firm adherence to the fundamentals of civil rights was one of Abraham Lincoln's most characteristic and persistent traits. The fact that these things were done in an emergency did not mean to him that they would be perpetuated in normal times. Even where using arbitrary measures he held those measures within bounds. If the Democratic party was unlucky to have Vallandigham infixed in

---

1 *Ann. Cyc.*, 1862, 696.

2 For the factor of Vallandighamism in the "politics" of 1863, see below, pp. 263 ff. After the war his influence within the Democratic party was negligible. Regretting Lincoln's assassination, he wrote to Horace Greeley, April 20, 1865: "We must lay aside for a time past & future differences, & associate upon the pressing questions of the moment." (Greeley MSS., N. Y. Pub. Lib.) Even when he advocated reasonable measures —peaceful relations between the sections and return to normal civil procedures—his fellow Democrats, interested in the same measures, seemed to avoid his coöperation as the kiss of death. Thus in August 1866, when a convention was held at Philadelphia to unite Northerners and Southerners in favor of non-vindictive restoration, there was a disposition to exclude Vallandigham from the convention. A Democrat of Hamilton, Ohio, L. D. Campbell, wrote to O. H. Browning (July 31, 1866): "We must *squelch* him. He means mischief. . . . He is as full of pure cussedness as an egg is of meat." Browning, *Diary*, II, xiv–xvi, 84 n., 89.

their organization, so was the President unfortunate in being subjected to blasts of abuse for what was untypical, what he did not do, and indeed for what he particularly opposed. He had not ordered Vallandigham's arrest. He was not overrating the man's influence. He never gave an order for severe treatment of the "wily agitator" whose safe protection, while soldier-deserters were being shot, he mentioned with stinging sarcasm. As for the order suppressing the Chicago *Times,* he disapproved of the order at the very outset and promptly ordered its revocation.

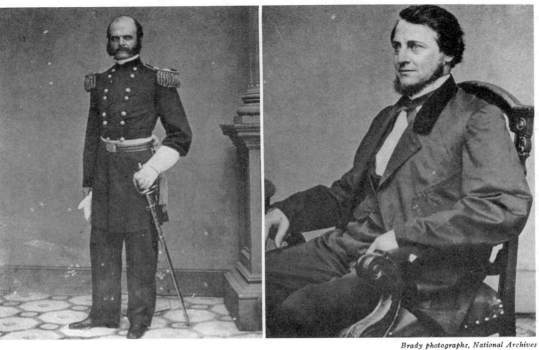

Brady photographs, National Archives

PRINCIPALS IN THE VALLANDIGHAM CASE

Vallandigham was an Ohio Democrat. For making a speech on May 1, 1863, he was arrested under General Burnside's command, tried by military commission, and sentenced to imprisonment during the war. Lincoln regretted the arrest, and the sentence was commuted to removal beyond Union military lines. Later in the war Vallandigham returned to Ohio and was unmolested. (Denial of freedom of speech was not the regular policy of the Lincoln administration.)

University of Rochester Library *Frederick H. Meserve*  *Brady photograph, National Archives*

MEN OF NEW YORK

Thurlow Weed, Horatio Seymour, and John A. Dix

CHAPTER X

POLITICS IN 1863

ONE thinks broadly of significant elections in the United States as belonging to even numbered years—a President elected every fourth year, members of Congress every two years. There is also the tendency to regard state elections as having only minor and local importance. It may be for these reasons, or perhaps from inadvertence, that insufficient attention has been given, in general histories and Lincoln biographies, to the numerous state elections in 1863. From Massachusetts to Kentucky, and from Iowa to Pennsylvania, the Union war policy was impressively sustained. Vallandigham was defeated for governor in Ohio by the war Democrat, John Brough; Curtin was re-elected as Republican governor of Pennsylvania; an opponent of Seymour was elected secretary of state in New York; Andrew was re-elected governor of Massachusetts; in addition, the Union forces also carried Connecticut, Maryland, Delaware, Kentucky, and other states.

I

In New England the political campaigns brought Republican victory without exception as to any state, though the contests were waged with great intensity. Three New England states voted in March and April: New Hampshire, Rhode Island, and Connecticut. In Rhode Island the Republicans triumphed for governor, legislature, and the state's two members of Congress.[1] There was a peculiar

1 *Ann. Cyc.,* 1863, 810–811. In this Rhode Island election (April 1863) the Republican candidate, James T. Smith, a cotton manufacturer, was chosen governor. In 1861 he had defeated the wealthy and handsome William Sprague. Sprague was a Democrat of the rich, conservative type that attracted Republican votes; he later became a Republican

situation in New Hampshire, where Justice Ira A. Eastman, Democratic candidate for governor, received nearly 33,000 votes as compared to 29,035 for the Republican contender, Joseph A. Gilmore; yet Gilmore was elected. This was because of an unimportant third ticket in the field, which took enough votes to leave Eastman without an overall majority; the choice of governor was consequently thrown into the legislature; that body, under Republican control, elected Gilmore.[2]

In Connecticut the 1863 contest was keen and exciting. It was, wrote Greeley, "chosen as the arena of a determined trial of strength . . . between the supporters and opponents . . . of the War for the Union." [3] William A. Buckingham, incumbent governor, contended for re-election against the popular former governor Thomas Hart Seymour, who could be described as a "peace Democrat," which implied avowed opposition, not to the Union, but to the Lincoln administration and the existing war policy. In the election, which was fairly close, and in which soldiers participated, success came to the Republicans, with 41,000 votes for Buckingham against 38,000 for Seymour. The Republicans also won control of the legislature and obtained three of the four seats in Congress.[4] It has been pointed out by W. B. Hesseltine that military intervention and presidential patronage were among the factors at work in this Connecticut election, that a wealthy gentleman vowed that he would raise $100,000 to "buy up the damned state," and that an ordnance official "put pressure on Connecticut's munitions manufacturers to force their workers to vote for Buckingham." [5]

A somewhat sensational feature of the contests in New England was the fervid stump speaking of the amazing girl orator from Philadelphia, Anna E. Dickinson. This female whirlwind, not much over twenty, stormed through New Hampshire and Connecticut especially, electrifying her audiences with rapid-fire speeches in the most approved radical style. Anna was not merely an abolitionist. Her speeches were not merely Republican. They were flaming tirades in

---

and as such served as senator, 1863–1875. He is best known as the husband of the brilliant and beautiful Kate Chase.

2 *Ann. Cyc.*, 1863, 681.

3 Greeley, *Amer. Conflict*, II, 486.

4 *Ann. Cyc.*, 1863, 330.

5 Hesseltine, *Lincoln and the War Governors*, 320.

which she gloried in bloody suppression, dished out hatred against Southerners, compared Jefferson Davis to a hyena, denounced "Democratic generals," and praised to the heavens such men as Frémont and Butler. At a time when Republicans were appealing to men of all parties to forget their differences and unite for the common cause, she habitually referred to Democrats as traitors, while her Republican sentiments were always voiced with an extreme radical accent. This factional emphasis was illustrated by her emphatic denunciation of Seward, whom she actually represented as somewhat of a traitor, while dubbing him "Fox of the White House."

Antislavery zeal was a strong stimulus to her tempestuous oratory. She soared the more easily for not being confined by solid information or temperate judgment. This was the climax of her career (1863–64); she liked applause; audiences gave her a heady thrill; Republican managers knew how to use her for their purposes. They knew that popular audiences, once they recovered from the un-Victorian spectacle of a political campaigner in petticoats, would be readier to take extravagant statements from feminine than from masculine lips. To hear Anna was a dramatic experience. There was something fascinating about her youthful presence, her voice, and her forward style of calling down Almighty thunderbolts upon rebels and Democrats. In appearance she was much like a female Henry Ward Beecher.

Anna had been coached by the secretary of the New Hampshire Republican state committee, Benjamin F. Prescott, "to use the method of attack, to point out the disloyalty of the Democrats . . . , the incompetence of their generals, the folly of their slogan prating of the Constitution as it is and the Union as it was . . . ." She was warned "against expecting too much of her audiences." [6] In both Connecticut and New Hampshire the Republicans were very grateful to this girl who was being compared to Portia, and whose vigorous championship of the colored race was warmly approved by men of good intent. In New Hampshire Prescott wrote that she had done "more good than any other speaker," Gilmore told her personally that her speeches had secured his election, and she received the un-

[6] James Harvey Young, "Anna Elizabeth Dickinson and the Civil War" (ms. doctoral dissertation, Univ. of Ill., 1941), 87–88.

precedented honor of being invited into that lofty masculine organization, the Union League.[7] Since the leading Democratic candidate in the Granite State had received almost four thousand more votes than Gilmore, and since Gilmore lacked a clear majority by about 8,000, the thanks of these Republicans indicated, and they said as much, that without the girl's oratory they would have suffered even a worse popular repudiation and would have lost the New Hampshire election.[8] That might well have happened had there been no third ticket.

II

Amid the agitations of politics—and with some relation to them—there occurred in the summer of 1863 an abortive effort toward negotiation between the governments of Richmond and Washington. Some writers have belittled this effort and there have been conflicting speculations as to its objectives, but since it involved an attempted mission to Washington on the part of Alexander H. Stephens, Vice President of the Confederacy, and required study by Lincoln and his cabinet, the episode should not be passed over too lightly.

After preliminary correspondence and consultation between Stephens and President Jefferson Davis, a steamer went down the James River under flag of truce bearing the Vice President together with Robert Ould, agent of the Confederate government for the exchange of prisoners.[1] These men were on their way to Washington if the Union authorities would permit the journey. Whatever broader objects may have been in mind, the stated purpose of the mission was to provide for the exchange of prisoners. This assuredly was no minor question. It proved one of the most wretched problems of the war, being hopelessly enmeshed with interrelated problems: the status of the Confederacy, Union use of Negro troops, dire threats of retaliation by the Confederacy, the proclamation of President Davis branding General ("Beast") Butler as an outlaw, the order for Butler's ex-

---

[7] *Ibid.*, 92.

[8] For an account of Miss Dickinson, see also James Harvey Young, "Anna Elizabeth Dickinson and the Civil War: For and Against Lincoln," *Miss. Vall. Hist. Rev.*, XXXI, 59–80 (1944).

[1] Moore, *Rebellion Record* (Diary), VII, 24; Stephens, *War Between the States*, II, 558–568.

ecution if caught (denying exchange), and the declaration (also by Davis) "that no commissioned officer of the United States, taken captive, shall be released on parole, before exchange, until the said Butler shall have met with due punishment for his crime." [2] (Among other things, Butler had caused a man to be put to death in New Orleans for tearing down the Union flag; it was urged that the general was disregarding the laws of war—indeed, that he was an "enemy of mankind.")

Earlier in the war a cartel for prisoner exchange had been worked out by General John A. Dix for the United States and General D. H. Hill for the Confederacy. Its object was to release all prisoners of war and to deal with an excess on one side by having surplus prisoners released on parole not to take up arms again.[3] After Davis's retaliatory proclamation—which came, by the way, after Lincoln had removed Butler from New Orleans—Secretary Stanton put an end to the Dix-Hill cartel. Union authorities were outdoing the Confederates in the number of prisoners taken, deriving an advantage all the greater in view of the over-all Union superiority in man power. With hundreds of thousands of prisoners suffering and thousands dying, and with each side accusing the other of brutal atrocity, the situation became a crying disgrace. Though need for redress was realized, nothing effective was done.

On July 4, 1863, the boat bearing Stephens and Ould was met by a Union boat under flag of truce, and Stephens conveyed the purpose of his trip to Admiral S. P. Lee, U. S. N., in Hampton Roads. Bearing a letter by Jefferson Davis to be put before Lincoln, the Vice President wished permission to go to Washington and present the communication in person. Though Ould was met by his opposite number, Colonel W. H. Ludlow (Union agent for prisoner exchange), and though the two men conferred, the mission failed on all counts, and on June 6 the Confederate steamer returned up-river with the unsuccessful Southern officials.

At Washington the problem of the Southern mission was discussed in cabinet meetings on July 5 and July 6. Welles has left a rather full account which is informative as to cabinet differences and sarcastic

---

[2] Randall, *Civil War and Reconstruction,* 438; Moore, *Rebellion Record* (Docs.), VI, 291–293.

[3] Hesseltine, *Civil War Prisons,* 32–33.

as to Seward who was disposed to manage the affair and to take it out of the hands of the navy department in which it had originated. Various alternatives were proposed for the answer to be sent to Hampton Roads, the President even suggesting at one point that "it would be well [so Welles quoted him] to send some one—perhaps go himself—to Fortress Monroe." [4]

It was decided, however, that no good could come of the proposed negotiation, upon which the only further question was the manner and phrasing to be adopted in communicating the answer to those concerned. Giving this matter his personal attention, with a combination of diplomatic caution and lawyerlike precision, Lincoln at first wrote out a draft of a statement—not a reply directed to Stephens, which would have involved what is now called "protocol" as to status, titles, and the like—but simply an order to Admiral Lee. In this autograph draft the President indicated that Stephens was not to be permitted to proceed to Washington and took occasion to reject any communication "in terms assuming the independence of the so-called Confederate States." He added that "anything will be received and carefully considered . . . when offered . . . in terms not assuming the independence of the so-called Confederate States." [5]

This earlier tentative form, which was of moderate length, was then reconsidered and the President wrote out a much briefer form (Welles to Lee) merely stating that the Stephens request was "inadmissable" and that "customary agents and channels" were "adequate for all needful communication . . . between the United States forces and the insurgents." [6]

Had Stephens been received, spokesmen for disunion (and anti-Lincoln spokesmen in the North) would have made the most of the occasion. Specifically the Confederate gentlemen were to confer as to exchange of prisoners, and no one could rightly deny the need for such a conference; but the evidence is pretty clear that larger problems were in Stephens's mind. He had written to President Davis: "While . . . a mission might be despatched on a *minor* point, the greater one could possibly . . . be opened to view . . . ." [7] All this was happening while the political campaigns of 1863 were rag-

[4] Welles, *Diary*, I, 359 (July 5, 1863).
[5] Nicolay and Hay, *Lincoln*, VII, 373; R. T. L. Coll., 24665.
[6] Nicolay and Hay, *Lincoln*, VII, 374.
[7] Stephens, *War Between the States*, II, 560.

ing in Northern states, and Confederates were counting on the Vallandigham type of partisan opposition to Lincoln as a factor working to their advantage. Stephens was one of the milder of the Confederate leaders, yet he was speaking not only of a permanently broken Union, but of the prospective defeat and overturn of the Lincoln government. (The idea that defeating Lincoln and putting a Democratic administration in its place would have meant Northern consent to disunion showed misunderstanding of Northern opinion, but misreading of public sentiment was a constant wartime factor; indeed, such misunderstanding had contributed to producing war.)

There could be no realistic discussion of the attempted negotiation on any assumption of accepting Confederate terms; [8] the mere thought, or wishful dream, of such acceptance was dashed even in Confederate minds by the coincidence of the mission with major military events. Assuming, or guessing, that the Lincoln government might have yielded to Confederate pressure if Lee had been successful and had threatened Washington, Stephens and other Confederate leaders realized how slight was any such prospect in the atmosphere of Gettysburg and Vicksburg. One need not criticize Stephens for the attempt, which had its humanitarian aspects and which President Lincoln considered carefully before rejecting it; but the Southern statesman was not bringing with him the essentials of peace. Then and thereafter Lincoln's terms for ending the war were simple and they were generous, but they included the indispensable factor of reunion and that was beyond Confederate acceptance.

III

After a considerable interval—a momentous one that included Morgan's raid as well as the victories at Gettysburg and Vicksburg—Kentucky voted in August. The situation there presented unusual features. It was a Southern state, a shifting battleground of Confederate and Union forces. At the same time it was shaken by guerrilla ac-

---

[8] Commenting on terms to be taken for granted, the Richmond *Enquirer* of July 7, 1863, outlined in part the following: "acknowledgment of the independence of every State now in the Confederacy"; "free choice" of Maryland to join it (Kentucky and Missouri being "already members" thereof), and navigation of the Mississippi "though lost to the United States by the trial of battle." Quoted in Moore, *Rebellion Record* (Diary), VII, 26–27.

tivity and constant disorder. It was under martial law.[1] There were elements that smacked of coercion. By proclamation of Governor Robinson a loyalty oath was required of voters. They had to swear Federal allegiance, pledge not to take up arms against the United States and to give no aid to its enemies, and disclaim fellowship with "the so-called Confederate States" and Confederate armies—all this under the threat that violation of the oath might lead to death or other punishment by judgment of a military commission.[2] It was claimed, but denied, that the result in Kentucky was due to military interference and the intimidation of Federal bayonets.

The contest in Kentucky was between Union Democrats and Peace Democrats. Thomas E. Bramlette, who had held a commission in the Federal army, was the Union candidate; Charles A. Wickliffe, also a Unionist (for he had opposed secession), headed the Peace Democratic ticket. The issue between the two candidates was not that of union against disunion; Wickliffe, for instance, would not have favored having the state join the Confederacy. Spokesmen for the peace party declared "this rebellion [to be] utterly unjustifiable . . . and the dissolution of the Union the greatest of calamities." [3] The parties differed in the fact that the Bramlette group was considered "entirely too subservient to Lincoln," while the Wickliffe group, bitter in denouncing Lincoln, was the party for those "who were looking for peace, and . . . who wished to register their protest against the military régime and the various unpopular acts of the National administration." (It was said also to be the party "for those . . . who favored secession, if any there should be," [4] but under all the circumstances the plain fact was that the secessionists had no ballot.)

Though Kentucky was predominantly Unionist (a fact which some Kentuckians seem to have forgotten), the Republican party had virtually no existence in the state. The Negro question was highly difficult and embarrassing; the men of the Bluegrass still thought unrealistically of conserving slavery, as of course they could do under existing law. This commonwealth of Lincoln's birth had some of the aspects of a region under military occupation. An "*unconditional union man* a General Jackson Democrat" has been quoted as saying

---

1 *Constitutional Problems Under Lincoln,* 171 ff.; E. M. Coulter, *Civil War and Readjustment in Kentucky,* 177.

2 Coulter, 177.

3 *Ibid.,* 174.

4 *Ibid.,* 174, 176.

that it would require tact and non-interference on the part of Federal officials to prevent a result in the state election that would be unfavorable to the Union Democrats. In the event of such an adverse result it was feared that a greatly increased Federal military force (the number 100,000 was even suggested) would be required "to hold the State." [5]

It was a light vote—a total of 85,000 as compared to 145,000 in the election of 1860—but, if the situation was not too closely analyzed, the figures looked well for the Union cause: 68,000 (round numbers) for Bramlette, 18,000 for Wickliffe.[6]

The peace party (one is using here the terminology of the time) took their defeat in bitter mood. They attributed it to flagrant military interference, but "It must . . . be remembered [writes E. M. Coulter] that many returned Confederates and Confederate sympathizers had counted on profiting by the profound discontent in the state and that precautions in the election were hence necessary." [7] Lincoln's special interest in the Kentucky outcome was shown in a letter to Mrs. Lincoln on August 8, 1863: "The election in Kentucky," he wrote, "has gone very strongly right." He added: "Old Mr. Wickliffe [well known in Kentucky in the days when Mary lived there] got ugly, as you know, ran for Governor, and is terribly beaten." Another well known Kentuckian, Brutus Clay, brother of Cassius, was, as Lincoln remarked, "largely elected" as a member of Congress.[8]

IV

There were no state or congressional elections in Illinois or Indiana in 1863, but nowhere was politics more heated and furious. In Illinois the party wrangle led to the proroguing of the legislature. In Indiana there occurred a collapse of constitutional government, resulting in a remarkable dictatorship by Governor Morton.

From the beginning Indiana Democrats had continually declared that only a restoration of their party could preserve or restore the Union, while Hoosier Republicans, albeit with a "no party" front, sought persistently to seize a partisan monopoly of both Unionism and patriotism. In 1862 Republicanism was "repudiated" by Indi-

---

[5] *Ibid.*, 175–176. [6] *Ibid.*, 178. [7] *Ibid.*

[8] Lincoln to his wife, Aug. 8, 1863, R. T. L. Coll., 25444.

ana voters. By an election in October of that year the Democrats triumphed largely as to state officials, congressmen, and members of the legislature.[1]

There followed a battle royal, leading to utter deadlock between the Republican governor, Oliver P. Morton, and the Democratic legislature. Morton was both a vigorous and a party-minded executive. He labored tirelessly for the war effort and for Indiana soldiers, but Democrats, and some Republicans, were irked by his habit of appropriating to himself too exclusively the sure-fire credit of being the "soldiers' friend." In the brief 1863 session of the legislature (January to March) each party was set to outmaneuver the other, with the result that the Democrats overplayed their hand and the Republicans, though in a minority, came through with the main advantage.

Though the Democrats had a majority in both houses, the Republicans wielded a powerful weapon of obstruction, since under the state constitution the session was limited to sixty-one days, no law could be enacted without a quorum, and that quorum was defined as two-thirds of each house. Indignant at Morton, who was treating the major party as a group of traitors, the Democrats sought to push through a series of bills to set up an executive council, reorganize the militia, and otherwise reduce the governor's power. The Republicans retaliated with a party bolt, absenting themselves from the legislature and leaving the majority powerless for lack of a quorum. Under these circumstances of complete frustration the session ended in early March with no appropriations and no revenue measures passed; there would not be another legislative session until January of 1865.

Throughout the rest of 1863 and all of 1864 the state of Indiana presented the spectacle of a virtual gubernatorial dictatorship. Kenneth Stampp refers to the situation correctly as "the collapse of constitutional government." [2] Disregarding the constitution and ignoring state officials such as treasurer and auditor, Morton practically took over the government, organized a bureau of finance, borrowed money on his own assurances, obtained loans from bankers, paid in-

1 Typical Democratic majorities in Indiana in 1862 were: for secretary of state, 9500; total popular votes for congressmen, over 11,000. The Democrats elected seven members of the House of Representatives, the Republicans, four. Some of the voting was close, but in certain districts the Democrats had majorities from two to four thousand.

2 Kenneth M. Stampp, *Indiana Politics during the Civil War,* chap. viii.

terest on the state debt, and enlisted the financial support of the Federal government.[3] It happened that Congress, with no thought of subsidizing a state government, had passed a statute appropriating $2,000,000 to be spent at the President's discretion in supplying arms and other aid to citizens of states where rebellion existed or was threatened. Since there was talk, or rumor, in Indiana that rebels would seize the government,[4] the congressional statute was stretched to cover the Hoosier emergency, and an order was issued by President Lincoln advancing $250,000, one-eighth of the total appropriation, to Morton, who was made accountable for the sum; he used $160,000 of it to pay interest on the state debt—i. e., on his own borrowings. The honesty and serious public purpose of the governor were evident, but here was a case where public funds were paid out from the United States treasury, without an appropriation for the special purpose, in order to assist a state whose financial system had broken down. By these and other measures the Morton administration succeeded in tiding over the emergency until in 1865 the legality of these proceedings was established by a Republican legislature. In the long run it was Morton and the Republicans who came out ahead.

It was, of course, a situation which ought never to have occurred. Party wrangling is not government. It was not true, as the Republicans would have it believed, that Indiana Democrats were traitors. Far from it. Though there were extremists in the state, and though there was "Copperhead" activity eventuating in the Milligan case, the careful study by Kenneth Stampp reveals that Republican rumors—as to the Democratic party conspiring to seize the arsenal, free Confederate prisoners, inaugurate a revolution, et cetera—were without substantial basis. Democrats held mass meetings and jubilees, as-

[3] When Morton was conferring with Lincoln and Stanton in Washington, according to a story that has come down to us, Stanton was told that Lincoln knew of no law by which Federal financial aid could be extended to Indiana. To this the secretary of war is said to have replied: "By God, I will find a law." W. D. Foulke, *Life of Oliver P. Morton,* I, 261.

[4] These rumors, sedulously cultivated by Republicans, had reached Lincoln's ears. In a conversation with Senators Hale of New Hampshire and Browning of Illinois on January 9, 1863, he mentioned that the Democratic party in Illinois and Indiana "was talking of a union with the lower Mississippi states." Browning, *Diary,* I, 611. At a time when the Indianapolis *Journal* (Republican) "saw a conspiracy in every Democratic move, a rebel plot in every criticism of war policy," Morton had telegraphed Stanton (January 3, 1863) that the Indiana legislature intended to recognize the Confederacy and urge the Northwest to dissolve all constitutional relations with the New England states. Stampp, 167; *Offic. Rec.,* 1 ser., XX, pt. 2, 297.

sailed Morton and Lincoln, opposed Burnside's militarism, criticized the extralegal Republican regime in their state, applauded Vallandigham, denounced arrests, and in times of military gloom urged pacification and armistice. Stampp, however, shows that, though "Republicans sought to misconstrue their purpose into a disloyal desire," the emphasis of peace men was upon "the nation's integrity." "Most Democrats," he writes, "never repudiated the war, but even those who did, generally favored only peace *and* Union." [5]

Times were changing, and much of the Democratic resentment was epitomized in the stirring personality of Daniel Voorhees who, like other "Jacksonian agrarians," resented current movements tending to "political and economic revolution." [6] It was, of course, a shameful misrepresentation that only Republicans in Indiana were loyal to their country. "Even in 1863," writes Stampp, "most Democrats continued to support the war and believe that only its vigorous prosecution could restore the Union." Governor Morton admitted that southern Indiana (overwhelmingly Democratic) was the most loyal part of the state, and the Indianapolis *Sentinel,* Democratic to excess, "spoke often for the suppression of the rebellion by force of arms." [7]

Indiana Democrats were not all of one faction. Some were like Senator Jesse Bright, some like Douglas. There were many thousands of Democratic enlistments, and men such as Voorhees did not fail to vote for supplies to sustain the army. They naturally could not accept the idea that Indianians in service were Morton's soldiers only. They saw real menace in the deliberate efforts to work up party feeling among Indiana troops, who were induced to pass angry resolutions and to threaten marching back and suppressing "treason" at home. This smacked too much of making the army the agent of a party, and earnest men could be pardoned for real alarm at "threats of military intervention in civil government." [8]

V

In Lincoln's own state the year 1863, though an off-year for elections, was a period of hot and furious political agitation. Hatred of

---

5 Stampp, 162. 6 *Ibid.,* 152, 211. 7 *Ibid.,* 210–211.
8 *Ibid.,* 175–176.

Lincoln's administration flared ominously in the North, and the word "Copperhead" sprang readily to the tongue. Many factors were working together. Friendship toward Southerners, defeatism, disgust toward a war which was considered a failure—all these elements, together with motives called "political," were operating to consolidate the opposition to Lincoln into what was coming to be known as a "peace party." Illinois was no exception to the statement that the election of 1862 in the Middle West had been a sharp blow to Lincoln's administration and an encouragement to his foes.[1] Under the ordeal of war this middle area had revealed itself as two sections (at least two): the prairie and lake regions farther north constituted a division distinct from the older areas of Egypt, Cincinnati, and the Ohio River counties. One finds it hard, therefore, to generalize about the Middle West as if it presented a clear pattern. Yet, writes H. C. Hubbart, "taken as a whole it had repudiated its own greatest man, Abraham Lincoln, and his administration at the polls."[2]

On top of this came 1863, the year of the emancipation proclamation—a glorious event to many, but a divisive factor in the North. To this was added the habeas corpus controversy, conscription, Union defeat until July, intensified "Copperhead" activity, huge Vallandigham excitement, the Chicago *Times* affair, sharp controversy between Lincoln and Seymour, and peace talk focusing on Alexander H. Stephens.

While Lincoln's opponents were becoming more bold and vigorous, the administration was meeting the challenge by a lenient policy, releasing some who had been imprisoned, and thus becoming weaker by its very effort to avoid too despotic an appearance. There was somewhat of a dilemma as to releases. Where men were arbitrarily held as political prisoners, they were rallying cries for those who denounced the President as a tyrant and a denier of civil liberties. Let them be released, however (the release being a mere executive act without trial, the kind of thing the President or secretary of war could do "on his own"), and the former prisoner, now a hero, made the utmost capital of his sufferings as he traveled about, regaling large audiences with accounts of his experiences and with denunciations of "bastilles, . . . of despotism, desolation and death."[3] In either case, released

[1] *Lincoln the President,* II, 232–237. [2] Hubbart, *The Older Middle West,* 190.
[3] *Ibid.,* 192.

or not, a man once arrested became an anti-Lincoln exhibit.

The overwrought wartime situation in Illinois was manifest in connection with the 1862 movement for a new state constitution. The constitutional convention elected for this purpose turned out to be fully under the control of the Democrats who made unwise use of a device of fundamental democracy which ought to have been above parties. The frame of government which the convention prepared, when submitted to popular vote, was defeated; one of the articles, however, prohibiting immigration of Negroes into the state, was overwhelmingly approved. This was at a time when Cairo witnessed the arrival of Negroes shipped by army officials from the South. As Republicans (some of them) urged farmers to employ this form of cheap labor, it became politically profitable to denounce the so-called "Africanization" of the state.[4] Lincoln might be freeing the slaves, but the people of his own state were decidedly not ready to receive free Negroes.

Lincoln was quoted as saying "that the democratic legislatures of Illinois & Indiana seemed bent upon mischief."[5] This was in January 1863. Governor Richard Yates of Illinois was like Morton of Indiana in Union loyalty, concern for soldiers, and party intensity. In Illinois the situation was constitutionally not so desperate as in Indiana, but the feuds of partisanship were equally as bitter. The bothersome anti-Yates and anti-Lincoln legislature proved so obnoxious to the Republicans that the legislators of that minority party withdrew so that a quorum was prevented. The business of legislation in the state was thus brought to a standstill, and Yates decided that he would prefer it so rather than yield to Democratic control. Finding a clause in the state constitution which had never been used before and has not been employed since, Yates declared the legislature prorogued. The two houses had disagreed on a matter of adjournment, and the governor, acting under article V, section 9, of the constitution of 1847, put an end to this session of the general assembly. Defending his action after the war, in a speech at Elgin, Illinois, on July 4, 1865, Yates explained that the enemy was fortified in the state house, that this enemy was starting "to run the government upon the . . . manner of the rebel states," and that under

[4] *Civil War and Reconstruction,* 601–602. [5] Browning, *Diary,* I, 611 (Jan. 9, 1863).

these circumstances he called his staff into consultation and resolved to attack the enemy in his stronghold.[6] There was thus, with differing legal devices, a collapse of representative government both in Indiana and Illinois. In each case it was the Republicans, with minorities in the heat of controversy, that gained ascendancy.

On June 17, 1863, Democratic agitation reached its culmination in a giant rally, a vast meeting held at Springfield. These great popular meetings, or "conventions," had been a familiar device since the days of Jackson. Those who attended this one, estimated at 40,000, had traveled long distances by a great variety of conveyances as well as by foot. They listened to Democratic orators, such as Senator William A. Richardson of Illinois, the old veteran John Reynolds who had been governor of Illinois in Black Hawk War days, Daniel W. Voorhees, and S. S. Cox. The most famous action of this meeting was the adoption of a resolution "in favor of peace upon the basis of a restoration of the Union." For the accomplishment of this object, continued the resolution, "we propose a national convention to settle upon the terms of peace, which shall have in view the restoration of the Union as it was, and the securing, by constitutional amendments, such rights to the several states and the people thereof as honor and justice demand." [7]

VI

As a foil to all this activity the Union men of Illinois planned their own huge demonstration. In August a call was issued to a mass assemblage to be held at Springfield on September 3, 1863. If only as a spectacle and a diverting entertainment, such an occasion was calculated to attract immense attention, but this one was heavily freighted with political interest. The call was for the "Unconditional Union men of the State of Illinois, without regard to former party associations, who are in favor of a vigorous prosecution of the war against this unholy and accursed rebellion." All such men were requested "to assemble together in a Grand Mass Meeting." Printed

[6] This speech is quoted in Richard Yates (the younger), *Richard Yates, War Governor of Illinois*, 24.

[7] John Moses, *Biographical Dictionary . . . of the Representative Men of the United States* (Illinois volume), 2d ed., II, 688; A. C. Cole, *Era of the Civil War*, 299–300; *Ill. State Register*, June 18, 1863.

repeatedly in the *Illinois State Journal* (Republican organ), the call was underwritten by an impressive list of signers arranged by counties. The names included Governor Richard Yates, Jesse Dubois, Charles W. Matheny, Owen Lovejoy, W. H. Herndon, W. H. Bailhache, and many others. In an editorial when the call was launched the *Journal* fell easily into superlatives, remarking that it would "require no persistent drumming . . . to render it the largest and most imposing popular demonstration ever held in the State." [1] Day after day the advertisement of this monster meeting was continued. The people liked a show, they liked a state fair, which was to coincide with the great meeting, and they liked excursions. Passengers bound for the rally could obtain railroad tickets at half price.

For this occasion, planned well in advance, the President was invited to attend as the main speaker, not merely to give "a few appropriate remarks," as later at Gettysburg. The committee on arrangements was headed by Lincoln's Springfield friend, James C. Conkling, who had married Mary Todd's chum Mercy Levering. On August 14 Conkling wrote to the President, telling of the grand mass meeting of unconditional Union men and asking him to gratify, by his presence, the "many thousands" who would attend.[2] To this Lincoln replied by cipher telegram (August 20): "I think I will go, or send a letter—probably the latter." [3] Next day the *Journal* ran an article headed: "President Lincoln will Probably be Here." The paper was "happy to announce . . . that [in answer to the committee's invitation] President Lincoln has given assurances justifying a strong hope that he will be here."

It is doubtful whether the President seriously expected to attend the meeting, though his secretaries state that for a moment he "cherished the hope of going to Springfield, and once more in his life renewing the sensation, so dear to politicians, of personal contact with great and enthusiastic masses, and of making one more speech to shouting thousands . . . ." [4] Advance publicity, of course, required that the supposed probability of Lincoln's attendance should be overplayed. In this connection the *Journal* editorialized: "It is

1 *Ill. State Jour.*, Aug. 17, 1863, p. 2, c. 3.
2 R. T. L. Coll., 25601-2.
3 Lincoln to Conkling, Aug. 20, 1863, photostat, A. Lincoln Assoc.
4 Nicolay and Hay, *Lincoln*, VII, 379–380.

now two years and a half since Mr. Lincoln bade adieu to his friends in Illinois to assume the vast responsibilities which attach to the office of President of the United States." There were words of eulogy and a reference to the dark times of '61; then the editorial continued: "Nothing could be more fitting . . . in this hour of national triumph and hope, than that he should visit his old home and receive the greetings of his friends of the Prairie State." [5]

At about the same time the Washington correspondent of the New York *Evening Post* wrote: "The President still resides at the Soldiers' Home. Every evening at about six o'clock, he can be seen leaving the Executive Mansion at the head of a mounted escort of 15 or 20 soldiers. The cares and responsibilities of his office are obviously telling upon the health of the President. He looks thin and feeble, and his eyes have lost their humorous expression. His friends entertain much solicitude about his health, and have endeavored to persuade him to leave Washington to recuperate, but so far the pilot sticks to his helm, and does not seem disposed to leave it so long as he has strength to hold it." [6] It was the hope of the editor of the *Illinois State Journal* that these considerations of Lincoln's friends "will be effectual in inducing him to be here on the 3d of September next." [7]

The huge Springfield gathering was but one of the popular rallies planned for this summer of 1863. There were small local ones, as at Virginia, Illinois, on August 25, where the redoubtable Dr. Peter Cartwright spoke of the "inconsistency of the Copperhead Democracy." [8] And in Indiana a big assemblage of "war Democrats" was planned for August 20, for which such prominent speakers as Henry S. Lane, Lewis Cass, John A. Logan, John A. McClernand, John

---

5 *Ill. State Jour.*, Aug. 21, 1863, p. 2, c. 3.

6 *Ibid.*, Aug. 22, 1863, p. 2, c. 1, quoting New York *Evening Post.*

7 Editor's comment in the *Journal*, same issue.

8 *Ill. State Jour.*, Sep. 2, 1863, p. 1, c. 2. Cartwright, Lincoln's opponent in the congressional election of 1846, took little active part in politics during the war, but there were several instances of his making Union speeches. In 1862, in exhorting brother preachers to sustain a church paper in St. Louis, he noted with commendation that its editor "advocates gradual emancipation and colonization . . . till the dark, damning sin of slavery is swept from our nation." *Central Christian Advocate* (St. Louis), May 15, 1862. The attitude of Cartwright was linked with that of Douglas. As the same editor wrote, "we thank God for the patriotism of Mr. Douglas and Dr. Cartwright, and of all others who are true to the Union of the United States." *Ibid.*, Jan. 8, 1863. On this matter the author has been assisted by Theodore L. Agnew, Jr., of Stillwater, Oklahoma, who is preparing a biography of Cartwright.

Brough, David Tod, James Guthrie, and Alvin P. Hovey, were announced as invited.

Meanwhile some of the plans of the so-called "Copperheads" had miscarried. A meeting of the grand castle of the K. G. C. was held at Chicago on August 4, attended by two delegates from each county containing as least one castle, said to be true of seventy-one counties. It leaked out, however, that "the Government had got hold of a member of the order and obtained such facts . . . as made it dangerous to transact any business." So all that was done was "to investigate the case of the supposed informer." It was reported that the knights returned to their castles "very much disappointed." [9]

The crescendo of excitement mounted as the day of the Union meeting approached. On September 2 loyal men were reported arriving in large numbers, with hotels overflowing and the people "determined to make the demonstration one which shall convince traitors abroad and sympathizers with traitors at home that the Government will be sustained and the rebellion crushed." "Partisanship," so ran the editorial of the *Journal,* "is discarded, and Democrats and Republicans will be found nobly burying their minor differences, and uniting heartily upon the platform of the Constitution and the Union." [10]

When the day arrived the editor wrote: "Thousands of loyal men will greet each other in the Capital of Illinois to-day. It is no ordinary occasion that calls them together. There is no election in immediate prospect—the interests of no particular candidate are to be urged or advanced. The object of the meeting . . . is to sustain the Government in the hour of its trial." The main issue was to defeat the effort to overthrow the government. "All minor issues should be forgotten." [11]

VII

While the plans for the Springfield rally were proceeding Lincoln had to think of many things—serious military developments in Tennessee, difficulties in army command, draft troubles on many sides, foreign affairs, and problems of a peace drive that could neither be ignored nor trusted for a favorable result. Elections were yet to come

[9] *Ill. State Jour.*, Sep. 2, 1863.

[10] *Ibid.*, p. 2, c. 1.

[11] *Ibid.*, Thursday morning, Sep. 3, 1863, p. 2, c. 1.

in the most critical states; reconstruction efforts were afoot in the South (especially in Louisiana and Tennessee); the President's unpublished opinion on the draft law was being carefully worked out; the debate with Seymour of New York was growing more intense; and the forces of Vallandighamism were working both openly and in secret.

It was, and this was typical, a time of petty or nagging details along with larger matters. What should be the compensation of Dr. Charles M. Wetherill, chemist in the department of agriculture? What about charges against (and by) John A. McClernand? How about the New Almedan mine in California, also the California land claim of General Daniel E. Sickles? And what was to be done about the persistent demand of Illinois that the Federal government refund to the state "two per cent. on the sales of public lands," a claim which the President considered (at such a time) "ungracious." Nor could the President ignore the importance of notifying Mrs. Grimsley of Springfield that he was "appointing Johnny to the Naval school." [1]

It was outrageous that the President's time had to be taken up with all such details, but in following the daily course of the Lincoln administration one needs constantly to bear in mind this persistent pressure of the trivial, the personal, and the miscellaneous along with grave and portentous problems of government.

In sending a letter to be read at the Springfield meeting,[2] Lincoln delivered by proxy what amounted to a political (though nonpartisan) address; it has been called his "last stump speech." [3] The sentences were short. The language was popular. There were applause lines interspersed with reasoned arguments. There were in fact two simultaneous letters to Conkling: the public letter to be read at the grand rally, and a transmitting letter in which the President briefly explained that he could not leave Washington, but added: "Herewith is a letter instead. You are one of the best public readers. I have but one suggestion. Read it very slowly. And now God bless you, and all good Union-men." [4] Lincoln wanted his absent per-

---

[1] Nicolay and Hay, *Works,* IX, *passim* (latter half of 1863).

[2] Paul Selby, "The Lincoln-Conkling Letter . . . An Explanation of Lincoln's Most Famous Epistle," *Transactions,* Ill. State Hist. Soc., 1908, 240–250.

[3] Nicolay and Hay, *Works,* IX, 95 (footnote).

[4] Lincoln's letter to be read at the rally was dated August 26, 1863, his letter of transmittal, August 27; photostats, A. Lincoln Assoc.

sonality and his message presented with due effect. He dated the letter August 26, but the matter remained in his mind, and five days later, thinking that the beneficial effect of the emancipation proclamation had not been sufficiently emphasized, he sent a third communication with an instruction for a substantial passage to be inserted.[5]

This Conkling letter belonged to presidential publicity on a national level. Lincoln was concerned not only as to the local occasion, which was no small factor; he was also interested in the wider reception in the press. It mortified him to find, on the day of the meeting, that the letter had been "botched up, in the Eastern papers."[6]

In the earlier portion of the address Lincoln was on the defensive, which shows how fully he was conscious of the criticism directed against his policy. There were those, he knew, who were dissatisfied with him. To them he put the question: You desire peace, but how can we obtain it? By three ways: (1) Suppress the rebellion by arms. That was what he was "trying to do." (2) Give up the Union. He said simply: "I am against this. Are you for it? If you are, you should say so plainly." (3) "If you are not for *force* [wrote the President], nor yet for *dissolution,* there only remains some imaginable *compromise.*" But, he said, the army was the strength of the rebellion: "no paper compromise to which the controllers of Lee's army [he meant the government at Richmond] are not agreed, can at all affect that army." He added: "In an effort at such compromise [with alleged negotiators who lacked full authority] we should waste time, which the enemy would improve to our disadvantage; and that would be all." He assured his hearers that no peace compromise had emanated "from that rebel army, or from any of the men controlling it." Insinuations to the contrary were "deceptive and groundless." He promised: "if any such proposition shall hereafter come, it shall not be rejected, and kept a secret from you." He was the servant of the people and responsible to them.

Still on the defensive, the President then passed to the controver-

5 This communication giving a passage to be inserted has been preserved in several forms: Lincoln's autograph (original at Brown Univ.); office copy in R. T. L. Coll., 25933–4; and the telegram as received (original in Ill. State Hist. Lib.).

6 Lincoln to Conkling, Sep. 3, 1863, photostat, A. Lincoln Assoc.

sial subject of the Negro; this he did with full awareness of the difficulty of that subject in Illinois and elsewhere. Here he differed with his "dissatisfied" friends. "I certainly wish that all men could be free," he wrote, "while I suppose you do not." He then launched into an argument on emancipation. He denied that his proclamation was unconstitutional (though this had been argued by so distinguished a man as the former justice of the Supreme Court, Benjamin R. Curtis).[7]

Then he said: "Some of you profess to think its retraction would operate favorably for the Union. Why better *after* the retraction, than *before* the issue? There was more than a year and a half of trial to suppress the rebellion before the proclamation issued, the last one hundred days of which passed under an explicit notice that it was coming, unless averted by those in revolt, returning to their allegiance. The war has certainly progressed as favorably for us, since the issue of the proclamation as before."

It was at this point that Lincoln, by a subsequent telegram, inserted a passage showing the effect of the proclamation on the progress of the war. Some of the commanders, he said, "believe the emancipation policy, and the use of the colored troops, constitute the heaviest blow yet dealt to the rebellion." "Among the commanders holding these views," he added, "are some who have never had any affinity with what is called abolitionism, or with republican party politics; but who hold them purely as military opinions. I submit these opinions as being entitled to some weight against the objections, often urged, that emancipation, and arming the blacks, are unwise as military measures, and were not adopted, as such, in good faith."

"You say you will not fight to free negroes," wrote Lincoln. "Some of them seem willing to fight for you; but, no matter." This was a justifiable thrust. It was also a deserved tribute to the colored race, emerging into the status of free men willing to bear the burdens that went with their new-found dignity. "Fight you, then," wrote Lincoln, "exclusively to save the Union. I issued the proclamation on purpose to aid you in saving the Union. Whenever you shall have conquered all resistance to the Union, if I shall urge you to continue fighting,

---

[7] *Lincoln the President,* II, 175–176.

it will be an apt time then for you to declare you will not fight to free negroes."

Was this a suggestion that emancipation was not one of Lincoln's war aims? Did it mean that emancipation might be dropped if the Union were made secure? Should it not rather be read in the light of the President's main argument—that, as of 1863, emancipation was vitally important for the Union and the Union for emancipation? The next passage clarified the point. Negroes, he said, "like other people, act upon motives." "Why should they do any thing for us, if we will do nothing for them? If they stake their lives for us, they must be prompted by the strongest motive—even the promise of freedom. And the promise being made, must be kept."

At this point in the Springfield letter it was as if a composer had changed the movement of a symphony. A different note was struck. After all, this was a Union meeting. It was time that an affirmative word should be said for the national cause. "The signs look better," wrote the President. "The Father of Waters again goes unvexed to the sea. Thanks to the great North West for it. Nor yet wholly to them. Three hundred miles up, they met New-England, Empire, Key Stone, and Jersey, hewing their way right and left. . . . The job was a great national one; and let none be banned who bore an honorable part in it. . . . Nor must Uncle Sam's Web-feet be forgotten. At all the watery margins they have been present. Not only on the deep sea, the broad bay, and the rapid river; but also up the narrow muddy bayou, and wherever the ground was a little damp, they have been, and made their tracks. Thanks to all. For the great republic—for the principle it lives by, and keeps alive—for man's vast future—thanks to all."

Then he closed: "Peace does not appear so distant as it did. I hope it will come soon, and come to stay; and so come as to be worth the keeping in all future time. It will then have been proved that, among free men, there can be no successful appeal from the ballot to the bullet; and that they who take such appeal are sure to lose their case, and pay the cost." Here he had a word for colored men who with steady eye and well-poised bayonet had helped mankind on to this great consummation, and white ones who had hindered it. He continued: "Let us be quite sober. Let us diligently apply the means, never doubting that a just God, in his own good time, will give us the rightful result." [8]

On the day after the huge Springfield meeting Lincoln's friend Conkling wrote a letter to the President. "Our Mass Meeting," he reported, "was a magnificent success. I should judge there were 50 000 to 75 000 present, and the largest meeting by far that ever assembled together in the State. Doolittle, Lane Chandler and Oglesby delivered splendid speeches. Seven stands were used during the day and on the most of them speaking continued without intermission from 11 o'clock to 5 P M. The most unbounded enthusiasm prevailed. The speeches were of the most earnest, radical and progressive character and the people applauded most vociferously every sentiment in favor of the vigorous prosecution of the war until the rebellion was subdued—the Proclamation of Emancipation and the arming of negro soldiers and every allusion to yourself and your policy." [9]

Not once in his Springfield letter did Lincoln claim credit for his party or use the language of partisanship. At the beginning he had addressed his "old political friends" and "those other noble men whom no partizan malice or partizan hope can make false to the nation's life." The call for the meeting had been to Union men "without regard to party associations." It has already been seen how the *Journal* declared that partisanship had been "discarded" and "minor differences" (between Republicans and Democrats) buried.

Yet mass meetings of this sort, in which Democratic participation was sought and obtained, were unhesitatingly used for Republican advantage. It was realized that effort in prosecuting the war, as well as ultimate victory in the war, however much it might be unpartisan in the factors and elements contributing to it, would inure to the benefit of the party in power. The name "Union" was appropriated and used for Republican triumph. Such was always the purpose of the Union League. And along with this there was the growing tendency to refer to Democrats as if they were the "peace party," the party of disloyalty, and of "Copperheads." This is not said lightly. It is unmistakably evident in the record of those times.

[8] For the letter to Conkling, Aug. 26, 1863, Lincoln's autograph draft has been followed (R. T. L. Coll., 25846–54); comparison with the letter as sent, in copyist's hand, shows only negligible variations (MS., Ill. State Hist. Lib.).

[9] James C. Conkling to Lincoln, Sep. 4, 1863, R. T. L. Coll., 26041.

This attitude was carried forward into later decades and became the pattern of Republican history writing. As to this very Springfield meeting, loudly advertised as including all Union men regardless of party, Nicolay and Hay wrote: "The meeting was an extraordinary one . . . ; it was addressed by the greatest orators of the Republican party; . . . . The speeches were marked by the most advanced and unflinching Republican doctrine; . . . and . . . every reference to Mr. Lincoln's name was received with thunders of applause . . . ." Having thus characterized it as a party meeting, which was the very opposite of its declared purpose, Nicolay and Hay wrote: "In this spirit the campaign [i. e., the party struggle in certain states] was fought through to its victorious close." They added: ". . . in this memorable contest the Republicans presented a united front to the common enemy . . . ." [10]

That common enemy—the Democratic party, as Nicolay and Hay understood it—was finding it hard to maintain itself as a party of opposition and at the same time promote the war for the Union. If it was a matter of party advantage—strictly that—they were as much entitled to it as the Republicans, but the wartime dilemma of the Democrats was obvious. As a writer of the time put it, "It does seem to me the most obvious folly . . . for an opposition to suppose that it can sustain the prominent measures of the party in power, without its support enuring to the benefit of that party altogether. . . . Common sense people at once say 'Will you uphold the main policy of the administration, why not let us vote for it . . . in preference to you, if we desire the spoils?' " [11] In reading this comment on a well recognized situation, one is led to the reflection that when great matters are at issue there is something essentially inadequate in the party motive. If men of differing political opinions pull together for the common cause, there is injustice in the two facts that the "ins" must gain party advantage, and the "outs" lose it, because of the common effort. If the occasion requires that partisanship be set aside in the interest of broader motives, the people and the leaders should make it so.

---

[10] Nicolay and Hay, *Lincoln,* VII, 380, 386, 388. Writing in the 1880's as Republicans, Nicolay and Hay showed a partisanship that was notably lacking in Lincoln's letter.

[11] James B. Walle to William Henry Hurlbut of New York, Burlington, Vt., no date (probably 1864), S. L. M. Barlow MSS.

CHAPTER XI

VALLANDIGHAM FOR GOVERNOR: FURTHER PHASES OF POLITICS, 1863

I

THOUGH citizens and soldiers in many states were balloting in 1863, and though all the votes were important, the most outstanding of these contests was in Ohio, where the Democratic campaign was pointed directly against Lincoln and where Vallandigham himself was candidate for governor. It would indeed have been a sensational occurrence had he been popularly chosen to that office. All the excitement and bitter resentment concerning military rule, arbitrary arrests, the "Vallandigham case," the quarrel with Seymour, the suppression of the Chicago *Times,* and the government's war policy were concentrated in the furious Ohio campaign.

When the Democratic state convention met at Columbus on June 11 the Vallandigham excitement was at its highest, the military situation prior to Gettysburg was full of gloom and uncertainty, and the agitation against conscription was vocal and menacing. It was a time when military measures *at home* were receiving special emphasis, as it was supposed on the one side that methods of free government were being cast aside, and on the other hand that subversive secret societies were seeking to undermine the army and leave the Union without adequate defense. These factors were associated with a peace drive which, though offering nothing for Union advantage, made its appeal to war-sick millions.

In its voluminous resolutions the Ohio Democratic convention expressed itself with strong indignation. The Democratic party, they declared, was the law-abiding party, favoring guarantees of public and private liberty. Their plea was for things which the American people held fundamental: free thought, free speech, and free government by the people's will. The emancipation proclamation, they protested, was unwise, unconstitutional, and void. Powers assumed by the President under the guise of military necessity were unwarranted. The arrest of Vallandigham "for no other pretended crime than . . . uttering . . . legitimate criticism upon the . . . Administration in power" was a "palpable violation" of the Constitution. Said arrest, furthermore, was "a direct insult offered to the sovereignty of the people of Ohio." It was an "unmerited imputation upon their intelligence and loyalty." At the time of the arrest Vallandigham was "a prominent candidate" for the Democratic nomination as governor [i. e., prominently considered; he was not yet nominated]. The Democratic party was "fully competent to decide whether he was a fit man for that nomination." [1]

The nomination of Vallandigham was unanimous by acclamation. By this act the Democratic convention was asking the people of Ohio to elect as their governor the man who, besides being probably the most famous and outspoken of Lincoln's critics in the North, was under sentence of a military commission which had found him guilty of aiding and encouraging the enemy, and of inducing in his hearers "a distrust of their own Government, sympathy for those in arms against it and a disposition to resist the laws of the land." [2]

It was conceivable that this Democratic politician could have been confined in Fort Warren or some other fortress of the United States and chosen governor of Ohio while so imprisoned. Instead of that, he was named as a candidate while in exile. His dramatic absence as a Federal prisoner-of-state under banishment added greatly to his importance, so much so that the people were moved more by sympathy for him as a "case" for civil rights than by agreement with his sentiments. This situation was illustrated when George Ellis Pugh, a Democrat who had resisted the extreme proslavery element of his party at Charleston in 1860, spoke in Vallandigham's stead, accepting the nomination for him. Pugh was not fully "a Vallandigham

[1] The convention that nominated Vallandigham met on June 11. He had been arrested on May 5, tried on May 6–7, and sentenced on May 7. For the resolutions see McPherson, *Hist. of the Rebell.*, 167–168.

[2] See the specifications, findings, and sentence of the military commission. *Offic. Rec.*, 2 ser. V, 635, 646.

man," since he had disagreed with the agitator as to procedures in deciding upon peace. Yet he considered the civil rights issue so important that he made "a speech many times more violent than any of Vallandigham's utterances," [3] for which he was not arrested. After this he was nominated on the Vallandigham ticket as lieutenant governor.

Out of this meeting there came a formal protest to the President, submitted by a committee of the convention, consisting of M. Birchard, Alexander Long, George H. Pendleton, and other Ohio Democrats. In a letter to the President, June 26, they "most respectfully" submitted the resolutions of their convention which, they said, was "one of the most earnest and sincere, in support of the Constitution and the Union, ever held in that State." Not "as a favor" but "as a right due to an American citizen" they prayed the President for "the revocation of the order banishing Mr. Vallandigham," whose arrest, trial, and exile had "created wide-spread and alarming disaffection among the people of the State, . . . impairing . . . confidence in the fidelity of your Administration to . . . free government . . . ." Noting that the President had been distressed at Vallandigham's arrest, the committee assured him that the public safety would be "far more endangered by continuing Mr. Vallandigham in exile than by releasing him."

The Birchard committee developed their argument at great length, using for the purpose the President's own letter on the same subject to the Albany committee.[4] Admitting that Vallandigham may have differed "with the President, and even with some of his own political party," they urged that this did not prove him unfaithful as an American citizen. They reminded the President that, during the Mexican War, opponents of the administration then in power opposed and denounced the war, which they declared to be unjust and unholy. With as much reason, they thought, as in Vallandigham's case, it might have been said of these opponents of President Polk that their discussions were calculated "to discourage enlistments, . . . to induce desertions . . . and leave the Government without an adequate military force to carry on the war."

They then touched upon Lincoln's answer to Corning. The Presi-

[3] G. H. Porter, *Ohio Politics during the Civil War Period*, 171.

[4] See above, pp. 226–228.

dent had admitted that if making a public speech were Vallandigham's only crime, the arrest was wrong, but had argued that his offense was more than that; he was laboring to prevent the raising of troops and to leave the rebellion without any adequate military force to suppress it. "He was warring upon the military, and this gave the military constitutional jurisdiction to lay hands on him." The committee argued that, if any one was discouraged from enlisting because of hearing Vallandigham's "views as to the policy of the war as a means of restoring the Union," and if Vallandigham was rightly subject to punishment on that account, then "upon the same grounds every political opponent of the Mexican war might have been convicted and banished from the country." (It was plainly implied, though not stated, that this would have included Lincoln himself.) After discussing habeas corpus, arrests, and summary trials, the committee put the President in the role of an unconstitutional ruler. Banishment, they urged, was "unknown to our laws"; they could not see the President's right to prescribe this, or torture upon the rack, or other unusual punishments.[5]

II

Lincoln was prompt and courteous in his reply to this Ohio committee. He began by referring the protesting gentlemen to his Albany letter which, he noted, had been used by the committee itself. On the Mexican War question, though reluctant "to waste a word on a merely personal point," he denied that he had "opposed, in discussion before the people, the policy of the Mexican war." It was only by implication that the committee was bringing Lincoln's own attitude of 1848 into the picture. They were pointing to the analogy between Vallandigham and the opponents of Polk's war policy. To mention the analogy was natural enough, but Lincoln, taking it as an accusation pointed at himself, answered it by denying that he had opposed the Mexican War in popular discussion. Lincoln's statements, of course, had been made in Congress.

Ohio opponents of the war policy of 1863 could hardly have been impressed by this argument. Lincoln in 1846–48 would have re-

[5] For the letter from the Birchard committee, see McPherson, *Rebellion*, 167–170; R. T. L. Coll., 24427–49.

sented it if his Whig friends—e. g., Thomas Corwin of Ohio or Daniel Webster of Massachusetts—had been imprisoned or banished for denouncing the Mexican War, whether in Congress or elsewhere. After treating the attitude and speeches of such men, the historian of the Mexican War writes: "Going far beyond the limits of reasonable criticism and helpful suggestions, and indulging in language calculated to dishearten and hamper the administration, they encouraged the enemy." [1] It must be added that many thoughtful, upright, and patriotic men in the time of Polk agreed with critics of the war against Mexico. Abolitionists did so with unanimity. It was a subject of complexities and difficulties, not a theme that lent itself to easy elaboration either for the President's purpose or otherwise. Lincoln knew that he had to touch it lightly.

The President then launched into a considerable discussion of the habeas corpus privilege under the Constitution and of the authority to suspend it. "You claim," he wrote, "that men may . . . embarrass those whose duty it is to combat a giant rebellion, and then be dealt with in turn, only as if there were no rebellion. The Constitution itself rejects this view. The military arrests . . . which have been made . . . have been for prevention, and not for punishment—as injunctions to stay injury, as proceedings to keep the peace . . . . The original sentence of imprisonment in Mr. Vallandigham's case was to prevent injury to the military service only and the modification of it was made as a less disagreeable mode to him of securing the same prevention."

The President was "unable to perceive an insult to Ohio in the case of Mr. Vallandigham," being quite sure "nothing of the sort was or is intended." He had been unaware that the gentleman was, when arrested, a candidate for the Democratic nomination for governor. He was grateful to Ohio "for many things, especially for the brave soldiers and officers she has given in the present national trial to the armies of the Union."

On the main question—Vallandigham's injury to the national cause—the President gave a convincing statement. He did not know that the orator had "by direct language advised against enlistments and in favor of desertion and resistance to drafting." But all knew,

---

1 Justin H. Smith, *The War With Mexico*, II, 280. Since Webster has been mentioned, it may be added that Major Edward Webster, his son, died in service near Mexico City.

he said, that combinations for that purpose existed "and that quite a number of assassinations have occurred from the same animus." This maiming and murder the President solemnly declared to be due to Vallandigham's course "in greater degree than to any other cause; and . . . to him in a greater degree than to any other one man." (Vallandigham was, in fact, to become early in 1864 supreme commander of the Sons of Liberty, this being the new name of the grandiloquent Order of American Knights, an organization similar to the Knights of the Golden Circle.) The whole burden of Vallandigham's speeches was to stir up men's minds against the prosecution of the war.

This, the President pointed out, was the man nominated for governor by the Ohio Democratic convention, while in their statement they showed no awareness of an existing rebellion. Since their nominee was known to have opposed using the army to suppress the rebellion, Lincoln wrote to the committee: "Your own attitude . . . encourages desertion . . . and the like . . . ." Such an attitude, he considered "a real strength to the enemy." The position of the Ohio men being a good deal weaker as to sustaining the Union than that of the Albany men, the President sought to pin them down, or to elicit a simple pledge. Would they sign their names as endorsing three propositions? If so, he promised Vallandigham's release. In brief these propositions were: (1) that there was in existence a rebellion to destroy the Union for whose suppression the army and navy were the constitutional means; (2) that they would not hinder the increase of the army or navy or lessen their efficiency; (3) that each of them in his sphere would labor to have the officers and men of the forces paid, fed, provided for, and supported. Let them sign these statements and their banished friend would be released.[2]

These signatures were not forthcoming. The purpose of the committee was to make a party issue against the President, to put him in the wrong, not to have him set up the conditions of Vallandigham's release or state the terms by which they should put themselves in the right. So they sent another letter, expressing surprise at the President's suggestions. The people of Ohio, they wrote, were concerned not so much because of Vallandigham's safety as because they visioned

---

[2] Lincoln to M. Birchard and Others, Nicolay and Hay, *Works,* IX, 1–10 (June 29, 1863). This text differs but slightly and not significantly from Lincoln's autograph draft (R. T. L. Coll., 24494–506).

an attack upon their own rights. They wanted his release as "an abandonment of the claim to the power of such arrest and banishment." However much the committee might feel inclined to endorse the President's propositions, they had no authority to bargain as to the conditions of release. Their pro-Union views were well known, but they resented the demand for a pledge which they regarded as an imputation upon their sincerity, as a concession of the legality of this instance of arrest, trial, and banishment. They asked the revocation of the order "not as a favor, but as a right due to the people of Ohio." The President's suggestion, they thought, was "a mere evasion," the more so as his letter had ended with an intimation that the presidential acts complained of might be repeated.[3]

Thus ended, with forensic banners waving on both sides, the Lincoln-Birchard debate. Both sides had appealed to high principles and neither side had given in. Ohio friends of Vallandigham were invoking time-honored traditions as if no desperate emergency existed and as if the processes of peace were appropriate to a tremendous civil war. They had a strong talking point in their stressing of civil rights, but they were unsatisfactory in their assumption that Vallandigham was doing no injury to the nation. As to this very question of civil rights they would have been in a stronger position had it not been that in previous years Ohio Democrats, though they were not the only ones, had scornfully denied basic rights to antislavery agitators. Toward such agitators they had been far indeed from allowing freedom of speech, of the press, of petition, of academic teaching, and the like.[4]

Lincoln was convincing in his insistence that the effect of Vallandighamism was to aid the enemy, but he was greatly embarrassed by Burnside's measures of which he did not approve. He would not have ordered Vallandigham's arrest and he promptly revoked the general's order suppressing the Chicago *Times*. He was ready to release Vallandigham, realizing that the "case" had given a handle to his critics and a continuing theme for denouncing his administra-

---

3 The President had closed his Birchard letter as follows: "Still, in regard to Mr. Vallandigham and all others, I must hereafter, as heretofore, do so much as the public safety may seem to require." Nicolay and Hay, *Works,* IX, 10. For the Ohio committee's rejoinder, see McPherson, 172–175.

4 These startling attacks upon civil rights and free expression of opinion are treated in Russell Nye, *Fettered Freedom*.

tion; but he realized that such release, if interpreted as a weakening of the military authority, would be an added embarrassment. Weighing one factor against another, the President stood ready to agree to the release, but he wanted some compensating assurance on the part of those who were making capital of what they were denouncing. He did not, of course, honestly intend that men should be imprisoned for criticising him—that was so evident that it hardly needed assurance—but he did believe, in a desperate civil war, that military arrests were a proper and constitutional emergency measure to prevent those activities behind the lines which injured the national cause and gave substantial aid and comfort to the enemy. It was not so much that he was prosecuting these men; he was intending to take such temporary measures as would "stay injury."

There was one point in the case which Lincoln left unstated. He said in the Birchard letter that, under the conditions indicated, the "order" as to Vallandigham would be revoked. This must have referred to the President's order of banishment. The assumption was, of course, that this would have allowed Vallandigham to go free. Then what about the sentence of imprisonment imposed by the military commission? In the 1863 situation—as also in the later action (or non-action) of the Supreme Court—there was nothing in law to check the enforcement of that military sentence. The President had the authority to set aside the sentence of a military commission if he thought best, but there was another way out, and in the Birchard letter Lincoln indicated that already, nearly at the outset of the case, his mind was disposed toward what was actually allowed to happen next year—i. e., to permit the sentence to become a dead letter. The order of banishment had provided reimprisonment according to the sentence of the military commission in case of Vallandigham's unauthorized return. For the prisoner to go free, it would have been expected that this part of the order as well as the banishment would be revoked if the prescribed conditions were met. Actually to have revoked the order or the sentence, however, especially in view of the obvious fact that it was proving an embarrassment to the government rather than an effective treatment for an ugly situation, would have been distasteful, and would have produced trouble in the war department. Publicity favorable to the Albany and Columbus committees was not the only kind to consider, for there were voices equally strong on the other side. After the imbroglio had developed as it did in 1863, there was no perfect solution. Realizing this, Lincoln looked the other way when, later, the notorious prisoner escaped and reappeared in the United States. The President did nothing, thus disregarding both the presidential order and the military sentence.[5] It was as if he had said: Here is that Vallandigham again—he's back. So what? Let him talk.

For the Ohioan's exile was brief. On July 5, two months after his arrest, he was reported as arriving at Halifax, N.S. He had escaped through the blockade to the British West Indies, whence he had sailed to Nova Scotia. On July 15, 1863, from Niagara Falls on the Canadian side just across the United States border, he vigorously entered the political campaign with an address to the people of Ohio. Recounting his hazards by land and sea, he declared that he found himself first a freeman when on British soil; under the British flag he enjoyed the rights which "usurpers insolently" denied him at home. "I return," he said, "with my opinions and convictions . . . not only unchanged, but confirmed and strengthened." It was not, in its wording, an anti-Union address, but rather a lofty political battle cry for liberty, popular government, and freedom of speech. Strongly denouncing the "party of the Administration," he warned that whoever voted its ticket would "forfeit his own right to liberty, personal and political, whensoever other men and another party shall hold the power." [6] (He was talking to the theme of freedom of speech, but this threat did not sound very much like freedom of voting.)

III

Not all the Ohio Democrats approved of Vallandigham. A small group known as "War Democrats" convened at Columbus on September 22 and took a stand declaring the nomination of Vallandigham a mistake and opposing any kind of peace except one that re-

[5] In a speech at Peru, Indiana, in the summer of 1864, Schuyler Colfax gave his interpretation of Lincoln's reason for not arresting Vallandigham on his return in 1864. According to Colfax, though not knowing "the details" of the movement, the President was aware of a dangerous secret conspiracy in the Northwest, and "knew the intention was to make Vallandigham's arrest a pretext for lighting the torch of civil war all over the Northwest." (This theory seems inconsistent with the fact that Lincoln never approved of the arrest at any time.) Buffalo *Morning Express*, Sep. 2, 1864, p. 2, c. 2.

[6] Frank Moore, ed., *Rebell. Rec.* (Docs.), VII, 438-439.

quired "unconditional submission to the Constitution and laws of the United States." [1] The effect of this splinter party was negligible. The Ohio Democratic banner had been appropriated by the Vallandigham forces. Managing politicians had put the party in a position which did not genuinely reflect the views of its supporters. Many Democrats resented this in 1863, just as millions of Democrats were to find bitter reason to resent the Vallandigham stigma in 1864.

Vallandigham's opponent, John Brough, "Union" candidate for governor of Ohio, was a Democrat, known not as a politician but as a business man, journalist, and orator. The campaign was spirited and angry. The Vallandigham men played their highest card—the issue of civil rights—but they overplayed their hand in announcing that in case of their hero's election a huge force of armed men would "receive their Governor-elect at the Canadian line and escort him to the State House to see that he takes the oath of office."

This bit of sensational theatrics was as badly misplayed as the statement by Daniel Voorhees of Indiana promising that such a move would be supported by the Democrats of his state.[2] These tactics enabled Brough's party to predict that Vallandigham's election would produce civil war in Ohio. Not that this was likely, any more than that Vallandigham's men, if victorious in the election, would have invited support in terms of a Confederate invasion of the state. Such things belong in the category of melodramatic predictions and are to be set down to the sometimes incredible and irresponsible intensity of political campaigning. There was enough reason for opposing Vallandigham without supposing that civil war within the state or a shift of allegiance of the whole commonwealth would have been the result if he had been chosen governor by a majority of Ohio voters. Predictions of this sort, however, did harm to the Democratic cause and probably added considerably to the vote for Brough. Just what "would have" been the result if Vallandigham had been elected can only be a matter of conjecture. As governor of a Union state, with actual responsibilities of office, he would have been less free to agitate than as a politician out of office. Perhaps he would have become simply a more vociferous Seymour. Yet with his record and personality, different from Seymour's, he would have been a menace to the cause for which Lincoln worked.

---

1 Porter, *Ohio Politics*, 181.

2 *Ibid.*, 182.

In commenting on the Ohio contest the *Republican* of St. Louis noted a curious fact: "neither of the candidates for Governor represents the party nominating him. Brough claims to be a Democrat, and in his speeches pretends that he has never left that party. The Democratic party of Ohio generally repudiate the doctrines of Vallandigham, so far as they relate to the war and . . . its prosecution." It was added that sympathy because of his arrest was the reason for the famous agitator's nomination.[8]

This somewhat confused situation as to candidates, labels, and organizations should not be taken as indication that party differences were being erased in Ohio. The "Union" party in that state was essentially the Republican party, while in the accounts of the time the group that nominated Vallandigham was regularly called the Democratic party. Thus the fact that many Democrats supported Brough, himself a "war Democrat," and the further fact that without such support Vallandigham would not have been defeated, never redounded to the advantage of the Democratic organization. It was quite the contrary. Democratic votes helped strongly to produce an election result which, *as interpreted in the party sense,* assisted only the Republicans.

One could, of course, speak of the Union cause, and Democrats did that; but it could not be overlooked that the word "Union" was appropriated for a party. It was not as if the Republican party had been abandoned, as if a new star had arisen in the party firmament, or as if a new political body, neutral in the party sense, had been created. One could not say that a Democratic-Republican organization, with dual party machinery working toward a strictly bipartisan effect, and with equal importance for both Democrats and Republicans under the combined name of "Union," had been brought into practical existence. The Republicans wanted Democratic votes, and they wanted the support (on election day) of those who earnestly favored the national cause but did not like Republicanism. Their managers, however, never intended that the victory for which the Union Leagues were springing into vote-getting action, should be otherwise treated than as a Republican triumph.

When the votes were counted in the Ohio election, which occurred on October 13, the result reflected the bitterness of the campaign

[8] St. Louis *Republican,* Oct. 13, 1863, clipping in R. T. L. Coll., 27197–8.

and the intensity of public concern. The dimensions of Brough's victory were striking. In the largest vote ever cast in the state, including about 43,000 soldier ballots, Brough was elected by a majority of 101,000. (These soldier votes were a contributing, but not a controlling, element.) It was also of significance that a legislature was elected which included large Union majorities in both houses.[4] It was generally recognized that the victories at Gettysburg and Vicksburg were important factors. It was, of course, a great advantage for the Republicans that it was their President who was in power in a desperate war where the vital cause of national survival was identified with the success of the administration. The fighting cause and the Lincoln cause could not be separated. This situation was evident in the overwhelming majority of the soldier vote that was cast for the Union candidate: 41,000 votes (round numbers) as compared to 2,000 for Vallandigham.

IV

Special interest attached to the 1863 contest in Pennsylvania. To take only one aspect, it involved a species of popular referendum (at least it might be so interpreted) on the legality of the draft. A. G. Curtin, somewhat reluctantly, was standing for reëlection against the judge who had issued a decision declaring the national conscription law unconstitutional. This judge was George W. Woodward of the Pennsylvania superior court; the decision (*Kneedler* versus *Lane*) became a topic of Democratic propaganda; the New York *Tribune* referred to it as a "partisan harangue." [1] The tone of the Democratic campaign was sharply critical of Lincoln, with emphasis upon arrests and with extension of thanks to Ohio Democrats for their vigorous stand. In contrast, Curtin, more than certain other Republican governors, was regarded as strongly pro-Lincoln. "It was hardly possible," wrote Greeley, "to make an issue more distinctly than was here made between the supporters and the contemners of the War for the Union." [2] It was vitally important from the party standpoint to win the 1863 contest as a prestige factor for the larger

[4] Porter, *Ohio Politics*, 183.

[1] New York semi-weekly *Tribune*, Nov. 13, 1863; for the decision, see 45 Pa. 238.

[2] Greeley, *Amer. Conflict*, II, 509.

struggle in 1864.[3] At the same time it was realized that Pennsylvania was a "doubtful" state and that chances of Republican victory were by no means sure. Curtin wrote to Lincoln, on September 4, 1863, that if the election were to occur then the outcome would be extremely doubtful. It was impossible, he added, to magnify the importance of the Pennsylvania result.[4]

An incident of the Pennsylvania campaign was a letter from General McClellan endorsing Woodward; this served to increase the imprecations against both Woodward and McClellan.[5] Before this, writes his biographer, the general had "kept clear of any partizan course"; what he now did in endorsing Woodward, though "intended by him merely as a personal act," was to prove a political blunder and a serious handicap to the general in 1864. It put him "not only with the most bitter opponents of the [Lincoln] administration but also with those who were opposing the war." This was entirely against McClellan's intent. He was, in fact, in no affinity with Copperheads; on the contrary, he was "strongly in favor of a vigorous prosecution of the war." [6] Only very recently, in fact, men favoring a vigorous war had earnestly urged the reinstatement of McClellan as head of the main army.

The Pennsylvania election was fairly close, but the Republicans gained a clear victory. Curtin came through with 269,000 votes to Woodward's 254,000; [7] the Republicans also gained a slight majority in the legislature. In this election David Agnew, Republican, was elected chief justice of the state. He promptly proceeded to re-

---

[3] A correspondent of Simon Cameron wrote telling why he wished Curtin reëlected: ". . . it will enable us to elect our President [he did not say Lincoln] next year. If we are defeated in the State this year it will take the prestige of success from us next year." (As for Cameron himself, he had worked against Curtin's nomination but had to support him in the election.) James S. Chambers to Simon Cameron, Phila., Oct. 9, 1863, R. T. L. Coll., 27067.

[4] *Ibid,* 26043–4.

[5] "I understand Judge Woodward to be in favor of the prosecution of the war with all the means at the command of the loyal States, until the military power of the rebellion is destroyed. . . . Believing our opinions entirely agree upon these points [McClellan had also mentioned regard for private rights, avoidance of military excess, etc.], I would, were it in my power, give to Judge Woodward my voice and my vote." McClellan to Charles J. Biddle, Oct. 12, 1863. (The Pennsylvania election occurred on October 13.) *Ann. Cyc.,* 1863, 740.

[6] William Starr Myers, *General George Brinton McClellan,* 427–428. Myers (p. 428) considers this letter "one of the greatest mistakes of McClellan's career."

[7] *Ann. Cyc.,* 1863, 740.

verse the Woodward decision which declared the conscription act unconstitutional. That decision, wrote Agnew, had been "made in a one-sided hearing . . . in a preliminary way, during a time of high excitement, when partisan rage was furiously assailing the law." [8]

Not all Pennsylvania Republicans were pleased with the result. The long-standing feud between Curtin and Cameron flared up, and the Cameron element had worked with intense determination to defeat Curtin's nomination, preferring John Covode, Republican radical famous for the Covode investigation-and-report assailing Buchanan's Kansas policy. When Curtin was nominated, Cameron (to quote William B. Hesseltine) "fumed in frustration and his cohorts hissed in the galleries." [9] Pennsylvania soldiers, while they did not possess the vote in 1863, made their influence felt by writing home, conveying "earnest appeals" for Curtin's reëlection. It has been remarked that this Republican governor was reëlected "by the votes of Democrats . . . influenced solely by their sympathy with . . . sons and brothers in the field . . . ." [10]

V

For its general significance in the complex, yet oversimplified, world of Republican politics, it is important to take a closer look at Governor Curtin, the victor in this hard-fought Pennsylvania contest. While Republican activity was being increasingly interpreted in terms of radical influence, the plain fact was that such Republicans as Curtin and such Union men as Brough, who carried important doubtful states in 1863, were most assuredly not of the radical type. For one thing, at least as late as June 1863, Curtin was understood to have favored McClellan for highest military command.[1] Leaving aside the controverted question as to McClellan's military leadership, this attitude of Curtin, which was shared by a great many people and soldiers at that time, shows conclusively that the governor was in the opposite camp from the radicals. The ugly antagonism

[8] 45 Pa. 310; *Constitutional Problems Under Lincoln* (revised ed.), 11–12, 32–33, 259.

[9] Hesseltine, *Lincoln and the War Governors*, 329.

[10] McClure, *Abraham Lincoln and Men of War-Times*, 266.

[1] "It was well known here that Govr Curtin had in June last . . . expressed himself favorable to the return of Genl McClellan to the Army of the Potomac or to the chief command in place of General Halleck . . . ." D. H. Williams to S. L. M. Barlow of New York City, Pittsburgh, Sep. 29, 1863, Barlow MSS.

of Cameron to Curtin was another evidence that such was the governor's position; this factor had importance for Lincoln, since Curtin sympathized with the President, while Cameron especially from about the end of 1861, directed his partisan activity along radical lines. It will be recalled that Cameron had caused keen embarrassment to Lincoln; few men had shown less genuine readiness to coöperate with the President in his difficult problems.

A. K. McClure, an authority on this subject, points to Curtin's "profoundly loyal" enthusiasm for the Union cause and shows the Pennsylvanian's great importance (with Lane of Indiana) in bringing about Lincoln's nomination in 1860. There "was not a . . . phase of the war," writes McClure, "at any time that did not summon Curtin to the councils of Lincoln." The governor's relations with Stanton were by no means cordial, and, when matters became difficult between these two men, Lincoln would interpose in Curtin's behalf, to the great irritation of the secretary of war.

For the 1863 story one of the most interesting episodes revealed by McClure is Curtin's willingness to retire as governor and the proposal he made in that connection. (Early in 1863 retirement from the severe burdens of his position seemed advisable because of ill health, but he improved later in the year and lived on with much active postwar service till 1894.) What Curtin proposed was the kind of thing that hardly ever happens in American politics but which in a critical situation would be of great public value. Curtin's suggestion was that he would retire as governor—i. e., not seek renomination—if the Democrats would nominate William B. Franklin, an able Pennsylvania general who had commanded a corps in the Army of the Potomac but had become the target of radical attack.

The plan was that the Republicans would also nominate Franklin, though he was a Democrat. McClure writes: "I was present when Curtin first made this suggestion to a number of his friends, and he made it with a degree of earnestness that impressed every one. He said that it was vastly more important to thus unite the whole Democratic party with the Republicans on an honest war platform than that any party or any individual should win political success." Less inspired counsels prevailed, however, and the plan fell through. The Democratic party was under the control of the "Bourbon" element; the judge who had ruled against conscription was nominated; partisanship was intensified; and Pennsylvania lost an opportunity to make the submerging of party politics not merely a matter of talk, but an actuality.[2] The career of Curtin gives evidence that devotion to the Union and loyalty to Lincoln were by no means synonymous with partisanship in the Republican sense.[3] He "sincerely sympathized with the Liberals" [4] of the party (1872) rather than the radicals and regulars; at important stages he was not in harmony with Republican leaders; furthermore, he realized in Lincoln's day the strength of the opposition to the Republicans in Pennsylvania.[5]

VI

In New York, though it was not a national election, nor for governor, the 1863 contest had unmistakable national significance. In the large it was a question of supporting either the administration of Lincoln or that of Seymour. The people were to vote for state officials other than governor—such as secretary of state, comptroller, and attorney general—but the declarations of the two parties spoke the language of Federal affairs. The Democrats favored united support of the national government for suppressing the rebellion and restoring the Union. They declared secession a false doctrine. At the same time they denounced conscription, favored conciliation, objected to infringement of state rights, assailed what were called illegal and unconstitutional arrests, and expressed highest approval of the administration of Governor Seymour.

The New York Republicans resolved in favor of maintaining the

---

2 McClure, *Abraham Lincoln and Men of War-Times*, 248 ff, esp. 251, 258, 261, 262.

3 Curtin supported Greeley instead of the regular Republican candidate, Grant, in 1872; later he went over to the Democratic party. In the 80's he served six years as Democratic member of the House of Representatives.

4 McClure, 275.

5 "I traveled in company with Gov Curtin from Harrisburg to Altoona & during the entire trip he spoke freely in regard to current politics. He stated in his recent interview with Lincoln and Stanton that Penna would be carried against them. . . . The whole tenor of his conversation was that nothing but the letter of Gen McClellan in favor of Woodward, prevents his coming out on our [Democratic] side. . . . I do believe an effort of a proper character would bring him to us . . . ." Jos. C. McKibbin to S. L. M. Barlow, Oct. 1 [no year given; probably 1864], Barlow MSS. There were comments in this letter which showed dissatisfaction with the Lincoln administration. To that extent the correspondent of Barlow gave a picture of Curtin very different from that of McClure; that correspondent, of course, was an intense Democrat. It should be added that where Curtin was displeased with doings at Washington his dissatisfaction was not so much with Lincoln as with Stanton.

integrity of the Union and the supremacy of the Constitution over the whole national domain, insisted on strengthening the armies, condemned all who embarrassed the government, denounced misleading tenders of peace, and specifically expressed "gratitude . . . to the administration of Mr. Lincoln" for steadfast courage, financial ability, preservation of peace with foreign nations, and splendid victories.[1]

When the votes were counted the result was revealed as a rebuke to Seymour and an endorsement of Lincoln. It is necessary only to note the totals for secretary of state, which were typical: Chauncey M. Depew of Peekskill, defender of Lincoln, received over 314,000 votes; his democratic opponent, Daniel B. St. John, less than 285,000. The Union ticket prevailed overwhelmingly in the choice of both houses of the legislature. In the senate the strength of this party was 21 as compared to 11 for the opposition; in the assembly the division was 82 to 46.[2]

In Massachusetts the Democrats strongly favored the Union, but with resolutions that slanted toward criticism of Lincoln. This was plainly evident in their declarations as to subjugation, martial law, and military usurpation; it appeared also in their expression of "thanks" to Seymour of New York. At the head of their ticket, for governor, they named a prosperous lawyer of little fame, Henry W. Paine.[3] The Republicans, strongly endorsing the emancipation proclamation and deprecating the idea of peace by negotiation with "rebels," renamed John A. Andrew for governor. On November 3, 1863, Andrew was "largely elected," as Lincoln would say; his vote was 70,000, Paine's 29,000. For the legislature strong Republican majorities were chosen.[4] Support of Andrew had the more significance

---

1 *Ann. Cyc.*, 1863, 688. 2 *Ibid.*, 689.

3 Henry William Paine (1810–1893) was a successful lawyer of Maine, later of Boston, and a teacher of law at Boston University. For a closely studied, though highly eulogistic, account, see the article by William Mathews in *New Eng. Mag.*, X, 189–197 (Apr., 1894). The author sets forth Paine's fine New England ancestry, learning, extraordinary memory, benevolence, "Websterian front," keen logic, and personal integrity. He states that "there was probably no one of his legal brethren who was engaged in so many and so important lawsuits . . . as Mr. Paine" (p. 191). Yet this man, the 1863 Democratic contender against Andrew, is so far forgotten that his name does not appear in the index of the voluminous life of Andrew by H. G. Pearson. His nomination shows that Massachusetts Democrats were offering, not a politician, nor a controversial figure, but a man of high ability and character.

4 *Ann. Cyc.*, 1863, 626; N. Y. *Tribune Almanac*, 1864, 58; report on return of votes in

by reason of his ardent antislavery policy and his enthusiastic efforts for raising Negro regiments.

As the months passed with state election days at staggered intervals all over the country, the smaller states gained considerable publicity. The result in Maine was not quite as easily predictable as might have been supposed. The election for governor and other state officials, was held on September 14. Samuel Cony, Union candidate, was elected governor by a vote of 67,916 against 50,366 for Bion Bradbury, Democrat.[5] On the day of the election J. G. Blaine, chairman of the Union committee for the state, telegraphed to Lincoln from Augusta: "Maine sustains your Administration by a majority of 15,000." The next day he sent word that the majority was greater than first estimated.[6]

VII

The situation in turbulent Maryland pertaining to the election of 1863 forced itself voluminously upon Lincoln's attention. The election was for members of Congress, members of the state legislature, and minor state officials (comptroller and commissioner of the land office). The state, so recently a battleground and so torn by riots in 1861, was shaken not only by the usual war agitation but by a combination of vexing factors: absconding slaves, colored soldiers, arbitrary arrests, citizens possessing arms, widespread accusations of disloyalty, and a series of suppressive military orders by General Robert C. Schenck. This officer, who commanded the "Middle Department" with headquarters at Baltimore, was of the radical type; he was not in full harmony with Lincoln, though the President had sought by careful personal approach to promote harmony.

The whole American Civil War was epitomized in Maryland as in Kentucky and Missouri. One has in mind here not so much the issue of secession, for Maryland was safely in the Union after the uncertainty of 1861, but those troublesome clashes by which brothers and neighbors were divided. It was in fact the divisions among pro-Union men that were agitating Maryland. Union Leagues, assuming

election of Nov. 3, 1863 (photostat from archives division, office of the secretary, Commonwealth of Mass.).

5 *Ann. Cyc.*, 1863, 604.

6 R. T. L. Coll., 26275, 26292.

to themselves a kind of exclusive function to organize "Union" men within the state, were pressing hard for state emancipation, for support of "the whole policy of the [national] Administration," and for having congressmen pledged to "abide by the Administration caucus for Speaker of the House of Representatives." This was plainly the language, not simply of the Union, but of the Republican radical machine. It was misleading language in the sense that people would suppose that the word "Administration" had to do with the President and his policy, while in reality the pledge to vote according to the "caucus" meant, being interpreted, to follow the dictates of Thaddeus Stevens.

After much sparring and dissension, with unsuccessful efforts to unite conflicting groups in conference, the position of affairs crystallized as a struggle between "unconditional Union men" (largely the radicals, the Union League group) and "Union men" who preferred the more moderate approach. Both groups strongly and unequivocally supported the Union and both opposed slavery. Their wordy "resolutions" and platforms need not detain us. The difference between them can, perhaps, be no better expressed than by noting that one type was personified by Henry Winter Davis; the other, less bitter, type, by Thomas Swann. Davis was driving hard for an "ultra" type of Republican control which was the opposite of Lincoln's. Though a Republican, he was an outspoken critic of the President and a close ally of Stevens and Wade. Swann, of the more moderate group, supported emancipation, having freed his numerous slaves, but favored the President's pattern for abolition and later for reconstruction. (Davis was a candidate for Congress; Swann the chairman of the Union State Central Committee.) Part of the trouble was the bitter storm raging over the head of Montgomery Blair, postmaster general, whom radicals vociferously denounced, but whom the President was retaining in his cabinet.

It was the moderate group that wanted unity. They tried to draw both groups together, but this did not appeal to the Union-League element. In seeking to eradicate "the evil of slavery" the moderates did not consider this an "excuse for violence"; they sought to avoid that "aggravation of feeling" which they believed would "have the effect of retarding rather than facilitating" the desired object.[1]

[1] *Ann. Cyc.*, 1863, 617.

The far-reaching repercussions of these political episodes were in evidence in connection with the activities of the Blairs. This famous family was persistent in its drive for influence, patronage, and all that went with political power. In one sense the contest was a phase of reconstruction development in a period when differences of policy as to restoration were causing savage factional disputes within the Republican party. It was ultras against conservatives, moderates against radicals, in clashes which proved to be but a foretaste of the long drawn out nation-shaking storm that was to come.

Of the principals in this struggle it could probably be said that the man who caused the greatest annoyance to the Blairs was Secretary Chase. This cabinet member with presidential ambitions was building up his influence with the radical element of the Republican party, and the tactics which he and his followers were using were intolerably distasteful to the Blairs. It was not easy to endure Chase's appointment of his partisans to treasury positions, but a far worse thing was the hawking of false charges of corruption against Frank Blair, Jr. There was also the question of the cotton trade within enemy lines, a shabby practice which Chase was promoting and the younger Frank Blair was stoutly denouncing and exposing. Being loyal to the President, the Blairs "regarded Chase as a traitor to the Chief." [2] Reading his motives and tactics, they perceived a scheme to achieve the presidency through encouraging the radicals and enabling them to control the Republican party.

It was under these circumstances that Montgomery Blair, on October 3, 1863, delivered at Rockville, Maryland, a speech in which the postmaster general, agitated by apprehensions as to radical schemes and angered by the Chase enmity, let himself go in emphatic warnings against ultras of the Republican party. The people of the country, he said, were "menaced by the ambition of the ultra-Abolitionists, which is . . . despotic in its tendencies, and which, if successful, could not fail to be . . . fatal to republican institutions." [3] The speech looked forward to the great problems of restoration and presented a dire picture of the dangers of a radical policy which would abolish state constitutions in the South and submerge that whole

---

[2] William Ernest Smith, *The Francis Preston Blair Family in Politics,* II, 235.

[3] *Ibid.,* II, 237.

broad section (under the designation of conquered territory) as a region to be governed by a radical Congress.

In his favoring non-radical reconstruction the views of Montgomery Blair were basically those of Lincoln, but that situation made it all the worse for the President, since the reaction to the Rockville speech, which was compared to a "bombshell," was highly unfavorable while at the same time it was supposed to be expressive of the President's sentiments. It was a matter of the President having an unskillful spokesman. In large part Blair's ideas did have the President's approval, but Lincoln would never have employed the Blair words nor used the Blair tone. Coming shortly before the President's launching of his main reconstruction policy (put before the country in early December of 1863) the intemperate speech was simply another of the many factors causing the vitally important question of a restored Union to be hung up and entangled in intraparty disputes.

It was the fate of the Blairs to be misunderstood. Frank Blair, Jr., for factional reasons, was actually called a "Copperhead," [4] which was false to the point of absurdity. Montgomery, for denouncing abolitionists—denouncing them because of their attitude toward the Southern people and states—was misrepresented as being friendly to slavery. The charge, of course, was slanderously false. Among the main elements of Montgomery's public service were his free-soil principle, his opposition to Buchanan, his service as counsel for Dred Scott, his prominence as an antislavery man in the Republican party in 1860, his firmness for the Union, and his readiness to uphold the antislavery standard in Maryland.[5] People were misled as to which men were supporting the administration. Readers of some of the newspapers were asked to believe that it was the radicals who were "administration men," while the Blairs were misrepresented as if they were warring against the administration.[6]

[4] *Ibid.*, II, 228.

[5] Among other evidences of his opposition to slavery was a letter which Montgomery Blair wrote on June 21, 1864, to William Lloyd Garrison. Addressing Garrison as a friend, he hoped that, despite differences as to method, their "one common object—emancipation" would be kept in mind. He explained that he had tried to buy an interest in the Baltimore *Clipper* in order to advocate the cause of abolition in Maryland. The letter was published in the *Liberator*. A rough draft is in the Blair MSS., Lib. of Cong. See also W. E. Smith, *Blair Family*, II, 268–269.

[6] Just after the Maryland election a Washington journalist wrote: ". . . measures have lately been taken to make General Blair [Frank P., Jr.], as well as his brother

There was also the difficulty that the Blairs were principals in a major cabinet split.[7] The savage opposition against Seward was brought into the picture, and people came to speak of the factional quarrels between the Chase-Stanton faction and the Blair-Bates-Seward faction. Seward was a special target of radical attack, while always the tendency was to include denunciations of the President in the same breath with criticism of Seward. The President was being injured by his friends. It was said that in Pennsylvania in 1863 the Rockville speech had cost the Republicans 20,000 votes.[8] Yet sincere Unionists who genuinely agreed with Lincoln and who supported his policy were friendly to Montgomery Blair. James Dixon, for instance, Republican senator from Connecticut, wrote the postmaster general expressing approval of his Rockville speech. "In the Senate I know you will find many supporters among the Republicans. It is impossible that the intelligence of that body should have sunk to so low a point as to permit the errors of the radicals to prevail there. In the House of Representatives you will also have much strength." [9]

VIII

As election day (November 3) approached, the hills of Maryland resounded to a clamorous war of words: protests to Lincoln by Swann and Governor Bradford, military orders, proclamations, letters by the President, and fulminations by the newspapers. In "Order No. 53" dated October 27 (modified, and first published on November 2), General Schenck declared that "evil disposed" (pro-rebel) persons were threatening disturbance. In view of this he gave a three-pronged command: (1) that provost marshals and other military officers should arrest "all such persons [i. e., those described in the preamble of his order as "evil disposed persons, . . ."] found at, or hanging about, or approaching" any polling place; (2) that a prescribed oath of al-

[Montgomery], understand that their warfare on the Administration from within . . . , had better be stopped." Cincinnati *Daily Gazette*, Nov. 9, 1863, p. 3, c. 4.

7 "Old Abe told me once that Fessenden & Hamlin remonstrated with him against allowing 'the Blairs' to rule everything." Montgomery Blair to S. L. M. Barlow, Montgomery Co., Md., Aug. 15, 1865, Barlow MSS.

8 Smith, *Blair Family*, II, 241.

9 James Dixon to M. Blair (private), Hartford, Oct. 7, 1863, R. T. L. Coll., 27009–10. As to Republican senators sharing Blair's moderate views, Dixon may have had in mind such men as Doolittle of Wisconsin, Collamer of Vermont, and Cowan of Pennsylvania.

legiance should have military support; (3) that military officers should report to Schenck's headquarters any state judge of election refusing to require the oath of allegiance of anyone whose vote should be challenged on the ground of "disloyalty or hostility to the Government." [1]

On October 31 Governor Bradford protested strongly against these measures. The right of suffrage, he thought, was being restricted, and detachments of soldiers, not residents of Maryland, were "expected to exert some control or influence" on the election. He could not but think that these things were being done without the President's personal knowledge.[2]

These Maryland difficulties took a distressing amount of Lincoln's time. Answering Governor Bradford at length (November 2) he pointed out that violence was "almost certain . . . at some of the voting places . . . unless prevented by . . . provost guards." The presence of troops was to make it possible to run a "Union" ticket. The oath, which had been represented as a restriction on suffrage, was intended, wrote Lincoln, to assure "the right of voting to all loyal men." He did not think that "to keep the peace at the polls, and to prevent the persistently disloyal from voting" constituted "just cause of offence to Maryland."

The President did, however, make one concession. He revoked the first of the three parts of Schenck's order. Where the general had ordered military arrest of a whole class of evil persons aiding the rebellion who might embarrass the election or foist enemies of the United States into power, Lincoln directed that the order be considerably modified: in the amended form the word arrest was not used; the injunction was "That all Provost Marshals, and other military officers do prevent all disturbance and violence at or about the polls, whether offered by such persons as above described or by any other person or persons whomsoever." [3]

This assurance and concession by the President did not satisfy the governor, who issued a lengthy proclamation on November 2, the day before the election, vigorously denouncing Schenck's "extraordinary order." The general then issued, on the day of election, an order strongly denouncing Bradford's "very extraordinary Proclama-

1 McPherson, 309. 2 *Ann. Cyc.*, 1863, 618.

3 Lincoln to Gov. Bradford, Nov. 2, 1863, photostat, A. Lincoln Assoc.

tion."[4] Also on the day of election the governor sent the President an intolerably long letter reviewing, calling attention, insisting, solemnly protesting, informing, hardly supposing, confessing himself unable to imagine, and, after nearly two thousand words, having "the honor" to conclude. A duplicate of his letter was sent to the press.[5]

These formidable documents are too voluminous to be quoted or summarized here. On one side there was uneasy dread of a clash between citizens and the military power, together with resentment of military interference where state judges of election were, as the governor said, "exclusive judges" of voters' qualifications. On the other side there were reported activities of disloyal men presaging trouble, petitions from "respectable and loyal citizens" imploring military protection, and Schenck's affirmation that his only purpose was to prevent collisions and secure peace and order at the polls. Lincoln was supporting Schenck whom he nevertheless restrained; he was giving ear respectfully to Maryland protests while not admitting all the Federal abuses that were charged. He was keeping his temper while seeing representatives of both sides personally.

Amid these verbal explosions the people of Maryland went to the polls on November 3 for the purpose, essentially, of choosing between "conservative" Union men and "unconditional" Union men. The latter were understood to be more earnest toward emancipation than the former. Anti-Union men and what were called "peace men" had no candidate. It was the "unconditional" men who won by strong majorities. Their candidate for comptroller (Goldsborough) received 36,000 votes; his opponent a bit less than 16,000. In the choices for Congress the "unconditional" ticket was successful in four of the five districts.[6]

As a kind of post-mortem on the 1863 campaign, Governor Bradford delivered a message to the legislature in January 1864, recounting abuses perpetrated by the military authorities and deploring that a "part of the army which a generous people had supplied . . . was . . . engaged in stifling the freedom of election in a faithful State, intimidating its sworn officers, [and] violating the constitutional rights of its loyal citizens, ..."[7] Another sequel to the election was the series of steps that led in 1864 to abolition of slavery as a matter

[4] *Ann. Cyc.*, 1863, 619–621. [5] *Ibid.*, 621–623. [6] *Ibid.*, 623.
[7] *Ibid.*, 624.

of Maryland law. Still another effect was that in the final Congress of the Lincoln administration—the Thirty-Eighth, which began its first session on December 7, 1863 [8]—the President had to contend with the forceful and unrelenting opposition of Henry Winter Davis, chosen without any rival candidate by 6200 Maryland votes in the third congressional district. It would be a mistake to suppose that the Maryland election was altogether an advantage to Lincoln.[9]

It is necessary to take another glance at the election of Henry Winter Davis as congressman. His third congressional district, consisting of thirteen wards of the city of Baltimore, contained a population of 138,040. (This included, as a minor factor, 1769 slaves, at a time when the population ratio for the apportionment of House seats among the states was based on the constitutional provision that two-fifths of the slaves were to be included in the calculation.)

For the Thirty-Eighth Congress (on the basis of the census of 1860) the formula called for one representative for 122,614 of population.[10] There was, of course, no strict conformity of particular districts to that overall formula; deviations among the districts were, and remain, quite common. The factor that does arouse wonder, however, is the small vote for Davis (6200) as compared to the general ratio (122,000). This was a remarkably small vote, made smaller, no doubt, by the fact that Davis had no competitor. If one were to suppose roughly that no more than one-fifth of the total population were entitled to vote (though some would figure it at approximately one-fourth),[11] the number of eligible voters in Davis's district would be over 24,000. Thus, for a Congress destined to deal with large national questions including reconstruction, this Republican opponent of

---

8 To present-day readers the practice of choosing congressmen in odd-numbered years seems unusual, but such was the system in Maryland in this period. In November 1863 Marylanders chose congressmen for a term that legally began in the previous March, though the actual session did not open until December. There was an obvious economy in choosing congressmen along with the regular state election.

9 "Davis never forgave the President for choosing Blair Postmaster-General instead of him." William Ernest Smith, *Blair Family,* II, 277. For election of Maryland congressmen in 1863, showing Davis's total of 6200, see *Ann. Cyc.,* 1863, 623.

10 *Historical Statistics of the U. S., 1789–1945* (U. S. Bur. of the Census, 1949), 294.

11 In an offhand estimate of the number of eligible voters one would have to make a large deduction from total population to exclude minors and then deduct about half of the remainder to exclude women. It should also be remembered that Negroes did not vote in Maryland in 1863. One does not need, however, to make all these calculations exactly in order to realize how small was the vote for Davis.

Lincoln, one of the sharpest of the "radicals," was chosen by about one-fourth of the potential voters of his district and by less than one-twentieth of that district's population. A small vote for Congress was characteristic of the 1863 election in Maryland, but in the first district, where there was competition, the total vote was 12,224, about twice the total vote in the Davis (third) district. Just how far Henry Winter Davis could have been said to represent the sentiment of Maryland, or Baltimore, is a question. The support he received was hardly a measure of the strength of sentiment for the Union in the Lincolnian sense. His heavily over-weighted influence in Congress was out of proportion to the constituency whose views he reflected.

IX

At the pitch of excitement in the 1863 campaigns President Lincoln took a step concerning one of the chief targets for his opponents —the question of arbitrary arrests. On September 15, 1863, he issued a formal proclamation, with the most careful legal wording, suspending the habeas corpus privilege "throughout the United States." [1] Why did he do this, seeing that he had already (September 24, 1862) proclaimed a general suspension of the privilege "now, or hereafter during the rebellion"? The answer would appear to be that the 1862 proclamation was on presidential authority only, resting on no statutory basis, and subject to the well known objection that the President was arbitrarily seizing power that should be exercised, if at all, by Congress. Though Lincoln did not accept the validity of this objection, which he refuted with legal chapter and verse, he recognized that the civil-rights issue was being potently used against him and that this issue was likely to be a strong factor in certain pending elections which his administration could not afford to lose. He had no intention of giving up military arrests, but if such arrests were formally placed on a statutory basis, that would be a factor of strength. This 1863 proclamation (September 15) was comprehensive and all-sufficient for any military arrests yet to come. The "privilege of the Writ of Habeas Corpus . . . throughout the United States" was suspended in all cases where officers under the President's authority were holding certain classes of persons as spies, aiders of rebellion, et cetera,

[1] Photostat, A. Lincoln Assoc.

or "for any other offense against the military or naval service." The suspension was to "continue throughout the duration of the . . . rebellion," or until modified or revoked by the President.

It is significant to note the preamble of this presidential document. In a series of "whereas" clauses the conditions justifying suspension and making it a matter of law, were recited: the constitutional provision, the fact that a rebellion existed, the statute of March 3, 1863, the provision of that statute which recognized (some would have said conferred) the authority for presidential suspension, and the controlling fact that, in accordance with both statute and Constitution, the "public safety" did require the setting aside of the privilege.

There was in this action of the President both a concession to legal objectors and a reënforcement of the administration's firm position. Arrests were to continue, but they were now placed squarely upon the foundation of a law of Congress. All the wording of the 1863 proclamation indicated that the President was then and thereafter to have the statute as a basis for the seizure and holding of prisoners without civil trial.

There remained, of course, several questions. Neither the executive nor the judicial branch was complying with that feature of the law of March 3, 1863, which required that lists of prisoners be furnished to the Federal district and circuit courts, and that, if grand juries brought no indictments, or if no lists were furnished and the judge was satisfied as to the allegations of the petition, prisoners were to be discharged *by judicial order.* In that respect the law was not being made effective. There was also the question of the six-months delay: a September proclamation issued in accordance with an act passed in March. One could have raised the point that the Vallandigham proceeding was not in accordance either with the congressional act or the pattern of executive conduct indicated in the President's proclamation of September 15, 1863. Nor was it in keeping with the President's above-mentioned instruction of September 17, 1863, prescribing the conduct of a military officer in giving a "return" to the judge when served with a writ of habeas corpus.[2] The method of that instruction, as we have seen, was not followed in the Vallandigham case.[3]

---

[2] See above, p. 223.

[3] Judge Leavitt in the Vallandigham case not only refused the relief sought by the

It should be noted that Lincoln issued this proclamation prior to the important October elections. This was not true, however, as to another proclamation—the call for further troops, by draft if necessary. Such a call was obviously on the agenda in September, but Lincoln "deemed it prudent to defer a fresh call for troops until after the October States had voted." [4] The elections in Ohio and Pennsylvania, favorable to Lincoln, occurred on October 13; on October 17 the President called for troops on a large scale; 300,000 men were called; the states were to raise their quotas if possible by volunteering; where enlistments were deficient, the required number was to be taken by drafting. Men so taken were "to serve for three years or the war, not however, exceeding three years." [5]

Officially the President held himself aloof from the state elections which we have been considering in this and the preceding chapter; yet no one doubted their national bearing. The Lincoln administration, the President's war policy—all this was an issue in these contests. In one sense, of course, Lincoln did take a hand in these canvasses. The political letters he wrote were not specifically addressed to the competition between parties; yet one could hardly overlook the import of his letters to Seymour, Corning, Birchard, and Conkling. If one were collecting political material pertaining to what could have been called the "campaign of 1863," Lincoln's statements would be among the most important documents to be included. People could not properly speak of these contests as if they were local. Behind the scenes the President was constantly advised as to the progress of party campaigns in the states and was influenced in the timing of executive acts for their bearing upon the elections. Whether people voted as they did because of party, or because of Lincoln's personality, or to sustain the national cause in a year of crisis, the various elections of 1863 had somewhat the same effect as Gettysburg, Vicksburg, and Chattanooga. They were victories, milestones, indicators of support for the main Union effort as directed from Washington. There were, of course, clouds soon to appear. While the Republican party, in the main, won these Northern elections, that party was not united.

---

writ; he refused the writ itself. He thus refused to inquire into the accusations and reasons for the military arrest.

[4] Rhodes, *Hist. of the U. S.*, IV, 417.

[5] Call for 300,000 volunteers, Oct. 17, 1863, photograph, A. Lincoln Assoc.

Moderates like Lincoln, examining the political scene carefully, could not but realize with growing regret that the radicals were insisting it was their party.[6]

On November 20, 1863, in a finely balanced letter to one of those radicals (Zachariah Chandler), Lincoln briefly related the 1863 elections to his own conduct. He wrote: "I am very glad the elections this autumn have gone favorably, and that I have not, by native depravity, or under evil influences, done anything bad enough to prevent the good result. [A modest statement—as if the President had been only a negative quantity in contests where his personality and policy had been vital and pivotal.] I hope to 'stand firm' enough to not go backward, and yet not go forward fast enough to wreck the country's cause." [7] This was not a mere colorless doctrine such as some noncommittal politicians would have counseled. Lincoln at this time was working out one of the most important programs of his whole career —his reconstruction plan, soon to be announced in his third regular annual message to Congress. That program was the very opposite of Chandler's. When the matter is considered not only in relation to the elections, but to basic policy at this midway stage, there were worlds of seasoned wisdom in Lincoln's statement that he would not go backward, yet not forward impulsively or too fast.

---

6 Immediately after reporting the results of the 1863 elections, with emphasis on Republican success, Lincoln's secretaries wrote that "within their own organization" the Republicans were experiencing "bitter differences." Nicolay and Hay, *Lincoln*, VII, 388. In the presence of these differences the outlook for the President's plans was not encouraging.

7 Lincoln to Chandler, Nov. 20, 1863, marked "private," photostat, A. Lincoln Assoc.

CHAPTER XII

LINCOLN AND SEYMOUR

IN A WAR situation in which the Federal government relied upon coöperation by the states, President Lincoln had to encounter persistent questioning in the Empire State of New York, largest of them all. In that commonwealth the Democratic governor, Horatio Seymour, boldly challenged the President's policy. This opposition was no minor episode. Seymour was Lincoln's major opponent, though not his only embarrassment, among the governors.

I

What about Seymour? Within the orbit of his own antecedents, associations, and experience, his views and predilections were understandable. In the excellent biography by Stewart Mitchell he stands forth as a consistent personality and a man of distinction—a conservative Democrat whose service went back to the "Albany Regency" days of Van Buren, eminently respectable, believing in the Democratic party, content with the "good life," distrustful of reformers, devoted to the Burkian concept of the expedient as the guiding rule of statesmen. This, together with his temperament, explained why he had never joined the crusade against slavery.[1]

Amid the divisive tendencies of the New York Democrats—to say nothing of their opponents, the Whigs and later the Republicans—Seymour had adhered to the "Hunker" (or less democratic) wing of the party, and had served his state as assemblyman, speaker of the house, and governor in prewar years. In 1860 he had enough prominent mention in connection with the Charleston convention (which

1 Stewart Mitchell, *Horatio Seymour of New York*, 229.

he did not attend) to enable his biographer to speculate as to the possibility that he might then have become the nominee of a united Democratic party. Though this should not be taken too seriously, it is presented as one of those fascinating "ifs": "a two-man contest between Abraham Lincoln and Horatio Seymour might have changed the course of American history." [2] In that campaign Seymour favored Douglas and in the election of that year he honestly regretted the minority-won success of a sectional party. Had his party remained united, and had it been successful in the election, he believed that war would have been averted.

In 1862 he was elected governor of New York in a hard-fought contest in which his opponent, General James S. Wadsworth, supported Lincoln and emancipation, while Seymour pointed to the danger of allowing the government at Washington to "continue unchecked by intelligent and active opposition." [3] If, in New York in 1862, it was a question of popular will expressed at the polls (though there may be error in oversimplifying this aspect of the problem), there was reason to claim that, as between Seymour and Lincoln, the mandate was in Seymour's favor. He reminded his hearers that "if northerners and southerners had taken the trouble to know each other well, the Civil War could never have occurred." [4] (To illustrate the complexities of the subject, it may be remarked that this sentiment—the need for mutual understanding, North and South—was also sincerely felt and repeatedly expressed by Lincoln.)

With all the immense and many-sided burdens of 1863, the President treated Seymour with great respect, patiently answered his complaints, and sought continually for a working adjustment of conflicting views. During these months of controversy the nation was going through severe ordeals as it watched the military news while also, in the states, the political pot was boiling in state elections spread out over a tiresome period from spring until late fall.

II

Prominent in all this Seymour discussion was the excitement and disturbance associated with resistance to the draft. This was not all agitation and threat; at times it broke out into violence; in New York

[2] *Ibid.*, 212. [3] *Ibid.*, 249. [4] *Ibid.*, 252.

City it came to a frightful climax in the bloody draft riots of July.

Draft disorders were not confined to any one area. Serious clashes of police with mobsters occurred in Boston,[1] and in New Hampshire there were reports of "a widespread and organized determination . . . to resist" enforcement and an unusual sale of fire-arms "significant of bad feeling and probably of bad action." [2]

The draft riot in New York City, mentioned in an earlier volume,[3] was unique as the only disturbance that reached large proportions. Raging for three days, it presented a ghastly contrast to the celebrations of July victory, but in its murderous destruction it was untypical. It was certainly not typical of New York, whose support of the war was a notable factor. It was typical of mobs, but that does not mean that mobs were typical of America. The New York episode was that of spasmodic impulse and undisciplined fury: mobs looting, killing, destroying enrollment lists, disarming soldiers in barracks, stoning a provost marshal, beating Negroes to death, burning a colored orphans' home leaving hundreds of children homeless, seizing rifles, destroying a police station, and engaging in a pitched battle with police. A summary of those days of disorder ran as follows:

> Thus the days wore on, with dust and smoke, with fire and flame; with sack of private dwellings and burning of charitable institutions, armories, and draft stations; with blood and wounds, and every imaginable instance of atrocity on the part of the maddened mob, till regiments, hurriedly withdrawn from the front, came speeding back to the city, and we saw the grim batteries and weatherstained and dusty soldiers tramping into our leading streets as if into a town just taken by siege. There was some terrific fighting between the regulars and the insurgents; streets were swept again and again by grape, houses were stormed at the point of the bayonet, rioters were picked off by sharpshooters as they fired on the troops from the house-tops; men were hurled, dying or dead, into the streets by the thoroughly enraged soldiery; until at last, sullen and cowed, and thoroughly whipped and beaten, the miserable wretches gave way at every point and confessed the power of the law. It has never been known how many perished in those awful days.[4]

Such was one picture of the draft riot, and a worse one was presented by Horace Greeley.[5] On the other hand, Stewart Mitchell de-

---

1 "Riots in New York, Boston, and Elsewhere," *Ann. Cyc.*, 1863, 811–818.

2 *Offic. Rec.*, 3 ser. III, 513, 565.

3 *Lincoln the President*, II, 294–295.

4 Morgan Dix, *Memoirs of John Adams Dix*, II, 75.

5 Greeley, *Amer. Conflict*, II, 501–507.

clares that the whole uprising was "magnified until it became a political myth" for the purpose of making out a case against the governor and the Democratic party.[6] Mitchell points out that much of this partisan use of the episode came out in the political campaign of 1868. Some of the atrocities—e. g., the burning of a colored orphan asylum—are admitted by Mitchell; he also admits collisions between mobs and police.[7] He points out that the disorder lasted three days—July 13, 14, and 15—not four, as sometimes stated. Mentioning a thunderstorm and downpour which scattered the crowds, he remarks that "nature did quite as much, if not more, than the forces of law . . . in restoring the city to temporary quiet." [8] As to the number who lost their lives in the riot Mitchell gives no specific answer; he finds that their "small number" cannot be exactly stated. Against the widely varying claims of anti-Seymour writers (ranging from three hundred to more than a thousand) the governor's biographer finds "no evidence that any more than seventy-four possible victims of the violence of three days died anywhere but in the columns of partisan newspapers.[9] The meaning of this is that Mitchell finds evidence of seventy-four deaths attributable to the riot—a significant conclusion, since he has done more than any other writer to sift the evidence critically. He does not, however, set up that figure, nor any figure, as the total number of those who lost their lives (such a total being impossible to ascertain), nor does he state the number of wounded. The historian must attach great value to Mitchell's careful analysis and must therefore discount the exaggerated accounts that were all too common. Even when all is said, however, the riot stands out as a serious and disgraceful episode. To associate Seymour with the riot or to insinuate (as partisan writers did) that he sympathized with the rioters—because, forsooth, he allegedly began an impromptu speech with the words "My Friends"—would be grossly unfair.

III

Riots are usually short lived. To put down the disturbance was to handle the problem on one plane, but on another plane—the higher

[6] Mitchell, *Seymour,* 306. Mitchell does not mean that it was promoting a "myth" to say that a riot occurred, but that extreme partisan statements as to what happened—e. g., as to the extent of bloodshed—overstepped the bounds of reality.

[7] *Ibid.,* 330. [8] *Ibid.,* 330, 335. [9] *Ibid.,* 333.

one of state-government protest—the labor and embarrassment to Lincoln was even greater. To send troops to prevent further mob action was one thing. To deal over many weeks with the serious challenge presented by Horatio Seymour, conscientious and dignified governor of New York, was quite a different thing. In the heavy strain of 1863, in a wretchedly difficult situation, the President had to muster up all his skill, courtesy, and tact toward the governor, whose opposition, though impressively justified by his defenders, was not unmixed with anti-Lincoln politics.

Lincoln never denounced Seymour, nor can a biographer explain the complicated situation by branding the governor, in the words of Nicolay and Hay, as having a "bitterly prejudiced mind"; these writers on another page have conceded his integrity and patriotism.[1] It was a matter of divisions in a democracy, of horror at the thought of civil war, of Americans being unready for conscription, of distress at the miserable system of compulsory service then in use, and of anxiety in contemplating a growing bureaucracy in Washington taking over functions of the states. The fact that the states were not performing nationwide functions adequately was the other side of the coin.

Lincoln's first letter to Seymour (March 23, 1863) was by way of a very human approach as one who introduces himself and wishes to make friends. "You and I," wrote the President, "are substantially strangers, and I write . . . that we may become better acquainted. I, for the time being, am at the head of a nation which is in great peril, and you are at the head of the greatest State of that nation. As to maintaining the nation's life and integrity, I assume and believe there cannot be a difference of purpose between you and me. If we should differ as to the means, it is important that the difference should be as small as possible; that it should not be enhanced by unjust suspicions . . . ." The President pleaded informally for "a good understanding." He asked: "Please write me at least as long a letter as this, of course saying in it just what you think fit." [2]

If ever there was a warm, hearty letter phrasing a friendly appeal, discarding official stiffness, and asking for a rising above differences,

---

1 Nicolay and Hay, *Lincoln,* VII, 11, 13.

2 Lincoln to Seymour, Mar. 23, 1863, autograph draft, R. T. L. Coll., 22581 (this text differs but slightly from Nicolay and Hay, *Works,* VIII, 230–231).

this was it. Seymour waited three weeks, then answered in much less cordial fashion, giving "pressure of official duties" as the excuse for not giving his views in the manner he intended. (The governor was then dealing with a legislative session, but it is hard to believe that his duties were pressing any more heavily than those of Lincoln.) Seymour went on to disclaim political resentment and promised support on all measures adopted "within the scope of . . . constitutional powers." [3]

The governor was not completely unresponsive, though he did fundamentally differ with Lincoln on peace-and-war and on conscription. That basic difference, after all, was the explanation of the trouble—that, and politics. Lincoln was asking for coöperation in terms of national conscription; Seymour was ready to give it in terms of New York's volunteer effort. The governor may have felt that the President wanted smooth relations on his own terms; from the gubernatorial point of view the advantage of the elimination of differences would have been one sided. Because of the historical attention given to Lincoln's letter of March 23, 1863, it might be supposed that the President had made the first overture, but as far back as January of that year, at the beginning of Seymour's administration as governor, he had sent his brother, John F. Seymour, to hold a friendly and coöperative conference with the President.

In that interview, as recorded by John Seymour, we see Lincoln laying aside official formality and conversing easily on matters of common interest with an opponent. Lincoln said that they, Governor Seymour and himself, "had the same stake in the country." Both were party men, and that brought up the question of the next President; but if the country were broken up, said Lincoln, "there could be no next President." There would be no presidency (of states united).

Lincoln admitted that he himself was a party man, yet he pointed out that "he had appointed most of the officers of the army from among Democrats." As to the main issue, Lincoln said (as reported) that there were but three courses to take: fight until enemy leaders were overthrown; give up the contest altogether; or "negotiate and compromise with the leaders of the rebellion." But he thought such compromise "impossible so long as Davis had the power"; Davis and the other

[3] Seymour to Lincoln, Apr. 14, 1863, Nicolay and Hay, *Lincoln*, VII, 11.

enemy leaders "would never consent to anything but separation and acknowledgment"—i. e., permanent disunion.

Seymour's brother told the President that, "while holding him [Lincoln] responsible," the governor "would sustain him against any unconstitutional attempts against his administration from any quarter." The rebellion, as the brother explained, was a great grief to the governor, though it was not his manner to indulge in loud denunciations. The benefit of the country was the governor's concern, but he was "especially vexed at some of the Republican party who claimed to have a patent right for all the patriotism." [4]

IV

Seymour asked Lincoln to do some things that the President could not agree to. He asked the suspension of the draft in New York. On August 3, 1863, he sent the President a lengthy letter. He mentioned the mob attack "which ultimately grew into the most destructive riot known in the history of our country." Though giving credit to Federal forces, military and naval, he asserted that the disturbance was put down chiefly by the city police. The general government, he said, could not "give any substantial aid." "It could not even man its own forts." The city of New York, he insisted, showed that they were able to put down the riot "without aid from any other quarter." He then went into the matter of quotas, credits, et cetera, for New York, charging partisan inequalities in the numbers demanded by districts. He mentioned state bounties and reported optimistically as to their effect in stimulating volunteering.

Then he wrote: "I ask that the draft may be suspended in this State . . . until we shall learn the results of recruiting which is now actively going on . . . ." He added: "It is believed by at least one-half of the people of the loyal States that the conscription act . . . is . . . a violation of the supreme constitutional law." The governor placed great confidence in New York volunteering, which he labored vigorously to promote. He wrote of ruinous results that would follow an attempt "to exact obedience at the point of the bayonet." His

[4] For the visit of John F. Seymour and the interview, see Mitchell, *Seymour,* 276 ff.; Alexander J. Wall, *A Sketch of the Life of Horatio Seymour,* 29–31.

argument was for "peace of the public mind," winning popular acquiescence, having "subordinate laws" square "with the supreme law of the land." [1]

That was Seymour's side of it, and it was well stated; but as long as the governor's willingness to support the enrollment act remained doubtful, the whole problem of the draft throughout the nation was in abeyance. Governor Kirkwood of Iowa wrote to Stanton, July 15, 1863: "The enforcement of the draft throughout the country depends upon its enforcement in New York City. If it can be successfully resisted there, it cannot be enforced elsewhere. For God's sake let there be no . . . half-way measures." [2] With the same idea in mind a Federal enrolling official wrote: "If New York [City] is excused from the draft the rest of the State will claim the same exemption, and if New York [State] is exempt, of course other States will claim as much. In other words, if the mob conquers in New York it will at least try as much throughout the land." [3] It was of necessity Lincoln's function to look at these matters from the standpoint of the nation, not of any one state. In a mild and conciliatory way he expressed that idea to the governor of New Jersey: "It is a very delicate matter to postpone the draft in one State, because of the argument it furnishes others to have postponement also. If we could have a reason in one case which would be good if presented in all cases, we could act upon it. . . . I beg you to be assured I wish to avoid the difficulties you dread as much as yourself." [4]

On the question of constitutionality Lincoln and Seymour differed in the manner that was to be expected. As Mitchell writes: "Seymour, like many Americans before and since, rationalized his dislike of a law into a conviction that it was contrary to the Constitution. He believed the draft was inexpedient and he persuaded himself that it was illegal." [5] Lincoln, who wrote an unpublished paper explaining that the conscription act was justified under the Constitution,[6] was ready to leave the question of constitutionality to the Supreme Court, but he could not suspend the law on any anticipation that the Court's de-

1 *Offic. Rec.*, 3 ser. III, 613–619.

2 *Ibid.*, 494.

3 *Ibid.*, 530.

4 Lincoln to Governor Joel Parker, July 20, 1863, R. T. L. Coll., 25011; Nicolay and Hay, *Works*, IX, 36.

5 Mitchell, *Seymour*, 345.

6 *Lincoln the President*, II, 298–300.

cision might be unfavorable. He was an executive and as long as the law stood it was his duty to enforce it. He wrote: "I do not object to abide a decision of the United States Supreme Court, or of the judges thereof, on the constitutionality of the draft law." [7]

What did Lincoln mean by the expression "or of the judges thereof," as if he were making a distinction between a statement of "the judges" and a decision of the Court? Supreme Court justices in the American system do not give advisory opinions (individually or otherwise), so that could hardly have been the meaning. Justices could have been consulted informally, but that would have been unusual and irregular. All the justices did duty on the circuit as well as on the highest Court, but it is not clear that this is what the President had in mind. There was also the fact that statements which constituted the very essence of the Dred Scott decision were said to be not "judicially decided"—i. e., were not technically before the Court.[8] It will be recalled that Lincoln did not go along with the idea of unquestionable finality attaching to decisions of the Supreme Court. In his first inaugural he had said: ". . . if the policy of the Government upon vital questions, affecting the whole people, is to be irrevocably fixed by decisions of the Supreme Court, the instant they are made, in ordinary litigation . . . , the people will have ceased to be their own rulers, having . . . practically resigned their government into the hands of that eminent tribunal." [9] The Court in 1863 was headed by Taney of Dred Scott fame; it was a close and doubtful matter how the tribunal would have decided on the constitutionality of the conscription act.[10]

---

[7] Nicolay and Hay, *Works*, IX, 60 (Aug. 7, 1863); photographic reproduction, A. Lincoln Assoc.

[8] G. T. Curtis, *Const'l Hist. of U. S.*, II, 268 ff.

[9] The variant versions of this inaugural address include many worksheets in the R. T. Lincoln Collection. In an earlier version, before final revision, Lincoln had used much stronger language concerning the Supreme Court. He had written: "if the policy . . . is to be irrevocably fixed by . . . the Supreme Court, it is plain that the people will have ceased to be their own rulers, having turned their government over to the despotism of the few life-officers composing the Court." R. T. L. Coll., 7743. At the suggestion of Seward the wording was revised and softened as shown in the text quoted above, which is taken from the address as officially printed in *Sen. Exec. Doc. No. 1*, p. 7.

[10] Taney not only opposed the view that the conscription act was constitutionally valid, but actually prepared an (undelivered) opinion denying such validity. *Lincoln the President, II*, 297–298; *Constitutional Problems Under Lincoln* (revised ed., 1951), 274.

V

Lincoln was acting within the changing American system while state-rights men of the North were unwilling to recognize and accept the changes. Under the impact of war the country was becoming less an aggregation of states and more fully a nation, though by no means a unitary state with all the leading functions consolidated at Washington. In this transitional period, with the nation's assumption of functions not fully realized and vigorously opposed, the President was in a trying position. The enrollment law was consciously intended to make the raising of the army a national function, but that did not mean that people ceased to think in terms of states. While administering this very law the President had to deal with governors all over the country, hearing their complaints when it was felt that burdens, as between states, were unequal.

Lincoln always showed respect for opponents and for men who differed with him. He never assumed the manner of a dictator. It is in this light that one should read his letter of August 7, 1863, in answer to Seymour's of August 3. He began with the heart of the matter. "I cannot consent," he said, "to suspend the draft in New York, as you request . . . ." He explained: "We are contending with an enemy, who, as I understand, drives every ablebodied man he can reach into his ranks, very much as a butcher drives bullocks into a slaughter-pen. No time is wasted, no argument is used. This produces an army which will soon turn upon our now victorious soldiers . . . with a rapidity not to be matched on our side, if we first waste time to reëxperiment with the volunteer system . . . , and then more time to obtain a court decision as to whether a law is constitutional which requires a part of those not now in the service to go to the aid of those who are already in it . . . ." He closed with a reference to his important duty "of maintaining the unity and the free principles of our common country." He signed his name, "Your obedient servant, A. Lincoln." [1]

On the very day that the President was writing this letter stating that the draft would proceed, Seymour, sincere as he was, was making further difficulty. He wrote on August 7 to the President: ". . . I can

---

1 Nicolay and Hay, *Works*, IX, 58–61.

never forget the honor of my country so far as to spare any effort to stop proceedings under the draft in this State—and more particularly in the cities of New York and Brooklyn—which I feel will bring disgrace not only upon your administration but upon the American name." He stated also that he would send tables to show that "errors, if . . . not shameless frauds" existed in fixing New York quotas.[2]

On August 8 Seymour wrote in answer to the President's letter of the 7th (the one, above summarized, in which he refused to suspend the draft in New York, though making a considerable concession to correct disparities). The main burden of this August 8 letter from the governor was a denunciation of the draft in New York and a defense of his state in its efforts to meet every call with volunteers. Putting responsibility on Lincoln for the unhappy situation, he wrote: "I regret your refusal to comply with my request to have the draft in the State suspended until it can be ascertained if the enrollments are made in accordance with the laws of Congress or with the principles of justice." Quoting the President's reference to the enemy's practice of driving men into the ranks as a butcher drives bullocks to slaughter, the governor said: ". . . even this . . . is more tolerable than any scheme which shall fraudulently force a portion of the community into military service by a dishonest perversion of law." Enclosing a lengthy report, replete with tables, by his judge advocate general, Nelson J. Waterbury (comparing quotas by districts) he imputed the whole difference to partisan motives, and closed by saying: "You cannot and will not fail to right these gross wrongs." [3]

The report by Waterbury, enclosed in Seymour's letter of August 8, is an example of the voluminous and complicated reading matter which burdened the President's desk. Supplied with statistics and exceeding four thousand words in length, the report constituted a kind of argument or brief to prove that the New York draft was unfair to New York City and especially to the Democratic party. The essence of the report is contained in the statement that "nine anti-Lincoln districts [were] required to furnish nearly as many conscripts as the nineteen Lincoln districts," and in the remark that "The enrollment is a partisan enrollment . . . ." [4]

To show the light-hearted manner in which one of Lincoln's staff

[2] *Offic. Rec.*, 3 ser. III, 636.
[3] *Ibid.*, 639–640.
[4] *Ibid.*, 648–649.

viewed this ponderous report, we have a "private and accidental" note (August 24, 1863) by John Hay to Fry, the provost marshal general. "The inevitable Waterbury is again upon us," wrote Hay. "His experience as a political ballot stuffer for twenty years comes up and troubles his dreams. He is afraid you are stuffing the draft on him. Read his wail if you don't think life is too short and Lee too near. If you do, file it. With a firm reliance on Providence and your waste-paper basket, you cannot fail." The secretary, then headed for the seashore, signed himself: "Yours, hilariously, John Hay." [5]

With regard to this controversy as to the unfairness of the New York enrollment, one should notice the following three points:

(1) In order to give every consideration to the Seymour claims, a commission was appointed with the President's full consent to inquire into the whole subject.[6] The report of this commission did not blame the Federal enrollment officers for intentional unfairness, but did assert that quotas should be adjusted so as to fix the number of drafted men in proportion to the *entire* population.

(2) Lincoln did not admit the correctness of this formula, since he considered that quotas should be determined with regard to the number of able-bodied men of military age. The President's view harmonized with the law as passed by Congress.

(3) In spite of this, the President nevertheless brought about a considerable "arbitrary reduction" of the quotas of certain disputed districts in 1863, following this also with a like reduction in 1864.[7]

Seymour's complaint, stated by his judge advocate general,[8] was that unjustifiably heavy quotas were demanded of the metropolitan districts (New York City and vicinity) where Democratic voters predominated, as compared to the rest of the state which had a larger proportion of Republicans. There were, however, so many points in dispute —both as to the proper proportion for determining quotas, and the correctness of numerical findings in applying whatever formula was used—that Lincoln, who was sensitive to the accusation of partisan

5 *Ibid.*, 712.

6 Mitchell, *Seymour,* 346; Nicolay and Hay, *Lincoln,* VII, 40–41. The commission consisted of William F. Allen of New York, a Democrat notably favorable to Seymour; General John Love of Indiana, a Democrat; and Chauncey Smith of Massachusetts, a lawyer not strongly committed to either party. It was recognized that Judge Allen dominated the commission.

7 Nicolay and Hay, *Lincoln,* VII, 40–42.

8 *Offic. Rec.,* 3 ser. III, 640–651.

unfairness, considered that it was best, without expecting perfection as to figures or formulas, to make the concession already noted—i.e., to reduce the New York quotas.

This haggling over comparative burdens as between states and groups within states was by no means limited to New York; it was one of the most uninspiring aspects of the conscription controversy. In such a dispute it is futile to look for finality of judgment. It makes the subject no easier to have one formula or finding supported by writers who defend Seymour and another by pro-Lincoln writers. Lincoln himself was not a stickler for the claims made on his supposed "side" of the dispute. There is a certain significance in the carefully balanced statements of the investigating commission (the Allen commission) above mentioned. This commission "acquitt[ed] the [Federal] enrolling officers of intentional unfairness," while on the other hand they made a good deal of the point that quotas should have been adjusted in proportion to the whole population. For New York and Brooklyn the commission found that the quotas were "excessive." [9]

It was on August 11, by way of answering Seymour's communication of the 8th, that the President reported the reduction of New York quotas. He made it clear that he had to get ahead with the job, which would not admit of endless delay. His main principle, he said, was "to proceed with the draft, at the same time employing infallible means to avoid any great wrongs." [10] He was making a practical adjustment, rather than seeking a scientific calculation for quotas of drafted men that would produce precise proportional equality among all districts, remembering that the correct basis of such equality was itself a matter of dispute.

VI

As the Lincoln administration looked forward to the renewal of the draft in New York City it became necessary to take preventive measures to avoid another riot. Just after the July riot the government

---

[9] Mitchell, *Seymour*, 346. There was nothing in the conscription law that required the determination of district quotas on the basis of total population. The law required an actual enrollment of able-bodied men of military age; this enrollment was the basis of the draft. In section 12 the law authorized the President "to assign to each district the number of men to be furnished by said district. . . ." *U. S. Stat. at Large*, XII, 731–737.

[10] Lincoln to Seymour, Aug. 11, 1863, R. T. L. Coll., 25521.

had sent a high-minded, reliable general, John A. Dix, to command the Federal forces in the New York area, succeeding the aged General Wool. Dix was a Democrat with a record for upholding the Union, a man who knew how to combine discretion with vigor. He had been a stanch member of Buchanan's cabinet. One can only speculate as to what would have been the outcome if a man of a different type—e. g., a fiery radical Republican—had been given the important New York assignment. It has been stated by Dix's son and biographer that certain Republican radicals had been "busily engaged . . . to get General Benjamin F. Butler sent to command in New York, in view of the draft." [1] It would be an obvious understatement to say that an orderly and peaceable situation could not have been anticipated with Butler in command. Since one of the important functions of an executive is that of appointment, it is worth while to judge the President's choice of Dix in contrast to the kind of choice that would have been made by men of less discretion within the dominant party. In choosing a Democrat, Lincoln was pointedly avoiding partisanship in this selection. (Butler had been a Democrat, but he was a Republican radical or extremist in the making. Such extremists were pushing him forward.) The value of Dix was in his well known character, and in recognition of the fact that "he could not be ruled in the interest of any faction, but occupied a broad, national ground." [2]

In the Dix-Seymour correspondence, which paralleled that of Seymour and Lincoln, one finds two New York Democrats who equally professed devotion to the national cause, but who differed strongly in their approach to the problem of the draft and of its enforcement in state and city. Dix inquired whether state military power would be used "to enforce the execution of the law in case of forcible resistance." [3] This was in the period when Seymour was assuming that the New York draft would be "suspended." The governor answered Dix, if it was an answer, by saying that he had sent Lincoln a letter on August 3 (it was in this letter that he had requested suspension of the draft); he thought this would avert the "painful questions growing out of an armed enforcement of the conscription law in this patriotic State." [4]

This did not satisfy Dix, who proved an emphatic spokesman for

---

1 Morgan Dix, *Memoirs of J. A. Dix,* II, 85.

2 *Ibid.*

3 *Offic. Rec.,* 3 ser. III, 592.

4 *Ibid.,* 619.

the national side in the controversy. The general made it clear that it was his duty to aid enrolling officers and to put down resistance to the law. He hoped the governor would assist with state troops; otherwise he would have to ask for an adequate Federal force. He regretted that the governor had characterized the law as "the conscription act." [5] This, said Dix, was a foreign phrase. There was danger, thought the general, that the chief executive of New York might "be understood to regard it as an obnoxious law which ought not to be carried into execution," thus throwing his important influence "against the Government in a conflict for its existence." The enemy were making heavy demands on their man power. "Shall not we," asked Dix, "do as much for the preservation of our political institutions as they are . . . to . . . destroy them?" Whatever the defects of the act, Dix urged that "it is the law of the land." He added: "Those, therefore, who array themselves against it, are obnoxious to far severer censure than the ambitious or misguided men [official secessionists] who are striving to subvert the Government," for the latter were acting "by color of sanction" under their legislatures and conventions. Dix concluded by an appeal at this late date (August 8) for the governor's early assurance that the state power would "be employed to enforce the draft." [6]

After a week's delay Seymour answered (August 15) in a manner which convinced the general that he had better look to Washington in making "arrangements for maintaining the law of Congress and keeping the peace in a city which had recently been the theatre of horrible scenes of riot, battle, pillage, and murder." [7] In this letter of August 15 Seymour expressed full confidence that volunteering in New York would adequately serve the need for troops and that no compulsion was necessary. Having said this, the governor added that state authorities could not perform duties "expressly confided to others," nor "relieve others from their . . . responsibilities." Nothing like a riot, however, could occur without infraction of state law; hence state officers would "perform their duties vigorously and thoroughly," if necessary with state military support. The governor, in this letter,

[5] Seymour could hardly have been blamed for calling it a "conscription" act. The whole system was so unfortunate in method and emphasis that if its supporters went into details, they were embarrassed in defending it. Under President Wilson, in contrast, the term used was not "conscription" but "selective service."

[6] *Offic. Rec.*, 3 ser. III, 652–654.

[7] Dix, *Memoirs of J. A. Dix*, II, 86.

was standing in a midway position; he was promising action by state authorities to keep order, but was not making it clear that General Dix would have his full coöperation.[8] An indication of Seymour's mood at this time appeared in his letter of August 6 to Samuel J. Tilden. He was satisfied, he said, that the government at Washington "means to go on in a spirit of hostility to this State; that it is governed by a spirit of malice in all things small and great." Under these circumstances, he wrote: "I look for nothing but hostility." It was Seymour's view that conscription would "make the [Lincoln] administration odious and contemptible." [9]

In the uncertain situation in which he found himself, Dix thought it best to apply to Washington for Federal troops to be sent to New York. Stanton replied (August 15) that 10,000 infantry and three batteries of artillery ("picked troops") were being sent. At the same time, Stanton submitted to Dix certain presidential orders, to be issued or not according to the general's discretion. By one order the President called forth the New York militia into national service (of which, of course, the President was commander in chief) in order to suppress "unlawful combinations." By the other order the state major-general of militia (Charles W. Sanford) was directed to "report forthwith to Major-general John A. Dix." [10]

It did not prove necessary to use this double-barreled order from Washington. The large force of Federal troops came, and the state militia was not summoned for the enforcement of the draft, which Seymour and his staff would have resented. Thus another possible misstep in the vexing New York situation was avoided as a matter of Federal policy.

Things were now set for going ahead with the draft. Dix was firmly but unprovocatively in command. Lincoln had made his concessions as to draft reductions. Reënrollment had been ordered, "employing infallible means to avoid any great wrongs." [11] United States troops were in New York by August 17. On that day General Dix issued an address "To the Citizens of New York." He insisted that there must be no resistance to "the law of the land" and earnestly exhorted the

[8] *Ibid.*, II, 82.

[9] Mitchell, *Seymour*, 344.

[10] Dix, *Memoirs of J. A. Dix*, 86–87. These two orders, worded in the manner of formal proclamations, were submitted (for possible issue) over Lincoln's name, but they apparently originated in the war department.

[11] Lincoln to Seymour, Aug. 11, 1863, R. T. L. Coll., 25521.

people to preserve the good name of their city, to maintain order, obey the laws, and quietly pursue their accustomed avocations. Should there be renewed disturbance, he clearly warned that violence would be "met by the most prompt and vigorous measures." [12]

When the draft was resumed (August 19) after all this prudent preparation, it proceeded in peaceable fashion.[13] In the long run the main significance of the whole episode was the demonstration that supremacy belongs to regularly constituted authorities when it is known that they are determined to maintain order. The part which Seymour had in this result should not be overlooked. It was Dix's belief that the presence of Federal troops accomplished the purpose, and that without violence; but it should be added that the governor issued a proclamation on August 18 in which he counseled the people to submit to conscription, despite his objection to the system. He admonished officials to enforce the law and preserve order, and declared that "Riotous proceedings must and shall be put down . . . and the lives and property of citizens protected at any and every hazard." [14]

VII

It would have been an advantage if, in the long-drawn-out New York controversy, a full stop could have been reached, a termination of complaint followed by smooth-working adjustment and absence of friction. Some writers consider the date August 19, the day of the unobstructed resumption of the draft in the state, as the settlement and quieting of the trouble, and in a sense it was. The draft proceeded and there was no further mob disturbance. After August 19, however, there were voluminous queries by the New York governor and his aides as to credits and the like, necessitating time-consuming study and replies by the President and other national officials. It was a high-policy matter, but it was also a tediously involved administrative problem.

There was, for instance, an elaborate letter from Seymour dated

---

12 Dix, *Memoirs of J. A. Dix*, II, 88–91.

13 "There is not the least symptom of disturbance in any part of the city. . . . The militia are all under arms co-operating perfectly." C. A. Dana to Stanton, New York, Aug. 19, 1863, *Offic. Rec.*, 3 ser. III, 693.

14 Wall, *A Sketch of . . . Horatio Seymour*, 51; *Public Record . . of Horatio Seymour* (campaign document, 1868), 147.

August 21.[1] The governor was unsatisfied as to credits for volunteers; he complained that he had not been informed of the exact dates of coming drafts, and he raised the objection that men in large numbers had been drawn off from New York "into the service of other States." Men enrolled in New York, he said, had been obtained as volunteers and substitutes for adjoining commonwealths. A question was raised as to finality in the determination of the number to be drafted for a district. This was a point that could not be left indefinitely open. Without too much delay there had to be, at some time, a fixing of the quotas and a closing of the books, after which further credits for volunteers could not be made till the next draft.

Lincoln had the Seymour protest studied by the United States provost marshal general, J. B. Fry, who supplied explanatory or refuting comments in the margin. The President then patiently explained to the governor that credits for volunteers would be allowed "up to the last moment which will not produce confusion or delay." [2] He also made it clear that the governor would be notified when the drawing of names was to occur in each district of the state. As he had already explained, he could not give up "a drafted man now" for a volunteer (or the "mere *chance*" of one) later. And, after a draft had actually been made, it would make trouble "to take any drafted man out and put a volunteer in; for how shall it be determined, which drafted man is to have the privilege of thus going out, to the exclusion of all the others?" It would disrupt the system too much "if every time a volunteer is offered the officers must stop and reconstruct the quota." [3]

As to the governor's protest concerning the loss of "credit" owing to a kind of raiding by "agents" of other states, that was one of the numerous headaches of the whole system. It appeared, wrote the provost marshal general, that "the practice complained of, which is general throughout the United States, was especially outraging in New York." A ruling on the subject had been requested of Judge Advocate General Holt, who gave the legal opinion that the state in which a drafted man is enrolled is credited with one soldier whether he serves or furnishes a substitute; if that substitute comes from an-

---

1 *Offic. Rec.*, 3 ser. III, 703–705.

2 Lincoln to Seymour, Aug. 16, 1863, photostat, A. Lincoln Assoc. See also Lincoln to Stanton, Aug. 26, 1863, R. T. L. Coll., 25857–8.

3 Lincoln to Seymour, Aug. 16, 1863, photostat, A. Lincoln Assoc.

other state, that could not be helped; the national government could not be debited with two soldiers when it received but one.[4]

One reason why Lincoln's wish for adjustment of draft difficulties was constantly hampered in New York was, of course, the unending maneuvering between parties. It was hard for partisans to bear the thought that friendly adjustment would have helped the Lincoln administration. It was of course known (though Lincoln was generous toward Democrats) that administration success would be proclaimed in the Republican sense. On October 27, a few days before the New York election of 1863, the subject of the draft was given the main emphasis in a printed circular issued by the Democratic state central committee. Expressing full confidence in success in the coming election, while at the same time urging that faithful and earnest work was required in every election district, the signers of the circular—Dean Richmond and Peter Cagger—made the accusation that the state was "charged . . . for every citizen who has paid the Three Hundred Dollars commutation—receiving no credit whatever therefor." They asserted that "the payment . . . only releases the conscript for the time being, and that the State still owes the Government a man." [5]

This circular was promptly answered by the provost marshal general, who declared the statement "untrue." In refutation of the "misrepresentations," it was pointed out that "every citizen who has paid the $300 commutation . . . is exonerated from military service for the time for which he was drafted, to wit, for three years." [6]

To illustrate another headache in the whole cumbersome administration of the draft, there was the question of where and when troops should be placed for maintaining order where mob disturbance was anticipated. The desired result was to prevent trouble before it started, which meant having soldiers already on hand at each district provost-marshal headquarters at which the need of soldiers was expected. But how could this be done? The suggestion was made that different drafting dates be set up for different districts, so that soldiers could be "moved from point to point as the draft progressed." [7] This was but another example of the awkward procedure of Civil War days. A much better system was used in 1917–18, where, instead of drawing

[4] *Offic. Rec.*, 3 ser. III, 729.
[5] Printed circular, R. T. L. Coll., 27528.
[6] *Offic. Rec.*, 3 ser. III, 981.
[7] *Ibid.*, 502.

names at various times by districts within the states, there was "a single national drawing [of serial numbers] for all registrants." [8]

VIII

The Lincoln-Seymour affair, in its many facets, stands out as a notable case study in wartime administration within a democracy, while it is also a study in personalities. The governor's difference with the President was, to him, a matter of great validity; it was not trumped up. He could not approve a sectional administration at Washington, he detested the war, and he honestly opposed conscription as a method of raising soldiers. He was nevertheless pro-Union and ready to see that New York, without compulsion, would do its part, both in sending troops and in keeping order. As to the preference for volunteering rather than drafting, that was evident even within the conscription system. The poorly devised draft law was itself a considerable factor in putting a stigma and a kind of badge of inferiority upon the drafted man. After the governor's death John F. Seymour remarked that "the only reproachful words he had ever heard his dead brother speak of the President with whom he had felt it was his duty to differ were these: 'Mr. Lincoln was not fair to me.' " [1] As shown earlier in this chapter in his letter to Tilden, Seymour wrote frankly of the "hostility" of men in Washington, but, while constantly expressing opposition to the President's policy, he said in October 1862: ". . . although I am politically opposed to him, never have I allowed myself to utter against him one disrespectful term, nor will I ever allow myself to do so." [2]

Yet Seymour's gentlemanly attitude and the uprightness of his sense of duty were not the whole story. Besides the hard core of the New York situation there was, in association with Seymour, a considerable fringe—a cluster of attendant influences inimical to Lincoln and, as the President believed, calculated to injure the national cause. Lincoln, too, was a gentleman on his side of the controversy. His position was not easy. He had a war to conduct, an army to raise, a whole cause

[8] *Second Report of the Provost Marshal General . . . to December 1918* (Washington, 1919), 41.

[1] Mitchell, *Seymour*, 382.

[2] Speech at Brooklyn Academy of Music, Oct. 22, 1862, *Public Record . . . of Horatio Seymour*, 77.

to promote. He had to adjust himself to the bitter problem of administration in a democracy amid powerful divisive forces. On both sides there were unreasonable partisan maneuvers and tricks. In this complex situation the historian can show that both men were patriotic and both of them sensible, but patriots differed as to measures. Factors at work in the crisis were abnormal. Politics was not adjourned during the war and the blame for that condition rested with both parties. The Democrats were at a disadvantage. They had reason to resent what a faction of the Republican party was doing. There were men in both parties who doubted the wisdom of the contemporary conscription law, one of the worst of its kind.

In the position in which he found himself, Lincoln played an honorable and a conciliatory, but not a weak, part. To show the President's lack of personal animosity, there is an interesting parallel between his attitude toward Seymour in 1863 and toward Douglas in 1858. In that year of the debate, in the very last speech of the long canvass, Lincoln had said: "I claim no insensibility to political honors; but today . . . [if the spread of slavery could be checked], I would . . . gladly agree, that Judge Douglas should never be *out,* and I never *in,* an office, so long as we both or either, live." [3]

We even have an indication or hint, in the recollection of Thurlow Weed, that Lincoln stood ready to support Seymour for the presidency looking forward to 1864, and that the President wished Weed to broach this subject to the governor. Not long before Weed's death (which occurred in November 1882) a New York journalist had, as he reported, an interview with the aged politician who was then quite feeble. The interview was at Weed's request. The journalist's account proceeded:

> His purpose in inviting me to call, he said, was to request me to see Horatio Seymour and extract from him a promise that, when he came to New York city again, he would give Mr. Weed an opportunity for a long-sought interview . . . . He said that in the latter portion of Mr. Lincoln's first term that statesman [Weed] became profoundly impressed with the conviction that the war could never be brought to a successful termination under a Republican President, nor probably under any partisan

---

[3] Speech, Oct. 30, 1858, photostat of autograph MS. A. Lincoln Assoc.; Oliver R. Barrett (name not given on title page), *Lincoln's Last Speech in Springfield in the Campaign of 1858,* 14.

President, and that some man must be sought out whose purity of character, statesmanship, exalted abilities and devotion to the Union would be recognized by all parties and all sections, so that he might be carried into the Presidency by acclamation. After long and anxious consideration and discussion, Horatio Seymour was settled upon as the only eligible citizen; that this gentleman was approached and made aware of these views of Mr. Lincoln . . . , and that the negotiations were not at first discouraged or repulsed, but as time passed on the proposed beneficiary of this extraordinary political movement became less inclined to regard the scheme as practicable or desirable . . . , and that the subsequent successes of the Union arms changed Mr. Lincoln's views and purposes, and made him desire and accept a renomination.[4]

There is good evidence that this was Weed's recollection. He mentions the matter in his memoirs and Seymour's biographer writes: "Weed was making use of this story as early as 1864, and in one form or another it has persisted to this day." [5] To contemplate such an "extraordinary political movement" was not unlike Lincoln and there were times in the war when the military and political outlook would have argued the desirability of a President who could have been placed completely above, and aside from, parties. Just who among the leaders of that day could have qualified in that respect is a matter of conjecture, but there are sufficient references to the "story" to indicate that it can be traced to Weed's recollection of what Lincoln said to him.[6]

As to the actual 1863 situation the fact of the President being of one party and the New York governor of another should not be misunderstood. Instead of treating this difference with a party slant as some writers have done, it would be more in keeping with Lincoln's thought to view the subject from a nonpartisan, or unpartisan standpoint. Lincoln felt that he and Seymour had much in agreement in that they had the same stake in keeping the government going. It was

---

[4] "Geneva, N. Y. Corr. of the Utica Observer," Washington *Post,* Feb. 4, 1883. The interview was reported as having occurred in the summer of 1882. For calling attention to this article and supplying a copy the author is grateful to David Rankin Barbee of Washington.

[5] Stewart Mitchell, *Horatio Seymour,* 273. Mitchell shows (273–274) that Lincoln's proposal to support Seymour as a kind of unpartisan successor was mentioned in such publications as the Albany *Evening Journal* (Weed's paper), the *Atlas and Argus* of Albany (with contemptuous comment), and the New York *Standard and Statesman.*

[6] Nicolay and Hay (*Lincoln,* VII, 12–13) mention the story as related in Weed's *Memoirs.*

like saying: We can agree to differ, but let's not allow the government to break down.

The challenge to Lincoln was serious, whether one has in mind his official authority or his capacity for human adjustment. In his management of the affair he succeeded in upholding the national authority while also avoiding a miserable explosion between the Federal government and a leading state. Indeed one of the significant points for the historian in the controversy is to note how a democracy functions when determined and seriously aroused groups are motivated by opposite intentions. Difficulties may become ominous and contention may become warm, but the time usually comes when some kind of working formula, some *modus vivendi,* becomes a necessity. If both sides ultimately realize this, such a realization is an indication that, amid strong diversity, a degree of basic unity is discernible. Such democratic unity was the theme of Lincoln's above-mentioned interview with Governor Seymour's brother. It may be regarded as the key to this chapter, and other chapters, of the Lincoln administration.

CHAPTER XIII

NATIONS UNDER STRESS: UNITED STATES AND BRITAIN

IN THE slowness of sea travel and communication in Lincoln's day the Atlantic Ocean might have seemed a vast wall of separation. However natural such an offhand assumption, the true situation was far otherwise. Imperfectly bridged though it was, the ocean was less a factor of isolation than a thoroughfare in which nothing was more certain than the contact of nations and the jostling of international interests. In the *Trent* affair an incident of ocean travel had quickly developed into a menacing crisis. It was only by restraint on both sides and by diplomacy in the valid sense that a war of untold proportions and fearful consequences between the United States and Britain was happily avoided. Statesmen breathed more freely when that severe crisis was passed; but the enveloping ocean was still there, and on its busy ships were laden those questions of commerce, blockade, prestige, international law, economic interest, recognition, and partisan assistance which carried through to the very core of the American conflict.

A small matter might involve the large issue: the repair of a rudder or the detention of a ship was likely to include the whole attitude that a foreign nation might take on the problem of recognizing, perchance of assisting, the forces of secession. Let one step be taken and others would follow. In the construction and fitting out of a single warship to serve against the United States there lurked again the possibility of war between Britain and America. Yet the chance of war has often lurked; in Lincoln's day the avoidance of actual conflict, with no loss of America's true interest, was the significant fact.

To treat the foreign outlook that confronted Lincoln and his administration would be to devote a complicated volume to that phase alone; nothing like an adequate coverage of the subject is possible here. There was Europe and here was the United States: Europe with its reactionary aristocracy, military castes, concepts of legitimate monarchy, predatory nationalism, frontier shibboleths, inflexible groupings, suppressed populations, and rumblings of revolution; the United States, less hampered with inhibitions and burgeoning with impulses of democracy, but threatened with dissolution and racked to its foundations with civil war. Peace on the old continent was inadequately organized. Indeed it was not organized at all. One aggressor might have the nations stymied. In Prussia's assault upon unoffending Denmark statesmen abroad might know well enough what was happening, but Bismarck seemed to have them hypnotized. And the minor Danish War led directly to war on a major scale. The compelling and all possessing impulse in Europe was for unity—unfortunately, however, not helpful human solidarity, but the militant unity of rampant nationalism. In contrast a vast proportion of America was thinking of separation. How could a Cavour, a Bismarck, a Palmerston, or a Gladstone understand what these Americans were about? Political leaders across the ocean might have formulas of peace for America, but they were heading toward wars on their own borders, and desires of certain groups for "mediation" in the American quarrel might bespeak not so much a helping hand as a meddling partisanship. With the fine word peace there went the words independence, freedom, and self government, but these honored words could be bandied about by those who would tear down the very basis of democracy.

I

Those who had to deal with Anglo-American relations in the days of Lincoln had full need of judgment, skill, and patience. There were pitfalls and danger spots, and at times such elements of instability as to cause statesmen to shudder. As one factor, there was on both sides an unreasonable readiness—among some—to rush into a fight supposedly for "honor" or for an idea, without forethought as to where such a fight would lead or whether the true idea or genuine honor required a fight. To the extent that passions were whipped up, such forethought would be left out of account. Englishmen were unfortunately ignorant of America and Americans of England. There is a record of an M. P. breakfasting with an American visitor in the summer of '63. The M. P. expected to hear next that Lee had entered Philadelphia, Baltimore, and Washington, "& then—a—a—he will just turn round and re-capture New Orleans—New Orleans is about 100 miles from Washington, I think?" [1]

There was always, in the minds of officials, the uncertainty as to what would happen next. What does Seward intend, would be a question in British minds. What about his alleged remark to Newcastle that insulting England was the only sure passport to popular favor in America? [2] Was the Secretary spoiling for a fight? Was Lincoln a boor and a brute? How would the next major battle turn out? Did Americans have aggressive designs upon Canada? What was the meaning of emancipation? Was it to stir up criminal violence against Southern whites?

In America the queries would indicate similar misunderstanding and uncertainty. Would Britain recognize the Confederates? What was the meaning of war preparations, what would Parliament do, how far did Parliament represent the people, why did British investors subscribe to the cotton loan? Sometimes a mere question or doubtful suspicion would become itself a provocative factor. To put a query into words, even though it lacked substance, would arouse distrust and deepen misunderstanding. Through all the speculations much would depend upon the basic good sense of both sides. Waters of diplomacy might be treacherous, but statesmanship might win though if the helmsman at the wheel could keep his bearings. To do so he had to remember that, while war talk was cheap and easy, yet amid popular clamor it was always necessary to keep in view the force of common inheritance, the stability of established relations, and the unquestioned importance of continued peace on both sides.

In Britain there were certain elements whose desire was not so much for "freedom" in America as for defeat and disintegration. It was the common men, the striving British millions, who wished success to the American nation and sensed a common cause with Lincoln. Among those abroad who desired the cracking of the American Union the

---

1 E. Schuyler to H. W. Bellows, Aug. 3, 1863, Bellows MSS.

2 C. F. Adams, Sr., to C. F. Adams, Jr., Dec. 20, 1861, W. C. Ford, ed., *Cycle of Adams Letters,* 88.

friends of democracy were few and far between. This is another way of saying that Lincoln's Gettysburg address had validity, and that, however imperfectly they might be fulfilled, the aspirations of democratically minded men were at one with the homely President at Washington.[3]

It was a stage in international relations in which neutrality was both an accepted principle and an imperfectly developed procedure. As a basic concept neutrality signified that if a conflict is alien and foreign, and if the issue of that conflict is not of concern to a nation, participation by that nation is unwise. As to procedures, baffling and difficult issues could arise in matters of reciprocal duties and rights of belligerents and neutrals. In the American struggle the very term "belligerent" was questioned; the rightful belligerency of the Confederate States of America was strenuously disputed by the government of Washington. There was also the inevitable embarrassment of any neutral in a huge and fiercely contested war. It was evident that neither Washington nor Richmond desired Britain to be guided by genuine neutrality. As Earl Russell's biographer put it, referring to the beginning of the conflict when British recognition of the mere belligerency of the Confederacy was resented by both sides: "Thus, even in these early stages of the war, the British Government was ascertaining by experience that strict neutrality in a struggle is never acceptable to either combatant."[4] The United States desired out-and-out denial of Confederate belligerency; this would have rendered pointless all the British emphasis upon the even balance between two conflicting governments in maritime and other matters. Since it was denied at Washington that two governments rightly existed, acceptance of governmental claims of the Confederacy, if only as one of two belligerents toward which Britain would hold an impartial course, was regarded as taking sides.

If one turns to Richmond he finds again that British neutrality was not desired. What President Davis and Secretary Benjamin wanted

---

[3] It is hard to reconcile this concept with actual American developments in the post-Lincoln period with its corruption, predatory exploitation, capitalistic abuse, and unenlightened treatment of the South. The imperfections of American democracy in the period after the Civil War cannot be overlooked, neither can they be explored here. Their significance for the Lincoln theme is obvious: it was the anti-Lincoln element that seized the reins of party and of government in the era of abuse that men have miscalled "reconstruction." And the democratic importance of saving the American nation from dissolution extended far beyond the immediate postwar period.

[4] Spencer Walpole, *The Life of Lord John Russell*, II, 342.

was that Britain should aid and abet their war; they desired unneutral intervention and assistance. The records of Confederate diplomats show that they were most hopeful at those moments when they could report, perhaps by wishful thinking, that Palmerston was about to "shake off his neutrality." [5]

In these trying circumstances it is worth remembering that the friendship of the United States with Great Britain was not in fact broken; on the other hand something equivalent to a breach—if one can speak of a breach where regular diplomatic relations never existed—did occur between England and the Confederacy in the latter part of 1863. Shaken and embarrassed though they were, statesmen at Washington and London did not forget the essential friendliness of nations. They did not overlook the comparative triviality of international disputes when weighed against the colossal disaster of war.

II

The conduct of international affairs was firmly enough in official hands, but it is surprising to notice how many Americans turned up abroad during Lincoln's administration and tried their hand—some of them semi-officially—at the business of diplomacy or of foreign propaganda. The idea of sending private citizens to serve as agents of good will abroad, occurred to Seward in 1861. After a number of declinations he obtained the services of Thurlow Weed the New York politician; Charles P. McIlvaine, Episcopal bishop of Ohio; and the Most Reverend John Hughes, Catholic Archbishop of New York. The government paid the expenses of Hughes and McIlvaine but not of Weed, whose brand of politics was unpalatable to certain groups, especially those of the antislavery persuasion. Weed was to use his journalistic contacts to combat Confederate propaganda, McIlvaine to make his appeal to the British clergy, Hughes to labor with the Papacy, with Napoleon III, and with other Catholic rulers.

Though somewhat baffled by the British impression that Seward was an ogre, Weed devoted himself to organizing a pro-American campaign in the press.[1] There was something about Weed's lack of enthusiastic fervor, his solidity, and his un-English manner which made

[5] *Offic. Rec.* (Nav.), 2 ser., III, 566.

[1] Glyndon G. Van Deusen, *Thurlow Weed: Wizard of the Lobby*, 275–281.

him an effective advocate. He discounted the Newcastle story, created a better attitude toward Seward, kept the secretary informed, and in the winter of 1861–62 played an important part in smoothing over the *Trent* affair. It was not to have been expected that Minister Adams would make the contacts with the English press which the Albany editor could make. Weed did, however, work well with Adams; it was remarked in this connection that politics made strange bedfellows.[2]

Though less was said of McIlvaine than of Weed, the bishop did his quiet work well. Chase thought he was "doing a great work and a good one." [3] Benjamin Moran of the American legation commented on his refinement and his activity in "correcting British opinion on our affairs." [4] As to Hughes, his position as a Catholic prelate caused special reliance to be placed upon his statements. His task was difficult since he encountered much pro-Confederate sentiment, but he refrained from argument with those whose minds were closed and carefully avoided trenching upon the proper domain of Minister Dayton in France. He reported foreign opinion to Seward, presented to Napoleon III the American position on the *Trent* case, and gave pertinent comment on the alleged grievances of the South. His letters to Seward were submitted to and highly appreciated by President Lincoln.[5]

Of importance in financial circles was August Belmont, a Democrat whose opposition to Lincoln did not check his sincere devotion to the Union cause. Visiting abroad in 1861 and 1863, and keeping up an active correspondence with friends in Britain and France, he wielded influence in foreign financial circles and offered timely advice to the Lincoln administration. Belmont was a man of influential family connections, being related to Matthew G. Perry of Japanese fame and to John Slidell. His eminence in finance was illustrated by his serving as American agent of the Rothschilds.

Other representatives of the business world were John Murray Forbes of Boston and William H. Aspinwall of New York, Forbes be-

---

[2] Charles Francis Adams, Jr. to his father, March 11, 1862, *Cycle of Adams Letters,* 118.

[3] Chase to McIlvaine, Feb. 17, 1862, MS., J. P. Morgan Lib. Interesting details concerning Bishop McIlvaine are given by David Rankin Barbee in *Southern Churchman,* Sep. 10, 1932, 12–14.

[4] Sarah A. Wallace and Frances E. Gillespie, eds., *Journal of Benjamin Moran, 1857–1865,* II, 920.

[5] *Cath. Hist. Rev.,* III, 336–339 (Oct. 1917).

ing a power in shipping, Aspinwall in railroad enterprise, and both in finance. Forbes was a man of many public-minded activities, such as helping Governor Andrew in war work, promoting Negro recruiting, and organizing the Loyal Publication Society. His service abroad, on secret mission, was especially valuable in the final adjustment of the affair of the Laird rams. In this enterprise his collaborator, Aspinwall, was respected by mercantile and financial groups and known for disinterested competence. It was specifically the business of Forbes and Aspinwall to undo the work in Britain of Captain James D. Bulloch of the Confederate Navy. Closely associated with this pair was William M. Evarts of New York, a lawyer of uncommon force who used his legal talents to prevent the ironclad rams from reaching the Confederates. It appears that Minister Adams did not relish Evarts's activities, nor did Moran; but the lawyer was of service in unexpected ways, as in making British leaders more familiar with the financial policies of Chase.

One of the most vigorous of the unofficial American advocates in Britain was the fluent preacher-orator Henry Ward Beecher, exuberant antislavery leader and mighty man of the pulpit. His speeches in the industrial city of Manchester and the shipping center of Liverpool were nothing less than sensational. Standing his ground against vociferous and persistent heckling at Liverpool, he felt "like a shipmaster attempting to preach on board a ship through a speaking trumpet with a tornado on the sea and a mutiny among the men." [6] But he did stand his ground, and his Liverpool performance stands out as a memorable feat of endurance against heavy odds. Not confining his talk to religious themes, he enlarged upon the cotton question, the American constitution, proslavery motives of Southerners, and tolerance in America (at least in his Brooklyn church) toward colored people.

Henry's famous sister, Harriet Beecher Stowe, had influential friends in England, having been honored with a remarkable welcome in her visits to that country in the fifties. An active letter writer, she used her pen in personal correspondence for the cause of Union and freedom. An example was an open letter to "many thousands of Women in Great Britain and Ireland." [7] The purpose of this letter was to fasten the guilt of slavery upon the Southern Confederacy and

---

[6] Lyman Abbott, *Henry Ward Beecher,* 256.
[7] *Atlantic Monthly,* XI, 120–133 (Jan., 1863).

to interpret favorably the Union policy of emancipation. In her letter of July 31, 1863, to the Duchess of Argyll she wrote: "Slavery will be sent out by this agony. We are only in the throes and ravings of the exorcism. The roots of the cancer have gone everywhere, but they must die—will." [8]

In a class by himself among Americans abroad was the former secretary of the treasury and governor of Kansas, Robert J. Walker, northerner by birth, Mississippian by residence, and propagandist in Britain for the Union. By his boldness and pranks in England he became one of the wonders of the age as when he rose in a balloon from the Surrey side of the Thames, sailed aloft over London, and descended in Hertfordshire. None of the upholders of the American cause in Britain was more active than this tireless Walker. Knowing quite a bit about finance and having a special relation to Chase, he was listened to with attention. In one of his pamphlets he struck at Confederate financial credit and made it appear, contrary to fact, that Mississippi's repudiation of its state bonds, largely in the hands of British creditors, was the work of Jefferson Davis. He ranged over the whole subject of the war, emphasizing Union victory, exposing Confederate weakness, denouncing Southern slavery as hostile to progress, and linking the Lincoln administration with the liberties of man. By his reports, as in his correspondence with Chase, the British working classes were "all for us," war with Britain was not to be feared, emancipation was enthusiastically hailed by the British people, and "rebel" agents could make but the poorest bargain with British subscribers for their loan. Walker was determined to break their loan, to make them odious, and to ruin their cause both in Britain and on the Continent. In one of his letters to Chase he wrote: "Please say to Mr. Lincoln, that, with steady perseverance in his emancipation policy, & successful results, he will have a higher European reputation than any American since the days of Washington & Franklin, will have exalted our country in the eyes of the world, & given a new & irresistible impulse to free institutions. . . . Please say this to Mr. Lincoln from one, who neither expects nor would accept office or emoluments . . . ." [9]

These men, and a number of others who could be mentioned, may

---

[8] Charles E. Stowe, *Life of Harriet Beecher Stowe*, 370.

[9] Walker to Chase, London, May 8, 1863, Chase MSS., Pa. Hist. Soc. (There are many such letters from Walker to Chase in this series.)

be thought of as Lincoln's unofficial ambassadors of good will. The full effect of their activity may be somewhat a matter of conjecture, but they served with zeal, each in his area of contact, and it may at least be said that good will was for the most part promoted during the time of their various and somewhat miscellaneous missions.[10]

As for diplomacy in the usual sense—international relations on the official level—that was handled by Charles Francis Adams, American minister at London. One could speak of his limitations: his inadequate appreciation of Lincoln's qualities, his imperfect contact with the British people, his failure to give due credit to Dudley at Liverpool, and so on. Yet for performance and results at the assigned task he proved one of the most successful of American servants abroad. British officials recognized in him a man of worth and force. He could play the game, perhaps not always with finesse, but by diligent watching to see that attainable tricks were not lost. To take three Adamses in lineal succession—John, John Quincy, and Charles Francis—and trace their international dealings, is to cover the major chapters in American foreign affairs in the first, and formative, century of American national history. Such a tracing, to give briefest mention of immensely important developments, would include the diplomacy of the Revolution, the treaty of independence, the signing of peace with Britain in December 1814, the formulation of the Monroe doctrine, and the steering of Anglo-American relations under Lincoln.

III

While in the large the American question abroad might involve the broadest interests, the situation at a given time was reducible to choices between concrete courses of action. So far as it concerned Britain, by far the most important country in American relations, the leading problems were two: (1) the basic issue that came to mind when one mentioned such related words as recognition, armistice, unneutral assistance, mediation, or intervention; and (2) the building of warships for the Confederate States of America. Other matters, such as recruiting in Ireland for Federal service and various forms of financial assistance, might be productive of friction; yet these two

10 For a comprehensive treatment of these unofficial diplomats, see August C. Miller, Jr., "Lincoln's Good-Will Ambassadors," *Lincoln Herald*, vol. 50, 17–27 (June, 1948).

main issues contained the core of the difficulty. As to the blockade and the cotton shortage, its serious potentialities were comprised within the ominous word "intervention." Also one might take the question of slavery, but it too was of vital effect chiefly as it bore upon possible intervention or recognition.

It is proper, therefore, to consider mediation and recognition, with its related question of the blockade and its threat of possible intervention, as the central issue, the more so as it occupied enormous space in British, continental, and American newspapers and in the diplomatic correspondence of the time. That Britain never did worse than hover on the brink in this matter when it seemed abroad that the Confederacy was sure to win, was a sufficient indication of the success of Union diplomacy, and of British also. That the imperial government of France made an offer of mediation early in 1863 was a matter of minor importance for several reasons: the offer was indignantly spurned by the United States government without untoward effect; the French government never carried its sympathy for the Confederacy to the point of effective substantial aid; and the mediation gesture from Paris was without British support. What could have made recognition and mediation serious would have been combined action by Britain and France. This was frequently mentioned as a possibility, but, as with many a specter of international trouble, it never materialized.

All nations, especially those newly formed, are sensitive as to international position and prestige. The Confederacy was poignantly eager for recognition. Its diplomats and semi-official emissaries were much in evidence. At the outset of its existence, even before the war, the Confederate government sent three of its hopefuls—William L. Yancey, Pierre A. Rost, and A. Dudley Mann—on a preliminary foreign mission. Later the two aces of cotton diplomacy were sent, James M. Mason to Britain and John Slidell to France. Lesser emissaries tried their hand in approaching foreign governments, including those of Spain, Belgium, the Papal States, Russia, the French-dominated Empire of Mexico, and even dependencies or subdivisions to which diplomats were not usually accredited, such as Ireland, Canada, West Indian colonies, and individual states within Mexico.

In the drive for British recognition the Yancey-Rost-Mann mission of early 1861 got no farther than an "informal interview" with Lord

Russell on May 3, in which his lordship had "little to say." [1] After that, and ultimately, their small degree of luck was shown by the following frigid communication under date of December 7, 1861: "Lord Russell presents his compliments to Mr. Yancey, Mr. Rost, and Mr. Mann. He has had the honor to receive their letters of the 27th and 30th of November, but in the present state of affairs he must decline to enter into any official communication with them." [2]

As early as August 24, 1861, in a letter addressed to Yancey and his colleagues, Russell had mentioned having received a communication from them "on behalf of the so-styled Confederate States of North America." [3] From the Confederate standpoint this was the unpardonable insult. In 1864 Secretary of State Benjamin took the ground that he would refuse to receive any communication in which the Southern government was addressed as "the so-styled 'Confederacy.'" [4] The failure of this preliminary mission to obtain the much desired recognition was definitely indicated in a despatch sent by Yancey and Mann to Richmond on January 27, 1862, when their preliminary mission was about to give way to Mason and Slidell. In this despatch they reported that Russell had informed Charles Francis Adams that such interviews as he had had with the Confederate emissaries were in line with the established British custom of receiving "such persons unofficially" with no implication of recognition, as in the case of "Poles, Hungarians, Italians, etc.," but that "he had no expectation of seeing them any more." [5]

Mason and Slidell did no better as to recognition than the Yancey mission. Mason enjoyed expressions of sympathy from unofficial groups of Englishmen, but Russell's attitude towards him was cold and cautious. Unsuccessful in his efforts to impress the British ministry, rebuffed in curt communications favoring the Washington view as to the effectiveness of the blockade, frustrated in overtures toward treaty relations, and unable even to obtain reception as an accredited diplomat near the British court, Mason announced to Russell as early as September 21, 1863, that he was withdrawing from the country.[6] It would be hard to think of a diplomatic mission that was a more com-

---

1 *Offic. Rec.* (Nav.), 2 ser., III, 214.

2 *Ibid.*, 310.

3 *Ibid.*, 247.

4 *Ibid.*, 1033. In this connection one may note a Confederate diplomat's reference to "the soi-distant [*sic*] United States." *Ibid.*, 758.

5 *Ibid.*, 320.

6 *Ibid.*, 904–905; see below, pp. 348–349.

plete failure. Though dealing with a flamboyant monarch given to reckless international ventures, Slidell at Paris did no better than Mason.

IV

Failing in recognition, the Confederacy failed also in mediation and intervention. Their desire was for the Lincoln government to become embroiled in international war, and to this end they were ready to accept as allies those foreign elements whose hostility to American progress and to the Monroe Doctrine was obvious. For this they would also have sacrificed the American tradition against that type of alliance that was known by the sinister word "entangling." There were times when their hopes were raised. In January 1862, despite official British rebuff, Yancey and Mann reported to Richmond a "prevailing and doubtless correct impression" in London that British and French interference would occur "in some way," there being "indications" that it would go to the extent of demanding an armistice with mediation as to boundaries.[1] This may have been wishful thinking of a sort constantly encouraged by certain British newspapers and private gentlemen, but in the coming months there were slight rumblings in the British Parliament that bore the same tone. In the summer and fall of 1862 the matter came to a head.

In September of that year Lord Palmerston, British prime minister, and Earl Russell, foreign secretary, were cautiously pondering the American question in terms of what seemed imminent Union defeat. Referring to General Pope's "complete smashing" and to the chance that "still greater disasters" were about to occur, with Washington or Baltimore falling into Confederate hands, Palmerston asked Russell: "If this should happen, would it not be time for us to consider whether . . . England and France might not address the contending parties and recommend an arrangement upon the basis of separation?" [2] Cau-

---

1 *Offic. Rec.* (Nav.), 2 ser., III, 320.

2 What this amounted to was that in the immediate sequel of Second Bull Run Palmerston and Russell were engaged in deliberation as to whether a change of course might become necessary. In Palmerston's query the key words were: "If this should happen:" If, for instance, the Confederates had taken and held Washington, that "would have" involved a drastic change in American affairs. The fact that in this event the British would have had to consider a reorientation of their attitude is significant as showing that their existing position was far from pro-Confederate.

tious as he was, Russell replied: ". . . I agree with you that the time is come for offering mediation to the United States Government, with a view to the recognition of the independence of the Confederates. I agree further, that, in case of failure, we ought ourselves to recognise the Southern States as an independent State." [3] Clear-cut statements of the United States government, together with instructions to Charles Francis Adams, show that such a proposal, if put into effect, would have been regarded as cause at least for a breach of relations between Washington and London, and that, had Britain sought to implement its mediation and recognition with measures of official assistance to the Confederacy, the result might have been war. Adams had seen to it that on this point the British government was left in no doubt.

In October Russell circulated among his colleagues of the British ministry a confidential memorandum concerning a type of European mediation which, because of its slanting toward Confederate success and victory, would certainly have been regarded by the Lincoln government as unjustifiable interference. Discussion of the matter in cabinet meeting was set for October 23. A dangerous moment indeed had been reached in Anglo-American relations, and the worst might have been expected if the British government had been less deliberate —for example if it had acted on the matter a bit earlier, say in the period just after reception of the news of Pope's defeat. (It will be remembered that an Atlantic cable did not then exist for prompt reporting of that defeat.) As it turned out, the crisis passed with no harm done. International dealing does not consist of what is conjectured at a particular moment in a changing situation or of what is tentatively contemplated, or posed as a question to be decided, in confidential memoranda. Actual decision or dealing is another matter, and in Britain that involved careful and extended consideration in cabinet. Such consideration led to the conclusion that mediation ought to be postponed, and while the British government was still pondering whether to take any steps in the matter it was seen that "the set of the tide was . . . against mediation." [4] This was not merely a failure to reach a decision; the main point was that after due consideration a decision was reached to avoid mediation, as shown by the fact that the

---

[3] For the Palmerston-Russell exchange of views, see Walpole, *Life of Lord John Russell*, II, 349.

[4] *Ibid.*, II, 351.

British government soon took the position of refusing joint mediation with France.

Various contributing factors were responsible for this clearing of the air: the cautious attitude of certain British ministers, the friendliness of the Duke of Newcastle who opposed mediation, the effect abroad of the emancipation proclamation, and the forthright yet skillful diplomacy of Charles Francis Adams. It would seem, however, that the most decisive of all factors was the marked change in the military situation produced by Lee's failure to crush McClellan at Antietam. The chance of his doing so had been the basis of the conditional and confidential Russell-Palmerston deliberations in September. To appreciate the significance of McClellan's contribution one must consider the matter from the London angle. Only if one remembers the possible effect of foreign recognition of the Confederacy and the evident hinging of that issue on military events, can the full measure of Antietam to the Union cause be assessed.

V

If questions of recognition and mediation were packed with dynamite, no less so was the building and equipping of naval vessels for the Confederacy. This furnishing of ships with the resultant strain on friendly relations, is one of the familiar topics in the diplomacy of Lincoln's day, but precisely because of being so widely "known" this phase of the problem is beclouded with stereotypes and misconceptions. For the avoidance of historical error, two points in particular need to be noted. (1) It is erroneous to suppose that a government policy of unfriendliness to the United States or of deliberate intervention for the Confederacy was involved in the case of the well known (or rather, the oft-mentioned) *Alabama* and those very few other naval ships in which British help to the enemies of the United States was supplied. A correct view of the facts by no means justifies this facile supposition. (2) It is as much to the point to remember Britain's favorable action in detaining ships intended for operation against the United States—e. g., the Laird rams—as to recall those few earlier cases where ships were not detained. Any review of the subject that emphasizes only the *Alabama* is therefore one-sided.

The famous *Alabama,* Confederate cruiser and sea raider extraordinary, began mysteriously, though perhaps with only a superficial mystery, as the "290," or "Enrica," being so designated while building in the Laird yard at Birkenhead opposite Liverpool.[1] There were warnings, protests, and impressive documents of evidence presented by Charles Francis Adams; there was delay while detention of the ship was dilatorily studied by the Queen's law officers; in these circumstances the vessel slipped out to sea.[2] Later it received various kinds of British help: [3] tug, armament, British seamen, and supplies. Off the Azores (on the high seas) the ship was taken into Confederate service as the *Alabama.* From that moment (August 24, 1862) it ranged the seas over vast areas, capturing more than sixty merchant ships of the United States. Needless to say, these noncombatant vessels were not sunk at sight with disregard of human life. Conditions of the Confederacy made it impossible for them to be brought into any port of the capturing government for court adjudication and forfeiture; they were therefore either burned *after the removal of persons on board,* or released on "ransom bond." This meant that the owner was pledged to pay a sum of money "unto the President of the Confederate States of America . . . within thirty days after the conclusion of the present war . . . ." [4] The *Alabama* was a formidable and dangerous raider, bent on damage to the commerce of the United States, but it was not an international outlaw.

The settlement of the *Alabama* case and that of vessels in like situation (the *Shenandoah, Florida, Tallahassee,* and *Georgia*) was deferred until after the war. Ultimately, during the administration of President Grant, the British government gave full satisfaction in terms of a treaty

---

1 "I presume that Mr. Dudley [U. S. consul at Liverpool] keeps the Government fully informed of the change of the chrysalis 290 into the butterfly Alabama on a piratical cruise against American shipping." C. F. Adams to Seward, London, Sep. 5, 1862, Diplomatic Despatches (Britain vol. 80), MSS., Department of State, National Archives.

2 "On Tuesday a . . . screw-steamer, . . . known to the initiated as the 'Enrica,' and to the ignorant as the '290,' built by Messrs. Laird, of Birkenhead, left the Birkenhead Docks, and steamed down the Mersey to sea, as it was understood, on her trial-trip, to test her sailing capabilities." Liverpool *Albion,* Aug. 4, 1862.

3 In one of his diplomatic documents John Slidell mentioned "the *Alabama* and *Florida,* Confederate cruisers, built and in a great degree fitted out in England, which have been freely admitted in various English ports, have there repaired damages and been supplied with fuel and provisions." *Offic. Rec.* (Nav.), 2 ser., III, 744.

4 *Ibid.,* 1 ser., I, 782.

of arbitration (involving an expression of "regret" by Her Majesty's government) and financial settlement as fixed by tribunal award.[5] A fact which is abundantly clear in the voluminous and complicated record of this international *cause célèbre,* and which can only be ignored by those unfamiliar with the case, is that the settlement, which was favorable to the United States, was promoted by the very terms of the treaty to which Britain agreed as a matter of negotiation; the whole outcome was a case of friendly adjustment rather than of forced retribution for wrongs committed. It should also be remembered that the British government had taken steps to detain the *Alabama,* but that before such steps could be effective the ship had already departed on its adventures. The ponderousness of lawyers may have been as much a factor in this result as deliberately unfriendly connivance. Lawyers take their time; they must have "proof" (legal evidence) of things that are unmistakably obvious to the layman.

VI

It is not, however, the *Alabama,* but the *Alexandra* and the Laird rams, that offer the clue to the controlling pattern of British policy in the war. Action at London in the case of these ships was such that no controversy developed and no postwar arbitration was necessary. In these instances the ambitious efforts of the Confederacy to obtain naval assistance from Britain were frustrated. Coming to a head in the spring of 1863, the case of the *Alexandra,* a sea raider being built in England for the Confederate navy, had significance as indicating whether the government of Britain, after letting the *Alabama* and other vessels slip through, would do likewise in other cases, thus making "connivance" at Confederate aid a continuing policy. In this sense it was a test case, and for that reason one should not underestimate the importance of British action in seizing the ship on April 5, 1863,[1] and preventing its ever being delivered into Confederate hands. The legal details of the case, which involved trial, appeal, and final decree by

---

[5] Randall, *Civil War and Reconstruction,* 839–846.

[1] Charles Francis Adams received on April 5, 1863, a note from Russell indicating that orders had been issued for the seizure of the *Alexandra.* Adams wrote: "I rejoice at this . . . disposition to defeat the machinations of those who hope to relieve the rebels by . . . a diversion from this side." Adams to Seward, London, April 7, 1863, *House Exec. Doc. No. 1,* 38 Cong., 1 sess., pt. 1, 228–229.

the House of Lords, may be omitted. The thing that stands out clear in the episode is the keen disappointment of Southern diplomats and the evident satisfaction of all who favored the cause of Lincoln. The Confederate propaganda agent Hotze referred to British official conduct in this case as proving "undoubtedly a strong desire to propitiate our enemies." [2] Concerning a somewhat similar question Mason wrote of "the determination of the [British] Government . . . to yield everything to avoid risk of collision [with the United States]." [3] When, asserting the doctrine of continuous voyage, the United States seized the *Peterhoff*, sailing from a British port to Matamoros, on the ground that its Mexican destination was fraudulent and its cargo intended for the Confederacy, Adams reported that he had mentioned to Russell the good effect produced in America by Britain's detention of the *Alexandra*, as well as of Russell's reply to the owners of the *Peterhoff*. "On his [Russell's] part," wrote Adams, "he expressed satisfaction at this as an indication that the . . . hostile spirit to England imputed to us was not entertained." [4] Essential friendliness toward America in Britain was promoted in spite of the chilling effect of Anglophobe sentiment among certain groups in the United States. Whenever a more amicable sentiment was expressed, its effect at London was both welcome and officially favorable.

Of like significance as to British attitude, but of even more importance in international relations, was the famous case of the Laird rams. These two ironclads, constructed by the Laird firm under contract arranged by Captain James Dunwoody Bulloch, Confederate naval officer and foreign agent, were intended to break the Union blockade, harass Northern ports, and assault merchant shipping. For their day they were formidable instruments of war. It was known for what purpose the ships were building, and as the case dragged on for anxious months the subject became one of great irritation to all concerned. Contradictory statements as to what Britain would do appeared from time to time, after the manner of diplomatic wishful thinking. Following months of pressure and controversy, a Confederate agent reported from London that Earl Russell was "said to be in a state of pitiable perplexity and in a ludicrously ill temper about

[2] *Offic. Rec.* (Nav.), 2 ser., III, 768. [3] *Ibid.*, 751.

[4] Adams to Seward, London, May 14, 1863, Diplomatic Despatches (Britain, vol. 83), MSS., Dep. of State, Nat. Archives.

the whole affair." [5] It is hardly too much to say that preservation of peace between Britain and the United States depended on the disposition of this question, a fact which Seward and Adams did not fail to impress upon British official minds. Had the ships departed for Confederate service, a breach of relations at the least seemed the certain result; if a breach had occurred, war was considered a probability. This being so, it was an ominous fact that on September 2, 1863, according to testimony taken at Liverpool, one of the rams had her masts in, her rigging completed, her engines and machinery in order, her funnel up, and everything in readiness to slip down the Mersey and out to sea.[6]

It was at this tense moment that Charles Francis Adams wrote his famous note to Russell (September 5, 1863) expressing "profound . . . regret" at developments, reminding the foreign secretary of Confederate threats against New York, Boston, Portland, and other ports, hinting at instructions of an ominous nature from Washington, and reaching a dramatic climax with the statement: "It would be superfluous in me to point out to your lordship that this is war." [7] To a superficial observer it might have seemed a clear instance of cause and effect when by a note under date of September 8 Russell informed Adams that "instructions . . . [had] been issued which . . . [would] prevent the departure of the two iron-clad vessels from Liverpool." [8]

The United States was satisfied and in this way the matter was settled; ultimately the warships were purchased by the British government. The historical error that must be avoided here is a misrepresentation of the episode as one of ultimatum by the United States followed by British surrender under threat. The real situation was far different. Adams and Russell were in fact working toward the same end; it was a mere accident—the absence of Russell from London (at his country home in Scotland)—that gave occasion for Adams's forthright note. As a matter of fact, Russell had decided upon the detention of the rams before Adams's note was written. He had caused the law officers to investigate the case, had been unconvinced by the evidence

[5] *Offic. Rec.* (Nav.), 2 ser., III, 915.

[6] Statement of Thomas Sweeney, sworn at Custom House, Liverpool, Sep. 2, 1863, Diplomatic Despatches (Britain, vol. 83), MSS., Dep. of State, Nat. Archives.

[7] *House Exec. Doc. No. 1*, 38 Cong., 1 sess., pt. 1, p. 418.

[8] *Ibid.*, 419.

(bearing the appearance of "legal" evidence) that the ships were intended for a French firm,[9] had given an instruction on September 1 that caused the vessels to be watched against departure,[10] and had actually directed them to be stopped on September 3, two days in advance of the American minister's stern note. On the very day of the note (September 5) he ordered detention; three days later he advised Adams that this had been done.[11]

The awkward thing was that written notes had to be used at all, since they crossed each other in such manner that Adams's statement had already ceased to have significance at the moment of being received. The whole episode illustrates the error of sensationalism in the treatment of historical material. When a public man coins a famous phrase and when superficially the event seems to show that the heroic phrase or gesture turns a trick, the temptation toward sensationalism is too hard for some writers to resist; in this case the overdramatization has passed into stereotyped history. If ever historical revision were needful, it is so here. There was no cause to overawe Russell with an ultimatum. Talking things over was all that was needed. Russell had indeed foreshadowed his friendly policy toward the United States the previous April in connection with the *Alexandra*. His government's amicable dealing with the rams was of a piece with that earlier case. Adams handsomely deserves credit for his persistent, watchful, and sagacious handling of his country's affairs, but in the case of the rams the leaving "no stone unturned" for peaceable adjustment could have been said as truly of Russell as of Adams. The nations that understood each other were the United States and Britain; the party that was checkmated and aggrieved, as the record amply shows, was the Confederacy.

In all this activity to prevent the ironclads from getting into Confederate hands, as in earlier efforts, the tireless work of Thomas H. Dudley, United States consul at Liverpool, was of great importance, and in most accounts the credit given to him has been inadequate. In continual watchfulness, secret investigations, the gathering of affi-

[9] Had the British government stood merely on the superficial legal aspects, it could have made out that the ships were not for the Confederacy at all. Bulloch had nominally sold them to a French firm; they were, of course, to be resold to the Confederacy after departure from Britain.

[10] Rhodes, *Hist. of the U. S.*, IV, 381.

[11] *House Exec. Doc. No. 1*, 38 Cong., 1 sess., pt. 1, 419.

davits, and the conveying of information to Adams, his service was of the highest value. This becomes clear when one examines, as the author has, the impressive and voluminous Dudley papers. William M. Evarts wrote to Dudley on September 26, 1863: "The merchants and shipowners of our country owe you a great debt . . . ." "You have had the greatest share of labor . . . in this business, and are entitled to the principal credit . . . for the invaluable result. I left England . . . with entire confidence that the British Government would not suffer these Iron-clads to come out." [12]

VII

Mention has already been made of the *Peterhoff* case, one of the troublesome questions between the United States and England in 1863. Though it has received inadequate attention, it was very revealing as to Lincoln's handling of international relations. It was significant also as showing how the President was pulled and tugged this way and that by strong disagreements within his cabinet. Though nearly forgotten now, this case was not a minor affair, since it involved talk of possible war with Britain. The *Peterhoff* was a British-owned merchant steamer captured in the West Indies in February 1863. It was on its way to Matamoros, a Mexican port close to the Atlantic Ocean (a little way inland), and across the Rio Grande from Brownsville, Texas. Mexico was a neutral country, but the question arose whether the "neutral" destination was genuine, especially in view of the contraband nature of part of the cargo and the close proximity of Matamoros to the Confederacy. In its supposed hazard of war with England, though war for such a cause was absurd, the case seemed like another *Trent* affair. The analogy was not complete, but the parallel was emphasized by the incidental fact that it was none other than Charles Wilkes of *Trent* fame who made the capture of the *Peterhoff*.

The matter was ultimately settled by freeing the captured ship, releasing the non-contraband cargo, and seizing such of the cargo as consisted of contraband goods. The case became historic because of the principle of "continuous voyage"—i. e., the right of a belligerent

---

12 Thomas H. Dudley MSS., Huntington Lib.

to seize cargo destined only nominally for a neutral port and plainly intended for an enemy.[1]

The point of interest here is not only the outcome of the case, which was fortunate, but what went on behind the scenes in an affair that offered a real challenge to the President's authority as well as to his skill in personal and official relations. The *Peterhoff* seizure was a bone of contention not only between Britain and the United States, but also between the secretary of the navy and the secretary of state. The President was caught in between, being under pressure from both secretaries though relying especially upon Seward.

The aspect on which Welles was particularly concerned was whether the United States, by a prize court, could legitimately seize the mails on board the captured ship. Emphatically, almost angrily, Welles favored the seizure, showing little regard for consequences, while Seward, giving attention to an adjustment through negotiation with Britain, strongly opposed such a measure.

The President wanted to know the usage as to the right of a belligerent to seize the mails of a captured ship, but all he got was a positive statement from Seward that the precedents did not favor such a "violation," which was flatly contradicted by Welles's statement of the opposite conclusion. The mails having been actually seized and taken into possession by a United States district court in New York, the question arose whether this amounted to lawful possession. Unhappy that Lincoln could not accept his view of the subject, Welles remarked that the "President . . . was a good deal 'obfusticated' in regard to the merits of the question." [2]

For week after week the unsolved problem dragged on, both secretaries continuing their pressure on the President, Welles's aides ransacking the books to get precedents, Welles himself becoming more and more emphatic, and Sumner, chairman of the foreign relations committee of the Senate, favoring the Welles position and making his senatorial views known to Lord Lyons. It angered Welles that Seward "conceded" the main point which Welles thought should have been left with the courts. The secretary of the navy looked on this as an unjustifiable interference, and so did the attorney general, when Seward

---

[1] J. B. Moore, *Hist. and Digest of International Law,* IV, 3838–3843; Peterhoff *vs.* U. S., 5 Wallace 28 (1867); *Offic. Rec.* (Nav.), 1 ser., II, 100 ff.

[2] Welles, *Diary,* I, 280 (April 21, 1863).

directed District Attorney Delafield Smith, an officer under the jurisdiction of the attorney general, to see that the mails were given up, which was done. It was Welles's view that the President was sincere and of right intention, but that he had been "imposed upon, humbugged, by a man in whom he confides." Welles added: "the Secretary of State is daily, and almost hourly, wailing in his ears the calamities of a war with England which he is striving to prevent. The President is thus led away from the real question, and will probably decide it, not on its merits, but on this false issue, raised by the man who is the author of the difficulty."

Here, as in the *Trent* case, Lincoln's conduct—for, after all, the President had to decide these things—was determined by the consideration that Britain would not consent to having their mail bags opened, their seals or locks broken; that war lurked as a possibility; and that, as Lincoln thought, "we were in no condition to plunge into a foreign war on a subject of so little importance in comparison with the terrible consequences which must follow our act." [3] Welles could see only his side, while the President weighed the great advantage of a friendly international adjustment against the minor factor of releasing a mail bag.

However Welles might characterize the President as "obfusticated" or a mere tool of Seward, the Chief saw the case through. He could not allow such a question between nations to dangle indefinitely in suspense. As Welles recorded it, Lincoln said to him, "I shall have to cut this knot." [4]

The case reached its climax on May 15, 1863. On that day the President called on Welles bringing "the basis of a dispatch which Lord Lyons proposed to send home." [5] Lyons had shown it to Seward; Seward turned it over to the President; the President was now submitting it to Welles. The dispatch involved a settlement by which the United States would give up any effort to hold the mails seized on the *Peterhoff*. This adjustment had been shaped up in a manner opposite to Welles's wishes.

Here were strong men of contrary views facing each other in the determination of an issue that had been hanging fire between them for months. A decision had to be made. Welles wanted the matter to rest

[3] *Ibid.*, I, 287 (April 28, 1863). [4] *Ibid.*, I, 289.
[5] *Ibid.*, 302.

with the courts and be adjudicated according to "law and usage." Seizing on that very point, Lincoln asked: "But have the courts ever opened the mails of a neutral government?" "Always," replied Welles, but with entire vagueness as to cases. "Why, then," said Lincoln, "do you not furnish me with the fact?" Welles made the weak reply that, to his knowledge, the matter had never been questioned, adding that the courts were independent of the departments. Lincoln was not satisfied: "if mails ever are examined," he said, "the fact must be known and recorded." He then pinned the secretary down: "What vessels have we captured, where we have examined the mails?" Welles's answer was again offhand where the President demanded specific citation. "All [vessels], doubtless," said the secretary, "that have had mails on board." The matter went on in this fashion till Welles was stumped. He could recall no actual case and when he sent for one of his staff, Watkins, who had charge of prize matters, that gentleman "could not call to mind anything conclusive." [6]

The President had given his secretary of the navy a respectful hearing, and now his position was all the stronger for having done so. The mails, also the noncontraband cargo, were released and an adjustment satisfactory to Britain, but in no way hurtful to the interest or honor of the United States, was thus arrived at. The President had taken sides with Seward, but the time was to come when Welles himself would come forward in print as one of the strongest defenders of Lincoln as President and statesman in the field of international relations.[7]

As for Wilkes, he was relieved of his West Indies command, where he had not captured the famous *Alabama,* but had repeatedly got his government into serious trouble. He incurred the strong dislike of Welles for negative results in defeating Confederate raiders as well as for insubordination, disobedience to orders, and use of the newspaper press for publicized self-vindication at the expense of superiors. For these offenses he was brought to trial before a naval court martial (1864) charged with insubordination and undue assumption of authority. He was found guilty and sentenced to a public reprimand and suspension from the service for three years.

The matters summarized in this chapter offer glimpses to suggest

[6] *Ibid.,* I, 303–304.
[7] Gideon Welles, *Lincoln and Seward . . .* (N. Y., 1874).

the nature of foreign affairs under Lincoln. Here was no dictatorship making decisions by irresponsible order or fiat. Here was a homely President of democratic habits at work in difficult situations. There were buffetings of popular excitement, misrepresentation, cabinet quarreling, and assertions of senatorial opinion. There was the hazard that a small incident might get out of hand and lead to untold consequences. There was the chance that rigid legality might come to the front and obscure the larger factors. Through it all ran the great fundamentals which it was Lincoln's function to keep always foremost. His eye was on the cause of American survival, which he identified with the cause of democracy in the world. While others were legalistic or litigious, he was careful not to be drawn into needless bickering or diverted from the great task as he saw it. He realized that it was not a question of winning a point against Britain (which, if won, might have proved of little value), but rather a matter of mutual interest as between the two nations; the cause of international adjustment was an equal benefit to both. He was shrewd enough to realize that the best victory in international dealing might be in terms of a concession, and that in the family of nations it becomes imperative for statesmen to see more than one narrow point of view. What we have been considering is the challenge of nations under stress; in the next chapter the unfolding pattern becomes steadily more clear in terms of the friendship of nations in a period of great crisis.

CHAPTER XIV

FRIENDSHIP OF NATIONS

FOR Britons to understand all that was involved in the American Civil War was not easy. It is therefore unwise to hazard generalizations in this field, as in other complex matters of public opinion and sentiment in international relations. Even at this date, with the records available, it is difficult to get a fully rounded picture of opinion in Britain toward the issue between the governments of Lincoln and of Jefferson Davis. When one points to British sympathy for the Confederacy, he is dealing with a socially prominent, class-conscious, vocal, and assertive element concerning whose activities vast quantities of historical material can be produced; nevertheless only a part of the picture—a minor part—is presented when this phase alone is considered.

I

British elements which opposed Lincoln were those which thought little of government of, by, and for the people. They were, for the most part, the London clubs, the silk-hatted folk of "society," the enemies of democratic rule, and the men who, from hostility or rivalry, dreaded the rise of the United States as a great and prosperous nation. As a qualification one must of course add that for a long time the Old South had been close to Britain in society and business and that during the war there were many Englishmen whose admiration of Southerners and sympathy for the Confederate cause was genuine. (Others in Britain would have preferred to keep their friendship for Southerners if only that sentiment could have been free from any anti-United-States involvement. If they had an interest in New Orleans friends, it was not by their wish that such an interest was transmuted into hatred of Boston.) Confederate propagandists and diplomats had ready access to social circles and to newspaper columns (some of them) in Britain, and they did not fail to pour out a story that sounded convincing to foreign ears. Lincoln's government was denounced for coercion, shutting off commerce, violating international law, and even, as in the case of an overadvertised and misrepresented order by General Benjamin F. Butler, of crass indecency.

The devil of misunderstanding, aided by a deliberate pro-Confederate effort to magnify it, was illustrated in the minor episode of Butler's "woman order." Having become the most hated Yankee in the South by reason of his administration of Union-occupied New Orleans, Butler had unfortunately issued a military order that any female insulting a Union soldier or officer would "be regarded and held liable to be treated as a woman of the town plying her avocation." The general explained that his action was based on reported insults to his soldiery by women in New Orleans, and that, in exaggerated denunciations, his order was misrepresented as to intent. The most charitable view of Butler was that he had committed a serious blunder. For this and other reasons he was called "Beast Butler" [1] and in the anti-Union propaganda sense in Britain the order was utterly misrepresented as having been directed from Washington and as typical of Northern depravity.[2] Benjamin Moran wrote in his diary on November 5, 1862: "This is Guy Fawkes' day, and at about 11 o'clock a crowd of men and boys brought a gigantic Guy in military dress, with a gallows at its side, past the [American] Legation, labeled 'The Brute Butler.' It was vociferously cheered . . . ."

The resources of the South, its harmony of economic interest with Britain, its military invincibility—all such themes were urged in speeches, editorials, pamphlets, and private conversation. Sometimes the Confederate propaganda theme abroad was the opposite of that at home. Domestically, secession leaders assailed the Lincoln government for its attacks upon slavery as upon Southern rights; abroad they

1 One of Butler's most unjustifiable acts was the military execution of a Southern citizen, Mumford by name, for tearing down a United States flag at New Orleans. The government at Washington was not enforcing the death penalty against participants or adherents of the Confederate cause. Randall, *Constitutional Problems Under Lincoln,* 227, chaps. iv, v.

2 B. F. Butler, *Private and Official Correspondence,* I, 490; James Parton, *General Butler at New Orleans,* 322–345; C. F. Adams, Jr., *Charles Francis Adams,* 243 ff.; W. Reed West, *Contemporary French Opinion on the American Civil War,* 80–81.

pointed out that slavery versus antislavery was not the issue at all and that the Lincoln government had disclaimed any intention to strike at slavery within the states. As to the blockade, they said both that it was ineffective and that it was a serious menace. In Confederate military historiography one of the familiar themes is the small number of soldiers that were doing battle for Lee, but George N. Sanders, in England on Confederate business, stated in the month of Antietam that the Confederate army east of Petersburg included about 200,000 men and four hundred pieces of field artillery.[3] Henry Hotze handled Confederate publicity abroad, publishing a weekly newspaper, the *Index* (nominally English but actually a Confederate organ) and carrying on a varied activity which included the supplying of articles to British newspapers, the circulating of brochures, and even the coaching of a few members of Parliament and the concealed authorship of a pamphlet entitled *La Question Mexicaine et la Colonization Française,* prepared with the aid of a translator and written "in the hope of its having some bearing on the Mexican debate in the French chamber." [4]

In Britain the Southern cause was served not only by diplomatic and unofficial agents of the Confederacy itself, but by Englishmen who formed the Southern Independence Association of London and other cities. This propagandist group concerned itself with holding public meetings, promoting sympathy for the Confederate cause, combating the arguments of Unionists, and seeking to relieve Southerners from the stigma of slavery by making it appear that slaves had a welcome and significant place in Southern armies. "This association," wrote J. M. Mason in December 1864, "is the largest, as it is the most active . . . of any . . . formed . . . in our behalf." [5] Not only at large gatherings, but more especially at select dinners or banquets, speeches were made which favored the enemies of the United States. British friends of the Confederacy were numerous, vocal, and well organized. In October 1863 Hotze asserted, though with the exaggeration of a propagandist: "Here [in England] there is scarcely a man eminent in letters, in politics, or in society, who dares profess friendship for the

[3] Liverpool *Daily Post,* Sep. 3, 1862. In the same issue it was mentioned that Sanders had been United States consul in London and that he had arrived in Liverpool from Richmond incognito "by underground railway."

[4] *Offic. Rec.* (Nav.), 2 ser., III, 1024.

[5] *Ibid.,* 1251.

North."[6] The boasts of Hotze were notorious, but one finds corroboration, at least in part, in a statement made privately by Henry Adams. Writing to his brother Charles Francis early in the war, young Adams indicated that Southerners in London were enthusiastic while Union men there were lukewarm, and that, in general, Americans could expect "no sympathy or assistance in Europe from any Government."[7]

It is unsatisfactory to attempt an enumeration of individual Britons who sought to aid the cause of secession or showed sympathy for it, but among them one would have to include James Spence (Liverpool merchant and author of *The American Union*), A. J. Beresford-Hope, the Marquis of Lothian, the Marquis of Bath, Lord Robert Cecil, Lord Wharncliffe, William S. Lindsay (shipping merchant), and John A. Roebuck. It will be seen on a later page how the parliamentary effort of Lindsay and Roebuck to promote a pro-Confederate movement in the British Parliament broke down completely. So also their somewhat farcical diplomatic contacts with Napoleon III. In fact the cause of the Confederacy in Britain always seemed brighter at dinners of the Southern Independence Association than in dealings with the British government.

Such men as Carlyle and Gladstone could be quoted on the Confederate side. Carlyle epitomized the attitude of a certain type of Britisher when he cynically referred to the American war as the burning out of a dirty chimney which could be regarded only with satisfaction by neighbors.[8] This expressed the view of those in Britain who desired the ruin of both the North and South, thus relieving Canada of an imagined menace and doing away with a cotton competitor of British India. Gladstone, chancellor of the exchequer, came into notoriety for a speech at Newcastle on October 7, 1862, in which he treated Southern military success as certain. He said: ". . . Jefferson Davis and other leaders of the South have made an army; they are making, it appears, a navy; and they have made what is more than either —they have made a nation. . . . We may anticipate with certainty the success of the Southern States so far as regards their separation

[6] *Ibid.*, 946.

[7] W. C. Ford, ed., *A Cycle of Adams Letters*, I, 61–62, 66. Henry Adams was writing of opinions in Britain as distinguished from actions. Of the latter he wrote, "There is no danger of any movement from England . . . ." *Ibid.*, 65.

[8] *Offic. Rec.* (Nav.), 2 ser., III, 506.

from the North."[9] This utterance was the more serious because it came at a critical moment of the war so far as British policy was concerned and because at the time Gladstone, being about the age of Lincoln, was a member of the British ministry, though in no sense its approved spokesman. Gladstone fraternized with Hotze, who, after meeting the statesman at dinner, wrote: "He is, of all the members of the cabinet, supposed to be the most friendly to us, and his manner and language . . . so impressed me." A feature of this conversation as reported by Hotze was Gladstone's "emphatic prediction that the war would speedily end in the acknowledged independence of the South."[10]

It is recorded that when Gladstone delivered his famous sentences concerning the success of Jefferson Davis and his Confederacy, his words produced a great sensation in his Newcastle audience. Sensations become events and in this case a momentary utterance became an international incident. In that sense, and in contrast to the whole large view which Gladstone could not then envisage, his phrases, all the more so because of their quotableness, exceeded the bounds of official discretion. Perhaps the main significance of the Newcastle speech was its revelation of the inability of a man so able and so well disposed as Gladstone to look at the contemporary American struggle and see it whole. Gladstone's limitation was simply that he could not foresee Union success at a moment when Confederate armies were riding high.

In a memorandum written in July, 1896, Gladstone stated that his Newcastle declaration "was not due to any . . . partizanship for the South or hostility to the North." It was simply that he thought the struggle was "virtually at an end" and that it was a matter of "friendliness to all America" to recognize the fact. He added that he "was not one of those who on the ground of British interests desired a division of the American Union" but that his view was "distinctly opposite."[11] Looking back from this memorandum to the speech itself, it is significant to read the passage which immediately preceded the sensational

---

[9] *The Times*, London, Oct. 9, 1862, pp. 7–8; John Morley, *Life of William Ewart Gladstone*, II, 79.

[10] Hotze to Benjamin, London, Aug. 4, 1862, *Offic. Rec.* (Nav.), 2 ser., III, 506.

[11] Morley, *Gladstone*, II, 81.

part; it puts the incident in a somewhat different light, at least to the extent of relieving Gladstone of any animosity toward the North. This part of the speech, hardly ever quoted, was as follows:

> . . . I would for a moment make an appeal to you on behalf of the people of the Northern States . . . . Great allowances are to be made for them. . . . let us bear with them all we can; let us maintain toward them a kindly temper; let us not allow ourselves to feel the smallest irritation when we see ourselves adversely criticized on the other side of the water; and let us be very cautious about indulging in adverse criticisms upon them on this side of the water. . . . They are our kin. They were . . . our customers, and we hope they will be our customers again. . . . they entertain warm affections toward England. Whatever momentary irritation may cross the mind of that people, let us not forget their reception of the Prince of Wales. (Hear.) Let every Englishman engrave upon the tablets of his heart the recollection of that memorable day; and, if occasionally he feels tempted to anger by seeing his country misapprehended, or, it may be, misrepresented, let him calm his tendency to excited sentiments by that recollection. (Hear, hear.) [12] It is the more necessary to do this because . . . the people of the Northern States have not yet drunk of . . . the cup which all the rest of the world see they nevertheless must drink of. We may have our own opinions about slavery; we may be for or against the South; but there is no doubt that Jefferson Davis and other leaders of the South have made an army . . . [then followed the sensational passage quoted above.] [13]

To bracket Gladstone with those who wished ill to the United States, therefore, seems hardly correct. It was rather that he was speaking somewhat hastily and out of turn and that, even then, the whole speech was in a different sense than the famous passage so often quoted. Even more does it give a wrong impression to quote outstanding British partisans of the Confederacy and leave the matter there. In so large a subject it is always possible to pick out instances. One therefore needs to be reminded that those in Britain who spoke in a manner inimical to the American Union were giving expression to a sentiment opposite to that which controlled the British government. Despite such statements reflecting the views of certain individuals or groups, the substantial action of the British ministry, supported by the Parliament, remains.

---

12 In these sections of his speech that urged a friendly attitude toward the North, Gladstone was frequently interrupted by shouts of approval.

13 *The Times,* London, Oct. 9, 1862, p. 7, c. 6.

II

Most influential among British newspapers favoring the Confederacy was the *Times* of London. In the summer of 1862 Charles Francis Adams wrote: ". . . I cannot fail to perceive a progressive consolidation of the popular prejudice against America, under the operation of the continuous denunciations of the London Times. The sympathies of the higher classes are decidedly enlisted in the struggle not from any . . . affection for either side, but from a longing to see the political power of the United States permanently impaired." [1] Readers who followed the issues and events of the American war through the pages of the *Times* were given a low opinion of the Lincoln government and of the cause for which it stood. The war was represented as a matter of "mob passions." [2] Methods of war employed by the United States, according to this oracle, were marked by "a cruelty which far surpasses anything that can be laid to . . . England." [3] Southern victories were emphasized even to the point of printing a dressed-up fable that McClellan was capitulating with his entire force.[4] Confronted two months later with the news of Antietam, the *Times* blandly remarked that "had it been the policy of the Confederates to have still held their ground in Maryland, they could have done so notwithstanding this battle." [5] It seemed actually painful to the editors of this impressive paper to record anything but Union defeats.

In its comments on Lincoln the superior tone of the *Times* was particularly evident. The American system was described as "a cheap and simple form of government, having a rural attorney for Sovereign and a city attorney [Seward] for Prime Minister." If, said the *Times,* such a "terrible exposure of incapacity had happened in England we should at the earliest moment possible have sent the incapables about

---

[1] C. F. Adams to Seward, London, July 31, 1862, Diplomatic Despatches (Britain, vol. 80), MSS., Dep. of State, Nat. Archives.

[2] *The Times,* Aug. 14, 1861, p. 8, c. 2. [3] *Ibid.,* July 5, 1864, p. 11, c. 5.

[4] "Such is the state of opinion here that a despatch incorporating it [the fable of McClellan's surrender] dressed up for the purpose . . . and published in . . . The Times was eagerly caught up and believed . . . ." Adams to Seward, London, July 19, 1862, Diplomatic Despatches (Britain, vol. 80), MSS., Dep. of State, Nat. Archives. The account to which Adams referred was under the heading "Reported Surrender of the Federal Army." It appeared in the *Times* of July 19, 1862, p. 14, c. 1.

[5] *The Times,* Oct. 1, 1862, p. 8, c. 3.

their business, and put ourselves in the hands of better men." [6] Lincoln's emancipation proclamation was misrepresented as the massacre of white women and children: "He will appeal to the black blood of the African; he will whisper of the pleasures of spoil and of the gratification of yet fiercer instincts; and when blood begins to flow . . . Mr. Lincoln will wait till the rising flames tell that all is consummated, and then he will rub his hand and think that revenge is sweet." [7] And again: "Is Lincoln yet a name not known to us as it will be known to posterity, and is it ultimately to be classed among that catalogue of monsters, the wholesale assassins and butchers of their kind? . . . We will attempt . . . to predict nothing as to . . . Lincoln's new [emancipation] policy . . . except that it certainly will not have the effect of restoring the Union. It will not deprive Mr. Lincoln of the . . . affix which he will share with . . . foolish . . . Kings and Emperors, Caliphs and Doges, that of being Lincoln—'the Last.' " [8]

The American President seemed to the *Times* unable to "emancipate himself from the shackles of a merely legal mind." [9] Prophesying (though making no "attempt . . . to predict"!) the effect of a Lincoln victory in the war, the *Times* warned that "the Executive of Washington . . . will, if successful, do what Saracens and Tartars spared to do—will unseat the population generally, and divide their lands among the conquering soldiery." [10] Asserting contrary to fact that Lincoln had "gone through the course of defying and insulting England, which is the traditional way of obtaining the Irish vote," the *Times,* though having no respect for McClellan either, deplored the President's reëlection in 1864, regarding it "as little less than an abdication by the American people of the right of self-government" and "an avowed step toward the foundation of a military despotism." By this time the editor was swinging his pen merrily. He added: "Future historians will probably date from the second presidency of Mr. Lincoln the period when the American Constitution was thoroughly abrogated, and had entered on that transition . . . through which Republics pass on their way from democracy to tyranny." [11]

---

[6] *Ibid.,* Nov. 4, 1862, p. 8, c. 6.
[7] *Ibid.,* Oct. 7, 1862, p. 8, c. 3.
[8] *Ibid.,* Oct. 21, 1862, p. 9, c. 1.
[9] *Ibid.,* Mar. 19, 1861, p. 9, c. 1.
[10] *Ibid.,* July 5, 1864, p. 11, c. 5. (It is needless to point out that this was completely opposite to Lincoln's intent.)
[11] *Ibid.,* Nov. 22, 1864, p. 6, c. 3. The reference to Lincoln "defying and insulting Eng-

By the very oppositeness of its slant, the *Times* went far forward substantiating Lincoln's own contention as to the fundamental cause for which the United States was struggling. That is to say, the *Times,* in revealing its dislike of democracy while assailing Lincoln, was unmistakably associating the opponents of Lincoln with the enemies of the democratic principle. "The real secret of the exultation . . . in the *Times,*" wrote John Lothrop Motley, ". . . over our troubles and disasters, is their hatred, not to America, so much as to democracy in England." [12] Though disclaiming any wish to "dogmatize about democracy," the *Times* delivered the obiter dictum that "the form which democracy has taken during the last 30 years [in America] . . . was not unlikely to lead to such consequences"—i. e., secession and civil war.[13] Foreign doubters, had they known it, were offering the most convincing corroboration of Lincoln's argument that his cause was "essentially a people's contest," that it embraced "more than the fate of these United States," that it was a testing of the democratic "experiment," and that success in the experiment would be a "great lesson of peace." [14]

III

Evidences of unfriendliness to the United States on the part of certain elements in Britain belonged, after all, to the Lost Cause; indeed it was a lost cause in England long before it became so at Appomattox Court House. It is a significant fact that midway in the war, in a manner of speaking, the Confederacy broke with England. It is true that regular diplomatic relations between London and Richmond never existed. There were, however, threads of connection or at least modes of attempted access; it was these which were severed in 1863.

By the latter part of that year Britain had proved receptive to the representations of Charles Francis Adams, had denied recognition to the Confederacy, had remained aloof from James M. Mason, had

---

land"—a complete misrepresentation of the President's attitude, for he did nothing of the sort at any time—is significant only as showing how far the anti-Lincoln press abroad strayed from the path of honesty and truth. It must be added that such straying has been characteristic of the anti-British press in America in our own day.

[12] J. L. Motley to his mother, Sep. 22, 1861, cited in E. D. Adams, *Great Britain and the American Civil War,* II, 280–281.

[13] *The Times,* Oct. 18, 1861, p. 6, c. 2.

[14] Nicolay and Hay, *Works,* VI, 304, 321–322 (July 4, 1861).

avoided a parliamentary resolution favorable to the South, and had detained both the *Alexandra* and the Laird rams. Olympian fulminations of journalists lose somewhat of their terror when one contemplates the rabid utterances of the *Times* in contrast to the habitual and growing aloofness of the British ministry toward secession leaders. Confederate diplomacy had always stopped short of persuasive contact with the British government. It was Seward, Adams, and Lincoln who took the tricks abroad. The Confederate secretary of state admitted Seward's "sagacity," his "penetration" into the "feelings of the British cabinet," and "the success of his policy of intimidation." This being interpreted meant his ability to convince leaders of Britain that the United States was ready, if provoked, to declare war on that country.[1] This should not be understood as a crude threat or a serious expectation that it would actually come to war. Rather it signified a kind of Anglo-American diplomacy that avoided rupture because mutuality, common interest, and statesmanlike intelligence were brought to play on both sides.

One finds in the summer and fall of '63 an increasing note of Southern bitterness toward England. Observing British sympathy bestowed upon Poland, "a people alien to them in every respect except that it belongs . . . to the European sisterhood," Hotze in March 1863 lamented that the Confederacy had not received one tithe of the same earnestness.[2] The previous summer Slidell had commented on the "tortuous, selfish, and time-serving policy" of England.[3] A. Dudley Mann in January 1863 bewailed the lack of courage of the British cabinet.[4] Next month Mason observed that both parties in Britain were "guided . . . by a fixed English purpose to run no risk of a broil, even far less, a war with the United States." [5]

It was but the logical outcome of events when Mason's mission to England was terminated that summer. On August 4, 1863, Secretary Benjamin, noting that "the Government of her Majesty has determined to decline the overtures . . . for . . . treaty . . . relations," instructed Mason that his continued residence in London was not "consistent with the dignity of this Government" and that the Southern President wished him to consider his mission at an end.[6]

---

1 *Offic. Rec.* (Nav.), 2 ser., III, 817. 2 *Ibid.*, 712.
3 *Ibid.*, 485. 4 *Ibid.*, 658. 5 *Ibid.*, 687. 6 *Ibid.*, 852.

On September 30 Mason left London for Paris, having given up his house and removed his archives.[7] The whole story of his effort in Britain was reduced to a nutshell in Secretary Benjamin's remark as early as January 1863 that the highest ranking Confederate diplomat had been "discourteously treated by Earl Russell." [8] Mason himself gave the gist of it by saying that he enjoyed "no intercourse, unofficial or otherwise, with any member of the [British] Government." [9]

Another unmistakable sign of the same breach was seen in the embittered controversy concerning British consuls in Southern cities. The fact of Britain having such consuls within the Confederacy—Moore at Richmond, Fullerton at Savannah, Cridland at Mobile, and Bunch at Charleston—bespoke an anomalous situation between nations that lacked diplomatic relations. They were, of course, merely a carry-over from prewar days when their presence was entirely regular within the pattern of the United States government. Complicating factors arose because these consuls, lacking exequaturs addressed to the Confederate government, took orders from British diplomatic officials accredited to Washington. Offended that Mr. Cridland carried a document signed by Lord Lyons appointing him acting English consul at Mobile,[10] the Confederate government adopted the policy of "prohibiting any direct communication between consuls . . . residing within the Confederacy and the functionaries of their Governments residing amongst our enemies." [11] Under these circumstances the consuls were annoyed and checkmated in their efforts to extend British protection over their nationals in the South. As the months passed, the matter of the consuls became increasingly acute. Finally, coming to the end of his patience in October 1863, President Davis took the decisive step of expelling these British officials from the country.[12] Commenting on these matters, Russell, though probably with no motive other than avoiding any commitment as to recognition, again referred to "the so-styled Confederate States." [13]

---

7 *Ibid.*, 934. 8 *Ibid.*, 656. 9 *Ibid.*, 715.

10 *Ibid.*, 797. On May 18, 1863, the Richmond *Whig* commented bitterly on the question of the consuls and referred to "the creation . . . of a Lincoln consul at Mobile [Cridland] by the English secretary of foreign affairs." *House Exec. Doc. No. 1*, 38 Cong., 2 sess., part 1, p. 802.

11 *Offic. Rec.* (Nav.), 2 ser., III, 801. 12 *Ibid.*, 922.

13 *Ibid.*, 928.

IV

An excellent indication of the attitude of the British government toward the American question is seen in the proceedings that were concerned with the parliamentary motion of the pro-Confederate Roebuck, to which brief allusion has already been made. Roebuck, with his co-worker Lindsay, both being members of Parliament, became conspicuous, not to say notorious, for their efforts in behalf of American disunion. In close touch with the Confederate agent A. Dudley Mann, they sought to promote their object by way of amateur diplomacy and parliamentary maneuver. Napoleon III,[1] with considerable impropriety, had conferred in person with them, after which they posed importantly in Parliament as spokesmen of the Emperor, as if that ruler were avoiding regular diplomatic channels, undercutting the British ministry, and making communications to the House of Commons through these two officious negotiators.

Roebuck's tone may be judged by a speech he made in Sheffield in the summer of 1862. Arguing that a "divided America will be a benefit to England," he declared: "The North will never be our friends. Of the South you can make friends. They are Englishmen; they are not the scum and refuse of Europe." At these words the mayor of Manchester interrupted: "Don't say that; don't say that." [2]

With this background of Confederate collaboration and self-promoted diplomacy, Roebuck argued his motion, that Her Majesty "be graciously pleased to enter into negotiations with the Great Powers of Europe, for the purpose of obtaining their co-operation in the recognition of the independence of the Confederate States of North America." [3] When this effort to commit the British government to the pro-Confederate cause was debated in Parliament, support for it was so slight as to approach the vanishing point. Robert Montagu moved an amendment favoring "impartial neutrality." [4] Then Bright pitched in and showed how small was Roebuck's understanding of the European as well as the British attitude. He "poured out on Roebuck a deluge of weighty ridicule from which he never fully recov-

[1] E. D. Adams, *Great Britain and the American Civil War,* II, 167; F. L. Owsley, *King Cotton Diplomacy,* 297 ff.

[2] E. D. Adams, II, 34 n.

[3] *Hansard's Parl. Debates,* 3 ser., vol. CLXXI, p. 1780 (June 30, 1863).

[4] *Ibid.,* p. 1797.

ered." One who heard the debate remarked: "He [Bright] shook him as a terrier shakes a rat." [5] Members of the British ministry sharply criticized Roebuck. Sir George Grey showed how faulty his tactics were,[6] while Lord Palmerston, realizing what a false step had been taken both by the unauthorized Lindsay-Roebuck team and by Napoleon himself, hoped that the debates would include no further mention of this pseudo-diplomatic episode. Fearing an adverse effect upon Anglo-French relations, he wrote to Roebuck: "No good can come of touching again upon this matter, nor from fixing upon the Emperor a mistake which amid the multiplicity of things he has to think of he may be excused for making. . . . Might I ask you to show this note to Mr. Lindsay, your fellow traveller." [7]

Though few persons were taking "Don Roebucco" [8] seriously, it was a relief when his motion faded out of the picture without having come to a vote. This happened on July 13, 1863,[9] when Roebuck withdrew his own motion after debate had shown how overwhelmingly it would have been defeated.

It will be noted that proceedings on the Roebuck motion occurred in the period of Lee's invasion culminating in the Gettysburg campaign, and at a time when some of the British newspapers were predicting that the Confederates would soon take Washington. It is a significant fact, however, that word of Union success at Gettysburg did not reach London until July 16,[10] and that the Roebuck motion had been disposed of three days earlier.

There is a further phase of this parliamentary episode that must not be overlooked: it brought into view the attitude of the opposition—i. e., the Conservative party—in Britain. Leaders of that party by no means associated themselves with the Roebuck type of pro-Confederate maneuver. On this point Lord Derby, the Conservative leader who would presumably have become prime minister if the Palmerston government had been voted down in Parliament, opposed the idea of recognition and mediation, which meant, of course, that he also op-

5 Trevelyan, *Bright*, 322–323. 6 E. D. Adams, II, 171. 7 *Ibid.*, 175.

8 The member was caricatured by *Punch* as "Don Roebucco, the smallest man 'in the House.'" W. C. Ford, ed., *A Cycle of Adams Letters*, II, facing p. 48.

9 *Hansard Parl. Debates*, 3 ser., CLXXII, p. 673. E. D. Adams (II, 177) explains that Roebuck "knew that if pressed to a vote it [his motion] would be overwhelmingly defeated."

10 E. D. Adams, II, 178.

posed any further step which would have led to intervention.[11] Confederate agents were disappointed with Derby. They wrote home that he would not agitate the American question during the period of the Queen's acute grief after Prince Albert's death, that he was careful not to commit himself on this problem, and that during the American war he was by no means anxious to take office. "Lord Derby," wrote the Confederate agent Hotze, "does not come as our ally." [12]

Nor could the Confederates count on Disraeli. That colorful gentleman, high in the leadership of the opposition, was said to have expressed an "interest" in secessionist affairs, yet like Derby he never committed himself to any pro-Confederate move. Few indeed of the opposition leaders showed a disposition to go "so far as to oppose the Government in power" on the American question.[13] In a gloomy letter to Secretary Benjamin on February 10, 1863, A. Dudley Mann wrote: "Many of our friends in England calculated largely . . . upon the opposition for the acknowledgment of our independence. I never for a moment indulged any such expectation. . . . Earl Derby and Mr. Disraeli, regard with the coldest indifference the successful struggles which we have made . . . ." [14] Whatever hopes may have been raised as to Disraeli's attitude, he certainly did not make the Confederate cause his own. Contemplating the prospects as to the opposition members, Hotze wrote on June 6, 1863, when there was much talk of the Roebuck motion: "As a party the Conservatives are inharmonious and cowardly on this question, as on most others." [15] Though it has been suggested that Disraeli thought the United States was breaking up, he kept quiet as to this view. He said not "a word from the front Opposition bench likely to create difficulty with America." [16] His biographers show that he was "determined that Great Britain should preserve neutrality." [17] There had been talk in the Roebuck camp of "turning to the Tories," but this was a total miscalculation. The debate, writes E. D. Adams, showed "a complete misunderstanding of the position of Tory leaders." [18]

What then becomes of the strange popular concept that Britain "sided with the Confederacy" and was unfriendly to the Lincoln gov-

---

[11] *Ibid.*, II, 51.
[12] *Offic. Rec.* (Nav.), 2 ser., III, 1023.
[13] *Ibid.*, 506.
[14] *Ibid.*, 689.
[15] *Ibid.*, 785.
[16] Monnypenny and Buckle, *Life of Benjamin Disraeli, Earl of Beaconsfield,* IV, 328. This statement is a quotation of the words of John Bright.
[17] *Ibid.*, IV, 329.
[18] E. D. Adams, II, 177.

ernment? Certainly that was not true of the British people, nor of the government (the ministry), nor of the Liberal party, nor of the prime minister, nor of the foreign secretary, nor of Parliament, nor even of the opposition (Conservative) party. One should not speak of the *Times,* of Roebuck and Lindsay, of the Southern Independence Association, and of certain other vocal elements, as if they were the same as Britain. The whole story shows the withholding of British support for the Confederacy, and this fact was nowhere more clearly realized than at Richmond.

V

This frigidity toward the enemy of the United States was no mere surface manifestation. Deep and underlying forces were working toward friendship between Washington and London. Men in office in Britain were not fire eaters, nor toward America were they international meddlers. At the outset of the war Lord Lyons, British minister at Washington, thought that "excitement" in South Carolina had "carried men . . . beyond the bounds of reason and common sense." [1] When in this same period an "honourable friend" mentioned that "the great Republican bubble in America had burst," the sentiment gave no satisfaction to Lord John Russell. He did not think it seemly to show "exultation at their discord." [2] Midway in the war, addressing the House of Lords on February 5, 1863, Russell spoke as follows: "For my own part, before this contest began, I rejoiced in the progress of the United States of America. The flourishing state of a people descended from the same ancestors as ourselves, and possessing laws of personal liberty similar to our own, was a sight in which Englishmen might rejoice." [3]

After nine months of war Charles Francis Adams noted in London that agitation "against us" did "not find its root deep in the heart of the community." [4] That the influential *Times* was unfriendly should not obscure the fact that other papers such as the *Morning Star* of London gave Lincoln's cause a better press. For example at the time of the congressional election of 1862 the *Morning Star* presented an analysis

---

1 Walpole, *Russell,* II, 340. 2 *Ibid.,* II, 338.

3 Reprinted in *House Exec. Doc. No. 1,* 38 Cong., 1 sess., pt. 1, p. 126.

4 W. C. Ford, ed., *Cycle of Adams Letters,* I, 107.

to show that the "opposition" had not "won" the contest.[5]

A number of factors were working to create that improvement in the climate of Anglo-American relations which was especially noted from 1863 onward: Confederate defeat, Lincoln's emancipation, the realization in the *Trent* affair that war could be avoided without loss of "honor" on either side, the sympathy of the common people, and the tireless work of John Bright. Emancipation meetings all over England in 1863, treated in a previous volume,[6] being unofficial, spontaneous and genuine, constituted a most impressive demonstration of like feelings between friendly nations. Commenting favorably upon the meeting at Manchester, the London *Daily News* of January 2, 1863, remarked upon the important role of the British working classes in showing Britain's attitude toward the American struggle. This attitude was held to be in keeping with "England's old attachment to the principles of freedom, and its undying hatred to oppression in any form." At this huge meeting, December 31, 1862, the Free Trade Hall, with a capacity of 6,000, was well filled and the address to the American President was adopted "with the greatest enthusiasm and unanimity." It was the sentiment of this meeting that Anglo-American relations "be knit more firmly, and that the people of the two nations may ever be united in the bonds of amity and fraternity." [7] The unemotional Adams was impressed by this meeting. He considered it "in every respect a most remarkable indication of the state of popular sentiment in Great Britain." He believed it would make "a strong impression everywhere" and would do much to promote amicable feeling between the nations.

Lincoln's reply to Manchester [8] combined a sympathy for the British working people with a strong assurance of "reciprocal feelings of friendship among the American people." Similar meetings, with like sentiments, were held at York, London (Exeter Hall), Blackburn, Leeds, Galashiels, Bath, Bromley, South London, Glasgow, Aberdeen, Edinburgh, Bristol, Sheffield, Birmingham, Leicester, Bolton, and many other places. The antislavery leader, George Thompson, wrote to Garrison that these meetings on the American question had been

---

[5] *Morning Star,* London, Jan. 2, 1863. [6] *Lincoln the President,* II, 176–180.

[7] Abel Haywood, Chairman, to C. F. Adams, Manchester, Jan. 1, 1863 (Britain, vol. 81), MSS., Dept. of State, Nat. Archives.

[8] *Lincoln the President,* II, 178–179.

"densely crowded, sublimely enthusiastic, and all but unanimous." [9] It would be "impossible," he wrote, "to give you a list of all the meetings which have recently been held [February 1863], for the purpose of expressing sympathy with the Anti-Slavery movement in the United States . . . . The men who a few months ago were so bold . . . in the advocacy . . . of the Southern Rebels, are now silent." [10] It was felt that these demonstrations showed clearly that the heart of England was not against the United States.[11] As one Englishman expressed it: "If our *nation* is consulted, it would rather vote down the House of Lords . . . than permit war with you." [12] These outpourings of British feeling kept the staff of the American legation busy. The diary of Benjamin Moran, one of the staff, in this period frequently mentions emancipation meetings "held very generally in England," addresses pouring in, and visits of numerous delegations. Minister Adams and his son Henry were kept busy in making suitable personal response.[13]

In the matter of these assemblages a book could be written on Manchester alone. The demonstration there had an effect like a series of widening circles. Not only did it call for the notable reply from Lincoln. Its sequel appeared in a visit of James William Massie who addressed audiences ranging from New England to the Middle West and Kentucky, delivering the message of good will committed to his charge at Manchester. Massie was a British clergyman of Irish birth, friendly to America and active in free-trade and antislavery agitation. He wrote: "I have always, everywhere, sought to express . . . an amicable and congenial sentiment, in Americans, toward their English kindred; giving assurance, that the Lairds, Roebucks, and *Times* are not England. . . . I can now assure my countrymen, that . . .

[9] George Thompson to W. L. Garrison, Feb. 5, 1863, Garrison MSS., Boston Pub. Lib.

[10] Thompson to Garrison, Feb. 27, 1863, *ibid.*

[11] W. C. Ford, ed., *Cycle of Adams Letters,* I, 107.

[12] Francis W. Newman to Epes Sargent, London, April 20, 1863, MS., Boston Pub. Lib.

[13] Sarah A. Wallace and Frances E. Gillespie, eds., *Journal of Benjamin Moran,* II, 1107 and *passim.* It was Moran's belief that Minister Adams was "determined to push his son to the front." Moran felt that the "boy" had "no business" doing such things, but that he was moved by a "love of distinction." *Ibid.,* II, 1120. In this connection one may note the unfavorable British reaction to Henry Adams's "Diary of a Visit to Manchester," which was published, not in the *Atlantic* as Henry had hoped, but in the Boston *Courier* on December 16, 1861. Especially did Englishmen dislike Henry's comparison of "society" in Manchester and in London to the detriment of the latter. See Arthur W. Silver, in *Am. Hist. Rev.,* LI, 74–89 (Oct. 1945).

there yet remains [among Americans] . . . . a partial [i. e., sympathetic] affection for Englishmen and a desire to live in the most cordial terms of international unity with Great Britain." [14]

VI

It was not merely the antislavery circles, but notably also the labor groups, then inadequately organized, which showed a marked sympathy for Lincoln's cause, as in Trades Unions gatherings in the spring of 1863.[1] If some among the "privileged classes all over Europe" were rejoicing at "the ruin of the great experiment of popular government," [2] it was also evident that the "old revolutionary leaven" was "working steadily in England" and that "the American question . . . [was] organizing a vast mass of the lower orders in direct contact with the wealthy" who were ready to "go our whole platform." [3]

Much could be written on "democratic and socialist" meetings, where Henry Adams noted a refusal to tolerate "interference against us." [4] Sentiment favorable to Lincoln and the Union came naturally to British labor and to socialist groups and there is no need to disclaim it, though as a threat "to the established state of things" agitation by such groups was as "alarming" to some English minds "as a slave insurrection would be in the South." [5] If British labor circles were hopeful toward the American experiment it is not to their discredit that such an attitude was identified with their own uphill struggles for political and economic opportunity at home. It belonged authentically to the history of the time and had its part in those varied manifestations which indicated, from early 1863 on, that popular British opinion was swinging toward Washington.[6]

---

[14] James W. Massie to Lincoln, Buffalo, Sept. 21, 1863, R. T. L. Coll. 26467–68.

[1] W. C. Ford, ed., *A Cycle of Adams Letters,* I, 296, 298.

[2] *Ibid.,* II, 65.

[3] *Ibid.,* I, 245. Considerable material on these meetings has been assembled in *House Exec. Doc. No. 1,* 39 Cong., 1 sess., part 1, pp. 59 ff., 141 ff., 214 ff.

[4] *Cycle of Adams Letters,* I, 244.

[5] *Ibid.*

[6] Writing from London in early '63, a Confederate leader noted that "the Radicals, under Bright and others" had the balance of power and that their opposition would be fatal to any ministry in England. He added: "These men are warm partisans of the United States, and have of late made a series of striking demonstrations by public meetings, speeches, etc." L. Q. C. Lamar to J. P. Benjamin, London, Mar. 20, 1863, *Offic. Rec.* (Nav.), 2 ser., III, 716–717.

To make a list of those in Britain who favored the American Union would be unfair to those omitted. Men so disposed were notable for their intellectual ability and human sympathy. One such person was "a curious looking man with a sharp nose, a wen on his forehead and a black cravat, . . . about the ablest man in England," John Stuart Mill. This portrait was drawn by Henry Adams, who referred to Mill as "a mighty weapon of defense for our cause" in England.[7] In *Fraser's Magazine* in February 1862 [8] Mill wrote favorably and convincingly of the Union cause. In his autobiography he records that his "strongest feelings were engaged in this struggle." Dreading what he deemed the "aggressive enterprise of the slave-owners to extend" slave territory "under the . . . influences of pecuniary interest, domineering temper, and the fanaticism of a class for its class privileges," Mill felt that success of the slave power "would give courage to the enemies of progress and damp the spirits of its friends all over the civilized world, while it would create a formidable military power, grounded on . . . anti-social . . . tyranny of men over men . . . ." [9]

There was also Richard Cobden. Though at first this outstanding British liberal was somewhat affected by Southern support for free trade in contrast to the Northern tariff, and also by his horror of war, he became "an earnest champion of the North," [10] as shown, for example, by his attitude in the *Trent* case.[11] Concerning Cobden's attitude Charles Francis Adams wrote: "In his [Cobden's] opinion, . . . the moral support of Europe [should have been] so far assured to the Government of the United States as to preclude any hope among the insurgents of possible assistance . . . ." [12] British friends of America included, of course, the antislavery leaders, notably George Thompson. There were also Prince Albert, the Duke of Argyll, Goldwin Smith, the evangelist Spurgeon, Leslie Stephen, and the journalist Frederick M. Edge, who expressed his passionate interest in the United

7 Henry Adams, in *Cycle of Adams Letters,* I, 253.

8 John Stuart Mill, "The Contest in America," *Fraser's Magazine,* LXV, 258–268 (Feb. 1862).

9 *Autobiography of John Stuart Mill,* 187.

10 Trevelyan, *Bright,* 302.

11 "During the *Trent* affair Lincoln's Government . . . received from Cobden the same counsels of moderation as from Bright." *Ibid.,* 316. (This was at a time when friends of the Confederacy hoped not for "moderation," but for a breach between America and Britain.)

12 C. F. Adams, to Seward, London, July 3, 1862, Diplomatic Despatches (Britain, vol. 80), MSS., Dept. of State, Nat. Archives.

States and his hope to assist "Americans in working out the . . . re-establishment of the Union's authority." [13]

VII

Finally, towering above them all, was John Bright. Never did a liberal have a clearer idea of where he was going than this sturdy champion of political and economic rights for the masses of laboring men in Britain. There was consistency in the totality of the causes which he led or sponsored. In addition to the American effort to survive as a whole nation, these causes included relief from the corn laws (that is, from injustices associated with landed privilege and monopoly), free trade, economic liberalism in general, outspoken opposition to the Crimean War, admission of Jews to Parliament, reform in India, and extension of the voting right to British workingmen.

In so busy a life it was a significant thing that Bright found time to devote so great an amount of energy and leadership to advocating the Union cause in Britain. He corresponded with Sumner, urged his thoughts upon Earl Russell, and promoted moderation on both sides in the *Trent* controversy, in which he did much to avert war. He kept at it constantly, exposing the one-sided nature of French "mediation," making vigorous speeches, and laboring successfully for the defeat of Roebuck's motion in Parliament looking toward recognition of the Confederacy. Stressing the cost and tragedy of war between Britain and the United States, the hollowness of British sympathy for secession, the stain of slavery, and the regularity of Lincoln's election,[1] he dwelt with moving eloquence upon the impressive example of American democracy, the effort of the slave power "to break up the most free government in the world," [2] and the unwisdom of recognizing "a new state intending to set itself up [as Bright saw it] on the sole basis of slavery." [3]

Economic interest in the superficial sense might well have caused Bright to favor the Confederacy.[4] Owner of a textile mill in Lanca-

---

[13] Frederick M. Edge to H. W. Bellows, Oct. 9, 1863, Bellows MSS., Mass. Hist. Soc.

[1] John Bright, *Speeches on the American Question,* 107.

[2] *Ibid.,* 27. [3] *Ibid.,* 113. See also pp. 7, 27.

[4] A bibliography of Anglo-American relations on the economic level cannot be attempted here. One should especially note W. O. Henderson, *Lancashire Cotton Famine, 1861–1865;* L. B. Schmidt, in *Iowa Jour. of Hist. and Pol.,* XVI, 400–439; and J. H. Clap-

shire, he found his business threatened with ruin by the blockade which shut off the supply of Southern cotton. It was precisely this economic dislocation, widespread and disastrous in British manufacturing districts, on which the leaders of secession banked in their drive for foreign intervention. Despite this motive of personal gain, Bright even favored the blockade, because to him the whole Union movement embodied the cause of broad economic opportunity and of political liberalism. Thousands of British laborers were thrown out of work, including employees of Bright, but British and American good will came handsomely to their relief. George Macaulay Trevelyan, biographer of Bright, writes that "all England came to the rescue with abundant generosity"; he adds that three large ships brought American flour as a token of friendship "tangible to eye and hand and mouth." [5]

Bright closely followed every event in the war, cultivated friendly British editors, kept privately in touch with persons in the Government, and expressed satisfaction at symptoms of "break up among the gang at Richmond." He approved a speech of Lord Russell which indicated an improved state of feeling on the state of American affairs, and wrote at one time, "whilst the [American] contest lasts, I seem able to think of nothing else." [6] A keynote to his attitude is to be found in a letter he wrote from Rochdale on July 9, 1863, to Consul Thomas H. Dudley: "I have kept my faith till now [i. e., regarding the outcome in the United States]—& I shall not part with it except as I would part with my life's hope." [7]

Between Lincoln and Bright there grew up a cordiality that was both a matter of personal regard and a factor of solid international import. It was a friendship based on political agreement. Harmony of views was its very essence. Lincoln was in America what Bright was in England. It was a long-range friendship. The two men never met, since Bright never visited America, nor was there direct correspond-

---

ham, *An Economic History of Modern Britain: Free Trade and Steel, 1850–1886.* In a doctoral thesis at the University of Illinois (1937) Martin P. Claussen has presented a careful study of economic factors in Anglo-American relations in the Lincoln period. His monograph is entitled: "The United States and Great Britain, 1861–1865: Peace Factors in International Relations."

[5] Trevelyan, *Bright,* 309.

[6] Letters of Bright to Thomas H. Dudley, Feb. 4, 1864; March 25, 1863; Aug. 27, 1863; Dudley MSS., Huntington Lib.

[7] Dudley MSS.

ence between them. For letters to have passed directly between the President of the United States and a prominent member of the British House of Commons might have seemed out of place. Yet by indirect communications, as through Sumner or Dudley, messages and friendly greetings were exchanged. A photograph of Bright, presented to Lincoln in 1864, was a significant item in these cordial exchanges. The gift is mentioned in a letter of Thomas H. Dudley to Congressman E. B. Washburne (March 14, 1864),[8] and the prominent displaying of the photograph in the White House in Lincoln's day is a matter of well attested record.[9]

A further item in the Lincoln-Bright story was a marble bust of Bright intended as a gift to Lincoln from Thomas G. Blain of Manchester; after Lincoln's assassination it was presented by Blain to the American nation. In a letter from Consul Dudley to President Andrew Johnson, Blain was described as a "warm friend of the United States and a great admirer of John Bright as well as of our late lamented President." [10]

One of Lincoln's many instances of clemency was associated with the Lancashire liberal. A British youth named Alfred Rubery, caught in a privateering escapade which amounted to conspiracy under the law of the United States, was befriended by Lincoln as a favor to Bright. In this rather freakish adventure about twenty men, Rubery among them, were caught in San Francisco Bay operating a schooner under Confederate letters of marque with designs against United States gold-carrying ships and with glittering hopes of private booty. The leader, a Kentuckian named Asbury Harpending, had taken oath as a member of a secret order. There was a dash of melodrama about

---

[8] Washburne MSS., Lib. of Cong.

[9] In the Bright MSS. in the British Museum there is a letter in which a correspondent of Bright named Henry Janney wrote (April 24, 1865) recalling how Lincoln told him of his pleasure in reading Bright's letters. Janney added that Bright's picture hung over the fireplace in one of the rooms of the White House. This is also attested by a letter of Schuyler Colfax under date of May 20, 1866 (Bright MSS., British Museum). Goldwin Smith, describing the ante-room to Lincoln's office, mentioned as a prominent ornament "a large photograph of John Bright." F. Lauriston Bullard, in *Amer. Bar Assoc. Jour.*, XXV, 219 (Mar., 1939).

[10] Information concerning this bust is found in the records of the commissioner of public buildings and in consular dispatches from Liverpool, National Archives, Wash., D.C. For a digest of this material the author is indebted to Dr. P. M. Hamer of the National Archives (P. M. Hamer to the author, Feb. 23, 1943).

the whole affair. The "pirates" were all brought to trial in the United States circuit court at San Francisco, Stephen J. Field being one of the justices, and three of the accused, including the Englishman Rubery, were sentenced to a fine of $10,000 and imprisonment of ten years. Interesting himself in the case as that of a young man of his Birmingham constituency who was adventurous rather than vicious, John Bright brought the matter to Lincoln's attention through Sumner, and Lincoln issued a pardon for Rubery in a formal proclamation, mentioning that in addition to other considerations the act was done "especially as a public mark of the esteem held by the United States . . . for the high character and steady friendship of . . . John Bright." [11]

If the Lincoln-Bright relation, neglected by most of Lincoln's biographers, has been emphasized in these pages, it is because the subject is basic. Regard for Bright was as fundamental with Lincoln as the Gettysburg address. Indeed the theme was the same: it was a question of democracy at large. One cannot write adequately of the American crisis without noting how Bright played his role: doing a man's part in averting war in the *Trent* case, eloquently developing British sympathy for the Union, tying the American cause to that of British liberals, making Lincoln's name a symbol of freedom to workingmen in England. Bright's countrymen by the many thousands realized that their interest and their philosophy was one with that of the rugged American President. If the two causes were of genuine identity, that made the friendship all the stronger. Not only did sympathetic British assemblages express Lincolnian convictions; it is even true that, through Senator Sumner, Lincoln sent to Bright in his own handwriting the draft of a resolution expressing the views which he wished to have adopted in such meetings.[12] In giving his own cue for resolutions of British sympathy, the American President knew well that Bright was the man to whom this cue should be directed. This does not mean that the expressions of sympathy were "inspired" in the propaganda sense; it means rather that the identity of political liberty

---

11 F. Lauriston Bullard, "Lincoln Pardons Conspirator On Plea of An English Statesman," *Amer. Bar Assoc. Jour.*, XXV, 220 (Mar., 1939); Jay Monaghan, *Diplomat in Carpet Slippers*, 297, 311, 337, 343, 346.

12 For facsimile see Trevelyan, *Bright*, 303.

with economic opportunity was a subject on which Lincoln and Bright could not be indifferent.[13]

While narrower ideas of gain and profit were voluminously agitated, and while in some quarters international relations were cast in a mold of twisted materialism, it was given to John Bright to assist in averting war, to disprove the economic thesis of "King Cotton," [14] to demonstrate that trade is not all, and to show that trade itself has its liberal and peace-promoting aspects.

Though the Anglo-American situation was at the forefront of Lincoln's international problems, his administration had to deal with nations the world over. In considering the diplomacy of that period —though these wider matters are not treated in the present volume— attention must be given to relations with Napoleon III, the Maximilian venture in Mexico, the Russian attitude toward the American struggle (including friendly visits of two Russian fleets), and complicated dealings in the Far East. A study of these oriental dealings brings into view the Lincoln-Seward policy toward China, and, for Japan, a highly difficult series of incidents in a period of stress, antiforeign feeling, and violence. In addition to all of Lincoln's other problems he and his department of state had to keep in mind the internal confusion of Mikado, Shogun (Tycoon), and feudal daimios. Not only the United States but other nations as well—notably Britain —were seriously embarrassed by the differences, and the challenge of adjustment, between the oriental and occidental mind, in language, background, mores, etiquette, worship, and national (in opposition to imperialistic) interests.[15]

---

[13] This subject is further discussed in "Lincoln and John Bright," Randall, *Lincoln the Liberal Statesman,* chap. vi.

[14] On the Southern economic concept of "King Cotton" in its relation to the Civil War, see F. L. Owsley, *King Cotton Diplomacy, passim* but especially pp. 562–578; Randall, *Civil War and Reconstruction,* 648–654.

[15] The author has prepared two chapters dealing with these further international problems, but their publication is being deferred to a later volume.

CHAPTER XV

THE CHATTANOOGA FRONT: DEATH OF HELM

WESTERN military operations in the latter part of 1863 form an elaborate and vacillating story. It was a changing situation: temporary Union defeat, serious menace of Confederate advance, decisions to be made as to relative strength in East and West, important shifts of command, and in November —the month of the Gettysburg address—Union triumph. Whether there was defeat or triumph there were always casualties, and to the Lincolns those casualties became close personal tragedy in the battle death of Mrs. Lincoln's brother-in-law. To contemplate the war in disregard of such tragedy, and write only of the movement of divisions and the winning or losing of battles, would be most unrealistic.

I

In the latter part of 1862, as already noted, there had occurred Bragg's ambitious but futile invasion of Kentucky. When, after the sanguinary battle of Perryville (October 8) the Confederate general pulled his forces back into Tennessee, the situation presented a disheartening anticlimax in Confederate plans. It was hardly to be expected that more than one major army enterprise could be launched in the West in any half-year; yet in the second half of 1862 the army of Bragg had shot its bolt, and the only result to show for it was that the "liberation" of Kentucky was abandoned. It was a cause which had elicited little response from the people of that state. Marching laboriously great distances, fighting indecisively with serious losses, separating and shifting positions—such was the procedure between the contending hosts. On the Union side dissatisfaction with Buell for not dealing more effectively with Bragg coincided with the success of Rosecrans over Price and Van Dorn at Iuka and Corinth. Buell was accordingly superseded by Rosecrans as the commander of the principal army in the West, the Army of the Cumberland.

At the turn of the year (December 31–January 2, 1862–63) there occurred an elaborate engagement between Bragg and Rosecrans at Stone's River (Murfreesboro) in central Tennessee. After this crippling but indecisive battle one heard little of Bragg and Rosecrans while Grant and his Army of the Tennessee were winning their slugging campaign against Vicksburg.

In the strategic planning for 1863 the question arose as to whether Lee should send troops west. Instead of doing so (after Chancellorsville) he spent his great effort in the ambitious but unsuccessful drive into Pennsylvania. There was consequently a great army-and-navy combination under Grant by which—with the surrender of Pemberton at Vicksburg on July 4 and the subsequent operation of Banks at Port Hudson—some of the most important stakes of the whole war were won by the Federals. The Mississippi River came completely within Union hands, western Tennessee was wrested from Confederate control, and the value of Southern trans-Mississippi forces was nullified. As to Vicksburg, three outstanding Confederate leaders—Generals Johnston and Pemberton and President Davis (not to mention Bragg)—had differed as to strategy. Basic orders had not been carried out and the concentration of Southern forces—union of Pemberton and Johnston to defeat Grant—had failed.

Bitter recrimination resulted from that failure, Davis sharply censuring Johnston's conduct and Johnston blaming the President for insufficient support to Pemberton. Looking back from Vicksburg to Perryville and attributing the unfortunate invasion of Kentucky to the Confederate chief executive, Johnston wrote: "If, instead of being sent on the wild expedition into Kentucky, General Bragg had been instructed to avail himself of the dispersed condition of the Federal troops in northern Mississippi and west Tennessee, he might have totally defeated the forces with which General Grant invaded Mississippi three months later. Those troops were distributed in Corinth, Jackson, Memphis, and intermediate points, while his own were united, so that he could have fought them in detail, with as much certainty of success as can be hoped for in war." [1]

II

After Vicksburg the strategic focus in the West shifted to Chattanooga. This important goal of contending armies was the key to eastern Tennessee and a good deal else, being both a river location and a vital railway point (on the Memphis and Charleston) between East and West. For a time after Murfreesboro it had seemed that the situation between the opposing commanders, Rosecrans and Bragg, had reached a kind of deadlock. There were months of inaction, and in June of 1863 Bragg's force in central Tennessee confronted that of Rosecrans in a confused stalemate. Then things began to happen and Rosecrans won the first round. Putting his divisions into motion on June 23, the Union commander maneuvered Bragg out of central Tennessee into Chattanooga. To maneuver him out of that position was the next task, and by early September this also was accomplished. Yet the great armies still faced each other, and the fate of the Chattanooga area was in the balance.

On September 9, in a despatch to Halleck, with something of a flourish, Rosecrans reported: "Chattanooga is ours without a struggle, and East Tennessee is free!!— Our move on the Enemy's flank and rear progresses while the tail of his retreating column will not escape unmolested. Our troops from this side entered Chattanooga about noon. Those north of the river there are crossing. Messengers go to Burnside tonight urging him to push his cavalry down. No news from him or his Cavalry." [1]

At that stage, while Grant and Sherman were not in the main spotlight (Grant contemplating a far flung movement to Mobile which never came off),[2] the fame of Rosecrans seemed on the point of bringing him to the top among commanders in the West. Iuka, Corinth, Murfreesboro (though a drawn battle), and now Chattanooga, stood

1 *Battles and Leaders of the Civil War,* III, 481–482.

1 Rosecrans to Halleck, Camp Near Trenton, Ga., Sept. 9, 1863, 8:30 p.m., R. T. L. Coll., 26166–7.

2 "After the fall of Vicksburg I did incline very much to an immediate move on Mobile. I believed then the place could be taken with but little effort, ..." Grant to Lincoln, Cairo, Ill., Aug. 23, 1863, R. T. L. Coll. 25799; see also Grant, *Memoirs,* I, 578; II, 19.

to his credit. As for Bragg, he had withdrawn into nearby Georgia.

As Rosecrans entered Chattanooga, Burnside, heading the Army of the Ohio, moved through Cumberland Gap and took possession of Knoxville, important center of a great mountain region whose inhabitants were predominantly Unionist in sentiment and whose interests were constantly in Lincoln's thought.

At this moment of high promise Rosecrans's luck, or strategic skill, or power of effective command, failed him. In the complicated and elaborate two-day battle of Chickamauga (September 19–20, 1863) a series of factors worked against him. He had not been reënforced by Burnside from Knoxville as Lincoln earnestly wished. On the other hand two corps had been detached from Lee's army on the Rapidan and sent West under Longstreet, whose part in the engagement was of great importance. Rosecrans had been thinking of Bragg as withdrawing deep into Georgia, not expecting that he would take the offensive against him. Bragg's forces were consolidated, while Rosecrans's dispositions were defective and his line weakened by over-extension.

Part of Rosecrans's preparation was a strengthening of the Union left; the result was a weakened right and a weaker center. On the second day of the battle, in a move which effective reconnaissance ought to have foreseen, Longstreet hurled six divisions forward in a powerful assault. Aiming his stroke at the Union right and the center gap, he poured his troops through the Federal line and Rosecrans suffered the "appalling demolition of his right wing." [3] Considering the battle lost, the Federal commander made his way into Rossville and then into Chattanooga to make suitable dispositions of his "disordered and defeated army." Charles A. Dana recalled that he "saw our lines break and melt away like leaves before the wind." He wrote that the whole Union right "had apparently been routed" and that "Everything was in the greatest disorder." [4]

On the Union left, however, it was a different story. In many hours of fierce and terrific fighting, in which the bayonet was used, George H. Thomas held fast, becoming known as the savior of the Union army and winning the sobriquet "Rock of Chickamauga." In addition to other points, the fact that Thomas was a Virginian who adhered to the Union gave him a special distinction. It should be added, of course,

---

[3] *Battles and Leaders,* III, 671.

[4] Dana, *Recollections of the Civil War,* 115.

Frederick H. Meserve of New York and Dr. R. Gerald McMurtry of Lincoln Memorial University

HARVEST OF WAR

Upper left and right: Col. Elmer E. Ellsworth of the 11th New York, "The First Fire Zouaves." Close friend of the Lincolns. On May 24, 1861, after tearing down a Confederate flag flying over the Marshall House in Alexandria, Virginia, he was shot dead by the hotel keeper. The President and Mrs. Lincoln were in deep grief at Ellsworth's death.

Lower left: Ben Hardin Helm, Confederate general, killed at Chickamauga, September 20, 1863.

Lower right: Helm and his wife. Emilie Todd Helm was a much younger half-sister of Mary Todd Lincoln. There is great poignancy in the shattering effect of Helm's death, in Emilie's visit to the White House in December 1863, and in the unbroken love, beating against the impassable barrier of war, between the Lincolns and Emilie, beloved "Little Sister."

Brady photograph, National Archives

GEORGE H. THOMAS

A Virginian who adhered to the Union cause; "Rock of Chickamauga"; successor of Rosecrans; it was Thomas's soldiers who carried Missionary Ridge. His decisive defeat of Hood's army in December 1864 was a highly important factor in final Union strategy.

that it was the building-up of the Union left under Thomas which had weakened the Federal right and center and had allowed Longstreet to rush through. (Considering the terrific punishment inflicted upon Thomas's wing and the dominant part he played, there was nothing unreasonable in the strengthening of his part of the line.)

In a cipher telegram Rosecrans reported the sad result to Halleck: "We have met with a serious disaster. . . . Enemy overwhelmed us. Drove our right, pierced our Center and scattered them. Thomas, who had seven divisions remained intact at last news. . . . Every available reserve was used when the men stampeded. . . . It seems that every available man was thrown against us." [5]

Major General John M. Palmer of Illinois, who commanded a division of Thomas L. Crittenden's corps at Chickamauga, wrote frequent letters in this period to his wife, who was in an agony of suspense as to his safety. On October 2, 1863, with due military restraint, he wrote his summary of Chickamauga: "The Army of the Cumberland has met with a reverse. Not severe relative to that of the enemy. We have had one of those terrific murderous conflicts between two masses of men guided and animated mainly by a mere determination to win and we were beaten by the bad conduct of Generals and the superior numbers of the enemy. Our communications are not safe. I will not therefore be more specific. Our glorious Army is in good spirits and ready to meet the enemy again." [6]

III

One finds a brief and optimistic comment on Chickamauga in a telegram which the President sent from Washington to Mrs. Lincoln who was then in New York: "We now have a tolerably accurate summing up of the late battle between Rosecrans and Bragg. The result is that we are worsted, if at all, only in the fact that we, after the main fighting was over, yielded the ground, thus leaving considerable of our artillery and wounded to fall into the enemie's [*sic*] hands, for which we got nothing in turn. We lost, in general officers, one killed and three or four wounded, all Brigadiers, while . . . they lost six

[5] Rosecrans to Halleck, telegram in cipher, Chattanooga, Sep. 20, 1863, 5 p.m., R. T. L. Coll. 26404–5.

[6] MS., Ill. State Hist. Lib.

killed and eight wounded. Of the killed one Major Genl. and five Brigadiers, including your brother-in-law, Helm; and of the wounded three Major Generals, and five Brigadiers." [1]

It was thus, almost parenthetically, that Lincoln broke the news to Mary of the death of the Confederate brigadier general, Ben Hardin Helm, husband of Emilie Todd Helm. (The announcement of the fact, in the necessary brevity of this message, was enough; Lincoln was not a man to put his emotions into a telegram.) None of Mary's sisters was closer to her or more beloved than Emilie. Both she and Helm had visited the Lincolns in Springfield and Lincoln had affectionately called her "Little Sister."

Toward this brother-in-law Lincoln at the outset of his presidency had shown a marked friendship. According to the account by Helm's daughter, Katherine, the President sent the young man a cordial invitation to Washington and handed him "a commission as paymaster in the United States Army with rank of major." [2] This was a great opportunity. "The rank of major at his age, thirty, was very exceptional in the army. Nothing had ever touched Helm like this." [3] Here was a fine career opening up for him if he would accept. It seems to have been assumed that, at least for a time, the position would have involved residence in Washington. To Helm the advantage appeared in terms of the rank and the chance to be transferred at an early date to one of the cavalry regiments. To Mary Lincoln, however, in need of having a member of her own family close to her, the great appeal was that her sister could be with her in Washington—a belle on social occasions in the White House, a source of pride, her husband a dignified officer. In this respect Helm had a decision to make that was not unlike that of Robert E. Lee—except, of course, that the great Virginian "went with his State" and the Kentuckian did not. Though grateful to his brother-in-law for the generous offer, Helm declined it.[4] It was a painful choice, and in that choice one may read the difficult problem of those men of the Blue Grass who, though regretting the breaking

---

1 Lincoln to Mrs. Lincoln, Sep. 24, 1863, MS. Ill. State Hist. Lib.

2 "Some time ago I requested that Ben. Hardin Helm might be appointed a paymaster, which I still desire." Lincoln to Sec. of War, Exec. Mansion, Apr. 16, 1861, Cameron MSS.

3 Katherine Helm, *Mary, Wife of Lincoln,* 184.

4 *Ibid.,* 183–188. See also R. Gerald McMurtry, *Ben Hardin Helm,* 17–24. John Hay made the erroneous statement that Helm "was made a paymaster by the President," implying that the offer was accepted. Dennett, . . . *Diaries* . . . *of John Hay,* 92.

of the Union, cast their lot with the Confederacy.

Commanding a brigade of the division led by his friend and neighbor J. C. Breckinridge (of the Confederate right wing under Lt. Gen. Leonidas Polk),[5] Helm's men had been brought under terrific cross fire from Union breastworks in a "portion of the line [which] proved to be one of the most hotly contested positions of the entire battlefield." [6] Struck while riding toward the enemy's works on the morning of September 20, Helm fell mortally wounded from his horse. He died that night. It was a fearful tragedy in the Todd family and a source of personal sorrow to the Lincolns. We are not speaking here of demonstrations of White House grief. Times were grim and feelings could not always be expressed. One could, of course, weep sincerely for Helm—as one could admire the character of Lee—without favoring the Confederacy. The general had done his Confederate duty. To prominent fellow-Lexingtonians his conduct was as "Kentuckian" as that of Breckinridge and Morgan. The fact that, to the Lincolns, Helm was an enemy had significance not as a matter of hatred between them, but as an added grief, a cause of Emilie's deep resentment, and a bitter, inscrutable token of the unnatural brothers' war. It made it no easier that the Lincolns were in such a position that their genuine grief could find no adequate expression.

The personal agony of war came now to the very White House, but without the sympathy and understanding of friends by which tragedy is customarily softened. Of the genuineness of the President's feeling there can be no doubt. David Davis had never seen him more moved "than when he heard of the death of his young brother-in-law." [7] And what of Mary's feelings? There were thousands of war-bereaved Americans, but the barriers to the expression of feeling made Mary's grief the harder; it was as if she was shut off from the right to feel as a human being and a sister. Devotedly loyal to the Union, she rejoiced in Federal victory, but with a poignant sense of what warfare meant in human terms on both sides. Having brothers in what she herself called the "rebel" army, she utterly disapproved of the cause which they served; yet the rightness of that Union disapproval, which she felt as sincerely as any, was denied her. She became the target of Northern suspicion; "a single tear shed for a dead enemy would bring torrents

[5] *Battles and Leaders,* III, 673.

[6] McMurtry, *Ben Hardin Helm,* 44.

[7] Katherine Helm, 216.

of scorn and bitter abuse on both her husband and herself." That she was a Southerner was true, but that a Southern origin made it necessary to war against the United States she, and many thousands of Kentuckians, denied. Yet Southerners judged her harshly as an enemy and thought of her as having a stony indifference to "the sufferings of her own people." [8] In all, she had four brothers in the Confederate army—George, Samuel, David, and Alexander. Of these only George survived the war. Sam was killed at Shiloh, David at Vicksburg, and Alec in 1862 in the fighting at Baton Rouge. If she wept for these of her kin on the other side, it had to be in secret. One cannot read her story as told by her niece, Katherine Helm, without realizing that there was no one in the land upon whom the unnatural hatreds and distortions of that day bore more relentlessly than upon her.

IV

Mrs. Helm had attended the last rites for her husband at Atlanta [1] and then stayed for a time in the home of E. M. Bruce in Madison, Georgia. At her request Mr. Bruce wrote to Lincoln reporting the manner of the general's death: "although opposed . . . to your forces, it will . . . be a satisfaction to you to know that he fell at the head of his Brigade—honorably battling for the cause he thought just and righteous—he was *leading* his 'Kentucky Brigade' to a charge which was successful . . . and I know you can but admire him for his deeds, and will regret that he could not have survived the conflict, and shared in the glories of the victory." (The reference here was evidently to the temporary Confederate victory in the battle of Chickamauga.) Mr. Bruce added: "Mrs Helm is crushed by the blow—almost broken hearted—and desires to return to her Mother and friends in Kentucky . . . ." He therefore asked the President to have a pass sent to her to enter the Federal truce boat at City Point: the pass to be sent in triplicate to Mrs. Helm, to William Preston Johnston at Richmond, and to Bruce himself at Madison, Georgia. The letter ended with a personal message from Emilie: "Mrs Helm desires to be affectionately remembered to her sister." [2]

Bound for Kentucky, Emilie made her way by sea to Fort Monroe,

[8] *Ibid.*, 217.

[1] *Ibid.*, 220.

[2] E. M. Bruce to Lincoln, Madison, Ga., Oct. 6, 1863, R. T. L. Coll., 26992–3.

but was informed that she could not proceed further unless she took the loyalty oath to the United States. Though faced with what seemed a helpless situation—in Union hands and "almost penniless"—she refused the oath. The officer in charge, not unfriendly but at a loss what to do, wired the President for instructions. Back came the answering telegram: "Send her to me." [3]

Thus it was that Emilie found herself spending a week at the White House under the affectionate care of her sister Mary and "Brother Lincoln." Yet in her diary she wrote: "Sister and I cannot open our hearts to each other as freely as we would like. This frightful war comes between us like a barrier of granite . . . ." [4] Not by words but by clasped hands of sympathy their griefs were joined—Mary grieving for her lost Willie, Emilie for her husband. Knowing they would hurt each other, they avoided the topic of the war. Emilie wrote of Mary: "Her fine tact and delicacy fill me with admiration." [5]

Emilie's arrival in Washington came shortly after the announcement of the President's broad plan of amnesty, in which an oath of allegiance was prescribed. Lincoln presented her with this oath, which he had prepared for her to sign,[6] but she refused, not with any air of bravado but simply because her loyalty was elsewhere; the Federal oath would have seemed to her and her friends a repudiation of the cause for which her husband had died.

At every stage Lincoln had done what he could. Where it was a matter of sending a pass,[7] facilitating the recovery of property in the South, or extending amnesty, he had given Emilie's situation his personal and considerate care, though always within correct conduct as Union President. He urged her to prolong her stay at the White House, despite the embarrassment that arose from outspoken people who could not understand, and hoped she would spend the summer of 1864 with the presidential family. In a statement in his own hand, "Whom it may concern," he expressed the wish that she might "have protection of person and property, except as to slaves." Back in Kentucky Emilie was again in the Todd fold and the Lexington scene but under poignantly hard times. A tone of bitterness now crept into her letters. On October 30, 1864, she wrote that her half-brother (Mary's

---

[3] Katherine Helm, 221. [4] *Ibid.*, 224. [5] *Ibid.*

[6] *Works,* IX, 255–256. For the refusal, see McMurtry, *Ben Hardin Helm,* 54.

[7] *Works,* IX, 169.

brother) Levi Todd was dead "from utter want and destitution." "I would remind you," she wrote the President, "that your *minnie* [*sic*] *bullets* have made us what we are." [8] It is needless to comment on Lincoln's hurt feelings, and Mary's, on reading those stinging and accusing words.

V

It was characteristic of the war that a "victory" might, in the long run or even in the immediate sequel, signify very little. The situation after Chickamauga was not as favorable to Bragg as would have seemed likely. He had won a battle marked by splendid fighting on the Southern side (indeed on both sides), but he had done so at tremendous cost; then, as his critics declared, he threw away the results. If there had been blunders on Rosecrans's part, the "great blunder of all," wrote D. H. Hill, was that of Bragg in not pursuing the enemy on the 21st. A breathing space was allowed to Rosecrans; he held Chattanooga; days of Confederate opportunity were wasted; it has been remarked that "the *élan* of the Southern soldier was never seen after Chickamauga." The "great battle of the West" as it was called has been described as a "barren victory." [1]

Thus failing to pursue the defeated enemy, Bragg contented himself with instituting a siege of Chattanooga, occupying the overlooking heights of Lookout Mountain and Missionary Ridge, together with Lookout Valley, and seeking, almost successfully, to bag the Union force or make its position untenable.

This siege was of no slight importance. It created a situation where the Union army was said repeatedly to be threatened with starvation. On the Confederate side it was felt that another quick blow close on the heels of Chickamauga would have finished Rosecrans. Since, however, there was no third or fourth day of the battle (such continuous fighting being most unusual in the Civil War), the question as to what "would have" been the result is no part of the actual story.

Both sides now seriously considered a change of commanders. In

---

[8] R. T. L. Coll., 37723.

[1] *Battles and Leaders,* III, 662. Bragg's failure to pursue was obviously due, at least in part, to his terrific losses at Chickamauga—a total of 18,000 with 2300 killed. (Union losses were about 16,000 with 1600 killed.) To rally Confederate units after such losses, push ahead immediately in pursuit, and fight another terrific battle was not so easy as Hill's words suggested.

that respect, if one accepts the unfavorable view of Rosecrans on which military writers usually agree, the long-range result of Chickamauga was favorable to the Union side: Bragg, the victor, was kept while the defeated Rosecrans was removed, thus setting the stage for later Union success. It was soon to be Grant and Thomas against Bragg instead of Rosecrans against Bragg. Another great campaign and then the Confederates, too late, were to let Bragg go.

On the Confederate side western generals, such as Forrest, Polk, Longstreet, D. H. Hill, Cheatham, and Buckner, so seriously differed with Bragg that some of them were sent off to other fronts, while others petitioned President Davis to find a new commander for the Army of Tennessee. Bragg, however, was a favorite, or pet, of Jefferson Davis, who now made a trip to the western front and by his erratic military intervention eased the problem for the hardly pressed Union army. Bragg was kept in command, and a large force (about 15,000) was sent off under Longstreet to operate without success against Burnside at Knoxville. (These were the troops that had recently been detached from Lee's army.) In the words of E. A. Pollard, Richmond editor and caustic critic of Davis, the Confederate President seems at this time to have contemplated "the visionary project of regaining East Tennessee, and perhaps . . . again penetrating Kentucky, and making the battle-ground of the Confederacy in this impossible country." [2] Davis was sharply criticized by Pollard not only for being "in furious love with the extraordinary design," but for "military conceit" and "vanity" as he boastfully told of Southern plans in public speeches, putting the Union side on its guard.

Lincoln, meanwhile, had been giving careful thought to the situation in terms of strategy, personalities among the generals, and friendliness to the people of Eastern Tennessee where Unionist sentiment (as in West Virginia and eastern Kentucky) was strong. Coördination of military progress with political reconstruction, with sufficient pace to make that reconstruction effective, was continually in his thought. This would have been true in any case, but the men of this region would not let him alone. When in August of 1863 the President was petitioned for greater military aid to eastern Tennessee (in the Knoxville area) he stated that he would do as much for these people as if his

---

[2] Pollard, *Lost Cause,* 456. See also *Battles and Leaders,* III, 693.

home and family were in Knoxville, but he stressed the "difficulties of getting a Union army into that region, and of keeping it there." Lines of supply, he explained, could be easily broken, a small force would be of no value because the enemy could match it, a large force would be "very difficult to supply, and [would] ruin us entirely if a great disaster should befall it." [3] It was painful to him to argue thus to a complaining group with whom he genuinely sympathized, since all the time the government was trying to increase its strength in east Tennessee. He alluded to his own efforts "to have a railroad built on purpose to relieve you," and added that Stanton, Halleck, Burnside, and Rosecrans were all at that time engaged in an effort to strengthen the region. After all, Knoxville was not the pivotal point, and the President was constantly receiving requests all over the map to strengthen this or that area for local reasons.

Rosecrans was proving militarily unsatisfactory and personally difficult. In the Union drive against Vicksburg Lincoln had felt that Rosecrans ought either to have attacked Bragg or have sent a force to strengthen Grant. When, however, the general showed that he was hurt by reports of presidential dissatisfaction, Lincoln wrote him a very frank letter stating certain elements of disappointment but assuring the general of his kind feeling. Having indicated that too much should not have been inferred as to any sense of dissatisfaction, the President wrote: "I am sure you, as a reasonable man, would not have been wounded, could you have heard all my words and seen all my thoughts, in regard to you. I have not abated in my kind feeling for and confidence in you." [4] In great anxiety for success on the complicated western front, Lincoln at first wanted Grant strengthened; later (after Vicksburg) he wanted Eastern Tennessee "occupied by us," while impressed with the difficulties involved. In early September he felt easier, since by that time Burnside had Knoxville, Bragg had withdrawn into Georgia, and the President could write: "All Tennessee is now clear of armed insurrectionists." Not a moment should be lost, he said, in reinaugurating a loyal state government; for that there should be "no such word as fail." [5]

---

[3] Lincoln to J. M. Fleming and R. Morrow, Aug. 9, 1863, R. T. L. Coll., 25468.

[4] Lincoln to Rosecrans, Aug. 10, 1863, R. T. L. Coll., 25486.

[5] Lincoln to Andrew Johnson, Sep. 11, 1863, "Private," photostat, A. Lincoln Assoc.

CHAPTER XVI

GRANT VERSUS BRAGG: MISSIONARY RIDGE: END OF 1863

I

THERE is a tendency to think of the war as forming itself into one grand pattern with strategy under central control in Washington, but for 1863 that would be far from the truth. It is a question how far Stanton had such over-all understanding and direction. Certainly Halleck did not, though that was supposed to be his function.[1] There were times when bad news was deliberately withheld from Lincoln despite his constant visits to the war office. The President carefully pondered eastern and western army problems, weighing them against each other, but he studiously avoided interference in military strategy. In this respect he presented a striking contrast to Jefferson Davis, to whose meddling Confederate failure has been largely attributed. Lincoln by no means considered himself the military genius or master of strategy which some of his eulogists have made him out to be. For one thing, Union armies were not always blessed with the notable success which this appraisal might imply; for another thing, correspondence emanating from Washington did not usually reveal answers as to strategic planning. Often it revealed obscurity in the fog of war and mystification of high command as to what the armies in the field were doing. Again and again it disclosed the

[1] Keenly anxious that Meade should pursue Lee after Gettysburg, Lincoln had spoken to Halleck in order to get action, but, according to Welles, the general in chief gave the President "a short and curt reply" and the President said, "I drop the subject." To Welles this seemed Lincoln's error. "His own . . . conclusions are infinitely superior to Halleck's . . . . I look upon Halleck as a pretty good scholarly critic of other men's deeds and acts, but as incapable of originating or directing military operations." Welles, *Diary,* I, 363–364 (July 7, 1863).

President's lack of military conceit. He deliberately kept himself in the strategic background. Repeatedly he wrote that he was not giving orders; field commanders must decide. Sometimes a dispatch from him would be one large question mark, as when he wired General Hurlbut at Memphis: "What news have you? What from Vicksburg? What from Yazoo-Pass? What from Lake Providence? What generally?" [2]

Though the military historian, trying to tell the whole story of the war, would emphasize the Tennessee front in the late summer and fall of 1863, Lincoln, a few days before Chickamauga, was writing, not of Rosecrans and Bragg, but of Meade and Lee. He was deeply concerned—not without reason—as to the chance of Meade getting action in Virginia against the main Confederate army. Recognizing Meade's uncertainty as to what he should do, the President wrote to Halleck (September 15): "My opinion is that he should move upon Lee at once in manner of general attack, leaving to developments whether he will make it a real attack." He thought this would develop Lee's real condition; it would have been something like a reconnaissance in force. He added: "Of course my opinion is not to control you and General Meade." Shortly after this he wrote to Halleck (September 19): "I am not prepared to order, or even advise, an advance in this case, wherein I know so little of particulars, and wherein he, in the field, thinks the risk is so great, and the promise of advantage so small." [3]

Thus in the situation immediately preceding Chickamauga the great problem—or question mark—in Washington was whether Meade should advance. Lincoln really wanted an advance, hoping for a decisive battle. To force the enemy slowly back into his intrenchments at Richmond was what he did not want. In contrast to the attitude of amateur strategists, the President clearly realized that Lee's army, not Richmond, was the "objective point." [4]

While Lincoln was trying to get answers, he had only uncertainty and hesitation from Meade and Halleck. To quote the Richmond *Sentinel* (as it misquoted Shakespeare): "Meade is making 'I would' wait upon 'I dare not.' " [5] Meade's own words confirm this attitude: "I

[2] Lincoln to Hurlbut, telegram in cipher, Mar. 20, 1863, photostat, A. Lincoln Assoc.

[3] Photostats, A. Lincoln Assoc.

[4] Lincoln to Halleck, Sep. 19, 1863, photostat, A. Lincoln Assoc.

[5] Richmond *Sentinel,* editorial, Sep. 22, 1863, quoted in letter of Meade to Halleck, Sep. 23, 1863, R. T. L. Coll., 26519.

do not feel justified in making a further advance without . . . more positive authority than was contained in your [Halleck's] last letter enclosing one from the President. . . . I am not in condition to follow Lee to Richmond and will be less so after being weakened by a severe battle. . . . I am reluctant to run the risks involved without the positive sanction of the Government." [6] In this difficult phase Lincoln trusted this delaying general (Meade) and was patient with him. He felt earnestly that a strong military move should be made, but he never wished his own judgment to become an embarrassment to a commander so far as a strategic or tactical matter was concerned. (If high policy was involved that was a different matter.) In mid-October the President wrote to Halleck urging that Meade should attack Lee. Then he added that if his suggestion should be adopted, "the honor will be his [Meade's] if he succeeds, and the blame may be mine if he fails." [7]

II

While the Virginia situation was a matter of uncertainty to Halleck, so also was the western situation. When Union forces had every need to concentrate in the region near Chattanooga, the general in chief was assuming that Rosecrans might occupy Dalton, Georgia, and was showing uncertainty regarding a report by deserters that "a part of Bragg's army is reënforcing Lee." This was September 11, 1863; on the 14th Meade correctly reported his "judgment" that Lee's army had been reduced by Longstreet's corps and perhaps by other troops. Where, however, were these men from Lee's army headed for? In fact they were reënforcing Bragg, but Halleck mentioned "suppositions" that they might attempt to capture Norfolk or to throw Meade off balance by threatening that place. Having mentioned Dalton at the southeast of Chattanooga on the 11th, Halleck sent word on the 13th indicating a possible turn to the west. If the enemy should trouble the Union right through Alabama, Chattanooga was to be turned over to Burnside and Rosecrans's army or a part thereof was to move west to prevent Bragg from entering middle Tennessee. Much of this was contingent planning (or suggestion) in uncertainty as to what the chief contingencies were. Bragg might be planning to pull back into Georgia

[6] Meade to Halleck, Sep. 18, 1863, telegram in cipher, *ibid.*, 26359–62.

[7] Lincoln to Halleck, Oct. 16, 1863, photostat, A. Lincoln Assoc.

(though probably not very far), or he might turn up in North Carolina.[1] Other Confederate forces in the West might push into middle Tennessee. And all the time Lee's army had to be watched. To weaken the front against Lee in order to strengthen Rosecrans might be hazardous, but to fail to do so might be more hazardous.

The Chattanooga story appears but slightly and inadequately in Lincoln's writings. Just after Chickamauga the President was thinking in cautious and defensive terms, cheering Rosecrans with "unabated confidence," advising Halleck that Rosecrans should "hold his position, at or about Chattanooga," and expressing the hope that Burnside would go to Rosecrans "without a moment's delay" to help him hold, and later to "turn the tide." [2]

It was realized that Rosecrans had been "whipped" but that "Thomas had held his own magnificently," [3] that Confederate losses had been terrifically heavy, that there had been no further Confederate assault, and that the shattered Union army had been able to re-form. The fact that a considerable force had gone from Lee's army to the western front raised a question as to how this could be countered on the Union side. This was the situation on Wednesday night, September 23, when a high-level conference was held at the war department, for which Lincoln was roused from his bed at the Soldiers' Home. Riding out to summon "the Tycoon," Hay took note of the "splendid moonlight"; it is in his diary that one finds brief mention of the conference whose deliberations, if they could be recovered in verbatim report, would be of considerable historical interest.

In addition to the President, the conference was attended by Stanton (who seems to have arranged the meeting), Halleck, Seward, Chase, and a few others. Among those in conference was General D. C. McCallum, superintendent of railroads in the United States. Military transportation would be a vital factor. The consultation ran on till after midnight; Hay's evening ended "with a supper by Stanton at one o'clock, where few ate." What must have been said about Rosecrans, about his subordinates such as Wood and McCook, and about Burnside for not joining him, can only be surmised. The main business

---

[1] *Offic. Rec.,* 1 ser., XXX, pt. 1, 34–36.

[2] Various telegrams of Lincoln on same day (Sep. 21, 1863) to Rosecrans, Halleck, and Burnside, photostats, A. Lincoln Assoc.; Nicolay and Hay, *Works,* IX, 131–133.

[3] Dennett, ed., . . . *Diaries . . . of John Hay,* 92.

of the conference was the important decision to send the 11th and 12th corps west (from Meade) under Hooker's command.[4]

This presented a major enterprise in troop movement in which the importance of engineering was impressively demonstrated. Railroads in the United States were under government control, and though this was a fact which existed chiefly on paper, key railroad officials had governmental status and much of the history of the time was in terms of rail transportation. Able men in the war department were in charge of railroad management—such men as Herman Haupt (till he retired from the army in mid-September 1863), Thomas A. Scott, and D. C. McCallum. Men high in the government were due for a surprise here. As Walter H. Hebert writes: "The 'profound' Halleck protested that it would take forty days [to shift these two corps under Hooker to the western front] and the President agreed with him, but finally Stanton won out when General McCallum . . . said it could be done in a week." [5]

As it turned out it took six days for "the trip." Nicolay and Hay are in error in saying that "the two corps, numbering some twenty thousand men, were brought from the Rapidan to Washington, . . . and carried . . . to the Tennessee . . . with their guns . . . and all their impedimenta . . . in the almost incredible time of eight days." [6] The better statement, detracting not at all from the efficiency of the enterprise, is that of Walter H. Hebert: the whole movement took two weeks (of course the men did not all entrain at once); the roundabout rail "trip" took six days; the total number in the two corps was about 15,000 rather than 20,000. There were several changes of cars because the roads did not all have standard gauge and bridges over the Ohio River were lacking. The project involved the movement of 700 wagons and almost 5000 horses over a distance of nearly 1200 miles. Hebert writes: "This was the most successful movement of so large a body of troops by rail during the entire war." [7] Of course no such thing, nor even any considerable military use of railroads, had happened in any previous war.

This shifting of the two corps from Meade to Rosecrans involved more than transportation. It set off a minor upheaval in the army, and

---

[4] *Ibid.*, 93.
[5] Hebert, *Fighting Joe Hooker*, 250–251.
[6] Nicolay and Hay, *Lincoln*, VIII, 112–113.
[7] Hebert, 251.

showed, as has been seen before, that conduct of war on all levels and especially that of the President is often a matter of human relations. In this case the difficulty as to feelings among generals developed into a hopeless split between Hooker, who was to lead this whole force, and Henry W. Slocum, who was in command of the Twelfth Corps. It was one of those instances when army leaders simply could not, or would not, work together, and when this kind of difficulty arose the appeal always went up to the President who was under the necessity of taking some kind of action, even if no real solution was possible.

Slocum had a considerable record with the Army of the Potomac, having served at Antietam, Chancellorsville, and Gettysburg, but he could not get along with Hooker. When it became known that the Eleventh Corps under Howard and the Twelfth under Slocum were being sent to the Tennessee front, both under Hooker, Slocum wrote a vigorous letter to Lincoln. He had his "opinion" of the general "both as an Officer & a gentleman"; it would be "degrading" to "accept any position under him." He therefore had "the honor" of respectfully tendering his resignation as major general of volunteers.[8] Here, as at other times, was a general quitting, or making a gesture of quitting, in the midst of a war crisis, though in military accounts the word quitting is not used as to generals. The assignment of Hooker to this command had been made and Lincoln did not undo it; neither did he accept Slocum's resignation. Not that the President had full confidence in Hooker either; he had a peculiarly mixed feeling toward this general and wanted always to give him a chance to show his qualities.

Suppressing his disgust at this kind of squabble, Lincoln untied the knot by having Slocum and Hooker detached from each other. He wrote to Rosecrans: "We are sending you two small corps, one under General Howard and one under General Slocum and the whole under General Hooker. Unfortunately the relations between Generals Hooker and Slocum are not such as to promise good, if their present relative positions remain. Therefore let me beg,—almost enjoin upon you—that on their reaching you, you will make a transposition by which Gen. Slocum with his Corps, may pass from under the command of Gen. Hooker . . . ."[9] As for Howard, he also suffered from unpleasant relations with Hooker but without thought of resignation.

---

[8] Slocum to Lincoln, Brandy Station, Va., Sep. 25, 1863, R. T. L. Coll., 26647–8.

[9] Lincoln to Rosecrans, Sep. 28, 1863, photostat A. Lincoln Assoc.

Grant wanted "both Hooker and Slocum removed from his command, and the Eleventh and Twelfth Corps consolidated under Howard." Hooker had "behaved badly," he felt, and Slocum had "sent in a very disorderly communication." All this was reported by Dana, who added: "He [Grant] would himself order Hooker and Slocum away, but hesitates because they have just been sent here by the President." [10] Hooker's position, wrote Grant, was "one that rather embarrasses the service than benefits it." Though being rid of both men was Grant's wish, his recommendation was that Hooker be assigned to the command of the Twelfth Corps and Slocum relieved of further duty.[11] What happened, however, was that Hooker was retained in the command Lincoln had given him, while Slocum, with only part of his corps, was sent off to an unimportant assignment in a distant section of Tennessee.

At this conference of September 23 there was no action toward removing Rosecrans. The President was bolstering him and trying to believe that the army had not been badly worsted.[12] Executive displeasure was directed chiefly against Burnside to whom Lincoln wrote the draft of a reproving letter which he did not sign or send. The letter expressed (for the historian) the President's complete mystification as to a message Burnside had sent promising assistance to Rosecrans; this message, thought Lincoln, contrasted strangely with the general's actions. In reading the despatch the President sarcastically doubted whether he was "awake or dreaming." [13] On Burnside's behalf it may be said that he was later to be the target of Longstreet's heavy force, that drawing off Longstreet turned out to be a Union advantage, and that the Unionists of eastern Tennessee could hardly have borne it to think of Knoxville being abandoned. "In the name of Christianity & humanity," they pleaded, "in the name of God and Liberty; . . . the loyal people of Tennessee appeal to you & implore you not to abandon them . . . ." [14] Yet in Washington minds anxiety for Ten-

[10] *Offic. Rec.*, 1 ser., XXXI, pt. 1, 73. [11] *Ibid.*, 740.

[12] Lincoln to Rosecrans, Sep. 21, 1863, photostat, A. Lincoln Assoc.

[13] "Yours of the 23d is just received, and it makes me doubt whether I am awake or dreaming. I have been struggling for ten days, first through Gen. Halleck, and then directly, to get you to go to assist Gen. Rosecrans in an extremity, and you have repeatedly declared you would do it, and yet you steadily move the contrary way." Lincoln to Burnside, draft of letter (not sent), Sep. 25, 1863, photostat, A. Lincoln Assoc.

[14] Telegram, John Williams and N. G. Taylor to Lincoln, Knoxville, Tenn., Oct. 15, 1863, R. T. L. Coll., 27282.

nessee required the strengthening of Chattanooga as a place of greater military importance than Knoxville.

III

In September and October 1863 drastic changes occurred in strategic plans, troop concentrations, and high army command, but it is not easy to pin down a statement as to who, in the last analysis, made these decisions. Who decided to put Grant in chief western command, to remove Rosecrans, to advance Thomas, and to move in full force upon Bragg? Who was it that caused the besieged and defeated Union army near Chattanooga to shake off the threat of starvation, seize the initiative, and win the decisive victory of Missionary Ridge? As to these decisions that set the stage for November victory the passive voice appears in much of the writing. We find it stated that "Grant was assigned" to his important command, that he "acquiesced" in the superseding of Rosecrans, and that Thomas "was made commander" of the Army of the Cumberland.[1] Nicolay and Hay state that "the Government" was convinced that Rosecrans must go, that it was "the intention of the Government" to put Grant in supreme command in the West,[2] and so on.

A writer seeking to give Lincoln credit for it all might be tempted to say that the President made these decisions, but evidence is lacking for that conclusion. Piecing together the information gathered by wading through many pages, it would seem that neither Lincoln nor Halleck was the fully controlling mind, and that the shape of things was brought about largely by Stanton among those in authority in Washington and by Grant in the field. It was Stanton who promoted the conference of September 23; he was in touch with the army before Chattanooga through Charles A. Dana, assistant secretary of war, whose reason for being in the West was to advise the secretary. Lincoln did not at this time "find" Grant, though he felt and expressed high regard for him and found his uncomplaining letters, and his lack of a personal ax to grind, refreshing in contrast to other military leaders. Grant had never been a self-promoting general, he had been the target of newspaper abuse, his performance at Shiloh had been severely de-

1 J. K. Hosmer, *Outcome of the Civil War,* 43.
2 Nicolay and Hay, *Lincoln,* VIII, 117, 119.

CONCERNED WITH ANGLO-AMERICAN RELATIONS

Upper left: Lord Palmerston, British Prime Minister. (From his last photograph, courtesy of New York Public Library.)

Upper right: Earl (Lord John) Russell, British Foreign Secretary. (Courtesy of New York Public Library.)

Center: John Bright, Liberal statesman and friend of United States. (Copy in Brady Collection, National Archives.)

Lower left: Charles Francis Adams, United States minister at London. (Photograph by courtesy of Massachusetts Historical Society.)

Lower right: His son and secretary, Henry Adams. (Courtesy of Massachusetts Historical Society.)

Brady photograph, National Archives

WILLIAM S. ROSECRANS

Led the Union forces against Bragg; concerned with important operations in Tennessee in 1863; after the battle of Chickamauga there were important shifts in command; Grant became supreme commander in the West, and Rosecrans was superseded by Thomas.

nounced, and his contacts with Lincoln, even by correspondence, had been slight. Lincoln, as of July 13, 1863, did not remember having ever met Grant, but he congratulated him handsomely on the victory at Vicksburg,[3] and at this time the Illinois warrior, whose career had in 1862 been in serious jeopardy, was advanced to the rank of major general in the regular army. Lincoln referred to him in writing as "a copious worker and fighter," [4] and was quoted as saying: "I can't spare this man; he fights." [5] It cannot be said that Lincoln planned or ordered Grant's November advance against Bragg. The President was thinking principally of "holding" Chattanooga, not of an attack, and was urging Burnside to go to that area, which Burnside did not do.

It would have been difficult to say which capital, Washington or Richmond, was the more troubled in the search for solutions. In reality the Confederacy was about to lose the war in the West, but on the Federal side the situation in October and November was beset with the greatest difficulty and hazard. The country was stunned—"paralyzed," wrote Sherman—by the defeat at Chickamauga, and the army of Rosecrans under siege in Chattanooga seemed to be "in actual danger of starvation." [6] The heights overlooking the city, Lookout Mountain and Missionary Ridge, were strongly held by the Confederates, and the morale of Rosecrans's men was at a low level. The Tennessee River was blocked by Confederate guns, and food—the opening of the "cracker line"—was the first consideration if the army was even to exist within its defensive position.

Then the balance of advantage was rapidly shifted, and in that shifting the trend of events may best be understood by focusing upon Grant. Stanton went west in person; Grant, coming from Cairo, met him at Indianapolis; and the two men rode together to Louisville. On this occasion one of the important bits of business was the decision as to Rosecrans. Stanton handed Grant two orders, saying he could take his choice. Both orders put Grant in broad western command (of the "Military Division of the Mississippi"); in one of the orders Rosecrans was to be retained "while the other relieved Rosecrans and assigned Thomas to his place." Grant laconically wrote in his *Memoirs:* "I ac-

[3] *Works,* IX, 26.
[4] Lincoln to Burnside, July 27, 1863, photostat, A. Lincoln Assoc.
[5] McClure, *Lincoln and Men of War-Times,* 196.
[6] Sherman, *Memoirs,* I, 346–347.

cepted the latter." [7] When this change was made the work assigned to Rosecrans (the department of the Missouri) was unimportant. The general was removed and the shifting of command was but a softening of the blow. Thus one of the leading generals of the war, who was considered a real strategist and a competent leader, was relieved of command as part of a whole series of significant changes. His good qualities were offset by a tendency to lose control of temper and an obstinate persistence in his own plans. Though proud and sensitive, he took his demotion in good spirit.

IV

Removing Rosecrans and putting Thomas in his place had not come easy.[1] There were those, according to Noah Brooks, who looked upon him as a "popular idol," a "consummate General," "the hero of . . . Murfreesboro and Corinth." Amid murmurs of discontent, "no man in the nation," wrote Brooks, "was more pained at the necessity of the removal . . . than was the President himself . . . ." Without stating all the reasons for the general's removal—reasons which he declared to be "weighty and all-sufficient" but which could not then be known—Brooks wrote: "It is enough to know that this Administration has never dismissed a valuable public servant or relieved any General of his command without good cause . . . ." Some of the accounts of the time tried to ease the fall by noting that Rosecrans outranked Grant and that it would have been a departure from military etiquette to retain him. "This," wrote Brooks, "is charitable, but it is not the reason . . . ." [2] After Chickamauga it was evident that new leadership was needed and that the team of Grant and Thomas (with Sherman, Hooker, and others) would make a better combina-

[7] Grant's command—division of the Mississippi—now included the department of the Ohio (Burnside), the Tennessee (Sherman), the Cumberland (Thomas), "and all the territory from the Alleghanies to the Mississippi River north of Banks's command in the south-west." The various orders making the necessary changes, which were made complete by October 20, were in the President's name. Grant, *Memoirs,* II, 18–19; *Offic. Rec.,* 1 ser., XXXI, pt. 2, 11; 1 ser. XXXI, pt. 1, 669.

[1] " 'Old Rosey' has left us, and sorry indeed we all were to have him go, for we 'swear by him'—To be sure he was beaten in his last move, but never, even for a moment has he lost the confidence of his Army." Letter by Dean R. Chester (copy of extract), Oct. 27, 1863, R. T. L. Coll., 27526. This writer goes on to refute the charge of intoxication against the commander as "the *vilest slander.*"

[2] "Castine" (Noah Brooks) letter from Washington, Oct. 24, 1863, in Sacramento *Daily Union,* Nov. 21, 1863.

tion than Grant and Rosecrans. The comments just quoted are of significance because Noah Brooks, more than the usual run of Washington correspondents, was in a confidential relation to the President.

One of the amusing things—if it could be called amusing—in the post-Chickamauga period was the comment of newspapers within the Confederacy. The "new Ulysses" was represented as distinguished in the old army "only for his love of strong drink." As for his victory at Vicksburg, as at Donelson, that was attributed "more to the Confederate Government than to his own genius." He was "a slow motioned General, and as a boaster [a most unusual comment on Grant] fully equal to Hooker or Pope." Thomas, probably because he was a Southerner, was the target of the most scorching sarcasm. He was described as "a fat, beefy man of forty," a "numbskull" in the old army, and such a "rabid and loud-mouthed Secessionist before the war" that Southern officers felt ashamed of themselves; yet he took up arms for the Union. It must have been due to his marrying "a Yankee woman, old enough to be his mother, and whose money has great influence over him." Rosecrans was ridiculed not only for his defeat but for "the art of gaining victories on paper," the reference being to his address to his army after the battle of Chickamauga. Not all the comments on "Rosy" were of this nature, however; the Richmond *Examiner,* now that he was down, characterized him as "the best General the Yankees have." In listing the Union generals who had lost their heads, the *Examiner* noted that Meade was "the only one left, and we predict for him a speedy decapitation." [3]

Accounts agree as to the serious plight of the Union army at the time when Grant took charge. With Confederate forces controlling the area before (i. e., south of) Chattanooga and the Tennessee River below that place, and with mountain roads back of Chattanooga almost impassable, the army was, as Grant wrote, "practically invested." It had been feared that Rosecrans, feeling himself in a trap, would withdraw to the north of the Tennessee River; such a move, thought Grant, would have meant "almost certain annihilation" when pursued as they "unquestionably" would have been. Yet supplies and food were cut off from the army; the "artillery horses and mules had become so reduced

---

3 Extracts from Southern newspapers of late October, 1863, Sacramento *Daily Union,* Nov. 26, 1863. The papers quoted are the Richmond *Whig,* Memphis *Daily Appeal,* and Richmond *Examiner.*

by starvation that they could not have been relied on for moving anything." [4]

Grant arrived at Chattanooga on October 23, and the depressing siege of the Union army was promptly lifted. This vitally important task was accomplished by an operation at Brown's Ferry (October 27–28) on the Tennessee River a few miles below Chattanooga, in which Confederate forces blocking the river were overpowered by surprise attack (troops having been stealthily concentrated and pontoons thrown into position), so that a regular line of supply was opened. The excellent work of General William Farrar Smith, chief engineer of the Army of the Cumberland, was evident here; but the planning of Rosecrans and Thomas, before Grant's arrival, should not be forgotten. It has been remarked that "Thomas would have made the same move . . . with the same results, had General Grant been in Louisville." [5]

The last word as to the assignment of multiple credit cannot be given here, but the effect on the army was unmistakable. Supplies could now be moved up the river from the rail point of Bridgeport, Alabama; the men had their "cracker-line"; within a week of Grant's arrival, "the troops were receiving full rations." [6] "From being an army in a condition in which it could not retreat, it became an army which . . . [soon] assumed the offensive, and under . . . Grant helped to win the battle of Missionary Ridge, inflicting a mortal blow upon the army under Bragg." [7]

V

In these weeks when the Chattanooga operation of November was shaping up Lincoln was giving thought to many problems. There was the visit to Gettysburg with its famous dedicatory address. A call for troops—referred to as a new draft because it was a call for 300,000 volunteers with deficiencies to be made up by conscription—had been issued on October 17.[1] Political campaigns of 1863 in the states were raging, with their partisan excess and menace of serious upset to the

4 *Offic. Rec.*, 1 ser., XXXI, pt. 2, 29.
5 *Battles and Leaders*, III, 717; *Offic. Rec.*, 1 ser. XXXI, pt. 2, 27.
6 *Battles and Leaders*, III, 689; *Offic. Rec.*, 1 ser., XXXI, pt. 2, 29.
7 *Battles and Leaders*, III, 714.
1 Nicolay and Hay, *Works*, IX, 172–174.

administration. This was also the formative period of Lincoln's reconstruction program, with Congress about to meet and a significant statement of broad policy to be formulated by the President. The whole cause, the great trend of events, was uppermost in his mind. Not that his published papers gave evidence of this, for in the Nicolay-Hay edition there is little to be found in the week after November 23 and up to December 1. This is to be sufficiently explained by Lincoln's illness following the Gettysburg address and by his preoccupation with his message to Congress.

During this illness of the President there occurred the three-day battle (November 23–25, 1863) in which Grant won a victory over Bragg which was parallel to the July triumph over Pemberton. The operation was famous for its mountain setting, its distinguished military names (Sherman, Thomas, Hooker, Sheridan, and so on), its decisiveness in the West, and its unusual interest in terms of soldier conduct.

Sherman's re-entry into the main strategic picture, taking his place as one of Grant's chief lieutenants at Chattanooga as he had been at Vicksburg, came at a time of bitter tragedy in his family. Having been permitted a long lull, a summer of inactivity, following the fall of Vicksburg, he was ordered to shift with the greatest rapidity to the Rosecrans front on the Tennessee River. He moved his troops via the Memphis and Charleston railroad, repairing it as he progressed. Just before that, traveling on a steamboat from Vicksburg to Memphis, he was accompanied by his wife and others of his family. When they arrived at Memphis on the second of October the general's son Willie was ill with typhoid; on the evening of the next day he died. "Of all my children," wrote Sherman, "he seemed the most precious. . . . Mrs. Sherman, Minnie, Lizzie, and Tom, were with him at the time, and we all, helpless and overwhelmed, saw him die."

The general referred to this child who bore his name as one in whose future he had more confidence than in his own plan of life. "Child as he was, he had the enthusiasm, the pure love of truth, honor, and love of country, which should animate all soldiers." He added: "God only knows why he should die thus young." [2]

Preparations had now been made for the assault upon Bragg. As

[2] Sherman, *Memoirs,* I, 347–349.

the Confederates faced Chattanooga, their left wing was at Lookout Mountain and their right wing on and before Missionary Ridge, with Lookout Valley between. In reverse direction, Grant's left was commanded by Sherman, who faced the north end of Missionary Ridge; his center by Thomas, east of Chattanooga and facing the west side of the Ridge; his right by Hooker before Lookout Mountain.

Grant's main plan was to turn Bragg's right, which meant that Sherman's action would be the pivotal part of the battle. Thomas's work in the center, while important, was planned to relieve Sherman. Hooker's assigned part was "the negative task of holding Lookout Valley." It was also expected that Hooker's Eleventh Corps was "to cross the [Tennessee] river and serve as a reserve for the attack on Bragg's right." [3]

Events developed differently from the details of Grant's scheme, though fortunately for the Union side. On the first day of the three-day struggle, November 23, the action was between Chattanooga and the Ridge at Orchard Knob, an outpost hill held by the Confederates. The Knob was taken by sharp fighting and then used as Grant's headquarters.

Now came the Hooker operation, November 24–25, which had been planned by Grant only as a "demonstration" against the enemy left. Hooker's achievement has been known as "the battle above the clouds"; its significance has been questioned but vigorously supported. Grant's postwar remark belittling the battle of Lookout Mountain has been met by answering claims as to the heavy odds, numerous Confederate losses, and "positive gains" of the engagement. As a result of this operation the Confederates abandoned the mountain and Lookout Valley. Hooker's men then swept across the Valley to Rossville (on the west side of Missionary Ridge) and successfully engaged the enemy in the closing phases of the complex battle.[4]

The main operation, however, was that of the center under Thomas; this was the battle of Missionary Ridge.[5] At this position the Confederates had strong entrenchments on the crest, further entrenchments midway down, and a line of rifle-pits at the base. In fierce fighting "like

[3] Hebert, *Fighting Joe Hooker,* 262. [4] *Ibid.,* 265.

[5] A full account of this charge is given in the grand military style by Sheridan, whose divisions were in the thick of the Union ascent. He tells how his men rushed the first line, moved prisoners to the rear, gained the crest, and pushed on in pursuit. That pursuit, however, was not supported. Sheridan, *Personal Memoirs,* I, 308 ff.

another Ætna" [6] the rifle pits were carried. At that point the men had done all that was ordered, having made the "demonstration" in the center that was intended to relieve pressure on the left under Sherman. Then, to the surprise of their officers, the men pushed up to the middle line of works and quickly up to the crest. Large numbers of Bragg's men were captured; "thousands threw away their arms in their flight." [7]

Grant wrote of this charge: "These troops moved forward, drove the enemy from the rifle-pits at the base of the ridge like bees from a hive—stopped but a moment until the whole were in line—and commenced the ascent of the mountain . . . They encountered a fearful volley of grape and canister from . . . the summit . . . . Not a waver, however, was seen in all that long line of brave men. Their progress was steadily onward until the summit was in their possession." He adds, however, that casualties were few probably because in the shock of the charge there was confusion and "purposeless aiming." [8]

The elation and exuberant demonstrations at the moment of triumph have been often described. Though quick in results the victory was not easy. It had been "won against great odds," and was due to Bragg's "grave mistakes." [9] That unfortunate general, a man of fine qualities and a favorite of Jefferson Davis, chagrined by inadequacies which he readily admitted, was now virtually at the end of his military services as he handed over his command to Joseph E. Johnston. Tennessee and the Tennessee River—with control of the West and with the power to drive deep into the heart of the Confederacy—had been won for the Union. In the military annals of 1863 Chattanooga ranked with Gettysburg and Vicksburg.

For the expression of national relief and satisfaction Lincoln was the restrained spokesman. On November 25, the day of Missionary Ridge, he wired Grant: "Well done! Many thanks to all." [10]

VI

In December 1863 the great dome of the Capitol was finished and its crowning statue—"Armed Freedom" was its warborn name—was

---

[6] *Battles and Leaders,* III, 725.
[7] *Ibid.,* III, 706–707.
[8] *Offic. Rec.,* 1 ser., XXXI, pt. 2, 34–35.
[9] Grant, *Memoirs,* II, 85.
[10] Lincoln to Grant, telegram, Nov. 25, 1863, photostat, A. Lincoln Assoc.

fastened in place.[1] It was a heartening symbol of coming triumph of the national cause, just as the jagged spectacle of the long unfinished dome had been a constant reminder of a broken Union. The public unveiling of the statue was to occur the following May, yet the statue was more of a fact than the unveiling and its completion was fittingly associated with the end of the notable year 1863.

The Lincoln administration and the people of the Union, though the war had shaken their democratic process, could have derived great encouragement from the contrast between the end of '63 and that of '62. The accomplishments of those twelve months were evident on virtually every front. So deeply had the President felt the significance of Gettysburg and Vicksburg that he had issued a proclamation for a day of national thanksgiving, setting the date at August 6, and hailing these victories as "reasonable grounds for augmented confidence that the union of these States will be maintained, their Constitution preserved, and their peace and prosperity permanently restored." [2] December of 1862 had been darkened by the gloom and stunning defeat of Burnside at Fredericksburg. In contrast, a year later (December 7, 1863) the President announced Union success in Tennessee, deeming it to be of such "high national consequence" that he again recommended that loyal people "assemble at their places of worship and render special homage and gratitude to almighty God for this great advancement of the national cause." [3] The Mississippi River had been completely opened, the area under enemy control had been reduced, and that diminished area had been "divided into distinct parts, with no practical communication between them." [4] Military discouragement would come again, and come hard, in the summer of '64, but the gains of '63 were never to be undone.

Favorable signs were not wanting in other fields. Politically the year 1863 had seen many a gain for the Lincoln cause. Partisan attacks upon the President had been repulsed in a series of state elections. In foreign relations, as shown in Britain and in the general European attitude toward interference, the situation was vastly improved. This could be measured on the one side by Confederate expulsion of

---

1 *National Intelligencer,* Dec. 1, 1863, p. 3, c. 3.

2 Proclamation of July 15, 1863.

3 Announcement of Union Success in Tennessee, Dec. 7, 1863, photostat, A. Lincoln Assoc.

4 Annual message, Dec. 8, 1863, Nicolay and Hay, *Works,* IX, 246.

Brady photograph, National Archives

SUPREME COMMANDER IN THE WEST, 1863

Conduct of war for Lincoln was often a matter of personal relations. There were many Union generals who, in relations with the President or with brother officers, proved difficult or impossible. Grant was a notable exception. Of prominent commanders it was he who gave the President the least personal annoyance. After his important command in the West in 1863, Congress, in addition to conferring a gold medal, revived the rank of lieutenant general to which in March 1864 Grant was elevated. As such he was supreme commander of the Union armies. Even yet there was to be hard fighting and long, disheartening delay, but Grant's leadership did not waver and the conditions of Union triumph had been achieved. Congressman Washburne said of him: "He fared like the commonest soldier in his command . . . ."

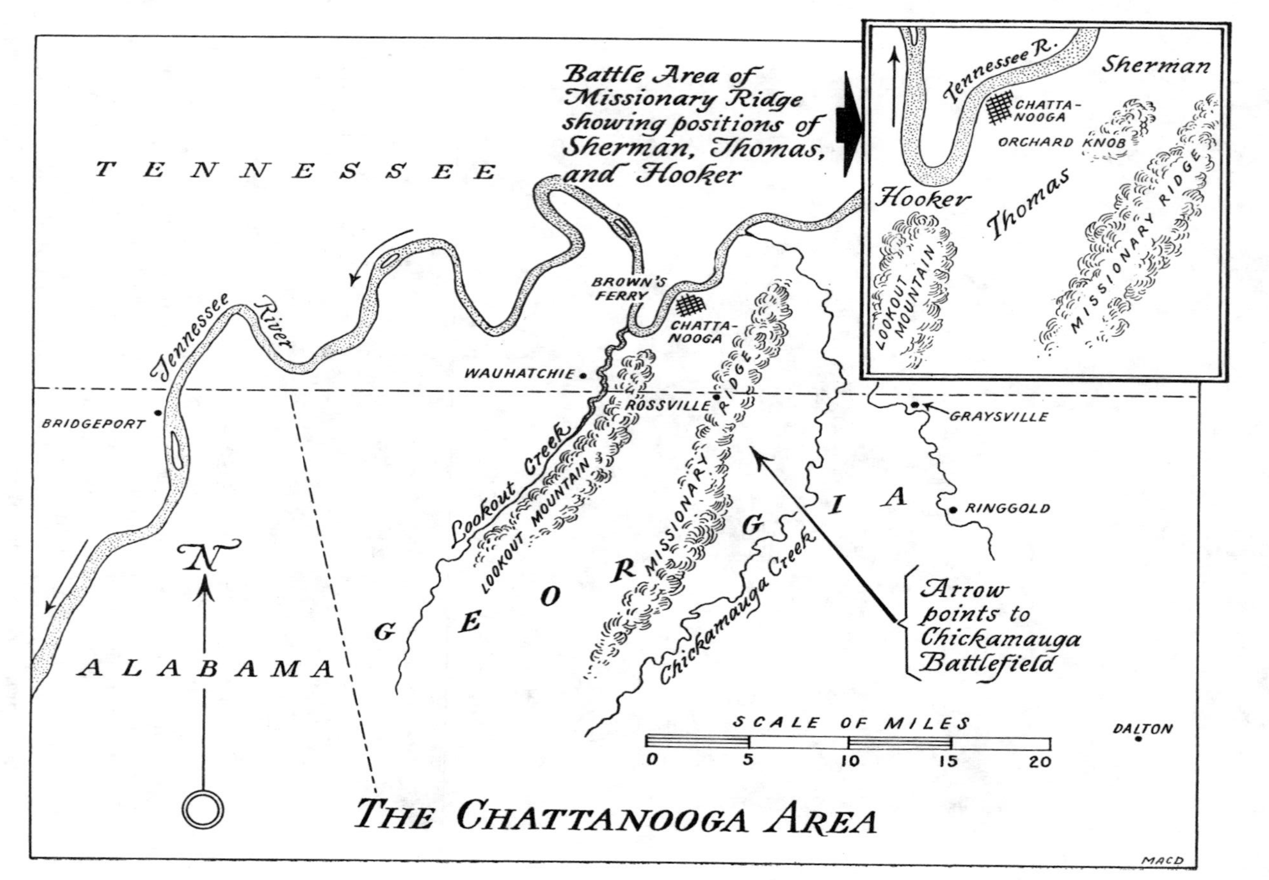

TENNESSEE
Battle Area of Missionary Ridge showing positions of Sherman, Thomas, and Hooker
Tennessee R.
Sherman
CHATTA-NOOGA
ORCHARD KNOB
Hooker
Thomas
LOOKOUT MOUNTAIN
MISSIONARY RIDGE
Tennessee River
BROWN'S FERRY
CHATTA-NOOGA
WAUHATCHIE
BRIDGEPORT
ROSSVILLE
GRAYSVILLE
RINGGOLD
Lookout Creek
LOOKOUT MOUNTAIN
MISSIONARY RIDGE
Chickamauga Creek
GEORGIA
ALABAMA
N
Arrow points to Chickamauga Battlefield
SCALE OF MILES
0 5 10 15 20
DALTON
MACD

THE CHATTANOOGA AREA

British consuls together with the withdrawal of Mason, and on the other side by Lincoln's statement that the country remained "in peace and friendship with foreign powers" and that international questions "of great intricacy and importance . . . [had] been discussed, and . . . accommodated, in a spirit of frankness, justice, and mutual good-will." [5]

Emancipation had moved forward with Union advance. Not alone had this been achieved by national action; measures had also been taken in the states which clearly indicated their reading of the signs of the times. By the end of '63 it was evident that border states were ready to "declare openly for emancipation." Three years before neither Maryland nor Missouri "would tolerate any restraint upon the extension of slavery into new Territories"; now, wrote Lincoln, they "only dispute . . . as to the best mode of removing it within their own limits." While making real strides, emancipation had come without servile insurrection, had been notably acclaimed abroad, and had produced a situation where "full one hundred thousand" former slaves were in the Union military service.[6]

Under fairer skies and with a nice sense of timing, the President now launched his scheme of reconstruction. He would not dally in the task of restoration nor waste valuable months in quibbling about abstruse theories. While writing of health and increasing prosperity, and of growing good will abroad, he wanted to rebuild at home even as the war progressed. He intended not only to have a plan of restoration and be clear about it; he wanted that plan to be understood, guaranteed, and launched into practical application. He cared more for action than for a volume of words.

That plan of restoration was the main burden of Lincoln's message to Congress of December 8, 1863, and of his simultaneous proclamation declaring on the President's part the terms of pardon, amnesty, resumption of allegiance, and reconstruction of loyal state governments.[7] What Congress would do, and how soon they would do it, was another matter; that would be tardily revealed in subsequent years. One of those long sessions of Congress was beginning; 1864 would be

[5] Same message, *ibid.*, IX, 224–225. [6] *Ibid.*, IX, 246–247.

[7] Treatment of Lincoln's design of reconstruction is deferred to a later volume. The present writer has dealt with the subject in *The Civil War and Reconstruction*, 689 ff.; *Lincoln the Liberal Statesman*, chap. vii; *Lincoln and the South*, 117 ff.

an election year with its tumult, distraction, and obstruction; troubles at home would become intensified as military and international prospects brightened.

Lincoln recognized that the processes of peace are not automatic. His statesmanship was purposeful yet flexible. It was coöperative with Congress if Congress would have it so. "I trust [he wrote in his third annual message] that Congress will omit no fair opportunity of aiding these important steps to a great consummation." Reaching into the future and concerned with making peace a reality, he faced the New Year with confidence as he wrote of "freedom disenthralled, regenerated, enlarged, and perpetuated." [8] The odd-year elections were over, Tennessee was safe, strategy and politics seemed to be working together, and the President, so recently in deep anxiety for his country, was now in hopeful mood.

---

[8] Concluding portion, annual message, Dec. 8, 1863.

CHAPTER XVII

"THIS STRANGE, QUAINT, GREAT MAN"

I

IF ONE seeks to make up a portrait of President Lincoln he will find the color and design endlessly varied, yet broadly consistent, in a wealth of descriptions that have come down to us. First impressions were sometimes disappointing. When A. K. McClure of Pennsylvania turned up in Springfield to confer with the new leader in January 1861, he went directly from the depot to the Lincoln home and rang the bell. Perhaps he was surprised to see the President Elect himself answer the summons and open the door. (Mrs. Lincoln had not been too successful in her efforts to break him of this habit.) "I doubt," wrote McClure, "whether I wholly concealed my disappointment at meeting him. Tall, gaunt, ungainly, ill clad, with a homeliness of manner that was unique . . . , I confess that my heart sank within me as I remembered that this was the man chosen by a great nation to become its ruler in the gravest period of its history. I remember his dress as if it were but yesterday—snuff-colored and slouchy pantaloons; open black vest, held by a few brass buttons; straight or evening dress-coat, with tightly-fitting sleeves to exaggerate his long, bony arms, and all supplemented by an awkwardness that was uncommon among men of intelligence. Such was the picture I met in the person of Abraham Lincoln."

They sat down in the parlor, and, according to McClure, talked without interruption for nearly four hours. (A record of that conversation would be of interest; it probably related to Pennsylvania politics, and especially to Cameron, whose appointment to the cabinet McClure opposed.) McClure continued: ". . . little by little, as his earnestness, sincerity, and candor were developed in conversation, I forgot all the grotesque qualities which so confounded me when I first greeted him. Before half an hour had passed I learned not only to respect, but . . . to reverence the man." [1]

Donn Piatt of Ohio, who, with his friend Robert C. Schenck, enjoyed a supper and a visit far into the night at the Lincoln home late in 1860, wrote: "Mr. Lincoln was the homeliest man I ever saw. His body seemed to me a huge skeleton in clothes. Tall as he was, his hands and feet looked out of proportion, so long and clumsy were they. Every movement was awkward in the extreme. . . . He had a face that defied artistic skill to soften or idealize." There follows a reference to the oft-mentioned contrast of the face in repose and in animation: "It brightened, like a lit lantern, when animated. His dull eyes would fairly sparkle with fun, or express as kindly a look as I ever saw, when moved by some matter of human interest." [2]

Lincoln had been so caricatured and misrepresented in second-hand descriptions that an exaggerated image of crudeness had been created in the public mind. "All sorts of stories had been told and believed about his personal appearance." [3] The face which later became the rugged delight of painters and sculptors was supposed to be coarse, backwoodsy, and boorish. The nickname "Old Abe" might be a title of endearment, but it bore also a connotation of crudity. He had not lived down the impressions of his seedy umbrella, his too-short pantaloons, his rough brogans, and his habit, when carrying books, of wrapping them in a bandanna handkerchief and impaling them on a stick in the manner of a tramp shouldering his baggage.

One returns by a kind of irresistible fascination to Herndon's voluminous descriptions, too long to be fully quoted. In a prodigality of adjectives and phrases, the verbose partner-biographer produced something of a *tour de force*. With his matter-of-fact literalness combined with originality of depiction he had the makings of Lincoln all measured, weighed, taken apart, tagged, and put together again. "Abraham Lincoln [wrote Herndon] was about six feet four inches high, . . . having good health and no gray hairs . . . . He was [a] thin—tall—wirey—sinewy, grisly—raw boned man, . . . standing he leaned forward—was what may be called stoop shouldered, ...

[1] A. K. McClure, *Abraham Lincoln and Men of War-Times*, 48–49.
[2] Allen Thorndike Rice, ed., *Reminiscences of Abraham Lincoln . . .* , 479–480.
[3] *Ibid.*, 49.

His usual weight was about 160 pounds. [Lincoln himself gave his average weight as 180.[4]] . . . His blood had to run a long distance from the heart to the tips of his frame, and his nerve force . . . had to travel through dry ground a long distance before the muscles & nerves were obedient to his will. His . . . build was loose and leathery. . . . The whole man . . . worked slowly—creakingly, as if it wanted oiling. Physically he was a very—very powerful man, lifting with ease 400—or 600 pounds. . . . When Mr. Lincoln walked he moved cautiously, but firmly, his long arms—his hands on them hanging like giants hands, swung down by his side. He walked with even tread . . . the inner sides of his feet were parallel, if not a little pigeontoed. He did not walk cunningly—Indian like, but cautiously & firmly. In walking Mr. Lincoln put the whole foot flat down on the ground at once, not landing on the heel. He lifted his foot all at once—not lifting himself from the toes, and hence had no spring or snap or get get [*sic*] up to his walk. He had the economy of fall and lift of foot, though he had spring or apparent ease of motion in his tread. Mr. Lincoln walked undulating up & down, catching and pocketing tire—weariness & pain all up and down his person, ... In sitting down on common chairs he was no taller than ordinary men from the chair to the crown of his head. A marble placed on his knee thus sitting would roll hipward, down an inclined plane. His legs & arms were abnormally—unnaturally long, & hence in undue proportion to the balance of his body. It was only when he stood up that he loomed above other men."

Herndon's inventory or bill of particulars, goes on unceasingly from Lincoln's head and brain to the size of his hat, (7⅛) the measure from ear to ear and from front to back, forehead, hair ("almost black and lay floating where the fingers or the winds left it"), cheek bones, jutting brows, heavy jaws, nose ("having the tip glowing in red, and a little awry toward the right eye"), chin, and eye brows ("like a huge rock on the brow of a hill"). "His face was . . . shriveled—wrinkled and dry, having here and there a hair on the surface. . . . His lower lip was thick—material and hanging undercurved while his chin reached for the lip up curved. . . . There was a lone mole on the right cheek and Adam's apple on his throat."

[4] Nicolay and Hay, *Works,* V, 288.

By this time Herndon's cataloguing—his curiously pictorial itemization—was well launched. In part his description has been quoted in an earlier volume.[5] He did not consider his hero pretty nor ugly, but "homely looking." He was plain, sad, and weighted with a "terrible gloom," yet "rather humorous by turns." We have already noted how, in Herndon's portrait, Lincoln walked the streets good humoredly, greeting his friends with a "good heart-soul welcome," "stalking and stilting it toward the market house . . . , his old gray shawl . . . around his neck, his little Willie or Tad running along at his fathers heels . . . ." When "lit up by the inward soul" all these features "sprang to organs of beauty . . . ."[6]

II

In a journalist's description just after the 1860 nomination we have a first-hand composite of Lincoln's physique, manner, and personality. "In walking, his gait . . . is never brisk. He steps slowly and deliberately, almost always with his head inclined forward and his hands clasped behind his back. In matters of dress he is by no means precise. Always clean, he is never fashionable; he is careless but not slovenly. In manner he is remarkably cordial, and, at the same time, simple. . . . At rest, his features . . . are not such as belong to a handsome man; but when his fine dark gray eyes are lighted up by any emotion, and his features begin their play, he would be chosen from among a crowd as one who had . . . the heavier metal of which full grown men and Presidents are made. . . . His head sits well on his shoulders, but beyond that it defies description. It nearer resembles that of Clay than that of Webster; but it is unlike either. . . . A slightly Roman nose, a wide-cut mouth and a dark complexion, with the appearance of having been weather-beaten, complete the description."[1]

The comparison to Clay occurs in a number of contemporary descriptions. William D. Kelley wrote: ". . . as I contemplated his tall, spare figure, I remembered that of Henry Clay, to whom I

[5] *Lincoln the President,* I, 28–29.

[6] "A Lecture [Dec. 12, 1865] by William H. Herndon," *Abr. Lincoln Quar.,* I, 356 ff. (Sep. 1941).

[1] Chicago *Press & Tribune* (author unidentified), May 23, 1860, reprinted in *Abr. Lincoln Quar.,* I, 207–209 (Dec. 1940).

noticed a more than passing resemblance; and that of General Jackson, as I had seen him in 1832 . . . ."[2]

Visiting the presidential nominee at his Springfield home in June 1860, a gentleman from Utica, New York, enjoyed the experience and left a glowing account. He found the "modest-looking two story brown frame house, with the name 'A Lincoln' on the door plate." He was impressed with the simple air of refinement in the home; there were flowers on the table; "everything was in its place, . . . [and] ministered to the general effect." He waited in the parlor while a servant carried his note to the master of the house. "Presently I heard footsteps on the stairs, and a tall, arrowy, angular gentleman, with a profusion of wiry hair, 'lying around loose' about his head, and a pair of eyes that seemed to say 'make yourself at home,' and a forehead remarkably broad and capacious, and arms that were somewhat too long and lank for a statue of Apollo, made his appearance."

The portrait continues: "The lips were full of character, the nose strongly aquiline, the cheek bones high and prominent, and the whole face indicative at once of goodness and resoluteness. In repose it had something of rigidity, but when in play, it was one of the most eloquent I have ever seen. None of the pictures do him the slightest justice." The visitor went on to record the effect of the whole personality: "His presence is commanding—his manner winning to a marked degree. After you have been five minutes in his company you cease to think that he is either homely or awkward. You recognize in him a high-toned, unassuming, chivalrous-minded gentleman, fully posted in all the essential amenities of social life, and sustained by the infallible monitor of common sense."

Lincoln took the visitor's hand with a warmhearted greeting, and talked of political topics. His knowledge of details proved surprising; he was "more conversant with some of our party performances in Oneida county than I could have desired, and made some pointed allusions to the great Congressional struggle which resulted in the election of Mr. Conkling in 1858."

Here it appears that the visitor must have changed the subject, asking if the candidate was not "very much bored with calls and correspondence." Lincoln made it clear that he liked to see his friends;

---

[2] Rice, 258.

"as to the letters, he took good care not to answer them." (This would be true in general of the great flow of incoming letters.) He went on to say that attempts on his life did not disturb him. His greatest grievance was "with the artists." It was in vain that he tried "to recognize himself in some of the 'Abraham Lincolns' of the pictorials." Summing up, the visitor wrote: "I found him to be one of the most companionable men I have ever met. Frank, hearty and unassuming, one feels irresistibly drawn toward him. In his conversation and bearing he reflects the gentleman." [3]

Cultured men who came from the East with preconceived notions as to Lincoln and the West, were often quite ready to confess that their minds were disabused as to the Illinoisan's crudity. At the time the notification committee from the Republican convention called on him in 1860 we have this record: "A neatly dressed New-Englander remarked . . . : 'I was afraid I should meet a gigantic rail-splitter, with the manners of a flat-boatman, and the ugliest face in creation; and he's a complete gentleman.'" [4]

Another close-up contemporary impression of the Lincoln of 1860 was that of Benjamin Francis Seaver, a business man of New York and Orange, New Jersey, who visited Springfield just after the election of 1860. In a slightly known letter of November 17, 1860, he told of meeting Lincoln. His letter has value as a first-hand record—not a flourish for posterity or a delayed memory, but a home letter written on the very day of his call on the new leader. He wrote: "Last evening we came here [Springfield] to see 'Old Abe' . . . . This too is a beautiful place & this forenoon we [Mr. Seaver and his brother] paid our respects to Mr. Lincoln & sat down & had a brief, but *very*, pleasant talk with him. Everybody goes to see him, at the Capitol, at certain hours of the day. As we entered, he was sitting with an immense pile of letters in his lap & seeing us, he jumped up with 'how do you do, sir' . . . . Altho an awkward looking large man . . . he had a free and easy manner which made us feel at home at once. There were several in the room when we entered, & before we left 3 or 4 real rough looking, half scared 'suckers' . . .

[3] Utica *Morning Herald,* June 27, 1860, reprinted in Sacramento *Daily Union,* Aug. 15, 1860. Recent reprint in *Lincoln Herald,* 46:26–27 (Feb. 1944). The writer has been identified as Ellis Henry Roberts, editor of the Utica *Morning Herald.* Rufus Rockwell Wilson, *Intimate Memories of Lincoln,* 299.

[4] "Mr. Lincoln and the Official Committee," New York *Daily Tribune,* May 25, 1860.

appeared & he shook hands with all, in the same easy style. Then a fine looking farmer held the door half open, hesitating to enter, when Mr. Lincoln stepped forward & said 'come in friend.' The latter replied 'here are some ladies to see the President elect'—4 or 5 real hale, large . . . corn fed looking country ladies in 'best bib & tucker'; one with a baby in arms!"

It was not a long account nor an important one, but its casualness and directness of record give it value. The ladies were admitted, and the letter continues: "His face is much better than the likenesses make him appear, but such long legs! They stick up in the air, as he sits in an ordinary chair!" There is a word or two describing the house, with broken panes and three broken blinds, then follows a reference to Lincoln's popularity. *"Everybody speaks well of Abe Lincoln* here." [5]

Often we have the adjective "homely" and sometimes "ugly," but a careful student of Lincoln, J. L. McCorison, Jr., who has studied direct descriptions from life, has written: "The stereotyped 'homely' Lincoln is due for revision." Referring to some of the better photographs Mr. McCorison adds: "[They] show a pleasing and personally attractive countenance." [6] If the stock adjectives "homely" and "ugly" are in need of revision, it should be added that the better informed men of that day were often aware of the need. One observer wrote: "The Pres. is not half so ugly as he is generally represented—his nose is rather long but he is rather *long* himself so it is a Necessity to keep the proportion complete." [7] There was, in fact, merit in homeliness so far as it connoted ruggedness.

It was the primal American, the rugged type, that admired Lincoln and described him best. We have, for instance, the description by Walt Whitman: ". . . his unusual and uncouth height, dress of complete black, stovepipe hat pushed back on the head, dark-brown complexion, seamed and wrinkled yet canny-looking face, his black, bushy head of hair, disproportionately long neck, and hands held behind as he stood observing the people." Whitman continued: "four mighty and primal hands will be needed to the complete limning

---

[5] J. L. McCorison, Jr., "Mr. Lincoln's Broken Blinds," *Lincoln Herald,* 50:43–46 (June 1948).

[6] *Ibid.,* 46, note 18.

[7] F. J. Bellamy to John F. Bellamy, in Pratt, *Concerning Mr. Lincoln,* 88.

of this man's future portrait—the eyes and brains and finger-touch of Plutarch and Aeschylus and Michael Angelo, assisted by Rabelais." [8]

Of Lincoln it was especially true that delineation of the features, in photographic time exposures, in pencil or paint, was inadequate. Frederick Seward wrote "how accurately" the newspapers "had copied his features [this accuracy could have been questioned], and how totally they omitted his careworn look, and his pleasant, kindly smile." [9] It is for this reason that the historian prizes those unstudied vignettes from life which are found in letters of the time, not written for publication. In one such letter (the time and scene being Albany, New York, February 18, 1861) we have this: "Mr. Lincoln looks much wearied & care worn. But his pictures do not do him justice. He is both a smarter & pleasanter looking man than his pictures represent. It was a thrilling scene to see him bowing in his carriage with head uncovered, while the ladies handkerchiefs waived [*sic*] from every window . . . ." [10]

III

Since, when he entered upon the presidency, Lincoln was hardly known at all outside the United States, descriptions by foreign observers sounded often like the report of some notable, or curious, discovery. The wholly unusual quality of the man appealed to English journalists, who have forever delighted in detailing to their readers the unusual and unbelievable things in America, and where these journalists had the knack of pictorial reporting the result was striking and memorable. An early account published in England was that of the famous British correspondent, William Howard Russell, of the *Times*. For March 27, 1861, Russell made a more than usually interesting entry in his *Diary*. He turned up at the department of state where Secretary ("Governor") Seward arranged to take him

---

8 Newspaper clipping identified as Whitman's, in the Walt Whitman papers, Lib. of Cong. In *Abraham Lincoln and Walt Whitman* by William E. Barton we have a none-too-favorable portrait of Walt, with here and there a *caveat* to the reader as to the reliability of the poet's autobiographical statements.

9 Frederick W. Seward, *Reminiscences of a War Time Statesman* . . . , 136.

10 Adoniram J. Blakely to Dan Blakely, Albany, Feb. 18, 1861, in Pratt, *Concerning Mr. Lincoln*, 53.

over a few steps and introduce him to the President in the White House. The minister from the new kingdom of Italy, the Chevalier Bertinatti, entered the mansion at the same time. They were received in "a handsome spacious room, richly and rather gorgeously furnished, and rejoicing in a kind of '*demi-jour*,' which gave increased effect to the gilt chairs and ormolu ornaments." Since this was a set occasion—a formal audience of the President to receive the new diplomat—Seward's son said to Russell: "You are not . . . supposed to be here."

The diary continued: "Soon afterwards there entered, with a shambling, loose, irregular, almost unsteady gait, a tall, lank, lean man, considerably over six feet in height, with stooping shoulders, long pendulous arms, terminating in hands of extraordinary dimensions, which, however, were far exceeded in proportion by his feet. He was dressed in an ill-fitting, wrinkled suit of black, which put one in mind of an undertaker's uniform at a funeral; round his neck a rope of black silk was knotted in a large bulb, with flying ends projecting beyond the collar of his coat; his . . . shirt-collar disclosed a sinewy muscular yellow neck, and above that, nestling in a great black mass of hair, bristling and compact like a ruff of mourning pins, rose the strange quaint face and head, covered with its thatch of wild republican hair, of President Lincoln."

The whole effect was by no means unfavorable upon this urbane Englishman. He continued: "The impression produced by the size of his extremities, and by his flapping . . . ears, may be removed by the appearance of kindliness, sagacity, and the awkward bonhommie of his face; the mouth is absolutely prodigious; the lips, straggling and extending almost from one line of black beard to the other, are only kept in order by two deep furrows from the nostril to the chin; the nose itself—a prominent organ—stands out from the face, with an inquiring, anxious air, as though it were sniffing for some good thing in the wind; the eyes dark, full, and deeply set, are penetrating, but full of an expression which almost amounts to tenderness; and above them projects the shaggy brow, running into the small hard frontal space, the development of which can scarcely be estimated accurately, owing to the irregular flocks of thick hair carelessly brushed across it. One would say that, although the mouth was made to enjoy a joke, it could also utter the severest sentences which the head could dictate, but that Mr. Lincoln would be ever more willing to temper justice with mercy, and to enjoy what he considers the amenities of life, than to take a harsh view of men's nature and of the world, and to estimate things in an ascetic or puritan spirit."

Since coming to the United States Mr. Russell had been supplied with doubting remarks as to whether Lincoln was a "gentleman." "I have heard," he wrote, "more disparaging allusions made by Americans to him on that account than I could have expected among simple republicans, where all should be equals; but . . . it would not be possible for the most indifferent observer to pass him in the street without notice."

The President's western cordiality was brought up short by the stiffness of Seward and the "profound diplomatic bows of the Chevalier Bertinatti." Then Lincoln "suddenly jerked himself back, and stood in front of the two ministers, with his body slightly drooped forward, and his hands behind his back, his knees touching, and his feet apart." When Seward presented the Italian diplomat, "the President made a prodigiously violent demonstration of his body in a bow which had almost the effect of a smack in its rapidity and abruptness." (We have here an impression quite different from Herndon's slow-motion picture.) After the ceremony of diplomacy the President was presented to Russell. "Conversation ensued for some minutes, which the President enlivened by two or three peculiar little sallies, and I left agreeably impressed with his shrewdness, humor, and natural sagacity." [1]

Starting to tell how Lincoln looked, men would glide into comment on his nature or temperament. Those who met him were aware that the man had more than was revealed at first glance, something of depth and at times of mystery. He was described as a man of "deep prudences," [2] a man of contrasts, "retired, contemplative," yet highly sociable, often in gay mood, yet given to a sadness that was impenetrable. The humorist, David R. Locke (Petroleum V. Nasby) wrote: "I never saw so sad a face." [3] Perhaps the briefest vignette

[1] W. H. Russell, *My Diary North and South,* 36–39.

[2] "Mr Lincoln was a secretive man—had great ambition—profound policies—deep prudences. . . . Lincoln was about as shrewd a man as this world ever had." Herndon to Ward H. Lamon, March 6, 1870, MS., Huntington Lib.

[3] Rice, *Reminiscences,* 442.

combining the inner and the outer personality is Donn Piatt's: "this strange, quaint, great man." [4]

The contrast between Lincoln's rugged and unfashionable appearance and the sometimes unexpected quality of his inner poise and dignity is well indicated in the following description by an English observer:

"Fancy a man six foot high, and thin *out of* proportion; with long bony arms and legs, which somehow seem to be always in the way; with great rugged furrowed hands, which grasp you like a vise . . . ; with a long, scraggy neck, and a chest too narrow for the arms at its side.

"Add . . . a head . . . covered with rough, uncombed and uncombable hair that stands out in every direction . . . ; a face furrowed, wrinkled and indented, as though it had been scarred by vitriol; a high, narrow forehead, and, sunk deep beneath bushy eyebrows; two bright, somewhat dreamy eyes, that seem to gaze through you without looking at you; a few irregular blotches of black bristly hair, in the place where beard and whiskers ought to grow; a close-set . . . mouth, . . . and a nose and ears which have been taken by mistake from a head of twice the size.

"Clothe this figure, . . . in a . . . badly-fitting suit . . . puckered up at every salient point . . . ; put on large, ill-fitting boots, gloves too long for the long bony fingers, and a fluffy hat, . . . ; and then add to all this an air of strength, physical as well as moral, and a strange look of dignity coupled with all this grotesqueness, and you will have the impression left upon me by Abraham Lincoln." [5]

Still another British description of unusual quality is that of the journalist, George Augustus Sala, who met the Emancipator early in 1864 at a reception in the White House. Steered through the crowd by Senator Sumner, he found himself face to face with the "Tallest Man of All." Next moment his hand was in the "cast-iron grip" of Abraham Lincoln, which made the handshaking painfully memorable. On this occasion the President wore gloves, "a pair of white

---

[4] *Ibid.*, 483. (This pithy and quotable phrase by Donn Piatt is part of a curious, and largely unfavorable, medley of comment on Lincoln.)

[5] *Macmillan's Magazine*, VI, 23 (May 1862).

kids, which the tallest of Barnum's four giants might have envied." Referring to the cartoon sketches in *Punch,* Sala noted that the artist, John Tenniel, had "seized upon that lengthy face, those bushy locks, that shovel beard, that ungainly form, those long, muscular, attenuated limbs, those bony and wide-spread extremities." Lincoln was so tall, according to this observer, "that, looking up in his face, you might, did not respect forbid you, ask, 'How cold the weather was up there.' He is so tall, that a friend who had an interview with him . . . [said] that when he rose there did not seem the slightest likelihood of his getting up ever coming to an end. He seems to be drawing himself out like a telescope." These touches might be second-hand, for we have the same remarks elsewhere.

The Englishman then commented on the President's "dark face, strongly marked, tanned and crows-footed, and fringed with coarse and tangled hair, . . . so uncouth . . . that it narrowly escapes being either terrible or grotesque." He hastened, however, to add that this impression was obviated "by a peculiarly soft, almost feminine, expression of melancholy, which . . . seemed to pervade the countenance of this remarkable man." This was the more striking because our British friend remembered that he was in the presence of "the great joker of jokes—the Sancho Panza made governor of this Transatlantic Barataria; but there the look was—the regard of a thoughtful, weary, saddened, overworked being; of one who was desperately striving to do his best, but who woke up every morning to find the wheat that he had sown growing up as tares; of one who was continually regretting that he did not know more—that he had begun his work too late, and must lay down his sceptre too early."

In a very brief interview Lincoln remarked upon the unfavorable impression which foreigners were apt to carry away from a country when they only saw it in a state of war; he hoped that the Englishman's sojourn would be pleasant. To this visitor the President told no stories, and talked no politics.

One more impression gained on this occasion is worth recording. "Mr. Lincoln," wrote Sala, "does not stand straight on his feet, but sways about with an odd sidelong motion, as though he were continually pumping something from the ground—say Truth from the bottom of her well—or hauling up some invisible kedge anchor. It gave me the notion of a mariner who had found his sea-legs, and could toe a line well, but who had to admit that there was a rough sea running." [6]

A valuable first-hand record was that of Mrs. Cornelia Perrine Harvey, who wrote an account of an undated wartime interview with Lincoln in which they discussed the establishing of military hospitals in the North. "I had never seen Mr Lincoln before," she wrote. "He was alone in a medium sized office-like room, no elegance about him, no elegance in him. He was plainly clad in a suit of black, that illy fitted him. No fault of his tailor however, such a figure could not be fitted. He was tall and lean, and as he sat in a folded up sort of a way in a deep arm chair, one would almost have thought him deformed. . . . When I first saw him his head was bent forward, his chin resting on his breast, & in his hand a letter, which I had just sent into him. He raised his eyes, saying, Mrs Harvey? I hastened forward . . . . The President took my hand, hoped I was well, but there was no smile of welcome on his face. It was rather the stern look of the judge who had decided against me."

Mrs. Harvey was promoting a plan for Northern hospitalization of wounded and sick soldiers, urging that Southern swamps were unhealthy and that the government was responsible for thousands of soldier graves in the South. Lincoln knew that the military authorities opposed the plan, and he feared that if the men were sent North they would never come back. As he spoke, wrote Mrs. Harvey, "a quizzical smile played over his face at my slight embarrassment." She filled in with further touches: "He threw himself around in his chair, one leg over the arm and spoke slowly." "His face was peculiar, bone, nerve, vein, and muscle were all so plainly seen, deep lines of thought, and care, were around his mouth, and eyes." [7]

A description of Lincoln by Seward has come down to us in a record written by Henry Bellows, head of the Sanitary Commission. In April 1863 Bellows dined with the secretary of state and on the next day he wrote his wife a full account of the conversation. "Mr. Seward," wrote Bellows, "had a great deal to say about the President. He always describes him as the most single-hearted, sincere, affectionate candid of men—patient to a fault—easy to get along with—

[6] George Augustus Sala, *My Diary in America in the Midst of War,* II, 145–150, quoted in *Journal,* Ill. State Hist. Soc., XLI, 438–440 (Dec. 1948).

[7] MS. of Mrs. Cornelia Perrine Harvey, Ill. State Hist. Lib.

doing ample & generous justice to each & all his ministers. He says his judgment & comprehension are admirable; his right-mindedness infallible. That he has an admirable intellect not invigorated by personal wilfulness, or ambition or intense earnestness—but a little weakened by gentle, mild & candid qualities & affections. That he is afraid of doing injustice, or hurting peoples' feelings. . . . He was most irregular as to his meals & took them *cold* usually—& in a hurry—after breakfast, he was shaved, probably at the time when, & as often as *it was convenient to the barber*—for his sense of justice & kindness made him consult his own comfort & convenience last—then, he rec'd, any & every body, as long as time held out—selecting from the hundreds applying those he thot best entitled to come—and except on Cabinet days Tuesday & Friday, he spent his day morning & evening till 11. in this way. The actual work thrown on him by his ministers was small. He had a notion he was a servant of the people & that he was there to hear their complaints & he spent his time at it." [8]

IV

It will be well to keep in mind two contrasts: Lincoln's rough-hewn exterior contrasted with a dignity that came from some inner source, and the seemingly casual informality of his demeanor as opposed to his exquisite handling of delicate or difficult situations.

The rail-splitter aspect has been overstressed. Lincoln was no stranger to cultured society. He was not ignorant or naïve. There was method in his simplicity, *savoir faire* in his bland unconventionality. This does not mean that his manner was artful in the sense of being affected or assumed. It means rather that he knew his way about. Seemingly artless, his behavior nevertheless amounted to skilled craftsmanship.

People were distressed at his lack of "style." He did not look like a President. He slouched in his chair. He hated gloves and wore them awkwardly. An acquaintance wrote that he had "a habit . . . of passing his right hand slowly around his head and through his unkept hair, when actively engaged in thought. His clothing was in

[8] Henry W. Bellows to his wife, Washington, Apr. 23, 1863, Bellows MSS., Mass. Hist. Soc.

THE FACE OF LINCOLN

". . . the homeliest man I ever saw." Donn Piatt.

"None of the pictures do him the slightest justice." Utica *Morning Herald,* June 27, 1860. "His presence is commanding—his manner winning to a marked degree." *Ibid.*

"Fancy a man six foot high, and thin out of proportion; with long bony arms and legs . . . always in the way . . . . Add . . . a head . . . covered with rough, . . . uncombable hair that stands out in every direction . . . a face furrowed, wrinkled and indented . . . ; and then add to all this an air of strength, physical as well as moral, and a strange look of dignity coupled with all this grotesqueness, and you will have the impression left upon me by Abraham Lincoln." *Macmillan's Magazine,* May 1862.

". . . his expressive face . . . now seeming almost to laugh outright in its grimaces of fun, and now as . . . sorrowful as a tomb." Mrs. Amanda Poorman, daughter of Dennis Hanks, in St. Louis *Post-Dispatch,* May 26, 1901.

Grateful acknowledgments to University of Nebraska Library (for picture, Beardstown 1858, in white coat), to Miss Charlotte Ward of Urbana, Illinois, for copy of 1860 ambrotype (upper right), and to Frederick H. Meserve.

hopeless disorder, and I thought him then, and think him now, the most ungainly man that I have ever seen." [1] Gamaliel Bradford, in his delightful but outdated essay on Mrs. Abraham Lincoln, wrote: ". . . it must always be remembered that she had the . . . most undomestic and unparlorable figure of Lincoln to carry with her, which would have been a terrible handicap to any woman." [2] To be *unparlorable* in the Victorian age was indeed a handicap. It was a day of fuss and feathers, of zouaves at home and monarchical trappings abroad.

What must the homespun leader have felt as Siam offered him several pairs of elephants? The offer came in a masterpiece of Siamese-English: "Somdetch Phra Paramendr Maha Mongkut,[3] by the blessing of the highest superagency of the whole universe, the King of Siam, the sovereign of all interior tributary countries adjacent and around in every direction, . . . to his most respected excellent presidency, the President of the United States of America . . . [etc.]."

The King wrote that he was sending a sword and a photographic likeness of himself, holding his daughter in his lap, to the President. He then offered to send several pairs of young elephants to the United States to propagate their kind and to serve as beasts of burden, "since elephants, being animals of great size and strength, can bear burdens and travel through uncleared woods and matted jungles where no carriage and cart roads have yet been made." He would have the United States send ships for the elephants, then added: "At this time we have much pleasure in sending a pair of large elephant's tusks, one of the tusks weighing 52 cents of a picul, the other weighing 48 cents of a picul, and both tusks from the same animal . . . that thereby the glory and renown of Siam may be promoted."

In reply Lincoln assured the King of his appreciation and accepted the gifts to be placed in the government archives as a token of Siam's friendship. As to the elephants, the monarch was informed: "Our political jurisdiction . . . does not reach a latitude so low as to favor the multiplication of the elephant." He also explained that

---

1 Statement of R. S. Rantoul, *Proceedings,* Mass. Hist. Soc., third series, II, 85.

2 Gamaliel Bradford, *Wives,* 26.

3 This was the potentate who appeared in *Anna and the King of Siam,* by Margaret Landon. For the more direct account see Anna Harriette Leonowens, *The English Governess at the Siamese Court: Being Recollections of Six Years in the Royal Palace at Bangkok* (Boston, 1870).

"steam on land, as well as on water, has been our best and most efficient agent of transportation in internal commerce." [4] After contemplating all this oriental magnificence it must have come as a relief to Lincoln to read a letter in which a group of French liberals praised him in earnest and scholarly fashion, addressing him simply as "Citizen Abraham Lincoln."

One may perhaps think of the President's job as legal or official, having to do with executing the laws, sending messages to Congress, serving as Commander in Chief of the army and navy, preserving, protecting, and defending the Constitution. It is all this, but it is much more. Beyond the duty that was official, Lincoln had to remember the adjustment that was personal. In addition to laws, orders, and constitutional matters, he had the constant challenge of human situations.

In his practice of the art of human relations Lincoln regularly and consciously applied that quality known as "tact." That is a way of conveying the idea, but tact is not one thing only. It is a number of qualities working together: insight into the nature of men, sympathy, self control, a knack of inducing self control in others, avoidance of human blundering, readiness to give the immediate situation an understanding mind and a second thought. Tact is not only kindness, but kindness skillfully extended. Charity does not always please, while even a reproof may be tactfully given. Human tact involves *savoir faire,* restraint, patience, ability to reach a person indirectly rather than by frontal attack, approaching a situation in terms of adjustment rather than by way of deadlock or "showdown." Tact requires poise, a potent factor in self control; it constitutes the opposite of brusqueness, clumsiness, or impulsive blurting out of one's feelings.

The finest tact is in terms of the greatest need, or the most intense provocation to be untactful. Lincoln was not only considerate. He was considerate toward Seward, who calmly planned to conduct his administration for him; toward Weed, whose grasping for Warwick-like power in 1861 was a serious embarrassment; toward Chase, who became the center of a radical drive to displace the President; toward Stanton, who was described by men of that day as "mercurial," "dis-

---

[4] *Sen. Exec. Doc. No. 23,* 37 Cong., 2 sess., 7 ff.

courteous," "unreliable," "brusque," "uncivil," "dictatorial," "disrespectful to the President," and almost impossible to deal with. Lincoln kept the most diverse and troublesome men in his cabinet; at least he kept them there so long as that was where they could do the least harm. It has been seen in an earlier volume that Lincoln dealt fairly with Frémont, whose conduct was painfully embarrassing and insubordinate in 1861, and with Mrs. Frémont, whose wrathful self-importance added to the Chief's difficulty in adjusting the Missouri imbroglio.

Lincoln's personal adjustment was suited to the special case. Toward Major Robert Anderson, a Kentuckian, whose duty had placed him at Fort Sumter, the unstable spot where the explosion began, he showed special favors, raising him to the rank of brigadier-general, assigning him to command in his native Kentucky, and later, when Anderson's health had failed, personally arranging for him a kind of nominal army assignment with soft duties at Newport, Rhode Island.

Writing on August 15, 1863, the President explained that he had been "through the War Department" that morning looking up the law in connection with the general's case. He found the current statute very restrictive as to the discretion of the President and other officials, but he concluded that the Newport assignment, while within the law, would serve the purpose—i. e., provide full pay with slight duties; for General Halleck said it would "require substantially no labor, or thought, whatever." Then, sensing that Anderson's spirit was hurt by what he had endured—but without spoiling the subject with too much attention—the President put in a final sentence: "And now, my dear General, allow me to assure you that we here are all your sincere friends." [5] The old warrior, approaching the age of sixty, did not accept the New England post, being placed on the retired list, but until the day of his death in 1871 he carried the mental satisfaction of the President's kindness.

Toward General Meade, Lincoln's kindness showed itself partly in what he refrained from doing; for Lincoln had that priceless wisdom to write a letter—an excellent one, carefully phrased—and then withhold it. At Gettysburg Meade had fought off Lee's invading host, which was a notable triumph, but Lincoln did not think it was

---

[5] Facsimile in New York *Times,* Dec. 26, 1926, p. 2, c. 4.

enough. As mentioned in an earlier volume, the President, with an intensity that must be recaptured if his feeling is to be understood, wanted the whole wretched war ended. For long years it had been a matter of stinging defeat (under McDowell, Pope, Burnside, Hooker) or of hope deferred. Then came Gettysburg with its shining opportunity. The President could hardly bear the realization that the retreating army was not being effectively pursued. He sat down and wrote out a letter to Meade. He used strong words. The letter was bitter because the President felt bitter, but if he had sent that post-mortem missive it would have seriously hurt the feelings of a high-minded general who had felt sufficient distress, whose services were needed, and who had asked to be relieved of his command. Lincoln thought it over; then he withheld the letter. On the envelope, in his own hand, he wrote: "To Gen. Meade, never sent, or signed." [6]

The President's almost unbearable distress was somewhat relieved by putting his thoughts on paper (a kind of mental therapy); but his wise second thought, as well as his patience and generosity, was shown in sparing Meade the pain of a presidential rebuke. When at a later time, General Sickles bitterly attacked Meade, who asked for a court of inquiry, Lincoln disapproved of such a court because it would have been a footless diversion of effort from the main business.[7] In this connection, however, he took occasion to refer to Meade's "good service." As for Sickles he did not agree with his ugly attitude toward Meade, yet, just after Gettysburg, he had sent him a word of praise for his courage and of deep sympathy for the loss of his leg.

That the management of a war, even on the military side, was more than a matter of recruitment and conscription, of strategy and tactics, of logistics *et cetera,* and that army matters were largely a question of personal relations, becomes evident by even the most cursory examination of the Lincoln record. It was Lincoln's human dealing with his generals that counted. So far was this true that the letters which Lincoln wrote to his chieftains—those highly individual communications which show such unusual distinction—belong together in a kind of series. They show the patient President, over and over,

---

[6] Lincoln to Meade, July 14, 1863, R. T. L. Coll., 24808; *Lincoln the President,* II, 288–289.

[7] *Offic. Rec.,* 1 ser. XXVII, pt. 1, 139.

putting in a word of caution, generous compliment, morale-building encouragement, explanation to avoid misunderstanding, and if necessary, rebuke, until the relation of the Chief Executive to his officers became that of a head of family dealing—by admonition, discipline, advice, and command—with difficult and temperamental children.

Viewed in this light the famous letter to General Hooker, when, after Burnside's failure, he was placed at the head of the Army of the Potomac, no longer stands by itself; it takes its place in a considerable category. To repeat the words of the Hooker letter here is unnecessary, since it has already been considered, but it must belong in any treatment of Lincoln's human relations. It was not a complimentary letter. The President was admonishing and criticising the man whom he was raising to the most important field command in the nation. What gives distinction to the epistle is the fatherly quality of the admonition. The President did not like Hooker's mixing politics with his profession, his attitude toward brother officers, nor his remark about the government needing a dictator. He was "not quite satisfied" with Hooker, yet he was promising him full support. Lincoln had to use such human material as he had. In using Hooker he thought that a little toning down would do no harm. Yet one will search in vain for any phrasing in the whole letter that was sharp or unfriendly.[8]

General Grant, who in the personal sense probably gave Lincoln the least trouble of any of the commanders, was the recipient of more than one gracious letter from the President, who did not reserve his tact for cases of antagonism. After Vicksburg, Lincoln wrote: "My dear General: I do not remember that you and I ever met personally. I write this now as a grateful acknowledgment for the almost inestimable service you have done the country." The President admitted that he had at an earlier time considered some of Grant's strategy defective. He concluded: "I now wish to make the personal acknowledgment that you were right, and I was wrong." [9]

---

[8] *Lincoln the President,* II, 255–256. The letter was dated January 26, 1863. It reads as if Lincoln were thinking out loud.

[9] Lincoln to Grant, July 13, 1863, facsimile in Albert D. Richardson, *A Personal History of Ulysses S. Grant,* 338–339.

V

Lincoln had often to deal with folks whose malady has recently been given its perfect name, "Injustice Collectors." The phrase is applied to "people who are looking for injustice in a friendly world, because they suffer from a hidden need to feel that this world has wronged them." [1] When Lincoln saw the symptoms of this human ailment, he put in a steadying word. On one occasion he wrote to a complaining general: "I regret to find you denouncing so many persons as liars, scoundrels, fools, thieves, and persecutors of yourself." [2]

When, for some reason that Lincoln knew not, the politician Thurlow Weed seemed offended, Lincoln wrote that he had no unkind thought toward him and concluded: "I am sure if we could meet we would not part with any unpleasant impression on either side." [3] Weed answered in like vein. He was a different sort from Lincoln, and Lincoln had had to watch carefully to see that Weed did not mar his administration; but after that frank exchange it would be unlikely for these two men to feel otherwise than as personal friends.

A prolific source of personal fretting among military men was the bothersome matter of rank and precedence among generals. On one occasion General Benjamin F. Butler's claim for precedence in rank over a number of generals (McClellan, Frémont, Dix, and others) made it necessary for an army board to investigate and report on the controversy. After a careful examination of the law, the facts, and the arguments, they solemnly reported that the other generals "have precedence respectively in point of rank over Major-General B. F. Butler, U. S. V." [4]

When this nursing of a sense of injustice became acute, Lincoln sometimes employed the device of a cooling-off period. General David Hunter, having served in Washington, at first Bull Run, and briefly in Missouri (succeeding Frémont), had been given a command in far off Kansas. He had expected a better assignment. He wrote to the President: "I am very deeply mortified, humiliated, insulted and disgraced. . . . I am sent into banishment with not three thousand

---

[1] Louis Auchincloss, *The Injustice Collectors,* foreword.

[2] Lincoln to General J. G. Blount, Aug. 18, 1863, photostat, A. Lincoln Assoc.

[3] Lincoln to Thurlow Weed, Oct. 14, 1863, photostat, A. Lincoln Assoc.

[4] Moore, *Rebellion Record* (Documents), VII, 340, July 1, 1863.

effective men under my command, while one of the Brigadier Generals, Buell, is in command of near one hundred thousand men in Kentucky." [5] It was another occasion to try the President's self control. He wrote to Hunter: "I am constrained to say it is difficult to answer so ugly a letter in good temper." He went into detail to show that he considered Hunter's assignment an honorable and responsible one, and added: "I have been, and am sincerely your friend . . . ."

But the reply of the President was not sent immediately. The Chief kept the letter on his desk for more than a month, and then sent it by a special conveyance, with directions to hand it to the general when he "was in a good humor." The effect was to administer a bit of gentle chiding along with a cordial expression of good will. The letter was signed: "Your friend, as ever, A. Lincoln." [6]

The sensitiveness of General James H. Lane as to the question of rank was equal to that of Hunter, and in the friction between these men Lincoln found one of his thousand difficulties in connection with western command. When in early 1862 an expedition into the southwest (with attention to Indian Territory and Texas) was contemplated—a project which was later abandoned—it was the President's wish "to avail the government of the services of both General Hunter and General Lane, and, so far as possible, to personally oblige both." His problem was comparable to having two prima donnas in an opera. He issued what amounted to an order to settle the issue, but he led up to it by way of suggesting a kind of modus vivendi to keep both generals satisfied. "Gen. Hunter [he wrote in a joint communication to the two men] is the senior officer, and must command when they serve together; though, in so far as he can, consistently with the public service, and his own honor, oblige Gen. Lane, he will also oblige me. If they can not come to an amicable understanding, Gen.

[5] Hunter added: "If you thought . . . that there was a political necessity for relieving me from command in Missouri, why should I not have been sent to Kentucky, where there was one hundred thousand men to command, and not to a wilderness [Kansas] with three thousand." Hunter to Lincoln, "Private," Ft. Leavenworth, Kas., Dec. 23, 1861, MS., Huntington Lib.

[6] Lincoln explained that he was losing confidence in Hunter, not from any official act or omission up to the time of his assignment to the Kansas command at Leavenworth, "but from the flood of grumbling despatches and letters I have seen from you since." The President considered the Hunter command "as responsible, and as honorable, as that assigned to Buell." Expressing full friendship for Hunter, he pointedly hinted that the general was "adopting the best possible way to ruin" himself. Lincoln to Hunter, Dec. 31, 1861, original MS., with Hunter endorsement, in Huntington Lib.

Lane must report to Gen. Hunter for duty, according to the rules, or decline the service." [7]

On this subject of rank Lincoln had occasion to write to Rosecrans, who had requested that his commission should have a certain date to give him superiority and precedence. Lincoln wrote that the general was asking for something that was "the right of other men." He gracefully added: "Truth to speak, I do not appreciate this matter of rank on paper as you officers do. The world will not forget that you fought the battle of 'Stone River' [Murfreesboro] and it will never care a fig whether you rank Gen. Grant on paper, or he so ranks you." [8] In this letter it will be noted that Lincoln refused the general's request in such a fashion as to pay him a compliment.

Once Gen. Robert C. Schenck called to see the President but departed without doing so. It was a small matter; Lincoln was ill that day; yet the President did not let it pass. He wrote to Schenck in his own hand to show how mortified he was that the general had left; he explained that he had gone downstairs expecting Schenck to await his return; he wanted it understood that no discourtesy was intended.[9]

While jealousy, recrimination, and answering self-justification among generals created constant and at times almost unbearable difficulties for Lincoln, it became an added cause of bitterness if, of two generals involved in dispute, one was an unprofessional volunteer soldier and another a West Point man. If the untrained officer disregarded the orders or advice of West-Point-trained superiors and, as a result, incurred disaster, the situation would be particularly painful. Such was the case of Major General Robert H. Milroy of Indiana, who had started by raising a volunteer company and had risen to colonel, brigadier-general, and major-general, serving chiefly in the Valley of Virginia. Having been among those luckless Union generals who were hit by Stonewall Jackson in the Valley campaign of 1862, Milroy was most unfortunate in Lee's pre-Gettysburg drive of June 1863, when at Winchester he suffered a serious disaster after having disobeyed orders. His position had not been considered capable of adequate defense, and he had been ordered to evacuate Winchester

---

[7] Lincoln to Major-General Hunter, Feb. 10, 1862, photostat, A. Lincoln Assoc. (same to General Lane).

[8] Lincoln to Rosecrans, Mar. 17, 1863, R. T. L. Coll., 22441–3.

[9] Lincoln to Schenck, July 23, 1863, photostat, A. Lincoln Assoc.

so that Union forces could be better concentrated at Harpers Ferry. Instead of this, he became needlessly engaged with far superior Confederate forces with smashing defeat.

What we are concerned with here for the moment is not so much the failure of Milroy, but the manner in which Lincoln handled it. After the capture of Winchester, while still in the service, Milroy was, as it were, on the shelf, and Lincoln refused to return him to command. The general had annoyed the President by letters he had written, and on June 29, 1863, Lincoln sent him a plain-spoken rebuke. "I have scarcely seen anything from you at any time [wrote the President], that did not contain imputations against your superiors, and a chafing against acting the part they had assigned you. You have constantly urged the idea that you were persecuted because you did not come from West Point, ... This, my dear general, is I fear, the rock on which you have split." The President referred to Milroy's disregard of orders calling him in from Winchester to Harpers Ferry, after which he was hopelessly beleaguered at Winchester. Though Milroy hated West Point in general and Halleck in particular, the President added that it had not been Halleck's fault that he was in Winchester against orders at the time of his disaster.[10] The Milroy instance shows that a complaining general whose own performance had been at fault was the kind of case in which Lincoln was disposed to be authoritative rather than too gentle.

VI

One of the most difficult persons to deal with was the high-minded Carl Schurz. He was forceful, strongly antislavery, tremendously in earnest, ambitious for personal distinction, and disposed to "collect" cases of injustice to himself. In a "Private" letter dated November 20, 1862, he simply tore Lincoln to pieces. The whole emphasis of the letter was that Lincoln was in error fundamentally, did not understand the true situation, and needed Schurz to set him right. The general feared that the Chief had "too favorable a view of the causes of our defeat in the [congressional] elections." He would have the

---

10 Lincoln to Milroy, June 29, 1863, "Private," photostat, A. Lincoln Assoc. On the previous day Milroy had written to Lincoln a letter full of self-justification and hurt feeling. R. T. L. Coll., 24484–85.

President know that *"the result of the elections was a most serious and severe reproof administered to the Administration."* He admonished Lincoln: "Do not refuse to listen to the voice of the people. Let it not become too true what I have heard said; that of all places in this country it is Washington where public opinion is least heard, and of all places in Washington the White House." He informed the President that the results of the election had "complicated the crisis," so that, "unless things take soon a favorable turn, our troubles may soon involve not only the moral power but the physical existence of the government." "Only relentless determination on your part," he warned, "can turn the tide. You must recognize the confidence of the people at any price, or your Administration is lost."

All this strong language, being interpreted, meant that Schurz wanted a Republican war: "between two Generals of equal military inefficiency [he wrote] I would . . . give a Republican the preference." "What Republican general," he asked, "has ever had a fair chance in this war?" Mentioning the doings of Democratic generals he pointed out: "There was consequently inefficiency, at the very least, in high quarters." Then, with a facility for coining words (a facility shared by his fellow German-American Francis Lieber) Schurz wrote: "it was unfortunate that you sustained them [Democratic officers] in their power and positions with such inexhaustible longanimity after they had been found failing."

With an unconscious egotism which pervaded the whole letter Schurz vindicated his own motives and attitude: "I pray you most earnestly not to attribute the expressions of grief and anxiety coming from devoted friends like myself to a pettish feeling of disappointment for not 'seeing their peculiar views made sufficiently prominent.' When a man's whole heart is in a cause . . . he may be believed not to be governed by small personal pride." With an implied hint that the President did not know, as he did, what war was, the general referred to the brave faces of the thousands whom he commanded. They were entitled to life and happiness "as well as the rest of us." When he saw their faces around the campfires and reflected "that to-morrow they [might] be called upon to die . . . for a cause which . . . is perhaps doomed to fail, and thus to die in vain"—when he thought of these and other things including the "wailings of so many widows and orphans" and realized that all this might "be for nothing," his heart sank within him. The implication of it all was that such serious matters would never occur to Lincoln's mind. He concluded: "I do not know whether you have ever seen a battlefield. I assure you, Mr. President, it is a terrible sight." [1]

It was a busy time for Lincoln (late November 1862), with a serious military situation looming up following the appointment of Burnside as commander of the Army of the Potomac; but the overburdened President had to take time out to read and answer this bitterly personal and partisan complaint from Schurz. He answered it with a reproof. He began by saying that he had received and read the complaining letter, the purport of which was "that we lost the late elections and the administration is failing because the war is unsuccessful, and that I must not flatter myself that I am not justly to blame for it." Touching upon the general's slap as to appointing men who had their "heart in it," Lincoln asked "who is to be the judge of hearts, or of 'heart in it'?" The President then remarked: "If I must discard my own judgment, and take yours, I must also take that of others; and by the time I should reject all I should be advised to reject, I should have none left . . . ." He remembered noble service unto death on the part of Republicans (Baker, Lyon, etc.), but they had done no more than Democrats such as Kearny, Reno, and Mansfield. Having said this, he declined "the ungrateful task of comparing cases of failure." The letter was stiff without being bitter. Lincoln meant it as a refutation and as an indication that unreasonable complaints would not go unanswered. He signed himself: "Very truly Your friend." [2]

One hesitates to report unfavorably on such a man as Schurz, for in the whole course of his changing (or adapting) career he was to bring an invigorating element of liberal thought into American political life. Schurz was more than a man: he was an outstanding representative of a great group—the large foreign-born group whom Lincoln sincerely respected and whose friendship he very much needed and valued. The question "What about Schurz?" usually brought up the corollary: "What about the Germans?" One needs to go back of this November correspondence, and then forward, in order

[1] Schurz to Lincoln, Hq., 3d Div., 11 Corps, Centreville, Va., Nov. 20, 1862, R. T. L. Coll., 19638–42.

[2] Lincoln to Schurz, Nov. 24, 1862, photostat, A. Lincoln Assoc.

to understand the relations between Schurz and Lincoln, which on the whole were those of close association, friendship, and almost of confidential intimacy. The distinguished German-American had been one of a committee which notified Lincoln of his nomination, and had campaigned strenuously for his election in 1860. On June 18 of that year Lincoln wrote assuring Schurz that his support of Seward at Chicago in preference to Lincoln was "not even remembered," to which the candidate added: "no man stands nearer my heart than yourself." [3] On July 4, 1860, Schurz was the speaker of the day at a large Republican meeting at Springfield. At that time he was a guest in the Lincoln home and received from the new nominee an autographed copy of the *Debates.*

Under Lincoln's appointment Schurz served briefly as minister to Spain, a diplomatic service which was significant chiefly because of his dispatch (from San Ildefonso, September 14, 1861) urging abolition of slavery for its international importance in placing the war "upon a higher moral basis," a move which he deemed of equal value with military victories. Having resigned his Spanish mission, he was appointed brigadier general and had an important command in a series of major engagements, including Second Bull Run, Chancellorsville, and Gettysburg. If he found himself at odds with the Lincoln administration in November 1862, that was but an episode which he later wished to forget. In his *Reminiscences* he tells what happened after Lincoln's rebuking letter of November 24, 1862 (which, to be sure, was not half so rebuking as Schurz's of November 20). A messenger, he said, brought a note from Lincoln asking that Schurz visit him. There was cordial and friendly talk on that visit, at which Lincoln is reported to have said: "Well, I know that you are a warm anti-slavery man and a good friend to me. Now let me tell you all about it." When they had had their talk Lincoln remarked: "I guess we understand one another now, and it's all right." [4]

Schurz was one of those generals who, while offering superior counsel, constantly tended to carry his advice over into the political sphere. Being the man he was, one could hardly have expected him to keep out of politics. The Lincoln papers are loaded down with his frequent and voluminous letters to the President. Lincoln was to

[3] Lincoln to Schurz, June 18, 1860, photostat, A. Lincoln Assoc.

[4] *Reminiscences of Carl Schurz,* II, 396.

learn in the election year of 1864 that Schurz wanted to leave the military front, to be invited to Washington, and to serve in the coming political canvass, but the President was to reply that it "would be detrimental to the public service." "Allow me to suggest [added the President] that if you wish to remain in the military service, it is very dangerous for you to get temporarily out of it; because, with a Major General once out, it is next to impossible for even the President to get him in again." Becoming more explicit, Lincoln explained: "quite surely speaking in the North, and fighting in the South, at the same time are not possible; nor could I be justified to detail any officer to the political campaign during its continuance and then return him to the army." [5]

That was how Lincoln felt in March 1864, more than two months before his renomination. As it turned out, however, Schurz did engage actively in the political campaign of 1864, making a number of speeches: [6] he was one of those military leaders—of whom the younger Francis P. Blair, Edward D. Baker, Robert C. Schenck, and John A. Logan were examples—whose interests and activities were divided between military duties and participation in politics. That Schurz had also the talents of an orator, author, and editor will indicate something of his vigor and versatility.[7]

It speaks well for both Lincoln and Schurz that they could differ so sharply, each with his own sincere nature, and yet remain good friends. It also speaks well for Lincoln's tactics in human affairs that he realized the value of a face-to-face talk. Schurz knew that the President was generous toward him; Lincoln knew that he could not afford to lose the services of so important a leader. Both men, so different in background and temperament, were devoted to the public service and were in agreement as to ultimate goals while favoring different methods. It was part of the greatness of Lincoln that such differences did not matter and that a personally irritating episode did not cause him, in a mood of resentment, to allow a hopeless breaking of relations with a difficult man whose sacrifice would have been a disadvantage to the nation's cause.

---

[5] Letters of Lincoln to Schurz, Mar. 13 and Mar. 23, 1864, photostats, A. Lincoln Assoc.

[6] *Reminiscences of Carl Schurz,* III, 106.

[7] For new light on Schurz as author, see *Charles Sumner: An Essay by Carl Schurz,* ed. by Arthur Reed Hogue, Univ. of Ill. Press, 1951.

VII

When one of the governors turned up "bristling with complaints in relation to the number of troops required from his State" the matter was referred from the provost marshal general, General James B. Fry, to the secretary of war, and from that stormy individual to the President. After an interview in which the state executive presented his "ultimatum" to the nation's Chief, "the Governor returned [to see Fry], and said with a pleasant smile that he was going home by the next train," making no reference to the session he had had with the President nor the business in hand. Fry continues the account:

"As soon as I could see Lincoln, I said: 'Mr. President, I am very anxious to learn how you disposed of Governor ——. He went to your office from the War Department in a towering rage. I suppose you found it necessary to make large concessions to him, as he returned from you entirely satisfied.'

" 'Oh, no,' he replied, 'I did not concede anything. *You* know how that Illinois farmer managed the big log that lay in the middle of his field! To the inquiries of his neighbors one Sunday, he announced that he had got rid of the big log. "Got rid of it!" said they, "how did you do it? It was too big to haul out, too knotty to split, and too wet and soggy to burn; what did you do?" "Well, now, boys," replied the farmer, "if you won't divulge the secret, I'll tell you how I got rid of it—*I ploughed around it.*" Now,' said Lincoln, 'don't tell anybody, but that's the way I got rid of Governor ——. *I ploughed around him,* but it took me three mortal hours to do it, and I was afraid every minute he'd see what I was at.' "[1]

Lincoln was tactful even when gently rebuking Governor Beriah Magoffin of Kentucky, though that official's attitude toward the President was that of antagonistic defiance. The governor was urging that the Union military force in Kentucky be removed beyond the limits of the state. Lincoln was not giving in. Though he could not comply with the governor's request, he did take occasion to explain all his reasons for not complying; then he put in a graceful rebuke: "I most cordially sympathize with your Excellency, in the wish to preserve the peace of my own native State, Kentucky; but it is with

[1] General James B. Fry, in Rice, 399–400.

regret I search, and cannot find, in your not very short letter, any declaration, or intimation, that you entertain any desire for the preservation of the Federal Union." [2]

This thoughtfulness in human situations was an integral part of Lincoln's technique as President. It is hardly too much to say that it enabled him to keep from being unhorsed. In September, 1862, some of the governors joined in a conference whose purpose, in the exaggerated statement of the New York *Herald,* was to "depose" Lincoln, or to request him to resign. This was after Pope's defeat at Second Bull Run and things were going badly.

The governors had their own meeting, then some of them called on Lincoln.[3] They thought it was their movement. Lincoln calmly associated himself with their patriotic purpose for a better prosecution of the war, clipping their wings and stealing their thunder; but he handled the whole matter so skillfully that the episode, which started as a formidable threat to the President's leadership, ended with a collective gubernatorial endorsement of the nation's Chief.[4]

Again, in December 1862 after Burnside's defeat at Fredericksburg, Lincoln was faced with a concerted attack by Republican senators who met in caucus; according to Senator Browning "enemies" were "doing all in their power to break him down." Lincoln conferred with his cabinet, then smilingly met the senators, never failing for a moment to keep the reins in his hands. Such was Lincoln's adroit planning and exquisite tact in this crisis that the complaining senators, who had planned a remaking of the cabinet, found after they had shot their bolt that the President was still in command, with the cabinet unchanged.[5] Yet all this was done without an explosion, without open hostility, and no one was humiliated. The prairie statesman had met the test.

Preservation of equanimity is usually conceived as a result, or a victory won, but it should rather be viewed as a process or a continuing contest. One does not conquer one's temper once and for all. Self-control is not a knockout, but succession of rounds. Lincoln was at it all the time. Can we see him at it?

---

2 Lincoln to Gov. Magoffin, Aug. 24, 1861, orig. autograph, Ill. State Hist. Lib. Lincoln kept a copy in his own hand; R. T. L. Coll., 11345.

3 *Lincoln the President,* II, 229–232.

4 W. B. Hesseltine, *Lincoln and the War Governors,* 249–272.

5 *Lincoln the President,* II, 238–249.

We can. One of Lincoln's secretaries came in one day to report that Gov. H. R. Gamble of Missouri had written a very irritable letter to the President. That letter is in the Lincoln Papers and it is a sizzler. Gamble accused Lincoln of insulting him and of saying things "unbecoming your station." [6] It was a moment that called for presidential self-control. In his own handwriting, as we find it in his papers, Lincoln wrote to Gamble: "My Private Secretary has just brought me a letter saying it is a very *'cross'* one from you, about mine to Gen. Schofield, recently published in the Democrat. As I am trying to preserve my own temper, by avoiding irritants, so far as practicable, I have declined to read the cross letter." Lincoln then added a few words on the subject-matter of the correspondence. This need not detain us, except that he said: "I was totally unconscious of any malice, or disrespect towards you, or of using any expression which should offend you." [7]

This incident affords almost a ringside view of the President's continuing struggle to avoid being thrown off balance by bad feeling. His mail had been screened. The governor's letter had been brought to him. He declined to read it, yet he answered it. By the very process of writing out the answer with his own pen he devoted himself deliberately and calmly to the effort for control. He overcame the impetuosity which, as a kind of involuntary reflex, would have seized and controlled a less disciplined mind. He disposed of the irritating factor in the incoming letter. Then he told Gamble that in his own feeling there was no element of malice or disrespect. That task was finished and the next item could be taken up. But if feelings had been allowed to boil over, the overburdened Chief could not so successfully have performed the day's work.

It has already become evident that one of Lincoln's traits was to give attention when a man's feelings were hurt and if possible to put in a healing word. This thoughtfulness was so often exhibited as to constitute a habit. An example was the case of General S. R. Curtis,

---

[6] It is unnecessary to quote at length from Gamble's letter. Here is a sample: "Occupying the position which I reluctantly accepted at the call of my State, animated by no desire but for the restoration of the Union and the prosperity of my country, I am obliged to say to you that your insult published over the land was most undeserved, and in our relations most unbecoming your station." Gamble to Lincoln, St. Louis, July 13, 1863, R. T. L. Coll., 24776–80.

[7] Lincoln to Gamble, July 23, 1863, R. T. L. Coll., 25067.

who occupied a "delicate position . . . in the Fremont embroglio [*sic*]." Curtis wrote to his brother after the service of Frémont in Missouri was closed, saying he had just received "the most exquisite little note" from the President, which he copied for his brother's perusal. "I snatch a moment," Lincoln had written, "to both thank you, & apologize to you. In all sincerity I thank you for the complete and entirely satisfactory manner in which you executed the trusts I confided to you . . . ." Referring to a general's report in which Curtis had been wronged, Lincoln added: ". . . it never would have been done, if I had had the least suspicion it was to be done." He concluded: "Being done I thought the maxim 'least said soonest mended' applied to the case."

There followed, in Curtis's letter to his brother, a tribute to Lincoln which ought to be better known. "I had always perceived," he wrote, "a cordial friendship was entertained by the President for me and I take this in the hurry and pressure of the times as a gracious legacy, a compensation for many jibes I have received . . . . The purity of our Revolutionary fathers is not universal in these latter days. The President is an exception, his purity is everywhere conspicuous." [8]

Mindful to avoid treading on others, Lincoln was, nevertheless, a man who felt keenly the cruel hurts that were inflicted upon him. When besmirched by men on whom he should have counted he was quoted as saying confidentially to a friend: "I would rather be dead than, as President, thus abused in the house of my friends." [9] Unlike other men, however, he did not make his feelings a matter of complaint.

That the colored people loved Lincoln, indeed the Lincolns, is a matter related not only to the enduring folklore of a people, but in particular to the personal dealing of the man himself. In his meeting with colored friends there was complete absence of condescension or embarrassment. Toward Frederick Douglass, eminent colored orator and antislavery leader, who took a hand in the recruitment of colored troops in Massachusetts, Lincoln showed a marked friendship. The Negro leader, by his own report, met Lincoln a number of

---

8 S. R. Curtis to his brother, Hq. St. Louis Dist., Dec. 16, 1861, Curtis MSS., Huntington Lib.

9 Ward H. Lamon, *Recollections of Abraham Lincoln*, ed. by Dorothy Lamon Teillard, 261.

times, once on an invitation to tea at Soldiers' Home. On a social occasion at the White House, amid a "sea of . . . elegance," Lincoln's face "lighted up" as he caught sight of Douglass. "In all my interviews with Mr. Lincoln," wrote the colored leader, "I was impressed with his entire freedom from popular prejudice against the colored race. He was the first great man that I talked with in the United States freely, who in no single instance reminded me of the difference between himself and myself, of the difference of color . . . ." [10] This attitude of the President has significance in race relations. As the two men conferred about important questions—use of colored troops, their uniforms, equal treatment with whites, proper respect for them as prisoners—Douglass was touched and heartened by Lincoln's genuine friendliness.

VIII

Lincoln had no use for hatreds and personal difficulties. Let "bygones be bygones," he said; "Let past differences as nothing be." [1] Late in the presidency he said: "For my own part I have striven and shall strive to avoid placing any obstacle in the way [of a nonpartisan effort to save "our common country"]. So long as I have been here I have not willingly planted a thorn in any man's bosom." [2] An opponent of Lincoln's policy wrote: "Mr. Lincoln had no resentments. He had kind words for men who bitterly assailed him. He joined in no outcry against men in civil or military life who went astray." [3] Hay wrote of him: "It seems utterly impossible for the President to conceive of the possibility of any good resulting from a rigorous and exemplary course of punishing political dereliction. His favorite expression is, 'I am in favor of short statutes of limitation in politics.' " [4]

It should not be supposed, however, that Lincoln was always gentle.

10 Frederick Douglass, in Rice, *Reminiscences,* 189–190, 192–193. As an example of direct contact between Douglass and the President we have the distinguished Negro's reference to "the interview with . . . your Excellency . . . a few days ago . . . ." Douglass to Lincoln, Rochester, N. Y., Aug. 29, 1864, R. T. L. Coll., 35652–53.

1 Speech at Republican banquet, Chicago, Dec. 10, 1856, *Ill. State Jour.,* Dec. 16, 1856.

2 Post-election response to serenade, Nov. 10, 1864, photostat, A. Lincoln Assoc.

3 George W. Julian, in Rice, 60–61.

4 This entry was made on a day of great political gloom for the President and his party—August 23, 1864. It was on that day that Lincoln wrote a memorandum expressing doubt of his re-election. Dennett, ed., *Diaries . . . of John Hay,* 239.

If a man's conduct called for reproof, he would let him have it. Some of those who sought to use Lincoln were referred to as "thieves, counterfeiters, blacklegs—the scum and curse of the earth." Lobbyists for special interests crowded the hotel bars and could by no means be kept out of the White House. One of these is pictured by one of Lincoln's secretarial staff as coming out of Lincoln's room propelled by a large foot.[5] Lincoln could not always conceal his irritation when men in responsible civil or military office would get their personal affairs in a snarl and then intrude their quarrels upon the President. On one such occasion he wrote to Senator Pomeroy of Kansas: "I wish you and [General James H.] Lane would make a sincere effort to get out of the mood you are in. I[t] does neither of you any good—it gives you the means of tormenting my life out of me, and nothing else." [6]

The subject of Lincoln's personal thoughtfulness, his tact and gracious dealing, runs on and on. As one goes into it fully, it becomes a significant series of case studies. Lincoln was tactful toward General Patterson, whom he refused to blame after Bull Run, and to whom he spoke, said Patterson, "with a manner so frank, candid, and manly as to secure my respect, confidence, and good-will." [7] He was exquisitely tactful toward the venerable General Scott, easing that veteran's retirement with unusual honors and marks of high respect.[8] McClernand, though an embarrassment to Lincoln, could have testified as to his graciousness. An eminent historian, who had written to the President on Divine Providence, was informed: "I esteem it a high honor to have received a note from Mr. Bancroft." [9] A certain Captain Young, in some difficulty as to his military service, had reason to be grateful to the President for intervening to give him "another chance." [10]

Another captain, J. Madison Cutts, Jr., had the honor—for it was such—of being reprimanded by the President in so exquisite a manner as to be not merely chastened, but personally cheered, uplifted in

---

[5] W. O. Stoddard, *Inside the White House in War Times*, 58.

[6] Lincoln to Pomeroy, May 12, 1864, photostat, A. Lincoln Assoc.

[7] F. B. Carpenter, *The Inner Life of Abraham Lincoln: Six Months at the White House*, 137.

[8] *Lincoln the President*, I, 394.

[9] Lincoln to Bancroft, Nov. 18, 1861, copy in Nicolay's hand, A. Lincoln Assoc.

[10] Nicolay and Hay, *Works*, VII, 61–62 (Dec. 6, 1861).

morale, and specially favored by the highest official in the land.

Cutts was the brother-in-law and close friend of Stephen A. Douglas. In compliance with Douglas's request, Lincoln had appointed him captain in the regular army; in his dying words (June 1861) Douglas had administered to the young man a special oath of loyalty to the United States. In the course of the war the young captain gave courageous and costly service to the cause and received severe battle wounds, for which in later years he was to be awarded a triple medal of honor. In spite of this, being a spirited and combative person, he had a stormy wartime career. Quarrels and feuds led him into personal difficulties, and in 1863 at Cincinnati he was subjected to court martial for two offenses, one of which was an altercation with a fellow officer, Captain Charles G. Hutton.[11] Cutts was charged with having used insulting words, putting his opponent in the category of "blackguards," "blacklegs," and "bullies." Found guilty, he was given the severe sentence: "To be dismissed the service."

The sentence of dismissal from the army was commuted and it was ordered that Cutts rejoin his regiment after a reprimand by the President. When the Lincoln papers were opened in July 1947 this Lincolnian gem came to light. Fragments from the document had been quoted in various places,[12] but it was not until that opening that the document in full, and in its true character, was known. It is a sheet of paper dimly written in pencil, a draft memorandum of an oral reprimand. It is only by following up the matter in the musty records in the National Archives that the attendant facts (Cutts's court-martial, the sentence, its commutation, Cutts's manuscript account of receiving the oral reprimand from Lincoln, etc.) are given. In the Lincoln memorandum the reprimand was worded as follows:

> Although what I am now to say to you is to be, in form, a reprimand, it is not intended to add a pang to what you have already suffered. . . . You have too much of life yet before you, and have shown too much

---

11 The other offense was that of peering through a transom at a lady undressing in a hotel in Cincinnati. The court-martial proceeding (in the National Archives) has the record. See also Dennett ed., *Diaries . . . of John Hay,* 53 (July 18, 1863).

12 Nicolay and Hay, *Complete Works,* I, 151–152 (footnote to Lincoln's letter to W. G. Anderson, Oct. 31, 1840); *Abr. Lincoln Quar.,* I, 91; Sandburg, *Prairie Years,* II, 277. For these references the common source is Nicolay and Hay, but they did not indicate what the document was, nor quote more than a fragment, nor mention Cutts. In the real sense the notable Lincoln reprimand was a discovery after the opening of the Lincoln papers in 1947.

of promise as an officer, for your future to be lightly surrendered. . . . The advice of a father to his son "Beware of entrance to a quarrel, but being in, bear it that the opposed may beware of thee" is good, and yet not the best. Quarrel not at all. No man resolved to make the most of himself can spare time for personal contention. Still less can he afford to take all the consequences, including the vitiating of his temper, and the loss of self-control.

Yield larger things to which you can show no more than equal right, and yield lesser ones, though clearly your own. Better give your path to a dog than be bitten by him in contesting for the right. Even killing the dog would not cure the bite.

In the mood indicated deal henceforth with your fellowmen, and especially with your brother officers, and even the unpleasant events you are passing from will not have been profitless to you.[13]

The patient President facing the young officer and administering a reprimand that became a gracious interview has been passed by in Lincoln biography, but this classic comment on quarreling, this supreme improvement on Polonius, will henceforth be kept in memory. It is so with many another neglected episode. One may take the more famous things that Lincoln did—the lofty eloquence of the Gettysburg address, the generous wisdom of his design for peace, the whole complex of leadership in a fearful crisis—and to all this must be added that priceless element of human thoughtfulness and personal understanding.

Such understanding did not come by chance. Like other things with Lincoln it was the result of planning and study. Where episodes of personal dealing were "unimportant" in that they touched no great public policy or well known individual, they nevertheless revealed much as to the type of man Lincoln was. The very fact that such dealing was close to earth and part of his everyday job is significant, for there is inspiration for more people in the thought of Lincoln working steadily at a hard job day after day than in matters that are remote and high-flown. Though applied in dealings that seemed small, his craftsmanship in the human art was one of his greatest achievements. It was an attribute to freedom and equality, to man's dignity, to self discipline, to the niceties of courtesy, to successful living with men—in a word, to democracy itself.

---

[13] Autograph document unsigned, R. T. L. Coll., 27496 (Oct. 26, 1863). Lincoln's handwriting, partly rather dim, starts in ink and continues in pencil.

APPENDIX

THE OPENING OF THE LINCOLN PAPERS

IN THE summer of 1947 a new domain was opened in the world of Lincoln research with the release of that vast treasure, the Robert Todd Lincoln Collection of the Papers of Abraham Lincoln. For all the years since Lincoln's death this great body of material had been denied to scholars in general; only Nicolay and Hay had used the documents for a life of Lincoln. Together with a feeling of frustration at this refusal of access to sources that historians needed, there had been added that lure of charm and conjecture that attaches to the unknown. Since, after being opened, the papers were found to constitute a most important and voluminous body of sources the nature of which is still imperfectly known, it is appropriate that some treatment of them be given in these pages.

I

What had happened to the papers, what were their travels, place of deposit, and guardianship through the years? This story is told with full information and unusual literary charm by David C. Mearns in *The Lincoln Papers* (2 vols., 1948). One must read that book to have the authentic details which can only be given in briefest summary here. Lincoln's home, his Springfield office, the lining of his hat, his pockets, and a rather famous carpetbag in 1861, may be mentioned in passing as temporary archival depositories; but the bulk of the collection during Lincoln's own lifetime reposed in those White House pigeonholes for which Lincoln prepared the labels and to which he often referred. Nor should one suppose that the President was neglectful of his documents or unmindful of their importance.

After Lincoln's death his papers were in the custody of David Davis, administrator of the Lincoln estate, who kept them for a time in a bank in Bloomington, Illinois. Some time in the 1870's John G. Nicolay took charge (though not ownership) of them in his office in the United States Capitol, he being marshal of the Supreme Court of the United States. Nicolay and Hay used them in preparing their ten-volume biography of Lincoln (1890), and in editing his so-called *Complete Works* (2 vols., 1894).

The idea that these "two everlasting angels" (Hay's phrase) had full freedom to use the manuscripts unreservedly is a misconception. The full Collection was open to them, but their work was done by the proprietary authorization of Robert Todd Lincoln and subject to his approval. From the time of Nicolay's resignation as marshal of the Supreme Court in 1887 to his death in 1901 the papers were kept in his home in Washington. Then they found their way to the state department while Hay was secretary of state (1901–1905). The first suggestion that they be deposited in the Library of Congress seems to have come in a letter from the Librarian, Herbert Putnam, to Robert Todd Lincoln, December 31, 1901. This letter, with its suggestion of the most reasonable disposition of the Collection, brought no result. For years after Hay's death in 1905 the papers were kept in Robert Lincoln's office in Chicago while he was president of the Pullman Company. When he resigned from that position in 1911 the Collection went with him, being kept in his residence in Washington (Georgetown), and at Hildene, his summer home at Manchester, Vermont. It was from the Georgetown home that the papers were secretly taken in a wagon to the Library of Congress on May 6, 1919. Eight trunks of them were thus received.

This placing of the papers was only a deposit; full ownership and control was retained by Robert Todd Lincoln. Meanwhile through the years one Lincoln biographer after another was refused access to the Collection, with Robert's brief explanation that the matter of using them had fully been attended to and the information which they contained had been "exhausted" by Nicolay and Hay.

Up to 1919, and from then on until 1923, there was no formal closing of the papers; it was simply that Robert had full command of their use or non-use, and, after Nicolay and Hay, all investigators were denied access. (The case of Katherine Helm, who had a brief peep at the Collection without using it, was the one exception, and this was unimportant.) In the years following 1919 Robert was a frequent visitor to the Library of Congress, where he permitted and watched over the preparation of an index. This project, however, was discontinued after no more than ten percent of the Collection had been covered.

Finally, on January 23, 1923, Robert executed a formal deed of gift, giving the Collection in perpetuity to the United States of America, to be deposited in the Library of Congress for all the people, on condition that the papers were to be put in a sealed vault and withheld from inspection until twenty-one years after the donor's death. He died on July 26, 1926. (On January 16, 1926, Robert had made a modification of his gift to permit his wife to grant permission to see the papers. This, however, was for a limited "special purpose," and it was never effective as a means of opening the papers to any investigator. At this time Robert also formally authorized the making of a complete index.)

Meanwhile, and thereafter, various garbled accounts and uninformed guesses arose to create a sad state of confusion as to the disposition and probable significance of the papers. There were reports that Robert had burned the manuscripts, that he had "purged" them, that they occupied only one trunk, that this was a kind of "mystery trunk," that the closing of the papers was to extend for fifty years, and that this closing was actuated by various alleged motives.

All such accounts were idle conjectures. Perhaps it was these guesses, along with uncomfortable pressure to learn the contents of the Collection, that caused statements to be made tending to play down the importance of the manuscripts and to create the impression that they contained, or were believed to contain, little of significant value.

From 1923 the story of the papers can be quickly told. During the Axis War they were temporarily kept at the University of Virginia at Charlottesville. Then they were brought back to Washington, arranged, repaired, indexed, mounted, bound, and locked up (all with great secrecy) in preparation for the opening in 1947.

II

What about the picture that has arisen in the popular mind of Robert Todd Lincoln burning his father's papers? Perhaps the obvious answer is simply to go to the Library of Congress and see the immense Collection, bound in 194 handsome volumes, with approximately 200 pieces, well preserved and very much intact, in each volume. One may then inquire: How did the story of the alleged burning get started? There are various versions, one of which is found in *Across the Busy Years* (II, 375–378), by Nicholas Murray Butler. In this book of "Recollections and Reflections" Butler tells of a visit in August 1923 to the home of Robert Lincoln at Manchester, Vermont. The President of Columbia University had just returned from a trip to Europe, and immediately after reaching Manchester, he was told by his and Robert's friend, Horace G. Young, that he must go and see Robert, who was said to be on the point of burning a lot of his father's papers.

According to this account, Butler went the following morning to Robert's home. There he saw "an old-fashioned trunk . . . near one of the bookshelves." Being questioned as to the trunk (as Butler told it), Robert said, "it contains only some family papers which I am going to burn." Continuing his recollection, Butler wrote that he remonstrated with Robert, reminding him that his father belonged to the nation and that these papers were therefore national property. In the strongest terms he admonished him, for heaven's sake, not to destroy the manuscripts. There was "excited and indeed difficult conversation," concluding with Butler's suggestion that the son should deposit the papers in the Library of Congress "and fix a date before which they shall not be opened." "That he did," added Butler.

One does not know fully what really happened at this visit of Butler to Hildene. The plain implication is that the trunk contained the famous collection of the papers of Abraham Lincoln (though this was not made clear), that Robert was about to burn a lot of them, that it was Butler who then and there persuaded the son to make the deposit in the Library of Congress with the time limitation, and that this disposition of the Collection occurred *after* and because of that interview. By this account the credit for placing the papers in the Library was represented as belonging to Dr. Butler.

One need not inquire into the dimming of Butler's recollections between the time of the event and the writing of his memoirs. It is sufficient to note the following facts. The interview, as related in *Across the Busy Years,* occurred just after Butler's return from Europe in August 1923; the date is further confirmed by his statement that he and Robert then had "a chat after a considerable absence abroad, during which time President Harding had died and Calvin Coolidge had succeeded to the presidency." (Harding died on August 2, 1923.) But the clinching fact is that the Lincoln papers had been deposited in the Library of Congress four years before that (1919), and Robert's deed of gift permanently bequeathing them with the twenty-one year limitation had been executed seven months previously (January 23, 1923). We do not know what to believe as to that "old-fashioned trunk" which Butler supposed to contain the papers of Abraham Lincoln. What we do know is that eight trunks of the actual papers had been put safely in the Library of Congress, which has ever since remained their permanent depository.

Butler himself was not sure of his own memories, as is shown by a letter he wrote to Herbert Putnam, Librarian of Congress, on December 18, 1928, asking as to the date when Robert sent to the Library "a box or trunk containing a collection of family papers, with the prescription that they should not be opened for a number of years, I think it was fifty." Butler added that he was "trying to reconstruct" the story of his talk with Robert, and a reminder of the date would help him do so. The facts were promptly transmitted to Butler, who nevertheless published the above-given account in the *Saturday Evening Post* on February 11, 1939. Later he used the same material in *Across the Busy Years.*

The only purpose of giving this summary here is to set the record straight as to the alleged intent to burn and the supposed role of Dr. Butler in the disposition of the Collection. After a careful survey, Mearns writes (*Lincoln Papers,* I, 127: ". . . it has been impossible to adjust that statement [concerning the "one trunk" and the Butler-Lincoln interview of August 1923] to any influence on, or relation with, the delivery of eight trunks [to the Library of Congress] in May 1919."

As to the motive for closing the papers, there is no evidence that it was done because of any family skeleton, which there was not, nor because of revelations of "treason" in the cabinet, however much of a headache Stanton may have been to his Chief. To reconstruct the motive as nearly as is possible, Robert is on record as having thought (contrary to fact) that Nicolay and Hay had made complete use of the papers. In addition—this also is a matter of record—he seems to have feared that some of the documents might give pain to persons yet living, which implies that he was not destroying such documents. Finally, there is no doubt that he was annoyed by incessant requests from investigators, particularly Beveridge, whose friendliness to the Herndon interpretation caused him to be distrusted.

Whatever may be said as to these motives, Robert's ultimate disposition of the Collection, except for the twenty-one year limitation, was admirable. If care had not been taken to guard the Collection and keep it intact, the papers might have become scattered, sold, lost, or mutilated by that miserable practice—all too common—of clipping off signatures of letters. Instead of that, the collection was, with the exception of a very few items, held together by Robert Todd Lincoln. An example of an item given away by Robert—and this was very unusual—was Lincoln's manuscript of the speech he gave from a White House window on the night of November 10, 1864. (The Library of Congress has a copy.) This valuable document was held in the family until April 18, 1916, when Robert presented the original to Congressman John W. Dwight of New York in gratitude for the congressman's service in the establishment of the Lincoln Memorial at Washington. Such instances, however, were very few. What the Library of Congress has is substantially the R. T. Lincoln Collection of his father's papers. In addition, it should be added that the Library has many other Lincoln documents either in originals or in copies.

The Library performed its task well, discreetly suggesting and keeping alive the idea of the Library as depository, fulfilling the terms of the deed of gift, holding the Collection in safe keeping, repairing the papers, mounting them, putting them in chronological order, preparing an "index" (or inventory), and binding them in handsome, permanent volumes. In addition the Library made ready for the opening as an occasion of importance and dignity, prepared many news releases, and served the needs of researchers in the following weeks and months. It is highly appropriate that the papers now occupy a revered place along with the voluminous manuscripts of Washington, Jefferson, and hundreds of other men, North and South, whose record has enduring significance in American history.

III

When the papers were opened, just after midnight in the earliest moments of July 26, 1947, the event was a mixture of high emotion and bustling excitement. The combinations were twirled and the safes unlocked to the clicking of news cameras. The volumes—194 of them—were brought out. More news pictures were taken as this or that Lincoln student was shown opening and reading some part of the collection. Then followed something rather unique: an all-night session as investigators pursued their searches, going from papers to index and back to papers, gathering in huddles to compare findings, and taking hurried notes for articles to be written or radio talks to be given that very day.

Through the night hours the labor was relieved by the booming laughter of Carl Sandburg. It was by his pen, in an excellent job of spot reporting published on the night of the opening day, that the public got the best immediate account of the occasion itself: the lighter moments at the dinner in the Whittall Pavilion of the Library of Congress, the repetition of last-minute conjectures as to what would be dug up, the battery of cameras, the floodlights, the Librarian's intoning of the deed of gift, the merriment with "a catch in it" as the significance of the occasion was borne in upon those present, the moment of unveiling, the samplings among the scores of volumes, the feeling of satisfaction as the mass of manuscripts came "out of its long hiding . . . into the public domain."

As one of the assembled students expressed it, quoting Keats, "Then felt I like some watcher of the skies, when a new planet swims within his ken." Yet, along with the thrill of the unveiling, there was something in the newspaper coverage of the event that was at least partly unfortunate. The wide public interest and desire for an instant report together with the fact that news writers have to work quickly, led to an over-extension of journalistic lines, with the result that incorrect ideas concerning the papers became well-nigh universal.

It should be remembered that the papers were opened on a Saturday morning—a monumental collection of them—and then one writer after another, writing no later than Saturday or Sunday, gave out sweeping generalizations which, whether intentionally or not, produced the impression that they had seen the whole collection. These premature pronouncements were quite misleading, and overnight, in addition to all the myths attaching to the Lincoln theme, another was added—the myth that the opening was a disappointment and that the Collection contains little of interest. Assuredly no one who has carefully worked with the papers—which requires long sustained labor—would give support to that legend.

For years an attitude had persisted concerning the papers and it was not readily sloughed off. The opening had occurred, but for hurried writers the cogitations that had been accumulated and intensified prior to the opening still lingered. In that long doubtful period a kind of synthetic answer had been supplied, often ignorantly, in efforts to satisfy the human mind in its unwillingness to tolerate a vacuum in any absorbing field of human knowledge. Months before the opening, various writers had been asked what they "expected to find." It was like the burlesque examination question: "Name the undiscovered islands of the Pacific Ocean." A variety of expectations and predictions came forth. Some who expressed themselves wondered if they might find things that no well informed student would have thought of looking for.

It was different, however, with the more serious student. He had maintained a healthy skepticism as to guesses and rumors. Now, as he became absorbed in the actual examination of the papers, all the miscellaneous and often amazing things that had been said as to what they might or might not contain seemed at once outmoded. Reality proved more exciting than any forecast.

And there was another feeling of the researcher—the sense of being a part of that age, living with Lincoln, handling the very papers he handled, sharing his deep concern over events and issues, noting his patience when complaints poured in, hearing a Lincolnian laugh, feeling a cumulative sense of unending presidential burdens and of hope deferred. This feeling that the age of Lincoln had come to life was nothing forced or imaginary; it was a real factor. If this suggests enthusiasm, the researcher must plead guilty to that charge, but it was an enthusiasm that came with that accent on reality that arises from being at the source of things, that realization of authenticity that accompanies the physical handling of original documents whose very penmanship revealed the haste, emotion, or urgency of a momentous period.

IV

To appraise the Collection would be to write an elaborate work, which would have to be a coöperative enterprise. An initial step toward such appraisal would be to discard certain superficial ideas and misconceptions. One is asked whether there is anything "sensational" in the papers. Certain unfavorable things are revealed as to the conduct of public men other than Lincoln. Would that be called "sensational"? When one asks for the sensational, what does he have in mind? After continued study of the documents in the original the present writer finds this kind of query a bit off key, as if a statesman's record or the inner history of the nation in an era of supreme crisis could be narrowed down to a short order of murder for breakfast or scandal for lunch. What one finds is significance, flavor, human interest, character revelation, grist for the historian's mill, not cheap sensation.

That other question which has become over-familiar—whether there is "anything new" in the papers—may be answered confidently in the affirmative. What we have in this Collection is the very essence of historical data. It is source material a thousand fold. It is the stuff out of which history is formed. It is original, not second-hand or retrospective. It is the impression of the event as it was happening or the thought or feeling as it was struck off or felt. The Collection is notable in that it knows not of the assassination. It knows only the living Lincoln. Despite the fact that Nicolay and Hay made use of the papers in their multi-volume biography, the newness of the Collection is largely unimpaired. Much of it—indeed the more flavorful part—was passed over by those writers. The papers are highly valuable for the kind of book that Nicolay and Hay did not write.

In sheer immensity the Collection is most remarkable. There are over 41,000 pieces, with millions of handwritten words. But the quality of the material is even more worthy of remark than its bulk. To exhibit the Collection illustratively by selection of particular samples is not easy. Many items could be chosen for that purpose, but that is the difficulty. After the culling out of a hundred specimens there would remain further hundreds, as truly typical or representative, that would be equally worthy of emphasis. Mention has been made of the "index," but the *contents* of these letters and documents have not been indexed. There is only an inventory of items by the surnames of those from whom and to whom they were written. The lack of any topical index makes it necessary for the researcher to turn the many pages of the Collection itself (in the original or in microfilm). The inventory just mentioned is highly useful, but there is no short cut—no concordance, calendar, or topical guide—by which one can be told where to look for material on a particular topic of research. For example, the Collection reveals much as to Unionists in the South, but, as with other subjects, the pertinent letters are not listed under that heading. (It should be added that for certain purposes the finding of material is assisted by the chronological arrangement.)

The papers are especially important for the presidency. Only about five per cent of the material belongs to the period before 1860, though the documents in this earlier group are often of special interest, among them a letter from Lincoln's stepbrother, John D. Johnston (May 25, 1849) telling that Thomas Lincoln, in expectation of death, "craves to see you all the time & he wonts you to Come if you ar able to git hure, for you are his only Child that is, of his own flush & blood . . . ." This letter with its backwoods spelling is assuredly of greater historical significance than trashy utterings in which Lincoln's paternity has been ignorantly challenged.

People will have different preferences as to their favorites among the riches of the Collection. The manuscript of Lincoln's farewell address at Springfield, February 11, 1861, would rank high on any list. What home meant to him as he departed "with a task . . . greater than that which rested upon Washington" is poignantly revealed in the jerky strokes of this document as it was written down on the train, partly in Lincoln's hand and partly in Nicolay's. There have been variant versions of this speech, but here we have the text as Lincoln wanted it remembered. High on the list of favorites also would be the draft of Lincoln's letter to Mrs. Gurney, his memorandum in reply to Seward's amazing "Thoughts for the President's consideration" (April 1, 1861), texts of his Mexican War speech, the worksheets of the 1861 inaugural, and the message to the special session of Congress, July 4, 1861. Public affairs, of course, were not all, and one finds special human interest in the letter of Lincoln to his wife (August 8, 1863), giving just the kind of familiar news and comment, including the latest about Tad's "Nanny Goat," which one would expect from an American husband writing to his wife who was away on a visit. And, for another choice item, few would exclude the President's exquisite reprimand to a spirited young captain, J. Madison Cutts, his personal friend and a brother-in-law of Senator Douglas.

One big factor showing the importance of the Collection is that of preliminary drafts which Lincoln made and kept. Even where the finished product has been long available it is of great interest to trace the document through those earlier stages which show Lincoln thinking out what he wrote, considering every word, striking out and inserting, recopying, and coming through with a result to which, not until then, he placed his signature. In this we see Lincoln the lawyer choosing his words for their unmistakable meaning, as well as Lincoln the literary artist seeking to summon forth the utmost rhythm and magic of the English language.

Not only did Lincoln weigh his sentences for their literary effect, which he unfailingly did in important papers as well as in ordinary intercourse; the Collection also shows his courteous effort in a personal situation to seek the utmost in skilled human relations. His letters have at times a classic quality in this respect. It has already been shown in this volume, and it is repeatedly illustrated in the Collection, that if Lincoln had a reproachful letter on his mind he would sometimes work it out with all the care devoted to a finished product, and then, on reconsideration, decide not to send it. He would not impulsively pull the trigger on a letter that was likely to misfire. One can yet read these unsent letters, for they were not thrown away.

An examination of the Collection is valuable for that kind of study which is concerned with the tracing of public speeches and papers to learn their provenance or the manner of their coming into being. By this is meant, not a mere textual investigation to determine the correct final wording, nor literary criticism alone, but, in addition to these, a kind of examination that seeks to bring together the factors that went into the preparation of a public speech, letter, or message. As to the notable first inaugural, for example, along with the literary and the strictly textual aspect, one needs to look into the whole wretched situation facing the country, the manner of Lincoln's approach to adjustment, the prudent consultation with his advisers, the numerous revisions of the address as it went through various handwritten and printed versions, and the ultimate product in which advice was taken and certain parts made over, yet without marring the whole effect of the speech in completed form. One could rewrite the story of secession and the plunge downward into war in terms of this speech of Lincoln's. Such an analysis would bring out Lincoln's emphasis on adjustment, non-provocation, and the utter needlessness of war between North and South.

Of course this inaugural was more than a speech. It was the announcement of a formulated policy, a solemn reminder of the need for second thought as the nation faced a terrible crisis. It was the setting forth of the pattern and design of a new administration taking the reins of government in Washington in an unprecedented threat to the nation's life. One might contrast it with some of the ill considered speeches of that general period—with Southerners in Congress firing off their parting shots, or with Gladstone's Newcastle speech of October 1862. Gladstone's utterance was not a well prepared and matured announcement of policy; Lincoln's inaugural was such an announcement. To re-read that inaugural of March 1861 is to realize anew how unfortunate was the lack of Southern understanding of Lincoln's intentions. It was regrettable that the speech in correct text and with appreciative comment, did not get across to the mind of the South. It is only when one turns the actual pages in its numerous worksheets as found in the Collection that one can properly understand what went on in Lincoln's mind as he phrased this exacting and difficult public declaration. The historian today can appreciate the speech better than the men of 1861.

In pursuing this kind of historical criticism it is well to remember that for every speech there are several versions—the speech as originally planned and (usually) written out in advance; the speech as revised, also in advance; the speech as spoken (for which in our day a sound recording would be necessary for preservation, and there were no phonographs in Lincoln's day); and the speech as reported in newspapers or elsewhere.

As the Collection conclusively shows, Lincoln did not make use of ghost writers. His speeches and letters were his own, unless in perfunctory intercourse a private secretary would produce a letter (by direction) for the President to sign. Sometimes Lincoln himself served as ghost writer for others. He prepared a message for Governor Bissell of Illinois, and in one case he wrote in his own hand a letter which went out over the signature of John Hay.

Of course, in annual messages to Congress—those voluminous documents that supposedly boxed the compass as to governmental problems down the line of departments and bureaus—Lincoln would put together the contributions of various cabinet members, Cameron or Stanton for the war department, Seward for foreign affairs, and so on. Yet even in these messages one can distinguish between those portions that amounted to a kind of catch-all of miscellaneous information and those paragraphs which constituted the President's own recommendations—for example, in December 1862 with respect to compensated emancipation—and which were written by Lincoln. In all these matters the historian can not restrain a feeling of regret that Lincoln did not employ the rather obvious but long unused technique of delivering the message in person before the houses of Congress in joint session. A half century later that governmental resource was used most effectively by Woodrow Wilson; still later by Franklin D. Roosevelt. In Lincoln's case the eloquent message of July 4, 1861, one of his great state papers, was perfunctorily communicated to Congress and unimpressively read by a clerk, while the "inaugural" of that forgotten man, Galusha A. Grow, then entering upon his duties as speaker of the House, was delivered in person.

The Sumter episode was Lincoln's most unhappy problem of state. In his papers we find no confirmation of the accusation that he was purposely provoking the lower South into firing the "first shot." There was no intent to make an attack from Sumter, and there was no element of hostile surprise in the relief expedition which the President sent simply because the alternative would have been the withdrawal of the garrison and evacuation of the fort. Instead of such evidence of intentional provocation we have just the opposite—the mildness of the first inaugural, the numerous concessions (as in the suggestion of offshore collection of duties and the avoidance of unfriendly appointments in the South), and the Chew message to Governor Pickens of South Carolina. This was the message which Lincoln sent for the perusal of the governor, carefully stating in advance what the Washington government was doing in "an attempt . . . to supply Fort Sumter with provisions only." To see that message (which came back to him) in Lincoln's handwriting is to have a new sense of the pressures, dangers, and cautionary measures of those critical days.

This reference to the inaugural and the Sumter problem illustrates a fact that runs through the whole subject—namely, that in studying the "Collection" one is reopening certain phases of American history. This could be further shown in Lincoln's firm but tactful handling of Seward's fools-day aberration as to foreign policy in 1861; in the replies to Greeley, Corning, and Birchard on matters of high policy; in his seeking of cabinet advice on the creation of West Virginia; in his non-provocative handling of the problem of retaliation between the United States and the Confederate States; and so on through hundreds of significant examples. It is thus that Lincoln's statesmanship must be studied and restudied at first hand.

There were abusive letters, expressions of a desire for Lincoln's scalp, and warnings of foul play. It was unhistorically asserted that the only other Whig Presidents—Harrison and Taylor—died in office of poison. (Lincoln, of course, was a former Whig.) Helpful souls offered an assortment of remedies. One writer recommended "a good Presbyterian Druggist, . . . and a good Republican." The President was warned of great danger in Baltimore in 1861 and was told of "a league of ten persons who had sworn that you shall never pass through that city alive." It was considered unsafe for Lincoln as President Elect to stay at a hotel, and Montgomery Blair offered a spare room in his city home, adding that it was "the one Genl Jackson intended to occupy after leaving the White House." (This was an interesting reference to the Blair House as a possible abode for a President.)

Over and over we find misunderstood subjects clarified in the papers. They show, for instance, how utterly untrue is the superficial idea that the British government "sided" with the Confederacy. Relations between the United States and Britain became increasingly friendly as the war progressed, and there are numerous expressions of friendship to Lincoln from Englishmen of the time. There is an unmistakable tone of sincerity in the British and French assurances of enthusiastic support for Lincoln and his cause. There is dignity in an address "To Citizen Abraham Lincoln" by a notable group of French gentlemen extending an enthusiastic greeting to Lincoln and assuring him of genuine support on the part of French liberals. This paper shows that in Lincoln's own day his cause was recognized as the cause of world freedom. These distinguished and thoughtful Frenchmen, intensely interested in liberty at home, realized that Lincoln's cause was theirs; if freedom failed in America, despotism would gain in Europe.

Some of the communications bear a cautionary injunction of secrecy, with such labels as "Private and Confidential" or "Read and Destroy." Now that those papers are available and the secrecy no longer holds, they have for the historian a now-it-can-be-told quality. Much of the information in the Collection was "off the record," such as inside comment on the cabinet or woeful forebodings of Republican defeat in 1864.

V

The Collection consists mainly of incoming material, but that word "mainly" in so immense a mass of papers leaves a considerable place for Lincoln's own writings, of which there are hundreds of examples. By no means all of these writings by Lincoln have been published, though most of them have. (Where they have been published by Nicolay and Hay, the editing is seldom precise.) Lincoln had a flair for pithy endorsements. Though many of these are in departmental archives as the President referred documents to cabinet secretaries for attention with brief comments, yet a considerable number of the endorsements in the R. T. Lincoln Collection will see the light of print for the first time in the new edition of Lincoln's works soon to be published under the editorship of the Abraham Lincoln Association.

Lincoln is revealed in the Collection in little things as well as great. Nothing seemed too small for his attention. He studied why a captain's commission was delayed, requested a physical examination for a private, dealt personally with innumerable cases of clemency, and in one case refused to consider a man's "excellent work for orphan children" a basis for exemption from the draft. While demands or requests for patronage ran into the thousands the large challenging problems constantly pressed upon him. As one of his correspondents expressed it: ". . . when I think of your Incessant Labours I wonder to myself . . . as you are not Superhuman and cannot any more do without Sleeping Eating and Rest than other men nor cannot extend the day & night Beyond twenty-four hours."

One could make up a composite of American types from the letters that came to Lincoln. Many of them reflected a selfish purpose. One writer reported the death of an office holder with the request that he have the job of the recently deceased. A gentleman of Alton, Illinois (October 10, 1861) gave a list of Federal offices he would "accept," including "Secretary of the Territory of Nebraska," the consulship at Glasgow, congressional librarian, and, lastly, "A Clerkship in Washington—3rd or 4th class preferred." Various successors of Roger B. Taney were offered before that aged Chief Justice passed away.

Many of those who wrote to Lincoln were prominent men—Everett, Bryant, Greeley, Grant, Scott, the Blairs, Beecher, Weed, Archbishop Hughes, Banks, Seward, Stanton, Sumner, Schurz, Frémont, Cassius M. Clay, and so on down a long roster of distinguished names of the time. Men of Congress sent letters to him by the scores, governors by the dozens, generals by the hundreds (over 1200), literary men and editors by more than a hundred. The Collection contains about 1100 letters from members of the cabinet.

Yet these missives from men of fame and high position are perhaps not the most interesting of the documents. The Collection is notable for the descent from the lofty to the lowly. There are family letters, including in-law letters from various Todds in Kentucky, Missouri, and Alabama, and communications from Lincoln's relatives in Coles County, Illinois. With quaint originality of spelling, that unforgettable country cousin, Dennis Hanks, from his backwoods home, tells of the state of health and feelings of Lincoln's stepmother. Another kinsman, John T. Hanks, wrote (July 22, 1860) from Douglas County, Oregon: "Dear unkel: while seting a lone in mi Cabing . . . I . . . write . . . to lete you no thate I was in the lande of the living . . . . it has ben a bout Ten years sense I saw you laste . . . ." "Billy the Barber" (William Florville), who served Lincoln in Springfield days, wrote a long missive (December 27, 1863) as of one neighbor to another. This home-town friend was sure of Lincoln's feeling for the Negro race. "My people," he wrote, "feel grateful to you for it." He went on to offer sympathy for the death of Willie and to inform Taddy "that his and Willy's dog is a live and kicking."

Friends of long ago New Salem days wrote to Lincoln and we have not a few of their letters preserved in the Collection. That backwoods entrepreneur Denton Offutt—now something of an authority on the horse, its treatment in sickness and in health—wrote one of those numerous begging letters asking for an appointment: "I hope you will Give me the Patten office or the office of Agricultural Department or the Commissary for Purchais of Horses Mules Beef for the Army or Mail agent . . . . I have to be looking out to live . . . ."

Since the impulse to write to the White House was well nigh universal, the papers reveal the relation of Lincoln to his people. Considering the comparative lack of conscious attention to presidential public relations or of studied contact between the White House and the American fireside, it is remarkable to note how unstintedly and spontaneously Lincoln was addressed as a confidential friend by individuals of all ranks. A deserter who had fought at Chancellorsville and Gettysburg but who had gone home to see wife and children, wrote of his readiness to rejoin his regiment. A prisoner in Castle Thunder, expecting to die, wrote as if putting himself on record before the world. Working people sent friendly appeals from England and America; they were acknowledged in like spirit.

That Lincoln stirred a response in the hearts of the people is shown by the many who requested locks of his hair, or who sent him gifts, from a pair of eagles to a tub of butter or a "Smoking pipe made expressly for you." Lincoln was told that thousands were praying for him. A freedman in the deep South, signing his name "don carlous Butler," wrote asking guidance as to how he should plan for his bit of land and the rebuilding of his house. The lady who wrote the letter for this ex-slave explained: "He, with others of the Freedmen, often expresses a wish to be able to speak to Massa Linkum feeling sure that he will listen to their plea for land & do what is best for them." Without these numerous letters from unfamed beings much of the feeling of the people for Lincoln would be hard to recover. One does not find it in the ponderous pages of the *Congressional Globe*. It existed as something in the air. It was not easily traceable. It spread abroad in the manner of the grapevine telegraph, but these papers show that it was a solid and unmistakable fact.

Recognizing that startling sensationalism is lacking (which is fortunate), one must avoid the mistake of underestimating the Collection. With these papers the portrait is now much fuller, the contemporary scene recreated, not as an album of tintypes but as a throbbing stage of actors who come alive in their own words. From the time the Collection was opened, and more especially after months had been devoted to its study, it became apparent that a new phase in the appreciation of Lincoln was upon us. Little of what was basically known has had to be discarded, but in vividness and glowing detail we have much more of Lincoln and his period than before.

Writers will continue to search, or skim through, these masses of material for divers purposes, though up to now the more careful investigators who have made penetrating and thorough use of the Collection are by no means numerous. The papers could be drawn upon for the lingo and patter of Lincoln's day, for an occasional earthy fable, for evidence of human folly or greed, for bygone excitements that seem stupid in retrospect, for glimpses or self-portraits of Lincoln's contemporaries, and for the psychological, or psychopathic, climate of a day when hate and illogical emotion ran wild and yet below the surface the foundations of sense and sanity remained somehow intact. One cannot easily enumerate the varying purposes for which the papers will yield their valuable product. They hold a mirror to American life.

LINCOLN THE PRESIDENT

LAST FULL MEASURE

Courtesy F. H. Meserve

THE LAST PORTRAIT

Taken by Alexander Gardner in Washington on April 10, 1865, the day after Appomattox and four days before the assassination.

To Ruth and Rose

PREFACE

AT THE TIME of his death, in early 1953, Professor Randall had finished about half of the manuscript for this, the fourth and final volume of his *Lincoln the President*. He had accumulated notes for most of the rest of the book, and he had made a series of trial lists of topics for the remaining chapters. Anticipating the end of his life, he had also indicated his preferences regarding the selection of an author to complete the work.

This honor having fallen to me, I have tried to carry on in his spirit and with his standards, yet I cannot claim to have succeeded in writing quite as he would have done. His mastery of the Lincoln subject was, of course, unique. Furthermore, he was able to hold in his mind the complex and subtle organization which he worked out for the biography as he went along, and he left on paper no outline for his successor to follow, except for the tentative jottings of chapter subjects. On one point he was explicit. "This biography," he noted, "knows only the living Lincoln." He did not intend to deal with the assassination or with the events following it.

The reader may be assured that the first eight chapters in this volume are "pure Randall." They were written and revised by him, and they stand as he left them, without any textual change. The only liberty I have taken with them has been to re-arrange the order slightly by moving from third to sixth the chapter entitled "Chase Is Willing." The last eight chapters are also in a real sense Professor Randall's, for they were written in the light of his interpretations and with the aid of his research. But I must assume the responsibility for the form they have finally taken.

I am sure that Professor Randall would desire here to thank again those many friends and helpers whom he acknowledged in the prefaces to his first and third volumes. I should like to express my personal indebtedness to several others whose aid and encouragement has been indispensable. I owe a great deal to various friends who happen to be authorities on the Civil War period, to William B. Hesseltine, Fred H. Harrington, T. Harry Williams, and Frank Freidel, and especially to Kenneth M. Stampp, who read and criticized my chapters. I owe a great deal also to Ruth Painter Randall, the foremost student of Mrs. Lincoln and the Lincoln family, who made me the beneficiary of her ripe wisdom; to Wayne C. Temple, who, as Professor Randall's research assistant and then mine, provided continuity for the project and who prepared the bibliography; and to my wife, Rose Bonar Current, who not only did most of my typing but also cheerfully put up with my preoccupation with Lincoln.

R. N. C.

LINCOLN THE PRESIDENT

LAST FULL MEASURE

CHAPTER I

THE STATE OF THE UNION: LINCOLN'S PLAN OF RECONSTRUCTION

IN HIS annual message to Congress in December 1863, in fulfillment of that provision of the Constitution which requires that the President shall "give to the Congress Information of the State of the Union," Lincoln addressed himself to the question of reconstruction. He did not deal in quibbles or generalities, but came up with a plan. Anyone who knew Lincoln would have known that his design for a restored Union would not be hateful and vindictive. It would not rule out the very spirit of reunion. His view had never been narrowly sectional. Born in the Southern state of Kentucky of Virginia-born parents, moving thence to Indiana and Illinois, he was part of that transit of culture by which Southern characteristics, human types, and thought patterns had taken hold in the West and Northwest.

In New Salem, in the legislature at Vandalia, and in Springfield he had remained in touch with men of Southern birth. His marriage into a cultured Kentucky family and his visits to Lexington, his wife's home town, had enabled him to understand the Southern—though here we do not mean the proslavery—viewpoint. (Among the Todd connections had been those who believed in gradual emancipation.) Southern understanding had also been assisted by his political career as a Whig, which greatly exceeded in duration his career as a Republican. His Whig friends had included good Southerners, and his Whig approach had been the opposite of sectional. When political alignments changed with the devil of discord in the 1850's, Lincoln had found no satisfaction in the formation of a sectional party. He obviously disliked being unwhigged. Though he was antislavery and of course antisecession, he was never anti-Southern.

I

One can pinpoint the launching of his plan in the month of December 1863, but back of that one must remember that Lincoln's earlier utterances bespoke a preference for conciliatory adjustment. In his Cooper Union speech of February 1860 he had stressed the wrong of slavery and had opposed its extension, but in doing so he had appealed to "the old policy of the fathers" and had strongly emphasized the unwisdom of doing anything "through passion and ill temper." He considered it "exceedingly desirable that all parts of this great Confederacy [the United States] shall be at peace, and in harmony with one another."

He had said in his first inaugural: "Physically we cannot separate," and on various later occasions he had returned to this theme. As he wrote in his annual message of December 1, 1862, to "separate our common country into two nations" was to him intolerable. The people of the greater interior, he urged, "will not ask where a line of separation shall be, but will vow rather that there shall be no such line." The situation as he saw it, in "all its adaptations and aptitudes . . . demands union and abhors separation." It would ere long "force reunion, however much of blood and treasure the separation might cost."

Thus Lincoln's fundamental adherence to an unbroken Union was the point of departure for his reconstruction program. One could find, in the earlier part of his presidency, other indications bearing upon restoration. In an important letter to General G. F. Shepley, military governor of Louisiana (November 21, 1862), he advised strongly against what came to be known as "carpetbagger" policy. He did not want "Federal officers not citizens of Louisiana" to seek election as congressmen from that state. On this his language was emphatic: he considered it "disgusting and outrageous" to "send a parcel of Northern men here as representatives, elected, as it would be understood (and perhaps really so), at the point of the bayonet." [1]

While in this manner disallowing the idea of importing Northern politicians into a Southern state as pseudo-representatives in Congress, he also repudiated the opposite policy of Fernando Wood of

[1] *Works,* VIII, 79.

New York which would accept Southerners in Congress prematurely—that is, before resistance to the United States was ended and loyalty assured.[2] To mention another point, he had, in considering the formation of the new state of West Virginia, expressed his view that, in the pattern of the Union, only those who were loyal—i. e., who adhered to the United States—could be regarded as competent voters.

To these points—the indispensable Union, loyalty, and the unwisdom of carpetbaggism—one must add Lincoln's fundamental policy of emancipation and his non-vindictiveness in the matter of confiscation. Taking these factors together the historian has, before December 1863, the ingredients of the President's reunion program.

In announcing that program on December 8, 1863, Lincoln issued two documents: a Proclamation, and a message to Congress. In his proclamation, having the force of law, he set forth the conditions of a general pardon and the terms of restoring a Southern state to the Union. In his accompanying message he commented upon his plan, telling more fully what was in his mind and defending his course by reason and persuasion. The offer of pardon (with stated exceptions) and restoration of rights (except as to slaves) was given to anyone in a seceded state who would take and keep a simple oath. Phrased by the President, this oath constituted a solemn pledge to support the Constitution of the United States "and the union of the States thereunder." The oath-taker would also swear to abide by and faithfully support all the acts of Congress and all the proclamations of the President relating to slaves unless repealed, modified, or declared void by the Supreme Court.[3]

So much for the oath, with pardon and restoration of rights. The next element in the proclamation was re-establishment of a state government. This again was intended to be simple and practical. Whenever, in a seceded state, a number not less than one-tenth of those voting in 1860, should re-establish a republican government,[4] such a

---

[2] *Ibid.*, VIII, 142 ff. [3] *Ibid.*, IX, 218–223.

[4] A writer need not be considered facetious if he calls attention to the lower case *r* in "republican." In all the tremendous efforts of those who disagreed with Lincoln the partisan motive was a constant factor; with such a man as Thaddeus Stevens, by his own admission, it was a controlling motive. In insisting that the state government be "republican" Lincoln had in mind that provision of the Constitution (article IV, section 4) which guaranteed to every state a republican—i. e., a non-monarchical or non-dictatorial—type of government, and to that end provided Federal protection for the state against invasion or domestic violence.

government, according to Lincoln's proclamation, would "be recognized as the true government of the State."

Turning from the proclamation to the simultaneous message, we find Lincoln setting forth the reasons and conditions of his policy. In this he addressed himself to various questions that he knew would arise. What about the oath? Why the ten per cent? What about state laws touching freedmen? Why preserve the state as it was? How about state boundaries? Why was the President assuming the power of reconstruction as an executive function? He started with the obvious unwisdom and absurdity of protecting a revived state government constructed from the disloyal element. It was essential to have a test "so as to build only from the sound." He wanted that test to be liberal and to include "sworn recantation of . . . former unsoundness." As for laws and proclamations against slavery, they could not be abandoned. Retaining so far as possible the existing political framework in the state, as Lincoln saw it, would "save labor, and avoid confusion." He did not, of course, mean by this that the system in any state was to be permanently frozen for the future in unchangeable form.

Lincoln gave attention at this point to a practical problem. In some states those ready for resumption of Union status might remain inactive for want of a plan of action. They needed a "rallying point." Potential unionism, or friendly Union sentiment, was not enough; unionist accomplishment must become actual. If a few should agree on a plan they might not know that it would be approved by the Federal government. To state the kind of plan for which acceptance could be assured, was an essential step; it would mean that those ready for restoration would be induced "to act sooner than they otherwise would." [5]

As to the specific formula of ten per cent, he said little; yet his simile of a rallying point held the key. The important object was to get a movement started. Acceptance of an initial electorate of ten per cent did not signify that Lincoln was favoring minority rule. It was not his thought that any minority should usurp the rights of the majority. Within his pattern of loyalty, Union, non-dictatorial government, and emancipation, he was putting the formation of any new state government in the hands of the loyal people of the state.

[5] For the message, see *Works,* IX, 224–252.

Government by the people was to him fundamental, but as a practical matter some loyal nucleus was essential; else time would pass, precious time, and nothing would be done.

There was precedent for the setting in motion of a popular government by a minority. That had been done in 1787–88 in the launching of the Constitution in which ratifying delegates had been chosen by a minor fraction of the population. Later Lincoln was to use a figure of speech to explain his meaning—the egg and the fowl.[6] One would sooner have the fowl by hatching the egg than by smashing it. It was as if majority rights were being temporarily administered in trust by a minor portion of the electorate. To administer them in trust was to keep them intact till a loyal majority could take over. The whole situation, of course, was abnormal. All beginnings, or rebeginnings, are difficult, especially rebuilding after or during a war, taking up the shattered pieces of a disrupted social and political order and putting them partly together so that ultimately they could be fully restored. Lincoln was willing to accept informality in order to accomplish the main practical purpose which he considered imperative. He was unwilling to throw away the cause while futilely waiting for perfection. Reconstruction, as he saw it, was a matter of stages. His "ten per cent plan" was easy to criticize. Yet it was the first step. As for those who were thinking up involved theories, looking for some unattainable formula of perfection, it was years before they were to take steps, and the steps they then took were to prove unworkable.

Lincoln would take his first step in the most available manner. A few states could be rebuilt and restored. This was to be done during the war, indeed as an important factor in waging and ending the war. Let people see that Lincoln did not intend an ugly and vindictive policy, and Southerners themselves, the President hoped, would set their own houses in order. Let one or two states do this, they would serve as examples for others as the armies advanced and national authority was extended. In time of war, prepare for peace, was Lincoln's thought. On the other hand, let the months pass, and let the Southern people witness only carpetbaggism, Federal occupation, and a repressive attitude as to the future, and victory itself would lose much of its value. It was Lincoln's intent that policy associated with

[6] Speech of April 11, 1865, *ibid.*, XI, 91.

victory should envisage willing loyalty while leaving free play for self government.

II

Lincoln's plan of reunion was greeted with a mixed response. The Washington *Chronicle,* regarded as a Lincoln "organ," naturally praised the President's announcement. The editor noted that the President gave out his statement in a setting of military and naval success: our armies victorious, our navy in control of Southern coasts, our cause strengthened by increased friendship of foreign nations. His generous offering of pardon was interpreted by the *Chronicle* as evidence of his kindness and sympathy toward the people of the South. The editor concluded: "Viewing his whole Administration and what he has done . . . we thank God that Abraham Lincoln is President of the United States." [1]

An English gentleman friendly to the United States wrote: "We have just received the news of President Lincoln's message, accompanied with his amnesty; also the message of . . . [Jefferson] Davis. The two documents coming together are doing an immense amount of good for the right cause." [2]

It is doubtful how many readers made the comparison of the two messages, but those who did must have noted a marked difference of tone. In general spirit Lincoln's message of December 8, 1863, was notable for its absence of war-engendered hatred toward the South, ending as it did on the note of "freedom disenthralled." In appealing for reunion the President was holding out the hand for genuine renewal of friendly relations. This attitude, however, was not reciprocated by the Confederate President. Though perhaps the comparison should not be overstressed, one finds quite the opposite note in the message (December 7, 1863) of Jefferson Davis to his Congress. After a depressing account of Confederate military reverses and of discouraging condition in foreign affairs and finance, the Southern Executive threw in bitter denunciations of the "barbarous policy" and "savage ferocity" of "our enemies." At one point he referred to them as "hardened by crime." (There were, of course, those in the

1 Washington *Daily Morning Chronicle,* Dec. 10, 1863, p. 2, cc. 1–2.

2 Frederick Edge to H. W. Bellows, London, Dec. 22, 1863, Bellows MSS.

North, though not Lincoln, who were saying equally hateful things of the South.) That enemy, wrote Davis, refused "even to listen to proposals . . . [of peace] of recognizing the impassable gulf which divides us." [3] This expression, the orthodox attitude of Confederate officialdom, must be remembered along with Lincoln's other problems. If anyone doubted why the President, in his reconstruction plans and his wariness toward "peace negotiations," realized the hopelessness of expecting high Confederate officials to consider a peaceable restoration of the Union, the reading of this message of Davis would have been enough to dispel such doubt. As was to be expected, this same attitude was reflected in the Congress at Richmond. When Lincoln's restoration plan came up for discussion in that Congress one member referred to "the imbecile and unprincipled usurper who now sits enthroned upon the ruins of constitutional liberty in Washington City," while another speaker suggested that silent contempt was the only treatment for "that miserable and contemptable despot, Lincoln." At about the same time the President's plan was denounced and spurned in the Virginia legislature as "degrading to freemen." [4]

Greeley's *Tribune* was favorable, expressing the view that the President answered the question as to how the "rebels" could "return to loyalty and fidelity"; this would "break the back of the Rebellion." [5] The Washington correspondent of the *Tribune* indulged in superlatives, remarking that "no President's Message since George Washington retired into private life has given such general satisfaction as that sent to Congress by Abraham Lincoln to-day." [6] The New York *Times* remarked apropos of the message that 1863 had become "the most eventful [year] since the Government began." "The process of reconstruction," said the *Times,* "is simple and yet perfectly effective." [7] It was not merely a plan, according to the *Times;* it was a program which "finds us already thoroughly committed to it in every essential particular." It "challenges at once the acquiescence of all truly loyal men." [8] "With regard to the fundamental is-

---

[3] Journal of the [Confederate] Congress (*Sen. Doc. No. 234* [U.S.], 58 Cong., 2 sess., 435–451, esp. 450–451.

[4] Moore, *Rebellion Record* (Diary), VIII, 21, 24.

[5] New York *Tribune,* Dec. 10, 1863 (editorial), p. 6, c. 2.

[6] *Ibid.,* Dec. 10, 1863, p. 1, c. 2.

[7] New York *Times,* Dec. 10, 1863, p. 6, c. 2.

[8] *Ibid.,* Dec. 11, 1863, p. 4, c. 2.

sues . . . ," writes Ralph R. Fahrney, "the sympathies of Greeley were with Lincoln . . . ." [9]

Some of the newspaper language, however, was stormy and vehement. Radical papers attacked the President and impetus was given to the movement in the Republican party which was already opposing his renomination. Conspicuous among these radical organs in New York were the *Independent* and the *Evening Post*. From an opposite partisan viewpoint the President's message was denounced by such New York papers as the *Journal of Commerce,* the *Daily News,* and the *World.* These papers, rather inconsistently, assailed both Lincoln and the radicals. Friendliness to the South on the part of these journals did not signify support of Lincoln's restoration policy or emancipation. Their attitude was a good deal like that of Vallandigham. In the *World* Lincoln's scheme was held to be "preposterous," without authority, and "the very height of absurdity." [10] The *Herald,* commenting on the ten per cent of the "rebellious" states, did not think there were "that many good men there." According to this widely circulating newspaper of Bennett, "Mr. Lincoln's plan will be a failure." This was the immediate reaction under date of December 9, 1863. Several weeks later, having grown in vituperation, the *Herald,* on January 31, 1864, denounced the plan as pettifogging, flimsy and incoherent.

It was obvious from the start that the President's plan would not have smooth sailing, but on several fronts steps were taken to make it known and put it into operation. Army officers were instructed to take copies of the proclamation and distribute them so as to reach soldiers and inhabitants within Confederate-held territory. Aid and protection was to be extended to those who would declare loyalty. On the occasion of raids into enemy territory a number of men were to be detailed "for the purpose of distributing the proclamation broadcast among rebel soldiers and people, and in the highways and byways." [11]

This matter of the handbills occasioned some correspondence across the lines between Confederate and Union officers. On the

---

[9] Ralph R. Fahrney, *Horace Greeley and the Tribune in the Civil War,* 175.

[10] Clipping from New York *World,* in Washington *Daily Chronicle,* Dec. 12, 1863, p. 2, c. 6.

[11] R. A. Alger to General Butler, Fort Monroe, Feb. 23, 1864, *Private and Official Correspondence of B. F. Butler,* III, 463–464.

Confederate side Longstreet in eastern Tennessee protested against the handbills, remarking that those who would desert under the promise held out would not be "men of character and standing." The Union cause, he urged, could not gain by the acceptance of such men. A complication in this connection was that going over to the Union side might turn out in some cases to be a mere trick. Union outposts and pickets reported that Confederate officers and men turned up as Union soldiers; in such cases, spying being suspected, the death penalty was enforced.[12]

On the legal or prosecuting front the effect of the pardon policy was explained in an instruction from the office of the attorney general of the United States to district attorneys throughout the country. It was made known that the "President's pardon of a person guilty of . . . rebellion . . . [would] relieve that person for the penalties" of that crime. District attorneys were therefore directed to discontinue proceedings in United States courts whenever the accused should take the oath and comply with the stated conditions.[13]

Such a statement would make it appear that the transition from a kind of rebellious guilt to complete relief from penalty was easy, automatic, and practically instantaneous, but it soon became evident that the matter was not so simple as that. Lincoln found that he had to make a distinction in applying his offer of pardon in return for the oath. What about Confederate soldiers held by Union authorities as prisoners of war? On this point the President issued a later clarifying proclamation, declaring that his pardon did not apply to men in custody or on parole as prisoners of war. It did apply, he explained, to persons yet at large (i. e., free from arrest) who would come forward and take the oath. It was also explained that those excluded from the general amnesty could apply to the President for clemency and their cases would have due consideration.[14]

What it amounted to was that Lincoln himself was generous in the application of his pardon both to soldiers and civilians, and the same was true of the attorney general's office; but army officers were not prepared, in return for the oath, to deliver prisoners nor give up pen-

12 Moore, *Rebellion Record* (Doc.), VIII, 296–297.
13 *Ibid.*, (Docs.), VIII, 383–384.
14 Proclamation about amnesty, Mar. 26, 1864, *Works*, X, 58–60.

alties for offences of various sorts, such as violation of rules of war. No one statement applies. Some enemies held as prisoners, on establishing loyalty, were discharged from custody by the President on assurance of good faith by three congressmen.[15] This showed, as in many cases, that Lincoln's general rules were subject to individual exceptions. In numerous instances Lincoln would write out in his own hand a slip of paper similar to the following, which was addressed to the secretary of war on March 15, 1864: "I shall be personally obliged if you will allow Silas H. Highley to take the oath of Dec. 8. and be discharged." [16] Where the President did not wish his pardon of a particular man to be taken as a precedent, he would make that clear. For example, in ordering the discharge (on taking the oath) of a prisoner held at Johnson's Island, he pointed out that this was a special case, not a precedent; the man had voluntarily quitted the enemy service, and was subject to fits.[17]

III

With a scorn of fine-spun theories and an urgent wish to get ahead with the job of reconstruction, the President proceeded, so far as possible, to make restoration a reality wherever, and as soon as, any reasonable opportunity offered in the seceded South. He was notably a patient man, but there was a touch of impatience when dilatoriness, confusion of authority, political intrigue, radical opposition, or mere inertia seemed to obstruct his program or threaten it with failure.

In Lincoln's plan of reconstruction the effort in Louisiana was of vital importance. From the time that New Orleans fell to Union arms on May 1, 1862, the President saw, in terms of Federal occupation, an early opportunity to make reconstruction a wartime reality. Let Louisiana be restored, he thought, let this be done in a reasonable manner with Washington approval, let it be seen that the plan

---

15 Angle, *New Letters and Papers of Lincoln,* 346.

16 *Ibid.,* 345. Lincoln collectors have long been familiar with the frequency, in the autograph market, of brief Lincoln originals—notes or endorsements—with the wording: "Let . . . [this man or men] take the oath of Dec. 8, 1863, and be discharged." Hundreds of such autographs—many of them shamefully clipped—i. e., robbed—from war department files, have become the possession of Lincoln collectors; it has been a method of obtaining a Lincoln autograph cheaply.

17 Angle, *New Letters and Papers,* 350.

would work, and other states would follow. To go into all the details of the Louisiana story, treating its complications month by month, would be a tedious process. These complications were numerous and vexatious: use of military power, attention of the same Union leader to military operations and govermental affairs, civil-and-military conflicts, cliquism, theories as to whether secession had ever really taken the state out of the Union, lack of co-operation between Federal leaders, doubts as to how slavery should be eliminated, transitional labor problems in the shift from bondage to freedom, social differences between the planter class and the common people, need for a promptness that was not forthcoming, constitution remaking in an era of revolution, and the depressing shadow of a great question mark as to what Congress would do or prevent from being done. It will be convenient to reduce this elaborate Louisiana story to four successive phases:

First Phase in Louisiana: Military Rule under Butler and Shepley. The first phase was that of army rule under General B. F. Butler. Immediate adjustments were of course necessary from the moment when New Orleans, largest city of the South, together with a large portion of Louisiana, came under the Union flag. Governmental officials in the occupied region, including merely local functionaries in city or parish, were now under Federal authority—not in terms of any deliberation as to procedure by Congress or the Executive, but simply by the fortunes of war. Where men in local office stood ready to co-operate with the occupying power, they had a good chance of being retained; if unco-operative, they were dismissed. For a time the mayor and council of New Orleans were continued in office subject to General Butler's authority with some relaxation of military pressure, but this situation did not last long. Within a month the mayor was deposed and imprisoned, and George F. Shepley, acting closely with Butler, took over mayoral functions. Then in June 1862 Shepley became military governor of Louisiana; soon afterward he had the rank of brigadier general.

This was military occupation, and of course it was intended only as a temporary condition. It amounted to martial law which has been defined as the will of the military commander; this meant that the sometimes eccentric will of General Butler was paramount. If nothing offered in the form of a re-established and recognized state government, the abnormal and temporary regime would continue. The distinction in the matter of authority between Butler and Shepley seems never to have been adequately worked out. It might have been supposed that army matters belonged to Butler and civil-government affairs to Shepley, but it was not so simple as that. Butler was not only the more famous—"as much a news item as any man except Lincoln"[1]—he was also the more domineering. In power he was ahead of Shepley and he had the military forces at his disposal. Louisiana was in fact under Butler, government and all; it was his regime, and it included such unfortunate acts of capricious severity or *gaucherie* as his "woman order" and his wanton execution of Mumford.[2]

It thus came about that Federal rule in Louisiana, the first step toward what Lincoln regarded as restoration of loyalty and normal conditions, got off to a bad start.[3] The name of "Beast Butler" became a hated by-word in the South, with far-reaching complications in Federal-Confederate relations;[4] it came as a considerable relief when President Lincoln removed him from his Louisiana command on December 16, 1862. His successor, as commander of the military forces stationed in Louisiana and Texas, was Major General Nathaniel P. Banks, with Shepley retaining his position as "military governor of Louisiana."

Under Butler little or nothing had been done toward wartime governmental reconstruction in the state, but this problem, dear to Lincoln's heart, was tackled under the President's urging during the Banks-Shepley regime.

A careful study of these matters reveals a problem as to top executive leadership locally applied—that is, the difficulty of achieving effectiveness in a particular area in terms of policy developed in Washington. Lincoln was President; he was the Chief; he made the appointments and formed decisions; presumably he would choose men to put his policies into operation. Yet so unpredictable were events and so complicated was the situation as to politicians' maneuvers that those who supposedly should have carried out Lincoln's

[1] Carl Russell Fish, *Dic. of Am. Biog.*, III, 357. [2] *Lincoln the President*, III.

[3] Randall, *Constitutional Problems Under Lincoln*, chap. x.

[4] These complications were especially bothersome as to threats of retaliation, denial of honorable officer status to Butler, exchange of prisoners, and the like.

purposes promoted their own factional and contrary schemes in such manner as to jeopardize the President's best laid plans.

George F. Shepley was a case in point. He had been a Maine Democrat, an appointee of Pierce and later of Buchanan as district attorney, and a supporter of Douglas in 1860. These factors in his background did not militate against him in Lincoln's view—the President often appointed Democrats—nor should they have been a drawback to successful service in Louisiana's reconstruction. There was, however, the further fact that Shepley became a Butlerite and a radical; remaining after Butler's removal, he played the radical game at a time when it was hoped that a more Lincolnian policy would be inaugurated. Thus Shepley stood as an obstacle to Lincoln's efforts to allay factionalism and to promote speedy and liberal restoration.

Unsatisfactory though this Butler-Shepley period was, Lincoln used it as best he could to push ahead the program of civil reconstruction in Louisiana. "I wish elections for congressmen to take place in Louisiana," he wrote to Shepley on November 21, 1862. He wanted it to be "a movement of the people . . . , and not a movement of our military and quasi-military authorities there." The President recognized that there were difficulties as to state law, but said: "These knots must be cut, the main object being to get an expression of the people." If necessary, Lincoln wanted Shepley to start proceedings. He did not want a day wasted. "Fix a day [he wrote] for an election in all the districts, and have it held in as many places as you can." [5]

Toward the end of the Butler-Shepley period an election was held within the Union lines on December 3, 1862, for members of Congress from Louisiana. Two men of different outlook, were elected: B. F. Flanders from New Hampshire, who was to become an instrument of the radical faction; and Michael Hahn, a citizen of Louisiana born in Bavaria, who was more in tune with Lincoln's purposes. When the question of admitting these gentlemen as members of the House of Representatives was brought before that body (February 9, 1863) a species of dog fight ensued, a forerunner of the rough treatment in store for Lincoln's whole reunion program. Few were ready for frontal attack and sidestepping was more in evidence; the result was confusion, unrelated motions, and postponement. Finally, on

[5] *Works,* VIII, 80–81.

February 17, 1863, the House voted, 92 to 44, to seat Flanders and Hahn.[6] By that time that particular Congress, the Thirty-Seventh, was about to pass out of existence.

Second Phase: Shepley and Durant versus Banks. In the next phase, while Banks was in top command in Louisiana with Shepley as military governor—i. e., governor as to civil affairs under military authority—certain groups in the state got to work, though at cross purposes, to seize control of the process of state remaking. It turned out to be a period of bickering and futility, a time of bitter disappointment to the President. Taking over the rebuilding task and attempting to do it in his own way, Governor Shepley proceeded to make a registry of voters, appointing T. J. Durant, a radical like himself, as commissioner of registration. An oath of allegiance was required (this was before the presidentially prescribed oath of December 8, 1863) and the registration of whites who would take the oath was ordered. It was Durant's idea that ten loyal men in a parish, if no more could be registered, would be a sufficient basis for an election. This was a period when Banks was preoccupied with military command in the Port Hudson and Texas areas, while Shepley was also absent from Louisiana, spending a large part of the summer of 1863 in Washington. Lincoln approved the Shepley-Durant registration and wanted it pushed.

Then, with a kind of fateful contrariness, the reconstruction movement, registry and all, was brought to a standstill. Provoked at the slowness of proceedings, Lincoln wrote to Banks on November 5, 1863. Mentioning the long delay, he said: "This disappoints me bitterly." Lose no time, was the President's injunction. "I wish him [Shepley] . . . to go to work and give me a tangible nucleus which the remainder of the State may rally around as fast as it can . . . . Time is important." Lincoln feared that disloyal men would "preoccupy the ground" and set up a government repudiating emancipation, in which case he could not recognize or sustain their work. He added: "This government in such an attitude would be a house divided against itself." [7]

What Lincoln had in mind was that so-called Louisiana "conserva-

[6] *Cong. Globe,* 37 Cong., 3 sess., 1036. The end of the Thirty-Seventh Congress came on March 3, 1863.

[7] *Works,* IX, 200–201.

tives," representing the proslavery planter class, were already organizing with a view to setting in motion the wheels of state government under the old Louisiana constitution of 1853 which recognized slavery and which was in other respects unsatisfactory. Lincoln wanted Union men to "eschew cliquism, and, each yielding something . . . , all work together." "It is a time now," he urged, "for real patriots to rise above all this." [8]

The President was trying to keep himself in the background, to avoid seeming to dictate, and to let things work themselves out as a Louisiana movement. Yet he soon found that a jurisdictional dispute or confusion as to control was spoiling everything. Shepley as military governor and Durant, his appointee, were claiming "that they were exclusively charged with the work of reconstruction in Louisiana," while Banks had "not felt authorized to interfere" with them. In a letter of December 16, 1863, Banks advised the President that he was "only in partial command," adding: "There are not less than *four* distinct governments here claiming . . . independent powers based upon instructions received directly from Washington, and recognizing no other authority than their own."

Judging by the context, the "four . . . governments" were the system of United States courts, the municipal government of New Orleans, the well-knit corps of treasury officials (radical, pro-Chase, and at cross purposes with Lincoln), and the authority of Shepley, who as "military governor" dealt with many matters of civil organization. In addition there was, of course, the army under Banks, but at the time that general was referring to ursurping influences that were working against him. The full story of this confused situation in Louisiana is too elaborate for treatment here, but Lincoln's intense distress because of all this lagging and (as he thought) wrong direction of reconstruction is a factor that cannot be overlooked.[9]

Though this unfortunate situation was due in large part to the activities of radical groups, another factor may have been a bit of inadvertence on the part of the burdened President: he had supposed all the time that Banks was in chief command but had not made that point sufficiently clear. He now wrote a strong letter to Banks

8 *Ibid.*, IX, 257.

9 On this point the author has benefited from the generous assistance of Professor Fred H. Harrington, biographer of Banks. For Banks's letter to Lincoln, Dec. 16, 1863, see R. T. L. Coll., 28710–16.

(December 24, 1863) with a fourfold repetition of the main theme: You are master. The President was seriously annoyed at the frustration and delay. Shepley, he wrote, was to "assist" Banks, not to "thwart" him. The desirable object, of course, was to have unity among pro-Union men and leaders, but a serious obstacle to such unity was the attitude of Shepley and his considerable faction. It became increasingly apparent that these radicals were unwilling to co-operate with the man whom Lincoln had placed in chief authority and whom he had plainly designated as "master." Treating delay and factionalism as if things of the past, Lincoln wrote to Banks: "give us a free State reorganization of Louisiana in the shortest possible time." The general was to do this while still conducting his military operation in Texas.[10] For getting ahead with the work, it was Banks's idea that the radicals—the Shepley-Durant element—should be relieved of all functions pertaining to reconstruction.[11]

Third Phase: The Louisiana Constitution of 1864. Under Lincoln's spurring Banks went into action. In January and February of 1864 he issued proclamations for two kinds of elections: an election for governor under the old Louisiana constitution of 1853, and an election of delegates to a convention to make a new state constitution.[12] In his proclamations, copies of which he sent to the President, Banks declared that officials then to be chosen were to govern unless they tried to change Federal statutes as to slavery. Voters were required to take the oath of allegiance to the United States.

Lincoln continued to prod and encourage. On the constructing of a free-state government he considered the words "can and will" exceedingly "precious." Proceed "with all possible dispatch," wrote the President. "Frame orders, and fix times and places for this and that . . . ." [13] Recognition of the death of slavery in Louisiana was causing less difficulty than might have been expected. While the planter class wanted to keep the institution, they were in the minority; the majority of the people were ready to accept emancipation. In doing so they preferred to treat abolition of the institution simply as a *fait accompli,* an unavoidable effect of the war. It was as if many of them wanted simply to look the other way and let the institution

---

10 *Works,* IX, 273–274.

11 Harrington, *Fighting Politician: Major General N. P. Banks,* 143.

12 *Ibid.,* 144.

13 *Works,* IX, 282–283.

die. Banks reported: "Not a word is heard from any one in favor of a restoration of slavery, and no objection is made to the free state basis upon which the election is based." [14]

Both of the elections were a success from the standpoint of Banks and of Lincoln. Not that Lincoln considered the outcome perfect, but the whole point of Lincoln's policy was that he was not expecting perfection. He wanted steps to be taken, a "free" government set up; modifications and improvements could come later. The vote for state officials was held on February 22, 1864. In a total of 11,411 votes (over a fourth of the normal peacetime vote of Louisiana) Michael Hahn, the moderate Union candidate acceptable to Banks and Lincoln, received 6183 votes and was elected; Flanders, candidate of the anti-Banks radical element, received 2232 votes; J. Q. A. Fellows, nominated by the proslavery conservatives, received the disturbingly large vote of 2996.[15]

Banks was using the psychology of significant dates. The election was on Washington's birthday; the inauguration of Hahn as governor, on March 4, 1864. There were imposing ceremonies for the inauguration which was described as a "magnificent" and enthusiastic demonstration of popular interest; it was reported by Banks that eight thousand public school children participated and that 50,000 people were present.

Amid all this gratification, however, a discordant note was struck. The radicals were organizing solidly to oppose and obstruct the reorganized government, and one of them, T. L. Durant, employed in the treasury department besides being a part of Shepley's machine as already noticed, wrote in dissatisfied mood to Secretary Chase. Casting a sarcastic slur at the "gorgeous pageantry" of the Hahn inauguration, the "stupid starers" and "loud huzzahers" of yesterday, he deplored the whole movement. Those promoting the Banks-Hahn reorganization, he reported, had muzzled the press, intimidated office holders, and debauched the voters.[16] On the same day George S. Denison, an official of the treasury department with important duties as collector in Louisiana, wrote to Chase that both of the defeated

---

14 Banks to Lincoln, New Orleans, Jan. 22, 1864, R. T. L. Coll., 29710–2.

15 Detailed returns of the Louisiana election are found in Reports to Lincoln: R. T. L. Coll., 30770. See also Harrington, 144; Nicolay and Hay, *Lincoln,* VIII, 432.

16 Thomas L. Durant to S. P. Chase, New Orleans, March 5, 1864, Chase MSS., Lib. of Cong.

factions (Flanders of the radicals and Fellows of the "proslavery" element) were forming a "coalition" to oust Hahn.[17]

At this point President Lincoln invested Hahn with the powers of civil government which had been temporarily entrusted to the presidentially appointed Shepley. Since the people had participated in this choice of governor, albeit imperfectly because of war, Lincoln could feel that the republican processes of civil government had been given a considerable impulse.

Next came the problem of constitution remaking. By Bank's proclamation an election was held on March 28, 1864, by which delegates were chosen (not a distinguished lot, but they represented the people rather than officials or politicians) to form a new instrument of government. From April to July the convention labored. Among its main acts was to abolish slavery by a vote of seventy to sixteen. Negro suffrage, then a new question and a difficult one, came harder. After voting it down, the convention reconsidered; it then "empowered" the legislature to grant the vote to colored persons; by the constitution it was provided that a militia be enrolled without distinction of color.[18]

On September 5, 1864, the people of Louisiana voted to ratify the constitution (6836–1566); members of congress were then chosen by popular election, after which the legislature set up under the new constitution chose two senators. If and when these men should be admitted by Congress—a big "if"—reconstruction for Louisiana, so far as essential political structure was concerned, would be complete. In the matter of preliminary steps—shaping up the situation so that Congress could act—the work of the executive branch for this pivotal state was done.

Fourth Phase: Trouble in Congress. Much water was to pass over the mill before one could know what Congress would do as to admitting Louisiana according to Lincoln's plan. The radical clique in Louisiana had opposed the measures taken in 1864 looking toward a new state government. This element made a break with the Lin-

---

17 Denison to Chase, U.S. Customs House, New Orleans, March 5, 1864, *ibid.*

18 Among the documents of the time (about March of 1864) is a printed petition of "free colored citizens of Louisiana." They pray that "the right of sufferage may be extended . . . [to Negroes] whether born slave or free . . . , subject only to such qualifications as shall equally affect the white and colored citizens." Andrew MSS., vol. 22, Mass. Hist. Soc.

coln administration, denounced the new constitution as null and void, and proceeded to make their influence felt in Congress. The radical element in Congress was working strongly against Lincoln's program in any case, and it was no surprise that the decision of the solons at Washington concerning Louisiana reorganization was negative. A long period of Federal occupation and troublous abnormality was to ensue. There were a number of uneasy years after Lincoln's death before the state was, one should not say restored, but outfitted with a carpetbag government. After that there was to be further delay—nearly a decade—before that unworkable carpetbag regime collapsed.

CHAPTER II

LINCOLN'S PLAN IN OPERATION: UNIONISM IN THE SOUTH

I

AS IN Louisiana, so in other regions of the Confederate South, Lincoln did his best to promote reorganization measures so that state governments could supersede Federal military rule, but wartime conditions made for obstruction and progress was slow. In Tennessee, where secession had been strongly resisted and where Union victories came in February and April of 1862, it might have seemed that a choice opportunity was offered for early restoration of civil government under unionist auspices. The pro-Confederate regime in Tennessee was brief; it extended only from May 7, 1861 (legislative ratification of the military league with the Confederacy) to March 3, 1862, when Lincoln appointed Andrew Johnson military governor of the state, a period of ten months. Johnson's attitude had been demonstrated by "violent opposition to slavery and secession" [1] and by retention of his seat in the United States Senate. His unionism was unassailable, but he could only perform the functions of civil government on an emergency basis and Lincoln's hopes for instituting a more permanent and regular regime were repeatedly deferred. There was heavy fighting in 1862 and 1863. Guerrilla warfare, raids by Forrest, agitation among discordant pro-Union elements, puzzlement as to what was "regular" by the old code of the state (nothing could be strictly regular in those war times), lack of popular interest when elections were held, complications as to soldier voting and military influence, divided leadership as between Nash-

[1] James W. Patton, *Unionism and Reconstruction in Tennessee, 1860–1869*, 30.

ville and Washington—these were among the factors that caused continual delay.

Not until February 1865 was an election held in Tennessee which had importance in terms of popular voting for fundamental state reorganization.[2] After that there loomed, as always, the serious obstacle of congressional opposition. Tennessee was not to be admitted to the Union until 1866. Yet as early as September 11, 1863, Lincoln had written to Governor Johnson: "All Tennessee is now clear of armed insurrectionists." Insisting that "Not a moment should be lost" in "reinaugurating a loyal State government," the President insisted, as in Louisiana, that prudent steps be taken without delay. Discretion was left with Johnson and "co-operating friends" as to ways and means, with the presidential injunction that the reinauguration should not be allowed to slip into the hands of enemies of the Union, "driving its friends . . . into political exile." "It must not be so," wrote Lincoln. "You must have it otherwise." [3] Yet Lincoln did not feel that specific measures of reorganization should emanate too much from Washington. Despite the delay Lincoln was satisfied, by the end of his administration, that Tennessee had been reconstructed sufficiently for executive recognition. To his mind the state was free and restored.[4]

In September 1863 Andrew Johnson said to his people: "Here lies your State; a sick man in his bed, emaciated and exhausted . . . unable to walk alone. The physician comes. Don't quarrel about antecedents, but administer to his wants . . . as quickly as possible . . . . This is no . . . metaphysical question. It is a plain, common sense matter, and there is nothing in the way but obstinacy." [5] Johnson's simile of the sick man and his suggestion as to the ineptness of

---

2 Local officials in Tennessee counties had been chosen in an election in March 1864. *Ibid.*, 43–44.

3 *Works,* IX, 116.

4 There was delay, confusion, and dispute as to reorganization in Tennessee, but at an election on February 22, 1865, amendments in the state constitution were ratified by which slavery was abolished and secession declared null; then an ardent unionist—W. G. ("Parson") Brownlow—was chosen governor. He was inaugurated on April 5, 1865. Thus Lincoln lived to see the re-establishment of a civil regime which he was willing to recognize as the true government of the state. Patton, *Unionism . . . in Tennessee,* 49–50. See also E. Merton Coulter, *William G. Brownlow: Fighting Parson of the Southern Highlands.* In his preface Coulter refers to Brownlow as "one of the most dynamic personalities of his times."

5 *Ann. Cyc.,* 1863, 828.

those administering to him could have covered a great deal more territory than Tennessee.

II

Events of 1863 and early 1864 in Arkansas proceeded with little difficulty so far as that commonwealth itself was concerned. It was a sparsely settled state, with 435,000 inhabitants in 1860, of whom 111,115 were slaves. Illinois, of comparable area, had nearly four times the population. It was chiefly in the southeastern part, in the plantation area near the Mississippi River, that slaveholding was concentrated. Throughout most of the state there were few slaves, in the northern portion hardly any. People of the Ozark mountain region had little in common with the few cotton-growing magnates. To the vast majority of the people the abolition of slavery would produce no serious reordering of their lives and economy.

The state had avoided secession until swept away by the post-Sumter excitement; when secession was adopted it was done reluctantly. Even after secession, considerable Union sentiment remained. According to a contemporary account, pertaining to the situation in 1863, "Citizens of distinction came forward to advocate the Union cause; among others, Brig.-Gen. E. W. Gantt, of the Confederate army, once held as a prisoner of war." The shift of General Gantt from Confederate to Union allegiance was, as he said, part of a popular movement; Union sentiment, he noted, was "manifesting itself on all sides and by every indication." [1] For many who were of like mind with Gantt the open declaration of loyalty to the Federal government, especially after the Confederate surrender of Vicksburg, came naturally. It was like snapping out of an abnormal situation. Gantt declared in 1863 that "loyalty to Jeff. Davis in Arkansas . . . [did] not extend practically beyond the shadow of his army . . . ." [2] Mass meetings were held, Union regiments were formed, Federal oaths were sworn without solicitation, and measures were set in motion, with less difficulty than in Louisiana and Tennessee, for a reorganization of the state government. Military events provided a considerable impulse toward Union reorganization, especially the Union victories at Vicksburg and Port Hudson, and the

[1] *Ann. Cyc.*, 1863, 15. [2] *Ibid.*

Helena-Little Rock expedition of General Frederick Steele, U. S. A., against Sterling Price, C. S. A., which resulted in Confederate evacuation of Little Rock on September 10, 1863. With this Confederate reverse a large part of the state was brought under Union control.

Lincoln kept in touch with Arkansas affairs, notifying General Steele that he, as in the case of Banks in Louisiana, was "master" of the reorganization process. "Some single mind," wrote the President, "must be master, else there will be no agreement in anything." [3] He had ample reason to realize the truth of this statement.

The pattern of the Arkansas movement reveals much as to Lincoln's plan in practical operation. Sentiment developed in meetings, with Union resolutions, in large parts of the state. Delegates were chosen in such meetings (by no more and no less authority than is usual in such popular movements under the stress of abnormal conditions) for a "convention" designed to make a new regime constitutional and legal. Lincoln encouraged the holding of the convention, welcoming it as a fulfillment of his plan as announced in December 1863. On January 20, 1864, he indicated that the reorganization emanated from citizens of Arkansas petitioning for an election, and directed Steele to "order an election immediately" for March 28, 1864.[4] When, on counting the votes for a Union-minded governor and for changes in the state constitution, the number should reach or exceed 5406 (that being ten per cent of the Arkansas vote of 1860), Lincoln directed that the governor thus chosen should be declared qualified and that he should assume his duties under the modified state constitution. (As a minor detail, when it was found that the Union convention in Arkansas was planning the election for March 14, not March 28, the President quickly acquiesced in the convention plan.)

In the President's mind a milestone had been reached in Arkansas affairs with that election of March 14. By an overwhelming majority (12,179 to 226) the voters, having qualified by taking the Federal oath of allegiance, approved those changes in the state constitution which abolished slavery, declared secession void, and repudiated the Confederate debt. Isaac Murphy, already installed as provisional governor by the convention, was now elected governor by "more than double what the President had required." [5] On April 11 the new state gov-

[3] *Works,* X, 11–12.
[4] *Ibid.,* IX, 289–291.
[5] Nicolay and Hay, *Lincoln,* VIII, 416–417.

ernment under the modified constitution was inaugurated at Little Rock. The reconstructed legislature chose senators (William M. Fishbach and Elisha Baxter); three members of Congress had already been chosen in the March election.

Obstruction in House and Senate prevented the admission of these representatives and senators, and for long years Arkansas remained outside the pale so far as Congress was concerned. Lincoln's view, however, both as to practical matters and as to his own function in promoting them, was shown in his executive measures to get these important steps taken, and in his advice to Steele (June 29, 1864) that, despite congressional refusal to give these solons their seats at Washington, the new state government should have "the same support and protection that you would [have given] if the members had been admitted, because in no event . . . can this do any harm, while it will be the best you can do toward suppressing the rebellion." [6] The President knew that admission of solons in Washington was only part of the process of reconstruction, that the setting up of a reorganized state government was indispensable, that Federal protection for such reorganization was essential, and that much of the value of such reorganization would be lost if matters were allowed indefinitely to drift.

III

A different type of situation presented itself in Florida, where the reconstruction effort was of a minor sort. Military accomplishment, so evident in Louisiana, Tennessee, and Arkansas, was lacking in this detached area, which was off the main line of strategy and unpromising as a field in which to commit any considerable body of troops. Aside from holding a few coastal points and maintaining the blockade, the United States paid little attention to the region of the St. John's, the St. Mary's, and the Suwannee. The war was to be decided elsewhere; and the fate of Florida, smallest in population of all the Southern states, would follow as a corollary of that decision. The only sizable engagement in the state during the war was the ill-starred "battle of Olustee," in the northeast corner, a short distance inward from Jacksonville, where a minor Union force under General Tru-

[6] *Works,* X, 139–140.

man Seymour, U. S. A., was defeated by somewhat superior numbers, with advantage of defensive position, under General Joseph Finegan, C. S. A. This engagement, February 20, 1864, was the futile anticlimax of an army-navy expedition of Seymour, a subordinate of General Quincy A. Gillmore who was in command of the "Department of the South" with headquarters at Hilton Head, S.C. Such was the sorry result that Gillmore put the blame upon Seymour, while at Washington Halleck disclaimed all responsibility for the operation.

Under these circumstances, though Union sentiment was held to be widespread in the state, the small-scale efforts to restore Florida were subject to the taunt that their motive was to give a plausible basis for sending pro-Lincoln delegates to the coming Republican convention; even the Seymour expedition was derided as a feature of the political campaign of 1864.

From Lincoln's standpoint the approach to reconstruction in Florida was like that in other Southern areas. On January 13, 1864, he wrote Gillmore advising that the general was to be "master" if differences should arise; in this letter the President urged that restoration be pushed "in the most speedy way possible," and that it be done within the range of the December proclamation. To handle some of the details John Hay was sent to Florida "with some blank-books [for recording oaths] and other blanks, to aid in the reconstruction." [1] This trip of Hay (February–March 1864) was not a brilliant success and the sum-total of the Florida gesture for reconstruction was far from impressive. Hay, now a major, wrote: "I am very sure that we cannot now get the President's 10th & that to alter the suffrage law for a bare tithe would not give us the moral force we want. The people of the interior would be indignant against such a snap judgment taken by incomers & would be jealous & sullen." [2] Hay also wrote of his own mission: "The special duties assigned him occupied little time; there were few loyal citizens to enroll; the most of his service was as an ordinary staff officer to General Gillmore, and there need be no further mention of him, except to say that the movement to restore a legal State government for Florida at that time failed for lack of material." [3] Florida's "delegates," chosen by a few in Jacksonville, did turn up at the Republican convention in June, 1864, but not until after the war

---

[1] *Ibid.*, IX, 283–284. [2] Dennett, ed., . . . *Diaries . . . of John Hay*, 165.

[3] Nicolay and Hay, *Lincoln*, VIII, 283.

did the commonwealth proceed to the making of a new state constitution within the range of the Union; readmission to the Union—i. e., inauguration of carpetbag government—occurred in 1868; restoration of home rule—the throwing off of radical Republican control—was deferred to 1877. It should be added that Lincoln never considered Floridan reconstruction complete according to his design and proclamation.

Small though it was, there was more in the Union effort in Florida than at first met the eye. One could treat the Seymour, or Gillmore-Seymour, expedition of 1864 as a sorry military enterprise, or as a disappointing phase of Lincoln's reconstruction plan, but in a realistic study one needs to enlarge the scope of inquiry. The episode must also be viewed in its relation to such subjects as the use of Negro troops (in which there was creditable performance), maneuvers in the pro-Chase sense, the opening of trade, and what has been called "carpetbag imperialism." In a detailed study George Winston Smith has pointed out that grandiose schemes or experiments were conjured up in connection with the Florida effort. There was, for example, the "extravagant plan" of Eli Thayer of Kansas emigrant fame—a well-intentioned plan to set up "soldier-colonists" and create model communities on the most approved New England pattern. The plan reached "only the blueprint stage," but it reveals much as to Yankee enterprise in the deep South. There was also injected into the wartime Florida scene the "machinations" of Lyman K. Stickney, "the most notorious of the early Florida carpetbaggers," who operated under Secretary Chase in the enforcement of a congressional act for collecting the Federal direct tax in the South. This law, writes Smith, was a "move to confiscate the real property of southern landholders" and was so administered as to become "an instrument of predatory corruption in Florida." [4]

These factors need to be borne in mind in judging Lincoln's approach to reconstruction. It was a complicated problem of many facets, with idealistic motives combined with profit-seeking greed. Lincoln tried to keep restoration on the main track and keep it unmarred, but it was part of the history of the time—the prelude to the "Gilded Age" —that debased and uninspiring maneuvers would creep in. Florida

[4] George Winston Smith, "Carpetbag Imperialism in Florida 1862–1868," *Fla. Hist. Quar.*, XXVII, 99–130, 260–299 (1948–49).

was only an example. When one remembers such influences, he can realize with fuller force the significance of Lincoln's rejection of the whole drive and tendency toward carpetbaggism.

IV

In Lincoln's planning for a restored Union he kept his eye constantly on a highly important factor, that of unionism in the South. Of course it could have been said by critics that Lincoln was not bothering with the opposition, that he was requiring an oath of Union allegiance as a prerequisite for the right to vote on any state reorganization, and that he was thus stacking the cards in his favor, working only with friends of the Union. This seemed the more striking because of his willingness to depend on a Union-minded minimum of ten per cent (of 1860 voters) for the initial steps of reconstruction.

Yet on closer study it will be seen that success for any reunion movement was dependent upon popular support in the state. Always at some point there had to be an election, a popular choice of a constitutional convention to remake the state constitution, and a vote for state officials and members of Congress. People who voted in these initial elections had to take the Union oath; but no one was to be coerced into taking it, and if the number of oath-takers was too insignificant, the plan would not get very far. Lincoln was starting with a loyal minority, but the quality and extent of that minority was never unimportant. Furthermore, the President was planning for peace, for the long years ahead after the war ended. This would involve withdrawing Federal forces and allowing Southerners to take over their state administrations. This was what Lincoln was looking forward to as the normal situation. The ten per cent "rallying point" was to be only a prelude to that restoration.

At all times the President felt assured that his plan would work for the whole South. He could hardly have proceeded with such confidence unless he genuinely believed that unionists in the South were, for the long run and for normal times, in the majority. In fact the validity of Lincoln's basic political philosophy depended upon self rule by the people. To impose a government upon an unwilling state —even a benevolent government—would have been contrary to this fundamental philosophy. There was a risk involved in Lincoln's scheme but it was a calculated risk. When there would come the hazard of an election, that would not merely mean that people should vote because of having sworn allegiance. It meant that such allegiance was expected to prove justified in the type of government set up, the working out of labor adjustment, the choice of well-disposed officials, the installing of honest government, and the like. If these things went wrong even after the initial steps had been taken in compliance with the President's plan, the broad policy would fail. Lincoln's feeling of assurance that it would not fail must have been based on more than wishful thinking. It is therefore of importance to look into the matter and find the basis for this assurance—in other words, to discover some of the evidences of unionism in the South which were known to the President. To give the whole body of such evidence is obviously impracticable, but a few items may be mentioned with the understanding that they were typical of a large and impressive total.

There was the element of war-weariness in the South; people were sick and tired of the continued slaughter. A captured Union general, the famous Neal Dow, wrote to Lincoln from Libby Prison, Richmond, on November 12, 1863: ". . . I have seen much of Rebeldom, behind the curtain, and have talked with a great many soldiers, conscripts, deserters, officers, and citizens. The result of all is, to my mind, that . . . the masses are heartily . . . anxious for its [the war's] close on any terms . . . ." He went on to mention numerous Confederate desertions, soldier infirmities, general debility, the worthlessness of conscripts, depreciation of the currency, flour at $125.00 a barrel, and "everything in the provision line . . . [bearing] a corresponding price." [1]

In Virginia the attitude of intelligent and patriotic unionists was typified by Alexander H. H. Stuart. Though not active against secession during the war, he had been fundamentally opposed to it as inexpedient, and stood ready to support early measures of reunion. Stuart defined his wartime attitudes as follows:

"During the war, I abstained from all participation in public affairs, except on two or three occasions when I was called to address public meetings to urge contributions for the relief of the suffering soldiers and the prisoners going to as well as returning from the North.

[1] Neal Dow, Brig. Genl. U. S. V., to Lincoln, Libby Prison, Richmond, Virginia, Nov. 12, 1863, R. T. L. Coll., 27980.

"My age relieved me from the obligation to render military service, and all the assistance I gave to the Confederate cause was by feeding the hungry and clothing the naked and nursing the sick Confederate soldiers, and making myself and urging others to make liberal donations for their relief." [2]

Another prominent Virginia unionist was the distinguished lawyer John Minor Botts. He had strongly opposed Southern Democratic disunionists, and, though disapproving also of abolitionists, had given support to the efforts of John Quincy Adams in the matter of antislavery petitions presented to Congress. When Lincoln was a Whig member of Congress from Illinois, Botts was a Whig member from Virginia (1847–49); indeed many of his views were similar to Lincoln's. Both in 1850 and in 1860 he was an earnest opponent of secession, his opposition to Jefferson Davis and to Governor Henry Wise of Virginia being especially marked. He greatly regretted the secession of his state in 1860, which he had tried to prevent. During the war he was so far out of sympathy with the Confederate government that he was arrested and confined for some months in jail. For the most part, however, he spent the war years in retirement. The collapse of the Whigs in the 1850's had left him without any adequate party outlet. Though not fully approving of Lincoln, he stood ready to assist in the reconstruction of his state. When elected United States senator by the "restored" Virginia legislature at Alexandria (the legislature of the Pierpoint government), he declined to serve, but he did not want this declination to be taken as evidence of any anti-Union attitude. It was rather that in his opinion the Alexandria regime lacked validity. On January 22, 1864, he wrote a long letter in which he gave consent to the publication of a certain letter he had previously written—i. e., the letter declining the senatorship but without prejudice to the cause of restoration. He wrote: "I think its publication would materially strengthen the Union cause with all Union men in the South, and especially in this state . . . ." [3] His later career showed the steadfastness of his Union loyalty.

[2] Alexander F. Robertson, *Alexander Hugh Holmes Stuart 1807–1891: A Biography*, 241.

[3] John Minor Botts to J. B. Fry, "Private and confidential," Auburn, Culpepper County, Jan. 22, 1864, R. T. L. Coll., 29714–27. (On April 12, 1864, Fry wrote to Lincoln enclosing the Botts letter.) In the crisis of 1861 Botts had been deeply disappointed by the failure of men like himself to hold Virginia in the Union. He differed with J. B. Baldwin, another

The fact that certain Southern areas had never left the Union was, of course, significant. That was true of Kentucky. It was remarked that the mountainous districts of that border state were "with very few exceptions . . . thoroughly union." The same observer noted derisively that in the central part of the state "most of the large slave holders, . . . the gamblers . . . all the decayed chivalry . . . all the fast & fashionable ones & nearly all the original Breckinridge Democrats are bitter to secessionists." [4]

From Little Rock, Arkansas, in March 1864 came a choice letter urging that members of Congress elected in the South be required to travel in the North and vice versa; "they would meet together at Washington in a better spirit." [5]

E. W. Gantt of Arkansas, whose wartime shift from Confederate to Union allegiance has been noted, issued a twenty-four page pamphlet (October 7, 1863) which belongs in any case study of unionism in the South. Much of his statement was a blistering denunciation of Jefferson Davis. With the whole cotton crop at his disposal, wrote Gantt, the Confederate President's foreign policy had been "a stupid failure," while at home he was "weak, mean . . . and supremely ambitious." Though supporting weak generals—such as Pemberton, Hindman, and Holmes—he had waged personal feuds against Joseph Johnston, Price, Pike, Beauregard, and even Stonewall Jackson. "We are whipped—fairly beaten," wrote Gantt. "Our armies are melting and ruin approaches us." Slavery, he said, was "doomed." Urging prompt steps for reunion—this was after severe military reverses in the southwest—he wanted no doubt to remain "that our people are loyal"; "let bygones be forgotten," he added, "and let us all unite to bring about peace . . . ." [6]

In the same month there appeared, in a printed broadside, the proceedings of a mass meeting of "Unconditional Union Men" of western Arkansas at Fort Smith, expressing a willingness to co-operate for re-establishing law and order and for promoting success to Union

---

unionist, in some of his statements, but the record of that time showed the sincerity, as well as the bitter frustration, of those who hoped for an understanding that would have averted secession in Virginia.

[4] W. Hamilton Stockwell to John P. Usher, Boyle Co., Ky., Aug. 28, 1863, R. T. L. Coll., 25903–04.

[5] C. C. Andrews to Lincoln ("Private"), Little Rock, Ark., Mar. 9, 1864, *ibid.*, 31396–97.

[6] Printed pamphlet by E. W. Gantt, Little Rock, Oct. 7, 1863, R. T. L. Coll., 27012–23.

arms.[7] And again from a citizen in Little Rock came the suggestion, months before the thing was done, that the President call upon the people "by proclamation of amnesty . . . to return to their allegiance," Federal protection being offered in return. "Do this," the President was assured, " and I venture to promise, that Arkansas, ere long, will be numbered among the loyal States of the Federal Union." [8]

V

Unionist voices were audible throughout the unhappy South. A clear sign of the times in Louisiana was the editorial of the *True Delta* of New Orleans (February 5, 1864) praising Lincoln, comparing him to Washington and Jackson, and favoring his re-election.[1] In Mississippi a local judge wrote: "I have *first, last and all the time,* been a Union man." Secession, he reported, had been put over without the people understanding what was involved.[2] In another report from Mississippi it was indicated that there were "thousands . . . who desire most ardently the restoration of the United States." [3]

In North Carolina peace movements were rife and it was reported early in 1864 that troops from the Old North State were deserting rapidly and extensively from the Confederate service.[4] In the previous year a group of North Carolina citizens had presented a petition to the President, asking him to "order an election day for this district for the purpose of electing a representative for the next Congress." These petitioners represented themselves as "loyal to the Constitution of our country anxious that it should be perpetuated." [5]

As to Alabama it was predicted that if the question of returning to the Union were submitted to a vote, the people would "vote aye,

7 Printed broadside, *ibid.*, 27599.

8 C. P. Bartrand to Lincoln, Little Rock, Ark., Oct. 19, 1863, *ibid.*, 27322–25.

1 New Orleans *True Delta,* Feb. 5, 1864, clipping in R. T. L. Coll., 30185. For a similar clipping, see no. 30057.

2 L. S. Houghton to Lincoln, Vicksburg, Miss., Aug. 29, 1863, *ibid.*, 25910 ff.

3 A. Burwell to Lincoln, St. Louis, Aug. 28, 1863, *ibid.*, 25884–85. The writer sent the letter after returning from Vicksburg. He expressed the view that there were *"more unconditionally Loyal or Union men in that state* [*Mississippi*], *in proportion to population, than in . . . Ohio or New York."*

4 Col. R. A. Alger to Nicolay, Washington, Feb. 9, 1864, *ibid.*, 30343–44. (One should not argue too much, of course, from the factor of army desertion; there were huge numbers of deserters on both sides. See Ella Lonn, *Desertion during the Civil War.*)

5 Petition signed by twenty-two names, Sept. 30, 1863, R. T. L. Coll., 26757.

five to *one*." The President was given the following assurance: "Could you know how deep and universal is the returning love for the union among the people of Ala & Geo you would discharge your great responsibilities with a hymn of joy in your heart." [6]

These evidences, and more of the same, were available to Lincoln. Since his day further material has come to light tending to reveal the extent of Union sentiment in seceded states. There is a wealth of information on the subject in Federal archives. One is not speaking here of the "amnesty papers"—that large body of written testimony emanating from numerous Southerners who sought special pardon under President Johnson and who in doing so reported their previous position as to secession and Confederate rule. Those papers, though still extant, have been closed to investigators. but there are similar letters outside the "amnesty papers" in various manuscript collections. A notable example was a letter of Alexander H. Stephens to President Johnson, written during the Georgian's brief imprisonment in Fort Warren: ". . . I clearly saw that the great objects in view by me . . . [in accepting Confederate office] were not likely to be obtained even by the success of the Confederate Arms . . . ." Stephens added that the war was inaugurated against his judgment and that he accepted its results.[7]

Of similar importance are the records of Federal agencies such as the United States Court of Claims and the Southern Claims Commission.[8] Since various claims, as for restoration of property, were brought before the Court of Claims, and since proof of loyalty was held to be essential, that court became the tribunal for judging the facts as to the conduct of thousands of professed unionists.[9] In the voluminous testimony which the court examined the historian of Civil War loyalists will find material rich in human interest and close to authentic cases. Naturally, men and women of Union sympathies in the South found existing conditions difficult for any expression of loyalty in active, organized form. Yet their restricted attitude was significant

[6] Edmund Fowler, M. D., to Lincoln, New York, Oct. 27, 1863, *ibid.*, 27529–30. The writer was a citizen of Montgomery, Alabama; he had served as surgeon to Union prisoners.

[7] A. H. Stephens to President Johnson, Ft. Warren, June 9, 1865, Johnson MSS., Lib. of Cong.

[8] Frank Wysor Klingberg, "The Southern Claims Commission: A Postwar Agency in Operation," *Miss. Vall. Hist. Rev.*, XXXII, 195–214 (1945).

[9] Randall, *Constitutional Problems Under Lincoln*, 335–338.

as they maintained a kind of passive resistance, avoided voluntary measures against the government at Washington, opposed the Confederate draft, carried provisions and medicines to Union soldiers, contributed money for the welfare of blue-coats, attended boys in hospitals, and performed other friendly acts for Federal troops. Such acts incurred persecution, and the Southern unionist moved often in an atmosphere of scorn and hostility not unaccompanied by threats and acts of personal violence. Of course, in various respects he was compelled to act against his will when it was a matter of serving as conscript, subscribing to a Confederate loan, contributing cotton, paying taxes, or performing labor. Since Southern wartime history has been largely remembered and recorded in Confederate terms, these details are still somewhat obscure; at least their full force is not generally recognized.

No history of Lincoln, however, can ignore them. His reports from the South were a vital element in policy making. When he made his broad appeal in December 1863, offering pardon, prescribing his simple oath, and opening the way for new state governments by genuine Southern effort looking toward peace with freedom and union, he had reason to know, at least in large part, the kind of support and fulfillment upon which he could count. His sense of his own function as leader was strengthened by his realization that Southern unionism did not signify willingness to accept the program and regime of congressional radicals. On the contrary, such union-mindedness was oriented in Lincolnian terms. In taking on the responsibility of launching and promoting reconstruction, Lincoln saw an opportunity which needed to be seized while its most fruitful results were yet possible. He was mindful of the fact that he had a Southern following, a support south of the line which was both actual and potential, and which needed to become more vocal and assertive. With that following in view, and with the interest of the whole nation at heart, he was making pledges and commitments. It would only have been a lesser man, or a do-nothing President, who would have held back and avoided such commitments.

CHAPTER III

PUBLIC RELATIONS

I

LINCOLN'S remark that he was "environed with difficulties" [1] could have related to a variety of vexations. He could have had in mind an unco-operative Congress, bickering among generals, factions in his own party, misguided peace efforts, unsought advice as to his cabinet, innumerable petty demands, patronage seekers, or perchance a muddled condition in Missouri.

Or it might have been newspaper trouble. In journalism it was the heyday of the "special" writer and the ubiquitous reporter. It was at once a time of remarkably active newspaper enterprise and of lax governmental control over the press. "No war," it has been said, "was ever before so waged in the world's eye." [2] Metropolitan dailies spent huge sums on their "war departments," half a million being spent by the *Herald* alone. Correspondents were seemingly on every march and at all fronts. They were accorded special privileges, eating at officers' mess, using army transportation for their baggage, enjoying the confidence of admirals and generals, unrestrained as they overheard camp talk or picked up snatches of military information. Usually they had army passes and sometimes they even carried military messages or orders. Though gestures were made toward governmental censorship, there was little effective curbing of reporters. Steps were taken early in the war to control the issue of telegraph news from Washington, and at the time of the *Trent* affair an effort was made to impose silence as to correspondence between Seward and Lord Lyons, but a committee of the House of Representatives raised charges of undue interference and the idea of a government censor, known

1 *Collected Works,* V, 438 (reply to serenade Sept. 24, 1862).

2 *Harper's Pictorial History of the Civil War,* I, 122.

as such, was found impracticable. It is true that during the war the telegraph system was under government control by congressional authorization and a special officer was set up with the title of assistant secretary of war and general manager of military telegraphs. This offered some chance for a sifting of news, while at the same time the government had taken over the railroads, so that an offending journal could be denied facilities for transporting papers by train.

Yet the mind of the American people was firmly conditioned against restrictions on the press, and efforts to protect the government proved to be no more than half-way measures. At no time were news channels fully or effectively closed. The mails were open to reporters, messengers could convey material to the home office, "leaks" from a general's headquarters were not uncommon, and confidential communications held up in Washington could be released from other points.

Generals differed in their treatments of journalists. Those ambitious for publicity petted and favored the reporters; if this was not done an offended journalist might vent his spite by misrepresenting a general or sending untrue reports of army conditions. The least effective generals were made to bask in newspaper glory, while abler commanders such as the laconic Grant or the peppery Sherman were basely abused. A Cincinnati editor, questioned as to the dissemination of the newspaper canard that Sherman was "insane," remarked that it was a news item of the day and that he had to keep up with the times. For this and many other reasons Sherman became probably the most severe of Union generals in his attitude toward reporters and editors. He despised the papers, declaring that they had "killed" able generals, incited jealousies, given notice of unexpected military movements, functioned as the "world's gossips," distorted their stories, and injected the names of generals into the political controversies of the day.[3]

Special coloration of certain newspapers in this and other countries is familiar to historians, though perhaps its full effect has not been measured. Francis Lieber, who knew much of European military politics, wrote: "I happen to think of what Joseph Bonaparte once said to me. I had mentioned the saying of Frederic II, that he who

---

[3] J. G. Randall, "The Newspaper Problem during the Civil War," *Amer. Hist. Rev.*, XXIII, 303–323 (Jan. 1918).

has the last shilling remains the master of the field. Joseph Bonaparte replied: Yes, but not because he can pay the last grenadier as Frederic believed, but because he can pay the last newspaper, within and without the country." [4]

In the newspaper world of the time there were great names—Greeley, Bowles, Bennett, Bryant, Raymond, Dana, Forney, and men of like caliber. Lesser men who nevertheless had potent influence included Whitelaw Reid of the Cincinnati *Gazette;* George Wilkes, interested in jockeying and sporting news, whose *Wilkes's Spirit of the Times* combined sports with political comments (seldom pro-Lincoln); George Alfred Townsend, a vigorous correspondent and prolific special writer with a flair for depicting personalities; the picturesque Ben: Perley Poore, notable for wide experience, travel, voluminous compilations, and descriptive column writing; and George William Curtis, influential in his Harper's "Easy Chair."

II

It could hardly be disputed that most of the newspapers were against Lincoln. Among the more partisanly virulent were the Chicago *Times,* the Columbus (Ohio) *Crisis,* the Baltimore *Exchange,* the New York *World,* and the New York *Daily News,* to mention but a few. The *World* characterized Lincoln's emancipation policy as "miserable balderdash"; the Chicago *Times* described his second inaugural as "slipshod," "loose-jointed," and "puerile." [1] Such journals as the Chicago *Times* and the New York *World* were Democratic sheets, but it was also true that Lincoln had a "bad press" among well known Republican publications such as the *Tribune,* and *Post,* and the *Independent* of New York. Bryant of the *Post,* angered by what he considered the monopoly of patronage by the Seward-Weed faction, wrote: "I am so utterly disgusted with Lincoln's behavior that I cannot muster respectful terms in which to write him." [2] Theodore Tilton was anti-Lincoln though pro-Republican. The Chicago *Tribune* was known as one of the stanch Republican papers, but John Hay wrote as follows of its editor: "I found among my letters here

[4] Francis Lieber to Gen. H. W. Halleck, New York, March 4, 1863, Lieber MSS., Huntington Lib.

[1] New York *World,* Feb. 7, 1863; Chicago *Times,* Mar. 6, 1865.

[2] Forbes, *Letters and Recollections,* II, 101.

. . . one from Joe Medill, inconceivably impudent, in which he informs me that on the fourth of next March [1865], thanks to Mr. Lincoln's blunders & follies, we will be kicked out of the White House." [3]

If to these few instances there were added a full coverage of newspaper opposition to Lincoln and his administration, one would find provocation for punitive and suppressive measures on the part of the government. Yet in general it was Lincoln's policy to avoid suppression and to endure abuse as the price, often a high price, of press freedom. To understand this statement one must remember that it is a generalization, and that in such a vast arena as the American Civil War, with its hundreds of newspapers and its array of generals and judges advocate, there could be enough exceptions to make a considerable list and yet the generalization would still hold good. In other words, after one has fully listed all the instances of governmental action against journals and editors, even though the list seems impressive in itself, the number untouched and unmolested would still constitute an overwhelming majority of the immense total.

The government was not lacking in potential methods of discipline. Newspaper men who moved with the armies were within military jurisdiction and were subject to the 57th Article of War which prescribed court-martial trial, with death or other punishment, for anyone "giving intelligence" to the enemy. It would, however, be hard to find any application of this part of the military code. Other possible methods of discipline were military arrest of editors, exclusion of offending correspondents from the bounds of a general's command, and the requiring of passes fortified by regulations for their issuance. As an ultimate punishment there remained the severe expedient of dealing with reporters as spies. It was Secretary of War Stanton who was responsible for one of the rare uses of this stern device. On February 10, 1862, he ordered that a Washington representative of the New York *Herald* "calling himself Dr. Ives" (Dr. Malcom Ives) be "arrested and held in close custody . . . as a spy." [4] The offending writer, according to Stanton, had "intruded" himself into a war department conference and Stanton ordered that no news gatherer could thus "spy out official acts." Ives was released after four months, his case not having been prosecuted in any regular manner; his con-

[3] Dennett, ed., . . . *Diaries* . . . *of John Hay*, 211–212.

[4] *Ann. Cyc.*, 1862, 509.

nection with the *Herald* was broken.[5]

On the question of whether newsmen could be considered spies there was one Union general who had no doubts. Sherman so pronounced them, and it was true that Confederate leaders perused Northern papers for the military information which they constantly supplied. Yet aside from the somewhat eccentric action of Stanton this form of punishment does not appear to have been enforced. To have done so properly would have required proof in each case that the offender was in the actual employ of the enemy.

If a newspaper was "suppressed," that usually meant that its publication was suspended for a period. In addition to the famous cases of the Chicago *Times,* the New York *World,* and the New York *Journal of Commerce,* which have already been treated, there were less known cases of "suppression," such as those of the Dayton (Ohio) *Empire,* the *South* of Baltimore, the *Maryland News* sheet of Baltimore, the Baltimore *Bulletin,* the Louisville *True Presbyterian.* Sometimes a single edition of a paper would be seized without the paper being suppressed, or the distribution of the paper would be checked.

A controversy arose as to whether offensive newspapers could be denied the use of the mails. Postmaster-General Blair, who had refused postal distribution for certain papers judicially condemned as disloyal, defended his legal right to do so. He disclaimed, however, any intent to strike against legitimate freedom of the press and he sharply denied a charge in the New York *World* that his department conducted a regular espionage against newspapers. The charge, he wrote, was "false in every particular." His department did not open papers to discover their contents, yet where evidence was clear he felt justified in excluding matters designed to stir up insurrection.[6]

There were cases of editors being put under military arrest as "prisoners of state," but where this was done there was a reasonable claim or suspicion of disloyalty against the editors, who were usually released after brief confinement. A notable case of such imprisonment was that of F. Key Howard, editor of the Baltimore *Exchange,* who was confined in Fort Lafayette. Immediately after the Howard arrest

---

[5] Robert S. Harper, *Lincoln and the Press,* 132–133.

[6] *Constitutional Problems Under Lincoln,* 501–502; Montgomery Blair to A. Wakeman, Aug. 2, 1864, Gist Blair MSS., Lib. of Cong.

the *Exchange,* which continued to appear, burst out with a denunciation of the Lincoln government, whereupon its publisher W. W. Glenn, was also put under military arrest.[7] In like fashion another Baltimore editor, Thomas W. Hall of the *South,* was consigned to Fort McHenry. Baltimore was indeed a kind of hotbed of anti-Lincoln journalism. It has been stated by Robert S. Harper that no newspaper other than the Baltimore *American* "made even a pretense of advocating the Union cause." [8] (Incidentally there is a bit of irony in the fact that this hostile city was the one in which the convention was held which renominated Lincoln for the presidency.) The net result in Baltimore, in view of the widely published denunciations of high handed military action, was unfavorable to the government, and Howard was released after confinement for several months.

Lincoln himself was no suppressor of journalistic freedom. It has been seen that he promptly revoked the Burnside order against the Chicago *Times,* and when General M. S. Hascall attempted a military policy of newspaper suppression in Indiana in 1863, word came from Washington of the President's disapproval of indiscreet assumption of "military powers not essential to the preservation of the public peace." Because of the harm done by an officer "issuing military proclamations and engaging in newspaper controversies upon questions that agitate the public mind" General Hascall was relieved of his provocative Indiana command.[9] Military arrest of editors belongs to the vast problem of arbitrary arrests and political prisoners, but the President's attitude stood out clearly. When the editor of the *Missouri Democrat* was arrested the President regretted the act. He wrote to General J. M. Schofield: "Please spare me the trouble this is likely to bring." [10]

In the matter of a dramatic "scoop" Lincoln stepped in to prevent severe action by Stanton against a news writer. A *Tribune* correspondent, Henry E. Wing, with great difficulty labored his way through to Grant at the time when the country and the government at Washington were without news of what was happening to the Commander and his great army at the time of the fighting in the Wilderness. Having achieved the notable feat of reaching and talking with the gen-

---

[7] Harper, *Lincoln and the Press,* 160. [8] *Ibid.,* 159.

[9] *Midstream,* 235–236; *Offic. Rec.,* 2 ser. V, 723–724, 759.

[10] *Collected Works,* VI, 326 (July 13, 1863).

eral, Wing made his painful way back, partly walking and running and partly by railroad handcar, and managed to send a wire to Charles A. Dana, assistant secretary of war, whom he knew and with whom he negotiated: if permitted to send one hundred words to the *Tribune,* he would tell the war department what he had so laboriously learned. Stanton threatened the writer with arrest, but the President, so goes the account, approved the transmission of Wing's despatch (New York *Tribune,* May 7, 1864), talked with him on arrival in Washington, and (uncharacteristically for Lincoln) rewarded him with a kiss on the forehead.[11]

When a *Herald* writer, Thomas W. Knox, was excluded from Grant's military command, Lincoln intervened in the newsman's favor. Being advised that the offense was "technical, rather than wilfully wrong," the President revoked the court-martial sentence of exclusion, though with the proviso that Knox's reinstatement would depend upon Grant's "express assent." [12] This seems to have been a matter of difficult relations among generals. The correspondent was acceptable to McClernand but unacceptable to Grant. Lincoln's maneuver was designed to placate both generals while undoing a measure of army discipline against a journalist.

III

While Lincoln found that it was best for him to avoid influencing the press by any of the coarser methods such as dictating editorial policy or imposing censorship, he could not ignore the effect of newspaper publicity. It has been remarked that it was "not uncommon" in the period "to place journalists in important military and political positions whence they could write for the papers with a view to directing public opinion." [1] It has been stated that "Lincoln seems to have chosen more newspaper men for official positions than any of his predecessors." [2] A Baltimore paper declared at the outset of the Lincoln administration: "Editors seem to be in very great favor with the party in power—a larger number of the fraternity having received

[11] F. Lauriston Bullard, *Famous War Correspondents,* 406–408; Welles, *Diary,* II, 25 (May 7, 1864).

[12] *Collected Works,* VI, 142–143 (Mar. 20, 1863).

[1] Dennett, ed., . . . *Diaries* . . . *of John Hay,* 56 n.

[2] Carman and Luthin, *Lincoln and the Patronage,* 125.

appointments . . . than probably under any previous Administration." [3]

John Bigelow, who had been connected with the New York *Evening Post,* was appointed consul general at Paris, which enabled him to exert influence upon European newspapers. Irish-born Charles G. Halpine, colorful and adventurous author-journalist with a varied record of service with the *Herald* and the *Times,* had military appointment leading up to that of brevet brigadier general. While with the army, on General Hunter's staff, he used his facile and poetic pen to influence sentiment; his pieces under the name of "Miles O'Reilly," fictitious Irish-American private, were popular and influential. John W. Forney, who supported the Lincoln administration with his Philadelphia *Press* and his Washington *Chronicle,* was close to the President. He had been a Pierce Democrat but his support of Douglas in 1860, which involved bitter antagonism to Buchanan, had deepened the split in the Democratic party, thus helping to promote Republican victory in Pennsylvania. Lincoln showed a marked friendliness to Forney and used presidential influence to have him chosen secretary of the Senate. When the editor dedicated his new printing establishment in Washington with a "blow-out" as Hay termed it, the President was in attendance.[4] Having spent an evening at Forney's in December 1863 with "political people," Hay reported that Forney "talked a great deal about the President," emphasizing the "unconditional confidence and the loyalty to his person that is felt throughout this land." [5] It would not be amiss to speak of the *Chronicle* as a pro-Lincoln organ. In one of its issues (December 7, 1864) the paper published an article written in full by the President. (For this purpose Lincoln used the good offices of his friend Noah Brooks who assisted in seeing that the article was printed.) The President's contribution pertained to certain wives' requests that their husbands, held in the North as prisoners of war, be released on the ground that each husband was "a religious man." The President gave his idea of a religion that sets men to fight against their Government in order to benefit by the "sweat of other men's faces." [6]

Among others in the newspaper profession who had governmental

[3] Baltimore *Evening Patriot,* Mar. 30, 1861, quoted in Carman and Luthin, 128.

[4] Dennett, ed., . . . *Diaries* . . . *of John Hay,* 74.

[5] *Ibid.,* 146.

[6] Harper, *Lincoln and the Press,* 181–182; *Daily Washington Chronicle,* Dec. 7, 1864; Brooks, *Washington in Lincoln's Time,* 299.

appointments were Scripps of the Chicago *Tribune* who became postmaster in Chicago (though Lincoln came to dislike his methods); Charles A. Dana of the New York *Tribune* (later of the *Sun*) who served as assistant secretary of war; and John D. Defrees, an Indianapolis editor who took a keen interest in pro-Lincoln politics and who became government printer by Lincoln's appointment.[7] There were also George Fogg of New Hampshire (minister to Switzerland), James S. Pike of the New York *Tribune* (minister to Holland), Bayard Taylor of the *Tribune* (secretary of legation at St. Petersburg), and James C. Welling of the Washington *National Intelligencer* (assistant clerk of the United States court of claims). But this brief enumeration gives no adequate impression of the great number of appointments given to journalists; the full number of such men is too long to be listed here.[8] Referring to a certain newspaper, Lincoln once wrote of the possible withdrawal of "the patronage it is enjoying at my hand." [9] The power of bestowal or withdrawal was his to be used at discretion; that power was not capriciously applied, but it was natural that one of the firms singled out for printing contracts was that of Forney, whose profits from this source were not inconsiderable.[10]

IV

The case of James Gordon Bennett the elder posed a special problem as to Lincoln's press relations. Though a thorn in the flesh to the President, it was felt that Bennett could possibly be won over. The *Herald* editor, born in 1795, was pre-eminent in Civil War journalism but stood apart in a class by himself. His complex personality and shifting positions cannot be defined in a word. His newspaper, known for its spicy journalism, was outstanding in success as judged by its circulation, estimated at about 77,000. The rising importance of this one journal was a kind of phenomenon, though earnest souls were often angered by its content. During the sectional crisis and the war the *Herald* shifted about, so that a chart of its attitude toward Lincoln and the government at Washington

---

7 Bates, *Diary*, 37 n. 8 Carman and Luthin, *Lincoln and the Patronage*, 125–128.
9 *Collected Works*, VI, 188 (Apr. 27, 1863).
10 Carman and Luthin, *Lincoln and the Patronage*, 120–121.

would show sharp peaks and deep troughs. In the crisis before Sumter the paper was pro-Southern (or pro-secessionist); then, as a diarist remarked, its "conversion . . . [was] complete" after the April firing started.[1] On May 22, 1863, Lincoln was represented as a strong candidate for the presidency in 1864. On May 28 the word was: "Give us Abraham Lincoln for the next Presidency." There followed suggestions that the President should "at once cut loose from his cabinet (June 6, 1863); on November 3 the verdict was that Lincoln was "master of the situation."

The tone then changed. On December 16, 1863, the *Herald* pronounced that Lincoln's administration had "proved a failure"; on December 18 the country had had "quite enough of a civilian Commander-in-Chief"; on December 21 Old Abe was "hopeless"; and on February 19, 1864, the acme of denunciation was reached in a long and stinging editorial in which the President was contemptuously mocked as this or that kind of joke; a "sorry joke," a "ridiculous joke," a "standing joke," a "broad joke," and a "solemn joke." The Bennett daily then took up for Grant for President in '64, overlooking the patent fact that Grant's indispensable function was that of military commander in the field.[2]

The idea of enlisting Bennett for the Lincoln cause had formed expression at an early date. A curious letter on the subject was written to Lincoln by Joseph Medill of the Chicago *Tribune* on June 19, 1860, who intended to sound out Bennett whom he considered susceptible to a "dicker." "Terms moderate," wrote Medill, "and 'no cure no pay.' " It was suggested that Medill or Ray of the Chicago *Tribune* go to New York taking Norman Judd along. Desiring an interview with his "Satanic Majesty" the Chicago editor reasoned that his "affirmative help" was not important, but he was "powerful for mischief." The journalistic giant did not want money. "Social position is what he wants. He wants to be in a position to be invited with his wife and son to dinner or tea at the White House and to be 'made of' by the big men of the party. . . . He has a vast corps of writers . . . at home and abroad and universal circulation North, South, East, West, Europe, Asia, Africa, and the Isles of the Sea."

---

1 Allan Nevins and Milton Halsey Thomas, eds., *The Diary of George Templeton Strong,* III, 122 (Apr. 16, 1861).

2 For instance, the *Herald* on January 6, 1864, carried an editorial entitled: "Why Grant is the Best Candidate for the Presidency."

This 1860 gesture came to nothing, but the President (who once wrote: "It is important to humor the Herald") [3] persisted in his efforts to enlist the support of the famous editor. As an intermediary he used Weed who is said to have remarked that "Mr. Lincoln deemed it more important to secure the *Herald's* support than to obtain a victory in the field." [4] That Bennett desired favors was shown when he offered the government his fine sailing yacht, the *Henrietta*. The offer was accepted and Bennett's son, at the father's request, was given a lieutenant's commission in the revenue cutter service under the treasury department.[5]

After many shifts the *Herald* support was belatedly given to Lincoln in 1864 and it has been supposed that this result was related to Lincoln's offer to appoint Bennett as United States minister to France. Lincoln's letter extending the offer was dated February 20, 1865.[6] Under date of March 6, 1865 Bennett wrote the President declining the offer but taking special pains to show his "highest consideration" of the President's attitude in "proposing so distinguished an honor." [7] Secretary Welles disapproved of the proffered appointment, referring to Bennett as "an editor . . . whose whims are often wickedly and atrociously leveled against the best men and the best causes . . . ."

Though Lincoln's offer was not written until February of 1865, it was the opinion of A. K. McClure that the President's tender of the French mission to Bennett was one of the "shrewdest of Lincoln's . . . political schemes." [8] This, together with the fact of Bennett's delayed support of the Lincoln ticket, implies that the prospect of the appointment was made known to the editor during the 1864 political campaign. It is known that the idea of such a presidential favor was pending in the pre-election period. Senator Harlan suggested that "it would pay to offer him a foreign mission." John Hay wrote on September 23, 1864, that Forney "had a man talking to the cannie Scot [Bennett] who asked plumply, 'Will I be a welcome visitor at the White House if I support Mr. Lincoln?' " [9] Bennett's biogra-

---

[3] R. T. L. Coll., 22036 (Feb. 28 [?], 1863).

[4] Autobiography of Thurlow Weed, 615–616; Carman and Luthin, *Lincoln and the Patronage*, 123.

[5] Don C. Seitz, *The James Gordon Bennetts*, 181–182; Carman and Luthin, *Lincoln and the Patronage*, 123–124.

[6] Draft in Lincoln's hand, R. T. L. Coll., 40843–44.

[7] R. T. L. Coll., 41070–1.

[8] A. K. McClure, *Abraham Lincoln and Men of War Times*, 90.

[9] Dennett, ed., . . . *Diaries* . . . *of John Hay*, 215.

pher, Don C. Seitz, quotes Thurlow Weed as saying that "two well-meaning friends" were responsible for the affair of the French offer. Seitz adds: "The surmise left open is that 'the two well-meaning friends' may have conveyed some word of the President's intention to honor the editor during the campaign and so brought about the switch in the *Herald's* attitude . . . ."[10]

V

Changing habits of the presidency have brought elaborate modern processes of "White House publicity," but it was quite a different matter under Lincoln. There were no "press conferences," no "White House spokesman," no speech writers, and but few speeches by the President. In 1864 he remarked: "It is not very becoming for one in my position to make speeches at great length."[1] His annual messages, though distinguished by eloquent passages, were not delivered to Congress in person, and throughout his presidency his principal speeches were his two inaugurals, his immortal Gettysburg address, and his last speech (April 11, 1865) pertaining to reconstruction. Showmanship was not congenial to Lincoln's temperament and there was little fanfare associated with the person or even the public duties of the Chief Executive.

This, of course, does not signify that the more important uses of presidential publicity were altogether ignored. Thought was given to public pronouncements and to their timing. When, after Gettysburg and Vicksburg, the fall of Port Hudson was expected, thus opening the entire Mississippi River, Halleck wrote to Grant: "The Prest will then issue a genl order congratulating the armies of the east & west on their recent victories. This consideration has prevented me from issueing [*sic*] one myself for your army. I prefer that it should come from the Prest."[2]

Such was the Halleck idea, but Lincoln did it in his own way. On July 13, 1863, he wrote a friendly personal letter to Grant expressing "grateful acknowledgment for the almost inestimable service you have done the country." Then on July 15 he issued, not a military "order," but a proclamation to the nation setting aside a special day

10 Don C. Seitz, *The James Gordon Bennetts*, 194–195.
1 *Collected Works*, VII, 302 (Apr. 18, 1864).
2 Halleck to Grant, Hq. of Army, Washington, July 11, 1863, MS. Ill. State Hist. Lib.

of thanksgiving for "victories . . . so signal and so effective as to furnish grounds for augmented confidence that the union of these States will be maintained . . . and their peace and prosperity permanently restored." On July 4 he had announced the news from Gettysburg as promising "a great success to the cause of the Union." It has already been seen (*Midstream*) that Lincoln made reluctant but effective use of serenades which were thrust upon him.[3]

The work of the Sanitary Commission—the Civil War counterpart of the Red Cross—made a special appeal to Lincoln's mind and he was called upon to speak at Sanitary Fairs held to raise money. At such a fair in Washington on March 18, 1864, he admitted that he was "not accustomed to the . . . language of eulogy," but added that "if all that has been said . . . in praise of woman were applied to the women of America, it would not do them justice for their conduct during this war." His speech at the Sanitary Fair in Baltimore on April 18, 1864, was somewhat of a major effort. He spoke of slavery, of the meaning of liberty, and of the knotty problem of wartime retaliation which he characterized as a "mistake." At the Sanitary Fair in Philadelphia on June 16, 1864, he made a moderately long speech, praising the Sanitary Commission and the Christian Commission for their "benevolent labors" and giving a word of encouragement for all voluntary activities to contribute to soldier comfort or relief of sick and wounded. He used the occasion for a morale-building word as to war aims. The conflict had taken three years for "restoring the national authority." So far as he was able to speak, he said "we are going through on this line if it takes three years more." For this he asked a "pouring forth of men and assistance." [4]

One technique of publicity was peculiarly characteristic of Lincoln: he made notable use of the occasional open letter, or the fine art of correspondence with a public purpose. Where an important matter needed to be presented to the people, in lieu of a speech, he would often write a careful letter to the appropriate person or group, intending it for the nation's ear. To Greeley on August 22, 1862, he wrote of his "paramount object . . . to save the Union." To Erastus

[3] *Lincoln the President,* III, 11–12.

[4] For these speeches, before Sanitary Fairs, see *Collected Works,* VII, 253–254, 301–303, 394–396.

Corning and others (June 12, 1863) he sent an extended argument concerning wartime executive measures which were being assailed as unconstitutional. To James C. Conkling he sent a public speech to be read at the elaborate Springfield rally of September 3, 1863. For a committee from the Workingmen's Association of New York (March 21, 1864) he wrote an important address on the fundamental relations of capital and labor. Recognizing that "Capital has its rights," he declared that "Labor is the superior of capital." He went on to show that the "strongest bond of human sympathy, outside of the family relation, should be one uniting all working people, of all nations, and tongues, and kindreds." To A. G. Hodges, of Kentucky (April 4, 1864) he wrote of his antislavery views, his official acts concerning slavery, his arming of the Negroes, and his challenge to those who doubted his policy. He did not claim credit for himself, but ended on the note "If God . . . wills." In general, it is in these occasional letters that one finds some of Lincoln's best turned passages of eloquent but unprovocative appeal to public sentiment.[5]

VI

To study Lincoln's letters of consolation is to find a blending of sentiment, uplift, and delicate, unaffected sympathy. When Colonel Elmer E. Ellsworth of the "Ellsworth Zouaves," a personal friend of the Lincolns, was killed at Alexandria in May 1861, the President's exquisite letter to the young warrior's parents, though innocent of effusiveness, came from the heart. Pointing out to the parents that "our affliction here, is scarcely less than your own," he wrote of the young man's indomitable yet modest qualities and his promise of usefulness to his country. It was not for him to remove the grief, but he could give assurance that both the pain and the appreciation of the son's gallant service were shared by the nation. He concluded: "In the hope that it may be no intrusion upon the sacredness of your sorrow, I have ventured to address you this tribute to the memory of my young friend, and your brave and early fallen child. May God give you that consolation which is beyond earthly power." The final

[5] For these occasional letters, see *Collected Works,* V, 388 (Greeley), VI, 260–269 (Corning); VI, 406–411 (Conkling); VII, 259–260 and V, 52 (Reply to Workingmen); VII, 282 (Hodges).

touch was in the subscribing of his name: "Sincerely your friend in a common affliction, A. Lincoln." [1]

It was characteristic that a Lincoln letter would be fitted to the case. In his words of sympathy to Fanny, daughter of Colonel McCullough of Bloomington, Illinois (December 23, 1862), Lincoln's old-time friend, the man in the White House talked as if face to face with the "young heart" that was suffering "beyond what is common in such cases." Sorrow comes to all, he wrote, but "to the young, it comes with bitterest agony, because it takes them unawares." Yet he told the girl, as if seeking to enter her inmost mind: "You are sure to be happy again . . . . The memory of your dear Father, instead of an agony, will yet be a sad sweet feeling in your heart, of a purer, and holier sort than you have known before." [2]

The most famous of Lincoln's letters of consolation was to Mrs. Bixby of Boston; it has taken a pre-eminent place as a Lincoln gem and a classic in the language. The letter reads as follows:

Executive Mansion,
Washington, Nov. 21, 1864.

Dear Madam,—I have been shown in the files of the War Department a statement of the Adjutant General of Massachusetts, that you are the mother of five sons who have died gloriously on the field of battle.

I feel how weak and fruitless must be any words of mine which should attempt to beguile you from the grief of a loss so overwhelming. But I cannot refrain from tendering to you the consolation that may be found in the thanks of the Republic they died to save.

I pray that our Heavenly Father may assuage the anguish of your bereavement, and leave you only the cherished memory of the loved and lost, and the solemn pride that must be yours, to have laid so costly a sacrifice upon the altar of Freedom.

Yours very sincerely and respectfully,
A. Lincoln.[3]

It is futile to paint the lily and it is always a question of how far one needs to comment on a literary classic. In the case of the Bixby letter the literature is tremendous. The subject is clouded by controversies, a deal of mythology has been thrown in, and commercialism has invaded the field. As a result the main significance of Lincoln's phrases has been obscured by irrelevant or unhistorical de-

1 *Collected Works,* IV, 385–386 (May 25, 1861).
2 *Ibid.,* VI, 16–17.
3 *Ibid.,* VIII, 116–117.

Brady Photographs, National Archives

THE BLAIR FAMILY

Upper: Francis P. Blair, Sr., once a member of Jackson's "Kitchen Cabinet," afterwards a self-appointed adviser to President Lincoln.

Lower left: Francis P. Blair, Jr., Army officer and Congressman, administration leader in the House of Representatives.

Lower right: Montgomery Blair, Postmaster-General, 1861–1864.

Executive Mansion,

Washington, September 4. 1864.

Eliza P. Gurney.

My ~~dear~~ esteemed friend.

I have not forgotten—
probably never shall forget—the very
impressive occasion ~~of the visit of~~ when yourself and friends visited me on a Sabbath
forenoon two years ago. Nor has your
kind letter, written nearly a year later,
ever been forgotten. In all, it has been
your purpose to strengthen my reliance
on God. I am much indebted to the
good christian people of the country for
their constant prayers and consolations;
and to no one of them, more than to-
yourself— The purposes of ~~God~~ the Almighty are perfect, and must prevail, though we
erring mortals may fail to accurately perceive them in advance. We hoped for
a happy termination of this terrible war
~~ere~~ long before this; but God knows best, and has
ruled otherwise. We shall yet ~~perceive~~ acknowledge
~~his~~ His wisdom, and our own error therein— Meanwhile we must work earnestly
~~only~~ in the best lights He gives us, trusting that

LINCOLN REVISES HIS LETTER—

working still conduces to the great ends He ordains. Surely He intends some great good to follow this mighty convulsion, which no mortal could make, and no mortal could ~~hinder~~ stay.

Your people—the Friends—have had, and are having, a very great trial. On principle, and faith, opposed to both war and oppression, they can only practically oppose oppression by war. In this hard dilema some have chosen one horn and some the other. For those appealing to me on conscientious grounds, I have done, and shall do, the best I could and can, in my own conscience, under my oath to the law. That you ~~know~~ believe this I doubt not; and ~~knowing~~ believing it, I shall still receive, for our country and myself, your earnest prayers to our ~~common~~ Father in Heaven.

Your sincere friend.

A. Lincoln

Robert Todd Lincoln Coll., Lib. of Cong.

—TO MRS. GURNEY, SEPT. 4, 1864

Brady Photographs, National Archives

PROFESSIONALS AND POLITICOS

Upper: Grant and Sherman, professional soldiers, in 1865.
Lower: B. F. Butler (standing) and N. P. Banks, political generals. The differences in pose and costume are revealing.

tails. If one reads the letter and appreciates its noble meaning and distinguished form, that after all is the prime consideration. For our present study, emphasizing Lincoln, a brief statement must suffice.

Amid the hundreds of thousands of casualties the Bixby boys were singled out in the following manner. William Schouler, state adjutant general of Massachusetts, gave a statement concerning the alleged death in battle of the five sons of Mrs. Lydia Bixby of Boston to Governor Andrew; the governor added his endorsement; the record came up to the war department in Washington; and the statement was communicated to Lincoln. It was on this evidence that Lincoln's letter of consolation was based.

The records themselves are confused. The report of five sons killed was erroneous; [4] Mrs. Bixby was an obscure person who frequently changed her residence; furthermore, there is evidence that her character was not that of respectability.[5] It must be added that the records clearly show two sons killed, this being truly enough a "costly . . . sacrifice."

Most troublesome of all has been the contention that it was not Lincoln, but John Hay, who composed the letter. If this could be proved to be true it would have to be accepted, but in so famous an instance readers on Lincoln will wish to know how the matter stands. The Hay-authorship theory depends not on clear evidence but on

---

[4] Two sons, according to reliable records, were killed in action: Sergeant Charles N. Bixby at Fredericksburg, May 3, 1863, and Private Oliver C. Bixby near Petersburg, July 30, 1864. Corporal Henry C. Bixby was captured at Gettysburg, held prisoner, and honorably discharged. (Also reported, less reliably, as "missing at Gettysburg" and "killed at Gettysburg.") In the case of Private George A. Way Bixby the records seem conflicting. According to one record he was captured, held prisoner, and died as a captive; he was also said to have been killed at Petersburg; by a third record (statement of Col. F. C. Ainsworth, U. S. Record and Pension Office, December 8, 1863) he was captured in July 1864, confined in Southern prisons, and "Deserted to the enemy." As to the youngest boy, Private (Arthur) Edward Bixby, William E. Barton has concluded that he was a deserter, and that he lived on until 1909. The summary by F. L. Bullard (33–34) reads: ". . . two . . . were killed in action, one was honorably discharged . . . , one may or may not have been a deserter and may or may not have died a prisoner . . . , and the youngest deserted . . . but apparently not 'to the enemy.' " On this subject the writer has studied, along with other material, the elaborate notebook of Dr. Barton in the University of Chicago Library, also the archives of the adjutant general's office of Massachusetts at Boston; in this office at Boston the author was ably assisted by Fred W. Cross.

[5] For a highly unfavorable account, reporting that Mrs. Bixby kept a house of ill fame, see L. Vernon Briggs, *History and Genealogy of the Cabot Family* (statement of Mrs. Andrew C. Wheelwright, formerly Sarah Cabot), I, 300–301.

an indirect and delayed transmission of reminiscence. One gets it from Nicholas Murray Butler, who wrote: "John Hay told Morley that he had himself written the Bixby letter . . . ."[6] This was not to be disclosed until after Hay's death. Morley, having talked with Hay in 1904, reported the matter to Butler in 1912, when again there was a pledge of secrecy; nothing was to be said of the matter until after Morley's death.

Some have accepted the Butler-Morley-Hay transmission (reading backward) and have bolstered it with supposed evidence that Hay was an imitator of Lincoln's style, of his handwriting, and of his signature. Butler makes the incredibly erroneous statement: "Abraham Lincoln wrote very few letters that bore his signature. John G. Nicolay wrote almost all of those which were official, while John Hay wrote almost all of those which were personal."[7]

With such flimsy statements as these and with various conjectures that Hay himself would never have approved, the subject has become artificially complex and hard to follow. A reader who wants a reliable analysis will do well to read the admirably thorough and fair minded study of the whole subject by F. Lauriston Bullard.[8] The notion that Lincoln wrote very few letters is a serious error. He wrote hundreds in his own hand while President. The statement that Nicolay wrote "almost all" the official ones and Hay the personal ones is demonstrably and astonishingly false. As for Hay imitating Lincoln's handwriting as stated by Butler, it has been shown by Bullard that no actual case of such an imitation can be found. "Nobody has brought forward any definite and convincing confirmation" of this claim,[9] to say nothing of the doubtful propriety of such an imitation on the part of a private secretary. Why should he have imitated Lincoln's handwriting and signature?

Hay did not compose Lincoln's personal letters though there may be found a few letters written for Lincoln in Hay's hand—that is, "routine run-of-the-mine documents"[10] which Lincoln signed though

---

6 Nicholas Murray Butler, *Across the Busy Years,* II, 390–393. 7 *Ibid.,* II, 390.

8 F. Lauriston Bullard, *Lincoln and the Widow Bixby*. For the argument supporting the Hay-authorship theory see the following pamphlets by Sherman D. Wakefield: *Abraham Lincoln and the Widow Bixby,* and *Abraham Lincoln and the Bixby Letter.* See also "Mr. Bullard's Reply to Mr. Wakefield," *Lincoln Herald,* Vol. 49, 45–46 (June, 1947); "Mr. Wakefield's Reply to Mr. Bullard," *ibid.,* Vol. 49, 27–29 (Dec., 1947).

9 Bullard, 79, 95. 10 *Ibid.,* 82, 86.

they were not holograph letters, and which did not require the special touch of Lincoln's personality. There is a considerable contrast in style between the writing of the young Hay and that of the President. Sometimes a Lincoln letter, if rather long, would be rewritten by a scribe to save labor for the President, but such a letter would be none the less Lincoln's own, probably being based on a draft or working copy in Lincoln's hand.

One of the factors on which careful historians are agreed is that reminiscence is not enough, and it must be repeated that the idea of Hay's authorship rests upon indirectly reported conversations.[11] Memories of honorable men are "fallible," as Bullard shows, and in the case of Hay it is a matter of record that when he talked to Morley in 1904 (eight years before Morley is reported to have talked to Butler), the former secretary of Lincoln was "heavily burdened with grief" from the death of his brother. Hay's own diary account reads: "I talked with him [Morley] hardly knowing what I was saying." [12] It should be added that in this contemporary diary record there is no mention by Hay of having chatted with Morley concerning the Bixby letter; what is more to the point is that one can trace no direct statement by Hay himself that he ever claimed Bixby-letter authorship.

The letter to Lydia Bixby is a genuine Lincoln document printed in the newspapers about the time of its delivery in person to the bereaved mother [13] in Boston and authenticated by inclusion in the *Complete Works of Abraham Lincoln* edited by Nicolay and Hay. On January 19, 1904, the very year of the statement later quoted to Morley, Hay wrote to W. D. Chandler: "The letter of Mr. Lincoln to Mrs. Bixby is genuine . . . ." [14] It must at once be added, however, that the familiar "facsimile" of the letter, or rather several differing facsimiles which have often been used for commercial advertising and for sale, are fakes. Lincoln scholars do not believe that the maker, or fabricator, of any "facsimile" had the actual handwritten letter of Lincoln before him. By comparison with genuine Lincoln letters of the late 1864 period one can see that the "facsimile"

11 *Ibid.*, 112.

12 *Ibid.*, 117.

13 Lincoln's letter was printed in the Boston *Transcript*, Nov. 25, 1864 (where it was reported as received "this morning"); in the Boston *Daily Advertiser*, Nov. 26, 1864; and in the *Army and Navy Journal*, II, 228 (Dec. 3, 1864).

14 Bullard, 122 ff.

lacks the easy flow and the vital quality of letters penned by Lincoln's hand. The writing is a labored and artificial, though superficially plausible, imitation of the President's handwriting. If any one of the facsimile makers had been in possession of the Lincoln original, or of an authentic photographic copy of it, the original would now in all probability be known to collectors, for the process of Lincoln collecting had gone far by the time these "facsimiles" were made. Yet the fact is that the original of this priceless letter has simply been lost,[15] and being a popular topic, it has been a likely subject of forgery. It must be emphasized, however, that it is the *facsimile* purporting to reproduce Lincoln's handwriting which is forged; the Lincoln letter, though long lost, is authentic and its printed form can be trusted as the recognized text.[16]

It is unnecessary to go fully into the mythology of the subject, but it may be briefly remarked that the original manuscript was never at Oxford University (Brasenose College), that it was never in the J. P. Morgan Collection, and that various and sundry "discoveries" of the "original" letter have proved erroneous. Mrs. Bixby did not preserve the letter nor did her family; what happened to it after she received it is unknown.

The vignette-like beauty of the letter, the tender reference to "a loss so overwhelming," the thanks of the Republic to the mother, are given with deep feeling and fitting expression as coming from the spokesman of the whole nation to a parent who stood in a representative capacity for all similarly afflicted parents. Then follows the lofty religious sentiment, the prayer to "our heavenly Father" to assuage the anguish, and the final complimentary mention of "solemn pride" in "so costly a sacrifice." The letter is sincere and heart-to-heart. It is a fine example of Lincoln's personal tact. It stands with the Gettysburg address as a masterpiece in the English language.

---

15 "Since the day of its delivery neither the original letter nor an undoubted facsimile of it has been seen, and yet it is perhaps the most sought-after letter in the world." Sherman Day Wakefield, *Abraham Lincoln and the Bixby Letter,* (pamphlet), 4.

16 For further treatment of the Bixby subject, see *Abr. Lincoln Quar.* III, 313 and IV, 35–39; Kendall Banning, "The Case of Lydia Bixby," *Bookman,* vol. 54, 516–520 (1922); William E. Barton, *A Beautiful Blunder;* Elmer Gertz, "Mrs. Bixby Gets a Letter," *Lincoln Herald,* Dec. 1942; Sherman D. Wakefield, in *Hobbies,* Feb. 1941. Numerous other titles are to be found in newspapers and magazines.

CHAPTER IV

LINCOLN'S GOOD NEIGHBOR POLICY: FRANCE, RUSSIA, MEXICO

IT WOULD make an interesting study to consider American leaders side by side with foreign contemporaries: John Adams with Talleyrand, Jefferson with Napoleon, John Quincy Adams with Metternich, and so on. Such a view presents divergences between the old world and the new which seem at times grotesque. Without laboring the point nor overplaying the superiority of new-world politics, one finds the contrast especially striking in the period when Abraham Lincoln stood forth in a world whose luminaries included a Son of Heaven, a Romanoff, a Hohenzollern, a Hapsburg, sultans and sheiks, daimios and rajahs, throned monarchs and dictators, a Napoleon, a Bismarck, a Garibaldi and a less dashing Cavour, a phantom-crowned Maximilian and an avenging Juárez.

Of some of these foreign elements little needs to be said except that they were contemporaneous; as to others their bearing upon America was vital. A President who had grown up in quiet and remote surroundings, and whose familiarity with foreign things was very slight, was thrown into a series of confused and delicate international situations which presented a constant demand for astute statesmanship. Toward Canada and Mexico, Britain and France, the importance of favorable relations was imperative; in any of these quarters a false step would have been disastrous. Any interruption of traditionally friendly relations with Russia would also have been deeply unfortunate. In dealing with Japan the oppositeness of East and West was startlingly revealed, though this seemed at the time a minor problem, while in the case of China the role of good neighbor in the days of Burlingame presented a challenge to the best and highest in American diplomacy. It was perhaps in the cases of Britain, France, Mexico, and China that the neighborly attitude of the Lincoln government stood out most noticeably; in these important areas especially, and in others also, the good will and foresight of Lincoln, Seward, and Company were weighed and found not wanting.

I

In considering the relation of France to the government of Lincoln one is dealing with an unnatural and abnormal situation. Genuine French opinion, as the documents amply reveal,[1] leaned heavily to the Union side. Accustomed to a unitary government and a concept of national solidarity, the people of France saw no fundamental wisdom in secession, while they were also powerfully influenced by their equalitarian views, their abhorrence of human slavery, and their remembrance of the traditional friendship between the lands of Lafayette and Washington. In contrast, however, to this natural harmony between the two nations was the fact that France was not herself under the Second Empire. The flamboyant dictatorship of Napoleon III, though unable completely to ignore public opinion, was under no specific democratic control, especially in those superficial attitudes that caused false ideas to arise. In following the tortuous diplomacy of the Tuileries one has a sense of unreality. In all the Empire's international dealing one notices an inconsistency between propaganda and fact, façade and main structure, promise and performance. While the war was yet raging violently the Confederacy suffered a collapse of gilded hopes as to French support, while on the other hand the cause of Lincoln and Seward, discouraged as it was by many a portent of French interference, came through with success in virtually every point at issue.

In France, as in Britain, the most serious difficulty was focused on the problem of mediation, with its menacing possibilities for an armistice, recognition of the Confederacy, and European intervention. Superficially a proffer of good offices might be phrased in terms of friendship for both sides, but the eagerness with which the government at Richmond hailed any foreign suggestion for a cessation of

[1] Lynn M. Case, *French Opinion on the United States and Mexico, 1860–1867* (contains a mass of official documents reflective of public sentiment); Owsley, *King Cotton Diplomacy*, 564.

the war in terms that envisaged an enduring Confederacy may be taken as sufficient evidence of the harm that such a plan would have brought to the Union cause. It was therefore an ominous fact that in the autumn of 1862 the French Emperor presented a proposal for joint mediation, asking the governments of Britain and Russia to join him in proposing to the American belligerents an armistice of six months. The proposal was understood (certainly by the Confederates) to imply the French imperial wish not only for "mediation," but also for recognition of the Confederacy.[2]

There had been a good deal of secret questioning as to the French proposal at St. Petersburg and London. On previous occasions Napoleon III had created the impression in Confederate minds that France was about to extend recognition. When, after considerable mulling in preliminary conversations, the French proposal for joint mediation came on November 10, 1862, it was published in the newspapers, and the matter was quickly brought to a head by the refusal of Russia and Britain to identify themselves with it. In a British cabinet meeting all present except Gladstone "proceeded to pick it to pieces." [3] In Russia the reaction, official and unofficial, was decisively unfavorable.

These were not snap judgments. Palmerston's cabinet gave the matter careful examination, remembering Adam's reminders of American hostility to the idea, while in Russia Prince Gorchakov [4] was given similar assurances. Seward's dispatches made it clear that "mediation," implying success of disunion (for otherwise no settlement would even have had a hearing by Confederate officials), was regarded at Washington as an alarming and unfriendly proposal.

In all these discussions nothing was more obvious than the propensity of those who favored mediation to misunderstand both American sides. The idea that the Lincoln government could make peace with an independent Southern Confederacy was but one aspect of this misreading of the American situation. Another aspect was seen in the Paris *Constitutionnel* of June 9, 1862, which misinterpreted a speech delivered the previous November in London by W. L. Yancey as a suggestion that the Confederacy might be willing to give

2 *Offic. Rec.* (Nav.), 2 ser., III, 601, 610–611.

3 E. D. Adams, *Great Britain and the American Civil War,* II, 63–64.

4 Vice chancellor and minister of foreign affairs of the Russian government. In contemporary American diplomatic correspondence the spelling is Gortchacow.

up slavery in order to gain foreign support for peace. The Confederacy made no such abolition move until the last phase of the war, and the inaccuracy of this French interpretation was shown by the Confederate diplomatic agent A. Dudley Mann who wrote: "The 'care of our honor' peremptorily forbade such a commitment . . . ." [5]

That "peace" by mediation, armistice, or any process that envisaged an undefeated Confederacy was equivalent to utter defeat of the Union cause must have been evident to an informed observer. Such a proposal necessarily implied normal continuing existence of two separate nations in America through an indefinite future. At no point did the representatives of the Richmond government leave any doubt as to their refusal to treat for the only kind of peace that the Lincoln government would consider—i. e., re-establishment of the American Union. A Frenchman who had visited the United States and had seen Seward, later conversed with Slidell in Paris, showing that he envisaged such a restoration of the Union as would allow "conditions and guarantees" favorable to the South, but Slidell resented his suggestion as pro-Northern and bluntly told him: "if Mr. Lincoln were to present us a blank sheet of paper on which we were to write our own . . . guaranties, we would never consent to live with the men from whom we had . . . forever separated." [6]

Despite the complete failure of joint mediation the government of Napoleon III made a strictly French move in isolated diplomacy in January 1863, when his foreign minister sent a dispatch to Washington, deeply deploring a "war, worse than civil," and extending a proffer of "good offices" in order to "shorten" the hostilities. If there was any doubt of Washington's attitude, that doubt was dissipated by Seward's emphatic answer (Feb. 6, 1863) and by a stinging resolution adopted by Congress (March 3, 1863). Though paying respect to the motive of friendship which, as he said, inspired the offer, Seward made it unquestionably clear that the government of Lincoln had "only one purpose— . . . to preserve the integrity of the country." [7] In sharper terms, for Seward kept the amenities of international intercourse, both houses of the American Congress on March 3, 1863, passed a concurrent resolution which did not require Lin-

[5] *Offic. Rec.* (Nav.), 2 ser, III, 443.

[6] *Ibid.*, 519.

[7] McPherson, *Hist. of the Rebellion,* 345.

coln's signature, denouncing "foreign interference" as "unreasonable and inadmissible," and declaring that any further step in this direction would be regarded as "an unfriendly act." [8]

There was evidence that French statesmen were sensitive to the lack of European support for their mediation proposal. Expressing the official attitude, the *Moniteur* declared on April 1, 1864: "if it had obtained the concurrence of . . . St. Petersburg and London, the idea of France might not have been either so fruitless or so badly received at Washington, as it was by remaining in the state of an isolated initiative." [9]

II

Dealings of Napoleon III's government with Confederate officials are suggestive of a kind of a pipe-dream diplomacy. Whether it was a financial deal, a bid for warships, or a quest for recognition, Confederate success seemed often to beckon, but substantial aid was an ever receding mirage. A loan was arranged with the French firm of Erlanger, but Confederate negotiators had to allow an unflattering discount, a one-sided deal as to the price of cotton on which the bonds were based, and enormous profits to the takers of the loan. Functionaries of Napoleon's government, openly sympathetic to the Confederacy, had built up Southern hopes; they had even served as Confederate propagandists. Certain ironclads were actually built, but they were never delivered; the Confederacy got no warships from France.

In receiving Confederate agents the French government had gone much further than the British government. Slidell was accorded the honor of personal interviews with the Emperor, as on July 16, 1862, when, by Slidell's account, the news of Union reverses near Richmond "appeared to give him [Napoleon] much satisfaction." [1] Napoleon might give a favorable gesture toward the South, as in the ludicrous episode of Lindsay-Roebuck diplomacy,[2] but such a move was

[8] *Cong. Globe,* 37 Cong., 3 sess., 1497–1498, 1541.

[9] The article in the *Moniteur* was a conspicuous reprint of an editorial published in the *Courrier des États Unis.* It was enclosed in a despatch of William L. Dayton to Seward on April 4, 1864, in which Dayton referred to the *Moniteur* as "exclusively an official paper." *House Exec. Doc. No. 1,* 38 Cong., 2 sess., pt. 3, 61–64.

[1] *Offic. Rec.* (Nav.), 2 ser., III, 482. For Napoleon's interviews with Slidell see *ibid.,* 481–487, 574–578, 808, 812–814, 1218–1219.

[2] See *Lincoln the President,* III, 350–353.

more likely to do the Confederacy harm than good. This episode [3] signified to the Confederate envoy Mason that Napoleon's "professions" had been reduced "to a mere shadow," and that the French monarch "held one language" to Roebuck and Lindsay and "a different language to his ambassador in London." [4]

Putting together the comments of Mason, Slidell, Mann, and Benjamin, one concludes that the Confederates themselves were not far misled by Napoleonic blandishment. Mann wrote in May 1863 that his side had "nothing whatever to expect . . . from . . . the Emperor of the French." [5] Hotze, Confederate propagandist, wrote in October 1863 that "the heart of France [beats] for our enemies." [6] After being shifted from one prospect to another, Secretary Benjamin had learned midway in the war to count on nothing as assured, remarking that European conduct was "so different from what was anticipated . . . that we no longer seek to divine their probable course of action." [7]

III

In the case of no other country did the United States under Lincoln enjoy such a marked demonstration of friendliness as in the case of Russia. It becomes necessary here, of course, to recall to mind the Russian-American situation of the nineteenth century. Seward wrote midway in the war: "In regard to Russia, the case is a plain one. She has our friendship, in every case, in preference to any other European power, simply because she always wishes us well, and leaves us to conduct our affairs as we think best." [1] That this good feeling was reciprocated at St. Petersburg was shown by Prince Gorchakov, Russian foreign minister, when the United States chargé d'affaires, Bayard Taylor, presented a friendly letter from Lincoln to Tsar Alexander II in October 1862. Gorchakov said: "We desire

[3] For Lindsay's interviews with Napoleon, see *Offic. Rec.* (Nav.), 2 ser. III, 392 ff.; Owsley, *King Cotton Diplomacy*, 298 ff.

[4] *Offic. Rec.* (Nav.), 2 ser., III, 825.

[5] *Ibid.*, 758. He had expressed the same sentiment before (*ibid.*, 516).

[6] Hotze was pointing out what he regarded as the antithesis between public opinion in Britain and in France. He wrote: ". . . the heart of England beats for us and the heart of France for our enemies." In noting Hotze's misreading of British public opinion it must be remembered that he was probably thinking of those Englishmen—such as James Spence—with whom he had been associating and working. *Ibid.*, 946.

[7] *Ibid.*, 656.

[1] *House Exec. Doc., No. 1*, 38 Cong., 1 sess., pt. 2, 851.

above all things the maintenance of the American Union, as one indivisible nation. . . . We have no hostility to the southern people. . . . There will be proposals for intervention. We believe that intervention could do no good at present. Proposals will be made to Russia to join in some plan of interference. She will refuse any invitation of the kind." [2]

A combination of circumstances joined to produce this friendly attitude. In the troubled diplomacy of nineteenth-century Europe France and Britain had been antagonistic to Russia, and in the Crimean War, 1854–1856, there had been armed hostility and bitter resentment. In that war the United States was, of course, neutral, but in feeling many Americans tended toward sympathy with Russia. This sympathy was shown by outspoken comments in the press and by efforts toward mediation on the part of distinguished Americans such as Sumner, Mason, and Fish, as well as by tentative official gestures.[3] The whole effect of the Civil War was to draw Washington and St. Petersburg "even closer together." [4]

This friendship was no less sincere because of being linked with Russian self-interest. The Russian minister at Washington, Edouard de Stoeckl, might fail to understand the Americans among whom he sojourned.[5] Yet distrust of Palmerston's Britain and Napoleon's France naturally strengthened the Russian wish to find, or keep, a friend in the New World. Early in the war it became obvious that Confederate diplomatic success, or even reception, at St. Petersburg was impossible, and it was promptly recognized that "a strong, united

---

2 *Ibid.*, 840.

3 "Numerous Russian well-wishers in Congress, among them Sumner, Mason, Clayton, Clingman, and Fish, introduced resolutions or sponsored petitions requesting the President to tender his good offices to end the war. . . . Marcy himself [secretary of state] informed Stoeckl [Russian minister at Washington] that mediation had been discussed in the cabinet . . . ." Benjamin P. Thomas, *Russo-American Relations, 1815–1867, (Johns Hopkins Studies*, ser. XLVIII, No. 2), 115. After noting the conciliatory efforts of Elihu Burritt, tireless crusader for international peace, Roy Franklin Nichols writes: "[President] Pierce did not take the steps to further the cause of arbitration [in the Crimean War] which Burritt had hoped, but he and his cabinet had ambitions to act as peacemakers." Nichols, *Franklin Pierce*, 346.

4 Benjamin P. Thomas as above cited, 120.

5 It appears that Stoeckl misjudged the American conflict, thought the war would be over soon, considered the old Union gone, and regarded the breach between North and South as irreparable. Lincoln seemed to him to have no far-sighted plan, and he had little respect for American leaders, or, in fact, for republican government. All this is revealed in Frank A. Golder, "The American Civil War through the Eyes of a Russian Diplomat," *Am. Hist. Rev.*, XXVI, 454–463 (Apr., 1921).

American state was an axiom of Russian foreign policy." [6]

For an understanding of these matters one must consider two principal episodes: Russian conduct in the drive toward European "intervention," and the visit of Russian fleets to American waters. Knowing that mediation was resented at Washington, the Russian government, despite its keen wish for a termination of hostilities, turned a cold shoulder toward those suggestions for negotiation which were actively promoted in late '62 and early '63. Especially did the Russian government throw a damper upon mediatory proposals emanating from Paris. Gorchakov besought Bayard Taylor to impress upon his government the feeling of Russia that permanent separation of the American sections would be a great misfortune. One separation, he feared, would be followed by another; the great American nation would break into fragments. He left no doubt in Taylor's mind as to the genuineness of Russian sympathy with the Lincoln government and the meticulous care of his government to maintain a strictly correct attitude in its dealings with Washington.[7] When by May 1863 American prospects abroad were seen to be "decidedly improving," [8] and when the tension as to mediation had noticeably relaxed, it was obvious that the Russian situation had much to do with this improvement.

The sending of the Russian fleets is a complex problem whose ramifications cannot be explored here. Because of a crisis in the perennial Polish question it seemed probable in 1863 that war might again break out between Russia on the one side and Britain and France on the other. Conferences dealing with this possibility were held in the Russian capital which involved anxious deliberation as to how Russia's naval forces could be best disposed. Not all the motives and complications in these conferences can be reconstructed,[9] nor can one say how much stress should be laid on the safety of the

---

[6] Thomas, 127. [7] *House Exec. Doc. No. 1,* 38 Cong., 1 sess., pt. 2, 839–841.

[8] "Our prospects are decidedly improving. The English antagonism has passed its climax, and I don't think intervention will again be hinted at." Bayard Taylor to Simon Cameron, St. Petersburg, May 12, 1863, Cameron MSS., Lib. of Cong.

[9] To set forth these complications is impossible here. Among the factors were the oft-expressed American interest in Polish claims, criticism of the Tsar's Polish policy by American newspapers (as far back as Jackson's administration), difficulties as to Russian America, refusal by the United States to adhere to the international abolition of privateering, the Federal blockade, and the privateering activities of the Confederacy. Thomas, *passim* (esp. 88, 92 ff., 108 ff.).

fleet or the chance of a problematical attack upon enemy colonies, but what the fleets did is a matter of history. One of them appeared in New York harbor under Admiral Lesovsky (Lisovskii) in September 1863; another turned up at San Francisco next month under Admiral Popov. The whole international situation made it seem advisable for Russia, in view of her own interests, to choose American ports for friendly visits, and from the Russian standpoint the episode can be sufficiently explained without supposing that the giving of specific aid to the Union side was the primary purpose. Nevertheless the arrival of the fleets, which amounted to an international sensation, was enthusiastically cheered by American citizens, newspapers, and officials. Russian officers were given elaborate high-society parties; the roster of gentlemen who constituted the committee on arrangements for the ball in New York City in honor of the Russian Naval officers reads like a social blue book.[10] While at New York the fleet enjoyed through Secretary Welles the facilities of the Brooklyn Navy Yard.

As Seward remarked, the American welcome to the Russians required no official prompting. It was "as universal as it was spontaneous." [11] When in December the fleet of Lesovsky sailed into the Chesapeake and up the Potomac Seward himself entertained the admiral and his associates, together with department heads and a large party of American naval officers at his home. This was but an incident of a series of social and official functions at Washington in which the courtesies of the United States were strengthened by the participation of foreign legations.[12]

While Popov's fleet was at San Francisco its assistance was given in extinguishing a fire. Furthermore, the fleet was ready, "simply in the name of humanity, but not of politics, to exercise . . . influence for the prevention of harm." [13] Some may have thought that this brought

[10] A printed list is found among the Tilden MSS. in the New York Public Library. Among the names that appear are W. H. Aspinwall, John J. Astor, Jr., Henry W. Brevoort, Hiram Barney, H. W. Bellows, George Bancroft, S. L. M. Barlow, August Belmont, Frederick E. Church, John A. Dix, Franklin H. Delano, Frederick De Peyster, William M. Evarts, Hamilton Fish, Cyrus W. Field, Moses H. Grinnell, Abram S. Hewitt, Francis Lieber, Robert Dale Owen, George Opdyke (Mayor), Edwards Pierrepont, Theodore Roosevelt, A. T. Stewart, John Austin Stevens, A. V. H. Stuyvesant, Samuel J. Tilden, and Alexander Van Rensselaer.

[11] *House Exec. Doc. No. 1,* 38 Cong., 2 sess., pt. 3, p. 279. [12] Welles, *Diary,* I, 481.

[13] The words of Stoeckl as quoted by E. A. Adamov in *Jour. of Mod. Hist.,* II, 600 (Dec. 1930).

Russia "very near [to] becoming our active ally." [14] Whether this is true may be doubted, for anything like specific assistance to the Union cause would have been interpreted as intervention. It was felt, however, that the presence of the fleet would have checked European warlike impulses against the United States had they existed in any serious degree, and such presence, in London and Paris no less than in Washington and St. Petersburg, was regarded as a gesture of Russian-American amity. After the naval squadrons returned home there occurred a renewed outpouring of Russian gratitude "for the hearty welcome and magnificent hospitality" which the fleet had enjoyed while in America.[15]

The "tradition" which accepted the motive of the Russian naval visit as a token of Russian-American friendship has been considerably tossed about in learned historical articles. Certain writers have shown (a) that in fact the Russians had other motives in terms of their own European situation, and (b) that these other motives—e. g., to avoid being bottled up in case war in Europe should break out—were sufficiently recognized at the time by the American people and press.[16] In a recent study, however, by Thomas A. Bailey [17] it is shown that there was real basis for the familiar tradition, and that in contemporary editorials the "most popular surmise . . . was the one relating to friendship, alliance, and succor." It is Dr. Bailey's conclusion that a "majority of interested citizens at the time—and certainly an overwhelming majority later—appear to have accepted the

---

[14] F. A. Golder, "The Russian Fleet and the Civil War," *Am. Hist. Rev.*, XX, 809 (July 1915).

[15] C. M. Clay to Seward, Oct. 12, 1864, *House Exec. Doc. No. 1*, 38 Cong., 2 sess., pt. 3, 290 ff.

[16] The following articles by Earl S. Pomeroy are helpful: "The Visit of the Russian Fleet in 1863," *New York History*, XXIV, 512–517 (Oct. 1943), and "The Myth After the Russian Fleet, 1863," *ibid.*, XXXI, 169–176 (Apr., 1950). In the latter article Mr. Pomeroy points out that contemporary American newspapers were aware of Russia's own strategic reasons for the naval visit.

[17] Thomas A. Bailey, "The Russian Fleet Myth Re-examined," *Miss. Vall. Hist. Rev.*, XXXVIII, 81–90 (June, 1951). Dr. Bailey takes note of the treatment by William E. Nagengast ("The Visit of the Russian Fleet to the United States: Were Americans Deceived?" *Russian Review*, VIII, 46–55 [Jan., 1949]), which emphasizes America's prompt and acute grasp of the true explanation of Russia's demonstration—e. g., that Russia's motives were to avoid the possibility of having the fleet "bottled up," and to enable the fleet to be used for commerce destruction. On the basis of a "wider coverage of the American newspaper press," Bailey finds less American attention to the Russian fleet than might have been expected; his careful research tends to reinstate the interpretation that "the friendship-alliance hypothesis was the one that took root" (p. 87).

visit of the fleets as primarily a gesture of friendship . . . ." [18]

Another element in promoting Russian-American community of feeling was the factor of slavery. On the one hand Confederate objections were raised to the prohibition of the international slave trade in any future treaty with the Richmond government (should its independence be recognized) on the ground that this was a problem belonging to the states.[19] On the other hand sympathy for Lincoln came naturally to a Tsar (Alexander II) who made a great point of social reform, of the breakdown of caste, and especially of his own notable emancipation of the Russian serfs. Whatever may have been the diversities of customs and institutions, it was felt by statesmen of this period that solidarity of peoples would find expression. In the words of a modern writer this solidarity was not "darkened because of the irreconcilable contradiction of the forms of the governmental order then existing in Russia and in the United States." [20]

IV

In relation to Mexico Lincoln's good neighbor policy moved unhurriedly toward its goal against alien forces that offered the utmost threat to the integrity of that important nation in its hour of revolution and hopeful change. When the United States of America was facing its own fiery ordeal the Mexican Republic was struggling with the greatest menace to its independence since the extinction of Spanish rule in 1821. That menace took the form of a full blown intrigue toward French imperial domination by way of conquest and the imposition of a foreign monarch upon an unwilling people.

If Spanish control in the land of Montezuma had brought civilization and enlightenment, it had also produced absolutism, peonage, and exploitation. With a grasping aristocracy and an avaricious clergy

---

18 *Ibid.*, 85, 90.

19 L. Q. C. Lamar, serving in March 1863 as Confederate emissary at St. Petersburg, indicated that, despite the strong insistence of European powers upon the suppression of the slave trade, no such arrangements should be inserted in a treaty with the Confederacy, since this function was not included within the treaty-making power. Bayard Taylor to Seward, St. Petersburg, March 3, 1863, *House Exec. Doc. No. 1,* 38 Cong., 1 sess., pt. 2, 861 ff. In Britain also there was Confederate objection to a treaty stipulation against the slave trade. Not that the British Government was contemplating any treaty at all; the matter was mentioned in conversation between Mason and Lord Donoughmore, cabinet member under the former Derby administration. *Offic. Rec.* (Nav.), 2 ser. III, 598.

20 Adamov, in *Jour. of Mod. Hist.,* II, 602.

the Spanish system had permitted, among other things, enormous land holdings by the church. Clerical privileges were jealously guarded and numerous fees were exacted from the peasants. Around this powerful influence clustered a political group known as the Church party which stood firm in opposition to nineteenth-century liberalism and in protection of agelong abuses. Not even the boon of governmental stability had been produced by this aristocratic domination. It was characteristic of Mexican politics since the days of liberation that every election tended to become a revolution.

In the period of the American conflict—some years in advance of it—a condition of civil war had existed in Mexico in which the reactionary Church party had contended unsuccessfully with the Liberal party, headed by the popular leader, Benito Pablo Juárez. Coming into power by hard won military success as the constitutionally elected President of Mexico, Juárez proclaimed a series of reforms including religious toleration, confiscation of church property and civil marriage. His government was formally recognized by the United States. Not all went smoothly, of course; hasty measures were unavoidable in the turbulence of the time; blunders were naturally committed by a country suddenly thrown upon its own resources without adequate political experience; adjustments in a radical change of regime were by no means easy. In addition to all these difficulties there was a deplorable weakness in Mexican finances.

Under these circumstances the Mexican Congress under Juárez suspended payment of obligations to foreign financiers for a period of time; this supplied the incident, if one were needed, for foreign intervention. On the side of Juárez it may be said that Mexico was not an opulent nation and that the obligations were considered fraudulent. For a joint enforcement of these outside financial claims a treaty was made between France, Spain, and Britain in October 1861. The United States was invited to join but declined, at the same time offering to guarantee the interest on Mexico's foreign debt if intervention were dropped. Seward did not let the episode pass without expressing his country's strong disapproval of any foreign acquisition of territory in a neighboring republic.

By January 1862 the three powers had put 10,000 troops into Mexico. The Juárez government proved reasonable to deal with, and by May 1862 Britain and Spain, concluding separate agreements in which they had obtained satisfaction from the Republic of Mexico, had withdrawn their forces and dissociated themselves from the joint armed intervention.

Contemporary sources reveal that Napoleon in this phase of his policy had grandiloquent ideas of race pride, religious domination, and what would later have been called *Geopolitik.* The vision of a powerful French monarchy in the New World originated as a kind of dream, then unfolded as an ambitious, flamboyant policy. Such a scheme was natural to a monarch who remembered the achievements and forgot the colossal failures of his spectacular uncle, and whose foreign policy ran easily to unsound foreign adventures. Forgetting the Monroe Doctrine, the Emperor's advisers conceived of a program in which they saw promise of commercial advantage and imperial greatness.

In this episode of power politics nothing is more clear than the contrast between British and French purposes. In a detailed study of the tripartite treaty of October 1861 between England, France, and Spain concerning Mexico, William Spence Robertson has shown that the joint intervention was intended as a means of obtaining satisfaction of financial claims and that British statesmen repeatedly insisted that there be no "forcible interference in the internal affairs of an independent nation." To this disclaimer the French minister for foreign affairs, Thouvenel, agreed, but with "mental reservations," while Napoleon III had secret designs toward a French-dominated monarchy before the treaty was signed. When French designs became unmistakably clear Britain was done with the violated treaty for good and all, while the Spanish government considered that the convention was only suspended. In the discussions pertaining to the whole transaction the Monroe Doctrine was of conscious influence.[1]

Thus after Spanish and British withdrawal in the spring of 1862 the Mexican enterprise was a French affair, evolving as a project in Napoleonic imperialism. More and more French troops were sent; hard campaigns were pushed against stealthy Mexican guerrilla resistance; Puebla yielded to siege in May 1863 after more than a year of fighting; Mexico City was entered by a French army in the following month. In the following year Maximilian of the Austrian house of

---

1 W. S. Robertson, "The Tripartite Treaty of London," *Hispanic American Hist. Rev.,* XX, 167–189 (May, 1940).

Hapsburg, more unsuspecting victim than designing conspirator, was installed as "Emperor of Mexico." In May 1864 Maximilian and his wife Charlotte landed at Vera Cruz and proceeded to the capital city where they were greeted by a synthetic ovation and crowned amid an artificial demonstration. A superficial legal form was contrived to make it appear that the crown was "offered" as the "gift of the Mexican people," but Juárez and his followers fought stubbornly on and it was obvious that the important rulers, however well disposed they might be personally, could not last a day without the protection of the French army.

Ignorant of Mexican affairs, isolated from true Mexican contacts, and utterly at odds with New-World trends, the ill-fated monarch soon found his Austrian associates becoming sullen toward the French, while the "pacification" of the country, to say nothing of the attitude of the United States, proved an insurmountable difficulty. Gradually he found also that Napoleon's glittering promises were not kept. Juárez, at war with both France and Maximilian but still recognized by the United States, suffered serious military setbacks. At the beginning of 1865 his visible support was so slight that his movement seemed about to collapse; yet he persisted in his claim as constitutional President of the Republic, and the authority of the French-sponsored monarchy was never completely recognized in the unhappy country. When in October 1865 an imperial "black decree" consigned all supporters of the Republic to sentence of death by court martial, so fierce a resentment was stirred up that reconciliation became impossible.[2]

V

In shaping American policy toward the Mexican affair the Lincoln administration took a course which may be described as moderate but firm. Having maneuvered France into a disavowal of any intention to establish permanent sway in Mexico, Seward blandly repeated his assurances of American confidence in this disavowal. Thus within the language of friendly diplomacy he contrived to give the most convincing expression of the American point of view as if it were both axiomatic and in harmony with the policy of France. In a

2 On the Mexican question, see Count E. C. Corti, *Maximilian and Charlotte of Mexico;* Dexter Perkins, *The Monroe Doctrine, 1826–1867;* J. Fred Rippy, *The United States and Mexico.*

strong despatch to Dayton, American minister at Paris, under date of September 26, 1863, Seward summarized the American position, stressing Mexican preference for republican government free from European interference, predicting the sure failure of any foreign attempt to control American civilization, and emphasizing the sympathy of the United States for the Mexican people in their determination to control their own affairs. Referring to rumors of incidents that might produce collision between France and the United States, he said: "The President . . . does not allow himself to be disturbed by suspicions so unjust to France . . . ; but . . . he knows . . . that it is out of such suspicions that the fatal web of national animosity is . . . woven." He made it clear that the United States would be ready for action if necessary (conveying this impression in non-aggressive phraseology), but added that assurances of the French Emperor's intentions were entirely satisfactory to the government at Washington.[1]

There is hardly room in these pages to treat the relation of the Confederacy to the Mexican venture. Leaders and agents of the Richmond government wanted the United States to get into foreign war. Forgetting the Monroe Doctrine, they recognized Maximilian as Emperor. They also showed a readiness to form an alliance with France, thus disregarding Jefferson's historic disapproval of "entangling alliances."[2] Just how a French imperial government in Mexico could have worked to the advantage of the Confederacy, supposing Southern independence to have been achieved, is hard to understand, but for its immediate effect in weakening the Washington government such a foreign embroilment would have been welcome.

In a situation of great delicacy the government of Lincoln continued its recognition of the Republic of Mexico, whose representative, Señor Matias Romero, was made welcome at Washington.[3]

---

[1] *House Exec. Doc. No. 1*, 38 Cong., I sess., pt. 2, pp. 781–783.

[2] Confederate recognition of the Maximilian government was indicated in the fact that President Jefferson Davis appointed William Preston of Kentucky "envoy extraordinary and minister plenipotentiary" to "His Imperial Majesty, Maximilian." (Preston's mission was a failure, as were also certain Confederate efforts to deal with the Juárez government.) As to the idea of an alliance with France, the Confederate agent A. Dudley Mann wrote on August 15, 1863, that he would "gladly see [his] Government entering into an offensive and defensive treaty with the Emperor of the French." F. L. Owsley, *King Cotton Diplomacy*, 541; *Offic. Rec.* (Nav.), 2 ser., III, 155, 871.

[3] In an official despatch dated at Washington, March 12, 1864, Seward referred to "Don

In these trying years Thomas Corwin of Ohio, an elder statesman whom Lincoln had appointed United States minister to the Mexican Republic, gave dignified evidence that friendship between the two countries was unbroken. This was especially significant in view of the notable scarcity of ranking diplomats in Mexico during the French occupation.[4] Not only did the United States decline to send or receive envoys to or from Maximilian, thus denying him international recognition; the American minister to France was instructed on the occasion of the Archduke Maximilian's appearance in Paris to "entirely refrain from intercourse with him." [5]

While the establishment of completely normal relations with Mexico was deferred, the correctness of the American attitude (looking forward to Mexican independence) was carefully watched. In the summer of 1863, with the French army installed in Mexico City, the question arose whether United States minister Corwin should move to San Luis Potosi, temporary seat of the government under Juárez. When Corwin decided not to move, this decision was approved at Washington (August 8, 1863), and at the same time permission was given for Corwin to take a leave of absence. For a time after this, Corwin remained in Mexico City, though accredited only to the government of the Republic; but in the spring of 1864 he left for New York, after which for some years the legation at the Mexican capital was maintained on a reduced basis, with no representative of full rank—i. e., minister—present. This was the situation until in July 1867 Marcus Otterbourg became United States minister at Mexico City. French intervention had by that time terminated and Juárez was back in the capital.

A memorandum of the department of state under date of July 17, 1865, gives significant indication of the attitude of the Lincoln-Johnson administration toward the Maximilian regime. On that date Secretary Seward refused to receive a special agent bearing a letter addressed by Maximilian to the President of the United States. Returning the letter, Seward informed the Marquis de Montholon, French minister at Washington, "that the United States are in friendly communication now as heretofore with the Republican Government

---

Matias Romero, the minister plenipotentiary of the Mexican republic residing at this capital." *House Exec. Doc. No. 1,* 38 Cong., 2 sess., pt. 3, p. 201.

[4] *House Exec. Doc. No. 1,* 38 Cong., 1 sess., pt. 2, 1229–1256 *passim.*

[5] Seward to Dayton, Feb. 27, 1864, *House Exec. Doc. No. 1,* 38 Cong., 2 sess., pt. 3, p. 45.

in Mexico and therefore cannot depart from the course of proceeding it has heretofore pursued towards that country . . . ." The minister was informed that the President declined to receive the letter or to hold intercourse with the agent of Maximilian.[6]

There were, of course, complicating elements in the situation: Yankees camped on the Texan border, Russia keeping a watchful eye and assuring the Union of its friendship, supplies given by Americans to Mexican guerrillas, rumors that Juárez would take refuge in Texas, repeated governmental difficulties within Mexico, the insertion of planks on the Monroe Doctrine in the National Union platform of 1864.[7]

It would have been far from the truth to suppose that the American people were detached or indifferent with reference to the Mexican question. In previous decades they had shown great concern for far-off nations such as Greece and Hungary; naturally the Latin-American world was of even greater concern. Here was a difficulty on the very border and newspapers in the United States kept the Napoleonic menace under constant discussion. A society at New Orleans known as "Defenders of the Monroe Doctrine" kept up its half-understood efforts. Ultimately, after the close of the Civil War, a military force of the United States appeared at the border. Meanwhile, on April 4, 1864, a resolution unanimously passed by the House of Representatives (109–0) declared opposition to "a monarchical government, erected on the ruins of any republican government in America, under the auspices of any European power." [8] It was not until after the war that the matter was cleared up under pressure from the United States by the ultimate withdrawal of French troops and the reinstatement of Juárez as president of Mexico.

In arriving at the complete achievement of United States objectives, Seward did not alienate the French. In a threatening and difficult situation the United States had maintained neutrality as between the French imperials and the Mexican armies; there was no American intervention, this being unnecessary; the Napoleonic Mexican project was allowed to collapse of its own top-heavy weight. It is true that the collapse came after Lincoln's death, but it came while

[6] Matters in this paragraph are based on records in the department of state; for a summary the author is indebted to Marcus W. Price and Carl L. Lokke of the National Archives.

[7] *Ann. Cyc.* 1864, 788.

[8] *Cong. Globe,* 38 Cong., 1 sess., 1408.

American procedures remained as the Lincoln-Seward government had shaped them. The American position was upheld none the less effectively because the method of that upholding was non-violent. The episode stands as an impressive testimonial that the Monroe Doctrine does not in practice necessitate the actual hostile use of American armies; the Doctrine is a force for peace, not for embroilment.

CHAPTER V

TYCOON, DAIMIOS, AND MIKADO

THE Lincoln government, of course, had business with the whole world. The administration had formal contact with the Sultan of Turkey and with that Ottoman functionary known as the "Sheik-ul-Islam," whose office was something like a combination of lord high chancellor and archbishop of Canterbury.[1] There were dealings, by no means unimportant, between the President of the United States and His Majesty the Sultan of Morocco, so that when complaints arose as to the treatment of Israelites in the Moroccan Empire, American influence was exerted in the direction of civilized amelioration.[2] On the Latin-American side (in addition to Mexican troubles) the Lincoln administration had to consider the Spanish-Cuban situation, "inter-oceanic transit through Nicaragua," troubles in Chile and Peru, and diplomatic relations with Colombia.[3]

As to Canada there were problems touching the St. Lawrence River at one geographical extreme and the Hudson's Bay Company at the other, and there was always the need of adjustment in the matter of trade. Irish groups, bent on involving America in their bitter anti-British movements, were a continuing embarrassment. The Fenian Society had conspiratorial projects involving designs upon Canada and would have welcomed American involvement in their schemes. Later in the war Confederate use of Canadian territory for anti-United-States intrigue seemed at certain stages to offer serious disturbances in Canadian-American relations. Canada has always had a double orientation, looking toward Britain, yet finding its policies and needs "largely determined by conditions indigenous to the Amer-

[1] *House Exec. Doc. No. 1,* 38 Cong., 2 sess., pt. 4, p. 375. [2] *Ibid.,* 425 ff.

[3] *Works,* IX, 225–227 (annual message to Congress, Dec. 8, 1863).

ican continent." [4] Through all these problems and difficulties the enduring factor was the continuance of peace on the "unguarded frontier" and the growing recognition that common and mutual interests were overwhelmingly more valid than temporary, local, or merely private matters of dispute and rivalry.[5]

Among the Japanese in this period the problems of contact with the western world produced one long continued crisis. Strains and stresses in that far-off realm were peculiarly difficult for occidentals to understand. There were times when a solution seemed impossible: Europe would not let Japan alone once Perry had broken the exclusion of centuries, while anything like a secure international adjustment seemed always to recede into the oriental mysteries of Yedo or Kyoto. In a period when Japanese foreign policy was in the making amid violent internal agitation it seemed to Europeans that the island empire of the East had no arbiter of its affairs, no single group or ruler who could speak with authority. At Yedo (Tokyo) there resided the Shogun or Tycoon, a kind of practical executive head of the government (if such a head existed); at Kyoto, in a kind of inaccessible mist, there existed the Mikado, awesome spiritual head, hereditary Emperor, supreme symbol, Son of Heaven. It was not sufficient to say that the Tycoon managed things while the Mikado lived in secluded grandeur surrounded by his impressive court. By rallying round the Mikado, certain aristocratic feudal lords (daimios) might threaten to undo the work of the Tycoon and even to conspire against his somewhat insecure official position. These daimios dreaded foreigners with their commercial exploitation and modern ways; they suspected the Tycoon's government of seeking to monopolize the benefits of foreign trade; they held to their feudal privileges; they felt constrained by no duty to obey orders issued by what foreigners considered the "government" of Japan. Rather they were little, or rather sizable, powers in themselves. If occidental diplomats reached an agreement after protracted negotiation, they might have need for all

[4] Edgar W. McInnis, *The Unguarded Frontier: A History of American-Canadian Relations,* 180.

[5] The book by McInnis (see preceding note) gives an excellent survey of relations between the United States and its northern neighbor. The author emphasizes the value of "broad vision and a comprehensive good will on both sides" rather than divergent tendencies on one side and economic nationalism on the other (p. 370). He shows that many Canadians enlisted in the Union army, and that "On the whole there was little positive support for the South in Canada" (p. 222).

their patience to obtain ratification and to know that something had been nailed down which would have effect within Japan.

That nailing down, or attainment of a workable understanding, was what westerners typically wanted, while to the oriental mind, in an age when concessions to the West were nothing less than startling, there was always a further barrier, if only a ceremony, which had to be surmounted before a commitment had been reached. The ceremony might not be the essence of the thing, yet it could not be ignored. A protracted chapter of diplomacy might come to naught for lack of it. And who could finally say that those who controlled ceremony and adulation were less effective or influential than those who tended the government machine? Any threat to the private interests of the princes might cause them to assert their will in the name of the Mikado.

In a day when it was doubted whether the Tycoon could maintain his throne, this was a serious matter. Under the impact of foreign penetration the nation of Japan was experiencing so serious a transition that its very government, as well as its international policy, was insecure and unpredictable. In the midst of assassinations, burnings, attacks on foreigners, interruptions of intercourse, and incidents of private war, pending international questions—rights of residence, opening of ports, promotion of trade, and protection of occidentals—were held in abeyance.

I

To draw together all these complicated factors of the Japanese situation is impracticable in these pages. The subject is unfamiliar to most American readers who seldom think of Japan at all in connection with Lincoln's foreign problems. To treat the Shogun (Tycoon) as practical head of state, or prime minister, seemed the reasonable course from the western point of view, but it was doubtful whether the Mikado's function could be considered merely nominal, for that would be to overlook the powerful position of the barons (daimios). These barons did not like the admission of foreigners to their land. The Emperor to them was an indispensable institution, an enduring conservative tradition, a source of power, and even a tool. With private armies at the disposal of rebellious lords, the Shogunate—the institution with which westerners were dealing—was under formidable attack. These cross currents within Japan were a constant difficulty, but equally disturbing were the differences among the western powers. Britain, France, and Russia were truculent and excessive in their demands, while the United States maintained an attitude of marked friendliness toward the Japanese people.

For this friendly attitude the credit lies largely with two New Yorkers—Townsend Harris, envoy until April 1862, then Robert H. Pruyn, his successor in that post. It has been said (by a British writer) that Harris's services were not "exceeded by any in the entire history of the international relations of the world." [1] Pruyn's conduct may be judged by the statement: "If Perry opened the gates of Japan, and Harris threw them open wide, then Robert H. Pruyn is entitled to no little credit for preventing their being closed again." [2]

In their policy of conciliation and peaceable adjustment, Harris and Pruyn labored amid hazardous conditions, buffeted as they were and almost overwhelmed by the explosive forces within the Empire. A bare enumeration of some of the leading international events in Japan, though inadequate as interpretative history, will at least convey an idea of the turbulent situation.

April 25, 1862: Pruyn, United States minister arrived in Japan. He was well received. *June 26, 1862:* A Japanese assassin killed two British sentries and then committed suicide.[3] The British legation (July 15) retired to Yokohama. Pruyn found himself the only foreign envoy remaining at Yedo. He seemed to be making progress with his demands for opening further treaty ports and did not consider that an unfortunate incident (in which guards of the British legation may have been partly to blame) should be magnified into an international disaster.

September 14, 1862: Another serious incident now occurred. A small party of British subjects was attacked on a road near Kanagawa, and one of them, C. L. Richardson, was murdered, apparently because the party had got into the way of a retinue of a Japanese noble.[4] To the Japanese mind they had committed a deliberate insult and an unforgivable offense against etiquette.

---

1 J. H. Longford, *The Story of Old Japan,* 302.

2 Payson J. Treat, *Diplomatic Relations Between the United States and Japan,* I, 131.

3 *Ibid.,* I, 135. 4 *Ibid.,* I, 137.

February 1, 1863: The British legation was burned.[5] After these unfortunate events Pruyn still relied on the Shogun for adjustment (the Shogun himself being greatly distressed by these outrages), but other foreign influences were pushing for the most severe measures. The British ultimatum for the Richardson affair (delivered at Yedo on April 6) demanded an indemnity or penalty of £100,000 from the Japanese government and £25,000 from the offending daimio. This led to further demonstrations.[6]

May 24, 1863: The United States legation was burned.[7] Though accepting the explanation that the fire was accidental, Pruyn reluctantly retired to Yokohama (June 1); it was two years before the legation was re-established in Yedo. There was now an interval in which the Shogun, summoned to the presence of the Mikado, agreed to the expulsion of foreigners. It was characteristic of the insecure situation that the agreement was not regarded as final or conclusive. The British demand for an indemnity was complied with.

June 26, 1863: Chosiu, a powerful daimio, strongly anti-Shogun, moved by an intense wish to expel the foreigners, now acted on his own by firing upon a small American merchant vessel, the *Pembroke*. This was followed by retaliatory bombardment by the U. S. S. *Wyoming*.[8] Matters had reached a serious pass. Could open war be averted?

In this critical situation the prestige of the Shogun took a temporary upward turn; he avoided enforcement of the expulsion decree (to which he had given only nominal consent); rebellious barons fell into disrepute; it now appeared that matters could be peaceably adjusted. Such, however, appears not to have been the intent of Sir Rutherford Alcock, British minister, who had the idea "to make war for the sake of forestalling war." [9]

August 28–29, 1864: There now occurred a joint expedition of the western powers (British, Dutch, French, American) resulting in a battle between the ships and shore batteries at Shimonoseki. This "punitive expedition" was not regarded as war, nor was it an attack upon the government of Japan. It was rather a punishing of Chosiu, the daimio of that region.[10] Chosiu quickly capitulated, the straits

[5] *Ibid.*, I, 155. [6] *Ibid.*, 157–162.

[7] Incendiarism was suspected, though the burning was "not an unusual incident . . . where houses are built of light wood and paper." *Ibid.*, I, 172.

[8] *Ibid.*, I, 184 ff. [9] *Ibid.*, I, 212. [10] *Ibid.*, I, 233.

were opened, and an indemnity was agreed to.

In Lincoln's annual message to Congress of December 1863 the Far Eastern situation was thus reported: "In common with other western powers, our relations with Japan have been brought into serious jeopardy, through the perverse opposition of the hereditary aristocracy of the empire, to the enlightened and liberal policy of the Tycoon designed to bring the country into the society of nations. It is hoped, although not with entire confidence, that these difficulties may be peacefully overcome."

II

Through all the intrigue, violence, and official evasions in the far eastern Empire the key to American policy was forbearance, avoidance of war, patient attention to the oriental point of view, and cultivation of friendly relations.

At length matters became easier as the Emperor, now becoming more of a power, agreed to the ratification of the international treaties which had been the subject of such long negotiation. As the Lincoln administration ended in 1865 the signs pointed to the success of American policy. This was evident in the abandonment of isolation by Japan (though this came hard) and the establishment of more normal economic and political relations between Yedo and Washington. Authorities writing of the situation as of 1865 have regularly commented on the subsidence of anti-foreign agitation within the Mikado's realm and the improvement in understanding and good will.[1] In the course of the years Lincoln was to become the subject of numerous Japanese books and to take an honored place in the island Empire's gallery of heroes and great men.[2]

Doings of the Lincoln government were important also in relation to China, whose pagodas and art treasures had long been familiar to Yankee mariners and shipowners. When the Emperor of China sent an autograph letter to the President of the United States,[3] or

1 In addition to the important study by Treat, already cited, the following works should be consulted for an understanding of the Japanese question under Lincoln: Tyler Dennett, *Americans in Eastern Asia; House Exec. Doc. No. 1,* 38 Cong., 2 sess., pt. 3, 445 ff.; Paul H. Clyde, *A History of the Modern and Contemporary Far East.*

2 For Japanese books on Lincoln, with illustrations, see Jay Monaghan, *Lincoln Bibliography, 1839–1939,* II, 405 ff., plates iii, iv, vi.

3 *House Exec. Doc. No. 1,* 38 Cong., 1 sess., pt. 2, p. 961.

when Chinese-American treaty provisions required negotiation and ratification, such matters called for studiously correct attention in diplomatic intercourse. While the relation of the United States to Japan in the Lincoln era was somewhat special—different from that of other nations—such a statement could have been made with equal significance as to China, where the American diplomat, Anson Burlingame, bore the high title of envoy extraordinary and minister plenipotentiary at Peking. In the days when the relations of China to the maritime powers called for great delicacy, and when the Chinese mind was decidedly apprehensive of the designs of foreign nations, the fruits of American oriental diplomacy were evident in those unusual marks of respect which that nation bestowed upon Mr. Burlingame. In the period of Lincoln's successor, so great was the confidence of the Chinese government in Mr. Burlingame that, on returning from the Orient, he was appointed by the Chinese government as its own envoy to the United States and other nations. Burlingame has been called "the most successful diplomat America has ever sent to Eastern lands." [4] In view of this high praise it is worth remembering that Burlingame went as Lincoln's envoy and that his influence was exerted not only toward China itself but also toward other powers, in the promotion of enlightened treaty relations and in opposition to Chinese dismemberment.

III

Relations with the Papacy at Rome, and with the newly welded Italian nation at Turin, may be omitted for lack of space to treat such subjects adequately, but there is one Italian episode that requires attention: an American offer of military command to Garibaldi in 1861. Such an offer emanated from Seward and involved considerable discussion. It led to no actual appointment for the distinguished Italian liberator, but it does form at least a curious minor chapter in Italian-American relations.

Briefly, the facts are as follows. Suggestions having been made in American newspapers that Garibaldi's services could be enlisted in the Union army, the American consul at Antwerp, J. W. Quiggle, presented the matter in a letter to Garibaldi himself, who replied in-

[4] L. M. Sears, *A History of American Foreign Relations*, 337.

dicating a "great desire" to serve the American cause. After the rude shock of Union defeat at Bull Run (July 21, 1861) Seward, possibly with an eye to incompetence in the Union army, wrote to Henry B. Sanford, United States minister at Brussels, instructing him to "proceed at once and enter into communication with the distinguished Soldier of Freedom." "Tell him [wrote Seward] that he will have the grade of major-general in the army of the United States, . . . with the cordial approval of the whole American People." [1]

There was more to the story, with letters passing between Garibaldi and his Italian friends on the one side and various American diplomats on the other. Not only was Quiggle involved, but also George P. Marsh, accredited to the new Kingdom of Italy at Turin, and Theodore Canisius, United States consul at Vienna, a German-American editor from Illinois.[2] Of Seward's assurance that Garibaldi might have a major generalship in the Union army, one of many, there is no doubt, and the illustrious foreign patriot seems to have been told, correctly enough, that he was being offered "a commission of the highest rank in the power of the President to bestow." [3] This of course meant that no army rank above that of major general lay at that time within the power of the President's appointment. Charles Francis Adams, however, was under the impression that Quiggle had led Garibaldi to believe that he would be invited "to *take the supreme command* in America," which, if true, would have been an egregious bit of bungling on Quiggle's part.[4]

From start to finish it was a queer business and one which illustrates how the same episode, or the same set of words, may produce one impression in foreign minds and another in American. In 1861 Garibaldi was a shining name; he had an immense world reputation as Italian liberator; he had lived in America; he had referred to himself inaccurately as an "adoptive citizen" of the United States. He considered his first allegiance due to Italy, but his services were not

---

1 Seward to Sanford, July 27, 1861, MS. (Dep. of State), National Archives.

2 In May 1859, with a view to the German vote, Lincoln had made a contract with Canisius for the publication of a German-language Republican newspaper at Springfield. *Lincoln the President,* I, 130–131.

3 Sanford to Seward, Sep. 12, 1861, MS. (Dep. of State: Belgium Despatches), National Archives.

4 *Proceedings,* Mass. Hist. Soc., 3rd series, I, 321 (1907–08).

being sought at home for further strokes toward nationhood and unification. He was in retirement, and his relations with the royal house and government of Sardinia were such that he may not have been unwilling to use an American offer as a kind of pressure upon his king, while at the same time being interested in the offer for its own sake. Sanford wrote an account of an interview which he had with Garibaldi in which the general said that "the only way he could render service . . . to the . . . United States, was as Commander-in-chief of its forces" and that he would also wish authority to emancipate the slaves. In treating this episode C. C. Tansill assumes that if Garibaldi had come it would have been as "head of one of the armies of the North," and indeed it would have seemed unreasonable to expect so distinguished a leader to accept a lesser role. Professor Tansill goes on to say (and this is no more than a doubtful conjecture) that Garibaldi "would at least have spared the Union cause the vacillating incompetence of McClellan, the costly blunders of Pope, and the pitiful collapse of Hooker." [5]

It is not likely, however, that historians will find it advisable to rewrite the history of the war on the basis of assumptions as to what would have happened "if" the highest Union command had been assigned to the Italian leader. The whole discussion as to what Garibaldi would have done is mere speculation: certainly it would have seemed strange for the Army of the Potomac to serve under a foreign general, no matter how illustrious. There is no evidence that this army would have welcomed Garibaldi as a substitute for the highly popular McClellan. It is not easy to transplant a celebrity or hero. Garibaldi's career had been in terms of the Italian milieu and environment. Transferred to America he might have suffered something of an anticlimax. If the documents were not before us, the offer from Seward, and in fact the whole episode, might seem hard to believe.[6]

---

[5] Charles C. Tansill, "A Secret Chapter in Civil War History," *Thought,* Fordham Univ. Quar., XV, 215–225 (June 1940).

[6] In addition to the items by Charles Francis Adams and by Tansill cited above, the Garibaldi episode is treated by H. Nelson Gay in *Century Magazine,* LXXV (new ser. XIII), 63–74 (Nov. 1907); by Carey Shaw, Jr., in *New York Times Magazine,* (Jan. 11, 1942); and by Howard R. Marraro in *Jour.,* Ill. St. Hist. Soc., XXXVI, 237–270 (Sep. 1943). Documents in the case are found among the manuscripts of the Department of State in the National Archives at Washington.

IV

Matters treated in this and preceding chapters lead naturally to the question: What of Lincoln himself in international matters? Did incidents and controversies merely occur during his administration, or did the man who was President put his stamp upon events and adjustments? In pondering this question one notes first that Lincoln had comparatively little to do with international affairs. In this respect the contrast with Woodrow Wilson is striking. Wilson was in large part his own secretary of state. Throughout his notable administration the course and pattern of international dealings was shaped by the President. Sometimes when a note was signed by Bryan or Lansing it was written by Wilson. Lincoln, however, left the foreign field to Seward. It is true that diplomatic dispatches emanating from Seward's office made frequent, almost constant, mention of the President. The reader of these despatches would be informed that the secretary of state had submitted a matter to the President or that he was conveying the President's wishes, reporting the President's concern, or expressing the President's satisfaction. He would be told that "the President thinks" this or that, that the President had engaged for a certain thing to be done, or that the secretary was doing a particular thing on the President's behalf. Such phrases, however, were so much a matter of mere form and usage that even if the matter involved had in fact been taken up in consultation with the President, the mention of such consultation in a Seward dispatch would not be adequate evidence that Lincoln's judgment had been sought.

With a prairie-lawyer President projected against a complicated world scene, two things were evident: the Chief was aware of his international limitations; and foreigners, both diplomats and citizens, did not at first expect much of the Illinois President. When his friend, John W. Forney, intending to visit foreign parts, asked for notes of introduction, Lincoln wrote in July 1864: "I have no European personal acquaintances, or I would gladly give you letters." [1] In addition to having not one personal acquaintance among Europeans, Lincoln admitted his lack of familiarity with the law of nations. In April 1861, when the President issued his first proclamation of blockade shortly

[1] Lincoln to John W. Forney, July 28, 1864, photostat, A. Lincoln Assoc.

after the firing on Fort Sumter, Thaddeus Stevens "packed up and went to Washington, to lecture the president on international law," urging that a blockade, bringing the conflict within the purview of regular international relations, was no way to deal with a domestic insurrection. According to Stevens's report of the interview Lincoln did not seek to defend his own official conduct. Instead, he admitted knowing nothing about the law of nations, remarking that his experience had been that of a "good enough lawyer in a western law court" where international law was not practiced. Seward, he thought, knew all about it; in any case, he said, the thing had been done, it could not be helped, and we must now "get along as well as we can." [2]

Nor did Lincoln claim any fullness of knowledge of the history of other countries. As the war neared its end in February 1865, in a peace conference at Hampton Roads, the question came up of a government entering into an agreement with persons in arms against constituted authority, and one of the Confederate Commissioners, R. M. T. Hunter, "referred to repeated instances of this character between Charles I . . . and the people in arms against him." Lincoln, as quoted, said in reply: "I do not profess to be posted in history. On all such matters I will turn you over to Seward. All I distinctly recollect about the case of Charles I, is, that he lost his head in the end." [3]

At the time of the 1860 nomination Lord Lyons commented with surprise on the Republican convention throwing out Seward and choosing "a man almost unknown." [4] After Lincoln's election Lyons showed distrust of both Lincoln and Seward: he thought "they would think it a safe game to bully us in words." [5] The war came and still the British minister had little confidence in Lincoln's ability; he thought the new leader had not shown "any natural talents to compensate for his ignorance of everything but Illinois village politics." [6]

On April 21, 1861, Archibald, British consul at New York, wrote unfavorably of the government's "vacillating and . . . objectless policy" and of the "ambiguity" of the President's inaugural address.[7]

---

[2] Richard N. Current, *Old Thad Stevens, A Story of Ambition,* 146–147.

[3] Alexander H. Stephens, *Constitutional View of the War Between the States,* II, 613.

[4] Lyons to Lord John Russell, May 22, 1860, Russell Papers, Public Record Office, London, G. D., 22/34.

[5] Lord Lyons to Lord Russell, November 12, 1860, Russell Papers, G. D., 22/34.

[6] Lord Lyons to Lord Russell, April 9, 1861, Russell Papers, G. D., 22/35.

[7] Archibald to Foreign Office, April 24, 1861, F. O., 5/778.

Richard Cobden considered Lincoln's serenity in the midst of war "really quite Pickwickian" and regarded his first regular annual message to Congress as "a quaint, droll affair." [8]

As time passed, however, Lyons, Cobden, and others developed increasing respect for the soundness of Lincoln's judgment in the actual business of foreign intercourse. In October 1863 Cobden was satisfied that Lincoln was determined to avoid a rupture with England or France and to steer clear of any meddling with Mexican politics. In all this he felt that the homely President's "strong common sense" was "much to be commended." [9] A year later Cobden's favorable view was confirmed. Lincoln, he thought, had "honesty, self-control, & common sense, in an eminent degree." [10] British appreciation of Lincoln's merits in international matters came with no less force because little had been expected. In the tense month of December 1862 it was reported from London that the "tone of the President's message in treating of the foreign relations is regarded with more favor, for the reason that something of a different kind had been anticipated in quarters where it was hoped an interpretation might be made of it to our disadvantage." [11]

Contemporary comments differ as to the character and manner of Lyons. To Edward Bates in September 1860 he seemed "unattractive and cold, with a countenance disturbed and uneasy, and an expression very like a suppressed sneer." [12] On the other hand William Howard Russell referred to the minister's discreet reticence, adding that when he did speak, he expressed "sentiments becoming the representative of Great Britain at the court of a friendly Power." [13] About to depart for England on sick leave in June 1863, Lyons had an "affectionate parting" with Lincoln. The two men talked face to face, and they must have conversed rather informally, because, according to Lyons, the President told "a number of stories more or less decorous." Then, coming to more serious matters, Lincoln said: "I suppose my position makes people in England think a great deal more

---

[8] Cobden to William Hargreaves, Midhurst, Dec. 18, 1862, Cobden MSS., British Museum, Add. MSS., 43655, pt. 4.

[9] Cobden to Bright, Oct. 12, 1863, Cobden MSS., Add. MSS. 43651, pt. 3.

[10] Cobden to Bright, Oct. 4, 1864, Cobden MSS., Add. MSS. 43650.

[11] C. F. Adams to Seward, London, Dec. 18, 1862. *House Exec. Doc. No. 1,* 38 Cong., 1 sess., pt. 1, p. 20.

[12] Bates, *Diary,* 148.

[13] W. H. Russell. *My Diary North and South,* 388.

of me than I deserve, pray tell 'em that I mean 'em no harm." Lyons went on to say: "He does not pay much attention to foreign affairs, and I suppose did not like to talk about them without Mr. Seward." [14]

V

Unfortunately Charles Francis Adams seems to have had a low opinion of the President's competence in the international field. Benjamin Moran wrote in his diary on November 19, 1862: "After business hours to-day Mr. Adams had a long talk with me about Lincoln. He thinks the recent political defeats [in the congressional election] a natural result of his management. His whole course from the beginning has been unstatesmanlike, and nothing in his Presidential career was more stupid than the selection of his Cabinet. He appointed Mr. Welles without knowing anything about him, and took the others in an equally hap-hazard way. The conversation satisfied me that Mr. Adams regards Lincoln as a vulgar man, unfitted both by education and nature for the post of President, and one whose administration will not be much praised in future." [1] One can also quote Moran's own view as to Lincoln's bad management. Referring to the 1862 election of Seymour of New York, he wrote: "This strikes me as a piece of bad luck. It is one of the consequences of the wretchedly bad management by Lincoln of this war . . . ." [2]

The question of Lincoln's qualities became the subject of sharp controversy when, after Seward's death, Adams delivered (at Albany on April 18, 1873) a panegyric on the secretary of state. It was fitting that Adams should praise Seward, for that was the specific purpose of this speech delivered at the invitation of the New York legislature; but, to quote Welles, "it was not anticipated that the occasion would be used to elevate the reputation of the deceased statesman . . . by depreciating or underrating the abilities of the President under whom he served." [3]

Welles was correct in his view that Seward's eulogist was less than

[14] Lord Lyons to Lord Russell, June 13, 1862, Russell Papers, G. D., 22/36.

[1] Sarah Agnes Wallace and Frances Elma Gillespie, eds., *The Journal of Benjamin Moran, 1857–1865*, II, 1092.

[2] *Ibid.*, II, 1091 (Nov. 17, 1862).

[3] Welles, *Lincoln and Seward: Remarks Upon the Memorial Address of Chas. Francis Adams, on the Late Wm. H. Seward*, iii–iv (preface).

just toward Lincoln. In his address Adams referred to "the . . . appalling . . . fact that we were about to have, for our guide through this perilous strife, a person selected partly on account of the absence of positive qualities . . . and absolutely without the advantage of any experience in national affairs" beyond a brief congressional term. Warming to his theme, he said: "I must, then, affirm without hesitation that, in the history of our Government down to this hour, no experiment so rash has ever been made as that of elevating to the head of affairs a man with so little previous preparation for his task as Mr. Lincoln. If this be true of him in regard to the course of domestic administration, with which he might be supposed partially familiar, it is eminently so in respect to the foreign relations, of which he knew absolutely nothing. Furthermore, he was quite deficient in his acquaintance with the character and qualities of public men, or their aptitude for the positions to which he assigned them. Indeed, he seldom selected them solely by that standard." [4]

With a good deal of outraged feeling Welles answered the Adams address at length in a book published in 1874. The former secretary of the navy wrote: "A greater error could scarcely be committed than to represent that Mr. Lincoln 'had to deal with a superior intelectual [*sic*] power' when he came in contact with Mr. Seward. The reverse was the fact." [5] The more sensible view is to disparage neither Lincoln nor Seward. Their diplomacy was the responsibility of both, with Seward in practical charge, and it is worth while to recognize the ability of the secretary of state, despite quirks which Adams seems to have overlooked, and in doing so to give due credit to the President who appointed him, and who, amid fearful complications gave him co-operation without meddling and constant support without embarassing interference.

This presidential support was no slight factor. Lincoln knew what it meant to operate with his secretary of state while that important official was under repeated sniping, especially by senators. The crisis of December 1862 was but one example of this kind of trouble. While responsibility for foreign affairs was vested in the President, and while the Senate had its proper function in this respect, yet these

---

[4] Charles Francis Adams, *An Address on . . . William Henry Seward . . . at Albany, April 18, 1873*, 47, 49.

[5] Welles, *Lincoln and Seward*, 7.

attacks, in the manner in which they came, placed pitfalls in Lincoln's path. Some of his most skillful steering had to do with persistent efforts to get rid of Seward. Lincoln knew how to work with his Senate, but if he had given in to this kind of pressure, the result would have been an unfortunate sense of cabinet insecurity and a disturbing interruption of international dealings. In terms of enduring historical appraisal the President was justified in the continued confidence he gave to his foreign minister.

One may admit Seward's merits while remembering also those of Lincoln, the more so since the President was needlessly belittled. The editorial comment of Charles A. Dana is worth noting here. At the time of Adams's eulogy of Seward, Dana wrote: "There are several things in this oration which are likely to excite dissent, and there is one especially which seems to require immediate correction. Having been absent from the country during . . . President Lincoln's administration, and never having enjoyed the advantage of personal intimacy with that remarkable man, Mr. Adams falls into the rather natural error of attributing to Mr. Seward a degree of influence with Mr. Lincoln and of control over his actions which he did not possess or exercise."

Dana continued: "No doubt the Secretary of State had his full share in the transactions of that time. He was much consulted by the President, who was fond of his conversation and his society; but the truth is—and this we say . . . from personal knowledge—no man was ever more entirely the master of his own affairs . . . than President Lincoln of the executive power of this Government. He was on friendly terms with all the members of his Cabinet, and gave them due latitude in the discharge of their proper duties; but when any one had to yield his opinion it was the Secretary and not the President . . . . This we say not to lessen the just glory of Mr. Seward or any of his colleagues, but to state the exact truth and do justice to Abraham Lincoln." [6]

Despite his small acquaintance with Europe and with international law, Lincoln came through his stormy presidency with painful crises averted and international matters wisely handled. Shrewdness, common sense (a phrase that often recurs), and the tact that goes with calmness and good will were elements that made up for lack of speci-

[6] Editorial, New York *Sun*, April 19, 1873.

fic experience in formal diplomacy. The picture of Lincoln's ineptness and of Seward's bluntness is after all superficial. In essential dealings the Lincoln-Seward team performed well; it is a pity that so much cannot be said of the Lincoln-Stanton team. In most matters Lincoln and Seward worked smoothly together. Differences between them appear never to have led to serious friction. Not always did Lincoln follow Seward's advice, but instances of clashes of will were exceedingly few. Other members of the cabinet resented the influence of the secretary of state over the President, as when Welles complained in August 1863 that Seward was yielding too much to the wishes of Lord Lyons.[7] In this there was the implication that both the President and his foreign secretary were easy going, which in a way was true. Bates felt much the same about it when he mentioned that the usual procedure was for "knotty cases" to be passed by without reaching a conclusion.[8]

Yet of course there were international decisions made by the Lincoln government, as preceding pages amply reveal, and while "concessions" were made to Britain, properly enough, equal or greater concessions were made to us by the British. Moreover, American concessions themselves were fruitful of results in international good will and in solid benefit. A stroke of international policy might amount to a "concession" and yet might constitute an actual advantage. Seward's tact in dealing with Lyons was as often associated with an American diplomatic victory as with a setback. When in 1861 the United States revoked the exequatur of Robert Bunch, British consul at Charleston, for his diplomatic negotiations with the Confederacy, the secretary of state, while fully upholding the American position, lost nothing in the process by coupling his victory with a compliment to Lyons.[9]

Lincoln's international contribution cannot be lightly dismissed. A President who appointed Charles Francis Adams to the mission at London, who put the tactful quietus on his secretary of state at the time of his April 1 aberration in 1861, who added touches of masterful revision to Seward's dispatch of May 21, 1861,[10] and whose mind turned to arbitration rather than truculent blustering in the *Trent* affair, was a President whose influence in foreign

[7] Welles, *Diary,* I, 409.

[8] Bates, *Diary,* 266.

[9] Bancroft, *Seward,* II, 201.

[10] *Lincoln the President,* II, 35-37.

matters was exerted in the direction of sanity and peace. The reply to the workingmen of Manchester was an example of the manner in which the democratic-minded President could speak to the millions in England. The overwhelming response of those millions to the head of the government at Washington was under no misguidance. The confidence of the liberal minded Bright was not misplaced. The friendliness of Bright and the appeals of British labor, though associated with politics at home, were not without significance as tributes to Lincoln's humanity.

In the matter of America's larger responsibility Lincoln held views that were not dissimilar to those of Woodrow Wilson. Each thought that democracy in the world, with peace and order, was at stake in the struggle. When Lincoln said that the issue embraced "more than the fate of these United States," [11] when he urged that we must demonstrate to the world that ballots are better than bullets, his thought was that to do so would be "a great lesson of peace." [12] With no grudge against the people of the South, he nevertheless felt that the "insurrection" constituted "a war upon the first principle of popular government." [13] In blue books and diplomatic dispatches Lincoln's role in international affairs is somewhat hidden, but the subject is not to be studied in these sources alone.[14] To deal fundamentally with Lincoln's significance in the larger world scene it is necessary to remember the man's whole confession of faith, his concept of democracy, his concern for growing economic opportunities for laboring people, and his deep sense of the enduring value of popular institutions.

---

11 Nicolay and Hay, *Works,* VI, 304 (message to Congress, July 4, 1861).

12 *Ibid.,* VI, 322.

13 *Ibid.,* VII, 56.

14 For a comprehensive and vividly written account of international relations under Lincoln, see Jay Monaghan, *Diplomat in Carpet Slippers: Abraham Lincoln Deals With Foreign Affairs.*

CHAPTER VI

CHASE IS WILLING

AS THE nation faced the presidential election of 1864 the political outlook was confused and the prevailing temper was that of disharmony. The "envenomed . . . spirit of party" [1] was rampant, whether the label was "Democrat," "Republican," or "Union" which being interpreted meant "Republican." Neither of the major parties was what conscientious Americans would have wished—that is, a consistent grouping of voters for a civic purpose. So strong was the tendency toward factionalism that adhesion within any major party remained less a matter of like-minded opinion than of organization pressure for winning elections and seizing or retaining governmental office. If party factions closed ranks for 1864, that would mean that there was political self-interest in victory under the party label and for the organization. It would not necessarily mean, for instance, that after the election the winning candidate could count on the support of those whose party name he shared.

I

The "next election" was, of course, on everyone's lips. The Republican party, a newcomer in politics, was torn by bitter internal dissension between the Chase-Butler-Frémont faction and the Seward-Blair-Welles-Bates faction, Lincoln being identified with the latter of these groups. It was not that the President was encouraging factionalism. He wished to avoid it, but the radical opposition to him was so intense and its drive for power so determined that anti-Lincoln maneuvers within the party were sure to arise. Against these maneuvers it was certain that support of Lincoln would also be expressed

[1] Welles, *Diary*, I, 211.

and organized.[1] If on Lincoln's part there was a wish for a kind of presidential neutrality between factions, the success of that attitude would depend on how it was taken or treated; it would have to be watched lest it be interpreted as surrender to the "radicals."

Political preferences determined the manner in which men of varying opinions read the signs. The 1863 elections, which were many and important, were regarded as notably favorable to the existing administration (as in the rousing defeat of Vallandigham),[2] but as the winds seemed to be taking a Republican turn the moves of this or that group to seize control of the party became intensified. There was disagreement as to the full meaning of those elections in which, though Lincoln was upheld, Henry Winter Davis was favored and Montgomery Blair was "repudiated." [3] It was not merely a question of Republican success in '64, but of how that success, once achieved, should be used.

The *pros* and *cons* of particular leaders were elaborately debated in the press. The New York *Herald,* in its issue of February 19, sounded off on the theme that "President Lincoln is a joke incarnated." His election, said the *Herald,* was a "ridiculous joke"; his secret manner of entering Washington "a practical joke"; his debut in Washington society and his inaugural address were "jokes"; his cabinet a "standing joke"; his military letters "cruel jokes," his reconstruction "another joke," and so. The climax of this devastating enumeration was reached with the statement that his hopes for renomination and reelection were "the most laughable jokes of all." Since the President had "nothing but jokes to recommend him" it was suggested that he ought "to make the most of them." Returning to the theme on March 7, the *Herald* came through with another scurrilous jibe at the President. After mentioning various factions in the Republican party (followers of Frémont, Chase, and Wendell Phillips), it added: "fourth, there are the smutty republicans, who go for Lincoln, the joker."

---

1 Lincoln's secretary-biographers assert that "from the opening of . . . 1864 the feeling in favor of the renomination of Lincoln grew so ardent and so restless that it was almost impossible . . . to hold the manifestations of the popular preference in check." Nicolay and Hay, *Lincoln,* VIII, 323. If this was an overstatement, it is nevertheless true that the Lincoln papers, open to scholars since July 1947, are full of enthusiastic letters expressing support for the President.

2 *Lincoln the President,* III, 239–291.

3 *Ibid.,* III, 287–288.

The whole tune of the *Herald* was that Lincoln was a failure and would "imperil our republican institutions if, by any chance, he should happen to be re-elected." The people were "tired of incapacity, tired of partisanship, tired of corruption . . . ." "The age of small politicians like Lincoln, Chase, Seward, Welles, Stanton, Weed, the Blairs or the Buncombes, is past and gone." [4] "Give us . . . a practical military man." [5] With the idea of getting clear of existing parties, the *Herald* offered its solution: "the independent ticket" of Grant and Dix with the understanding that General McClellan would be identified with this ticket and would be "our future General-in-Chief." [6]

Quite different was the policy voiced by Greeley's *Tribune*. This distinguished newspaper did not go "all out" against Lincoln. It admitted (February 23) that the President had "well discharged the responsibilities of his exalted station," and noted that he was "the first choice . . . of a large majority of those who have . . . supported the Administration and the War." Yet in the *Tribune's* reasoning it did not follow "that Gov. Chase, Gen. Frémont, Gen. Butler, or Gen. Grant, cannot do as well."

In a careful study of Greeley's wartime attitude, Ralph R. Fahrney shows how the famous editor persisted in his opposition to a second term for Lincoln. He "lost faith in the ability of Lincoln to weather the crisis," sought repeatedly to postpone the 1864 Republican national convention (an anti-Lincoln move), gave support to Chase and repelled attacks upon that statesman, discouraged the formation of Lincoln clubs, advocated "the good old Harry Clay 'One Term' principle," and, on the collapse of the Chase boom, turned with other radicals to Frémont.[7]

II

Lincoln's strait-laced secretary of the treasury and presidential rival had not been lacking in courage and forthrightness. Not only did he appreciate with a burning earnestness the moral importance of the antislavery cause; he had held this moral principle to be of

4 New York *Herald,* Mar. 2, 1864, p. 4, c. 3.

5 *Ibid.,* Mar. 5, 1864, p. 4, cc. 2–3.

6 *Ibid.,* Feb. 22, 1864, p. 4, cc. 2–3.

7 Ralph Ray Fahrney, *Horace Greeley and the Tribune in the Civil War,* 139–140, 184–185, 187.

more validity than party adherence. Though formerly a Whig, he was prominent in the 1840's as a zealous leader in the Liberty and Free Soil parties. Then, convinced that a party could not live on antislavery alone, he operated with the unrealistic hope of capturing the Democratic party for the antislavery cause. It was partly with the help of Democratic votes in the Ohio state legislature that he was elected United States senator in 1849. When later he joined the "anti-Nebraska" (Republican) party, that was because of its free-soil stand. Having made the shift, he was genuinely pained, as were Giddings and others, when it seemed at times that his adopted party was slipping in its adherence to principle. In the disunion crisis he had not been inflexible against the right of secession. For a time he favored letting the erring sisters go in peace.[1] He considered this preferable to a compromise that would have sacrificed principle; he also seems to have held it preferable to war.

Lincoln did not satisfy him. As of 1860 the Ohioan was a man of more prominence, with a longer record in public office and in party leadership, than the Springfield lawyer. He had been governor of his state and senator at Washington. Disappointed in his efforts for the presidential nomination in 1860, he had worked for Lincoln, and his appointment to the cabinet was not only natural; it was a matter on which Lincoln's mind was clearly made up as it had not been, for example, in the case of Cameron. Lincoln felt that he simply had to have Chase in the cabinet, as, for a balancing reason, he also had to have Seward. In the opposition of these two men and their followers—beginning at the very outset of Lincoln's administration in 1861—the long-standing cleavage within the Lincoln team had its inception.

Chase had always been uncomfortable in the Lincoln cabinet and people wondered how two men of such different temperament and outlook could wear the same yoke. Often he expressed dissatisfaction with "the whole state of things" along with regret that he could do so little outside his own department.[2] He was pained at what he saw: "irregularity, assumptions beyond law, deference to Generals and reactionists. . . . ." [3] He visualized himself as alone in his high-

[1] *Lincoln the President,* I, 320–321.

[2] Chase to Murat Halstead, Washington, May 24, 1862, copy in Chase MSS., Pa. Hist. Soc.

[3] Chase to Greeley, May 21, 1862, copy in *ibid.*

minded motives. Referring to the attitude of "the old laborers for freedom" who complained that Chase had not done more, he wrote: "They forget that I am but one member of the administration, and the only one who has any special sympathy with them." [4] Considering the President's methods slipshod, he referred scornfully to the "so-called cabinet," whose meetings he deemed "useless." He "chafed" under Seward's management and resented the New Yorker's patronizing and superior manner. According to Welles, Lincoln felt that both of these men were serviceable. "He is friendly to both. He is fond of Seward, who is affable; he respects Chase, who is clumsy. Seward comforts him; Chase he deems a necessity." [5] The tense situation led to repeated efforts (or gestures) on Chase's part toward resignation, the most striking of which was in the "cabinet crisis" of mid-December 1862. This had been a time of senatorial attack upon the secretary of state and of deep distress to the President, but Lincoln's self control and shrewd tact had overmatched the clamorous pressure against him, so that he succeeded in keeping in his cabinet not only the target of senatorial displeasure (Seward), but also the embarrassed member (Chase) who had become a center of anti-Lincoln intrigue.[6]

Cabinet methods were "all wrong," thought Chase; he was "mortified that things were so conducted." [7] This attitude was genuine. Chase honestly believed that Lincoln was wanting in energy, inefficient in military leadership, unsystematic in method, needlessly willing to compromise, and in general inadequate to the fearful demands of the emergency. Being a vigorous man and tremendously in earnest for the cause as he saw it, the secretary of the treasury, more than any colleague in the cabinet other than Seward, often took a hand in the management of affairs. He took up for particular generals such as Frémont and Hooker, visited Hooker's headquarters, and assumed a kind of direction of Hooker's future.[8] He told Butler what to do at New Orleans.[9] He sought frequently to exert influence in military matters. "Please let me hear from you . . . frequently," he wrote to General N. B. Buford. "Give me all the facts . . . es-

[4] Chase to Thomas Heaton, June 21, 1862, copy in *ibid.* [5] Welles, *Diary,* I, 205.

[6] *Lincoln the President,* II, chap. XXV.

[7] Chase to Greeley, Sep. 7, 1862, Greeley MSS., New York Pub. Lib.

[8] Welles, *Diary,* I, 335–336, 349.

[9] Diary and Letter Book of S. P. Chase, Lib. of Cong., May 16, 1862.

sential to forming a correct judgment. . . . Tell me who are your best officers old and young, and in all ranks . . . ." [10] He had a way of writing as to what he would do if he "were in the field." [11] He had not only joined with a cabinet clique to have McClellan dismissed but had been opposed to the President's action in reinstating the general in the critical pre-Antietam phase.[12] When Frémont and Hunter seemed prematurely to be taking emancipation policy into their own military hands, out of the hands of the President, Chase sympathized with the generals and was supposed to have encouraged them. He opposed Lincoln's revocation of the Hunter order.[13] At times, though it need not be supposed that this was beyond his duty, he told the President what to do. For example, he earnestly regretted the removal of Rosecrans from command in the Chattanooga area.[14] Welles remarked that he made himself "as busy in the management of the army as the Treasury." [15]

III

The more Chase thought of presidential matters the more did his distrust of Lincoln color his views. As an example one could note his changing attitude toward Cameron. In 1860–61 he had opposed the Pennsylvanian's entry into the cabinet, but after Cameron became associated with anti-Lincoln groups Chase wrote favorably of him. The other side of the same coin was that Chase disliked men, such as Frank Blair, Jr., who were championing the President. The one cabinet member toward whom Chase's feeling gravitated was Stanton. Men who wrote statements friendly to Lincoln were not likely to couple them with praise of Chase. Those two thoughts did not go together. An Ohioan in December 1862 wrote: "It is a comfort . . . to know that there is one honest man in the Administration. . . . That man is Abraham Lincoln himself." This state-

---

10 Chase to N. B. Buford, Oct. 11, 1862, copy in Chase MSS., Pa. Hist. Soc.

11 "If I were in the field I would let every man understand that no man loyal to the Union could be a slave. We must come to this." Chase to John Pope, Aug. 1, 1862, copy in *ibid.*

12 Welles, *Diary,* I, 93 ff.; *Lincoln the President,* II, 112.

13 Chase to Greeley, May 2, 1862, copy in Chase MSS., Pa. Hist. Soc.; Diary and Letter Book of S. P. Chase, Lib. of Cong., May 16, 1862.

14 Chase to Lincoln, Oct. 31, 1863, R. T. L. Coll., 27610.

15 Welles, *Diary,* I, 108 (Sep. 3, 1862).

ment was significantly joined with strong denunciation of Chase: Ohio owed him nothing, it was said; there were worthier men in the state; the weakest thing Lincoln had done was to call such rivals into his cabinet.[1]

It may be footless to speculate as to the bounds or dimensions of Chase's self esteem. When a man is prominently mentioned for the presidency he naturally has some concept of himself in relation to that position. Chase appears to have believed that, in the existing circumstances, his availability for the high office had to be taken into account. Believing that Lincoln was falling short while the nation's interests were in gravest peril, he had definite views as to broad policies, presidential techniques, and specific measures. Not only was he regarded as one of the outstanding leaders of the Republican party; in the eyes of his admirers he was its principal leader. He had ability, experience, and a knack for administration. Many in the party who could see no compelling reason to renominate Lincoln in 1864 were urging upon Chase that he was the man. Bates wrote in 1863: "I'm afraid Mr. Chase's head is turned by his eagerness in pursuit of the presidency." [2] Wade's comment, as quoted by Hay, was: Chase "thinks there is a fourth person in the Trinity." It was also noted that Chase desired to injure the Lincoln administration.[3] The secretary "wished others to believe him omniscient," wrote Welles; he "lamented the President's want of energy"; anti-administration remarks in the Senate had "their origin in the Treasury Department." He had, continued Welles, "inordinate ambition, intense selfishness for official distinction and power to do for the country, and considerable vanity." Welles thought that these traits impaired his moral courage; "they make him a sycophant with the truly great; and sometimes arrogant towards the humble." [4]

It was significant that in February 1864 the treasury head was writing long "autobiographical letters" to J. T. Trowbridge who in that election year, obeying the vogue for self-made heroes, brought out a campaign biography with the Alger-like title, *The Ferry Boy*

[1] Editorial by Lyman W. Hall, *Portage County Democrat:* undated clipping, Chase MSS., Lib. of Cong., no. 9302.

[2] Bates, *Diary,* 310 (Oct. 17, 1863).

[3] Dennett, ed., . . . *Diaries* . . . *of John Hay,* 53, 231.

[4] Welles, *Diary,* I, 494, 520, 525; II, 121.

and the Financier.[5] In the treasury department, with Jay Cooke's support, the unprecedented expenses of war were met, though the high interest rate bespoke a none-too-high credit for the government, while much of the financing was a matter of forced bank-borrowing, suspension of specie payments, and greenback issues. Yet the treasury was holding up and superficially its management bespoke great administrative skill. Chase himself wrote: "I am astonished at my own success, financially. The public credit is now established." Again he wrote: "Would you believe it? In spite of all embarrassments, I yet raise a million a day!" [6]

Naturally Chase's attitude was influenced by incoming letters in which his name was featured for the presidency. "All things considered," wrote one correspondent, "my opinion is that you ought to be our next President. . . . The country demands that our best and only our best, men should be placed in nomination . . . ." [7] As he read his mail Chase found a Wisconsin man urging that pro-Chase "wires" be laid; [8] an Ohio man declaring: "You are head and shoulders above any other statesman in America." [9] His papers show that he was getting a stream of such letters.

To set a date for the beginning of Chase's 1864 aspirations for the presidency is not easy. A competent scholar has written: "It would . . . be difficult to say at just what point Chase began to think seriously of himself as a rival to Lincoln for the Republican-Union nomination of 1864, but certain it is that by September, 1863, he was actively doing just that." [10] What might be called a specific "boom" for Chase was launched—or an organization for launching

[5] The Trowbridge letters are among the Chase MSS. in the Pa. Hist. Soc. One of Chase's admirers wrote: "Every body—friend and foe, ascribe all the good work of the administration to you & all its weak doings where they belong. You may never be our president, but you may well be content with the honor of having the people everywhere feel that you deserve to be. The children are learning this . . . from the 'Ferry Boy.' A delightful book. We have enjoyed it exceedingly," H. B. Walbridge to Chase, Toledo, May 16, 1864, Chase MSS., Lib. of Cong.

[6] Chase to E. D. Mansfield, May 31, 1862, and to James Watson Webb, Oct. 21, 1862, copies in Chase MSS., Hist. Soc. of Pa.

[7] J. R. Freese to S. P. Chase, *State Gazette* office, Trenton, N.J., Dec. 18, 1863, Chase MSS., Lib. of Cong.

[8] E. A. Spencer to Chase, Madison, Wis., Dec. 8, 1863, Chase MSS., Lib. of Cong.

[9] M. F. Conway to Chase, Atchison, Kan., Dec. 8, 1863, *ibid.*

[10] George Winston Smith, "Carpetbag Imperialism in Florida, 1862–1868." *Florida Hist. Quar.*, XXVII, 275 (Jan. 1949).

it was mapped out—at a meeting in Washington on December 9, 1863, significantly the day immediately following Lincoln's message outlining his restoration program. The conference then held was designated as "a meeting of the friends of Freedom and the Union," and a set of "committees," Central and State, or Local, was "appointed." It is not certain what this appointing meant, but one can look down the list of names and find those Republicans who were—or were understood to be—uncommitted to Lincoln and friendly to Chase. The list included General Schenck and Congressman Rufus P. Spaulding of Ohio; Roscoe Conkling and John Austin Stevens of New York; Andrew Johnson and W. G. Brownlow of Tennessee; Henry Wilson and Governor Andrew of Massachusetts; Hannibal Hamlin of Maine; "Gov. Pierpont" of "E. Va."; John Wentworth of Illinois; David Wilmot, A. H. Reeder, and Jay Cooke of Pennsylvania; O. P. Morton of Indiana; Charles D. Drake of Missouri; Samuel R. Curtis and Governor Samuel Kirkwood of Iowa; and Charles Durkee of Wisconsin. There were other names. The list was tentative as indicated by question marks attached to the names of Conkling, Wilmot, Henry Wilson, Reeder, and others; certainly Andrew Johnson and "Parson" Brownlow had not consented to inclusion in the enumeration. For some states—Rhode Island, New Jersey, Kansas, Minnesota, and Michigan—no one was named. The idea was to set down a list of men who could, conceivably, as it was supposed, become part of an organized Chase movement. The endorsement on the memorandum of proceedings read: "Organization to make S. P. Chase President: Dec. 9, 1863: Important." The advisory committee consisted of Schenck, Spaulding, Conness of California, Henry Wilson, L. E. Chittenden, Whitelaw Reid, and D. Taylor. The letter-head was that of D. Taylor, "Paymaster, U. S. A." [11]

That the Chase effort was not confined to managers at Washington was indicated by a statement (quoting Doolittle of Wisconsin) in Welles's diary for December 28, 1863: ". . . there is an active, zealous, and somewhat formidable movement for Chase." He added: "Chase clubs are being organized in all the cities to control the nominating convention."

[11] The manuscript report of this Chase organization meeting is in the Library of Congress.

As with all such movements politicians got out their pencils to figure prospects, not so much in terms of popular support, but in the hard currency of delegates at the coming Republican national convention. In one such prediction, arrived at in January 1864, the one who made the calculation placed New York, Pennsylvania, Indiana, Illinois, and a scattering of others in the Lincoln column, while in the Chase column he included all of New England along with Ohio, Missouri, Wisconsin, Michigan, Iowa, and other commonwealths. The final conjectural result came out as almost a tie: 119 delegates for Lincoln, 118 for Chase. Some of those set down for Lincoln were mentioned as doubtful.[12]

To study the reports of willing workers for Chase would be to learn much, if not of the way Presidents are chosen, at least of the manner in which presidential bees are encouraged. "Under all . . . circumstances, I desire to see you the next President of the United States," wrote a gentleman from New York: "Try me, assign me any part in securing your nomination, and see how well I will perform it." [13] On February 18 an editorial leader in the New York *Independent* indicated that the Tilton publication, with more than 50,000 subscribers, was working for Chase. The editorial did not proclaim any candidate by name, but declared oracularly that the nominee's credentials should be "a sublime allegiance to God, Liberty, and Human Rights." Reprinting the editorial the New York *Tribune* explained: ". . . it *means* Mr. Chase; it describes him without mentioning his name." It was known that Theodore Tilton, ardent antislavery editor of the *Independent,* did not prefer Lincoln. The proprietor, Henry Chandler Bowen, wrote calling attention to the leader which he hoped would please Chase. "You see," he wrote, "that our article . . . contemplates a change in Presidents . . . ." [14] A newspaper publisher in a small Ohio town wrote: "You ought to have the nomination, because you have done more, in the management of our fiscal affairs, to carry on the war than Lin-

---

12 S. H. Boyd to S. P. Chase, Washington, D.C., Jan. 16, 1864, Chase MSS., Lib. of Cong. The endorsement reads: "Hon S. H. Boyd . . . His calculation as to complexion of Rep. Nat. Convention."

13 W. C. Cooke to S. P. Chase, "Strictly Confidential," Feb. 19, 1864, Chase MSS., Lib. of Cong.

14 Henry C. Bowen to S. P. Chase, *Independent* office, New York, Feb. 17, 1864, Chase MSS., Lib. of Cong.

coln and all the Generals in the field."[15] Another laborer in the cause, whose motto should have been that newspapers are not what they seem, proposed to start a journal to run with "gratuitous circulation" from February to November 1864. It could advocate whatever cause Chase might direct, "while the real object of the paper would be attained without any ostensible effort to that end being made." The writer of the letter, who seems to have supposed that Chase would be the next President, added that he made the offer "with the earnest . . . desire of serving you, and, of course, collaterally of serving myself."[16]

IV

In the month of February 1864 the Chase drive for the Republican nomination came quickly to a head with the "Pomeroy Circular," a printed letter put out over the name of Senator S. C. Pomeroy of Kansas. This senator, originally from Massachusetts, had come up through the turbulent years of jayhawkers and ruffians—and, it should be added, of normal pioneers—in Kansas Territory. He had been active in free-state efforts and was chosen senator when the state was admitted to the Union. Accusations in connection with his political activities led to various investigations; as a result, his record could hardly have been described as stainless.[1] His position as senator was that of a "Jacobin" or anti-Lincoln radical. After opposing colonization as the solution of the emancipation problem, he became a promoter of a scheme to set up a colony of Negroes in Central America (Chiriqui); a fellow-radical admitted that the project "was simply an organization for land-stealing and plunder."[2]

Pomeroy's colleague in the Senate, vigorous and military-minded James H. Lane, was the opposite of Pomeroy.[3] Yet Lane was such a fiery individual, so involved in Kansas feuding, that the President was sorely tried by both these senators. On May 12, 1864, Lincoln

15 W. H. P. Denny to Chase, Circleville, Ohio, Jan. 29, 1864, Chase MSS., Lib. of Cong.

16 From J. F. Brennan, Fort Monroe, Va., *ibid.*, Jan. 18, 1864. This correspondent, in the quartermaster department, seems to have been close to the influence of B. F. Butler.

1 *Dic. of Amer. Biog.*, XV, 54.

2 George W. Julian, *Political Recollections*, 226–227. See also Browning, *Diary*, I, 577; *Lincoln the President*, II, 139 n.

3 "The feud between Pomeroy and Lane centered, in the last analysis, around the question of Lincoln's renomination for a second term. While Lane was satisfied with Lincoln, Pomeroy was not." H. J. Carman and R. H. Luthin, *Lincoln and the Patronage*, 229.

wrote to Pomeroy: "I wish you and Lane would make a sincere effort to get out of the mood you are in. It does neither of you any good. It gives you the means of tormenting my life out of me, and nothing else." [4]

The Pomeroy Circular was a movement of Chase's friends (Lincoln's opponents) to rally their forces and create a nation-wide organization to promote the nomination of their favorite. It was printed, issued from Washington, marked "Private," and signed by S. C. Pomeroy, "Chairman, National Executive Committee." It read in part: "The movements recently made throughout the country, to secure the renomination of President Lincoln, render necessary some counter-action on the part of those unconditional friends of the Union, who differ from the policy of his administration." It was then stated that those who demanded "a change" had "no choice but to appeal at once to the people, before it shall be too late . . . ."

Point by point the argument was elaborated. Re-election of Lincoln was "practically impossible." If re-elected, "temporary expedients" would become stronger and the war might "continue to languish during the whole administration." Government patronage had become so enormous and "so loosely placed" as "to render the 'one-term principle' absolutely essential to the certain safety of our Republican Institutions." Salmon P. Chase possessed "more of the qualities needed in a President" than any other available candidate. Finally, it was asserted that Chase's developing popularity was "unexpected even to his warmest admirers." For these reasons a "Central organization" had been effected with connections in all the states in order "most effectually to promote his elevation to the Presidency." All who wished to further this object, and thus "make our American nationality the fairest example for imitation which human progress has ever achieved" were therefore urged to join in the work of organization in their sections of the country and to apply to the Chairman for "receiving or imparting information." [5]

---

[4] *Works,* X, 98.

[5] Copies of the circular appear in various manuscript collections—e. g., as enclosure in letter from Jesse Dubois of Springfield, Illinois, to Lincoln, Feb. 25, 1864, R. T. L. Coll., 30936. Philip Speed of the U. S. internal revenue collector's office, Louisville, Ky., also sent the President a copy he had received; it bore the frank of Henry T. Blow of Missouri. The Anna E. Dickinson MSS., and the Simon Cameron MSS., both in the Lib. of Cong., also contain the document.

In some quarters the famous circular was treated as a kind of anti-Lincoln conspiracy. To others it seemed that, since Lincoln's friends were organizing in his favor, some such move was but natural on the part of politicians who preferred another candidate. The *Tribune,* while disapproving the "invidious comparisons" between Lincoln and Chase, declared that the latter's friends had "a perfect right to present his name" which was entitled "at least to respectful and generous consideration." [6]

Lincoln's attitude toward the Chase movement was that of a patient but also a shrewd though unprovocative leader. His friends wrote numerous letters showing their resentment and reporting their observations as to activities in the Chase camp. From Springfield the President's old friend Jesse Dubois sent the document with the suggestion that Chase would "have his head in the basket if he does not take heed . . . ." J. P. Usher, Lincoln's secretary of the interior, thought that Chase had knowledge of the Circular. He added: "It contains reflections upon the President of such an offensive character that there will have to be explanations and will I think cause a rupture in the cabinet. There is much caballing & plotting going on here all dangerous to the government . . . ." As to the President's attitude, Usher observed: "Lincoln says but little finds fault with none & judging from his deportment you would suppose he was as little concerned as any about the result." [7]

Welles wrote: "It will be more dangerous in its recoil than its projectile. That is, it will damage Chase more than Lincoln. . . . Were I to advise Chase, it would be not to aspire for the position, especially not as a competitor with the man who has given him his confidence . . . ." [8]

Correspondence between Chase and Lincoln, though revealing embarrassment, showed that matters were carefully watched in order to avoid, at that time, a break in official relations. Chase explained that he had no previous "knowledge of the existence" of the communication from Pomeroy until he saw it (Feb. 20) in the *Constitutional Union.* He maintained that friends had urged the use of his name

[6] New York *Tribune,* Feb. 24, 1864, p. 4, c. 3.

[7] These comments are found in two manuscript letters of J. F. Usher to R. W. Thompson both from Washington: Feb. 17, 1864, MSS., Lincoln Nat. Life Foundation, Ft. Wayne, Ind.

[8] Welles, *Diary,* I, 529.

in connection with the approaching election, that there were "several interviews," but that he told them he "could render . . . no help, except . . . from the faithful discharge of public duties." He asked them to withdraw his name whenever the "public interest" would require it. After more of the same, he declared: "I do not wish to administer the Treasury Department one day without your entire confidence." [9]

The letter in itself, while not stating the whole truth, showed dignity, correctness of attitude, and "affection" despite differences.

After some delay Lincoln answered the secretary, though admitting that he found "very little to say." He had been aware of the "existence" of the Pomeroy Circular but had not read it. He had known as "little of these things" as his friends had allowed him to know. "They bring the documents to me, but I do not read them; they tell me what they think fit to tell me, but I do not inquire for more." Whether Chase should remain at the head of the treasury department, he wrote, "is a question which I will not allow myself to consider from any standpoint other than my judgment of the public service." He perceived no "occasion for a change." [10] Later (March 4) the President wrote that he had no wish for the publication of the correspondence between himself and Chase in regard to the Pomeroy Circular.[11]

Chase had noted a certain omission in the correspondence: "there was no response in his letter to the sentiments of respect & esteem which mine contained." [12] Such a sentiment would not have been inappropriate in Lincoln's letter. Perhaps the President, from his relations with the stiffly dignified secretary, did not realize that the omission of affectionate or appreciative comment would have been noticed. He was thinking rather of the public interest and the official relationship. He was, of course, not a man to dissemble or express an attitude he did not feel, yet his personal relations were regularly characterized by unusual, often exquisite, tact and personal friendliness. The correspondence was published and the Washington *Chronicle* (March 8, 1864) remarked: "nothing in them [the Chase and Lincoln letters] shows the slightest abatement of mutual respect and confidence." So Chase remained in the cabinet.

---

9 Warden, *Chase,* 573–574.

10 Lincoln to Chase, Washington, Feb. 29, 1864, *Works,* X, 25–26.

11 Lincoln to Chase, Mar. 4, 1864, *ibid.,* X, 29–30.

12 Chase to Greeley, Washington, Mar. 4, 1864, typed copy, Chase MSS., Lib. of Cong.

Welles had been right. The Chase boom hurt the secretary more than Lincoln. Chase's biographer, J. W. Shuckers, noted that the movement "fell . . . into bad hands; it was badly officered and . . . badly managed. . . . With a surprising want of tact and sense, this circular was marked 'confidential' and was sent to perhaps a hundred persons. . . . If at any previous time the 'Chase movement' had been attended by the least likelihood of success, that likelihood was promptly and utterly extinguished by the appearance of the 'Pomeroy Circular.' "[13]

V

The vigorous and explosive Frank Blair Jr. now played his part by delivering severe attacks upon the secretary of the treasury in the House of Representatives (February 5 and February 27, 1864), and the resulting outcry became an angry tempest of feuding within the President's official family. Blair spoke of the "odium" attaching to the ideas of Lincoln's rivals. He defended the President's policy of amnesty and restoration and asserted that the whole anti-Lincoln business, especially in Missouri and Maryland (Blair territory), had been "concocted for purpose of defeating the renomination of Mr. Lincoln." He sarcastically asked whether the radical discontents who were needling the President had either a valid grievance or a reason for gratitude to Chase.

These speeches of Frank Blair occurred at the time when the short-lived Chase "boom" was at its peak. Thus, in addition to all the other subjects of angry difference, the provocative incident entered into the intraparty warfare that was raging not only for the presidency but for basic policy. Part of the trouble was that Blair, a major general, was alternating between army service, commanding a corps in the Chattanooga area, and membership from Missouri in the House of Representatives. Lincoln needed all the help that could be mustered in Congress and after the close of the Chattanooga campaign it was agreed by Lincoln and Stanton that Blair should temporarily resign his army commission in order to assist in the important business of organizing Congress in view of the highly significant work of implementing the President's program of restoring the Union.

[13] Shuckers, *Chase,* 476.

Only the most extreme doctrine of isolating the President from the vital work of Congress would have militated against some executive effort to find a spokesman in the national legislature. This is not to imply that Blair, or any general, was the most suitable agent for the President's purpose, but it is fundamental in Lincoln's whole administration to remember that he was poorly supplied with instruments for promoting that executive-legislative co-operation which is always essential and was especially so in these critical times. There had been a promise that, after a period of congressional service, Blair could go back into the army; but when this was actually put into effect after the broadsides against Chase, the secretary's friends bitterly resented it, feeling that the President was rewarding the fiery Missourian, thus becoming himself a party to what was considered undeserved abuse of a highly placed cabinet member.[1]

A friend of Chase wrote: "A deep seated feeling of indignation . . . is manifested every where, at the attack on the Secretary by that pup, Blair;—and the course pursued toward him by Mr. Lincoln, after that attack." It was mentioned that Blair was helping Jeff Davis. The writer continued: "You can judge, then, of the indignation . . . against Blair, for the dastardly course he has pursued; and . . . it is even more bitter against Lincoln, because it is unmanly in him thus to endorse what he dare not do in person." It was also charged that the appointment of Blair without the action of the Senate was "a high handed measure" and "the first dawning of a Dictatorship." [2]

The flare-up became quite a tempest and there was considerable speculation as to whether Chase's resignation would follow. President Lincoln, however, explicitly "disavowed . . . all connection with, or responsibility for, Blair's assault, and expressed his decided disapproval of it." Chase hoped that his "every friend" would denounce "these vile calumnies" and express their honest resentment "by voice, pen, and press." [3] A. G. Riddle, who left a full account of the episode, showed how excessive was the abuse of the President at the time. Explaining that "it was impossible that the President could have been a party to Blair's assault," Riddle took a hand in reassuring Chase and inducing him not to resign. "There really was," wrote

1 *Works*, X, 83–84; 87–89.

2 Letter of John Wilson, Chicago, May 2, 1864, Chase MSS., Lib. of Cong.

3 Warden, *Chase*, 584.

Riddle, "a very unpleasant state of feeling among thoughtful men of both parties, the old abolitionists generally were in a rage." [4] The whole unfortunate imbroglio showed how the President was misrepresented within his own party (so far as it was a party), being equally embarrassed by the barbs of his opponents and the awkward maneuvers of his friends.

VI

What may be called the Chase "machine" for 1864 was found in the wide-flung personnel of the treasury department with its collectors, assessors, customs officials, assistants, clerks, and agents scattered over the land. A New Jersey gentleman wished to be appointed a revenue collector in his district in the place of the incumbent who was a "warm supporter of Mr. Lincoln for the next nomination." Pointing out that he could still run his paper while serving as collector, this office seeker wrote: "I could so arrange the appointment of my subordinates as to make the influence available for *our* candidate at the proper time. Besides, the duties of the position would give me reason & *excuse* [italic in the original] for visiting all parts of the District, and State, during which time I could use my personal exertions (in connection with my Journal) to forward your wishes." [1]

From friends over the country Lincoln had word of the workings of the Chase machine. An assessor in Indiana wrote the President that overtures had been made to him by a revenue agent to organize a Chase movement in Indiana. This friend, favoring Lincoln, wanted the President's protection if the treasury department should make trouble for him.[2]

A rather wretched but widespread practice of the time was the issuing of permits to profit-seeking individuals wishing to trade across enemy lines. When permits were applied for, so it was reported, an agent close to Chase would question the applicant as to his presidential preference. If the applicant favored Chase, full privileges would be readily granted; if not, there would be reservations and curtailed advantages.[3] Samuel Galloway of Ohio, well known friend

---

4 Riddle, *Recollections of War Times,* 267 ff.

1 Jacob R. Freese, of the *State Gazette & Republican,* to Chase, Trenton, N.J., Jan. 23, 1864, Chase MSS., Lib. of Cong.

2 William A. Bradshaw, Feb. 22, 1864, R. T. L. Coll., 30725–26.

3 John Donnally, Louisville, Nov. 26, 1863, *ibid.,* 28237–8.

of Lincoln, wrote: "The fact is notorious that the officials of the Treasury Dept are using every false and foul effort to suppress the voice . . . of the people." Noting that the people desired Lincoln's renomination and re-election, Galloway explained: ". . . these minions of a madly ambitious aspirant have been laboring with all their wicked zeal to prevent utterance of the popular voice." [4]

Dr. A. G. Henry, old-time intimate friend of the Lincolns, wrote from Washington Territory that the "whole influence of the Treasury Department" was used against Lincoln and for Chase.[5] William Pickering, governor of Washington Territory wrote on the same date giving similar information.[6] Thus Lincoln was kept informed of maneuvers which were by no means intended for his knowledge.

It was in Louisiana that the activity and intrigue of the Chase "machine" was most strikingly exemplified. Under Federal occupation, that state was serving as proving ground for testing the plan of reconstruction which Lincoln had earnestly favored and which the radicals were stoutly and angrily opposing. There was yet another factor: because of wartime laws concerning captured property and the like the state was covered with an expanded army of treasury agents. Without going into all the details of this widespread Chase instrument, one may note that Shepley, Flanders, and Durant were working for him. Shepley was military governor; Flanders and Durant were officials of the treasury department who devoted much of their time to politics. The Chase forces gained control of the New Orleans *Times* and it became their organ. The tone of this newspaper appears from the following statement of March 11, 1864: "We turn with sorrow from the contemplation of the evils that are to result from Mr. Lincoln's friends bringing him out for the second contest." [7] Following the pattern of Chase argument, the *Times* praised the secretary, criticized Frank Blair,[8] expressed fear that Lincoln's powers would be "despotic," deplored the prospect that the party would be "Tylerized"—e. g., seized for un-Republican purposes as under Tyler for un-Whig purposes—and sarcastically referred to the amnesty proclamation of the President as a kind of

4 Samuel Galloway in a letter of stinging indignation to Lincoln, Columbus, Ohio, Feb. 25, 1864, *ibid.*, 30938.

5 A. G. Henry, Olympia, W. T., to Benj. F. James, Feb. 20, 1864, R. T. L. Coll., 30699.

6 R. T. L. Coll., 30706–8.

7 New Orleans *Times*, Mar. 11, 1864.

8 *Ibid.*, Feb. 25, 1864.

trick to get the Southern states back into the Union "in time for the June convention . . . [and] recruit votes for Uncle Abraham in that body." [9]

Lincoln, of course, also had some strength in Louisiana. Michael Hahn was an earnest supporter, Cuthbert Bullitt served as president of the "Lincoln club," General Banks worked for the Lincoln type of state reorganization, and the New Orleans *True Delta* came "out for Lincoln." When Hahn, purchaser of the *True Delta,* was elected governor in the first "free-state election" the event, coinciding in time with the Chase boom, indicated that, for the time, the pro-Lincoln forces had popular support and were moving, but the sulking attitude of the radical element among the Republican leaders in the state gave warning of trouble ahead.

It became increasingly evident that people were taking sides—pro-Chase or pro-Lincoln. Greeley's feeling for the secretary was, whether rightly or not, attributed to "selfish motives." [10] The attitude of the Cincinnati *Gazette* and particularly of Whitelaw Reid, was resented, and John Hay took steps to have Reid removed from his assignment as correspondent of the Western Associated Press because he was "so outrageously unfair to the President and so servilely devoted to Mr. Chase." [11] The feeling that Lincoln was but going halfway in support of emancipation was a big factor in causing distrust. In Dubuque, Iowa, a German-American editor, favoring Chase for President, noted that he had lost the support of Lincoln men; he expected Chase to offer "compensation for said loss." [12] The situation seemed to be getting so far out of hand that some of Chase's friends cautioned him against getting out on a limb. James Freeman Clarke sounded a warning: ". . . your friends who are bringing you forward for the Presidency . . . are not doing you any service." [13] Justice Swayne of Ohio wrote to his friend Samuel Tilden that the "current is altogether in favor of honest and glorious Old Abe." [14] David Tod, ex-governor of Ohio, wrote that he favored Lincoln and

---

[9] *Ibid.,* Feb. 27, 1864.

[10] James M. Scovel to Lincoln, London, Dec. 30, 1863, R. T. L. Coll., 29007–08.

[11] Dennett, . . . *Diaries* . . . *of John Hay,* 138.

[12] Gustavus Grahl, publisher and editor of the Dubuque *Staatszeitung,* to Chase, Mar. 7, 1864, Chase MSS., Lib. of Cong.

[13] James Freeman Clarke to Chase, Boston, Feb. 26, 1864, Chase MSS., Lib. of Cong.

[14] Justice Noah H. Swayne of the United States Supreme Court to Samuel J. Tilden, Washington, Feb. 19, 1864, Tilden MSS., New York Pub. Lib.

was mortified to be set down as a Chase man.[15] The radicals themselves did not all favor Chase, some of them going for Frémont or Butler or Grant, while some who would otherwise have been inclined toward Chase felt that he did not "remember his friends" and had not bestowed sufficient favors.[16]

VII

When all was said the Chase "boom" was remarkable for its short life. On March 5, 1864, about two weeks after the opening of the drive for the presidency first became a matter of formal publicity in the newspapers, Chase wrote a letter asking that "no further consideration be given to my name." [1] The letter was addressed to James C. Hall of Toledo, to whom the presidential aspirant had written on January 18 explaining in typical Chasian phraseology that, while he had no objection to the use of his name by a committee for the chief magistry, "whenever any consideration, either by them or by the friends of the cause, thought entitled to weight, should indicate the expediency of any other course, no consideration of personal delicacy should be allowed to prevent its being taken." [2]

Chase's announced withdrawal may have been largely motivated by embarrassment arising from the boom itself and especially by the action of the party caucus of the Ohio general assembly, which on February 25 voted in favor of the President's renomination. Similar resolutions were issued elsewhere in the country, which showed that the effect of the clumsy Pomeroy Circular had been to bring out formal and open declaration of support for Lincoln. At the moment of withdrawal it was obvious that Chase was giving up something he did not have. In such papers as the New York *Tribune* and the Washington *Chronicle* the withdrawal was coupled with praise of the secretary's distinguished service and appreciation of "the honorable disinterestedness which has prompted this noble letter." [3] This disinterested pose ran through Chase's own correspondence, as

---

15 David Tod to Lincoln, Youngstown, Ohio, Feb. 24, 1864, R. T. L. Coll., 30902–3.

16 S. M. Booth to Chase, Milwaukee, Mar. 7, 1864, Chase MSS., Lib. of Cong.

1 Chase to James C. Hall of Toledo, Mar. 5, 1864, in Shuckers, *Chase,* 497, 502–503; New York *Tribune,* Mar. 11, 1864, p. 4, c. 3; *Daily Washington Chronicle,* Mar. 11, 1864, p. 2, c. 1; R. T. L. Coll., 31306.

2 Shuckers, 497.

3 *Daily Washington Chronicle,* Mar. 11, 1864.

when he wrote to Hiram Barney, prominent but uncomfortable collector of the port of New York: "I no longer have any political side save that of my country; and there are multitudes who like me care little for men but everything for measures." [4]

After years had passed and Chase had died (1873) there came further light on the "boom," the Circular, its actual authorship, and the imperfectly understood relation of the secretary of the treasury to the movement. One finds a revealing now-it-can-be-told story on this subject in the New York *Times* of September 15, 1874, which carried a letter to the editor by J. M. Winchell of Hyde Park, New York, dated September 14. Having read the *Times* extract from Shucker's life of the secretary, Winchell felt compelled to refute the biographer's statement that Chase had been "ignorant of the preparation of this circular, and was as much surprised at its appearance as anyone, and regretted it as deeply . . . ."

Shuckers was "quite mistaken," wrote Winchell. He explained: "Before the preparation of the circular the committee had spent a good deal of effort in trying to give the 'movement' some coherency and life. Mr. Chase had manifested no reluctance whatever to be a candidate against Mr. Lincoln, whom he honestly believed to be totally unfit to the crisis; his only reluctance was to be connected with a failure. . . . His most earnest friends were greatly depressed by the general timidity of the politicians in opposing the President, ... Mr. Chase was himself vacillating to a painful degree; moved alternately by aspirations and fears. Finally, . . . the writer hereof [Winchell], who was acting as Secretary of the committee during the period of suspense, conceived that it would be better to take some action *which would determine Mr. Chase's pluck and popularity,* and either place him at once before the country as a candidate, or withdraw him definitely from the attitude of rivalry which the President, as well as all Washington politicians, knew him to hold."

Winchell concluded: "To this end I wrote this circular . . . . *Mr. Chase was informed of this proposed action and approved it fully*. He told me himself that the arraignment of the Administration made in the circular was one which he thoroughly indorsed and would sustain. The circular was, therefore, sent out. No one expected it long to remain a secret."

[4] Chase to Hiram Barney, May 24, 1864, Chase MSS., Pa. Hist. Soc.

At the time of the brief pre-convention excitement there had been knowing persons all along who had refused to take Chase's withdrawal very seriously and who doubted that it was real or final. Attorney General Bates remarked: "This forced declention of Mr. Chase is really, not worth much. It proves only that the *present* prospects of Mr. Lincoln are too good to be openly resisted . . . . The extreme men who urged Chase . . . will only act more guardedly . . . with the hope of bringing in Mr. C, at least, as a compromise candidate." Bates thought that in the meantime these men would try "to commit Mr. L. to . . . their extreme measures." [5]

Just before the withdrawal letter to Hall, the secretary had conferred with Mr. Winchell. On that occasion (March 4, 1864), though regretting the withdrawal, Winchell indicated that it "may . . . enable you to give your friends aid which you cannot now bestow." [6] This probably meant that stepping out of the race would relieve Chase of embarrassment, give him a kind of independent position, keep the question open while radicals searched, and allow an option by which the secretary might later head a presidential movement or not as circumstances should suggest. It was indicated editorially in the *Herald* that Chase's declination was a feint; open electioneering would have required his withdrawal from the cabinet; though he "allegedly" did not want his candidacy, the people still desired it.[7] At any rate Chase's friends still hoped he would somehow remain available. Governor Andrew of Massachusetts regretted the Ohioan's "supposed purpose" of withdrawing from the cabinet though perceiving the "discomfort" of his official position in view of "being in a sense complicated with the policy and non-policy of the administration touching many grave . . . affairs which you would gladly influence to the better." [8] The confidential comment of David Davis, political-minded regular, to Thurlow Weed on March 14, 1864, showed that this expectation of Chase's friends was held also by his opponents. Davis wrote: "Mr. Chase's declension is a mere sham, and very *ungracefully* done. The plan is to get up a great opposition to Lincoln through Frémont and others, and represent when the convention meets, the necessity of united effort and that anybody can unite, ex-

[5] Bates, *Diary,* 345 (Mar. 9, 1864).

[6] J. M. Winchell to Chase, Washington, Mar. 4, 1864, Chase MSS., Lib. of Cong.

[7] New York *Herald,* editorial, Mar. 12, 1864, p. 4, c. 3.

[8] John A. Andrew to Chase, May 2, 1864, Andrew MSS., Mass. Hist. Soc.

cept Lincoln, and then, to present Chase again." With a quip about Micawber hoping for something to "turn up" Davis added that his informant on this matter was Henry D. Cooke. Davis concluded his letter with the remark that Lincoln must have been "obstinately pacific." [9] The President, of course, had his methods. He was not blundering into any explosion. For his own reasons he was keeping Chase in the cabinet, though it could not be denied that relations were undergoing severe strain.

[9] David Davis to Weed, confidential, Mar. 14 [1864]. Thurlow Weed MSS., Univ. of Rochester Lib. If Henry D. Cooke, brother and partner of Jay Cooke of the Philadelphia banking firm, was Davis's informant, he was getting his information, or interpretation, from a source which involved confidential relations with Chase.

CHAPTER VII

THE RENOMINATION OF LINCOLN

AFTER the collapse of the Chase movement events on the 1864 political front moved through a series of changing phases. There was the pre-nomination period with threats of angry radical opposition to the President, the launching of an independent party headed by Frémont, and in early June (many thought, too early) the Republican convention in which Lincoln's renomination was neatly and easily achieved. Then followed a long discouraging summer of defeatism and discontent in which many men of Lincoln's party despaired of his re-election. After three years of war the atmosphere was darkened by military operations which were at the same time shocking in human cost and deeply disappointing as to result. It was not until September and October that the auguries brightened for the Union cause; with these changing currents the withdrawal of Frémont registered a concession of Lincoln's strength on the part of his bitter opponents; finally, in November came the decision of the people to sustain the President for another four years. Some of these political difficulties of Lincoln were like bumps or ruts in the highway; others were serious road blocks. The most serious road block of all would come not so much in the problem of votes for the presidency, but in the process of obtaining congressional support for carrying out the basic programs which Lincoln favored and for which, in all sincerity and reason, his candidacy was significant.

I

The expressions of dissatisfaction with Lincoln constituted a medley of radical displeasure, uncertainty among friends who desired patronage changes, misgivings as to what men would "control" him, and doubts as to how in each state the national cause could be co-ordinated with that of local office holders or seekers. Such a thing as the unpopularity of certain Federal appointments and the dread of having incumbents continue in office might cause hesitation or might defer commitment on the part of Lincoln's friends. It was not merely a matter of supporting Lincoln but of seeing which men in a particular state would get "credit" for such support and would consequently wield what politicians called "influence." In such a situation one Republican faction might seek to gain superior control by accusing leaders of another Republican faction of being the President's enemy.

The period prior to the meeting of the Republican national convention was not the most propitious for inspiring confidence in national leadership. The sickening disappointment in the slow progress of Union arms under Grant, the cumulative load of war weariness, and the constant talk of peace efforts, combined to set the stage for a presidential campaign that became unique for dark foreboding and open disunity. A book could be made up of letters expressing distrust of the President. Mark Howard of Hartford, Connecticut, had been a follower of Lincoln. "But now [he wrote] I am unable to see our way out of our National troubles through the drifting, conciliatory and temporizing policy of Mr. Lincoln, but believe its continuance would ruin us." [1] From a more unfriendly source came the complaint that if Lincoln's policy did not change, "there are a very large class of earnest men who will feel very little interest in this contest." The writer continued: "It makes me sick to think what we have lost & the prospect of having nearly five years more of this thing." [2] Another observer, who referred to the President's policy as "muddy," wrote: "I pray God we may have a change, as anything positive can hardly be worse." [3] "Mr. Lincoln may mean well," wrote another, "but he has far greater faculty for perpetuating evil than good, he is a politician never a statesman, he lives, breathes, and has his being in the brief hour that fortune—ever blind—has allotted to him. . . . Vacillating in policy, undecided in action, weak in intellectual grasp, he writhes in contortions of dissimulation that

1 Mark Howard to Gideon Welles, Hartford, May 30, 1864, Welles MSS., Lib. of Cong.

2 John A. Hiestand to Thaddeus Stevens, Lancaster, Pa., May 29, 1864, T. Stevens MSS., Lib. of Cong.

3 A. Wattles to Horace Greeley, Washington, D.C., Feb. 6, 1864, Greeley MSS., New York Pub. Lib.

would do Blondin honor." [4] Striking the same note of gloom, the wife of General Butler wrote her husband: "I think the country is doomed if Lincoln is again elected." [5]

II

In the effort to find a focus for all this scattered opposition, the names of political rivals, or supposed rivals, of Lincoln were put forward. Most prominent among these was Chase whose name was still on the radical horizon though temporarily in the background. To take the next step and inquire as to who besides Chase were to be seriously regarded as available presidential timber is to reveal the poverty of high-power leadership in the radical camp. To answer that question is to mention Frémont and Butler and then to take the somewhat preposterous step of naming Grant, though this was hard to believe, as the man to supplant Lincoln. It was in Missouri, on fire with radical agitation, that actual moves in the party sense took definite shape in terms of offering a substitute in the drive to prevent a second term for Lincoln.

By May 1864 it was known that the plan to put Frémont forward had reached the stage where a nominating convention was scheduled to be held in Cleveland. Frémont was out of the military picture, being no longer an active general. In the summer of 1862 he had resigned and for the rest of the war he remained on the shelf. His friends, always ready to magnify a grievance, put the blame for this lack of command upon Lincoln's unfriendliness or upon West Point influence. In reality the actual factors were Frémont's military failure in the campaign against Stonewall Jackson, his refusal to serve under Pope whom he detested, his declination of offers which Lincoln would have given, and his well known tendency toward insubordination. The army question, however, was but one factor in the confused situation. In the background was the old Frémont-Blair feud, the complex Missouri imbroglio, and, especially the whole radical attitude of discontent because Lincoln did not favor the proce-

4 S. Wolf to Rev. Dr. McMurdy, Washington, D.C., Mar. 7, 1864, *Private and Official Correspondence of Gen. Benjamin F. Butler,* III, 497. (Blondin performed the amazing feat of walking a tight-rope across Niagara Falls, varying his technique with theatrical and incredible handicaps and contortions.)

5 Mrs. Butler to Gen. Butler, Fort Monroe, June 11, 1864, *ibid.,* IV, 342.

dures which the extremists were demanding. They favored not only abolition of slavery but wholesale immediate abolition by processes which Lincoln deemed unconstitutional; they also favored confiscating in sweeping fashion all the lands of Southern "rebels," and they advocated a drastic policy of reconstruction which was the opposite of Lincoln's and which in his view would have perpetuated a condition of disunion after the conclusion of a war whose object was to restore the Union.

The Chase people favored the Frémont drive, not so much for approval of the general as for disapproval of Lincoln. The "Missouri radicals" gave their support, and the Germans of the Middle West (from a strong antislavery motive and a feeling that Lincoln was dragging his feet as to emancipation) were drawn into the movement. Many German papers of Illinois and Missouri had hoisted Frémont's name as early as March 1864. Medill of the Chicago *Tribune* wrote: "There is no use in concealing the fact that the Germans are deeply offended [by the "treatment" of Frémont and Sigel] and feel very bitter towards Lincoln and we cannot afford to have them alienated from our party." As a remedy, better army commands for Sigel, Schurz, and Osterhaus were suggested, climaxed by Frémont to the West Virginia department.[1]

In addition, many ardent abolitionists of New England were denouncing Lincoln as they had been for years and demanding Frémont for President. Apropos of a meeting for woman's rights, W. L. Garrison expected that its leaders would "turn their meeting into a Frémont conclave, showing no mercy to Lincoln or his administration." [2]

With obvious lack of political experience but with a quick impulse to get their man nominated before the meeting of the Republican national convention, the representatives of what was called the "radical Democracy"—a Republican offshoot—met at Cleveland, listened to oratorical and epistolary outbursts, set up an extreme platform, and adopted their ticket for 1864: Frémont for President, John Cochrane for Vice President. Cochrane was in that year attorney general of New York. The turns and shifts in his career serve as a kind of

---

1 Joseph Medill to E. B. Washburne, Chicago, Feb. 12, 1864, Washburne MSS., Lib. of Cong.

2 W. L. Garrison to Oliver Johnson, May 5, 1864, Garrison MSS., Boston Pub. Lib.

mirror of the stresses of America in the mid-century. Though a Democrat friendly to Southern attitudes, he favored neither slavery nor secession. His support of the Union was demonstrated by his raising a regiment and his service as colonel and later as brigadier general until his retirement because of ill health in February 1863. He was not as vociferous and impulsive as Frémont, but it was enough that in May 1864 he was at odds with Lincoln's policy. His very unlikeness to Frémont, together with the hope that he could garner disparate votes including those of Democrats, may have been factors in his selection for second place on a ticket that was never taken too seriously even by its promoters. (Since both Frémont and Cochrane were residents of New York, they could not have been legally chosen President and Vice President. The Constitution provides that these two officials may not come from the same state.)

The Frémont convention, like the drive for Chase, showed the ineptitude of the anti-Lincoln radicals when it came to political action. With the nominees openly in the field, people speculated with some confusion as to their real intentions. Did this radical enterprise have a definite program, or was it a catch-all for diverse elements of discontent? How would a practiced politician expect to draw dividends from such a movement? How far could it be expected even to rally the radicals? It was observed that Greeley was not present and that the *Tribune* had no reporter to cover the Cleveland convention.[3] According to one report there were no more than two hundred men in the hall at any time, and no crowds in streets or hotels.[4] The proceedings were cut and dried, Frémont being nominated by acclamation and Cochrane with only three opposing votes. People questioned whether the Cleveland affair was oriented to the Baltimore (Republican) convention or the Chicago (Democratic) convention. To the *Herald* it seemed that nineteen-twentieths of the gathering were planning with a view to the Democratic convention.[5] The *Herald* writer may have had in mind that Frémont men, looking far ahead, contemplated joining with Democrats to nominate Grant. This should be regarded as meaningless in terms of realities as to Grant; it was rather a kind of wishful thought as to how the Frémont drive

[3] Cincinnati *Daily Gazette,* June 1, 1864, p. 3, cc. 4–5, (special dispatch dated Cleveland, May 31).

[4] *Ibid.*

[5] New York *Herald,* June 2, 1864, p. 5, c. 3 (a dispatch dated Cleveland, June 1).

could work mischief for the Lincoln cause, especially at a time when the renomination of the President seemed virtually certain, so that his defeat would depend on Democrats. Out of all these puzzled speculations the only clear conclusion seemed to be that the object of the Cleveland convention was not the election of Frémont, but the defeat of Lincoln on the alleged ground that he had "proved false to the cause of 'human freedom' " and that "a new President . . . [was] essential to the salvation of the country." [6]

Welles found it hard to understand Cochrane's part in the scheme. "A Democrat, a Barnburner, a conservative, an Abolitionist, an Anti-abolitionist, a Democratic Republican, and now a radical Republican. . . . It will not surprise me if he should change his position before the close of the . . . campaign, and support the nominees of the Baltimore Convention." Welles believed that "weak and wicked" men in the party "would jeopard and hazard the Republican and Union cause," and that "many of them would defeat it and give success to the Copperheads [he meant Democrats] to gratify their causeless spite against the President." [7]

In its platform the Cleveland group took a stand for limiting the President to one term, electing President and Vice President by direct vote of the people, and intrusting the question of reconstruction to Congress but "not to the Executive." Finally, there was a declaration in favor of "confiscation of the lands of the rebels, and their distribution among the soldiers and actual settlers." [8]

One of the incidents of the convention was a long letter from Wendell Phillips expressing the hope that if Lincoln was renominated, "we shall fling our candidate's name . . . to the breeze"; otherwise, he hoped that "some plan" could be arranged so that all could unite on a "common basis." The Phillips letter was full of denunciation of Lincoln and especially of his plan of reconstruction. With many of the elements of a sincere liberal and with the commendable motive of elevating the Negro, Phillips favored only that type of restoration which would "admit the black to citizenship and the ballot." For this reason he favored "quick and thorough reorganization of States on a democratic basis" but not in acceptance of

[6] Editorial, New York *Herald,* June 2, 1864, p. 4, c. 3.

[7] Welles, *Diary,* II, 43 (June 1, 1864). Welles's surmise was correct; as it turned out, Cochrane did support the Republican candidates.

[8] McPherson, *Hist. of the Rebellion,* 413.

Lincoln's plan. "If Mr. Lincoln is re-elected," he wrote, "I do not expect to see the Union reconstructed in my day, unless on terms more disastrous to liberty than even disunion would be." [9] Though Phillips thus earnestly advocated Negro suffrage, which Lincoln himself was coming to accept in part, the Cleveland platform made no reference specifically to the subject, though broadly demanding that the Constitution should "secure to all men absolute equality before the law." There was a declaration for an amendment to abolish slavery, but that abolition was also to be favored both by the President and the Republican national convention.

In his letter of acceptance General Frémont defended himself against "the reproach of creating a schism in the party with which I have been identified." No schism would have resulted, he said, if Lincoln had "remained faithful to the principles he was elected to defend." The general laid it on heavily in denouncing the Lincoln administration for military abuse, disregard of constitutional rights, feebleness, incapacity, alienating true friends, and making "humiliating concessions." The principles of the platform had the general's "cordial approbation," yet he could not concur in all the measures proposed. Confiscation of the property of all "rebels" he did not consider either practicable or sound policy; at the beginning of the war he could understand it, "but not as a final measure of reconstruction." As to the intent of his candidacy, Frémont declared that if the Baltimore convention should put up a man favorable to what he called "our cardinal principles," he would support him (which meant withdrawal), but if Lincoln should be nominated, it would be "fatal to the country" to give him renewed power and there would be "no other alternative but to organize against him . . . with the view to prevent the misfortune of his re-election." [10]

III

Republicans of the anti-Lincoln drift looked to the party's convention with doubt and discontent. With wearisome sameness the familiar complaints were repeated. Lincoln was slow, weak, not sufficiently decisive and active against slavery, too friendly to Seward and the Blairs, incompetent, unsatisfactory as to patronage, influenced

[9] *Ibid.*, 412.

[10] *Ibid.*, 413–414.

or controlled by "dishonest" men, and far too lenient in plans for reconstruction. To some he was a coarse joker, an imbecile, susceptible to the advice of "that arch criminal" (Seward), guilty of "damnable blunders," and "too angelic for this devilish rebellion." He lacked backbone, it was said, encouraged corruption, squandered millions, failed in the military task, and was using Southern delegates, set up under his reconstruction scheme, to insure his own renomination. It was stated in April 1864 that overwhelming majorities of both houses of Congress were opposed to the President's re-election.[1] Horace Greeley felt "a very strong desire to see some man besides Old Abe nominated for President." [2] Greeley's *Tribune* declared: ". . . we are known not to favor his [Lincoln's] renomination . . . ." [3] Even when conceding Lincoln's good points, the *Tribune* would go on to oppose him.

The call having gone out in February for the Republican national convention to meet at Baltimore on June 7,[4] there were loud and urgent demands for postponement. The desire was for "a suspension of judgment until this question of renominating Mr. Lincoln is first fully discredited." [5] In nearly every case the insistence on a later date came from anti-Lincoln men. Better not act in June, they urged. Wait till September. Give the disaffected time to defeat the administration. If the convention were postponed, it was argued, Lincoln would not be nominated. Chase called it a "Blair-Lincoln Convention." [6] Joseph Medill of the Chicago *Tribune* wrote: "I don't care much if the Convention is put off till August. . . . If Lincoln loses the nomination thereby he will have nobody but himself to blame. . . . I am free to say . . . that if it shall be known to be his intention to continue his present cabinet I don't believe we could elect him if nominated." The points of dissatisfaction on which Medill focused were Lincoln's attachment to the three Blairs, "old granny Bates," and Halleck; also his giving the "cold shoulder" to the Missouri radicals. The Chicago editor continued: "Lincoln has some

1 Editorial, New York *Herald,* Apr. 2, 1864, p. 4, c. 2.

2 Greeley to Brockway, New York, Apr. 9, 1864, Greeley MSS., Lib. of Cong., misdated 1861.

3 New York Semi Weekly *Tribune,* Apr. 29, 1864, p. 4, c. 1.

4 McPherson, *Rebellion,* 403.

5 James W. White to Horace Greeley, Albany, Jan. 15, 1864, Greeley MSS., New York Pub. Lib.

6 Chase to Brough, May 19, 1864, Warden, *Chase,* 593.

very weak and foolish traits of character." [7]

Eminent men in New York, including W. C. Bryant and George Opdyke, joined in a published statement (March 25, 1864) objecting to the seventh of June as the date of the coming national convention. These men—an impressive list—argued that unity for a single candidate was important but that such unity could not be reached at the early date named. Events in the spring and summer should be awaited, for upon them would "depend the wish of the people to continue in power their present leaders, or to change them for those from whom they may expect . . . more satisfactory results." [8] It was suggested by the Washington correspondent of the Cincinnati *Gazette* that to make Lincoln the Union candidate would be "most perilous, if not suicidal." If there were defeat in the field, it was urged, the President's popularity would vanish. If the seat of government were in any large city, the imbecility of the Administration would provoke a revolution in thirty days. (This was a strange suggestion—the idea that a revolution to overthrow the government could be started by the populace of a large American city.) It was also reported that prominent leaders were considering the propriety of demanding Lincoln's resignation as the only means of saving the government.[9] Charles Sumner, though cautiously non-committal as to candidates, opposed the June date. He wrote: "I regret very much that the Baltimore Convention is to be at so early a day. I see nothing but disaster from mixing our politics with battle and blood." [10]

IV

Despite strong protest the Republican national executive committee headed by Edwin D. Morgan of New York went ahead with its plan for opening the Baltimore session on June 7, and in the months prior to that date the friends of the President saw many encouraging signs. The radical effort was brushed off as a minor factor. "The great majority," wrote a party worker, "are in favor of the re-election of Mr. Lincoln . . . . [He] can get more votes than any

7 Joseph Medill to E. B. Washburne, Chicago, Apr. 12, 1864, Washburne MSS., Lib. of Cong.

8 *Ann. Cyc.*, 1864, 785.

9 Cincinnati *Daily Gazette*, Apr. 13, 1864, p. 3, c. 8.

10 Charles Sumner to Charles Eliot Norton (private), Senate Chamber, May 2, 1864, *Proceedings, Mass. Hist. Soc.*, LVIII, 135 (1925).

other man." [1] There were numerous similar comments, running true to what was considered a prevailing pro-Lincoln pattern. From Illinois came the report, *"A. Lincoln* is the first choice of the great body of the people." [2] From Concord, New Hampshire: ". . . I think Mr. Lincoln is the strongest man we can take and the *best* man." [3] From New York: "My business calls me among a great many people . . . in all parts of the country . . . and a large majority are for you [Lincoln] for the next four years." [4] From Kentucky: "If Old Abe is nominated for re-election I am strongly inclined to the belief that he can carry this State against any named man . . . ." [5] From Cincinnati: "I intend to go to the State Convention and see to it that Lincoln is endorsed. . . . He is the only man." [6] From Philadelphia: "The masses have an abiding faith in his honesty and ability." [7]

Granted this popular support, it was also true that much of Lincoln's strength was in party organization. Each state had its Republican party; that party had its conventions, officials, and committees; dissident groups could be overridden by the sheer power of political machinery. The men who operated that machinery had executive party positions; they had much to do in controlling the choice of paymasters, collectors, postmasters, and the like; they took a hand in obtaining government contracts; finally, through state or district conventions they managed the choice of delegates to the national nominating convention. These politicians foresaw Lincoln's renomination and wanted to keep their influence in the party. Thus it happened that while radicals freely expressed their discontent, the party "regulars" or managers somehow saw to it that pro-Lincoln resolutions were passed by state legislatures or conventions, setting in motion the process by which men were pledged to support the President.

This practical process of actually committing official groups to support of the President was evident as early as January of 1864. In

[1] J. D. Defrees to R. W. Thompson, Washington, Feb. 2, 1864, MS., Lincoln National Life Foundation, Fort Wayne, Ind.

[2] Thomas Gregg to E. B. Washburne, Hamilton, Ill., Dec. 23, 1863, Washburne MSS., Lib. of Cong.

[3] B. F. Prescott to Anna E. Dickinson, Concord, N.H., Mar. 13, 1864, Anna E. Dickinson MSS., Lib. of Cong.

[4] C. M. Smith to Lincoln, New York, Feb. 7, 1864, R. T. L. Coll., 30277–8.

[5] John Jay Anderson to H. C. Adams, Side View, Ky., Jan. 24, 1864, R. T. L. Coll., 29805.

[6] Will Cumback [to Nicolay], Cincinnati, Feb. 11, 1864, R. T. L. Coll., 30449–50.

[7] J. W. Stokes to Isaac Newton, Philadelphia, Feb. 10, 1864, R. T. L. Coll., 30427–28.

New Hampshire the state Republican convention took early action, the movement for Lincoln was off to an early start, and on January 6 the state convention of the Granite State registered its support for the President's renomination.[8]

From Pennsylvania came a like wave of Lincoln endorsement. In the legislature of the Keystone State a paper was passed around on January 6, addressed to the President and urging him to accept another term as President. Within a few days the full Republican strength in the legislature had been mustered and every member of both houses had signed the paper. It was pointed out in this address that a change of national administration would be most undesirable and that support of Lincoln was needed in order to crush the rebellion. On January 14, 1864, Simon Cameron wrote the President: "You are now fairly launched on your second voyage, and of its success I am . . . confident . . . ."[9]

Thus even before the February call for the convention there were actual pledges for Lincoln, but especially from February on through May the process of building up votes for him was evident throughout the North. The call itself, of course, could have been interpreted as a pro-Lincoln maneuver, since, as has been seen, those who preferred another candidate were solidly opposed to so early a date. February declarations for Lincoln—by Republican members of the legislature or by state party convention—occurred in New Jersey, Indiana, Maryland, Colorado, and California. As the weeks passed, the movement, thus aided by an early start, steadily gained momentum. In March Rhode Island was added to the Lincoln column, and in the same month a pro-Lincoln declaration of Republicans in Ohio signalized the end of the Chase boom, for a candidate who could not "carry" the party men of his own state would have a hopeless prospect as national leader. This decisive action came when in early March a large majority (90 out of 107) of Republican legislators in Ohio passed a resolution favoring Lincoln's renomination.[10] Prior to this, in late February, a caucus of Republican members had declared for Lincoln. It was not until May, however, that the state convention in Ohio took similar action.[11]

[8] Nicolay and Hay, *Lincoln,* IX, 52–53; New York *Times,* Jan. 7, 1864, p. 4, c. 6.

[9] Nicolay and Hay, *Lincoln,* IX, 53.

[10] New York *Herald,* Mar. 9, 1864, p. 5, c. 2.

[11] Cincinnati *Daily Gazette,* May 26, 1864, p. 3, c. 4; Eugene H. Roseboom, *The Civil War Era 1850–1873* (*Hist. of the State of Ohio,* IV), 430.

Kansas also made an early pro-Lincoln commitment. Its legislature by concurrent resolution on February 2 called for the nomination of Abraham Lincoln and Andrew Johnson "by general acclamation, without the formality of a National Convention." [12] Confirming this attitude, the Kansas state convention meeting at Topeka in April unanimously instructed its delegates to support Lincoln.[13] Another April state in which pro-Lincoln action was unanimous, was Wisconsin.[14]

Thus the ball rolled on. States that had not acted by May were influenced by the commitments of those which had done so. Men who belonged to the managing wing of the party, even if not enthusiastic for the President, were swept along with the Lincoln tide. In Maine the renomination of the President was given party endorsement on May 5,[15] while similar action was taken in Vermont on May 17 and in Massachusetts (at the state convention in Boston) on May 19.[16]

To elaborate the detailed methods by which these results were achieved in the state conventions would be to reveal in some cases the strategy—some would have said the questionable tricks—by which the opposition was overridden. Such a complaint was made as to the procedure in Indiana. Throughout that state it could not have been said that in February the party was united for Lincoln. Dissatisfaction with the President and support for Chase were by no means lacking. For this reason it was likely that if the matter had been presented for debate and deliberation, the State Republican convention at Indianapolis would have resolved in favor of sending an uninstructed delegation to Baltimore. Among Republican workers there was more ardent support for Governor Morton than for Lincoln, the more so since the movement to renominate the governor had been sedulously nurtured among local and district groups. Morton himself was somewhat cool toward Lincoln and favored an uninstructed delegation, which would have been entirely satisfactory to Lincoln's opponents. With eleven districts in the state, only five of the district

[12] Kansas *Concurrent Resolution No. 2,* Topeka, Feb. 2, 1864, R. T. L. Coll., 30121–2.

[13] Editorial, Washington *Daily Morning Chronicle,* Apr. 26, 1864, p. 2, c. 1.

[14] *Ibid.,* Apr. 2, 1864, p. 2, c. 3.

[15] Cincinnati *Daily Gazette,* May 7, 1864, p. 1, c. 5 (special dispatch from Bangor, Me., May 5).

[16] Washington *Daily Morning Chronicle,* May 20, 1864, p. 2, c. 6.

conventions had acted as to any declaration on the subject of a presidential nomination, and these had voted for uninstructed delegations.

Under such circumstances a quick maneuver was employed by which the Indiana convention, in the manner of a popular mass meeting, was swept off its feet. A delegate from Knox County, friend of Lincoln and bitter opponent of Morton, stepped on the stage at the outset of the meeting before the chairman was seated, and read resolutions to an audience of thousands who were prepared to cheer every allusion to the Union cause. The first resolution praised Lincoln and declared that the convention "instruct the delegates" (yet to be appointed) to vote for his nomination. By the second resolution Governor Morton, who was sure to be supported in any case, was then and there declared the candidate for re-election as governor. In a burst of enthusiastic cheers and without debate, both resolutions were passed by a shouting affirmative. By this scheme the gathering was committed before it had time to catch its breath and the convention was put on record. Naturally the Chase men were disgusted. Renomination of Morton was unopposed, yet there was no such agreement on the presidency or on debatable public issues. Endorsement of Lincoln was tied to the sure-fire endorsement of the governor and the whole thing was done by a mass-meeting proceeding in which discussion was impossible.[17] It was reported that the German element especially was stirred up by the maneuver.

In New York, despite political cross currents and intraparty feuds, the strength of organized Republican support was decisively added to the Lincoln cause. Though the *Tribune*, the *Independent*, and the *Post* worked against Lincoln in the prenomination phase, and though a huge meeting was held in favor of Grant, such men as Henry J. Raymond, Edwin D. Morgan, and Thurlow Weed held the Republican forces together for the President, and the state convention of the party, meeting at Syracuse on May 24, resolved by acclamation to approve the Lincoln administration and to favor his renomination.[18]

In Lincoln's own state there were ample evidences of difference within the Republican party, but anti-Lincoln efforts were more a

---

17 Indianapolis *Daily Journal*, Feb. 24, 1864, p. 2, c. 2; H. B. Carrington to Chase, Indianapolis, Feb. 27, 1864, Chase MSS., Lib. of Cong.

18 Sidney D. Brummer, *Political History of New York during the . . . Civil War*, 379.

matter of agitation than of management; dominance and political guidance were held by supporters of the President. It is true that the strength of the radicals could not be brushed off, and the Chicago *Tribune* showed an attitude of caution and a tendency to accompany its endorsement of Lincoln with insistence upon the need for recognizing the radicals. Germans in Illinois were strongly moved by radical doctrine, which meant displeasure with the President, and when the state convention met at Springfield on May 25 it was far from a harmonious body. A radical effort was made in opposition to an endorsement of Lincoln, but this movement failed; for one thing, there was no satisfactory alternative to Lincoln on the score of availability. When action was taken on the question of a presidential candidate, it was done by including a rather mild pro-Lincoln declaration in a long series of resolutions passed by the convention. By this method the Illinois Republican delegates were "instructed to use all honorable means to secure his [Lincoln's] renomination." The unusually late date of party action in Illinois (May 25) was but one indication of the difficulty of uniting the party solidly behind the President.[19]

In addition to regular party conclaves various agencies or citizen organizations worked for the President. This was true of the Union Lincoln Association of New York, the Union Leagues in many states, and the New England Publication Society. Of the widely influential newspapers that came out for Lincoln's renomination one should mention the New York *Times,* the Washington *Chronicle,* the Philadelphia *Press,* and the Springfield (Mass.) *Republican.* It was remarked by A. K. McClure that the *Times* was "the only prominent New York journal that heartily supported Lincoln." [20] His renomination was not favored by such powerful New York papers as the *Tribune,* the *Post,* the *Independent,* the *Herald,* and the *World.* In that important publicity organ, the Loyal Publication Society, sentiment among the leading managers was divided. Charles Eliot Norton favored Lincoln's renomination but such men as John A. Andrew and John Murray Forbes agreed with the radicals in opposing the

---

19 The attitude of Illinois Republicans toward the renomination of Lincoln is treated in A. C. Cole, *Era of The Civil War,* esp. 315–317, with full citations of newspapers and other material, and in Paul G. Hubbard, "The Lincoln-McClellan Presidential Election in Illinois," doctoral dissertation, 1949, Univ. of Ill.

20 McClure, *Abraham Lincoln and Men of War-Times,* 121; see also Francis Brown, *Raymond of the Times,* 218 ff.

President and urging a postponement of the convention. The Society, however, did not swing to their anti-Lincoln point of view.[21]

V

The gathering which in 1864 performed the important and uniquely American quadrennial function of nominating a President and Vice President consisted of somewhat more than five hundred delegates, not counting alternates, assembled in the Front Street Theater at Baltimore on the seventh of June. The scene was enlivened by a "splendid band," "graced by the presence of many ladies," and honored by the attendance of distinguished guests including the commanding general of the department, Lew Wallace.[1] There was excitement because of the crowds and the interest which a presidential nomination always produces, but there was virtually no contest as to the head of the ticket and the occasion presented no such dramatic situation as that in Chicago in 1860. The whole emphasis was pro-Lincoln, in spite of the New York *Herald* which declared on June 4 that if nominated Lincoln would not be elected. J. W. Forney is said to have remarked that the convention had no candidate to choose; the choice had already been made.[2]

For two days these delegates talked, raised points of order, considered and reconsidered, offered and withdrew motions, called the roll, and, in the result, managed somehow to get ahead with their appointed business. Some of the proceedings were confusing and hard to follow. Members would at times be in doubt as to the rules under which they were operating and uncertain as to what motion or amendment was before the house. A rule or motion would be "adopted," and some would immediately ask what the action meant and where they stood. Amid the five hundred, most of whom might as well have been nameless, it devolved upon a few men to steer the course and evoke order out of what looked at first like unorganized chaos. Thaddeus Stevens spoke authoritatively as an expert on procedure, but a more important function was performed with special

---

21 George Winston Smith, "Broadsides for Freedom: Civil War Propaganda in New England," *New England Quarterly*, XXI, 305–307 (Sep. 1948).

1 *Proceedings of the First Three Republican National Conventions of 1856, 1860 and 1864*, 176.

2 Nicolay and Hay, *Lincoln*, IX, 63.

skill, yet unobtrusively, by Henry J. Raymond, who remarked that the gathering began as nothing more than a mass meeting, and that the problem was to organize that mass meeting and convert it into a convention of authorized delegates.[3] It was no easy job for the permanent presiding officer, William Dennison of Ohio (chosen after considerable delay) to focus the action of the meeting amid a maze of conflicting motions, personal explanations, parliamentary sparring, and "out of order" rulings. At one of the awkward moments the distinguished and honored Robert J. Breckinridge, having been told that, under the rule, he could not speak on the pending question, declared: "I wish to say a single sentence . . . . I do not wish to be gagged." [4] (Breckinridge persisted and managed to have his say.)

After the preliminaries the report of the committee on credentials was presented and this started the only ripple of dissent in the matter of the nomination. Missouri had sent two delegations—one pro-Lincoln, the other radical and anti-Lincoln. The committee on credentials recommended seating the radical group; those who were steering the convention were opposed in sentiment to this group so far as the presidency was concerned, but to recognize and admit them was a concession that could well be afforded. This Missouri question, the most controversial of all the convention's problems, had produced earnest and animated debate in which George William Curtis wanted it to "ring out" over that land "that we recognize the radicals of Missouri," while Robert J. Breckinridge objected that the convention, in so doing, would be refusing seats to "a delegation from a party in Missouri, whose main business . . . has been to support . . . the President of the United States, whom we are about to nominate by acclamation." By such action, added Breckinridge, the convention would "come as nigh to playing the devil as any set of gentlemen ever did with their eyes blindfolded." [5]

There was a confusing proposal to admit both delegations: the idea was that where they agreed they should cast the Missouri vote, but if they disagreed the vote of the state should be lost. This proposal, which would have pleased neither side, was rejected, and the convention voted to follow the lead of the credentials committee and admit the Missouri radicals as official state delegates.

[3] *Proceedings . . . Republican National Conventions,* 185, 210.
[4] *Ibid.,* 215. [5] *Ibid.,* 213–216.

Questions then arose as to other delegations—those of Tennessee, Louisiana, Arkansas, Virginia, Florida, and South Carolina. It was complained that the presence of some of these state groups at Baltimore was too closely related to the President's controversial reconstruction scheme and was therefore distasteful to the radicals. The controversy involved degrees of recognition: some thought that certain delegations should be given "seats" but without the right to vote. As to three important states—Tennessee, Louisiana, and Arkansas (all pro-Lincoln)—the decision was to admit them with the voting right. (This was not accomplished without opposition; there were negative votes in considerable number from Massachusetts, Pennsylvania, Kentucky, and Michigan.) In the case of Virginia and Florida, where the restoration process was clouded and incomplete, the delegates were admitted without the right to vote; in the case of South Carolina the delegates were rejected. These troublesome matters were handled smoothly and in such a manner as to allow dissenting opinions to be expressed, yet to keep explosive factors in the background.

VI

For this efficient yet unprovocative handling of the convention's business a considerable share of credit should attach to Henry J. Raymond of the New York *Times*. In addition to being fully steeped in the politics of New York and specially gifted for political journalism, Raymond was also known as a champion of the President. His *History of the Administration of President Lincoln*,[1] an elaborate volume crowded with speeches, messages, and other documents, was completed in manuscript in May 1864 and was "designed wholly and frankly to promote his [Lincoln's] nomination and reelection."[2] Throughout the war Raymond had regularly defended Lincoln and his policies, though showing his concept of press freedom by occasional blame and criticism where this was considered appropriate. His arguments on reconstruction showed fundamental agreement with Lincoln and his support of the President for another term had been indicated in the *Times* at the beginning of 1864.

1 A similar but longer book by Raymond appeared in 1865 under the title *The Life and Public Services of Abraham Lincoln . . . Including his Speeches . . .* [etc.] *and the Closing Scenes Connected With His Life and Death.*"

2 Francis Brown, *Raymond of the Times*, 249.

With its tendency to slip off the track the convention needed guidance and at awkward times it was Raymond who offered the steadying touch, though in no sense taking over or seeming to dominate the proceedings. At an early stage when Cameron moved to call for a roll of the states so that some one from each state should present a list of its delegates (before any committee of credentials was even appointed), the Pennsylvanian's motion became "so tangled in amendments, withdrawal of amendments, votes of approval and disapproval, motions and counter-motions, that the bewildered Breckinridge confessed that he had no idea where matters stood." [3] In this well nigh impossible situation it was Raymond who offered the clarifying word and sensible procedure which enabled the convention to "organize" and get ahead with its task.

With this background it can be understood why Raymond became the "natural choice to draft the platform" of the convention.[4] Without clashing with anti-Lincoln radicals he managed to keep the resolutions comparatively harmless. This part of the business gave the convention no trouble. In fact, after being read, the resolutions were adopted "by acclamation" without debate; one of the members remarked that they were "their own argument." [5] In Raymond's hand the platform was so framed as to elicit sure-fire applause while sidestepping or ignoring some of the burning controversies which agitated the nation and on which the Republicans were far from united. For example, though broadly pledging the party to prosecute the war and punish the "rebels," the platform contained no formula or plan for reconstruction, whether the moderate and practical plan of Lincoln or the vindictive program of the radicals. Thus the keenest political question of the day was avoided.

There had been vigorous pressure for a radical platform, the more so as the radicals were unable to prevent the renomination of the President. If they swallowed Lincoln, they insisted that the platform should suit them, while from the standpoint of pro-Lincoln men the

---

[3] *Ibid.*, 253. Breckinridge's bewilderment becomes easy to understand when one reads the confused proceedings on the Cameron proposal. Progress to a reasonable result seemed impossible in the parliamentary maze until Raymond straightened out the tangle.

[4] *Ibid., Raymond of the Times,* 254.

[5] *Proceedings . . . Republican National Conventions,* 227.

acceptance of such a platform was regarded as a maneuver to check the Frémont movement.[6] In the result it may be said that the 1864 resolutions had a radical tone and emphasis but were free from any specific or clear-cut radical plank. The soldiers were thanked in glowing terms and paragraphs were included favoring an antislavery amendment to the Constitution, a railroad to the Pacific, and full national faith for the redemption of the debt. The tariff was not even mentioned, nor the national banking system, nor the use of paper money on which the government was largely relying. Some of the declarations, while phrased in a generalized wording, were intended, among those who knew, to have a specific and partly hidden application. This could have been said of the sixth resolution which indicated that none could be trusted except "those who cordially endorse the principles proclaimed in these resolutions." This was announced as being essential to "harmony," but it could have been interpreted somewhat in the sense of a "purge"; instead of giving the Republican blessing to differing shades of opinion, the declaration signified that moderates were not "worthy of public confidence" and that radicals were to take over. This specific meaning was not spelled out, for lack of clarity is often the fashion in party platforms, but those who knew the cross currents of the time understood well enough what was the intent and meaning. In particular, this part of the platform, called the "denunciatory" clause was "aimed . . . at the Blairs, primarily, though Welles and Bates were included." [7] There were many who understood that the declaration as to those who could and could not be trusted was directed also against Seward.

The striking and distressing fact was that the men who were thus denounced as unworthy, and as if they should have no support from the party, were moderates who on essential points agreed with the President. The sixth resolution really implied, if its purpose were to have been put into effect, that pro-Lincoln moderates should get out of the government and the party; yet all this was set forth in the supposed cause of "harmony." As part of this clamor for alleged harmony there was a lively demand in the convention, though it was not expressed in the proceedings, to get rid of Seward. In frustration

---

[6] Cincinnati *Daily Gazette,* June 6, 1864, p. 3, c. 6.

[7] William E. Smith, *The Francis Preston Blair Family in Politics,* II, 267.

of this effort "the managers, under the contrivance of Raymond, . . . so shaped the resolution as to leave it pointless," [8] as to any particular cabinet member.

When the states were polled in the balloting for the presidential nomination, every delegation cast its full total for Lincoln except that of Missouri whose radical vote, under instruction, was given to Grant. Mr. J. F. Hume, however, speaking for the Missouri radical delegation, carefully explained that they were with the Union party, would assist in carrying its banner to victory, and would support its nominees. He further explained that in voting for "the head of the fighting Radicals of the Nation, Ulysses S. Grant" the Missouri delegates were bound by instructions from their state convention and could not do otherwise than obey that instruction on the first balloting.[9] On the roll call Lincoln thus received 484 votes and Grant 22 (all from Missouri), after which, on motion by Hume of Missouri, the nomination of Lincoln was made unanimous. When one considers all the factors of opposition to the President and all the maneuvers to block his nomination, this result, so easily achieved, stands out as an impressive demonstration of Lincoln's popularity and of the practical force of party organization and steering.

VII

In terms of unforeseen history one of the most important functions of the Baltimore convention was the nomination of a candidate for Vice President. Numerous names were suggested for this post, including Hannibal Hamlin, Simon Cameron, Andrew Johnson of Tennessee, Joseph Holt of Kentucky, B. F. Butler, Daniel S. Dickinson of New York, Schuyler Colfax of Indiana, and even Horatio Seymour of New York.[1]

In the actual balloting for the vice-presidential nomination there was no Butler movement and support for him was minor, yet he received 28 votes: they included twenty from the Missouri faction and eight from New England, thus indicating the radical flavor of his following. Only three names were prominent in this voting: John-

[8] Welles, *Diary*, II, 174.

[9] *Proceedings . . . National Republican Conventions*, 232–233.

[1] Alfred Churchill to Richard Yates, Kanesville, Kane Co., Mo., June 11, 1863, Yates MSS., Ill. State Hist. Lib.

son who received 200 votes on the first roll call, Hamlin with 150 votes, and Dickinson with 108. When the trend toward Johnson became clearly evident several delegations changed their votes, and when the first and only ballot was finally recorded Johnson had 494 votes, Dickinson 17, and Hamlin 9. A highly important part of the convention's work was thus smoothly concluded. Of the winning candidate for second place the Washington *Chronicle,* which was understood to be in sympathy with Lincoln wrote: "Of this noble Unionist, who has been selected as a Union candidate for Vice President, we cannot speak in terms of sufficient commendation. A son of poverty and obscurity, he has won his way, by dint of energy and superior ability, to the highest offices in the gift of his adopted State [legislator, congressman, governor, senator]." [2] There were, of course, Republicans who had no love for Johnson. That was true of Thaddeus Stevens, but then he had no love for Lincoln either.

On the floor of the convention the choice of Andrew Johnson was rather quickly accomplished, but the nomination was to become the theme of lively speculation and controversy, particularly as to the part said to have been played in Johnson's favor by the President. There had been considerable feeling that it would be appropriate to renominate the incumbent, Hannibal Hamlin of Maine, but the friends of Hamlin were "safe"; they could be counted on to support the ticket in any case, and convention support for him, though substantial, decreased as attention focused on sturdy Andrew Johnson of Tennessee. The main argument for Johnson was that by his nomination the party would be reaching out for "War Democrats." (Hamlin had formerly been a Democrat but had joined the Republican party in 1856. In contrast, Johnson was a Southern Democrat of 1860, though differing strongly from Democratic colleagues of the South who favored secession.) Openly and on the surface Lincoln avoided interference with the work of the convention on the vice-presidency and otherwise [3] and the statement has been made that he did not favor Johnson.[4] On the other hand, Ward H. Lamon, old friend of Lincoln, stated in reminiscence that Lincoln "was decidedly in favor of a Southern man for Vice-President" and that "his preference, as he expressed

[2] Editorial, Washington *Daily Morning Chronicle,* June 9, 1864, p. 2, c. 1.
[3] See below, p. 133, note 7.
[4] Noah Brooks, *Washington in Lincoln's Time,* 152, 160.

himself to prudent friends, was for Andrew Johnson."[5] Those who in later years thus reported that the President favored Johnson the Tennessean explained that he did not wish this preference to become public; it was a delicate question, and, according to Lamon, Lincoln did not want to give offense to Hamlin's New England constituency.

The acrimonious dispute as to Lincoln's vice-presidential preference was revived in postwar years. After Hamlin's death in 1891 the Philadelphia *Times* stated that Lincoln had favored Johnson's nomination. This statement was contradicted by J. G. Nicolay, who asserted that Lincoln's "personal feelings" were for Hamlin's renomination but that he carefully avoided any move to influence the action of the convention. This Nicolay statement was in turn emphatically contradicted by A. K. McClure who criticized Nicolay for his "ignorance" and for presuming to speak for Abraham Lincoln. McClure commented that "Nicolay was dress-parading at Baltimore and knew nothing of the President's purposes." "He [Nicolay] saw and knew President Lincoln [wrote McClure]; the man Abraham Lincoln he never saw and never knew." As the newspaper controversy went on it became ugly and vituperative. Nicolay referred to McClure's "personal abuse" and his "rage and wounded vanity at being exposed in a gross historical misstatement." He quoted Lincoln's written statement at the time of the convention: "Wish not to interfere about V. P. Cannot interfere about platform. Convention must judge for itself." This exceedingly brief jotting by Lincoln, a June 6 endorsement on a letter which Nicolay wrote to Hay from Baltimore on June 5,[6] was no more than a bit of advice as to the President's official attitude or open position. It would hardly be accepted by critical writers as a full statement of the whole truth as to behind-the-scenes comments. Lincoln knew that a statement given through his private secretary would have somewhat the character of an official statement by the President himself. In rejoinder to Nicolay, McClure declared that Nicolay did not know fully what was going on in June 1864, that some of his statements were "flagrantly . . . false," and that Mr. Hay "refused to sustain" Nicolay's interpretation of the President's brief non-committal note. Without dwelling further on the unseemly

[5] A. K. McClure, *Abraham Lincoln and Men of War-Times,* 477.

[6] Nicolay and Hay, Lincoln, IX, 73; Works, X, 115 (endorsement dated June 6, 1864); Helen Nicolay, *Lincoln's Secretary,* 323.

controversy it is sufficient to observe that in the nature of the case Lincoln's confidential understandings were not revealed in his public declarations. He talked with politicians without making all his thoughts known to his secretaries.[7] McClure was a knowledgeable politician, and his account of Lincoln's unpublicized preference deserves historical attention, especially since it has confirmation from other sources.[8] That Lincoln managed the matter so as not to offend Hamlin and his followers was another example of the President's handling of human relations. On this point McClure praised the President's "curiously characteristic diplomacy." [9]

In a careful study focused on Ward Lamon, Clint Clay Tilton confirms the report that Lincoln favored Andrew Johnson as having greater appeal at the polls than Hamlin. Leonard Swett and A. K. McClure, according to Tilton, personally favored Hamlin but yielded to Lincoln's insistence that they should work for the defeat of the incumbent Vice President in favor of Johnson. These "master politicians" apparently worked to promote Joseph Holt of Kentucky, but this was only a "smoke screen" behind which the maneuver for Johnson was successfully managed. Tilton states that Ward Lamon was present when McClure and Swett conferred with Lincoln at the White House, and that the President gave a letter to Lamon embodying his views. The letter, however, (as Tilton states), was not used "and later was returned to the writer at his request." So far as the convention was concerned, Lincoln's confidential attitude was not revealed.[10]

Much of the discussion on this subject was colored in later years by fierce radical hatred of Johnson in reconstruction days, but on that aspect of the subject it is sufficient to say that Johnson's restoration policy was essentially the same as Lincoln's and that, in the considered

---

[7] Nicolay's side of the controversy is supported by his daughter, Helen Nicolay. She repeats that Lincoln gave a personal word favoring Hamlin and that the President at the time of the convention wrote that he wished "not to interfere about V. P." She treats McClure's postwar statements in disagreement with Nicolay as untrue, but in general her account leaves the controversy about where it stood in the Philadelphia *Times* correspondence between Nicolay and McClure in 1891. Helen Nicolay, *Lincoln's Secretary: A Biography of John G. Nicolay,* 207–208, 322–325.

[8] For the documents on the Nicolay-McClure controversy, with material also from Lamon, see A. K. McClure, *Lincoln and Men of War-Times,* appendix, 457 ff.

[9] *Ibid.,* 16, 119 ff.

[10] Clint Clay Tilton, "Lincoln and Lamon: Partners and Friends," *Transactions* Ill. State Hist. Soc., 1931, 212.

opinion of contemporary leaders and of historians the same type of postwar radical opposition and bitter congressional obstruction would have confronted Lincoln if he had lived and had adhered to his policies as stated during his presidency and on down to the time of his last speech on April 11, 1865.[11]

VIII

Of all the aspects of the 1864 vice-presidential candidacy the most sensational (in its possible implications) was the effort to put Benjamin F. Butler in second place. The details are given in the recollections of A. K. McClure and in an article by Louis Taylor Merrill. McClure recounts how "Lincoln's first selection for Vice-President was General Butler," how in March 1864 he explained this purpose to Simon Cameron, and how he made Cameron his messenger to Fort Monroe to "confer confidentially with Butler." [1] Despite all the heated antagonism attaching to his personality and career, Butler was a real political force. This was demonstrated by the enthusiastic ovation that greeted him (after his removal from the New Orleans command) when he spoke in his home town of Lowell, Massachusetts, while similar popular approval was also shown at a speech in Boston's Faneuil Hall and in a reception in New York. He was spoken of as a presidential prospect, also as a cabinet officer, "especially Stanton's place." [2] The man evoked emotional acclaim; he inspired headlines; he had unusual publicity value; he was one of the most prominent of those men around whom it was believed the radicals could rally. There was a persistent effort on his part, though without success, to enhance his military importance; he was one of the most "political" of the Union generals.

To resume the story of this reported 1864 offer, when Cameron turned up at Butler's headquarters at Fort Monroe the general decisively rejected the opportunity. It is stated that the President

11 The biographer of Henry J. Raymond gives that New York journalist and Republican leader considerable credit for the nomination of Johnson. It is known that Raymond was acting in Lincoln's interest. Francis Brown, *Raymond of the Times,* 255.

1 McClure, *Abraham Lincoln and Men of War-Times,* 118 ff.

2 Louis Taylor Merrill, "General Benjamin F. Butler in the Presidential Campaign of 1864," *Miss. Vall. Hist. Rev.,* XXXIII, 541 (Mar. 1947).

planned to visit Fort Monroe with Mrs. Lincoln to confer with Butler, but the plan was never carried out and about this time the President's mind was directed favorably toward Andrew Johnson as his running mate.

This account of the Butler offer through Cameron—a rather unlikely go-between for Lincoln—has not been verified on the Lincoln side, and as it stands the story has features which are undocumented and other features which are of the tongue-in-cheek quality. Yet it should be added that Butler himself confirmed the story in later years. In an article published in 1885 he wrote that "a gentleman who stood very high in Mr. Lincoln's confidence" came to see him at Fort Monroe to convey the message from Lincoln that the President desired Butler to serve as candidate for Vice President. At this point Butler reported a bit of misplaced humor on his part. "Please say to Mr. Lincoln that . . . I must decline. Tell him . . . I would not quit the field to be Vice-President, even with himself as President, unless he will give me a bond with sureties, in the full sum of his four years' salary, that he will die or resign within three months after his inauguration. Ask him what he thinks I have done to deserve the punishment . . . of being made to sit as presiding officer over the Senate . . . [etc.]." [3]

It is known that Butler's real interest in 1864 was in the first, not the second, place. The Cameron visit was reported as having been made at a time in the spring of 1864 when Republican maneuvering for the presidency was highly active; people who knew the radical anti-Lincoln game at that time and who knew Butler's ambition, would hardly have expected him to make an advance commitment which would have kept him out as presidential candidate and at the same time have placed him in support of Lincoln.

There has been speculation as to Butler's possible thoughts when further pages of history were unfolded and he heard of Lincoln's assassination. As Dr. Merrill puts it, " 'bold Ben' Butler had muffed the highest prize." [4] There were, however, matters of greater importance than Butler's feelings, and the historian may well ponder the

---

[3] B. F. Butler, "Vice-Presidential Politics in '64," *North Amer. Rev.* CXLI, 333 (Oct. 1885).

[4] Merrill, as above cited, 570.

possible situation that would have resulted if the explosive, unpredictable, flamboyant, and radically vindictive Butler, of all Union generals the most hated in the South, had been the executive head of the nation in the confused and viciously partisan days of so-called "reconstruction."

IX

As a sequel to the convention Lincoln received committees and delegates, addressing them with brief responses. On June 9, the day after his nomination, he spoke to a committee of notification. In a sentence that was characteristically Lincolnian (in its attitude of caution as to a pledge or commitment) the President stated that perhaps he "should not declare definitely before reading and considering what is called the platform." He made it clear, however, that he approved the anti-slavery amendment to the Constitution as "a fitting and necessary conclusion to the final success of the Union cause." [1] Eighteen days later Lincoln issued a more formal acceptance indicating that the platform was "heartily approved." He did, however, offer one qualifying statement. The plank upholding the Monroe Doctrine and denouncing any effort to overthrow republican government on the western continent could have been interpreted, by reading between the lines, as a rebuke of Seward as secretary of state. Consequently Lincoln, while concurring in the declaration, took occasion to announce that "the position of the government . . . as assumed through the State Department" would be "faithfully maintained." [2]

Reactions to the results of the Baltimore convention varied. The Union Leagues loudly approved of the convention's work, though radical rumblings in those leagues had not been lacking. Some dissent and dissatisfaction was expressed shortly after the convention, but most of it was withheld. Later in the summer it would become abundantly evident. There were, it should be added, withdrawals, resignations, and replacements, but these will be discussed at a later period. One member of the cabinet, Attorney General Bates, wrote on June 10: "The Baltimore Convention . . . has surprised and mortified me greatly." Many of the delegates, he remarked, though they were

1 *Works,* X, 116–117 (June 9, 1864).

2 *Ibid.,* X, 136–137 (June 27, 1864).

instructed to vote for Lincoln, "hated to do it." He added: "I shall tell the Prest. in all frankness, that his best nomination is not that at Baltimore, but . . . by the People, by which the convention was constrained to name him." [3]

[3] Bates, *Diary*, 374–375 (June 10, 1864).

CHAPTER VIII

WAR FRONT AND PEACE TALK

AS THE armies renewed their fighting with fierce intensity in the spring of 1864, a new situation presented itself. In three years of indecisive warfare a certain repetitive pattern had become familiar: advance by one or the other side (usually the Federal), concentration on a one- or two-day battle, "victory" by one side or the other (usually the Confederate), Union withdrawal, change of Union commanders, then considerable delay for each side, neither being really defeated, to reorganize for the next concentrated push and sanguinary though indecisive engagement. Seemingly, the war could have gone on indefinitely in such fashion. Now, however, came a kind of struggle that was different as to broad strategy, as to method in the field, and as to pace. These changes coincided with the shifting of Grant from the field of his western triumphs to the main area of operations against Lee in Virginia; moreover, the shift involved the placing of general command of the Union armies in Grant's determined hand. The strategy was now for co-ordinated forward drives, continued assaults though producing no immediate advantage, killing and wounding at a thousand a day, emphasis on fighting and slaughter rather than on this or that battle—in a word, a "war of attrition."

As the doubtful spring gave way to a summer of deepest gloom, the Union cause appeared to be in a hopeless stalemate, while the mounting casualties produced a wave of shock and indignation in the North. The "political" result of all this was a rising tide of anti-Lincoln sentiment in the President's own party, while at the same time the nation's attention was continually focused on unofficial and misguided "peace" maneuvers which the President could not ignore, though they offered no tangible hope for genuine peace.

I

On February 29, 1864, Lincoln signed an act of Congress reviving the grade of lieutenant general, a rank so high that it had been used only for Washington and (as brevet) for Winfield Scott. It was understood that this high rank was to be conferred upon U. S. Grant, who arrived in unspectacular fashion in Washington to become the sensational center of interest and the cynosure of social eyes at a White House reception remarkable for the presence of the nation's notables (May 8). There was an unusually large attendance in expectation of Grant's presence and a considerable "stir and buzz" (as Welles recorded) when the "short, brown, dark-haired man" appeared. As the general passed into the East Room escorted by Seward, there was clapping and "a cheer or two"; to Welles it "seemed rowdy and unseemly." [1]

Next day, March 9, there occurred a formal ceremony of military investiture at the White House. As Lincoln and Grant had met for the first time on the evening of the reception, the President, with tactful thoughtfulness toward the diffident hero, explained the nature of the coming occasion, giving him a copy of his (the President's) speech and adding a friendly suggestion that a brief response would be in order. In the presence of the cabinet, specially summoned for the purpose, the military notables gathered (Grant and his staff with Stanton and Halleck) and Lincoln presented the unusual commission. It was remarked that the general was "somewhat embarrassed" as he gave his response.[2] On March 10 the President and Mrs. Lincoln invited Grant and Meade to dinner at the White House. Lincoln was omitting nothing that could improve the social and personal as well as the official recognition of the officer who was now regarded as the man of the hour.

For this dinner there was a special courtesy in the inclusion of General Meade; if either Meade or Grant had been of smaller stature, the new situation might have developed into an awkward rivalry of the kind so common among Civil War generals, or at least a sense of hurt feelings. It was not merely that Grant was elevated to supreme military "rank." He was at the same time "assigned to the

---

1 Welles, *Diary,* I, 538–539 (Mar. 9, 1864).

2 *Ibid.,* I, 539.

command of the Armies of the United States." Though in a sense this high general command had been held by Scott, McClellan, and Halleck, yet it had been exercised with so little effectiveness that the investiture in the case of Grant came with all the force of something new and untried. Lincoln had found Halleck unsatisfactory in the role of general in chief and his dissatisfaction on that score was well known. Halleck, with the best of motives, now offered his resignation, not for the first time, but the President, as previously, made it clear that "Old Brains" was to remain at his post.

To appreciate the extent of the change now instituted it must be remembered that general direction of the armies was to be no longer in the hands of a lofty desk commander in Washington. If Grant had so chosen he might have continued the old system, but the "new" general from the West, now the main leader in the East but with authority for all the fronts, promptly decided that his headquarters would not be in Washington, but with the Army of the Potomac, with himself as leader of that army in the field. Yet he never became its appointed commander; that office was retained by Meade. It augured well for the Union cause, and it revealed much as to the personalities of these generals, that they could stand in this unusual and potentially difficult relation to each other—the one the official commander, the other the effective leader of the main army—without personal friction and without detriment to efficiency.

If lesser personalities had been involved the feuding might have disrupted the team as in the case of Hooker and Slocum in the fall of 1863. Or another possible result might have been that any successes would have been credited to Grant, who was wearing an aura of military triumph, while failures would have been Meade's. As explained, however, by Meade's chief staff officer, Colonel Theodore Lyman: "In point of reality the whole is Grant's: he directs all, and his subordinates are only . . . executive officers having more or less unimportant functions." [3] Lyman also wrote: "he [Grant] is a man who does everything with a specific reason; he is eminently a *wise* man." The colonel added: "He knows very well Meade's precise capacity and strong points. For example, if Meade says a certain movement . . . should be made, Grant makes it, almost as a matter of course,

[3] George R. Agassiz, ed., *Meade's Headquarters, 1863–1865: Letters of Colonel Theodore Lyman from the Wilderness to Appomattox,* 224.

because he is so wise as to know that there is one of Meade's strong points." [4] This statement only partly covers the subject. Fully to understand the unusual relationship which was nevertheless made workable, one must remember Grant's statement of his own feeling: "Meade's position . . . proved embarrassing to me if not to him. . . . All other general officers occupying similar positions were independent in their commands so far as any one present with them was concerned. I tried to make General Meade's position as nearly as possible what it would have been if I had been in Washington or any other place away from his command. I therefore gave all orders for the movements of the Army of the Potomac to Meade to have them executed." [5]

In person and temperament, Grant was "different." He lacked style, made an undistinguished appearance, showed carelessness of dress, and appeared bored by unusual attention. Describing him at the time of his arrival in Washington, Ben: Perley Poore wrote: "He wore a plain, undress uniform and a felt hat of the regulation pattern, the sides . . . crushed together. He generally stood or walked with his left hand in his trousers pocket, and had in his mouth an unlighted cigar, the end of which he chewed restlessly." From these externals Poore proceeded to points of personality and character. "His square-cut features, when at rest, appeared as if carved from mahogany, and his firmly set under-jaw indicated the unyielding tenacity of a bull-dog, while the kind glances of his gray eyes showed that he possessed the softer traits." It also seemed to Poore that the general "seemed always preoccupied." He "would gaze at any one who approached him with an inquiring air, followed by a glance of recollection and a grave nod of recognition." [6]

An observer wrote: "He is rather under middle height, of a spare, strong build; light-brown hair, and short, light-brown beard. His eyes of a clear blue; forehead high; nose aquiline; jaw squarely set, but not sensual. His face has three expressions: deep thought; extreme determination; and great simplicity and calmness." [7] Other details have

---

[4] *Ibid.*, 359.

[5] Grant, *Memoirs,* II, 117–118. More than two weeks after the White House ceremony putting Grant in full command, Bates wrote in his diary (March 27, 1864): "Day before yesterday, Lt. Genl. Grant went to the front—Hd. Qrs. A. P. It seems not known whether he will supersede Genl. Meade, or only supervise him, as all the rest."

[6] Poore, *Perley's Reminiscences,* II, 150.

[7] Agassiz, ed., *Meade's Headquarters,* 80.

been added to the portrait. "He is a man of a natural, severe simplicity, in all things—the very way he wears his high-crowned felt hat shows this: he neither puts it on behind his ears, nor draws it over his eyes; much less does he cock it on one side, but sets it straight and very hard on his head. His riding is the same: without the slightest 'air' . . . he sits firmly in the saddle and looks straight ahead, as if only intent on getting to some particular point." [8] Again we have the following: "He is an odd combination; there is one good thing, at any rate—he is the concentration of all that is American. He talks bad grammar, but talks it naturally, as much as to say, 'I was so brought up and, if I try fine phrases, I shall only appear silly.' " [9]

II

The military planning for 1864 soon unfolded itself in terms of a grand scheme by which the Union armies on all major fronts would be co-ordinated in a series of encircling or squeezing operations. By simultaneous movements on several fronts Federal numerical superiority would be brought into play while the resulting Confederate necessity of manning a number of distant points would be sure to leave some area exposed to attack.

Just after receiving his commission as lieutenant general and before taking up his headquarters at Culpepper, Grant had gone West for about ten days conferring with Sherman at Nashville, after which the two generals rode together from Nashville to Cincinnati. They laid plans for the major features of what Grant called "sanguinary war." [1] They pored over maps and planned simultaneous attacks with Richmond and Atlanta—the armies of Lee and Johnston—as targets. Thus they proposed to nullify the enemy's advantage of interior lines; incidentally they hoped to prevent Confederate soldier furloughs for the planting of crops. The new strategy was reducible to two points: unity of command and "attrition to powder of the Confederate armies by a continuous series of battles." [2] In addition to the two most prominent commanders—Grant and Sherman—other campaigns were intrusted to such commanders as Butler in Virginia and Banks in the far Southwest.

---

[8] *Ibid.*, 83.

[9] *Ibid.*, 156.

[1] Grant, *Memoirs*, II, 119.

[2] *Harper's Pictorial History of the Civil War*, II, 600.

While at Culpepper in late March and April, Grant planned the spring and summer offensive of the eastern army, keeping in touch with Lincoln by occasional personal visits to nearby Washington. Lincoln gave Grant a free hand, but it would be a mistake to suppose that the President had nothing to do with strategy or that he was passively inattentive to military matters. Too much should not be made of Lincoln's statement to Grant, as to other generals, disclaiming military expertness while leaving the field commander to act as the effective military leader. It is true that on the eve of the Virginia campaign the President wrote: "The particulars of your plans I neither know nor seek to know." [3] In his *Memoirs* Grant records that Lincoln "told me he did not want to know what I proposed to do." [4] (This was probably a misinterpretation of the Chief's statement that he did not seek to know the "particulars" of the general's plans.) In those same *Memoirs,* written long after the war, the general related that the President "submitted a plan of campaign of his own," illustrating it with a map. The general "listened respectfully," but knew that the President's plan was unworkable.[5] The full truth as to the respective attitudes of Lincoln and Grant is not easy to state. In a careful study T. Harry Williams discounts the validity of some of the general's comments in his *Memoirs.* The general, he said, wrote "under the influence of the postwar Grant and Lincoln myths." "Grant had forgotten much in the years after the war, and his account [of Lincoln's unworkable plan] was wide of the truth." [6]

On May 4, 1864, Grant moved out from his Culpepper headquarters, crossed the Rapidan, and began a slugging campaign of forty days, in which the most frightful and bloody slaughter of the war brought little apparent success while it produced agony and heartache by its terrific Union casualties. The chief phases of these forty days were: (1) the battle of the Wilderness, May 5 and 6; (2) the shifting of the armies to Spottsylvania and the engagement there; (3) operations on the North Anna River; (4) the unsuccessful and shockingly costly assaults at Cold Harbor, June 1–3; and (5) the Union change of front as Grant's army crossed the James River and attempted the quick taking of Petersburg. Each of these operations could be set down as a Union failure, beginning with the confused struggle in the Wil-

[3] *Works,* X, 90 (Apr. 30, 1864). [4] Grant, *Memoirs,* II, 123.
[5] *Ibid.* [6] T. Harry Williams, *Lincoln and His Generals,* 304–305.

derness, where Grant had not intended to fight, and ending with the shifting of the "line" which he had said he would not do. At the end of the forty days the assault on Petersburg failed, so that the Union effort against that Confederate stronghold resolved itself, much to Lincoln's disappointment, in a long siege.

Yet such was war: it looked like failure, but because of ceaseless pounding while Union soldier morale kept at high pitch, the enemy was not only prevented from conducting an offensive operation (had that been Lee's purpose), but was progressively weakened for the (as yet unforeseen) final chapter. Grant was sustained both by his basic character and by his star. He seems to have had a reserve of endurance as well as a surplus of prestige. Otherwise his lack of success in the spring and summer of '64 might have relegated him to the fate of McDowell, Pope, Burnside, and Hooker.

As for the Wilderness, the obvious disadvantages of that impossible area will serve to confirm the reasons why McClellan, two years before, had preferred the Peninsular approach. The two-day battle (May 5 and 6) has been described as "a battle which no man saw or could see."[7] It was a series of attacks and repulses without co-ordinated control, fought in brush and thickets which made artillery ineffective and made it almost impossible to find the wounded who remained lying in the field, with a renewed engagement about to begin.[8] Neither side claimed victory; on the Union side the only justification for the encounter was that the Confederates brought on the operation before Grant's dispositions could be developed, and that by hammering continuously, "by mere attrition, if in no other way," the enemy would be forced into "submission."[9]

III

Despite Grant's over-all leadership and the much emphasized principal of co-ordinated strategy there were two fairly ambitious operations in 1864 which resulted in sorry fiascos: the Red River expedition of General N. P. Banks in the Southwest and the frustrated advance of B. F. Butler on the James River in Virginia. Only a brief mention of these episodes can be allowed.

The Union expedition up the Red River in western Louisiana,

[7] *Offic. Rec.,* 1 ser., XXXVI, pt. 1, 218. [8] *Ibid.,* 218, 231. [9] *Ibid.,* 13.

Ten Reasons why Abraham Lincoln should not be elected President of the United States a second term.

1. Because after having taken an oath to support the Constitution, he falsified his oath, and trampled the Constitution under foot, by adopting the slaveholders' *construction* of it, instead of the plain language of the instrument itself.

2. Because he did not "let the oppressed go free" when, according to his own theory he had the power, as in the Border States, but *pretended* to emancipate in those States and parts of States where he had not the power, the rebels having military possession.

3. Because his Emancipation and Amnesty proclamations, taken together and translated into plain Saxon-English, mean just this: "If you will come back into the Union and help elect me President for another term I will agree that your slavery shall be guaranteed to you and your posterity forever, but if you will not, I will then emancipate your slaves."

4. Because during the time this billing and cooing was going on with the slaveholding rebels, our President was spending two millions of dollars a day and allowing our brave soldiers to be sacrificed at the rate of a hundred thousand lives per annum, in the criminal attempt to drive a sharp bargain with the rebels, that would put him in the Presidential chair for a second term, against which he was virtually pledged.

5. Because he returned to slavery 50,000 slaves, embraced in Gen. Fremont's proclamation of emancipation, and superceded him and every other General in favor of emancipation.

6. Because, after the rebels—mean and cruel as they are—had spurned the bribe, Pres. Lincoln would neither emancipate their slaves himself nor allow any of his Generals, so disposed, to do so, but permitted others of them, without let or hindrance, to return fugitive slaves to their former masters, and *compel* our soldiers to stand guard over rebel property, and act as slave catchers generally, for the miserable scamps in rebellion.

7. Because he hypocritically *says* he is "naturally anti-slavery," while *really* he *chooses* to *establish* slavery where he has the power to *abolish* it, (as in the Border States), thus *acting* in *favor* of slavery while *professing* to be *against* it.

8. Because he has used the major part of his *first* presidential term, more to conserve slavery, and get himself elected a *second* term than to *conquer* the rebellion.

9. Because after Congress passed a law excluding the States in rebellion from the Electoral College, and making a republican form of government (of course, without slavery) a condition of readmission to the Union, the President coolly pocketed the bill without signing or vetoing it, until Congress had adjourned, so that it could not be passed by a Constitutional majority of two thirds over his veto, but left the door open for him to reconstruct, before election, the States in rebellion, on his old plan of one tenth of the people, and by that means obtain a majority of Electoral votes.

10. Because his plan of re-constructing the Slave States on a slaveholding basis, is now so transparent that the wayfaring man though a fool need not err in the matter.

Robert Todd Lincoln Coll., Lib. of Cong.

THE CASE OF THE RADICALS

A pro-Fremont, anti-Lincoln campaign circular issued by Radical Republicans in the summer of 1864.

Courtesy Ill. State Hist. Lib.

FOR McCLELLAN

A lithographic broadside issued by Currier & Ives for sale to Democrats during the campaign of 1864. McClellan is trying to prevent Lincoln, on the left, and Jefferson Davis, on the right, from tearing the United States apart.

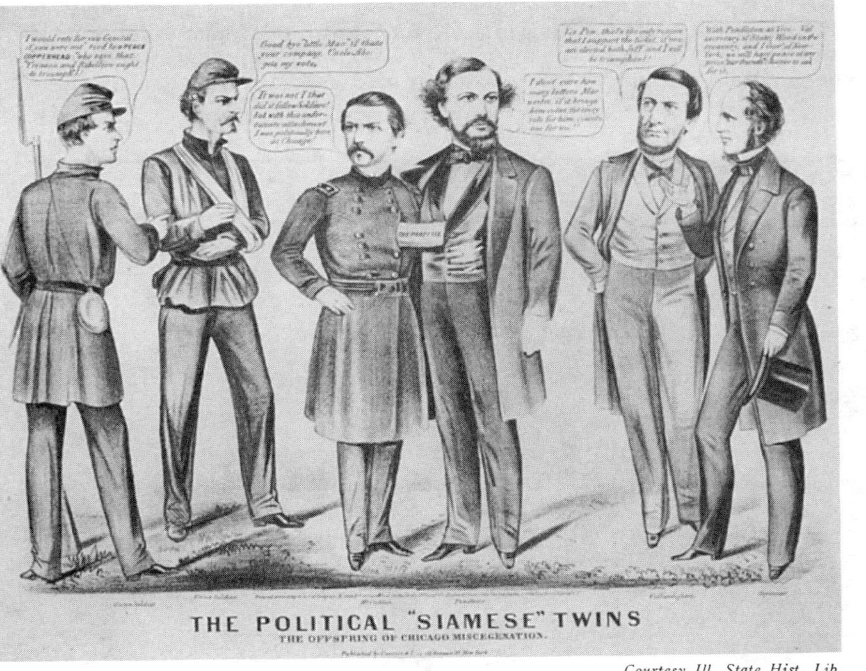

THE POLITICAL "SIAMESE" TWINS
THE OFFSPRING OF CHICAGO MISCEGENATION.

Courtesy Ill. State Hist. Lib.

AGAINST McCLELLAN

Currier & Ives sold their lithographs to Republicans as well as Democrats. In this one the two Union soldiers on the left say good-bye to "little Mac" because of his "party tie" with Pendleton. On the right Vallandigham and Seymour tell Pendleton that they support the ticket because a victory for him will also be a victory for the Peace Democrats and for Jefferson Davis.

FREEMAN AND FREEDMAN

Left: John H. Rock, a Boston lawyer, the first Negro to be admitted to practice before the U. S. Supreme Court (on Feb. 2, 1865). Never a slave, Rock exemplified the successful freeman. From *Harper's Weekly,* Feb. 25, 1865.

Right: Frederick Douglass, abolitionist and friend of Lincoln. Born in slavery on the Eastern Shore of Maryland, Douglass was an outstanding freedman.

March to May 1864, was designed as a combined army-navy operation in which Banks had (presumably) the military command while Admiral D. D. Porter was called upon to assist with a formidable fleet of gunboats. Sherman reluctantly "loaned" 10,000 of his men under General A. J. Smith for the purpose, while General Frederick Steele, moving from Arkansas, added a fourth unit to the clumsy enterprise. The purposes of this far-off trans-Mississippi adventure were political, military, and economic: if successful, it was expected that the operation would promote Lincoln's free-state organization in Louisiana (very dear to the President's heart), extend the line of Union occupation, discourage the French in their imperial Mexican designs, encourage Unionists in eastern Texas, capture Shreveport, and result in Union seizure of immense quantities of cotton. By getting started in March, it was expected that the operation would require only a month, after which Sherman's troops could be returned for use in the Atlanta campaign. The plan was largely Halleck's, though Lincoln approved it. It was vigorously opposed by Grant, yet this was supposed to be the period of unified Grant strategy on all fronts.

From first to last the execution of the operation went wrong. The army and navy were distrustful of each other; Porter disliked Banks; no one commander had recognized authority in the field; Sherman himself did not participate; commanders criticized each other; professionals of the army had little confidence in the politically minded Banks who was not of West Point; and the whole scheme brought into play the bitter antagonism between the pro-Lincoln plan of reconstruction personified in Banks and the radicals who detested him and were determined to undo his efforts.

Faulty marching arrangements, a miserable surplus of wagons on narrow roads, unwise tactics, and failure of the diverse units to concentrate—such factors as these contributed to what has been called "one of the most humiliating and disastrous [expeditions] . . . to be recorded during the war." [1] At Sabine Cross Roads (April 8, 1864), some miles south of Shreveport, the Confederates struck when Union forces were at a serious disadvantage. Artillery was useless and the Union line falling back was hampered by wagons clogging the road; Federal retreat was covered and the army mainly

[1] *Battles and Leaders of the Civil War,* IV, 366.

"saved" but all hope of taking Shreveport was destroyed. On April 9 the Union army did better at the battle of Pleasant Hill, but Banks was now in retreat. Moreover, a new complication had arisen; the drying river had fallen to such an extent that Porter's gunboats were in serious danger of being grounded and lost; this misfortune was narrowly averted by brisk and expert engineers who built dams to raise the water level and allow the fleet to get through in the nick of time. Losses were heavy—about 2200 army casualties in the one day of Sabine Cross Roads; the navy lost a few gunboats and over 300 men.[2] Banks was demoted—i. e., superseded in military command by E. R. S. Canby—and the force under A. J. Smith was sent, not to Sherman, but to the Army of the Potomac in the war's main theater. As to the cotton, many of the speculators came back "without their sheaves";[3] their disappointment as to profits had much to do in spreading false reports concerning Banks. Much of the cotton had been burned by the Confederates, and the emphasis on speculators getting cotton behind enemy lines was not so much a policy of Banks as of Lincoln and the government at Washington. The whole enterprise was one of the sorry episodes which tended to discredit the Lincoln administration in an election year.

IV

Simultaneously with Grant's Wilderness drive, B. F. Butler made his contribution, if such it could be called, to the Union effort. Having been for some months established at Fort Monroe in command of the Army of the James (about 36,000 men), he now moved up that river, pointing toward Richmond, and hoping to achieve a spectacular result by entering the Confederate capital, though at times it appeared that Petersburg was his objective. The scheme was conceived in terms of Grant's broad strategy of concerted Union attacks from different directions. Yet the effort was poorly co-ordinated with the work of the Army of the Potomac. Moreover, Butler being the man he was, the adventure cannot be judged apart from the general's prominence as a frequently mentioned rival of Lincoln for

---

[2] Fred H. Harrington, *Fighting Politician; Major General N. P. Banks,* 156; *Battles and Leaders,* IV, 366.

[3] *Battles and Leaders,* IV, 361.

the presidential nomination. All this, of course, was in terms of radical support. Had Butler been able to "take" or enter Richmond in May of 1864, it is hard to believe that such an event would not have been exploited for political advantage.

As it turned out, this subsidiary operation of Butler was a fiasco. On May 5 he "occupied" City Point and Bermuda Hundred on the James River less than twenty miles southeast of Richmond; this was easily done without opposition. Moving slowly up the river, and giving his antagonist, Beauregard, time to improve his defensive arrangements, Butler reached Drewry's Bluff, but soon withdrew and "intrenched" in "a position" which he could "hold," assuming he received supplies.[1] Little more need be said of Butler's part in the campaign. Beauregard, unharmed by Butler, was able with an inferior force to keep him penned in at Bermuda Hundred, in a corner between the Appomattox and James Rivers, where the much-advertised general was useless to Grant, who wrote: "His [Butler's] army . . . , though in a position of great security, was as completely shut off from . . . Richmond as if it had been in a bottle strongly corked. It required but a . . . small force of the enemy to hold it there." [2]

For this phase of the war one finds elaborate and important sounding military dispatches in Butler's published correspondence, but when they are boiled down they relate to such things as failure of an "attempt on the railroad," orders "for the purpose of" cutting communications between Richmond and Petersburg, criticisms of his corps commanders (Quincy A. Gillmore and William Farrar Smith), requests to Washington for reinforcements, references to his orders not being executed, comments on the safety of his force, and repeated mention that he had not taken Petersburg.[3]

---

1 *Battles and Leaders of the Civil War,* IV, 147.

2 This was Grant's statement in his official report (*Offic. Rec.,* 1 ser., XXXVI, p. 1, 20; *Battles and Leaders,* IV, 147). Years later, in writing his Memoirs, he softened his words. Without substantially modifying the impression as to Butler's ineffective position, he showed that the simile of the bottle and the cork, which caused annoyance to Butler, was not his own, but was only a repetition without quotation marks, of the words of his "chief engineer, General Barnard." *Memoirs,* II, 150–152. There is no reason to believe that in this effort to "correct history" and rectify an "injustice," the famous general had undergone any change of opinion as to the facts.

3 *Private and Official Correspondence of B. F. Butler,* IV, *passim,* especially 168, 169, 171, 411, 417, 426.

V

In the shift to the North Anna the superiority of Lee's maneuvering was demonstrated. In the operations on that river the Confederates, contrary to usual procedure in this campaign, took the offensive and made unsuccessful assaults. Aside from the slaughter little was accomplished in this battle.

Meanwhile, in addition to Grant's shifting and pounding with the main army, there were ambitious cavalry operations in which Sheridan, Hunter, and Custer were active on the Union side, against Confederate commanders Stuart, Early, and Mosby. One of the most striking of the cavalry episodes, though minor in results, was Sheridan's raid toward Richmond in the period of Grant's severe fighting against Lee's army. With the idea of cutting Lee's communications and diverting Confederate cavalry, Sheridan pushed rapidly toward the Southern capital, destroying railroad equipment, seizing food supplies, and releasing Union prisoners. At Yellow Tavern on May 11, six miles north of Richmond, a sharp engagement between Sheridan's force and that of the redoubtable J. E. B. Stuart resulted in Union repulse, yet sadly for the Confederates it resulted also in the fatal wounding of Stuart. The Union cavalry leader then swept back toward the Army of the Potomac without attempting to enter Richmond. Had he made that entry, it would have been only for a quick raid and prompt withdrawal.

After the continued slaughter in the Wilderness, at Spottsylvania, and on the North Anna, there was more of the same, though intensified, at Cold Harbor, where in a series of assaults Union troops were hurled against solid enemy defense positions. The enemy were taking no risks and the human sacifice was tremendous. In this battle, which was a failure, Grant lost 12,000 men in killed and wounded.[1] Charging bravely but hopelessly, the troops were simply mowed down at close range. If this was Grant's type of warfare, he nevertheless admitted that Cold Harbor was a mistake. In his *Memoirs* he wrote: I have always regretted that the last assault at Cold Harbor was ever made." [2] He was conducting a seemingly reckless "war of attrition,"

---

1 Thomas L. Livermore, *Numbers and Losses in the Civil War in America, 1861–1865*, 114.

2 Grant, *Memoirs*, II, 276.

yet even in terms of that kind of "strategy" he realized that such losses could not be continued. Beginning with the Wilderness (May 5) and running on through Cold Harbor and the cavalry raids, the total of Grant's casualties have been figured at 54,000 men, of whom 7621 were killed.[3] Casualties were running far above a thousand a day, much more for days of actual fighting, and Grant could not point to sufficient advantage to justify the excessive human cost. He wrote: "Without a greater sacrifice of life than I was willing to make, all could not be accomplished that I had designed north of Richmond." [4]

It was part of Grant's fitness for the grim business of war that he did not permit his emotions to be revealed. At the time of Cold Harbor an observer wrote: "His is a face that tells no tale—a face impassive in victory or defeat; face of stone; a sphinx face! Not of him can it be said, as Lady Macbeth to her lord: 'This face, my thane, is as a book, wherein one may read strange things.' Rather it is a *palimpsest,* whose obscured characters escape the scrutiny of the keenest-eyed searcher."

The writer then thought of Meade and added: "Nothing, indeed, could be more striking than the contrast presented by the two commanders, as they stooped in consultation on that bare hill, with their faces turned Richmond-ward. The small form with the slight stoop in the shoulders, sunken gray eyes; still, reserved demeanor, impassive face, and chin as of a bull-dog or close-set steel-trap—that is Grant; the tall figure, with the nervous, emphatic articulation and action, and face as of antique parchment—that is Meade—and the antipodes could not bring together a greater contrast." [5]

With a fundamental shift of plan Grant decided to cross the James River, place the Army of the Potomac south of Richmond, and pursue his further operations against Lee's army from Petersburg in the hope that that place could be quickly reduced. At the outset of his 1864 campaign he had written (May 11) Halleck: "I . . . propose to fight it out on this line if it takes all summer." [6] Yet after weeks of incessant hammering and ghastly losses he changed his "line." The shift was successfully made in mid-June. The crossing by bridge and ferry occupied several days beginning on June 14. In this movement

[3] *Offic. Rec.,* 1 ser., XXXVI, pt. 1, 188.
[4] *Ibid.,* 22.
[5] Moore, *Rebell. Rec.* (Doc.), XI, 560–561.
[6] *Offic. Rec.,* 1 ser., XXXVI, pt. 1, 4.

Lee was surprised, but on the other hand Grant's expectations were not fulfilled. His first effort south of the James was to conduct assaults upon Petersburg which failed, after which his great army settled down to a long-drawn-out siege, which was the type of war that he had hoped to avoid.

Lincoln was always generous toward Grant, and when the Army of the Potomac was in the thick of its death grapple with Lee, the President wrote: "My previous high estimate of General Grant has been maintained and heightened by what has occurred in the remarkable campaign he is now conducting . . . . He and his brave soldiers are now in the midst of their great trial . . . ." [7]

The President, with his beloved son Tad, visited Grant's army for several days at City Point in late June, leaving Washington on June 20 and returning to Washington on the 23rd. At this stage in the war the President was "deeply disappointed" that the costly campaign had resolved itself into a siege of Petersburg; he may then have felt "perhaps some doubts of Grant's generalship." [8] The shocking extent of the slaughter was weighing upon the President's mind. Shortly before his visit to the army, he had wired to Grant: "I do hope you may find a way that . . . shall not be desperate in the sense of great loss of life." [9] The war had now reached an unprofitable stage; it would be months before the burdened Chief could see prospects of ending the conflict.

VI

Military failure and national anger produced, or gave occasion for, grave and sometimes sensational manifestations behind the lines. Because of the overwrought feelings of the time a newspaper hoax in New York which should have stirred up a mere ripple, was magnified into a kind of tidal wave. In two of that city's newspapers there appeared on May 18, 1864, a purported proclamation of President Lincoln, allegedly dated May 17, in which, because of "the general state of the country," the President set a day for "fasting, humiliation, and prayer"; called forth an additional 400,000 men, and ordered that the troops "be raised by an immediate and peremptory

[7] *Works,* X, 112 (June 3, 1864).

[8] Williams, *Lincoln and His Generals,* 320.

[9] *Works,* X, 160 (June 17, 1864).

draft." The author of this daring forgery was one Joseph Howard, Jr., a prolific writer who had been private secretary to Henry Ward Beecher and had floated about on various journalistic assignments. His motive apparently was to make money by a disturbance in the stock market. He has been identified by Nicolay and Hay as having perpetrated the disgustingly false report that Lincoln, on his way through Baltimore to Washington in February 1861, had worn a Scotch cap and long military coat as a disguise, an invented yarn which led to caricatures belittling the President Elect and holding him up to ridicule.[1]

Though the effort was made to play the trick upon all the leading New York papers, only two of them—the *World* and the *Journal of Commerce*—permitted the issuance of editions containing the bogus proclamation. The *Herald* discovered the forgery after its edition had been put through the press; the edition was then destroyed and a new one printed.[2] As for the papers that were tricked, it was but a coincidence that they were both strongly hostile to the Lincoln administration. What happened to them was a matter of deception; there was no intention of fraud on the part of editors and proprietors. The false document came in by messenger at night, written on the kind of thin manifold paper used for Associated Press dispatches. In handwriting and physical appearance it looked like a regular news report. A boy opened the envelopes with the A. P. dispatches and the bogus telegram between three and four o'clock and handed them to the night editor who thought they were all from the same legitimate source. When the fraud was discovered it was too late to stop the edition in the case of the *World* and the *Journal of Commerce*.

At this point the stern and impulsive secretary of war, Stanton, entered the picture. Without waiting for an investigation, Stanton caused the immediate issuance of a sharp order, for which he obtained Lincoln's signature, which soon became revealed as a serious executive blunder. The order declared that the proclamation had been "wickedly and traitorously . . . published" with the "design to give aid and comfort to the enemies of the United States." Gen-

1 Nicolay and Hay, *Lincoln,* III, 315 n.

2 Typed memorandum by Frank A. Flower to accompany an original of Joseph Howard's bogus proclamation sent to C. F. Gunther, MS., Chicago Hist. Soc.

eral Dix was accordingly "commanded forthwith to arrest and imprison" the editors and proprietors, to hold them "in close custody until they can be brought to trial before a military commission," to take forcible military possession of the printing establishments of the papers, and to "prohibit any further publication thereof." [3]

This was indeed an amazing order. It was issued on snap judgment without knowledge of the facts, though on that very day General Dix was instituting an investigation which would promptly reveal that the papers and their publishers were not guilty. It was done in the arrogant fashion and with the peremptory language of a military despotism most uncongenial to the mind and nature of Lincoln. It was an attack on freedom of the press, and was inconsistent with the prevailing policy of the Lincoln government, which was to leave opposition newspapers unmolested—a policy of which the *World* and the *Journal of Commerce* were standing examples. It opened up a wretched conflict of state against Federal power and of civil against military procedures. In its mention of trial before a "military commission" it seemed to presage a proceeding which could have subjected the Lincoln administration to serious embarrassment and censure. Finally it gave a handle to Lincoln's unfair partisan critics who used the episode for much more than it was worth; it seemed to give validity to their attacks upon the President as a tyrant and a destroyer of civil rights.

What made it more amazing was that the action taken was quite unnecessary. Neither of the papers concerned was so blind to its own self interest as to publish a fake proclamation of the President intentionally for a treasonable purpose. The accusation was preposterous, however hostile the papers had been to the Republican administration. The *World* managers promptly discovered the fraud; they announced the fact in their bulletin; they withheld copies of the May 18 edition from the steamer which took dispatches to Europe and offered a reward of $500 for information leading to detection of the perpetrator. The angry and elaborate sequel to the affair was due not so much to the forgery, which had its brief hour, but to the post-mortems and voluminous legal proceedings against Dix and his officers, but with Lincoln, Stanton, and the Republicans, as the ultimate targets.

[3] Randall, *Constitutional Problems Under Lincoln,* 496–497.

The suppression, or suspension, was very brief. General Dix, whose attitude differed notably from that of Burnside in the cases of Vallandigham and of the Chicago *Times,* reluctantly executed the Stanton order (for so it should be called) so far as arresting some of the editors and proprietors. This was a military arrest and if a trial had been sought it would presumably have been a military trial, but on discovering that the men were innocent, Dix released them on May 20 and on May 23 the papers were allowed to resume publication.

It might now have been supposed that there had been enough ado about the freakish occurrence, and the matter would have been dropped so far as the Washington authorities were concerned, but Governor Seymour of New York would not allow the episode to be so terminated. By instruction of the governor accusations were brought against Dix and other officers before a New York grand jury. That body refused to vote an indictment and recommended that it would be inexpedient to pursue the case further. Even then the governor would not let the matter drop, and indeed if appropriate legal procedure could be found here was a flagrant misuse of military authority and a shocking violation of the freedom of the press, which the governor, with his anti-Lincoln attitude, would quite naturally wish to expose and exploit, as he could do with civil rights on his side. Seymour now instructed A. Oakey Hall, district attorney of the County of New York, to have the case further prosecuted.[4] Accordingly elaborate proceedings were begun before a local magistrate, Judge A. D. Russell, city judge in New York City.

The case was titled: *The People of New York* versus *John A. Dix and Others,* in which the defendants were charged with kidnaping and inciting to riot; it was thus a somewhat eccentric hearing in that the charges were whittled down to fit a merely local court and to be comprehended within state law, though in reality large Federal issues were at stake. Dix and his men were not in fact imprisoned; they were free on verbal recognizance while arguments long enough to fill a book were presented to the judge. On the side of the prosecution were A. Oakey Hall and John Cochrane, the latter being attorney general of New York; the defense was conducted by Edwards Pierrepont and William M. Evarts. Weighty questions were brought

[4] Stewart Mitchell, *Horatio Seymour of New York,* 358.

into the long discussion: the war power, martial law in relation to civil government, the habeas corpus act, application of military rule outside the area of war, the duty of an officer to execute the order of a superior, and the problem whether an officer of the general government acting under an order from Washington could be rightfully arrested by local authority and subjected to trial before a state judge.

When at last Judge Russell issued his decision the result was an anticlimax. It is true that portentous words were used on broad points of law. The Federal authorities were strongly criticized and the habeas corpus act was denounced, but after the decision the defendants were free, with the possibility of any follow-up in an actual trial remaining a matter of doubt.

In the strict sense this was not a "trial" of Dix and the others; the judge was giving out a statement in a preliminary hearing. The question was whether the case could and should come to trial in a New York court in spite of the habeas corpus act of March 3, 1863 (especially the indemnity feature of that law) by which those who made military seizures or arrests under the President's order were protected from prosecution in any court for such acts, with the further provision that such cases belonged within Federal, not state, jurisdiction.[5] As showing the preliminary nature of the proceeding Judge Russell explained that he did not "deem it proper" to state his views on the legal principles involved; then he added: "Such an exposition of the law would be more appropriate should this case come before the court for trial." In the whole proceeding the judge's words were stronger than his judicial deeds. He could not approve the "very novel and startling doctrine" of the Federal indemnity (habeas corpus) law, since in his opinion it made the President "an absolute monarch . . . incapable of doing any wrong." The existing war, he argued, did not justify a system by which "the President can direct anything to be done in this state he pleases." The government, he declared "must not only enforce but obey the laws." Having so expressed himself, the judge ended somewhat harmlessly by announcing that "The complaints will . . . pass to the grand jury in the usual way for its action." A verbal recognizance was accepted; no written one being required. Though the decision has a certain dignity in its treatment of fundamental matters of government, it was

[5] Randall, *Constitutional Problems Under Lincoln,* chap. ix.

probably intended less for a showdown with the Federal government than for a public declaration in the heat of a presidential campaign.[6]

Thus the case in the courts was closed, but the criticism of Lincoln, which may be regarded as one of the motives of the New York proceedings, continued. For this criticism the *World* was the main spokesman; on August 8, 1864 that newspaper declared "The liberties of the people have been invaded. The war . . . has been made the instrument of usurpation and oppression . . . ."

In judging official Washington it must be concluded that the real blunderer was Stanton, who had seen to it that an order was issued in Lincoln's name. It was a hasty order based upon mere suspicion of wrongful intent; its wording was excessive and inappropriate; it made accusations that were soon found to be baseless; and the Lincoln administration felt that the arrests and seizures were unnecessary and ill advised. Welles commented that the seizure of the papers was "hasty, rash, inconsiderate, and wrong." As for Howard, author of the miserable forgery, Welles remarked: "He is of a pestiferous class of reckless sensation-writers for an unscrupulous set of journalists who misinform the public mind."[7] On May 20 Howard had been arrested; he was thrown into Fort Lafayette and kept for three months; he was then released by special intervention of the President. Howard had gone wrong, but he had influential friends, chief of whom was Henry Ward Beecher. On August 2, 1864, Beecher wrote earnestly to another man of influence, John D. Defrees, superintendent of public printing in Washington. The preacher felt that the sting and prostration of his punishment would be a lesson to the young man. He continued: "He was the tool of the man who turned states evidence and escaped; & Joe, had only the hope of making some *money,* by a stock broker, he had not foresight or consideration enough to perceive the relation of his act to the Public Welfare." Admitting his personal interest, Beecher wrote: "You must excuse my earnestness. He has been brought up in my parish & under my eye and is the *only* spotted child of a large family." Defrees wrote promptly to Lincoln[8] and on August 22 the President wrote to Stanton: "I very much wish to oblige [Henry Ward] Beecher by relieving Howard

6 Russell's opinion is given in the New York *World,* August 8, 1864, p. 1, c. 6.

7 Welles, *Diary,* II, 38 (May 23, 1864).

8 Henry Ward Beecher to John D. Defrees, New York, Aug. 2, 1864, R. T. L. Coll., 35002–3; John D. Defrees to John Hay, Washington, Aug. 3, 1864, *ibid.,* 35025.

. . . ." Several communications were exchanged between the President and the secretary of war; then on August 23 came Lincoln's order: "Let Howard, imprisoned in regard to the bogus proclamation, be discharged." [9] In compliance with this order the actual release came on August 24 and Howard continued to float about in the journalistic world for many years. The President himself had had but little to do directly with the affair, though it was "said to have angered Lincoln more than almost any other occurrence of the war period." [10]

VII

In the despair that hung over the nation in July 1864, with the certainty that the country's heavy woes would be capitalized for partisan or factional advantage, there occurred a remarkable episode of peace agitation. That irrepressible editor, Horace Greeley of the New York *Tribune* was now cast in the prominent role of attempted "negotiator" between Confederate emissaries and the President of the United States. As Greeley himself wrote, "the very darkest hours of our contest . . . were those of July and August, 1864." [1] Grant's campaign seemed a failure; the North was horrified by casualties such as those at Cold Harbor; attacks upon Petersburg were unavailing; the mine explosion there was a flash in the pan; and the whole war, though greatly intensified, seemed to have degenerated into an unprofitable stalemate. Increasing war weariness of the Northern people could be exploited by opponents of the Lincoln administration; this might give a considerable advantage to Northern Democrats in this year of a presidential election, to be held in the midst of a shattering war. Added to all this were two factors not to be overlooked: Greeley's ardent if eccentric personality, and his deep distrust of Lincoln.

To give an appraisal of this peacemaking episode one should seek to understand the whole Greeley and that is not easy. The problems of the age were a challenge and a disturbance to his active mind and sympathetic heart. He felt social ills so keenly that one could think

---

9 Stanton MSS., 54446, Lib. of Cong.
10 F. A. Flower to C. F. Gunther, Washington, Feb. 14, 1904, MS., Chicago Hist. Soc.
1 Greeley, *Amer. Conflict*, II, 664.

of the Greeley quest for solutions as the quest, or dilemma, of the age. He had the restless instinct of the reformer. In the depths of his nature there was Christianity, deep Puritan respect for moral virtue, and a consuming interest in humanitarian advance and achievement. Others were complacent, or inattentive, toward the needs of the time, but not Greeley. He could not help thinking earnestly and writing prolifically. If the demands of quick journalism led to superficiality in some of his declarations, it was nevertheless true that few editors could match him in informed study of the stresses of a changing industrial America. Though he had known the cruel hard knocks of life, he was notable for the uplift of his thought and the optimism of his fundamental outlook. In his friendliness toward socialism and his concern for the working man he did not slip off the track into Marxian radicalism or economic excess. His interest in Fourierism and in Brook Farm was genuine, yet he kept an element of conservatism in his idealistic nature. He decisively rejected communism. Though he should not be set down as a mere utopian dreamer, he burned with righteous discontent as he saw the working of the greedy capitalism of mid-century America. If the times were out of joint, his sense of mission prompted him to set them right.

His intense opposition to human slavery was an authentic part of his humanitarian concept; it was in harmony with his transcendentalism, his strong religious (yet not dogmatic) sense, his universalist viewpoint, his thought of the Over-Soul, and his deep devotion to the democratic faith.[2] Despite his "On to Richmond" drive and his earlier belief that war was necessary to rid the country of slavery, the bent of Greeley's mind was toward hatred of war and friendliness to peace crusades. He had once favored letting the cotton states "go in peace," and though his attitude on this question was complex and a bit hard to define, the result was that the editor was associated with the concept of peaceable separation.[3]

In addition to all his other qualities and outshining them all, Greeley was a great power in journalism. As a newspaper to give the people what they wanted, the *Tribune* had become a notable success. No one had done more to give importance to the editorial page

[2] The mind of Greeley, in a wide range of social and intellectual attitudes, is presented in Theodore Fisch's scholarly and readable treatment entitled "Horace Greeley: A Yankee in Transition," ms. doctoral dissertation, Univ. of Ill., 1947.

[3] David M. Potter, *Lincoln and His Party in the Secession Crisis,* 52–55.

as a force for shaping, not merely reflecting, opinion. In his editorial capacity Greeley had outstanding eminence as a pundit; his words were accepted by thousands of readers, including many in the West, as political gospel.

The Baltimore convention had not been to Greeley's liking. No political solution had materialized in terms of his radical preferences. He doubted whether Lincoln could lead the country either to military triumph or to terms of peace. He did not, nor did others in the country, foresee that a more favorable situation would be reached later in the year; these were the defeatist days of dark July. As a man keenly devoted to politics without being a politician, he desired the success of the Republican party; he did not relish the prospect that the Democrats might have, in their own peace drive, a popular and perchance a winning issue. It was not that his ultimate motives were so different from Lincoln's—they had in fact much in common—but if the President needed prodding in order to turn motives into accomplishment, Greeley stood ready to apply the editorial spur.

VIII

Such were the factors at work when, in early July, Greeley received word that "two Ambassadors of Davis & Co." were in Canada "with full & complete powers for a peace."[1] His informant was William Cornell ("Colorado") Jewett, a man notorious for wild schemes, an agitator in America and abroad who had been bombarding Lincoln with unpleasant letters giving vociferous advice and demanding that the war be terminated. There were indeed commissioners or emissaries of the Confederate President operating in Canada—Clement C. Clay of Alabama, Jacob Thompson of Mississippi, and J. P. Holcombe who had been a professor at the University of Virginia—but their instructions, which were not fully known, were vastly different from what was implied in recommending them to Greeley as promising peace negotiators. They had no authority whatever to confer on terms of peace in the name of the Confederate

1 William Cornell Jewett to Greeley, Niagara Falls, July 5, 1864, R. T. L. Coll., 34281. Next day (no. 34298) Jewett wired Greeley: "Will you come here? Parties have full power." Jewett's numerous letters to Lincoln, reposing in the R. T. L. Collection, might have been a considerable annoyance, except that, according to Hay, the President did not read them.

government. They were part of the Confederate secret service and their purposes were to cause mischief by a variety of means to the Union cause, as for instance by rigging the gold market, creating Northern disaffection, subsidizing newspapers, making contact with "Copperheads," plotting the release of Confederate prisoners in the North, and building up for a major revolt in the Northwest. (Not that a revolt in terms of a "Northwest Confederacy" to withdraw from the United States and join the Southern Confederacy was feasible, but it was among the anti-Union schemes that were agitated and on which hopes were built.) Later in the year 1864 there would be fantastic Canadian-based efforts of Confederate agents to stir up violence and insurrection behind the lines in the United States, promoted with small concern for Canadian neutrality. Though these schemes involved more of melodramatic intrigue than real menace, they were part of the hidden history of the time and it was for such purposes that the Confederate secret service in Canada was set up.

Among these agents in Canada was George N. Sanders of Kentucky who was concerned with business matters on behalf of the Confederate government, such as arranging for the building of ships abroad, to be paid for in cotton deliverable at any port of the Confederacy.[2] Sanders had a considerable Canadian acquaintance and had made it his business to invite citizens of the United States to take part in various conferences at Niagara Falls, such invitations being given only to those understood to be hostile to the Lincoln administration. Thus Sanders offered a kind of liaison between Americans and Confederate agents, while Jewett in his self-made capacity assisted Sanders in obtaining contact with Greeley.

On hearing of these Confederate "ambassadors" (Jewett's word) ready to talk peace, Greeley was sufficiently impressed to undertake an appeal to Lincoln. On July 7 he wrote the President urging him to invite these gentlemen to Washington, "there to open their budgets." Referring to the Confederate desire for peace, he reminded the nation's Chief "that our bleeding, bankrupt, almost dying country also longs for peace—shudders at the prospect of fresh conscriptions, of further wholesale devastations, and of new rivers of human

---

[2] *Offic. Rec.* (Nav.), 2 ser., III, 529, 1235. For the general subject of these schemes and maneuvers from across the Northern border, see John W. Headley, *Confederate Operations in Canada and New York.*

blood." [3] From that point there followed an elaborate series of communications, letters, telegrams, and interviews, in which on Lincoln's part a safe conduct was offered to "any person, anywhere," bringing from Jefferson Davis a proposition for peace with Union and abolition of slavery.[4] On the other side, however, it was soon revealed that the "commissioners" were utterly lacking in credentials as Confederate agents authorized to negotiate peace.

Lincoln not only agreed to confer with accredited Confederate representatives, promising them safe conduct; he went farther in an adroit maneuver by assigning to Greeley himself the task of bringing the emissaries to see the President. For this purpose the editor was expected to meet the Confederates at Niagara Falls and accompany them to Washington. To have done so would have been understood as signifying that Greeley was vouching for these men as authorized negotiators. The editor, now greatly embarrassed, dallied and seemed disposed to pass the ball to the President. In a letter of July 13 he informed him of the names of the agents and expressed the hope that the President would take appropriate action.[5] At that rate the matter would have dragged on indefinitely, since the Confederate gentlemen were reluctant to show their hand, but Lincoln decided not to have it so. A famous editor was sponsoring a peace movement; the matter was being widely discussed; the national government was being distrusted or misrepresented; and the President could not afford to allow the question to remain dangling in uncertainty. Accordingly he sent John Hay to see Greeley, bearing a communication expressing disappointment that nothing had been done to produce the commissioners and concluding "I not only intend a sincere effort for peace but I intend that you shall be a personal witness that it is made." [6]

Greeley was now annoyed, feeling that the President had put him at a disadvantage. Proceeding to Niagara Falls and acting through Jewett, he sent a note addressed to Clay, Holcombe, and Thompson.

---

[3] *Ann. Cyc.*, 1864, 780; Horace Greeley to Lincoln, New York, July 7, 1864, R. T. L. Coll., 34316–18.

[4] *Works*, X, 154 (July 9, 1864); R. T. L. Coll., 34278.

[5] Nicolay and Hay, *Lincoln*, IX, 189; Horace Greeley to Lincoln, New York, July 13, 1864, R. T. L. Coll., 34458–9.

[6] *Works*, X, 159; Lincoln's draft of this letter, all in his own hand, is in R. T. L. Coll., 34492 (July 15, 1864).

Being "informed," he wrote, that these gentlemen were "duly accredited from Richmond as bearers of propositions . . . [for] peace," he extended safe conduct to them on authority of the President and offered to accompany them to Washington.[7] In this proceeding there was a strange omission: Greeley said nothing to the Southern agents about Lincoln's essential conditions of peace. The President had stated these conditions clearly enough in his letter to Greeley of July 9: "the restoration of the Union and abandonment of slavery." [8] Lincoln knew that no "negotiation" was worth trying if it did not presuppose these simple but indispensable terms. Lincoln's understanding with Greeley was not that the Commissioners should be asked merely to talk peace, but that they should come to Washington with Greeley "on the terms stated" in his letter of July 9.

At this point there came a hitch in the proceedings. The motive of the Confederate gentlemen was not to take constructive measures toward peace by negotiations at Washington, but to cause all possible trouble to the Lincoln administration and the Union cause. Clay and Holcombe now informed Greeley truly enough that Lincoln's safe conduct had been tendered them under a "misapprehension," inasmuch as they had "not been accredited to him (Lincoln) from Richmond as the bearers of propositions looking to . . . peace." [9] Greeley then telegraphed Washington for "fresh instructions," though Lincoln's previous statement of terms had been clear enough.

The President was now determined to see the thing through, to crystallize the trying situation for what it might signify, and to close the episode with national dignity if no favorable results were possible. He now entrusted Hay, for delivery to the appropriate persons, a paper which is of such significance that it may be quoted in full:

Executive Mansion, July 18, 1864

Whom it may concern

Any proposition which embraces the restoration of peace, the integrity of the whole Union, and the abandonment of slavery, and which comes by and with an authority that can control the armies now at war against the United States, will be received and considered by the Executive government of the United States, and will be met by liberal terms on other

[7] *Ann. Cyc.*, 1864, 780 (July 17, 1864).

[8] *Works*, X, 154.

[9] *Ann. Cyc.*, 1864, 781 (July 18, 1864).

substantial and collateral points; and the bearer or bearers thereof shall have safe-conduct both ways.

Abraham Lincoln [10]

There followed a fruitless interview at the Cataract House, Niagara Falls, between Hay and Greeley on one side and Holcombe on the other. Nothing came of the interview except that the Confederates now had the President's statement of minimum terms. As for a Confederate reply, that was delayed until Holcombe and Clay could prepare a rather ambitious paper which turned out to be an elaborate manifesto in the manner of Confederate propaganda. (This reply was prepared by the agents without consulting the Confederate government at Richmond, but such consultation was impracticable and if it had occurred the result would hardly have been different.) The commissioners had been assured of safe conduct, they declared, and they had expected a "most gratifying change in the policy of the President." It had seemed "that the President had opened a door . . . previously closed" against the Confederate States. Then came Lincoln's "To whom it may concern." They could not claim safe conduct "in a character . . . [they] had no right to assume." They could only express "profound regret" that the peace spirit "had not continued to animate the counsels of the President." Instead of the requested safe conduct, they received (so they declared) a document which provoked "as much indignation as surprise." It precluded negotiation; it constituted a "sudden and entire change in the views of the President." This "rude withdrawal of a courteous overture for negotiation" meant only "fresh blasts of war to the bitter end."

The President, as they represented it, was fully to blame. They therefore concluded that they could publish the correspondence and if any Confederate citizen still hoped that peace was "possible with this administration," the documents in the case would "strip from his eyes the last film of such delusion." [11]

Greeley had departed for New York with some haste, Hay left at about the same time, the Niagara "conference" was terminated, Jewett was left to receive any further Confederate communication, the *Tribune* carried a report, and the incident was closed. Lincoln, of

10 *Works,* X, 161; Lincoln's autograph draft, with his notation: "Copy of Doc sent by John Hay," is in R. T. L. Coll., 34536.

11 *Ann. Cyc.,* 1864, 782.

course, had never been inconclusive as to conditions of peace. He had not changed as the Confederate agents asserted, but the President's side of the controversy had not been adequately impressed upon the alleged negotiators and it was they, with Greeley, who captured the journalistic headlines. In the words of E. C. Kirkland, excellent historian of these peace moves: "The public was furnished with no evidence to dispute the charge of the Confederates that the President had, in bad faith, changed his policy in the course of negotiations." [12]

As for these Confederate gentlemen in Canada, it is to be noted in the first place that they never were authorized negotiators for peace,[13] and in the second place that their purpose—namely, to forestall peace drives in the South while sowing defeatism and anti-Lincoln sentiment in the North—was the opposite of Lincoln's. There was ample reason for Lincoln's attitude, which combined full willingness for genuine peace with a clear statement of the indispensable national aims of Union and abolition of slavery. The non-vindictiveness of the President's position was well expressed in his July 18 statement that Union and emancipation would "be met by liberal terms on other substantial points." Once the essential conditions were met, there would be no reprisals, no undue punitive measures, and no postwar policy of revenge so far as the President was concerned.

When Greeley was well started he was hard to stop, and thus it happened that the Niagara conference discussion did not end when the conference ended. Greeley's demand now was for publication of the correspondence between himself and Lincoln and his letters on this subject made a vexatious sequel to the July episode.

Misunderstood by his friends and under fire from his enemies, the troubled editor felt that such publication would help his case. The subject of peace, which he deemed imperative, still burned in his soul, and besides, the permission to publish would afford reading matter for the *Tribune*. He wrote to Hay broaching the idea of publication, and the next day his *Tribune* suggested that the whole of the correspondence be made public.[14] Lincoln saw a danger here; he therefore proposed that, in the event of publication, some of

---

[12] Edward Chase Kirkland, *The Peacemakers of 1864*, 85.

[13] *Offic. Rec.* (Nav.), 2 ser., III, 1194, 1236.

[14] Greeley to Hay, Aug. 4, 1864, R. T. L. Coll., 35055.

Greeley's phrases, of the sort that would disturb public thought, be omitted. Since the matter had become tense and personally difficult between them, Lincoln further proposed that Greeley come to Washington and talk the matter over, but to this Greeley demurred. Perhaps he felt that the meeting would put him at a further disadvantage; what he wrote was that it might "only result in farther mischief, as at Niagara." [15] The editor then launched into a reproach of Lincoln, bringing up old scores and telling him that he had made a great mistake in not letting Alexander H. Stephens come to Washington for consultation on peace in 1863.[16] Next day the editor continued in the same vein in another letter to the President. He feared that his usefulness had passed, but he knew that "nine-tenths of the whole American People, North and South, . . . [were] anxious for Peace—Peace on almost *any* terms." He knew that "to the general eye" the "rebels" were "anxious to negotiate, and that we repulse their advances." So the people understood it, and if that impression were not removed he feared "we shall be beaten out of sight next November." He therefore begged and implored the President "to inaugurate or invite proposals for peace forthwith." He thought that a national convention should be held, and if peace could not be at once made, he favored an armistice for a year. If this were done he thought that "at all events" (which meant regardless of terms or conditions of settlement) "there will surely be no more war." [17]

There came one more Greeley letter. On August 11 he wrote the President again suggesting that the entire correspondence be published.[18] This, however, was at variance with the President's wish who wanted certain "discouraging and injurious parts" deleted.[19] As a result, the correspondence that preceded the Niagara conference "was not published until after the President's death." [20] Having to choose between two undesirable things, Lincoln thought it was better to allow a false impression as to his own position to continue than to incur consequences (in terms of Greeley's phrases) which would

15 Horace Greeley to Lincoln, New York, Aug. 8, 1864, R. T. L. Coll., 35139.

16 *Lincoln the President: Midstream,* 242–245.

17 R. T. L. Coll., 35171.

18 *Ibid.,* 35228.

19 Lincoln to H. J. Raymond, Aug. 15, 1864, *Works,* X, 191–192. In the Lincoln Papers (R. T. L. Coll., 34277–80) there is a printed pamphlet giving the correspondence of Jewett, Greeley, Lincoln, etc. and ending with the statement "To Whom it May concern." Parts have been crossed out in red pencil. Did Lincoln make these deletions?

20 Nicolay and Hay, *Lincoln,* IX, 199.

have been unfortunate for the nation. Thus the North was largely misjudging Lincoln at the same time that Southern foes were assailing him in almost the same terms, as shown by the following statement in the Richmond *Sentinel:* "We want to treat, to bargain, to negotiate for peace, and Mr. Lincoln will not deign to show his face to us . . . but slams the door rudely in our faces." [21]

IX

Simultaneously with the Greeley fiasco there occurred a minor peace effort which at least resulted in an interview between Jefferson Davis and two unofficial Northerners. One of these was Colonel James Jaquess of Illinois, a preacher of great piety, a commander of a regiment under Rosecrans, and a soldier of gallant record. In his combination of military fervor with religious enthusiasm he has been compared to Cromwell's Ironsides. He had been president of a small Methodist college and it burned deeply into his conscience that Christians, especially Methodists, North and South should be killing each other. The other amateur diplomat was J. R. Gilmore, a man of business and of literature who had visited the South and had become known as the colorful author of *Among the Pines,* under the pseudonym of Edmund Kirke. He had written much else and was regarded as an authority on Southern conditions. Yet he was anti-slavery and by no means shared pro-Confederate views in the existing war. In 1863 Colonel Jaquess was given a furlough, was passed through the military lines with Lincoln's permission, and reached Richmond; at that point his mission broke down in that he failed to obtain an interview with President Davis.

The effort was renewed in 1864, and in July of that year Gilmore and Jaquess, with Gilmore in responsible charge, reached the Confederate capital by passes through the lines. From President Lincoln's standpoint there was little to be expected from such a mission, but on the experimental principle that no harm would be done and that no well meant effort for peace should be rebuffed, possibly also with the intent of exposing false representations of peace prospects at the North, the President gave his consent, though not his official accrediting, to the mission. On reaching Richmond the peacemakers con-

[21] Quoted in New York *Daily News,* Aug. 9, 1864; clipping in R. T. L. Coll., 35173.

ferred with the Confederate secretary of state, Judah P. Benjamin, and through him obtained an interview with President Davis which occurred on July 17 in Benjamin's office in the old customs house. Lincoln's terms were presented—reunion, abolition of slavery, amnesty, restoration of the rights of the states, and generous compensation for emancipated slaves.[1] (These terms had been drawn up by the President before the peacemakers had left Washington.)

The result of the pious effort was a decisive refusal on the part of Davis whose actual words at the interview are a matter of some doubt (there having been no verbatim report on the spot), but the essential point was that Lincoln's demand for a reunited country was indignantly spurned by the Southern leader as the equivalent of defeat and surrender.[2] Gilmore published his report of the episode in the Boston *Transcript* of July 22, 1864, but this was denounced by Confederate authorities as grossly inaccurate; it was a matter of coincidence that the Gilmore report appeared on the same day as Greeley's account (in the *Tribune*) of the unsuccessful Niagara Falls conference.

No better result followed when in midsummer of 1864 the names of three former members of Buchanan's cabinet—Jeremiah S. Black, Edwin M. Stanton, and Jacob Thompson—were involved in a footless conference in Canada between Black and Thompson. Black had been attorney general and later secretary of state under Buchanan; Thompson had been secretary of the interior (until he withdrew in the sharp secession crisis); and Stanton had been appointed in the last phase of Buchanan's administration as attorney general. Stanton's part in the 1864 affair consisted in the fact that he had a talk with Black in Washington, but the stern secretary of war, denying that Black was his envoy, avoided all responsibility for the episode.

In an elaborate letter to Stanton, August 24, 1864, Black reported the conversation to the secretary of war. Thompson, according to this

---

1 Kirkland, *Peacemakers of 1864*, 92; *Offic. Rec.* (Nav.), 2 ser., III, 1193.

2 "The President [Davis] answered that . . . the offer was in effect a proposal that the Confederate States should surrender at discretion, admit that they had been in the wrong from the beginning of the contest, submit to the mercy of their enemies, and avow themselves to be in need of pardon for crimes; that extermination was preferable to such dishonor." Report of Judah P. Benjamin, Confederate secretary of state, to James M. Mason, "Commissioner to the Continent" (circular), *Offic. Rec.* (Nav.), 2 ser., III, 1193. Coming from a high Confederate source, this may be considered a more authentic report of Davis's statement than that which Gilmore caused to be published in the Boston *Transcript* of July 22, 1864.

account, expressed fear of subjugation, insult, degradation, control by enemies of the South, confiscation, spoliation, military execution of the best men, and total suppression of free speech and personal liberty. (In so expressing himself he was certainly not speaking with understanding of Lincoln's views.) He spoke bitterly of the abolitionists, and opposed forcible emancipation of Negroes. On one important point there was doubt as to what was really said and intended. Black reported that the terms indicated by Thompson did "not mean the separate nationality of the South" but rather Southern control of their own domestic affairs. Yet in a postscript Black stated that "nothing positive" was said as to the restoration of the Union. Then he added: "My desire to see a restoration may have helped me to the conclusion. If you wish you may cross-examine me . . . ."

The main point of Black's letter was a suggestion to Stanton to "advise the President to suspend hostilities for three or six months and commence negotiations in good earnest . . . ." Stanton's reply was entirely negative as to the prospect of any favorable result to come from dealings with Thompson. The secretary was all the more convinced that the "rebels" would accept no peace except with dissolution of the Union. He had no wish to cross-examine Black, he would not give the President the suggested advice, and he made it clear that Black's conversation with the Confederate gentleman was not in accord with his (Stanton's) wishes. As to an armistice, he considered it "fatal to the Government and the national existence." [8] The Thompson-Black conversation was informal and unofficial. It seemed that the two men were not so far apart as, for instance, Lincoln and Davis, but neither man had authority in the premises, and it would be a mistake to consider the episode as a "negotiation." Whatever Thompson may have said, he was not authorized to speak for the Confederate government and Lincoln knew that so long as that government remained intact and its armies unbeaten, any agreement for reunion was impossible.

---

[8] The Black-Thompson episode is treated in E. C. Kirkland, *Peacemakers of 1864*, 118–124. The letter of Black to Stanton and Stanton's reply are in the Stanton MSS., Lib. of Cong. nos. 57801–57822.

CHAPTER IX

CONGRESS: MEANS AND ENDS

THE first session of Lincoln's second Congress adjourned on July 4, 1864, after having done less, and more, than the President had hoped. Necessarily he had looked to the lawmaking branch for money and men, for the means of carrying on the war to a successful conclusion. With him, victory and reunion were the main considerations in such matters as conscription and public finance. With many congressmen, however, there were other considerations, including the protection and promotion of the profits of Northern business. Going beyond means and looking toward ends, some in Congress attempted to dictate the President's choice of cabinet advisers and to thwart his reconstruction program. In the Wade-Davis Bill they presented their alternative to his "ten per cent" plan, and though he disposed of the bill with a pocket veto, he did not silence all his congressional critics. Already a climax was approaching in the conflict between Congress and President—a conflict that was to eventuate in deadlock between congressional Radicals and Lincoln's successor during the "tragic era" of postwar reconstruction.

I

As summer approached in 1864, with Grant fighting his stubborn and costly campaign in northern Virginia, the Union government faced a crisis in regard to military manpower. In replenishing the armies the procedure was for the President first to issue a call for volunteers, designating a period of time within which each locality was to fill a specified quota. Then, in those areas which failed to meet their quotas by volunteering, he set going a draft. As a means of recruiting, the draft was a last resort; its main purpose was to threaten men into volunteering. The conscription threat was supplemented by rewards in the form of bounties (local, state, and national) held out to volunteers. Despite both the threat and the rewards, Lincoln's call for troops in the summer of 1863 yielded disappointing results, and so did his three additional calls during the winter of 1863–64.

The conscription law itself (even as amended on February 24, 1864) was defective. Its most serious faults were its provisions for commutation and substitution, by which a drafted man had the privilege, if he had the money, of buying exemption or procuring a substitute. Such discrimination in favor of the rich and against the poor was not only undemocratic: it was also inefficient, for it caused the poor to resent the calls to military service, and it enabled the rich to escape such service entirely. So the number of men willing and eligible to serve was decreasing at the very time when the needs of the army—its ranks depleted by the expiration of short-term enlistments and by desertion, disability, and death—were reaching new heights.[1]

In June, 1864, Lincoln received an appeal for new legislation which Provost-Marshal-General James B. Fry had submitted to the secretary of war. Fry cogently demonstrated the faults in the existing law (of February 24, 1864) with figures on the returns from the latest draft. Too many men were buying their way out. The congressional session now drawing to a close, Lincoln hastily added his endorsement to Fry's recommendations and submitted them, without change, to the Senate and the House. A bill "to prohibit the discharge of persons from liability to military duty by reason of the payment of money" happened to be in Congress already, having been introduced by Senator Edwin D. Morgan, of New York. Within two days the Morgan bill, embodying the essence of the administration's own proposal, was under debate.[2]

The Democrats in Congress generally opposed this plan, as they did any plan, for strengthening the conscription act, and the Republicans divided in regard to it, most of them unwilling to compel the businessman to fight. Such Radicals as James G. Blaine and Thaddeus Stevens voted consistently with the opposition and against a repeal of the commutation or the substitution clause. Blaine believed that

---

1 Fred A. Shannon, *The Organization and Administration of the Union Army, 1861–1865*, II, 34–36.

2 *Ibid.*, 35.

commutation was indispensable to "the great 'middle interest' of society—the class on which the business and the prosperity of the country depend." He warned: "Just let it be understood that whoever the lot falls on *must go,* regardless of all business considerations, all private interests, all personal engagements, all family obligations; that the draft is to be sharp, decisive, final, and inexorable, without commutation and without substitution, and my word for it you will create consternation in all the loyal States." Stevens urged a generous bounty policy, rather than an inexorable draft, as the proper means for raising adequate troops. He insisted that volunteers should be allowed to enlist not only in their home district but in whatever district paid the highest bounty. "If one [district] is willing to pay $500, and another refuses to pay anything," he said, "why should not these poor men be permitted to go and take the $500 for the benefit of their families? In that way you will fill the army with volunteers instead of drafted men." As Fred A. Shannon has remarked, Stevens' argument "centered on the discrimination against the poor, as if the whole mercenary system were intended as a device for the dispensation of national charity." [3] Of course, if Stevens had been sincerely opposed to discrimination, he might have sought to eliminate the rich man's privilege of buying personal safety rather than to insure the poor man's opportunity of selling his military service to the highest bidder.

Nevertheless, the view prevailed in Congress that the business class must not be compelled, and that the working class must be enticed, to enlist. The Morgan bill, after being emasculated, was set aside entirely and replaced by another measure (June 28, 1864) which was passed just before the end of the session. In this bill the President was authorized to call for volunteers for terms of one, two, or three years, and the volunteer was granted (in addition to local bounties) a war department bounty of one hundred dollars for each year of his enlistment period. Commutation was abolished, except for conscientious objectors, but the right to furnish substitutes, without restriction, was expressly guaranteed. Though it fell far short of the recommendations he had submitted to Congress, Lincoln signed this bill and made it a law on the last day of the session, July 4.[4]

---

[3] *Ibid.,* 32, 38–40, 89. On the question of the repeal of the commutation clause, see also *Lincoln the President,* III, 127–130.

[4] Shannon, *Union Army,* II, 37, 38, 87.

On July 18, under the new law, the last conscription act to go into effect during the war, he issued the third of his draft calls. His proclamation asked for a half million men and allowed fifty days for them to volunteer, setting September 5 as the date for the beginning of the draft.[5]

His call could not have been expected to be popular, nor was it. Some critics thought the proclamation should have been couched in language more eloquent and less matter of fact, though, as *Harper's Weekly* commented, the country needed soldiers, not rhetoric. Other critics thought that a military leader, General Sherman or General Grant, should have appealed directly to the people for troops.[6] The *New York Herald* argued that the people, at least in New York, would have responded more eagerly if Lincoln first had restored McClellan to a command. One small-town newspaper editor in New Jersey was arrested for publishing articles tending to discourage enlistments.[7]

State governors of both political extremes, such as John A. Andrew of Massachusetts and Horatio Seymour of New York, objected to the terms of the President's new call. On the day of the proclamation Andrew telegraphed Lincoln urging him to make a succession of calls for two hundred thousand men at a time, rather than one call for five hundred thousand.[8] After the proclamation Seymour resumed his complaints of the unfairness of the quotas for New York, even though Lincoln had gone to great lengths to appease Seymour after the governor's contest with the federal government the previous summer. In response to Seymour's original grievances Lincoln had authorized a special commission to look into the New York quotas, and the commission had drawn up a new table for the state, increasing the quotas in some districts and decreasing them in others. "For the now ensuing draft," Lincoln had instructed the secretary of war, February 27, 1864, "let the quotas stand as made by the enrolling officers, in the Districts wherein this table requires them to be increased; and let them be reduced according to the table, in the others." But Seymour was not to be appeased. In a letter dated August 3, 1864, addressed to

---

5 Nicolay and Hay, *Works,* X, 164–166.

6 *Harper's Weekly,* VIII, 514 (Aug. 13, 1864); Shannon, *Union Army,* II, 130–131.

7 New York *Herald,* July 19, 1864, p. 4, c. 2; Washington *Constitutional Union,* Aug. 13, 1864.

8 Andrew's telegram was not received at the War Department until 8:45 p. m., July 18. R. T. L. Coll., 34537.

the secretary of war, and printed as a campaign circular, the governor repeated his familiar objections against the "draft lately ordered by the President" that the quotas for New York State, and especially for New York City and Brooklyn, were "unequal and oppressive," a "heavy drain," and a "great injustice." [9]

Lincoln's call of July 18, 1864, produced less volunteering than his calls under the two previous drafts. According to Provost-Marshal-General Fry, volunteering was discouraged by a growing fear of Confederate brutality to prisoners. "Men who would cheerfully enlist in the cause of the Union and would take all the chances of civilized warfare," said Fry afterwards, "were not so willing to expose themselves to the protracted torture that awaited them if, by the fortunes of war, they fell into the hands of the enemy." By this time, stories of Andersonville prison were circulating throughout the North.

If, for whatever reason, the new call raised fewer troops through voluntary enlistment than either of the previous calls, it raised more by direct conscription than both of them combined. More than half of the conscripts, however, were substitutes. The price of substitutes, now that commutation had been abolished, rose so high that only the very well-to-do could afford them. "Men of wealth served in the army," as Professor Shannon has said, "but never by compulsion." [10]

II

The army's need for men was but one of Lincoln's worries in connection with the draft. He also faced the problem, less serious for the Union cause but equally trying to him personally, of what to do with the unwilling conscript, the conscientious objector. The law allowed no exemption on grounds of conscience. The objector could keep from shouldering arms if he could afford to pay the commutation fee of three hundred dollars and if his conscience would permit him to pay it; otherwise he had no choice but to join the army when he was drafted. Once in uniform, he ran into hardships of more or less severity, depending upon the attitude of his superior officers, and his only recourse was an appeal to the secretary of war or to the President.

Seldom, if ever, did Lincoln fail to provide relief in some way for conscientious objectors whose cases were brought to his personal at-

[9] R. T. L. Coll., 5407–8–9, 35096.

[10] Shannon, *Union Army*, II, 42, 131.

tention.[1] One of the earliest cases was that of Henry D. Swift, a Quaker of South Dedham, Massachusetts, who was drafted in 1863. Refusing to take part in military drills, Swift was court-martialed and sentenced to be shot. When prominent members of the Society of Friends appealed to Lincoln and Stanton, the President directed the issuance of an honorable parole, which was delivered to Swift shortly before his execution was to have taken place.[2]

A more fully reported case was that of Cyrus Pringle, another Quaker, from Vermont. When conscripted, Pringle would neither pay commutation money nor allow anyone else to pay it for him. He was hustled into a railroad car along with other conscripts and taken to a camp near Boston, where he was put into the guardhouse for refusing to perform fatigue duty. Later he was transported to Alexandria, Virginia, to be equipped, but he would not handle a gun, even to clean it. "Two sergeants soon called for me," he recorded in his diary, "and taking me a little aside, bid me lie down on my back, and stretching my limbs apart tied cords to my wrists and ankles and these to four stakes driven in the ground somewhat in the form of an X." Still he would not give in, would not "purchase life at the cost of peace of soul." He was not merely being stubborn but was holding to his principles, resisting the military way of life, in which, as he said, "the man is unmade a man" and "is made a soldier, which is a man-destroying machine." As he lay in the hot sun, staked down on the rainsoaked ground, the cords cutting his wrists, he wept not from his own suffering but "from sorrow that such things should be in our own country, where Justice and Freedom and Liberty of Conscience have been the annual boast of Fourth-of-July orators so many years."

Already a group of Friends had interceded with Lincoln, who had agreed to detail Pringle and some Quaker companions to hospital duty or to the care of colored refugees, but Pringle and his fellows had declined to accept either of these alternatives, since acceptance would have released other men for active service. Then, on the same morning as he was staked down (October 6, 1863), Pringle received orders to report to the war department in Washington. There he learned from one of the Friends who again had interceded for him:

"That the Secretary of War and President sympathized with

[1] *Ibid.*, 252.

[2] Edward N. Wright, *Conscientious Objectors in the Civil War,* 124–125.

Friends in their present suffering, and would grant them full release, but that they felt themselves bound by their oaths that they would execute the laws, to carry out to its full extent the Conscription Act. That there appeared but one door of relief open,—that was to parole us and allow us to go home, but subject to their call again ostensibly, though this they neither wished nor proposed to do. That the fact of Friends in the Army and refusing service had attracted public attention so that it was not expedient to parole us at present. That, therefore, we were to be sent to one of the hospitals for a short time, where it was hoped and expressly requested that we would consent to remain quiet and acquiesce, if possible, in whatever might be required of us. That our work there would be quite free from objection, being for the direct relief of the sick; and that there we would release none for active service in the field, as the nurses were hired civilians."

A month later, after further repeated visits at the White House, Pringle's sponsor reported that Lincoln had exclaimed to him: "I want you to go and tell Stanton that it is my wish that all those young men be sent home at once." And they were.[3]

Lincoln's action in the Pringle case became a precedent for the regular policy thereafter in dealing with conscientious objectors. A war department instruction, issued on December 15, 1863, directed that such objectors, if they declined to pay commutation or provide substitutes, should be put on parole, "to report when called for." [4] They continued to be drafted under the amended enrollment act of February 24, 1864, which did not exempt them, though it made service or commutation easier for them to accept. It provided that, if they served, they should be considered as noncombatants and assigned to hospital work or the care of freedmen; or, if they chose commutation, their money should be used for medical purposes and not for hiring substitutes. Since many conscientious objectors continued, as Pringle had done, to reject these alternatives, Lincoln found it necessary to go on granting individual paroles.

His heart, as the Hicksite Friends of Philadelphia gratefully resolved after his death, was "imbued with a regard for conscientious scruples in relation to war." [5] He felt, as his own, the dilemma of a

---

[3] Rufus M. Jones, ed., *The Record of a Quaker Conscience: Cyrus Pringle's Diary*, *passim*.

[4] *Offic. Rec.*, 3 ser., III, 1173.

[5] Wright, *Conscientious Objectors*, 125.

religious people who shrank from a bloody conflict while they embraced its presumably righteous aims. "Your people—the Friends—have had, and are having, a very great trial," he said in his well-known letter to Eliza P. Gurney, a letter written (September 4, 1864) on the eve of a new draft. "On principle and faith, opposed to both war *and* oppression, they can only practically oppose oppression by war. In this hard dilem[m]a some have chosen one horn and some the other." Lincoln himself managed to keep from grasping either horn, though with him the dilemma was complicated by his oath of office. As he had protested, when he first received an appeal in Pringle's behalf, he had sworn to execute the laws, including the conscription act. "For those appealing to me on conscientious grounds," he now repeated to Mrs. Gurney, "I have done, and shall do, the best I could and can, in my own conscience, under my oath to the law." [6] It was, of course, an evasion of the law for him to release conscripted men and let them go home, there to remain subject ostensibly though not actually to recall at some future time. He never tried to resolve his dilemma by requesting Congress to change the law so as to grant outright exemption to conscientious objectors.

III

As summer came in 1864 Congress had to cope with serious emergencies in public finance as well as military manpower, with problems of finding ways and means to uphold the national credit, restore confidence in the currency, and carry on the war. Wartime finance, as evolved during the three years since the firing on Fort Sumter, was a hodgepodge of expedients. There were loans on a great variety of terms, paper money issues and national banknotes, and taxes on almost every taxable object, though much the greater part of the government's income was derived from borrowing. Now the government's currency was depreciating badly, the national banking system (as established in 1863) was proving defective, and the public credit was in jeopardy. In dealing with these problems, as with that of raising troops, congressmen and their constituents were inclined to confuse their special interests with the national interest.

The most drastic, and the least successful, of the financial reme-

[6] R. T. L. Coll., 35907–8.

dies proposed by Congress was a measure to prevent speculation in gold. This evil had arisen as a perhaps inevitable consequence of the issuance of irredeemable paper money, to which Congress first had resorted as an emergency expedient at the end of 1861, when a bank crisis led to the suspension of specie payments and left the country flooded with state banknotes not exchangeable for cash. Congress then (February 2, 1862) authorized an issue of "United States notes," and in succeeding years authorized two further issues, a total of $432,000,000 actually being put into circulation. These notes, popularly dubbed "greenbacks," were declared legal tender for all debts public and private but not for the payment of customs duties or interest on government bonds. Though the greenbacks were, in a vague sense, promises to pay hard money, no provision was made for their redemption in gold.

The way was open for fluctuations in the price of gold as expressed in greenbacks, and on the Gold Exchange in New York dealers bought and sold "gold futures" as they did those of other commodities on other exchanges. The daily gold quotations became an index of Union morale: the worse the prospects for the armies in the field, the higher the price of gold in New York. During June, 1864, as the casualty lists lengthened, the price rose to a point where nearly two dollars in greenbacks were needed to buy an ordinary dollar's worth of the precious metal.[1]

Congress reflected a popular demand to do something about this gambling in gold, which looked like gambling on the lives of Union soldiers. On June 17, 1864, a "gold bill" was enacted forbidding speculative trading in gold futures and making it illegal for anyone to contract for the delivery of gold not actually in his possession.[2]

This did not go far enough in the opinion of some congressmen, such as Thaddeus Stevens, who was later to demand legislation simply prohibiting the acceptance of legal-tender notes for less than their face value.[3] Doubtless such a law would have been unenforceable, but certainly the one actually passed was inadequate. After the enactment the price of gold rose even faster than before, so that by June 29 two and a half dollars in greenbacks were necessary to buy an ordinary

---

1 Randall, *Civil War and Reconstruction*, 450–453; Horace White, *Money and Banking*, 5th ed., 126–127.

2 *U. S. Stat. at Large*, XIII, 132–133.

3 Current, *Old Thad Stevens*, 205.

dollar's worth of gold. Though the bankers, brokers, merchants, and money-changers of Wall Street disagreed among themselves as to whom the law was hurting or helping the most, they united in sending a committee to Washington to lobby for its repeal.[4] On July 2, after only a day more than two weeks of the experiment, Congress decided to abandon it. The price of gold fell suddenly, then rose again, and thereafter fluctuated wildly for several weeks.

Despite this experience the congressional advocates of paper money, including Stevens, desired to authorize another issue of greenbacks, but the majority chose instead to rely on a new loan. The wartime loans, through a personal arrangement made by Secretary of the Treasury Chase, were handled exclusively by the country's foremost investment banking firm, Jay Cooke and Company. By means of high-pressure selling methods, including newspaper advertisements and appeals to workingmen to invest their savings in government bonds, Cooke succeeded in disposing of the loans readily enough—for a handsome profit to himself as the "financier of the Civil War." The largest purchasers were not day laborers, of course, but bankers and men of wealth who acquired government securities on terms which made them an unusually attractive investment.[5] The bonds, though purchasable in greenbacks, paid interest in gold, and some of them the principal as well. The government paid its other creditors, among them its officers and soldiers of the armies, in mere "legal currency," that is, in greenbacks. According to Stevens, who repeatedly insisted that all the government's creditors should be treated alike, the government's own demand for gold, to pay its bondholders, accounted for the exorbitant prices on the Gold Exchange.[6]

To provide a large market for bonds, and at the same time to create a uniform and stable national currency, Chase had planned and Congress had authorized (in an act of February 25, 1863) the establishment of a national banking system. Further legislation was needed, however, and Congress supplied it in the law of June 3, 1864, on which the system, as it was to operate from the Civil War to the first World War, was actually based. Under the system, federally chartered banks purchased United States bonds and, with these as

4 New York *Herald,* June 23, 1864, p. 4, c. 5.

5 Randall, *Civil War and Reconstruction,* 444-448, 454-455; E. P. Oberholtzer, *Jay Cooke: Financier of the Civil War* (2 vols., 1907).

6 Current, *Old Thad Stevens,* 195.

security, issued national banknotes guaranteed by the Federal government. The banknotes circulated as money, and unlike the greenbacks they were accepted at par, since they were exchangeable for gold.

The national banking system, at least as it operated in the beginning, should not be viewed as a purely fiscal instrument, free from politics or favoritism. As George La Verne Anderson has said, it "soon developed into something that was neither national nor a banking system." Instead, it was a "loose organization of currency factories" designed to serve "commercial communities" and confined "almost entirely to the New England and Middle Atlantic States." [7] Even within these states, as for example in the vicinity of Stevens' home in Pennsylvania, the system discriminated against certain areas, and here businessmen were hard put for money, especially after a prohibitory tax on state banknotes went into effect in 1866. In this light Stevens's partiality for greenbacks becomes understandable. "In my judgment this whole national banking system was a mistake," he was finally moved to say. "I think every dollar of paper circulation ought to be issued by the Government of the United States." [8]

While legislating on gold, loans, and banks, Congress did not neglect the perennial problem of taxes but made a successful effort to increase considerably the proportion of Federal income derived from tax revenues. Early in the war (act of August 5, 1861) Congress had provided for an income tax, imposing a flat rate of 3% on all incomes over $800. Now (act of June 30, 1864) the base was broadened and the rate increased and made progressive. The new law put a tax of 5% on incomes from $600 to $5,000, one of 7½% on those from $5,000 to $10,000, and one of 10% on those over $10,000.[9] Though this was a graduated tax, it was not by modern standards very steeply graduated, and it placed a relatively heavy burden on citizens with low and moderate incomes.

During the second year of the war (act of July 1, 1862) Congress also had levied a wide range of excise taxes. These fell on manufactures of all sorts: liquor, tobacco, stamps, cotton, wool, flax, hemp, iron, steel, wood, stone, earth, carriages, billiard tables, yachts, gold and silver plate, and so forth. The taxes also had to be paid as a price of doing business by every butcher, baker, pawnbroker, lawyer, horse

[7] Randall, *Civil War and Reconstruction*, 455-458.

[8] Current, *Old Thad Stevens*, 246.

[9] *U. S. Stat. at Large*, XII, 309; XIII, 223, 281.

dealer, physician—indeed, by practitioners of almost every calling except that of minister of the gospel. Having cast this very broad net, Congress in subsequent years had only to raise the rates in order to increase the yield, and with the new rates of 1864 the excise along with the income tax produced the unprecedented sum of $209,000,000 for the ensuing fiscal year. If the excise was a hardship to many producers and to most consumers, it was nevertheless a boon to commodity speculators who managed to get advance notice of forthcoming tax boosts and consequent price increases.[10]

The excises, payable as they were by domestic but not by foreign manufacturers, put the former at a competitive disadvantage and gave them a pretext for demanding increased protection in the form of "countervailing" duties. Such compensatory protection was the chief feature of the tariff of June 30, 1864. American manufacturers now "found their opportunity in the necessity of the government"; they "had only to declare what rate of duty they deemed essential, and that rate was accorded to them." [11] Most of the new duties were outrageously high, some as high as 100%, the average being 47%, or approximately double the average rate of the last prewar tariff act, that of 1857. After the war this high level was maintained even after the wartime excise taxes, which ostensibly justified it, had been eliminated. A habit of protectionist thinking had been established.

The wartime tariffs, including that of 1864, received the signature of Lincoln as President, but that fact does not necessarily indicate that he favored extreme protectionism as a permanent principle. During the war years the government was indeed confronted with what a later President, with connotations of his own, was to call a "condition" and not a "theory." The government desperately needed revenue, and whatever else they may have been, the tariff bills were also revenue measures. No one can say what stand Lincoln might have taken on the protectionist issue in later years if he had lived. "For decades following his death, however," writes Reinhard H. Luthin, "protectionists, in summoning testimony from 'the Fathers,' made full use of Lincoln's high-tariff record to bolster their claims that huge duties on imports were economically sound and socially desirable; at

---

10 Blaine, *Twenty Years of Congress*, I, 433; Report, Sec. of the Treas., *House Ex. Doc. No. 3*, 39 Cong., 1 sess., p. 18; Current, *Old Thad Stevens*, 192.

11 Stanwood, *American Tariff Controversies in the Nineteenth Century*, II, 129–130.

times the more zealous, in combating free trade, misquoted Lincoln and even concocted orations which they attributed to him." [12]

In Lincoln's own party there were a number of critics of extreme protectionism during and right after the war. The scholarly Francis Lieber, for example, writing to Senator Sumner soon after the final Emancipation Proclamation, insisted that New England in fairness to the rest of the country should give up her demands for unreasonable protection, and he argued that there could be "no better accompaniment for *the Proclamation* than *Free Trade*." [13] Many practical businessmen themselves opposed high tariffs, at least on certain products.

The promoters of railroads in the West objected to protection for iron rails, though otherwise they could hardly complain that they were being neglected by the Federal government. Congress (in an act of July 2, 1864) further extended the largess already granted in the form of public lands and loans (act of July 1, 1862) to the Central Pacific and Union Pacific railroads for constructing a line from the Missouri River to California,[14] and Congress was yielding readily enough to the demands of other enterprisers for similar favors. As a congressional agent of both the railroad and the iron interests, Stevens found himself in a rather difficult position, but he managed to satisfy both groups fairly well. Himself an ironmaster, he included in a bill for land grants to the projected People's Pacific railroad a stipulation against the use of imported rails. "I go for nothing but American iron, of course," he frankly explained. On the other hand, when the tariff bill of 1864 was impending, he assured the worried president of the St. Croix and Lake Superior Railroad Company that the company's recently imported rails, on which the duties had not yet been paid, would be exempt from the new rates.[15]

While using his position as Ways and Means chairman to further the railroad schemes of Eastern capitalists, Stevens also exerted his power to thwart the internal improvements projected by certain Western interests. On behalf of his Illinois constituents Congressman Elihu B. Washburne repeatedly introduced a bill for a Federal appropriation to improve the Illinois-Michigan canal, and each time Stevens brought to bear his sarcastic eloquence and his mastery of

[12] Luthin, "Abraham Lincoln and the Tariff," 49 *A. H. R.* 629 (1944).

[13] Lieber to Sumner, Jan. 10, Jan. 16, 1863, Lieber MSS., Huntington Lib.

[14] *U. S. Stat. at Large*, XII, 492; XIII, 358.

[15] Current, *Old Thad Stevens*, 195–196.

parliamentary rules to defeat it.[16] Many Westerners, more interested in access to markets than in tariff protection, accumulated a sense of outrage which seemed likely to provoke a sectional controversy between East and West as soon as the one between North and South had been disposed of. "The South cannot be kept out of Congress forever," Horace White, an editor of the *Chicago Tribune,* was to threaten early in 1866. "When the south does come back the south & west will join hands & rule this country." [17]

So the question of economic measures—of tariff protection, money, the banking system, and the public debt—was linked to the question of the future of the seceded South, the question of reconstruction. However seriously the interests of various groups in the Northeast might conflict, these groups had a common concern in preventing an early restoration of political power to the South. This consideration, underlying many of the maneuvers of Congress against President on the reconstruction issue, gives meaning to legislative stratagems not easily explained otherwise.

IV

At the end of June, 1864, the final resignation of Treasury Secretary Chase raised new questions about government finance and complicated the relations between Congress and President. His resignation climaxed the long-raging feud in Congress between his adherents and those of Seward, Welles, and the Blairs.

After Frank Blair's repeated philippics in the House against the treasury secretary, the friends of Chase twice demanded that Lincoln dismiss Montgomery Blair as postmaster general in order to repudiate his brother. But Lincoln not only declined to get rid of Montgomery; he also showed favor to Frank by telegraphing Grant, late in April, to restore him to his position as major general. Infuriated, Chase thought of resigning, going home to Ohio, and rallying the people to support him against Lincoln and the Blairs. The Governor of Ohio, John Brough, talked him into withholding his resignation —for the good of the country.[1]

Though Chase was quieted for the moment, his adherents in both

[16] *Ibid.*, 165–166, 175, 185–186, 195–196.

[17] White to Justin S. Morrill, Feb. 15, 1866, MS. in Cornell Univ. Lib.

[1] Smith, *Blair Family in Politics,* II, 258–260.

houses of Congress were not. Some of the representatives muttered about impeaching the President, and the Senate approved a resolution, introduced by Garrett Davis of Kentucky, which rebuked Lincoln along with Stanton for violating the Constitution by permitting Blair to serve as a military officer while a member of Congress. Unable to get at the cabinet representative of the hated Blair family, the Radicals became the more determined to make an example of his more vulnerable brother. Stevens introduced and the House passed a resolution calling on the Executive to provide information about Frank Blair's dual character, military and congressional. Responding fully and yet somewhat defiantly, Lincoln gave Congress a complete report, including a copy of a letter he had written the previous December advising that Blair give up his military commission temporarily, aid in organizing the House of Representatives, and then remain in Congress if elected Speaker. Their fury redoubled by this revelation, the Radicals took occasion at the Baltimore convention to strike at the Blairs by seating the anti-Blair delegation from Missouri and by inserting in the platform the sixth resolution, which called for a reorganization of the cabinet in the interests of harmony. In Congress they succeeded in unseating Blair before the end of the session.[2]

Blair's ouster did not entirely appease Chase and his friends, for Chase was already encountering the Blair charges of corruption and mismanagement from another quarter, and these charges became involved in and gave added bitterness to a deadly patronage fight. Thurlow Weed, replying in his Albany *Evening Journal* to attacks on Seward in the pro-Chase New York *Evening Post,* elaborated on the alleged corruption of Chase's treasury appointees in New York. In the midst of this journalistic bickering the Assistant Treasurer in New York, John J. Cisco, decided to leave his job. Chase was ready to name as Cisco's successor the Assistant Secretary of the Treasury, Maunsell B. Field. But Weed objected to Field's appointment.

Lincoln faced a dilemma. If he appointed Field he would antagonize not only Weed and Seward but also the New York senators, one of whom was Edwin D. Morgan, chairman of the Republican National Committee. The rule of senatorial courtesy as well as relations with the New York machine was at stake. Lincoln regularly consulted with

---

[2] *Ibid.,* 250–251, 259, 265, 267, 268. On the Blairs and Lincoln, see also *Lincoln the President,* III, 280–284.

Republicans in the Senate before making major appointments in their respective states.[3] After consulting with Senator Morgan, who protested against Field and suggested three others as possibilities for a compromise appointment, Lincoln submitted the three names to Chase and requested him to approve one of them or suggest someone else not obnoxious to the senators.[4] Chase refused to consider anyone except Field for Cisco's job but, rather than force the issue, he persuaded Cisco to withdraw his resignation for the time being. Lincoln meanwhile was putting pressure on Chase by hinting that, if Field was to be appointed, another Chase man, Hiram Barney, might have to be removed from the lucrative and powerful position of collector of the port of New York.[5]

Chase replied in a two-page letter with a couple of enclosures which Lincoln received on the evening of June 29. Hastily scanning the first page, Lincoln noticed the words: "The withdrawal of Mr. Cisco's resignation, which I enclose, relieves the present difficulty . . . ."[6] This was most welcome news, and happy that the troublesome matter was thus disposed of, Lincoln put the papers in his pocket without finishing the letter. Hours later, sitting down to pen a congratulatory note to the secretary, he looked at the letter and the enclosures again. He now discovered that, while Cisco was taking back his resignation, Chase was putting forth his own! [7]

That same evening Lincoln happened to see Governor Brough, visiting in Washington, and invited him into the White House to discuss Chase's resignation. Brough thought he could get the Ohio congressmen together and, with them, prevail upon Chase to retract it. "But," protested Lincoln, as Brough quoted him in a memorandum he dictated two weeks afterward, "this is the third time he has thrown this at me, and I do not think I am called on to continue to beg him to take it back, especially when the country would not go to destruction in consequence." [8] The next day Lincoln penned a note to Chase

[3] Carman and Luthin, *Lincoln and the Patronage,* 264–265.

[4] Dennett, . . . *Diaries* . . . *of John Hay,* 198–199 (entry for June 30, 1864); Nicolay and Hay, *Works,* X, 137–138.

[5] Carman and Luthin, *Lincoln and the Patronage,* 265–266; Nicolay and Hay, *Works,* X, 138–139.

[6] R. T. L. Coll., 34119–20–21.

[7] Dennett, . . . *Diaries* . . . *of John Hay,* 199 (entry for June 30, 1864).

[8] MS. transcription of shorthand record, dictated by John Brough and dated July 12, 1864, Vol. 20, Letters and Papers of William Henry Smith, Ohio State Arch. and Hist. Soc.

—"you and I have reached a point of mutual embarrassment in our official relations which it seems can not be overcome"—accepting the resignation.[9]

In naming Chase's successor Lincoln at first seemed to be most concerned about appeasing the Ohio Republican organization rather than Congress or Wall Street. He promptly thought of David Tod, Brough's predecessor as Ohio governor. "Dave Tod. He is my friend, with a big head full of brains," the President told John Hay. True, he lacked experience in government finance, but, said Lincoln, "He made a good Governor, and he has made a fortune for himself. I am willing to trust him." The Senate finance committee, however, was not willing. Headed by William Pitt Fessenden, the committeemen called on the President to tell him Tod had too little experience and was too little known. Lincoln assured them of his own confidence in Tod, acknowledged their duty and responsibility of passing on Tod's fitness, and declared that he could not "in justice to himself or Tod" withdraw the nomination.[10]

In another talk with Governor Brough the President emphatically repeated his refusal to withdraw it. "The Governor," according to Brough's own account, "advised him to request the Senate Committee to delay their report until the next morning, as he was satisfied Tod w[d] decline the appointment, and in that way the President, the Senate, Tod and the country would be relieved from embarrassment." Lincoln wanted to know Brough's reasons for thinking Tod would decline. Brough gave his reasons: "the state of his [Tod's] health, and the fact that in the nomination he got all the honor without the hard work; and that Tod was a man of good common sense and would not willingly place himself in a position which he was not capable of filling" Lincoln "accepted this advice, and apparently with great pleasure." [11]

Tod did decline, but Lincoln continued to talk of appointing an Ohioan, either former Governor Dennison or Governor Brough himself. Brough, again according to his own story, argued against any such appointment and recommended Senator Fessenden instead.[12]

The next morning, July 1, Lincoln sent Hay to the Senate with

---

[9] Lincoln to Chase, June 30, 1864, R. T. L. Coll., 34148.

[10] Dennett, . . . *Diaries* . . . *of John Hay*, 198–199 (entry for June 30, 1864).

[11] Brough MS.

[12] *Ibid.*

Fessenden's nomination. It was "instantly confirmed, the executive session not lasting more than a minute," as Hay recorded. At this very moment, unaware of his appointment, Fessenden was in the White House in conversation with the President. "I could not help being amused," Lincoln told Hay afterwards, "by seeing him sitting there so unconscious and you on your way to the Capitol." When Fessenden began to speak of the qualifications of Hugh McCulloch for the treasury office, Lincoln answered: "Mr. Fessenden, I have nominated you for that place. Mr. Hay has just taken the nomination to the Senate." Fessenden sputtered in protest, but Lincoln closed the interview by saying firmly: "If you decline, you must do it in open day, for I shall not recall the nomination." [13]

If, in this business of finding a new secretary of the treasury, Lincoln's behavior seems rather airy and impulsive, one should not forget his characteristic and habitual shrewdness in such matters. It is possible, indeed probable, that he all along expected Tod to refuse the job. By insisting at first on naming an Ohio man, he could expect to disarm much of the opposition that might otherwise have arisen in behalf of Chase. He was doubtless pleased at Brough's impressions because they confirmed his own, and he doubtless had Fessenden in mind even before Brough recommended him, if indeed Brough did so. (Hay quoted Lincoln as remarking: "It is very singular, considering that this appointment of F's is so popular when made, that no one ever mentioned his name to me for that place." [14]) Fessenden was as nearly an ideal choice as could have been made in the circumstances, and Lincoln knew it, summarizing Fessenden's qualifications in Hay's presence as follows: 1. "he knows the ropes"; as chairman of the Senate finance committee, he was as well informed as Chase on financial questions; 2. he had a national reputation and the confidence of the country; 3. he was "a radical—without the petulent [*sic*] and vicious fretfulness of many radicals." [15]

The inner meaning of the cabinet change was interpreted in various ways, even by Chase himself, who provided a whole series of explanations for his departure from the administration. Surprised and hurt when his resignation actually was accepted, he complained of Lincoln's ill will toward him. "Had his feelings been kind," he told a

---

[13] Dennett, . . . *Diaries* . . . *of John Hay*, 201–203 (entry for July 1, 1864).

[14] *Ibid.*, 202.

[15] *Ibid.*

friend, ". . . he would have invited an interview and all might have been harmonized." [16] He attributed this ill will to the Pomeroy Circular. "Then the course of some of my friends in making my name prominent in connection with the Presidential canvass tended to cool his regard for me; and the shameless assaults of the Blairs upon whom a Jacksonian 'down!' from him would have silenced the hounds cooled my regard for him." [17] He also blamed the President for the "embarrassment" in their official relations, saying: "I had found a good deal of embarrassment from him but what he could have found from me I could not imagine unless it has been created by my unwillingness to have offices distributed by spoils or benefits with more regard to the claims of divisions, factions, cliques and individuals than to fitness of selection." [18] Besides: "He had never given me the active and earnest support I was entitled to & even now Congress was about to adjourn without passing sufficient tax bills, though making appropriations with lavish profusion, and he was notwithstanding my appeals taking no pains to assure different results." [19] The administration, Chase further complained, had failed to support him earnestly in his efforts to "give the people a uniform currency, made in the end equivalent to gold everywhere." [20] Whatever the explanation for his departure—whether it was personal jealousy, the Blairs, the patronage, or differences about fiscal policy—Chase was sure that the fault was the President's.

His admiring and sympathizing correspondents confirmed Chase in his conviction that he had been grossly wronged.[21] Some other observers, however, thought they saw a different meaning in his separation from the cabinet. The task of a treasury secretary—"the great practical problem regularly recurring," as Congressman Samuel Hooper put it, "to raise one hundred millions a month"—was most difficult. Chase had been widely criticized as personally responsible for the financial ills of the nation, and, according to Hooper, he had been "attempting to throw unfair responsibilities on Congress." Then came

---

16 Chase to Col. R. C. Parsons, July 8, 1864, Chase MSS., Box 15, Pa. Hist. Soc.

17 *Ibid.* 18 Chase MS. diary, June 30, 1864, Lib. of Cong. 19 *Ibid.*

20 Chase to Joseph Cable, July 11, 1864, Buffalo *Morning Express,* Aug. 15, 1864, p. 2, c. 3.

21 See letters to Chase from M. C. Meigs, June 30; R. D. Mussey, July 1; H. G. Stebbins, July 1; E. T. Carson, July 4; M. Goodrich, July 7; E. G. Cooke, July 11, 1864, Chase MSS., Lib. of Cong.

the acceptance of his resignation, "to relieve him of all responsibility." [22] So Hooper said, and an English journalist expressed a similar opinion. This writer, observing that "Mr. Chase's strategic movement" had occurred "just when gold had risen to 270 per cent," called it a "timely retreat from overwhelming difficulties," a retreat which might save Chase's reputation and his presidential availability.[23]

For a while some of Lincoln's friends as well as Chase's partisans feared that the loss of Chase might prove disastrous to the administration and to the Union cause. At a time of "military unsuccess, financial weakness," and "Congressional hesitation on question of conscription," Representative Washburne said, Lincoln's acceptance of the resignation would be "ruinous." [24] The financiers in Wall Street, however, did not consider Chase an indispensable man. Though distressed by Tod's nomination, they were reassured by Fessenden's appointment and by the coincident repeal of the gold bill.[25] Nor was Lincoln himself inclined to fear for the public finances. All along he had disagreed with some of Chase's policies and had agreed with the Blairs that the trade in Southern cotton should not be monopolized by favored agents holding treasury department permits. On the day he accepted the resignation he told Hay "he had a plan for relieving us to a certain extent financially: for the Government to take into its own hands the whole cotton trade and buy all that [was] offered; take it to New York, sell for gold, & buy up its own greenbacks." [26]

The political consequences of the cabinet change were more dangerous for the administration than the financial consequences. So far as Lincoln's re-election prospects were concerned, Abram Wakeman, the New York postmaster, believed that Chase's departure would be a help rather than a hindrance, for "henceforward the fifty thousand Treasury agents would be friends of the President instead of enemies." [27] But a newspaper correspondent warned that, if the people

---

22 Dennett, . . . *Diaries . . . of John Hay,* 199–200. For criticism of Chase's conduct of finances, see for example New York *Herald,* June 20, 1864, p. 2, c. 1.

23 London *Saturday Review,* July 23, 1864, quoted in Boston *Daily Advertiser,* Aug. 12, 1864, p. 2, c. 4.

24 Dennett, . . . *Diaries . . . of John Hay,* 198 (entry for June 30, 1864).

25 New York *Herald,* July 1, 1864, p. 2, c. 1; July 2, 1864, p. 2, c. 1; July 4, 1864, p. 2, c. 1; July 6, 1864, p. 2, c. 1; New York *Post,* quoted in Cincinnati *Daily Gazette,* July 2, 1864, p. 3, c. 4.

26 Dennett, . . . *Diaries . . . of John Hay,* 203 (entry for July 1, 1864).

27 *Ibid.,* 201.

generally should get the impression that Chase had been "wrongly treated," then Lincoln, though re-elected, might "find himself *in a minority of Congress*" during his second term.[28]

Certainly the affair did bode ill for Lincoln's relations with Congress, immediately as well as remotely. Though Fessenden was a Radical of sorts and "the Senate's man," the Radicals in Congress did not consider him a sufficient offset to such cabinet Conservatives as Montgomery Blair. With Chase out, the Radicals were to increase their clamor for Blair's removal. Already one of the most extreme among them in the House, Blair's Maryland rival Henry Winter Davis, was preparing in collaboration with Benjamin F. Wade in the Senate an explosive challenge to the President's authority over the reconstruction of the Southern states.

V

While the President was beginning the re-establishment of Southern state governments with his "ten per cent plan," many of his fellow partisans in Congress were denouncing it, frustrating its purposes, and preparing an alternative of their own. "We may conquer rebels and hold them in subjection," Stevens told the House in reply to Lincoln's message of December, 1863, but it was a "mere mockery" of democratic principles to say that a "tithe" of the inhabitants of a conquered state could carry on government because they were "more holy or more loyal than the others." Stevens refused to hear of giving seats in Congress to representatives seeking admission from states reorganized under the presidential plan. The record of Republicans, he said, should not so "entangle" them that later they might be "estopped from denying the particular condition of those states." [1] When, before the end of the session, senators elected by the reconstructed legislature of Arkansas appeared in Washington, they were turned away.

Meanwhile Henry Winter Davis had induced the House to refer the reconstruction passages of the President's message to a special committee, of which he became chairman. From the committee he reported a bill (February 15, 1864) to guarantee a "republican form of government" to certain states whose governments had been "usurped or overthrown." A preamble to the bill implied that these

[28] Cincinnati *Daily Gazette,* July 8, 1864, p. 1, c. 2.
[1] Current, *Old Thad Stevens,* 189–190.

states were no longer in the Union: they were entitled neither to be represented in Congress nor to take any part in the national government. Some of the bill's provisions coincided with features of the President's plan, but others ran counter to it. As in his program, slavery was to be prohibited, the post-secession public debts disavowed, and representation in Congress permitted only with congressional assent. A majority of the white male citizens, however, and not a mere ten per cent of the 1860 voters, was to start the remaking of a state government—a majority taking an oath to support the Constitution of the United States. Not all members of this majority were to be allowed actually to participate in the creation of a new state constitution: only those who could swear that they had never voluntarily borne arms against the United States, nor given aid to persons in armed hostility thereto, nor supported any hostile "pretended government." Nor was any former officeholder under a "usurping power" to vote or hold office in the recreated state.[2]

In support of his bill Davis made a characteristically fiery speech in the House. He asserted that only Congress, not the President, had the constitutional authority to provide for the reorganization of state governments. He argued—as if the President's plan did not already include abolition—that slavery was "really, radically inconsistent with the permanence of republican governments" and must be eliminated. By denouncing those who, he said, clamored for "speedy recognition of governments tolerating slavery," he left the implication that he opposed speedy recognition of any governments, since those being restored under the Lincolnian process did not, in fact, tolerate slavery, and it was the recognition of such governments as these to which he was objecting.[3]

On May 4, by a strict party vote of 73 to 59, the House passed the Davis bill. Extreme though it was, it still did not go far enough to suit all the Radicals who voted for it. Stevens, for one, desired a measure providing for the reversion to the Federal government of all lands, in the "so-called states" or "territories" of the South, belonging to rebels who owned a hundred acres or more. When a colleague voted for the Davis bill under protest, Stevens spoke up: "I ought to say that I refused to vote, under protest." [4] Other Radicals agreed with him that

[2] *Cong. Globe*, 38 Cong., 1 sess., 3448–3449. [3] *Ibid.*, App., 82–85.
[4] *Ibid.*, 38 Cong., 1 sess., 2108; *Old Thad Stevens*, 198, 201.

the bill should embody more explicitly the principle that the Southern states, once recovered from the Confederacy, were no more than conquered provinces, which Congress might dispose of as it pleased, even with a general confiscation of rebel property.[5]

In the Senate Ben Wade took charge of the bill. Wade tried, without success, to strike the word "white" from the clause directing provisional governors to enroll "all white male citizens" for taking the loyalty oath. Sumner tried, without success, to add an amendment by which the Emancipation Proclamation would have been "adopted and enacted as a statute of the United States." Other Senators succeeded in attaching amendments, none of them drastic, and the minor differences between the House and Senate versions had to be reconciled by a conference committee. The Senate finally passed the bill on July 4, 1864, within an hour of the *sine die* adjournment of the session.[6]

The last hours of any session were confused and chaotic, and the last hours of this one were unusually so. Though both houses had agreed to adjourn at noon, they found it necessary to make three ten-minute postponements, in order to take care of the final rush of business. Toward the very end important bills were still being "pitchforked into shape"—not only the reconstruction measure but also a bill amending the Pacific Railroad Act so as to increase the compensation of the railroad builders, and another bill providing for a whiskey tax. "Cabinet ministers were numerous on the floor of the House," as Noah Brooks recalled, "and lobbyists in the general disorder slipped in through the doors and buttonholed members, while the mill of legislation slowly ground out its last grist." [7] A clerk of the House droned out the Declaration of Independence, which was being read in observance of the Fourth of July, despite the objection of the congressional jester, the Democrat "Sunset" Cox, who said the Declaration was an insurrectionary document and would give aid and comfort to the rebels.[8] As the hands of the clock neared the closing time, some of the congressmen began to wonder whether the President was going to sign the Wade-Davis bill. Word came that he had no further communication for the House, and Speaker Colfax adjourned the

5 Williams, *Lincoln and the Radicals,* 319.
6 S. S. Cox, *Three Decades of Federal Legislation,* 341.
7 Brooks, *Washington in Lincoln's Time,* 166–167.
8 Dennett, . . . *Diaries . . . of John Hay,* 204.

session and dismissed the members to their homes. "In the disorder which followed, Davis standing at his desk, pale with wrath, his bushy hair tousled, and wildly brandishing his arms, denounced the President in good set terms." [9]

The President all the while was in the room set apart for his use in the Senate wing of the Capitol, where he had been conferring with members of the cabinet and the Congress as he considered newly passed bills for his signature. During the morning Zachariah Chandler had warned him not to veto the Wade-Davis measure, for, he said, a veto would have a disastrous political effect in the states of the Northwest. Lincoln, who had made no move to discourage Congress from passing the bill, now patiently explained to Chandler his constitutional doubts about it. As Lincoln left the Capitol that day he told John Hay that Chandler and the Radicals could "do harm" politically on the reconstruction issue. "At all events," he went on, "I must keep some consciousness of being somewhere near right: I must keep some standard of principle fixed within myself." [10]

Unless the President signed the bill within ten days, it would fail to become law, no positive veto being necessary after the adjournment of Congress. Lincoln could have let the ten days pass in silence on his part. Instead, he chose the unusual course of issuing a proclamation on the subject, and a most remarkable proclamation it proved to be. He announced (July 8, 1864) that he was "unprepared, by a formal approval of this bill, to be inflexibly committed to any single plan of restoration," and that he was "also unprepared to declare that the free-State constitutions and governments already adopted and installed in Arkansas and Louisiana" should be "set aside and held for nought." Nevertheless he was "fully satisfied with the system for restoration contained in the bill as one very proper plan for the loyal people of any State choosing to adopt it," and he was "prepared to give the executive aid and assistance to any such people." [11] That is to say, he was willing to give effect to a mere proposal—a bill that had not become law—and he left the Southern people to take their choice between his plan and that of Davis and Wade.

"What an infamous proclamation!" exclaimed Old Thad Stevens

---

9 Brooks, *Washington in Lincoln's Time,* 168.

10 Dennett, . . . *Diaries* . . . *of John Hay,* 204–206.

11 Nicolay and Hay, *Works,* X, 152–154.

in a letter to an intimate. "The idea of pocketing a bill and then issuing a proclamation as to how far he will conform to it . . . ." Though Lincoln had intended to mollify the Radicals, he had succeeded only in exasperating them with his conditional approval of their plan. "But what are we to do?" Stevens asked his friend, then answered his own question: "Condemn privately and applaud publicly!" [12] His colleagues Wade and Davis, however, were in no mood for applause, and in a month the President and the nation were to hear from them.

VI

Lincoln based his ten per cent plan on his assumption of a strong potential unionism in the South. He counted upon the good will of his countrymen, even in their hour of defeat, and he intended to nourish that sentiment rather than take for granted, and thereby foster, the perpetuation of wartime hatreds. But the Radicals did not share his faith in this regard. Stevens, for one, expected guerrilla warfare to go on indefinitely even after the Confederate armies should all have surrendered.[1] And Winter Davis declared: "There is no fact that we have learned from any one who has been in the South and has come up from the darkness of that bottomless pit which indicates . . . repentance." There was no fact "at all reliable," he went on, which indicated that "any respectable proportion of the people of the southern states" were willing to accept even such terms as the Northern Democrats might grant them.[2] Davis and his associates in Congress looked for continuing disunionism and strife; the President hoped for peace.

The differing approaches of President and Congress, in planning for the defeated South, followed naturally from their differing assumptions. Lincoln aimed to conciliate the recent rebels and to adapt his program, if necessary, to meet conditions that might vary from state to state. He was unprepared, as he said in his proclamation on the Wade-Davis bill, "to be inflexibly committed to any single plan of restoration," and he was also unprepared to see the free-state constitutions of Arkansas and Louisiana set aside, "thereby repelling and

---

12 Stevens to Edward McPherson, July 10, 1864, Stevens MSS.

1 Current, *Old Thad Stevens*, 207.

2 *Cong. Globe*, 38 Cong., 1 sess., App., 84.

discouraging the loyal citizens" in those states.[3] The bill, by contrast, would have provided a fixed and invariable program for all areas of the South, regardless of differences in the time and circumstances of the rebuilding of state governments.

The difference in spirit between the presidential and the congressional plans is clearly seen in the different oaths the two required. The Wade-Davis bill prescribed the "ironclad oath" that a man had not willingly supported the rebellion, before he could participate in politics or government. Thus, in the bill, loyalty was made a matter of past conduct, not of present attitude or future promise, and no allowance was made for a possible change of heart. In Lincoln's plan the concept of loyalty was forward and not backward looking. "On principle I dislike an oath which requires a man to swear he *has* not done wrong," Lincoln explained. "It rejects the Christian principle of forgiveness on terms of repentance. I think it is enough if the man does no wrong *hereafter.*" [4]

Whether or not Lincoln's was the more Christian way, the Radicals argued that it was the less democratic. As Stevens said, to allow a "tithe" of the people to govern the rest was a "mere mockery" of democratic principles. Of course the Wade-Davis bill did require a majority and not merely a tenth of the loyal voters to start the constitution-making process. But Lincoln intended his tenth as a nucleus around which a loyal majority might, with his simple oath, soon develop. His was a minority that had possibilities of rapid growth. The majority principle of Wade and Davis, on the other hand, was deceptive. Under their program no one could participate in politics who could not take the ironclad oath, which would eliminate hundreds of thousands and very likely leave political power in the hands of a minority. And this minority could grow only with the aging and death of former Confederates and the rise of a new generation too young to have participated in the war. (A majority could have been created, of course, by the enfranchisement of former slaves, but the Senate had defeated Wade's proposal to strike the word "white" from the bill's provision for enrolling all "adult white males.")

The President and the Congress disagreed on issues of constitutionality as well as loyalty. Could a state secede from the Union? Had some of the states actually done so? The Wade-Davis bill implied that they

[3] Nicolay and Hay, *Works,* X, 152–153.

[4] *Collected Works,* VII, 169.

had, and Radicals like Stevens made the point explicit. "This bill and this position of these gentlemen seems to me," Lincoln commented in Hay's presence, "to make the fatal admission (in asserting that the insurrectionary States are no longer in the Union) that States whenever they please may of their own motion dissolve their connection with the Union." Lincoln thought the Federal government could not survive such an admission. "If that be true," he said, "I am not President, these gentlemen are not Congress." He preferred not to argue about the question whether certain states were in or out of the Union. To him this was a "merely metaphysical question." The real problem was a practical one—how to "restore the Union"—and he believed the Union could best be restored without a quarrel over abstractions.[5] In discussing the future of the Southern states he habitually used the term "restoration" in preference to "reconstruction," with its connotations of change drastic, forcible, and delayed.

Both Lincoln and the Radicals, including Davis himself, favored an amendment to the Federal Constitution as an ultimate measure for disposing of slavery in the states of the South. Pending the adoption of such an amendment, there were sharp differences of opinion about presidential and congressional powers in the sphere of abolition. In urging Lincoln to sign the Wade-Davis bill, Senator Chandler said: "The important point is that one prohibiting slavery in the reconstructed States." Lincoln: "That is the point on which I doubt the authority of Congress to act." Chandler: "It is no more than you have done yourself." Lincoln: "I conceive that I may in an emergency do things on military grounds which cannot be done constitutionally by Congress." After Chandler had left and Fessenden had come in, Lincoln continued: "I do not see how any of us now can deny and contradict all we have always said, that Congress has no constitutional power over slavery in the States." Fessenden agreed, but added that he had doubts about the "constitutional efficacy" of the President's own emancipation decree.[6]

Lincoln inclined to the belief that, in time of war, the Constitution restrains the President less than it does Congress. Yet the Supreme Court was later to rule that Congress may exercise belligerent powers in disregard of the ordinary restraints of the Constitution.[7] This opin-

5 Dennett, . . . *Diaries* . . . *of John Hay*, 204–205. 6 *Ibid.*, 205.

7 Randall, *Constitutional Problems under Lincoln*, 514–515.

ion (though the Court was not deciding the specific question of the war power of Congress to abolish slavery) suggests that the abolition clause of the Wade-Davis bill was based on constitutional grounds no more dubious than those on which stood the Emancipation Proclamation or the presidential order prohibiting slavery under the ten per cent plan.

As for the practical consequences of the presidential and congressional programs, there would have been no immediate difference in respect to slavery, at least within the states of Louisiana, Arkansas, and Tennessee, where Lincoln's plan was being put into operation. There might (theoretically) have been a difference later on. That is, if Radical fears were justified, pro-slavery governments might eventually have come into power and re-established slavery in the restored states. Or, in other states yet to be restored under the presidential plan, flexible and variable as it was, Lincoln conceivably might have made concessions to slavery—might, for example, have directed gradual rather than immediate emancipation. Such fears were idle. The President was, in fact, already committed to an antislavery constitutional amendment (and was, within a year, to press it upon Congress). Wade and Davis were only confusing the issues when they tried to give the impression that their bill was an antislavery alternative to proslavery policies on the part of the President.

Their bill, if enacted would have had other consequences very different from those of the President's plan, if he had been free to carry it out. His kind of "restoration" would have meant the early return of the Southern states to a normal and natural place in the Union. The Radicals' brand of "reconstruction," however, might have delayed the return indefinitely. Even to begin the process would have been difficult, if not impossible, so long as a majority of adult white males, willing to take an oath of loyalty to the Constitution of the United States, was required. And after the process was begun, the disfranchisement of the former political leaders would doubtless have led to complications, conflicts, and delays.

On the part of some of the Radicals the postponement of restoration was deliberately intended. As Stevens was to say, the Southern people must "eat the fruit of foul rebellion" before receiving all the rights of citizenship again. He was to calculate that, as soon as Southern representatives should be readmitted to Congress, they along with the

Northern Democrats would have a clear majority there. His own aim, he was frankly to state, was to "secure perpetual ascendancy to the party of the Union," that is, to the Republican party. If Republicans should lose the ascendancy, then their entire economic program—the protective tariff, the national banking system, the subsidization of railroads—would be jeopardized.[8]

But the Wade-Davis bill was not nearly so effective an instrument for perpetuating disunion and Republican supremacy as the Radicals later were to devise. Radical reconstruction, in the fullness of its development, was to include military rule, Negro suffrage, and hopelessly complicated procedures for reorganizing and recognizing new state governments in the South. Indeed, as the Radical Congressman George W. Julian was to say, the "somewhat incongruous bill" of Wade and Davis, if the President had accepted it, would have become "a stumbling-block in the way of the more radical measures which afterwards prevailed." [9]

Even without achieving the enactment of the bill, the Radicals accomplished at least part of their purpose in passing it. "It was commonly regarded," Blaine later recalled, "as a rebuke to the course of the President in proceeding with the grave and momentous task of reconstruction without waiting the action or invoking the council of Congress." [10] The bill was also a rebuke to Lincoln for his presidential aspirations, or so it was intended by some of the Radicals, who intimated that his real purpose in hastening the restoration of Southern state governments was to use them in building a personal political machine which would assure his renomination and re-election in 1864.[11] The rebuke was the perhaps inevitable outcome of his habit of playing scant regard to the prerogatives and sensitivities of Congress. If he had sedulously cultivated congressional support, he might possibly have avoided the rebuke and the impasse to which it led. But that is doubtful, in view of the fundamental divergences in spirit and purpose between him and the majority of his fellow partisans in Congress.

This much is certain, that in consequence of the bill's passage and pocket veto, Congress and the President had reached a stalemate in

---

[8] Current, *Old Thad Stevens,* 207, 226–229.

[9] Julian, *Political Recollections,* 247–248.

[10] Blaine, *Twenty Years of Congress,* II, 42.

[11] Current, *Old Thad Stevens,* 190.

the conflict over policy with regard to the Southern states. And this conflict boded ill for the success of the party in general and the President in particular in the coming political campaign. Some of the bills recently passed and signed—tax laws, the conscription act—were dubious party assets in an election year, but the bill passed and not signed was likely to make far more trouble for the party. Congress adjourned with worse relations between legislative and executive than at any time since the foundation of the Republic under the Constitution, or at least since the days of Andrew Jackson. The prospects for fruitful co-operation between Congress and President, even if Lincoln should be re-elected with a Republican majority in both houses, seemed rather poor.

CHAPTER X

DARK SUMMER

DURING all the four years of the Civil War there were, for President Lincoln, no darker months than those from the summer solstice to the autumnal equinox in 1864. In September the skies were to brighten for him, but in July and still more in August the days brought little but increasing gloom. These were the days of abortive peace missions, of lagging recruitments, of cynical speculation in gold, of widespread defeatism throughout the North. The war dragged on, and Grant made no noticeable dent in the great ring of earthworks that kept him from Richmond and Petersburg. While the enemy Capital remained beyond the reach of Union troops, Washington itself was threatened by the Confederates.

I

Besieged as he was in Richmond and Petersburg, General Lee looked for relief, as he informed Jefferson Davis on June 20, 1864, from a stratagem for drawing the attention of the Federals to their own territory. Thereby he might induce Grant to weaken his besieging force by sending part of it northward or, better yet, to bleed his army further by assaulting the strong Confederate defenses. So Lee sent Jubal A. Early with nearly twenty thousand men up the Shenandoah Valley, that convenient approach to the unguarded rear of Washington, a route already well worn by Confederate raiders, who had used it every summer of the war. The Union forces under David Hunter having previously retreated out of the way, over the mountains into West Virginia, Early advanced unopposed through the Valley. During the first days of July his troops crossed the upper Potomac. On July 11, just a week after the adjournment of Congress, his army was on the northern outskirts of Washington, in sight of the Capitol dome.[1]

For a couple of days Washington had a small taste of what was becoming familiar and routine in Richmond—a state of siege—but Washington knew far less than Richmond about the nature and intentions of the besieging force. Communications with the North by rail and telegraph were cut off. No one in the city, not even the President and his cabinet, could do more than guess how large the enemy force was, precisely where it was concentrated or whether it was concentrated at all, and when or whether it was going to attack. In his diary Secretary Welles railed against the "dunderheads" at the War Office, the stupid Stanton and the confused Halleck, and expressed no satisfaction when told that intelligence was poor because fresh cavalry was lacking.[2] Grant himself suffered from defective information, though from his own intelligence and from Washington reports he had a broadly accurate picture of Early's movement. Unaware that Hunter had removed himself from the possibility of effective action, Grant counted upon him to pursue and entrap Early's army.[3]

Fortifications dotted the circumference of Washington, but most of the garrisoning troops had been sent to Grant as replacements for his heavy losses, and the forts were manned by a motley collection of invalids and raw militiamen. At the enemy's approach, civilian employees of the navy and war departments were called into service.[4] When Grant offered to come to the relief of the city, Lincoln suggested but did not order that he do so. On second thought Grant decided to send two corps but not to go himself, and Lincoln calmly accepted this arrangement.[5]

Much alarmed about the President's personal safety, Stanton on July 9 sent Lincoln a note telling him his carriage had been followed by a mysterious horseman and warning him to be "on the *alert.*" Nevertheless Lincoln with his family went out as usual on the next evening to spend the night at the Soldiers' Home, in the northern part of the city, where the enemy was expected to appear. At ten that evening Stanton drafted another warning note, in which he started to tell Lincoln to "come into town at once," then corrected the last two

---

1 Nicolay and Hay, *Abraham Lincoln: A History,* IX, 158, 160, 169–173; Williams, *Lincoln and His Generals,* 324.

2 Welles, *Diary,* II, 69–70, 72–74.

3 Williams, *Lincoln and His Generals,* 325–326.

4 Nicolay and Hay, *Abraham Lincoln: A History,* IX, 163–164; Welles, *Diary,* II, 72.

5 Williams, *Lincoln and His Generals,* 325–326.

words to read, a little less peremptorily, "tonight." [6] The President, though reluctant, did return with his family that night, in a carriage which Stanton had sent for him, but he was considerably annoyed. He was further annoyed to learn that a gunboat was being readied so that he might flee the city.[7]

The next day he determined to "desert his tormentors" and make a tour of the city's defences. He went out to Fort Stevens, beyond the Soldiers' Home, near the northern corner of the District of Columbia, on the 7th Street Road. He was on the parapet when the Confederates, advancing through heat and dust from Silver Spring, first opened fire on the fort. A soldier standing beside him—long afterward identified as Oliver Wendell Holmes, Jr.,—"roughly ordered him to get down or he would have his head knocked off." [8] The expected assault did not develop, as Early spent the afternoon in feeling out the strength of the works.

On the following day the President again was under fire at Fort Stevens. Though Early still ordered no attack, he kept up his reconnaissance, and a "continual popping" of gunfire came from pickets and skirmishers on both sides. An officer a few feet from Lincoln on the parapet fell with a mortal wound. A few minutes later Secretary Welles and Senator Wade entered the fort together and found the President sitting in the shade, his back against the parapet towards the enemy. Shells fired from the fort were setting fire to houses in which rebel sharpshooters were hiding.[9] Learning that "the military officers in command thought the shelling of the houses proper and necessary," Lincoln, as he afterwards stated, "certainly gave" his "approbation to its being done." [10]

Smoke arising in the distance indicated that the Confederates also were burning houses, and one of these was the mansion of Montgomery Blair at Silver Spring. "The Rebels have done him this injury," Welles was to reflect later, on viewing the blackened walls of Blair's house, "and yet some whom they have never personally harmed denounce him as not earnest in the cause, as favoring the Rebels and their views." One of Blair's foremost detractors, personally unharmed by the rebels, was of course Welles' uncongenial companion on the

---

6 R. T. L. Coll., 34399, 34405. 7 Brooks, *Washington in Lincoln's Time,* 175.
8 Dennett, . . . *Diaries* . . . *of John Hay,* 208 9 Welles, *Diary,* II, 72, 74–75.
10 Lincoln Memorandum, Oct. 10, 1864, Box 162, House of Rep. Coll., Lib. of Cong.

Fort Stevens visit, Senator Wade.

From the fort, after the shelling had let up, Lincoln had a chance to see at first hand a little of the drama of soldiers in action. There, only a few hundred yards away, in the broad valley below, were men in blue (newly arrived veterans) advancing across open fields, and ahead of them were men in grey running for the wooded cover on the brow of the opposite hills. And here, nearer at hand, were Union stretcher bearers bringing in their wounded comrades. By nightfall the action had ceased, and campfires lighted up the woods around the fort, while the road was clogged with Union stragglers, some weary and worn out, others drunk.[11] In the darkness to the north Early was withdrawing his troops.

All the while Lincoln had worried little if at all about his own safety or that of the city. "With him," as Hay noted on July 11, "the only concern seems to be whether we can bag or destroy this force in our front." And when the force had begun to leave, he became doubly anxious lest it get away. On July 13 Hay recorded again: "The President thinks we should push our column right up the River Road & cut off as many as possible of the retreating raiders." But there was no one to give the necessary orders in time. Grant was too far away. Halleck, never a man to assume responsibility, declined to act without instructions from Grant. And Lincoln, unwilling to interfere with the general-in-chief, restrained whatever impulses he may have had to take personal command in the emergency. Finally a telegram from Grant started General Wright in pursuit with all available forces. "Wright telegraphs that he thinks the enemy are all across the Potomac but that he has halted & sent out an infantry reconnoissance [*sic*], for fear he might come across the rebels & catch some of them." So, on July 14, Lincoln said to Hay. And Hay observed to himself, "The Chief is evidently disgusted." [12]

Wright, of course, was not really to blame for his delayed and seemingly timid pursuit. As T. Harry Williams has written, "Early got away because the tangled command system in the Washington military area did not make anybody responsible for catching him." Both Lincoln and Grant soon recognized this fact and saw the necessity

---

11 Welles, *Diary*, II, 74–75, 80.

12 Dennett, . . . *Diaries . . . of John Hay*, 209–210; Brooks, *Washington in Lincoln's Time*, 177.

for reorganizing the command system so as to put the troops in the Capital and the adjacent departments under the control of a single general. Otherwise Early could threaten Washington again and again, Grant would have to keep on detaching troops from the Richmond and Petersburg area, and Lee would never be finally hemmed in and compelled to surrender.[13] This military lesson for the President and his general-in-chief was one of the important consequences of the Early raid.

Another consequence, less favorable to the Union cause, was an aggravation of the defeatism prevailing throughout the North. The people of the country did not realize how little panic, how little sense of real danger, the raid had aroused in Washington itself. After communications had been reopened, however, the people got from the Washington papers, such as the *Chronicle* and the *National Intelligencer,* the impression that there had been a miraculous deliverance from imminent peril and that the narrow escape was cause for national humiliation.[14] Prophets of disaster drew what seemed to them an obvious moral from the idea that, even at this late date in the war, the Capital, the government records and treasures, and the person of the President were not safe.[15]

II

The Lincoln government had to deal not only with overt military threats, such as the Early raid, but also with threats, rather obscure and ill defined, of what in a later day would have been called "fifth column" activity. Confederate plotters were full of schemes for exploiting defeatism and disloyalty in the North during the gloomy summer of 1864. Though the exact dimensions of the conspiracy were not known to Lincoln and his advisers at the time, there were signs and rumors aplenty which both exaggerated and underestimated its extent.

In Peoria and Springfield, Illinois, in Syracuse, New York, and in other cities of the North the Peace Democrats during August sponsored mass demonstrations which to Republicans seemed sinister and ominous. At the Peoria "Copperhead Convention" on August 3 there

13 Williams, *Lincoln and His Generals,* 326–327.

14 Welles, *Diary,* II, 77.

15 Brooks, *Washington in Lincoln's Time,* 179–180.

was a crowd of between ten and twenty thousand, according to the estimate of the sympathetic Chicago *Times*. Conspicuous at the meeting were such prominent Democrats as Clement L. Vallandigham, George H. Pendleton, and Fernando Wood. The resolutions of the convention condemned Lincoln for his reply to the Niagara peace proposal and demanded an immediate armistice to end the war.[1]

Governor Richard Yates of Illinois saw in the peace movement signs of serious trouble for his state. Already, as in Coles County during the spring, mob violence had flared up between critics and defenders of the Lincoln administration, and passions still were simmering. After the Peoria demonstration Yates feared a general uprising might begin in Illinois. He said, privately, that if he had only himself to consider, he would be for "shooting the home traitors" as he would "so many dogs." He refrained from giving guns to loyal citizens, however, because his doing so might give rise to the accusation that he was "arming the abolitionists," and this might be made a "pretext for arming the copperheads." Then "hostilities might be provoked & civil war precipitated." [2]

From time to time President Lincoln received warnings of a "great conspiracy" which extended far beyond the borders of Illinois. He sent Hay to Missouri to find out what General Rosecrans knew. The general gave Hay some papers to take back, and dispatched others by another courier—documents giving "the details of evidence covering a thousand pages of foolscap." This detailed report, the general said (in a letter of June 22), would show the following:

"1. That there exists an oathbound secret society, under various names but forming one brotherhood both in the rebel and loyal states, the objects of which are the overthrow of the existing national government, and the dismemberment of this nation.

"2. That the secret oaths bind these conspirators to revolution and all its consequences of murder arson pillage and an untold train of crimes, including assassination and perjury under the penalty of death to the disobedient or recusant.

"3. That they intend to operate in conjunction with rebel movements this summer to revolutionize the loyal states, if they can.

---

1 *Weekly Illinois State Journal* (Springfield), Aug. 10, 1864, p. 2, c. 7; New York *Herald*, Aug. 19, 1864, p. 5, c. 4.

2 Yates to J. Berden and others, Aug. 12, 1864, Reavis MSS., Chicago Hist. Soc.

"4. That Vallandingham [*sic*] is the Supreme Commander of the Northern wing of this society . . . .

"5. That the association is now and has been the principal agency by which spying and supplying rebels with the means of war are carried on between the loyal and rebel states, and that even some of our officers are engaged in it.

"6. That they claim to have 25000 members in Missouri, 140000 in Illinois, 100000 in Indiana, 80000 in Ohio, 70000 in Kentucky and that they are extending through New York New Jersey Penn[a] Delaware & Maryland." [3]

A Canadian wrote to Lincoln on July 7 to give additional information about the plot. His country and many of his countrymen, this man said, were involved in it. Vallandigham while in exile in Canada had organized Union deserters and draft dodgers, together with thousands of Canadians and Irishmen living in Canada, into a force which, together with civilians in the Northern states and officers and men in the Union army, totalled at least three hundred thousand, "all anxiously waiting for the time to arrive to strike a deadly blow." Arms were being cached against the day of revolution. "It is not intended to make any demonstration before the presidential election comes on if the South can hold out successfully until that time and then they will concentrate their forces and commence their work of destruction on the lakes and the frontiers." [4]

From other sources also the war department was warned that Confederate agents in Canada were "setting on foot expeditions of the most dangerous character," and Republican newspapers published rumors of Confederate and Copperhead intrigue.[5] In these stories there was a considerable element of truth.

The Confederate government was in fact carrying on a campaign to exploit the war weariness of the Northern people, the organized peace movement, the partisan opposition to Lincoln, and the financial difficulties of the Union government. The peace offensive (as a later generation would have termed it), which Jacob Thompson and his colleagues launched from Canada during the summer, was only a part of a large and ambitious enterprise. From Jefferson Davis, in

---

[3] R. T. L. Coll., 33944–45. [4] M. C. Moe to Lincoln, R. T. L. Coll., 34323–24.

[5] Maj. Gen. S. A. Hitchcock (Sandusky, Ohio) to Stanton, Sept. 23, 1864, *Offic. Rec.*, 1 ser., XXXIX, 448; New York *Tribune*, Oct. 29, Nov. 5, 1864.

Richmond, Thompson had received oral instructions to proceed at his discretion to do what would "seem most likely to conduce to the furtherance of the interests of the Confederate States of America." [6] From Thompson other agents got unwritten instructions.[7] Most colorful and resourceful of these agents was a young Kentuckian, Thomas Henry Hines, who is said to have shaken hands with Lincoln once, while the bonds that were to finance his efforts stuck boldly out of his pockets.[8] Despite the poor condition of Confederate finances, Thompson was fairly well supplied with funds.

The Confederate conspirators counted on the co-operation of the Sons of Liberty in Illinois, Indiana, Ohio, and other states of the North. The Sons of Liberty—a name adopted early in 1864 for its patriotic connotations from Revolutionary days—were successors of the Knights of the Golden Circle. Thompson enjoyed the confidence of some of the leading Liberty men, and through them he helped to finance the Peoria peace demonstration. He also managed to gain interviews with Vallandigham, Pendleton, and other prominent Peace Democrats. Thompson and his fellow plotters hoped, through their connection with the Sons of Liberty, to do more than merely stimulate pacifist demands. At the most, the Sons were expected to rise up in rebellion, "throw off the galling dynasty at Washington," and create an independent Confederacy of the Northwestern states. At the least, the Liberty men were expected to collaborate in various undertakings for the harassment of the Union.[9]

If the conspiracy had succeeded, a United States gunboat on Lake Erie would have been captured and the rebel prisoners on Johnson's Island freed. Prisoners at other camps from Illinois to New York also would have been turned loose. River boats on the Mississippi would have been sabotaged or destroyed. Fires would have been started in New York, Boston, Philadelphia, Chicago, Pittsburgh, Washington, and other cities, all of which would have been reduced to ashes. Chicago would have been captured. Settlements along the

---

[6] *Offic. Rec.,* 4 ser., III, 278, 322.

[7] J. W. Headley, *Confederate Operations in Canada and New York,* 221, 227.

[8] For a recent and exaggerated account of the conspiracy in general and of Hines's career in particular, see James D. Horan, *Confederate Agent: A Discovery in History* (New York, 1954).

[9] *Offic. Rec.,* 1 ser., XLIII, pt. 2, 930–931; 2 ser., VIII, 523–525; *Offic. Rec.* (Nav.), 2 ser., III, 1235.

Canadian border would have been plundered. And the Union government would have been forced to make peace on the basis of the independence of the Confederate States of America.[10]

The actual accomplishments of the conspirators fell somewhat short of this grand design. In September an attempt on Johnson's Island failed. In October a band of raiders from Canada fell upon St. Albans, Vermont, a border town of about five or six thousand, and attempted to burn the place after robbing the three local banks. In November arsonists set fires in several New York hotels and on vessels on the North River, but all the fires were put out before significant damage was done. The hoped-for revolt of the Sons of Liberty did not even start.[11]

The idea of revolutionizing the Northwest and establishing a new Confederacy was never more than a fantastic dream. Only a few of the Sons of Liberty themselves were implicated in the plot, and still fewer outsiders would have been willing to have anything to do with it. From the outset even the conspiring leaders of the Liberty organization recognized the futility of an armed uprising. "We are willing to do anything which bids fair to result in good," one of them wrote to Thompson and his associates on August 8, "but shrink from the responsibility of a movement in the way now proposed." The writer added: "You underrate the condition of things in the Northwest." [12] Thompson's partner C. C. Clay informed Judah P. Benjamin, the Confederate secretary of war, in September, that the Northern people showed little sympathy for the Liberty men.[13]

Nothing was done except when the Confederates themselves did it, and all their efforts failed except for the St. Albans raid, which was only a partial success. The other undertakings were frustrated by the vigilance and the prompt counteraction of Union authorities.

Meanwhile, though the President had not been able to ignore the rumblings of the Confederate underground, he had refused to give them any more attention than they deserved. At the time of Rose-

---

10 Headley, *Confederate Operations,* 230; *Offic. Rec.,* 1 ser., XLIII, pt. 2, 229–230, 932, 934.

11 Headley, *Confederate Operations,* 259–261, 274–277; *Offic. Rec.,* 1 ser., XLIII, pt. 2, 932–933; XLV, pt. 1, 1077–1079; Welles, *Diary,* II, 152; New York *Herald,* Oct. 21, 1864, p. 5, c. 4; Oct. 23, 1864, p. 5, c. 1; New York *Tribune,* Dec. 16, 1864; *Ann. Cyc.,* 1864, 588.

12 Quoted in Headley, *Confederate Operations,* 225.

13 *Offic. Rec.,* 4 ser., III, 639.

crans' warning, he had stated "in reply to Rosecrans' suggestion of the importance of the greatest secrecy, that a secret which had already been confided to Yates, Morton, Brough, Bramlette, & their respective circles of officers could scarcely be worth the keeping now," as Hay noted. Hay observed further: "He treats the Northern section of the conspiracy as not especially worth regarding, holding it as a mere political organization, with about as much of malice and as much of puerility as the Knights of the Golden Circle." [14] His calmness and sanity in that time of wild rumor and equally wild plot make a refreshing contrast to the hysteria of men like General Rosecrans, with his make-believe of mystery, and Governor Yates, with his mutterings about shooting down home traitors like dogs.

III

A month and a day after the adjournment of Congress the authors of the Wade-Davis bill replied to Lincoln's pocket veto and his proclamation with a joint statement published in the New York *Tribune*. Their "manifesto" was a most remarkable document for two so prominent Republicans to hurl at the candidate of their own party in the midst of a presidential campaign.

Mincing no words, Senator Wade and Representative Davis savagely denounced Lincoln for proceeding with his own reconstruction plan in disregard of the aims of Congress. They charged him with "grave Executive usurpation" and with the perpetration of a "studied outrage on the legislative authority." They condemned his "shadows of governments" in Arkansas and Louisiana as "mere oligarchies" and "mere creatures of his will." Referring to his "personal ambitions" and his "sinister" motives, they insinuated that his real purpose in hastening the readmission of Southern states was to assure himself of additional electoral votes. They questioned whether the Supreme Court sooner or later would not disapprove his plan. Then they turned to strong hints of immediate retaliation against him. They declared that his pocket veto—"this rash and fatal act"—had been "a blow at the friends of his Administration" as well as a blow at the "rights of humanity" and the "principles of Republican Government." He "must understand that our support is of a cause and

14 Dennett, . . . *Diaries . . . of John Hay*, 192.

not of a man," and "if he wishes our support" he must "confine himself to his Executive duties" and "leave political reorganization to Congress." [1]

Throughout the North the Wade-Davis Manifesto made sensational news. The immediate reaction among many of the Radical Republicans was highly favorable, though Greeley himself, on publishing it, said only that it was "a very able and caustic protest." "Better late than never," crazy old Adam Gurowski told his diary. "Two *men* call the people and Mr. Lincoln to their respective senses." [2] The *National Anti-Slavery Standard* opined that the Wade-Davis bill had been well devised (and left the implication to be drawn that Lincoln's plan had *not* been) to accomplish the triple aim of eliminating slavery, forestalling traitors, and disavowing rebel debts in the reorganized states. "We certainly shared in the general regret that the bill was not permitted to become law," the *National Anti-Slavery Standard* now observed.[3] To Wade and Davis the old abolitionist Gerrit Smith sent a letter of congratulation, saying Lincoln had "good intentions" but lacked "nerve" and "stern justice," and this letter was published in John W. Forney's Philadelphia *Press*.[4]

Generally Republicans who approved the manifesto discussed the subject of congressional and presidential relations in bitterly personal terms. In a few cases, however, they based their approval of it on fairly sober constitutional grounds. "Our government is strictly a government of law," one Republican paper reminded its readers. Procedures and policies not prescribed by legislation but laid down by arbitrary executive action were "alien and repugnant" to the Constitution, the *Evening Post* went on. Congressmen were entitled to protest when the President, at his own whim, "put aside action of Congress" and "left the restoration of the rebel states to their proper place in the Union wholly unprovided for, except by methods which the Executive might think proper to dictate." [5]

Some conservative Republicans came wholeheartedly to the Presi-

---

1 New York *Tribune*, Aug. 5, 1864; *Ann. Cyc.*, 1864, 307–310.

2 Gurowski, *Diary, 1863–1864*, 309–310.

3 Quoted in the New York *Times*, Aug. 13, 1864, p. 3, c. 4.

4 Smith to Wade and Davis, Aug. 8, 1864, Philadelphia *Press*, Aug. 17, 1864, p. 2, c. 4.

5 New York *Evening Post*, Aug. 6, 1864. Welles listed the *Evening Post* as one of the "Administration journals" in New York. Welles, *Diary*, II, 104 (Aug. 13, 1864).

dent's defense. The New York *Times,* edited as it was by Lincoln's campaign manager, Henry J. Raymond, deplored the "ultra radicalism and barbarism" of "these gentlemen," Wade and Davis. They were dangerous revolutionaries, the *Times* alleged. "They have sustained the war not as a means of restoring the Union, but to free the slaves, seize the lands, crush the spirit, destroy the rights and blot out forever the political freedom of the people inhabiting the Southern States." [6] A Buffalo newspaper saw the issue as one of patronage, not revolution. "It is suggested that if Mr. Lincoln had granted Winter Davis what he modestly asked a year ago—the control of all the military and civil appointments for Maryland—Winter wouldn't have issued his protest." [7]

"As President of the United States he must have sense enough to see and acknowledge he has been an egregious failure," was the moral that James Gordon Bennett's New York *Herald* drew on the day after the publication of the protest in the rival *Tribune.* "One thing must be self-evident to him, and that is that under no circumstances can he hope to be the next President of the United States." [8] The Democratic New York *World* observed: "Wade's charge amounts to an impeachment, and may be followed by one." [9]

Among members of Lincoln's cabinet the protest aroused as much alarm as it did rejoicing in extreme Radical circles. Welles assumed that Wade had been motivated by presidential aspirations of his own.[10] J. P. Usher, the secretary of the interior, noted that, except for Chase, everyone in the cabinet had approved the President's amnesty proclamation. Usher thought that Wade and Davis were seeking to "gratify their malignity" at the expense of Republican success in the election. Lincoln, he wrote, had tried to "oblige this class of men," had given them little "cause & reason to assail him," but they were unappeasable and would never be satisfied.[11] Montgomery Blair saw them as enemies of the Union and the administration, which had to face Jefferson Davis, R. E. Lee, and the rebels on one side and

6 New York *Times,* Aug. 18, 1864, p. 4, c. 3; Williams, *Lincoln and the Radicals,* 325.
7 Buffalo *Morning Express,* Aug. 24, 1864.
8 New York *Herald,* Aug. 6, 1864, p. 4, c. 3.
9 Quoted in Washington *Constitutional Union,* Aug. 13, 1864, p. 2, c. 1.
10 Welles, *Diary,* II, 95–96.
11 Usher to R. W. Thompson, Aug. 14, 1864, MS., Lincoln Nat'l Life Foundation, Fort Wayne, Ind.

"Henry Winter Davis & Ben Wade and all such hell cats on the other." [12]

Seward read the manifesto to Lincoln on the night of August 5, and the President (as a state department visitor heard the next day, apparently from Seward himself) commented: "I would like to know whether these men intend openly to oppose my election—the document looks that way." [13] Not long afterward he said to Noah Brooks: "To be wounded in the house of one's friends is perhaps the most grievous affliction that can befall a man." He felt that he had done his best to meet the wishes of Wade and Davis while also keeping in mind his "whole duty to the country." Their bill, however, seemed to him like the bed of Procrustes: "if a man was too short to fill the bed he was stretched; if too long, he was chopped off"; and if any state "did not fit the Wade-Davis bedstead, so much the worse for the State." Grieved though he had been by the passage of the bill, the President was even more distressed by the manifesto, "so needless" and "so well calculated to disturb the harmony of the Union party," as Brooks reported, doubtless expressing Lincoln's attitude as well as his own.[14]

IV

Lincoln had guessed right about the intentions of Davis and Wade when he suspected that these men meant openly to oppose his reelection. Their "protest" was, in fact, the first public sign of a move to replace him as the Republican candidate in mid-campaign. Davis soon was circulating among prominent party men, for their signatures, a paper calling for a new national "Union" or "Peoples" convention to meet in September and nominate another candidate. This document, said to be a "powerful arraignment" of the administration's "shortcomings in the conduct of the war," demanded the nomination and election of a President who could and would "save the country from anarchy and rebellion." [1] If the "call" gained the support of enough politicians, it was to be brought out into the open at a suitable time.

[12] J. K. Herbert to B. F. Butler, Aug. 6, 1864, *Private and Official Correspondence of Gen. Benjamin F. Butler during the Period of the Civil War,* V, 8–9.

[13] *Ibid.*

[14] Brooks, *Washington in Lincoln's Time,* 170–171.

[1] Albany *Journal,* Aug. 12, 1864, p. 1, c. 4; Washington *Constitutional Union,* Aug. 16, 1864, p. 1, c. 5.

Once launched, the movement was directed (in so far as it had any central direction) by a secret council of party leaders who met on August 14 and from time to time thereafter in New York. The chief conspirators included not only such chronic dissidents as Davis and Greeley, but also the Mayor of New York, George Opdyke; the prosperous merchant, David Dudley Field; and the president of the New York Bank of Commerce and treasurer of the Union (i. e., Republican) National Committee, John Austin Stevens.[2] Among other schemers were three outstanding Massachusetts politicians: Senator Sumner, Governor Andrew, and General Butler. Chase was expected to co-operate, and so were Seward's friend Weed and Lincoln's campaign manager Raymond. As the project attracted both numbers and respectability, it developed into something far more serious than a mere gesture of Lincoln haters and party irresponsibles.

What gave it sense, during those dark days of August, was the seeming hopelessness of Lincoln's chances for re-election in the fall. Republican politicians gloomily assured one another that the people would have no more of him. "Among the masses of the people a strong reaction is setting in, in favor of the Democrats & against the war," said one. "I have been among the mechanics, and the high prices . . . are driving them to wish a change." [3] Said another, in upstate New York: "It is certainly true that in this region the President has lost amazingly within a few weeks, and if the public sentiment here affords a fair indication of the public sentiment throughout the country, the popular suffrage today would be 'for a change.' " [4] And still another wrote: "Things in a political way do not look so favorable as they did some time ago. Pennsylvania, New York, and all the New England States are getting down on *Old Abe* as they call him." [5] Many others found, or thought they found, that Republican voters were "utterly spiritless," [6] were "sick and dispirited," [7] were

[2] The New York *Sun,* June 30, 1889, p. 3, published a collection of documents illustrating the "secret movement to supersede Abraham Lincoln in '64." Actually, the movement was not entirely secret, since news of it was given in contemporary newspapers, such as those cited in the footnote above.

[3] A. Brisbane (Buffalo, N.Y.) to H. Greeley, Aug. 2, 1864, Greeley MSS., N. Y. Pub. Lib.

[4] G. Martindale (Rochester, N.Y.) to Butler, Aug. 16, 1864, *Private and Official Correspondence of Gen. Benjamin F. Butler during the Period of the Civil War,* V, 54–55.

[5] G. C. Rice to E. B. Washburne, Aug. 14, 1864, Washburne MSS., Lib. of Cong.

[6] Schurz, *Reminiscences,* III, 102.

[7] J. W. Grimes to C. H. Ray, Aug. 3, 1864, Ray MSS., Huntington Lib.

completely apathetic,[8] and would either stay away from the polls or mark their ballots for Frémont or for the Democratic candidate. To some Republican leaders it seemed hardly worth while to bother with campaigning for Lincoln. Senator Grimes, of Iowa, wondered whether Senator Trumbull, of Illinois, would take the stump. "There was not a very great inclination among Senators to do so when I left Washington," Grimes believed.[9]

Who, if not Lincoln, could inspirit Republicans, unite the party, and salvage victory on election day? On this question the malcontents disagreed. Davis himself was said to favor some man like Charles Francis Adams,[10] but most of the others preferred a military man like General Grant or, if he was unavailable, then some lesser general like Sherman, Hancock, or Butler.[11] Grant, endorsing the re-election of Lincoln, refused to allow himself to be made a rallying point for political opposition to his commander-in-chief. Butler however, was willing enough, as always. To Andrew's friends he was unacceptable, but to Wade he appeared available enough. To his wife, to his admirer J. K. Herbert, and to some men on his staff Butler seemed an ideal candidate—indeed, to one of them, he was "the greatest Intelligence on this continent." The Butler men visited and corresponded with dissaffected politicians to boom the general's cause, while their hero himself remained discreetly at Fort Monroe, until late in August, when he visited his home in Lowell and conferred with politicians in New York on the way back.[12]

The leaders of the anti-Lincoln movement disagreed on questions of tactics as well as personnel. Some of them wished to go ahead with a new nomination regardless of Lincoln's attitude. Others, like Sumner, were willing to proceed only if Lincoln first could be induced voluntarily to resign as the party's candidate.[13] Most of them came to agree that both Lincoln and Frémont should withdraw, so that the followers of both could reunite behind a single nominee, who might be expected also to attract many of the War Democrats if the Demo-

---

8 D. Dickinson to S. Cameron, July 26, 1864, Cameron MSS., Lib. of Cong.

9 Grimes to Ray, Aug. 3, 1864, Ray MSS., Huntington Lib.

10 W. J. Gordon to S. J. Tilden, Aug. 25, 1864, Tilden MSS., N. Y. Pub. Lib.

11 Albany *Statesman,* quoted in Baltimore *Daily Gazette,* Aug. 23, 1864, p. 2, c. 1.

12 Louis Taylor Merrill, "General Benjamin F. Butler in the Presidential Campaign of 1864," *Miss. Valley Hist. Rev.,* XXXIII, 558–562.

13 Sumner to Andrew, Aug. 24, 1864, Andrew MSS., Mass. Hist. Soc.

cratic party, at its forthcoming convention, should choose a peace man or a peace platform.

Frémont indicated his willingness to consider the plan when he replied to an appeal from six Bostonians. "You must be aware of the wide and growing dissatisfaction, in the republican ranks, with the Presidential nomination at Baltimore; and you may have seen notices of a movement, just commenced, to unite the thorough and earnest friends of a vigorous prosecution of the war in a new convention which shall represent the patriotism of all parties," the six had written. "Permit us, sir, to ask whether, in case Mr. Lincoln will withdraw, you will do so, and join your fellow citizens in this attempt to place the Administration on a basis broad as the patriotism of the country and as its needs." In reply, Frémont said he could not resign his nomination without consulting the party that had nominated him at Cleveland, but he suggested that his correspondents confer with leaders of both his own and Lincoln's party, then organize a "really popular convention," one broader than factions or cliques. This exchange of letters was published on August 27.[14]

Meanwhile the proponents of a new convention found reason to believe that Lincoln also would co-operate. Lincoln's political expert Weed, his former law partner Swett, and his campaign manager Raymond all seemed to think so. After a two-hour conversation with Weed, Butler's man Herbert wrote to the hopeful general on August 11: "He says Lincoln can be prevailed upon to draw off. Swett, who I sent to Maine for, is of the same opinion." Herbert added: "Raymond says Lincoln has gone up, all we can expect of him is to get him to help choke [others] off the track." [15]

On or about that same August 11 Weed told Lincoln frankly "that his re-election was an impossibility," and he repeated this conviction in a letter of August 22 to Seward. "Mr. Swett," he added, in confirmation of his own view, "is well informed in relation to the public sentiment. He has seen and heard much." [16] While Weed was writing to Seward, Raymond wrote to Lincoln a letter detailing the hopelessness of the outlook. Said Raymond:

---

14 Boston *Daily Advertiser,* Aug. 27, 1864, p. 1, c. 6. The letter to Frémont was signed, by George L. Stearns, S. R. Urbino, James M. Stone, Elizur Wright, Edward Habich, and Samuel G. Howe.

15 *Correspondence of Gen. Benjamin F. Butler,* V, 67–68.

16 Weed to Seward, Aug. 22, 1864, R. T. L. Coll., 35490–91.

I feel compelled to drop you a line concerning the political condition of the country as it strikes me. I am in active correspondence with your staunchest friends in every State and from them all I hear but one report. The tide is setting strongly against us. Hon. E. B. Washburne writes that "were an election to be held now in Illinois we should be beaten." Mr. Cameron writes that Pennsylvania is against us. Gov. Morton writes that nothing but the most strenuous efforts can carry Indiana. This State [New York], according to the best information I can get, would go 50,000 against us to-morrow. And so of the rest.[17]

But neither Weed nor Raymond proposed to Lincoln, at this time, that he should step out of the presidential race. Instead, Raymond urged upon him a stratagem by which, as Raymond thought and Weed concurred, the President might yet save the day for the party and for himself. "Two special causes are assigned for this great reaction in public sentiment," Raymond explained, "—the want of military successes, and the impression in some minds, the fear and suspicion in others, that we are not to have peace *in any event* under this administration until Slavery is abandoned. In some way or other the suspicion is widely diffused that we *can* have peace with Union if we would." Now, said Raymond, the thing for Lincoln to do was to disperse these fears and suspicions with a shrewd propaganda stroke. The President should appoint a special commission *"to make* [a] *distinct proffer of peace to* [Jefferson] *Davis, as the head of the rebel armies, on the sole condition of acknowledging the supremacy of the Constitution,"* all other questions to be settled later in a convention representing the people of the states North and South. This offer, which would require no armistice, would put Davis and the Confederate government into a dilemma. If they accepted, the war would be ended and the Union saved. If, as was much more likely, they rejected the proposal, they would thereby "plant seeds of disaffection in the South" and "dispel the delusions about peace that prevail in the North." They would "unite the North as nothing since the firing on Fort Sumter" had done. "Even your radical friends could not fail to applaud it when they should see the practical strength it would bring to the common cause." [18]

In fact, however, the Radicals were most unlikely to applaud an offer of peace on the basis of Union alone, with such matters as slavery to be postponed for discussion at some later time. The Radi-

---

[17] Raymond to Lincoln, Aug. 22, 1864, R. T. L. Coll., 35478–79–80–81.

[18] *Ibid.*

cals were pressing Lincoln in exactly the opposite direction, that is, in the direction (to use the hackneyed phrase of the time) of a "vigorous prosecution" of the war. Some of them urged upon him a quite different strategem by which, if he did not delay too long, he might presumably save himself and also the Republican cause. They were merely repeating the familiar demand that he purge his cabinet of lukewarm advisers and replace them with "sound, energetic, reliable" men.[19] Thaddeus Stevens, for one, called at the White House in mid-August and tried to argue him into forming a new cabinet with Montgomery Blair left out. Otherwise, said Stevens, party workers in his state could not put their hearts into the campaign. Lincoln answered that he desired re-election but not on terms which would make him a mere puppet. Returning unsatisfied to his home in Lancaster, Stevens let it be known that he could no longer canvass for the President. "If the Republican party desires to succeed," he was heard to say, "they must get Lincoln off the track and nominate a new man." [20]

Lincoln was caught between extremes. The Radicals complained because, they said, he was too friendly with Conservatives. And Conservatives "who have been acting with us," as Blair heard from a Missouri correspondent, intended to go for the Democratic candidate "because the President countenances the Radicals." [21]

He knew of the movement against him within his own party, as he also knew of the consensus among political experts that his chances of re-election were slim, at best. Yet, rather than make concessions to the politicians who beset him on either side, he was willing to accept defeat, if defeat must come. On August 23, the day after Raymond had penned his pessimistic letter on "the political condition of the country," Lincoln wrote the remarkable memorandum which he folded, pasted, and gave to his Cabinet members to endorse, sight unseen. In it he put himself on record thus:

> This morning, as for some days past, it seems exceedingly probable that this Administration will not be re-elected. Then it will be my duty to so co-operate with the President elect, as to save the Union between the

---

19 N. G. Upshur to Butler, Aug. 12, 1864, *Correspondence of Gen. Benjamin F. Butler,* V, 43–44.

20 Current, *Old Thad Stevens,* 202.

21 M. Blair to B. Able, Aug. 22, 1864, Blair MSS., Lib. of Cong.

election and the inauguration; as he will have secured his election on such ground that he can not possibly save it afterwards.[22]

This, as Lincoln was to recall after the election, was at a time "when as yet we had no adversary, and seemed to have no friends." [23] The Democratic convention was six days away. Even when defeat seemed most probable, however, Lincoln had not quite abandoned hope. Earlier he had been reported as saying that the people blamed him for Grant's failure to take Richmond, and that he knew as well as anyone that he was going to be *"badly beaten"*—unless "some great change" occurred in the military situation.[24] Pessimistic though he became, he still counted on that great change. "Lincoln said," according to a letter of August 26, citing a recent White House visitor, "the public did not properly estimate our military prospects, results of which would change the present current," but he himself "relied on this confidently." [25]

V

The gloomier the Republicans became, the more hopeful the Democrats had reason to be as they looked ahead to the meeting of their own nominating convention, scheduled for the unprecedentedly late date of August 29, in Chicago. They ran the risk, however, of exposing fissures in their own party as wide and deep as any in administration ranks. To win, they must unite, War Democrats with Peace Democrats. "The greatest danger of Mr. Lincoln's succeeding in another term of office, whether by fair or foul means, and thus dragging our poor country still deeper down his road to Ruin seems to consist in the . . . possible division of the Democratic Party," one worried Democrat believed. Unless the Democrats could agree upon a popular candidate and a "people's" platform, they must expect a second and possibly a third term for the man in the White House—"another four years, *or more,* of Lincolnism." [1]

The pre-convention favorite was the erstwhile hero of the Army of the Potomac, General George Brinton McClellan. Would Mc-

---

22 *Collected Works,* VII, 514.

23 *Ibid.*

24 Herbert to Butler, Aug. 11, 1864, *Correspondence of Gen. Benjamin F. Butler,* V, 35-37.

25 H. A. Tilden to S. J. Tilden, Aug. 26, 1864, Tilden MSS., N. Y. Pub. Lib.

1 W. R. Skidmore to W. Kelly, Aug. 18, 1864, Tilden MSS., N. Y. Pub. Lib.

Clellan run? "It is very doubtful whether anything would now induce me to consent to have my name used," he wrote as late as June 25.[2] But he must run, the War Democrats told one another. Only he could "control any large portion of the army vote in the field and at home"; only he could "prevent the use of the army by Mr. Lincoln" to deprive the opposition of free expression at the polls.[3] McClellan was not the choice, however, of such party leaders as Vallandigham, Pendleton, and Wood. These men stood to gain by the long delay in the opening of the convention. "The democrisy have postponed their convenshun till it is ascertained how Lee *agt* Grant comes out," explained Petroleum V. Nasby, one of Lincoln's favorite humorists. "Ef Lee whales Grant—Peace Platform." [4] And the Ohio Congressman S. S. Cox grew "really mortified, vexed, and discouraged" at the postponement, which he feared would give the extreme peace men a chance to "dirk" McClellan. Cox thought there was "no denying that since Grant's failure or seeming failure," there had been "an increase of the peace sentiment—irrespective of consequences." [5]

Some Republican as well as Democratic politicians believed that McClellan, if nominated, could beat Lincoln in the campaign. During the darkest days of July and August the Blairs, Cameron, and others toyed with a stratagem for nullifying the general's supposed popularity or converting it into an administration asset. Here was another of those last-minute schemes for salvaging Lincoln's chances. In pursuance of it the elder Frank Blair called upon McClellan in New York, about July 20, and told him he would be restored to command if he would disavow any presidential aspirations he might have. McClellan was noncommittal.[6] When Blair returned to Washington the President listened to him without comment, though, according to Frank Blair, Jr., the President himself "had concluded with Genl Grant to bring again into the field as his adjunct Gen McClellan if he turned his back on the proposals of the peace junto at Chicago." [7]

---

[2] McClellan to Manton Marble, June 25, 1864, Marble MSS., Lib. of Cong.
[3] S. L. Barlow to Manton Marble, Aug. 21, 1864, Marble MSS.
[4] Buffalo *Morning Express,* Aug. 26, 1864, p. 2, c. 4.
[5] Cox to Manton Marble, June 20, 1864, Marble MSS.
[6] Smith, *Blair Family,* II, 280–281.
[7] F. P. Blair, Jr., to the editor of the *National Intelligencer,* Oct. 15, 1864, Blair MSS., Lib. of Cong.

Despite the failure of Blair's mission, some Republicans continued to hope that Lincoln might appease McClellan and the War Democrats.[8] On August 26 Cameron was reported as having recently said that Lincoln could not win against McClellan and so was "disposed to be friendly" toward him. "He [Cameron] also says, which is even more important, that Lincoln told him last week that if McClellan was not nominated he should at once appoint him to his 'old place.' Whether he means in command of the army of the Potomac, or in Hallecks place I do not know." [9]

Nothing came of all this, except for some campaign propaganda later on,[10] and McClellan still led all contenders when the Democratic convention finally met. The delegates disposed of their business within a remarkably few days. Vallandigham, dominating the resolutions committee, saw to it that the platform denounced the war and declared for an early peace, though he insisted that a "dishonorable peace" was not to be considered. "Whoever charges that I want to stop this war in order that there may be Southern independence and a separation," he declared, "charges that which is false, and lies in his teeth, and lies in his throat!" [11] The key plank, as reported and adopted, read in part: ". . . after four years of failure to restore the Union by experiment of war . . . justice, humanity, liberty, and the public welfare demand that immediate efforts be made for a cessation of hostilities, with a view to an ultimate convention of the states, or other peaceable means, to the end that at the earliest practicable moment peace may be restored on the basis of the Federal Union of the States." After the adoption of the platform, McClellan was nominated on the first ballot. Then, unexpectedly, and as another sop to the peace faction, Pendleton was selected as his running mate.

These Chicago proceedings had the close attention of the politician in the White House. His secretary Nicolay gave instructions: "Save all the Chicago papers so that we may have a full report of the convention." [12] His journalist friend Brooks attended the convention

---

8 J. D. Kellogg to S. Cameron, Aug. 6, 1864, Cameron MSS., Lib. of Cong.

9 S. L. Barlow to Manton Marble, Aug. 26, 1864, Marble MSS.

10 See Washington *Daily National Intelligencer,* Oct. 3, 1864, p. 3, c. 1; Oct. 20, 1864, p. 2, c. 4; Oct. 21, 1864, p. 3, c. 1.

11 Cincinnati *Daily Commercial,* Aug. 27, 1864.

12 Nicolay to Mr. Neill, MS., Lib. of Cong.

and, "agreeably to the expressed wish of the President," sent back letters in which he gave facts and insights which the newspapers overlooked. In one of his letters Brooks reported that, at every stop west of Pittsburgh, crowds "attracted by the music and the cannon on our train" were "blindly and ignorantly bawling for 'Peace.' " In Chicago most of the delegates were similarly peace-minded, even though the majority of them clearly favored the war man, McClellan. The Democrats seemed confident as they began their work. "These men are making the most of our own dissensions and have published as a campaign document the Wade-Davis manifesto . . . ," Brooks wrote. "These things create a great deal of despondency among our own people, of course, and many of the weak-kneed already predict defeat and disaster . . . ." In a second letter, written from Dixon, Illinois, after the adjournment of the convention, Brooks was able to report a more optimistic spirit among Republicans. First, he detailed the complicated deals to which the Democrats had had to resort in completing their work, and he made clear the bitter intra-party feeling which nevertheless persisted. He had gathered from Democrats themselves that "McClellan's nomination was made for the soldiers' vote, which, they think, will be the decisive power in the next election," and that only this consideration had enabled Vallandigham to "swallow the bitter pill, which he did with a very ill grace." Finally Brooks noted: "Our people hereabouts are confident and hopeful. The nomination has already served to unite them, and I feel more encouraged than when I left Washington." [13]

Another observer, in not-so-distant Naperville, got a very different impression of the reaction among Illinois Republicans. "Since I came home," this man wrote to Senator Trumbull, "I learn of a number who have been, *and are,* Republicans, who have been supposed to be all right for Lincoln, who declare, since the Chicago Nomination, that as between Lincoln and McClellan, *they are for McClellan.*" [14] But Lincoln heard directly from Governor Dennison, in Columbus, Ohio: "The Chicago nominations are welcomed with no enthusiasm here, nor, so far as I can learn, anywhere in the State." [15] And he heard from Henry Wilson, in Natick, Massachusetts, that the nomination

---

[13] These letters were dated Aug. 29 and Sept. 2, 1864. R. T. L. Coll., 35638–39 and 35828–29.

[14] G. Marton to Lyman Trumbull, Sept. 2, 1864, Trumbull MSS., Lib. of Cong.

[15] Dennison to Lincoln, Sept. 2, 1864, R. T. L. Coll., 35833–34.

had aroused "our friends" to action and that they were now "fighting up in New England." [16]

Whether or not it served to unite and inspirit Republicans, the Chicago convention had the effect of exacerbating the factional quarrel among the Democrats. They had nominated McClellan because of his war record but had provided a peace platform for him to run upon. Now they would be handicapped by a fundamental contradiction in their position—unless McClellan somehow could resolve their dilemma for them.

In composing his letter of acceptance he faced that impossible task. The issue between the factions of his party was not one of peace *or* union, since even Vallandigham insisted that no cessation of hostilities should be considered on the basis of a separation of the states. The question was, which should come first—union, or peace? Vallandigham and his followers desired an armistice without prior stipulations in regard to reunion; they took it for granted that reunion would follow. The other faction demanded that reunion be made a precondition of any cease-fire agreement. For days, prominent men of both groups pelted McClellan with contradictory advice. On the one hand, August Belmont, the Prussian-born New York banker who was chairman of the Democratic National Committee, told him he must stand squarely and unequivocally upon Union ground.[17] On the other hand, Vallandigham urged him not to listen to his Eastern friends, not to "*insinuate* even a little war" into his letter of acceptance, lest he lose at least a hundred thousand votes in the West.[18] Thus beset, McClellan wavered as he drafted and redrafted his letter. For a time he seemed willing to accept an armistice even at the risk of disunion. At last, in the fourth and final version, dated September 8, he came out for union as the prerequisite of peace.[19]

The publication of his letter provoked new disagreements within his party, setting the separate factions to quarreling among themselves. Some of the peace men desired to repudiate him and reas-

---

[16] Wilson to Lincoln, Sept. 5, 1864, R. T. L. Coll., 35963–64.

[17] Belmont to McClellan, Sept. 3, 1864, cited by Charles R. Wilson, "McClellan's Changing Views on the Peace Plank of 1864," *Amer. Hist. Rev.*, XXXVIII, 503.

[18] Vallandigham to McClellan, Sept. 4, 1864, McClellan MSS., Lib. of Cong.

[19] Wilson, *Amer. Hist. Rev.*, XXXVIII, 498–505. McClellan's biographer William Starr Myers is "not able to agree entirely" with Wilson that McClellan "really wavered." Rather, "he merely was trying shrewdly to meet the *political* necessities of the campaign, but without any compromise of principle." Myers, *McClellan*, 455 n.

semble the convention for nominating a new candidate.[20] Others preferred to make the most of a bad situation by endorsing him, acceptance letter and all. The Ohio Sons of Liberty, in a meeting at Columbus on September 12, decided by a majority of only two to adhere to the ticket as it was.[21] George N. Sanders, the Confederate agent in Canada, assured Benjamin Wood, a New York Peace Democrat, that the peace plank would be binding on McClellan, no matter what he had said in his acceptance letter. "Genl McClellan has accepted the nomination," Sanders said, "and he cannot as an honorable man, and will not, reject a suspension of hostilities and a convention of the states; so clearly marked out, and required by the platform." [22]

At least a few of the War Democrats declined to support McClellan for the same reason that Sanders urged Peace Democrats to stay with him, namely, that he would be bound to carry out the party resolutions, even the peace plank. While McClellan's own statement was a "manly declaration," there was serious doubt "whether he would be permitted to pursue the line of policy indicated in his self-constructed platform." Lincoln often had been forced to give way to extremists within the Republican party. McClellan, if elected, would "have as violent and unreasonable men to deal with" in the Democratic party. So declared one group of War Democrats who announced their decision to vote for Lincoln.[23] Other War Democrats gave thought to the possibility of reassembling the convention and getting "Genl McClellan's letter adopted as their manifesto." [24] Still others considered calling a convention to present to the voters a new candidate as well as a new platform.[25] The party seemed about to split again, as it had done in 1860.

As September came in 1864, Democrats were bickering among themselves at least as bitterly as Republicans lately had been doing. The Democrats, too, were troubled by factious enterprises for setting aside their duly nominated candidate. Yet, though increasingly defeatist, they were not defeated. They had declared the war a failure, as conducted by the Lincoln administration, and if the news of battle

20 New York *Herald,* Sept. 11, 1864, p. 4, c. 2; Cincinnati *Daily Gazette,* Sept. 12, 1864, p. 1, c. 5.

21 Washington *Evening Star,* Sept. 15, 1864, p. 2, c. 5.

22 Sanders to Wood, Sept. 11, 1864, Tilden MSS.

23 Buffalo *Commercial Advertiser,* Oct. 5, 1864, p. 2, c. 2.

24 D. E. Sickles to Dem. Union Club, N. Y., Sept. 19, 1864, Sickles MSS., N. Y. Pub. Lib.

25 Bates, *Diary,* 421.

should continue to bear them out, they could expect success on election day. In this sense bad news would be good news for them. But not for Lincoln.

VI

Focusing most of their attention on the fortunes of the Army of the Potomac, the Northern people during the summer of 1864 kept looking for news that Grant had taken Richmond. They were inclined to measure Federal success or failure in terms of this objective, and hence their growing pessimism as the August days went by. They might and did read reports of victories by the Union Navy, but these alone were not enough to change the Northern temper, so long as Grant still faced an undefeated Lee. Finally, before the summer's end, news came of land engagements which, in outcome, seemed so spectacularly favorable to the Union cause that Northerners at last began to revise their hopes, even without any significant change in the opposing lines of Lee and Grant.

Early in the summer the most dramatic naval duel of the war—except, perhaps, for the duel of the *Monitor* and the *Merrimac*—was fought and won by a Union ship, the *Kearsarge,* against the most notorious and most successful of the Confederate commerce raiders, the *Alabama*. This vessel was one of those built for the Confederate Navy in a British shipyard. Its captain was the doughty sea fighter and confirmed Yankee-hater, Raphael Semmes, but its officers and men were mostly English. Roving the oceans for two years, the *Alabama* destroyed the U. S. S. *Hatteras* (one hundred tons larger than herself) and captured sixty-two merchant ships, burning or sinking most of them after taking off the persons on board. The actual destruction by this and other such raiders was only a small part of the damage done by them, for they created a hazard which raised insurance rates to prohibitive heights, caused the transfer of hundreds of ships from the American to the British flag, and helped to set the American merchant marine upon a decline lasting until the first World War. The Union cruiser *Kearsarge,* Captain John A. Winslow, finally trapped the *Alabama* in the port of Cherbourg, France, and (June 19, 1864) ended her career in a blazing fight which sent her to the bottom, leaving 26 of her complement of about 146 dead and

70 others as prisoners (the rest being taken off on a British steam yacht and a French pilot boat).[1] Gratifying though this news was to Northern hearts, it was soon overshadowed by reports of action much closer to home, by reports of Early's raid and the supposedly narrow escape of the national Capital itself.

Less than a month after Early's raid, the Navy gained another notable victory in the battle of Mobile Bay (August 5, 1864). Here Admiral David G. Farragut forced his large wooden ships, monitors, and gunboats through the difficult channel and into the bay defended by shore forts and a fleet including the famous ram *Tennessee*. The old admiral, lashed to the rigging of his flagship, the *Hartford,* damned the torpedoes and ordered full speed ahead into a fatal storm of shot and shell. He maneuvered so skillfully that the *Tennessee* failed to ram any of his vessels, and the torpedoes did little damage, though "the fire of the Confederate fleet and of Fort Morgan fell with butchering precision upon the Union decks, piling them with mangled fragments of humanity." Mobile fell, the Confederacy lost one of its few remaining ports, and the Union blockade was drawn tighter by another notch.[2] Significant though the victory was, it did not suffice to dispel the August gloom in the North nor even to lessen the effect of the Wade-Davis manifesto, published on the very same day.

The capture of Atlanta, a few weeks later, made far more glorious news than did the capture of Mobile. Atlanta was the reward for a long, strenuous, and expertly conducted campaign by General Sherman. At first he had been held in check by the defensive skill of his opponent, General Joseph E. Johnston, who had the disadvantage of an army only a little more than half as large as Sherman's but had the partly conmpensating advantage of a rough and mountainous terrain. "His resistance to Sherman was comparable to Lee's performance in delaying Grant." In mid-July, however, the Confederate war department, disliking his Fabian tactics, replaced him with the less cautious J. B. Hood, who promptly exposed his army to unequal battle. Hood had to withdraw to Atlanta and then (September 1, 1864) had to evacuate the city. The next day Sherman occupied it. The effect of this news, immediately and throughout the North, would be hard to exaggerate.[3] "The good news from Atlanta has set the

---

1 Randall, *Civil War and Reconstruction,* 587–590.

2 *Ibid.,* 592–593.

3 *Ibid.,* 551–554.

people wild," General Butler, stopping in New York on September 5, wrote to his wife in Massachusetts.[4]

After a few weeks more, news almost as cheering came from the Shenandoah Valley in Virginia. There, after Early's retreat from Washington, Grant had sent his ablest cavalry commander, Sheridan, to dispose of Early and devastate the farmland which comprised the chief Confederate granary. In a campaign of quick movement and sharp fighting, with frequent costly engagements, Sheridan outpointed Early in the battles of Winchester (September 19, 1864) and Fisher's Hill (September 22), then drove him southward up the Valley. A little later, returning from Washington after consulting with Halleck and Stanton, Sheridan was to make the ride that became famous in song and story.[5] Already his exploits, coming as they did on top of Sherman's occupation of Atlanta, were enough to convince many of the Northern people that the tide of the war was turning fast. To some of them, the battle of Winchester alone seemed like an "overwhelming defeat for the rebs." [6]

VII

While McClellan was being nominated and Atlanta was about to fall, the anti-Lincoln movement within the Republican party reached a climax. On August 30 a council of the malcontents in New York concluded that it was "useless and inexpedient" to run Lincoln "against the blind infatuation of the masses in favor of McClellan." They agreed to call a new convention, which was to meet in Cincinnati on September 28 "and, if need be, to nominate some candidate who can unite the entire loyal vote." [1] Before publishing the call, however, they decided to reassure themselves that Lincoln's prospects were indeed hopeless. To all the Republican governors they dispatched copies of a circular letter—signed by Horace Greeley, Parke Godwin, and Theodore Tilton—inquiring whether the governors could carry their respective states for Lincoln and whether he could be elected or whether another candidate should be nominated.

"The fall of Atlanta puts an entirely new aspect upon the face of

[4] *Correspondence of Gen. Benjamin F. Butler,* V, 125.
[5] Randall, *Civil War and Reconstruction,* 569–570.
[6] J. Galt to E. B. Washburne, Sept. 23, 1864, Washburne MSS., Lib. of Cong.
[1] George Wilkes to E. B. Washburne, Aug. 31, 1864, Washburne MSS., Lib. of Cong.

affairs," a New Yorker who professed to be a student of public opinion said on September 3, just three days after he had insisted that Lincoln had no chance and should withdraw.[2] "If you want to know who is going to vote for McClellan," the Albany *Journal* suggested, also on September 3, "mention Atlanta to them. The long face and the low muttered growl is sufficient. On the other hand, every Lincoln man bears a face every lineament of which is radiant with joy." [3] The war now seemed to be a success, yet the Chicago platform of the Democrats called it a failure. Disaffected Republicans were beginning to admit to one another that the Chicago platform had made Lincoln's re-election possible and McClellan's defeat necessary.[4] As Sumner put it, "Lincoln's election would be disaster, but McClellan's damnation." [5]

The governors had a chance to read the war news before they replied to the letter of Greeley, Godwin, and Tilton. Governor Yates, in his reply, declared that the re-election of Lincoln was a "strong probability," that Illinois could be carried for him and "not for any other man," and that any substitution would be "disastrous": "It is too late to change now." [6] Yates sent copies of his own letter to the other governors.[7] Governor Andrew was less positive and enthusiastic. He feared that, with a candidate like Lincoln, "essentially lacking in the quality of leadership," the party could not be so certain of success as it could be "under the more energetic influence of a positive man, of clear purpose and more prophetic nature." Nevertheless, said Andrew, "Massachusetts will vote for the Union cause at all events and will support Mr. Lincoln so long as he remains its candidate." [8]

The war news, together with the opinions of the governors, caused the arch-plotters in New York to abandon their project for a new convention within a week after deciding to go ahead with it. On September 5 they held their last council meeting, most of them agreeing that

---

[2] H. H. Elliott to G. Welles, Sept. 3, 1864, Welles MSS., Lib. of Cong.

[3] Albany *Journal*, Sept. 3, 1864, p. 2, c. 2.

[4] W. Dennison to Lincoln, Sept. 2, 1864, R. T. L. Coll., 35833–34; Anna E. Dickinson to "My dear friend," Sept. 3, 1864, Dickinson MSS., Lib. of Cong.; C. Sumner to F. Lieber, Sept. 3, 1864, Pierce, *Memoirs and Letters of Charles Sumner,* IV, 198; G. W. Julian to Sumner, Sept. 4, 1864, Sumner MSS., Widener Lib.; B. F. Butler to Mrs. Butler, Sept. 5, 1864, *Correspondence of Gen. Benjamin F. Butler,* V, 125; Henry Wilson to Lincoln, Sept. 5, 1864, R. T. L. Coll., 35963–64.

[5] Lillie B. Chace to Anna E. Dickinson, Sept. 19, 1864, Dickinson MSS.

[6] Yates to Greeley *et al.,* Sept. 6, 1864, Mass. Hist. Soc. *Proceedings,* LXIII, 86–87.

[7] James Conkling to Lincoln, Sept. 6, 1864, R. T. L. Coll., 35983–84.

[8] Andrew to Greeley *et al.,* Sept. 3, 1864, Andrew MSS., Mass. Hist. Soc.

recent developments had made it "the duty of all Unionists to present a united front." [9] On the same day Tilton wrote to Andrew: "*The Tribune* and *The Independent* [Tilton's own paper], and I suppose *The Post* also, will take the ground that all the Republican forces ought to rally round the Baltimore platform & candidates (not because these candidates are the best) but because we cannot afford to run the risk, by division, of giving a victory to the outrageous principles put forth at Chicago." [10] A few days later Seward heard from Weed: "The conspiracy against Mr. Lincoln collapsed on Monday last." [11]

The state elections in Vermont and Maine, held during the second week in September, seemed to confirm the belief that Lincoln would have a good chance to win in November. The New York *Herald* had conceded that, if the Republicans should carry those states, McClellan would have little if any chance. And the Republicans did carry both states, by majorities considerably larger than in the previous elections.[12]

Even after these returns were in, a few diehards among the malcontents still wanted and thought they could get a new candidate. Sumner, for one, "had not quite given up the hope that someone else might be substituted for Lincoln." [13] George Wilkes, fanatic editor of the *Spirit of the Times,* remained reluctant to abandon the proposed convention and, unlike Sumner, continued to think that Lincoln should be forced to retire. Winter Davis, he informed Butler on September 15, would send a delegation to Cincinnati, and so would others. But, Wilkes went on, even if the convention plan should fail, mass meetings could be held in every state, and these, "as a *dernier resort,*" could denounce Lincoln and endorse another man, presumably Butler. "I confess, however, the prospect now looks very slim." Greeley, said Wilkes, was deserting the cause, and so was John Austin Stevens, one

---

9 Tilton to Anna E. Dickinson, Sept. 5, 1864, Dickinson MSS.

10 Tilton to Andrew, Sept. 5, 1864, Andrew MSS.

11 Weed to Seward, Sept. 10, 1864, R. T. L. Coll., 36155–56. Weed now attempted to dissociate himself entirely from the conspiracy, writing: "It was equally formidable and vicious, embodying a larger number of leading men than I supposed possible. Knowing that I was not satisfied with the President, they came to me for co-operation, but my objection to Mr. L. is that he has done too much for those who now seek to drive him out of the Field."

12 New York *Herald,* Sept. 2, 1864, p. 4, c. 2; Sept. 15, 1864, p. 4, c. 2.

13 Lillie B. Chace to Anna E. Dickinson, Sept. 19, 1864. Dickinson MSS.

of the original arch-plotters.[14] Indeed, Stevens soon gave up the movement as dead and pronounced an autopsy on it. The replacement of Lincoln, he said on September 19, had become an impossibility because of "the outrage to the nation offered at Chicago, the glorious result of the Georgia campaign, the steady attitude of Vermont and the vote of Maine." [15]

All along, loyal Republican politicians had kept the President well informed of the plot against him. He had watched it rise and grow and die down, without his having to lift a hand to appease anybody. No longer did he need to fear that dissident Republicans might put up a new rival candidate. One rival, however, was already in the field, and that of course was Frémont. Some of the Radical leaders, Wade and Davis among them, though not intending to campaign for Frémont, remained unwilling to come out for Lincoln. "You must lose no time in the work of putting all our friends in the fight," Henry Wilson advised the President. Wade and Davis in particular "should be brought in if possible," Wilson said, so as to "take the force" out of their late manifesto.[16] But Wade and Davis and others like them would probably go on sulking unless Lincoln should make a gesture toward conforming with the plank in the Baltimore platform that called for a reorganization of the cabinet. Chase had gone: Blair must go.

VIII

Finally, on September 22, Frémont announced his withdrawal from the presidential race. The next day Lincoln requested and received Blair's resignation from the cabinet. This conjuncture has given rise to a story that the President, to insure his re-election, had made a "bargain" with Frémont. "To prevent almost certain defeat," the biographer of the Blairs has written, "he entered into a bargain with the Frémont Radicals, they to support the Union National ticket in exchange for the decapitation of Postmaster-General Blair." [1] Some historians, including Frémont's biographer, have questioned the bargain story, and one of Lincoln's biographers has dismissed it as a

[14] Wilkes to Butler, Sept. 15, 1864, *Correspondence of Gen. Benjamin F. Butler,* V, 134–135.

[15] Stevens to Andrew, Sept. 19, 1864, Andrew MSS.

[16] Henry Wilson to Lincoln, Sept. 5, 1864, R. T. L. Coll., 35963–64.

[1] Smith, *Blair Family,* II, 284.

myth.[2] To find what truth there is in it, the rather fragmentary bits of evidence must be re-examined.

The chief source for most of the accounts of the supposed Lincoln-Frémont deal is the official biography of Senator Zachariah Chandler, of Michigan, who undertook to serve as the go-between. Himself one of the most extreme Radicals, Chandler was an intimate of Wade and a friend of both Davis and Frémont, but he was also on fairly good terms with Lincoln, who allowed him to dispose of an ample share of the federal jobs in Michigan.[3]

At the end of August, according to his official biography, Chandler left home to mediate among the party factions. Stopping in Ohio, he found Wade apparently willing to take the stump for the Union cause if Lincoln would "make some sacrifices" in concession to the Radicals and if Davis was satisfied. Going on to Washington, "he obtained from the President what were practical assurances that Mr. Blair would not be retained in the Cabinet in the face of such strong opposition if harmony would follow his removal." In Baltimore he consulted Davis, who "promptly recognized the logic of the situation, and expressed his willingness to accept Blair's displacement as an olive branch and give his earnest support to the Baltimore ticket." Proceeding to New York, he "opened negotiations there with the managers of the Frémont movement," and after much delay they finally "agreed that, if Mr. Blair (whom General Frémont regarded as a bitter enemy) left the Cabinet and all other sources of Republican opposition to the Baltimore nominees were removed, the Cleveland ticket should be formally withdrawn from the field." Hastening back to Washington to see Lincoln and "ask the fulfillment of the assurances," he was "admitted to an immediate private interview with the President in preference to a great throng of visitors, and reported in detail the successful result of his labors." That was on September 22, the day the newspapers published Frémont's letter of withdrawal.[4]

This account, at certain of its significant points, is borne out by contemporary correspondence. Thus Butler's man Herbert wrote in Washington on September 3 that he had had a long conversation with

[2] Nevins, *Frémont,* II, 665; Stephenson, *Lincoln,* 507–508 n.

[3] See Winfred A. Harbison, "Zachariah Chandler's Part in the Reelection of Abraham Lincoln," *Miss. Valley Hist. Rev.,* XXII, 267–270.

[4] *Zachariah Chandler: An Outline Sketch of His Life and Public Services* (Detroit, The Post and Tribune Company, 1880), 273–276.

Chandler. "But, briefly, he is sent here by Wade and others from the west to say to Mr. L., & he & Washburn & Harlan did say to him to-day, throw overboard your Cabinet or we can't save you." Herbert added: "He is to see Mr. L. tomorrow again to get his ultimatum." [5] Presumably Lincoln's "ultimatum" sent Chandler to New York to confer with Frémont. From New York he wrote to his wife, on September 8, that Wade had disappointed him by not joining him there. "If he were here I could accomplish all I started to do but without him I fear I shall fail," Chandler complained. "The President was most reluctant to come to terms *but came* & now to be euchered is hard. I saw Frémont yesterday & shall see him again today when the matter will be decided one way or another." [6] The "terms" to which Lincoln and Chandler had come, implicit in this last sentence, were more definitely implied in the subsequent correspondence of Chandler and Wade. A week after Frémont had withdrawn, that is, on September 29, Chandler wrote to Wade and rebuked him for his non-appearance in New York. Wade replied: ". . . I did not understand that in your opinion it was essential that Frémont should withdraw from the canvass." He explained: "I mentioned that thing to you while here and that I ought to have some influence with Frémont and thought I could persuade him to withdraw, but concluded from your manner that you attached but little importance to the idea . . . ." [7] From all these interchanges, it seems safe to infer that Lincoln did agree to remove Blair on the condition that Frémont be persuaded to quit. Lincoln made a bargain, all right, at least with Chandler, or so Chandler certainly understood.

That Frémont himself entered into the bargain is not so clear, in the light of other contemporary evidence. Rather, it appears, from McClellan's correspondence, that he was more willing to make a deal with McClellan than with Lincoln. McClellan was informed, on September 20, that Frémont had authorized an agent to make whatever arrangement the Democrats considered best for themselves in regard to his withdrawing or continuing to run.[8] McClellan was told further,

5 Herbert to Butler, Sept. 3, 1864, *Correspondence of Gen. Benjamin F. Butler,* V, 120–121.

6 *Miss. Valley Hist. Rev.,* XXII, 273.

7 Wade to Chandler, Oct. 2, 1864, Chandler MSS., Lib. of Cong.

8 Charles R. Wilson, "New Light on the Lincoln-Blair-Frémont 'Bargain' of 1864," *Am. Hist. Rev.,* XLII, 71–78.

in a cipher telegram a few days later, that Chase and Wilson had promised Frémont a place in Lincoln's cabinet and the dismissal of both of the Blairs, Frank from the army as well as Montgomery from the cabinet, "if he would withdraw and advocate Lion [Lincoln]. He replied that it was an insult." [9] After his withdrawal, Frémont denied that he had been motivated either by a guarantee of Blair's removal or by promises of political favors for himself. He also insisted that his "only consideration was the welfare of the Republican party." [10] This does not seem to have been his only consideration, for, as Charles R. Wilson concludes from his study of the McClellan manuscripts, "Frémont came very close to withdrawing in favor of McClellan and the Democrats rather than in favor of [Lincoln and] the Republicans." [11]

In the public letter announcing his retirement, Frémont did not mention such a possible alternative. On the contrary, he now denounced McClellan's candidacy, though he did not quite endorse Lincoln's. He was stepping aside, he declared, "not to aid in the triumph of Mr. Lincoln" but to do his part toward "preventing the election of the Democratic candidate," which because of the Chicago platform would signify "either separation or re-establishment with slavery." He did hint, however, that he and his followers would not give Lincoln their wholehearted support unless he reformed his cabinet. "I consider," he said, "that his administration has been politically, militarily and financially a failure, and that its necessary continuance is a cause of regret to the country." [12]

Lincoln took the hint. Commenting in cabinet, the day Frémont's statement was published, he said the remark that his administration was a failure—"politically, militarily, and financially"—included at least the secretaries of state, treasury, and war, and the postmaster-general.[13] In asking, the next day, for the postmaster-general's resignation, he reminded Blair of Blair's repeated assurance that it was at his disposal whenever it would be a "relief" to him. "The time has come," Lincoln wrote. "You very well know that this proceeds from no dissatisfaction of mine with you personally or officially." [14] The inference to be drawn was that he was dissatisfied politically, and

[9] Fragmentary telegram from General Rosecrans, Sept. 23, 1864, McClellan MSS., Lib. of Cong.

[10] Nevins, *Frémont,* II, 665.

[11] Wilson, *loc. cit.*

[12] Quoted in Smith, *Blair Family,* II, 286.

[13] Welles, *Diary,* II, 156.

[14] Lincoln to Blair, Sept. 23, 1864, R. T. L. Coll., 36580.

Blair and his friend Welles both drew that inference. Welles believed, and Blair agreed, that Lincoln would not have yielded to the pressure for "pacifying the partisans of Frémont" if Seward and Weed had not advised him to do so. Lincoln assured Blair, however, that Washburne had recommended it, and Welles thought it strange that Lincoln should listen to such a man. "But Washburne thinks it will help the President among the Germans." [15]

If Frémont had not withdrawn, Lincoln possibly might have dismissed Blair anyhow, to conciliate such Radicals as Davis and Wade.[16] But probably not. For, if Chandler understood aright, Lincoln had come to "terms" most reluctantly and had presented the "ultimatum" that Frémont must give up if Blair was to go. To the last, he remained extremely loath to sack Blair. As he told Blair's father, not long before the dismissal, Blair was a good and true friend who should not be sacrificed for false friends.[17] The day came, however, when Lincoln apparently felt that he had to choose between imposing on the one and antagonizing the other. His decision can be criticized, as Rhodes has criticized it, as beneath the dignity of a President of the United States, though worthy of a shrewd politician.[18] Or it can be defended as Nicolay and Hay have defended it. "He felt," they wrote of Lincoln, "that it was his duty no longer to retain in his Cabinet a member who, whatever his personal merits, had lost the confidence of the great body of Republicans." [19]

IX

The sacrifice of Blair was not in vain. True, it outraged some of Blair's political friends, one of whom wrote to him to exclaim: "Great God has it come to this. That a man who is . . . Honest cannot . . . hold an office under this administration. . . . I had concluded to vote for Mr. Lyncoln but I cannot support him any longer . . . ." [1] But Blair himself loyally took the stump and doubtless won back most of those among his admirers who at first might have been tempted to stray from the Lincoln party.

[15] Welles, *Diary,* II, 156–157.

[16] So believes Wilson, *loc. cit.*

[17] F. P. Blair, Sr., to Montgomery Blair [Sept., 1864], Blair MSS., Lib. of Cong.

[18] Quoted in Smith, *Blair Family,* II, 284.

[19] Nicolay and Hay, *Lincoln,* IX, 340. These authors evince a strongly anti-Blair bias in their account of the dismissal.

[1] R. W. Y. to Blair, Sept. 30, 1864, Blair MSS.

As September turned to October the sulking Radicals one by one indicated a renewed optimism and a determination to carry the election for the regular candidate as well as the Radical cause. "Everybody who voted for him four years ago will vote for him now, while others, like Edward Everett, who voted against him before, will gladly range among his supporters," Charles Sumner assured a cheering crowd in Faneuil Hall on September 28.[2] Winter Davis wrote to Sumner the next day: "The Chicago platform compelled people to swallow their disgust and elect Lincoln: but," he added ominously, "will the Senate hold him to a proper responsibility & compel respect for the will of the nation . . . ?" [3] Theodore Tilton wrote to Anna E. Dickinson at the end of September: "As to politics, the field grows clearer—the prospect brightens." He confessed: "I was opposed to Mr. Lincoln's nomination; but now it becomes the duty of all Unionists to present a united front." [4] Early in October, Ben Wade assured "Brother" Chandler that Lincoln could be elected "by an overwhelming majority" and that he was "doing all for *him*" that he could have done "for a better man." [5] Ben Butler, in a public letter to Simon Cameron, averred that it was "the plain duty of every loyal man to support the election of Lincoln and Johnson." [6] Thad Stevens began to tell the Pennsylvania voters that Lincoln had risen above "the influence of Border State seductions and Republican cowardice" and would make no peace with slavery. "Let us forget that he ever erred, and support him with redoubled energy." [7]

Now, with the election hardly more than a month away, it was time for every good man to come to the aid of the party, and every good man came. At last the campaign got seriously under way.

---

2 Sumner, *Works,* VIII, 68.
3 Davis to Sumner, Sept. 29, 1864, Sumner MSS., Widener Lib.
4 Tilton to Anna E. Dickinson, Sept. 30, 1864, Dickinson MSS., Lib. of Cong.
5 Wade to Chandler, Oct. 2, 1864, Chandler MSS., Lib. of Cong.
6 Cincinnati *Daily Gazette,* Oct. 5, 1864, p. 3, c. 7.
7 Current, *Old Thad Stevens,* 203.

CHAPTER XI

RE-ELECTION

"IF WE come triumphantly out of this war, with a presidential election in the midst of it," Francis Lieber wrote to Charles Sumner at the end of August, 1864, ". . . I shall call it the greatest miracle in all the historic course of events." [1] There was, indeed, something marvelous if not miraculous in the very fact that a presidential election was being held, and still more in the fact that its being held was taken pretty much for granted. In all the historic course of world events, there had been few if any examples of a great people doing what the American people were now about to do. In the midst of a desperate civil war they were about to assess their leadership and, if they so decided, to change their rulers by the same orderly processes as in times of peace. If these processes, as usual, involved a certain amount of "dirty" politics, the dirt must not be allowed to obscure the shining truth that American democracy now met and surmounted one of its supreme tests of all time.

I

When, in September, the Republicans reunited themselves and began their campaign in earnest, the outcome of the election in November was still far from a foregone conclusion. The polling was to be by no means a mere formality or a manipulated plebiscite, even though the administration with the powers of government at its disposal could powerfully influence the behavior of the people at the polls. If Lincoln, weeks ahead of time, could have foreseen the final returns, he could have spared himself much troubling of spirit.

Political forecasting, even in this present day of public opinion

[1] Freidel, *Francis Lieber*, 351.

polls and "scientific" sampling, is a somewhat hazardous business. In 1864 no such techniques were known. One could attempt prediction by appraising the reports of politicians with their ears to the ground, but, in the fall of 1864, the wiseacres were hearing uncertain and contradictory noises. The New York financier and Democratic leader August Belmont bet $4,000 that his state would go for McClellan; at the same time James Gordon Bennett was positive that the state would go for Lincoln, though "by a very close vote." [1] In Indiana, Republicans breathed confidence while Democrats quoted a "very shrewd politician" who regarded Lincoln's chances as *"very doubtful."* [2] As for Pennsylvania, John W. Forney gave Lincoln alternately optimistic and pessimistic estimates, Simon Cameron was consistently sanguine and Alexander K. McClure cautious most of the time, yet as late as November 1 a Democratic worker found the prospect "exceedingly encouraging"—for McClellan.[3]

If such politicians' guesses were undependable, there was in those days an indicator of election trends in several of the states which was much more reliable, even more reliable than modern samplings of public opinion seem to be. In Maine and Vermont the voters chose various state officers in September, and, by the time the national campaigning got seriously under way, these states already had gone Republican by increased majorities. In Indiana, Ohio, and Pennsylvania the state elections were to be held in October, and the results would give an even more significant indication of the voting trend—at least in those three important "October states."

On the night of October 11 Lincoln watched anxiously for the returns from Indiana and Pennsylvania, both of which balloted that day. At eight o'clock he went to the telegraph office in the war department. The place was locked, and Stanton had taken the keys upstairs, but "a shivering messenger was pacing to and fro in the moonlight over the withered leaves," and he let the President and his party in at a side door. When there was a lull in the dispatches coming in over the wires, Lincoln—as he so often did in worried moments—took a volume of Petroleum V. Nasby from his pocket and read aloud several chapters. Later the good news from Indiana became better, but the

---

1 W. O. Bartlett to Lincoln, Oct. 20, 1864, R. T. L. Coll., 37390–91.

2 G. W. Adams to Manton Marble, Sept. 21, 1864, Marble MSS., Lib. of Cong.

3 Dennett, . . . *Diaries . . . of John Hay,* 230; McClure, *Lincoln and Men of War-Times,* 183; G. W. Adams to Manton Marble, Sept. 20, 1864, Marble MSS.

fat reports from Pennsylvania began to be "streaked with lean." When, a few days afterward, the final returns were in, Indiana like Ohio had gone Republican by a gratifying margin but Pennsylvania by a less satisfactory one. The "wild estimates of Forney & Cameron" were not fulfilled, "but we did not expect them to be," Hay reflected.[4]

After the October elections Lincoln was by no means overconfident about his own chances in November. On October 13, again at the war department's telegraph office and writing on its stationery, he jotted down his estimate of the forthcoming electoral vote. In the Democratic column he listed the states of New York, Pennsylvania, New Jersey, Delaware, Maryland, Missouri, Kentucky, and Illinois, and tallied 114 electoral votes. In the Republican column he listed the rest of the states and got a total of 117.[5] The conclusion thus was that he probably would win—but by the very narrow majority of three in the electoral college.

Yet, even if this probable majority had been an absolutely certain one, he would not have been satisfied with it. He longed for a decisive vindication of his party and his administration, for a victory made glorious by the numbers of Republican congressmen and governors elected as well as by the size of the popular and electoral votes for himself. McClure, having talked with him just after the October returns, went away impressed with the idea that it was "of the utmost importance" to gain such a "majority on the home front" as would "give moral force and effect to the triumph." [6] At about the same time Hay told Lincoln that the defection of two such states as Indiana and Illinois would be "disastrous and paralyzing," and that, as for himself, he would be willing to sacrifice some votes in Pennsylvania if those states could be held. Lincoln, however, could approve no such sacrifice. "He said he was anxious about Pennsylvania because of her enormous weight and influence which, cast definitely into the scale, w^{d} close the campaign & leave the people free to look again with their whole hearts to the cause of the country." [7]

There was a device by which the President could have tried to swell his electoral vote—the device of hastening the admission of new states or the readmission of old ones before election day. In the West the

[4] Dennett, . . . *Diaries . . . of John Hay,* 227–229.
[5] Lincoln, *Collected Works,* VIII, 46.
[6] McClure, *Lincoln and Men of War-Times,* 184.
[7] Dennett, . . . *Diaries . . . of John Hay,* 229–230.

territories of Nebraska, Colorado, and Nevada had enthusiastic aspirants and sponsors for statehood. In the South the conquered states of Louisiana and Tennessee were in different stages of Lincolnian reconstruction. If a couple of states—say, Tennessee and Nevada—could be hurried into the Union, Lincoln would be assured of several additional votes in the electoral college, since Republican majorities could be counted on in both. But Lincoln himself expressed little interest in such schemes, apparently feeling that, at best, they would give him only a contrived and not a real vindication.

In Tennessee, on September 30, the military governor and vice-presidential candidate Andrew Johnson issued a proclamation setting forth plans, authorized by the constitutional convention, for the election of presidential electors in that state. A group of Tennesseeans protested to Lincoln against the announced proceedings. In reply to them Lincoln, on October 20, refused to disavow what Johnson and the convention had done, and he also refused to interfere in any way.[8] The votes of Tennesseans were not to be counted in the presidential election of 1864.

Nevada was a different case. The territorial governor, James W. Nye, was eager for the territory to be made a state in time for its electoral vote to be counted, and so was his intimate friend Seward. To Lincoln's own list of probable electoral votes, someone (possibly it was Seward) added the prospective three votes of Nevada, making a total of 120 instead of 117 and a victory margin of six instead of three. If the final result should have proved as close as Lincoln had calculated, the three Nevada votes, few though they were, would have been of considerable comfort to him. So that there would be ample time to make it possible for Nevadans to vote, Congress, in response to Governor Nye's appeal, had moved the date for the territory's constitutional referendum ahead from October 11 to September 7. After the constitution had been thus early ratified, Seward was eager for Lincoln to proclaim Nevada as a state,[9] but, as Earl S. Pomeroy has written, Lincoln "was curiously slow to take advantage of the change." He refused to act until he had seen a copy of the constitution as ratified, even though he had already seen a copy as sent to him before ratification. Finally the governor telegraphed him the full text of the ratified constitution, at an expense of $4,303.27. This long telegram

8 Cincinnati *Daily Gazette,* Oct. 24, 1864, p. 3, c. 7.

9 Welles, *Diary,* II, 163–164.

was received in Washington on October 28. "Lincoln did not issue the proclamation until October 31—eight days before the election!" The oft-repeated story that the admission of Nevada was instigated by the President and was a pet project of his is, as Professor Pomeroy has shown, a fabrication put forth by the journalist Charles A. Dana.[10]

Lincoln was little concerned about the three votes of Nevada, but he was intensely interested in the twenty-six votes of Pennsylvania and the thirty-three votes of New York.

II

Lincoln once protested that he could not see personally to all the details of his campaign. "Well, I cannot run the political machine; I have enough on my hands without *that,*" he wrote. "It is the *people's* business—the election is in their hands." [1]

The people and the politicians pursued the business with elaborate organization. As chairman of the Union (that is, Republican) National Committee, Henry J. Raymond provided general direction in the management of the campaign. Members of his committee, such as Simon Cameron in Pennsylvania, ran the party organization within their respective states and provided a link between the national chairman and the local workers. "We have had our County Committee appointed for some time," one of these workers informed Cameron in September, "and we are trying to have an organization in every township—so that we may hold meetings in every school district." [2] Nowhere was any prospective voter likely to escape the over-arching influence of the party hierarchy.

Supplementing the regular machinery were other campaigning groups. The Republicans in Congress set up their own Union Executive Congressional Committee consisting of three senators, headed by James Harlan of Iowa, and three representatives, headed by Elihu B. Washburne of Illinois. Lest this committee duplicate some of the work of the national committee, Raymond early sounded out Washburne on ways to "arrange matters so as not to have the two organizations go over the same ground." [3]

[10] Earl S. Pomeroy, "Lincoln, the Thirteenth Amendment, and the Admission of Nevada," *Pac. Hist. Rev.,* XII, 366–368.

[1] Hertz, *Abraham Lincoln: A New Portrait,* II, 941.

[2] G. E. Minor to Cameron, Sept. 7, 1864, Cameron MSS., Lib. of Cong.

[3] Raymond to Washburne, June 20, 1864, Washburne MSS., Lib. of Cong.

The Union Leagues, those secret societies which had appeared in time to serve the Republican party in 1862, were strengthened and expanded for 1864. "It is all important to the success of the Union cause," an organizer declared, ". . . that Union Leagues be established in every County, and if practicable in every Township in the District." [4] Though not so universal as the Union Leagues, there were in many localities organizations of War Democrats supporting Lincoln and Johnson, such as the War Democratic General Committee of the City and County of New York. Also active throughout the North were the Lincoln and Johnson Clubs and such miscellaneous groups as, in New York, the Young Men's Republican Union. And the Loyal Publication Society now devoted itself to electioneering.

All the various Republican organizations, in their efforts to outdo the Democrats, had enough work to keep their members fairly busy for a couple of months. They staged the usual torchlight processions, the ward rallies, the great meetings with fireworks, cannon, bells, brass bands—and speeches.[5] In the small town of Polo, Illinois, the local Republicans built a Wigwam of their own, a building over a hundred feet long, "to accommodate a crowd as well as any place west of Chicago," in which to hold their meetings during the campaign.[6]

Speakers were routed through this or that state or district in response to the appeals of local leaders. Joshua Giddings, of Ohio, went into Illinois and Wisconsin. Frederick Douglass, the famous Negro abolitionist, was steered into some areas and away from others as prejudice and prudence seemed to dictate. "I think he would do pretty well in some parts of Wisconsin," a Chicago worker informed Washburne, but "for fear that our people would be driven off by the cry of 'Nigger' and a prejudice be raised in the Southern portion of the State," he should postpone his appearance in Illinois.[7] Thaddeus Stevens not only stumped his own district in Pennsylvania but also addressed a monster rally in Philadelphia. Naturally the Democrats noted with some concern the peregrinations of Republican orators, which amounted at times to something like a mass movement. "Indi-

---

[4] E. H. Berry (Indianapolis) to R. W. Thompson, April 20, 1864, Lincoln National Life Foundation, Fort Wayne, Ind.

[5] See, for example, Baltimore *Sun,* Sept. 2, 1864, p. 1, c. 5; Washington *Daily Morning Chronicle,* Oct. 6, 1864, p. 1, c. 4.

[6] H. Norton to E. B. Washburne, Sept. 19, 1864, Washburne MSS.

[7] Z. Eastman to Washburne, Sept. 19, 1864, Washburne MSS.

ana has sent up a Republican cry for help!" a Hoosier Democrat exclaimed early in the campaign. "The Republicans have sent out *twenty* new speakers. *Gov. And. Johnson,* candidate for V. P. is among them." [8]

Campaign literature was distributed in such tremendous quantities and such numerous varieties that, if it was all read, the voters must have had little time for several weeks to do anything but read it—and listen to speeches. "We are now sending out from fifty to a hundred thousand documents a day," Washburne reported on September 15, when his congressional electioneering committee had scarcely begun its work.[9] Between early September and early November the Loyal Publication Society alone broadcast more than a half-million pieces of literature, mostly among the German voters of New York City.[10] The publisher of the campaign biographies of Lincoln (which Raymond had authored) and of Johnson offered the books for circulation as campaign documents at twenty dollars the hundred, a price low enough to encourage wide distribution.[11] Another publisher, Mason & Company, of Philadelphia, was ready with a Lincoln campaign songbook, "containing a number of good songs, set to the most popular tunes," the whole collection being "excellent to circulate throughout the country," and the price only "$25 per 1000 copies." [12] Oliver Ditson, of Boston, published "Liberty's Call, or Hurrah for Abe and Andy," a piece of sheet-music widely sold during the campaign. A celebrated composer, publisher, and songster of the time, James D. Gay, of Philadelphia, entertained hundreds of crowds with his "Abe Lincoln's Union Wagon" and his "Abe Lincoln's Battle Cry." [13]

The election was indeed, as Lincoln said, in the hands of the people, but despite his protestations he was not content to leave it entirely in their hands. While burdened with his duties as the country's President, he did not evade his obligations as the party's leader. He was himself the master strategist of his own campaign. He did not al-

---

8 G. W. Adams to Manton Marble, Sept. 25, 1864, Marble MSS.

9 Washburne to E. D. Warner, Sept. 15, 1864, Warner MSS., Illinois Historical Survey, Urbana, Ill.

10 Freidel, *Francis Lieber,* 351–353.

11 Derby & Miller to E. B. Washburne, Sept. 13, 1864, Washburne MSS.

12 Mason & Co. to Simon Cameron, Oct. 15, 1864, Cameron MSS.

13 Philip D. Jordan, "Some Lincoln Civil War Songs," *Abr. Linc. Quar.,* II, 133–134.

ways leave even the details to Raymond or Washburne or the workers in the field, many of whom reported directly to him about ordinary tactical questions. Little that went on escaped his eye, and certainly nothing of significance.

He sometimes took a hand in the management of the Republican speakers' bureau, as when he requested General John A. Logan to leave his command in Sherman's army and miss the march to the sea, in order that he might apply his talents as a colorful and persuasive stump speaker in Indiana and Illinois.[14] Apparently Lincoln also suggested to Gustav Koerner that he, as a leading German-American of Illinois, might do much good among the German voters of the Midwest. "My German friends seem to agree with me that I can do a great deal more good by not taking a prominent stand on the stump," Koerner wrote, at Belleville, Illinois, to Lincoln. "The opposition papers have already charged that I had been called home by you to the great detriment of public bussiness [*sic*], to regulate the Dutch, and set them right." [15]

Lincoln did not hesitate to interfere in the operations of the regular party organization when he thought they were being poorly carried on. After the somewhat disappointing results of the October election in Pennsylvania he had reason to believe, from the complaints of Pennsylvanians returning to Washington after having gone home to vote, that Cameron had "botched the canvass badly" in that state.[16] He promptly called Cameron's factional foe Alexander K. McClure from Harrisburg to Washington, discussed the Pennsylvania situation carefully with him, and requested him to devote himself to aiding the state committee. McClure objected that his own participation would antagonize Cameron, but Lincoln promised to take care of that difficulty. Two days later McClure got a letter from Cameron inviting him to join in the committee's work. From that time on, Lincoln kept in close touch with McClure and, through him, with the progress of the Pennsylvania campaign. He even sent Postmaster General Dennison to Philadelphia to talk confidentially with McClure.[17]

---

14 McClure, *Lincoln and Men of War-Times,* 83.

15 Koerner to Lincoln, Sept. 22, 1864, R. T. L. Coll., 36559–60.

16 Dennett, . . . *Diaries* . . . *of John Hay,* 232.

17 McClure, *Lincoln and Men of War-Times,* 184–185. In the *Collected Works,* VIII, 81, there is a telegram from Lincoln to McClure, Oct. 30, 1864: "I would like to hear from you."

Brady Photographs, National Archives

WOULD-BE PEACEMAKERS

Upper left: Alexander H. Stephens, Vice President of the Confederacy.
Upper right: William H. Seward, Lincoln's Secretary of State.
Lower left: John A. Campbell, Ass't. War Secretary of the Confederacy.
Lower right: Robert M. T. Hunter, Confederate Senator from Virginia.

The three Confederates, as peace commissioners, met with Lincoln and Seward in the abortive Hampton Roads Conference of February, 1865.

NORTH AND SOUTH.
"Now, Jeffy, when you think you have had enough of this, say so, and I'll leave off."—(Vide President's Message.)

UNCLE ABE'S VALENTINE SENT BY COLUMBIA.
AN ENVELOPE FULL OF BROKEN CHAINS.

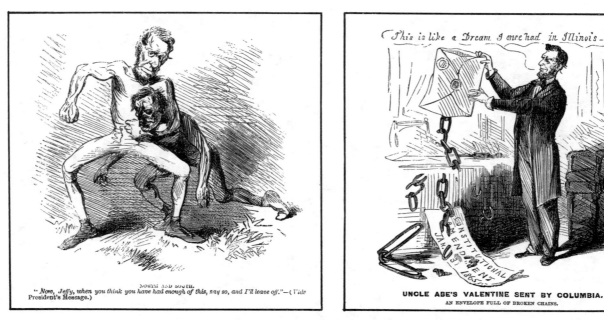

CARTOON COMMENT FROM *LESLIE'S*

Left: A comment on Lincoln's message to Congress of Dec. 6, 1864. Lincoln, pummeling Davis, says: "Now, Jeffy, when you think you have had enough of this, say so, and I'll leave off." *Frank Leslie's Illustrated Newspaper,* Dec. 24, 1864.

Right: A comment on the House of Representatives' passage of the resolution for a thirteenth amendment, Jan. 31, 1865. *Leslie's,* Feb. 25, 1865.

THE PEACE COMMISSION.
Flying to ABRAHAM'S Bosom.

FROM OUR SPECIAL WAR CORRESPONDENT.
"CITY POINT, VA., *April* —, 8.30 A.M.
"All seems well with us."—A. LINCOLN.

CARTOON COMMENT FROM *HARPER'S*

Left: The Confederate peace commissioners—Stephens, Hunter, and Campbell—fly to Abraham's bosom. *Harper's Weekly*, Feb. 18, 1865.

Right: Lincoln at City Point writes: "All seems well with us." This was published in the issue of *Harper's* for April 15, 1865, the day Lincoln died.

THE SECOND INAUGURATION

Chief Justice Chase administering the oath to Lincoln, March 4, 1865. This drawing, published in *Harper's Weekly* for March 18, 1865, was made from an Alexander Gardner photograph which has since disappeared.

In the disposal of the federal patronage Lincoln participated in the campaign more intimately and more continuously than in any other way. He did not always consult or even inform his party leaders about his use of job offers. When Senator Harlan suggested to Hay that the pro-McClellan editor James Gordon Bennett be offered a foreign mission, Hay reflected that Bennett was "too pitchy to touch" and that Lincoln probably thought so, too.[18] Yet Lincoln apparently did touch him.

Lincoln did not go out and campaign for himself: he could not have done so, of course, because of the taboo which, as late as 1864, still showed no signs of breaking down. He would not even "write a general letter to a political meeting" when requested to do so.[19] And yet, when delegations of soldiers or civilians appeared from time to time in the White House yard, he addressed them with remarks which were intended to influence the voters who heard them and the many more who read them in the newspapers. Indeed, he could scarcely have done or said anything without its having, consciously or unconsciously, some electioneering effect. He, after all, was the President and a candidate for re-election. More than that, he was himself the foremost issue of the campaign.

III

In addition to the personalities of the candidates, the issues most frequently and most thoroughly discussed during the campaign were those of Union and disunion, freedom and slavery, war and peace. These were not really discrete questions but, rather, closely intertwined themes. Nor were the differences between the two parties made entirely clear by the stump speakers, pamphleteers, and journalists on either side.

In the contest of semantics the Republicans held a distinct advantage as a result of their appropriation of the term "Union." Their official name, for the duration of the campaign, was the "National Union Party," and the word "Union" appeared prominently on their tickets and throughout their literature. Often the politicians forgot themselves, however, and reverted to the term "Republican," espe-

18 Dennett, . . . *Diaries . . . of John Hay,* 215.
19 Lincoln to I. M. Schermerhorn, Sept. 12, 1864, *Collected Works,* VIII, 2.

cially in their private correspondence, but sometimes in their public pronouncements. A Massachusetts circular calling for the formation of a "Union Club" in every town bore the heading "Headquarters, Republican State Committee." [1] Of course, the existence of a coalition ticket of Lincoln and Johnson, the latter a man of Democratic antecedents, lent some color to the Republican claim to the "Union" designation, as did the support which many War Democrats gave to the ticket. But even Lincoln, in a passing reference to it after the election, spoke of it as "the Union ticket, so called." [2]

To reinforce the implication that the Democrats, in presuming to oppose the administration, were advocates of disunion and treason, the Republicans during the campaign, as before and after it, commonly referred to them as "Copperheads," without discriminating between War and Peace factions or between innocent Sons of Liberty and actual plotters of sedition. In Indiana, Governor Morton drove home the "treason" issue by bringing about military trials of leaders of the Sons at election time. "The most ludicrous aspect of this 'secret' society," writes Kenneth M. Stampp, "was the fact that it was never able to conceal its secrets, and that, so far from aiding the Democracy, its very existence was a source of infinite satisfaction to the Republicans." [3]

The Democrats also tried to benefit from the magic in the "Union" name. At the time of the regular Democratic convention in Chicago, a group of prominent party members staged a "Union Conservative National Convention" in the same city, to denounce the Lincoln government. Later the Democrats organized a series of "Young Men's Democratic Union Clubs," whose members adopted McClellan's letter of acceptance as their manifesto.[4] Democratic speakers appealed again and again to "the friends of the Union and the Constitution." [5] A Tammany Hall broadside—printed in patriotic colors: red and blue ink on white paper—declared for the "preservation of the Union," the "perpetual Union." [6] But the Democrats were never able to identify themselves with the Union cause so convincingly as the Republicans did.

---

[1] John A. Andrew MSS., Mass. Hist. Soc. [2] Nicolay and Hay, *Works,* II, 613.
[3] Stampp, *Indiana Politics During the Civil War,* 241.
[4] H. Liebenau and others to S. J. Tilden, Sept. 15, 1864, Tilden MSS., N. Y. Pub. Lib.
[5] F. H. Churchill and others to S. J. Tilden, Sept. 1, 1864, Tilden MSS.
[6] Tilden, MSS.

The Chicago Platform, which McClellan's letter could not entirely cancel, put the Democrats on the defensive. That platform, the Republicans kept insisting, "gives a silent approval of the Rebellion itself, and an open condemnation of the war waged for its suppression." [7] And many Democrats themselves feared, as one of them expressed it: "That platform will cost the Democratic party the defeat of McClellan. Tens of thousands of Republicans & War Democrats votes would have been polled for McClellan, who will now vote for Lincoln unpleasant as it may be." [8] That platform gave Republican orators golden opportunities, and they took advantage of them. "There is but one question before the country in the approaching canvass," General John A. Dix told a Philadelphia mass meeting. "Shall we prosecute the war with unabated vigor until the rebel forces lay down their arms; or shall we, to use the language of the Chicago Convention, make 'immediate efforts' for 'a cessation of hostilities,' with a view to an ultimate convention of all the States, etc." [9] General James A. Garfield, addressing a Cincinnati crowd, found apt alliteration in the names of the Democratic candidates for governor and vice president as he declaimed against those Ohioans who were "for Pugh and Pendleton, and Peace at any price." [10]

A number of Republican papers harped incessantly upon the charge that every rebel and every sympathizer with rebellion was working and praying for Lincoln's defeat. But the opposition press could quote Southern opinion to show that the Confederacy could hope for no advantage from a victory by the Democrats. "They would like peace on condition of our return to the Union, and they are fools enough to believe that a majority of the people in the Confederacy are in favor of reunion," the Richmond *Dispatch* had said, long before the campaign of 1864 began. "But they are as bitterly opposed to separation as Lincoln himself, or any of the thieves and murderers who lead his armies." [11] Robert C. Winthrop, an eloquent Boston Democrat, once a Whig friend of Daniel Webster, turned the Republican charge back upon the Republicans by insinuating that Southerners preferred Lincoln for President of the United States. "We all know that the seces-

[7] "Appeal of the National Union Committee to the People of the United States," circular dated N. Y., Sept. 9, 1864.

[8] J. W. Rathbone to Manton Marble, Nov. 4, 1864, Marble MSS.

[9] Cincinnati *Daily Gazette,* Oct. 12, 1864, p. 1, c. 3.

[10] *Ibid.,* p. 1, c. 4.

[11] Quoted in *ibid.,* Jan. 27, 1863.

sion leaders of the South . . . exulted in the election of Abraham Lincoln," Winthrop declared at a great New York "ratification" meeting, harking back to 1860, ". . . because it supplied the very fuel which was needed for kindling this awful conflagration." [12]

Democrats repeated their familiar cry that the war, as carried on by the Republican administration, was not a war for the preservation of the Union. "If Lincoln is re-elected, the war will last at least four years longer," one of their journals said. "He is waging it, sacrificing the white population of the North, to free the degraded negro slaves of the South." [13] Such Radical Republican spokesmen as Salmon P. Chase frankly avowed abolition as a leading war aim. "People are resolved on Union & Freedom & recognize in Lincoln & Johnson the representatives of these great ideas," Chase averred.[14] In Missouri, where he had gone as Lincoln's personal mediator, John G. Nicolay appealed to the quarreling factions, as he reported back to Lincoln, to patch up their differences so as to elect Republican congressmen and help "get a two-thirds vote in the House and thus be able to pass the Constitutional Amendment about Slavery." [15]

In an effort to get the labor vote, some Republicans sought to define the issue of freedom in broader terms than the mere abolition of Negro slavery. The wealthy Boston merchant J. M. Forbes urged "bringing into prominence the great Issue—*Democratic Institutions against Aristocratic ones.* Mr. Lincoln must not depend upon the rich or aristocratic classes." The party must concentrate upon "appealing to the *plain people.*" [16] One of Cameron's correspondents suggested a different approach to the laboring man. "But Pa. has a peculiar class of interests, mining, manufacturing & rail road, deeply interested in the reelection of Mr. L.," Cameron was reminded, "& a combination of which, by securing funds, & also by influencing the operatives in their employ, would secure a very decided success in the Octr election." [17] The tariff issue was the means thus to get the operatives' vote, and at least in Pennsylvania the perennial protection-

---

12 Pamphlet in McClellan MSS., Lib. of Cong.

13 Pittsburgh *Daily Post,* Sept. 9, 1864.

14 Chase to Z. Eastman, Oct. 24, 1864, Chicago Hist. Soc.

15 Hay to Lincoln, Oct. 18, 1864, R. T. L. Coll., 37371–76.

16 J. M. Forbes to F. P. Blair, Sept. 18, 1864, R. T. L. Coll., 36422–23.

17 M. Ryerson to Cameron, Sept. 10, 1864, Cameron MSS.

ist arguments were not entirely neglected during the campaign. But the Democrats outdid the Republicans in workingclass appeal. They made the most of such labor grievances as the high cost of living, which they blamed upon the Lincoln administration.[18]

Lincoln stated his own view of the interconnection between the issues of Union, freedom, and war when he was interviewed, in August, by Governor Alexander Randall and Circuit Judge John T. Mills of Wisconsin. This interview, first reported in the Grant County, Wisconsin, *Herald,* was afterward reprinted by Republican newspapers and was also circulated as a campaign broadside throughout the North. "There is no programme offered by any wing of the Democratic party but that must result in the permanent destruction of the Union," the President told his Wisconsin visitors at the Soldiers' Home. "But, Mr. President," one of them protested, "General McClellan is in favor of crushing out the rebellion by force. He will be the Chicago candidate." Then Lincoln patiently explained how "arithmetic" would prove his point. There were, he said, nearly two hundred thousand able-bodied colored men in the service of the United States, most of them under arms. "Abandon all the posts now garrisoned by black men; take 200,000 men from our side and put them into the battlefield or cornfield against us, and we would be compelled to abandon the war in three weeks." His enemies pretended, Lincoln went on, that he was carrying on the war for the sole purpose of abolition, but this was not true. "So long as I am President it shall be carried on for the sole purpose of restoring the Union. But no human power can subdue the rebellion without the use of the emancipation policy, and every policy calculated to weaken the moral and physical forces of the rebellion." [19]

When, on the evening of October 19, a group of Marylanders serenaded Lincoln at the White House, his impromptu response reinforced the standard Republican argument that a Democratic victory would mean unconditional peace with disunion and slavery. He said he believed the people were "still resolved to preserve their country and their liberty," but how they voted was their own business. "If they should deliberately resolve to have immediate peace even at the

18 New York *Herald,* July 26, 1864, p. 5, c. 4.

19 Clipping from Grant County *Herald* as reprinted in unidentified newspaper, R. T. L. Coll., 36047; Republican broadside, n. p., n. d.

loss of their country, and their liberty, I know not the power or the right to resist them." [20]

IV

Even those who saw little difference in issues between the two parties, asserted that there was a vast difference in the personal fitness of the two candidates for the high office of President. Partisans of both sides considered as woefully unfit the candidate they opposed. So a good deal of the campaigning consisted of sheer defamation.

Among Republicans the favorite epithets for McClellan were "traitor" and "coward," and they ransacked his military record for evidences of his craven ways and his downright villainy. In search of new scandal the zealous editor John W. Forney looked to Lincoln. "Can you tell me whether the arrest of the members of the Maryland Legislature [in 1861] was opposed by General McClellan, or whether it was recommended by him?" Forney inquired. "A single word in reply to this will enable me to complete what I think will be a most damaging article for him for to-morrow's paper." [1] But Lincoln was not the man to abet such a campaign of vilification. "I never heard him speak of McClellan in any other than terms of the highest personal respect and kindness," testified another editor, Alexander K. McClure, who spent a fair amount of time with the President during the electioneering season. "He never doubted McClellan's loyalty to the government or to the cause that called him to high military command." [2]

Lincoln was a target for even more mud than McClellan was. Lincoln was a power-mad dictator, a "scoundrel" and a "tyrant," according to indignant stump speakers, who seemed to think that his opponent would be far less dangerous in the presidency, though that opponent was a military man who once had shown some signs of a Napoleonic complex. The former Whig President, Millard Fillmore, now a McClellan supporter, admitted that he did not favor the election of "military chieftains" as a general rule, but he believed that a "military man of disinterested devotion to his country" (meaning

---

20 *Collected Works,* VIII, 52–53.

1 Forney to Lincoln, Sept. 1, 1864, R. T. L. Coll., 35800.

2 McClure, *Lincoln and Men of War-Times,* 207.

McClellan) could "do more to save it from ruin than any other" (meaning Lincoln).[3] Certainly, in the view of Democrats, Lincoln was not an indispensable man.

The Republicans did not exactly say he was, but they did advise the voters: "It is no time to change leaders when you are confronting a powerful and wily foe—'No time to swap horses in the middle of the stream.' "[4] Lincoln himself had put this "swap horses" expression into currency, when the Baltimore convention was meeting in June. And he did seem to think that, in the circumstances, his continued services were indispensable to the nation. In running for re-election he was motivated not by "personal vanity or ambition," as he told his Wisconsin visitors in the well-publicized August interview, but by "solicitude for his great country."[5]

When not denouncing him for his alleged dictatorial proclivities, the Democrats condemned him for what they considered his loutish ways. The New York *World* characterized the Lincoln-Johnson ticket as made up of "a rail-splitting buffoon and a boorish tailor, both from the backwoods, both growing up in uncouth ignorance."[6] And the New York *Herald,* while editor Bennett was still in an anti-Lincoln phase, had this to say: "Mr. Lincoln is a country lawyer of more than average shrewdness, and of far more than the average indelicacy which marks the Western wit."[7] McClellan, on the other hand, was a gentleman with the dignity becoming to the White House, at least according to the Democrats. When installed in the presidential mansion, he would see that callers would "put on their best clothes & make themselves clean," as one of his admirers wrote to Mrs. McClellan. "It is the cultivation of the feeling that the President is no better than any other citizen, that has brought us to the election of such ordinary men as Abraham Lincoln."[8]

Such phrases as "rail-splitting buffoon," the "indelicacy" of his "Western wit," and "Abe, the vulgar joker" were intended to turn against Lincoln one of the traits that most endeared him to the people

[3] Fillmore to Mrs. McClellan, Mar. 24, 1864, McClellan MSS.

[4] Union League circular, dated Washington, Oct. 18, 1864, R. T. L. Coll., 37382.

[5] Clipping from Grant County, Wisconsin, *Herald,* as reprinted in unidentified newspaper, R. T. L. Coll., 36047.

[6] Quoted in Washington *Daily Morning Chronicle,* June 20, 1864, p. 2, c. 3.

[7] New York *Herald,* Sept. 9, 1864, p. 4, c. 2.

[8] J. S. Fay to Mrs. McClellan, Sept. 22, 1864, McClellan MSS.

—his sense of humor. A more elaborate piece of propaganda, adorning the theme of his crudeness and insensitivity, was an old story about the "Antietam song-singing," which the Democrats revived, elaborated, and then repeated, with variations, throughout the campaign.

One version of the canard, published in the New York *World,* was this: "While the President [after the battle of Antietam in September, 1862] was driving over the field in an ambulance, accompanied by Marshal Lamon, General McClellan, and another officer, heavy details of men were engaged in the task of burying the dead. The ambulance had just reached the neighborhood of the old stone bridge, where the dead were piled highest, when Mr. Lincoln, suddenly slapping Marshal Lamon on the knee, exclaimed: 'Come, Lamon, give us that song about Picayune Butler; McClellan has never heard it.' 'Not now, if you please,' said General McClellan, with a shudder; 'I would prefer to hear it some other place and time.' " But Lamon went ahead and sang the funny song, and Lincoln relished it.[9]

Another version, printed in the *Essex Statesman* and (like the *World's* version) reprinted by other Democratic papers, told how, "soon after one of the most desperate and sanguinary battles," Lincoln was being shown over the field by an unnamed commanding general, who was of course McClellan. Finally, Lincoln said, "This makes a fellow feel gloomy." Turning to a companion, he asked, "Jack, can't you give us something to cheer us up. Give us a song, and give us a lively one." Obligingly, Jack "struck up, as loud as he could bawl, a comic negro song," and he kept it up until the general, in deference to the feelings of his soldiers, requested the President to quiet his friend. "We know that the story is incredible," commented the *Essex Statesman* as it proceeded to point the moral of the tale. "The story can't be true of any man fit for any office of trust, or even for decent society; but the story is every whit true of Abraham Lincoln." [10]

Referring to the anecdote as given in the New York *World,* a Democrat wrote to McClellan and asked if it was true.[11] What reply McClellan gave to this inquiry, if any, is not on record, but he issued no public denial to scotch the story.

[9] Quoted in Lamon, *Recollections of Abraham Lincoln,* 141–142.

[10] Clipping from *Essex* [Massachusetts] *Statesman,* as reprinted in unidentified news paper, R. T. L. Coll., 35007.

[11] J. S. Philip to McClellan, Oct. 1, 1864, McClellan MSS.

A Republican appealed to Lamon for a repudiation. Already Lamon had begged Lincoln to refute the slander, but Lincoln had said: "Let the thing alone." Now Lamon took it upon himself to write out a refutation and a protest, which he showed to Lincoln. Lincoln criticized Lamon's remarks as too belligerent and thought it would be better simply to state the facts. The facts were that the incident had occurred sixteen days after the battle and several miles from the battlefield (and, as Lamon recalled in his reminiscences, Lincoln had requested "a little sad song," not a comic one). "Let me try my hand at it," said Lincoln, and he himself wrote out a statement, then told Lamon to keep it until the proper time to make it public. But Lincoln never found the proper time.[12]

At the close of the campaign he remarked to John Hay: "It is a little singular that I, who am not a vindictive man, should have always been before the people for election in canvasses marked for their bitterness: always but once; when I came to Congress it was a quiet time." [13]

V

"The Democrats will enter the coming canvass," the New York *World* complained on August 25, 1864, "under the great disadvantage of having to contend against the greatest patronage and the greatest money-power ever wielded in a presidential election." [1] And an Indiana Democrat predicted confidentially that Lincoln would "in all probability be re-elected," because the group that controlled "legitimately nine hundred millions of Dollars a year," and would control "corruptly" much more than that, could hardly be dislodged.[2] There was considerable justice in these Democratic complaints. As the campaign got under way, Lincoln and his campaign directors proceeded with a determination that Federal jobholders and other beneficiaries of the government must do their part for the administration party and all its candidates.

After removing the Chase man Horace Binney from the New York

[12] Lamon, *Recollections of Abraham Lincoln,* 142–146.

[13] Dennett, . . . *Diaries* . . . *of John Hay,* 233.

[1] Quoted in Carman and Luthin, *Lincoln and the Patronage,* 293.

[2] W. S. Holman to Allen Hamilton, Mar. 17, 1864, MS., Lincoln Nat'l Life Foundation, Fort Wayne, Ind.

Custom House, Lincoln rapidly brought into line the employees of this politically most important of all such establishments. The new collector, Simeon Draper, had to dismiss only a few of the deputy collectors, weighers, inspectors, and debenture officers in order to discipline the rest. In September Lincoln himself removed the surveyor of the port, Rufus F. Andrews, and appointed the New York postmaster, Abram Wakefield, in his place. Then he named James Kelly as postmaster. "The appointment of Draper as collector, Wakeman as surveyor, and Kelly as postmaster of New York City," say the two most thorough students of Lincoln's patronage policies, "indicated that Lincoln fully realized that the Seward-Weed faction of Republicans must be awarded more recognition if the Empire State was to be made secure for Lincoln in November." [3]

He used his patronage power not only in his own behalf but also on behalf of those members of Congress who were loyal to his administration. He rebuked the Philadelphia postmaster for restraining a couple of hundred postal employees from aiding in the renomination of William D. Kelley. He checked the Chicago postmaster, who was working against Isaac N. Arnold. When George W. Julian, of Indiana, complained to him that Commissioner of Patents David P. Holloway, also a Hoosier, refused to recognize Julian as the regular party nominee, he replied to Julian: "Your nomination is as binding on Republicans as mine, and you can rest assured that Mr. Holloway shall support you, openly and unconditionally, or lose his head." [4]

Lincoln expected officeholders to act as loyal party workers, and the great majority of them did. They performed the lowly chores necessary for holding rallies, distributing campaign documents, and otherwise garnering votes. At a big meeting at the Cooper Institute in New York, the Federal officials in that city turned out "almost *en masse*," according to the New York *World,* which listed the names of many of them. And, according to the Indianapolis *Daily State Sentinel,* a hundred government clerks were kept busy in congressional committee rooms with mailing out Lincoln propaganda. They "continue to draw their salaries while engaged in re-electing Abraham Lincoln. They neglect the business of the country, for which only they ought to be paid." [5]

---

[3] Carman and Luthin, *Lincoln and the Patronage,* 280–281.

[4] *Ibid.,* 282–285. See also R. T. L. Coll., 34600.

[5] Carman and Luthin, 287, 296–297.

Some of the government employees balked, presenting touchy problems to Lincoln and his deputy dispensers of the patronage. The most serious problem of this sort arose at the Brooklyn Navy Yard, and it was an especially urgent one because of Lincoln's desperate need for votes in the crucial state of New York. The chairman of the Union State Committee, Charles Jones, reported in August to campaign-manager Raymond: "It cannot be questioned that nearly one half of the employees of the Govt. in the Brooklyn Navy-Yard are hostile to the present Administration, and will oppose the reelection of Mr. Lincoln. Of this number there are Mechanics in the different departments who must be retained, but I have no doubt that of the 6,000 to 7,000 employed it will not be necessary for the efficient working of the departments to retain as many as 1,000 who are opposed to us." [6]

Wholesale dismissals were needed to rid the Navy Yard of men who were "actually loud mouthed and insulting in their expressions of hostility to what they call the Black Republican Administration." But the existing rules of employment stood in the way, and the President or the secretary of the navy would have to intervene. Raymond went to Washington and "explained these matters" to Lincoln and Gideon Welles and, according to his own account, "received from the Secretary assurances of a disposition to remedy all these evils." [7] But Welles, a month later, left a different impression in his diary: "I am not sufficiently ductile for Mr. Raymond, Chairman of the National Executive Committee, who desires to make the navy yard a party machine." Welles indicated a disinclination to aid Raymond "by the arbitrary and despotic exercise of power" from his own office.[8]

At last, a few weeks before election day, a number of workmen were discharged—not thousands of them but enough (fifty-one out of a total of fifty-three employed in one particular shop) to serve, perhaps, as a healthy example to the rest. When the Democratic papers protested that the only grounds for the dismissal of the fifty-one was their avowed intention to vote for McClellan, the Republican Brooklyn *Daily Eagle* explained that only loyal men should be allowed to work on Union ships, and added: "The only questions asked were,

[6] Jones to Raymond, Aug. 2, 1864, MS., N. Y. Pub. Lib.

[7] Raymond to Seward, Aug. 5, 1864, MS., N. Y. Pub. Lib.

[8] Welles, *Diary*, II, 136.

whether they were loyal men or not, and whether they were Union men or Democrats, which amounted to just the same thing." [9]

Federal employees, from the highest to the lowest, were expected not only to work and vote for Lincoln but also to contribute to the Republican campaign chest. The various committees—national, state, and congressional—all gave considerable attention to money-raising activities. "Does your State Committee expect to make *exclusive* assessments upon Federal officeholders within the State for the purpose of the canvass," Raymond inquired of Cameron, "or is our Committee to go over the same ground?" [10] Raymond collected five hundred dollars apiece from cabinet members, directed the assessing of employees in all the departments, and levied "an average of three per cent of their yearly pay" on the workers in the New York Custom House. Senator Harlan, on behalf of the congressional campaign committee, franked letters to postmasters throughout the North, demanding from them sums ranging from two to one hundred and fifty dollars, depending on the size of the post office. When a jobholder declined to pay, the campaign directors used their influence to have him discharged. "Pressure was brought to bear upon Lincoln, who," say Professors Carman and Luthin, "seems to have had full knowledge of this expedient and at least did nothing that served to discourage it." [11]

The fund-raisers did not confine themselves to Federal employees but also turned to individuals and firms doing business with the government. Raymond sent out a circular appealing to war contractors, and from one of them alone—Phelps, Dodge and Company, New York dealers in metals—he received at least $3,000. Cameron got large sums from a Philadelphia businessman who expected him to secure government contracts in return.[12] "Simonds, a fortunate contractor and builder of wagons for Govt. has given $50,000," an envious Democratic worker reported to one of his own party's strategists. "An officer has been detailed both at Phila. and New York, to ascertain from Quarter Masters in charge of those places, the names of those who have been favored with Govt. patronage, for the purpose of levying assessments upon them." [13] Jay Cooke and Company, the bankers and

9 Carman and Luthin, *Lincoln and the Patronage,* 298.

10 Raymond to Cameron, July 17, 1864, Cameron MSS.

11 Carman and Luthin, *Lincoln and the Patronage,* 288–289, 292–293.

12 *Ibid.,* 290–292.

13 Samuel North to Manton Marble, Sept. 28, 1864, Marble MSS.

sellers of government bonds, gave Cameron a checking account of $1,000, to be drawn upon as needed for his committee's expenses.[14]

How much money the Republicans raised and spent, all together, would be impossible to guess. One Democratic worker thought they had a fund of a million dollars exclusively for the October election in Pennsylvania, but another Democratic worker estimated the true figure as being nearer a half million.[15] The Democrats themselves, by their own accounting, spent only $32,475 in that same October election.[16] There can be no doubt that, whatever the exact sums, the Republicans received and disbursed a tremendous and unprecedented total and one far larger than the Democrats could aspire to. Lincoln certainly had the advantages of patronage and the purse.

VI

If the President's appointive powers comprised an asset in a political campaign, so too, in war time, did his powers as Commander-in-Chief of the Army and Navy. The Democrats were "impressed with the opinion that Lincoln's best prospects of re-election" were "based on his power to control the votes of the army." [1] To politicians on both sides it seemed that the votes of soldier citizens might prove decisive, and to Lincoln himself the utilization of those votes was a matter of deep personal interest.

Politicians both Republican and Democratic hoped to get a party endorsement from leading army officers, for this presumably would influence both civilian and soldier voters. The officers whose commitments were most eagerly sought were, of course, Sherman and Grant. Sherman inclined toward McClellan, or so at least some of the Democrats thought, and one of them, a Boston cotton broker, wrote McClellan to ask whether they could outflank the Republicans "by getting a letter from Gen Sherman (who it is very generally believed here advocates your election) endorsing the Chicago nominations?" [2] But Sherman remained noncommittal. Grant favored Lincoln,

---

[14] J. K. Moorhead to Cameron, July 22, 1864, Cameron MSS.

[15] S. North to Marble, Sept. 28, 1864, and H. M. Phillips to Marble, Sept. 30, 1864, Marble MSS.

[16] H. M. Phillips to R. E. Randall, Nov. 5, 1864, Marble MSS.

[1] Washington *Daily Constitutional Union,* Aug. 10, 1864, p. 1, c. 6.

[2] E. H. Kettell to McClellan, Sept. 24, 1864, McClellan MSS.

or so Republicans said, but Lincoln himself seems to have doubted whether he really had Grant's wholehearted support.[3] At any rate, the Republicans were able to make extensive use of a letter which Grant and written in August opposing the election of any "Peace candidate." [4] Among the officers in the Army of the Potomac, the Democrats started a subscription to buy a testimonial gift for McClellan, but abandoned the project because their opponents "misconstrued" it and because they themselves feared it might offend McClellan's successor as commanding officer, Meade, whom they aspired to win over.[5] "Genl. Meade is on the fence as far as I can learn," a Democrat in the Army of the Potomac reported to McClellan, "but the prevailing sentiment at his Hd. Qrs. is in your favor." [6] Rosecrans also wavered, sometimes talking like a McClellan man, but Nicolay, after seeing Rosecrans in Missouri, advised Lincoln on ways to bring him definitely to the administration side.[7]

Whatever the consensus among Army officers may have been, Republicans became more and more confident, as the campaign progressed, that the overwhelming majority of the men in the ranks were for Lincoln. "There were in the Western Army many McClellan men at the time of his nomination," an Illinois soldier in Sherman's army reported from Atlanta at the end of September, "but since the platform has been read and then to know that the nomination of McClellan was made unanimous on the motion of that Traitor Valindlingham [*sic*] is more than the admirers of little 'Mac' could stand and I can assure that 'Mac' has lost thousands of votes within three weeks." [8] A straw vote in this soldier's regiment, the 45th, produced 329 votes for Lincoln and only 16 for McClellan. A few weeks later a test ballot in one corps of the Army of the Potomac gave "3,500 votes Union and 500 for McClellan," and soldier ballotings elsewhere yielded similar results.[9]

---

[3] "Well, McClure," Lincoln is quoted as saying late in October, "I have no reason to believe that Grant prefers my election to that of McClellan." McClure, *Lincoln and Men of War-Times,* 185–187.

[4] Washington *Evening Star,* Sept. 9, 1864, p. 2, c. 1.

[5] Arthur McClellan to George B. McClellan, Sept. 26, 1864, McClellan MSS. See also Washington *Daily Morning Chronicle,* Sept. 25, 1864, p. 2, c. 2.

[6] M. F. McMahon to McClellan, Oct. 10, 1864, McClellan MSS.

[7] Nicolay to Lincoln, Oct. 12, 1864, R. T. L. Coll., 37168–69.

[8] Evans Blake to Washburne, Sept. 30, 1864, Washburne MSS.

[9] Cincinnati *Daily Gazette,* Oct. 18, 1864.

But Republican party workers did not take the soldier vote for granted. Their congressional campaign committee sent an agent to scatter "Union" literature among the soldiers, and he reported shortly before election day that he had "distributed nearly a million of documents, nearly all to the Army from Maine to La." [10] McClellan's brother, at the Harrisonburg headquarters of the 6th Army Corps, complained to McClellan: "Nothing is seen by the troops but Republican papers and the Democrats seem to be afraid to open their mouths or do anything." [11] A Democratic worker in the Army of the Potomac, pleading for "papers, tracts and so forth," said that the Republicans were "sending them down by the wagon loads" while there was "not one yet for our side." [12] But some Democratic officers found ways of dealing with the excess of Republican propaganda. "Maj. Hancock (brother of the General) tells us that the McClellan colonels destroy whole boxes of Republican documents sent to them," a Democrat proudly informed his own national committee. "They don't allow the soldiers to see them." [13]

Lincoln himself was careful not to offend soldier opinion. Whenever he addressed groups of uniformed men in Washington, as he did on several occasions during campaigning season, he praised them for their labors and sacrifices in upholding the Union.[14] And he gave heed to soldier feelings when, late in September, he faced the difficult question of going ahead with the scheduled new draft. Some of the frightened politicians, especially Governor Morton of Indiana, begged him to postpone the draft until after election day. Otherwise, the Indiana Republicans insisted, they would lose their state.[15] But Lincoln had a dispatch from Sherman, dated September 17, 1864, which he recopied in his own hand and which he no doubt pondered carefully. "The Secretary of War tells me the draft will be made on Monday next. If the President modifies it to the extent of one man, or wavers in its execution," Sherman had warned, "he is gone over. The Army would vote against him." [16] Lincoln went ahead with the draft.

---

[10] G. T. Brown to Lyman Trumbull, Nov. 5, 1864, Trumbull MSS.

[11] Arthur McClellan to G. B. McClellan, Oct. 2, 1864, McClellan MSS.

[12] Unsigned letter to Manton Marble, Sept. 22, 1864, Marble MSS.

[13] G. W. Adams to Marble, Sept. 27, 1864, Marble MSS.

[14] Cincinnati *Daily Gazette*, June 13, 1864, p. 3, c. 6; Baltimore *Sun*, Aug. 23, 1864, p. 2, c. 1, and Sept. 2, 1864, p. 1, c. 7.

[15] Stampp, *Indiana Politics during the Civil War*, 250–251.

[16] R. T. L. Coll., 36417.

Well before the election every Northern state (except Oregon) considered the matter of amending its constitution or passing legislation so as to make possible the counting of soldier votes cast in the army. Most of the states—those with Republican-controlled legislatures—made provision either for voting in the field or for voting by proxy at home, but none of the states with Democratic-controlled legislatures did so.[17] In these states, only those soldiers home on furlough at election time could legally vote. Lincoln watched with keen interest the action of the various states on soldier voting, and when, in California, the voting arrangement was declared unconstitutional, he "was sorry to see the Courts there had thrown *out* the soldier's right to vote," and he thought "it a bad augury for the success of the loyal cause on Nov. 8th." [18]

He was prepared to co-operate fully with his party's managers when they undertook, in accordance with state laws, to gather in the votes of men in the armed forces far from home. These votes were especially needed in New York. When the chairman of the New York state committee appealed to Lincoln "to obtain facilities for taking the votes of Seamen & Sailors," Lincoln obliged him with a note to Secretary of the Navy Welles: "Please do all for him in this respect which you consistently can." [19] The next day Lincoln, with Seward, called personally at Welles' office. "Wanted one of our boats to be placed at the disposal of the New York commission to gather votes in the Mississippi Squadron," Welles noted. Welles did not like the idea, "and yet," he thought, "it seems ungracious to oppose it." He gave his permission.[20]

Some of the Democrats were even more eager than Lincoln and Seward to get the New York soldier vote, so eager indeed that they were willing to steal it. According to the New York proxy system, a soldier in the field sealed up his ballot and sent it to his home county to be opened for him on election day. A couple of zealous Democratic workers in Washington intercepted large numbers of these ballots, unsealed the envelopes, put in ballots marked for the Democratic ticket, and sent them on. These "ballot-box stuffers" were said to have had more than twenty men at work for them and to have been "sending off the ballots, as fabricated by them, in dry-goods boxes full."

[17] Benton, *Voting in the Field,* chap. xxx.

[18] H. Bellows to his son, Nov. 2, 1864, Bellows MSS., Mass. Hist. Soc.

[19] Lincoln to Welles, Oct. 10, 1864, Lincoln Coll., N. Y. Pub. Lib.

[20] Welles, *Diary,* II, 175.

Before election day the two ringleaders were apprehended, tried, and sentenced to long prison terms, with the approval of Stanton and Lincoln.[21]

Although Pennsylvania had authorized its soldiers to vote in the field, "as fully as if they were present at their usual place of election," [22] Lincoln after the rather unsatisfactory returns in October was unwilling to depend on their absentee ballots for victory in November. "He knew that his election was in no sense doubtful," according to McClure, "but he knew that if he lost New York and with it Pennsylvania on the home vote, the moral effect of his triumph would be broken and his power to prosecute the war and make peace would be greatly impaired." McClure told him there was no reasonable prospect of carrying Pennsylvania on the "home vote." Lincoln asked: "Well, what is to be done?" McClure advised him to see that Meade and Sheridan each furloughed five thousand Pennsylvania troops in time to vote at home. Lincoln did so.[23]

In Indiana, where the unamended state constitution forbade voting in the field, Governor Morton and Representative Colfax desperately sought soldier votes for the October election. Colfax repeatedly begged Sherman to send his Indiana soldiers home, but Sherman wrote him that this was "impossible." Colfax was not satisfied, and he wrote to Lincoln. "About ⅓ of each Regiment are minors," he pointed out to the President. "Why not leave them, & let the voters come . . . ?" Lincoln endorsed Colfax's letter and turned it over to Stanton.[24] Still Sherman did nothing. Finally Morton went to Washington to see Lincoln, and Lincoln sent a note direct to Sherman, suggesting that he let some Indiana men go home. Even then, Sherman's response was far from satisfactory to the Hoosier politicians.[25]

In Illinois, where (as in Indiana) there was a stalemate between governor and legislature and no arrangement had been made for absentee balloting, Governor Yates became frantic about furloughs as the November election approached. In response to his appeals Secre-

---

21 Cincinnati *Daily Gazette,* Oct. 27, 1864, p. 3, c. 5; Oct. 31, 1864, p. 3, c. 3; Nov. 3, 1864, p. 1, c. 8; Nov. 5, 1864, p. 3, c. 4 and 8.

22 Washington *Daily Morning Chronicle,* Mar. 12, 1864, p. 2, c. 1.

23 McClure, *Lincoln and Men of War-Times,* 185–187.

24 Colfax to [Lincoln], Aug. 29, 1864, Stanton MSS., Lib. of Cong. On the back of the letter is the endorsement: "Submitted to the Sec. of War Sept. 3/1864 A Lincoln."

25 Stampp, *Indiana Politics during the Civil War,* 251–252.

tary Stanton on October 28 ordered General Rosecrans to furlough several regiments of Illinois troops to enable them to vote. But on October 30 the war department, faced with a military emergency on top of a political one, ordered these troops sent to Nashville to reinforce General Thomas, who expected an attack from the approaching Confederate army of Beauregard. Immediately, on November 1, Yates sent a long and frenzied telegram directly to Lincoln. "Defeat in Illinois is worse than defeat in the field," Yates argued, "and I do hope that you will immediately order that these Regiments may be allowed to remain and vote, on the route to Tennessee." Lincoln did not flatly turn down this candid appeal from Yates. He directed that a reply be wired to him saying merely that, until the Illinois regiments had reached St. Louis on their way from Missouri to Tennessee, his telegram could not be "fully answered." [26]

VII

In some parts of the country the Republicans, expecting violence, awaited election day with apprehension. In Illinois, Stanton was informed, more than five thousand armed Confederates were roaming at large. "They intend to vote at the coming election and by terrorism to keep from the polls more than 5,000 *citizens.*" [1] In the city of New York, Stanton heard, the rebels intended not only to jam the polls with "enemies" but also to start a general conflagration.[2] From New York and a number of other cities the War Department received appeals for troops to protect the polls, and a regiment was sent to New York, but General Halleck exclaimed that if the army were to respond to only half of the requests, "we would not have a single soldier to meet the rebels in the field!" [3]

When November 8 came, however, no serious disturbances interfered with the polling anywhere. In Illinois the qualified voters—white men over twenty-one with a year's residence in the state—patiently waited their turns to vote, standing single file in long lines

---

26 Yates to Lincoln, Nov. 1, 1864, and T. M. Vincent to Yates, Nov. 2, 1864, *Offic. Rec.,* 3 ser., IV, 871–872.

1 H. E. Payne to Stanton, Sept. 8, 1864, Stanton MSS.

2 Stanton to Dix, October 23, 1864, and Grant to Dix, October 24, 1864, *Offic. Rec.,* 1 ser., XLIII, pt. 2, pp. 463–464.

3 Halleck to Lieber, Oct. 26, 1864, Lieber MSS., Huntington Lib.

at many polling places. Saloons were closed, and in Springfield, where it rained steadily most of the day, the *Illinois State Journal* noted that "fewer drunken people were seen upon the streets than usual." [4] From New York, General Butler, in command of the Federal troops, telegraphed laconically to the war department at noon: "The quietest city ever seen." [5]

But Butler had not seen Washington that day. It was even quieter. The day was dark and rainy, and the city was considerably depopulated by the homeward exodus of more than eighteen thousand voters, mostly government employees. "The rush to the cars of those going home to vote was too much for the railroads," a news dispatch reported two days before the election. "Some four hundred were left behind, but by the aid of extra trains, all have been able to get off to-day." [6] The White House was almost deserted, and the President, beginning to look "care-worn and dilapidated," [7] was by himself when Noah Brooks called at noon. Lincoln did not attempt to hide his anxiety about the election. "I am just enough of a politician to know that there was not much doubt about the results of the Baltimore convention," he told Brooks; "but about this thing I am very far from being certain. I wish I was certain." [8]

In the evening, the weather still rainy and "steamy," Lincoln went with a party including Brooks and Hay to the telegraph office, to get the returns as they came in. "We splashed through the grounds to the side door of the War Department where a soaked and smoking sentinel was standing in his own vapor with his huddled-up frame covered with a rubber cloak." Upstairs, the President was handed the reports of the early returns, which were extremely favorable. He sent out the "first fruits" to Mrs. Lincoln. "She is more anxious than I," he explained.[9] Later in the evening the reports began to come in slowly because of the rainstorm, which interfered with the telegraph, and during the lulls he entertained the group around him with anecdotes.

By midnight, though to his great disappointment he had not heard

---

4 Paul G. Hubbard, The Lincoln-McClellan Presidential Election in Illinois (MS. doctoral dissertation, Univ. of Ill., 1949), 191–192, 196–197.

5 Dennett, . . . *Diaries* . . . *of John Hay,* 233.

6 Cincinnati *Daily Gazette,* Nov. 7, 1864, p. 3, c. 3.

7 L. D. Campbell to Andrew Johnson, Nov. 12, 1864, Johnson MSS., Lib. of Cong.

8 Brooks, *Washington in Lincoln's Time,* 216–217.

9 Dennett, . . . *Diaries* . . . *of John Hay,* 233–234.

from Illinois (or Iowa), Lincoln could be "tolerably certain" that Maryland, Pennsylvania, most of the Middle West, and all of New England would go for him.[10] A midnight supper was brought in, and Hay observed how "The President went awkwardly and hospitably to work shovelling out the fried oysters." [11] As he received congratulations on what looked like a sure and decisive victory, Lincoln appeared utterly calm, with no trace of elation or excitement. He did say "he would admit that he was glad to be relieved of all suspense, and that he was grateful that the verdict of the people was likely to be so full, clear, and unmistakable that there could be no dispute."

About two o'clock in the morning a messenger brought the information that a crowd of Pennsylvanians were serenading the White House. Lincoln went home and, in response to cries for a speech, he talked for a few minutes, concluding: "If I know my heart, my gratitude is free from any taint of personal triumph. I do not impugn the motives of any one opposed to me. It is no pleasure to me to triumph over any one, but I give thanks to the Almighty for this evidence of the people's resolution to stand by free government and the rights of humanity." [12]

VIII

Slightly more than four million votes were cast, and counted, for presidential electors in 1864. Of these, Lincoln's electors received approximately 55 per cent, or about four hundred thousand more than McClellan did (but McClellan got practically as many popular votes as Lincoln had got in 1860). Lincoln's majority of the electoral vote was even more impressive—234 to 21—as he carried every state in the Union except Delaware, New Jersey, and Kentucky. Yet, as an analysis of the voting will show, the election was actually closer than it seemed, and the worries that beset Lincoln even as late as election day were by no means far-fetched.

His strength varied considerably from place to place. The state he carried by the largest proportion of the votes cast was Massachusetts, where he got more than 125,000 of a total vote of 175,000. The state he carried by the smallest proportion was New York, the most popu-

---

10 Brooks, *Washington in Lincoln's Time,* 217–218.

11 Dennett, . . . *Diaries* . . . *of John Hay,* 235–236.

12 Brooks, *Washington in Lincoln's Time,* 218–219.

lous of all, where he had a margin of fewer than 7,000. He made his poorest showing in the big cities. The heaviest majority against him in any city was that in New York, where McClellan got nearly two-thirds of the approximately 100,000 votes. In Chicago and Cincinnati, Lincoln did best in the wards with a predominantly German population and worst in those where the Irish were most numerous.[1] In Detroit, McClellan captured nearly three-fourths of the votes in the heavily Irish eighth ward and carried both the city and Wayne County, although the county had gone for Lincoln in 1860.[2]

Lincoln "received an almost unanimous vote," as Frank Blair believed, from the army.[3] Indeed, it has been calculated that Lincoln was given roughly three-fourths of the ballots cast by soldiers in the field or through proxies at home. The total of this vote—not more than 235,000—was relatively very small, both in proportion to the size of the army (it contained at least ten times as many men as voted in the field or by proxy) and in proportion to the size of the popular vote as a whole.[4] But this does not mean that soldier voting had little or no effect upon the outcome of the election. It should be remembered that, in addition to the soldiers who voted in the field or by proxy, many others on furlough voted at home (their numbers cannot be determined, since their ballots were not counted separately from those of civilians). It should be noted also that most of the votes of soldiers on furlough were concentrated in certain large and pivotal states. William B. Hesseltine has estimated that in New York, Pennsylvania, Illinois, Indiana, Maryland, and Connecticut the Republican majorities—which ranged from 2,000 (Connecticut) to 30,000 (Illinois)—resulted from the presence of soldiers as guards or as voters at the polls. "Without the soldiers' vote in six crucial states," concludes Professor Hesseltine, "Lincoln would have lost the election."[5]

Just what factors (other than habitual party allegiance) were most important in making up the minds of the more than four million voters, soldier and civilian, it would be difficult to say. Frank Blair believed that "no effort upon the part of any officer of rank" had been

1 Cincinnati *Daily Gazette*, Nov. 22, 1864, p. 1, c. 4.

2 W. A. Harbison, "Detroit's Role in the Re-Election of Abraham Lincoln," *Bulletin of the Detroit Hist. Soc.*, V, No. 6, pp. 8–9.

3 Frank Blair to F. P. Blair, Sr., Nov. 10, 1864, Blair MSS., Lib. of Cong.

4 Benton, *Voting in the Field*, chap. xxx.

5 Hesseltine, *Lincoln and the War Governors*, 384 n.

made to "influence the votes of the troops," and that they had "voted their own unbiased sentiments." [6] (Democrats charged, however, "the War Department and our commanding generals" had "adopted a rule to refuse furloughs to Democratic soldiers and to grant them *ad libitum* to those of Republican proclivities." [7]) As for civilian voters, many who marked their ballots for McClellan doubtless were influenced more by anti-Negro prejudice and by dislike of high prices, high taxes, draft calls, and arbitrary arrests than by the arguments of Democratic politicians. On the other hand, large numbers of habitual Democrats, at least in the Northwest, voted for Lincoln because they did not like the "peace plank" in the Democratic platform. They were for "war to the knife and the knife to the hilt," as a Detroit Democrat told McClellan after the election. "The Chicago Platform . . . defeated us in this state." [8] Very likely the Chicago platform, together with the news of victories on the battlefield, refuting the resolution that declared the war a failure, also confirmed many Republicans in their inclination to support Lincoln and the "Union" party. Yet considerations of patronage and personal gain seem to have had as much influence on many Republicans as did political issues.

The real issues, as between Lincoln and McClellan, were much less sharp than they had been made to appear to the voters. There was no question of Union or disunion. As Lincoln himself put it (in his message to Congress, December 6, 1864): "There has been much impugning of motives, and much heated controversy as to the proper means and best mode of advancing the Union cause; but on the distinctive issue of Union or no Union the politicians have shown their instinctive knowledge that there is no diversity among the people." [9] Certainly McClellan did not think that the Union had been at stake. As he looked back upon the election, it seemed to him "a struggle of honor, patriotism & truth against deceit, selfishness & fanaticism." [10] The truth is that he, like Lincoln, had been a Union candidate. In his attitude toward the war he had much more in common with Lincoln than with the Peace Democrats. And Lincoln, in his attitude toward

[6] Blair to F. P. Blair, Sr., Nov. 10, 1864, Blair MSS.
[7] Washington *Daily Morning Chronicle*, Nov. 3, 1864, p. 2, c. 2.
[8] R. McClelland to W. Wright, Nov. 10, 1864, McClellan MSS.
[9] Nicolay and Hay, *Works*, X, 305.
[10] McClellan to Manton Marble, Nov. 28, 1864, Marble MSS.

the South, had much more in common with McClellan than with the Radical Republicans.

What difference would it have made, for the Union cause, if McClellan had won? It is inconceivable that he would have considered peace on the basis of disunion. Even the so-called "peace plank" of his party's platform did not sanction such a thing. That plank called for peace discussions with a view to restoration of the Union, and the man who wrote it, Vallandigham, in supposing that the rebel leaders would make peace without the independence of the Confederacy, was not traitorous but misinformed. Anyhow, there is little reason to suppose that McClellan, if elected, would have been guided by Vallandigham. It is possible, of course, that McClellan's anti-emancipation views, if he had put them into effect, would have weakened the Union Army by depriving it of Negro troops and auxiliaries (as Lincoln had argued in his August interview). It is also possible that a change in Presidents, with a kind of four-month interregnum between election and inauguration, might have unsettled policies and jeopardized the Union cause. But Lincoln stood ready, if he lost, to co-operate fully with McClellan in minimizing the break between administrations. After the election Lincoln showed the cabinet his memorandum of August 23, which the secretaries had signed without reading, and in which he recorded his intention of inviting McClellan's co-operation if McClellan should be elected. Seward commented that McClellan would have said yes, yes, and would have done nothing about it.[11] But Seward, for all his perspicuity, was something less than a fair and impartial judge in this case.

Yet the election did hold a profound meaning for the future of both the Union and democracy, a meaning that occurred simultaneously to Grant, to Lincoln, and to dozens of newspaper editors throughout the North. The election showed, according to the Detroit *Free Press,* that "in the very midst of the most gigantic revolution" the American people could "execute a freeman's will with the same dignity and respect, with the same quiet and regard for the forms of law witnessed in the most ordinary peaceful times." [12] Grant, in a telegram congratulating Lincoln, said: "The election having passed off quietly,

[11] Dennet, . . . *Diaries . . . of John Hay,* 237–238.

[12] Quoted by Harbison, *Bull. of the Detroit Hist. Soc.,* V, No. 6, p. 9.

no bloodshed or riot throughout the land, is worth more to the country than a battle won." [13] Addressing a crowd that surged about the White House two nights after the election, Lincoln said: "It has long been a grave question whether any government, not *too* strong for the liberties of its people, can be strong *enough* to maintain its own existence, in great emergencies." The election, "a political war," had "partially paralyzed" the loyal people and so had weakened them, temporarily, for the war against the rebellion. And yet the election had been a necessity. "We can not have free government without elections; and if the rebellion could force us to forego, or postpone a national election, it might fairly claim to have already conquered and ruined us." [14]

---

[13] Grant to Stanton, Nov. 10, 1864, *Correspondence of Gen. Benjamin F. Butler,* V, 336.
[14] *Collected Works,* VIII, 100–101.

CHAPTER XII

POLICY, POLITICS, AND PERSONNEL

RE-ELECTED, Lincoln would have liked to end his first term and begin his second with as little change as possible in the personnel, both high and low, of his government. He was weary of the interminable demands of friendship and faction, which he had to try to reconcile with his needs for competence and for loyalty to the administration. After more than three years of shuffling men and places, he had achieved a fair balance between his needs and the politicians' demands. But he had not set up a stable equilibrium, nor could he. Vacancies continued to occur through resignation, dismissal, or death, and hungry politicians continued to clamor for patronage. So the President, while wrestling with problems military and financial and diplomatic, still had to concern himself with the problem of re-adjusting personnel in such a way as to serve the ends of both politics and policy.

I

Of all the places that Lincoln now had to fill, the most important was the Chief Justiceship of the Supreme Court, which had become vacant only a few weeks before election day, when John Marshall's successor Roger Brooke Taney finally died. His death broke the tension which, ever since Lincoln's inauguration, had existed between the Republican President and the Republicans in Congress, on the one hand, and the Democratic Chief Justice on the other.

Taney's infamy among Republicans dated back to the Dred Scott case (1857). He and a majority of the Court then held that a Missouri Negro could not be an American citizen and therefore could not sue in the Federal courts, but they had gone on to say in an *obiter dicta* that Congress could not constitutionally exclude slavery from the territories. This opinion struck at the key plank of the Republican platform, the Free Soil plank. Republicans denounced Taney and the concurring judges as tools of slavery, and Lincoln in the debates with Douglas intimated that he and his party, once in power, would somehow set aside the decision of the Supreme Court.

At Lincoln's inauguration it was of course this same Taney who, by virtue of his office, administered the oath to the new President, in the presence of the other justices. And Lincoln, in his inaugural address, gave a word of warning to Taney and the court when he said: ". . . if the policy of the government, upon vital questions affecting the whole people, is to be irrevocably fixed by decisions of the Supreme Court, the instant they are made, in ordinary litigation between parties in personal actions, the people will have ceased to be their own rulers . . ." [1] Soon Taney defied Lincoln when, sitting as a circuit judge in *ex parte Merryman,* he denied the constitutionality of the President's suspension of the writ of *habeas corpus.*[2] And Lincoln, in his message to the special session of Congress (July 4, 1861), again answered Taney. He noted that the Federal laws were being violated wholesale in almost a fourth of the states, then asked whether "all the laws but one" (the one concerning the *habeas corpus* writ) were "to go unexecuted, and the government itself to go to pieces lest that one be violated." [3]

Neither then nor later did Lincoln call upon Congress to curb the Supreme Court, but when the first regular session of Congress met, he did suggest that the circuit courts be reorganized so as to provide a circuit of approximately equal population for each of the Supreme Court justices. The congressional Radicals, led by Senator John P. Hale of New Hampshire, took it upon themselves to eliminate the judiciary as an obstacle to their program. After debating at length Hale's proposal to abolish the Court and set up a new one, they had to be satisfied with nothing more than the President's re-organization plan, most of which became law. The Conservative Republicans were willing to wait for the President to capture the Court by appointing new judges.[4]

---

1 Nicolay and Hay, *Works,* II, 5. 2 See *Lincoln the President,* III, 161 ff.

3 Nicolay and Hay, *Works,* II, 59–69.

4 David M. Silver, "The Supreme Court during the Civil War" (doctoral dissertation, Univ. of Ill., 1940), 40–50.

When the Court convened for the first time under Lincoln, there were already three vacancies on it, and some of the remaining justices appeared to be too old to last much longer. The three oldest came from slaveholding states and two of them from seceding states—Taney from Maryland, James M. Wayne from Georgia, and John Catron from Tennessee. The rest had been appointed by Democratic (and two of them by Southern) Presidents—Samuel Nelson, of New York, appointed by Tyler; Robert C. Grier, of Pennsylvania, by Polk; and Nathan Clifford, of Maine, by Buchanan. One vacancy existed already when Lincoln was inaugurated, Buchanan having been unable to get Senate approval for his last appointee. Another vacancy occurred when, exactly a month after Lincoln's inauguration, the seventy-six-year-old John McLean died. And the third vacancy arose when John A. Campbell, of Alabama, resigned to go with his state into the Confederacy.[5]

Lincoln was in no hurry to appoint new justices but preferred to wait until Congress had rearranged the circuits. When the Court met in December, 1861, however, there was no quorum, Taney and Catron being ill. So, in January, 1862, Lincoln nominated Noah H. Swayne, a Virginia-born Ohio lawyer who had once been a Jacksonian Democrat and who possesed no judicial experience of any kind. He was so little known in the East that the newspapers there usually misspelled his name as "Swain." But he was the choice of the Ohio Republican leaders, including Senators Sherman and Wade and Governor Dennison, and that was enough.[6]

Lincoln made his second appointment in July, 1862, on the day after the circuit reorganization had become law. Samuel F. Miller, the new justice, born in Kentucky, had taught himself law while practicing medicine there, then had moved to Iowa and gone into law and politics. Before his Supreme Court appointment, when the Iowa congressman, John A. Kasson, visited Lincoln in his behalf, Lincoln had confused him with a Daniel F. Miller he had known, and after his appointment some of the eastern newspapers kept referring to him as Daniel F. rather than Samuel F. Miller. He was the nominee of the Iowa Republicans, of Senators Harlan and Grimes and Governor Kirkwood.[7]

Not till October, 1862, did Lincoln get around to naming a third

[5] *Ibid.*, 13 ff., 108 ff. [6] *Ibid.*, 37–39, 68 ff. [7] *Ibid.*, 76–82.

Supreme Court justice, though the friends of David Davis had been urging his appointment ever since the death of McLean. David Davis, a Maryland-born cousin of the Marylander Henry Winter Davis, had been a judge of the eighth Illinois circuit where Lincoln used to practice and had been Lincoln's manager at the Chicago convention of 1860. His friends, among them Leonard Swett, expected him to be rewarded for his part in making Lincoln President, and they became increasingly impatient at Lincoln's long delay. Davis himself said that so many friends were mentioning him for a Supreme Court position that he was beginning to feel a desire for one. Finally they and he got their wish.[8]

Except for Davis, none of Lincoln's three appointees had had judicial experience or was known outside his own state. All of them, including Davis, had been born in slave states. All were chosen primarily for political reasons. Yet all were men of ability, all were strongly pro-Union and antislavery, and all could be depended upon to uphold the administration. But they comprised only a minority of the Supreme Court, and when the first test of the President's war powers came up, in the *Prize Cases* (decided in March, 1863), the legality of Lincoln's blockade proclamation during the first three month's of his administration could have been sustained only with the aid of at least two of the older justices. Two of them—Justices Grier and Wayne—did join with the three Lincoln appointees in the five-to-four decision.[9]

Meanwhile Congress was enlarging the Supreme Court by adding a tenth justiceship and a tenth circuit. Lincoln signed the bill and it became law on March 3, 1863. He named a judge to fill the new place, Stephen J. Field, on March 6. The Court's decision in the *Prize Cases* was announced on March 10 (Field did not, of course, participate in this). It has been said that the creation of the additional judgeship and the appointment of the extra judge were closely related to the *Prize Cases,* though the timing of the events indicates that the actual vote in this decision could not have been the cause of the action by Congress and the President. Nevertheless, the President and Congress, anticipating a close vote or possibly an adverse one, may have been "packing" the Court so as to lessen the danger of judicial "sabo-

---

[8] *Ibid.*, 86–94.

[9] See Randall, *Constitutional Problems under Lincoln,* 51–59, and *Lincoln the President,* III, 153–156.

tage."[10] Or Congress may have been merely following through on the President's earlier recommendation that it provide a circuit for each justice and a justice for each circuit. The new circuit, bringing California and Oregon into the regular court system, needed a judge familiar with the tangled land laws and land claims of California. Stephen J. Field—one of the famous family of brothers, including David Dudley, Cyrus W., and Henry M.—was such a man. He had gone to California as a forty-niner and had served for several years on the Supreme Court of that state. Incidentally, while on the California court, he had written an opinion which impugned Federal authority to the extent of arguing that the legal-tender act did not apply to state debts.[11] If Lincoln had been deliberately packing the Court, he might have picked a man with fewer qualms about the greenbacks than Field.

Some members of Congress had a continuing interest in increasing the number of Republicans on the Court, as was indicated by the bill which Senator Harlan introduced in December, 1863. This would have made it possible for a justice to retire on a pension which, depending on the length of his service, would range from $4,000 to $6,000 (as compared with the salaries of $6,000 for the associate justices and $6,500 for the Chief Justice). If Harlan's bill had passed, a few of the older judges—including Unionists like Wayne and Grier—might have been lured from their positions by the promise of generous retirement pay. "The 4 seniors, Taney, Wayne, Catron, and Grier, are evidently failing . . ." Attorney-General Bates noted on April 11, 1864. "I think all four of them would gladly retire, if Congress would pass the proposed bill—to enable the justices to resign, upon an adequate pensi[o]n."[12] But Congress never passed the bill. Even without it, the preponderance of age on the Court was considerably reduced by Lincoln's appointments, the average age of the judges being 71 years in 1861 and 62 in 1864.

The Taney Court had been converted into a Lincoln Court, with a majority generally loyal to the administration. "If it could not sustain the administration in war cases," as David M. Silver has written, "it denied that it had jurisdiction."[13] The greatest danger of judicial sabotage had already passed by the time of Taney's death, but Repub-

---

10 Swisher, *Taney*, 652–663, and *Stephen J. Field*, 115–116.

11 Silver, "Supreme Court during the Civil War," 99–105.

12 Bates, *Diary*, 358.

13 Silver, "Supreme Court during the Civil War," 138.

licans had not forgotten the case of Dred Scott, and there were questions regarding slavery which they expected the Court yet to pass upon.

II

From week to week during 1864 Chief Justice Taney, going on eighty-seven, feeble, incapacitated much of the time, was expected to die. The Radicals could hardly wait. Senator Wade quipped: "No man ever prayed as hard as I did that Taney might outlive James Buchanan's term, and now I'm afraid I have overdone it." [1] So efficacious had been Wade's prayers that it looked as if Taney might outlive Abraham Lincoln's term also!

During one of Taney's illnesses Lincoln made up his mind that the next Chief Justice should be Salmon P. Chase, then secretary of the treasury.[2] He did not change his mind when he accepted Chase's resignation from the treasury department. Chase learned of the President's intention from Representative Samuel Hooper, of Massachusetts, who reported to him on June 30 (the day after Chase resigned) a recent White House conversation. As Chase recorded the gist of it in his diary: ". . . the President expressed regret that our relations were not more free from embarrassment . . . . At the same time he expressed his esteem for me & said that he had intended in case of vacancy in the Chief Justiceship to tender it to me & would now did a vacancy exist." [3] The next day Lincoln remarked privately that Chase ought to "go home without making any fight and wait for a good thing hereafter, such as a vacancy on the Supreme Bench." [4]

Taney held out for more than three months longer, until October 12. Few mourned him, even among the Conservative Republicans. Attorney-General Bates, who had been with him on the night of his death, was the only cabinet member who attended the funeral. Secretary of the Navy Welles "felt little inclined to participate" in any ceremony, for he believed that by the Dred Scott decision Taney had "forfeited respect" both as a man and as a judge.[5] President Lincoln himself, along with Secretary of State Seward and Postmaster-General Dennison, "attended the body from the dwelling to the cars" after

---

1 Nicolay and Hay, *Lincoln,* IX, 386. 2 Browning, *Diary,* I, 687.

3 Chase MS. diary, entry for June 30, 1864, Lib. of Cong.

4 Dennett, . . . *Diaries . . . of John Hay,* 203. 5 Welles, *Diary,* II, 176–177.

services in Washington, but did not go on to the burial in Frederick, Maryland.[6]

Meanwhile some of the rejoicing Radicals got busy on behalf of Chase. Secretary of War Stanton sent him a terse telegram: "Chief Justice Taney died last night," [7] and Chase promptly replied that for three or four months he had been "afraid" it was the President's intention to appoint him; he thought he would accept, but he wondered whether he should.[8] Professor Lieber, the moment he heard the glad news in his Columbia College classroom, sat down in front of his students and dashed off a note to his friend Senator Sumner, suggesting that the Senator go at once from Boston to Washington. "The subject is so vitally important," Lieber wrote, "and we ought to show our gratitude, practically, for God's having removed at last this fearful incubus." [9] But Sumner needed no prodding. Already, on the very night of Taney's death, he had written to Lincoln a whole-hearted endorsement of Chase. "Thus far the Constitution has been interpreted for Slavery," he said. "Thank God! it may now be interpreted solely for Liberty." [10]

After a week Lincoln let Chase know, through Secretary of the Treasury Fessenden, that he had not forgotten what he had said about appointing him, "but as things were going on well he thought it best not to make any appointment or say anything about it, until after the election was over." [11] Meanwhile Chase kept on campaigning for Lincoln, amid rumors of a "bargain" by which Lincoln had persuaded Chase to support him in return for a promise of the Chief Justiceship.[12] Election day came and went, and still Lincoln sent no nomination to the Senate. Chase's friends became impatient. "The President, in my opinion, errs by his delay," Sumner said. "The appointment ought to have been made on the evening of Taney's funeral; but sooner or later Mr. Chase will be nominated." [13] Chase himself also became restless. He needed to go to Washington on business but,

6 Bates, *Diary*, 418–419.

7 Stanton to Chase, Oct. 13, 1864, Chase MSS., Hist. Soc. of Pa.

8 Chase to Stanton, Oct. 13, 1864, Stanton MSS., Lib. of Cong.

9 Lieber to Sumner, Oct. 13, 1864, Sumner MSS., Harvard Coll. Lib.

10 Sumner to Lincoln, Oct. 12, 1864, R. T. L. Coll., 37179–80.

11 Fessenden to Chase, Oct. 20, 1864, Chase MSS., Hist. Soc. of Pa.

12 J. K. Herbert to Butler, Sept. 26, 1864, *Correspondence of Gen. Benjamin F. Butler*, V, 167–168.

13 Pierce, *Sumner*, IV, 208.

rather than give the impression that he would "solicit or even ask such an appointment as a favor or as a reward for political service," he stayed at home in Cincinnati, hoping from day to day that the President would act.[14]

Meanwhile strong opposition to Chase was arising in several quarters, even in Lincoln's own household, on the part of his wife. Several other candidates were being urged, or were pressing their own claims, among them Associate Justice Swayne, Secretaries Stanton and Bates, the New York legal light William M. Evarts, and the former Postmaster-General, Montgomery Blair.[15] Stanton himself did not seek the job, but Mrs. Stanton sought it for him, and at her request O. H. Browning interceded with Lincoln. The President "said nothing . . . except to admit Mr. Stantons ability, and fine qualifications," and also to confide that Bates "had personally solicited the Chief Justiceship" for himself.[16]

Having been sacrificed to appease the Radicals, Blair deserved the Chief Justiceship as his consolation, or so his father thought. Old man Blair wrote to everyone he could think of who might possibly appeal to Lincoln in the son's behalf.[17] He had no trouble in enlisting Mrs. Lincoln's support. "Mr. Blair," she told him, as he reported their conversation, "Chase and his friends are beseiging my Husband for the Chief-Justiceship. I wish you could prevent them." The elder Blair finally went to Lincoln himself and, though the President was noncommittal, came away with great expectations. "From the tenor and manner of his remarks I infer that he is well disposed to appoint Montgomery." [18]

The Supreme Court was to meet on December 5, and when that day arrived, the Court still lacked a Chief Justice. No one knew—unless Lincoln himself did—when it would have one or who he would be. Welles remained confident that, while the President sometimes did "strange things," he would not make such a "singular mistake" as to appoint Chase.[19] Welles thought Blair was the man, and the New York *Times* predicted that Blair probably would be ap-

[14] Chase to John Sherman, Nov. 12, 1864, Sherman MSS., Lib. of Cong.
[15] Silver, "Supreme Court during the Civil War," 208–214.
[16] Browning, *Diary*, I, 687–688.
[17] Silver, "Supreme Court during the Civil War," 211–214.
[18] Blair to John A. Andrew, Nov. 19, 1864, Mass. Hist. Soc. *Proc.*, LXIII, 88–89.
[19] Welles, *Diary*, II, 187.

pointed. The New York *Herald* predicted that Swayne would be.[20]

On December 6, without an advance word to the cabinet or to anyone else, Lincoln sent the name of Chase to the Senate. The Senate, as it usually did with appointees who were or had been senators, promptly and unanimously confirmed the appointment.[21] Republican newspapers hailed it as marking a revolution in the history of the Court and the Constitution. "Five years ago, had any one suggested Salmon P. Chase as the probable successor of Roger B. Taney," observed the New York *Tribune,* ". . . he would have been regarded as in need of a straight jacket." [22]

Chase wrote to Lincoln on the day of the nomination: "Before I sleep I must thank you for this mark of your confidence, and especially for the manner in which the nomination was made." [23] The next day the new Chief Justice paid a brief social call at the Executive Mansion.[24] Whatever Lincoln may have told him at that time, Lincoln told another visitor at about the same time, as Welles had it, "that he would rather have swallowed his buckhorn chair than to have nominated Chase." [25]

Why, then, did he nominate him? He explained to Representative George S. Boutwell, of Massachusetts, that there were three reasons. First, Chase was a prominent figure with a considerable following. Second, as Chief Justice he would uphold the administration on the issues of emancipation and the legal tenders, if and when these issues came before the Court. Third: "We cannot ask a man what he will do, and if we should, and he should answer us, we should despise him for it. Therefore we must take a man whose opinions are known."

But Lincoln added that there was a strong reason against the appointment of Chase. "He is a candidate for the Presidency, and if he does not give up that idea, it will be very bad for him and very bad for me." [26] Chase's overweening ambition doubtless accounted for Lincoln's long hesitation. Blair did not suffer from the same defect; he was certainly as deserving on account of political services as was Chase; and he could have been counted on as well or better to sustain the administration. One consideration alone, however, was enough

20 Silver, "Supreme Court during the Civil War," 219–220.

21 Washington *Daily Chronicle,* Dec. 7, 1864.

22 Silver, "Supreme Court during the Civil War," 222.

23 Schuckers, *Chase,* 513.

24 New York *Herald,* Dec. 8, 1864, p. 4, c. 5.

25 Welles, *Diary,* II, 196 (Dec. 10, 1864).

26 Boutwell, *Reminiscences,* II, 29.

to disqualify Blair. He was anathema to the Radicals, and his nomination would never have been confirmed by the Senate. Whatever other motives Lincoln may have had, his naming of Chase was a concession to the Radicals.

For them, the first of February, 1865, was an epoch-making date. On that day Sumner moved in the Supreme Court that John S. Rock be admitted to practice before it. Chase, consulted in advance by Sumner, had made sure of favorable action on the motion. It carried, and Rock was admitted. The Dred Scott decision was indeed a thing of the past, for Rock was a Negro, the first of his race to appear as a lawyer before the Supreme Court.[27] Here was an auspicious beginning, from the Radical point of view, and the Radicals expected other great things in the new era under Chase.

However reliable Chase might be on questions involving the Negro and emancipation, Lincoln soon was told that he could not be depended upon when such questions as the constitutionality of the greenbacks came up. Chase, it was said, would "fail the Administration," but Lincoln, recalling the "committals of Chase," refused to believe it.[28] Chase was indeed to fail the administration, after Lincoln was dead, when he ruled the legal-tender act unconstitutional, even though, as secretary of treasury, he had been largely responsible for its passage in the first place. And Chase was to justify Lincoln's fear that he would never give up his intriguing for the Presidency.

He was also to disappoint the hopes of the Radicals—as when, presiding at the impeachment trial of President Johnson, he behaved with judicial impartiality instead of abetting the impeachers. Once he was on the Court he seemed to grow more conservative—or perhaps only more independent—than he formerly had been. He did not agree with the Radicals in Congress who refused even to let money be spent to provide the Supreme Court chamber with a bust of Taney, that "wicked" man.[29] At least in private conversation, he was willing to be generous and just to his predecessor. He once remarked to Browning "that he, Taney, had been cruelly misrepresented in regard to his opinion in the Dred Scott case—that what he said about the rights of negroes was but the statement of a historical fact, and that there was nothing in it derogatory to the Judges integrity or hu-

[27] Pierce, *Sumner*, IV, 209. [28] Welles, *Diary*, II, 245–246 (Feb. 22, 1865).
[29] Silver, "Supreme Court during the Civil War," 230–231.

manity—that he was a man of great talents and attainments—a very able jurist—unusually kind and gentle in his nature, and of very pure and exalted character." [30]

III

Though the Radicals hailed the Chase appointment as a victory for themselves, they were not content with that alone. In the sixth plank of the Baltimore platform they had called for a reorganization of the Cabinet in the interests of "harmony," which meant of course the interests of Radicalism. The removal of Blair, as they saw it, was only a beginning. After the election of 1864 they renewed their old criticisms of the Lincoln ministry, and—though not for the same reasons—reformers with Conservative leanings joined them in the demand for changes in the cabinet.

All kinds of rumblings and rumors about the cabinet were to be heard on the streets and in the offices and salons of Washington during the fall and winter of 1864–65. One visitor in the Capital reported with heavy irony his "joy" at finding that, among some of Lincoln's friends, his re-election was taken to mean "the people were overwhelmingly in favor of trusting the Government in the hands of the Administration! and this, notwithstanding the unpopularity of many members of the Cabinet, Stanton & Welles particularly. Seward is by no means wholly satisfactory to the people. Lincoln himself lacks the power to content the fastidious & the highly conservative, or the strongly radical." [1] Another observer in Washington predicted that the cabinet would "all bust up" soon after Lincoln's re-inauguration in March. Stanton was "worse than ever," or so Blair was swearing "on corners of the streets"; Welles was "listless"; Seward was "devilish"; and the observer himself was "disheartened—disgusted." [2] The President did have defenders, such as the eloquent Edward Everett, who in a Boston speech replied to the charge that Lincoln's administration "wanted unity of counsel" by pointing out that George Washington's had included "the heads of two radically opposite parties," Hamilton and Jefferson. "It rarely happens," protested Everett, "that

---

30 Browning, *Diary,* II, 54 (Dec. 22, 1865).

1 H. W. Bellows to his son, Nov. 13, 1864, Bellows MSS., Mass. Hist. Soc.

2 L. G. Hews to J. A. Andrew, Dec. 17, 1864, Andrews MSS., Mass. Hist. Soc.

any other course is practicable in difficult times."[3] Yet the gossips persisted in saying that Lincoln's cabinet was a "solemn failure" and that the President himself had come to realize it. "Having violated what is known to have been his original intention to make no changes till the close of his Administration, by accepting Mr. Chase's resignation and requesting Mr. Blair's, he may be reasonably presumed to be contemplating others."[4]

He was indeed. When Congress met, early in December, he was ready with two names to send to the Senate. Neither of these names attracted much attention, since they were overshadowed in the news by the nomination of Chase to the Chief Justiceship at the same time.[5] One was that of William Dennison, an interim appointee already designated (September 24) to replace Blair as Postmaster General.[6] The choice of Dennison, a former Ohio governor, implied that the President had both geographical and factional considerations in mind. Dennison, a loyal Lincoln campaigner, was "preaching the gospel to the heathen" of southern Ohio at the moment he received word of his nomination.[7] He was also a Radical and a friend of Chase, and his accession to the cabinet would presumably compensate to some degree for Chase's departure, so far as Ohio Republicans were concerned.

The other place which Lincoln was ready to fill when Congress met was that of the Attorney General. Edward Bates, viewing himself as the last of the old Whigs, had begun to feel that he was "among strangers." During the campaign of 1864 Bates told Lincoln he wanted to retire after the election, and at the end of November Lincoln accepted his resignation.[8] Since Bates was a Missourian, Lincoln looked for a successor from a border state, first offering the job to Joseph Holt, the Judge Advocate General, a Kentuckian. When Holt declined, Lincoln sent a telegram (December 1) to another Kentuckian, James Speed.[9] For this selection, Lincoln had personal as well as geographical reasons, James being the brother of Joshua F. Speed, Lincoln's intimate of the early Springfield days. "The appointment of James

3 Washington *Daily Chronicle,* Nov. 18, 1864, p. 1, c. 5.
4 Cincinnati *Daily Gazette,* Nov. 23, 1864, p. 1, c. 4.
5 Washington *Daily Chronicle,* Dec. 7, 1864.
6 Dennett, . . . *Diaries* . . . *of John Hay,* 216.
7 Carman and Luthin, *Lincoln and the Patronage,* 277–278.
8 Bates, *Diary,* 428.
9 *Collected Works,* VIII, 126.

Speed, of Louisville, to the vacant Attorney-Generalship," said a Washington commentator, "is owing rather to the President's old friendship and high appreciation of his abilities, than to any specific political interest." [10] In fact, a "political interest" also was involved, at least incidentally, since Speed could be expected to help balance the cabinet on the Conservative side.

A third and more important vacancy appeared in the offing when, in February, 1865, William Pitt Fessenden indicated his intention of resigning as secretary of the treasury. After entering the cabinet reluctantly, Fessenden soon had become anxious to leave it, so as to return to the Senate, for which his talents better fitted him. In anticipation of his departure, several Radicals were mentioned for his place, among them George S. Boutwell, John W. Forney, and Thaddeus Stevens.[11] As chairman of the House committee on appropriations—corresponding to the Senate finance committee, of which Fessenden had been chairman—Stevens seemed, to the Pennsylvania Republicans in Congress, to be logically next in line for the treasury post. If, by his inflationary views, he had pleased many of the manufacturers of his own state, he had antagonized the "sound money" men of Wall Street. His latest gaucherie in their eyes was a bill to prohibit any greenback from being "received for a smaller sum" than was specified on its face, a proposal which led the New York *World* to sneer at him as one who expected to "legislate fair weather in finance." Even had Lincoln been inclined to appoint him in appeasement of the Radicals, Stevens would have been disqualified because of his monetary aberrations.[12]

But Lincoln was not inclined to appoint him, anyhow. Apparently he did consider naming Hannibal Hamlin, the retiring Vice President, whose ambition for a Senate seat from Maine was frustrated by Fessenden's desire for the same seat. According to Hamlin's son, Fessenden objected to his rival's succeeding him in the cabinet, and so Lincoln promised him the Boston collectorship as a consolation prize (and President Johnson later gave him the Boston job).[13] Lincoln then called in Thurlow Weed for a consultation, and Weed recommended Senator Edwin D. Morgan, of New York, for the treas-

[10] Cincinnati *Daily Gazette*, Dec. 5, 1864, p. 3, c. 3.

[11] *Ibid.*, Feb. 25, 1865, p. 1, c. 1.

[12] Current, *Old Thad Stevens*, 205–206.

[13] C. E. Hamlin, *Hannibal Hamlin*, 495.

ury.[14] Morgan had no special qualifications as a financial expert, but he was thought to deserve a cabinet place on account of his political services—"for," as Washington gossips asked, "was he not Chairman of the National Executive Committee that insured Mr. Lincoln's nomination by refusing to postpone the call for the National Convention?" [15] But Morgan could not be persuaded to accept.

His reiterated refusals left Hugh McCulloch as Lincoln's favorite candidate. McCulloch was a banker, not a politician. Chase as treasury secretary had brought him to Washington from Indianapolis to serve as comptroller of the currency. Both Chase and Fessenden recommended McCulloch to head the treasury department, though McCulloch did not entirely approve the policies of either of them. He thought Chase had erred in consenting that the government paper money should be made a legal tender, and he thought Fessenden had erred in attempting to dispense with the services of the middleman Jay Cooke in the sale of government bonds. Indeed, he feared that the treasury had become "considerably embarrassed" and the government credit considerably "impaired" as a result of Fessenden's timidity and administrative incompetence. McCulloch was "taken aback" when, a day or two after the second inauguration, Lincoln called him by messenger to the Executive Mansion, grasped his hand, and told him he was needed as secretary of the treasury. McCulloch protested that he doubted his own capacity to do what the "existing financial condition of the Government" would make necessary. "I will be responsible for that," said Lincoln, as McCulloch afterward recalled, "and so I suppose we will consider the matter settled." [16]

Lincoln had one final cabinet change to make. He had been growing more and more dissatisfied with John P. Usher's administration of the interior department. Early in 1865 he conferred with Governor Yates and Senator Trumbull, of Illinois, about a successor to Usher. They recommended Senator Harlan, of Iowa.[17] Others, however, urged the appointment of Representative Isaac N. Arnold, of Illinois. "Representative Arnold insists that he is a candidate for no place and wants nothing; but his position as peculiarly the President's man in Congress entitles him to something; and the arrangers of the

[14] Carman and Luthin, *Lincoln and the Patronage,* 310.
[15] Cincinnati *Daily Gazette,* Feb. 25, 1865, p. 1, c. 1.
[16] McCulloch, *Men and Measures,* 190–191.
[17] Carman and Luthin, *Lincoln and the Patronage,* 311–312.

Cabinet hold that he would make as good a Secretary of the Interior as anybody." [18] Arnold was fighting the President's fight for the Thirteenth Amendment in the House at this time, and the President thought highly of him. But Lincoln thought highly also of Harlan, who was a loyal political lieutenant, having headed the congressional campaign committee in 1864, and a family friend as well. Harlan escorted Mrs. Lincoln to the second inauguration, and his daughter was often escorted by her son, Robert Todd Lincoln (who later married Miss Harlan). When Usher submitted his resignation, to take effect May 15, Lincoln named his friend Harlan as secretary of the interior (March 9), but Lincoln was dead a month before Harlan took office.

By the personnel changes he made after his re-election, Lincoln probably improved and certainly did not impair the administrative efficiency of the departments. But he did not succeed in adding political strength to his administration, nor did he achieve greater unity, though he managed to maintain a fairly even Radical-Conservative balance. McCulloch was a Conservative in politics as much as a conservative in finances. Speed, however, who as a Kentuckian was originally thought to be a Conservative, aligned himself with the Radicals Stanton and Dennison before Lincoln's death.[19]

The policy-making significance of the appointments, apart from their bearing on the broad issue of Radicalism and Conservatism, was not very clear. By his choice of a new treasury secretary the President might have been expected to indicate his own financial preferences. The fact is, however, that Lincoln disagreed profoundly with McCulloch about the relation of government finances to the national economy.

McCulloch was bearish. He had the dour outlook proverbially associated with a man of his Scotch ancestry. As comptroller of the currency he had issued to the National Banks in December, 1863, a circular embodying his pessimistic views. The states of the North, he then warned, appeared to be prosperous but actually were not, for the war was "constantly draining the country of its laboring and producing population, and diverting its mechanical industry from works of permanent value to the construction of implements of warfare."

---

18 Cincinnati *Daily Gazette*, Feb. 25, 1865, p. 1, c. 1.

19 Carman and Luthin, *Lincoln and the Patronage*, 312.

The "seeming prosperity," he explained, was due primarily to "the large expenditures of the Government and the redundant currency." He advised the bankers to prepare for a depression: "manage the affairs of your respective banks with a perfect consciousness that the apparent prosperity of the country will be proved to be unreal when the war is closed, if not before . . . ." When he received the offer of the treasury position, McCulloch assumed that Lincoln had been motivated by "the impression which was made upon him" by this gloomy circular.[20]

But Lincoln in his message to Congress of December, 1864, expressed an entirely different spirit. Part of the message was a paean to wartime progress and prosperity. "It is of noteworthy interest," the President declared, "that the steady expansion of population, improvement and governmental institutions over the new and unoccupied portions of our country have scarcely been checked, much less impeded or destroyed, by our great civil war, which at first glance would seem to have absorbed almost the entire energies of the nation." Sales of public land soared high, the Pacific railroad was being pushed to completion, new sources of gold and silver and mercury were being opened in the West. The popular vote in the recent election—larger in the free states, despite the non-voting of most of the soldiers, than it had been in 1860—demonstrated an important fact: "that we have *more* men *now* than we had when the war *began* . . . ." Besides: "Material resources are now more complete and abundant than ever." [21]

IV

William H. Seward (who, with Welles, was to remain in the cabinet from the beginning of Lincoln's administration to the end of Johnson's) was doing a thoroughly satisfactory job as secretary of state, and Lincoln's working relations with him were excellent, the secretary's foreign-war panacea of 1861 long since forgotten. The President still took an occasional hand in diplomatic affairs, as in such ceremonials as the presentation of the credentials of the Baron de Vetterstedt, the first fully accredited Envoy Extraordinary and Minister

[20] McCulloch, *Men and Measures,* 195–198. [21] *Collected Works,* VIII, 145–146.

Plenipotentiary ever sent from Stockholm to Washington. In a rather quaint interchange of pleasantries the President told the Baron: "My memory does not recall an instance of disagreement between Sweden and the United States." [1]

With respect to few other countries could Lincoln honestly have said such a thing, but he could and did announce, in his annual message of December 6, 1864, that the United States was on fairly good terms with most of the world. He went so far as to suggest that, "if it were a new and open question," the maritime powers "would not concede the privileges of a naval belligerent to the insurgents," as Great Britain and others had done at the start of the war.[2] But he and Seward did face two serious problems of diplomacy in the winter of 1864–65. One, the problem of the French intervention in Mexico, he passed over lightly in his message to Congress. The other, the problem of the use of Canadian soil for Confederate raids across the border, he discussed more fully.

He announced that, because of the border threat (he did not refer specifically to such recent events as the St. Alban's raid), it had been "though proper to give notice that after the expiration of six months, the period conditionally stipulated in the existing arrangement with Great Britain, the United States must hold themselves at liberty to increase their naval armament upon the lakes." While thus denouncing the Rush-Bagot agreement of 1817, he also indicated that he was ready to modify the reciprocity treaty of 1854, so as to raise tariffs on Canadian goods and discontinue certain privileges of transit from Canada through the United States.

He made these announcements in no bellicose tone. He wished to be understood that the Canadian authorities were "not deemed to be intentionally unjust or unfriendly" and that they, "with the approval of the imperial government," would "take the necessary measures to prevent new incursions across the border." [3] In British government circles his remarks were received in the spirit in which he had intended them. "The resolution of the Federal government to place an additional force on the great lakes is not to be complained of," said the authoritative *Times* of London. "So long as the war lasts

1 Washington *Daily Chronicle,* Jan. 21, 1865, p. 2, c. 1.

2 *Collected Works,* VIII, 136, 140.

3 *Ibid.,* 141.

it will be the object of the Confederates to make the British provinces the basis of some kind of operations against their enemy." [4]

Lincoln was careful to see that zealous Americans did not go beyond the intent of his Canada policy. When General Dix, in command in New York, instructed all military commanders on the frontier to shoot down raiding groups on sight, whatever their nationality, and to cross the boundary in pursuit of them if necessary, Lincoln disapproved the order and it was revoked.[5] He also declined an offer of the Fenian Brotherhood, a revolutionary organization of armed Irish-Americans, to prevent invasions from the North.[6] (A few years later the Fenians were to reverse the border problem by themselves undertaking incursions into Canada.) Lincoln did order that crossings into the United States be denied to all who lacked appropriate passports. The Canadian authorities co-operated by providing a few thousand militia to patrol the border, at an estimated expense of $100,000 per month.[7]

No patronage matter arose to complicate relations with Canada and Great Britain, but such a matter did momentarily jeopardize relations with France. In December, 1864, the American minister in Paris, the rather ineffectual William L. Dayton, died. Fortunately there was an ideal successor to Dayton already on the ground, namely, John Bigelow, the American consul general, who already was performing many of the functions of an ambassador, who in fact was more nearly than Dayton the equivalent in France of Minister Charles F. Adams in England.[8] But, unfortunately, Lincoln during the presidential campaign had promised the French mission to the newspaperman whose help he then had needed—James Gordon Bennett.

And Bennett was not likely to be *persona grata* in Paris. Though Bigelow sometimes was impatient with Seward's policy of speaking softly on French intervention in Mexico, Bennett was becoming fanatical on the subject. His New York *Herald* criticized Lincoln's annual message for its neglect of the Monroe Doctrine.[9] Reviving the essence of the forgotten Seward formula—reunion at home through a war abroad—the *Herald* kept hammering at the theme of combining the Blue and the Gray into an army that would drive the puppet em-

[4] Quoted in Cincinnati *Daily Gazette*, Jan. 10, 1865, p. 1, c. 3.

[5] *Ann. Cyc.*, 1864, IV, 360–361.

[6] New York *Herald*, Dec. 19, 1864, p. 5, c. 6.

[7] *Ann. Cyc.*, 1864, IV, 178.

[8] See Margaret Clapp, *John Bigelow*.

[9] Dec. 7, 1864, p. 4, c. 2.

peror Maximilian out of Mexico and at the same time reconcile the North and the South in a common cause. "In the struggles and triumphs of a foreign war," as the *Herald* bluntly put it, "we shall re-cement the sundered sympathies of loyal and rebellious states." [10]

Even though Bennett as minister to France could thus be expected to work against Seward's temporizing policy, Lincoln was not a man to forget his political promises. Of course, he may have counted upon Bennett's declining the appointment. If so, he was taking a risk, for he had no way of knowing for sure that Bennett would decline it. On the contrary, Bennett seemed eager for the offer, if not also for the position itself. In any case, when Lincoln offered it he turned it down.[11] Later Lincoln nominated Bigelow, another experienced newspaperman, a former part owner of the New York *Evening Post*. The French mission thus happened to fall into able hands.

V

With U. S. Grant as general-in-chief, the army was led by a man whom the President could depend upon. From time to time Lincoln still "interfered" in military affairs, though the myth persists that he allowed Grant to have his own way completely. As late as August, 1864, for example, he insisted that the general come to Washington for consultation about the pursuit of Early's army after the raid on Washington. "In the remaining months of 1864," T. Harry Williams writes, "Lincoln watched intently and sometimes anxiously over the conduct of the vast Union war effort, but he intervened in the management of it only at rare intervals because in general he was satisfied with Grant's direction." [1]

During these months the most spectacular military activity was conceived and initiated by General W. T. Sherman, with the somewhat doubtful approval of Grant and Lincoln. With the capture of Atlanta, Sherman had not won his main objective, which was the capture or destruction of the opposing army under General J. B. Hood.[2] Moreover, Sherman had lost the initiative. To recover it, he proposed to divide his forces and, with about 60,000 men, strike out

---

10 Nov. 8, 1864, p. 4, c. 3; Nov. 9, 1864, p. 4, c. 4.

11 See above, pp. 42–45.

1 Williams, *Lincoln and His Generals*, 336.

2 Randall, *Civil War and Reconstruction*, 554.

boldly from Atlanta to some point on the coast, effecting a "devastation more or less relentless" [3] on the way, while he sent General George H. Thomas back with about 30,000 men to hold Tennessee. Grant thought Sherman should dispose of Hood's army before he started off. Lincoln let Grant know that he himself had doubts about the plan. Yet he accepted it when Grant told him that nothing better seemed available.[4]

Early in November Sherman's men moved out of Atlanta and headed southeast, with orders to advance fifteen miles a day by four parallel roads, foraging on the country and laying waste mills, houses, cotton gins, public buildings, and especially railroad tracks and bridges.[5] Sherman did not attempt to maintain lines of communication or supply, and the North had little news of his three-hundred-mile march while it was in progress. The President referred to it cautiously in his annual message on December 6. "It tends to show a great increase in our relative strength that our General-in-Chief should feel able to confront and hold in check every active force of the enemy, and yet to detach a well-appointed large army to move on such an expedition," he said. "The result not yet being known, conjecture in regard to it is not here indulged." He left out of the address one sentence which would have revealed to the people his own very real fear of possible disaster. In this sentence he had written that the general-in-chief must have concluded that "our cause could, if need be, survive the loss of the whole detached force." [6]

Before Sherman left Atlanta, Hood had moved northward into Tennessee, in the hope of maneuvering Sherman out of Georgia, but Sherman relied on Thomas to deal with Hood. Though defeated at Franklin, Hood pushed stubbornly on to Nashville and besieged Thomas there. Lincoln, as he anxiously watched events from Washington, kept expecting Thomas to come out and fight. Finally he directed Stanton to consult with Grant about Thomas's failure to attack, and he got more of a reaction from Grant than he had bargained for. Grant advised that Thomas be removed from command and, despite Lincoln's unwillingness to approve such a drastic step, sent General John A. Logan to supersede him.[7] Finally Grant went to

[3] Sherman, *Memoirs,* II, 175. [4] Williams, *Lincoln and His Generals,* 339–340.
[5] Sherman, *Memoirs,* II, 171–172, 175. [6] *Collected Works,* VIII, 148.
[7] Williams, *Lincoln and His Generals,* 341, 345; Randall, *Civil War and Reconstruction,* 675–676.

consult Lincoln, intending to go on from Washington to Nashville to see personally that Thomas was relieved.

On December 15, Lincoln presided at a conference of Grant, Stanton, and Halleck. The President was now in the position, unusual for him, of arguing for the retention of a general who seemed to be afflicted with what, in the case of McClellan three years earlier, he had called the "slows." Lincoln pointed out that Thomas, on the ground, was better able to judge the tactical situation than was Grant, hundreds of miles away. Angrily and stubbornly Grant persisted in demanding Thomas's removal, and at last Lincoln gave in.

That night, before Grant had left Washington, a telegram came to the war department with news of a great victory at Nashville. Stanton immediately drove to the White House, where Lincoln in a nightshirt and with a candle in his hand appeared at the head of the main stairway to hear the news. He smiled and went back to bed.[8]

Next day he telegraphed his congratulations to Thomas on the "good work." Remembering other "victories" which had proved abortive, he also admonished: "You made a magnificent beginning. A grand consummation is within your easy reach. Do not let it slip." [9]

Thomas did not let it slip. He followed up the shock of his first assault with a vigorous pursuit of Hood, who escaped across the Tennessee River with only a sorry remnant of the fine army he had taken out of Atlanta several weeks before. "The victory at Nashville was the only one in the war so complete that the defeated army practically lost its existence," says T. Harry Williams. "It was also a complete vindication of Lincoln's faith in Thomas. Again the President had been more right than Grant." [10]

Grant as well as Lincoln had complete faith in Sherman, who was approaching the end of his march to the sea at the time of the battle of Nashville. He took Savannah in time to give it to Lincoln as a Christmas present. On December 26 the President sent his thanks to Sherman and his whole army. "When you were about leaving Atlanta for the Atlantic coast," Lincoln confessed to him, "I was *anxious,* if not fearful; but feeling that you were the better judge, and remembering that 'nothing risked, nothing gained' I did not interfere. Now, the undertaking being a success, the honor is all yours; for I believe

---

[8] Williams, *Lincoln and His Generals,* 343–344. [9] *Collected Works,* VIII, 169.
[10] Williams, *Lincoln and His Generals,* 344–345.

none of us went farther than to acquiesce. And, taking the work of Gen. Thomas into the account, as it should be taken, it is indeed a great success." [11]

As the year 1864 ended and the fateful new year began, the President had reason to be satisfied with Thomas, Sherman, and Grant. The army now was commanded by professional soldiers—with one very notable exception—and the professionals were doing excellent work.

VI

The last of the politician-generals to hold important army commands were Nathaniel P. Banks and Benjamin F. Butler, whose careers provide interesting comparisons and contrasts. Both men were former Democrats with backgrounds as labor champions in Massachusetts, Banks as the "Bobbin Boy" of Waltham and Butler as an agitator for the ten-hour day in Lowell. Both had become Radical Republicans and, like many another politico when the war was young, had received commissions in the army by virtue of their political influence rather than their military skill. In the spring of 1864 each had demonstrated his unfitness for a field command, Banks in the fiasco of his Red River expedition into Texas, Butler in allowing his Army of the James to be "as completely shut off from further operations directly against Richmond as if it had been in a bottle strongly corked" (to quote Grant's report of Butler's withdrawal into Bermuda Hundred, at the forks of the James and the Appomattox). Both Banks and Butler had had experience in administering occupied territory, Banks having succeeded Butler as military commander in occupied New Orleans. But Banks had proved a much better administrator, at least from Lincoln's point of view, and he was willing to co-operate loyally in carrying out the presidential plan for restoring loyal state governments. Butler, equipped with a kind of audacity and a talent for publicity which Banks lacked, devoted his truly remarkable talents to sabotaging the presidential plan while continuing his military blunders. Of all Lincoln's many personal problems, this man Butler must be singled out as the most persistently troublesome.

By comparison, Banks was a minor nuisance. During the fall of

[11] *Collected Works*, VIII, 181–182.

1864, in Washington on leave from his command of the Gulf Department, where he no longer exercised more than civil functions, he tried for weeks to persuade Lincoln to restore the military powers of which Lincoln had deprived him in May. "I cannot . . . ," said the President. Referring presumably to Grant, he explained: "He whom I must hold responsible for results, is not agreed." Banks then offered to resign, but Lincoln dissuaded him, needing him to continue working in behalf of the new state government of Louisiana, the launching of which Banks had already overseen. "I know you are dissatisfied, which pains me very much," said Lincoln, "but I wish not to be argued with further." [1] In November he extended Banks' leave indefinitely,[2] and Banks stayed on in Washington throughout the winter to lobby, ex-congressman that he was, in behalf of the reconstructed Louisiana government. He became a source of comfort rather than pain to the President.

Butler, however, continued as the storm center of one personality clash after another. While in New York, where with his troops he was supposed to prevent violence at the November polls, he got into a controversy with General John A. Dix, the commander of the Department of New York, by insisting on precedence over Dix even though he did not outrank him.[3] As commander of the Department of Virginia and North Carolina, a position he had held since late in 1863, he was continually at odds with Francis H. Pierpont, the governor of the "Restored Government" of Virginia, with presumed authority over what was left of that state after West Virginia and the Confederate-controlled area were subtracted from it. General Butler, in Norfolk, repeatedly challenged the authority of Governor Pierpont, in Alexandria, and Lincoln finally had to step in to decide the issue of military as against civilian rule.

In the spring of 1864 Pierpont published in pamphlet form a long letter, addressed to the President and Congress, in which he described the "abuses of military power" in Virginia and North Carolina. According to Pierpont's indictment, Butler was guilty of an imposing list of arbitrary actions, most of them intended to line his own pockets or those of his friends. He levied taxes on oyster boats in Chesapeake Bay and on other vessels using the port of Norfolk. He set up a pro-

[1] Harrington, *Fighting Politician*, 159–160, 163–164. [2] *Collected Works*, VIII, 106.
[3] F. E. Howe to John A. Andrew, Nov. 6, 1864, Andrew MSS.

vost marshal's court in competition with the courts of the Pierpont government, and his provost marshal turned out of jail prisoners awaiting trial in the state courts. Setting up a monopoly of the liquor traffic, he placed it in the hands of his associates from Boston, as he also did the management of the Norfolk gas plant. He issued an order that every fourth dog should be killed; any dog-lover desiring to rescue a pet had to pay two dollars which, along with other Butler exactions, went into a "provost marshal's fund." [4]

In reply, Butler dismissed Pierpont as "the *soi disant* Governor of Virginia." During the summer of 1864 he further showed his contempt for Pierpont by holding a referendum in Norfolk on the question of abolishing the civil government there. The vote favored Butler and military rule. He then put forth an order forbidding any exercise of authority by "persons pretending to be elected to civil office" in Norfolk. Pierpont protested to Lincoln and assured him that most of the loyal voters had boycotted the election, that Butler's majority had come chiefly from "Uncompromising seceshinists" and "Non residents Mostly liquor sellers." [5] Attorney-General Bates took up Pierpont's cause and wrote a long letter to Lincoln.[6] Butler, also writing to Lincoln, attacked Bates and Pierpont as men of doubtful loyalty and defended his own assumption of civilian powers as necessary for the preservation of order and the protection of his troops.

"This subject has caused considerable trouble, forcing me to give a good deal of time and reflection to it," Lincoln wrote at last, on August 9, in a letter he intended to send to Butler. Pierpont and Bates were as loyal as Butler himself, the President patiently reassured the general. True, Pierpont did not actually govern much of Virginia, and the "insignificance of the parts" which were "outside of the rebel lines" gave a "somewhat farcical air to his dominion." But Pierpont, as well as Lincoln himself, had "considered that it could be useful for little else than a nucleus to add to" a nucleus, in other words, for the reconstruction of Virginia. "Coming to the question

[4] *Letter of Governor Peirpoint, to His Excellency the President and the Honorable Congress of the United States, on the Subject of Abuse of Military Power in the Command of General Butler in Virginia and North Carolina* (Washington, D. C.: McGill & Witherow, Printers and Stereotypers, 1864), *passim.* The Governor then spelled his name *Peirpoint* but in 1881 changed it to *Pierpont* to conform to an earlier spelling which had been corrupted. See Ambler, *Pierpont,* 3–4.

[5] Peirpoint to Lincoln, July 8, 1864, R. T. L. Coll., 34359.

[6] Ambler, *Pierpont,* 232 ff.

itself," Lincoln went on, "the Military occupancy of Norfolk is a necessity with us." If Butler, as commander of the department, found it necessary to take complete control of the city and provide such services as street cleaning and lighting, fire protection, wharfage, and poor relief, he could of course do so. "But you should do so on your own avowed judgment of military necessity, and not seem to admit that there is no such necessity, by taking a vote of the people on the question." And then Lincoln added a sentence which was more than an afterthought: "I also think you should so keep accounts as to show every item of money received and how expended." [7] The President finished the letter, then laid it aside. The time was not auspicious for sending it, this being dark August, the Wade-Davis Manifesto still fresh, and Butler himself the Radical favorite for replacing Lincoln on the presidential ticket. Grant wanted Butler removed as unfit for command, but Lincoln for the time being would not assume personal responsibility for removing him, though willing to let Grant do it on his own. For Lincoln to remove Butler, or even to rebuke him, would be most impolitic until after the election. And, as Lincoln thought, the Pierpont-Butler controversy was dying down anyhow.

Before the end of the year it flared up again. On December 21, 1864, Lincoln finally sent Butler a copy of his letter of August 9 and with it a note: "I now learn, correctly I suppose, that you have ordered an election, similar to the one mentioned, to take place on the Eastern Shore of Virginia. Let this be suspended, at least until conference with me, and obtaining my approval." On December 27 Butler wired back that the inhabitants of the Eastern Shore (the peninsula above Norfolk and east of Chesapeake Bay) had petitioned for such an election but he had not ordered it.[8]

Just as this old issue was coming to a head again, Butler was busy with his final enterprise as a military commander. This was a joint army-navy expedition against Fort Fisher on the Cape Fear River, near Wilmington, the only port of any size still accessible to Confederate blockade-runners. For some time the navy department had contemplated such an undertaking but had delayed it because of difficulties in enlisting army co-operation. Then Butler came forth eagerly with an original plan of his own. He had read in the newspapers about the terrible damage recently done by the accidental explosion of a gunpowder dump in England. This gave him the idea

[7] R. T. L. Coll., 35159–62.

[8] *Collected Works,* VIII, 174.

that, "by bringing within four or five hundred yards of Fort Fisher a large mass of explosives, and firing the whole," he could do such damage that "the garrison would at least be so far paralyzed as to enable, by a prompt landing of men, a seizure of the fort." Welles agreed to provide naval assistance in carrying out Butler's scheme, and Grant consented to Butler's participation as commander of the troops to be landed. The navy prepared a "powder boat," packed with 235 tons of explosives, through which ran a complicated fuse designed to set off the whole mass at once. After repeated delays the expedition finally got under way.[9]

At a cabinet meeting on December 27 Lincoln was "very pleasant over a bit of news in the Richmond papers, stating that the fleet appeared off Fort Fisher, one gun boat got aground and was blown up," as Welles noted. "He thinks it is the powder boat which has made a sensation." Welles himself expected little from Butler's stratagem but trusted that the expedition itself would succeed, in spite of Butler's presence. Welles's doubts were confirmed and Lincoln's hopes were dashed two days later, when dispatches arrived from Rear Admiral David D. Porter, the naval commander in the Fort Fisher assault. "The powder-ship was a mere puff of smoke, doing no damage so far as is known," said Welles, summarizing the admiral's report. The navy nevertheless had succeeded in silencing the fort's batteries, but Butler had not gone ahead with the landing of his troops. Welles and his assistant secretary, Gustavus Vasa Fox, took Porter's dispatches to the President, and the President read them carefully. What now? Welles asked. Lincoln referred him to General Grant.[10]

For Lincoln, the Butler problem had now become a complication in the larger problem of co-ordinating the army and the navy. Butler himself blamed the navy—which, he said, had put too much powder into the boat and had exploded it too soon and in water too deep—and was convinced that *"Porter did not intend that the attack of the army should succeed."* [11] The secretary of war did not try to justify Butler to the President but did say that Porter was no better. The naval officers denounced Butler while Lincoln "listened calmly," and Welles sided with them, while regretting to himself that he had ever sanctioned the powder boat. "That was not regular military," he re-

[9] Butler, *Autobiography . . . Butler's Book,* 775 ff.
[10] Welles, *Diary,* II, 210.
[11] Butler, *Autobiography . . . Butler's Book,* 808.

flected, "and had it been a success, the civilian General would have had a triumph." [12] Grant telegraphed that he would immediately organize another expedition, and Lincoln told Welles to see that the navy co-operated better this time.[13] The second attack by combined land and naval forces brought the capitulation of Fort Fisher, on January 15, 1865.

The Butler question remained. A possible way to dispose of it was to shift the trouble-making general from Virginia to Kentucky. The commander in the Kentucky area, General S. G. Burbridge, was unpopular with many Republicans, one of whom complained to the President: ". . . he lost us the vote of Kentucky by his offensive manner of carrying into effect your orders as to Coloured troops." [14] On January 2, 1865, a delegation of Kentuckians asked Lincoln to assign Butler to the command including their state. "Somebody has been howling ever since his assignment to military command," Lincoln replied. "How long will it be before you, who are howling for his assignment to rule Kentucky, will be howling for me to remove him?" [15]

A couple of days after that, Grant wrote to Stanton and requested that Butler, for "the good of the service," be removed as commander of the Department of Virginia and North Carolina. "In my absence General Butler necessarily commands, and there is a lack of confidence felt in his military ability, making him an unsafe commander for a large army," Grant explained. "His administration of the affairs of his department is also objectionable." Learning that Stanton was out of town, Grant on January 6 telegraphed directly to Lincoln and asked for "prompt action." Next day an order came from the war department relieving Butler "by direction of the President of the United States" and instructing him to "repair to Lowell, Mass." When Butler asked Lincoln for permission to publish his own report of the Fort Fisher assault, Lincoln replied that he could not grant permission until he had seen the report, "and not then, if it should be deemed to be detrimental to the public." So, as Butler later complained, "while the newspapers of the country were filled with extract's from Porter's reports and abusive criticisms of my conduct, I

---

12 Welles, *Diary*, II, 212–217.

13 Williams, *Lincoln and His Generals*, 348.

14 T. Ewing to Lincoln, Dec. 1, 1864, Ewing MSS.

15 New York *Tribune*, Jan. 4, 1865, quoted in *Collected Works*, VIII, 195.

could not say one word as to what that conduct had been." [16]

Butler soon had an opportunity to air his whole collection of grievances and to defend his record from beginning to end. The committee on the conduct of the war moved quickly to investigate the Fort Fisher failure and invited Butler to be heard. Lincoln, after having ordered him home to Lowell, had little choice but to grant him leave to come to Washington, though as Welles observed: "Allied with Wade and Chandler and H. Winter Davis, he will not only aid but breed mischief. This is intended." [17] When Butler arrived in Washington (on the day after the fall of Fort Fisher) the Radicals gave him a hero's reception and asserted that they would restore both his reputation and his command.[18] On the floor of the House Thaddeus Stevens was heard to mutter that Congress would rather have Butler than Lincoln for President.[19]

The Butler question now embraced not only the issue of Radical as against Conservative politics but also the issue of the civilian general—the latter-day Cincinnatus—as against the professionals, both military and naval. Given wide latitude on the witness stand, Butler assured the sympathetic committeemen that Admiral Porter and the navy were entirely responsible for the repulse from Fort Fisher and that he himself and also Grant, whom he exculpated, were victims of a clique of West Pointers who had conspired to disgrace him because he was the last of the civilian generals in an important command.[20] In the committee's unanimous report, Chairman Wade declared that, under the circumstances, "the determination of General Butler not to assault the fort" seemed to have been "fully justified." [21]

Though the Radicals thus cleared Butler's name, at least to their own satisfaction, they did not succeed in getting his command restored to him. He retired to Lowell, whence he kept Wade supplied with documents incriminating Porter, while the committee continued its investigation by calling Grant to testify and then going to Fort Fisher to look for evidence on the spot.[22] At least, Lincoln's Norfolk

---

[16] Butler, *Autobiography . . . Butler's Book,* 827–830; *Collected Works,* VIII, 207; Williams, *Lincoln and His Generals,* 347–348.

[17] Welles, *Diary,* II, 223–224 (Jan. 14, 1865).

[18] Williams, *Lincoln and the Radicals,* 366.

[19] Current, *Old Thad Stevens,* 206.

[20] Williams, *Lincoln and the Radicals,* 367–368.

[21] Butler, *Autobiography . . . Butler's Book,* 820–821.

[22] Williams, *Lincoln and the Radicals,* 368–372.

headache was gone. Civil government was restored in the city, and Pierpont had no difficulty in collaborating with Butler's successor, General E. O. C. Ord.[23]

VII

The removal of the bold political general, the partial reorganization of the cabinet, the appointment of a Chief Justice—these personnel changes at the policy-making level Lincoln could not well have avoided after his re-election. With respect to presidential patronage at a lower level he would have liked to maintain the *status quo* almost intact. "Can't you and others start a public sentiment in favor of making no changes in office except for good and sufficient causes?" he appealed to Senator John B. Clark of New Hampshire not long after election day. "It seems as though the bare thought of going through again what I did the first year here, would *crush* me." [1] So as to win a decisive victory in the late campaign, he had been willing to use his appointing power vigorously, even ruthlessly. Once the victory had been won, however, he was unwilling to use that power punitively. When Henry J. Raymond, "breathing fire and vengeance," demanded the dismissal of certain employees of the New York custom house, who he thought had been disloyal to him and to the party, Lincoln refused to comply, saying: "I am in favor of a short statute of limitations in politics." [2]

Yet the President could not ignore entirely the well-established patronage rule of punishing enemies and rewarding friends. The pressure on him was too great. From November throughout the winter and spring jobseekers crowded into Washington in numbers inferior only to those of 1860–61. Some friends of Lincoln worried lest he, like Presidents Harrison and Taylor before him, suffer a physical breakdown as a result of his hounding by the spoilsmen. Despite his determination against a large-scale shift of officeholders, he had a number of political debts arising from the campaign, and he paid off many of them.[3] Up to the day of his death in April, 1865, he was busy with appointments of collectors of internal revenue and other

[23] Ambler, *Pierpont,* 243.

[1] Carpenter, *Six Months in the White House,* 276.

[2] Dennett, . . . *Diaries* . . . *of John Hay,* 239.

[3] Carman and Luthin, *Lincoln and the Patronage,* 301–302.

such officers, sometimes making the appointments in batches.[4] On the eve of his assassination he penned a note to the secretary of the treasury in which he said he "would like to oblige Gen. Schenck by the appointment of his nephew" to a collector's job in California.[5]

If Schenck had a nephew to place, Lincoln had a son: Robert Todd, twenty-two, fresh out of Harvard. "Could he, without embarrassment to you, or detriment to the service, go into your Military family with some nominal rank, I, and not the public, furnishing his necessary means?" Lincoln wrote diffidently to Grant, after beginning his letter with a request that it be read as though he were not the President "but only a friend." Whether as a favor to a friend or as a response to the suggestion of his superior, Grant consented gracefully to accepting Robert Todd as a captain on his staff.[6] This was a family affair. Mrs. Lincoln could not stand the thought of her son's being exposed to death in battle, and Lincoln had tried to calm her fears and save her sanity by having him put into a relatively safe army berth, though she persisted in seeing him as any other soldier, exposed to all the risks of war.[7]

The case of John G. Nicolay and John Hay, the President's private secretaries, was also a family matter. Mrs. Lincoln did not like them, and they did not like the "hellcat," as they called her. She was fond of Noah Brooks, a dapper young newspaperman and literateur, much like John Hay except that his sense of humor was less cruel than Hay's. Hay, technically, was never Lincoln's secretary, but first as a pension office clerk and then as an army officer, was assigned to special service at the White House as Nicolay's assistant.[8] He and Nicolay slept at the White House and were practically members of the presidential family, too much so to please the President's wife. Early in 1865 she undertook a campaign to get Nicolay out and Brooks in.[9] Nicolay and Hay, tiring of their secretarial routine, were glad to accept Lincoln's offer to send them off to Paris, Nicolay as consul general and Hay as secretary of the legation under Minister Bigelow.[10] Brooks, the Wash-

[4] Cincinnati *Daily Gazette,* Apr. 8, 1865, p. 3, c. 6.

[5] *Collected Works,* VIII, 408.

[6] Lincoln to Grant, Jan. 19, 1865, *ibid.,* 223. Robert Todd Lincoln was appointed on February 11, 1865.

[7] Ruth Painter Randall, *Mary Lincoln,* 333–334, 367–368.

[8] Dennett, *John Hay,* 35 ff.

[9] A. G. Henry to Mrs. Henry, Mar. 13, 1865, Henry MSS., Ill. St. Hist. Lib.

[10] Dennett, *John Hay,* 57.

ington correspondent of the Sacramento *Union,* had already accepted from Lincoln "the promise of a lucrative place in San Francisco," and Lincoln hesitated to ask him to sacrifice this in order to become the President's private secretary. He told Brooks he could continue his work as a correspondent to supplement the secretary's income, and Brooks accepted the less remunerative position, though he never served in it, since Lincoln died before the change was actually made.[11]

Among the applicants for government jobs who filled the streets and hotel lobbies of Washington were numerous one-armed or one-legged men, disabled veterans of the war which still was adding daily to the total of the seriously scarred or maimed. A United States Sanitary Commission committee, headed by the former general-in-chief, Winfield Scott, set itself to the task of finding employment for such men as these. If the Federal government would hire as many as possible, a part of the growing total would thus be taken care of, and the rest might then get work from state governments and from private employers who, presumably, would follow the fine example which the Federal government should set.[12] Scott's committee looked to the President, not to Congress. In a public letter Scott asked Lincoln to recommend to the heads of departments that they give preference to badly crippled soldiers for whatever jobs these men could fill. Lincoln replied on March 1, 1865, with "hearty concurrence," saying he would be glad to "make these suggestions" to his department heads.[13]

So, in the last months of Lincoln's administration, much of the patronage (so far as the President personally could direct it) went to disabled soldiers, to his own relatives and friends, and to deserving politicians. Yet his most frequent and most serious consideration was neither war sacrifice nor friendship and family nor, in the usual uncomplicated sense, political service. As always, he had to consider the needs of factional harmony, the ways of bridging over that never-ending dichotomy of his administration, the division between Radicals and Conservatives. Much of the impetus to the new rush for offices came from Radicals who hoped, at last, to control the personnel as well as the policy of the government. Indeed, the quarrel between

11 Brooks to Isaac P. Longworthy, May 10, 1865, published as *The Character and Religion of President Lincoln* (Champlain, N.Y., 1919).

12 Philadelphia *Public Ledger,* Jan. 10, 1865, p. 2, c. 1; Apr. 1, 1865, p. 2, c. 1; Cincinnati *Daily Gazette,* Apr. 1, 1865, p. 3, c. 7; Apr. 5, 1865, p. 1, c. 8.

13 *Collected Works,* VIII, 327.

Republican factions arose not only from differences over Reconstruction programs but also from differences over the distribution of the patronage.[14]

In 1864–65 there was a factional quarrel in almost every state, but none so bitter and so demanding of the President's attention as the one in Maryland. There it was the familiar story of the fight, now more fierce than ever, between Henry Winter Davis and Montgomery Blair. The resurgence of Davis's factional bitterness came as a special disappointment to Lincoln. From the beginning, Davis's conduct had seemed "strange" to him, for he had "heard nothing but good" of Davis and had expected nothing but friendliness from the man who was a cousin of his good friend Judge Davis. Then, on election night, Lincoln was inclined to think that Davis's hostility toward him was at last about to disappear. "It has seemed to me recently that Winter Davis was growing more sensible to his own true interests and has ceased wasting his time by attacking me," the President commented. As for himself, he was ready to forgive and forget. "A man has not to spend half his life in quarrels," he said. "If any man ceases to attack me, I never remember the past against him."

The very next day, however, Blair visited the White House and complained bitterly against the "Davis clique." [15] Each side considered the other as the aggressor. The Davisites believed that "little minded men," who had worked against emancipation in the state, were about to "come forward as 'Lincoln men' under the leadership of M. Blair to claim at the President's hands a redistribution of the offices." The Davis group feared that Senator Thomas H. Hicks would be given the Baltimore collectorship, which was both pecuniarily and politically the most valuable job in the state. "Blair is then to be engineered into the U. S. Senate to take Hicks's place. This after his repudiation by the Baltimore Convention and his futile effort to get even meagre support in his application for a seat upon the Supreme Bench!" [16] Lincoln did not have time to show whether, for his second term, he intended to make Senator Hicks the Baltimore collector, for Hicks suddenly died in February. In the Maryland legislature Blair immediately had to fight for Hicks's Senate seat against a Davis man,

[14] Carman and Luthin, *Lincoln and the Patronage,* 321.
[15] Dennett, . . . *Diaries* . . . *of John Hay,* 234–236.
[16] J. S. Stewart to Simon Cameron, Dec. 27, 1864, Cameron MSS.

Congressman John A. J. Creswell. Though Blair was thought to have Lincoln's favor, Creswell held an advantage in government patronage, since Stanton and the pro-Chase employees of the treasury department were backing him. Blair lost. Davis, as if crowing over Creswell's triumph, which was also his own, promptly challenged the Lincoln policy with a tirade in the House on reconstruction in Louisiana.[17]

Finally Lincoln acted to check the Davis faction and strengthen that of Blair. The latter would have been glad to see Hicks at the head of the Baltimore custom house, and now that Hicks was dead and he himself defeated for the Senate, he was more determined than ever that the President should remove the pro-Davis collector of the port. Lincoln decided to re-deal the Baltimore patronage so as to provide a more even factional balance. He suggested that Blair meet with a representative of the Davisites and draw up a compromise slate of officeholders for the city. On April 14 he received and approved the slate.[18]

From day to day, to the very end, Lincoln thus had to concern himself with the distribution of the spoils. Only by doing so could he hold his party together, and only by holding the party together could he hope to accomplish his program. He did not succeed perfectly but, considering the magnitude and complexity of his tasks, he did extremely well. If his predecessor and his successor had handled the patronage as carefully, they might have been more nearly as successful in the presidency. He accomplished more than James Buchanan or Andrew Johnson partly because he was more of a politician. "In being a competent politician, he became a statesman." [19]

---

[17] Welles, *Diary*, II, 243; Carman and Luthin, *Lincoln and the Patronage*, 325–326.
[18] *Collected Works*, VIII, 411.
[19] Carman and Luthin, *Lincoln and the Patronage*, 336

CHAPTER XIII

THE THIRTEENTH AMENDMENT

THE Radicals of his own party insinuated that Lincoln was willing to see slavery survive the war, and sincere friends of the slave often felt he was too slow and hesitant in striking at the institution. Democrats, on the other hand, portrayed him as a "nigger lover" and fanatical abolitionist.[1] The truth is, he had shared some of the anti-Negro prejudices of the people among whom he lived in Kentucky and southern Indiana and Illinois. But, in the White House, he outgrew his prejudices. He also had possessed anti-slavery feelings which were rather rare among his early neighbors, and these feelings he did not outgrow during his Presidential years. But he doubted whether, as President, he should act upon his personal impulses in disregard of the powers of his office and the demands of statecraft. "I am naturally anti-slavery. If slavery is not wrong, nothing is wrong. I can not remember when I did not so think, and feel." Thus he wrote in April, 1864. "And yet I have never understood that the Presidency conferred upon me an unrestricted right to act officially upon this judgment and feeling." He had moved toward emancipation, he explained, only as it became an "indispensable necessity" for winning the war and saving the Union. "I claim not to have controlled events, but confess plainly that events have controlled me." [2] During the final year of his life, influenced by events and also influencing them, he devoted himself to seeing that slavery, every last remnant of it, should be eliminated from the land, forever.

---

[1] Quarles, *The Negro in the Civil War,* 132–162, 255–257.

[2] Lincoln to A. G. Hodges, Apr. 4, 1864, R. T. L. Coll., 32077–78.

I

Already much had been done toward eliminating it. "When the war commenced, three years ago," Lincoln told the crowd at the Sanitary Fair in Baltimore, April 22, 1864, "no one expected that it would last this long, and no one supposed that the institution of slavery would be modified by it. But here we are. The war is not yet ended, and slavery has been very materially affected or interfered with." [1] It had been and was still being materially affected by acts of Congress, by Presidential decree, and by the actions of several states.

Congress had begun the work less than four months after the firing on Fort Sumter. The first confiscation act, of August 6, 1861, provided that slaveowners should forfeit those of their slaves whom they used in military service against the United States. The second confiscation act, of July 17, 1862, went much beyond that: it declared "forever free" all slaves of owners who committed treason or supported the rebellion. In other acts of 1862 Congress abolished slavery in the District of Columbia, with compensation to the owners, and in the territories, without such compensation. Also in 1862 Congress provided that enemy-owned slaves serving in the Union armies should be free, and their families as well, and in 1864 Congress also gave freedom to slave-soldiers (with their families) belonging to loyal owners. In 1864 Congress finally repealed the fugitive-slave laws of 1793 and 1850 which, up to that time, had continued to provide an indirect sanction for slavery in the Federal statute books.[2]

President Lincoln, with his Emancipation Proclamation of 1863, actually did not go so far as Congress already had gone in the second confiscation act, but he did assert and dramatize the antislavery policy of his own administration. Though in itself the Proclamation did not free a single slave, it appealed to slaves who heard of it and thus brought thousands within the Union lines, where they were freed according to existing laws.[3] How it operated Lincoln was reminded

1 Cincinnati *Daily Gazette,* Apr. 22, 1864, p. 3, c. 8.

2 Randall, *Civil War and Reconstruction,* 480–481, 481 n.

3 On the Emancipation Proclamation and its consequences, see *Lincoln the President,* II, 151–203. At the Hampton Roads Conference in February, 1865, Lincoln agreed with Seward's estimate that, up to that time, a total of about 200,000 slaves had gained their freedom under the Proclamation. Alexander H. Stephens, *A Constitutional View of the Late War Between the States,* II, 611.

when, on January 1, 1864, the first anniversary of the Proclamation, General R. H. Milroy wrote to him about the use he had made of it in the Shenandoah Valley. First, Milroy announced it to his men, who cheered and sang "We are coming, Father Abraham" and "John Brown's Body" to the accompaniment of the regimental band. Then he posted and distributed over the countryside a handbill, headed in large type "Freedom to Slaves," which contained a summary of the Proclamation and commanded obedience to it. "That hand-bill order," Milroy now told Lincoln, "gave Freedom to the slaves through and around the region where Old John Brown was hung." [4]

Lincoln himself acted in a manner somewhat reminiscent of John Brown when, in August, 1864, he invited the former slave Frederick Douglass to the White House to discuss ways of encouraging slaves to heed the call to freedom. Lincoln suggested to Douglass that he organize a kind of government-sponsored Underground Railroad.[5] Soon afterward Douglass reported back to Lincoln: " . . . I have freely conversed with several trustworthy and Patriotic colored men concerning your suggestion that something should be speedily done to inform the slaves in the Rebel States of the true state of affairs in relation to them." Douglass outlined a plan according to which Lincoln would appoint a number of Negroes as "agents," with a "general agent" over them, to circulate in the South, talk to slaves, and persuade them to cross the line into Union-held territory.[6] But Lincoln soon lost interest in the plan. He had proposed it in the middle of the dark August when his re-election seemed unlikely. After the clouds lifted, he concentrated on other and more effective ways of extending and confirming the work of emancipation.

He still hoped to see it carried on by the slaveholding states themselves. West Virginia had been admitted to the Union in 1863 with a gradual-emancipation clause in its constitution. In those states being "restored" under Lincoln's ten per cent plan, slavery was duly abolished with the adoption of new constitutions—in Arkansas, March, 1864; in Louisiana, September, 1864; and in Tennessee, February, 1865.[7] He kept watching the border states and encouraging them to act upon his proposal of 1862 for gradual and compensated

---

4 R. H. Milroy to Lincoln, Jan. 1, 1864, R. T. L. Coll., 29147–48.
5 Quarles, *The Negro in the Civil War,* 258–259.
6 Douglass to Lincoln, Aug. 29, 1864, R. T. L. Coll., 35652–53.
7 See above, chaps. i and ii.

emancipation, but he ceased to insist upon either compensation or gradualness. "I am very anxious for emancipation to be effected in Maryland in some substantial form," he wrote to Representative A. J. Creswell on March 7, 1864. "I think it probable that my expressions of a preference for *gradual* over *immediate* emancipation, are misunderstood." He had thought "the *gradual*" would produce less confusion and destruction, but if those who knew best preferred "the *immediate*," he would have no objection to it. The important thing was that all favoring emancipation *"in any form"* should co-operate with one another and not delay or jeopardize the movement by bickering among themselves.[8] After the Republican victory of 1864 Maryland did act, merely repealing the slave code, an ordinary law, on which slavery had been based in that state. On January 11, 1865, Missouri also acted, abolishing slavery by means of a special ordinance passed by a state convention. But Delaware, though within its boundaries in 1865 there were about 20,000 free Negroes and fewer than 2,000 slaves, refused to let these people go. And Kentucky also clung to slavery.[9]

For all that the President, the Congress, and the states had done, the great majority of those who had been slaves in early 1861 remained in bondage at the beginning of 1865. Their future status was uncertain and, indeed, so was the future status of those who were already exercising their freedom. The Emancipation Proclamation was based avowedly on the President's war powers; once the war was over, its claim to legality would disappear. The various emancipatory acts of Congress were yet to be tested in the courts; though the antislavery champion Salmon P. Chase was now Chief Justice, the constitutional validity of the laws was not absolutely certain. Moreover, these laws conflicted with those of some of the states, and a man claiming freedom under the former might have difficulty in asserting his claim as against the latter. In Kentucky, for example, various state judges held that the Federal law giving freedom to the families of slave-soldiers was unconstitutional, and white employers hiring such persons were prosecuted in the state courts for the offense of harboring slaves. If, when the nation was reunited, slavery were to be permanently and unquestionably abolished everywhere in the United

8 Lincoln to Creswell, Mar. 7, 1864, R. T. L. Coll., 31334–35.

9 Randall, *Constitutional Problems under Lincoln,* 388–390.

States, abolition would have to be written into the Federal Constitution.[10]

II

When the Thirty-Eighth Congress (1863-65) first met, there seemed little likelihood that a proposal for an antislavery amendment would ever emerge from its sittings. The Republicans, Conservative and Radical, anti-administration and pro-administration, agreed upon the desirability of such a resolution. The Democrats, almost as unanimously, were opposed to it. Its passage would require a two-thirds majority in both chambers. In the Senate the Republicans controlled more than enough votes, but not in the House. When the measure was considered in the first session (1863–64) it met the fate expected of it. When it was reconsidered in the second session (1864–65) it passed, even though the party composition of the House remained essentially unchanged. Its success at that time was due largely to the exertions of the President, acting upon what he considered a mandate from the people in the election of 1864.

Lincoln needed to concern himself little about the action of the Senate, even though rivalries among the Republican leaders seemed at times to jeopardize the party program. Charles Sumner, the antislavery veteran, "whose pride of erudition amounted almost to vanity" (in the words of Nicolay and Hay), threatened at first to divide the majority by insisting upon his own wording for the proposed resolution.[1] A month after John B. Henderson, of Missouri, had introduced a resolution, Sumner (February 8, 1864) introduced another one, to the effect that "everywhere within the limits of the United States, and of each State or Territory thereof, all persons are equal before the law, so that no person can hold another as a slave." He desired this proposal referred to the Committee on Slavery, of which he himself was chairman, but finally consented to let it go to the judiciary committee, to which Henderson's resolution already had gone.[2] Lyman Trumbull, chairman of the judiciary committee, reported back a substitute with wording different from that of either Henderson or Sumner, wording adapted from the Northwest Ordinance of 1787. Sumner now tried to reinsert his "equal before the

[10] *Ibid.*, 385–388.

[1] Nicolay and Hay, *Lincoln*, X, 75–76.

[2] *Cong. Globe*, 38 Cong., 1 sess., 521, 1313; New York *Tribune*, Feb. 9, 1864, p. 5, c. 1.

law" phrase, which he had derived from the constitution of revolutionary France. The Senate managed, however, to pass the Trumbull substitute without change: "Neither slavery nor involuntary servitude, except as a punishment for crime whereof the party shall have been duly convicted, shall exist within the United States, or any place subject to their jurisdiction." [3]

Meanwhile Lincoln closely watched the progress of a similar measure in the House, hoping against hope that it might get enough Democratic support to pass. Again and again, consulting with Republican members, he added up the possible votes in its favor, but he could never make a total of two-thirds. After conferring with him, his friend Isaac N. Arnold tested the calculations of Lincoln and the Republicans by introducing a resolution which did not propose an actual amendment but merely declared "that the Constitution should be so amended as to abolish slavery." The vote on this test confirmed Lincoln's apprehensions.[4] When the proposed amendment itself came to a vote (June 15, 1864) only one Democrat supported it with a speech and only four with their ballots. One Republican, James M. Ashley, of Ohio, changed his vote from yea to nay so that, in accordance with the House rules, he could move for a reconsideration of the resolution at the next session of Congress.[5]

III

Though doubtless influencing few votes, the congressional debates on the proposed amendment revealed the kind of case that could be made for or against slavery in the United States in the years 1863–65.

The Republicans denounced the institution on principle, as an evil in itself. Yet in the same breath they urged the amendment as a measure of expediency, as a necessary means for winning the war and making a lasting peace. This argument of expediency was the Lincolnian approach—the President himself stressing the need for the amendment in order to "bring the war to a speedy close" [1]—and it represented the lowest common denominator of Republican thought.

[3] Blaine, *Twenty Years of Congress,* 504 ff., 535 ff. [4] Arnold, *Lincoln,* 351–352.

[5] Nicolay and Hay, *Lincoln,* X, 77–78; McClure, *Lincoln and Men of War-Times,* 109 ff.

[1] Arnold, *Lincoln,* 358–359.

Senator Henry Wilson, a veteran antislavery man like his Massachusetts colleague, Sumner, made one of the strongest attacks on slavery as a moral wrong. He referred to "its chattelizing, degrading, and bloody codes; its dark, malignant, barbarizing spirit," and the "moral degradation" with which it had "scarred" the face of the nation. But he also stressed the charge that slavery had caused the war, and left the "bosom" of the country "reddened with the blood and strewn with the graves of patriotism." And he neatly combined in one sentence the twin indictment of slavery when he said: "Sir, this gigantic crime against the peace, the unity, and the life of the nation, is to make eternal the hateful domination of man over the souls and bodies of his fellow men." [2] Senator Trumbull made the gravamen of his charge the pragmatic argument: "No superficial observer even of our history, North or South, or of any party, can doubt that slavery lies at the bottom of our present troubles." [3]

Most of the Democrats, on the other hand, made no attempt to justify slavery as an institution, though a few of them did so. Senator Willard Saulsbury, of Delaware, put forth the hoary proslavery argument based on carefully selected passages from the Bible, citing both the Old Testament and the New. He said "the Almighty immediately after the Flood condemned a whole race to servitude," the Negro race presumably being descended from Noah's accursed son Ham. He also said that one of "God's own apostles," Paul himself, had sanctioned slavery in sending the slave Onesimus back to his master.[4]

Occasionally one of the Democrats, such as Representative J. A. McDougall, of California, attempted to refute the Republican's main contention by denying that the amendment would make for victory or peace and insisting that it would only arouse "the fiercer animosity of an already violent foe." [5]

Still others took refuge in Constitution-worship. "Let the Constitution alone. It is good enough," begged Representative Randall, of Pennsylvania. In defense of the good old Constitution, he quoted the sentimental song, popular in that day:

> Woodman, spare that tree!
> Touch not a single bough.

---

[2] *Cong. Globe,* 38 Cong., 1 sess., 1320, 1323–24.

[3] *Ibid.,* 1313.

[4] Henry Wilson, *Rise and Fall of the Slave Power,* III, 439.

[5] *Ibid.*

In youth it sheltered me,
And I'll protect it now.[6]

While the Democrats reiterated their familiar campaign slogan—"The Constitution as it is and the Union as it was"—they urged most strongly and most repetitiously the argument that the abolition of slavery was outside the scope of the Constitution altogether, that an antislavery amendment would be itself unconstitutional. Senator Saulsbury conceded that all the states, when they made the Constitution, could have prohibited slavery in it. He maintained, however, that after all the states had signed the "contract," a mere three-fourths of them could not alter it in such a way as to destroy a domestic institution that antedated the contract.[7] Representative Pendleton, of Ohio, the Democratic vice-presidential candidate in 1864, put the matter this way: "neither three-fourths of the States, nor all the States save one, can abolish slavery in that dissenting State; because it lies within the domain reserved entirely to each State for itself, and upon it the other States cannot enter." [8] Representative John Pruyn, of New York, added: "The Constitution would never have been ratified had it been supposed by the States that, under the power to amend, their reserved rights might one by one be swept away. This is the first time in our history in which an attempt of this kind has been made, and should it be successful it will . . . be an alarming invasion of the principles of the Constitution." Pruyn went on to say that the disposition of slavery ought to be left to the separate states, or else there ought to be passed "a supplementary article to the Constitution, not as an amendment, but as the grant of a new power based on the consent *of all the States, as the Constitution itself is.*" [9]

That such objections and counterproposals made sense to their authors is understandable, perhaps, when one remembers that the Constitution had not been amended for some sixty years, not since the Twelfth Amendment was proposed in 1803 and ratified in 1804, and that the proposed Thirteenth Amendment was different in a significant respect from any of the preceding twelve. All the others had dealt with "constitutional" matters in a strict sense, that is, with governmental powers and functions. The new amendment would be

[6] Arnold, *Lincoln,* 355.

[7] *Cong. Globe,* 38 Cong., 1 sess., 1441.

[8] *Ann. Cyc.,* 1865, p. 207.

[9] *Cong. Globe,* 38 Cong., 2 sess., 154.

the first to effect a sweeping social reform by means of the amending process. Yet the objecting Democrats, if they truly had been motivated by constitutional considerations, might have concluded that such an amendment dealt as properly with "constitutional" matters as any article of the bill of rights, concerned as it was with the great subject of human freedom. They might also have reflected that the reserved rights of the states, for which Pruyn and others of them were so solicitous, were guaranteed not in the original text of the Constitution but in one of the amendments, the Tenth. They were on weak ground in making any distinction between the Constitution *and the amendments;* they would have been on better ground if they had thought of the Constitution *as amended.*[10] And they should have recognized that (at least after 1808) the Constitution contained no limitations, expressed or implied, on its own amendability.

These are not merely the reflections of a later generation of historians and political scientists. That the Constitution could be amended freely, if the appropriate procedures were followed, was the common-sense view of that time. "After all," observed a Washington newspaper in January, 1865, "the Constitution is but the legally expressed will of the people, susceptible of amendment whenever they choose to exercise the power." [11] As recently as 1861, less than six weeks before the firing on Fort Sumter, Democratic as well as Republican politicians had given indisputable evidence of the general understanding that the Constitution could be amended for any purpose, even for the purpose of abolishing slavery within the states. By a two-thirds vote in the Senate and the House, they proposed for ratification by the states a thirteenth amendment which provided: "No amendment shall be made to the Constitution which will authorize or give to Congress the power to abolish or interfere within any State with the domestic institutions thereof, including that of persons held to labor or service by the laws of said State." [12] If the Senators and Congressmen had not thought that the Constitution, lacking this proposed amendment, could have been amended so as to abolish slavery, there would have been no point in undertaking to add the amendment. Since the amendment failed of adoption, the

---

10 Randall, *Constitutional Problems under Lincoln* (rev. ed.), 394–396.

11 Washington *Daily Chronicle,* Jan. 11, 1865, p. 2, c. 2.

12 *Cong. Globe,* 36 Cong., 2 sess., 350 (Mar. 2, 1861).

Constitution remained as before, with no limit on the ways in which it might be amended. And even if that amendment had been adopted, it of course could have been repealed by another one.

IV

The question was not to be decided by the mere oratory of congressmen but by persuasions of a more powerful kind, by the voice of the people as expressed in the election of 1864 and by the President's efforts to see the popular mandate promptly carried out.

Lincoln had done all he could to make the antislavery amendment a campaign issue. From the outset he intended to run on a platform favoring the proposition. In June of 1864, while the proposition was still before the House of Representatives, he called to the Executive Mansion the chairman of the National Republican Committee, Senator E. D. Morgan, and gave him instructions for his speech opening the Baltimore convention. "Senator Morgan," he is reported to have said, "I want you to mention in your speech when you call the convention to order, as its key note, and to put into the platform as the key-stone, the amendment of the Constitution abolishing and prohibiting slavery forever." [1] At Baltimore Senator Morgan did as the President wished him to do, and the delegates responded in adopting the third plank of the party platform, which stated the prevailing Republican view that slavery was the cause of the rebellion and added that the President's proclamations had aimed "a death blow at this gigantic evil" but that a constitutional amendment was necessary to "terminate and forever prohibit" it.[2] In his statements which were used during the ensuing campaign, Lincoln stressed the indispensability of an antislavery policy as a means of winning the war. On this point, rather than the issue of Union or of peace, he differed most sharply with the rival candidate, McClellan.

When Lincoln was overwhelmingly re-elected, he therefore was justified in feeling that his antislavery program had the sanction of the popular will. When, along with him, so many Republican candidates for Congress also were elected that the party would control more than the needed two-thirds majority in the next House of Representatives, he could look forward confidently to the ultimate con-

[1] Arnold, *Lincoln,* 358. [2] Nicolay and Hay, *Lincoln,* X, 78–80.

version of the popular will into a constitutional amendment. But the newly elected Congress, the Thirty-Ninth, would not meet in the usual course of events for over a year, that is, not until December, 1865. The President could call a special session of the new Congress to meet at any time after his own re-inauguration on March 4, and he was prepared to do so if the old Congress, the Thirty-Eighth, should fail to act at its last regular session (1864–65).[3] This Congress contained, in the House, the same sizeable minority of Democrats who previously had blocked the passage of the resolution which the Senate had passed. Many of these Democrats now were lame ducks. Lincoln was eager to get the work done, and he counted on enough lame-duck support to get it done before he finished his first term. He stated his views on the subject in his message to the Thirty-Eighth Congress when it met for its final session in December, 1864:

"At the last session of Congress a proposed amendment of the Constitution abolishing slavery throughout the United States, passed the Senate, but failed for lack of the requisite two-thirds vote in the House of Representatives. Although the present is the same Congress, and nearly the same members, and without questioning the wisdom or patriotism of those who stood in opposition, I venture to recommend the reconsideration and passage of the measure at the present session. Of course the abstract question is not changed; but an intervening election shows, almost certainly, that the next Congress will pass the measure if this does not. Hence there is only a question of *time* as to when the proposed amendment will go to the States for their action. And as it is to so go, at all events, may we not agree that the sooner the better? It is not claimed that the election has imposed a duty on members to change their views or their votes, any further than, as an additional element to be considered, their judgment may be affected by it. It is the voice of the people now, for the first time, heard upon the question. In a great national crisis, like ours, unanimity of action among those seeking a common end is very desirable —almost indispensable. And yet no approach to such unanimity is attainable, unless some deference shall be paid to the will of the majority, simply because it is the will of the majority. In this case

[3] Lincoln was reported as saying that if the proposal failed to pass the second session of the Thirty-Eighth Congress he intended immediately to call a special session of the Thirty-Ninth Congress. Philadelphia *Public Ledger,* Jan. 7, 1865, p. 1, c. 4.

the common end is the maintenance of the Union; and, among the means to secure that end, such will, through the election, is most clearly declared in favor of such constitutional amendment."[4]

Here the President was appealing to the Democratic members of the current Congress, and especially to the numerous lame ducks among them. Other Republicans besides the President were thinking of the possibility of winning over some of the opposition and thus passing the proposal soon, during the winter of 1864–65. "The majority against it in the House was I think *eleven*," a correspondent advised Senator Sumner, "& in view of the feeling of the people, as evidenced by the Presidential vote, I think that a sufficient number of Democrats might be brought over without difficulty to carry it thro at once without waiting for the new Congress."[5] Lincoln did not leave it to his party leaders in Congress to persuade these Democrats to change their votes. He invited a number of them individually to the White House for informal interviews in January, 1865.

One of those he interviewed was James S. Rollins, a representative from the strongest slave district in Missouri and himself one of the largest slaveowners in his county, who had voted against the amendment in the previous session but who had not been re-elected to Congress. Lincoln said to him (as Rollins afterward reported the conversation): "You and I were old whigs, both of us followers of that great statesman, Henry Clay, and I tell you I never had an opinion upon the subject of slavery in my life that I did not get from him. I am very anxious that the war should be brought to a close at the earliest possible date, and I don't believe this can be accomplished as long as those fellows down South can rely upon the border states to help them; but if the members from the border states would unite, at least enough of them to pass the thirteenth amendment to the Constitution, they would soon see that they could not expect much help from that quarter, and be willing to give up their opposition and quit their war upon the government; this is my chief hope and main reliance to bring the war to a speedy close, and I have sent for you as an old whig friend to come and see me, that I might make an appeal to you to vote for this amendment." Rollins replied that he already had made up his mind to vote for it. Lincoln then

4 *Collected Works,* VIII, 149.

5 J. Jay to Sumner, Nov. 15, 1864, Sumner MSS., Harvard Coll. Lib.

asked him to see and talk with other members of the Missouri delegation, and Rollins cheerfully agreed to do so.[6]

Possibly, in talking with some of the Democratic holdovers in the House, Lincoln used the more substantial argument of patronage. At least one of the Democrats who changed their votes—Moses F. Odell, of New York—went into a Federal job as navy agent in New York City after leaving Congress at the end of the session in 1865.[7] Representative George W. Julian, Republican from Indiana, may have had patronage deals in mind when he wrote, enigmatically, that the success of the measure "depended upon certain negotiations the result of which was not fully assured, and the particulars of which never reached the public." [8] In any event, Lincoln declined to go as far as he might have done in "negotiations" with Congressmen. Representative Ashley, in charge of the amendment in the House, urged upon him a scheme to get the aid of the New Jersey Democrats. A bill was pending which was intended to curb the monopoly of the Camden and Amboy Railroad in New Jersey, and the railroad company apparently controlled the congressmen from that state. Senator Sumner was behind the anti-monopoly bill. If Sumner would postpone it—so Ashley informed Lincoln—the company "would in return make the New Jersey Democrats help about the amendment, either by their votes or absence." But Lincoln felt he could do nothing with Sumner. He told Ashley that the Senator would become "all the more resolute" if he tried to persuade him to give in.[9]

V

On January 6, 1865, Representative Ashley moved the reconsideration of the resolution for the Thirteenth Amendment and reopened the debate, which occupied the House off and on until the end of the month. As before, the Republicans were solidly in favor of the resolution, but the Democrats were no longer so nearly unanimous against it. Some of them, moved by Lincoln's persuasions as well as by the election returns, had come to the conclusion that for political

6 Arnold, *Lincoln,* 358–359.

7 See the brief sketch of Odell in *A Biographical Congressional Dictionary . . . 1774–1911.*

8 Julian, *Political Recollections,* 250.

9 Memorandum of Nicolay, dated Jan. 18, 1865, Nicolay and Hay, *Lincoln,* X, 84–85.

reasons alone, for the salvation and revival of their party, they would be wise to turn about and support the amendment.

The issue on which many Democrats relied for future success was the issue of public finance. They generally favored a program of easy money and continued inflation, and with this program they hoped to attract not only farmers and wage-earners but also many small businessmen, who feared the deflationary effect to come from the elimination of state banknotes and the retirement of the greenbacks. Though these voters, in the North, could be expected to respond to the promise of abundant currency, they could not be expected to rally to a proslavery party. "You cannot present the issue of the finances till the slavery question is settled, & that question can be settled but in one way." So George Bancroft, the historian and prominent party intellectual, advised Congressman Samuel S. Cox, of Ohio, a few days before the question came to a final vote. "Do away with slavery & the democrats will be born[e] into power on the wings of their sound principles of finance." [1]

Cox himself was not much impressed by Bancroft's advice, not enough impressed to decide to change his vote. But some of Cox's Democratic colleagues were influenced by a similar line of argument. Representative Anson Herrick, a Democrat from New York, addressed his fellow partisans with a frank appeal to party interest. "It has been our seeming adherence to slavery, in maintaining the principle of State rights, that has, year by year, depleted our party ranks," he said. "Looking at the subject as a party man, from a party point of view, as one who hopes soon to see the Democratic party in power, this proposition seems to present a desirable opportunity for the Democracy to rid itself at once and forever of the incubus of slavery." [2]

Representative Rollins, of Missouri, presented the essence of Lincoln's own argument, as Lincoln had given it to him. "We can never have an entire peace as long as the institution of slavery remains as one of the recognized institutions of the country," Rollins declared in the course of one of the more eloquent speeches of the entire debate. "It occurs to me that the surest way to obtain peace is to dispose of the institution now." Rollins went on to say that the border states had missed an opportunity in not accepting Lincoln's suggestion of

[1] Bancroft to Cox, Jan. 28, 1865, Bancroft MSS., Mass. Hist. Soc.

[2] *Cong. Globe,* 38 Cong., 2 sess., 526.

1862. "And, sir, if ever a people made a mistake on earth, it was the men of Kentucky, by whom I was somewhat governed myself, when three years ago they rejected the offer of the President of the United States, who, wiser than we were, seeing the difficulties before us, but seeing the bow of promise set in the sky, and knowing what was to come, proposed to us to sweep the institution of slavery from the border states, offering the assistance of the United States, to aid in compensating the loyal men of those states for their losses in labor and property." [3]

Another Democratic Congressman, however, cited the words of Lincoln to dissuade his fellow Democrats from reversing themselves. "It is not many months since the President of the United States, above his own signature, publicly stated that if he could save the Union he would do so, irrespective of slavery," said Representative Kalbfleisch, of New York. "I am for leaving open to him the opportunity of redeeming the pledge thus given to the country." [4] Like Kalbfleisch, the great majority of the Democrats in the House had no intention of voting for the amendment. Many more of them spoke against it than spoke in favor of it. They tried to postpone or prevent a decision by their stalling tactics.

Thaddeus Stevens got the floor repeatedly to reply to the Democrats and to urge Ashley and the Republicans to press ahead on schedule. Stevens made himself one of the most insistent of the champions of the amendment, saying that he had devoted his whole life to attacking social inequalities wherever he found them. "I will be satisfied," he declared, "if my epitaph shall be written thus: 'Here lies one who never rose to any eminence, and who only courted the low accomplishment to have it said he had striven to ameliorate the condition of the poor, the lonely, the downtrodden of every race and language and color.' " But while he, along with the rest of the Radicals, joined in pushing Lincoln's amendment, he did so in an un-Lincolnian and even an anti-Lincoln spirit. While the President was thinking of peace and reconciliation, the congressman was talking about the "desolation of the South" and the necessity of giving the Southerners "just retribution for their hellish rebellion." [5] The slaveholder Rollins, rather than the self-proclaimed egalitarian Ste-

[3] Arnold, *Lincoln*, 360. [4] *Cong. Globe,* 38 Cong., 2 sess., 528.

[5] Current, *Old Thad Stevens,* 204–207.

vens, was the real spokesman for Lincoln in the House.

On January 31, 1865, the proposal came to a final vote in the House. Stevens had set the hour at three o'clock, but Ashley allowed the Democrats to go on speaking until half past three. A group of angry Republicans gathered around Ashley's seat, Stevens among them. His eyes blazing, he shook his finger at Ashley and read him a lecture for giving way, while Ashley's face, according to a witness, looked "as red as a fresh cut of beef." Though a few minutes behind schedule, the roll call duly began.[6]

As the clerk came to the names of the Democrats who the previous session had voted *nay*, and one after another several of them—Baldwin, Coffroth, McAllister, English, Ganson—now voted *aye*, the crowded galleries burst out with repeated and growing applause, and many of the Republicans on the floor joined in it. All together, thirteen Democrats this day voted in favor of the amendment, besides the four who also had voted for it previously. The resolution carried with more than the necessary two-thirds majority. When Speaker Colfax announced the result, renewed and intensified cheering was heard, and parliamentary order was forgotten. The House quickly adjourned for the day. Outside, cannon boomed.[7]

VI

From Capitol Hill, Representative Arnold with a group of Lincoln's personal friends went at once to the White House to exchange congratulations with the President. "The passage of the resolution filled his heart with joy," Arnold later recalled. "He saw in it the complete consummation of his own work, the emancipation proclamation."[1]

The next day, February 1, 1865, when the resolution was brought to him for his signature, Lincoln signed it, as seemed perfectly natural for him to do. He, along with Speaker Colfax and Vice President Hamlin, had forgotten that the President need not sign a resolution of that kind. On second thought the Senate resolved that "such approval was unnecessary," since the Supreme Court had decided in a case arising in 1798 that the President had "nothing to do" with

6 *Ibid.*, 206.

7 *Cong. Globe*, 38 Cong., 2 sess., 531.

1 Arnold, *Lincoln*, 365–366.

either the proposal or the adoption of constitutional amendments.[2] Only in a technical sense, however, did Lincoln have nothing to do with this one.

The crowd who, on the evening of the day he signed the resolution, marched to the White House to felicitate him, certainly thought that he had had something to do with it. He had done what he could to eradicate slavery by issuing his proclamation, he told the marchers, but the proclamation "did not meet the evil," or so its critics might maintain. "But this amendment is a King's cure for all the evils. It winds the whole thing up." He could not help congratulating everyone in the crowd, himself, the country, and the whole world upon this "great moral victory." [3]

As the news spread, the old abolitionists were among the most enthusiastic of all who rejoiced throughout the North. To them the President long had seemed timid and ineffectual in dealing with slavery. Now, at last, they could give him unstinted and wholehearted praise. "And to whom is the country more immediately indebted for this vital and saving amendment of the Constitution than, perhaps to any other man?" So William Lloyd Garrison asked in the course of a speech to a meeting of celebrators in Boston. "I believe I may confidently answer," he went on, "—to the humble railsplitter of Illinois—to the Presidential chainbreaker for millions of the oppressed—to Abraham Lincoln!" [4]

"The great job is ended," Lincoln himself declared.[5] That is, the first great obstacle had been overcome. "But," as he told the serenaders on February 1, "there is a task yet before us—to go forward and consummate by the votes of the States that which Congress so nobly began yesterday." He was proud to inform the crowd that his own state of Illinois, this very day, had led off by ratifying the amendment. And Maryland was "about half through." [6]

Ratification proceeded apace. After Illinois came Rhode Island and Michigan on February 2, then Maryland, New York, and West Virginia on the next day. Before the end of the month Maine, Kansas, Massachusetts, Pennsylvania, Virginia, Ohio, Missouri, Indiana, Nevada, Louisiana, and Minnesota also acted. By the end of the first

---

[2] *Collected Works,* VIII, 253–254. [3] *Ibid.,* 254–255.

[4] *The Liberator,* Feb. 10, 1865, quoted in Nicolay and Hay, *Lincoln,* X, 79 n.

[5] Arnold, *Lincoln,* 366. [6] *Collected Works,* VIII, 254.

week in April three more states—Wisconsin, Vermont, and Tennessee—had joined the list. Thus a total of twenty ratified while Lincoln was still alive.

Two of the loyal states, Delaware and Kentucky, refused to ratify, and both expressed their refusal in more forceful terms than mere inaction. The General Assembly of Delaware resolved (February 8, 1865) that the proposed amendment was "violative of the reserved rights of the several States," and, if adopted, would "form an insuperable barrier to the restoration of the seceded States to the Federal Union." [7] In Kentucky (also on February 8) Governor Bramlette recommended that the state legislature ratify but provoked more antagonism than support. To the last, a majority of the Kentucky legislators remained sullen and defiant. Like those of Delaware, they declared that the amendment encroached upon the reserved rights of the states, which were "above and superior to the Constitution." They denied that the amendment would be binding upon their state, and they hinted strongly at nullification.[8]

Since Kentucky and Delaware refused to approve it, the amendment would have to have the favorable action of at least four states of the Confederacy, if it was to receive the approval of three-fourths of all the states. In the end, on December 18, 1865, Secretary Seward counted the ratifications of eight ex-Confederate states, in addition to nineteen others, when he proclaimed the Thirteenth Amendment as in full effect. At that time the Radicals in Congress had excluded the Senators and Representatives from the seceding states and had refused to recognize their reconstructed governments. These governments were competent to ratify a constitutional amendment but incompetent, in the eyes of Congress, for anything else.[9]

VII

It would be an oversimplification to say that the Thirteenth Amendment made freemen out of slaves, or even that it was intended to do so. The amendment grew out of a variety of motives, as Henry Wilson said. Some who favored it were motivated by a sense of "re-

[7] *Delaware Senate Journal,* 1865, pp. 126, 128; *Delaware House Journal,* 1865, p. 148.
[8] Chicago *Tribune,* Dec. 23, 1865, p. 2.
[9] Randall, *Constitutional Problems under Lincoln,* 396–401.

ligious obligation" or by "humane considerations," but others by "feelings of resentment" against slaveholders, whom they blamed for starting the war. The largest number were moved by "prudential considerations merely," Wilson believed (and, though Wilson did not say so, Lincoln himself was moved by such considerations mainly). "They accepted emancipation not so much from any heartfelt conversion to the doctrine of anti-slavery as from the conviction that the removal of slavery had become a military, if not a political, necessity." The "foul spirit of caste" still "lurked within the hearts of many" who applauded the progress of emancipation.[1] So long as the former slaves suffered from the prejudice of the white community, they would not be free *men* but only free *Negroes*.

The Negroes freed during the war, like those already free when the war began, had to make their way against serious handicaps, whether as soldiers or as civilians and whether as residents of the North or of the South. The plight of the new freedmen was sometimes desperate. Before the end of 1863 fifty thousand of them, mostly women and children, were adrift in the lower Mississippi Valley, with little shelter and practically no food, except occasional army rations of crackers and dried beef. "At present, hundreds of the blacks would gladly return to slavery, to avoid the hardships of freedom," Lincoln was informed.[2] Even the most fortunate of the freedmen faced hardships and dangers to which white men were immune. Negro soldiers ran an added risk (if captured, they could not count upon the usual protection of the laws of war) and Negro laborers in the army were paid, at first, according to their color and not according to their work. Even Negroes born free and living in the so-called free states lacked many of the privileges ordinarily associated with freedom. They could not enter certain occupations, they could not always travel without restriction, and they could not vote or hold office in most of the states, including Illinois.

Before the end of the war the free Negroes and their white friends began a campaign in the state legislatures and in Congress to free the colored population from discriminatory laws. Most of the anti-Negro legislation of Illinois (but not the restriction of suffrage to the

---

1 Wilson, *Rise and Fall of the Slave Power*, III, 453–454.

2 Western Sanitary Commission to Lincoln, Nov. 6, 1863, A. A. Lawrence MSS., Mass. Hist. Soc.

whites) was repealed early in 1865. At about the same time Congress passed and the President signed a bill setting up the Freedmen's Bureau to care for refugees. Senator Sumner, who had got Negroes admitted to practice in the Federal courts, tried to obtain for them the privilege of riding on the Washington street cars. Representative Stevens began to talk of confiscating Southern estates and dividing them among the freedmen—"forty acres and a mule" to each family head. The Fourteenth Amendment, presumably designed to protect Negroes in their civil rights, and the Fifteenth Amendment, to guarantee their right to vote, were to be adopted in the early post-war years. These were only the beginning steps in an undertaking which, nearly a century later, was still to fall short of complete success.

The Negro's advancement was hindered less by laws or the absence of laws than by popular attitudes—the "foul spirit of caste," as Henry Wilson called it. Lincoln himself had yielded to this spirit when, in 1862, he urged the resettlement of freed Negroes in foreign lands, with the argument that the white and black races could not be expected to live together in harmony within the United States. While some Negro leaders approved the idea of colonizing their people outside the country, others denounced it, and one wrote impertinently to the President: "Pray tell us is our right to a home in this country less than your own?" [3] Lincoln not only abandoned the colonization idea but also proceeded to give repeated demonstrations that, whether or not Negroes and whites could mingle harmoniously in the country at large, they could certainly do so within his own official home.

He opened the White House to colored visitors as no President had done before, and he received them in a spirit which no President has matched since. At his New Year's Day reception in 1864 "four colored men, of genteel exterior and with the manners of gentlemen, joined in the throng that crowded the Executive Mansion, and were presented to the President of the United States," as the Washington *Morning Chronicle* reported the unprecedented news. There was no scene. "We are neither amalgamationists nor advocates of the leveling of all social distinctions," the *Chronicle* commented; "but we rejoice that we have a President who is a democrat by fact as well as

[3] Quarles, *The Negro in the Civil War,* 150.

by nature." [4] On the Fourth of July that same year Lincoln gave permission to the colored schools of the District of Columbia to hold a celebration on the White House grounds, and on August 6 he allowed Negroes to assemble on the grounds in day-long ceremonies observing the national day of humiliation and prayer which he had ordained.[5] In these and other ways he set an example of tolerance for all his fellow countrymen.

Lincoln invited and welcomed prominent individual Negroes. Frederick Douglass met him several times at the Soldiers' Home and paid at least three calls at the White House. He made his last visit as a guest at the reception on the night of the second inauguration. As he approached the door that night he was seized by two policemen and forbidden to enter, but managed to bolt past them. On the inside two other policemen took hold of him. He thought they were going to lead him to the President; instead, they led him out through a window on a plank. At the door again, he appealed to a guest going in to tell Lincoln he was there. In a moment he was invited into the East Room. There, in the presence of an elegant company of ladies and gentlemen, Lincoln said in a voice heard all around: "Here comes my friend Douglass." He shook hands cordially with him and immediately engaged him in conversation. Afterwards Douglass recalled:

"In all my interviews with Mr. Lincoln I was impressed with his entire freedom from popular prejudice against the colored race. He was the first great man that I talked with in the United States freely, who in no single instance reminded me of the difference between himself and myself, of the difference of color, and I thought that all the more remarkable because he came from a state where there were black laws." [6]

Another former slave, the remarkable Sojourner Truth, had a friendly and unstrained conversation with Lincoln when she dropped into see him, October 20, 1864. He obliged her by signing his name in her autograph book, for "Aunty Sojourner Truth," as he wrote. When a delegation of Negro Baptist clergymen sought an appointment with him, he had them shown in and nodded his head in assent

---

[4] Washington *Morning Chronicle,* Jan. 2, 1864, p. 3, c. 2.

[5] Quarles, *The Negro in the Civil War,* 253–254.

[6] Rice, *Reminiscences of Abraham Lincoln,* 188–193.

as they requested permission to preach to colored soldiers.[7] He gave hearty encouragement to another Negro preacher who wished to send missionaries among the escaping slaves, the "contrabands." [8] Numbers of other colored people also came to him, and all went away gratified at their cordial and respectful treatment.

He did more than send his Negro supplicants away with kind words. When a thousand New Orleans Negroes sent a two-man delegation to Washington (in January, 1864) he responded by assigning James A. McKaye, of the American Freedmen's Inquiry Commission, to look into their needs and wants. McKaye went to New Orleans, attended a colored mass meeting, and learned that they desired public schools, recognition as human beings, and the abolition of the black codes.[9] Lincoln, apparently impressed by the behavior of the Louisiana Negroes, was willing to grant them a little more than they demanded. In March he sent a private letter to Michael Hahn, congratulating him on his inauguration as the first free-State governor of Louisiana, and adding: "Now you are about to have a convention, which, among other things, will probably define the elective franchise. I barely suggest to your private consideration, whether some of the colored people may not be let in—as, for instance, the very intelligent, and especially those who fought gallantly in our ranks. They would probably help, in some trying time to come, to keep the jewel of liberty within the family of freedom." [10]

In the presence of his Negro visitors Lincoln was careful not to use expressions or tell stories which might offend them. In the presence of white men approaching him in the Negro's behalf he was not always so careful, but he was equally responsive to their appeals. "Sometime during the year 1864," according to a memoir left by Henry Samuels, several representatives of the Committee for Recruiting Colored Troops were ushered into the President's private room by Secretary Stanton. "The President was seated at his desk with his long legs on the top of it, his hands on his head and looking exactly like a huge katydid or grass-hopper." He quietly listened until his petitioners had finished, then "turned his head and jocularly said, with one of those peculiar smiles of his": "Well, gentlemen,

---

[7] Quarles, *The Negro in the Civil War*, 252–253.

[8] Cincinnati *Daily Gazette*, June 23, 1863, p. 3, c. 4.

[9] Quarles, *The Negro in the Civil War*, 251.

[10] Nicolay and Hay, *Works*, X, 39.

you wish the pay of 'Cuffie' raised." The youthfully brash and earnest Samuels objected: "Excuse me, Mr. Lincoln, the term 'Cuffie' is not in our vernacular. What we want is that the wages of the American Colored Laborer be equalized with those of the American White Laborer." Lincoln replied: "I stand corrected, young man, but you know I am by birth a Southerner and in our section that term is applied without any idea of an offensive nature. I will, however, at the earliest possible moment do all in my power to accede to your request." About a month later the war department issued an order requiring that Negro teamsters and other laborers employed by the army be paid at the same rate as white men doing the same kinds of work.[11]

Though relatively few Negroes ever saw Lincoln, and still fewer talked with him, Negroes everywhere came to think of him as their friend. They were not backward in expressing their regard for him. The colored people of Baltimore, to show their appreciation of the "distinguished services of President Lincoln in the cause of human freedom," contributed $580.75 to have a copy of the Bible bound in purple velvet, mounted in gold, engraved with a representation of Lincoln striking the shackles from a slave, and enclosed in a walnut case lined with white silk. This imposing volume they presented to the President at the White House in September, 1864. "I can only say now, as I have often said before, it has always been a sentiment with me that all mankind should be free," Lincoln remarked, in thanking the colored delegation. "In regard to the great book, I can only say it is the best gift which God has ever given man." [12] The action of the Baltimore colored people, he told Frank B. Carpenter, gave him more real satisfaction than any other public testimonial he ever received.[13]

In the mail that came to Lincoln from colored correspondents, no letter was more touching than the one signed "don carlous Butler," on St. Helena Island, off the coast of South Carolina, who begged the President to see that his plot of ground, with his improvements on it, was not taken away from him. Don Carlos dictated the letter to Laura Towne, a devoted teacher of the freedmen, and she added a postscript. She said that he had formerly been a confidential servant in

11 Henry Samuels, "My Interview with Lincoln," typescript dated "3/8/89," Ill. State Hist. Soc.

12 Baltimore *Sun,* Sept. 8, 1864, p. 1, c. 5.

13 Quarles, *The Negro in the Civil War,* 254.

the famous Alston family (he had been acquainted with Theodosia Burr Alston before her mysterious disappearance at sea in 1812) and explained that he could read and write but was too old to do it with ease. "He, with others of the Freedmen, often expresses a wish to be able to speak to Massa Linkum, feeling that *he* will listen to their plea for land & do what is best for them." [14]

Lincoln, dead, was nearly deified by many Negroes. "There were no truer mourners, when all were sad, than the poor colored people who crowded the streets, joined the procession, and exhibited their woe, bewailing the loss of him whom they regarded as a benefactor and father." So wrote Secretary Welles, after the funeral ceremonies in Washington.[15] And many years later a Negro historian wrote: "The deep, nation-wide grief of the Negroes was an outward sign that their generation would hold the name of the martyred President in everlasting remembrance. The colored people beheld in Lincoln a father image; he was 'the chieftest of ten thousand, and altogether lovely.' His death burdened every black with a personal sense of loss . . . ." [16]

---

[14] Don Carlos Butler and Laura Towne to Lincoln, May 29, 1864, R. T. L. Coll., 33391.

[15] Welles, *Diary,* II, 293.

[16] Quarles, *The Negro in the Civil War,* 345.

CHAPTER XIV

ANOTHER PEACE BUBBLE

EVENTS appeared to be hurrying to a climax as January ended and February began, in 1865. Not only was the Thirteenth Amendment approved by Congress and sent out to the states for ratification. Peace feelers also were being extended from Washington to Richmond, and these culminated in President Lincoln's going to Hampton Roads to meet commissioners from the Confederacy on February 3. Northern newspaper readers assumed for a few days that the war was about to end. Then the peace bubble burst. The Hampton Roads conference left both President and people (with some exceptions) convinced that actual peacemaking must wait upon the final military victory.

I

Victory could not be deferred for long, or so most Northerners believed during the winter of 1864–65. "The people seem to have settled since the election into perfect confidence," a Washington visitor wrote in mid-February, "that the end is sure, that the South must submit and come back, that slavery is dead, & that Grant & Sherman & Thomas are masters of the situation & guarantors of their security." [1]

This confidence was justified by news from the Confederacy. Defeatism was spreading in the ranks of the Confederate armies. Disaffected states, such as North Carolina and Georgia, were threatening to withdraw from the war. President Jefferson Davis was losing more and more of his little popularity among the Southern people, and his critics in high places, including the Vice President himself, Alex-

[1] H. Bellows to his son, Feb. 12, 1865, Bellows MSS., Mass. Hist. Soc.

ander H. Stephens, were becoming increasingly outspoken against him. Some talked merely of impeachment, others of overthrowing the Davis regime and replacing it with a military dictatorship, headed by Robert E. Lee. Lee was finally made, not dictator, but general-in-chief of all the Confederate armies (heretofore he had commanded only the Army of Northern Virginia), giving the Confederacy a unified military command—too late. As a last desperate expedient, Confederate leaders began to take steps toward the recruitment of slave soldiers, which probably would have led to the abolition of slavery itself—if the Confederacy had lasted long enough.[2]

As they looked hopefully ahead to a Confederate collapse, the Northern people (or some of them, at least) began to think about the kind of peace that should be made. How many favored a lenient and how many a vengeful settlement, it was impossible to know. The only poll of public opinion was the one provided by the elections of 1864, and those elections gave no clue to popular preference as between Lincolnian and Radical reconstruction. Lincoln had been triumphantly re-elected, of course, but at the same time the Radical strength in Congress had been increased. Nevertheless, if no cross-section of opinion was available, at least the extremes could be delimited clearly enough.

At one extreme were men like Lieutenant Colonel H. B. Sargent, of Massachusetts. As early as 1862, while on active duty, he had concluded that the South would have to undergo a long period of military occupation after the war. By the end of 1864, as a permanently disabled veteran, he had come to believe, further, that the war should be made "a universal and effective scourge" and should lead to "the precipitation of a new civilization on the South." [3] A similar view was elaborated in an anonymous handbill, circulated in Massachusetts, which listed eight "Conditions of Peace Required of the So-Called Seceded States." These conditions were "unconditional surrender," the hanging of "one hundred of the arch traitors," disfranchisement of all other traitors, confiscation of rebel property, collection from the rebels of the costs of the war, collection of an additional indemnity to compensate the North for its time and trouble in

[2] Newspaper clipping, unidentified and undated, in Meigs Diary, 1866, MS., Lib. of Cong.; New York *Herald*, Feb. 1, 1865.

[3] Sargent to John A. Andrew, Apr. 13, 1862, Dec. 10, 1864, Andrew MSS., Mass. Hist. Soc.

having had to fight the war, abolition of slavery, imposition of territorial government upon the seceded states.[4]

At the other extreme were men like Clement L. Vallandigham, Fernando Wood, and other so-called Copperheads, who desired peace without any condition except the return of the seceded states to their old places in the Union.

Probably the majority of Northerners held views which fell somewhere in between the two extremes. The attitude of the moderates was exemplified by the numerous Philadelphians who contributed money for the relief of the citizens of conquered Savannah. The Philadelphia *Public Ledger* approved this generous treatment of the beaten rebels. "All we ask is their submission to the laws," the *Public Ledger* said. "When they are ready to do this they cease to be enemies, and it is our duty to act so as to make them our friends." [5]

There was not only the question of the kind of peace ultimately to be made; there was also the question, very closely related to it, of the procedure for making peace. This was not a case where the President was to negotiate and, with the consent of the Senate, to ratify a treaty, as with a foreign power. What should be the President's role, and what the role of Congress?

The newspapers were full of suggestions for the President after his re-election. Deal with the rebellious states as so many independent nations, beginning with North Carolina, whose legislature seems eager for peace and reunion. Or combine the Union and Confederate armies and send them to the Canadian and Mexican borders, to settle accounts with England and France, thus terminating the Civil War by means of a foreign war, or a couple of foreign wars. Or send a peace embassy to Richmond and promise a liberal amnesty to the rebels and the prompt readmission of Southern senators and representatives to the United States Congress.[6]

Lincoln meanwhile was pondering the peace problem in his own way. On November 25, 1864, he raised the question in cabinet. "He says he cannot treat with Jeff Davis and the Jeff Davis government," Secretary Welles noted, "but whom will he treat with or how commence the work?" Welles had an answer. Though the Confederate

4 Handbill, undated, in Mass. Hist. Soc.

5 Philadelphia *Public Ledger,* Jan. 11, 1865, p. 2, c. 1.

6 New York *Herald,* Aug. 27, 1864, p. 4, c. 1; Nov. 9, 1864, p. 4, c. 2; Nov. 17, 1864, p. 4, c. 3; Nov. 18, 1864, p. 4, c. 3; Nov. 20, 1864, p. 4, c. 3.

government itself could not be approached, for it was a "usurpation," and to negotiate with it would be to recognize it, nevertheless the separate states of the Confederacy were "entities" and could be "recognized and treated with." Welles agreed with Stanton's advice that the President should make no offer to any Confederate authority but should approach the Southern people as individuals. He should "hold open the doors of conciliation and invite the people to return to their duty." [7]

In his annual message to Congress, December 6, 1864, Lincoln made a clear statement of his own considered views on peacemaking procedures and peace terms. As for a peace mission to Richmond: "On careful consideration of all the evidence accessible it seems to me that no attempt at negotiation with the insurgent leader could result in any good. He would accept nothing short of severance of the Union—precisely what we will not and cannot give." As for the people of the South: "They can, at any moment, have peace simply by laying down their arms and submitting to the national authority under the Constitution." As for the roles of President and Congress: "Some certain, and other possible, questions are, and would be, beyond the Executive power to adjust; as, for instance, the admission of members into Congress, and whatever might require the appropriation of money. The Executive power itself would be greatly diminished by the cessation of actual war. Pardons and remissions of forfeitures, however, would still be within Executive control."

As for the President's use of his pardoning power: "A year ago general pardon and amnesty, upon specified terms, were offered to all, except certain designated classes; and it was, at the same time, made known that the excepted classes were still within contemplation of special clemency." During the year many had availed themselves of the general provision, and many others had received special pardons. "Thus, practically, the door has been, for a full year, open to all . . . . It is still so open to all. But the time may come—probably will come—when public duty shall demand that it be closed; and that, in lieu, more rigorous measures than heretofore shall be adopted." As for slavery: "I repeat the declaration made a year ago, that 'while I remain in my present position I shall not attempt to retract or modify the emancipation proclamation, nor shall I return

[7] Welles, *Diary,* II, 179.

to slavery any person who is free by the terms of that proclamation, or by any of the Acts of Congress.' "

In sum: "In stating a single condition of peace, I mean simply to say that the war will cease on the part of the government, whenever it shall have ceased on the part of those who began it." [8]

To most of the Northern people these terms seemed, on the whole, remarkably lenient. "Taken altogether, no such executive emanation has ever proceeded from the Chief Magistrate of the American Republic," declared the Washington *Chronicle*. "It is an olive branch, a pardon, a welcome to return to the old household, to the penitent." [9] To impenitent Southerners, however, the terms seemed hypocritical, since they actually required complete submission to the authorities of what was to them an enemy power. The Richmond *Enquirer* commented sarcastically: "But 'the good wine is reserved for the last,' and the 'conditions of peace' close the message, and herein the amiability, mercy, and goodness of Mr. Lincoln stick out 'like the ears of an ass.' " [10]

II

Lincoln's message, despite his remark about the futility of his approaching the Confederate authorities, did not put an end to peace rumors or to schemes for opening negotiations. The Peace Democrats continued to insist that peace, with Union, could be had at an early date. Among Republicans, Horace Greeley still made himself the center of peacemaking plans, as he had done the previous summer. Yielding a little to the clamor, Lincoln allowed two separate unofficial peacemakers to cross the Union lines and go to Richmond. The upshot was an abortive peace conference in which the President himself took part.

The first of the unofficial missions was that of Francis P. Blair, Sr., and the impetus to it came from Greeley. On December 15, 1864, he wrote a long letter to Blair in which he suggested that the old man go South and use his talents to play upon the defeatism and disaffection there. If he was "at Raleigh with large powers," he "could pull North Carolina out of the Rebellion in a month." At any rate,

[8] *Collected Works,* VIII, 151–152.

[9] Washington *Morning Chronicle,* Dec. 7, 1864, p. 2, c. 2.

[10] Richmond *Enquirer,* Dec. 10, 1864, quoted in *ibid.,* Dec. 14, 1864, p. 1, c. 6.

by offering peace he could weaken the Confederacy. Lincoln ought to let him go. Lincoln ought to learn from the example of Napoleon, who never fought a war "without *seeming* to try hard to avoid it." Lincoln had done this in his first inaugural, but in his more recent public statements there was "no exhibition of the same spirit." His recent management of affairs was "worse on its civil or diplomatic than in its military aspect," and that was "quite bad enough." [1]

Old man Blair needed no urging. He promptly replied to Greeley that he had been thinking of a peace plan for some time and that Greeley's letter tempted him to reveal it to the President very soon.[2] He did hint repeatedly to Lincoln that he wanted to see him, but Lincoln put him off by saying: "Come to me after Savannah falls." [3] On December 28, a few days after Savannah had fallen, Blair got from Lincoln a pass through the Union lines,[4] without telling him what he intended to do. From the Confederate secretary of war he gained permission to enter the Confederate lines on the pretext that he was seeking certain family papers which had been taken from his Silver Springs house at the time of the Early raid.[5]

His destination was Richmond, not Raleigh. Once inside the Confederacy, he sent two letters to Jefferson Davis. One, intended as a cover-up, referred to the lost papers. The other stated his real purpose: to discuss with Davis the "state of the affairs of our country." Blair explained that he was "wholly unaccredited except in so far as I may be by having permission to pass our lines and to offer you my suggestions—suggestions which I have submitted to no one in authority on this side of the lines." [6] Davis, who knew something of the devious language of diplomacy, took these words to mean that Lincoln was, of course, privy to Blair's plans and would espouse them officially in due time. So Davis admitted Blair to a private conference in Richmond on January 12, 1865, to hear his scheme.

And a remarkable scheme it proved to be. It was nothing less than the plan, long familiar in the pages of the New York *Herald,* to end the Civil War by means of a foreign war. Blair talked to Davis about the French in Mexico, about their puppet emperor Maximilian, and about the danger to American republicanism from European mon-

1 Greeley to Blair, Dec. 15, 1864, Blair MSS., Lib. of Cong.

2 Blair to Greeley, Dec. 20, 1864, Greeley MSS., N. Y. Pub. Lib.

3 Nicolay and Hay, *Lincoln,* X, 94.

4 *Collected Works,* VIII, 188.

5 Seddon to Blair, Dec. 31, 1864, Blair MSS.

6 Nicolay and Hay, *Lincoln,* X, 94–95.

archy. "Jefferson Davis is the fortunate man who now holds the commanding position to encounter this formidable scheme of conquest," Blair intimated to him, "and whose fiat can at the same time deliver his country from the bloody agony now covering it in mourning." Suppose "secret preliminaries to armistice" should enable Davis to send part of his armies to Mexico to aid in driving out the invader. Then, very likely, "multitudes" from the Union armies would join in the patriotic enterprise. Not only would the Monroe Doctrine be vindicated, but also the United States might be expanded by the annexation of Mexico and most of Central America. Jefferson Davis would thus have credit for completing the work of Thomas Jefferson by "rounding off our possessions on the continent at the Isthmus."

To Davis, this project must have sounded like one of Seward's brainstorms, and he expressed to Blair his suspicions of Seward, whom Confederate leaders generally considered as a crafty and unprincipled schemer. Blair replied that, whatever Seward's failings, Lincoln was trustworthy. "The transaction is a military transaction," he went on, "and depends entirely upon the Commander-in-Chief of our armies." Whatever Davis may really have thought of the Mexican project—he professed to be interested in it—he could see possible gains for the Confederate cause from the appointment of commissioners to a peace conference. He gave Blair a letter, for Lincoln to see, in which he indicated his willingness to appoint such commissioners, "with a view to secure peace to the two countries." [7]

These words, "the two countries," caught Lincoln's eye when, on January 18, Blair brought him Davis's letter and an account of the conversation with Davis. What Lincoln then said about Blair's Mexican project, if he said anything, is not recorded. Doubtless he was more interested in what Blair had to say about the despondency and defeatism of prominent Confederates, with many of whom Blair had talked while in Richmond. Anyhow, Lincoln gave Blair a note to take back to Davis. In it he said he was ready to receive any agent whom Davis might informally send to him "with the view of securing peace to the people of our one common country." [8]

On the day he called on Lincoln, Blair wrote to Greeley that the success of his mission depended upon absolute secrecy, and he did not tell even Greeley what he had in mind, but only that he had

[7] *Ibid.*, 95–105.

[8] *Collected Works,* VIII, 275–276.

"great hopes." [9] Greeley kept his *Tribune* fairly free of news on the subject, but other newspapers reported Blair's goings and comings in considerable detail and, with no inhibitions, speculated about the significance of his mission.[10] Many Republicans criticized the President for permitting "the journeyings of Mr. Blair." One of Stanton's correspondents wrote, from Ohio: "The opinion of our thinking men and the masses is, that there should be no negotiation, or discussion or official communication, or understanding with the rebels in regard to peace or a cessation of hostilities, or their condition after peace is established, until there is an unconditional surrender." [11] And one of Washburne's Illinois constituents likewise deplored the rumor of peace. "It does not strike the country favorably here," he wrote. "We think rebels should be made to submit to the government." [12]

Amid wild rumors, South as well as North, Blair reappeared in Richmond and had a second interview with Davis. He tried to explain to Davis that Lincoln, because of Radical opposition, could not approve the Mexican venture. He made a new suggestion—that "political agencies" might be by-passed by the military, Generals Lee and Grant arranging a suspension of hostilities. After returning to Washington, however, Blair sent word to Davis that the idea of a military convention also was unacceptable.[13]

Davis was left with nothing except Lincoln's agreement to an informal discussion of ways to bring peace to "our one common country." He conferred with his cabinet and decided to go ahead with the appointment of commissioners. Alexander H. Stephens thought Davis himself should serve, but Davis appointed Stephens and two other strong peace advocates: the president *pro tem* of the Confederate Senate, R. M. T. Hunter, and the assistant secretary of war (formerly associate justice of the United States Supreme Court), John A. Campbell.[14] The Confederate secretary of state, Judah P. Benjamin, prepared a commission for the three which read: "In com-

9 Smith, *Blair Family,* 311.

10 See, for example, the Cincinnati *Daily Gazette,* Jan. 10, 1865, p. 3, c. 4; Jan. 19, 1865, p. 3, c. 3; Jan. 21, 1865, p. 3, c. 3.

11 James L. Bates to Stanton, Jan. 23, 1865, Stanton MSS.

12 W. Talcott to Washburne, Feb. 4, 1865, Washburne MSS.

13 Davis, *Rise and Fall of the Confederate Government,* II, 616–617.

14 Stephens, *A Constitutional View of the Late War between the States,* II, 594–595.

pliance with the letter of Mr. Lincoln . . . you are hereby requested to proceed to Washington City for conference with him upon the subject to which it relates . . . ." But Davis changed the commission to read: ". . . for the purpose of securing peace to the two countries." [15]

After the three commissioners, on the basis of Davis' instructions, had applied (January 29) for entrance into the Union lines, Lincoln sent a messenger, Major Thomas T. Eckert, with directions to admit them only if they would state in writing that they came for the purpose specified in his note of January 18 to Blair. They then addressed a second application to Grant, and in it they referred to Lincoln's note. Grant accordingly admitted them, and Lincoln sent Seward to meet them at Fortress Monroe, with instructions to make clear to them the peace terms (reunion, emancipation, no armistice) and to hear and report what they had to say, but not to "assume to definitely consummate anything." As Seward left Washington (February 1) Lincoln repeated to Grant instructions which Stanton already had sent him: to proceed with his military movements and agree to no armistice.[16] Before Seward arrived, Eckert met the commissioners. When they presented their commission from Davis, Eckert refused to allow them to proceed to Fortress Monroe. "Thus," as Lincoln's secretaries have written, "at half-past nine on the night of February 1 the mission of Stephens, Hunter, and Campbell was practically at an end." [17]

III

In Washington, on the evening of that same February 1, Lincoln received at the White House a second man who, like Blair, had gone to Richmond as a self-appointed agent to feel out the chances for peace. This White House visitor was General James W. Singleton, a Democratic congressman from Illinois and a member of the Sons of Liberty.

On January 5, 1865, Lincoln had written out cards authorizing Singleton "to pass our lines with ordinary baggage, and go South," and (on return) "to pass our lines, with any Southern products, and

[15] Davis, *Rise and Fall,* II, 617.

[16] *Collected Works,* VIII, 279–280.

[17] Nicolay and Hay, *Lincoln,* X, 116.

to go to any of our trading posts."[1] Before departing, Singleton conferred with Greeley, and after he had gone a friend of his wrote to Greeley that he had "started for Richmond under direction of the President."[2] His mission was supposed to be secret but, along with Blair's, provoked much comment in the Northern press. "The President has given a pass to the notorious Copperhead of Illinois, General J. W. Singleton, to go to Richmond to have a talk with Jeff Davis," one Washington correspondent reported. "It is understood that he has [had] the assurance to tell the President that the rebels would talk freely with him (Singleton) although they will not 'with you Abolitionists.' "[3] Singleton arrived in Richmond (January 13) on the same boat that Blair boarded to return from his first visit. He remained there a couple of weeks and talked with Davis, Lee, and other prominent men of the Confederacy.Then he came back and talked with Lincoln.

Regarding the White House interview on Singleton's return, it was reported: "The President was not carried away by his suggestions as to the best way to restore harmony between the two 'nations.' "[4] Yet, in fact, there was something in the suggestions which must have impressed the President. Singleton's chief conclusions were the following: (1) "The Southern people are all anxious for peace." (2) It is "in the power of the North to reconstruct by an offer of liberal terms—to be considered and acted upon during an armistice of sixty days." (3) "The South will not consent to reconstruction on any other basis than the clearest recognition of the rights of States respectively to determine each for itself all questions of local and domestic government, slavery included." (4) "They will not permit slavery to stand in the way of Independence—to that it would be promptly surrendered, but to nothing else—unless it should be a fair compensation coupled with other liberal terms of reconstruction secured by Constitutional Amendments."[5] This "unless" clause was important. If correct, it meant that there was a possibility of an early peace with reunion and with the abolition of slavery—Lincoln's minimum terms—provided that Lincoln could assure the Southerners that they would be compensated for the loss of their slaves.

1 *Collected Works,* VIII, 200.
2 Alexander Long to Greeley, Jan. 11, 1865, Greeley MSS.
3 Cincinnati *Daily Gazette,* Jan. 13, 1865, p. 3, c. 4.
4 *Ibid.,* Feb. 2, 1865, p. 3, c. 5.
5 *Ibid.,* Feb. 8, 1865, p. 3, c. 9.

IV

On the morning after Singleton's visit, Lincoln received a telegram from Seward at Fortress Monroe saying "Richmond party not here," and then a telegram from Eckert at City Point explaining why he was detaining the three commissioners there. Lincoln was about to recall both Eckert and Seward, when another telegram—from Grant to Stanton—was shown to him. ". . . I am convinced, upon conversation with Messrs Stevens & Hunter that their intentions are good and their desire sincere to restore peace and union," Grant said. "I am sorry however that Mr. Lincoln cannot have an interview with the two named in this despatch if not all three now within our lines." This despatch changed Lincoln's mind, and he telegraphed to Grant and Seward that he personally would meet the Richmond "gentlemen" at Fortress Monroe as soon as he could get there.[1]

By this decision Lincoln took certain risks, especially the risk of antagonizing Radical opinion in his cabinet, in Congress, and among the Northern people. But he also stood to gain something. At the least, he might silence the Peace Democrats and the Peace Republicans, among the latter the influential journalists Horace Greeley and James Gordon Bennett. At the most, he might actually discover a basis for peace by conceding everything possible except his minimum conditions, Union and emancipation.

The Confederate commissioners themselves might have been satisfied with those conditions, if combined with liberal concessions on collateral points, and if embodied in a formal agreement. Stephens, for one, did not believe that the success of "the Cause" necessarily required independence for the Confederacy or even the permanence of slavery. With him, the Cause depended upon the establishment of a principle, the principle of state rights and constitutional liberties as he viewed them, and this principle might be established regardless of battles won or territory held. He would be satisfied with a peace recognizing his theory and enabling Southern libertarians and Northern Democrats to combine and put it into practice.

Stephens could hope, however, to win more immediate and more concrete gains for the Confederacy. Like Davis, he was convinced

[1] *Collected Works,* VIII, 281–282.

that Lincoln was actually behind Blair's suggestion of a truce during which the Confederate armies, with Northern aid, should drive the French out of Mexico. Now, Stephens and his fellow commissioners had no intention of accepting this proposal in the precise form in which Blair had put it forth. They intended to turn it against Lincoln: they would urge a truce during which the *Union* armies, but not the Confederate, might go about enforcing the Monroe Doctrine.[2] At the end of the truce the Lincoln government might or might not be able to resume the war against the South, and the Confederacy would have gained a respite if not final success.

On this point the interests of the Confederate President coincided with those of the Vice President. Davis, too, would have liked to see a truce. But he was not ready to accept a permanent peace that recognized only the theory of secession and state rights; so far as he was concerned, the peace must also embrace the fact of Confederate independence. Not that he expected this kind of peace to come from the mission of his three agents. The most he could hope for was an armistice; the least he could expect was an opportunity to discredit the Confederate peace men—in particular, his agents themselves, who were three of the foremost of Southern peace advocates. He might also get a new argument for appealing to the Southern people to fight on to the last.

The aims of Davis and his three commissioners, considered separately, were realistic enough, but peace did not mean quite the same thing to all these men. The aims of Lincoln and Seward also were realistic, but neither did these two agree precisely on all matters, such as the concessions to be made in regard to slavery. And the Confederates persisted in assuming that Blair's ideas were really Lincoln's. So there developed a curious air of unreality, and the discussion proceeded not only at cross purposes but also on different levels, when Lincoln and Seward met with Stephens, Hunter, and Campbell on board the *River Queen,* anchored off Fortress Monroe in Hampton Roads, for about four hours on the morning of February 3, 1865. It was an informal conference and, as Seward made clear at the outset, no official record was to be kept. Except for the summary reports afterwards made in Washington and in Richmond, the only sources for what was said are the recollections of the Confederate commis-

[2] Stephens, *Constitutional View,* II, 589, 592.

sioners, and Stephens left much the most circumstantial account. Our knowledge of the Hampton Roads Conference must depend, for most of the details, upon the memory and the veracity of Stephens.[3]

Once acquaintances had been renewed, and old recollections recalled, Stephens set out to commit Lincoln to the truce that was to give the Confederate armies a rest while occupying the Union armies in Mexico. "Well, Mr. President, is there no way of putting an end to the present trouble . . . ?" Stephens began. Lincoln said there was only one way he knew of, and that was for those who were resisting the laws of the United States to cease their resistance. "But," hinted Stephens, is there no other question that might divert the attention of both parties, for a time . . . ?" Lincoln got the hint. He explained that Blair's ideas had not been revealed to him in advance and had never received the least authority from him. "The restoration of the Union is a *sine qua non* with me," he said, "and hence my instructions that no conference was to be held except upon that basis."

Stephens took this to mean merely that the Mexican project was conditional upon a previous pledge that the Union would be restored. He tried to argue that, after the armistice and the vindication of the Monroe Doctrine, reunion was bound to follow, whether or not there was an advance commitment regarding it. "A settlement of the Mexican question in this way," it seemed to Stephens, "would necessarily lead to a peaceful settlement of our own." Lincoln repeated that he could make no treaty or agreement of any kind with the Confederate states, jointly or separately, until the question of reunion had been satisfactorily disposed of. Seward clinched the point by reading the relevant passages of the President's last message to Congress, concluding: "In stating a single condition of peace, I mean simply to say that the war will cease on the part of the Government whenever it shall have ceased on the part of those who began it." [4]

That ended that. There remained, besides the issues of political

---

[3] Stephens' account is in *ibid.*, 599–619; Hunter's and Campbell's are in *So. Hist. Soc. Papers,* n. s., III, 168 ff. and IV, 49 ff. The report of the Confederate commissioners to the Confederate President may be found in Davis, *Rise and Fall,* II, 619–620. Lincoln's report to Congress, with the correspondence relating to both the Blair mission and the Hampton Roads Conference, is given in *Collected Works,* VIII, 274–285.

[4] Stephens, *Constitutional View,* II, 599–602, 608–609.

and property rights for Southerners, the question of slavery. Stephens wanted to know whether, after the war had ended, the Emancipation Proclamation would be held to have freed all the slaves of the South or only those who actually had become free during the war. Lincoln said his own opinion was that it was a war measure and would become inoperative once the war had stopped, but he said the courts might decide otherwise. Seward then broke the news that, only a few days before, Congress had passed the proposal for a constitutional amendment abolishing slavery. He went on to say that this also was a war measure, and he left the commissioners to infer that, if the Confederate states would quit the war, they could defeat the amendment by voting it down as members of the Union.[5]

Lincoln himself did not suggest that they could defeat the amendment, but he did suggest (according to Stephens) that they could postpone its adoption. He advised Stephens to induce Georgia to recall its troops, then to "ratify this Constitutional Amendment *prospectively,* so as to take effect—say in five years," and thus to avoid the evils of immediate emancipation. He added, later, that he thought there was a good chance slaveowners might be compensated. "He believed that the people of the North were as responsible for slavery as the people of the South, and if the war should then cease, with the voluntary abolition of slavery by the States, he should be in favor, individually, of the Government paying a fair indemnity for the loss to the owners. He said he believed this feeling had an extensive existence at the North." But he could not guarantee compensation.[6]

What about confiscated property other than slaves? Would confiscation continue? Lincoln answered that the enforcement of the confiscation acts was up to him, and he gave full assurance that he would exercise his power with the utmost liberality. What about property already confiscated? Would it be returned? Seward explained that this was up to Congress and the courts, and he said they would no doubt make restitution or pay indemnity after the excitement of the times had passed. Would the seceded states be readmitted to representation in Congress if they abandoned the war? Lincoln said he could enter into no stipulations on the subject (Congress being, of course, the judge of its own membership). "His own opinion was, that when the resistance ceased and the National Authority

[5] *Ibid.,* 610–614.

[6] *Ibid.,* 614, 617.

was recognized, the States would be immediately restored to their practical relations to the Union." [7]

Such was the kind of peace that Lincoln would have made in February, 1865, if the insurgent leaders and his own Congress and people had permitted him to make it. Let the Southern people lay down their arms and acknowledge the laws of the United States. Let them be represented again in the national Congress. Let them emancipate their slaves—gradually perhaps—and be paid for the loss. Let their other property be restored as soon as possible, and their civic rights at once. These terms, however, were much too generous for the Radical Republicans of the North, and they were much too severe for even the most sincerely peaceminded leaders of the South. "No treaty, no stipulation, no agreement, either with the Confederate States jointly, or with them separately, as to their future position or security!" exclaimed Hunter. "What was this but unconditional submission to the mercy of conquerors?" [8]

V

The American people, both North and South, wanted peace in February, 1865, but peace meant different things to them. In the North it meant reunion at the very least and various degrees of reconstruction besides. In the South it generally meant separation and independence. The popular reactions to the Hampton Roads Conference varied according to the different definitions of peace.

While awaiting the return of the Confederate commissioners, newspapers in Richmond undertook to prepare the Southern people for fighting on. The *Sentinel,* frankly concerned lest the mission should "enfeeble us with injurious expectation," urged its readers to keep in view the aim of independence for which they had drawn the sword, and to consider no peace which would compromise that aim. The *Enquirer* adopted a more positive tone. "We think it likely to do much good for our people to understand in an authoritative manner from men like Vice-President Stephens, Senator Hunter, and Judge Campbell the exact degree of degradation to which the enemy would reduce us by reconstruction," the *Enquirer* said. "We believe that the so-called mission of these gentlemen will teach our people that the

[7] *Ibid.,* 610, 617.

[8] *Ibid.,* 616.

A WHITE HOUSE RECEPTION

This lithograph, entitled "Grand Reception of the Notabilities of the Nation at the White House, 1865," and copyrighted by Frank Leslie in 1865, should be viewed as a generalized conception rather than a depiction of a specific event. The artist apparently confused a reception of March 1864, honoring General Grant, with the inaugural reception of March 4, 1865. Andrew Johnson was absent from the first of these occasions and Grant from the second, yet both men are pictured here. The drawing is interesting for its accurate representation of the East Room and its faithful likenesses of many "notabilities" who at one time or another were there. Among them, in the right foreground, the President and the First Lady are greeting Mrs. Grant. Near by are General Grant, Vice President Johnson, Chief Justice Chase, Secretary Stanton, Chase's daughter Kate, and Secretary Seward.

CLOTHING

LINCOLN IN RICHMOND

April 4, 1865. The drawing reproduced on the preceding page shows the President riding through Richmond "amid the enthusiastic cheers of the inhabitants." The one on this page shows him entering the "White House of the Confederacy," lately vacated by Jefferson Davis. From sketches drawn by Leslie's special artist on the scene, Joseph Becker, and published in *Frank Leslie's Illustrated Newspaper*, April 22 and 29, 1865.

Head Quarters Armies of the United States,
City Point, April 7. 11 AM 1865

Lieut. Gen. Grant.

Gen. Sheridan says "If the thing is pressed I think that Lee will surrender." Let the *thing* be pressed.

A. Lincoln

The original dispatch sent by Mr. Lincoln to me, Apl. 7th 1865,
U. S. Grant

Courtesy Chicago Hist. Soc.

A WORD TO GRANT

Lincoln's dispatch from City Point, April 7, 1865, admonishing Grant: "Let the *thing* be pressed." Note Grant's endorsement underneath.

terms of the enemy are nothing less than unconditional surrender." [1]

After the commissioners had returned, Davis appeared to be disappointed at Lincoln's repudiation of the Mexican project, and he attributed it to bad faith on Lincoln's part. Yet he thought something could be salvaged from the results of the conference. "Mr. Davis's position was," according to Stephens, "that inasmuch as it was now settled beyond question, by the decided and pointed declarations of Mr. Lincoln, that there could be no Peace short of *Unconditional Submission* on the part of the People of the Confederate States, with an entire change of their Social Fabric throughout the South, the People ought to be, and could be, more thoroughly aroused by Appeals through the Press and by Public Addresses, to the full consciousness of the necessity of renewed and more desperate efforts, for the preservation of themselves and their Institutions." Davis proceeded to make what propaganda he could. From the commissioners he demanded a written report, despite Stephens's protest that the *"real objects"* of the conference could not properly be disclosed, and he promptly transmitted the report (which was brief and matter-of-fact) to his Congress and to the newspapers. Then he made a fiery speech at a public meeting in Richmond.[2]

As among Southerners, so also among Northerners the news of the conference had some effect in uniting opinions and strengthening the will to fight. Reports from Washington, which gave a fairly accurate overall account of the day-to-day progress of the negotiations, indicated after the conference that it had "resulted in no change of attitude either of the Government or of the rebels. In other words, it was a failure." But the reports also said: "The Administration leaders hold the peace negotiations to have had a highly successful result in this, that they have shown authoritatively and conclusively the baseless character of arguments of opposition against our prosecution of the war. To have obtained from the proper rebel sources an authentic and authorized statement that they are fighting for independence and will consent to nothing less, is in itself a great success." [3] The news undoubtedly had a galvanizing effect upon Peace Democrats. Their leader in the House of Representatives, Fernando Wood, who for

---

[1] Quoted in Cincinnati *Daily Gazette,* Feb. 4, 1865, p. 3, c. 4 and 5.

[2] Stephens, *Constitutional View,* II, 619–623; Davis, *Rise and Fall,* II, 618–620.

[3] Cincinnati *Daily Gazette,* Feb. 6, 1865, p. 3, c. 5.

some time had been urging Lincoln to make overtures to the enemy,[4] said in the House on the day after the Hampton Roads Conference that he was no disunionist and that his complaint against the administration was based on its refusal to accept peace proposals from the rebels. "But," he was now reported as saying, "if the door had now been thrown open by the President, and if the answer to that was that *they would accept recognition and separation, and nothing else, then he desired to say, with his humble efforts, he should aid the conquering efforts of his country to obtain by force what it has been unable to obtain by peace*." And, with more italics, the Washington *Chronicle* concluded: ". . . *the action of the President of the United States has united the North*." [5]

The action of the President was, however, less pleasing to Radical Republicans than to Peace Democrats. A few of the Radicals approved the conference. "I am glad Lincoln was there in person," one of them wrote. "Now we shall have no more talk about commissions. He is shrewd and far seeing, I think." [6] But the Radicals in the cabinet and indeed all the members of the cabinet except Welles and Seward disapproved. "None of the Cabinet were advised of this move," Welles noted, "and without exception, I think, it struck them unfavorably that the Chief Magistrate should have gone on such a mission." [7] The Radicals in Congress also disapproved. "There are ultras among us who do not favor the cessation of hostilities except on terms and conditions which make that event remote," Welles noted further. "They are determined that the States in rebellion shall not resume their position in the Union except on new terms and conditions independent of those in the proposed Constitutional Amendment." [8]

The Radicals in the House called upon the President for information, and he responded by submitting copies of the correspondence relating to Blair's mission and his own. There was no document on the conference itself, and Lincoln's summary of the conversation was extremely brief. "On our part, the whole substance of the instructions to the Secretary of State, herein before recited, was stated and insisted upon, and nothing was said inconsistently therewith," he reported; "while, by the other party it was not said that, in any event, or on any

---

[4] Wood to Lincoln, Nov. 18, 1864, R. T. L. Coll., 38496–97.

[5] Washington *Daily Morning Chronicle*, Feb. 6, 1865, p. 2, c. 2; Feb. 7, 1865, p. 2, c. 1.

[6] B. F. Prescott to Anna Dickinson, Feb. 13, 1865, Dickinson MSS., Lib. of Cong.

[7] Welles, *Diary*, II, 235 (Feb. 2, 1865).

[8] *Ibid.*, 239 (Feb. 10, 1865).

condition, they *ever* would consent to re-union, and yet they equally omitted to declare that they *never* would so consent. They seemed to desire a postponement of that question, and the adoption of some other course first, which, as some of them seemed to argue, might, or might not, lead to re-union, but which course, we thought, would amount to an indefinite postponement." [9]

So Lincoln only hinted at the Mexican project, and he said nothing at all about his discussion of slavery. Yet that subject had been much on his mind since his return from Hampton Roads. Apparently Singleton's opinion that the South might accept abolition with compensation, then the reaction of the Confederate commissioners to his own suggestions along that line, had made a deep impression on him. He was also driven to reconsider compensation by demands from Maryland. At Annapolis both the outgoing and the incoming governor, in January, 1865, recalled the pledge which Congress had made in 1862 to give pecuniary aid to those states that should liberate their slaves. In February the Maryland legislature, after resolving that the people of the state had acted in response to the offer of Congress, sent a committee to confer with the President and see whether he could get an appropriation.[10]

On February 5, the day after he arrived home from Hampton Roads, Lincoln presented his ideas on compensation to an evening session of the cabinet. He had prepared a message to Congress, recommending the passage of a joint resolution, and a proclamation to be issued in pursuance of it. The resolution would have empowered him to pay four hundred million dollars in government bonds to the slaveholding states, half of the amount when they ceased their resistance to the national authority, if they did so by April 1, 1865, and the other half after they had ratified the Thirteenth Amendment, if they ratified it in time for it to become law by July 1, 1865. (He had abandoned the idea of a "prospective" ratification, to take effect in five years, if indeed he had proposed that idea at Hampton Roads, as Stephens reported.) The proclamation would have announced "that all political offences will be pardoned; that all property, except slaves, liable to confiscation or forfeiture, will be released therefrom, except in cases of intervening interests of third parties; and that liberality

[9] *Collected Works,* VIII, 284–285.
[10] Randall, *Constitutional Problems under Lincoln* (rev. ed.), 402.

will be recommended to congress upon all points not lying within executive control." [11]

This was a proposal to buy peace and, with it, the ratification of the Thirteenth Amendment. The way Lincoln presented the plan, it sounded reasonable enough. The war could be expected to last another two hundred days, at least, and the cost of fighting that much longer would amount to four hundred million. Why not spend for peace what the nation was willing to spend for war? But the cabinet unanimously opposed the plan, and Lincoln put it aside. "The earnest desire of the President to conciliate and effect peace was manifest, but there may be such a thing as so overdoing as to cause a distrust or adverse feeling," Welles commented. "In the present temper of Congress the proposed measure, if a wise one, could not be carried through successfully." [12] And even if Congress had been inclined to adopt it, there is no reason to suppose that Jefferson Davis, judged by his reaction to the Hampton Roads Conference, would have been willing to accept it.

---

11 *Collected Works,* VIII, 260–261.

12 Welles, *Diary,* II, 237 (Feb. 6, 1865).

CHAPTER XV

WITH CHARITY FOR ALL

AS OF March 4, 1865, the old Congress had met for the last time, and the new one would not meet for several months (until December) unless the President meanwhile should choose to call it into special session. Lincoln now began his second term, which was not expected necessarily to be his last—gamblers soon were betting that he would be re-elected in 1868.[1] After four years as a war President, he could look ahead to nearly four more, at least, as a peace President. More immediately, with no Congress in session to hinder him, he could look ahead to a few months of peace-making on his own. He could hope, within that time, to complete the preliminaries of the kind of settlement that he desired.

I

Inauguration day dawned dark and rainy, and rain fell steadily throughout the morning. The streets of Washington, especially Pennsylvania Avenue, were filled with soft mud which oozed up between the bricks even where there was pavement. Before the inaugural ceremonies began, the rain stopped, but most of the spectators, standing in the mud around the east entrance of the Capitol, already were thoroughly bedraggled.[1] The ceremonies themselves were poorly planned, or so they seemed to Secretary Welles, who wrote: "All was confusion and without order,—a jumble." [2] As if the weather and the planning were not bad enough, the new Vice President, Andrew Johnson, made something of a scene when he was inaugurated. Those who heard or read his rambling and maudlin speech wondered whether he was

1 New York *Herald,* Mar. 19, 1865, p. 4, c. 5.

1 Cincinnati *Daily Gazette,* Mar. 9, 1865, p. 3, c. 8.

2 Welles, *Diary,* II, 251.

crazy or only drunk.[3] In fact he was unwell. Having been strongly urged by Lincoln to be present, he had fortified himself with whiskey beforehand, and because of his illness and his temperate habits, the effect was only too noticeable.

Lincoln's own inaugural address was short, the shortest any President had ever made. Its opening lines gave the impression that Lincoln had nothing to say. So many public declarations had been made during the war, he remarked, that "little that is new could be presented." He went on to remind his hearers of the circumstances of his first inaugural, then restated the central issue of the ensuing struggle as he saw it: "Both parties deprecated war; but one of them would *make* war rather than let the nation survive; and the other would *accept* war rather than let it perish. And the war came." Then he elaborated upon the basic issue by speaking of the "peculiar and powerful interest" of slavery. "All knew that this interest was, somehow, the cause of the war." He proceeded to describe the sufferings of the people, both North and South, as divine punishment for the sin of slavery, of which both were guilty. He concluded with the paragraph which made the address forever memorable (except to a later President, who in 1945, in characterizing his own war aims, distorted its spirit by omitting the first two phrases): "With malice toward none; with charity for all; with firmness in the right, as God gives us to see the right, let us strive on to finish the work we are in; to bind up the nation's wounds; to care for him who shall have borne the battle, and for his widow, and his orphan—to do all which may achieve and cherish a just, and a lasting peace, among ourselves, and with all nations." [4]

This second inaugural, like the Gettysburg address, was not hailed unanimously as a classic at its birth. Lincoln himself expected it to "wear as well—perhaps better than" anything he had produced, but he believed it was "not immediately popular." [5] Yet (like the Gettysburg address again) it was not entirely unappreciated by contemporaries.[6] The New York *Herald,* misquoting the phrase "the nation's wounds" and making it read "the nation's *wound,*" found aptness and significance in Lincoln's supposed use of the singular noun. On

[3] *Ibid.,* 252; Lincoln to Johnson, Jan. 24, 1865, *Collected Works,* VIII, 235; Philadelphia *Public Ledger,* Mar. 8, 1865, p. 2, c. 1.

[4] *Collected Works,* VIII, 332–333.

[5] Lincoln to Thurlow Weed, *ibid.,* 356.

[6] On the reception of the Gettysburg address, see *Lincoln the President,* II, 311 ff.

the whole, the *Herald* approved the speech while expressing some puzzlement at the personality of its author, "this remarkable rail-splitter." But the *Herald* was disappointed at its brevity and its generality, its failure to spell out peace terms, a failure which might cause the address to be taken as an "unconditional surrender" manifesto in the South.[7] The Washington *Chronicle,* contrasting the second with the first inaugural, thought the second one much superior, for it was "solemnly affirmative" where the other had been "deprecatory, apologetic, explanatory." [8]

At least one American citizen, however, was ashamed of the speech as a literary production. "Lincoln's Inaugural, while the sentiments are noble, is one of the most awkwardly expressed documents I ever read—if it be correctly printed. When he knew it would be read by millions all over the world, why under the heavens did he not make it a little more creditable to American scholarship?" So wrote a Pennsylvanian to Simon Cameron. "Jackson was not too proud to get Van Buren to slick up his state papers. Why could not Mr. Seward have prepared the Inaugural so as to save it from the ridicule of a Sophomore in a British University?" [9] But Cameron's correspondent knew nothing of the actual response in England, and if any British sophomore was inclined to ridicule the address, the Duke of Argyll certainly was not. "I . . . congratulate you both on the good progress of the war, and on the *remarkable speech* of your President," the Duke wrote to his friend Charles Sumner. "It was a noble speech, just and true, and solemn. I think it has produced a great effect in England." [10] The *Times* of London, for all its pro-Southern record, commented favorably on the address, and some of the British reviews gave it superlative praise, the *Spectator* declaring: "No statesman ever uttered words stamped at once with the seal of so deep a wisdom and so true a simplicity." [11] If anything, the second inaugural received even greater immediate acclaim in England than in the United States.

After delivering the address, Lincoln took the oath of his office, kissing the Bible which Chief Justice Chase presented to him. At that

---

[7] New York *Herald,* Mar. 4, 1865, p. 4, c. 3; Mar. 5, 1865, p. 1, c. 1–3, and p. 4, c. 2.

[8] Washington *Daily Morning Chronicle,* Mar. 6, 1865, p. 2, c. 1.

[9] A. B. Bradford to Cameron, Mar. 8, 1865, Cameron MSS., Lib. of Cong.

[10] Mass. Hist. Soc. *Proc.,* XLVII, 87.

[11] Various English newspaper and magazine reactions to the address are given in *Littell's Living Age,* LXXXV, 86–88 (April 15, 1865).

moment the sun burst forth above the actors and the crowd of spectators. Doubtless many of them, like the Chief Justice himself, looked for a symbol in the sudden change of weather. Later in the day, sending to Mrs. Lincoln the ceremonial Bible, with the kissed page carefully marked. Chase wrote in a note to her: "I hope the Sacred Book will be to you an acceptable souvenir of a memorable day; and I most earnestly pray Him, by whose Inspiration it was given, that the beautiful sunshine which just at the time the oath was taken dispersed the clouds that had previously darkened the sky may prove an auspicious omen of the dispersion of the clouds of war and the restoration of the clear sunlight of prosperous peace under the wise and just administration of him who took it." [12]

II

As Lincoln began his second term, the war was entering upon its final phase. Sherman's army, having left Savannah, was advancing northward through the Carolinas but had yet to meet the enemy under General Joseph E. Johnston, newly restored to command. Grant's forces were increasing their pressure upon Petersburg and Richmond. If Lee should escape and join with Johnston against Sherman, the end of the war might be delayed for some time. If, on the other hand, Sherman should get past Johnston and combine with Grant against Lee, the Confederate Capital would be isolated from the rest of the Confederacy, and Lee would have to surrender fairly soon.

Lincoln, glad for an opportunity to flee the cares of Washington and observe the fighting from near at hand, eagerly accepted Grant's invitation of March 20 to visit the front. With his wife and his son Tad he left Washington, March 23, on the steamer *River Queen* and arrived the next day at City Point, on the south side of the James River, several miles below Richmond. After a week Mrs. Lincoln went home and brought back a party including Senator Sumner and Senator and Mrs. Harlan and their daughter, the bride-to-be of Robert Todd Lincoln, who was on Grant's staff.[1] But Lincoln himself did not return to Washington for more than two weeks. Making the *River*

[12] Chase to Mrs. Lincoln, Mar. 4, 1865, R. T. L. Coll., 41949.

[1] *Collected Works,* VIII, 372–373, Washington *Daily Morning Chronicle,* Apr. 6, 1865, p. 2, c. 3.

Queen his home, he conferred with Grant and other officers—most significantly, with Sherman, who made a quick trip from his new base at Goldsboro, North Carolina. He visited the various camps, chatted with soldiers and was cheered by them. All the while he watched with great interest and with intelligent comprehension the progress of the fighting.

Grant kept him informed by frequent telegrams, which Lincoln forwarded to Stanton at the war department, with his own summaries and comments. But Grant, according to his memoirs, did not confide to Lincoln the fullness of his intentions, which were to capture Richmond and Petersburg and dispose of Lee's army without waiting for Sherman's men to join in the final assault. Grant intended to send Sheridan with his cavalry around to the southwest of Petersburg to take Five Forks and thus cut off Lee's lifeline, the railroad leading to Danville and the south. Lee, in an effort to save his communications and protect his flank and rear, could be expected to weaken his defenses before Petersburg and leave them vulnerable to a breakthrough.[2]

Lincoln, from day to day expecting (and fearing) a great and bloody battle, was not sure just when it would come or what form it would take. On March 30 he telegraphed to Stanton from City Point: "Last night at 10:15, when it was dark as a rainy night without a moon could be, a furious cannonade, soon joined in by a heavy musketry-fire, opened near Petersburg and lasted about two hours. The sound was very distinct here, as also were the flashes of the guns upon the clouds. It seemed to me a great battle, but the other hands here scarcely noticed it, and, sure enough, this morning it was found that very little had been done." On April 1 he learned from Grant that, on this day, something had been done indeed: Sheridan had taken Five Forks. The next day the dispatches came to Lincoln thick and fast. "All going finely," he telegraphed to Stanton. The Union troops had broken through the Petersburg intrenchments at several places, and Sheridan's cavalry was busy tearing up the tracks of the Danville railroad.

"This morning Gen. Grant reports Petersburg evacuated; and he is confident Richmond also is," Lincoln wired again, on the morning of April 3. "He is pushing forward to cut off if possible, the re-

[2] Grant, *Memoirs,* II, 440, 459–460.

treating army. I start to him in a few minutes." [3] Lincoln found Grant waiting for him in Petersburg on the piazza of a deserted house. The streets were empty, not a person, not an animal in sight. "I had a sort of sneaking idea all along that you intended to do something like this," Lincoln said, as he shook hands with Grant and thanked him, "but I thought some time ago that you would so maneuver as to have Sherman come up and be near enough to cooperate with you." The tactful General replied: "I had a feeling that it would be better to let Lee's old antagonists give his army the final blow and finish the job." [4] He explained that, if the Western soldiers of Sherman's army should deliver the final blow, Western politicians in after years might taunt the Eastern soldiers of the Army of the Potomac with the charge that the latter had won no important victories in the war, and thus sectional bitterness might arise between the East and the West. Lincoln remarked that, as for himself, he had not cared where aid came from, so long as the work was done.[5]

On his return to City Point he found a telegram from Stanton warning him against visiting Petersburg and exposing his life to rebel assassins. "Thanks for your caution," Lincoln answered; "but I have already been to Petersburg, stayed with Gen. Grant an hour and a half and returned here. I am certain now that Richmond is in our hands, and I think I will go there to-morrow. I will take care of myself." [6]

And to Richmond he went on the following day, by gunboat up the James to where the river was obstructed, then by a boat rowed by twelve sailors to Rockett's wharf. There he landed and, with his son Tad at his side and an escort of army and navy officers around him, proceeded to walk up Main Street a mile or so to the executive mansion of the Confederacy, the house occupied until two days before by Jefferson Davis. On the way the tall President, in his long black overcoat and high silk hat, stood out above those with him. Negroes left the river bank to follow along and crowd around him, many of them singing and shouting their praises. Soldiers white and black cheered as he entered the mansion and took a seat in Davis' chair.[7] His appearance among the people of what had been, until so recently, the enemy capital, deeply moved a Boston newspaper correspondent, who wrote:

---

[3] *Collected Works,* VIII, 377, 379–380, 382, 384. [4] Coolidge, *Grant,* 193.
[5] Grant, *Memoirs,* II, 459–460. [6] *Collected Works,* VIII, 385.
[7] Richmond *Evening Whig,* Apr. 6, 1865, quoted in Washington *Daily Morning Chronicle,* Apr. 8, 1865, p. 1, c. 6.

"He came among them unheralded, without pomp or parade. He walked through the streets as if he were only a private citizen, and not the head of a mighty nation. He came not as a conqueror, not with bitterness in his heart, but with kindness. He came as a friend, to alleviate sorrow and suffering—to rebuild what had been destroyed." [8] In the Davis house he received a number of Union officers and Richmond citizens. He also received and conversed with the only member of the Confederate government who remained in Richmond—John A. Campbell, lately the assistant secretary of war and two months previously one of the Confederate peace emissaries at Hampton Roads. Then he rode about the city in a carriage, to review the troops and to see the sights, especially the extensive ruins left by the great fire which the Confederate authorities accidentally had set at the time of their evacuation.

Back again at City Point, during the next few days he received heartening news of Grant's pursuit of Lee. Grant sent him batches of telegrams, in which the various commanders reported the chase in picturesque detail—"the Road for over 2 miles is strewed with tents baggage cooking utensils some ammunition some material of all kinds"—and in one of which a line of Sheridan's particularly caught the President's eye. "Gen. Sheridan says 'If the thing is pressed I think that Lee will surrender,' " he wired to Grant on April 7. "Let the *thing* be pressed." He would gladly have stayed on for news of the surrender itself, but he decided to go back to Washington because of word from Stanton that Seward had been injured badly in a carriage accident.[9]

He arrived in Washington late in the afternoon of April 9, the day that Lee finally surrendered to Grant near Appomattox Court House, ninety miles west of Richmond. Next morning the news was known to everyone in Washington. The people of the Capital, like those of other towns and cities throughout the North, already had indulged themselves in uproarious celebrations at the tidings of the evacuation of Richmond. Now they outdid themselves. In Washington a crowd, swelled by government employees who had been given a holiday, swarmed into the White House grounds and called for the President, while a band played "Hail to the Chief," "Yankee Doodle," and

---

8 Boston *Journal,* quoted in *Littell's Living Age,* LXXXV, 137–138 (Apr. 22, 1865).
9 *Collected Works,* VIII, 390–392.

"America." Lincoln, busy with a cabinet meeting, at first declined to appear but finally yielded to the cries of the crowd. He told the people that he supposed arrangements were being made for a formal celebration either that night or the next. "I shall have nothing to say then," he said, "if I dribble it all out before." Then he suggested that the band play "Dixie." The "adversaries over the way" had tried to appropriate that song, but now the Union forces had captured it, and it was a lawful prize. So the band played "Dixie." [10]

On April 11 Lincoln made, from an upper window of the White House, the speech he had promised. "We meet this evening, not in sorrow, but in gladness of heart," he began. It was to be his last public speech. On the morning of the 14th he held another cabinet meeting—his last. Meanwhile, assuming that the war was over (though Johnston was yet to surrender to Sherman, and Confederate commanders farther south and west were still to lay down their arms), he took several steps signifying the end of hostilities. He issued a proclamation terminating the blockade of Southern ports but closing certain specified ones to foreign commerce. He prepared a memorandum proposing that the size of the regular army be reduced—to a ratio of one soldier for every thousand of the population. After having written a number of passes for individuals desiring to go South, he gave up that chore and noted: "No pass is necessary now to authorize any one to go to and return from Petersburg and Richmond. People go and return just as they did before the war." On that final 14th of April, just four years to the day after the evacuation of Fort Sumter, its former commander, Major Robert Anderson, ran up the Stars and Stripes again over the fort, in ceremonies the President had approved.[11]

The war was over, but peace was yet to be made.

III

During the preceding weeks, while the war was drawing to a close, some people in the North (and some in the South) thought that peace should be made by the military men and not by the politicians. The Peace Democrats clamorously said so, and Greeley and his New York

10 Washington *Daily Morning Chronicle,* Apr. 10, 1865, p. 1, c. 3–5; Cincinnati *Daily Gazette,* Apr. 11, 1865, p. 3, c. 5.

11 *Collected Works,* VIII, 375–376, 396–397, 399, 408, 410, 412.

Tribune agreed with them. Certain generals in both the Union and the Confederate armies took up the idea of ending the war by means of a military convention. Before the beginning of March, 1865, General Longstreet, C. S. A., gathered from a conversation with General Ord, U. S. A., while under a flag of truce for the exchange of prisoners, that Grant would welcome an interview with Lee to discuss peace terms with him. On March 2 Lee proposed such an interview to Grant, and Grant telegraphed to Washington for advice.[1]

When Stanton brought Grant's telegram to the Capitol, where Lincoln was signing bills as Congress finished its work, Lincoln wrote out, word for word, a telegram for Stanton to send back to Grant. "The President directs me to say to you that he wishes you to have no conference with General Lee unless it be for the capitulation of Gen. Lee's army, or on some minor, and purely military matter," Stanton wired. "He instructs me to say that you are not to decide, discuss, or confer upon any political question. Such questions the President holds in his own hands; and will submit them to no military conference or convention." [2] Unfortunately, neither Lincoln nor Stanton nor Grant directed that a copy of this message be sent to Sherman.

The Peace Democrats kept on with their agitation. "We are not little surprised that Seward should stand in the way of peace, and that his organ here, The Times, should now as heretofore, resist any attempt to accomplish this end, save by continued slaughter," two of them in New York wrote to Greeley on March 24. "How can the administration refuse any longer to invest Lt. Gen. Grant with ample powers to meet Gen. Lee in this conference for peace, and here we trust you will stand firm and *drive* the administration, if need be, to accept the opportunity to close if possible, this devastating war." These men trusted that the President was going to the front in order to authorize the conference.[3] Greeley, in his *Tribune,* also interpreted Lincoln's visit to Grant as a sign of possible military negotiations. "The sword in one hand and the olive branch in the other," observed the *Tribune* approvingly, "are always found to work mutually in aid of each other." [4]

Disagreeing with Greeley and the Peace Democrats, Lincoln

[1] Nicolay and Hay, *Lincoln,* X, 157–158. [2] *Collected Works,* VIII, 347–348.

[3] L. G. Capers and V. W. Kingsley to Greeley, Mar. 24, 1865, Greeley MSS., N. Y. Pub. Lib.

[4] New York *Tribune,* quoted in Philadelphia *Public Ledger,* Mar. 31, 1865, p. 2, c. 2.

thought the generals were likely to make neither an early nor a generous peace. "He had been apprehensive that the military men are not very solicitous to close hostilities," Welles noted, "—fears our generals will exact severe terms." [5] Indeed, he could hardly expect Sherman, in war the scourge of the South, to act as an angel of mercy in peace (though Sherman later was to do just that). He had little reason to think that Grant would be much better, for Grant had a reputation as an unfeeling and unsparing commander. Besides, Grant was inclined to question Lincoln's liberal exercise of the pardoning power.

Lincoln was, of course, a pardoning President. He was human enough that he always found it hard to resist a tearful appeal on behalf of a prisoner or a condemned man. And yet his pardoning proclivities have often been exaggerated and misunderstood. As a rule he was moved by considerations of policy rather than by sentimentality when he granted a pardon. When he refused clemency, he was motivated by similar considerations, and (what is commonly overlooked) he turned down numerous appeals. In the case of John Y. Beall, a Confederate secret agent who had been operating on Lake Erie, Lincoln faced tremendous pressure from influential men desiring to save the prisoner from the gallows. Ninety-one members of Congress, among them Thaddeus Stevens, petitioned for clemency to Beall. Nevertheless, Beall was hanged, late in February, 1865.[6] And, if Lincoln daily released large numbers of captured Confederate soldiers, on condition only that they take an oath of allegiance to the United States, he was responding to the demands of congressmen, mostly from the border states, who requested the release of their constituents and certified to their loyalty.

For military reasons, Grant thought it wrong to free so many prisoners who were willing to take the oath. These men, if they had loyal inclinations, were the very ones to keep and later to exchange for captured Union soldiers. The United States would lose little in exchanging these converted rebels: "They can afterward come into our lines," Grant explained, "if they do not wish to fight." [7]

---

[5] Welles, *Diary,* II, 269.
[6] Dorris, *Pardon and Amnesty under Lincoln and Johnson,* xvii, 77.
[7] *Collected Works,* VIII, 347–348.

At City Point, in conferences aboard the *River Queen* with Grant and Sherman on March 27 and 28, Lincoln went to great lengths to impress the generals with his desire to see the war ended quickly and humanely. "Must more blood be shed! Can not this last bloody Battle be avoided!" So he "more than once exclaimed," as Sherman recalled afterward. He said that "he wanted us to get the deluded men of the Rebel Armies disarmed, and back to their homes, that he contemplated no revenge, no harsh measures, but quite the contrary." [8] More specifically, "he distinctly authorized me to assure Governor Vance and the people of North Carolina that, as soon as the rebel armies laid down their arms, and resumed their civil pursuits, they would at once be guaranteed all their rights as citizens of a common country; and that to avoid anarchy the State governments then in existence, with their civil functionaries, would be recognized by him as the government *de facto* till Congress could provide others." [9] Such, at least, was the impression of the conversation that Sherman took back with him to North Carolina.

About two weeks later Grant presented his terms to Lee at Appomattox. He generously allowed Lee and his officers to keep their horses and their side arms once they had sworn oaths, for themselves and for their men, not to take up arms again against the United States. So far, so good. But Grant added: "This done, each officer and man will be allowed to return to his home, not to be disturbed by U. S. authority so long as they observe their paroles and the laws in force where they may reside." [10] Thus Grant, in effect, extended amnesty to Lee himself and to every officer and man in the Army of Northern Virginia. In doing so, he went beyond Lincoln's amnesty proclamation of December 8, 1863, which excluded officers above the rank of colonel and everyone who had resigned from Congress or the army or the navy to participate in the rebellion. Grant also violated Lincoln's order of March 3, 1865, which prohibited him from deciding upon any political questions, for his amnesty was a political as well as a military matter. But he did not disregard the spirit of Lincoln's recent remarks at City Point. Nor did Lincoln repudiate the terms to Lee. On the contrary, he endorsed them, according to newspaper

---

[8] Sherman to I. N. Arnold, Nov. 28, 1872, MS., Chicago Hist. Soc.

[9] Sherman, *Memoirs*, II, 324–327.

[10] *Offic. Rec.*, 1 ser., XLVI, 58.

reports at the time.[11] Some of the Radical papers denounced Grant for them, but the pro-administration press praised him. Said the Washington *Chronicle,* in publishing his correspondence with Lee, "We cannot omit our almost unutterable gratitude to him for proclaiming this truth to his defeated antagonist, and to all mankind: *'I am equally anxious for Peace with yourself, and the whole North entertain the same feeling.'* "[12]

Sherman, meanwhile, was preparing to put into effect what he thought were Lincoln's policies. If the victors adopted a humane approach, he declared soon after returning to North Carolina, "the State would be the first to wheel into the line of the old Union."[13] He was confirmed in his belief that Lincoln intended to recognize the rebel legislatures, at least temporarily, when he read newspaper reports that on April 6 Lincoln had authorized the reconvening of the Virginia legislature. Grant's terms to Lee on April 9, when Grant informed Sherman of them, seemed to him to be still further evidence that Lincoln intended his generals to exercise broad powers in making a peace of reconciliation.[14]

Lincoln was dead when, on April 18, Sherman finally came to terms with Johnston, at Bennett's farm house, near Durham, North Carolina. Assuming that he was carrying out what had been the President's wishes, Sherman then made with Johnston what amounted virtually to a treaty of peace, subject to the approval of the political authorities in Washington. Sherman not only provided for a general amnesty, as Grant had done. He also guaranteed to the Southern people their political and property rights and, as if that were not enough, he recognized the existing state governments in the South.[15]

It should be emphasized (as Grant emphasized in his memoirs) that Sherman's terms to Johnston were *conditional* upon the approval of the authorities in Washington.[16] Sherman did not pretend to be able to bind the United States by his own say-so. But the authorities in Washington—General Grant, Secretary Stanton, and President Johnson—ruled that Sherman had exceeded his powers. What was worse, Stanton gave to the press a collection of documents and statements

---

11 Philadelphia *Public Ledger,* Apr. 12, 1865, p. 1, c. 5.

12 Washington *Daily Morning Chronicle,* Apr. 10, 1865, p. 2, c. 1.

13 Philadelphia *Public Ledger,* Apr. 3, 1865, p. 1, c. 4.

14 Sherman, *Memoirs,* II, 329; McClure, *Lincoln and Men of War-Times,* 221.

15 Sherman, *Memoirs,* II, 356–357.

16 Grant, *Memoirs,* II, 514–516.

which made it appear that Sherman had deliberately flouted his orders. Throughout the North the Radicals denounced him as no better than a traitor.

Had he really been proceeding according to Lincoln's wishes? Would Lincoln, if alive, have approved the Sherman-Johnston convention? Sherman himself believed so, of course. His brother, Senator John Sherman, agreed with him, as did Admiral Porter.[17] Grant believed that, at least, Sherman *thought* he was doing what Lincoln would have wanted done.[18] Welles conceded that Sherman might have been in error. "But this error, if it be one, had its origins, I apprehend, with President Lincoln, who was for prompt and easy terms with the Rebels," Welles noted. "Sherman's terms were based on a liberal construction of President Lincoln's benevolent wishes and the order to Weitzel concerning the Virginia legislature, the revocation of which S. had not heard [of]." [19]

IV

Whether or not Lincoln made his intentions clear to Sherman, he certainly failed to make them clear to those with whom, on April 4 and 5, he discussed the question of the reassembling of the Virginia legislature. In the executive mansion in Richmond and aboard the gunboat *Malvern* in the James, he then conferred with John A. Campbell, two months previously one of the peace commissioners at Hampton Roads, and with Gustavus Myers, a Richmond attorney and a member of the Confederate Congress. Also present was Major General Godfrey Weitzel, in command of the occupation forces in Richmond. "The result of the conferences cannot be made public," a New York *Herald* correspondent reported from Richmond at the time, "but auspicious results are known to be about to accrue from them." [1] In fact, however, only the most inauspicious results were to accrue—misunderstanding, repudiation, and charges of bad faith which, long afterward, were still to be repeated against Lincoln.[2]

We do not know all that he said to the Virginians, or all that they said to him, at the meetings on April 4 and 5. We do know part of

[17] McClure, *Lincoln and Men of War-Times,* 220 n; Sherman, *Memoirs,* II, 330.

[18] Grant, *Memoirs,* II, 515.

[19] Welles, *Diary,* II, 296 (Apr. 23, 1865).

[1] Quoted in Washington *Daily Morning Chronicle,* Apr. 10, 1865, p. 1, c. 5.

[2] William M. Robinson, Jr., *Justice in Grey* (1941), 592–593, revives the contemporary charge by Southerners that "Lincoln broke faith with the Virginians."

what he said, however, since he presented to them a written statement, copies of which have been preserved. For the rest of the conversation, we must depend mainly on two letters which Campbell wrote, one of them a couple of days afterward and another several months later. We can find confirmation for a portion of Campbell's account in remarks which Weitzel made to Charles A. Dana, Lincoln's assistant secretary of war, and which Dana relayed from Richmond to Washington.

The conferences began with Campbell's requesting terms of peace. In response, Lincoln gave him a paper stating the same indispensable conditions as he had insisted upon at Hampton Roads: "The restoration of the national authority throughout all the States"; "No receding by the Executive of the United States on the slavery question . . ."; "No cessation of hostilities short of an end of the war, and the disbanding of all forces hostile to the government." The paper added that confiscations of property, except for slaves and except where the interests of third parties intervened, would be remitted to the people of any state which promptly should withdraw its troops and other support from resistance to the government.[3]

The conferees also discussed oaths of allegiance, pardon and amnesty, and the calling into session of the Virginia legislature. "The conversation," wrote Campbell in his letter of April 7, "had relation to the establishment of a Government for Virginia, the requirements of oaths of allegiance and the terms of settlement with the United States." Lincoln "assented to the application, not to require oaths of allegiance from the citizens." While he did not offer a general amnesty (as Grant was to do at Appomattox on April 9) he "intimated that there was scarcely any one who might not have a discharge upon the asking."[4] Or, as Weitzel informed Dana, "the President did not promise the amnesty, but told them he had the pardoning power, and would save any repentant sinner from hanging."[5] Campbell also, according to his letter of April 7, "strongly urged" upon Lincoln the "propriety of an armistice." Lincoln "agreed to consider the subject" (though, of course, his written terms had ruled it out). As for the Virginia legislature, Campbell in his nearly contemporary report said

[3] *Collected Works*, VIII, 386–387.

[4] Campbell to Joseph A. Anderson and others, Apr. 7, 1865, Stanton MSS., Lib. of Cong.

[5] Dana to Stanton, Apr. 5, 1865, Stanton MSS.

that Lincoln agreed to "send to Genl Weitzel his decision upon the question of a Government for Virginia." [6] On this point Campbell provided additional details in a later account, dated August 31, 1865. Lincoln, according to this account, said he thought he might recall the legislators who had been convening in Richmond and have them vote the return of Virginia into the Union.[7]

On April 6, the day after his last conversation with Campbell, Lincoln sent to Weitzel the following message for him to show to Campbell: "It has been intimated to me that the gentlemen who have acted as the Legislature of Virginia, in support of the rebellion, may now now [*sic*] desire to assemble at Richmond, and take measures to withdraw the Virginia troops, and other support from resistance to the General government. If they attempt it, give them permission and protection, until, if at all, they attempt some action hostile to the United States . . . ." [8] It should be noted that this message was sent three days before Lee's surrender, at a time when it looked as if Grant might yet have to fight that last great bloody battle which Lincoln so much dreaded. Certainly one of the motives that prompted Lincoln to send the message was the hope that the Virginia legislators might obviate such a battle by simply ordering Lee and his Virginia troops out of the war. The next morning Lincoln remarked to Dana "that Sheridan seemed to be getting Virginia soldiers out of the war, faster than this Legislature could think." [9]

With Virginia confused and distracted in the days following the evacuation of Richmond, it is perhaps surprising that Lincoln should have expected the legislature to think or to act very fast. In fact, considerable time would have to be allowed for the legislators even to assemble. Already, on April 7, Campbell was taking the first, preliminary steps. On that day he met with five of the legislators to consider the President's proposal. He presented them with copies of Lincoln's

---

[6] Campbell to Anderson and others, Apr. 7, 1865.

[7] Campbell to J. S. Speed, Aug. 31, 1865, *So. Hist. Soc. Papers,* new ser., IV, 66–74.

[8] *Collected Works,* VIII, 389.

[9] Dana to Stanton, Apr. 7, 1865, Stanton MSS. On the previous day, in reporting to Grant his arrangement with Campbell, Lincoln had indicated his military motive. "I do not think it very probable that anything will come of this; but I have thought best to notify you, so that if you should see signs, you may understand them," he informed Grant. "From your recent despatches it seems that you are pretty effectually withdrawing the Virginia troops from opposition to the government." *Collected Works,* VIII, 388.

terms and the message to Weitzel and with his own letter in which he gave his version of the recent conversations. He had much more in mind than merely the withdrawal of Virginia troops. "The object of the invitation," he stated to the five, "is for the Government of Virginia to determine, whether they will administer the laws in connection with the authorities of the United States, and under the Constitution of the United States." [10] And on the same day, in a communication to Weitzel, he again asked for an armistice, arguing that peace and the disbandment of the Confederate armies would follow soon. He also suggested to Weitzel that he provide for South Carolina the same facilities as for Virginia, so as to permit the reassembling of the legislature in that state, too. The South Carolinians, like the Virginians, should be "invited to send commissioners to adjust the questions that are supposed to require adjustment." [11] Campbell, obviously, was thinking of a series of peace negotiations between the authorities of the United States and the legislators of the various states of the Confederacy!

In just two days, with Lee's surrender on April 9, Campbell's request for an armistice ceased to have much meaning, and so did Lincoln's plan for the withdrawal of Virginia troops by the action of their own legislature. If Lincoln had known that the surrender would come so soon, he never would have made the arrangement with Campbell. That, at least, was what he told Francis H. Pierpont, the governor of the Restored Government of Virginia, when he summoned him from Alexandria to Washington on April 10 (according to Pierpont's recollection years afterward). Lincoln also told him that Campbell had suggested the idea of the Virginia legislature's meeting in Richmond to take Virginia soldiers out of the army and Virginia itself out of the Confederacy. Lincoln now said he all along had kept in mind the Pierpont government at Alexandria as the rightful government of Virginia and intended eventually to recognize it as such.[12] (According to Campbell, however, Lincoln recently had said that "he had a government in Northern Virginia—the Pierpont government—but it had but a small margin, and he did not desire to enlarge it.") [13]

---

[10] Campbell to Anderson and others, Apr. 7, 1865, Stanton MSS.

[11] *Collected Works,* VIII, 407–408.

[12] Ambler, *Pierpont,* 255–259.

[13] Campbell to Speed, Aug. 31, 1865, *So. Hist. Soc. Papers,* new ser., IV, 66–74.

In Richmond, on April 11, eight legislators and twenty-five other officeholders and prominent citizens met and issued a request for the governor and the legislature to assemble there on April 25. General Weitzel, General Shepley, and Assistant War Secretary Dana all approved this call before it was published in the Richmond *Whig* and distributed on handbills.[14]

In Washington, on that same April 11, Lincoln met with his cabinet. None of the members liked the idea of the assembling of the Virginia legislature, but Stanton and Speed especially were disturbed by it. They saw Lincoln individually after the cabinet meeting and protested to him. Lincoln then saw Welles, the Conservative stalwart among the secretaries (Seward being still incapacitated by his recent carriage accident), "said Stanton and others were dissatisfied," and asked Welles's frank opinion. Welles confessed that he himself doubted the wisdom of convening rebel legislators, for they might conspire together against the Union, or they might demand terms which would seem reasonable but which would prove unacceptable. Lincoln, however, thought the Southerners were too badly beaten, too exhausted, to make much trouble. "His idea was, that the members of the legislature, comprising the prominent and influential men of their respective counties, had better come together and undo their own work." In the critical transition from war to peace, what was needed was some temporary authority which the Southern people would obey. "Civil government must be reestablished, he said, as soon as possible; there must be courts, and law, and order, or society would be broken up, the disbanded armies would turn into robber bands and guerrillas, which we must strive to prevent. These were the reasons why he wished prominent Virginians who had the confidence of the people to come together and turn themselves and their neighbors into good Union men." But Lincoln said he could not go ahead when all his advisors were opposed to him. He might be wrong, he admitted.[15]

This conversation, as reported by Welles, took place on April 12 and 13—three and four days after the surrender of Lee. In it Lincoln gave no indication that his only purpose, in permitting the as-

---

14 Robinson, *Justice in Grey*, 592.

15 Welles, *Diary*, II, 279. Welles elaborated somewhat in his article on "Lincoln and Johnson: Their Plan of Reconstruction and the Resumption of National Authority," in *Galaxy*, XIII, 524–525 (April, 1872).

sembling of the Virginia legislature, was to have that legislature withdraw the Virginia troops. So far as Welles's record goes, he did not mention that phase of the subject at all. Indeed, if he had lost interest in the plan because of the surrender, he would have had no issue with the cabinet on April 11 and no occasion for the discussion with Welles on the following two days. Apparently he decided to drop the plan in consequence of the criticisms from his cabinet. He did not avow this opposition as a reason for his change of mind, however, when he informed Weitzel of the change.

At nine o'clock on the morning of April 12 he telegraphed to Weitzel: "Is there any sign of the rebel legislature coming together on the basis of my letter to you? If there is any such sign, inform me what it is; if there is no such sign you may as [well] withdraw the offer." At three in the afternoon of the same day Weitzel wired his reply: "The passports have gone out for the legislature, and it is common talk that they will come together." At six on the evening of the same day Lincoln telegraphed again:

"I have just seen Judge Campbell's letter to you of the 7th. He assumes as appears to me that I have called the insurgent Legislature of Virginia together, as the rightful Legislature of the State, to settle all differences with the United States. I have done no such thing. I spoke of them not as a Legislature, but as 'the gentlemen who have *acted* as the Legislature of Virginia in support of the rebellion.' I did this on purpose to exclude the assumption that I was recognizing them as a *rightful* body. I dealt with them as men having power *de facto* to do a specific thing, to wit, 'to withdraw the Virginia troops, and other support from resistance to the General Government,' for which in the paper handed Judge Campbell I promised a specific equivalent, to wit, a remission to the people of the State, except in certain cases, the confiscation of their property. I meant this and no more. In as much however as Judge Campbell misconstrues this, and is still pressing for an armistice, contrary to the explicit statement of the paper I gave him; and particularly as Gen. Grant has since captured the Virginia troops, so that giving a consideration for their withdrawal is no longer applicable, let my letter to you, and the paper to Judge Campbell both be withdrawn or, countermanded, and he be notified of it. Do not allow them to assemble; but if any have come, allow them safe-return to their homes." [16]

If Lincoln "meant this and no more," and if he had made his intention as clear a week earlier as he did now, neither Campbell nor Weitzel could very well have misunderstood him. If he meant a little more than this, if he intended for the leading Virginians themselves to undo their act of secession and to prevent chaos until some new state government could be established, as Welles's record indicates, then he could have attempted to clarify his purposes instead of cutting Campbell off so peremptorily. But his own purposes seem to have changed somewhat—after his return to Washington and his troubles with his cabinet.[17]

In Richmond, General E. O. C. Ord, Butler's successor and Weitzel's superior, gave the actual notice to Campbell to call off his project, on April 13.[18] The next evening Ord telegraphed to Lincoln that Campbell and his Hampton Roads colleague, R. M. T. Hunter, wished to visit Washington at once with important and urgent communications for the President. The telegram was received in Washington at half past nine.[19] Lincoln already had gone to Ford's Theater.

V

The many-sided problem of reconstruction, of which the question of the Virginia legislature was only one aspect, was a subject of con-

16 *Collected Works,* VIII, 405–407.

17 Robinson, *Justice in Grey,* 592–593, writes: "In the face of such determined resistance from his advisers, Lincoln renounced his liberal policy and the next day withdrew his permission for the assembling of the State government, attempting to quibble out of his original sanction." Lincoln's reference to Campbell's mere request for an armistice does seem like a rather weak excuse. On the other hand, Campbell was guilty of downright distortion when he said, in his letter to Speed of August 31, 1865, that Lincoln "never for a moment spoke of the Legislature, except as a public corporate body, representing a substantial portion of the State." Also, whether wilfully or not, Campbell certainly had gone beyond Lincoln's original intentions. In giving permission for the Virginia legislature to assemble, Lincoln most likely had two main objectives in mind: one, weakening the military resistance of the enemy; the other, providing a means of governmental transition from war to peace. The first objective lost its importance with Lee's surrender. The second became hopeless both because of the cabinet opposition in Washington and because of Campbell's misunderstanding of the role the Virginia legislature was expected to play. Undoubtedly Lincoln was himself largely at fault in not making himself better understood, but he cannot justly be charged with sanctioning Campbell's plans or with quibbling out of his agreement.

18 *So. Hist. Soc. Papers,* new ser., IV, 75.

19 Ord to Lincoln, Apr. 14, 1865, *Offic. Rec.,* ser. 1, XLVI, pt. 3, p. 748.

tinual debate in the North from 1863 on. After reaching a furious pitch in the summer of 1864, the debate had been toned down during the final weeks of the presidential campaign, to be renewed fitfully and shrilly as the final military victory approached. Lee's surrender brought the issue to a climax again. Then, temporarily at least, Lincoln and the Radicals found themselves even farther apart than before. For a while, in early April, 1865, he seemed willing to readmit the Southern states on terms more generous than those he had announced in his ten-per-cent plan and in his amnesty proclamation of December, 1863. But the Radicals were prepared to demand terms even more rigorous than those they had embodied in the Wade-Davis bill, which Lincoln had refused to sign in July, 1864.

With a new sense of urgency the Radicals began to consult with one another and to speak out. On the day after Appomattox, in Washington, General Butler made a speech in which he recommended, on the one hand, that the leaders of the rebellion should be disfranchised and disqualified for public office and, on the other, that the masses including the Negroes should be given immediately all the rights of citizenship.[1] The next evening, in Baltimore on court duty, Chief Justice Chase dined with Henry Winter Davis and other Maryland Radicals, then wrote a letter to the President.[2] "It will be, hereafter, counted equally a crime and a folly," Chase said, "if the colored loyalists of the rebel states shall be left to the control of restored rebels, not likely, in that case, to be either wise or just, until taught both wisdom and justice by new calamities." [3]

That same evening, April 11, Lincoln made his own, last contribution to the public debate when he addressed the crowd gathered on the White House grounds. After a few congratulatory words on Grant's recent victory, he proceeded to defend at some length his own reconstruction view.

The problem, as he saw it, was essentially one of re-establishing the national authority throughout the South. This problem was complicated by the fact that there was, in the South, "no authorized organ" to treat with. "Nor is it a small additional embarrassment that we, the loyal people, differ among ourselves as to the mode, manner, and

1 Philadelphia *Public Ledger,* Apr. 11, 1865, p. 1, c. 7.

2 David Donald, ed., *Inside Lincoln's Cabinet: the Civil War Diaries of Salmon P. Chase,* 265.

3 *Collected Works,* VII, 399.

means of reconstruction." He had been criticized, he said, because he did not seem to have a fixed opinion on the question "whether the seceded States, so called," were "in the Union or out of it." He dismissed that question as "a merely pernicious abstraction" and went on to declare: "We all agree that the seceded States, so called, are out of their proper practical relation with the Union; and that the sole object of the government, civil and military, in regard to those States is to again get them into that proper practical relation."

He had been criticized also for setting up and sustaining the new state government of Louisiana, which rested on the support of only ten per cent of the voters and did not give the franchise to the colored man. He confessed that the Louisiana government would be better if it rested on a larger electorate including the votes of Negroes—at least "the very intelligent" and those who had served as soldiers. "Concede that the new government of Louisiana is only to what it should be as the egg is to the fowl, we shall sooner have the fowl by hatching the egg than by smashing it?" The loyalists of the South would be encouraged and the Negroes themselves would be better off, Lincoln argued, if Louisiana were quickly readmitted to the Union. An additional ratification would be gained for the Thirteenth Amendment, the adoption of which would be "unquestioned and unquestionable" only if it were ratified by three fourths of *all* the states.

What Lincoln said of Louisiana, he applied also to the other states of the South. "And yet so great peculiarities pertain to each state; and such important and sudden changes occur in the same state; and, withal, so new and unprecedented is the whole case, that no exclusive, and inflexible plan can safely be prescribed as to details and colatterals." (Virginia was not mentioned.) In concluding, Lincoln said enigmatically that it might become his duty "to make some new announcement to the people of the South. I am considering, and shall not fail to act, when satisfied that action will be proper." [4]

In Washington and throughout the country the speech aroused much speculation about Lincoln's undisclosed intentions, and it provoked mixed feelings about his general approach to reconstruction. The editor of the Philadelphia *Public Ledger* noted that the President had indicated his "feelings and wishes" rather than his "fixed opin-

[4] *Ibid.*, 399–405.

ions," then commended him for his lack of "passion or malignancy" toward the late rebels.[5] The Washington correspondent of the Cincinnati *Gazette* believed that Lincoln's position was generally approved except among the Radical Republicans, who were saying that the rebel leaders must be punished and the rebel states subjected to "preliminary training" before being restored to their rights as members of the Union. "The desire of the people for a settlement—speedy and final—upon the easiest possible terms, will, it is believed, sustain the President in his policy foreshadowed in his speech." [6]

Whatever the people might have approved, it was again made clear to Lincoln, when the cabinet met on the morning of April 14 (with General Grant present), that some of his own advisers would not approve a settlement upon easy terms. Secretary Stanton came to the meeting with a project for military occupation as a preliminary step toward the reorganization of the Southern states, Virginia and North Carolina to be combined in a single military district. Secretary Welles objected to this arrangement on the grounds that it would destroy the individuality of the separate states. He said that, in the case of Virginia, there was nothing to do but recognize the Pierpont government, which had been recognized throughout the war, its consent having been necessary for the erection of the new state of West Virginia. The President sustained Welles's objection but did not completely repudiate Stanton's plan. Instead, he suggested that Stanton revise it so as to deal with Virginia and North Carolina separately, and that he provide copies of the revised plan for the members of the cabinet at their next meeting.[7]

Attorney-General Speed got the impression that Lincoln was coming over to the Radicals. "He never seemed so near our views," Speed told Chase the next day. "At the meeting he said he thought [he] had made a mistake at Richmond in sanctioning the assembling of the Virginia Legislature and had perhaps been too fast in his desires for early reconstruction." [8]

Before the cabinet meeting adjourned, Lincoln said he was glad that Congress was not in session. The House and the Senate, he was aware, had the unquestioned right to accept or reject new members

[5] Philadelphia *Public Ledger,* Apr. 13, 1865, p. 2, c. 1.

[6] Cincinnati *Daily Gazette,* Apr. 13, 1865, p. 3, c. 4.

[7] Welles, *Diary,* II, 281; Welles, "Lincoln and Johnson," *Galaxy,* XIII, 526–527.

[8] Donald, *Diaries of Salmon P. Chase,* 268.

from the Southern states; he himself had nothing to do with that. Still, he believed, the President had the power to recognize and deal with the state governments themselves. He could collect taxes in the South, see that the mails were delivered there, and appoint Federal officials (though his appointments would have to be confirmed, of course, by the Senate). He knew that the congressional Radicals did not agree with him, but they were not in session to make official objection, and he could act to establish and recognize the new state governments before Congress met in December. He did not intend to call a special session before that time, as he told the speaker of the House, Schuyler Colfax, later on the day of that final cabinet meeting, as he was entering his carriage to go to Ford's Theater.[9]

When, in December, 1865, the regular session of Congress finally began, Andrew Johnson had been President for nearly eight months. At first, in the days of terror following Lincoln's assassination, Johnson talked like a good Radical. He also acted like one when he ordered the arrest of Jefferson Davis and other Confederate leaders on the charge of complicity in the assassination. But Johnson and the Radicals soon disagreed on reconstruction. During the summer he succeeded in the restoration of state governments according to a plan which required them only to abolish slavery, retract their ordinances of secession, and repudiate their debts accumulated in the Confederate cause. In December the Radicals in Congress refused to seat the senators and representatives from these restored states. After checking Johnson's program, the Radicals proceeded to undo it, while impeaching the President. Eventually they carried through their own program of military occupation, similar to the one Stanton had proposed at the cabinet meeting of April 14, and they undertook to transfer political power from the old master class to the freedmen, as Chase and other Radicals long had advocated.

Whether Lincoln, if he had lived, would have done as Johnson did, is hard to say. Certainly Lincoln would not have hounded Jefferson Davis or other Confederate officials (but, then, the presupposition here is that there would have been no assassination to seem to justify it). At the City Point conversation in March, Lincoln had given Sherman to believe that he would not mind if Davis escaped from the country, "unbeknownst" to him. To his cabinet in April he had

[9] Welles, *Diary*, II, 281; *Galaxy*, XIII, 526–527.

indicated his hope that there would be no persecution, no bloody work, with respect to any of the late enemy. "None need expect he would take any part in hanging or killing those men, even the worst of them," Welles paraphrased him. "Frighten them out of the country, open the gates, let down the bars, scare them off, said he, throwing up his hands as if scaring sheep."

As for the restoration of state governments, it is impossible to guess confidently what Lincoln would have done or tried to do, since the very essence of his planning was to have no fixed and uniform plan, and since he appeared to be changing his mind on some points shortly before he died. In the states already being reconstructed under his program of December, 1863, he doubtless would have continued to support that program, as he did to the last. In other states he might have tried other expedients, no doubt accepting the Pierpont government (as Johnson did) in Virginia. In no state did he seem inclined, at the very end, to accept the going government as a temporary authority, and the probability is that he would have overruled the Sherman-Johnston convention just as his successor did. In general, Lincolnian reconstruction probably, but not certainly, would have been very similar to Johnsonian reconstruction.

Whether, if Lincoln had lived and had proceeded along Johnson's lines, he would have succeeded any better than Johnson, is another "iffy" question, impossible to answer. It seems likely that, with his superior talent for political management, Lincoln would have avoided the worst of Johnson's clashes with Congress. Yet he could scarcely have escaped the conflict itself, unless he had conceded much more to the Radicals than Johnson did.

Another poser is the question whether Lincoln's approach to peace, if he had lived and had carried it through, would have advanced the Negro toward equal citizenship more surely than did the Radical program, which degenerated into a rather cynical use of the Negro for party advantage. One is entitled to believe that Lincoln's policy would have been better in the long run for Negroes as well as for Southern whites and for the nation as a whole.

CHAPTER XVI

GOD'S MAN

AT FIFTY-SIX Lincoln had not yet arrived at the full development and use of his personal powers. Such was Herndon's firm belief, and while many of Herndon's judgments must be discounted, there is little reason for doubting this one.

Certainly, as the President entered upon his second term, he still possessed a sturdy and resilient physical constitution, one capable of withstanding the cares of his office and recovering from the shocks of ordinary disease. A week or so after his re-inauguration he stayed in bed for a few days, refusing to see visitors, while it was reported on the one hand that he had "no serious illness" but was "only suffering from the exhausting attentions of office hunters" [1] and, on the other hand, that his case had been diagnosed as a "severe attack of influenza." [2] Even after he had improved enough to receive "hosts of visitors," and then to go out with Mrs. Lincoln to a German opera, he remained rather feeble for several days. When he left Washington for his two weeks' stay at City Point, he was seeking to escape the bothersome jobseekers and to rest and convalesce, as well as to oversee the closing of the war. He returned to the White House with renewed vigor and buoyant spirits.[3] At his final cabinet meeting he looked better than ever, at least to Secretary Speed, who remembered vividly his "shaved face well brushed clothing and neatly combed hair and whiskers." [4]

If Lincoln's physical capacity for further accomplishment was great, his mental and spiritual capacities seemed even more so. Mentally, he had grown to a remarkable extent since first becoming President.

1 Cincinnati *Daily Gazettte,* Mar. 15, 1865, p. 3, c. 6.
2 New York *Herald,* Mar. 15, 1865, p. 4, c. 5.
3 Washington *Daily Morning Chronicle,* Apr. 18, 1865, p. 1, c. 7.
4 James Speed to Joseph H. Bennett, Apr. 16, 1885, Barton MSS.

As the London *Spectator* said (March 25, 1865), comparing his debates against Douglas and the second inaugural, to "apprehend truly the character of Mr. Lincoln" one should notice the tremendous "growth of his mind." [5] Spiritually, as Herndon afterwards observed, Lincoln "grandly rose up" year after year.[6] No doubt the circumstances of his untimely death contributed to his later apotheosis, yet his fame might possibly have had an even more substantial foundation in true greatness if he had lived at least another four years.

I

The heroic image of Lincoln, so familiar to later generations, was not entirely a by-product of his martyrdom. While yet alive he became one of the most admired and best loved Americans of all time—a rival of George Washington for the place of first in the hearts of his countrymen, though there was then no such consensus as was afterwards to give him a clear priority over Washington.[1]

The living Lincoln seemed a hero most of all to the Negroes who hailed him as their deliverer and, among the white people of the North, to women and children. Miss Sarah B. Howell, of Trenton, New Jersey, requesting a lock of his hair "to be woven into a bouquet for the 'Sanitary Fair,' " told him in June, 1864, "no other President has come so near our hearts." [2] Other women sent him even more touching letters. "I only wish to thank you for being so good—and to say how sorry we all are that you must have four years more of this terrible toil," Miss Mary A. Dodge wrote him from Hamilton, Massachusetts, on the day of his second inauguration. "You can't tell anything about it in Washington where they make a noise on the slightest provocation. But if you had been in this little speck of a village this morning and heard the soft, sweet music of unseen bells rippling through the morning silence from every quarter of the far-off horizon, you would have better known what your name is to this nation." [3] Doubtless many children shared the aspiration of

[5] Quoted in *Littell's Living Age,* LXXXV, 135–137 (Apr. 22, 1865).

[6] Herndon MSS.

[1] The latter-day consensus has been indicated by such polls as that which in 1940 asked six thousand New Yorkers the question, "Who is the greatest American, living or dead?" Lincoln led in the returns, and Washington was second. New York *Times,* Apr. 20, 1940.

[2] Miss Howell to Lincoln, June 6, 1864, R. T. L. Coll., 33565.

[3] Miss Dodge to Lincoln, Mar. 4, 1865, R. T. L. Coll., 41055–56.

Governor Thomas H. Hicks' little son who was "anxious to see" the President and shake hands with him, as Hicks explained in the note he sent along with his servant who, on a May day in 1864, took the boy into the White House.[4]

The living Lincoln seemed a great man also to certain contemporary journalists. Some of these had partisan motives for praising him, no doubt; but others, writing for English publications, viewed him with relative detachment. And, whether English or American, these observers analyzed the elements of greatness in his character as perceptively as any historian or biographer afterwards could do.

An editorial in Henry J. Raymond's New York *Times,* endorsed and reprinted in John W. Forney's Washington *Chronicle,* described Lincoln in the summer of 1863 as resembling Washington in "perfect balance of thoroughly sound faculties," "sure judgment," and "great calmness of temper, great firmness of purpose, supreme moral principle, and intense patriotism." [5] An editorial in the Buffalo *Express,* about a year later, noted Lincoln's "remarkable moderation and freedom from passionate bitterness," then went on to say: "We do not believe Washington himself was less indifferent to the exercise of power for power's sake. Though concentrating in his hands a more despotic authority, in many respects, than had Napoleon, he has never used it for his personal ends, and we believe the verdict of history will be that he has far less frequently abused it than he has failed to use it as terror to evil-doers despite the clamor about arbitrary arrests." [6] The *Spectator* of London, in March, 1865, commented that Lincoln's task was lighter than Washington's but Lincoln had had to meet it without the advantages of Washington's education and experience. Lincoln was great because of his growth to meet his responsibilities. He had outgrown "the rude and illiterate mould of a village lawyer's thought" and had attained "a grasp of principle, a dignity of manner, and a solemnity of purpose, which would have been unworthy neither of Hampden nor of Cromwell," and he had acquired a "gentleness and generosity of feeling toward his foes" which one would hardly have expected from either Cromwell or Hampden.[7] The *Times* of London at about the same time observed

[4] Thomas H. Hicks to Lincoln, May 30, 1864, R. T. L. Coll., 33420.

[5] Washington *Daily Morning Chronicle,* Sept. 17, 1863, p. 2, c. 2.

[6] Buffalo *Morning Express,* Aug. 30, 1864, p. 1, c. 1.

[7] *Spectator,* Mar. 25, 1865, quoted in *Littell's Living Age,* LXXXV, 135–137 (Apr. 22, 1865).

that Lincoln, "placed in the most important position to which a statesman can aspire, invested with a power greater than that of most monarchs," fulfilled his duties "with firmness and conscientiousness, but without any feeling of exhiliration." [8]

The Liverpool *Post* (October 1, 1863) believed that, to judge from external appearances, "no leader in a great contest ever stood so little chance of being a subject of hero worship as Abraham Lincoln," with his long legs and long pantaloons, his shambling figure and his general awkwardness, which made him an easy target for caricature and ridicule. "Yet a worshiper of human heroes might possibly travel a great deal farther and fare much worse for an idol than selecting this same lanky American," the Liverpool *Post* continued. His inner traits—his truthfulness, resolution, insight, faithfulness, and courage, together with his equanimity, which was such that none of the bitter personal attacks upon him had ever "drawn from him an explanation of ill humor, or even an impudent rejoinder"—all these qualities would "go a long way to make up a hero," whatever his outward appearance.[9]

II

The concept of Lincoln the hero was inverted in the minds of many of his contemporaries, Northerners as well as Southerners, who thought him no hero but a villain whose death would be a good riddance. A number of them took the trouble to tell him so. One, who signed himself "Joseph," wrote (January 4, 1864): "The same who warned you of a conspiracy, Novr. 18th 1862, is now compelled to inform you, that,—'Your days are numbered,' you have been weighed in the balance & found wanting. You shall be a dead man in six months from date Dec. 31st, 1863." [1] Assassination threats appeared not only in the privacy of crank letters but also in some of the public prints, such as the LaCrosse, Wisconsin, *Democrat,* which avowed during the campaign of 1864: "If Abraham Lincoln should be re-elected for another term of four years of such wretched administration, *we hope that a bold hand will be found to plunge the dagger into*

[8] London *Times,* Mar. 17, 1865, quoted in *Littell's Living Age,* LXXXV, 86–88 (Apr. 15, 1865).

[9] Quoted in Washington *Daily Morning Chronicle,* Oct. 19, 1863, p. 1, c. 7.

[1] R. T. L. Coll., 29176.

the Tyrant's heart for the public welfare." [2]

To kidnap or kill the President would be easy, the New York *Tribune* cautioned. A band of rebels or rebel sympathizers might fall upon him at home, on the way to church, on one of his visits to the front.[3] In February, 1865, Stanton was warned: "The President could be seized any reception evening, in the midst of the masses assembled round him, and carried off by fifty determined men armed with bowie knives and revolvers, and once out could be put into a market wagon guarded by a dozen horsemen, and borne off at will,—the conspirators having first set a dozen or twenty hacks in motion to distract attention. Look out for some such dash soon." [4]

No such dash came, but a story of another kind of assassination plot made news a few weeks later. Raving and cursing in the Washington jail, Thomas Clements boasted that he and an accomplice had made the trip from Alexandria to kill the President on inauguration day. Clements said they had arrived just a half hour too late, and his Savior would never forgive him. As for his motive, he explained that the President had robbed him of a large amount of money.[5]

The men around Lincoln, among them Stanton in particular, worried continually about his safety. Seldom was he allowed out of the sight of his personal bodyguard, Ward Hill Lamon, or of other guards, including details of cavalry or infantry and sometimes both.[6] But the President was not inclined to co-operate with the custodians of his welfare, and he frequently disregarded Stanton's advice against exposing his life, as on his visits to Petersburg and Richmond at the end of the war.

His own attitude seemed to vary with his moods. Sometimes he discounted the danger, saying that he did not share his friends' apprehension about his life.[7] On the last day he was alive, when told there had been much uneasiness in the North during his Richmond visit, he cheerfully replied that he would have been alarmed, himself, if someone else had been President and had gone there, but in

---

2 Quoted, with the italics, in the Buffalo *Commercial Advertiser,* Nov. 5, 1864, p. 2, c. 2.

3 New York *Daily Tribune,* Mar. 19, 1864, p. 1, c. 1.

4 T. Weing to Stanton, Feb. 22, 1865, Ewing MSS., Lib. of Cong.

5 Cincinnati *Daily Gazette,* Mar. 8, 1865, p. 3, c. 6.

6 New York *Herald,* Jan. 3, 1865, p. 1, c. 2.

7 J. D. Defrees to Hugh McCulloch, Apr. 20, 1865, Lincoln National Life Foundation, Ft. Wayne, Ind.

his own case he had not felt any peril whatsoever.[8] In his more gloomy moments he confessed he did not expect to survive the Presidency. One evening, riding from the White House to the Soldiers' Home, he told an Illinois acquaintance that his cavalry escort had been more or less forced upon him by the military men, but he thought such an attempt at protection rather futile. "He said it seemed to him like putting up the gap in only one place when the fence was down all along." [9] On another occasion a representative of the United States Sanitary Commission, who had walked freely through an unguarded door into the White House, ventured to protest to the President about the latter's lack of protection at a time when assassination was openly threatened. "Well," Lincoln answered, "you know that it is as well to have but one trouble of it. Assassination would be one, but continual dread would make two of it!" [10]

No use in worrying. What is to be, must be. If anyone is really determined to kill me, I shall be killed. So Lincoln generally reacted to the thought of personal danger. His reaction was perfectly in keeping with his profoundly fatalistic outlook.

III

Though Lincoln's fatalism grew and developed while he was in the White House, it was in itself nothing new with him, not a product of his Presidential years. It may have derived from the predestinarian doctrines of his parents and of the Kentucky and Indiana communities in which he was reared. Anyhow it was firmly fixed in his mind by the time he ran for Congress in 1846. In that election his opponent, the revivalist Peter Cartwright, "was whispering the charge of infidelity" against him,[1] and he replied with a fairly forthright statement of his personal philosophy. Admitting he was no church member, but denying he was a scoffer, Lincoln said that "in early life" he had been "inclined to believe in" what was called the "Doctrine of Necessity"—the doctrine that the human mind was moved by some power over which it had no control. He added that, in the past, he sometimes had tried to maintain this doctrine by argument, though

8 Washington *Daily Morning Chronicle,* Apr. 17, 1865, p. 2, c. 1, 2.
9 Gillespie to Herndon, Dec. 8, 1866, Herndon MSS.
10 Undated memorandum by R. Pearsall Smith, Nicolay-Hay MSS., Ill. St. Hist. Lib.
1 Lincoln to Allen N. Ford, Aug. 11, 1846, *Collected Works,* I, 383.

not in public, but for more than five years he had "entirely left off" his "habit of arguing." [2] He did not say he had abandoned the belief itself: he only said he had quit arguing it.

The power that controlled the human mind and the human destiny might be called *God,* and Lincoln as a young man sometimes referred to it that way, though he did so apologetically, as when he wrote (in 1842) to his recently married friend Joshua F. Speed: ". . . I was always superstitious; and as part of my superstition, I believe God made me one of the instruments of bringing your Fanny and you together, which union, I have no doubt He had foreordained. Whatever he designs, he will do for *me* yet." [3] Here was an expression of Lincoln's fatalistic philosophy with religious (or, as he said, "superstitious") overtones. God had designs. He foreordained events. He worked through human agents, and Lincoln on occasion was one of them.

Lincoln as President held to the same belief, but he held to it with a far deeper religious assurance and with an appropriately grander conception of his own role in the divine plan. He came to view the war as God's way of removing slavery and punishing the people, both North and South, for the sin that all shared on account of slavery. And he came to look upon himself, humbly, as God's man, God's human agent in the working out of His mysterious providence.

Lincoln's clearest expression of this religious, predestinarian interpretation of the war is found in his second inaugural. "If we shall suppose that American slavery is one of those offences which, in the providence of God, must needs come, but which, having continued through His appointed time, He now wills to remove, and that He gives to both North and South, this terrible war, as the woe due to those by whom the offence came, shall we discern therein any departure from those divine attributes which the believers in a Living God always ascribe to Him?" [4] If Lincoln had said such things only on public occasions, his sincerity might be questioned, but he expressed similar ideas in private letters and conversations, and he did so with the ring of true conviction. "Men are not flattered by being shown that there has been a difference of purpose between the Al-

---

[2] Handbill addressed "To the Voters of the Seventh Congressional District," July 31, 1846, *ibid.*, 382.

[3] Lincoln to Speed, July 4, 1842, *ibid.*, I, 289.

[4] *Ibid.*, VIII, 333.

mighty and them," he wrote to Thurlow Weed in response to the latter's congratulations upon the second inaugural. "To deny it, however, in this case, is to deny that there is a God governing the world. It is a truth which I thought needed to be told; and as whatever of humiliation there is in it, falls most directly on myself, I thought others might afford for me to tell it." [5] Once he wrote to Eliza P. Gurney: "The purposes of the Almighty are perfect, and must prevail, though we erring mortals may fail to accurately perceive them in advance. We hoped for a happy termination of this terrible war before this; but God knows best, and has ruled otherwise." [6] In conversation at the White House he spoke feelingly of God's will and his own submission to it.[7] Thus, before the end of his life, he had substituted the idea of "God's will" for his earlier concept of a "necessity" abstract and mechanistic.

But Lincoln found room within his predestinarian scheme for human will, human choice. He once told Congressman Arnold how, years earlier, he had declined an offer of the governorship of Oregon Territory. "If you had gone to Oregon," Arnold commented, "you might have come back as senator, but you would never have been President." Lincoln agreed, then said with a musing, dreamy look: "I have all my life been a fatalist. What is to be will be, or rather, I have found all my life as Hamlet says:

> There is a divinity that shapes our ends,
> Rough-hew them how we will.[8]

Or, as Lincoln told Mrs. Gurney, we must acknowledge God's wisdom and our own error. "Meanwhile we must work earnestly in the best light He gives us, trusting that so working still conduces to the great ends He ordains." [9]

IV

Since Lincoln's death, more words have been wasted on the question of his religion than on any other aspect of his life. Many preachers in their obituary sermons described him as a true, believing Christian, and one of them obtained from the presumably authorita-

[5] Lincoln to Weed, Mar. 15, 1865, *ibid.*, 356.
[6] Lincoln to Mrs. Gurney, Sept. 4, 1864, R. T. L. Coll., 35907–8.
[7] Carpenter, *Six Months at the White House*, 86. [8] Arnold, *Lincoln*, 81.
[9] R. T. L. Coll., 35907–8.

tive Noah Brooks an assurance of "Mr. Lincoln's saving knowledge of Christ; he talked always of Christ, his cross, his atonement." [1] Some of the preachers seemed desperately eager to get Lincoln on the side of Christianity, so eager that the Reverend James A. Reed, one of the staunchest defenders of Lincoln's orthodoxy, was constrained to remind the public that "the faith and future of the Christian religion in no wise depends upon the sentiments of Abraham Lincoln." [2] The earliest biographers—Josiah G. Holland, Isaac N. Arnold—pictured their subject as a paragon in every respect, especially in Christian piety. All this was too much for Herndon, the aggressive freethinker of Springfield, and he set out to prove that his former law partner had been an infidel and very nearly an atheist.[3] Lincoln himself had left off arguing religion some thirty years before he died, but afterward countless volunteers took up the argument for him, and they never left it off. Sectarians of all kinds, from spiritualists to biosophers, claimed him as one of them.[4]

In fact, however, Lincoln had never signed any creed, never joined any church. After about 1850 he went to Sunday services regularly, at the First Presbyterian Church in Springfield and then at the New York Avenue Presbyterian Church in Washington. In Springfield he was a friend of the Rev. Dr. James Smith, the Presbyterian minister, and he read with interest Dr. Smith's book designed to lead skeptics to the Christian faith by rational argument. In Washington he was again a friend of his minister, the Rev. Dr. Phineas D. Gurley. But neither Smith nor Gurley won him to the fold.[5]

If Lincoln was no professing Christian, neither was he in any sense an atheist. Indeed, even Herndon did not really think he was. Herndon was driven to overstatement by his zeal against the cant of pious moralizers, yet he sometimes qualified his statements and contradicted

---

1 Brooks to the Rev. Isaac P. Langworthy, May 10, 1865, printed as *The Character and Religion of President Lincoln* (Champlain, N.Y., 1919).

2 Douglas C. McMurtrie, ed., *Lincoln's Religion . . . Addresses . . . by William H. Herndon and Rev. James A. Reed . . .* (Chicago, 1936).

3 Benjamin P. Thomas, *Portrait for Posterity: Lincoln and His Biographers,* chap. i. See also Albert V. House, Jr., "The Genesis of the Lincoln Religious Controversy," *Proceedings of the Middle States Association of History and Social Science Teachers,* XXXVI (1938), 44–54.

4 See, for example, Paul Miller, "Was Abraham Lincoln a Spiritualist?" *Psychic Observer,* Feb. 10, 1945, and Arthur E. Briggs, "Lincoln the Biosopher," *Biosophical Review,* Spring-Summer, 1936.

5 William E. Barton, *The Soul of Abraham Lincoln,* 73–75, 87, 156, 255–256.

himself. "I affirm that Mr. Lincoln died an unbeliever—was not an evangelical Christian," he said in rebuttal against the Rev. James A. Reed.[6] On another occasion Herndon declared that Lincoln *"was in short an infidel*—was a universalist—was a Unitarian—a Theist. He did not believe that Jesus was God nor the son of God etc." [7] Of course, a theist is not an atheist and, except by fundamentalist standards, a universalist or a unitarian is hardly an infidel. Nor is a person necessarily an unbeliever simply because he is not an "evangelical" Christian.

Doubtless Lincoln did share some of the basic Universalist and Unitarian attitudes. Like the Universalists he apparently believed in salvation for all and disbelieved in hell, and like the Unitarians he seems to have rejected the supernatural account of the birth of Christ. While, in private letters and state papers, he referred often to God or the Almighty, he very seldom mentioned Jesus as the Savior, very seldom mentioned Jesus at all (despite Brook's unsupported testimony that he "talked always of Christ, his cross, his atonement").

Lincoln also was inclined toward the Quaker point of view, and he acknowledged that his ancestors had been Quakers. Some of the Friends believed, as his correspondence with Mrs. Gurney reveals, that like them he felt a "true concern" laid upon him by the Heavenly Father.[8] There is no need to look for proof of the as yet unproved story that one of Mrs. Gurney's letters, carefully treasured by him, was found in his breast pocket after the assassination.[9] There is ample evidence, in the correspondence itself, to show that he deeply sympathized with the Quakers and did indeed treasure their good wishes.

In common with the Friends he felt a kind of mysticism, a sense of direct communion with the unseen. He did not carry this so far as to become a spiritualist. True, he permitted a few seances in the White House, after the death of little Willie, but these were Mrs. Lincoln's doing, not his. He commented that the seances reminded him of his cabinet meetings: the voices of the spirits, he said, were as contradictory as was the advice of his secretaries. Nevertheless he had a superstitious belief in various kinds of mysterious signs and

[6] McMurtrie, *Lincoln's Religion*, 23.
[7] Herndon to Lamon, Feb. 25, 1870, Herndon MSS.
[8] Mrs. Gurney to Lincoln, Sept. 8, 1864, R. T. L. Coll., 36053–56.
[9] *Friends Intelligencer*, Feb. 12, 1944, p. 102.

portents, especially dreams. Once in 1863, when Mrs. Lincoln with Tad was visiting in Philadelphia, Lincoln thought it important enough to telegraph her: "Think you had better put Tad's pistol away. I had an ugly dream about him." [10] On several occasions the President thought his dreams so significant that he brought them to the attention of his cabinet. On the morning of his final cabinet meeting he related the poignant recurring dream in which he was upon the water and, as Welles recorded, "seemed to be in some singular, indescribable vessel" and "was moving with great rapidity towards an indefinite shore." [11]

A believer in dreams, a mystic with some affinity for the Quakers, a rationalist with Universalist and Unitarian views, a regular participant in Presbyterian services—Lincoln cannot easily be categorized as to religion. Yet it is possible to construct a personal creed from his own statements, as William E. Barton has done.[12] Lincoln believed in God. He believed that God was intimately concerned with human affairs, that nations as well as men were dependent upon Him, that men and nations were punished for their sins, in this world as well as the next. He believed in the Bible as the best gift ever given by God to men. And he believed with all humility that he himself was an instrument in the hands of God.

Indeed, Lincoln was a man of more intense religiosity than any other President the United States has ever had. He had not demonstrated this trait very noticeably during his Illinois years. Reacting perhaps against the backwoods religion of his Baptist father, he had turned to skepticism, read such iconoclastic authors as Volney and Paine, and gained a reputation as a scoffer—a reputation which he felt he must deny when running for Congress in 1846. This early Lincoln was the Lincoln that Herndon knew, or thought he knew, and Herndon insisted that the later Lincoln was exactly the same. For this, Herndon got confirmation from Nicolay. "Mr. Lincoln, did not, to my knowledge, change in any way his religious views, beliefs, or opinions from the time he left Springfield to the day of his death," Nicolay replied to Herndon's query.[13] But Nicolay vitiated his testimony as to Lincoln's unchanging religious beliefs when he added that he did "not know just what they were." And in Lincoln's writings and

[10] Barton, *The Soul of Abraham Lincoln,* 232–236. [11] Welles, *Diary,* II, 282–283.
[12] *The Soul of Abraham Lincoln,* 300. [13] McMurtrie, *Lincoln's Religion,* 41.

speeches, there is plenty of evidence, whether or not Nicolay could see it and appreciate it, to indicate that Lincoln as President gained a more and more pervasive consciousness of God.

Almost invariably students of Lincoln have noted his spiritual growth, but some have differed in their efforts to account for it. Ruth Painter Randall has explained it as his response to a series of crises both personal and public—the deaths of his sons Eddie and Willie, the awesome responsibilities of his wartime office.[14] Charles W. Ramsdell has suggested that the President's deepening sense of melancholy and charity may have been due in part to a sense of guilt for having contributed to bringing on the war.[15] There may be some truth in Ramsdell's guess—at times Lincoln seemed to make a special point of protesting that not he but God was responsible, as when he wrote: "Surely He intends some great good to follow this mighty convulsion, which no mortal could make, and no mortal could stop." [16] Richard Hofstadter has found a clue to Lincoln's tragic sense of life in an antithesis between Lincoln the ambitious politician and Lincoln the sensitive and humble man of the people. "Lincoln's rage for personal success, his external and worldly ambition, was quieted when he entered the White House, and he was at last left alone to reckon with himself," Hofstadter writes. "To be confronted with the fruits of his victory only to find that it meant choosing between life and death for others was immensely sobering." [17]

Whatever the source of Lincoln's religious feeling, it became a vibrant force in his thought and action as President. It transformed him, even in the view of Herndon, who once wrote: "Do you not see Lincoln's Christ like charity—liberality—toleration loom up & blossom above all." [18] It moved Lincoln's friend Jesse W. Fell to say that, though Lincoln subscribed to no sectarian dogma, "his principles and practices, and the spirit of his whole life, were of the kind we universally agree to call Christian." [19] It led John Hay to call him "the greatest character since Christ." [20] Surely, among successful American

14 Ruth Painter Randall, "Lincoln's Faith was Born of Anguish," *New York Times Magazine*, Feb. 7, 1954, pp. 11, 26–27. See also Harlan Hoyt Horner, *The Growth of Lincoln's Faith* (1939).

15 Ramsdell, "Lincoln and Fort Sumter," *Journal of Southern History*, III (1937), 288.

16 Lincoln to Mrs. Gurney, Sept. 4, 1864, R. T. L. Coll., 35907–8.

17 Hofstadter, *American Political Tradition*, 133.

18 Herndon MSS.

19 Fell to Lamon, Sept. 26, 1870, J. S. Black MSS.

20 Hofstadter, *American Political Tradition*, 92.

politicians, Lincoln is unique in the way he breathed the spirit of Christ while disregarding the letter of Christian doctrine. And the letter killeth, but the spirit giveth life.

V

Lincoln's tastes in literature provide something of a clue to the nature of the inner man. He did not read widely, but he read deeply. He re-read over and over the things he liked, and he liked a rather odd assortment of things. He did not care for philosophical works as such. Though fond of the essays of John Stuart Mill, particularly the famous one on liberty, he considered the tomes of Herbert Spencer and Charles Darwin as "entirely too heavy for an ordinary mind to digest," if Herndon is to be believed. Metaphysical books he considered even worse. "Investigation into first causes, abstruse mental phenomena, the science of being," says Herndon, "he brushed aside as trash—mere scientific absurdities." [1] He liked poetry, including that of Lord Byron and Robert Burns, but his favorite poem was one written by the otherwise undistinguished William Knox, and he often recited it: "Oh! Why should the spirit of mortal be proud?" [2] Among his favorite authors were, at one extreme, the comic writers who went by the names of Petroleum V. Nasby, Orpheus C. Kerr, Artemus Ward, and Joe Miller of the famous jokebook and, at the other extreme, William Shakespeare.[3] Lincoln conformed to the accepted convention of a great man's proper literary tastes in his sincere love of Shakespeare's plays and the Bible.

According to Arnold, he knew the Bible almost by heart. "There was not a clergyman to be found so familiar with it as he." And there is "scarcely a speech or paper prepared by him" from 1834 to 1865 "but contains apt allusions and striking illustrations from the sacred book." [4] According to Brooks, he "would sometimes correct a misquotation of Scripture, giving generally the chapter and verse where it could be found." And, according to Brooks, he much preferred the Old Testament to the New.[5]

Actually, Lincoln did not quote the Bible in his state papers quite so often as Arnold believed, nor in his quotations did he indicate such

1 Daniel K. Dodge, *Abraham Lincoln: The Evolution of His Literary Style,* 17.

2 *Littell's Living Age,* LXXXV, 239–240 (May 6, 1865).

3 Dodge, 16–17.

4 Arnold, *Lincoln,* 45.

5 Brooks, "Recollections of Abraham Lincoln," *Harper's Magazine,* XXXI (1865), 229.

a preference for the Old Testament as Brooks reported. A sampling of Lincoln's works has shown that, in twenty-five speeches from 1839 to 1865, he alluded to the Bible a total of twenty-two times—to the Old Testament eight times and to the New Testament fourteen. A few of the speeches contain several references each, others contain none at all, and there is a good deal of repetition, as for example of the "house divided against itself" passage.[6] From this it does not necessarily follow that Lincoln was less familiar with the Bible than he has been credited with being or that he preferred the New Testament. Apparently there is no close correlation between, on the one hand, his interest in and familiarity with the Bible, either in whole or in part, and, on the other hand, the frequency of his references to it in public addresses.

The same is true also in regard to Shakespeare's plays. In public addresses Lincoln quoted or paraphrased them even less often than the Bible. In private conversations, however, he not only used a great many Shakespearean allusions but he also discussed problems of interpretation, with remarkable insight, and gave effective performances of his own. Doubtless he would have made a powerful tragic actor as well as a discerning drama critic.

"Unlike you gentlemen of the profession," he wrote to the actor Hackett, "I think the soliloquy in 'Hamlet,' commencing 'O, my offense is rank,' surpasses that commencing, 'To be or not to be.' "[7] The first of these soliloquies—spoken by the King after the murder of Polonius—was a favorite with Lincoln. In the presence of Carpenter he once recited the entire passage from memory, and with more feeling and better understanding than Carpenter had ever heard it done on the stage. Lincoln complained that the passage usually was slurred over by professional actors, and so, he said, was another of his favorites, the opening lines of "King Richard the Third," beginning "Now is the winter of our discontent." This soliloquy, too, Lincoln repeated in Carpenter's presence, "rendering it with a degree of force and power that made it seem like a new creation" to Carpenter. While at Fortress Monroe, in 1862, the President read feelingly from "Hamlet" on the theme of ambition.[8] On shipboard returning from City Point, in 1865, he delighted his fellow passengers, including the

[6] Dodge, 18–19. [7] Cincinnati *Daily Gazette,* Sept. 30, 1863, p. 1, c. 6.

[8] Carpenter, *Six Months at the White House,* 49–52.

Marquis de Chambrun, with Shakespearean readings which lasted for several hours. He was especially moved, and moving, with the verses in "Macbeth" in which Macbeth speaks of Duncan's assassination:

> Duncan is in his grave;
> After life's fitful fever he sleeps well;
> Treason has done his worst: nor steel, nor poison,
> Malice domestic, foreign levy, nothing
> Can touch him further.[9]

With Lincoln, the play was the thing, not the acting, and in the play it was the thought that counted. "It matters not to me whether Shakespeare be well or ill acted," he once remarked; "with him the thought suffices." [10] Unless the acting was unusually good, Lincoln preferred his own reading and interpretation of the play. After seeing Edwin Booth as Shylock he said to Brooks: "It was a good performance, but I had a thousand times rather read it at home, if it were not for Booth's playing. A farce, or a comedy, is best played; a tragedy is best read at home." [11]

At home, in the White House, there was little rest for Lincoln during those tumultuous days and nights of celebration following the surrender at Appomattox. Now, as always, the theater offered him an escape in a physical as well as a psychological sense. It was a place to go to get away from people and be alone while in their midst. Time and again in the past he had sat with an audience and had remained abstracted and unmoved as scene after scene passed.[12] On the evening of April 14, 1865, he planned to seek that accustomed relaxation, this time at Ford's Theater, where a comedy, "The Country Cousin," was playing. At dinner he complained of being worn out from the toils of the day, and he looked forward eagerly to an opportunity to laugh. Mrs. Lincoln, troubled with a headache, suggested that they stay home, but he insisted on their going out; otherwise, he said, he would have to see visitors all evening as usual.[13] And so they went.

---

[9] James Speed to Joseph H. Barrett, Sept. 16, 1885, Barton MSS. The Marquis de Chambrun's account is in *Scribner's Magazine,* XIII (1893), 34.

[10] Carpenter, *Six Months at the White House,* 49–52.

[11] Brooks, "Personal Recollections of Abraham Lincoln," *Scribner's Monthly,* XV (1877–1878), 675.

[12] Forney, *Anecdotes of Public Men,* 272.

[13] A. G. Henry to Mrs. Henry, Apr. 19, 1865, MS., Lib. of Cong. See also Ruth Painter Randall, *Mary Lincoln,* 381.

BIBLIOGRAPHY[1]

Anon., "As Lincoln Knew New Salem." 36 *Life* 79–81 (Feb. 15, 1954).

Abbott, Martin, "Southern Reaction to Lincoln's Assassination." 7 *A. L. Q.* 111–127 (1952).

Adams, George Worthington, *Doctors in Blue: The Medical History of the Union Army in the Civil War.* New York: Henry Schuman, 1952. 253 pp.

Agar, Herbert, *Abraham Lincoln.* New York: The Macmillan Co., 1952. 143 pp. *Brief Lives,* No. 6.

Anderson, Frank Maloy, *The Mystery of "A Public Man:" A Historical Detective Story.* Minneapolis: Univ. of Minnesota Press, 1948. 256 pp. For another version, see Lokken, Roy N.

Anderson, George L., "The South and Problems of Post-Civil War Finance." 9 *Jour. So. Hist.* 181–195 (1943).

Angle, Paul M., "The Changing Lincoln," *The John H. Hauberg Historical Essays,* ed. by O. Fritiof Ander. Rock Island, Ill.: Augustana College, 1954. Pp. 1–17.

———, ed., "The Recollections of William Pitt Kellogg." 3 *A. L. Q.* 319–339 (1945).

———, *A Shelf of Lincoln Books: A Critical, Selective Bibliography of Lincolniana.* New Brunswick: Rutgers Univ. Press, 1946. 142 pp.

———, ed., *The Lincoln Reader.* New Brunswick: Rutgers Univ. Press, 1947. 564 pp.

———, comp., *Abraham Lincoln: His Autobiographical Writings Now Brought Together for the First Time . . . .* Kingsport, Tenn.: Privately printed at Kingsport Press, Inc., 1947. 67 pp.

———, ed., *Herndon's Life of Lincoln.* Cleveland: World Pub. Co., 1949. 511 pp.

———, ed., *Abraham Lincoln by Some Men Who Knew Him . . . .* Chicago: Americana House, 1950. 123 pp.

Arena, Frank C., "Southern Sympathizers in Iowa during the Civil War Period." 30 *Ann. Iowa* (3 ser.) 486–538 (1951).

[1] This list is intended to supplement the bibliography in *Lincoln the President,* II, 343–400. Included in the list are, for the most part, items published since that earlier bibliography was prepared. Also included here are certain items of earlier date which are relevant to the subjects treated in volumes III and IV of the biography but not relevant to volumes I and II. This bibliography was prepared by Wayne C. Temple.

Auer, J. Jeffery, "Lincoln's Minister to Mexico." 59 *Ohio Arch. and Hist. Quar.* 115–128 (1950).

Bailey, Thomas A., "The Russian Fleet Myth Re-Examined." 38 *M. V. H. R.* 81–90 (1951).

Ballard, Colin R., *The Military Genius of Abraham Lincoln.* Cleveland: World Pub. Co., 1952. 246 pp.

Banks, N. P. See Harrington, Fred Harvey.

Barbee, David Rankin, "President Lincoln and Doctor Gurley." 5 *A. L. Q.* 3–24 (1948).

———, "The Musical Mr. Lincoln." 5 *A. L. Q.* 435–454 (1949). For the correction of this story, see 6 *A. L. Q.* 37–39 (1950).

Baringer, William E. and Marion D. Bonzi [Pratt], "The Writings of Lincoln." 4 *A. L. Q.* 3–16 (1946).

———, "The Birth of a Reputation." 4 *A. L. Q.* 217–242 (1947).

———, *Lincoln's Vandalia: A Pioneer Portrait.* New Brunswick: Rutgers Univ. Press, 1949. 141 pp.

———, "On Enemy Soil: President Lincoln's Norfolk Campaign." 7 *A. L. Q.* 4–26 (1952).

Barrett, Oliver R., "Lincoln and Retaliation." 49 *Lincoln Herald* 2 ff. (Dec., 1947).

Barton, Robert S., "William E. Barton—Biographer." 4 *A. L. Q.* 80–93 (1946).

———. See also Spears, Zarel C.

Barton, William E., *Lincoln at Gettysburg: What He Intended to Say; What He Said; What He Was Reported to Have Said; What He Wished He Had Said.* New York: Peter Smith, 1950. 263 pp.

Basler, Roy P., *Abraham Lincoln: His Speeches and Writings.* Cleveland: World Pub. Co., 1946. 750 pp.

———, "Lincoln and People Everywhere." 4 *A. L. Q.* 349–355 (1947).

———, "Lincoln in Politics, 1948." 5 *A. L. Q.* 216–233 (1948).

———, "What Did Lincoln Say?" 5 *A. L. Q.* 476–479 (1949).

———, "Isaac Harvey or Samuel Haddam." 6 *A. L. Q.* 353–357 (1951).

———, "'Beef! Beef! Beef!' Lincoln and Judge Robertson." 6 *A. L. Q.* 400–407 (1951).

———, Marion D. (Bonzi) Pratt, and Lloyd A. Dunlap, eds., *The Collected Works of Abraham Lincoln.* New Brunswick: Rutgers Univ. Press, 1953. 8 vols. Index vol. to follow.

Baxter, Maurice G., "Encouragement of Immigration to the Middle West during the Era of the Civil War." 46 *Ind. Mag. Hist.* 25–38 (1950).

Beale, Howard K., "On Rewriting Reconstruction History." 45 *A. H. R.* 807–827 (1940).

———, "What Historians Have Said about the Causes of the Civil War." In *Theory and Practice in Historical Study . . . .* Ed. by C. A. Beard and others. Social Science Research Council Bulletin No. 54. New York: Social Science Research Council, 1946. Pp. 55–102.

Beck, Warren A., "Lincoln and Negro Colonization in Central America." 6 *A. L. Q.* 162–183 (1950).
Bernard, Kenneth A., "Lincoln and Civil Liberties." 6 *A. L. Q.* 375–399 (1951).
———, "Glimpses of Lincoln in the White House." 7 *A. L. Q.* 161–187 (1952).
Binkley, Wilfred E., *President and Congress.* New York: Alfred A. Knopf, 1947. 312 pp.
Black, Robert C., III, *The Railroads of the Confederacy.* Chapel Hill: Univ. of North Carolina Press, 1952. 360 pp.
Blum, Virgil C., "The Political and Military Activities of the German Element in St. Louis, 1859–1861." 42 *Mo. Hist. Rev.* 103–129 (1948).
Bonner, Thomas N., "Horace Greeley and the Secession Movement, 1860–1861." 38 *N. V. H. R.* 425–444 (1951).
Bonzi, Marion D., "A Sparks Debate Variant." 4 *A. L. Q.* 140–144 (1946).
Briggs, Harold E. and Ernestine B. Briggs, *Nancy Hanks Lincoln: A Frontier Portrait.* New York: Bookman Assoc., 1952. 135 pp.
Brown, Charles Leroy, "Abraham Lincoln and the Illinois Central Railroad, 1857–1860." 36 *Jour. Ill. S. H. S.* 121–163 (1943).
Brown, Richard A. See Miers, Earl Schenck.
Brown, Virginia Stuart, *Through Lincoln's Door.* Springfield Li-Co Art & Letter Service, 1952. 79 pp. Revised edition 1953.
Bullard, F. Lauriston, *Abraham Lincoln & the Widow Bixby.* New Brunswick: Rutgers Univ. Press, 1946. 154 pp.
———, "Lincoln's Copy of Pope's Poems." 4 *A. L. Q.* 30–35 (1946).
———, "Abraham Lincoln and Harriet Beecher Stowe." 48 *Lincoln Herald* 11–14 (June, 1946).
———, "Abraham Lincoln and George Ashmun." 19 *New Eng. Quar.* 184–211 (1946).
———, "Abe Goes down the River." 50 *Lincoln Herald* 2–14 (Feb., 1948).
———, "When—If Ever—Was John Wilkes Booth in Paris?" 50 *Lincoln Herald* 28–34 (June, 1948).
———, "Anna Ella Carroll and Her 'Modest' Claim." 50 *Lincoln Herald* 2–10 (Oct., 1948).
———, "Church and State in Lincoln's Time." 50–51 *Lincoln Herald* 28 ff. (Dec., 1948–Feb., 1949).
———, "A Friend in France in '61." 51 *Lincoln Herald* 33–37 (June, 1949).
———, "Garfield and Chase—Their Ideas of Lincoln." 51 *Lincoln Herald* 2 ff. (Dec., 1949).
———, "How Much Did Abraham Lincoln Owe to 'Luck?'" 52 *Lincoln Herald* 44–45 (Feb., 1950).
———, "A Correction of 'The Musical Mr. Lincoln.'" 6 *A. L. Q.* 37–39 (1950).
———, "Again, the Bixby Letter." 53 *Lincoln Herald* 26 ff. (Summer, 1951).

———, *Lincoln in Marble and Bronze*. New Brunswick: Rutgers Univ. Press, 1952. 353 pp.

Cannon, M. Hamlin, "The United States Christian Commission." 38 *M. V. H. R.* 61–80 (1951).

Carr, R. T. and Hugh Morrow, "We Found Lincoln's Lost Bank Account." 225 *Sat. Eve. Post* 22 ff. (Feb. 14, 1953).

Carruthers, Olive and R. Gerald McMurtry, *Lincoln's Other Mary*. Chicago: Ziff-Davis, 1946. 229 pp.

Catton, Bruce, *Mr. Lincoln's Army*. Garden City: Doubleday & Co., 1951. 372 pp.

———, *Glory Road: The Bloody Route from Fredericksburg to Gettysburg*. Garden City: Doubleday & Co., 1952. 416 pp.

———, *A Stillness at Appomattox*. Garden City: Doubleday & Co., 1953. 438 pp.

Chambrun, Marquis Adolphe de, *Impressions of Lincoln and the Civil War: A Foreigner's Account*. Trans. by Gen. Aldebert de Chambrun. New York: Random House, 1952. 174 pp.

Chase, Salmon Portland. See Donald, David.

Chester, Giraud, *Embattled Maiden: The Life of Anna Dickinson*. New York: G. P. Putnam's Sons, 1951. 307 pp.

Clary, William W., *How Abe Lincoln Went to Oxford*. Claremont, Cal.: Claremont College, 1948. 16 pp.

Claussen, Martin P., "Peace Factors in Anglo-American Relations, 1861–1865." 26 *M. V. H. R.* 511–522 (1940).

Coleman, Charles H., "The Use of the Term 'Copperhead' during the Civil War." 25 *M. V. H. R.* 263–264 (1938).

———, "The Half-Faced Camp in Indiana—Fact or Myth?" 7 *A. L. Q.* 138–146 (1952).

Cramer, J. H., "Lincoln in Cincinnati." 3 *Bulletin Hist. and Philosophical Soc. of Ohio* 11–16 (1945).

———, "The Great and the Small." 49 *Lincoln Herald* 14–20 (Feb., 1947).

———, "A President-elect in Western Pennsylvania." 71 *Pa. Mag. Hist. and Biog.* 206–217 (July, 1947).

———, "Abraham Lincoln Visits with His People." 57 *Ohio Arch. and Hist. Quar.* 66–78 (1948).

———, *Lincoln under Enemy Fire: The Complete Account of His Experiences during Early's Attack on Washington*. Baton Rouge: Louisiana State Univ. Press, 1948. 138 pp.

Craven, Avery O., "The Civil War and the Democratic Process." 4 *A. L. Q.* 269–292 (1947).

———, "The Price of Union." 18 *Jour. So. Hist.* 3–19 (1952).

Cresson, Margaret French, *Journey into Fame: The Life of Daniel Chester French*. Cambridge: Harvard Univ. Press, 1947. 316 pp.

Cross, Jasper W., "The Civil War Comes to 'Egypt.'" 44 *Jour. Ill. S. H. S.* 160–169 (1951).

Current, Richard Nelson, *Old Thad Stevens: A Story of Ambition.* Madison: Univ. of Wisconsin Press, 1942. 344 pp.

Cuthbert, Norma B., ed., *Lincoln and the Baltimore Plot, 1861: From Pinkerton Records and Related Papers.* San Marino: Henry E. Huntington Library, 1949. 161 pp.

Daugherty, James, *Lincoln's Gettysburg Address: A Pictorial Interpretation.* Chicago: Albert Whitman & Co., 1947. 42 pp.

Donald, David, "The Folklore Lincoln." 40 *Jour. Ill. S. H. S.* 377–396 (1947).

———,"The True Story of 'Herndon's Lincoln.'" 1 *The New Colophon* 221–234 (1948).

———, *Lincoln's Herndon.* New York: Alfred A. Knopf, 1948. 392 pp.

———, ed., *Divided We Fought: A Pictorial History of the War 1861–1865.* New York: The Macmillan Co., 1952, 452 pp.

———, "Getting Right with Lincoln." 202 *Harper's Mag.* 74–80 (April, 1851).

———, ed., *Inside Lincoln's Cabinet: The Civil War Diaries of Salmon Portland Chase.* New York: Longmans, Green & Co., 1954. 342 pp.

Donald, Henderson H., *The Negro Freedman: The Life Conditions of the American Negro in the Early Years after Emancipation.* New York: Henry Schuman, 1952. 270 pp.

Dorris, Jonathan Truman, *Pardon and Amnesty under Lincoln and Johnson.* Chapel Hill: Univ. of North Carolina Press, 1953. 459 pp. Introduction by J. G. Randall.

Drake, Julia A., "Lincoln Land Buying." 50–51 *Lincoln Herald* 32–35 (Dec., 1948–Feb., 1949).

Dunlap, Lloyd A., "President Lincoln and Editor Greeley." 5 *A. L. Q.* 94–110 (1948).

———, "Lincoln Saves a Son." 7 *A. L. Q.* 128–137 (1952).

———. See also Basler, Roy P.

East, Ernest E., "Lincoln and the Peoria French Claims." 42 *Jour. Ill. S. H. S.* 41–56 (1949).

Ehrmann, Bess V., *Lincoln and His Neighbors.* Rockport, Ind.: Democrat Pub. Co., 1948. 44 pp.

———, *The Lincoln Pioneer Village: A Lincoln Memorial, Rockport, Indiana.* Rockport, Ind.: Democrat Pub. Co., 1949. 7 pp.

Eisendrath, Joseph L., Jr., "Lincolniana in the Official Records." 4 *A. L. Q.* 201–204 (1946).

———, "Suggestions that Inspired Immortal Words." 5 *A. L. Q.* 212–215 (1948).

Eisenschiml, Otto and Ralph Newman, comps., *The American Iliad: The Epic Story of the Civil War as Narrated by Eyewitnesses and Contemporaries.* Indianapolis: Bobbs-Merrill Co., 1947. 720 pp.

——— and E. B. Long, *As Luck Would Have It: Chance and Coincidence in the Civil War.* Indianapolis: Bobbs-Merrill Co., 1948. 285 pp.

———, "Addenda to Lincoln's Assassination." 43 *Jour. Ill. S. H. S.* 91–99; 204–219 (1950).

———, *The Celebrated Case of Fitz John Porter: An American Dreyfus Affair.* Indianapolis: Bobbs-Merrill Co., 1950. 344 pp.

Elliott, Claude, "Union Sentiment in Texas 1861–1865." 50 *Southwestern Hist. Quar.* 449–477 (1947).

Fatout, Paul, "Mr. Lincoln Goes to Washington." 47 *Ind. Mag. Hist.* 321–332 (1951).

Fehrenbacher, Don E., "The Nomination of Lincoln in 1858." 6 *A. L. Q.* 24–36 (1950).

Fisch, Theodore, "Horace Greeley: A Yankee in Transition." (MS) Ph. D. thesis, Univ. of Ill., Urbana, 1947.

Fischer, LeRoy H., "Lincoln's Gadfly—Adam Gurowski." 36 *M. V. H. R.* 415–434 (1949).

Foster, Genevieve, *Abraham Lincoln: An Initial Biography.* New York: Chas. Scribner's Sons, 1950. 111 pp.

Frank, Seymour J., "The Conspiracy to Implicate the Confederate Leaders in Lincoln's Assassination." 40 *M. V. H. R.* 629–656 (1954).

Freeman, Douglas Southall, *Lee's Lieutenants: A Study in Command.* New York: Chas. Scribner's Sons, 1942–1944. 3 vols.

Freidel, Frank, "General Orders 100." 32 *M. V. H. R.* 541–556 (1946).

———, *Francis Lieber: Nineteenth-Century Liberal.* Baton Rouge: Louisiana State Univ. Press, 1947. 445 pp.

Garraty, John A., "Lincoln and the Diplomats." 46 *Ind. Mag. Hist.* 203–204 (1950).

Geyl, Pieter, "The American Civil War and the Problem of Inevitability." 24 *New Eng. Quar.* 147–168 (1951).

Gillespie, Frances. See Wallace, Sarah A.

Glonek, James F., "Lincoln, Johnson, and the Baltimore Ticket." 6 *A. L. Q.* 255–271 (1951).

Gorgas, Josiah. See Vandiver, Frank E.

Greenbie, Sydney and Marjorie Barstow Greenbie, *Anna Ella Carroll and Abraham Lincoln: A Biography.* Manchester, Me.: Univ. of Tampa Press, 1952. 539 pp. For an evaluation, see Kenneth P. Williams, 54 *Lincoln Herald* 54–56 (Summer, 1952).

Grierson, Francis, *The Valley of Shadows.* Boston: Houghton Mifflin Co., 1948. 278 pp.

Griffith, Albert H., *The Heart of Abraham Lincoln.* Madison: Lincoln Fellowship of Wisconsin, 1948. 16 pp.

Gunderson, Robert Gray, "Lincoln and Governor Morgan: A Financial Footnote." 6 *A. L. Q.* 431–437 (1951).

Hagen, Richard S., "Back-Yard Archaeology at Lincoln's Home." 44 *Jour. Ill. S. H. S.* 340–348 (1951).

Hambrecht, George P., *Abraham Lincoln in Wisconsin.* Madison: Lincoln Fellowship of Wisconsin, 1946. 17 pp.

Hamilton, Holman, "Abraham Lincoln and Zachary Taylor." 53 *Lincoln Herald* 14–19 (Fall, 1951).

Hammand, Lavern Marshall, "Ward Hill Lamon: Lincoln's 'Particular Friend.'" (MS) Ph. D. thesis, Univ. of Ill., Urbana, 1949.

Harkness, David J., "Lincoln and 'The Ship of State.'" 53 *Lincoln Herald* 28–30 (Spring, 1951).

Harnsberger, Caroline Thomas, *The Lincoln Treasury*. Chicago: Wilcox & Follett Co., 1950. 372 pp.

Harper, Robert S., *Lincoln and the Press*. New York: McGraw-Hill Book Co., 1951. 418 pp.

Harrington, Fred Harvey, *Fighting Politician: Major General N. P. Banks*. Philadelphia: Univ. of Penn. Press, 1948. 301 pp.

Harris, Alfred G., "Lincoln and the Question of Slavery in the District of Columbia." 51–53 *Lincoln Herald* 17–21; 2–16; 11–18 (June, 1949–Spring 1951).

Harwell, Richard Barksdale, "Lincoln and 'Dixie:' The Yankee Conversion of Some Southern Songs." 53 *Lincoln Herald* 22–27 (Spring, 1951).

Hawley, Charles Arthur, "Lincoln in Kansas." 42 *Jour. Ill. S. H. S.* 179–192 (1949).

Hays, Roy, "Is the Lincoln Birthplace Cabin Authentic?" 5 *A. L. Q.* 127–163 (1948).

Heathcote, Charles William, "Lincoln's Funeral Train in Pennsylvania." 48 *Lincoln Herald* 13 ff. (Dec., 1946).

———, "Three Pennsylvanians and Lincoln's Nomination—1860." 51 *Lincoln Herald* 38–41 (June, 1949).

———, "The Lincolns of Massachusetts, New Jersey and Pennsylvania." 51 *Lincoln Herald* 17–19 (Dec., 1949).

———, "President Lincoln and John Burns at Gettysburg." 53 *Lincoln Herald* 31–33 (Spring, 1951).

Heintz, Michael G., "Cincinnati Reminiscenses of Lincoln." 9 *Bulletin Hist. and Philosophical Soc. of Ohio* 113–120 (1951).

Hendrick, Burton J., *Lincoln's War Cabinet*. Boston: Little, Brown & Co., 1946. 482 pp.

Hesseltine, William B., "Lincoln's War Governors." 4 *A. L. Q.* 153–200 (1946).

——— and Hazel C. Wolf, "The Cleveland Conference of 1861." 56 *Ohio Arch. and Hist. Quar.* 258–265 (1947).

———, *Lincoln and the War Governors*. New York: Alfred A. Knopf, 1948. 405 pp.

Hewitt, John Hill, *King Linkum the First: A Musical Burletta*. Emory Univ. Library: Higgins-McArthur Co., 1947. 32 pp. Reprint of a play presented at Concert Hall at Augusta, Ga., on Feb. 23, 1863.

Hildner, Ernest G., Jr., "The Mexican Envoy Visits Lincoln." 6 *A. L. Q.* 184–189 (1950).

Hobeika, John E., *The Sage of Lion's Den: An Appreciation of . . . Lyon Gardiner Tyler and of His Writings on Abraham Lincoln . . . .* New York: The Exposition Press, 1948. 64 pp.

Hochmuth, Marie, "Lincoln's First Inaugural." In Wayland Maxfield Parrish and Marie Hochmuth eds., *American Speeches.* New York: Longmans, Green & Co., 1954. pp. 21–71.

Horner, Harlan Hoyt, "Lincoln Replies to Horace Greeley." 53 *Lincoln Herald* 2–10; 14–25 (Spring–September, 1951).

———, "Lincoln Rebukes a Senator." 44 *Jour. Ill. S. H. S.* 103–119 (1951).

———, "Lincoln Scolds a General." 36 *Wis. Mag. Hist.* 90 ff. (1952–1953).

———, *Lincoln and Greeley,* Urbana: Univ. of Illinois Press, 1953. 432 pp.

Howard, Oliver Otis, "Some Reminiscences of Abraham Lincoln." 55 *Lincoln Herald* 20 ff. (Fall, 1953). This sketch was written by Howard on March 1, 1895; MS at Bowdoin College, Brunswick, Me.

Howe, Mark De Wolfe, ed., *Touched with Fire: Civil War Letters and Diary of Oliver Wendell Holmes, Jr. 1861–1864.* Cambridge: Harvard Univ. Press, 1946. 158 pp.

Hubbard, Freeman H., *Vinnie Ream and Mr. Lincoln.* New York: Whittlessey House, 1949, 271 pp.

Hunt, Eugenia Jones, "My Personal Recollections of Abraham and Mary Todd Lincoln." 3 *A. L. Q.* 235–252 (1945).

Isely, Jeter A., *Horace Greeley and the Republican Party, 1853–1861: A Study of the New York Tribune.* Princeton: Princeton Univ. Press, 1947. 368 pp.

James, H. Preston, "Election Time in Illinois, 1860." 49 *Lincoln Herald* 12–21 (June, 1947).

———, "Lincoln and Douglas in Their Home State." 49 *Lincoln Herald* 2–9 (Oct., 1947).

———, "Political Pageantry in the Campaign of 1860 in Illinois." 4 *A. L. Q.* 313–347 (1947).

———, "Lincoln and Douglas in Their Home State: The Election of 1860 in Illinois." 49 *Lincoln Herald* 12–20 (Dec., 1947).

Jillson, Willard Rouse, *Abraham Lincoln in Kentucky Literature.* Frankfort, Ky.: Roberts Printing Co., 1951. 75 pp.

Johannsen, Robert W., "National Issues and Local Politics in Washington Territory, 1857–1861." 42 *Pacific Northwest Quar.* 3–31 (1951).

———, "Spectators of Disunion: The Pacific Northwest and the Civil War." 44 *Pacific Northwest Quar.* 106–114 (1953).

"John, Evan" [Capt. E. J. Simpson], *Atlantic Impact, 1861.* New York: G. P. Putnam's Sons, 1952. 296 pp. This is a history of the *Trent* affair.

Jones, Edgar DeWitt, *The Greatening of Abraham Lincoln.* St. Louis: The Bethany Press, 1946, 38 pp.
———, "Abraham Lincoln Still Walks at Midnight." 48 *Lincoln Herald* 28–31 (Oct., 1946).
———, *Lincoln and the Preachers.* New York: Harper Bros., 1948. 203 pp.
———, "A Preacher at Lincoln's Tomb." 50 *Lincoln Herald* 28–29 (Oct., 1948).
Judson, Clara Ingram, *Abraham Lincoln: Friend of the People.* Chicago: Wilcox & Follett Co., 1950. 205 pp.
Kennedy, Kaywin, "If Lincoln Were Alive Today." 35 *Ill. Bar Jour.* 229–230 (1947).
Kincaid, Robert L., "Kentucky in the Civil War." 49 *Lincoln Herald* 2–12 (June, 1947).
Klement, Frank L., "Jane Grey Swisshelm and Lincoln: A Feminist Fusses and Frets." 6 *A. L. Q.* 227–238 (1950).
———, "Economic Aspects of Middle Western Copperheadism." 14 *The Historian* 27–44 (1951).
———, " 'Brick' Pomeroy: Copperhead and Curmudgeon." 35 *Wis. Mag. Hist.* 106–113 (1951).
———, "Middle Western Copperheadism and Genesis of the Granger Movement." 38 *M. V. H. R.* 679–694 (1952).
Klingberg, Frank Wysor, "James Buchanan and the Crisis of the Union." 9 *Jour. So. Hist.* 455–474 (1943).
———, "The Case of the Minors: A Unionist Family within the Confederacy." 13 *Jour. So. Hist.* 27–45 (1947).
Korn, Bertram W., *American Jewry and the Civil War.* Philadelphia: The Jewish Pub. Soc. of America, 1951. 331 pp.
Korngold, Ralph, *Two Friends of Man: The Story of William Lloyd Garrison and Wendell Phillips and Their Relationship with Abraham Lincoln.* Boston: Little, Brown & Co., 1950. 425 pp.
Kramer, Sidney, "Lincoln at the Fair." 3 *A. L. Q.* 340–358 (1945).
Kunhardt, D. M., "Lincoln's Lost Dog." 36 *Life* 83–86 (Feb. 15, 1954).
Kyle, Otto R., "Mr. Lincoln Steps Out: The Anti-Nebraska Editors' Convention." 5 *A. L. Q.* 25–37 (1948).
Landon, Fred, "Canadian Appreciation of Abraham Lincoln." 3 *A. L. Q.* 159–177 (1944).
Lawson, Elizabeth, *Lincoln's Third Party.* New York: International Pub., 1948. 48 pp.
Lewis, Lloyd, "Lincoln and Pinkerton." 41 *Jour. Ill. S. H. S.* 367–382 (1948).
———, "Lincoln's Legacy to Grant." 5 *A. L. Q.* 75–93 (1948).
Lewis, Montgomery S., *Legends that Libel Lincoln.* New York: Rinehart & Co., 1946. 239 pp.
Lieber, Francis. See Freidel, Frank.

Lincoln, Mary Todd. See Randall, Ruth Painter.

Lincoln, Nancy Hanks. See Briggs, Harold E.

Lockwood, Theodore D., "Garrison and Lincoln the Abolitionist." 6 *A. L. Q.* 199–226 (1950).

Lokken, Roy N., "Has the Mystery of 'A Public Man' Been Solved?" 40 *M. V. H. R.* 419–440 (1953).

Long, E. B. See Eisenschiml, Otto.

Lonn, Ella, *Foreigners in the Union Army and Navy*. Baton Rouge: Louisiana State Univ. Press, 1951. 725 pp.

Lorant, Stefan, *The Life of Abraham Lincoln: A Short, Illustrated Biography*. New York: McGraw-Hill Book Co., 1954. 256 pp.

———, *Lincoln: A Picture Story of His Life*. New York: Harper & Bros., 1952. 256 pp.

Ludwig, Emil, *Abraham Lincoln: The Full Life Story of Our Martyred President*. Trans. by Eden and Cedar Paul. New York: Liveright Pub. Corp., 1949. 505 pp.

Lufkin, Richard Friend, "Mr. Lincoln's Light from under a Bushel—1850." 52 *Lincoln Herald* 2–20 (Dec., 1950).

———, "Mr. Lincoln's Light from under a Bushel—1851." 53 *Lincoln Herald* 2–25 (Winter, [1951]). This issue is misprinted as "Winter 1952."

———, "Mr. Lincoln's Light from under a Bushel—1852." 54 *Lincoln Herald* 2–26 (Winter, 1952).

Luthin, Reinhard H., "Lincoln the Politician." 48 *Lincoln Herald* 2–11 (Feb., 1946).

Macartney, Clarence Edward, *Lincoln and the Bible*. New York: Abingdon-Cokesbury, 1949. 96 pp.

———, *Grant and His Generals*. New York: The McBride Co., 1953. 352 pp.

McClure, Stanley W., *The Lincoln Museum and the House Where Lincoln Died*. Washington: Nat. Park Service, 1949. 42 pp.

McCorison, J. L., Jr., "Mr. Lincoln's Broken Blinds." 50 *Lincoln Herald* 43–46 (June, 1948).

———, "The Great Lincoln Collections and What Became of Them." 50–51 *Lincoln Herald* 2 ff. (Dec., 1948–Feb., 1949).

McGlynn, Frank, *Sidelights on Lincoln*. Los Angeles: Wetzel Pub. Co., 1947. 335 pp.

McMurtry, R. Gerald, *Why Collect Lincolniana?* Chicago: Abraham Lincoln Book Shop, 1948. 19 pp.

———, "The Kentucky Delegation that Attended Lincoln's Funeral, May 3–4, 1865." 53 *Lincoln Herald* 38–40 (Summer, 1951).

———. See also Carruthers, Olive.

Maher, Edward R., Jr., "Sam Houston and Secession." 55 *Southwestern Hist. Quar.* 448–458 (1952).

Malone, Dumas, "Jefferson and Lincoln." 5 *A. L. Q.* 327–347 (1949).

Marsh, Raymond, "Lincoln Patriotics." 52 *Lincoln Herald* 48–53 (Dec., 1950).

Massey, Mary Elizabeth, *Ersatz in the Confederacy*. Columbia: Univ. of South Carolina Press, 1952. 233 pp.

Mayhew, Lewis Baltzell, "The Clay-Thompson Mission into Canada." (MS) A. M. thesis, Univ. of Illinois, Urbana, 1946.

Maynard, Douglas H., "Union Efforts to Prevent the Escape of the *Alabama*." 41 *M. V. H. R.* 41–60 (1954).

Mearns, David C., "The Lincoln Papers." 4 *A. L. Q.* 369–385 (1947).

———, *The Lincoln Papers*. Garden City: Doubleday & Co., 1948. 2 vols.

———, "Our Reluctant Contemporary: Abraham Lincoln." 6 *A. L. Q.* 73–102 (1950).

Meredith, Roy, *Mr. Lincoln's Camera Man: Mathew B. Brady*. New York: Chas. Scribner's Sons, 1946. 368 pp.

———, *Mr. Lincoln's Contemporaries: An Album of Portraits by Mathew B. Brady*. New York: Chas. Scribner's Sons, 1951. 233 pp.

Merrill, Louis Taylor, "General Benjamin F. Butler in the Presidential Campaign of 1864." 33 *M. V. H. R.* 537–570 (1947).

Miers, Earl Schenck, *The General Who Marched to Hell: William Tecumseh Sherman and His March to Fame and Infamy*. New York: Alfred A. Knopf, 1951. 349 pp.

———, "Lincoln as a Best Seller." 5 *A. L. Q.* 179–190 (1948).

——— and Richard A. Brown, eds., *Gettysburg*. New Brunswick: Rutgers Univ. Press, 1948. 308 pp.

Miller, August C., Jr., "Lincoln's Good-Will Ambassadors." 50 *Lincoln Herald* 17 ff. (June, 1948).

Monaghan, Jay, "Was Abraham Lincoln Really a Spiritualist?" 34 *Jour. Ill. S. H. S.* 209–232 (1941).

———, "Did Abraham Lincoln Receive the Illinois German Vote?" 35 *Jour. Ill. S. H. S.* 133–139 (1942).

———, "The Growth of Abraham Lincoln's Influence in Literature Since His Death." 51 *Lincoln Herald* 2–11 (Oct., 1949).

Moore, Guy W., *The Case of Mrs. Surratt: Her Controversial Trial and Execution for Conspiracy in the Lincoln Assassination*. Norman: Univ. of Oklahoma Press, 1954. 142 pp.

Moran, Benjamin. See Wallace, Sarah A.

Morrow, Hugh. See Carr, R. T.

Nevins, Allan, *Ordeal of the Union*. New York: Chas. Scribner's Sons, 1947–1950. 4 vols.

——— and Milton Halsey Thomas, eds., *The Diary of George Templeton Strong 1835–1875*. New York: The Macmillan Co., 1952. 4 vols.

———, *The Statesmanship of the Civil War*. New York: The Macmillan Co., 1953. 82 pp.

Newman, Ralph. See Eisenschiml, Otto.

Nicolay, Helen, *Lincoln's Secretary: A Biography of John G. Nicolay.* New York: Longmans, Green & Co., 1949. 363 pp.

———, "Lincoln's Cabinet." 5 *A. L. Q.* 255–292 (1949).

Nichols, Roy Franklin, "1461–1861: The American Civil War in Perspective." 16 *Jour. So. Hist.* 143–160 (1950).

Noble, Hollister, *Woman with a Sword.* New York: Doubleday & Co., 1948. 395 pp. A biographical novel about Anna Ella Carroll.

Packard, Roy D., *The Riddle of Lincoln's Religion.* Mansfield, O.: The Midland Rare Book Co., 1946. 12 pp.

———, *The Love Affairs of Abraham Lincoln.* Cleveland: Carpenter Printing Co., 1947. 14 pp.

———, *A. Lincoln: Successful Lawyer.* Cleveland: Carpenter Printing Co., 1948. 14 pp.

———, *The Lincoln of the Thirtieth Congress.* Boston: The Christopher Pub. House, 1950. 52 pp.

Page, Elwin L., "Franklin Pierce and Abraham Lincoln—Parallels and Contrasts." 5 *A. L. Q.* 455–472 (1949).

Parker, Owen W., M. D., "The Assassination and Gunshot Wound of President Abraham Lincoln." 31 *Minnesota Medicine* 147–149 (Feb., 1948).

Parkinson, Robert H., "The Patent Case that Lifted Lincoln into a Presidential Candidate." 4 *A. L. Q* 105–122 (1946).

Pauli, Hertha, *Lincoln's Little Correspondent.* Garden City: Doubleday & Co., 1951. 128 pp.

Peterson, Henry J., "Lincoln at the Wisconsin State Fair as Recalled by John W. Hoyt." 51 *Lincoln Herald* 6–10 (Dec., 1949).

Pollard, James E., *The Presidents and the Press.* New York: The Macmillan Co., 1947. 866 pp.

Pond, Fern Nance, "Two Early Lincoln Surveys." 6 *A. L. Q.* 121–125 (1950).

———, *New Salem Village: Photographic Views and Brief Historical Sketch of New Salem State Park* . . . . Petersburg, Ill.: Ira E. Owen, 1950. 16 pp.

———, "A. L. and David Rutledge." 52 *Lincoln Herald* 18–21 (June, 1950).

———, "New Salem's Miller and Kelso." 52 *Lincoln Herald* 26–41 (Dec., 1950).

Potter, David M., *The Lincoln Theme and American National Historiography.* Oxford: Clarendon Press, 1948. 24 pp.

Pratt, Fletcher, *Stanton: Lincoln's Secretary of War.* New York: W. W. Norton & Co., 1953. 520 pp.

Pratt, Harry E., "Abraham Lincoln in the Black Hawk War," *The John H. Hauberg Historical Essays,* ed. by O. Fritiof Ander. Rock Island, Ill.: Augustana College, 1954. Pp. 18–28.

———, "The Springfield Mechanics Union 1839–1848." 34 *Jour. Ill. S. H. S.* 130–134 (1941).

———, *Lincoln in the Legislature.* Madison: Lincoln Fellowship of Wisconsin, 1947. 16 pp.

———, "A Beginner on the Old Eighth Judicial Circuit." 44 *Jour. Ill. S. H. S.* 241–248 (1951).

———, "Our Growing Knowledge of Lincoln." 39 *Ill. Bar Jour.* 627–629 (1951).

———, "Springfield's Public Square in Lincoln's Day." 40 *Ill. Bar Jour.* 480–488 (1952).

———, "Lincolniana in the Illinois State Historical Library." 46 *Jour. Ill. S. H. S.* 373–400 (1953).

——— and Wayne C. Temple, "James Garfield Randall 1881–1953." 46 *Jour. Ill. S. H. S.* 119–131 (1953). This sketch includes a bibliography of the writings of J. G. Randall.

———, "Lincoln Autographed Debates." 6 *Manuscripts* 194–201 (1954).

Pratt, Marion D. Bonzi. See Basler, Roy P. and Baringer, William E. See also Bonzi, Marion D.

Quarles, Benjamin, *The Negro in the Civil War.* Boston: Little, Brown & Co., 1953. 379 pp.

Randall, J. G., *Lincoln and the South.* Baton Rouge: Louisiana State Univ. Press, 1946. 161 pp.

———, *Lincoln the Liberal Statesman.* New York: Dodd, Mead & Co., 1947. 266 pp.

———, "Lincoln and Thanksgiving." 49 *Lincoln Herald* 10–13 (Oct., 1947).

———, "In Lincoln's Words: Great Issues that Live." *N. Y. Times Mag.*, July 27, 1947, p. 8 ff.

———, "A. Lincoln: A Clearer and Fuller Portrait of Lincoln Is Emerging from a Study of His Papers." *N. Y. Times Mag.*, Aug. 10, 1947, p. 10 ff.

———, "Dear Mr. President." *N. Y. Times Mag.*, Aug. 24, 1947, p. 33.

———, " 'Living with Lincoln'—A New Impression." *N. Y. Times Mag.*, Dec. 14, 1947, p. 13 ff.

———, "The Great Dignity of 'the Rail Splitter.' " *N. Y. Times Mag.*, Feb. 8, 1948, p. 7 ff.

———, *Living with Lincoln and Other Essays.* Decatur, Ill.: Tippett Press, [1949]. 34 pp. The title page is in error, listing the date as "1948."

———, "President Lincoln: Tactician of Human Relations." 28 *Elks Mag.* 10 ff. (1950).

———, *Constitutional Problems under Lincoln.* Urbana: Univ. of Illinois Press, 1951. Revised edition. 596 pp.

———, Lincoln and the Governance of Men." 6 *A. L. Q.* 327–352 (1951).

Randall, Ruth Painter, *Mary Lincoln: Biography of a Marriage.* Boston: Little, Brown & Co., 1953. 555 pp.

Rawley, James A., "Lincoln and Governor Morgan." 6 *A. L. Q.* 272–300 (1951).

Renne, Louis Obed, *Lincoln and the Land of the Sangamon.* Boston: Chapman & Grimes, 1945. 140 pp.

Richardson, Harriet Fyffe, *Quaker Pioneers.* Milwaukee: Privately printed, 1940. 129 pp. Treats Lincoln's friendship with Jesse W. Fell.

Richardson, Robert Dale, *Abraham Lincoln's Autobiography: With an Account of Its Origin and History and Additional Biographical Material.* Boston: The Beacon Press, 1947. 45 pp.

Riddle, Donald W., *Lincoln Runs for Congress.* New Brunswick: Rutgers Univ. Press, 1948. 217 pp.

Ridley, M. R., *Abraham Lincoln.* London: Blackie & Son Limited, 1944. 208 pp.

Roberts, Octavia, "We All Knew Abr'ham." 4 *A. L. Q.* 17–29 (1946).

Robinson, William M., Jr., *Justice in Grey: A History of the Judicial System of the Confederate States of America.* Cambridge: Harvard Univ. Press, 1941. 713 pp.

Roseboom, Eugene H., "Southern Ohio and the Union in 1863." 39 *M. V. H. R.* 29–44 (1952).

Roske, Ralph J., "The Post Civil War Career of Lyman Trumbull." (MS) Ph. D. thesis, Univ. of Ill., Urbana, 1949.

———, "Lincoln's Peace Puff." 6 *A. L. Q.* 239–245 (1950).

Ross, Earle D., "Lincoln and National Security." 22 *Social Science* 80–85 (Jan., 1947).

Russell, Don, "Lincoln Was Tough on Officers." 34 *Jour. Ill. S. H. S.* 344–348 (1941).

———, "Lincoln Raises an Army." 50 *Lincoln Herald* 2–16 (June, 1948).

Sandburg, Carl and J. G. Randall, 'Lincoln Reprimand Becomes a Classic." *Chicago Sun and Times,* Oct. 5, 1947, p. 32.

———, *Lincoln Collector: The Story of Oliver R. Barrett's Great Private Collection.* New York: Harcourt, Brace & Co., 1949. 344 pp.

———, "Abraham Lincoln." 179 *Atl. Mo.* 62–65 (Feb., 1947).

———, *Abraham Lincoln: The Prairie Years and the War Years.* One-volume edition. New York: Harcourt, Brace & Co., 1954. 762 pp.

Santovenia, Emerterio S., *Lincoln in Marti: A Cuban View of Abraham Lincoln.* Trans. by Donald F. Fogelquist. Chapel Hill: Univ. of North Carolina Press, 1953. 75 pp.

Scanlan, V. M., "A Southerner's View of Abraham Lincoln." 43 *Ind. Mag. Hist.* 141–158 (1947).

Schaefer, Carl W., "Lincoln, the Lawyer." 51 *Lincoln Herald* 10–16 (June, 1949).

Schlesinger, Arthur M., Jr., "The Causes of the Civil War: A Note on Historical Sentimentalism." 16 *Partisan Review* 969–981 (1949).

Scott, Kenneth, "Lincoln's Home in 1860." 46 *Jour. Ill. S. H. S.* 7–12 (1953).

Searcy, Earle Benjamin, "A Dead Pig Goes to Court—With Lincoln." 51 *Lincoln Herald* 26–28 (Oct., 1949).

———, "The Lincoln Voice." 51 *Lincoln Herald* 28 (Oct., 1949).

Segal, Charles M., "Lincoln, Benjamin Jonas and the Black Code." 46 *Jour. Ill. S. H. S.* 277–282 (1953).

Seiler, Grace, "Walt Whitman and Abraham Lincoln." 52 *Lincoln Herald* 42 ff. (Dec., 1950).

Shaw, Archer H., ed., *The Lincoln Encyclopedia: The Spoken and Written Words of A. Lincoln* . . . . New York: The Macmillan Co., 1950. 395 pp.

Shutes, Milton H., "Republican Nominating Convention of 1860: A California Report." 27 *Cal. Hist. Soc. Quar.* 97–103 (1948).

———, "The Happy Lincoln." 53 *Lincoln Herald* 19–22 (Spring, 1951).

Sigaud, Louis A., "When Belle Boyd Wrote Lincoln." 50 *Lincoln Herald* 15–22 (Feb., 1948).

Silver, David Mayer, "The Supreme Court during the Civil War." Doctoral dissertation (MS), Univ. of Ill., 1940.

Singmaster, Elsie, *I Speak for Thaddeus Stevens.* Cambridge: Houghton Mifflin Co., 1948. 446 pp.

Simpson, Capt. E. J. See "John, Evan."

Skinner, James G., "Lincoln the Strategist Statesman." 36 *Ill. Bar Jour.* 506 ff. (1948).

Smith, Bethania Meradith, "Civil War Subversives." 45 *Jour. Ill. S. H. S.* 220–240 (1952).

Smith, George Winston, "Some Northern Wartime Attitudes toward the Post-Civil War South." 10 *Jour. So. Hist.* 253–274 (1944).

———, "New England Business Interests in Missouri during the Civil War." 41 *Mo. Hist. Rev.* 1–18 (1946).

———, "The National War Committee of the Citizens of New York." 28 *N. Y. Hist.* 440–458 (1947).

———, "Broadsides for Freedom: Civil War Propaganda in New England." 21 *New Eng. Quar.* 291–312 (1948).

Smith, T. V., *Abraham Lincoln and the Spiritual Life.* Boston: The Beacon Press, 1951. 95 pp.

Smith, Willard H., *Schuyler Colfax: The Changing Fortunes of a Political Idol.* Indianapolis: Indiana Hist. Bureau, 1952. 475 pp.

Snigg, John P., "The Great Prairie Lawyer." 37 *Ill. Bar Jour.* 234–235 (1949).

———, "A Real Lincoln Pilgrimage." 51 *Lincoln Herald* 47–48 (June, 1949).

———, "Edward Dickinson Baker—Lincoln's Forgotten Friend." 53 *Lincoln Herald* 33–37 (Summer, 1951).

Spears, Zarel C. and Robert S. Barton, *Berry and Lincoln, Frontier Merchants: The Store that "Winked Out."* New York: Stratford House, 1947. 140 pp.

Squires, J. Duane, "Some Enduring Achievements of the Lincoln Administration, 1861–1865." 5 *A. L. Q.* 191–211 (1948).

Stampp, Kenneth M., "Lincoln and the Strategy of Defense in the Crisis of 1861." 11 *Jour. So. Hist.* 297–323 (1945).

———, *Indiana Politics during the Civil War.* Indianapolis: Ind. Hist. Bureau, 1949. 300 pp.

———, *And the War Came: The North and the Secession Crisis, 1860–1861.* Baton Rouge: Louisiana State Univ. Press, 1950. 331 pp.

———, "The Historian and Southern Negro Slavery." 57 *A. H. R.* 613–624 (1952).

Stanton, Edward M. See Pratt, Fletcher.

Starr, Thomas I., "The Detroit River and Abraham Lincoln." 3 *Bulletin of Detroit Hist. Soc.* 4–6 (Feb., 1947).

Steen, Ralph W., "Texas Newspapers and Lincoln." 51 *Southwestern Hist. Quar.* 199–212 (1948).

Stoddard, William O., Jr., "Face to Face with Lincoln." 135 *Atl. Mo.* 332–339 (1925).

Strong, George Templeton. See Nevins, Allan.

Stutler, Boyd B., " 'We Are Coming, Father Abra'am.' " 53 *Lincoln Herald* 2–13 (Summer, 1951).

Sumner, G. Lynn, *Meet Abraham Lincoln: Profiles of the Prairie President.* Chicago: Privately printed for Abraham Lincoln Book Shop, 1946. 78 pp.

Taylor, Edgar C., "Lincoln the Internationalist." 4 *A. L. Q.* 59–79 (1946).

Tegeder, Vincent G., "Lincoln and the Territorial Patronage: The Ascendancy of the Radicals in the West." 35 *M. V. H. R.* 77–90 (1948).

Temple, Wayne C., "The Date of the Alschuler Ambrotype of Lincoln." 6 *A. L. Q.* 446–447 (1951).

———, "Lincoln's Fence Rails." 47 *Jour. Ill. S. H. S.* 20–34 (1954).

———. See also Pratt, Harry E.

Thomas, Benjamin P., *Portrait for Posterity: Lincoln and His Biographers.* New Brunswick: Rutgers Univ. Press, 1947. 329 pp.

———, "Our Lincoln Heritage from Ida Tarbell." 6 *A. L. Q.* 3–23 (1950).

———, *Theodore Weld: Crusader for Freedom.* New Brunswick: Rutgers Univ. Press, 1950. 307 pp.

———, *Abraham Lincoln: A Biography.* New York: Alfred A. Knopf, 1952. 548 pp. This is the best one-volume biography of Lincoln.

———, *Lincoln's New Salem.* New York: Alfred A. Knopf, 1954. 166 pp. Revised edition.

———, "Abe Lincoln: Country Lawyer." 193 *Atl. Mo.* 57–61 (1954).

Thomas, Milton Halsey. See Nevins, Allan.

Thornbrough, Emma Lou, "The Race Issue in Indiana Politics during the Civil War." 47 *Ind. Mag. Hist.* 165–188 (1951).

Townsend, William H., *Abraham Lincoln, Defendant: Lincoln's Most Interesting Lawsuit.* Boston: Houghton Mifflin Co., 1923. 40 pp.

———, "Bullard's Bixby Book." 48 *Lincoln Herald* 2–10 (Oct., 1946).

———, " 'The Sage of Lion's Den:' A Review and Rejoinder." 51 *Lincoln Herald* 40–44 (Dec., 1949).

Turner, George Edgar, *Victory Rode the Rails: The Strategic Place of the Railroads in the Civil War.* Indianapolis: Bobbs-Merrill Co., 1953. 419 pp.

Vandiver, Frank E., *Ploughshares into Swords: Josiah Gorgas and Confederate Ordnance.* Austin: Univ. of Texas Press, 1952. 349 pp.

Vasvary, Edmund, *Lincoln's Hungarian Heroes: The Participation of Hungarians in the Civil War, 1861–1865.* Washington: Hungarian Reformed Federation of America, 1939. 171 pp.

Voigt, David Quentin, " 'Too Pitchy to Touch'—President Lincoln and Editor Bennett." 6 *A. L. Q.* 139–161 (1950).

Wagenknecht, Edward, ed., *Abraham Lincoln, His Life, Work, and Character: An Anthology of History and Biography, Fiction, Poetry, Drama, and Belles-Lettres.* New York: Creative Age Press, 1947. 661 pp.

Wallace, Sarah A. and Frances E. Gillespie, eds., *The Journal of Benjamin Moran 1857–1865.* Chicago: Univ. of Chicago Press, 1948–1949. 2 vols.

Warren, Louis A., *Abraham Lincoln's Gettysburg Address: An Evaluation.* Columbus, O.: Charles E. Merrill Co., 1946. 32 pp.

———, *Sifting the Herndon Sources.* Los Angeles: Lincoln Fellowship of Southern California, 1948. 19 pp.

———, "Herndon's Contribution to Lincoln Mythology." 41 *Ind. Mag. Hist.* 221–244 (1945).

———, "The Woman in Lincoln's Life—With Special Emphasis on Her Cultural Attainments." 20 *The Filson Club Hist. Quar.* 207–219 (1946).

Wayland, John W., *The Lincolns in Virginia.* Staunton, Va.: John W. Wayland, 1946. 299 pp.

Weber, Thomas, *The Northern Railroads in the Civil War, 1861–1865.* New York: Columbia Univ. Press, 1952. 318 pp.

Weisberger, Bernard A., *Reporters for the Union.* Boston: Little, Brown & Co., 1953. 316 pp.

Wessen, Ernest J., "Debates of Lincoln and Douglas—A Bibliographical Discussion." 40 *The Papers of the Bibliographical Soc. of America* 91–106 (1946).

Wheare, K. C., *Abraham Lincoln and the United States.* New York: The Macmillan Co., 1949. 286 pp.

Whitton, Mary Ormsbee, *First First Ladies, 1789–1865: A Study of the Early Presidents.* New York: Hastings House, 1948. 341 pp.

Wiel, Samuel C., *Lincoln's Crisis in the Far West.* San Francisco: Privately printed, 1949. 130 pp.

Wiley, Bell Irvin, *The Life of Johnny Reb: The Common Soldier of the Confederacy.* Indianapolis: Bobbs-Merrill Co., 1943. 444 pp.

———, "Billy Yank and Abraham Lincoln." 6 *A. L. Q.* 103–120 (1950).

———, *The Life of Billy Yank: The Common Soldier of the Union.* Indianapolis: Bobbs-Merrill Co., 1952. 454 pp.

Wiley, Earl W., " 'Governor' John Greiner and Chase's Bid for the Presidency in 1860." 58 *Ohio Arch. and Hist. Quar.* 245–273 (1949).

———, "Ohio Pre-Convention Support for Lincoln in 1860." 52 *Lincoln Herald* 13–17 (June, 1950).

———, "Behind Lincoln's Visit to Ohio in 1859." 60 *Ohio Arch. and Hist. Quar.* 28–47 (1951).

Williams, Kenneth P., *Lincoln Finds a General: A Military Study of the Civil War.* New York: The Macmillan Co., 1949–1952. 3 vols.

———, "The Tennessee River Campaign and Anna Ella Carroll." 46 *Ind. Mag. Hist.* 221–248 (1950).

———, Review of *Anna Ella Carroll and Abraham Lincoln.* 54 *Lincoln Herald* 54–56 (Summer, 1952). In this issue, pages 54 and 10 are interchanged in the magazine.

Williams, T. Harry, "The Committee on the Conduct of the War: An Experiment in Civilian Control." 3 *Jour. Am. Military Institute* 139–156 (1939).

———, "The Attack upon West Point during the Civil War." 25 *M. V. H. R.* 491–504 (1939).

———, "Voters in Blue: The Citizen Soldiers of the Civil War." 31 *M. V. H. R.* 187–204 (1944).

———, *Lincoln and His Generals.* New York: Alfred A. Knopf, 1952. 363 pp.

———, "Abraham Lincoln—Principle and Pragmatism in Politics: A Review Article." 40 *M. V. H. R.* 89–106 (1953).

William, Wayne C., *A Rail Splitter for President.* Denver: Univ. of Denver Press, 1951. 242 pp.

Wilson, Rufus Rockwell, "Abraham Lincoln and Ben Montgomery." 48 *Lincoln Herald* 2–5 (Dec., 1946).

———, "Mr. Lincoln's First Appointment to the Supreme Court." 50–51 *Lincoln Herald* 26 ff. (Dec., 1948–Feb., 1949).

———, "President Lincoln and Preacher Luckett." 51 *Lincoln Herald* 42–43 (June, 1949).

———, "President Lincoln and Emancipation." 51 *Lincoln Herald* 43–46 (June, 1949).

———, *Lincoln in Caricature.* New York: Horizon Press, 1953. 327 pp.

Wingfield, Marshall, "The Likeness of Lincoln and Lee." 49 *Lincoln Herald* 21–26 (Feb., 1947).

Woldman, Albert A., *Lincoln and the Russians.* Cleveland: World Pub. Co., 1952. 311 pp.

———, "Lincoln Never Said That." 200 *Harper's Mag.* 70–74 (May, 1950).

Wolf, Hazel Catherine, *On Freedom's Altar: The Martyr Complex in the Abolition Movement.* Madison: Univ. of Wisconsin Press, 1952. 195 pp.

———. See also Hesseltine, William B.

Woodward, William E., *Years of Madness: A Reappraisal of the Civil War.* New York: G. P. Putnam's Sons, 1951. 311 pp.

Zornow, William Frank, "The Attitude of the Western Reserve Press on the Re-Election of Lincoln." 50 *Lincoln Herald* 35–39 (June, 1948).

———, "Indiana and the Election of 1864." 45 *Ind. Mag. Hist.* 13–38 (1949).

———, "Treason as a Campaign Issue in the Re-Election of Lincoln." 5 *A. L. Q.* 348–363 (1949).

———, "Lincoln's Influence in the Election of 1864." 51 *Lincoln Herald* 22–32 (June, 1949).

———, "Lincoln and Chase: Presidential Rivals." 52 *Lincoln Herald* 17–28; 6–12 (Feb.–June, 1950).

———, "The Missouri Radicals and the Election of 1864." 45 *Mo. Hist. Rev.* 354–370 (1951).

———, "The Unwanted Mr. Lincoln." 45 *Jour. Ill. S. H. S.* 146–163 (1952).

———, "The Democratic Convention at Chicago in 1864." 54 *Lincoln Herald* 2–[10] (Summer, 1952).

———, *Lincoln and the Party Divided.* Norman: Univ. of Oklahoma Press, 1954. 264 pp.

INDEX TO PART ONE

INDEX TO PART TWO